THE OXFORD HANDBOOK OF

THE HISTORY OF
LINGUISTICS

OXFORD HANDBOOKS IN LINGUISTICS

The Oxford Handbook of Applied Linguistics
Second edition
Edited by Robert B. Kaplan

The Oxford Handbook of Case
Edited by Andrej Malchukov and Andrew Spencer

The Oxford Handbook of Cognitive Linguistics
Edited by Dirk Geeraerts and Hubert Cuyckens

The Oxford Handbook of Comparative Syntax
Edited by Gugliemo Cinque and Richard S. Kayne

The Oxford Handbook of Compounding
Edited by Rochelle Lieber and Pavol Štekauer

The Oxford Handbook of Computational Linguistics
Edited by Ruslan Mitkov

The Oxford Handbook of Compositionality
Edited by Markus Werning, Edouard Machery, and Wolfram Hinzen

The Oxford Handbook of Field Linguistics
Edited by Nicholas Thieberger

The Oxford Handbook of Grammaticalization
Edited by Heiko Narrog and Bernd Heine

The Oxford Handbook of the History of Linguistics
Edited by Keith Allan

The Oxford Handbook of Japanese Linguistics
Edited by Shigeru Miyagawa and Mamoru Saito

The Oxford Handbook of Laboratory Phonology
Edited by Abigail C. Cohn, Cécile Fougeron, and Marie Hoffman

The Oxford Handbook of Language Evolution
Edited by Maggie Tallerman and Kathleen Gibson

The Oxford Handbook of Language and Law
Edited by Peter Tiersma and Lawrence M. Solan

The Oxford Handbook of Linguistic Analysis
Edited by Bernd Heine and Heiko Narrog

The Oxford Handbook of Linguistic Interfaces
Edited by Gillian Ramchand and Charles Reiss

The Oxford Handbook of Linguistic Minimalism
Edited by Cedric Boeckx

The Oxford Handbook of Linguistic Typology
Edited by Jae Jung Song

The Oxford Handbook of Translation Studies
Edited by Kirsten Malmkjaer and Kevin Windle

THE OXFORD HANDBOOK OF

THE HISTORY OF LINGUISTICS

Edited by

KEITH ALLAN

OXFORD

UNIVERSITY PRESS

OXFORD
UNIVERSITY PRESS

Great Clarendon Street, Oxford, OX2 6DP,
United Kingdom

Oxford University Press is a department of the University of Oxford.
It furthers the University's objective of excellence in research, scholarship,
and education by publishing worldwide. Oxford is a registered trade mark of
Oxford University Press in the UK and in certain other countries

Published in the United States of America by Oxford University Press
198 Madison Avenue, New York, NY 10016, United States of America

British Library Cataloguing in Publication Data
Data available

Library of Congress Cataloging in Publication Data
Data available

ISBN 978–0–19–958584–7

To my partner, Alexandra

&

In memory of Anna Maria Siewierska,
my friend for more than thirty years,
who still had so much to give the world when she was
tragically killed in a traffic accident on August 6, 2011:
niech spoczywa w pokoju.

Contents

CONTRIBUTORS

Keith Allan is Emeritus Professor of Linguistics at Monash University, Fellow of the Australian Academy of Humanities, and editor of the *Australian Journal of Linguistics*. His research interests focus mainly on aspects of meaning in language, with a secondary interest in the history and philosophy of linguistics. He is the author of several books, of which the most relevant here is *The Western Classical Tradition in Linguistics*, second expanded edition (2010; first edition 2007).

Catherine Atherton holds appointments in the Departments of Philosophy and Classics at UCLA, having previously been Tutorial Fellow in Classical Philosophy at New College, Oxford. She works on a broad range of topics in ancient philosophy, with a special interest in logic, the philosophy of language, and the philosophy of mind.

David Blank is Professor of Classics at UCLA. A specialist in Greco-Roman philosophy, he has written extensively on philosophy of language and grammar in antiquity. His current major project is a new edition and commentary of the *Rhetoric* of the Epicurean Philodemus from the papyri found at Herculaneum.

James P. Blevins received his Ph.D from the University of Massachusetts, Amherst, in 1990. He later taught at the University of Western Australia before coming to the University of Cambridge, where he has taught since 1997. His current research interests include information-theoretic approaches to morphology, constraint-based treatments of discontinuous dependencies, and the history of morphological and syntactic models.

Kate Burridge is Professor of Linguistics in the School of Languages, Cultures and Linguistics, Monash University, and a fellow of the Australian Academy of the Humanities. Her main areas of research are grammatical change in Germanic languages, the Pennsylvania German spoken by Amish communities in North America, the notion of linguistic taboo, and the structure and history of English. She is a regular presenter of language segments on radio and has appeared as a panellist on ABC TV's *Can We Help?* Her books include *Syntactic Change in Germanic* (1993), *English in Australia and New Zealand* (with Jean Mulder, 1998), *Blooming English: Observations on the Roots, Cultivation and Hybrids of the English Language* (2004), *Weeds in the Garden of Words: Further Observations on the Tangled History of the English language* (2005), *Forbidden Words: Taboo and the Censoring of Language* (with Keith Allan, 2006), *Introducing English Grammar* (with Kersti Börjars, 2010), and *Gift of the Gob: Morsels of English Language History* (2010).

Karen Steffen Chung (史嘉琳 Shǐ Jiālín), originally from St Paul, Minnesota, USA, has taught English and linguistics in the Department of Foreign Languages and Literatures of National Taiwan University since 1990; she is currently Associate Professor. She has a BA in East Asian Languages from the University of Minnesota (1976), an MA in East Asian Studies from Princeton University (1981), and a Ph.D in Linguistics from Leiden University (2004), for which her dissertation was entitled 'Mandarin Compound Verbs'.

Peter T. Daniels earned degrees in linguistics from Cornell University and the University of Chicago. His interests in Semitic languages and calligraphy led inexorably to the neglected field of the linguistic study of writing systems; his first forays into history of linguistics concerned the stories of little-known decipherments—whether untold (Palmyrene, Himyaritic) or mistold (Mesopotamian cuneiform). More recently he has been exploring the modern development of understanding of the languages written with cuneiform scripts.

Ana Deumert (Linguistics, University of Cape Town) has studied, worked, taught, and researched on three continents: Africa, Europe, and Australia. Her research programme is located within the broad field of African sociolinguistics and has a strong interdisciplinary focus (with particular attention to anthropology, sociology, and economics). She has authored and edited several books and is editor of *IMPACT—Studies in Language and Society* (John Benjamins).

Robert Freidin is Professor of Linguistics in the Council of the Humanities at Princeton University. His research concerns syntax and semantics, focusing on the foundations of syntactic theory (the central concepts of syntactic analysis and their evolution) and their role in the study of language and mind. Some of this work is collected in *Generative Grammar: Theory and its History* (2007). His most recent publications include 'The Roots of Minimalism' (with Howard Lasnik) in *The Oxford Handbook of Linguistic Minimalism*, 'A Brief History of Generative Grammar' in *The Routledge Companion to the Philosophy of Language*, and *Syntax: Basic Concepts and Applications* (forthcoming).

Alan Garnham is Professor of Experimental Psychology at the University of Sussex, UK. He studied for his doctorate at Sussex with Phil Johnson-Laird, and has spent most of his academic life there. His main academic interests are in text comprehension, particularly inference and anaphor resolution. His work is situated in the mental models framework, which he helped to develop.

Dirk Geeraerts is Professor of Linguistics at the University of Leuven and head of the research group Quantitative Lexicology and Variational Linguistics. He is the author of *The Structure of Lexical Variation* (1994), *Diachronic Prototype Semantics* (1997), *Words and Other Wonders* (2006), and *Theories of Lexical Semantics* (2010), and the editor, with Hubert Cuyckens, of *The Oxford Handbook of Cognitive Linguistics* (2007).

Giorgio Graffi is Professor of Linguistics at the University of Verona, Italy. His research topics include methodology of linguistics, general syntax, and history of linguistics. In the latter field, he has published *200 Years of Syntax: A Critical Survey* (2001) and *Due secoli di pensiero linguistico* (2010). He is also author of the chapter 'The Pioneers of Linguistic Typology: From Gabelentz to Greenberg', in *The Oxford Handbook of Linguistic Typology*.

Patrick Hanks is a lexicographer and corpus linguist. He is a Visiting Professor at the Universities of Wolverhampton and the West of England. He was editor of the first edition of the *Collins English Dictionary* (1979), managing editor of the first edition of Cobuild (1987), and chief editor of current English dictionaries at Oxford University Press (1990–2000). His research interests are: corpus pattern analysis of lexical collocations; the relationship between word meaning and word use; metaphor and figurative language; and the origin and history of personal names.

Andrew Hardie is a Lecturer in Corpus Linguistics at Lancaster University. His research interests include corpus construction and annotation; the relationship between collocation and grammatical theory; and studying the languages of South Asia. He is one of the lead developers of the widely used Corpus Workbench software for indexing and analysing corpus data. He is the author, with Tony McEnery, of the book *Corpus Linguistics: Method, Theory and Practice* (2012).

Graeme Hirst's research in computational linguistics includes topics in lexical semantics, anaphora resolution, discourse structure, and text analysis. Hirst is the author of two monographs: *Anaphora in Natural Language Understanding* (1981) and *Semantic Interpretation and the Resolution of Ambiguity* (1987). He was elected Chair of the North American Chapter of the Association for Computational Linguistics for 2004–5 and Treasurer of the Association for 2008–2017.

Harry van der Hulst (Ph.D 1984, University of Leiden) specializes in phonology with interests in feature systems and segmental structure, syllable structure, word accent systems, vowel harmony, and sign language phonology. He has published four books, two textbooks, and over 140 articles, and has edited 23 books and six journal theme issues. He has been editor-in-chief of *The Linguistic Review* since 1990. He is Professor of Linguistics at the University of Connecticut.

Esa Itkonen (born in 1944) has been since 1982 Professor of General Linguistics at the University of Turku, and since 1986 Dozent of Philosophy at the University of Jyväskylä. His research interests are philosophy of linguistics, history of linguistics, and linguistic typology. His book publications include *Grammatical Theory and Metascience* (1978), *Causality in Linguistic Theory* (1983), *Universal History of Linguistics: India, China, Arabia, Europe* (1991), *What Is Language? A Study in the Philosophy of Linguistics* (2003), *Analogy as Structure and Process: Approaches in Linguistics, Cognitive Psychology, and Philosophy of Science* (Benjamins 2005), *The Diversity and* *the Unity of the World's Languages* (3rd edn, in 3 vols (in Finnish), 2008–10). He is co-editor of *The Shared Mind: Perpectives on Intersubjectivity* (2008).

Kurt R. Jankowsky studied German, English, Philosophy, Latin, and Greek at the University of Münster (Germany). He spent four years, from 1958 to 1962, as DAAD (German Academic Exchange Service) Postgraduate Lecturer in German at the University of Poona, where he conducted the first German Ph.D programme in India. In 1962 he started teaching German linguistics at Georgetown University, Washington, DC, first as Assistant Professor, from 1972 as Full Professor, until his retirement in 2008. Apart from numerous scholarly articles he is author of more than a dozen books, including *The Neogrammarians: A Reevaluation of their Place in the Development of Linguistic Science* (1972) and *Multiple Perspectives on the Historical Dimensions of Language* (1996).

Adam Kendon studied at Cambridge and Oxford (D.Phil. 1963), and has worked in the United States, Australia, and Italy on face-to-face interaction, sign languages, and gesture. His books include *Sign Languages of Aboriginal Australia* (1988); *Conducting Interaction* (1990); *Gesture: Visible Action as Utterance* (2004); *Gesture in Naples and Gesture in Classical Antiquity* (2000), a translation of Andrea de Jorio's 1832 treatise on Neapolitan gesture.

Andrew Linn is based at the University of Sheffield, UK, where he is Professor of the History of Linguistics and Director of Research and Innovation in the Faculty of Arts and Humanities. He is the author of books and articles on the history of English and Scandinavian linguistics and also in the field of language policy and language planning. He is an elected member of the Norwegian Academy of Science and Letters.

Edward Lipiński, born at Łódź (Poland) in 1930, is a Professor Emeritus of the Katholieke Universiteit Leuven (Belgium) and *doctor honoris causa* of Lund University (Sweden). He taught Semitic linguistics and epigraphy, as well as history of Ancient Near Eastern religions and institutions. He continues to work in both fields, linguistic and historical. His bibliography up to 2010 was published in *The Polish Journal of Biblical Research* 9 (2010).

Deborah Loakes is a postdoctoral fellow at the University of Melbourne. She has a Ph.D from the University of Melbourne, and an undergraduate degree from Monash University. Her current work involves analysis of variation and change in the phonetics of Australian English spoken in Melbourne, and in border and near-border regions of Victoria. As well as fine-grained analysis of acoustic features of speech, she is also exploring the interrelationship between accent and identity.

Anneli Luhtala is University Lecturer in the Department of Classics at the University of Helsinki. Her interests include ancient and medieval grammar, especially syntactical theory and philosophy of language. She is the author of *On the Origin of Syntactical*

Description in Stoic Logic (2000) and *Grammar and Philosophy in Late Antiquity* (2005), and of many articles on the development of medieval grammatical theory.

Jaap Maat is a lecturer at the Department of Philosophy, University of Amsterdam, and a member of the Institute for Logic, Language and Computation (ILLC). He has published widely on seventeenth-century artificial languages. His main interests are in the history of ideas, history of logic, history of linguistics, and modern philosophy of language and mind.

Michael K. C. MacMahon is Emeritus Professor of Phonetics at the University of Glasgow. He is a member of Council of the International Phonetic Association, and Archivist of the British Association of Academic Phoneticians. His publications focus on the history of phonetics and linguistics, including the first major study of the state of English pronunciation from the mid-1770s to the present day (in *The Cambridge History of the English Language*, vol. IV, 1999).

Margaret Magnus began her doctoral work in 1981 at MIT and in 1984 co-founded the linguistics software house Circle Noetics, which created natural language software. In 1997 she founded the Linguistic Iconism Association and its peer-reviewed journal *Iconicity in Language*, which was active online until 2000. In 2001, she completed her Ph.D at the University of Trondheim with a dissertation on sound symbolism. She is currently Principal Software Engineer with the linguistics group at Nuance Communications.

Kirsten Malmkjær holds a BA in English and Philosophy (1981) and a Ph.D (1984) from Birmingham University. She lectured there until 1989, when she moved to the University of Cambridge, Research Centre for English and Applied Linguistics. In 1999 she moved to Middlesex University as Professor of Translation Studies. Since September 2010 she has been Professor of Translation Studies at the University of Leicester. She has published widely in Translation Studies.

Tony McEnery is Professor of English Language and Linguistics at Lancaster University. He is the author or editor of sixteen books, including *Corpus Linguistics* (1996/2001, with Andrew Wilson), *Corpus-Based Language Studies* (2006, with Richard Xiao and Yuko Tono), and *Corpus Linguistics: Method, Theory and Practice* (2012, with Andrew Hardie). His research interests are wide-ranging, but all focus on the application of corpus-based methodology to new problems in linguistics and beyond.

Jacob L. Mey (born 1926) is Professor Emeritus of Linguistics at the University of Southern Denmark. Previously, he has taught at the University of Oslo, the University of Texas at Austin and numerous other institutions. His research interests concern all areas of pragmatics, with an emphasis on the social aspects of language use, the pragmatic impact of computer technologies, and the pragmatic use of literary devices. Among his most recent publications are: *Pragmatics: An Introduction* (2001); *When Voices Clash: A Study in Literary Pragmatics* (2001); and *Concise Encyclopedia of*

Pragmatics (ed., 1994; 2nd edn 2009). In 1977 he founded the *Journal of Pragmatics*, of which he was editor-in-chief until 2009, when he founded the new journal *Pragmatics and Society*. He holds honorary D.Phil. degrees from the Universities of Zaragoza, Spain (1993) and Bucharest, Romania (2006). In 2008 he was presented with a lifetime award from the University of Southern Denmark for his work in pragmatics.

Salikoko S. Mufwene is the Frank J. McLoraine Distinguished Service Professor of Linguistics and the College at the University of Chicago, where he also serves on the Committee of Evolutionary Biology and on the Committee on the Conceptual and Historical Studies of Science. He spent the 2010–11 academic year at the Collegium de Lyon (Institute for Advanced Study) in Lyon, France. His publications include: *The Ecology of Language Evolution* (2001); *Créoles, écologie sociale, evolution linguistique* (2005); and *Language Evolution: Contact, Competition and Change* (2008).

Peter M. Scharf specializes in the linguistic traditions of India, Vedic Sanskrit, and Indian philosophy, and has devoted considerable attention recently to Sanskrit computational linguistics and building a digital Sanskrit archive. After teaching Sanskrit for nineteen years in the Department of Classics at Brown University, he is currently laureate of a Chaire Internationale de Recherche Blaise Pascal in the Laboratoire d'Histoire des Théories Linguistiques, Université Paris Diderot, and Director of the Sanskrit Library.

Pieter A. M. Seuren started out as a classicist (Latin, Greek, Ancient History) at Amsterdam University, graduating in 1958. After a brief period as a teacher of classical languages, he entered Academe, as an assistant in various Dutch universities. In 1967 he became Lecturer in Linguistics at the University of Cambridge, and in 1970 at Oxford University. From 1974 till 1999 he was professor of Philosophy of Language and Theoretical Linguistics at the Radboud University of Nijmegen. Since his retirement in 1999 he has been a research fellow at the Max Planck Institute for Psycholinguistics at Nijmegen.

Anna Siewierska studied linguistics in Gdansk and Monash University, Melbourne, where she did her MA and Ph.D. She was a lecturer in Gdansk, where she did her Habilitation, and in Amsterdam. In 1994 she became Professor of Linguistics and Human Communication at Lancaster University. She coordinated the group on constituent order of the EuroTyp project, and was president of both the Association of Linguistic Typology and the Societas Linguistica Europaea. Anna's major publications are on the passive, word order, transitivity, and person.

Linda R. Waugh is Professor of French, English, Anthropology, Linguistics, and Language, Reading, and Culture; a faculty member in the Interdisciplinary Ph.D Program in Second Language Acquisition and Teaching; Co-Director of the Center for Educational Resources in Culture, Language, and Literacy (CERCLL) at the University of Arizona; and Executive Director of the Roman Jakobson Intellectual Trust.

Her recent research has been focused on discourse and textual analysis, identity, iconicity, metonymy, and the history of linguistics. Linda Waugh's co-contributors: **José Aldemar Álvarez Valencia** is a doctoral student in the Interdisciplinary Ph.D program in Second Language Acquisition and Teaching at the University of Arizona. Before enrolling for the Ph.D he was a faculty member at Universidad de la Salle in Bogotá, Colombia. He has published in the areas of discourse analysis and foreign language teacher education. His current research focuses on the intersection between multimodal social semiotics and Computer Assisted Language Learning. **Tom Hong Do** is a doctoral student in Rhetoric, Composition, and the Teaching of English at the University of Arizona. His research investigates the impact of assimilation and literacy on ethnic identity construction among first-generation Asian-Americans. **Kristen Michelson** is a doctoral student in the Interdisciplinary Ph.D program in Second Language Acquisition and Teaching at the University of Arizona. Her research centres around second language acquisition and the development of intercultural competence in study abroad programmes, culture and language teaching, and semiotic representations of cultural values through media such as virtual spaces and literature. **M'Balia Thomas** is a doctoral student in the Interdisciplinary Program in Second Language Acquisition and Teaching at the University of Arizona. Her research critically investigates the role of social discourses in second language learning and literacy.

Bencie Woll is Professor of Sign Language and Deaf Studies and also the Director of the Deafness Cognition and Language Research Centre (DCAL) at University College London. Her research and interests embrace a wide range of topics related to sign language. These include the linguistics of British Sign Language (BSL), the history and sociolinguistics of BSL and the Deaf community, the development of BSL in young children, sign language and the brain, and developmental and acquired sign language impairments.

ACKNOWLEDGEMENTS

I am very grateful to Keith Brown for inviting me to co-edit this volume with him and for his contribution towards the planning of its content. Sadly, the ink was barely dry on the contract with Oxford University Press when my would-be co-editor withdrew for health reasons (though I am pleased to report he has by now fully recovered). So I became sole editor.

I would like to thank John Davey at OUP for being extraordinarily supportive throughout the gestation and birth of this volume. A couple of the contributors we initially engaged pulled out and a third ceased all communication with us; warm thanks to Bob Freidin, Graeme Hirst, and especially to Karen Steffen Chung for stepping into the breaches. My deepest gratitude to all those contributors who submitted work on time. If I am tempted to wish a pox on those who were tardy, perhaps it was to guarantee the excellence of their content. So I warmly thank all of the contributors to this volume for their outstanding work.

On a very sombre note, Anna Siewierska sent in her chapter a few months before I visited with her in Lancaster; three weeks later I was devastated to learn she had been killed in a traffic accident while holidaying in Vietnam. My profound thanks to Anna's husband, Dik Bakker, for acting as her literary executor under these dreadful circumstances.

As this volume has been steadily pulled together, I have treasured the constant cheerfulness, love, and support of my partner, Ali. Together we are 陰陽, but which of us is yin and which yang I really don't know; maybe we are both, both.

Keith Allan

INTRODUCTION

THE *Oxford Handbook of the History of Linguistics* offers comprehensive coverage of the history of linguistics in a single volume and will serve as an introduction to the understanding of countless topics within the history of linguistics. This project began immediately after I had completed *The Western Classical Tradition in Linguistics* (Allan 2010a), which contains pretty much all I wanted to write on that subject; but even on topics within the history of linguistics that I covered in that book, there are other perspectives to be presented and, on many matters, much greater expertise than mine to be tapped. In addition there are the non-western traditions to consider. So the present volume was conceived[1] as a book that would make a significant contribution to the historiography of linguistics on a very wide range of topics. Thirty-four chapters, many covering a variety of issues, were commissioned from scholars who are expert in the field outlined in the title for each chapter. The size of the book necessarily favours concision over expansiveness, but there is a vast bibliography pointing to sources for further inquiry in all the fields covered in the book for readers wishing to pursue a special interest.

The readership envisaged for the handbook includes those already knowledgeable about the history of linguistics, but it is principally intended for students of linguistics and those (not necessarily professional linguists) with an interest in a history of investigations into language, language origins, the media through which language is delivered, and the purposes to which language is put. The book chronicles centuries of explanations for language structures, language meanings, and language use, as well as the history of some applications of linguistics.

The *Oxford Handbook of the History of Linguistics* is loosely organised into six thematically grouped parts. Part I contains four chapters which look at linguistic studies of the basics of human communication: the origins of language (Chapter 1), the invention of writing (Chapter 2), the nature of gesture (Chapter 3), and of sign languages (Chapter 4). Part II consists of five chapters that examine the history of the analysis and description of sound systems used in human languages. Chapter 5 looks at the development of phonetics from earliest times; Chapter 6 focuses on instrumental

---

[1] Originally together with Keith Brown: see the Acknowledgements.

phonetics; Chapter 7 deals with the discovery of sound change laws in the nineteenth century; Chapter 8, the history of phonology; Chapter 9 chronicles the history of ideas about sound symbolism. Part III comprises three chapters dealing with non-western traditions. Chapter 10 is about linguistics in East Asia, with the focus on China, which has the richest history, but briefly commenting on linguistic events in Korea and Japan. Chapter 11 discourses on the superbly worked out and comprehensive linguistic tradition in Ancient India which influenced linguistic events in China, the Middle East, and, from the end of the eighteenth century, Europe. Chapter 12 is on Semitic and Afro-Asiatic linguistics. Part IV surveys the history of grammar and morphology in Europe and North America, proceeding from Ancient Greece and Rome (Chapter 13) to late antiquity and the Middle Ages (Chapter 14), the Renaissance and beyond (15), morphology throughout the ages (16), universal grammar from the medieval scholastics to Chomsky (17), American structuralism (18), Chomsky's contribution and legacy (19), European linguistics in the twentieth century (20), and the characteristics of functional and cognitive grammars (21). Part V comprises six chapters that survey lexicography (22), aspects of semantics (chapters 23–25), pragmatics (26), and text/discourse studies (27). Part VI offers histories of the application of linguistics to the comparison and classification of languages (Chapter 28), within the fields of social and cultural theory (29) and psychology and brain sciences (30); Chapter 31 deals with applications of linguistics in education and translation, Chapter 32 the use of computers, and 33 the development of corpora; finally, Chapter 34 is a history of the philosophy of linguistics that is something of a summary of many topics discussed earlier in this volume.

I'll now review the chapters in a little more detail, offering a handful of my own comments on the way, without precluding the much richer experience of reading each chapter for yourself. In Chapter 1, 'The Origins and the Evolution of Language', Salikoko S. Mufwene discusses the phylogenetic emergence of language and questions the probable time of the emergence of the ancestor, or ancestors, of modern language. Are individuals or populations the agents in the emergence of language? Mufwene reviews relationships between language and thought, language and the brain, language and our anatomical architecture, as well as the social conditions that favour oral communication.

In 'The History of Writing as a History of Linguistics', Chapter 2, Peter T. Daniels shows that the language constituents most accessible to conscious control (words, syllables, tone, etc.) are most likely to be represented in orthography. All writing systems utilize a sequence of symbols that reflects the temporal order of utterance. The earliest writing functioned as a kind of memory prompt and was to some extent pictographic; but when Sumerian script was adapted to the unrelated language Akkadian, it (mostly) used the sounds of the characters to spell out words phonetically. Similar patterns of development are found elsewhere.

In Chapter 3, Adam Kendon records the 'History of the Study of Gesture'. Gesture is bodily action, usually integrated with speech during the process of communication, and was first described as an accompaniment to oratory. During the Renaissance, contact with exotic peoples led to a better appreciation of the communicative value of gesture, pantomime developed as a form of entertainment, and the mistaken idea arose that gesture is a universal language. Come the eighteenth century, gesture in sign language for the deaf was studied and taught. In the nineteenth century Wundt suggested that gesture is the first modality of language, an idea that persists today.

In 'The History of Sign Language linguistics', chapter 4, Bencie Woll explores the similarities and differences between signed and spoken languages and among sign languages. Sign languages are largely mutually unintelligible, and where iconicity is present, it does not produce identical lexicons: even the English-based sign languages of Ireland, the UK, and the USA are distinct. Sign languages are a semi-autonomous gestural medium that exploits three-dimensional space, simultaneous combinations of a location where the sign is articulated, a configuration and movement of the hand, and additional bodily gestures. Sign languages were ignored by linguists until the late twentieth century.

Part II opens with Michael K. C. MacMahon's 'Orthography and the Early History of Phonetics' (Chapter 5), reviewing the growth of phonetics in Europe, the Middle East, and Asia. It began when phonetic markers, syllabaries, and alphabets were invented; later, 'correct' pronunciation was of interest in the delivery of venerated texts (religious, poetic, etc.) and for orating. MacMahon contrasts 'the acumen of phoneticians such as Pāṇini and Patañjali' in Ancient India with the virtual absence of any significant work on phonetics in Europe before the Renaissance. Interest in reforming orthography inspired Martianus Capella (c.470 CE), the Icelander known as the 'first grammarian' (c.1135), Charles Butler (c.1633), the seventeenth-century inventors of 'real character' (c.1647–68), and Henry Sweet (c.1877) to phonetic analysis. Instrumental phonetics developed from primitive beginnings in the late eighteenth century, and flowered in the twentieth.

Deborah Loakes reviews its history in Chapter 6, 'From IPA to PRAAT and Beyond'. The International Phonetic Alphabet was established in 1886 by a group of language teachers in Paris, based on an alphabet designed by Pitman, of shorthand fame, with Ellis, who had studied British dialects. By the end of that century, sound could be recorded. Early instruments for recording speech and articulatory gestures (e.g. linguagrams, palatography, filming, X-rays) were comparatively crude, but there was a great leap forward with the development of computer-aided systems such as PRAAT and EMU that allow for all sorts of articulatory and acoustic analyses of the segmental and prosodic characteristics of speech. Loakes gives examples of their use in dialect research and for forensic purposes. The nineteenth century saw great strides made in phonetics, concomitant with the study of relationships among Indo-European languages that led to the postulation of sound-change laws.

In Chapter 7, 'Nineteenth-Century Study of Sound Change from Rask to Saussure', Kate Burridge reports on the era when the study of language moved once again from description to explanation with the rise of the comparative method. It stemmed from the proposals of Sir William Jones, via Rask's identification of systematic sound correspondences improved upon by Germanicist Jacob Grimm with his notion of

Kreislauf ('rotation'), the exceptions to which were explained away by Grassmann and Verner. Neogrammarians demonstrated insightful interactions between the phonological and morphological levels of language (see also Chapter 28). Meanwhile, Bopp adopted an organic view of languages (they are born, flourish, and degenerate), while Schleicher pictured a tree as the model for family relationships among languages. To this period belong modern linguistic canons like the primacy of speech; recognition that sound change is phonetically conditioned and regular, permitting proto-forms to be reconstructed; and the aphorism that yesterday's syntax is today's morphology.

Harry van der Hulst in 'Discoverers of the Phoneme', Chapter 8, writes that the development of alphabetic systems presupposes some recognition of phonology. With the possible exception of Pāṇini, early grammarians in the Indian, Chinese, Greek, Roman, and Arabic traditions discussed speech sounds without explicit recognition of the phoneme. In the mid-1870s the Kazan school (Baudouin de Courtenay and Kruszewski) studied phonemic alternations (morphophonology). They influenced the Prague School (*c*.1928–39), who focused on what were later called the 'distinctive features' of phonemes. For them, as for de Courtenay, the phoneme was a psychological unit, but for Trubetzkoy it was an abstract functional unit of phonological opposition. Later, in America, Jakobson elaborated the theory of distinctive features, breaking with the idea that phonemes are the smallest elements of phonological structure. Generative phonology adopted distinctive features, with the modification that they are articulatory rather than abstract functional units.

Part II ends with Chapter 9, 'A History of Sound Symbolism', in which Margaret Magnus shows that although the arguments of the 'naturalist' Cratylus were dismissed by Socrates in Plato's *Cratylus*, the distribution of phonemes across semantic classes is not random as Hermogenes would hold because there are phonesthemes in every language (e.g. the onset to *flash, flare, flame, flutter, flicker*, and the rhyme in *flutter, stutter, clutter*). Humboldt recognized the existence of sound symbolism, as did Jespersen and Jakobson. However, if sound determines meaning, we should know what a word means just by hearing it, yet we don't. Locke sided with Hermogenes, but Leibniz pointed out there must be some rationale behind the forms of names. We don't normally think of Bloomfield as a romantic, but he wrote: 'to study the coordination of certain sounds with certain meanings is to study language' (1933: 27).

Part III is on non-western traditions. In Chapter 10, 'East Asian Linguistics', Karen Steffen Chung notes that the earliest linguistic records in China are fifth-millennium BCE symbols on pottery that might be precursors in modern Chinese script; Oracle Bone Inscriptions (*jiǎgǔwén*) from as early as the fourteenth century BCE certainly are. The *Ěryǎ* (second century BCE) explains characters found in earlier texts. Xu Shen's *Shuōwén Jiězì* (121 CE) is China's first dictionary. In Chinese lexica, items are arranged by subject category and usually paired with a phonetically related definition, either a homophone or an alliterative or rhyming gloss; such entries are more useful as a prompt for the correct form of a word than a means to discover meaning. Because Chinese has very little morphological marking, syntacticians from the third century CE simply divided content words from function words. The most notable linguistic event in Korea was the invention in 1446 of *Hangul* to replace Chinese script.

In Chapter 11, 'Linguistics in India', Peter M. Scharf examines the tradition of linguistic analysis that grew up around the preservation of the oral language of the ancient Vedic hymns composed between 1900 and 1100 BCE. In the first millennium BCE commentators often used faulty etymology when interpreting terms in ritual liturgy (something similar happened later in Europe: see Chapters 13 and 24). From the sixth century BCE, systematic analyses of phonetics, phonology, and prosody often reveal dialect variation. Some phoneticians recognized component features of segments as distinct from both articulatory processes and the segments themselves—which directly inspired feature analysis in twentieth-century Europe (see Chapter 8). In the early fourth century BCE, drawing on existing work, Pāṇini composed a precise and fairly complete description of late Vedic Sanskrit. There are phonetic, morphological, syntactic, and semantic rules and conditions, rule ordering, metarules, lexical and phonological lists. Commentaries and developments continued through to the Middle Ages.

In Chapter 12, 'From Semitic to Afro-Asiatic', Edward Lipiński suggests that Proto-Semitic, a branch of Afro-Asiatic, probably originated in the present-day Sahara. Bilingual Semitic word lists date from the third millennium BCE, and tabled equivalences between Sumerian and Akkadian phrases from the eighteenth century BCE. The earliest extant Syriac grammar dates from the late seventh century; the earliest Arabic grammar, that of Sībawayhi, from the eighth century; Hebrew tri-radicalism was noted in the tenth century. In the nineteenth century, decipherment of Egyptian hieroglyphs, Akkadian cuneiform script, and South Arabian and Ugaritic inscriptions was followed by grammatical studies that had a great impact on the analysis and perception of Semitic languages, and research extended to Egyptian connections with Beja and the Ethio-Semitic relations with Cushitic languages of the Horn of Africa.

Part IV consists of nine chapters that narrate the history of grammar and morphology in Europe and North America. The story begins with Chapter 13, 'From Plato to Priscian: Philosophy's Legacy to Grammar' by Catherine Atherton and David Blank. In Ancient Greece, language study grew out of philosophy: language enables truth-bearing presentations of the internal and external world and is also a vehicle of persuasion and education. The basics for the parts of speech can be found in Plato and Aristotle, but it was the Stoics who noted regularities and irregularities indicating underlying rules of grammar and norms of behaviour governing the use of language. In the second century BCE Aristarchus of Samothrace refers to all eight traditional parts of speech and to some of their subcategories; these were propagated in the *Tekhnê grammatikê* (attributed to Dionysius Thrax) which was a model for the pedagogical grammar of Donatus—a cornerstone of Latin instruction throughout the Middle Ages. Although very little original material has survived, the Stoics were a major influence on Varro, Apollonius, and Herodian, and—indirectly—their disciple Priscian[2].

---

[2] Unfortunately there's not a great deal on Priscian in this book; for more extensive treatment see Allan (2010a: 111–27) and references cited there.

Donatus and Priscian figure in Anneli Luhtala's 'Pedagogical Grammars before the Eighteenth Century', Chapter 14. Luhtala identifies four types of word and paradigm grammars in late antiquity. Those, like Donatus' school grammar, cover the parts of speech and are often cast in question-and-answer form. Then there are those, like Priscian's *Institutes*, which closely examine one or more parts of speech. Parsing grammars, which also favour the question–answer method, go for exhaustive analysis of the grammatical properties of words on the model of Priscian's *Partitiones Duodecim Versuum Aeneidos Principalium*. Commentaries undertake critical discussion to flesh out the terse structure of the typical school grammar, enabling new ideas to be launched with the stamp of authority from what was commented upon. The mnemonic value of verse grammars made them popular from the twelfth to sixteenth centuries. A major novelty in the medieval period was the integration into pedagogical grammars of practical techniques for construing and constructing sentences.

Chapter 15, 'Vernaculars and the Idea of a Standard Language' by Andrew Linn, builds on the pedagogical theme of the previous chapter with the idea that underpinning language teaching is a presumption that the goal of learning is mastery of the standard vernacular language alongside, and later in place of, Latin. The oldest grammar of a vernacular is the Irish *Auraicept na n-Éces* 'The Scholar's Primer', perhaps composed in the seventh century, though the oldest surviving manuscript is *c.*1160. Grammars of Italian and Castilian appeared in the fifteenth century, and other languages followed. The Bible was translated into vernacular languages from the fifteenth century.

In Chapter 16, 'Word-Based Morphology from Aristotle to Modern WP (Word and Paradigm Models)', James P. Blevins identifies a tradition that has roots in Ancient Greek and Pāṇini. Both classify words into paradigms in which sub-word elements are inflections; in the western model, no unit intervenes between sound and word. Aristotle and the Alexandrians focused on the systematicity of inflectional morphology, where the Stoics and Varro emphasized the irregularities of derivational morphology. Even though the Neogrammarians recognized morphological roots in the late nineteenth century, they went little further than Priscian (sixth century); there was no advance until the rise of morphemic theory in the early twentieth century. Today, analysis is an interpretive process in which bundles of morphosyntactic features are spelled out by realization rules.

Jaap Maat, in 'General or Universal Grammar from Plato to Chomsky', Chapter 17, reminds us that Plato concluded, after systematically considering the relationships among language, knowledge, and the world, that investigating language is not a suitable method for investigating reality. Aristotle's logic provided a rigorous framework for the analysis of meaning and for studying the relationships between language, mind, and the world. He demonstrated that the structure of meaning will often differ from the structure of language. Most importantly, he pointed the way to universal grammar by pointing out that, though languages may differ, human minds and the world around us are (broadly speaking) the same for all humankind. Scholars in the Middle Ages, assuming that all languages are basically structured in the same way, sought to explain the grammatical categories found in Priscian using Aristotelian notions of universal concepts of reality. These Modistae proposed modes of signifying that specify features of the denotata for the different parts of speech. In 1587 Sanctius proposed his *doctrina supplendi*, an elaborative structure making explicit the meaning of a surface sentence;[3] this idea recurs in the Port-Royal grammar of 1660 on the basis that it is present in the mind—a position later held by Chomsky.

In Chapter 18, 'American Descriptivism ("Structuralism")', James P. Blevins says the 1940s–1950s saw the rise of a distinctive American school of linguistics that emphasized synchronic analysis. Focus shifted from description of languages to the investigation of methods, techniques, and inductive theories about languages. Bloomfield initiated a rigorous methodology and taxonomic representations of language structures that include abstract units as well as segmental material. Post-Bloomfieldians took morphemes to be composed of phonemes, but this was not sanctioned by Bloomfield; the travesty was mitigated by the introduction of morphophonemics. Bloomfield was agnostic about the place of meaning in linguistics, but Harris excluded it completely. It was Harris who defined grammar 'as a set of instructions which generates the sentences of a language' (1954b: 260), and Chomsky who shifted interest from language description to theory construction.

In 'Noam Chomsky's Contribution to Linguistics: A Sketch', Chapter 19, Robert Freidin recounts that Chomsky's work on generative grammar began with his honours thesis in 1949, revised in a master's thesis and developed in *The Logical Structure of Linguistic Theory*, written 1955–6 and amended for publication in 1975. Ever since, Chomsky has continuously revised the formulations and developed his theories of grammar. He has controversially linked his linguistic theory first to psychology and later to biology. From the start he was defining grammar as the recursive specification of a denumerable set of sentences along with their structural descriptions. The Minimalist Program proposes a simplified theory of grammar that presupposes language is a component of the human mind/brain with substantial biolinguistic innate content from Universal Grammar (UG).[4]

Chapter 20, by Giorgio Graffi, surveys 'European Linguistics since Saussure'. Saussure's *Cours de linguistique générale* was reconstructed from student notes in 1916, revised in subsequent editions, and much later augmented by his own rediscovered notes (Engler 1967–74). For Saussure, a linguistic element is structurally and semantically defined in terms of its relations with other elements. Although the Prague School was influenced by Saussure's view of *la langue* as a system of reciprocal values, they also believed that language change is systematic and that at every stage language bears traces of earlier states—in other words, contra Saussure, diachrony is relevant to synchrony (an idea found in Paul 1880). The Prague School distinction between the physical phone and the phoneme as an element of a functional system distinguishes phonetics

---

[3] There is a similar idea in the *Syntax* of Apollonius Dyscolus (2nd century CE): see Chapter 34 below and volume, and Allan (2010a: 106f.).

[4] Kibbee (2010) has some interesting chapters critical of Chomsky, his ideas, and his work.

from phonology (though the insight had occasionally appeared earlier[5]). They emphasized that the functions of language must be accounted for within a grammar. Thereafter European linguistics was fragmented and, with the exception of functonalism, had
little effect on later developments in syntactic or morphological theory.

In Chapter 21, 'Functional and Cognitive Grammars', Anna Siewierska recounts that,
for functionalists (inspired by the Prague School), the communicative function of
language structures grammar; for cognitivists, language reflects the way we conceptualize the world and so create meaning through language. Whereas Chomskyans treat
grammar as autonomous, functionalists and cognitivists believe that cognitive and
discoursal factors shape grammars, both diachronically and synchronically—though
neither camp seeks support from psycholinguistic experimentation. Functional grammars are essentially process-oriented whereas cognitive grammars are construction-
based. In cognitive grammars there is no sharp division between lexicon and syntax:
the notion of construction subsumes all linguistic units irrespective of their size and
complexity.

Part V is concerned with studies of meaning. In several traditions there was
lexicography; semantics was primarily occupied with word meaning and, among
etymologists, lexical networks. The Stoics recognized illocutionary types and, perhaps
under Stoic influence, Apollonius Dyscolus identified the link between clause type,
mood, and illocutionary force (see Chapter 34 and Allan 2010a: ch. 6). Otherwise
the meaning of clauses was the province of logicians rather than grammarians until
the late twentieth century. Also in the late twentieth century, ancient studies of rhetoric
and oratory were supplanted by developments in pragmatics and discourse analysis.

Chapter 22, 'Lexicography from Earliest Times to the Present', by Patrick Hanks,
begins by describing decisions a lexicographer must make when deciding on the
character of an entry: the choice between polysemy and homonymy, how to accommodate nominal phrases, whether to include rare or specialized words, etymological
detail, and/or citations; how should entries should be organized and what metalanguage used? Hanks recounts the history of lexicography and lexicographical method in
China, India, Persia, Greece, Rome, the Semitic world, and Europe, then reviews the
different functions of a dictionary: to be polyglot or monolingual; (supposedly) to act as
a standardizing force for a language; to record language change; or to act as a resource
for language learners.

Chapter 23, 'The Logico-philosophical Tradition', by Pieter A. M. Seuren, opens with
an account of Plato's notion of 'proposition' implicit in the discussion of truth as
correspondence between the idea of an entity and its (not-)being. For Aristotle, the
truth of a proposition is the mental act of assigning properties to entities. Where
Aristotle had a semantic notion of *hupokeímenon* 'subject' and *katēgoroúmenon*
'predicate', when these terms were used by Alexandrine grammarians they became
syntactic constituents. The discourse relevance of such terms came to be recognized

---

[5] According to Allan (2004), as early as Aristotle's *Poetics* (4th century BCE).

again in the later nineteenth century, and then—decades later—the Prague School reinterpreted them in terms of information structure. Aristotle recognized a 'law of the excluded middle' which was questioned in his lifetime by Eubulides, author of some famous paradoxes including the liar paradox and the sorites ('heap') problem. If Aristotle were right and if *the morning star* denotes Venus and *the evening star* also denotes Venus, then *the morning star is the evening star* would be necessarily true; but, as Frege pointed out, this is not so. It led him to separate *Bedeutung* 'extension' from *Sinn* 'intension'. Russell's theory of descriptions led to questions about the nature of presupposition; Geach's rediscovery of Burleigh's donkey sentences led to the invention of Discourse Representation Theory, able to capture the incrementation of information in a system of logic.

In Chapter 24, 'Lexical Semantics from Speculative Etymology to Structuralist Semantics', Dirk Geeraerts dismisses the etymology in Plato's *Cratylus* and Isidore of Seville's *Etymologiae* as speculative guesswork and very often wrong. However, if we understand the Ancient etymologists to be exploring lexical relations rather than undertaking etymology in today's sense, their endeavours seem less absurd. The development of diachronic lexical semantics marks a shift from speculative etymology to comparative historical linguistics. In nineteenth-century Europe, study of the historical development of words and meanings gave rise to dictionaries that charted the development of language.

Chapter 25, 'Post-structuralist and Cognitive Approaches to Meaning', also by Geeraerts, continues the history with Katz and Fodor's introduction of componential analysis into generative grammar that combines 'a structuralist method of analysis, a formalist system of description, and a mentalist conception of meaning'. Geeraerts reviews Wierzbicka's Natural Semantic Metalanguage, Jackendoff's Conceptual Semantics, Pustejovksy's Generative Lexicon, prototype semantics, and frame theory.

According to Jacob L. Mey in Chapter 26, 'A Brief Sketch of the Historic Development of Pragmatics', pragmatics studies acts of linguistic communication in particular social situations, wherein face maintenance is highly important. There is a communicative presumption that if a person is apparently trying to communicate, it is worthwhile to expend effort trying to understand them. The Sophists in Ancient Greece advocated language as a tool for action and not merely a vehicle for truth and falsity. Humboldt, Peirce, Vendryes, and Bühler all emphasized the importance of language in use—which determines truth values and implicatures. The Gricean maxims are practical applications of some of Aristotle's proposals to get an intended meaning across.

Part V ends with 'Meaning in Texts and Contexts' by Linda Waugh et al. This chapter focuses on the switch from the structuralist tradition of sentence-level grammar and concern with lexical meaning (continued in the Chomskyan paradigm) to a consideration of meaning in use within conversations and written texts. The switch was inspired by the ideas of Wittgenstein and speech act theorists, the Prague School functionalists, the work of Firthian contextualists under the banner of Systemic Functional Linguistics, and analysts of real conversations, their structures, and the flow of information within them. This was a coming together of ideas from linguistics, philosophy, sociology, anthropology, ethnomethodology, and later narratology, critical discourse analysis, and the like, so that the wider panoply of linguistic history has come to examine the interplay of speaker/writer, hearer/reader, their belief systems, and the contexts in which language is produced and construed.

Part VI is a historiography of comparative, typological, sociolinguistics, psycho-/ neurolinguistics, computational, and corpus linguistics, translation, and the philosophy of linguistics.

In Chapter 28, 'Comparative, Historical, and Typological Linguistics since the Eighteenth Century', Kurt R. Jankowsky credits Francis Bacon with promulgating practical empiricism over philosophical speculation, and Leibniz with applying this to the study of language. In the late eighteenth century Pallas and Adelung compiled comparative vocabularies and Sir William Jones launched discussion of the relationship of Sanskrit and Persian to European languages. Humboldt thought that the comparison of languages should look beyond vocabulary to the world view of language speakers. Rask, Grimm, Grassmann, and Verner mapped sound changes showing that careful attention to facts reveals regularities and genealogical relationships among languages. Comparative linguistics went hand-in-hand with historical linguistics, which then spawned typological linguistics. The Schlegel brothers and Humboldt began to inquire into morphological typology in the first quarter of the nineteenth century; in the twentieth century Sapir took it up and Greenberg went much further.

In 'Language, Culture, and Society', Chapter 29, Ana Deumert says that sociocultural linguistics emerged in incremental steps. For Humboldt, language is the formative organ of thought, such that cognition and perception are embedded in the inner structure of languages, reflecting a multiplicity of ways of conceptualizing the world around us—an idea that recurs in the Sapir–Whorf hypothesis. Humboldt emphasized individual agency and creativity, but for Whitney, language was consensual within society, a matter taken up by Saussure and others[6]. Dialectology flourished in mid-nineteenth-century Europe and often encompassed social variation. From 1966, Labov's *The Social Stratification of English in New York City* became the model for sociolinguistic methodology.

In Chapter 30, 'Language, the Mind, and the Brain', Alan Garnham reports that the mind/body distinction was made in Plato's *Phaedo*. Aristotle referred to the cognitive mechanisms attendant on language, but neither these nor the crucial role of the brain in mental functioning were investigated until modern times. Brain trauma reveals that some language functions are localized in the left (primary language) hemisphere and some supported in the other hemisphere (usually the right). Brain imaging reveals brain activation in response to language, but there is no evidence at all of a language-dedicated part of the brain and thus no empirical evidence for Chomsky's 'language organ'; furthermore, it has never been explained how such an organ could possibly have evolved. Chomsky also denies that language learning is like other cognitive

[6] See Allan (2010a: 259).

learning systems; however, connectionist experiments and work in AI show that this is probably wrong. Psychologists working within lexical semantics find that meanings are not stored in the mind as abstract symbols but embedded in encyclopedic knowledge; and neurologists find that, for example, when action verbs are understood, areas of the brain that control movement are activated. In other words: cognition is dependent on the way the human body interacts with the rest of the world.

Chapter 31, 'Translation: The Intertranslatability of Languages; Translation and Language Teaching' by Kirsten Malmkjær, shows that functionality is an important part of language learning and understanding. It is uncertain that any two people understand the same thing even if they speak the same language; so although languages are intertranslatable, they are rarely ever precisely equivalent, with poetic and figurative language more difficult to translate than plain language. Translation is possible because meaning is a relation between the utterance and its context, and because humans share mental processes, somatic relations, and the ability to accommodate to the behaviours of others. Translation requires that readers of the target language text respond the same way as readers of the source language text. Malmkjær reports that translation exercises only aid the learning of languages if the learner is persuaded they are purposeful and rewarding.

In 'Computational Linguistics', Chapter 32, Graeme Hirst opens with 'The field of computational linguistics (CL) has its origins in research on machine translation (MT) in the early days of computing in the post-Second World War 1940s.' Except in places like the Cambridge Language Research Unit (founded 1954), assumptions about language structure were naïve. Bar-Hillel said that fully automatic high-quality translation was impossible because of the encyclopedic knowledge needed; this became the standard view from the 1960s. Determining the intent, goals, and plans of a human interlocutor became an important theme in computational linguistics in the mid-1970s. Schank's 'conceptual dependency' and then his 'scripts' sought to solve the problem for artificial intelligence and natural language understanding, which they almost did for tiny fragments of language. Computational linguistics rejects the need for formal syntax and semantics, except lexical meaning and frames, finding greater use for complex representations of encyclopedic knowledge. Google Translate functions on purely statistical criteria.

In Chapter 33, 'The History of Corpus Linguistics', Tony McEnery and Andrew Hardie tell us that corpus linguistics began with the compiling of frequency lists in the late nineteenth century. Field linguists and those studying language acquisition compile corpora, usually very small. Chomsky correctly claimed that no corpus can completely represent a language, but a carefully assembled corpus will contain a representative sample of the language. Corpora often show that reported native intuitions about grammaticality are false. The Brown Corpus assembled before 1964 was one of the first; such early corpora contained little speech data, but recently that has changed. With the increased power of computers and capacity of data storage media, corpora have grown in size so that, today, corpus linguistics has become the computer-assisted analysis of very large bodies of naturally occurring text. Automated tagging has been standard in most corpora since 1971. Corpora are a major resource for lexicographers, functionalists, cognitivists, psycholinguists, and computational linguists; they readily permit cross-language, diachronic, sociolinguistic, and stylistic comparisons to be made.

The 34th and final chapter, 'Philosophy of Linguistics' by Esa Itkonen, retraces, with a different perspective, some of the ground covered elsewhere in the volume. In addition there is a long discussion of Aristotle's syllogistic, which went almost unchallenged for 2,200 years. Whereas Aristotle was interested in language only as medium for logic, poetry, or rhetoric, the Stoics investigated language for its own sake, perhaps influencing the valuable contributions of Varro and Apollonius. Apollonius has a notion of underlying structure being transformed into surface structure, and also an idea very much like that of illocutionary force.[7] In today's re-evaluation of the importance of diachronic linguistics as a means of explaining the connection between successive states of the language, Itkonen sees a return to beliefs similar to those of Schleicher and Paul in the nineteenth century.

That ends my brief overview of all the chapters in the *Oxford Handbook of the History of Linguistics*—with the caveat that the foregoing sketches barely scratch the surface of the treasure to be found in the pages of this volume.

The western tradition in linguistics is substantially sketched in my *The Western Classical Tradition in Linguistics*, 2nd edn (Allan 2010a). Rivals to that include *A Short History of Linguistics* (Robins 1997), *Western Linguistics: An historical Introduction* (Seuren 1998), and *The History of Linguistics in Europe: From Plato to 1600* (Law 2003). Works that go beyond the western tradition include *Universal History of Linguistics: India, China, Arabia, Europe* (Itkonen 1991), *Concise History of the Language Sciences: From the Sumerians to the Cognitivists* (Koerner and Asher 1995) and the three-volume *History of the Language Sciences* (Auroux et al. 2000–2006). There are, of course, many other highly respected works referred to elsewhere in the *Oxford Handbook of the History of Linguistics*—which I confidently and unreservedly recommend to the reader.

Keith Allan
Sunshine Coast, Australia
April 2012

---

[7] See also Householder (1981); Allan (2010a: ch. 6).

CHAPTER 1

....

THE ORIGINS AND THE EVOLUTION OF LANGUAGE

....

SALIKOKO S. MUFWENE

1.1 INTRODUCTION[1]

....

ALTHOUGH 'language evolution' is perhaps more commonly used in linguistics than 'evolution of language', I stick in this chapter to the latter term, which focuses more specifically on the phylogenetic emergence of language. The former, which has prompted some linguists such as Croft (2008) to speak of 'evolutionary linguistics', applies also to changes undergone by individual languages over the past 6,000 years of documentary history, including structural changes, language speciation, and language birth and death. There are certainly advantages in using the broader term, especially to uniformitarians who argue that some of the same evolutionary mechanisms are involved in both the phylogenetic and the historical periods of evolution. For instance, natural selection driven by particular ecological pressures putatively applies in both periods, and social norms emerge by the same principle of the 'invisible hand' or 'self-organization' (e.g. Hurford 2006, Mufwene 2008). However, I focus here only on phylogenetic evolution.

In this chapter I provide a selective history, since antiquity, of this complex but still largely speculative topic which, over the past two decades alone, has prompted numerous publications and has aroused much controversy among linguists and informative exchanges between them, primatologists, psycholinguists, anthropologists, neurolinguists, evolutionary biologists, paleontologists, and computational linguists. This

[1] I wrote this chapter while I was a fellow at the Collegium de Lyon, from 15 Sept. 2010 to 15 July 2011. I am very grateful to the Institute and its administrative staff for the financial and logistic support that enabled me to pursue my research on the phylogenetic emergence of language. I am also indebted to Keith Allan, Barbara Davis, Paul Keyser, and Ioana Chitoran for constructive comments on my first draft. I am alone responsible for all the remaining shortcomings.

intellectual engagement has been in sharp contrast with most of the twentieth century, during which linguists appear to have abided by the the Société de Linguistique de Paris' 1866 ban on discussing the subject at its meetings. It appears also to have resurrected several positions by—and controversies among—especially eighteenth- and nineteenth-century European philosophers and philologists. I show below that the differences between the two periods lie especially in the stronger empirical founda- tions of some recent hypotheses, and in the realization by their authors of the need for interdisciplinary scholarship.

My discussion is organized around the following questions (which do not necessarily determine the section structure of the chapter):

1. Was language given to humans by God or did it emerge by Darwinian evolution?
2. From a phylogenetic perspective, did language emerge abruptly or gradually? If the emergence of language was protracted, what plausible intermediate stages can be posited and what would count as evidence for positing them? Assuming that the structure of modern languages is modular, would gradual evolution apply to any of the modules, only to some of them, or only to the overall architecture? What is the probable time of the emergence of the first real ancestor of modern language?
3. Does possessing Language, the non-individuated construct associated exclusively with humans, presuppose monogenesis or does it allow for polygenesis? How consistent is either position with paleontological evidence about the evolution of the *Homo* genus? How did linguistic diversity start? Assuming Darwinian (vari- ational rather than transformational) evolution, can monogenesis account for typological variation as plausibly as polygenesis?
4. What is the chronological relationship between communication and language? What light does this distinction shed on the relation between sign(ed) and spoken language? Did some of our hominin ancestors communicate by means of ape-like vocalizations and gestures? If so, how can we account for the transition from them to phonetic and signed languages? And how can we account for the fact that modern humans have favoured speaking over signing? Assuming that language is a communication technology, to what extent are some of the structural properties of languages consequences of the linearity imposed by the phonic and signing devices used in their architecture?
5. Is the evolution of language more biological than cultural? Or is it the other way around, or equally both? Are languages as cultural artifacts deliberate inventions or emergent phenomena? Who are the agents in the emergence of language: individuals or populations, or both?
6. What is the relationship between language and thought? Did these entities co-evolve or did one cause the other?
7. Is there such a thing as 'language organ' or 'biological endowment for language'? How can it be characterized relative to modern humans' anatomical and/or

mental makeups? What are the anatomical, mental, and social factors that facilitated the emergence of language?

8. Can we learn something about the evolution of language from historical language change, especially from the emergence of creoles and pidgins? Can we learn something from child language and/or from home sign language? And what can be learned from 'linguistic apes'? Does it make sense to characterize these particular communicative 'systems' as fossils of the human protolanguage (cf. e.g. Bickerton 1990)? In the same vein, what can modelling contribute to understanding the evolution of language. This is definitely the kind of thing that scholars could not do before the twentieth century; it is important to assess its heuristic significance.

As noted by Kirby (2007), the subject matter of the origins and evolution of language is very complex. It lies at the intersection of several academic disciplines and requires an interdisciplinary approach. I have listed all the above questions, which are still but a subset of the larger range of questions one can address in a book, so that the reader may empathize with the daunting task I have accepted in writing this synopsis, and appreciate the synthetic approach I adopt in focusing on noteworthy positions and issues, aiming at the big picture. Unfortunately, this strategy entails omitting many equally relevant references, aside from forcing me to be topically selective. The positions of the scholars I discuss may not even be presented in their entirety, due largely to space limitations. More interested readers are encouraged to read recent publications such as Fitch (2010) and Hombert and Lenclud (in press) for complementary and/or alternative accounts. I must also apologize for focusing exclusively on Western scholarship, which reflects my embarrassing ignorance of the other traditions. I will seek no excuse for the fact that European colonial expansion, which has shaped me intellectually, has generally downplayed what we could be learning from the other scholarly traditions.

1.2 A HISTORICAL SYNOPSIS

Speculations about the origins of language and linguistic diversity date from far back in the history of mankind. Among the most cited cases is the book of Genesis, in the Judeo-Christian Bible. After God created Adam, He reportedly gave him authority to name every being that was in the Garden of Eden. Putatively, God and Adam spoke some language, the original language, which some scholars have claimed to be Hebrew, the original language of Bible. Adam named every entity God wanted him to know; and his wife and descendants accordingly learned the names he had invented.

Although the story suggests the origin of naming conventions, it says nothing about whether Adam named only entities or also actions and states. In any case, it suggests that it was necessary for Adam's wife and descendants to learn the same vocabulary to facilitate successful communication.

Up to the eighteenth century, reflecting the impact of Christianity, pre-modern Western philosophers and philologists typically maintained that language was given to mankind, or that humans were endowed with language upon their creation. Assuming that Eve, who was reportedly created from Adam's rib, was equally endowed with (a capacity for) language, the rest was a simple history of learning the original vocabulary or language. Changes needed historical accounts, grounded in natural disasters, in population dispersals, and in learning with modification, to which I return below.

The book of Genesis also deals with the origin of linguistic diversity, in the myth of the Tower of Babel (11: 5–8), in which the multitude of languages is treated as a form of punishment from God. According to the myth, the human population had already increased substantially, generations after the Great Deluge in the Noah's Ark story. To avoid being scattered around the world, they built a city with a tower tall enough to reach the heavens, the dwelling of God. The tower apparently violated the population structure set up at the creation of Adam and Eve. God brought them down (according to some versions, He also destroyed the tower), dispersed them around the world, and confounded them by making them speak in mutually unintelligible ways. Putatively, this is how linguistic diversity began.[2] The story suggests that sharing the same language fosters collaboration, contrary to some of the modern Darwinian thinking that joint attention and cooperation, rather than competition, facilitated the emergence of language (see e.g. Tomasello 2008).

Another story often reported in linguistics is the following:

> According to Herodotus (*Histories* 2.2) Pharaoh Psammetichus I [also known as Psamtik, of the 26th dynasty, seventh century BC] wanted to determine the oldest nation and establish the world's original language. For this purpose, he ordered two children to be reared by a shepherd, forbidding him to let them hear a single word, and charging him to report the children's first utterance. After two years, the shepherd reported that on entering their chamber, the children came up to him, extending their hands, calling *bekos*. Upon enquiry, the pharaoh discovered that this was the Phrygian word for 'wheat bread', after which the Egyptians conceded that the Phrygian nation was older than theirs. (*Wikipedia*, Jan. 2011)

The story may be interpreted to suggest monogenesis, according to which a single language was the ultimate ancestor of all modern languages. This would correspond to a protolanguage, such as proto-Bantu or proto-Indo-European, in genetic linguistics. However, this is not the theme we find in Plato's *Cratylus*, which focuses on how the

---

[2] Hombert and Lenclud (in press) identify another, less well-recalled account also from the book of Genesis. God reportedly told Noah and his children to be fecund and populate the world. Subsequently, the descendants of Sem, Cham, and Japhet spread all over the world and built nations where they spoke different languages. Here one also finds an early, if not the earliest, version of the assumption that every nation must be identified through the language spoken by its population.

first words emerged (in Greek). According to the dialogue with two disciples, Cratylus and Hermogenes, Socrates (the teacher and Plato's mouthpiece) claims that names originally captured the essence of the entities they denote; transmission from generation to generation has affected their transparency, making them (rather) opaque, reducing them to conventional, arbitrary signs. Opaqueness is accordingly more obvious in words borrowed from other languages, then considered 'barbarous,' especially since their roots are harder to trace. Socrates' comparison of the putative initial baptismal practice with the work of a painter makes his account a precursor of modern synesthetic approach, as he associates particular sounds with specific meanings. He thus anticipated some eighteenth- and nineteenth-century philologists who saw the origins of language in 'natural sounds' produced by animals and other entities in nature.

Anticipating Johann Gottfried Herder, Socrates rejects the hypothesis that names had divine origins because, according to him, they are so imperfect that they could not have been made by the gods. The *Cratylus* is also one of the earliest works that associate language change with imperfect learning and language contact. The latter phenomenon complicates the evolutionary trajectories of particular languages, which, in contemporary metalanguage, need not be considered as unilinear.

Recently, the significance of population movements and language contacts in the evolution and diversification of languages has been underscored especially by Cavalli-Sforza (2000). Assuming that the exodus of *Homo sapiens sapiens* out of East Africa was protracted, he argues that some of the later migrant populations came in contact with earlier ones. Though he says nothing about monogenesis vs polygenesis, the idea appears to be that the original language changed as human populations migrated away from the homeland. Later contacts between the dispersing populations produced even more changes. No more reason other than population dispersal is given for the change, which is also problematic in typical accounts of speciation in language families such as Bantu and Indo-European.

The dominant trend in genetic linguistics, which inspired Cavalli-Sforza (2000) but had been disputed by Trubetzkoy (1939), has indeed been for monogenesis, positing a proto-language from which all the members of a language family can be derived. This account of the evolution of language has also been adopted in particular by Ruhlen (1994), who attempted to reconstruct the ultimate phylogenetic protolanguage since *Homo sapiens*, on the model of proto-Indo-European or proto-Bantu. This 'protolanguage,' identified by some as 'proto-world,' should not be confused with the 'protolanguage' (without a hyphen) posited by Bickerton (e.g. 1990) and discussed below.

Writing in the first century BC, the Roman poet and philosopher Titus Lucretius Carus questioned one particular brand of monogenesis that is not necessarily Adamic:

> [...] to think that one individual then distributed names to things and that humans learned the first words from him is absurd. For why would he be able to mark everything with utterances and emit different sounds of the tongue, and at the same time others not being capable of having done it? Besides, if others too had not

used their voices with one another, from where was the notion of utility implanted, and from where was this power first granted to him, to know what he wanted to do and conceive of it in his mind? Similarly, one person could not have prevailed and forced so many to want to learn the names of things so thoroughly [. . .] (Lucretius Carus 2003 [?54 BC]: ll. 1041–51).

Lucretius thereby suggests that language emerged and evolved from the collective communicative acts of individuals interacting with each other. We may, in modern terms, think of different interactants innovating on different occasions and the successful innovations being copied by others. This is the position articulated by Michel Bréal in the late nineteenth century (see below), in contrast with the vast majority of scholars who have simply ignored the question.

There doesn't seem to have been much speculation on the origins of language since Lucretius until the eighteenth century, 'the (Age of) Enlightenment.' The contribution of the Renaissance period appears to be negligible, as the focus was on (the logic of) the structure of language, epitomized by the Port-Royal Grammar, published in 1660 by Claude Lancelot and Antoine Arnauld. It's not evident what the reason for this return to the subject matter of the origins of language was, except perhaps that the post-Renaissance social philosophers, so interested in defending the natural rights of people and freeing fellow citizens from superstition and the creationist dogma of Christianity, may have wanted also to have a better understanding of the origins of mankind. Convinced that rationality distinguishes mankind from other animals, they were interested in the apparent chicken-and-egg connection between humans' mental capacity and language.

A name that was particularly influential in the eighteenth century was Étienne Bonnot de Condillac, who, according to Aarsleff (1982), then launched debates on the origins of language with his *Essai sur l'origine des connoissances humaines* (1746). He argued that language is a consequence of humans' being rational and needing this tool to express their thoughts. Although he saw language as constrained by its phonetic architecture to linearize thought, he also claimed that language gives more structure to thought processes and is the foundation of (the growth of) human knowledge. This sounds similar to Bickerton's (e.g. 1990) claim that the emergence of language, especially syntax, enhanced human capacity for thought (see below).[3]

Contrary to the received doctrine of the Catholic Church, the dominant one at his time, Condillac, an abbot, concluded that language was man-made, the product of humans' capacity for creative thought, and not God-given, a position adopted by other eighteenth century philosophers. He is also reported to have contributed to, if not started, the hypothesis that language emerged from natural cries. Although it would be derided by Friedrich Max Müller in the nineteenth century (see below), this position addresses the question of how humans evolved from the mere production of 'natural

---

[3] Yet one can argue that syntax, also phonology and morphology, are just a consequence of linearity, constrained though it is by other, cognitive or pragmatic factors.

cries,' identified today as holistic vocalizations, to phonetic ones, which Condillac characterized as 'vocal signs,' at least according to Aarsleff (1982). This is a question that still awaits a conclusive answer (see esp. Wray 2002, Tallerman 2007, and Bickerton 2010) and on which MacNeilage (2008) contributes some significant insights (see below).

The hypothesis that the original ancestor of language lies in the natural cries and gestures was also developed by Jean-Jacques Rousseau in his 1755 essay on the origin of language, in *Discours sur l'origine et les fondements de l'inégalité parmi les hommes*. For him, cries and gestures are the language most expressive of humans' passions, which dominated in the earliest phylogenetic stages of mankind. The evidence can allegedly still be found in 'savage' or less advanced populations, particularly in southerly, warmer climates, where humans are, according to him, closer to nature. It is not that those populations are still in the primordial or less evolved stages of human evolution,

> the order of their progress is different. In southern climates, where nature is bountiful, needs are born of passion. In cold countries, where she is miserly, passions are born of need, and the languages, sad daughters of necessities, reflect their austere origin. (1755; Moran and Gode's translation, 1966: 46)

According to Rousseau, the passions are still best expressed through tones (and intonation) and gestures, and thus in tonal languages. However, 'while visible signs can render a more exact imitation, sounds more effectively arouse interest' (Moran and Gode 1966: 9), which is why, as communication became less and less passionate and more and more referential/rational, speech prevailed as a means of communication. Like most philosophers and philologists of the eighteenth century, Rousseau did not realize that tones play a contrastive lexical and/or grammatical function in many languages, although this is not the case in most European languages. On the other hand, like some modern students of the origins of language (e.g. Tomasello 2008, MacNeilage 2008, Corballis 2010, Dor and Jablonka 2010, Mufwene 2010b), Rousseau also assumed that modern language emerged under social ecological pressures, especially out of the need to help each other understand what they had to do in order to survive danger (pp. 47–8). On the other hand, unlike today's scholars, Rousseau interpreted evolution as progress towards a more explicit architecture meant to express reason more than emotion. According to him,

> Anyone who studies the history and progress of tongues will see that the more words become monotonous, the more consonants multiply; that, as accents fall into disuse and quantities are neutralized, they are replaced by grammatical combinations and new articulations. [...] To the degree that needs multiply [...] language changes its character. It becomes more regular and less passionate. It substitutes ideas for feelings. It no longer speaks to the heart but to reason. (Moran and Gode 1966: 16)

Thus, Rousseau interpreted the evolution of language as gradual, reflecting changes in the *Homo* genus's mental, social, and environmental structures. He also suggests that consonants emerged after vowels (at least some of them), out of necessity to keep 'words' less 'monotonous.' Consonants would putatively have made it easier to identify transitions from one syllable to another. He speaks of 'break[ing] down the speaking voice into a given number of elementary parts, either vocal or articulate [i.e. consonantal?], with which one can form all the words and syllables imaginable' (p. 17). This account appears to anticipate Peter MacNeilage's notion of 'syllabic variegation' (see below).

Like his contemporaries and predecessors, Rousseau did not (always) distinguish sounds from the letters, but he also had curious positions about the latter. He associated pictographic writing with 'a savage people, signs of words and propositions [with] a barbaric people, and the alphabet [with] civilized peoples' (p. 17).

This stratification of populations was a common belief until the early twentieth century (see below). However, it is not out of place to discuss, in the context of the evolution of language and of writing systems as technology designed to overcome some of the shortcomings of speech and signing. Writing does not just extend our capacity to remember and carry to longer distances what was or could have been spoken or signed. For instance, Chinese ideograms are additionally efficient in enabling speakers of mutually unintelligible Sinitic language varieties to understand each other. In this particular respect, they also illustrate why evolution should not be thought of in rectilinear and unilinear terms, as there is room for variation. While alphabetic writing systems, designed to capture speech, may be preferred (by the principles of economy and productivity) for their simplicity, they cannot accomplish the role Chinese ideograms play in bridging dialectal differences with regard to meaning. Scholars who think of language as technology (Smith and Szathmáry 1999, Lee et al. 2009, Mufwene 2010a) will hail Rousseau for bringing writing as derivative technology into the picture. It's undoubtedly also relevant to ask to what extent writing has influenced language evolution during the historical period (Wang 2011).

Rousseau questioned the Adamic hypothesis on the origins of modern language, arguing that the language that God had taught Adam and was learned by the children of Noah perished after the latter abandoned agriculture and scattered. Modern language is therefore a new invention (Moran and Gode 1966: 36). Rousseau may have been concerned more about the diversification of the language that Noah's children had spoken before they dispersed than about the origins of language itself. He assumed the speciation to have happened before the Tower of Babel explanation in the Judeo-Christian tradition.

Language diversification is a topic that has not been sufficiently discussed in today's literature on the evolution of language(s). The focus has typically been language as a common endowment of all humans, thus obviating the question of whether the origins of modern languages were monogenetic or polygenetic. If they evolved ultimately from one language, was this original language internally variable or not? Accounts of how linguistic diversity emerged should vary, depending on whether one assumes monogenesis without internal variation or polygenesis with the possibility of variation from one hominin colony to another.

It is thus noteworthy that, unlike most of his contemporaries and somewhat anticipating variational evolutionary theory, Rousseau also addressed the question of the consequences of inter-idiolectal variation in the emergence of language as a communal phenomenon:

> [E]ach individual is unique, possessed of, even in some ways identical with, his own nature or 'essence' while participating in the whole of nature, the whole of reality, so speak. In so far as there is plurality of individuals, and one individual (or group) practices any of the arts on others, there is a basis for contrasting nature (the nature of one) and art (the art of another). (Moran and Gode 1966: 76)

In modern terms, every idiolect differs from others. This situation raises the interesting question of how they converge toward the same communal norm (Mufwene 2008, 2010b). Does normalization as emergence of a communal norm entail elimination, or just reduction, of variation? What does it really mean when two or more individuals are said to speak the same language? One should also ask: what role has inter-idiolectal variation played in the evolution of language?

A contemporary of Jean-Jacques Rousseau, the German philologist Johann Gottfried Herder contributed to the debates on some of the above issues, with his *Über den ursprung der Sprache* (1772), translated and published in Moran and Gode (1966) as *Essay on the origin of language* (which is cited here). Herder especially argued that human language was not God-given, and that it started in animal communication (p. 94). Like Lucretius, he thought that even Hebrew, assumed then to be the oldest language, was too imperfect to be God's creation (pp. 94, 96), though he could have made allowance for change, which normally disturbs the original design, over time. Likewise, he observed:

> Now trace, if you can, divine order in the fact that a god, who saw the plan of language as a whole, invented seventy words for the stone and none for all the indispensable ideas, innermost feelings, and abstractions, that in one case he drowned us in unnecessary abundance while leaving us in the other in the direst need which obliged us to steal and usurp metaphors and talk half nonsense, etc. (p. 153)

The distribution of the vocabulary within and across languages appeared to Herder to be too inconsistent for the latter to be God's creation(s). Like Rousseau, he concluded that such varying reality could only reflect the work of mankind.

Herder was ambivalent about the origins of language. On the one hand, he argued against Rousseau's and Condillac's position that it evolved from emotional cries (p. 102). On the other, he admitted that it may have started as animal-like cries, with the difference that human utterances in the form of speech are volitional and driven by reason (p. 99). He concludes several pages later that early human language 'was an expression of the language of all creatures within the natural scale of the human voice' (p. 137).

Herder also argued that knowledge of particular languages is not instinctive; the child learns the language of its social environment. Anticipating modern linguists, he clarified that what is being discussed is the capacity for language, what Ferdinand de Saussure referred to as the *faculté de langage* and generativists as Universal Grammar or biological endowment for language. He observed that this capacity, which is also shared by the deaf (p. 118), enables humans to learn naturalistically, through interactions or by immersion, whatever language they have been exposed to. This of course leaves unanswered the question of how in the first place this particular capacity for language evolved in mankind and in what form. It also leaves open the question of how particular languages displaying both structural diversity and common/universal features evolved (see below).

Herder also speculated that language started with the practice of naming. He claimed that predicates, which denote activities and conditions, were the first names; nouns were derived from them (pp. 132, 160). He thus partly anticipated Heine and Kuteva (2007), who argue that grammar emerged gradually, through the grammaticization of nouns and verbs into grammatical markers, including complementizers, which make it possible to form complex sentences. An issue arising from Herder's position is whether nouns and verbs could not have emerged concurrently. Not quite in the same way, Allan (2010a: 230) comments that Herder was more concerned with proving that 'God could not have invented human language because, as the Western Classical Tradition affirms, the logical order is to name entities first and then predicate acts and attributes of them.'

On the other hand, as hypothesized by William Dwight Whitney (discussed below), the original naming practice need not have entailed the distinction between nouns and verbs and the capacity to predicate. At that time, naming may have amounted to pointing with (pre-)linguistic signs; predication may have started only after hominins were capable of describing states of affairs compositionally, combining word-size units in this case, rather than holophrastically. This issue cannot be addressed independently of what Bickerton's (1990) 'protolanguage' is and when it may have emerged. The question of the order in which other grammatical categories emerged remains open, there being no conclusive evidence in support of the particular order proposed by Heine and Kuteva (2007). In any case, Herder also argued that language was 'the child of reason and society' (p. 91). He thought that 'vowels are the first, the most vital things, the hinges of language' (p. 95), which appears to suggest evolution from primate-like vocalizations.

Another important philosopher of the eighteenth century was Pierre Louis Moreau de Maupertuis, author of *Réflexions sur l'origine des langues et la vie des mots* (1748). Among other things, he sought to answer the question of whether modern languages can ultimately be traced back to one single common ancestor or whether current diversity reflects polygenesis, with different populations developing their own languages. Associating monogenesis with the Tower of Babel myth, which needs a *deus ex machina*, God, to account for the diversification of languages, he rejected it in favour of polygenesis. Note, however, that his position needs Cartesianism, which assumes that all humans are endowed with the same mental capacity and suggests that our hominin ancestors could have invented similar communicative technologies at the same or similar stages of our phylogenetic evolution. This position makes it natural to project the existence of language as the common essence of languages beyond their differences. Saussure (1962 [1916]) may be credited with similar thinking when he observed that *le langage* 'language' is heteroclitic, anterior to languages and more natural than them, and yet deriving its unity from the latter (pp. 25–26). These considerations provide the background for speaking of universals in the architecture of language and of (constraints on) parametric typological variation.

In the nineteenth century, scholarship on the origins of language was enriched with an alternative perspective. Charles Darwin commented in *The Descent of Man* (1871) that the evolution of language was in several ways reminiscent of that of mankind itself. He hypothesized that it had emerged gradually, had not been given by God or invented by design by humans, and could also be explained by natural selection. He was among the first to correlate the evolution of language with that of the human mind (see also Müller 1880 [1861]), thus accounting for why parrots cannot produce original spoken messages intentionally, although they can imitate human speech fairly accurately. Showing what an important driver role the human mind has played in the evolution of language, he argued that it was for the same reason that other primates do not use their buccopharyngeal structure to speak.

We now know that Charles Darwin was only partly right. The other primates' buccopharyngeal structure is not shaped in exactly the same way as that of humans, although, based on the parrot's phonetic accomplishments, we must wonder how critical this particular structure was for the emergence of language (not speech!) in the first place. After all, humans who cannot speak produce signed language, which is just as adequate for communication. This argument may be claimed to support the position that the emergence of the capacity for language must be distinguished from the emergence of languages. However, one must also wonder whether the two questions can be considered independently of each other (see below).

On the other hand, like eighteenth-century philosophers, Charles Darwin also claimed that complex thought could not 'be carried on without the aid of words.' Many modern linguists doubt that the language of thought is structured just like spoken or signed language. It does not appear to be constrained by linearity (see below). In fact, in its most fundamental form it does not appear to depend on these communication media and is ontologically anterior to them. Just because the language of fundamental thought is probably structured differently, it does not follow that it is less complex than spoken or signed language. The evidence appears to be lacking regarding the role that speech and signing allegedly play in structuring human thinking. It seems so natural to claim that complex language evolved in response to the communicative needs of social minds that were becoming more and more complex.

Charles Darwin should be credited for subsuming the topic of language vitality, as it should be under the umbrella of language evolution (Mufwene 2001, 2008). He paid attention to the spread of some languages at the expense of others, a topic that linguistics has dealt with recently under the heading of 'language endangerment.' However, he also thought of some populations and their languages as less evolved than others, although he did not establish any obvious correlation between the alleged less evolved populations and less evolved languages. This is a recurrent claim throughout the eighteenth and nineteenth centuries, whereby non-Europeans are often described as 'savages' and the position of their languages on a putative evolutionary trajectory as 'primitive,' simply because their morphologies are too complex (the case of agglutinating and polysynthetic languages), or they have no morphophonology (the case of isolating languages), and/or they are tonal. Though Charles Darwin also concluded that races are probably the counterparts of subspecies in biology, he was still a prisoner of the social prejudices of his time (Mufwene 2008: ch. 6). His hypotheses on the evolution of language were thus tainted by them.

It is worth mentioning in this context the contribution that George Howard Darwin, Charles Darwin's son and an accomplished astronomer and mathematician, made to the subject of the evolution of language. He defended his father and Dwight Whitney against Friedrich Max Müller, both of whose views are discussed below. In his essay titled 'Professor Whitney on the Origin of Language' (1874), George Darwin especially supported the idea that human language may have started from 'the imitational and interjectional sources of [Aryan] roots,' that the number of initial roots must have been very small at the early stages of true language and everything else developed later. He elaborates:

> It is surely probable that many generations of quasi-men passed away, who used a small vocabulary of conventionalised cries, that these cries became more and more conventionalised, by departing more and more from the sounds of exclamations, from which they took their origin. Many roots would probably propagate themselves by fission, and give rise to new roots, gradually to become entirely separate from their onomatopoeic originals. (Harris and Pyle 1996: 288)

Max Müller had ridiculed as 'bow-wow theory' the hypothesis that human language had started from imitations of animal sounds, interjections, etc. In his essay titled 'The theoretical stage and the origin of language' (1861), Müller argues that what distinguishes humans from other animals is not so much speech but the 'inward faculty which is called the faculty of abstraction, [. . .] which is better known to us by the homely name of Reason.' Against Charles Darwin's unjustified assertion that there are languages without abstract terms (of course spoken by 'savages'), he observes that every (denoting?) word 'contains a predicative root' which 'expresses a general concept' (Harris and Pyle 1996: 197). Against the 'bow-wow theory,' Müller argues that although there are interjections and onomatopoeic terms in every language, 'as yet no language has been discovered that was so formed.' According to him, 'interjections are only the outskirts of real language,' which begins where they end (Harris and Pyle 1996: 23). Although it is conceivable that 'some kind of language might have been formed' based on onomatopoeias and interjection, it could not have been 'a language like that which we find in numerous varieties among all races of men' (p. 24).

In his 1873 'Lectures on Mr. Darwin's Philosophy of Language,' Müller is undecided about whether the roots emerged in a protracted fashion or all at the same time. His overall position raises the question of when grammar emerged in the phylogeny of human language and whether, in the first place, our hominin ancestors were capable of producing phonetic sounds at the time they developed the initial vocabulary. Nonetheless, the original roots evolved gradually into the vocabulary of modern spoken languages, some of them becoming grammatical terms, as argued today by Heine and Kuteva (2007).[4]

On the other hand, Müller also thought that some languages are primitive and simpler, especially those with an isolating morphosyntax. Within the context of complexity/simplicity in language, this is fundamentally the thesis defended recently by McWhorter (1998, 2001), according to whom creoles are not only young languages but also the world's simplest. According to the latter, creole 'prototypes' lack derivations, inflections, and tones, all being features that older languages have putatively acquired through much longer histories of evolution and accretion. Independent of the forceful and extensive rebuttal provided by DeGraff (2001), how ironical it is that, for reasons that are no sounder, much of the eighteenth- and nineteenth-century literature on the evolution of language considered inflections and tones to be primitive features! As we will see soon in the discussion of Otto Jespersen's views, creoles could thus be considered more evolved than their European lexifiers and other languages.

Objecting to Charles Darwin's hypothesis that human languages, like different races of man, have evolved from a common ancestor, Müller (1873) states:

> [B]ecause the merest tyro in anatomy knew that the different races of man constituted so many species, that species were the result of independent creative acts, and that the black, brown, red, yellow, and white races could not possibly be conceived as descended from one source. (Harris and Pyle 1996: 175)

This remark is reminiscent of objections made by some scholars such as Maine (1875) and Freeman (1881, 1886) to Sir William Jones's 1786 hypothesis that Sanskrit, Greek, Latin, and other Indo-European languages had all evolved ultimately from the same protolanguage, Proto-Indo-European. They thought that the Indians were too 'barbaric' to share genetic ancestry, racially and linguistically, with Europeans. Otherwise, Müller's objection conjures up the question of whether monogenesis and transformational evolution, as typically suggested in linguistics, can account adequately for the emergence of linguistic diversity, especially if no allowance is made for internal variation in the protolanguage *à la* Bickerton (1990). In this respect, modern linguists would be remiss to overlook the fact that Charles Darwin invoked natural selection as applying to variation which he assumed to obtain in any population (see below).

---

[4] Note that, although the book is titled *The Genesis of Grammar*, Heine and Kuteva offer no plausible hypothesis of how the overall grammar evolved, beyond the emergence of free grammatical morphemes and a few inflections.

Müller thought that 'collateral development' (polygenesis) was more likely to account for some of the differences between dialects and languages. According to him, there is no reason why different individuals at different places and/or different times would have solved the same communicative challenges in identical ways, even when they are endowed with the same 'instinct, gift, talent, faculty, *proprium*' for language (1873: 228–9). He was clearly not Cartesian! Nonetheless, he maintained that language was a means 'for the formation of thought' (pp. 231–2), oddly in agreement with Darwin in this case.

Müller was also strongly opposed to the hypothesis that humans are phylogenetically related to the great apes and monkeys. He concluded that Darwin must have been confused, ignoring the fact that human language is unattainable by other animals (p. 183). The question is whether this state of affairs is a consequence of Müller's suggestion that the great apes are not phylogenetically related to humans. One wonders what he would think of today's attempts to get some great apes to communicate with humans in approximations of sign language or with lexigrams, or even of claims that they understand speech.

Like Jean-Jacques Rousseau, Müller stipulated a distinction between 'emotional language' and 'rational language.' Accordingly, the former is something that humans share with animals and in which imitations of 'natural cries' fit, whereas the latter is the outer side of the mind and is unique to mankind. Müller was curious how one may account for the evolution from 'emotional' to the 'rational language' (1873: 225). This question has remained hard to answer, though one may suggest that our hominin ancestors may have started with modulating their vocalizations into sequences of contrasting syllabic peaks, thus producing different vowels. However, as discussed below, more was involved in the process; we need to learn from paleontology and other relevant disciplines about how we evolved mentally, anatomically, and socially from *Homo habilis* to *Homo sapiens sapiens* to be able to account adequately for the transition.

William Dwight Whitney responded to Müller in his article titled 'Nature and Origin of Language' (1875), by first articulating a distinction between the 'capacity for language,' with which every normal human is endowed, and 'speech.' The critical point is that the 'capacity' has made it possible for humans to develop language or learn whatever is spoken and/or signed in their social environment. This 'capacity' distinguishes mankind from animals, although, as recent findings about bird songs have made clear (e.g. Margoliash 2010), the observation should be mitigated (see below). Whitney argues that 'the only conscious motive' for developing language was communication, which is certainly at odds with Bickerton's (1990) claim that it was made to enhance human capacity for thought. Then he reformulates the 'bow-wow theory' as follows:

> Spoken language began [. . .] when a cry of pain, formerly wrung out by real suffering, and seen to be understood and sympathized with, was repeated in

imitation, no longer as a mere instinctive utterance, for the purpose of intimating to another, 'I am (was, shall be) suffering.' (Harris and Pyle 1996: 298)

Whitney thus saw the foundations of language in the intentional use of the cries and other sounds. Then he proceeded to address the question of how spoken language has emerged as the dominant mode of explicit communication in mankind:

> [I]t is simply by a kind of process of natural selection and survival of the fittest that the voice has gained the upper hand, and come to be so much the most prominent that we give the name of *language* ('tonguiness') to all expression. There is no mysterious connection between the thinking apparatus and the articulating apparatus, whereby the action that forms a thought sets the tongue swinging to utter it. (Harris and Pyle 1996: 300)

As we shall see below, 'natural selection' is not much of an explanation if one does not mention the factors that influenced the resolution of the competition in this particular direction. On the other hand, like Charles Darwin, Whitney seems also influenced by the social prejudice of his time, as in the following passage that should not resonate well to speakers of tone languages:

> [T]one, and still more gesture, has assumed the subordinate office of aiding the effectiveness of what is uttered. And the lower the intellectual condition of the speaker and the spoken-to, the more indispensable is the addition of tone and gesture. (Harris and Pyle 1996: 302)

The bias against non-Indo-Europeans is equally strong in the following passage:

> An infinity of things can be said in English which cannot be said in Fijian or Hottentot; a vast deal, doubtless, can be said in Fijian or Hottentot which could not be said in the first human language. (Harris and Pyle 1996: 307)

A great deal can be said in Fijian, Hottentot, and other non-European languages that cannot be said in European languages either, just as there are things that can be said in English but cannot be readily expressed in French, for instance, and vice versa. Whitney also claimed that the earliest form of linguistic communication must have been holographic, consisting of one-word utterances, without a formal distinction between entities and actions; parts of speech and predication emerged later, and even later the combinations of words belonging in different lexical categories into complex utterances (Harris and Pyle 1966: 306, 308). As noted above, this comes as an apt rejoinder to Herder's speculations, although, as with everything else, this must be verified by future research. Like his contemporaries, Whitney thought that inflectional or fusional languages represent a high level of 'cultivation.' However, he also thought of the evolution of language as the 'accidental [. . .] product of forces and circumstances so numerous and so indeterminable that we cannot estimate them and could not have predicted their result' (pp. 312–13). In this respect, he is like today's emergentists, for whom evolution is largely driven by self-organization.

Several other scholars, many of them anonymous, published on the origins of language in the nineteenth century. One of the non-anonymous was the social anthropologist Edward Burnett Tylor. In a 1866 paper titled 'On the Origin of Language', he attempted to support the 'bow-wow theory' by invoking the ways in which 'savages' in the colonies named the goods the Europeans brought, using words based on sounds associated with the goods. For instance, the Sea Islanders in the Pacific allegedly used *pu* for musket, *puhi* for 'to blow' (as they thought the European blew in the gun), *puff* for the smoke coming out of the musket, and *pupuhi* for the barrel of a gun. He concluded:

> If several languages have independently chosen like words to express like sounds, then we may reasonably suppose we are not deluding ourselves in thinking that such words are highly appropriate to their purpose. Thus we have such forms as *pu*, *puf*, *bu*, *buf* recurring in the most remote and different languages with the meaning of blowing or puffing. (Harris and Pyle 1996: 91)

In a note, he illustrates his claim with the following list: 'Tongan *buhi*, Mahjori *pupui*, Zulu *pu*, Hebrew *puach* &c.' He likewise finds evidence for the common origin of language in the cross-linguistic similarities among words used for 'father' and 'mother', words which, according to him, vary more in their consonants than in their vowels (p. 95). It did not matter at all to him that some terms that are phonetically similar sometimes denote opposite entities. It is striking how nineteenth-century scholars really thought that the colonized populations were apparently less evolved anatomically and/or mentally and therefore may provide evidence for how language evolved. Nowadays, we have to deal with Bickerton's (1990) controversial claim that pidgins (typically those based on European languages) represent fossils of his 'protolanguage.'

Nobody articulates the above thesis as explicitly as the Revd Frederic William Farrar, who, in his 1865 book *Language and Languages*, asserts:

> Savage languages are [. . .] the best to show us what *must* have been the primitive procedure; but we can trace the same necessary elements of words in languages far more advanced. (Harris and Pyle 1996: 59)

Arguing that language is too imperfect to be God's creation, he also interpreted the multiplicity of languages as evidence that language is an invention of mankind, 'developed by intelligence and thought. [. . .] It may be *unable to keep pace with* the advancing power of abstraction, but it can never by any possibility anticipate or outstrip it' (p. 45). He adduced evidence for humans' ability to invent languages from what is now known as 'home sign language' and from the ability of abandoned children living in groups to develop a language of their own (pp. 54–5). This evidence should actually be used to highlight the fact that, from an evolutionary perspective, the language phenomenon under discussion is a communal one, which does not emerge unless there is population of individuals, at least two, who interact with each other. (See also Lieberman 2006: 354ff.) Unless a situation such as the Nicaraguan boarding school for the deaf arises, no particular communal sign language emerges from the practices of isolated home signers interacting only with their speaking relatives.

Not unlike Bickerton (1990) with pidgins and creoles, Farrar thought that the modifications of European languages in the colonies might shed light on how language evolved, just like the invention of 'Argots' by 'the dangerous classes throughout Europe' (Harris and Pyle 1966: 66). According to him, because they are not intelligible to speakers of the languages from which they have evolved or been developed, they 'must, from their very nature, remain uncultivated' (p. 66). Although he assumed that language emerged gradually, he discussed the complexity of 'savage languages' in a way that reveals again strong prejudice against non-Europeans. This was indeed the century of 'la mission civilisatrice' or 'the white man's burden' ideologies developed by the French and the British respectively to justify exploitation colonization. Being non-European, isolating languages and, according to Farrar, also agglutinating and polysynthetic languages were deemed primitive. Putatively, the 'apparent wealth of synonyms and grammatical forms is chiefly due *to the hopeless poverty of the power of abstraction*' (Farrar's italics, p. 78). This would allegedly be obvious in languages that lack the copula. All such remarks that are undoubtedly offensive today, at least to some of us, underscore how cautious we must be in how we use our findings about some modern linguistic systems to make inferences about the evolution of language.

We should, of course, not ignore Friedrich Wilhelm Christian Karl Ferdinand Freiherr von Humboldt, who conceived of language dynamically in terms of the 'energeia' that translates the 'inner linguistic sense' into the outer expression, in which the universe of experience is categorized differently from one community to another. He may be considered a forerunner of the Sapir–Whorf hypothesis. What is especially relevant to the study of the evolution of language (a topic on which Humboldt did not say much) is the individuality of the inner sense, which makes every idiolect different but also every dialect and every language different, as the dynamics leading to social norms vary from one community to another. Humboldt also claimed that different populations have not evolved identically in developing their linguistic individuality. He characterized the evolution of language as what Harris and Taylor (1989: 177) paraphrase as 'the continuous outcome of [the] dialectic between the inner linguistic sense and sound-form; that is, between *energeia* and *ergon*.' Every individual speaker contributes to this process, as they reshape in not reproducing perfectly, the language of their social environment.

Then we must now ask how the different individuals, innovators and copiers, ultimately converge toward shared communal norms (Mufwene 2008). Note that invoking either the 'invisible hand' or 'self-organization' is simply admitting that we cannot yet articulate explicitly how the mutual accommodations that speakers/signers make to each other, in their ever-changing dyadic and triadic interactions, evolve to these 'conventions.' It is like saying that languages take on lives of their own when in reality the agents and hosts are the speakers or signers (Mufwene 2001). The conclusion does not take us farther than Saussure's 1916 correct observation that 'la parole fait évoluer la langue' ('speech makes language evolve'), without explaining how it does it.

The foregoing gives us a representative canvas of the state of the art in the eighteenth and nineteenth centuries concerning the evolution of language. It also gives us a sense of the kinds of controversial speculation that led the Société de Linguistique de Paris in 1866 to ban any linguistic discussions on the subject matter at its meetings. Only one more scholar is worth noting from the period, the semanticist Michel Bréal, who argued against the French ban on the ground that it impoverished the subject matter of linguistics. Bréal saw languages as being reshaped constantly by their speakers, and rejected his contemporaries' organic approach to them. He thought the approach was inaccurate in casting some languages not only as less evolved than others but also as decaying or dying. He would undoubtedly have opposed the present discourse about language birth, vitality, and endangerment, as well as about moribund languages, though it can be argued that languages conceived of as species (Paul 1880, Mufwene 2001) are born and may die in the same protracted ways biological species do, unlike individual organisms (Mufwene 2008: 208–9).

As noted above, the French ban appears to have been respected even outside France. It became almost taboo to discuss the evolution of language throughout most of twentieth century, until the 1990s, which I discuss in the next section.[5] Among the exceptions to the rule are the Dane Otto Jespersen, in his book *Language: Its Nature, Development and Origin* (1922a) and the American Morris Swadesh, whose book *Origin and Diversification of Language*, written in 1967 but published posthumously in 1971, also changed the nature of the discourse.

Otto Jespersen's contributions to the study of the origins of language include his argument that the 'bow-wow' theory (claiming the origins of language in the imitation of sounds in nature), the 'pooh-pooh' theory (based on human interjections), and the 'yo-he-yo' theory (based on human sounds during collective physical work) need not dismissed offhand. 'Each of the three chief theories enables one to explain *parts of language* but still only parts, and not even the most important parts—the main body of language seems hardly to be touched by any of them' (1922a: 416).

A more important and relatively uncontroversial contribution of Jespersen's is his position that we can learn indirectly about the origins of language by focusing on infant language during the first year of what is still nonlinguistic interaction with the caretakers, focusing on its cooing, babbling, and gestures. Later scholars such as Tomasello (2008) have suggested the development of joint attention, observable in human infants but not in great apes, as an important determinative factor in the evolution of language. Babies' ability to take turns in vocalization games also appears to be evidence of joint attention.

---

[5] According to Hombert and Lenclud (in press), much of this practice has to do with what the linguists thought was the subject matter of their discipline. Ferdinand de Saussure was allegedly more interested in languages (*les langues*), which consist of systems, are unified, but are not organic. He was less interested in language (*le langage*), which he putatively considered 'multiform and heteroclitic' (as noted above), straddling domains that are 'physical, physiological, and psychic' [i.e. mental?].

Jespersen also advocated paying attention to trends in how human languages have evolved in documented history, though the conclusions he suggests are controversial. He points out that European languages such as English and French have evolved from more complex morphosyntax to simpler, analytic ones and from structures putatively harder to learn and full of irregularities to more regular and systematic ones. 'The direction of the movement is toward flexionless languages (such as Chinese, or to a certain extent Modern English) with freely combinable elements' (1922a: 425). If, like Jespersen, one adopted from the misguided nineteenth century the view that some languages and related populations are less evolved than others, this would not rank German (which Jespersen does not discuss in this context) very high on the scale, nor Basque, which he finds excuses for not lumping into the category of 'primitive languages.' His conclusion is that the initial language must have had forms that were more complex and non-analytic; modern languages reflect evolution toward perfection which must presumably be found in languages without inflections and tones. It is not clear what Jespersen's position on derivational morphology is. In any case, his views are at odds with Bickerton's (1990) hypothesis that the protolanguage, which allegedly emerged by the late *Homo erectus*, was much simpler and had minimal syntax, if any. While Bickerton sees in pidgins fossils of that protolanguage and in creoles the earliest forms of complex grammar that could putatively evolve from them, Jespersen would perhaps see in them the ultimate stage of the evolution of language to date. Many of us today find it difficult to side with one or the other position.

Rather outrageous is Jespersen's claim that languages of 'savages' in Africa and the Americas could inform us about the origins of language, not only because they have longer words (with complex morphology, 1922a: 421), but also because they use difficult sounds such as clicks and rely on tones (p. 419), which, according to him, suggests that their speakers are 'passionate' (p. 420). 'Primitive languages' were accordingly sung, poetic, and figurative (p. 432). Being tonal and using numeral classifiers (pp. 429–30), Mandarin would be low on Jespersen's scale of evolved languages, though it might be better off than languages that are both tonal and have complex morphological structures. It is of course worse for languages that have no terms such as 'colour' for abstract concepts or general categories. Jespersen concludes, among other things: 'Primitive units must have been more complicated in point of meaning, as well as much longer in point of sound, than those with which we are more familiar' (p. 425). As pointed out in Mufwene (2008: ch. 6), it is noteworthy how late race lingered as a factor in accounts of language evolution in linguistics.

In contrast, Morris Swadesh's arguments are grounded in the then state of the art concerning phonetic and morphological properties of several languages around the world, as well as in paleontological and archaeological evidence. The examination of these led him to draw (among others) the following conclusion, which anticipated Mufwene's 2010b comparison of the pace of the evolution of language with that of computers, in shorter and shorter intervals of time as we near the present: 'It seems probable that language developed in the same general lines as other aspects of human culture: very slowly at first and gradually faster and faster' (Swadesh 2006: 45).

However, like many others before him, Swadesh hypothesized that language started with naming. The words may originally have been imitative of sounds heard in nature; then they were allegedly replaced by 'exclamative' ones, and later by 'a purely expressive paradigm and an attention-calling or demonstrative one' (p. 182). He believed that numerals 'were among the last to take on their present character' (p. 183). His worldwide comparison of demonstrative forms led him to the conclusion that 'before the neoglottic period, perhaps in the paleoglottic, fewer phonemes were differentiated than in contemporary languages' (p. 199), suggesting that even the phonetic inventories of modern languages must have evolved gradually, not becoming fully modern until as late at the emergence of agriculture.

Philip Lieberman (2002) believed phonetic language to have emerged earlier with the late *Homo erectus* or archaic *Homo sapiens*. Although this position has been revised (see below), the most relevant point here is that different parts of language appear to have evolved incrementally and no particular module seems to have emerged abruptly. It does not appear likely that *Homo erectus* or archaic *Homo sapiens* waited until a complete phonetic inventory was in place before producing their first words, or waited until there was a complete vocabulary with identifiable morphemes before producing phrases and sentences. Although ontogeny does not recapitulate phylogeny, child language acquisition discourages us from speculating about the phylogenetic emergence of language in strictly linear terms. Then, as now, early lexical and phonetic developments must have proceeded concurrently. One may also speculate that the expansion of the lexicon drove the elaboration of a wider phonetic inventory, as this enables more lexical distinctions.

In the style of evolutionary biology, Swadesh proposes a monogenesis account which assumes inter-individual variation in the 'vocal behavior' of the relevant hominins: 'in addition to individual differences, there could have been variations by sub-species and by locality, but all within essentially 'one language'' (1971 [2006 edn: 213]). Putatively, hominin populations equipped with similar anatomical and mental structures, living in different localities, and having developed comparable communities in which they experienced similar pressures to interact explicitly, would have developed comparable but non-identical means of communication. This sounds quite plausible, as East Africa, where most of the hominin fossils have been found, is a vast geographical area; to date no paleontological evidence suggests that an early *Homo habilis* or *Homo erectus* population dispersed out of one single locality to the rest of the world.

As argued in Mufwene (2008, 2010b), different individuals endowed with the same capacity for language need not have innovated exactly the same strategies for the same communicative needs.[6] Locally and regionally, there must have been plenty of

---

[6] According to Dor and Jablonka (2010: 139), this variation 'is inevitable given genetic differences, anatomical differences between brains, differences among ontogenies, and differences of processes of socialization,' which amount to 'different developmental trajectories.' Mufwene (2008) underestimated the consequences of biological variation across individuals when he invoked 'different interactional histories' (pp. 120, 126) in his account of inter-idiolectal variation.

variation, as argued by Johann Gottfried Herder, which set the innovators' productions up for competition among their imitators. This would have set things up for variational evolution, through competition and selection among available alternatives even within the same language, as members of the relevant populations converged toward their respective norms. Dor and Jablonka (2010: 138) call this normalization process 'canalization.'

Swadesh assumed that in the earliest, longest stages of the emergence of language, communication among hominins remained instinctive and did not vary significantly from one locality to another; therefore it is normal to assume that our hominin ancestors spoke the same language. According to him, significant diversity started to emerge about 'half a million or so years ago,' when the earliest forms of phonetic and symbolic communication, which he calls 'formal language,' started to emerge (2006: 214–15). The estimated period is consistent with that proposed by Corballis (2002) and Lieberman (2002), though they now think otherwise (see below). This is a stage when Swadesh believes it was possible for different individuals to innovate different linguistic forms for the same denotata and presumably different structures for the same propositions. (Which is reminiscent of Herder's account of the origin of synonyms in various languages.)

Swadesh's hypothesis raises the question of whether his monogenesis position is not really polygenesis; it leaves open the possibility that two late *Homo erectus* or archaic *Homo sapiens* populations developed languages that were not structurally identical and/or mutually intelligible. As is obvious from Bickerton's (1990) hypothesis of the protolanguage from which 'true language' putatively evolved, all may depend on what particular stage in the evolution of the *Homo* genus and what particular phase of its vocal communication one decides to identify as the beginnings of modern language. This entails particular assumptions about the size of the phonetic inventory and the nature of grammar, which are captured eloquently by Ray Jackendoff's 2010 title 'Your Theory of Language Evolution Depends on Your Theory of Language.'

Swadesh is also one of the very few scholars who have considered the implications of population movements for language evolution. As the migrants' languages come into contact, often coexisting in competition with each other for the same communicative functions within the same larger population, some may drive others to extinction. Typically, the prevailing language undergoes structural changes and can even speciate into separate languages. Seldom have linguists who are concerned with language endangerment and loss today cast the subject matter from this perspective, which Mufwene (2001, 2008) articulates in his ecological approach. The contact-based approach to language birth, endangerment, and death makes language evolution more similar to biological evolution, especially regarding the consequences of language practice under differing ecological pressures. The relevant ecology includes not only the mental and anatomical structures of hominins and humans but also the socioeconomic conditions that determine their population structures and their particular interactional dynamics. Indeed, the latter also trigger migrations, which history has shown to affect both the vitality and structures of languages.

1.3 RECENT DEVELOPMENTS

As a research topic, the evolution of language has expanded into a productive and stimulating, though diverse, area of scholarship since the 1990s. The scholarship has also expanded beyond the origins of language to include language birth and death, as well as language speciation. While philosophers and philologists no longer appear to deal with it, linguists can hardly claim it as a private domain. No insightful or informative linguistics publication on the subject matter is based exclusively on linguistic data. Interestingly, this is also an area where generative syntax, which has claimed centre stage since the late 1950s, has probably been unable to prevail over other areas, especially since the notion of Universal Grammar (UG), or 'biological endowment for language,' or 'language organ' (Chomsky 1986, Anderson and Lightfoot 2002), or 'bioprogram' (Bickerton 1981) is still a black box whose contents have not been articulated in sufficient detail and whose capacity to account for how language works and/or is learned has increasingly been disputed (see below).

Noam Chomsky's occasional contributions to the discourse (e.g. Hauser et al. 2002, Chomsky 2010) have aroused controversy, primarily for not considering much of the non-linguistic evidence and for ignoring objections to his claim that recursion is the most important characteristic of the capacity for language that is not shared by other animals. Others have objected that recursion distinguishes human languages from other animals' means of communication only to a degree. For instance, Margoliash and Nusbaum (2009) argue that some form of it occurs in some bird songs. Moreover, it may be a general cognitive, problem-solving strategy, as it is attested outside language, such as in mathematics and musical scores, unless the latter domains are claimed to be consequences of language. According to Lieberman (2006: 4–5; 2010: 164), it can be identified in dancing too. In addition, some scholars argue that there is little, perhaps nothing, in the structure of the human brain that exists only for language and is not part of the general learning adaptation. Language has also increasingly been interpreted as the gradual cumulation of exaptations of particular mental capacities and anatomical organs for communication (Hurford 2006, Oudeyer 2006).

Chomsky's (2010: 51) stipulation 'The study of the evolution of language is specifically concerned about UG and its origins' is questionable. An important reason why several scholars have raised issues with it has to do with whether language boils down to UG only, to the exclusion of the physical architecture of language(s). Chomsky's usual equivocations with the disjunctive phrase 'mind/brain' has not been informative about the nature of UG. Neurolinguistics has revealed that there is no particular part of the brain that can be identified as the 'language organ.' The fact that the parts of the brain implicated in language are not only situated in different regions but also associated with domains other than human communication precludes the possibility of a discontinuous modular language organ. The fact that UG appears to be mental, a property of the mind rather than of the brain as physical matter, clearly leaves open the possibility that it is a (by)product of something else in the many brain activities, including its capacity to produce language. Anderson and Lightfoot (2002) do not address these issues, although the book is specifically on this topic. Taking the notion for granted, they decide to define it 'in functional rather than in anatomical terms,' as it is 'not localized in the manner of the kidney' (p. xiii). As a matter of fact, they sometimes identify language itself, like the 'knowledge of language,' as the language organ (e.g. p. 8).[7]

One must also note an important difference between, on the one hand, how 'modularity' is invoked here in reference to concurrent engagements of different parts of the brain during the production of utterances and, on the other, the way the concept is used in technology to characterize the way different parts of a complex machine just complement each other. While complementarity is also true in the case of language, it is not evident that the brain parts are specialized for language only. For instance, Broca's area plays a central part in coordinating sensorimotor activities that have nothing to do with language. Mirror neurons, which have been invoked recently as playing a role in the reproduction of sounds, also play an important part in the reproduction of other physical activities and have been identified in other primates. The lateralization of the brain is not exclusively associated with language either. According to Lieberman (2010: 171), the FOXP2 gene, which was initially too hurriedly associated with language alone, also appears to facilitate 'learning and precise motor control in human and other species.'

If UG contains no properties that are unique to language, then we are perhaps back to the interest of Condillac and other eighteenth-century philosophers in the evolution of language as a way of learning about the evolution of mankind and their mind. Thus some linguists such as Jackendoff (2010) justifiably object to focusing on a questionable notion of FACULTY OF LANGUAGE, especially 'in the narrow sense' (Hauser et al. 2002). It impedes investigating the evolution of language in relation to that of, say, human cognition in general and animal communication.

Several scholars appear to align themselves with Pinker and Bloom's (1990) position that an all-purpose mental capacity, or various phases of its development, at a particular stage (or stages) of the *Homo* phylogeny, would have sufficed to produce language.[8] Assuming that what emerged are individual languages but not Language *per se* (a position consistent with Saussure's 'la parole [...] est nécessaire pour qu'une langue s'établisse', 1962 [1916]: 37), an alternative interpretation of UG is that it is the common denominator of the properties and architectures of the different languages. Thus, UG may not be a particular mental infrastructure that emerged at some particular

---

[7] MacNeilage (2008) doubts that the notion of UG is worth positing at all. He suggests that it is a consequence of language emergence rather than its cause. According to him, '*there is currently no validity to the claim that UG has a specific genetic basis*' (p. 298, MacNeilage's italics).

[8] Hombert and Lenclud (in press) state more specifically: 'The capacity for language is considered as a derivative capacity and its emergence as the secondary or induced effect of the emergence of a general cognitive competence. It may have followed from the aptitude that only humans would have been endowed with to read and share the other's intentions' (my translation).

phylogenetic stage of the *Homo* genus and enabled or facilitated the emergence of language, but simply a consequence of this evolution (MacNeilage 2008: 298).

Subscribing to the distinction between I-language and E-language, Chomsky correctly dismisses the hypothesis that language emerged in the form of 'language of thought' (LOT), citing lack of linguistic evidence and the fact that 'we have almost no idea what LOT would be' (2010: 226, n. 24). However, he associates language diversification with the externalization of language. According to him, the reason why there are so many languages 'might be that the problem of externalization can be solved in many different and independent ways, either before or after the dispersal of the original population [out of Africa]' (p. 61).

Consistent with some remarks in §1.2, one may want to justify this position by invoking the Cartesian view that the mind is the same in all members of *Homo sapiens sapiens* and would work the same way (allowing a limited number of alternatives) in speaking or signing. However, this position does not entail that they must of necessity be endowed with a language-specific UG in order to accomplish this. We just do not know yet. A general-purpose problem-solving cognitive capacity can lead to the same results, if interactants develop similar technologies for communication. UG could amount to common properties of these technologies, i.e. languages of particular communities, properties that are tantamount to universals of language and typological variation on particular parameters. Alternatively conceived of as a body of constraints on the architecture of language, UG can boil down to specifications of what the general-purpose problem-solving cognitive capacity permits and does not permit, bearing in mind that some of the constraints may simply be consequences of the materials used in the technology.

Chomsky too speculates that the externalization 'might have been a process of problem-solving using existing cognitive capacities' (2010: 61). This appealing position need not be wedded to his assumption of UG. Those who believe that modern language emerged to facilitate communication among humans can ask why I-language, associated with UG, need be considered anterior to E-language; it may also be conceived of as patterns emerging from successful utterances, as suggested in Construction Grammar or by Complexity Theory. In other words, 'knowledge of language' may be considered as internalization of what the communicator can(not) do vocally and/or with manual signs in his/her attempts to express meaning, i.e. a mental representation of the technology developed by a particular population for communication. As hypothesized by Saussure (cited above), the internalization may be considered as a consequence of practice.

Chomsky also argues that only I-language should be in the domain of investigations on the evolution of language. In his own words, 'any approach to the evolution of language that focuses on communication, the SM [sensory–motor interface] system, or statistical properties of spoken language, and the like may well be seriously misguided' (2010: 61). This position raises the issue of whether in some cases students of the evolution of language should not start by agreeing on the particular conception of LANGUAGE they are assuming. This is especially important because Chomsky's reaction to the question of 'why languages appear to vary so widely' is that this phenomenon 'is an illusion, much like the apparent limitless variety of organisms' (p. 62). He is of course driven to this remark by his strong minimalist theory, which appears to treat typological variation as a linguistic epiphenomenon less important than the core of language putatively determined by UG.

Could language really have originated as an abstract and uniform UG, thanks to the brain-rewiring event Chomsky hypothesizes? Or, as surmised above, is UG only the consequence of similarities among the ways members of the *Homo* genus have gradually solved their communicative problems? As remarked above, this evolution would have been enabled by the same general-purpose mental capacity that evolved gradually in them, and would have led them to coopt their anatomical structures to produce the relevant technology for communication, but not necessarily in identical ways.

It is certainly necessary to agree on a particular definition of language, so that we may determine whether or not we seek to explain the same subject matter. As pointed out in Mufwene (2001, 2008), the Saussurean conception of language as 'system,' which still prevails in linguistics, is at odds with the folk notion of language as the particular way a population speaks. In fact, lay people speak of languages, not Language (which is a philosophical concept); for them a language is just a way of speaking. It is not evident that the earliest speculations about the origins of human communication were not about languages but about Language, hence the long-held belief among some that Hebrew was the original language.

A problem in linguistics about what is language also arises from the status of phonetics. It is not obvious that linguists agree on whether it is part of language proper or is just a modality, as suggested, for instance, by Hombert and Lenclud (in press). This is a legitimate question, as some like to focus on rules and constraints seemingly ignoring the fact that these apply to physical items called words, which couple meanings (abstract entities) with forms. The architecture of language is built on them. It is hard to imagine that any grammar at the UG level or at the specific-language level, say I-language, could exist without physical entities that it applies to.

The above considerations make it natural to investigate how typological diversity emerged between languages and sometimes within individual languages. The diversity regards, among other things, the specific phonetic inventories that different populations of speakers have chosen and whether or not they made tones phonemic. It also has to do with whether they chose agglutination, polysynthesis, inflections, or isolating morphosyntax to code information around the main verb, whether the verb comes second or in another position in the sentence, whether they use Nominative/Accusative or Ergative/Absolutive syntax to code agency, what strategies they use to specify and track reference (for instance, do they use noun classifiers or genders?), how they articulate tense distinctions, etc. (See Hurford 2008 for a complementary discussion.)

Although syntax has long been privileged in formal linguistics, it has by no means claimed centre stage in the scholarship on the evolution of language, despite all of Bickerton's (1990) claims about the nature of his phylogenetic protolanguage. Very little has been written, for instance, about the evolution of combinations of words,

constraints on the positions of particular constituents within larger units, and movements of constituents to particular positions in sentences. If Chomsky is correct in
claiming that typological variation is an illusion, then something should be said about
how the common aspects of these syntactic phenomena evolved.

The above question may be more difficult to answer than that of why delimiters such
as TENSE, ASPECT, and MOOD for the verb as well as NUMBER and CLASS for the noun
evolved in language. One can surmise that for communication to be more precise, or
less vague, events and conditions must be situated in time and reported differently
according to whether they are facts or not, and whether the referents of nouns must
be specified according to cognitive requirements that interest particular populations.
It must be equally informative to find out why, for instance, the verbal complements of
volitional verbs in inflectional languages are more likely to be used in the subjunctive or
infinitive. Are the constraints purely linguistic or cognitive?

An answer to the question of why predication emerged, one that Herder considered
to be central to the study of the evolution of language, can also be attempted here. We
can resort to the way the distinction between TOPIC/SUBJECT and PREDICATE has been
traditionally explained in grammars, viz. what the utterance is about (the TOPIC) and
what state of affairs (ACTIVITY or STATE) is associated with the topic. However, much
more is involved in predication than just having a head of the predicate phrase. The
evolution of the organization of an utterance into TOPIC/SUBJECT + PREDICATE
PHRASE for most languages needs some explanation, as much as the ways in which
materials are structured into the predicate phrase. Would a UG-based account be
satisfactory? Or would it be more informative to invoke general-purpose problem-
solving cognitive capacity to explain how different populations developed their communicative technologies which nonetheless share similar principles? We probably need
considerations not exclusively grounded in linguistic theory to answer this question.

As pointed out by Jackendoff (2010: 69), an important problem with 'syntactocentr-
ism' is that is does not account for 'the evolutionary source of the lexicon.' Questioning
the centrality of syntax in generative grammar, Bolinger (1973) had argued, along
with generative semanticists, that syntax was a consequence of the lexicon, being a
body of generalizations from the ways that individual lexical items behave in utterances. It captures morphosyntactic similarities that lexical items display among themselves. Jackendoff (2010: 70) is also right on the mark in pointing out that Chomsky's
approach makes it hard to explain how lexical categories (and presumably the ensuing
syntactic categories) emerged. Were they arbitrarily predetermined? Why do they not
all occur in all languages or in identical ways? Is it also an illusion that some languages
have articles while others do not, or that inflectionless languages may not have a
FINITE/NONFINITE distinction for the verb, or that the INFINITIVE may not have an
identical syntactic status from one language to another?

Ideologically germane to Chomsky's reliance on UG but drawing very different
conclusions is Derek Bickerton's work since his book *Language and Species* (1990).
Bickerton started with the claim that modern human language evolved almost abruptly
from a 'protolanguage' used by our hominin ancestors up to *Homo erectus*. The

protolanguage putatively consisted of a (limited) vocabulary without much grammar, and may have combined both words and gestures.[9] The protolanguage 'is not a true language, but it's made up of languagelike elements' (2010: 40). Its users produced 'short and shapeless and disconnected utterances,' as one may encounter in especially child language and incipient pidgins, which he considers to be its modern fossils (p. 40). They lack the kinds of syntactic rules and constraints one finds in a 'true language.'

Like Slobin (2002), Mufwene (2008, 2010b) argues against this characterization of particularly pidgins and child language, products of humans endowed with *Homo sapiens sapiens*'s mind. Moreover, one must be cautious; the human child is not creating a language but learning the language of its social environment. The producers of a pidgin did not start from the absence of a language. Nor did their minds regress to the state of *Homo erectus*'s mind when faced with the challenge of communicating with another population in a language other than their own and without sufficient exposure to the target language. If anything, pidgins tell the extent to which a modern language can be reduced without losing the status of a language, therefore what are the most central/essential architectural materials a language cannot do without. Assuming that language has evolved gradually, they also tell us what in the architecture of language is so deeply entrenched that it cannot be dispensed with (Wimsatt 2000). Gradual emergence assumes a lot of scaffolding (Wimsatt and Griesemer 2007), a position quite implicit in grammaticization hypotheses, in which later developments are built on earlier ones. That order of evolution would more or less determine what can be dispensed with, in a less costly manner, if the system must be reduced to an earlier functional modern stage. We also learn that the architectural complexity of a language can be correlated with the communicative needs of its creators/users, not necessarily with the complexity or sophistication of their mental structure. Pidgins are by-products of contact settings where communication was minimal and sporadic (Mufwene 2008).

Bickerton also hypothesizes that language must have started with labels that were iconic. Symbolic communication would evolve later, making human language more different from animal means of communication. It's not clear whether symbolic items were already present in the putative protolanguage or whether they emerged in 'true language.' I am not sure that his quoting Terrence Deacon's assumption that 'symbolism' emerged 'probably not until *Homo erectus*' (Bickerton 2010: 50) answers the question, though he concedes to Deacon (1997) that symbolism, rather than syntax, is what distinguishes humans from animals (Bickerton 2010: 49). Symbolism enabled what Hockett (1959) identified as 'displacement,' the ability to talk about entities and states of affairs that are not in the *hic et nunc* of interactions, and thus the ability to talk also about the past and the future, as much as about fictional scenarios. All human

---

[9] Note that some scholars, including Corballis (2010) and Lieberman (2010), now think that modern language may not have originated before 50,000 years ago or so, thus much later than *Homo erectus*, apparently during *Homo sapiens sapiens*, and this event may have coincided with the last exodus out of East Africa. (I return to this below.)

populations have developed the capacity to narrate stories and even construct myths of all kinds thanks to the world-creating power of language. This is not possible in animal communication, even after they have been taught to communicate with humans. The reason appears to lie not so much in our invention of symbolic language as in our being endowed with the mental capacity that enabled us not only to produce it but also to do more with it.

On the other hand, Bickerton appears to contradict himself in some ways, when he elaborates on the architecture of his 'protolanguage':

> [T]he words of protolanguage, even if vocal, could not have been divided into component parts [i.e. sounds], and would likely sound to us like meaningless grunts or squawks. But, like today's words, each would have a fairly well-defined range of meaning, and that meaning, rather than relating directly to the current situation, would refer to some relatively stable class of objects or events, regardless of whether or not these were present at the scene. (2010: 66)

This sounds very much like symbolic communication minus phonetics and syntax. Except for symbolism, protolanguage would be a more elaborate version of primates' calls and gestures, raising the question of why Bickerton compared it to child language and incipient pidgins, which have human linguistic properties. These varieties have basic syntax, variable as it may be in the case of pidgins. In addition, it is not clear how consistent he is with the concession he makes to Deacon. If the latter version is right, reference would have started before 'true language' emerged, though 'true language' would refine reference by the addition of specifiers such as demonstratives and articles, as well as possessive constructions. The question of when such strategies developed is as worth investigating as that of when parts of speech emerged, and what the emergence entailed regarding the complexification of the architecture of grammar.

One of Bickerton's most problematic positions is his claim, like Condillac's, that language emerged to enhance human capacity for thought. In addition to Chomsky's (2010) observation that 'we have almost no idea what LOT would be' (p. 226, n. 24), we must ask why anybody would need a language of thought that would slow down their thinking process with the constraints of linearity? What is so more efficient about conceptual categories that are labelled linguistically when they can be identified non-linguistically, as is often obvious when speakers do not have words for ideas they want to express? Granted, human languages have a world-creating capacity; but isn't language more for sharing conceptualizations across speakers rather than for conceiving the scenarios that are shared?

In a different vein, some linguists such as Croft (2000), Wang and Minett (2005), Mufwene (2008, 2010b), Beckner et al. (2009), and Lee et al. (2009) also now conceive of languages as complex adaptive systems, which presuppose no permanent sets of rules that guide linguistic behaviour. Instead, linguistic rules are interpreted as emergent patterns produced by self-organization, in a way similar to other natural phenomena involving complexity. This position does not remove from mankind its agency in the emergence of language; it simply means that, throughout the *Homo* genus phylogeny, the individual acts of solving communicative problems did not include anticipation or a plan to develop what Antoine Meillet identified as a 'système où tout se tient'. The interactants never had/have any foresight of what their communicative 'system' will be like in the future or once it is presumably completed. The focus is always on the *hic et nunc* ecological pressures for adequate or successful communication.

Patterns, which linguists have identified as 'rules,' are therefore consequences of habits that the interactants have developed, based largely on analogies that obtained among items (Mufwene 2008), as when, in English, verbs of intention combine with verbal complements in the subjunctive or the infinitive but verbs of prohibition (such as *prevent* and *discourage*) combine with verbal complements in the gerund, sometimes preceded by the preposition *from*. Because there are cross-linguistic similarities across languages, though the patterns are not identical, it is interesting in terms of evolution to understand why such variation is the case.[10] Thus, are there any particular cognitive pressures that impose on speakers only the typological options that have been attested in human languages but not others? Why would such a mood as the SUBJUNCTIVE, as opposed to the INDICATIVE, have emerged, even if it is not universal? Why didn't some other kinds of strategies develop for complements of verbs of intention and prohibition?

Would such constraints provide evidence for Charles Darwin's hypothesis that mental evolution drove the evolution of language rather than the other way around? This kind of question has generally not been addressed, though it arises as an issue from Bickerton (1995). He could not address it, because he assumes that language emerged to enhance human capacity for thought; therefore the conceptual infrastructure could not possibly influence how language would evolve. Is there any hope that cognitive grammar, functional grammar, construction grammar, or any other approach to syntax that does not rely overly on what Lieberman (2006: 61) calls 'theories of data' may help us address the question adequately? Or are the approaches that assume that language is primarily a means of communication misguided? In any case, emergence is antithetic to design. If the claim that language emerged out of hominins' attempts to communicate at various stages of their evolution is correct, then it may be misguided to continue using Hockett's (1959) term/concept 'design features.'

Much of the current scholarship on the evolution of language has been more global, focusing on the correlation between, on the one hand, the different stages of the evolution of the mental and anatomical structures of the *Homo* genus and, on the other, the apparently gradual emergence of language, especially since *Homo habilis*. These include but are not limited to Bickerton (1990, 1995, 2007, 2010), Lieberman (1984, 2002, 2006, 2010), Corballis (2002, 2010), MacWhinney (2002), Fitch (2002,

---

[10] Dor and Jablonka (2010: 140) comment on this as follows: 'as more and more elements came to be canalized, and the language came to assume a certain architectural logic, the logic gradually imposed system constraints on what the next viable innovation would be.' This underscores Wimsatt and Griesemer's (2007) idea that current forms and/or structures provide the scaffold for innovations. From the point of view of the evolving system, they refer to this extension of the notion as 'self-scaffolding.'

2010), Tomasello (2008), Tomasello et al. (2005), McNeill (2005), McNeill et al. (2008), MacNeilage (2008), Mufwene (2008, 2010b), and Hombert and Lenclud (in press). All but Bickerton argue for gradual, protracted evolution. Tomasello stresses the significance of ecological pressures exerted on hominins by their increasingly more complex social lives, which required management by means of efficient and explicit communication. Modern language would provide this, driven by the same mind that was ready to handle the corresponding complex social interactions. He argues that cooperation and joint attention played as important a role in the emergence of language as in social organization. He shares with Sperber and Wilson (2002) (see also Sperber and Origi 2010) the 'theory of mind,' which enables interactants to second-guess each other and thus to infer the intended meaning. All these factors enabled the emergence of symbolic language, the characteristic that indeed led Deacon (1997) to identify mankind as the 'symbolic species.' As noted above, symbolic communication is, according to the latter, the characteristic that clearly distinguishes human communication from animal communication. Sperber and Origi (2010: 131) conclude:

> From a pragmatic perspective, it is quite clear that the language faculty and human languages, with their richness and flaws, are only adaptive in a species that is already capable of naïve psychology [i.e. mind-reading ability] and inferential communication.

Corballis, MacWhinney, and McNeill also argue that the earliest ancestors of human language could not have been vocal. Whereas Corballis and MacWhinney originally estimated that the embryonic forms of speech may have started as early as 500,000 years ago, Corballis (2010: 115–16, 119, 123) argues that only language, using gestures, may have started that early, with some complex grammar for that matter, and that the contribution of *Homo sapiens* since about 100,000 years ago was the introduction of speech. This may not have evolved to its modern forms until about 30,000 years ago. To be sure, Corballis does not claim that the switch was abrupt or that no phonetic vocalizations occurred before *Homo sapiens*. What he means is that gestural communication was dominant and verbal communication did not prevail as the dominant means of communication until *Homo sapiens*. It still took tens of thousands of years to evolve to modern phonetic norms.

Corballis' new position is echoed by Lieberman (2010: 175):

> McCarthy, Strait, Yates and Lieberman (forthcoming) found that the necks of the Middle Paleolithic fossils who lived about 100,000 years ago were too short to have a pharyngeal SVTv [vertical supralaryngeal vocal tract] that was equal in length to SVTh [horizontal SVT]. A similar constraint rules out Neanderthals having a human SVT. Surprisingly, neck lengths that would support a fully human SVT are not apparent in the fossil record until the Upper Paleolithic, some 50,000 years ago, when a blossoming of complex tools and art appears in the archeological record [. . .] the sudden appearance of an array of advanced artifacts has been taken to be a sign of cognitive advance. [. . .] The presence of a human SVT in a fossil hominid can be regarded as an index for the reiterative neural substrate that

makes voluntary speech possible. And that neural substrate also plays a critical role in making syntax, cognitive flexibility, and, yes, dancing possible. Speech, language, and some degree of cognitive flexibility surely were present earlier, but the presence of a SVT specialized for speech at the cost of choking places a date stamp on when brains like ours definitely existed [and presumably on when, or after which, modern languages did too].[11]

McNeill's work certainly indicates that speech has not become the exclusive means of communication to date, as it is usually complemented or supplemented by gestures. Kegl et al. (1999, on Nicaraguan Sign Language), Goldin-Meadow (2003b, on home sign language), and the rest of the literature on sign language (see Woll, Ch. 4 below) suggest also that mankind could have evolved to become predominantly signers rather than speakers.[12] It appears to me that biology-style natural selection *did* drive the evolution of language conceived of as the cumulative manufacture of particular communicative technology under specific ecological pressures that favoured speech as its medium. Givón (1998, 2002) cites advantages such as the ability to work and communicate at the same time and the ability to communicate in the dark or in spite of barriers to vision. MacNeilage (2008) and Allan (2010a: 233) also invoke the broadcast capacity of speech, a factor that, according to Dunbar (1996), fostered the emergence of speech, as it enables the speaker to 'groom' (interpreted here charitably in the sense of 'socialize with') several rather than one other person at a time.[13] Broadcasting certainly widens the radius of message transmission. Corballis (2010: 122) and Mufwene (2010b: 305) invoke, in addition, the fact that speaking uses less energy, as it depends on compact articulators that move in a much smaller space and proceeds faster. To be sure, signing compensates for this in not being absolutely linear, though the signer's hands probably cannot keep up with the speed of a normal speaker's speech organs.

These considerations are nonetheless not the full story. Signing has its advantages too. As John W. Wenzel (p.c., 24 Jan. 2009) pointed out to me, signing is useful when silence is required, such as during group hunting, or in situations where speaking would place the speaker in danger (such as before a carnivorous predator), or when one is diving. It looks as though our hominin ancestors would have weighed the pros and cons of speech vs signing as the primary technology for communication. All these

---

[11] [McCarthy, Strait, Yates, and Lieberman (forthcoming) is still being revised as we go to press, and its title is not yet determined.–Editor] The shift from Corballis' (2002) and Lieberman's (2002) early conclusion about when phonetic language emerged underscores the stronger empirical foundations of today's speculations on the evolution of language. New paleontological discoveries and a better understanding to modern humans' neural circuitry will shed more light on the subject matter.

[12] MacNeilage argues against this perspective, citing not only the assumption that the ability to vocalize started before *Homo habilis* but also 'the greater organizational similarity between speech and birdsong than between speech and sign language' (2008: 309).

[13] Bickerton (2010: 28) disputes this account, on the grounds that 'it fails the ten-word test, what you might call the test of immediate utility.' To be sure, grooming falls in the category of ecological explanation; it provides actuation for the emergence of language but says nothing about how the emergence occurred. It is undoubtedly one of the many social reasons and is not mutually exclusive with any particular account of how things proceeded, including Bickerton's own account.

dangerous situations are not part of humans' default mode of existence, in safe environments and interacting in dyads or triads rather than in large groups. If Tomasello (2008) is right about the significance of social life as an ecological pressure on the emergence of language (see also Corballis 2010: 116), then interactions in situations of no danger must have favoured the advantages that speech offers over signing, though we now know that one can express in signed language anything that can be expressed in spoken language. Interactions in situations of danger might explain why gestures have not been completely eliminated, especially if one factors in their tendency to be iconic.

However, Fitch (2010: 442–5) articulates more explicitly some of the counterarguments developed since Hewes 1996 about this evolution, highlighting more advantages of signing over speech. Auditory attention is freed while signing, and gestures can be more efficient while teaching a partner to make tools (aside from the fact that actions are more often learned by observation and imitation than from somebody else's verbal teaching). Speech may be more energy-efficient, as it depends on articulators that are smaller than those involved in signing. However, as MacNeilage (2008) points out, the latter is not structured in exactly the same way. So, according to Fitch, there is still no convincing explanation for why speech has prevailed as the demographically dominant medium of human language.

It appears that the study of the evolution of language will be enriched by a better understanding of changing ecologies of the *Homo* genus, within and outside the species, during its protracted evolution. It will be informative to learn more about the role played by obvious major ecological factors such as its neural, mental, and anatomical structures, the evolving social structure, and all the pressures they exerted on the emergence and evolution of language. It is crucial to identify individuals as the most direct ecology that filters the external ecological pressures, because the structures and vitality of languages are determined not by concerted behaviours of populations but rather by accumulations of individual behaviours, which occur without foresight of consequences but just happen to converge toward certain outcomes. (See also Dor and Jablonka 2010 for a related discussion.) Each communicative act is determined by particular ecological pressures to which the communicator responds in the *hic et nunc* of the interaction.

Much of the recent scholarship has focused just on the emergence of speech, especially regarding the transition from ape-like holistic vocalizations to phonetic communication, and the relation of this aspect of the evolution of language to that of the relevant neural circuitry and anatomical structure. This is probably also an area that is less abstract than syntax and semantics and easier to speculate on with more paleontological evidence. Space and time constraints force me to focus here on Philip Lieberman, Peter MacNeilage, and Alison Wray, though many others deserve attention.

MacNeilage (2008) presents perhaps the most extensive discussion to date, which, as noted above, also questions, like Lieberman (2006), the empirical justification for the notion of UG and its relevance to accounting for the emergence of language. According to him, speech evolved in several steps, starting with the cooption for phonation of organs that had evolved for ingestion. The rhythmic pattern of the relevant organs was subsequently exapted for vocalization in CV syllables, which could be reduplicated as in child language; but reduplication was abandoned for 'syllabic variegation and (the related) restrictions on VC co-occurrences' in the production of words, as 'pressures on speech systems to expand the size of their message sets' increased (MacNeilage 2008: 320). Eventually, longer utterances corresponding to sentences would evolve, but MacNeilage does not discuss this particular aspect of the evolution of language. However, he leaves 'some latitude for different dialects and for individual differences' to have been part of the emergence process. (He does not specifically tackle the monogenesis/polygenesis issue.) Against the role that UG, he writes:

> For language in particular, mirror neurons provide the foundation for a more encompassing embodiment-based neuro-cognitive alternative to UG, one that goes beyond the mechanisms that lie between meaning and sound, considered separately, by including meaning and sound in the same picture, and giving us a better basis for the relationship.
> The embodiment perspective was primary in my attempt to say how the first words were made. I suggested that the phonetic structure of the first words resulted from the cognitive pairing of an observed *action* [. . .] with a concept. (p. 326)

To be sure, MacNeilage brings us closer to articulating Wray's (2002) hypothesis that the *Homo* genus evolved from holistic vocalizations to phonetic communication. However, it is difficult to link both scholars here, largely because they do not start from the same working assumptions. MacNeilage does not subscribe to Bickerton's protolanguage any more than to UG. A natural bridge between them is Carstairs-McCarthy (1999), who, not unlike Jean-Jacques Rousseau, argues that Wray-style vocalizations would have been articulated into syllables first and later into the segments that these consist of. This evolution would have resulted in phonetic communication, though, as noted in §1.2, it raises the question of whether vowels and consonants arose at the same time, and whether 'syllabic variegation' started in the way hypothesized by Rousseau and by MacNeilage (with CV syllables) or initially just with variation in the quality of vowels—which would raise the question of how long the initial polysyllabic words consisting only of vowels could be. In the relevant passage quoted in §1.2, Rousseau suggests that the initial vocalizations consisted of vowels only, and consonants were innovated to mark syllabic boundaries. The fact that in all languages around the world the vast majority of syllabic peaks consist of vowels makes these considerations an interesting question for students of the evolution of language.

An informative complement of the above discussion on speech comes from Fitch's (2010: §8.3) summary of the state of the art about the evolution and functions of what linguists call 'speech organs,' which, based on the foregoing, are but exaptations of anatomical structure that evolved primarily for breathing and ingestion of food and liquids. Their use for speech is a perfect illustration of exaptation as defined by Gould and Vrba (1982):

A character, previously shaped by natural selection for a particular function (an adaptation), is coopted for a new use—cooptation. (2) A character whose origin cannot be ascribed to the direct action of natural selection (a nonadaptation), is coopted for a current use—cooptation. (Gould and Vrba, copied from *Wikipedia*, 1 Mar. 2011)

Fitch starts by noting, 'Many animals open and close their jaw in the course of a call [. . .] and changes in lip position are almost as common' (2010: 311). The role of the descent of the larynx in the emergence of speech has been exaggerated, especially also in the interpretation of the feature as uniquely human. It is attested in other animals too, though in many of them the descent is not permanent. Its role in non-humans is to exaggerate size, and humans too exploit this feature: 'it is really the descent of the tongue root [. . .] that is the critical factor in speech production, rather than the descent of the larynx *per se*' (p. 312). Fitch agrees with Lieberman et al. (1972) that 'hominids *must* have had some form of speech [intended as 'language'] before the descent of the larynx' (p. 313)—which does not mean that they had modern language.

Based on Lieberman (2006, 2010), discussed above, one must ask when (i.e. at what stage of hominin evolution) the larynx descended. According to Lieberman (1984, 2006), this otherwise maladaptive phenomenon (which puts humans at the risk of choking while ingesting) was probably a consequence of the reconfiguration of the basicranial structure after the hominins became bipedal. This says nothing about the phylogenetic time of the emergence of the feature. However, it is informative to know more specifically that the descent of the larynx was a consequence of the descent of the tongue root down the pharynx, pushing the larynx down, as happens now in human infants (Lieberman 2007: 46). This anatomical feature must have been selected because of the advantages it conferred to the further evolution of speech into its modern form. Fitch concludes:

> Not only does the descent of the larynx enlarge our phonetic repertoire, but it does so in a way that enhances speech encoding and decoding [. . .] and it give[s] us the point vowels [/i/, /a/, /u/] that are found in all human languages, particularly the 'supervowel' /i/, which plays a central role in the vocal tract normalization. (2010: 315)
>
> [T]here must be functions of a descended larynx other than increased phonetic versatility [. . .] leaving size exaggeration as the most plausible explanation. (p. 321; Fitch's italics)
>
> [T]he primary evolutionary changes required for [modern] spoken language were neural, not changes in vocal anatomy. (p. 362)

This conclusion confirms Darwin's (1871) position that the mind drove the emergence and evolution of human language, as it enabled hominins at successive stages of their phylogeny (mental and physical) to coopt parts of their anatomy to develop various stages of the language technology. In other words, with the increasing power of their minds, hominins and humans gradually domesticated their anatomies to produce the communicative technologies called languages. I submit again that the mind is really the most important feature that distinguishes mankind from other primates, and certainly other animals, although it does not function identically in all individuals, not any more than their physiologies are identical. Language is after all a collective gradual invention (by emergence).

The implications of this position are worth exploring further, since no two speakers have identical competences in any language they speak and/or sign. This interpretation is consistent with the notion of IDIOLECT, whose features, as noted above, are determined as much by the variation in the interaction histories of speakers/signers (Mufwene 2008: 120, 126) as by their individual learning capacities as determined by their mental and anatomical singularities (Dor and Jablonka 2010: 139).

It should be obvious by now that students of the evolution of language do not share identical working assumptions. Nor have they focused on the same research questions. Some have been more interested in the particular interactive dynamics that made it possible for language as a communal phenomenon to emerge. This is especially the case for Croft (2000, 2003b, 2008), Tomasello (2008), Tomasello et al. (2005), and Mufwene (2001, 2005). Croft and Mufwene have patterned their approaches on biological evolution. Assuming an emergentist construction grammar, Croft has assumed that utterances are replicators, which vary across individuals and are in COMPETITION, which is explained by Mufwene 2008 as a situation in which the variants are not equally rated by users. The competition is resolved by SELECTION, which can be interpreted as in biology, when a variant prevails over another or others, for any number of reasons in the relevant ecology.

Mufwene has gone as far as to argue that individual languages are the counterparts of viral species, with their organisms being the idiolects of particular speakers/signers. He posits a FEATURE POOL in which the variants produced by different speakers/signers are in competition and the machine that runs selection lies in the ecologies in which languages are used. The challenge is to define ECOLOGY, which has usually been understood as the social environment, with all the pressures emanating from population structure. I now think that, regarding the evolution of language, the ecology that matters the most lies in the different evolutionary stages of the mental and anatomical structures of the *Homo* genus. They determine what forms the relevant means of communication could assume.

Where both Croft and Mufwene hope to inspire those focusing on strictly phylogenetic topics and issues is especially the way they invoke INNOVATORS and SPREADERS/COPIERS (concepts also used by Tomasello 2008 and Tomasello et al. 2005) to account for the emergence of new linguistic features, which can, for convenience, be explained roughly here as applying to forms and constructions. As different innovators need not introduce the same features, competition arises, and various ecological factors determine which variants will prevail for which specific functions, there being room for free variation too. Selection is not made consciously, but is the cumulative outcome of choices made at different times by speakers/signers in their utterances. Since most interactions are dyadic or triadic, and since speakers do not normally hold meetings to state which particular variants they prefer, the question arises of how norms emerge.

Both linguists have at times invoked the 'invisible hand' but have been invoking 'self-organization' in their recent works, after familiarizing themselves with complexity theory.

EXAPTATION has been a recurrent concept in the literature, underscoring the (self-) scaffolding aspect of language evolution. This has been implicit in many of the discussions above, but the term has increased in currency especially regarding the emergence of speech (see Oudeyer 2006 for an extensive discussion.) It is also applicable to the emergence of grammar, especially in the process called 'grammaticization' or 'grammaticalization,' whereby some verbs or nouns are exapted to be used as function words, such as complementizers or prepositions. Regarding the emergence of grammar itself, the boldest attempt is to be found in Heine and Kuteva (2007), who, in the footsteps of Herder and Max Müller, claim that the initial language consisted just of nouns and verbs; all the other categories are derivatives from these. They do not explain how, among other aspects of grammar, predication and different strategies for specifying reference and time evolved, or under what particular ecological pressures, though they explain, on the basis of synchronic linguistic evidence, how particular markers may have acquired grammatical meanings.

I will conclude this selective survey of topics addressed in the past two decades on the evolution of language with a brief discussion of the emergence of linguistic diversity. It is particularly significant because universals and typological variation have been central in linguistics since Greenberg's (1966) landmark publication on the subject. Even the generative linguists' preoccupation with principles and parameters as they are constrained by UG is a consequence of the pioneering work of Greenberg, though UG is not synonymous with language universals. The question is critical especially because most of the literature has assumed or suggested monogenesis; it has typically not mentioned variation in the protolanguage or the earliest ancestor of modern language. As a matter of fact, as noted above, Swadesh (2006 [1971]) assumed that because the original ancestor of modern language was instinctive, there could not be significant variation in it. Let's thus focus on when speech started to emerge. Here is what Jim Hurford, one of the veteran students of the evolution of language, has to tell us:

> Summarizing the factors contributing to linguistic diversity, (1) the fact that languages are learned, rather than coded into the genes, (2) the arbitrariness of the sign, and (3) the prevalence of horizontal transmission allow for great diversity, but this is significantly constrained by (4) biological factors such as memory and processing limitations, which may or may not be specific to the Language domain. (Hurford 2008: 251).

These factors account more for idiolectal variation, as there is no faithful replication in language learning (Lass 1997), than for the emergence of typological variation across languages. If populations can choose to build their languages on different words and only on overlapping phonetic inventories, what should keep them from developing different combination patterns of these units into larger utterances and therefore different grammars? If we interpret phonology as the grammar of sounds and assume that grammars are consequences of the ways units are combined together and structured into larger and larger (hierarchical) units, why should we expect the relevant hominin/human populations at the different stages of the evolution of language to have done exactly the same thing?[14] After all, the paleontological evidence does not suggest that *Homo sapiens sapiens* dispersed to the world out of one village in Africa; hominin fossils have been found in a vast area of East (and South) Africa. Shouldn't it be normal to assume that, having reached the same stage of mental and anatomical evolution, hominin populations developed languages that were comparable but not identical in their architectures? They did not have to package information in identical ways, no more than they developed identical cultures.

Another dimension of the scholarship on the evolution of language today lies in computer modelling, which I will not discuss here, due to lack of space. The rewards depend largely on the assumptions that underlie the models. When they are empirically grounded, they become important research tools, such as when used by Philip Lieberman and his associates to determine whether the Neanderthal was capable of speaking. When accurately informed and well designed, modelling can help empirical research reformulate some of its questions about a distant past that cannot be recreated. (See e.g. Oudeyer 2006 on self-organization in the emergence of language and Steels 2011 on the emergence of communal norms.)

Last but not least, there is all the research on animal communication, especially intraspecifically among non-human primates and between humans and some great apes. It is expected to inform research on the evolution of language insofar as scholars can identify both behaviours that may have been inherited from our common ancestors millions of years ago and later homologous evolutions from features shared earlier in our common phylogenetic ancestry. Unfortunately, I can do even less justice to this topic here than to those discussed above. Comparisons by Tomasello (2008) regarding joint attention and cooperation highlight the significant role which these social factors that we do not share with the other primates played in the phylogenetic emergence of human language. Fitch's and Lieberman's comparisons regarding primates' supralaryngeal vocal structures also reveal important differences that rule out the possibility that they would have developed human-like speech even if they were endowed with the same kind of mind as we have. On the other hand, discoveries that non-human primates share with us mirror neurons, the FOXP2 gene, and some of the specialized functions associated with Broca's area suggest that the human mind had a greater role to play in the emergence of language than may have been assumed before, which is precisely why our phylogenetic cousins have not even developed some symbolic-iconic system similar to sign language. Language may be a more cultural phenomenon than some of us have assumed. I submit that language is indeed one of the facets of human culture,

---

[14] A convenient nonlinguistic illustration of this may be found in how engineers using similar algorithms constrained by the same principles produce technologies (such as computers and derivative products) that are not identical in their architectures and functionalities.

and that both linguists and anthropologists may have been misguided in speaking of language and/in culture as if they were opposed to each other on the same plane.

On the other hand, there is a growing literature suggesting that differences between animals and humans are more a matter of degree than dichotomy. Some of the capacities having to do with mirror neurons and mind-reading are very similar, which raises the question of whether human intelligence is not a consequence of the particular ways various parts of the brains and modules of the mind interact.

It has long been assumed that animal means of communication are innate but that of humans are not. However, it has also become evident that a certain amount of learning is involved in, for instance, bird songs (Margoliash 2010). Past the critical period, the bird does not develop the right song for its con-specifics! Besides, some birds exposed to alter-specifics' songs acquire it rather than that of their con-specifics. This and other factors raise the question of whether there is such a thing as language or cultural 'transmission,' analogous to gene transmission in biology, especially among humans. Unlike transmission, which, in the absence of mutations, guarantees faithful mainten-ance of inherited traits, learning by inference almost ensures modification of the target features, which is more consistent with language 'acquisition,' interpreted as system reconstruction (Mufwene 2001, 2008). Students of cultural evolution, such as Richerson and Boyd (2005), Mithen (2005), and Mesoudi et al. (2004), have kept up impressively with the scholarship on language evolution. We have everything to learn in reading them too.

Some of the more popular studies of animal communication have focused on what can be learned from teaching human language or an artificial system made by humans to primates (e.g. Segerdahl et al. 2005). It appears that lexigrams constitute a seriously impoverished system that does not go beyond the telegraphic stage in child language. Although great apes such as Kanzi have been credited with the ability to understand human speech, it is not obvious that they can follow a narrative the way a human child can. This highlights mental differences between non-human primates and us, though differences in mental capacities are also a matter of degree. Nonetheless, it appears that the less than 2 per cent genetic differences between chimpanzees and humans have entailed exponential cultural, and more specifically language-related, differences.

The overall approach has assumed that humans are more evolved than non-human primates, rather than just being different from them. We have not yet accounted for why we cannot learn to communicate the way they do! Answers to this question may equally well inform us about how different our minds really are from theirs or, more accurately, about how communication in all species is jointly constrained by their respective mental and anatomical ecologies. We have discussed culture as if it were peculiar to humans, whereas it can be interpreted as customary ways in which members of a particular population behave and do things. Cultural differences can also inform us about how different social structures have influenced what needs to be communicated and what kinds of systems are needed to convey the relevant pieces of information.

1.4 Conclusions: Older vs Current Approaches to the Evolution of Language

As aptly expressed by Fitch (2010: 389),

> regarding language evolution, there are very few new hypotheses under the sun, and current debates can and should pick up where our scholarly predecessors left off. [... T]here are real insights in the older literature which remain unappreciated.

Hombert and Lenclud (in press) note likewise that a number of the positions assumed today were already defended by philosophers of the eighteenth century. For instance, the claim that language is what distinguishes mankind the most clearly from the animal kingdom is already evident in Condillac. It is also hard to sharply distinguish eighteenth-century arguments for the emergence of human language out of instinctive cries and gestures from Bickerton's position that the predecessor of his 'protolanguage' consisted of holistic vocalizations and gestures. The idea of gradualism in the evolution of language is not new either; and Rousseau had already articulated the significance of social interactions as a prerequisite to the emergence of language. And one can keep on identifying a number of current hypotheses which are hardly different from earlier speculations on the subject.

An important difference between us and those philosophers and philologists before the nineteenth century, and in some cases up to then, is that we no longer assume that our hominin ancestors up to 200,000–100,000 years ago were just like us, except that they were either created by God or just happened to inhabit our planet long before we did, or just were mentally inferior to us. We now approach the subject taking into account what communicative architecture would have been possible at various stages of hominin evolution. We ask: since *Homo habilis* was anatomically different from *Homo erectus*, what kind of language would those remote ancestors of ours have been capable of developing even if they were equipped with the same kind of mental capacity as us? The same applies to *Homo erectus* and archaic *Homo sapiens*. A similar question arises regarding the complexity of utterances relative to the complexity of the hominin mind and/or social organization. What kinds of ecological pressures did they exercise on the evolution of language? Lieberman (1984), Bickerton (1990), Tomasello (2008), Corballis (2002, 2010), MacNeilage (2008), and Fitch (2010) are good illustrations of this ecological approach, although they do not draw identical conclusions.[15]

Another important difference between us and philosophers and philologists before the nineteenth century is that, better than Socrates in Plato's *Cratylus*, we are more

---

[15] As a matter of fact, Bickerton (2010) now discusses the evolution of language from the point of view of 'niche construction,' which Laland (2007: 35) characterizes as 'the process whereby organisms, through their metabolism, their activities, and their choices, modify [their] niches.' (See also Odling-Smee et al. 2003 for a more elaborate discussion.) The subtitle of Bickerton (2010) captures the idea adequately: *How Humans Made Language, How Language Made Humans.*

aware of the speculative nature of our hypotheses in this research area. With few exceptions, scholars have generally been more critical and more cautious, revealing more awareness of the limitations of the state of the art.

Whether or not we acknowledge it, Charles Darwin has also exercised a long-lasting impact on us: most scholars today do not assume that language was God-given (presuming creationists to be in the minority). Even Chomsky's account that UG emerged by some rewiring of the brain is a Darwinian explanation, because Darwin made allowance for mutations, and UG could have emerged only at a particular stage of hominin evolution, quite late. Besides, mutations are probably also the best explanations from all the changes in hominin evolution, with the mutants prevailing and the rest evolving as consequences of those mutations.

We also now think of the architecture of languages as modular. This is an idea that does not appear in the earlier literature. It also frees scholars from having to assume that every component of modern language must have evolved at the same time as the others. Nor do we have to assume that the anatomical and mental structures that were coopted in the apparently gradual emergence of language all evolved at the same time. Even in assuming that the mind domesticated hominin and human anatomy for the production of language, it need not have coopted the different organs concurrently. This is the kind of evolution suggested by the paleontological evidence that experts have adduced, leading both Michael Corballis and Philip Lieberman to now conclude that speech-dominated communication must have emerged more recently, 50,000–30,000 years ago, not 500,000 years ago. This thinking is consistent with Hombert and Lenclud's (in press) conclusion that the capacity for language is a derivative and consequence of hominins'/humans' evolving cognitive capacity.

It is more and more evident that the subject matter of the evolution of language is multifaceted, having to do with the mechanical/architectural aspects of language, with the particular anatomical organs coopted for its production and perception, with the mental aspects of the technology (including the formation of concepts and their combinations into larger chunks), and with the apparently social motivation for producing the technology. It would be difficult, if not impossible, to explain how modern humans' linguistic communication got where it is now without answering various questions that pertain to these different facets of the subject matter. It is part of understanding how the *Homo* genus has evolved over the past two or three million years biologically, anatomically, mentally, and socially.

CHAPTER 2

....

THE HISTORY OF
WRITING AS A HISTORY
OF LINGUISTICS

....

PETER T. DANIELS

> The invention of writing itself may well be considered testimony of
> linguistic analysis of the spoken language. (Reiner 2000: 1)

A generation ago, Michael Patrick O'Connor (1983) introduced the concept of writing
systems as 'native speaker analyses.' They reveal what people know about their
language from learning to write. His principal concern is the West Semitic consonan-
tary (the type I have called the *abjad*; Daniels 1990), but it is obvious—so obvious that it
has remained unnoticed—that *any* writing system is in that sense a native speaker
analysis of a language and thus an aspect of linguistics. This source of people's
knowledge of their language has not otherwise been exploited by linguists or historians,
except in a few incidental cases. §§2.1 and 2.2 of this chapter briefly present some
principles observed in the origins and development of writing respectively;[1] §2.3
provides examples of what writing indicates of speakers' knowledge of language.

Francesca Rochberg (2011) cautions against taking the history of science as a searching
for early or ancient antecedents of modern approaches; thus studies like Miller (1994) and
even O'Connor (1983), which find 'evidence' for the Sonority Hierarchy and for Jakob-
sonian distinctive features (respectively) in the non-alphabetic Greek scripts and the
Ugaritic script (respectively) are rather beside the point. Such approaches are a legacy of

---

[1] The two classic English-language works on the history of writing have not been superseded.
Diringer (1968) is more readable, Jensen (1969) provides a very full bibliography. The only two reliable
handbooks (Février 1959, Friedrich 1966) are even older. Cohen (1958) brings sociological insight (the
discipline of sociolinguistics had not yet been identified) to the full range of the subject. Daniels and
Bright (1996) is not intended as a history of writing but includes historical notes where appropriate; it is
the source for information in this chapter not otherwise referenced.

mid-twentieth-century positivism, the prevailing mindset of the time when the academic discipline of History of Science was becoming established: it results in an equivalent of spuriously teleological 'Whig history' (Butterfield 1931) or 'presentism' (Jardine 2003). Also of lesser interest is explicit graphonomic[2] work by orthographers and orthoepists; rarely did it filter down to common use (Haugen 1950: 56 §5.1), and when it did (Korean hangul; several nineteenth-century shorthand systems, see §2.3.1.2 below), the special properties of the resulting scripts remain generally unknown to their users.

For Rochberg (p.c., Mar. 2011), the history of science must be the history of how earlier peoples understood their environment: it 'can never be about how the ancient[s] understood science, but only about what their study and understanding of phenomena can tell us about what *we* think science is.' Ordinarily, speakers have no insight into the nature of their language or what they are doing when they are speaking. But when a language is written, it is *consciously* written, and every writing system embodies an analysis of its language. And that analysis is known not only to the deviser of the writing system (however great an accomplishment the act of devising a writing system may be), but also—consciously—to everyone who learns to write, and even read, that writing system. Ergo, every writing system informs us of 'native speaker analysis' of every written language, and such analyses have touched on virtually every level of analysis known to modern linguistics.

2.1 Origins of Writing

Alfred Schmitt (or his posthumous editor) did well to arrange his *Origin and Development of Writing* (1980) with the modern inventions in the first half and the ancient inventions in the second, for it is careful study of the former that illuminates the latter (Daniels 1992a).[3]

2.1.1 Modern Grammatogeny

Traditional surveys of writing systems treat the two best-known script inventions (what I have called 'grammatogeny') of North America, Cherokee, and Cree, together, because they both successfully serve Native American communities and both

---

[2] Adopting Hockett's (2003 [1951]) term 'graphonomy'; by the time it saw print (Hockett 1958: ch. 62), Gelb's (1952) 'grammatology' had already caught on, but its hijacking (with acknowledgment) by Derrida (1976) renders the alternative desirable.

[3] My approach to the origins of writing was shaped by psycholinguistic research of the 1970s and 1980s showing that the syllable, rather than the segment, is the most accessible unit of the phonological structure of the mental lexicon. The psychologist Peter MacNeilage (2008), casting his net more widely but into work of that era too, finds that the syllable is prior in both phylogeny and ontogeny as well.

denote CV syllables of their languages. But their inventions were quite different activities with quite different results. The differences trace to the intellectual background of the inventors: the inventor of Cree Syllabics was English-literate and familiar with the phonetic science of his day; the inventor of the Cherokee Syllabary was literate in no language and knew only that the surrounding Americans could communicate at long distances by marks on paper. I have characterized the former's knowledge of writing and phonetics as 'sophisticated' and the latter's lack thereof as 'unsophisticated'.[4]

2.1.1.1 *Sophisticated Grammatogeny*

James Evans (1801–46) was a Methodist missionary in Manitoba who, having heard of the success of Sequoyah's Cherokee syllabary (§2.1.1.2), devised a script for Cree with a small number of simple geometric symbols that, by 90° rotations or reflections, denote the four vowels alone or preceded by a consonant. The shapes are said to be taken from English shorthands based in 'phonotypy' (the phonetician and shorthand-deviser Isaac Pitman's term for letter shapes that denote phonetic features), showing that Evans was aware of the nascent science of phonetics. Each consonant is embodied by a series of symbols of the same shape, each vowel by a series of symbols in the same orientation.

Further successful examples of sophisticated grammatogeny include the 'Phags-pa of the Mongol empire (1269; §2.2.3.2), Korean Hangul (1446; §2.3.1.2), the Fraser and Pollard scripts created by Christian missionaries for several Southeast Asian languages (early twentieth century), and the Nko script (1949) serving Manding languages of West Africa (Wyrod 2008).

2.1.1.2 *Unsophisticated Grammatogeny*

Sequoyah (*c.*1770–1843) is the first known inventor of a writing system *ex nihilo*. Wishing to provide the boon of writing to his own people, after attempting and rejecting the notion that a symbol could be invented for each word, he analysed the words into the smallest components he could identify and devised a symbol for each CV syllable.[5] There is no resemblance between symbols embodying the same consonant or the same vowel.

Further examples of unsophisticated grammatogeny include the Vai script of Liberia (1840s) and a number of other scripts of West Africa that may have been inspired by it; similar projects are known from North America and Oceania as well. In each case, whatever the graphic source of the images used, the result is a CV syllabary.

---

[4] In the only place I am aware of where this distinction has been acknowledged, it is ridiculed because the labels are misunderstood and taken in a colloquial sense as an assertion that Chinese culture was 'unsophisticated' (Houston 2004).

[5] The Cherokee characters resemble in shape (not sound) roman and other letters, but these were choices by the first printer of Cherokee from the type available to him, choices approved by Sequoyah.

2.1.2 Ancient Grammatogeny

Ancient grammatogeny must be viewed through the lens of unsophisticated grammatogeny. It is thus not surprising that in the three known instances—for Sumerian, for Chinese, and for Mayan—what was denoted was syllables. But, differing from the modern grammatogenies, these were syllables with meanings: monosyllabic morphemes. Where Sequoyah had tried, and failed, to create a symbol for each (polysyllabic, multimorphemic) word—because the word is the unit of language one is most aware of—the monosyllabic nature of words (morphemes) in these three languages made these attempts not futile. The three societies concerned had arrived at a degree of urbanization (necessitating some sort of economic records), and it is most significant that other societies of similar complexity kept records with tallies, sometimes of great sophistication (in the ordinary sense) like the Incan *quipu*, that did not give rise to writing systems. The inescapable implications are that undeciphered independent ancient grammatogenies (notably Indus writing: Parpola 1994, Wells 2011) encode monosyllabically organized languages as well; and that the encoded stretches of speech are syllables, and not anything smaller or larger.

2.1.2.1 *Mesopotamia*

Among the earliest written records yet discovered, from late fourth-millennium Sumer, are lists of words representing the start of a scholarly tradition that survived for some 3,000 years, so that their interpretation is assured. Most of the clay 'tablets' bearing the pictographic antecedents of cuneiform writing, however, are economic documents recording commodities, quantities, and personal names; they are not connected prose texts; they are not 'read.'[6] The characters ('signs'), numbering some 800, for the most part represent monosyllabic words with both a pronunciation and a meaning.

The recalcitrant medium of stylus dragging on clay soon led to the pictographs being replaced by abstracted and then abstract signs, comprising wedge-shaped ('cuneiform') indentations in the surface of the clay, that did not resemble their representational origins—although the fact that the signs originated as pictures of what they stood for was not forgotten, their original shapes were unknown (Daniels 1992b).

Not until Sumerian cuneiform writing had been adopted for writing the unrelated Semitic language Akkadian, around the mid-third millennium, and writing it largely phonetically, using only the sounds of the characters and only to a limited extent their semantic values (as 'logograms'),[7] were the grammatical affixes notated in Sumerian

---

[6] 'Sumerian writing, in its original conception particularly, held economy as its topmost priority. There was a considerable gap between the natural, spoken language and what is represented by the early Uruk script. Most of the morphological information of speech, such as pronouns, adverbial markers, and other elements that convey grammatical meaning, is simply not recorded' (Woods 2010: 44).

[7] In both Sumerian and Akkadian, logograms could be specified with the occasional 'phonetic complement' (helping indicate whether a sign meant 'leg' or 'walk', for instance), and a small number of signs served as 'semantic determinatives', tagging words with a category such as 'man', 'bird', 'city', wooden object'.

texts, so that they could be read rather than simply consulted as an *aide-mémoire* (Cooper 1999). It seems unlikely that the early Sumerian scribes were unaware of the grammatical affixes in their speech; in recent decades, Sumerologists have realized that the language is not as strictly agglutinative as had been assumed and have identified a range of morphophonemic alternations. Is it possible that the lack of single surface forms of affixes made it impossible for the scribes to assign signs to them on a solely phonetic basis—they could not recognize an underlying form—until they were at home notating purely phonetic information about utterances in a different language?

2.1.2.2 *China*

The earliest known Chinese texts, the Oracle Bone Inscriptions of the later Shang dynasty (thirteenth century BCE), already use a writing system exhibiting the characteristics of the modern script; it has remained in continuous use for more than three millennia. The characters' pictographic origins are in many cases somewhat more recognizable than they are today, albeit hardly transparent. Importantly, many characters representing a monosyllabic morpheme comprise a semantic component and a phonetic component, providing indications of both the meaning and the pronunciation of the morpheme (the pronunciation indicators were much more reliable when the system was standardized some 2,000 years ago than they are now, after two millennia of language change and virtually no script change).

After less than one millennium of language change, phonetic keys to the script proved necessary. They first took the form of *fanqie* (Bugarski 1970, Downer 1963), pairs of characters selected from a limited inventory written small alongside the character being keyed, one giving the 'initial' sound, the other giving the 'rime' (the rest of the sound), e.g. 耐_{奴代}: 耐 *nài* 'endure' explained as 奴 *nú* + 代 *tài* (Coulmas 1996: 150); and subsequently of the 'rime tables' from many eras (Branner 2006), which are charts of rhyming characters as needed by poets.

Chinese writing was adopted by various peripheral peoples, but the only such place where it remains in use is Japan. Pure logography was ill suited to the inflectional Japanese language, and within a few centuries of the first attempts at writing, a small group of characters had come to be used for their sound alone; by modern times they had simplified into two syllabaries with distinct uses (§§2.3.2.2, 2.3.3.2, 2.3.5.1): cf. 耐: 耐 *tai* 'endure' explained as た *ta* + い *i*.

2.1.2.3 *Mesoamerica*

Maya writing's ancestry is unclear (other script-like graphic systems may likewise prove to be true writing), but with the accomplishment of its decipherment in the late 1970s it became clear that, like Sumerian and Chinese writing, its source was the recording of monosyllabic morphemes with acrophonic pictograms and their rebus reuse for unpicturable syllables (Mora-Marín 2003, 2010).

2.2 TRANSMISSIONS OF WRITING

It has often happened that a writing system comes to be used in a new way only when it is taken over for a new language. These takeovers happen by accident, by adoption, or by adaptation.

2.2.1 Accident: Transmissions by Misunderstanding

It is my opinion that the three changes in the nature of writing systems that led to the present-day assortment of writing types were due, accidentally, to misunderstandings.

2.2.1.1 *Egyptian Logoconsonantary*

The first was that a vague acquaintance with Sumerian logographic writing reached Egypt (Daniels, in press, b). In early Sumerian, the morphemes that were written did not change their phonological shape, so each character always represented both the same sound and the same meaning; and the first Egyptian scribes tried writing each morpheme with the same character every time it appeared (we now have notations that can have provided the graphic basis of the characters; Dreyer 1998). The problem is that Egyptian uses internal flection or apophony like the distantly related Semitic languages—so that only the consonants are the same in every use; the vowels vary with inflection and derivation. It thus came about that Egyptian hieroglyphs represent only consonants. But each hieroglyph was always used for however many consonants its morpheme happened to have—one, two, or three. Egyptian scribes in the very earliest surviving texts did not notate affixes, but that is a brief and ill-attested stage. As well as content morphemes, grammatical morphemes too were soon written; pictograms could denote unrelated words for related unpicturable concepts, and phonetic complements took on an important role. Moreover, a semantic determinative followed nearly every word, taken from a considerably larger inventory than was used in cuneiform. The Egyptians, however, never took the step of recognizing consonants as such: the so-called 'hieroglyphic alphabet'—a presentist invention—is just a random list of monoconsonantal signs; they were not used as a set to write Egyptian.

From almost the beginning of Egyptian writing, a more swiftly penned form of the script ('hieratic') was used for most papyrus records, a cursive variety with a one-to-one relationship of characters with the hieroglyphs. Any hieratic scribe could presumably read (though probably not paint or carve) any hieroglyphic inscription, and the connection with the pictographs, unlike in Mesopotamia or China and like in Mexico, was never lost. (A late—i.e. early first millennium BCE—popular, 'demotic,' highly cursive script records a much-developed stage of the Egyptian language and lost its connection with the hieroglyphs.)

2.2.1.2 *West Semitic Abjad*

It is the next transmission-by-misunderstanding from which we can determine that scholars became capable of and conscious of phonological analysis. In the 1990s it suddenly became less clear who was responsible for this step, when two inscriptions were discovered at Wadi el-Hol in Egypt (Darnell et al. 2005) that use what certainly looks like the same script as had been known for nearly a hundred years from Serabit el-Khadem in the Sinai, dubbed Proto-Sinaitic. The latter used shapes taken from Egyptian characters (Hamilton 2006), but with sounds based on words in a Semitic language, to write what seems to be a Semitic language—with exactly one sign for each presumed consonant of Proto-Semitic. The Wadi el-Hol inscriptions cannot be inter-preted as either Semitic or Egyptian. From about the eighteenth century BCE, then, there were no fundamental changes in the Semitic abjad, even as its shapes began to diversify as it came to be used for a variety of Northwest Semitic languages across the Fertile Crescent. There were two main varieties: the Phoenician, which remained consonant-only until it died out, and the Aramaic, where around 1000 BCE, probably as a result of the contraction of diphthongs into long vowels (*ay* to *ē* and *aw* to *ō*) while spelling remained traditional, semivowel letters came to be used for certain long vowels, at first word-finally, and eventually internally as well. (They are called *matrēs lectionis*, 'mothers of reading'.) By the time such letters could be used freely, awareness had grown of vowels as something distinct from consonants.[8]

One of the most successful scripts ever is the Arabic descendant of the Aramaic branch: as the script of the Islamic scripture, the Qur'ān, it became the vehicle for literacy wherever Islam succeeded, adapting in its flexibility (§2.3.2.3) to the phono-logical systems of many languages, only once being replaced (by an adaptation of the roman alphabet) as part of the secularization of modern Turkey in 1928.

2.2.1.3 *Greek Alphabet*

The third transmission-by-misunderstanding is the addition of vowel letters to the Phoenician variety for Greek, producing the first alphabet. It probably happened in a commercial setting, probably *c.*800 BCE, certainly where Greeks and Phoenicians interacted, perhaps in an Anatolian or Levantine port. A Greek merchant (who did not speak Phoenician well) might have observed a Phoenician keeping accounts and, realizing what a boon that was for business, asked how it was done. Phoenician has several consonants absent from Greek, and when the Phoenician pronounced the letter names beginning with those consonants, the Greek heard not the consonants, but the vowels that followed them—and used those letters for *a*, *e*, *i*, *o*, and *u* instead: segmental phonology had been fully grasped. Thereafter the development of the alphabet in Europe is merely a matter of detail—it changed shape, for Latin, Armenian, Georgian, Slavic, taking on additions for phonemes not present in the donor language. These

---

[8] This is an additional obstacle to Gelb's proposal to regard the Northwest Semitic abjad as a 'syllabary with unspecified vowel' (Gelb 1952, Daniels 2000b).

additions are made in a variety of ways (Daniels 2006), but they do not represent further refinement of linguistic understanding.

2.2.2 Adoption: Transmissions by Tradition

Phonographic writing progressed across Asia by two historic routes, in both cases emerging from varieties of the Aramaic abjad plus *matrēs* (Daniels 2007). Across the north, roughly speaking, there has been a continuous nearly 3,000-year scribal tradition, from chancery to chancery, that saw Aramaic writing transferred by instruction from Aramean to Assyrian to Achaemenid Persian to Parthian[9] to Sassanian to Sogdian to Uyghur to Mongolian to Manchu courts. The letter shapes changed, the direction of writing turned from sinistrograde[10] to vertical, and *matrēs lectionis* notated more and more of the vowels, but the basic principles remained the same. The Iranist Nicholas Sims-Williams (1981) shows on the basis of the phonology of Sogdian that the Sogdian script was adapted for the Turkic language Uyghur not by analytic reflection, but through gradual, casual reuse of the characters and orthographic principles in ways suited to the rather different phonology of Uyghur. Careful study may reveal similar activities in the many other transfamilial adaptations over the centuries.

2.2.3 Adaptation: Transmissions by Scholarship

The southern route of transmission of the Aramaic script, by contrast, involved several passes through grammatically sophisticated civilizations. Where there has been a tradition of thinking about language, scripts are improved or invented that reflect the cumulated insights.

2.2.3.1 *India*

There is no evidence in the work of Pāṇini that writing was used in India in his time (or, if it was, that it played any part in grammatical analysis). When, however, Aramaic language and script (replete with generous use of *matrēs lectionis*) came to the northwest frontier of the Subcontinent with Achaemenid adventurers, the abjad was taken over for recording the Gandhari Prakrit of the area in a script known as Kharoṣṭhi. The pandits, attuned to the segmental phonology of their own Prakrit, found a script where hardly any /ă/, but very many /ī ē/ and /ŭ ŏ/, were notated. Their

---

[9] The Parthian and Sassanian empires wrote several Iranian languages using, essentially, Aramaic logograms (content words spelled with the Aramaic abjad but read in Iranian, as shown by the inflections and syntax) with remarkably uniform orthography across lands and centuries, evidencing rigorous traditional scribal training (Henning 1958: §11).

[10] *Sinistrograde* = 'leftward', *dextrograde* = 'rightward'.

language used only CV syllables, and they economically took the Aramaic C symbols to represent the unmarked C*a*, while inventing appendages (*mātra*s) to the letters for *e i o u* (I label the type *abugida*). Grammatical theory (Patel 2007) came to the fore[11] when Kharoṣṭhi was reformed into Brahmi in the time of Aśoka (mid-third century BCE): it turns from sinistrograde to dextrograde, the lettershapes are geometricized, *mātra*s for long vowels and diphthongs are added, and over the generations ways were found for notating the consonant clusters found in Sanskrit (illustrated in the modern Devanagari script: त *ta*, ता *tā*, ति *ti*, ती *tī*; त + क *ka* → त्क *tka*, ट *da* + ट → ड *dda*, क + ष *ṣa* → क्ष *kṣa*; क्षि *kṣi*; त् *t#*, क् *k#*); each such graphic unit is called an *akshara*.

2.2.3.2 *Tibet*

Another grammatically informed people then took over an Indic writing system, but their language, Tibetan, is isolating, so disregarding syllable boundaries could impede comprehension. In Tibetan, the consonant letters are grouped horizontally and vertically within each syllable, the four vowel *mātra*s appear above or below the consonant(s), and a dot follows each syllable. A short-lived offshoot of Tibetan is the 'Phags-pa script of the Mongol empire, intended for writing all the languages of the realm (Nakano 1971: 1–58; Svantesson et al. 2005: ch. 8), though in the event it seems to have been used more for Chinese than for other languages (Coblin 2007). Here the sequence of letters is vertical and each vowel *mātra* (*a* is still inherent in each letter) follows below its consonant.

2.2.3.3 *Korea*

The Korean alphabet[12] reveals familiarity with both 'Phags-pa and Chinese phonological theory; the five letter shapes (§2.3.1.2) are almost certainly based on the corresponding 'Phags-pa letters (Ledyard 1997), which could more generally have provided the notion of separate treatments of consonants and vowels. The mid-fifteenth-century documents promulgating the script are couched in Chinese linguistic terms, and the letters are grouped into square (C)V(C(C)) syllable blocks that superficially resemble Chinese characters (§2.3.3.4).

2.3 KNOWLEDGE OF LANGUAGE EVIDENCED IN WRITING SYSTEMS

Because writing is a learned process always under conscious control, whatever analysis is embodied in the script and the orthography is necessarily part of the writer's and

---

[11] The opposite, I claim, is found in the Arab grammarians, where the notion of the vowel-less triconsonantal root is grounded in the consonants-only script (cf. رمى ⟨rmy⟩ *ramā* 'throw', سار ⟨sʔr⟩ *sāra* 'start', where three letters are written for two consonants); when Arabic grammatical theory began to influence Syriac grammarians, one concept they did not import into their work was the triconsonantal root (Bohas 2003).

[12] See also §10.3 below.

reader's explicit knowledge about the structure of their language. Virtually every level of analysis used in modern linguistics has been reflected in some writing system.

2.3.1 Phonetics

2.3.1.1 *The Speech Stream*

A most salient fact about language is that it is, by and large, temporally linear, and all writing systems impose a direction of setting down and reading symbols, usually unidimensional, reflecting the temporal order of utterance of the units to which they correspond. Reasonably straight lines are the norm (violations are due to considerations of aesthetics or of the space or surface available), vertical or horizontal, proceeding in either direction, occasionally in both directions alternately (*boustrophedon*), and rarely symmetrically (ancient Egyptian architectural display). Outward spirals occur in special circumstances (such as on Mesopotamian 'incantation bowls' in several languages); inward spirals would seem to be impractical.

Most Brahmi-derived scripts violate the congruence of temporal and spatial dimension by placing the ⟨ĭ⟩ *mātra* before (to the left) of the *akshara* of the consonant after which the vowel /i/ is pronounced (and similarly with ⟨ĕ⟩ and derivatives from it in scripts for languages with a larger complement of vowel phonemes). The other *mātras* are written above, below, or right of the consonant(s). Kandhadai and Sproat (2010) suggest that the incongruence between visual and temporal ordering impacts reading speed, but with suspect methodology and assumptions. Presumably an entire sequence of consonant((s) and vowel) is apprehended in a single act of perception.

2.3.1.2 *(Allo)phones*

Including sub-phonemic information in an alphabet is rare, but it has happened at least twice: the Avestan alphabet, which was devised (using Iranian and Greek letter shapes) probably in the fourth or fifth century CE to record the Zoroastrian scriptures, with its plethora of letters e.g. for vowels and sibilants, remains difficult to interpret in full detail apparently because the distinctions being recorded are sub-phonemic. And the Masoretic vowel (and other) notation added to the Hebrew abjad in the second half of the first millennium of the modern era (§2.3.2.3) also only makes sense if it is understood to represent subphonemic distinctions: in particular the wide variety of uses of the symbol for *šǝwa* ְ, which at times marks a reduced vowel, at times marks silence, and at times in combination with other vowel symbols marks reduced vowels whose colour is not entirely indistinct. All three are found in the word לְזַרְעֶךָ *lǝzar'ǎkɔ* 'to thy seed' (Gen. 48: 4).

A different matter is the inclusion of information about phonetic features in the letters of an alphabet. In Korean Hangul, five basic lettershapes ㄱ ㄴ ㅅ ㅁ ㅇ ⟨k n s m

Ø/ŋ⟩ are said to be iconic representations of vocal-tract anatomy[13] and the other letters are built from them somewhat systematically, e.g. ㄴㄷㅌㄸ,ㅁㅂㅍㅃ ⟨n t th tt, m p ph pp⟩.

Phonetic features are also the basis of a variety of successful shorthand systems (Pitman, Duployan, Gabelsberger, Gregg). In neither Korean nor shorthand are the phonetic connections explicitly taught. One iconic phonetic transcription was devised that saw some success in the later nineteenth century (Bell 1867),[14] but its very iconism (entailing very intricately drawn characters) may have contributed to its early abandonment in favour of Roman-alphabet-based phonetic transcriptions.

2.3.2 Phonology

Implicit in the definition of writing—*a system of conventional visible signs by which an utterance can be conveyed to and understood by a reader without the intervention of the utterer*—is the requirement that it be or include a means of encoding the sounds of its language (to be able to convey stretches of speech with no semantic content, such as proper names, foreign proper names in particular).

2.3.2.1 *Syllables*

While syllabography underlies all unsophisticated grammatogenies, only a few true syllabaries are used by literate communities today: Cherokee, Vai, and Yi (a Tibeto-Burman language of China).

2.3.2.2 *Moras*

The term 'mora' was introduced into modern linguistics by McCawley (1968) to render a term (equivalent to 'letter') for the characters in the two Japanese 'syllabaries' ('kana'), *hiragana* and *katakana*, which denote not merely the (C)V syllables of the language but also a syllable-closing nasal or length.[15] The following examples contain four moras each but varying numbers of syllables: Hiragana ながさき ⟨na-ka-sa-ki⟩ *Nagasaki*, しんぶん⟨shi-N-fu-N⟩ *shimbun* 'newspaper', おおさか ⟨o-o-sa-ka⟩ *Ōsaka*; Katakana ロケット⟨ro-ke-Q-to⟩ *roketto* 'rocket', ローソク ⟨ro-:-so-ku⟩ *rōsoku* 'candle' (only the last two of these would normally be written with kana; cf. §2.3.3.2).

Another script that obligatorily notates moras is Arabic, where each letter represents C(V), the second portion of a diphthong, or vowel length: يكتب ⟨yktb⟩ *yaktubu* 'he

---

[13] The conceit of iconic representation of lips, teeth, or throat may have arisen from an incidental observation in one or two cases that was extended, perhaps wishfully, to the rest.

[14] I have seen one large-scale 19th-century English dictionary whose pronunciations were given in Bell's Visible Speech, but I have been unable to recover the reference.

[15] 'Mora' in recent phonological theory is quite different, as segments can be 'extra-moraic'; different again in the well-known albeit unpublished suggestion by Poser (1992) (cf. Miller 1994: 1, Rogers 2005) that nearly all syllabaries be termed 'moraographies.'

writes', يوم ⟨ywm⟩ *yawm^{un}* 'a day', مكتوب ⟨mktwb⟩ *maktūb* 'written' (Daniels, in press, a) and notation of consonant length is all but obligatory (see §2.3.2.4).

2.3.2.3 *Segments*

We do not say that West Semitic writing omits vowels (that is a presentist approach); West Semitic writing writes consonants.[16]

Consonants. The Arabic abjad developed from a variety of Aramaic script, the Nabatean. Several of the letter forms had converged to near-identicalness; moreover, Aramaic has only 22 consonants, whereas Arabic has preserved 27 of the 28 Proto-Semitic consonants. Unlike many scribes, the Arabs chose to rectify this mismatch, and they did so by affixing dots to the basic linear consonant shapes. About half the cases of differentiating dots are based on phonetic similarity (س *s* and ش *š*, for example) but about half are based on etymology: the letter ث *θ*, for example, is a dotting of the letter ت *t*. In Aramaic, **θ* merged with **t* as *t*, and arguably *θ* is most phonetically similar to ف *f*; but the graphic correspondence reflects the etymology of the sound. This demonstrates awareness of cognates between Aramaic and Arabic (Daniels 2000a). On the other hand, a few generations after the dotting became obligatory and universal, the founding Arabic grammarian Sībawayhi did not extend the dotting pattern when he needed to talk about allophones or about foreign sounds like *ž*: he resorted to circumlocutions like 'the sound between Šīn and Zā'' (Al-Nassir 1993).

Phonemic split sometimes brings new letters or spellings (e.g. Middle English ⟨v⟩ alongside ⟨f⟩ when French loans caused voicing to become significant; cf. also ⟨vision⟩ vs ⟨mission⟩), sometimes not—English used ⟨ð⟩ and ⟨þ⟩ indifferently, even in a single manuscript, for both the voiced and voiceless interdentals, a situation persisting with Modern English ⟨th⟩ due to low functional load. Japanese, on the other hand, uses diacritics on certain *kana* for the same purpose.

Vowels. As we have seen (§2.2.1.3), the 'discovery' of vowels and the 'invention' of vowel letters in the West was accidental. While all the Greek-derived alphabets of Europe (which have spread by mission and conquest around the world) continue(d) to use symbols of equal status for both consonantal and vocalic segments, the Aramaic-derived scripts of Asia continued to use *matrēs lectionis*, in fact more and more lavishly (§2.2.3), though ⟨w y⟩ did not cease being used for /w y/ alongside /ŭ ĭ/.

In the languages of scripture, Jewish Tanakh, Christian Bible, Islamic Qur'ān, the written form of the text was sacred. With their demise as spoken languages, vowel letters could not simply be interpolated on the Greek model, and ways (called 'pointing') were found to notate vowels in phonemic detail. First was the Christian Aramaic variety Syriac, where the large number of Greek loanwords that arrived with Christianity and Iranian loanwords that arrived with the civil administration may have

---

[16] Similarly, in my accounts of decipherments I do not tot up the number of characters each investigator 'got right,' because as far as any individual investigator was concerned, they were *all* right.

made this especially necessary.[17] It happened gradually (Segal 1953)—at first a dot for a 'fuller' vowel was placed above the consonant letter: ܥܒܕܐ ⟨ʕbdʔ⟩ ʕḇoḏɔʔ[18] 'a work' and below for a 'weaker' vowel: ܥܒܕܐ ⟨ʕbdʔ⟩ ʕaḇdɔʔ 'a servant'. Over time, combinations of dots became associated with specific vowel qualities.[19] Syriac vocalization may have been the inspiration for several Hebrew pointings devised in various rabbinic centres across the Fertile Crescent; the one associated with Tiberias in Galilee is exclusively found in modern editions. Arabic pointing comes about with the establishment of the text of the Qur'ān in the early decades AH, but in this case because the consonantal text was established on the basis of a dialect that had lost /ʔ/, consonant length, and final short vowels (but notated every /ā ī ū/ with *matrēs*) and the standard language retained them (Versteegh 1997: 54–7). In all three cases, pointing is restricted almost entirely to the sacred text itself and is thoroughly optional in all other writing.

For languages of southern India with more vowels than Sanskrit, additional *mātra*s were devised. Alphabetically written languages can resort to diacritics (German ⟨ä ö ü⟩), to digraphs (Greek *ου* [u] vs *υ* [y]), or to new letter shapes (especially favoured for minority languages of the Soviet Union using expansions of the Russian alphabet). The Vietnamese letters ⟨ă â ê ơ ô ư⟩ [a ə e ɤ o ɯ] should be considered new letters, not letters with diacritics, because they have no systemic relation with ⟨a e i o u⟩ [ɑ ɛ i ɔ u] as does the *Umlaut* relationship in German.

2.3.2.4 *Suprasegmentals*

Length. Vowel length can be marked by distinct symbols (Classical Greek ε ⟨ĕ⟩ vs η ⟨ē⟩, Devanagari ि⟨ĭ⟩ vs ी⟨ī⟩); by presence vs absence of a symbol (Hungarian a ⟨ă⟩ vs á ⟨ā⟩, Devanagari ○ ⟨ă⟩ vs ा ⟨ā⟩); by doubling a symbol (as in Finnish or Somali orthography); or by nothing at all (Classical Greek α ⟨ă⟩ or ⟨ā⟩, any Latin vowel).

Consonant length[20] can be marked by doubling a symbol (Finnish *Kokkola*, Sanskrit सुदृशीकसंदृग्गवाम् *sudṛśīkasaṁdṛg gavām*, cf. Whitney 1879: §87c) or with a diacritic. Arabic ّ (*šadda* or *tašdīd*) is the least omissible optional point (§2.3.2.2): كتّب ⟨kt:b⟩ *kattaba* 'he made (someone) write (something)'. Hebrew ⊙ (*dāḡēš*), like *šəwa* (§2.3.1.2), has a dual function. In pointed text, it marks both consonant lengthening and the non-fricative (= not postvocalic) pronunciation of the six simple stops. Both are illustrated in the expression לֹא פִלָּלְתִּי *lô p̄illaltî* 'I did not expect' (Gen. 48: 11). It appears to be the

---

[17] Unlike in Arabic, they tended not to be assimilated to Semitic derivational patterns.

[18] In transcriptions of Aramaic and Hebrew, an under- or over-bar marks fricative (i.e. postvocalic) pronunciation and a circumflex marks the presence of a *mater lectionis*.

[19] In the western Syriac-use area, a few late manuscripts were vocalized by inserting Greek vowel letters alongside the consonantal text. This has misleadingly become the preferred introductory system in European pedagogical materials.

[20] Weingarten (2011) gathers much data on long consonants and their representations in modern orthographies.

case that consonant length is not marked in a script unless vowels are individually marked.[21]

Accent. In languages with non-constrastive stress (word-initial, word-final, penultimate, etc.), stress position indication is concomitant with word division. In Spanish, stress is largely predictable, but where it is not, it is marked with an acute accent. In Greek, the former pitch-accent was marked for both position and quality (high or rising, and falling). In Hebrew, word stress is predictable, but in a fully pointed biblical text each word bears an 'accent' mark that performs two additional functions as well (cf. §2.3.4.1).

Tone. It is fairly unusual to mark tone, and in scripts with a long history, obligatory tone marking usually reflects historical tonogenesis (Thai, Burmese; Sawada 2003). Lexical tone can be marked in newly devised alphabets (in Vietnamese, the symbols for the tones are to an extent iconic: o ó ò ỏ õ ọ [level, high rising, low (falling), dipping-rising, high rising glottalized, low glottalized]). The diacritics provided for downstep tone in missionary roman alphabets are often omitted as superfluous by native writers,[22] but they are apparently obligatory in Nko.

2.3.3 Morphology

2.3.3.1 *Words*

Quite a few orthographies incorporate means of isolating words. This is generally not done in (logo)syllabaries, but it is more the rule than the exception in (logo)segmental scripts. In ancient Egyptian, the semantic determinative (chosen from a limited inventory) that follows nearly every word serves the purpose. The earliest sizeable corpus in an abjadic script, the Ugaritic, uses a vertical stroke (slightly smaller than the vertical stroke used in the letter forms). Many epigraphic North Semitic scripts use a dot or vertical bar. In some cursive Aramaic scripts, letters within a word began to be connected so that whole words could be written with no or few lifts of the pen. In many Aramaic scripts a pause at the end of writing a word led to a prolongation of a penstroke: in Hebrew five 'final forms' became standardized—ך ף ן ם ץ for כ מ נ פ צ ⟨k m n p ṣ⟩ respectively—but a Hebrew word can end with any letter, so word spacing is used as well. In Arabic, on the other hand, almost all letters have distinctive word-final forms—e.g. ح س ع ه for ـحـ ـسـ ـعـ ـهـ ⟨ḥ s ʕ h⟩ respectively—so that in careful manuscripts little or no more space is left between words than within words that contain non-connecting letters. Space between words is otiose in Greek texts because very few letters can end a word. Space between words in roman-alphabet texts was a gradual medieval

---

[21] An implicational universal to be added to those noted in Justeson (1976).
[22] Roberts (2011) surveys tone indication in roman-alphabet orthographies.

innovation whose introduction coincided with the introduction of silent reading (Saenger 2000). Brahmi-derived scripts tend to space only after breath-groups or full clauses, though with Western influence in India, it became more usual to space after words (Thai continues not to space).

An advantage of an orthography that is not (fully) phonemic is that homophones can be graphically distinguished. Among the most successful such systems are the Chinese—aptly characterized by Hockett (1997b) as a syllabary 'but with homophones distinguished,' cf. 炸彈 'bomb', 詐彈 'fake bomb', 炸蛋 'deep-fried egg', all ⟨zhà dàn⟩ (Lee Sau Dan, Usenet group sci.lang 28 Jan. 2011)—and English *bough~bow, sew~sow, son~sun*; such pairs are usually the result of orthographic change not keeping up with linguistic change (which can also have pernicious effects, as in *bow~bow, sow~sow*, and *ear~ear*).[23] This sort of homophony is found in orthographies with long histories, including French,[24] Thai, and Tibetan.

2.3.3.2 *Inflection*

The most familiar example of distinctive writing of an inflectional category is the English possessive, where near-total homophony is resolved by an apostrophe: ⟨Socrates, Socrates'; cat's, cats, cats'⟩. Syriac adopted the 'fuller/weaker' vowel pointing (§2.3.2.3) to identify inflectional categories in biconsonantal verbs: given ܩܛܠ ⟨qtl⟩ *qṭal* (perfect) ܩܛܠ⟨q̣tl⟩ *qoṭel* (participle) ܩܛܠ⟨q̣tl⟩ *qaṭel* (intensive) 'kill', cf. ܣܡ⟨sm⟩ *sɔm* (perfect) 'set' with underdot despite the 'fuller' vowel (Nöldeke 2001 [1904]: 6–7).

It is in Japanese that the graphic expression of inflection has reached its acme. The inherited Chinese characters (*kanji*) denote only the bases of verbs, substantives, and adjectives (communicating, unlike in Chinese, the meaning only);[25] inflections and function words are written with *hiragana*, the 46-character (plus diacritics) syllabary: 断る ⟨KOTOWA-ru⟩ or 断わる ⟨KOTO-wa-ru⟩ 'to refuse'.

2.3.3.3 *Derivation*

Graphic representation of derivation—uniform writing of bases even as their phonological shape changes, usually the result of conservative spelling—is the foundation of classic generative phonology (Chomsky and Halle 1968), which celebrates the fact that ⟨photograph⟩ does not change its spelling when *-ic* (changing the stress) or *-y* (changing both stress and vowel pattern) is added. Arabic and French orthography, too, lent themselves to such treatment (Brame 1970, Schane 1968).

---

[23] Cf. German *Bogen~Bug, säen~Sau, Ähre~Ohr*. Cf. also n. 25 on Japanese homography.

[24] French also makes a few purely lexical distinctions with diacritics: *a* 'has', *à* 'to'; *ou* 'or', *où* 'where' (plus *août* 'August').

[25] Almost all *kanji* have both a native Japanese reading (*kun*) and a borrowed, Sino-Japanese, reading (*on*), and the consonant of the first-following *kana* can disambiguate. Rogers (2005) uses the *on/kun* distinction to characterize any borrowed vs native orthographic system, e.g. Eng. ⟨phase/faze⟩.

2.3.3.4 *Morphophonemics*

The tendency to morphophonemic spelling of Korean is documented. Fifteenth-century NIMKUM-*i* 'lord (nom.)' changed from 님그미 ⟨nim.ku.mi⟩ via 님금미 ⟨nim.kum. mi⟩ to 님금이 ⟨nim.kum.i⟩, the modern orthography. Compare the treatment in English over time of the past tense morpheme |D|. For a time, it was often spelled phonetically, ⟨ed⟩ or ⟨'d⟩ or sometimes ⟨'t⟩, but now (in American English) it can only be ⟨ed⟩ for all three allomorphs.

2.3.4 Syntax

2.3.4.1 *Constituent structure*

The forty Hebrew 'accents' or 'cantillation marks,' one on every word, fully parse the biblical text into strictly binary syntactic structures (Aronoff 1985) and also identified the melodies to which the text was to be chanted (their musical interpretation is unknown today).

2.3.4.2 *Discourse structure*

The fairly crude systems of punctuation of European languages (Parkes 1993), ⟨, ; : . ¿ ? ¡ !⟩ and a variety of delimiters for interpolations and, especially, direct quotations (which have been adopted into Hebrew and Arabic to an extent, and to a lesser extent into East Asian scripts), pale beside those described for Syriac (Segal 1953). Many devices for paragraphing have been used over the millennia, from straight lines ruled on cuneiform tablets presumably with a taut string, to signs equivalent to ⟨¶⟩ embedded within a text, to an enlarged and probably decorated initial letter, to ending a paragraph before a margin is reached and indenting and/or spacing before the next begins.

2.3.5 Pragmatics

2.3.5.1 *Emphasis*

The European use of capital letters to mark sentence openings, proper nouns (e.g. French), proper nouns and adjectives (e.g. English), or all nouns (e.g. German) emerged from manuscript practice in Late Antiquity, where Latin scripts of greater antiquity and formality of structure (such as inscriptional majuscules) were taken as more appropriate for prominent text elements such as titles, and a hierarchy emerged through uncial, half-uncial, and minuscules. Roman typefaces based on Petrarch's revival of the Carolingian minuscule were developed in Italy in 1470–71. Italic typefaces, narrower and thus more economical of expensive paper, based on the contemporary bookhand, appeared in 1501 in Venice; their use for special material within roman text was a French innovation of the late sixteenth century (Morison 1973: 67–71) and received a boost in England through their use for interpolated material in the Author-ised ('King James') Bible of 1611: by the mid-1800s, authorities were complaining of overuse of italics in the previous century. In German printing, until the mid-twentieth century Fraktur ('black letter,' Textura), inherited from Gutenberg, was usual for popular material (though roman appears in technical work already in the early nine-teenth century); quoted words in Latin, French, etc. were set in roman, and emphasis was noted by letter-spacing words rather than by italics. Japanese uses the *katakana* syllabary, which stands out from a text as more angular than *hiragana*, for similar purposes: emphasis, foreign words, onomatopoeia (Hadamitzky and Spahn 1981).

2.3.5.2 *Politeness*

The Javanese abugida includes a partial set of 'capital' letters any of which can be used anywhere in a word that is to be distinguished for some purpose (typically proper names), and the script also incorporates a set of introductory text markers that signal the relative status of writer and addressee. This reflects the social stratification that also makes Javanese one of the original type specimens of diglossia.

2.4 CONCLUSION

What emerges from this survey is the unsurprising conclusion that aspects of linguistic structure that are most salient to the language user—the most accessible to conscious control: words, syllables, discourse, emphasis—are the most likely to be taken into account in their orthographies. Other features have emerged more or less incidentally over the centuries, and have either been incorporated into common usage or have dropped out of fashion. Needed is investigation of the origin and persistence of all these features in all the world's orthographies (vs the prevailing concentration on the evolution of the *shapes* of characters and beyond the recent attention to the *acquisition* of orthographies). It may show that imposition of script *reform* outside the context of adoption or adaptation of a script to a new language is an otiose and even futile exercise. The twin examples of Sassanian conservatism and Turkish innovation reveal that only in extraordinary circumstances can either of these extremes succeed. In every case, a writing system must be understood through the pens of those who write it.

CHAPTER 3

....

HISTORY OF THE STUDY OF GESTURE

....

ADAM KENDON

3.1 INTRODUCTION

....

THIS chapter discusses the history of the study of gesture in the Western tradition. In other traditions, for example in India, there are discussions of gesture, some of great antiquity, but these will not be treated.

'Gesture' here refers to the wide variety of ways in which humans, through visible bodily action, give expression to their thoughts and feelings, draw attention to things, describe things, greet each other, or engage in ritualized actions as in religious ceremonies. 'Gesture' includes the movements of the body, especially of the hands and arms, often integrated with spoken expression; the use of manual actions, often conventionalized, to convey something without speech; or the manual and facial actions employed in sign languages. All this is part of 'gesture', broadly conceived. Expressions such as laughing and crying, blushing, clenching the teeth in anger, and the like, or bodily postures and attitudes sustained during occasions of interaction, are less likely to be so considered. 'Gesture' is not a well-defined category. Although there is a core of phenomena, such as those mentioned, to which the term is usually applied without dispute, it is not possible to establish clear boundaries to the domain of its application, and some writers are inclined to include a much wider range of phenomena than do others.[1]

---

[1] Footnotes will provide guides to further reading. As the literature is very large, citations from it are quite selective. Chs 1 and 2 in Kendon (2004) and esp. ch. 2 in Andrén (2010) discuss the problem of defining 'gesture'. Chs 3–6 in Kendon (2004) and Kendon (2002, 2007) provide more extended accounts of the history of the study of gesture.

In what follows, studies of gesture that are most relevant to the study of language will be emphasized. Gesture in relation to neurological disorders (such as aphasia) and work on the neurological foundations of gesture, which has greatly expanded since the 1990s, will not be covered. The role of gesture in the human–computer interface, an increasingly active field of research, will also not be covered.

3.2 FROM CLASSICAL ANTIQUITY UNTIL THE EARLY MODERN PERIOD

In the Western tradition, gesture is first discussed in relation to oratory. Although mentioned by the Greeks (in Plato's dialogue known as the *Cratylus*, gesture is mentioned as a form of language used among the deaf), extended discussion begins with Latin authors, most fully developed in Quintilian's *Institutio Oratoria* (first century AD). Book XI of this work deals with *actio*, the art of delivery. There are detailed accounts of the use of the voice, the pose of the body, the management of glance, how to handle clothing, and, most notably, descriptions of how the hands should be used: what handshapes and motions are appropriate to different stages of the oration, and how the hands can express emotions and attitudes such as joy, anger, fear, sorrow, penitence, hesitation, and actions such as demanding, promising, summoning, dismissing, threatening, questioning, or asserting; how they can mark different points in the discourse, rounding off the steps in a syllogism, indicating when one is stating facts or reaching a conclusion.[2]

In the Middle Ages, the practical aspects of rhetoric, including *memoria* and *actio*, were not given much attention, the emphasis being upon discourse structure and how to organize topics and develop arguments. Bodily expression and comportment, including gesture, in this period was discussed mainly from what has been called an ethical point of view. How one moved one's body, the manner in which one employed one's hands when speaking, were seen as indices of piety and the goodness of one's soul. Gesture in church ritual and prayer was carefully managed and prescribed. During this period, also, monastic orders were founded in which gesture largely replaced speech. However, although books were written explaining how the body should be used and how gestures were to be employed in communication in these communities, gesture was not a topic of scholarly inquiry.[3]

---

[2] For studies of gesture in classical antiquity, see Sittl (1890), Brilliant (1963), Corbeill (2004), Aldrete (1999). Quintilian's account of gesture is in his *Institutio Oratoria*, Book XI.III. 85–123 (see Butler 1922). For discussion of gesture in Quintilian, see Maier-Eichorn (1989), Graf (1992), Dutsch (2002, 2007).

[3] For gesture in the medieval period see Schmitt (1990), Davidson (2001), Burrow (2002), Dodwell (2000). For monastic sign languages, see Umiker-Sebeok and Sebeok (1987), Kendon (1990b), Bruce (2007).

3.3 FROM THE FIFTEENTH TO THE EIGHTEENTH CENTURY

Early in the fifteenth century certain texts by Cicero and a complete manuscript of Quintilian's book were rediscovered. When, first among Protestants and then among Catholics, the priest's role as a persuasive teacher and preacher as well as a manager of ritual came to be emphasized, delivery or *actio* was taught once again, and much use was made of these rediscovered texts. Changes in the organization of teaching in schools and universities led to a redefinition of the scope of rhetoric to include only delivery, the other aspects being incorporated into grammar and logic. This meant that delivery received more elaborate discussion, including much discussion of gesture. Later, as the merchant classes became more wealthy and powerful, an interest in the idea of the finished gentleman or gentlewoman developed that would be acceptable in courtly circles. Beginning in Italy but spreading rapidly through the rest of Europe, books such as Castiglione's *Il libro del cortigiano* (1527) and Della Casa's *Il Galateo* (1558), promoted the idea of universal modes of conduct appropriate to a given class of person. Conduct became a way to enhance one's social status. This contributed to an interest in the question of how people expressed themselves, focusing attention on forms of behaviour and their meaning.

The expansion of contacts between Europeans and peoples of other lands, especially in the New World, led to an enhanced awareness of the diversity of spoken languages, and because explorers and missionaries had reported successful communication by gesture, the idea arose that gesture could form the basis of a universal language. The idea of a universal language that could overcome the divisions between peoples brought about by differences in spoken languages was longstanding. However, interest in it became widespread, especially in the sixteenth and seventeenth centuries, in part because, as Latin began to be replaced with vernaculars, the need for a new lingua franca was felt. There were philosophical and political reasons as well, and there developed the idea that a language should be created whose meanings were fixed, which could be written or expressed in forms that would be comprehensible, regardless of a person's spoken language. The idea that humans share a 'universal language of the hands,' mentioned by Quintilian, was taken up afresh by Bonifaccio. In his *L'arte dei cenni* ('The art of signs') of 1616 (perhaps the first book ever published to be devoted entirely to bodily expression); see Knox 1996), he hoped that his promotion of the 'mute eloquence' of bodily signs would contribute to the restoration of the natural language of the body, given to all mankind by God, and so overcome the divisions created by the artificialities of spoken languages.

This idea is again expressed in John Bulwer's *Chirologia or the Naturall Language of the Hand* and *Chironomia or the Art of Manual Rhetorick*, which appeared together in a single volume in London in 1644. The *Chironomia* elaborated the principles of manual rhetoric, following Cicero and Quintilian. Bulwer argued that the natural uses of the hand described in his *Chirologia*, for the purposes of rhetoric, must be refined and shaped by aesthetic principles. The 'natural language of the hand,' however, was universal and could be understood by all peoples 'without teaching.' As the original language, it had 'escaped the curse at the confusion of Babel.'[4]

When, in the eighteenth century, discussion of a natural origin for human language began, the idea that the original language was gestural was already current.[5] It was discussed by the Neapolitan philosopher and jurist Giambattista Vico in his *Scienza Nuova* of 1744, but it was the work of Étienne Bonnot de Condillac that promoted its wider discussion. In his *Essai sur l'origine des connaissances humaines* ('Origins of human knowledge') of 1746, Condillac proposed that if a boy and a girl (after the Deluge) were lost in the desert, neither with any knowledge of language, they could create modes of communication by elaborating their natural actions as they strove to obtain what they needed. These actions, being mutually recognized, could form the basis of communicative acts, and thus the first forms of linguistic expression. Condillac termed this a *langage d'action*. This idea was elaborated upon and modified in various ways in the work of others, for example by Diderot, in his *Lettre sur les sourds et muets* (1751), by Rousseau, in his *Essai sur l'origine des langues* (written in 1761 but published posthumously in 1782), as well as by several other authors in entries in the *Encylopédie* of Diderot and D'Alembert (1751–2). These discussions reflected the development of a philosophical interest in gesture. At the same time, new forms of theatre, emphasizing pantomime, developed. There was, too, a movement to reform pedagogy by using gesture to link objects and the expressions for them more directly (rather than concentrating on the analysis of purely verbal expressions). The idea that gesture could form the basis of a new kind of language was promoted especially by the work of the Abbé L'Epée, whose public demonstrations of his successes in teaching deaf persons to read and write French and other languages by means of his system of 'methodical signs' were widely attended by the Parisian elite. Condillac was interested in L'Epée's methods and, following this, in his *Cours d'etude pour l'instruction du Prince de Parme* (1775) he said that the *langage d'action* is not a primitive form of expression (his view in the *Essai* of 1746) but can undergo development and form a system of expression sufficient 'to render all the ideas of the human mind' (quoted in Fischer 1993: 433).

---

[4] For gesture in the early modern period, see Knox (1990a), Burke (1992). On Castigliano, see Burke (1992). For Bonifaccio see Benzoni (1970), Knox (1996). For Bulwer, see Cleary (1974, 1959), Wollock (1996, 2002). For gesture and the idea of a universal language, see Knowlson (1965, 1975), Knox (1990b).

[5] For discussion of language origins in 18th-century France, see Stam (1976), Wells (1987), Aarsleff (1982); for L'Epée, see Lane (1980, 1989). Gesture and the French Enlightenment is treated in a most interesting manner in Rosenfeld (2001), which contains an excellent bibliography. See also Fischer (1990, 1993). Engel (1785–6), a work addressed in the first place to actors, was of great influence. For the art of gesture as it developed in the 18th century, see Barnett (1987). Austin (1966 [1802]) is an excellent source for the rhetorical approach to gesture, as this developed to the end of the 18th century. Stocking (1982) is a useful essay on French anthropology in the 18th century.

By the late eighteenth century, therefore, especially in France, gesture and pantomime as forms of expression were much discussed, and the possibility of gesture
forming the basis for a highly sophisticated system that could be universally understood was often entertained. Abbé L'Epée strongly championed his idea that his system
of 'methodical signs' could form the basis of a universal language, an idea also
advocated by his pupil and successor at the National Institute for Deaf-Mutes in
Paris, the Abbé Sicard. De Gerando, in his *Des signes et de l'art de penser* (1800) showed
rather conclusively, however, that because a language of signs would become conventional like spoken language, it could not form the basis of a universal language.

3.4 THE NINETEENTH CENTURY

The idea that gesture is a universal and primitive form of expression which can be
elaborated to form a language (although developing different forms or 'dialects' in
different parts of the world), the possibility that it may have played a crucial role in the
origin of language, and the significance of language systems created in gesture (i.e. sign
languages) for a more general theory of language remained themes into the nineteenth
century. However, discussion now took advantage of the numerous observations of
gesture in use that were becoming available from many parts of the world from the
accounts of travellers, missionaries, colonial officials of all kinds, many of whom were
the precursors of anthropologists.

   This is exemplified in the work of Edward Tylor (1832–1917). In his *Researches into
the Early History of Mankind* (1865) he explored the question of whether cultural
similarities found in diverse parts of the world were to be explained by diffusion or
by parallel processes that depended upon the 'psychic unity' of mankind. He also
sought to combat the anti-evolutionist stance that had developed in a reaction to
Darwinism, then setting in, that maintained that the savage state of many peoples
was the result of a degeneration, rather than indicating earlier stages in the development of civilization. Tylor begins his book with language. He equates this with the
'power . . . of . . . uttering thoughts' which he sees as the most essential element of
civilization. 'Utterance' for him means a putting forth of one's ideas, something done
in speech, but also in gesture and in picture writing. His first three chapters investigate
'the gesture language,' including its relationship to 'word language'; the fourth is on
picture-writing. Tylor seeks to establish four main points. First, that detailed observations of sign language as used by the deaf show that it is a form of linguistic communication. Second, reviewing available information on North American Indian sign
language, deaf sign language, accounts of deaf persons communicating with 'savages,'
gestures used by speakers in everyday life, including gestures of greeting and submission, he concludes that gestural expression follows universally shared principles.
Third, he argues that the processes by which gestures or signs come to be established
as meaningful are the same as those by which word meanings are established. The

arbitrary relation between a word and its meaning is to be understood as an outcome of a process of schematization and conventionalization, as seen in sign languages and in picture writing. Fourth, Tylor argues that gesture language and speech language are not independent of one another, for it is by means of pointing and nodding and other gestures that a child first comes to know what words mean. He concludes that gesture language and spoken language are different expressions of the same underlying capacity. Although he does not commit to the idea that gesture was the first form of language, he does agree that this is plausible. Tylor thus shows how understanding gesture, including sign language, can throw light upon fundamental questions about the human capacity for language. His arguments are remarkably similar to those often put forward today.[6]

Another figure prominent in the study of gesture in the nineteenth century is Garrick Mallery (1831–94). As Chief of the Signalling Division of the US Army, he became interested in the gesture systems in use among the Indians he encountered during his tours of duty in the American West. He was eventually reassigned to the Smithsonian Institution in Washington, where he devoted himself full time to the study of Plains Indian Sign Language and also to their systems of picture writing. His book, *Sign Language Among the North American Indians Compared with that Among Other Peoples and Deaf Mutes* (1881), remains one of the most comprehensive books on gesture ever written. Like Tylor, he demonstrates that gesture can serve as well as speech as a medium for conceptual expression. He sees the study of gesture as relevant for the question of language origins, but argues that in the evolution of language both voice and gesture must have been used from the beginning, with perhaps gesture as more important at first. He did not regard the signing of the Plains Indians as a primitive form of language, but insisted that it had undergone an evolution. He believed that gestural and spoken expression are adaptive alternatives. An elaboration of gesture was not an indication of poverty in spoken language. He provides a thorough survey of what was then known of gesture and sign, drawing upon Andrea de Jorio's account of Neapolitan gesture (see below), among other sources, and he discusses the use of gesture on the stage. He concludes with lengthy extracts from the Plains Indian Sign Language Dictionary he had worked on. Like Tylor, Mallery believed that by studying Indian Sign Language light would be thrown on the processes that underlie the formation of meaning in language in general.[7]

Also of importance in this period is Wilhelm Wundt (1832–1920) of Leipzig. He wrote a very large work on *Völkerpsychologie* ('folk psychology' or 'anthropological psychology') covering all aspects of human life, including magic, myths, and religion. The first two volumes of this book are concerned with language. Here he puts forward ideas on the origins and psychological foundations of language discussing gesture in some detail, because he sees it as a precursor to spoken language. He argued that

---

[6] See Bohannan's useful introduction in Tylor (1964) and Stocking (1982: chs 4 and 5); see Stocking (1992) for a broader discussion.

[7] See Mallery (1972 [1881]), Davis (2010).

language had developed from the basic patterns of behaviour that are characteristic for different affective states. These movements, when observed by others, induce similar feelings in others, and this provides a basis for communication. However, because humans can conceptualize their experience they can employ expressive bodily movements as symbolic representations of feelings. Thus gesture is the first modality of language.

Having laid out this position, Wundt then discusses sign language among the deaf, the sign language used by the Plains Indians of North America (drawing on Mallery), signing used in monastic orders where use of speech was restricted or forbidden, and gesture among Neapolitans (drawing on de Jorio). He argued, much as did Tylor and Mallery, that the study of these sign languages and gesture systems could provide insight into the psychological processes that make language possible, in a way that the study of words could not. This is because there is often a direct connection between a gestural expression and what it signifies, which is not found with words. He divides gestures broadly into demonstrative (deictic), depictive, pantomimic, and symbolic forms, the latter being forms in which meaning is extended by various processes of association. He presents some very interesting observations on the syntax of gestured or signed discourse, sometimes anticipating recent insights into syntactic processes from modern research on sign languages.[8]

The works of the three authors just considered focus mainly upon the use of gesture as an autonomous communication medium, which they believe can serve all the fundamental functions of language. All three think gesture is suited to be the first modality in which linguistic expression could have developed, although neither Tylor nor Mallery commit strongly to a 'gesture first' theory of language origins. However, like twentieth-century writers on this topic, they are attracted to the apparent transparency of the relationship between the forms of gestural expression and their meanings, and find evidence for how arbitrary symbolic forms of expression could have come into being through historical processes of progressive abstraction and schematisation.

Although the writers just considered make no direct reference to Darwin, both Mallery and Wundt refer to the idea that gestural expression in humans shows continuities with expressive movements in other animals, as Darwin argues in his *Expression of the Emotions in Man and Animals* of 1872. This book says little about gesture (as here understood), but in *The Descent of Man* (1871), where the nature and origin of language is discussed, Darwin acknowledges that linguistic expression can be manual. He otherwise mentions gesture only as a form of expression that might have aided vocal expression in the emergence of speech. On page 54, Darwin adds a footnote drawing attention to Edward Tylor's 'very interesting work' on gesture in his *Researches* of 1865, but he does not otherwise discuss it.

---

[8] My summary of Wundt is based on Wundt (1973 [1921]), which also contains discussions by Blumenthal, George Herbert Mead 1934, and an extract in English from Karl Bühler 1933.

All three of the authors just considered make reference to gesture in Naples and refer to the work of Andrea de Jorio (Tylor only indirectly). Andrea de Jorio (1769–1851) was a Neapolitan ecclesiastic and archaeologist who published works on Pompeii and Herculaneum. He believed that the traditions and modes of expression of his contemporary Neapolitans preserved much of the ancient Greek culture of which they were, historically, the inheritors (Naples was founded by Greek colonists in the fourth century BC and remained mainly Greek in language and culture for a long time after it was absorbed by Rome). He thought that many of the gestural expressions depicted on the vases and in the frescos and mosaics emerging from the excavations undertaken in the buried cities nearby could be better interpreted if they were compared with the gestural expressions then in common use among Neapolitans. To demonstrate this, he wrote *La mimica degli antichi investigata nel gestire napoletano* ('Gestural expression of the ancients in the light of Neapolitan gesturing'), published in Naples in 1832.[9] In this book he described in detail the gestures in everyday use among Neapolitans so that these could be matched against the images of gestures found on ancient objects. Although nowadays not considered useful for archaeologists, the book is of considerable interest for understanding Neapolitan gesture use in the early nineteenth century. De Jorio considered gestural expression as a part of Neapolitan culture, and sought to understand it from this point of view. This was relevant for his archaeological concerns since, according to him, the ancients, like the moderns, are ordinary human beings who lived as humans do today. As a work on the anthropology of everyday life (and on the application of ethnography to archaeology), this book was ahead of its time.

The book also included a discussion of a number of theoretical issues regarding the nature of gesture as a form of expression, and discussions of methods to be followed in the study of gesture. De Jorio insisted on careful description of gestures as actions, and maintained that gesture meaning could not be given unless contexts of use were known. He did not think gesture was a language, but since it could meet many language functions it was appropriate, in analysing it, to apply concepts derived from the study of language. He shows how grammatical features such as number, person, comparison, tense, and aspect may be expressed in gesture, how gestures may combine to form compound expressions, and how they work as rhetorical devices such as metaphor, metonymy, synecdoche, or irony and may thus be a part of discourse. Most of what he has to say is concerned with how Neapolitan speakers use gestures together with speech, although he alludes to their use as an autonomous form of communication in some conditions, as in noisy circumstances, across big distances, or when communication must be concealed.

---

[9] For an English translation and for an outline of his life and analysis of his work by Kendon, see de Jorio (2000). De Jorio (1832) was reprinted in 1964 and has since been issued in facsimile at least twice.

3.5 THE FIRST HALF OF THE
TWENTIETH CENTURY

By the end of the nineteenth century gesture was well understood, for the most part with regard to how it functions on its own, as in sign languages, and its significance for theories about the origins of language seemed clear. Gesture continued to be described by some of the pioneers of anthropology. H[enry] Ling Roth 1889 published a study of greeting gestures, and in Australia, Alfred William Howitt, Walter Edmund Roth, Walter Baldwin Spencer, Francis James Gillen, and Carl Strehlow provided details of the gesture systems in use among the Australian Aborigines (see Kendon 1988b: chs 2 and 3, 2008a. Alfred Cort Haddon, who led the Cambridge University expedition to the Torres Straits Islands, included gesture as a topic to be studied (see Stocking 1992: ch. 1). Some linguists, following Wundt, also recognized gesture as important. For example Leonard Bloomfield, in his first general book on language published in 1914, followed Wundt's approach closely and begins his book with a discussion of language origins which includes a consideration of gesture, which he believes will throw light on the origin of symbolic expression.

After this, however, interest in gesture among anthropologists and linguists declined. This was due to several different factors. By the end of the nineteenth century sign language as a medium for educating the deaf had fallen out of favour, which depressed serious interest in it by others. Discussion of the problem of language origins, where the phenomena of gesture had been considered relevant, was no longer regarded as worthwhile, so an interest in gesture from this point of view came to seem somewhat quaint. In linguistics, furthermore, as in other social sciences such as anthropology, there was a shift away from an historical, evolutionary approach. Saussure's proposal that linguistics should focus on *langue* changed the interest of linguists away from historical studies to the problem of describing the structure of language as a synchronous system. In social and cultural anthropology the emphasis came to be laid on studying the functioning of societies as self-contained systems, rather than investigating particular social practices and their origins. In the United States especially, linguistics was to be established as an independent discipline. Leonard Bloomfield, in his influential *Language* (1933), rejects his earlier indebtedness to Wundt, and seeks to free linguistics from its ties to psychology. As a result, gesture is treated as peripheral or derivative and not of interest to linguistics. Gesture was not studied by psychologists, however, for psychology was dominated by behaviourism or by Freudian theory, and research was mainly concerned with learning theory, with the unconscious, or with perception and psychophysics. Gesture would have been regarded as being, like speaking, a form of wilful, conventionalized expression and was not attractive as a topic for study by psychologists in this period.[10]

Some linguists, nevertheless, did retain interest in gesture. In North America, linguistics developed as a part of anthropology, and two of its most prominent pioneers, Franz Boas (1858–1942) and Edward Sapir (1884–1939) recognized that expressive behaviour beyond the boundaries of what was included in speech was important for meaning and, being governed by social convention, could be partly structured in ways similar to language. Boas, in the late 1930s, encouraged one of his students, David Efron, to undertake a systematic comparative study of gesture, comparing its use among first-generation Italians and Yiddish-speaking East European immigrants living in Manhattan, with its use among their descendants who had assimilated to English-speaking American life. Boas wanted to demonstrate that differences between gesturing among Italians as compared to the Jews were cultural, learned differences, and not due to racial inheritance, as Nazi anthropologists maintained. Efron showed that the marked differences between Italian and Jewish gesturing largely disappeared in their Americanized descendants. This was taken as conclusive proof that gesture is patterned by cultural tradition. Efron undertook field observations, was assisted by the artist Stuyvesant Van Veen, who made many brilliant drawings, and, unusually for the time, he analysed in detail 16mm films of spontaneous interactions in the streets. Although he could not use sound-film, he is perhaps the first student of gesture to attend to how gestures and speech are employed together. His work, published in 1941, was considered important at the time for showing that gestures are culturally patterned. It was re-published in 1972 on the initiative of Paul Ekman, because of its wider relevance for the study of gesture.

Edward Sapir always maintained that spoken language was but a component of communication. He wrote of how 'the unwritten code of gestured messages and responses, is the anonymous work of an elaborate social code and tradition.' The idea that this 'unwritten code' has an intimate relationship with language and that, at least to a degree, its structure could be analysed in a systematic way, much as spoken language can be, was quite influential and, as noted below, was to influence a number of linguists who came to agree that there is no sharp boundary between what is 'linguistic' and what was later to be called 'paralanguage' and 'kinesics.'[11]

[10] Nevertheless, there were a few publications, notably Cocchiara (1932) and Critchley (1939). For an account of the varying attitudes toward sign language, especially in the US, see Baynton (1996, 2002). See also Lane (1980, 1989). On the decline of interest in the discussion of language origins, see Stam (1976). On Bloomfield and the shift to an autonomous linguistics, see Bloomfield (1914), which contains a useful introductory essay by Kess. See also Hymes and Fought (1975), Andresen (1990).
[11] For Franz Boas see Ruby (1980, 1983) and Norman Boas (2004); for Sapir see 'The Unconscious Patterning of Behavior in Society' in Mandelbaum (1949: 554–9); see also Darnell (1990). See Efron (1972 [1941]).

3.6 FROM AFTER THE SECOND WORLD WAR UNTIL THE 1980S

In the first years following the Second World War, certain changes eventually produced a climate in which gesture again became relevant for theoretical issues related to language and thought. First, information theory and cybernetics, developed as solutions to problems in communication engineering, were applied in the study of communication within and between living systems, with the result that much thought and investigation came to be devoted to social communication. Not unrelated was the emergence of semiotics which, especially in North America, greatly broadened attention to sign processes, enhancing an interest in visible modes of signification, including gesture.[12] Further, the question of language origins once again began to be taken seriously. When experiments with chimpanzees suggested that they might use gesture symbolically, as in a sign language, the idea of gesture as a first form of language was discussed once again (as we shall see).

At the same time, in psychology, complex mental processes once again became legitimate objects of investigation. Psychologists took an interest in language and the field of psycholinguistics was established. Noam Chomsky's work was especially important. He showed the inadequacy of a behaviourist approach to language and argued that linguistics should focus on 'competence', the mental apparatus making the acquisition and use of any language possible, rather than on descriptions of specific languages. Although neither Chomsky himself nor his followers showed interest in gesture, their mentalistic orientation was influential. When, later, psycholinguists looked at gesture, they did so for what it might reveal about the mental operations of utterance production.[13]

Some linguists, many influenced by Boas and Sapir, saw that gesture might be studied as a part of language—or, at least, it should not be sharply separated from it.

---

[12] For developments in information theory and cybernetics in their application to social interaction, see Ruesch and Bateson (1951), von Foerster et al. (1949–53), Schaffner (1956), Heims (1975, 1977). For the early development of semiotics and the broadening of interest in communication to include visible bodily action, see Sebeok et al. (1964). This volume is the proceedings of a conference held in Bloomington, Indiana, in 1962. The preface to the volume gives a brief history of the term 'semiotics' and how it came to be proposed, apparently for the first time at this conference, to mean 'patterned communication in all modalities.' Sebeok was a powerful promoter of this idea and did a great deal for the development of the general field of semiotics, and he was very important in promoting an interest in the role of visible bodily action in human communication. He published several collective works concerned with this, was responsible for the re-publication of works such as those by David Efron and Garrick Mallery, and provided important support for the birth of the journal *Sign Language Studies*, founded by William Stokoe in 1972. The journal *Semiotica*, under Sebeok's editorship, often published papers on gesture and related matters.
[13] 'Psycholinguistics' was first named as a field in Osgood and Sebeok (1954); Noam Chomsky's impact on linguistics and psychology in America (and elsewhere) has been widely discussed; for one account see Newmeyer (1986). See also Ch. 19 below.

For example, Dwight Bolinger (1946) maintained that language as studied by linguists is an arbitrary, though convenient, abstraction. He said that we should not insist upon what this abstraction excludes before the implications of phenomena that accompany speaking, such as gesture, are fully understood. Similarly, Kenneth Pike argued that 'verbal and nonverbal activity is a unified whole and theory and methodology should be organized or created to treat it as such' (Pike 1967: 26). Zellig Harris (1951) said that the boundaries between what is linguistic and what is not are to be drawn only at the point where it is no longer possible to apply methods of linguistic analysis. Until gestures have been systematically studied in this way, therefore, the nature of their relationship to spoken language must remain an open question. Hockett, who originally wanted to maintain a sharp boundary between language and other communicative modalities, revised his view and agreed that there are no sharp boundaries between what is 'linguistic' and phenomena such as paralangage and kinesics. Rather, there are just 'zones of gradual transition' (Hockett 1987: 26–7, 140).

The implication of this is that there should be aspects of visible bodily action associated with utterance that could be shown to be structured. The attempt to explore this explicitly was undertaken by Ray Birdwhistell, an anthropologist from Chicago who, inspired by Sapir and encouraged by George Trager, established what he called 'kinesics.' In developing this, Birdwhistell proposed applying methods analogous to those used in linguistic analysis, and went some way towards describing the repertoire of 'kinemes' in use among American speakers, and how these were assembled into more complex constructions which he termed 'kinemorphs.'[14]

Important for the development of kinesics was Birdwhistell's participation in a project known as 'The Natural History of an Interview', undertaken at the Institute for Advanced Study in the Behavioral Sciences at Stanford in 1955–6. For the first time, an episode of interaction as recorded on 16mm film was studied to see how its verbal, paralinguistic, and kinesic aspects interrelated. This project, initiated by the interpersonal psychiatrist Frieda Fromm-Reichman, included two linguists, Norman McQuown and Charles Hockett, the anthropologist Gregory Bateson, Birdwhistell, and Henry Brosin, a psychiatrist. Although there was, ultimately, no publication, the interplay of ideas among the participants had important consequences for their subsequent thinking, and was seminal for the development of a new way of thinking of human communication in co-presence as a continuous multi-level process, mediated by multiple communication systems involving linguistic, vocal, kinesic, and spatial-orientational (or proxemic) systems in a complex interplay. Gregory Bateson was especially influential here, for he introduced concepts from information theory and cybernetics and showed how these could be applied in the study of social interaction.[15]

[14] See Birdwhistell (1970). For evaluations of Birdwhistell see Kendon (1972a) and Kendon and Sigman (1996).

[15] For the 'Natural History of an Interview' project see Leeds-Hurwitz (1987). Ch. 2 in Kendon (1990a) provides a broad overview of many of the developments referred to in this period. For Bateson see Bateson (1972), Bateson and Mead (1942), and Lipset (1980). The collection of documents stemming from

The linguistic-kinesic analysis in this project was possible because a film of the interaction studied was available. Gregory Bateson, in his work with Margaret Mead in Bali a decade before, had pioneered the use of film (and also still photography) for the analysis of human interaction. At the time of the 'Natural History' seminar Bateson was an ethnographer at the Veterans Administration Hospital in Palo Alto, where he used film to study interaction in disturbed families, and it was he who provided the film for this seminar. Film, more easily available and cheaper after the Second World War, had already been used by several psychiatrists interested in analysing communication in psychotherapy sessions, and this had revealed how much besides speech was important for communication. The features important for communication besides speech came to be called 'non-verbal communication.' The term caught on, even though it is in many ways unfortunate, for it puts together as one kind of communication a wide range of phenomena which are semiotically very diverse.

Under the rubric of 'nonverbal communication' (sometimes 'nonverbal behaviour'), a vast literature developed, produced mainly by psychologists, who investigated such topics as how facial expression, patterns of gaze in interaction, interpersonal spacing, and bodily posture could provide indices for emotional predispositions, interpersonal attitudes, and personality characteristics, or how the perception of them by observers influenced how they judged others. This work was mainly experimental, very different from the ethnographic and linguistic approach. Probably because interest was so much directed toward the psychological significance of 'nonverbal behaviour,' rather than toward the study of the structure of communication, gesture received little attention.[16]

An influential publication from this period is Ekman and Friesen (1969). This paper, written in an attempt to show that 'nonverbal behaviour' was not a simple, unified phenomenon, proposed several categories which differ according to their origins, their use, and in their coding or semiotic properties. These included 'affect displays' (facial expressions), 'adaptors' (actions such as scratching an itch, patting the hair, and the like), 'regulators' (actions that played a role in regulating interaction), and two kinds of actions performed as explicit communicative acts: highly conventionalized forms said to be equivalent to 'a word or two or a phrase,' termed 'emblems'; and 'illustrators,' the complex hand movements made when people speak which, in different ways, 'illustrate' what is being said. The concepts of 'emblem' and 'illustrator' were specifically inspired by Efron. Because this paper offered an apparently well-articulated conceptual structure for phenomena which many psychologists had only just become aware of, it had great success and has been widely cited. The term 'emblem,' especially, has been adopted by many, although it is by no means generally accepted.

---

this project, intended as a volume to be edited by Norman McQuown, is available from the Regenstein Library, University of Chicago.

[16] For a critique of the term 'nonverbal communication,' which probably originated with Ruesch, see Ruesch (1955) and the influential Ruesch and Kees (1956), see Kendon (1981b). Extremely useful bibliographical surveys for this period are Key (1975, 1977), Davis (1972), Davis and Skupien (1982).

Ekman and Friesen later published other papers on methods for the study of emblems, and a few publications by others followed, inspired by these. However, gestures of this sort, also referred to as 'symbolic gestures,' 'conventional gestures,' or simply as 'gestures,' had long been studied by folklorists, foreign language teachers, and some anthropologists, among others. Many studies took the form of lists, vocabularies, or dictionaries of gestures in use in a particular language community. Often semi-popular in nature, containing little theoretical, ethnographic or methodological back-ground and discussion, they do not cohere as a tradition of inquiry.[17] However, one study of gestures of this type took a step in the direction of greater ethnographic sophistication. Desmond Morris, whose ethologically oriented book *Manwatching* (1977) had been influential in promoting interest in gesture, undertook a study com-paring the history and meanings of twenty gestures, as recognized by informants in forty different locations distributed through western Europe, from the British Isles to the countries of the Mediterranean. This book, although addressed to a general audience, contains much interesting information and includes an extensive bibliog-raphy. The studies just referred to, which focus on individual gestures, including the study of Morris and colleagues, have little to say about the circumstances in which these gestures are used, by whom they are used, how they are employed in relation to speech, and what roles they may play in their occasions of use. De Jorio, discussed above, was an important early exception, but studies of conventionalized gestures within a communication ethnography perspective have been very few.[18]

Another development that had positive consequences for the study of gesture was a renewed interest in the question of language origins.[19] This began with the publication, in 1964, in *Current Anthropology* of Hockett and Ascher's paper 'The Human Revolu-tion.' Here the authors brought together the then new findings in human palaeontology and historical climatology in Africa, comparative analysis of the properties of human language, and several animal communication systems, to make a persuasive case that a serious, empirically grounded discussion of the origin of language was possible. Gesture was not discussed in this paper, but it soon entered the picture after the announcement by the Gardners that they had succeeded in teaching elements of a sign language to the chimpanzee Washoe (Gardner and Gardner 1969). This announce-ment, which seemed extraordinary, especially after previous efforts to teach chimpan-zees to speak had all ended in failure, impressed Gordon Hewes, among others, as providing important support for the old idea that the first form of language was gestural rather than vocal. Hewes (1973), which argued explicitly for the gestural origins position, was published in *Current Anthropology*, attracting much discussion

---

[17] A comprehensive bibliography of work of this sort is Hayes (1957). See also Barakat (1969).
[18] For discussions of work on highly conventionalized gestures, see Kendon (1981a, 1984). For a useful survey of Hispanic work, see Payrató (2008). For recent ethnographically grounded work on such gestures, see Brookes (2001, 2004, 2005). See also Sherzer (1972, 1991, 1993).
[19] See Ch. 1 above.

and served to put gesture firmly on the agenda of subsequent language origins discussions.[20]

The announcement by the Gardners also drew new attention to sign languages. If a chimpanzee could acquire a sign language, it was threatening to cross the Rubicon that was supposed to separate Man from Beast. It became a matter of urgency to investigate the nature of sign language. Although William Stokoe had demonstrated in 1960 that the sign language he studied had structural and functional properties quite comparable to those of spoken language, his work had been slow in gaining acceptance. After Washoe, however, the question of the linguistic nature of sign language aroused much wider interest. Ursula Bellugi, directly inspired by the work with Washoe, set up a research unit on sign language at the Salk Institute in California. This led to the publication of *The Signs of Language* (Klima and Bellugi 1979), a book which did more than any other to set sign language linguistics on its way. This book demonstrated the linguistic character of sign language; it also contained interesting and insightful discussions on the transition from pantomime to linguistic sign, the nature and importance of iconicity, and the nature of the gestural modality as a linguistic medium, among other topics. Since its publication, the linguistic study of sign languages has expanded to become a major branch of linguistic study.

Sign languages are *languages*, but formed within the gestural medium. Because disdain for 'mere gesture' in deaf education circles had gathered strength from the end of the nineteenth century, those studying sign language following Stokoe and Klima and Bellugi found they had to overcome considerable prejudice against the idea that gestural expression could be a language. For this reason, many maintained a sharp distinction between 'sign' as in sign language and 'gesture' as used by speakers. From a more neutral perspective, it will be seen that many features of speakers' use of gesture are shared with signers. Speakers, furthermore, in circumstances where speech is not usable (whether for ritual or environmental reasons or because of an experimenter's manipulations) may very rapidly develop use of gestures as alternatives to speaking, and when this happens, the manual expressions quickly acquire features like those found in sign languages. Sometimes, as among the Plains Indians of North America or the central desert Australian Aborigines, elaborate 'alternate sign languages' develop which may have much in common with sign languages as used by the deaf, which may be termed 'primary sign languages.' This puts into question how we may understand any distinction between 'sign' and 'gesture.' It may be better to approach the issue by way of comparative studies of the range of semiotic properties visible actions used in utterance may have, and the circumstances which govern the appearance of these

---

[20] For the emergence of origins of language discussions in which gesture is important see Hewes (1973), Hewes et al. (1974), Harnad et al. (1976). For the work with Washoe see Gardner and Gardner (1969) and Gardner et al. (1989). For the controversy surrounding this and other ape language work, Sebeok and Umiker-Sebeok (1980) and Wallman (1982) are representative. For later developments regarding gesture and language origins see Donald (1991), Armstrong et al. (1995), Stokoe (2001), Corballis (2002), Arbib (2005).

properties. It is to be noted that collaboration between students of gesture in speakers and students of sign language has become more frequent since the beginning of the twenty-first century, and the idea of a 'semiotic gradient' linking the gesturing of speakers and signing in sign language is gaining acceptance.[21]

We turn now to developments in psychology and psycholinguistics. As noted above, from the fifth decade of the twentieth century, psychologists began studying complex mental processes; in particular, many were interested in language. Chomsky was soon to have a very important influence. One consequence of Chomsky's ideas was an expansion in the study of language acquisition. Chomsky had proposed that language acquisition involved a biologically given module, the Language Acquisition Device, which guided the child in its interpretation of whatever linguistic input it received, allowing it grammatical understanding and production competence without these features being taught. This controversial idea led to many studies of children's first sentences. However, many investigators realized that to understand how language begins, one must look at what happens before speech. Studies were initiated that, using film (later video), examined interactions between mothers and infants. These showed that meaningful conversations occurred with babies well before they could use speech, the interaction being mediated by visible actions, including identifiable gestures, as well as by vocalizations. Observers such as Colwyn Trevarthen, Jerome Bruner, Elizabeth Bates, and colleagues showed that symbolic expression emerged as much in visible action as in speech. Such work led to a wider awareness of the importance of gesture in the language process, and much work has since been undertaken on the development of gesture use in very young children. This includes studies of pointing, studies of the acquisition and use of specific symbolic gestures, the symbolic use of objects in play, and how these developments appear to be linked to the emergence of verbal mastery.[22]

There have also been studies, mainly by Susan Goldin-Meadow and colleagues, of children who were born deaf, but who were reared by hearing parents who wished the child to have no exposure to sign language. It was found that such children employed gestures in their efforts to communicate and that the gestural utterances these children produced showed consistent patterns suggesting spontaneously created grammatical structures. Goldin-Meadow's view that these children demonstrate that linguistic

[21] For the importance of the Washoe work for prompting research on sign language, see Bronowski and Bellugi (1970), Bellugi (1981), and Kendon (2002). For the first developments in analysing a sign language in linguistic terms see Stokoe (1960), Klima and Bellugi (1979), Friedmann (1977). For alternate sign languages among the Plains Indians of North America, see Mallery (1972 [1881]), Sebeok and Umiker-Sebeok (1978), Farnell (1995), Davis (2010). For alternate sign languages among Australian Aborigines see Kendon (1988b). For the problem of the relationship between 'gesture' and 'sign', see Kendon (2004: chs 14, 15; 2008), Andrén (2010).

[22] For early studies of pre-speech interactions with infants and studies of the importance of gesture preceding and at the beginning of language acquisition, see Lock (1978), Bullowa (1979), Bates et al. (1979), Volterra and Erting (1990). For reviews of later work on gesture and language development, see Capone and MacGregor (2004), Gullberg et al. (2008).

structures emerge without linguistic input is controversial, but her work has under-scored the importance of gesture for understanding the nature of language.[23]

3.7 ONWARDS FROM THE 1980S

The apparently intimate relationship between visible bodily movement and speaking became a focus of particular interest for Ray Birdwhistell, largely as a consequence of his involvement with the 'Natural History of an Interview' project described above. This work prompted the micro-analytic studies of Condon and Ogston and, somewhat later, the work of Kendon, in which films of persons speaking and gesturing simultan-eously were closely analysed. This led to the explicit formulation that speech and gesture are 'two aspects of the process of utterance' (Kendon 1980), and that therefore spoken expressions and the gestures associated with them are the outcomes of a single production plan.

David McNeill, arriving (independently) at this view in 1985, went on to emphasize how, with gestures, speakers use a holistic, imagistic mode of expression simultan-eously with verbal language, which he refers to as a 'categorial arbitrary analytic system.' He argued that a speaker's co-speech gestures may be directly shaped by the speaker's meanings, revealing dimensions of thought not accessible if only verbal expressions are taken into account. For him, this duality of expression challenged current theories of language and cognition. Drawing on ideas from Vygotsky, he proposed a theory according to which the 'idea unit' (or 'growth point'), from which an utterance is unpacked, contains both imagistic thinking and linguistic categorial thinking which combine in a dialectic relationship to produce the speaker's actual expression. Central is the idea that an utterance emerges as if it is unpacked from a unit that contains all its content at once. In this way it contrasts with the linear information processing models of speech production proposed by other theorists. These ideas were elaborated in McNeill's *Hand and Mind* (1992). This book linked the study of gesture to central problems in cognition and psycholinguistics, and following its appearance there have been many publications (often by former students of McNeill) that look at gesturing in speakers from a cognitive or psycholinguistic point of view. For example, gesture is examined for the light it might throw on issues such as the nature of conceptual metaphor or the processes of 'thinking for speaking,' or how the grammat-ical structure of a language may shape a speaker's gestures.[24]

[23] These studies are summarized in Goldin-Meadow (2003a, b).
[24] Early studies on the gesture–speech relationship include Condon and Ogston (1967) and Kendon (1972b, 1980). See McNeill (1985, 1992, 2000, 2005). Duncan et al. (2007) is a collection of papers including many that reflect themes inspired by McNeill's work. Cienki and Muller (2008) is a collection of papers on metaphor and gesture. See also Müller (2008).

Work on gesture by those influenced by the anthropological linguistic tradition, and by work on the micro-organization of interaction, also greatly expanded from the beginning of the 1990s. This work has emphasized the study of the properties of gesture as a form of expression, the different ways in which it is shaped by social convention, its semiotic diversity, the origins of the various forms observed, and how these are orchestrated with other modalities, especially speech, in the construction of turns or moves within occasions of interaction. Here we find attempts to describe the different forms that gestures may take, their contexts of use, and their semiotic functions. Included in this tradition is the work of Adam Kendon, and also that of Charles Goodwin, Christian Heath, and Jürgen Streeck, among others, which reflects the influence of micro-ethnographic research on interaction practices as developed in ethnomethodology, conversation analysis, and the work of Erving Goffman.[25] Also important is the work of Geneviève Calbris, which approaches gesture from a semiotic point of view. Her work has been known in English from her book *Semiotics of French Gesture* (1990), which, while not ignoring the work on gesture in the North American linguistic tradition, has been much influenced by Ivan Fonagy and is indebted to Karl Bühler and Roman Jakobson. Calbris was an important influence on Kendon in relation to his work on pragmatic gestures.[26] A second major work by Calbris, also in English, is *Elements of Meaning in Gesture* (2011). This expands her arguments and provides many analyses of examples derived from video recordings—a feature that was absent from her earlier book, and which puts her arguments on a much surer footing.

These research trends, ethological, ethnographic, linguistic, and semiotic in their orientation, aim to provide better systematic understanding of the part gesture plays in the construction and management of communicative conduct. In this work, audio-visual recordings made in all sorts of natural, everyday settings are analysed. This has led to a recognition of the importance for interaction not just of speech and gesture, but also of how participants are oriented to one another and to their physical environment, how they make use of this environment and of the objects it contains, and how their expressive actions may derive from and be shaped by the ways in which relevant physical objects are handled and the role they play in the current interactional focus. Interesting questions are raised about the boundaries between gesture and manipulatory action, and how action related to the immediate physical setting may become a part of the symbolic actions out of which occasions of interaction are constructed.

[25] Publications by Kendon such as Kendon (1981a, 1983, 1986, 1997) have been influential in helping to define the field of gesture studies. Kendon (2004) is an integrated presentation of his approach. Important papers for gesture studies by Goodwin include Goodwin (1984, 1986, 2000, 2003, 2007), Goodwin and Goodwin (1986). For Christian Heath see Heath 1984, 1986, 1992. For Streeck, see esp. *Gesturecraft* (Streeck 2009). Erving Goffman, although he did not contribute studies of gesture as such, has been of great importance in showing how actions of all sorts must be understood within the frame of the occasion of interaction of which they are a part. See e.g. Goffman (1963, 1971, 1974, 1981).

[26] Calbris (1990). For an evaluation see Kendon (1992). See also Fonagy (2001). For work on gestures with pragmatic functions see n. 27, below.

There are also studies of the different movement patterns of gesture, showing how visual forms are used that exploit parallelisms between content and form, moving from concrete representations of acts of object manipulation of various kinds, toward abstract meanings through processes of visual metaphor. These forms may become recurrent and conventionalized and repertoires of gestures may develop. Of interest is the observation that gestures which express such aspects of the utterance as its illocutionary force, which function to draw attention to the topic structure of the speaker's discourse, or which indicate the topic focus are often recurrent in form and conventionalized. Analyses of utterances constructed using both speech and gesture reveal how gesture collaborates with speech in the creation of multi-modal expressions. Studies of occasions of interaction following methods derived from context analysis and conversation analysis show how participants incorporate visible bodily actions in how they construct and manage orderly occasions of interaction together.[27]

3.8 CONCLUSION

Gesture is of interest for students of language because it straddles the boundary between spontaneous, uncodified expression, and modes of expression that belong to socially shared communication systems. It is as if, by examining gesture, we are able to look in two directions: inward to the mental operations involved in symbolic expression and outwards to the social processes by which communication codes become established. It should be clear why gesture has, at various times in the history of its study, been seen to be of great relevance and importance for the study of the central communication processes of the human species.

---

[27] For studies that address parallelisms between content and form, see Calbris (1990, 2003, 2011); on the development of conventionalized forms, especially among gestures with mainly pragmatic functions, see Kendon (1995, 2004), papers by Seyfeddinipur, Neumann, and Müller in Müller and Posner (2004), a collection with many other interesting papers, and Streeck (2009). On the construction of multimodal utterances, see Enfield (2009).

CHAPTER 4

....

THE HISTORY OF SIGN LANGUAGE LINGUISTICS

....

BENCIE WOLL

4.1 INTRODUCTION

....

BEFORE the beginning of linguistic research in the field, sign languages were regarded as exemplifying a primitive universal way of communicating through gestures. In the modern period of linguistic research on sign languages, with the recognition that sign languages were real human languages, the emphasis initially swung to the opposite view: that sign languages differed substantially from each other, with an emphasis on the mutual unintelligibility of different sign languages. This approach undoubtedly arose from the desire to emphasize the equivalence of the linguistic status of signed languages and spoken languages, despite the differences in modality, and was certainly an essential stage in the development of the field.

The field has moved on again, and studies have now turned to an exploration of the similarities and differences among sign languages, and between signed and spoken languages. This chapter reviews the history of research on sign language, concluding with a consideration of the implications of recent approaches for our understanding of sign languages and of the nature of human languages.

Research undertaken in the past half century has identified three key features of the sign languages used by Deaf[1] communities:

---

[1] Deaf with an upper-case 'D' refers to linguistic communities characterised by the use of sign languages. Lower-case 'deaf' refers to an individual's audiological status.

- Sign languages are complex natural human languages.
- Sign languages are not related to the spoken languages of the surrounding hearing communities.
- Sign languages can be compared and contrasted in terms of typology and modality with spoken language.

§4.2 will provide a brief description of the characteristics of sign languages, their history, development, and distribution. This will serve as a background to the central part of the chapter: the history of sign linguistics research, §4.3. The final section will describe the importance of sign linguistics for linguistics research more generally.

4.2 WHAT IS SIGN LANGUAGE?

Spoken language is clearly the preferred modality for human language. There are no communities of hearing people who use a sign language as a primary language. However, there do exist complex sign systems used by hearing people. These 'secondary' sign languages are largely outside the main remit of this chapter but are nevertheless of interest.

The Plains Indian Sign Language of North America has been described in some detail. Plains Indian Sign Language was used as a lingua franca among the tribes of the North American plains, who spoke many different languages. Tomkins (1969: 7) describes it as '[t]he first and only American universal language.' In 1885, it was estimated that there were over 110,000 'sign-talking Indians,' including Blackfoot, Cheyenne, Sioux, and Arapahoe. By the 1960s, there remained a 'very small percentage of this number' (p. 7). This sign language had its own syntactic rules and Tomkins makes it clear that it differed from the American Sign Language used by Deaf people at that time, both lexically and grammatically.

Other communities of hearing people may use sign languages for specific cultural and social reasons. Kendon (1988b) has documented the sign language of the Warlpiri people in Australia, who use this language at points in their life when speech is not allowed. Religious orders that seek to limit the use of speech also use sign languages. Barakat (1987) has researched the sign language used by Cistercian monks in the USA, Banham (1991) has described signs used in medieval Anglo-Saxon monasteries, and Quay (1998) has reported on signs used by Trappist monks in Japan and China.

Most sign languages used by Deaf communities have only emerged over the past 300 years. Just as all languages need a community of users, sign languages need a Deaf community. Deaf communities can only exist where there is a large enough concentration of deaf people. The development which triggered the creation of large Deaf communities and sign languages as we know them today came when schools were set up for deaf children, starting in the late eighteenth century in Europe. At these schools, children were able to use a single form of a language, rather than the widely varying 'home signs' characteristic of isolated deaf individuals. In many countries today, education for deaf children has only recently begun, and this can still be seen to provide an environment in which sign language can develop. Linguists (e.g. Kegl et al. 1999) have described how the establishment of the first school for deaf children in Nicaragua in the 1980s led to the beginnings of a national sign language. There are also communities where an unusually high incidence of deafness results in a sign language used by both deaf and hearing people (see Woll and Ladd 2011 for a review of a number of these).

It is commonly assumed that sign language is universal. The history of this belief will be described later in this chapter. However, the belief is a myth, most likely arising from the pervasive iconicity found in sign languages. Even where iconicity is present, it does not of itself produce identical lexicons, since there are numerous ways to create a visual link with a referent (Taub 2001). For example, signs for 'woman' in various sign languages represent earrings, breasts, long hair, lips, soft cheeks, etc. The sign for 'man' in British Sign Language (BSL) represents a beard; the same configuration and movement of the hand in American Sign Language (ASL) means 'old'.

Although sign languages use hands and body as articulators and are perceived visually, they are different from gestures, in linguistic, psychological, and neurological terms. Sign languages are left-lateralized and processed in the classical language areas of the brain (see MacSweeney et al. 2008 for a review). Nevertheless, the nature of the relationship between sign and gesture is still of research interest today.

It is difficult to know how many different sign languages exist, since counts of the world's languages almost always exclude sign languages. However, Ethnologue (www.ethnologue.com: Lewis 2009) lists 170 different sign languages, while the Hamburg bibliographic database of sign language research (www.sign-lang.uni-hamburg.de/bib-web) lists thousands of entries on over 100 of these languages. Since sign languages are independent of the spoken languages that surround them, we cannot assume a parallel relationship between national spoken and signed languages. In many cases the same sign language is used by Deaf communities located in different spoken language communities (e.g. the sign language used by Quebecois and Anglo Deaf people in Canada). There are also Deaf communities with different sign languages within surrounding hearing communities which use the same spoken language. For example, English is the dominant spoken language of Ireland, the USA, and the UK, but the Deaf people living in these countries use three different sign languages for reasons related to the history of deaf education.

4.3 HISTORICAL VIEWS OF SIGN LANGUAGE

Writers and researchers on sign languages have taken a variety of positions regarding the similarities and differences between signed and spoken languages, and the similarities and differences among sign languages themselves. In the period before the beginning of linguistic research in the field, sign languages were regarded as exemplifying a primitive universal gesture language.[2] The conflation of sign language and gesture was reinforced by the use of 'sign' to refer both to elements in communication used by deaf people and to what would now be called 'co-speech gesture' (Kendon 2008a).

Although descriptions of the use of signs by deaf people are found in the Mishnah (first-century compilation of Jewish law) and earlier, the first systematic observations of sign language use by deaf people in Europe date from the seventeenth century. In Britain, John Bulwer was the earliest writer on sign language in Britain; his second book, *Philocophus* (1648), was dedicated to two deaf brothers and reveals both Bulwer's familiarity with sign language and his belief that signing was universal.

Bulwer's two books, *Chirologia* (1644) and *Philocophus: or the deafe and dumbe man's friend* (1648), while describing signing and discussing the independence of sign language from spoken language, express the belief that signs and gestures are natural, and hence universal. This belief is found in virtually every text on the subject published up to the middle of the twentieth century.

> What though you cannot express your minds in those verball contrivances of man's invention; yet you want not speeche; who have your whole body for a tongue, having a language more naturall and significant, which is common to you with us, to wit, gesture, the general and universall language of human nature. (Bulwer 1648: introductory dedication)

In conjunction with the view of sign language as representing a universal language, it was recognized that sign language was unrelated to the spoken language of the community. Although not regarding sign language as universal, George Dalgarno, an early educator of the deaf and the inventor of the first manual alphabet used in Britain, noted:

> The deaf man has no teacher at all and though necessity may put him upon ... using signs, yet those have no affinity to the language by which they that are about him do converse among themselves. (Dalgarno 1680: 3)

The notion of universality persisted for centuries. Rée (1999) and Mirzoeff (1995) provide descriptions of eighteenth- and nineteenth-century beliefs about the international nature of 'gesture languages.' Wundt sought to discover the universal properties underlying all languages by studying the signing of deaf children. He ascribed the universality he perceived in sign language to the concreteness of its concepts:

> Systems of signs that have arisen in spatially separate environments and under doubtlessly independent circumstances are, for the most part, very similar or indeed closely related: this, then enables communication without great difficulty between persons making use of gestures. Such is the much lauded universality of gestural communication. Further, it is self-evident that this universality extends only to

---

[2] See Ch. 3 above.

those concepts of a generally objective nature. [. . .] Objects and actions perceived according to their basic features. (Wundt 1973 [1921]: 58)

After the establishment of the first schools for deaf children in the eighteenth century, educators began to contribute to the literature on sign language. Joseph Watson, headmaster of the school for the deaf in London in the first quarter of the nineteenth century, while still believing in the basic universality of signing, did note processes of sign language change in Deaf communities:

> The naturally deaf do not always stop here with this language of pantomime. Where they are fortunate enough to meet with an attentive companion or two, especially where two or more deaf persons happen to be brought up together, it is astonishing what approaches they will make towards the construction of an artificial language. (Watson 1809: 78)

There are striking disconnections in writings on the subject which simultaneously claim that sign language is universal while describing processes of change and increasing abstraction. Edward Tylor, a nineteenth-century anthropologist, in interviews with deaf signers, noted how sign language changed and developed into progressively more complex language. He was impressed by the memoirs of Kruse, a deaf teacher.

> What . . . makes a distinction to him between one thing and another, such distinctive signs of objects are at once signs by which he knows these objects and knows them again; they become tokens of things. And whilst he silently elaborates the signs he has found for single objects . . . he develops for himself suitable signs to represent ideas . . . and thus he makes himself a language . . . a way for thought is already broken and with this thought as it now opens out the language cultivates and forms itself further and further. (Kruse 1853, in Tylor 1870: 51)

However, Tylor also claimed that sign language is universal both in lexicon and grammar.

> [T]here is a great deal of variety in the signs amongst particular tribes, but such a way of communication is so natural all the world over, that when outlandish people, such as Laplanders, have been brought to be exhibited in our great cities they have been comforted in their loneliness by meeting with deaf-and-dumb children, with whom they at once fall in conversing with delight in this universal language of signs. This 'gesture language' is universal not only because signs are 'self-expressive' (their meaning is self-evident) but because the grammar is international. (Tylor 1881: 118–19)

Such titles as Long's *The Sign Language* (1910) and Nevins' *The Sign Language of the Deaf and Dumb* (1895) imply the existence of only one sign language. Mallery (1972 [1881]), who studied American Indian signing, reported that the sign language of Indians, of deaf people, and of everyone else 'constitute one language—the gesture speech of mankind, of which each system is a dialect.' Berthier, who was himself deaf, stated: 'For centuries scholars from every country have sought after a universal language and failed. Well, it exists all around, it is sign language' (quoted in Battison and Jordan 1976: 54).

4.4 Linguistics and Sign Language

4.4.1 Historical Perspectives

The development of linguistics as a discipline in the late nineteenth century had two major impacts on interest in sign language. The first was the Saussurean emphasis on the arbitrariness of the word–referent relationship. As well as marginalizing those words in spoken language which exhibited sound symbolism or onomatopoeia, this view placed sign languages with their pervasive iconicity outside the scope of linguistics. Linguists also held to a new belief that sign languages were somehow derived from spoken languages. This view, expressed by Leonard Bloomfield, must be understood in the context of the emphasis in linguistics on the primacy of spoken language as the core form of human language.

> Gesture languages have been observed among the lower-class Neapolitans, among Trappist monks ... among the Indians of our western plains ... and among groups of deaf-mutes. It seems certain that these gesture languages are merely developments of ordinary gestures and that any and all complicated or not immediately intelligible gestures are based on the conventions of ordinary speech. (Bloomfield 1933: 39)

Sign languages remained ignored by linguists until Tervoort (1953) and Stokoe (1960) 'rediscovered' them in the middle of the twentieth century. Mainstream linguistics regained an interest in sign language in the 1970s. The major expression of this interest was research designed to demonstrate that apes were capable of using human language. Because apes are unable to articulate speech, signing was used instead, most often in the form of spoken English accompanied by individual lexical signs of American Sign Language (i.e. without any ASL grammar: see Patterson 1978, Savage-Rumbaugh et al. 1985, Fouts and Waters 2001). It is beyond the scope of this chapter to discuss these studies in greater depth, but there is little evidence that any of the apes acquired any form of communication resembling the sign languages of Deaf communities.

4.4.2 Modern Approaches

In 1960 William Stokoe published his pioneering work on American Sign Language (ASL), working within a Bloomfieldian structuralist model. Stokoe was the first to recognize that sign languages had an internal 'phonological' structure comparable to that of spoken languages, and hence duality of patterning. This led to an explosion of interest in the linguistics of sign language, with Klima and Bellugi's *The Signs of Language* (1979) being hugely influential, and there is now a substantial literature in the field. This new interest was accompanied by an attempt to overthrow the beliefs both of the pre-linguistic era and of the early linguists and demonstrate: (1) that sign languages are not universal, (2) that they differ substantially from each other and (3) that they are mutually unintelligible. These claims are found extensively in the literature from this period (see e.g. Fischer 1974, Lane 1977, Klima and Bellugi 1979, Baker and Cokely 1980, Kyle and Woll 1985).

This approach undoubtedly arose from the desire to emphasize the equivalence of the linguistic status of signed languages and spoken languages, despite the differences in modality, and was certainly an essential stage in the development of the field. It is from this perspective that one should, for example, understand the minimization of the importance of iconicity in sign languages. As Johnston notes:

> It has often been taken as a defining characteristic of languages that the relationship between signifier and signified is completely arbitrary and the 'language-likeness' of nonverbal signifying systems has been judged according to the degree of this arbitrary relationship. Systems in which the signifiers are highly motivated have been suspect and considered to be pseudo-linguistic. (Johnston 1989: 326)

Vermeerbergen (2006) points out that the methodology of research itself may lead to this view. For example, researchers conventionally use written glosses, usually arranged linearly, to represent sign language data, in the absence of a writing system or widely used notation system (although such systems exist). Apart from the fact glosses can never capture the full complexity of sign language data, the use of glosses may result in transfer of the characteristics such as word class from the word to the sign: using an English adjective to gloss a BSL sign does not necessarily mean the BSL sign is also an adjective.

4.5 SIMILARITIES AMONG SIGN LANGUAGES

It has been noted by many researchers that the grammars of unrelated sign languages are more similar than the grammars of unrelated spoken languages. Johnston 1989 and Woll (2003) suggest several reasons for the patterns of similarities among sign languages.

- The relative youth of sign languages (including creolization). Sign languages are relatively young languages; indeed, the recent studies of Nicaraguan Sign Language (Kegl et al. 1999) suggest that sign languages can arise and develop spontaneously in deaf communities over three generations.

- The relatively low percentage of signers who are themselves the children of signers results in continual recreolization with resulting similarity of grammar (Fischer 1978).
- Iconicity as an organizing factor may result in greater similarity at all linguistic levels.
- The linear syntax found in spoken languages may intrinsically allow greater differences than spatial syntax.
- Sign languages are fused linguistic/gestural systems.

There is evidence for all of these, but a great deal of research remains to be done in this area.

4.5.1 Typology and Modality

Early modern research on sign languages emphasized the underlying structural similarities of spoken and sign languages, but more recent research has moved towards a recognition that there are systematic typological differences between signed and spoken language. These arise mainly from the interaction of language form with modality. Observation of such differences has led to active consideration of the extent to which the contrasting typological properties of spoken and signed languages indicate that linguistic theory may need to take greater account of modality (Meier et al. 2002).

There are also consistent grammatical features in which sign languages differ from spoken languages. These all relate to iconicity and to links between sign languages and gesture. The most important areas of current research interest are the use of space, and the relationship of phonology and morphology to iconicity. Other differences arise from the properties of the articulatory systems used for spoken and signed language. Sign languages make use of both hands (one hand being dominant). These can be used simultaneously at the lexical level (e.g. two-handed signs) and at the grammatical level (e.g. one hand articulating the head of a phrase and the other simultaneously assigning a locus in space). See Fig. 4.1, which shows a series of still images of the BSL sentence *The woman hands the cup to the boy* as produced by a left-handed signer. In (a) she produces the lexical sign BOY with her right hand. In (b), she assigns a locus to BOY using the classifier 'small entity' (i.e. 'boy is located at x'). She maintains this sign throughout the remainder of the sentence. In (c) she shifts to using her right hand to produce the lexical sign WOMAN. In (d) she assigns a locus to WOMAN. In (e) she produces the lexical sign CUP, and in (f) she produces the classifier 'curved object', moving it from the locus assigned to WOMAN to the locus assigned to BOY (i.e. 'she hands cup to him').

Additionally, the face and body provide prosodic (e.g. distinguishing interrogatives from declaratives and marking conditional clauses) and adverbial information. Mouth actions are also used to disambiguate manual homonyms (e.g. in BSL, manually

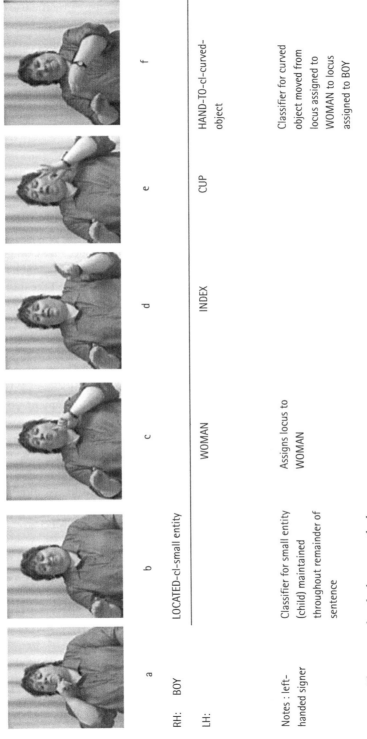

	a	b	c	d	e	f
RH:	BOY	LOCATED-cl-small entity				
LH:			WOMAN	INDEX	CUP	HAND-TO-cl-curved-object

Notes : left-handed signer	Classifier for small entity (child) maintained throughout remainder of sentence	Assigns locus to WOMAN			Classifier for curved object moved from locus assigned to WOMAN to locus assigned to BOY

FIG. 4.1 The woman hands the cup to the boy

identical signs such as BATTERY and UNCLE are distinguished by the use of mouth-
ings derived from English. The differences between the visual and auditory perceptual
systems also impact on language structure. For example, the temporal resolution of
auditory processing is much higher than that of visual processing (i.e. we can distinguish very rapid changes in sound) while spatial resolution is much higher in visual
processing (we can identify very small spatial distinctions visually but have much
poorer ability to localize sounds.

4.5.2 Phonology and Morphology

Since Stokoe (1960), linguists have seen signs as consisting of simultaneous combinations of configuration of the hand, a location where the sign is articulated, and
movement—either a path through signing space or an internal movement of the joints
in the hand. Each is understood to be a part of the phonology, because changing one of
these parameters can create a minimal pair. There have been considerable modifications to Stokoe's framework since 1960, but this model has remained the basic description of sign language phonology.

Sign language morphology tends to manifest itself in simultaneous combinations of
meaningful handshapes, locations, and movements. In derivational morphology, for
example, handshape can change to reflect numbers—for example BSL n-WEEKS,
n-O'CLOCK, and n-YEARS-OLD are articulated with conventionalized location and
movement while the handshape indicates the number (e.g. 3-WEEKS, 5-YEARS-OLD).
Signs referring to objects and actions may also differ only in movement, so the verbs
LOCK, READ-NEWSPAPER, and EAT are made with a single, long movement,
compared to the nouns KEY, NEWSPAPER, and FOOD, which have short, repeated
movements.

Inflectional morphology is also shown by changes in movement and location. Thus,
degree is shown through size, speed, onset speed, and length of hold in a movement,
with, for example, LUCKY having a smaller, faster, and smoother movement than
VERY-LUCKY. The movement changes conveying temporal aspect are frequently
visually motivated, so that repeated actions or events are shown through repetition
of the sign, duration of an event is paralleled by duration of the sign (signs for shorter
events being articulated for less time than signs for longer events), and when an event is
interrupted suddenly, the movement of the sign is interrupted. Signs can also change
handshape to indicate how the direct object is handled. So (I) HAND-OVER-A-
FLOWER-TO-EACH-OF-YOU has the same movement as (I) HAND-OVER-AN-
ICECREAM-TO-EACH-OF-YOU but a different handshape.

Both spoken and signed languages articulate lexical items sequentially. Spoken
languages can give some linguistic information simultaneously (as in e.g. tone languages), and prosody adds further grammatical and affective information to the
lexemes uttered. Essentially, though, humans have only one vocal apparatus, so spoken

languages must use sequential structures. The availability of two hands (and head and face) enables sign languages to use simultaneously articulated structures (Vermeerbergen et al. 2007). Two hands can be used to represent the relative locations of two referents in space, and their spatial and temporal relationships. It should be noted, however, that simultaneity is an option exercised differently by different sign languages (Saeed et al. 2000).

4.5.3 Syntax

Sign languages exploit the use of space for grammatical purposes, preferring three-dimensionality and simultaneity in syntax, while spoken languages prefer linearization and affixation. In earlier literature, on American Sign Language in particular (e.g. Poizner et al. 1987; Padden 1988), two uses of space for linguistic purposes are contrasted. Topographic space is described as being used to depict spatial relationships and to map referents onto a representation of real space, while syntactic space is conceived of as an exploitation of space for purely grammatical purposes, without any mapping to real-world spatial relationships. In this model, referents are localized in space by establishing arbitrary loci for referents between which verbs move. Different semantic classes of verbs are described as exploiting syntactic space (e.g. verbs of transfer such as GIVE, TELL, ASK, PAY, SUPERVISE) and topographic space (verbs of location and movement, such as PICK-UP, TRAVEL, FALL-DOWN). In the 1970s and 1980s, the descriptions of uses of syntactic space are expressed in terms (morpheme, cliticization, pronouns, agreement in person and number, etc.) that suggest a resemblance to agreement in spoken languages. Also in this approach, in topographic space the handshapes in verbs of motion and location are described as representing object features or classes (how objects are handled, their size and shape, or their function). These were termed 'classifiers' to indicate their parallels to classifiers in spoken languages (Supalla 1986).

In the 1990s, this clear-cut distinction between 'spatial mapping' (topographic space) and 'spatialized syntax' (syntactic space) was questioned by researchers working on a number of sign languages, who argued that the spatialized representations of syntactic space are not based on abstract linguistic properties but on the inherent locative relationships among real-world people, objects, and places. Engberg-Pedersen (1993) and Liddell (1990) challenged the interpretation of loci as arbitrary, abstract points in space, arguing instead that loci should be seen as 'referent projections' (Engberg-Pedersen) or as based on the real-world location and extension of imagined referents (Liddell). Liddell (2003) went further, proposing that verbs such as GIVE are a mix of gesture and linguistic elements, and analysing such signs as being composed of a linguistic part expressed by the handshape, the type of movement, and certain aspects of the hand's orientation, and a gestural part relating the sign to a locus.

An increasing number of researchers also consider the possibility of dealing with mixed forms, i.e. structures involving both linguistic and nonlinguistic components, in classifier constructions. Schembri (2003) has argued that the use of the term 'classifier' is inappropriate for sign languages. Schembri et al. (2005) compared the representation of motion events by hearing non-signers using gesture without speech and by native signers of three different sign languages. They found that the classifier constructions in the three sign languages compared were strikingly similar, but also that the motion events produced by the hearing gesturers show significant points of correspondence with the signed constructions. In both cases the location and movement parameters are similar, and the handshape component shows most differences. They argue therefore that these data are consistent with the claim that classifier verbs of motion and location are blends of gestural and linguistic elements.

Whether or not researchers accept the Liddell model, sign language linguistic research has contributed to consideration of the interrelationship of language and gesture. From the traditional point of view, gestures are seen as nonlinguistic features of human interaction. In parallel with the development of research on sign languages, an increasing number of researchers have started to look at gesture as an integrated part of face-to-face spoken language communication.

4.6 BILINGUALISM

Until recently, all studies of bilingualism were studies of individuals and communities in which two spoken languages are used. With the development of research on sign languages, it has become clear that bilingualism can exist in two forms: cross-modal (or bimodal) bilingualism and unimodal bilingualism.

Unimodal bilingualism occurs when either two spoken or two sign languages are used (e.g. Irish and British Sign Language); cross-modal or bimodal bilingualism occurs when the two languages are perceived by different sensory systems and there are two different output channels; they thus exist in different modalities: one signed and one spoken. Recognition of bimodal bilingualism leads to a necessary re-evaluation of models of bilingualism. Cross-modal bilingualism differs from unimodal bilingualism with respect to the temporal sequencing of languages. Bimodal bilinguals often produce code *blends*, rather than code *switches*, producing sign and speech simultaneously when in a bilingual mode of communication (Emmorey et al. 2008). Since in unimodal spoken-language bilingualism, just one production system (the vocal tract) is utilized, there is a bottleneck in processing, which has been identified both in behavioural and in neuroimaging studies. For production, this is evident in constraints on serial output: only one utterance can be produced at any one time: selection between two competing languages with respect to the common output path may impose a greater cognitive burden than selection of items within one language. For perception, similar constraints may apply—the speaker's utterances are usually processed through the ear and require serial analysis to be understood. For cross-modal bilinguals, vocal-tract (speech) and manual actions (signing) can—in principle—be processed simultaneously, as they use separate sets of articulators which are seen to be spatially separated. The processing of speech and sign, within a single proficient user of both languages, can therefore offer a unique insight into core language processes (Emmorey et al. 2008; Emmorey and McCullough 2009).

4.7 EVOLUTION OF LANGUAGE

Spoken languages are believed not to arise independently, spontaneously, and rapidly. Some linguists believe that spoken language only emerged once and that all spoken languages are descended from a single ancestor. Others believe that it arose independently in several locations around the world. In general, however, the spoken languages we see today are all assumed to have histories of many thousands of years. Sign languages, on the other hand, clearly arise spontaneously and independently in many parts of the world. They have therefore been used as data to support theories about the origins of human language. However, sign languages are the creation of humans with 'language-ready' brains. Thus it is inappropriate to view sign languages as comparable to the communication of pre-linguistic humans. Perhaps the most important contribution of sign linguistics to language evolution theory is the recognition that human communication is essentially multi-channel.

In the Research Review prepared for the UK government's Foresight Cognitive Systems Project, William Marslen-Wilson wrote (2005: 9): 'A more dramatic type of cross-linguistic contrast that may be uniquely valuable in elucidating the underlying properties of speech and language, comes through the comparison between spoken languages and native sign languages, such as BSL.' He went on to identify the investigation of features common to how the brain processes spoken language and sign language as one of six key questions facing researchers in language.

The relevance of linguistic research into sign language can thus be seen to extend well beyond this specific subdomain of linguistics. If the gestural-visual nature of sign languages does indeed have an impact on their linguistic structure, this means that at least some of the differences between sign and spoken languages are related to their different modalities. The relationship between modality and linguistic form is, of course, as important to linguists working with spoken languages as to sign linguists.

Studies of atypical sign language and deaf children creating 'language' on their own also provide new perspectives. It is clear that within the domain of linguistics the study of manual–visual languages offers an important supplement to the analysis of oral–auditive languages. The findings of sign language studies have led and can lead to a revision of assumptions which were believed to be basic tenets about language. A better understanding of different aspects of their structure and usage and the application of the outcomes of sign linguistics to spoken-language research will contribute to a better understanding of human language and linguistics in general. In this regard it is encouraging to see that international recognition of and appreciation for sign linguistics is growing, and that this research domain is increasingly becoming part of the field of linguistics in general. Sign linguistic research thus has a unique part to play in linguistics in the future. Only sign language research can help to establish what the real universals of human language are, and also to illuminate for all linguists how the instantiation of language in a particular modality shapes language itself.

CHAPTER 5

ORTHOGRAPHY AND THE EARLY HISTORY OF PHONETICS

MICHAEL K. C. MacMAHON

5.1 OVERVIEW

THE study of the analysis of speech sounds can be traced back to at least 500 BCE, to the work of certain Sanskritic grammarians. Yet this time-frame belies the idea of a continuous engagement with the topic. What evidence we have indicates that interest in questions of phonetics has waxed and waned depending on local circumstances. For example, the legacy of phonetic studies in the Graeco-Roman period was relatively limited, and in Europe in the first millennium CE hardly any work on phonetics was pursued—or, if it was, no evidence of it has survived. Compare this with the situation in India, where the acumen of phoneticians such as Pāṇini and Patañjali produced work of such quality that it easily bears comparison with comparable studies within twenti-eth-century linguistics.[1]

Sometimes, instead of long time-gaps between one relevant work and the next, one also finds clusters of work on phonetics produced by more than one person and within a relatively short time. An example is the publishing activity of several members of the Royal Society in Britain in the mid-seventeenth century. Another example is the noticeable growth of publications on phonetic topics in the mid to late nineteenth century in Europe, primarily by German scholars, scientists, and medical personnel.

---

[1] Other studies of the history of phonetics include: Essen (1962), Fischer-Jørgensen (1974), Grammont (1933), Jespersen (1933), Kemp (1994a, 1994b, 2001), Koerner (1994), Kohler (1981), Meinsma (1983), Ohala et al. (1999), Panconcelli-Calzia (1941, 1957, 1994[1941]), Pompino-Marschall (1995), Robins (1967), Stammerjohann et al. (2009).

Looking at the time-frame of three and a half millennia as a whole, one sees a range of interest within phonetics. Some authors describe a particular language or languages, usually a 'standard' form, but occasionally a vernacular dialect. Some highlight differences between the written and spoken forms of a language. Some concentrate on the anatomical and physiological processes of speech production in the light of contemporary scientific and clinical knowledge. The reforming of the spelling conventions of a language is another topic. The application of concepts in phonetics to the audiolingual education of deaf persons is one particular example of applied phonetics in Britain in the seventeenth century and later. The place of phonetics in the description and treatment of speech and language disorders should be noted, too. Other users of phonetics have been concerned with developing an elocutionary standard for a language. Discussions of the techniques of rhetoric have sometimes included insights from phonetics.

During the nineteenth century, there is a discernible pattern of acceleration of interest. Moses (1964) lists by year the growth of interest from 1829 to 1899 (see also Panconcelli-Calzia 1921). Much of the development was unrelated to phonetics itself, but instead to advances in medicine and physics, especially the availability of appropriate instrumentation. Some examples are Benjamin Babington's invention of the laryngoscope in 1829; Babington was a scholar of Tamil. In 1847 Carl Ludwig introduced the concept of the 'recording method,' with its accompanying instrumentation, into physiology. Further examples are more obviously focused on phonetics: Erasmus Darwin's limited forays in speech synthesis (Darwin 1803: 119–20); Robert Willis's work on sound synthesis in the context of organ pipes (Willis 1830); and Manuel García's observation of the vocal folds in action in a living subject—done by means of a dental mirror onto which light was directed—carried out in 1854 (see García 1855).

5.2 ANCIENT INDIAN PHONETICS

In the context of linguistics, 'Ancient Indian' is a general term for the period from about 800 BCE to about 100 BCE. It parallels the period in Greek linguistics of Plato, Aristotle, and the Stoic philosophers.[2] Initially, phonetics was an aspect of the study of Sanskrit concerned with the preservation and propagation of the Vedas, a large corpus of religious literature associated with Hinduism and Buddhism (*véda* is one of the words for 'knowledge' in Sanskrit).[3] Vedic texts date from about 1500 BCE and originate in north-west India; they continued to be composed over about the following 1,000 years. Contact between Sanskrit and other languages and a growing mismatch between the language of the texts and contemporary pronunciations was one of the reasons for the scholarly interest in Sanskritic phonetics.[4] In the manuals or

---

[2] See Ch. 13 below.   [3] See Ch. 11 below.
[4] See further Allen (1953).

commentaries on Vedic texts, one finds material on the pronunciation of sounds, on metrical patterns—as well as on etymology and grammar. The specifically phonetics sections deal in detail with the pronunciation of Vedic texts, rather than generally with Sanskrit. Phonetic terminology and analytic tools are part of the metalanguage that came to be developed.

By about 700 BCE, a standardized phoneme-based alphabet for Sanskrit had come into use. Phonetic analysis distinguished between vowels and consonants, with the consonants then divided into three groups corresponding to stops (plosives and nasals), approximants and related categories, and voiceless fricatives. There is clear evidence that the scholars were aware of the patterning of sounds as well as their articulatory characteristics. An example of the modernity of the analysis is revealed in this quotation: 'Sounds are distinguished from each other on the basis of accents, time or duration, point of articulation, manner, and type of phonation' (from a verse in the Pāṇiniya-siksa (Deshpande 1994: 3056)). There was no necessary agreement between one scholar and the next, and hence different commentators can and do vary in their analyses and terminology.

The analysis of a later form of Sanskrit, 'Classical Sanskrit' as it is often called, is primarily associated with the work of Pāṇini in the period from about 400 to about 350 BCE. Clear evidence of the use of the phonemic concept can be found in both Vedic and Classical Sanskrit, but it is not always carried through consistently. In Vedic Sanskrit, some allophonic matters are included. However, there are examples of what would now be called minimal pairs and contextually determined allophonic variants of phonemes. An intuitive concept of the phoneme was used; there is nothing that anticipates the discussions of differing concepts of the phoneme in twentieth-century phonological theories.

Of the Sanskritic linguists, the most famous was Pāṇini; another was Patañjali, the author of *Mahābhāsya*, younger than Pāṇini by two centuries. Pāṇini was from northwest India, but little else about his personal circumstances is certain, including the dates of his birth and death. His major work is a reference grammar (which includes material on phonetics and phonology), known by various names but usually referred to as his *Aṣṭādhyāyī* 'eight chapters'. It is one of the early grammars of Sanskrit, yet it is the most erudite and sophisticated of them all. Although it exemplifies a form of descriptivist linguistics, yet it also anticipates by millennia, not just centuries, certain aspects of a generative approach to the analysis of language. There is no equivalent or parallel to it in later Graeco-Roman linguistic studies, nor in western Europe until the twentieth century. The quality of Pāṇini's analysis of pronunciation in the *Aṣṭādhyāyī* bears immediate comparison with works in twentieth-century linguistics, from the point of view of both classificatory principles and an understanding of the interrelation of phonology/phonetics and grammar.

5.3 GREEK PHONETICS

The interests of the Greek linguists from approximately the third to the first centuries BCE lay far less in matters of pronunciation than grammar, and so the style and depth of analysis does not bear comparison with that of, for example, Pāṇini.[5] One looks in vain for anything that approaches his understanding of pronunciation as part of the wider structure of language. Even so, one finds anticipations of a more familiar vocabulary for the analysis of speech. There is an intuitive sense of the phoneme by the originator(s) of the first alphabetic writing system for Greek, and the later adjusters of the system. The first explicit classification of sounds into vowels and consonants can be found in the writings of Plato and Aristotle. There are comments on (in today's terminology) vowels, stops and approximants. Further, albeit limited, comments on particular sounds are set out in Dionysius Thrax's *Tékhnē grammatikē* 'Art of Grammar' from the second century BCE.[6] These include some prescriptivist remarks about the phonetic niceties to be observed when reading aloud—especially prosodic matters. The ambiguity of the concept and word 'letter' to represent both a written character and a spoken sound is noted.[7] Plato and Aristotle not only drew attention to the differences between vowels and consonants: they also commented on different categories of consonant—for example, between those with lingual or labial contacts—and on the nature of accent, word-stress, and phrase-stress patterns.[8] Later philosophers, the Stoics, identified the syllable as a unit of description; this led to discussions of phonotactic patterns within the syllable and word: actual, improbable, and impossible sequences.

5.4 ROMAN PHONETICS[9]

Marcus Tullius Cicero's *De Oratore* (55 BCE) deals partly with the techniques of rhetoric (cf. Fantham 2004). A more informative work, which provides firmer evidence of a serious interest in phonetic matters, is Marcus Fabius Quintilian's *Institutio Oratoria* from the early first century CE; it deals with practical aspects of rhetoric (cf. Smail 1938). He comments on how arguments should be presented in order to achieve the most

[5] See also Allen (1987) for a discussion of the pronunciation of Classical Greek in the light of contemporary sources.

[6] See Salmon (1995), Allan (2010a).

[7] The varying interpretations of the Latin word *litera* 'letter' in relation to *nomen, potestas*, and *figura* are discussed by Abercrombie (1949).

[8] See e.g. Plato's *Theaetetus* (Plato 1987: 118). For recent remarks on Plato and Aristotle's understanding of phonetics, see Ademollo (2011: 283–85) and Robins (1967: 23–4).

[9] See also Allen (1965).

appropriate form of communication; other remarks relate to the choice of lexical and syntactic styles when presenting arguments. Pronunciation, and how it should be used to achieve an appropriate communicative effect, is also dealt with. A section of one of the books deals with orthography and the differences between speech and writing. In Quintilian's words, 'What shall I say, too, of words that are written otherwise than they are pronounced? *Gaius* is spelled with the letter *c*, which, inverted, means a woman; for that women were called *Caiae*' (Book 1, ch.7). Other comments on pronunciation relate to, for example, speakers' voice qualities, their choice of intonation, key, and rhythmical structures. It is obvious that Quintilian was fully familiar with the essential features of rhetorical choices in communication, and he was able to describe them without recourse to technical details.

5.5 ARAB AND PERSIAN PHONETICS

The emergence of Islam as a religious and cultural movement from the seventh century CE onwards created conditions for the formal study of language, too. The Qur'ān, written in Arabic, became a focus of epistemological work, initially in order to achieve an appropriate writing system for Arabic. Throughout, questions of the correct recitation of the Qur'ān are important: one of the principal reasons for the development of Arab phonetics. Particular features of Arabic, such as the symbolization of short vowels, derive from the eighth century CE.[10] Similarly in the eighth century a major statement of not only Arabic grammar but also phonology was provided by the Persian grammarian Sībawayhi. His analysis included broad division of consonants into 'tense' and 'slack,' corresponding to 'stops' and 'fricatives.' He comments on places of articulation, articulatory variants of certain phonemes, the classification of the teeth, and manners of articulation; he uses a finer classification of part of the tongue than would be deemed necessary even today. There are also comments on phonotactics, morphophonemics, and assimilation. This strong and relatively sophisticated tradition continued throughout the tenth and eleventh centuries CE.

Sībawayhi's work formed much of the basis for that of Ibn Jinnī on phonetics. In the latter's phonology, he advanced the subject with, for example, descriptions of morphophonemics. More generally, the interest in speech led to studies of what has been described as the 'speech mechanism, physics of speech, articulatory, auditory, pulmonic, and mental processes' (Bakalla 1994: 189).

The study of the anatomy of the speech mechanism became a major topic, the first book on it being written in the late eighth or early ninth century CE; others followed in the tenth century and beyond. The work of Ibn Sīnā (known also as Avicenna, a prolific author on a wide range of subjects including medicine, theology, and astronomy) is

---

[10] See Ch. 2 above.

especially important for his book on the mechanism of speech production early in the eleventh century CE.

5.6 CHINESE PHONETICS

The development of Chinese studies of phonetics amongst certain Buddhists in China was in part determined by their awareness of the contents of Indian texts and the classificatory framework of Sanskritic language structure that had been elaborated within them. It was Buddhism that brought Sanskritic literature to the attention of the Chinese in the 400 years from about 200 BCE to about 200 CE. Certain consequences of this contact include the recognition and naming of four tones—first attributed to Shěn Yuē, a poet and historian.

The Chinese Buddhists' knowledge of the Indian alphabet led also to comparable studies of the phonetics of Chinese. Tables of sounds, 'rhyme tables,' were created. In very broad terms, what was developed was a method for classifying consonant sounds according to the categories of lips, tongue (with subdivisions), molar teeth, incisor teeth, and throat. The specific inspiration for this work is most likely to have come from the five vargas (i.e. classes or groups) of traditional Indian alphabets, which then formed the basic framework for the analysis of Chinese phonology. Additional classification of consonants by phonation type followed, e.g. 'clear' and 'muddy' corresponding to voiceless and voiced.[11] Overall, Chinese phonetic studies in the period following the creation of Sanskrit-inspired work on Chinese itself led to a 'sophisticated knowledge both of acoustics and of the physiology of speech production' (Wang and Asher 1994: 525), to which one should add the study of speech anatomy. Much later in the history of Chinese phonetics, in the sixteenth century CE, attempts were made to reconstruct the pronunciation of poetry composed in the sixth century CE. A later example of the excellence of much Chinese phonetic scholarship is the work of the linguist Duan Yucai in the eighteenth century CE, who created a major commentary, which included phonetics, of the famous second-century CE dictionary of Chinese, the *Shuōwén Jiězì*.

5.7 KOREAN PHONETICS

In the absence of more recent research into the history of phonetics in Korea, the only example that can be quoted of phonetic studies of Korean is the programme of language reform that was initiated by the fifteenth-century CE King Sejong. His

---

[11] For a detailed exposition and critical discussion of the Chinese classificatory principles of sounds, see Pulleyblank (1994: 3095–6).

alphabet was intended to be partly iconic and partly classificatory. Thus there is a common graphic feature in all the 'incisor' consonants, all the 'labials,' and so on.[12]

5.8 JAPANESE PHONETICS[13]

Like China, Japanese phonetic studies benefited from a knowledge of Ancient Indian sources, but also from Korean studies. Factors in the development of Japanese phonetics and phonology included the introduction of a Chinese script (and its development for Japanese, *kana* syllabaries) and the arrival of Buddhist monks who were conversant with Indian scholarship. There exists an eleventh-century CE sound chart set out in the form of a matrix, and showing a series of minimal contrasts between syllables. Even so, the study of phonetics and phonology was of more limited interest to scholars, compared with the study of grammar. From the nineteenth century CE onwards, developments in European phonetics and phonology became part of the intellectual landscape of Japanese phonetic studies, with younger scholars spending time in the West to acquire expertise and knowledge in phonetics.

5.9 PHONETICS IN EUROPE DURING THE MIDDLE AGES

In western Europe, there is a long hiatus of about 1,000 years before one finds evidence of interest in phonetics and phonology: this time in twelfth-century Iceland and England. (The Icelandic work did not become accessible in published form until the early nineteenth century, however.[14]) The person traditionally referred to as the 'First Grammarian' aimed to produce a better alphabet for contemporary Icelandic—better in the sense of a direct relationship between the written characters and the phonemic system. Its most notable feature is the systematic use of certain diacritics to aid the identification of certain phonological distinctions which had been obscured by the orthography. Thus the First Grammarian uses an acute accent to signal a long vowel ('fár' (danger) vs 'far' (vessel)), and an overdot to signal a nasalized vowel. (The positing of nasalized vowel phonemes which contrast with oral vowels is debatable.) Small-capital Latin letters (e.g. ʙ) are used to indicate geminate consonants. The intentions of the grammarian and the quality of the analysis do not approach the analytical quality displayed by the Sanskritic grammarians many centuries earlier, but

---

[12] For further, detailed information, see ibid. 3097–9. See also Chs 2 and 10, this volume.
[13] See also Kaiser (1994).
[14] Two important discussions of the text are Benediktsson (1972) and Haugen (1972).

they reflect a different utilitarian aspect of applied phonetics—spelling reform rather than the exegesis of the language of religious texts—as well as evidence that the principle of phonemic contrastivity was understood many centuries before the publications of various nineteenth-century phoneticians and language teachers with whom its development has traditionally been associated.[15] (See further below.)

The medieval English material on spelling reform is the *Ormulum* (*c.*1180 CE), an extensive verse commentary on texts from the Bible by a twelfth-century monk, Orm, from an abbey in Lincolnshire (see Holt 1878). One of his aims was to produce material that could be used by others in Christian worship in the vernacular, not in Latin; a logical and consistent orthography, reflecting current sounds, not traditional written characters, was deemed necessary for this purpose. Orm was especially concerned to aid in the avoidance of what he considered to be mispronunciations of certain words. One solution was to use systematically such features as doubling of consonants to signal a preceding short vowel, with a singleton consonant signalling a preceding long vowel. (His approach is not always consistent, and there are revisions to his choice of phoneme markers at various places in the text.) Writing in verse, and adhering strictly to his metrical patterns, Orm also provides us with valuable evidence about patterns of accentuation in his dialect of Middle English.

5.10 RENAISSANCE PHONETICS

The growing preference for studies of vernacular languages instead of only the classical languages is a feature of phonetic studies in the period before and during the European Renaissance, especially in Italy, Spain, and France. Examples are Dante Alighieri's *De vulgari eloquentia* (early fourteenth century; cf. Botterill 1996), Elio Antonio de Nebrija's *Gramática de la lengua castellana* (1492), Gian Giorgio Trissino's *Epistola de le lettere nuovaments aggiunte alla lingua italiana* (1524), and Louis Meigret's *Traité touchant le commun usage de l'escriture françoise* (1542). The latter includes the first example of phonetic spelling in French. (One notes too the interest that Leonardo da Vinci took in the anatomy of the speech mechanism.)

The period of nearly 200 years from 1492 (Nebrija) to 1686 (Lodwick) saw the production of several key works on phonetics and spelling reform. The sixteenth-century scholar and diplomat Sir Thomas Smith, who had long been interested in questions of Greek pronunciation—primarily because of contemporary arguments over the style of pronunciation to be used—turned his attention to the question of reforming the spelling of English: his *De recta & emendata linguae anglicae scriptione, dialogus* (1568) presents different sides of the argument for the reform. Smith was one of a number of eminent sixteenth-century scholars engaged in such matters. Another

---

[15] The work of the so-called Second Grammarian in Iceland is discussed by Raschellà (1982).

was John Hart, who authored series of works on English orthography over a twenty-year period from 1551 (see Dobson 1968: 63). Hart sets up only five vowels, but he describes them in terms of their tongue height and lip position; he also distinguishes between short and long varieties of the five. Similarly, his description of consonants is on an articulatory basis. In short, he was as much a phonetic observer as a proponent of the need for spelling reform.

A few years later, the Danish theologian and scholar Jacob Madsen Aarhus adopts a similar approach to Hart's in the description of vowels and consonants—except that his analysis is more detailed, especially of consonant sounds. The work in which he sets out his views, *De literis libri duo* (1586), is not restricted to a consideration of only one language, but is rather an essay in general phonetics (Møller and Skautrup 1930). Some of Madsen's ideas about phonetics derive from the work of the sixteenth-century French grammarian Petrus Ramus.

Petrus Montanus (various non-Latin forms of his name exist) was a Dutch minister of religion, with a particular interest in speech. His *De spreeckonst* (Montanus 1964 [1635]) aimed to provide a description of phonetics from a general, not a language-dependent, point of view. In this he was only partly successful. Some of the terminology he uses is opaque, at least to begin with. One noticeable merit of the work is the anticipation of the principle of distinctive features, and even of aspects of articulatory phonology.

Questions of spelling reform and phonetics in the seventeenth century engaged the attention of several leading figures, including Wallis, Holder, Dalgarno, and Wilkins.[16] Most publications on phonetics and phonetic-related matters went into some detail about the organs of speech, but an understanding of the operational mechanism of the larynx (voicing etc.) eluded them. Interest in spelling reform and aspects of phonetics (especially the organs of speech and their role in creating sound segments) were features of the work of a number of scholars in Britain, particularly over the period lasting more than 25 years from 1617 to 1644. (The term 'English School of Phonetics' is often applied to them.) Some scholars who were pre-eminent in other areas contributed to the interest. The first—and one of the most important—was Robert Robinson, a London schoolmaster. His *The Art of Pronuntiation* (1617) is an essay in descriptive phonetics and questions of transcription. He introduces new symbols, many of which have little in common with those of traditional orthography; he pairs sounds and letters together, examples being <s> and <ꜩ> for /u:/ and /ʊ/, and <ɛ> and <ɜ> for /æ/ and /a:/. The transcription of a poem in Latin, with its contemporary pronunciation by an English speaker, illustrates some of the varying pronunciations of the language in the seventeenth century. Some of his unpublished material illustrates patterns of change in the pronunciation of English during his lifetime.

Other contributors to the growing literature on phonetics were Alexander Gil (1619), Charles Butler (1634)—his work concerns bee-keeping, but it is printed in an easily

---

[16] See further the papers in Subbiondo (1992).

readable reformed orthography (see Allan 2010a: 200)—Simon Daines (1640), and Richard Hodges (1644).[17]

John Wallis, the mathematician and one of the founding members of the Royal Society, published his *Tractatus de Loquela* in 1653. He had more than a passing interest in matters to do with the education of deaf users of English, and this is evidenced in the work. His schema of description and classification of sounds is fairly rudimentary: it has, for example, only three places of articulation.[18]

Francis Lodwick was a London merchant of Dutch ancestry and a member of the Royal Society. One of his publications (1686) was a proposal for a 'universal alphabet'— a general phonetic alphabet—in which sounds that were related in terms of articulation were given related symbols. Thus, the initial consonants of *dark, tart, name, this, thing,* and French *danse* are allocated to a category equivalent to 'apical' in today's terminology.

William Holder, an Anglican divine and physicist, and another member of the Royal Society, had, like Wallis, a concern for the education of deaf speakers. In his *Elements of Speech* (1669), he presents a more detailed and more reliable account of general phonetics than Wallis had done. For him, the contemporary and older grammarians of English had achieved only 'faulty alphabets.' Notably, his discussion of the sounds of speech is with reference to meaning differences—he was adopting an intuitive phonemic approach. And he took as his remit not just the sounds of English but a wider, more general anthropophonic analysis of speech.

The speech education of the deaf is the focus of George Dalgarno's *Didascalocophus, or, The Deaf and Dumb Man's Tutor* (1680), a work that is important for its positioning of deaf language within a general theory of signs—'sematology' is Dalgarno's term. But phonetically important is an original excursus on an aspect of phonotactics, namely the analysis of consonant clusters.

5.11 EIGHTEENTH-CENTURY PHONETICS

One of the most detailed descriptions of the speech mechanism is by the Swiss-Dutch physician Jan Coenraad Amman. One of his publications is on teaching the deaf (1692), the other, far better known, is a treatise on speech (1700). His concept of 'latitude,' or the latitude allowed in the pronunciation of a sound, equates to the concept of contextual variants of a phoneme.

In the first half of the eighteenth century one finds a series of papers in the medical literature specifically to do with aspects of the speech mechanism. Two authors in particular deserve to be noticed: the French physician and botanist Denis Dodart and the French anatomist Antoine Ferrein. In a paper of 1741 Ferrein adduces evidence

[17] For an authoritative discussion of these and other writers, see Dobson (1968).
[18] The standard work of reference on Wallis and his *Grammar* is Kemp (1972).

from experiments with larynxes from cadavers, and concludes that it is airflow from the lungs that is responsible for setting the vocal folds in motion. Over the course of the next 150 years, other studies confirmed the correctness of Ferrein's conclusions.

In Britain, the activities of elocutionists such as Joshua Steele (1775, 1779), Thomas Sheridan (1780), and John Walker (1791) led to the publication of pronouncing dictionaries and other works. Steele's description of the prosodic features of English is important for the manner in which intonation and rhythm are analysed. His influence is evident in the publications on speech by later authors well into the twentieth century.

The concept of the 'vowel triangle' in phonetics derives from Christoph Hellwag's *Dissertatio physiologico-medica de Formatione Loquelae* (1781). Hellwag was a small-town physician in Germany, but, very possibly because of his professional work, he took a particular interest in aspects of phonetics. His comments on vowels show that he recognized the need to base any description on both auditory and articulatory criteria. Unlike many of his contemporaries, he was not misled by the concept of orthographic vowels, and commented on the myriad number of vowel sounds that can be found in the world's languages.

The year 1781 was also important for another reason: the publication by Christian Kratzenstein of his studies of speech synthesis, which moved the nature of phonetics beyond criteria of audition and articulation into acoustics and instrumentally derived evidence. (He had demonstrated his findings in 1779.) Amongst other things, Kratzenstein gives an excellent account of vowel sounds.

Ten years later, in 1791, the Hungarian Kempelen Farkas, better known by his German name of Wolfgang von Kempelen, published his *Mechanismus der menschlichen Sprache*... together with a working model of a synthetic vocal tract. It was the culmination of work on speech synthesis that had been in progress over the previous twenty or so years. Critically, there is evidence that he could detect the formants of vowels, albeit by auditory criteria.

The emergence of experimental (instrumental) phonetics in the late eighteenth century was consolidated during the nineteenth.[19] It was associated with the interests of medical professionals, physicists, and linguists. The instrumentation varied in quality and quantity. Examples of later nineteenth-century work include palatography (Coles 1872, Grützner 1879, Kingsley 1879, 1880, Lenz 1887; see also Abercrombie 1957, 1965). The technique was relatively straightforward: the tongue or the hard palate was painted with a marking agent, and the areas of wipe-off as the articulators met were observed. A second technique, kymography, for registering changes in air pressure in speech, required rather more sophisticated equipment.

---

[19] See esp. Tillmann (1994). The gradual development and achievements of experimental (instrumental) phonetics are summarized in various publications by Pierre-Jean Rousselot, but primarily in his *Principes de phonétique expérimentale* (1897 and later edns).

5.12 NINETEENTH-CENTURY PHONETICS

A key feature of nineteenth-century work on phonetics is the increasing use of instrumentation—primarily that of the physicist and the physician. Ernst Chladni was a professional physicist and an amateur musician, and speech was one of his interests. In his publications (e.g. 1802, 1827), he was able to demonstrate (using less complex equipment than Kratzenstein had used) connections between harmonics and the formant frequencies of vowels. The publications in a similar vein by men like Robert Willis (1830) and Hermann von Helmholtz (1863) added to a finer understanding of the physics of speech.

Interest in the physical properties of vowels is further evidenced by the work of Ernst von Brücke. His *Grundzüge der Physiologie und Systematik der Sprachlaute* (1856) contains a system of vowel classification which is based on the auditory perception of resonances; he sets it out in the shape of a triangle, corresponding in part to the sort of formant frequency-location diagram in use today. By contrast, his discussion of consonants, in terms of place and manner of articulation, harks back to an earlier descriptive tradition uninformed by concepts in physics. A similar schema for the representation of vowel sounds appears in Félix Du Bois-Reymond's *Kadmus oder allgemeine Alphabetik vom physikalischen, physiologischen und graphischen Standpunkt* (1862).

Von Brücke's work should be compared with that of Carl Merkel, whose *Anthropophonik* appeared the following year, in 1857. The focus is strictly on sounds, not on the anatomy and physiology of the vocal tract or the acoustic dimension of speech production. In a sense, the two works, Brücke's and Merkel's, illustrate the still differing conventions for studying phonetics, and yet the emergence of an emphasis on sounds as units of language—linguistic phonetics, in other words—and less on the standard anatomy of the vocal tract. A later work by Merkel, *Physiologie der menschlichen Sprache* (1866), is a vast compilation of knowledge about speech, though heavily restricted in its choice of languages for exemplification, and with some gaps, but the discussion of suprasegmentals is impressive. By contrast, one sometimes finds examples of where an author, despite his academic background, chooses to comment on speech in an unpredictable way: Karl Rapp's *Versuch einer Physiologie der Sprache* (1836) is less concerned with the physiology of speech than with the history of particular languages.

The Englishman Alexander John Ellis had many linguistic interests, including acoustics—he was the translator of von Helmholtz's *Die Lehre von den Tonempfindungen* (1863)—but he is remembered best for his extensive series of alphabets for English; some were devised in cooperation with Isaac Pitman, the inventor of one of the century's foremost shorthand systems. Ellis saw a clear connection between the requirements of the linguist *per se* in notating speech (some decades before the founding of the IPA) and the immature reader of English, who struggled to overcome the irregularities and inadequacies of the spelling system. Like several other linguists, Ellis supported schemes for reforming the orthography of English.[20] His Palaeotype—'old type'—utilized the traditional units of orthography, supplemented by inverted. reversed, and italicized forms of some of them, together with roman-based diacritics, with a more logical distribution of sound values. Palaeotype allows the user to notate at a much deeper level of accuracy than could normally be expected of a set of phonetic symbols created from the roman repertoire.

The name of Alexander Melville Bell (the father of Alexander Graham Bell of telephony fame) is associated with a major publication in 1867 on categories of general phonetics and on phonetic notation, *Visible Speech, or the Science of Universal Alphabetics*. Speech is notated by means of an iconic alphabet, and one which is usually initially baffling to most readers, but which logically captures the various features, or gestures, that constitute a sound. Bell saw a very practical use of his system in aiding deaf speakers to achieve a more natural, and less marked, style of pronunciation.

Henry Sweet, one of the foremost phoneticians (and more generally, linguists) of the nineteenth century, maintained that phonetics has to be accorded a central place in the study of a language. His *Handbook of Phonetics* (1877) includes some general phonetics, though the main focus is English and other European languages. The type of phonetics he describes is articulatory-auditory, with little on the anatomical or acoustic aspects of speech production. His views on phonetic notation, and types of notation, are important: partly because of the distinction he draws between 'broad' and 'narrow' notation (similar to, but not identical with, phonemic and allophonic notation), his choice of a Latin-based notation ('Romic' is his term), and his exposition of the difference between those sounds 'which actually correspond to differences of meaning in language' and those that do not: in other words, every sound in a language is either phonemic or non-phonemic.[21] Sweet was an early supporter of Melville Bell's 'Visible Speech' alphabet, but he later adopted large parts of it and published the result as his own 'Organic Alphabet' (1880–81).

In Continental Europe, one finds growing interest in a style of phonetics from the 1870s onwards which had begun to move away from investigations of the physiology and acoustics of speech towards that of the sounds and the systems they form in individual languages, i.e. linguistic phonetics, in other words. The differing titles of the four editions of Eduard Sievers' work on phonetics, between 1876 and 1893, highlight a shift in orientation and content: from 'Sound Physiology' (Sievers 1876) to 'Phonetics' (Sievers 1893). Phonetics—at least for him—was moving from the earlier position of its roots in the medical sciences and physics to a more autonomous and linguistically informed one, in which the core of the subject is constituted by the sounds and sound systems of languages and dialects of languages (cf. Kohler 1981). Moritz Trautmann,

---

[20] Ellis (1845) is a relatively early work on spelling reform, but it illustrates the direction that Ellis was to pursue in this area.

[21] See further Jakobson (1966), which discusses not only Sweet's ideas but those of some of his contemporaries.

however, intended that phonetics should consciously move away from an articulatory description of vowels to an acoustic one (1884–6), but the result was not particularly successful. Wilhelm Viëtor's introduction to phonetics, *Elemente der Phonetik* (1884) married the theoretical with the practical sides of phonetics, and encapsulated the ideas on phonetics of both Bell and Sweet.

Friedrich Techmer edited a journal of general linguistics from 1884 until his death in 1891. An equivalent publication for phonetics was *Le maître phonétique*, founded by the French scholar and language teacher Paul Passy, in 1886, and which quickly moved to publish material on phonetic theory—including notation—as distinct from the role of phonetics in language-teaching.

In Britain, the work of Daniel Jones and the Department of Phonetics at University College London is synonymous with the study of speech during the twentieth century; it set a benchmark for future developments elsewhere. The Department's activities covered not only the phonetics of English and many other languages but questions of phoneme theory, intonational analysis, and clinical phonetics.[22]

5.13 NINETEENTH-CENTURY PHONOLOGY

Sweet's distinction in 1877 between what would nowadays be considered the phoneme and the speech sound had parallels in the work of two other phoneticians: the Swiss Jost Winteler and the Pole Jan Baudouin de Courtenay. In his study of a dialect of eastern Switzerland, Winteler distinguished between distinctive differences that could differentiate meaning and those that were merely variants (1876). Baudouin de Courtenay, a Polish linguist and Slavist, was the senior figure of a group of linguists working at Kazan's Imperial University in Tatarstan in Russia from the mid-1870s. He distinguished between the phoneme as a psychological concept and the speech-sound as the physical manifestation of that concept.[23]

5.14 ALTERING THE ORTHOGRAPHY: SEVERAL EXPERIMENTS

Over the centuries, the motives for altering the contemporary form of orthography have varied. Sometimes there has been a connection between the desire to adjust (or replace) the current orthography and other, related activities. In the seventeenth

---

[22] The fullest description of phonetics in London is by Collins and Mees (1999).
[23] See Bandouin de Courtenay (1972a). His work is discussed in detail by Mugdan (1984) see also §8.3.1 below.

century, it was the design of shorthand systems; in the eighteenth century, it was to do with establishing standards of pronunciation, and/or elaborating a theory and practice of elocution and rhetoric. In the twentieth century and earlier, the motive has often been to simplify the spelling system in order to make the process of learning to read more reliable and faster.

An early example of a proposal to alter, but not completely replace, the current orthography was Sir Thomas Smith's study of English pronunciation, *De recta et emendata linguae anglicae scriptione dialogus* (1568). He uses the <¨> diacritic to indicate long vowels; he also re-introduces the Old and Middle English <þ> and <ð> for dental fricatives (as in *breath* and *breathe*).

The following year, 1569, John Hart, in his *An Orthographie*, introduces completely new symbols for five phonemes. In William Bullokar's *A short introduction or guiding* (1580), one finds forty new symbols. Admittedly, almost all are modifications of standard characters: for example, <ŕ> and <ȝ>. Similarly, Alexander Gil's revised version (1621) of his *Logonomia Anglica* utilizes modified standard characters (e.g. <ħ>), older symbols (e.g. <Ð>) and diacritics (e.g. ¨). Three lines of poetry will illustrate some of the changes Gil wanted to make:

> Nou mai yï âl sï plain
> Ðat trvth iz strong, and trv lvv möst of mjħt
> Ðat for hiz trusti servants duth so strongly fjħt (Gil 1621: 113).

Charles Butler (1634) follows Gil in his use of horizontal strokes through certain letters to create new ones: thus <sh> (in 'ship') is 'ʃ'. The <th> of 'thin', however, is <ꞇ>. John Wilkins' excellent study of phonetics (and other linguistic topics) in *An Essay towards a Real Character . . .* (1668) includes various notations which involve modified Latin characters as well as novel sequences (e.g. <dh>). The following example is taken from 'The Lord's Prayer' (Wilkins 1668: 373):

> . . . byt deliver ys frɑm ivil, fɑr dhyn iz dhe cingdim, dhe pyɣër and dhe glɑrı, fɑr ever and ever. Amen.

The eighteenth century saw other attempts to create an orthographic system that would either be an improvement on the standard one or a tool that could be used by quasi-phoneticians in their analysis of speech. Benjamin Franklin, one of the founding fathers of the United States, experimented with a partially different alphabet and some rearranged spelling conventions for the phonology of his variety of American English. He uses mostly conventional characters, with a small number of new ones created from already existing characters: for example, <h> for the voiceless dental fricative /θ/ in 'that' (Franklin 1972 [1768]). His novelties harmonize well visually alongside the other characters.

John Walker, the author of an excellent pronouncing dictionary (1791), opts for a system of re-spelling with small numbers on the tops of vowels: <hȧt> with the number 1 on top of the <a> signals the /æ/ phoneme; <hȧte> retains the final <e>, but the <a> has a number 4 on top, thus signalling the /eː/ phoneme.

William Thornton (1793) uses a Latin-based symbol system, but with some modifications, to notate the 'distinct sounds' (i.e. the phonemes) of American English. The result is a reformed orthography, well described and illustrated. Examples of the changes he proposed include the use of small capital letters (<G>, <H>, <I>, <L>, <R>) variants of standard characters (<ɑ>, <ɒ>), and older characters (<Ð>).

The question of how to establish a romanized, or partly romanized, orthography for several languages, especially those structurally distant from English, was tackled by various linguists: for example, by Sir William Jones for Indian languages; Count Constantin Volney for Arabic, Persian and Turkish; and John Pickering for Native American languages. In his *Dissertation on the Orthography of Asiatick Words in Roman Letters* (1786), Jones prefers an organic notation, in which there is a visual connection between the formal lines of the symbol and the mode in which the sound is made. The driver for the choice of a roman-based orthography was, clearly, to facilitate an easier learning procedure for the languages of India, especially in the context of developing commercial and administrative systems between the English-speaking and writing world and India. A few years later, Volney (1795) put forward a roman-based system for transliterating Arabic, Persian, and Turkish, on the advice of William Thornton, who introduced him to Sir William Jones's alphabet. His later publication on the same topic (Volney 1819) uses a further set of roman-based symbols. In his will, he left money for Le Prix Volney, to be awarded for an 'harmonic alphabet.' This stimulated further interest in the general issue of spelling reform and the creation of a more 'scientific' alphabet—and one for all languages (Leopold 1999). The first winners of the prize, in 1822, were Josef Scherer and Andreas Schleiermacher. The latter's version, only published posthumously in 1864, spelled out his aims: the alphabet had to be useable for the notation of all languages; it also had to be roman-based, and without any digraphs. As a result, a set of diacritical marks has to be employed to signal particular phonetic features. For example, there are acute accents below as well as above characters; similarly, there are dots and hačeks below and above.

Pickering (1820) had a more restricted aim: a notational system that could be used in the description of Native American languages. The characters are mainly roman; the remainder are handled by means of digraphs and diacritics. Erasmus Darwin's analysis of 'letters' led him not to a new alphabet, but to suggestions as to how particular sounds should be symbolized. For example, he felt that the /uː/ vowel of *cool* and *school* 'ought to have an appropriated character as thus ∞' (Darwin 1803: 117).

The needs of the Christian church in producing Bibles and prayer books in many overseas countries led to the Church Missionary Society publishing an alphabet in 1848 consisting of roman characters, which was designed primarily for the benefit of missionaries in Africa (Venn 1848). Furthermore, users of a new (or modified) orthography could expect to be presented with a method of transcription that would remain permanent, rather than be subject to the whims of the publishing trade. Hence one finds publications with words like 'Rules', 'Standard,' and 'Uniform' in their titles during this period. Several linguists heeded this requirement, and in 1854 the German linguist and Egyptologist Carl Lepsius convened a meeting of linguists and others to decide on a recommended system of notation. It had very specific aims, one of which was that it should not attempt to notate anything other than 'typical' sounds. (This can be construed as a further example of an awareness, albeit somewhat imprecise, of the phonemic principle.) The alphabet was published in German (1854) and English (1855); a second English edition followed in 1863. It uses the roman alphabet, but has to be supplemented by a large array of diacritics. It enjoyed some support in the shorter term, but ultimately it fell into neglect. Yet the roman base for any new orthographic system was to remain—as it still does.

Karl Rapp (1836) uses a roman alphabet, with additional items from Greek and Old English, and some diacritics; von Brücke (1856, 1863) more or less likewise. The non-roman alphabet by Carl Merkel (1857, 1866) was unsuccessful. Critics pointed out that in places it was very difficult to read. Another failure was the system of Félix Henri Du Bois-Reymond (1862), despite being roman-based. Samuel Haldeman's roman-based orthography (1860) inevitably includes some diacritics, some new letters, and even some broken ones. The result is a more complex looking style of notation, despite its obvious roman base. Examples are: *six* <sɪcs>, *nine* <nʌjn>, and *three* <˥rɪ> (Haldeman 1860: 140).

To a non-specialist, Alexander Melville Bell's 'Visible Speech' system (1867) is unreadable and quite unlike the standard orthography of English, or IPA—or any other language. It is an iconic alphabet whose forms represent, if sometimes tenuously, the shape and position of the articulators. Bell believed that he could persuade the British government to adopt it as an official orthography for English, yet its usefulness lies in its ability to notate subtleties of pronunciation, both segmental and non-segmental. Sweet's 'Organic Alphabet' is a partial modification of Bell's Visible Speech (Sweet 1880–81: 207–16).

So-called 'analphabetic' (or 'antalphabetic') schemes have been devised at various times. These are not necessarily predicated on the concept of the sound segment (phonemic or non-phonemic) as a defining feature of the system. Thus Jespersen 1889 uses a variety of notational devices (roman characters, Greek characters, numbers) to describe the feature composition of sounds. So [t], rather than being considered simply a voiceless alveolar plosive and notated as such, is treated as 'a pulmonic egressive slightly breathy voiceless oral tongue-blade medio-alveolar non-labialized stop.' For each of the named features there is a symbol or diacritic. The resulting transcription becomes, effectively, unreadable, and perhaps counterintuitive, without the help of a key. Kenneth Pike's 1943 system is based on the same principle, and leads to a yet more complex notation. His notation of [t] runs to 34 characters.

The growth of phonetics as a university-level subject in some countries from the second half of the nineteenth century onwards altered the nature of any new orthography: the needs of the phoneticians and linguists were different from those of devisers of orthographic systems for general use. Notations for non-standard ('dialect') forms of a language were needed with the growth of dialectological studies in the nineteenth century: two examples are the Swedish dialect alphabet of 1879 (Lundell) and the

Danish alphabet of 1890 (Jespersen). Both are alphabets for phoneticians, not the general public.

By the late 1880s, the International Phonetic Alphabet (IPA), founded only a few years earlier, had quickly established itself as the preferred method for phoneticians and language teachers to notate speech, both in Europe and much further afield. Yet alternative proposals continued to be made. Wilhelm Schmidt's 'Anthropos Alphabet' (1907; revised 1924) harked back to Lepsius and the 'Standard' alphabet of the mid-1850s, to which some IPA symbols and diacritics were added. A second example of the incorporation into an alphabet of parts of IPA, together with Sweet's 'Romic' alphabets, is the Boas–Goddard–Sapir–Kroeber report in 1916 on native North American languages (Boas et al. 1916). Jörgen Forchhammer's 'Weltlautschrift' (1928) is largely IPA, but the diacritics are mostly his own.

Given the continuing interest and concern over questions of notation, twelve linguists met in Copenhagen in 1925 to discuss possible new phonetic symbols and diacritics (Jespersen and Pedersen 1925). Their recommendations gave priority to the choice of symbols for a phonemic representation of speech; and they argued that no further iconic notations should be devised. A long series of proposals was presented for alterations to be made to certain of the IPA's set of symbols and diacritics, primarily by adjusting the appearance of particular symbols rather than by replacing them. The end result, however, was that the IPA made scarcely any alterations to its notational practices.[24]

---

[24] See §6.1 below.

CHAPTER 6

....

FROM IPA TO PRAAT AND BEYOND

....

DEBORAH LOAKES

In the late nineteenth century, the development of the International Phonetic Alphabet and the inception of acoustic analysis together were the starting point for phonetic analysis and interpretation as it is carried out today. From making a record of an utterance using an IPA transcription, to analysing the vocal fold vibrations in a voiced consonant using speech analysis software, to assessing tongue–palate contact using articulatory tracking devices—the possibilities for transcribing and analysing spoken language are multitudinous. In this chapter, some of the tools used in modern-day phonetic research, as well as their progress over time, are reviewed.

6.1 TRANSCRIPTION SYSTEM: SPOTLIGHT ON THE IPA

....

Phonetic transcription has been described as 'the use of phonetic symbols to represent speech sounds [where] each sound . . . is represented by a written phonetic symbol, so as to furnish a record sufficient to render possible the accurate reconstruction of the utterance' (Wells 2006: 366). It has been said that some form of transcription system has always existed (Kemp 2006). For example, poets have long required transcription systems to represent verse, and transcription systems are needed for written representations of speech such as dictionaries and grammars (examples are provided in Abercrombie 1981). Within linguistics today, phonetic transcription is used for varying purposes, from describing the speech sounds of a language to making a record of an utterance produced by a speaker on a particular occasion. Depending on the needs of the analyst, these transcriptions range from broad (recording only the contrasts in the language) to narrow (including fine-grained phonetic detail); see for example the discussion in Wells (2006).

While the International Phonetic Alphabet (IPA) is only one of many orthographic systems that exist for transcribing speech sounds, it is the most commonly used system by phoneticians (Wells 2006), 'the most widely relied on international standard for the phonetic transcription of dictionary entries' (Esling 2010: 678, and references therein), and it is also considered the main system in use across the world (MacMahon 1996).

Last revised in 2005, the International Phonetic Alphabet consists of approximately 100 mostly alphabetic symbols, as well as approximately 30 diacritics (Wells 2006, Esling 2010). The alphabet itself is today represented on a chart,[1] and categorized according to a number of features. Pulmonic consonant symbols are arranged horizontally according to their place of articulation in the vocal tract, and vertically according to their manner of articulation. Place of articulation is arranged according to the sequence of articulators in the vocal tract, from the lips (bilabial sounds such as /m, b/) to the glottis (glottal sounds such as /h/). Manner depends on stricture in the vocal tract and how it relates to airflow, and includes complete obstruction (plosives) through to a state where two articulators approach one another (approximants). Non-pulmonic consonants (clicks, voiced implosives and ejectives) are contained in a separate chart. Vowel symbols in the IPA are represented on a quadrilateral, where symbols are arranged according to vertical (from close to open) and horizontal (front to back) dimensions. The IPA also has a range of diacritics that can be used to modify primary symbols such as aspiration, palatalization, and creakiness, as well as symbols for suprasegmentals, tones and word accents. There is also a category of 'other symbols' which represent sounds made by more than one articulator; for example /w/ is listed in this section because it is a labio-velar approximant.

Outside of the full IPA chart, there is also a separate alphabet called the 'ExtIPA chart for disordered speech,' which contains a range of symbols for consonant sounds that may need to be transcribed in clinical settings (see Nolan, Esling, et al. 1999: 186–93). For example the consonant /ﬀ/ is a velopharyngeal fricative often used by speakers with a cleft palate. The ExtIPA chart contains extra diacritics, with one example being the symbol / \ /, used for reiterated articulation (as in stuttered speech). In practice, [m\m] would be a reiterated bilabial nasal. There are also symbols for connected speech phenomena such as pausing (and relative pause length), timing, and relative loudness, and a section on voicing which has symbols for factors such as pre-voicing, post-voicing, and pre-aspiration. Finally, there are 'other symbols' as in the main IPA chart, including those for indeterminate sounds and extraneous noise. Factors occurring in disordered speech are also accounted for in the other symbols section; for example, silent articulations are symbolized with parentheses, so [(m)] would be a silently articulated bilabial nasal, and sounds produced by speakers which have no available symbol may be transcribed /*/.

---

[1] Esling (2010) discusses historical aspects of the arrangement of IPA symbols in a chart format.

A book containing information specifically about the IPA, as well as illustrations of its use in twenty-nine languages, was produced by the International Phonetic Association in 1999 (Nolan, Esling, et al. 1999). This is the *Handbook of the International Phonetic Association: A Guide to the Use of the International Phonetic Alphabet* (the 'IPA handbook'), which replaced an earlier edition of 1949. According to the foreword, it is intended for those who will use the alphabet: 'language teachers and phoneticians interested in the sounds of different languages ... speech technologists, speech pathologists [and] theoretical phonologists' amongst others (Nolan, Esling, et al. 1999: vii). Aside from the IPA handbook, another resource which exemplifies the IPA in use is Ladefoged and Maddieson's *The Sounds of the World's Languages* (1996). This book uses primary data to explore articulations across the world's languages, covering consonants, vowels, secondary articulations, phonation types, and suprasegmentals using IPA transcription.

While phonetic transcription has 'always' existed, the International Phonetic Alphabet has its origins in the nineteenth century with Sir Isaac Pitman, who was involved in the reform of alphabet and spelling systems—essentially to make them easier to use and more accessible. In 1842 he collaborated with Alexander J. Ellis, who had an interest in transcribing languages encountered in his travels. The two developed an alphabet in 1847, and it is this alphabet which formed the basis for the IPA (Kemp 2006, Nolan, Esling, et al. 1999; see also Kelly (1981) for discussion of issues surrounding the 1847 alphabet, and Kemp (2006) for information on the history of other transcription systems). This particular alphabet was essentially chosen by members of the International Phonetic Association (also IPA) which began in Paris in 1886.[2] The group was initially composed of eleven language teachers whose aim was to use, in schools, phonetic notation for 'a realistic pronunciation of foreign languages,' by 1914 the group had grown to 1751 members (Nolan, Esling, et al. 1999: 194). Over time, the primary focus of the association became phonetic-related matters rather than teaching-related. Further information on the history of the International Phonetic Association is available in MacMahon (1986).

Ellis and Pitman's alphabet was altered and revised by the (precursor to) the International Phonetic Association from 1887 through the 1890s (Nolan, Esling, et al. 1999: 196). Changes are still occasionally made to the alphabet, which is progressive in the sense that when a new symbol is needed, one will be created. This must be proposed by members of the International Phonetic Association, and then voted upon (see Nolan, Esling et al. 1999: 196). For instance, the most recent addition to the IPA was the labiodental flap (see Nikolaidis 2005). Prior to its inclusion in the IPA chart, Olson and Hajek (1999) argued that the labiodental flap should be awarded a place because it is easily describable, occurs in the phonology of many languages, including at least two independent languages.[3] Despite the fact that the IPA has had some developments such

---

[2] The Association initially began under the name *Dhi Fonètik Tîcerz' Asóciécon*, and has had various names prior to the current one (see Nolan, Esling et al. 1999: 194).

[3] Principles governing the IPA, including the addition of new symbols, are outlined in the IPA handbook (Nolan, Esling, et al. 1999: app. 1).

as this, Esling (2010) notes that the latest edition of the chart, updated in 2005, looks remarkably similar to the 1926 version. Additionally, it is reported in the IPA handbook: 'The development of the Alphabet has not been without controversy'—however, the handbook also adds that the aim is to have a 'healthy cycle of renewal . . . as new knowledge is brought to bear' (Nolan, Esling, et al. 1999: 197). Further discussion regarding revisions to the IPA is available in Ladefoged and Roach (1986), and some examples of early versions of the IPA are given in MacMahon (1996).

Given its place in history, the IPA system is couched in classical phonemic theory. As discussed in the IPA handbook, the use of an alphabetic system for transcribing speech sounds is a theoretical construct which in fact 'underlines the conceptualization of speech as a sequence of sounds' (Nolan, Esling, et al. 1999: 37). That is, the system is based on a one-to-one mapping between phones and phonemes, as opposed to their being overlapping (coarticulated) and highly variable, the direction in which phonological theory has now moved. In discussing the analysis and transcription of English vowels, Wells points out further theoretical issues with the widespread use of the IPA: 'it is possible for analysts who disagree on the phonological treatment [of a data set] to use the same transcription system, or conversely, for analysts who agree on the phonology to use different notations' (Wells 2006: 391). While this is the case, benefits of the IPA are its traditional nature, the fact that the principles on which it is founded are generally well understood by those using the alphabet, and that the system is robust and stable (see Nolan, Esling, et al. 1999: 38). Wells 2006 also notes that even though many users disagree with the IPA's basis in classical phonemic theory, the system is used today for its convenience.

6.2 SOFTWARE PROGRAMS: PRAAT AND EMU

So far, we have addressed one tool used in phonetic research, that of notation using the IPA. We have seen that the International Phonetic Alphabet has changed very little since the symbols were decided on in the late nineteenth century, and that any change today must be discussed and voted upon by members. In the current section, the focus is on selected software used to analyse speech instrumentally. In stark contrast to the IPA, the nature of these phonetic tools is that they change rapidly.

Since Edison developed the phonograph in 1878 (see Edison 1878), the possibilities for recording and analysing speech signals have continued to advance. Recording systems used for linguistic analysis, including a comparison of old and new technologies, are reviewed by Ladefoged (2003: 16–21, 25–6). The most striking change over time is the ability now to both record and store high-quality speech samples on personal computers. It is really the development of personal computers which has led to the advent of new technologies enabling phoneticians to answer vastly different types of questions about speech.[4] For example computer programs such as *Praat: A System for Doing Phonetics by Computer* (hereafter 'Praat') and *The EMU Speech Database System* ('EMU') now mean that spectrograms and accompanying displays such as Fo (first formant) contours, waveforms, and intensity traces are instantly available on laptop or desktop computers. Today, spectrograms can be produced almost instantly for a single utterance through to dialogue in multi-speaker corpora. These easily produced images (such as that shown in Fig. 6.1 below) contrast with one of the earliest systems used at Bell Telephone Laboratories, where researchers worked on understanding spectrographic patterns so that hearing impaired people would have access to 'visible speech'[5] (see Potter et al. 1947).

Early spectrographs were large devices consisting of two shelves, with an analyser and recorder unit on the top shelf and a power unit, speaker, microphone, pre-amplifier, and filter on the bottom shelf. Only a maximum of 2.4 seconds of speech could be represented on a spectrogram, which was printed on magnetic tape contained in the analyser unit (Potter et al. 1947: 11–15). Anecdotes regarding these older devices are given by Ladefoged (2003: 105, 109).

Just as the IPA is one of many notation systems for transcribing speech sounds, Praat is just one (popular) system for analysing speech signals. Some examples of other systems used for phonetic analysis and annotation on personal computers are EMU (discussed in more detail below), Snack, Speech Analyser, Computer Speech Lab (CSL),

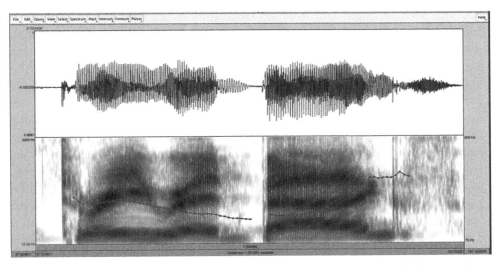

FIG. 6.1 Screen shot of the spectrographic display in Praat (version 5.1.31), including waveform and pitch trace

---

[4] As pointed out by Hardcastle and Gibbon (2005: 40) with respect to electropalatography.
[5] This term was also used by Melville Bell, Alexander Graham Bell's father, to describe an orthography similar in principle to the IPA (see Potter et al. 1947: 3), but which was never as popular (Nolan, Esling, et al. 1999: 197).

PCquirerX (or MacquirerX depending on the platform), and PitchWorks (for intonational analyses). Praat enables acoustic analysis and annotation of speech data, and is used widely for phonetic and phonological research. The program is freely downloadable (Boersma and Weenik 2012), and is also regularly updated. Praat was designed in 1992 by Paul Boersma from The Institute of Phonetic Sciences at the University of Amsterdam, who saw a need for such a program and so created it. He developed it from a similar undistributed program called Kal which he designed for the Vax computer in 1990; parts of the program were also inspired by the MATFUN program designed in the Department of Medical Physics and Biophysics by at the University of Nijmegen in the 1980s. When the program was moved to another platform in 1992 (SGI Irix), Boersma distributed it and renamed it 'Praat' ('talk' in Dutch). A version was designed for Apple Macintosh in 1993, the year that David Weenink (also of the University of Amsterdam) became involved in development of Praat, and versions continue to be made for various other platforms, most recently Mac OSX (Boersma, p.c., 2010).

An example of the spectrographic display in a recent version of Praat, also showing a waveform and a pitch trace, can be seen in Fig. 6.1. This example shows a record of the utterance *three red bags* produced by a female speaker of Australian English. A high-rising intonation pattern is clearly visible from the pitch trace.

In Fig. 6.1, the toolbar in the top left-hand corner shows various options, 'spectrum,' 'pitch,' 'intensity,' etc. Users can alter the default settings; for example, this spectrogram shows frequencies up to 5000 Hz, but this can be changed up to a maximum of 20,000 Hz. The window length and dynamic range (dB) of the spectrogram can also be changed, as well as various other settings such as analysis method and window shape (default settings for these are Fourier and Gaussian, respectively). Users may segment and annotate the data according to the focus of the analysis. Praat has been used in phonetic research for measuring duration (e.g. Patterson and Connine 2001 for alveolar flaps in American English, Hirata and Tsukada 2009 for vowel length in Japanese), formant frequencies (e.g. Hay et al. 2006 for diphthongs in New Zealand English; Ferragne and Pellegrino 2010 for accents in the British Isles), and fine-grained phonetic detail (e.g. Dalton and Ní Chasaide 2005 for intonation in Irish Dialects; Stevens and Hajek 2007 for pre-aspirated consonants in Siennese Italian). Praat can also used for prosodic investigation, for example measuring tone (e.g. Yu 2007 for tone in Cantonese), intonation (e.g. Ladd and Schepman 2003 for pitch accents in English), and stress (e.g. Remijsen and van Heuven 2005 for a dialect of Papiamentu). Praat may also be used for phonological description of sound systems in languages—that is, for measuring contrasts in phonation types, vowels and consonants, as well as tonal and intonation systems (e.g. Abramson et al. 2004 for phonation types in Suai; McDonough and Wood 2008 for stop contrasts in Athabaskan languages). Another way in which Praat may be used is for running experimental listening tests, and the program also allows for acoustic aspects of tokens to be synthesized (see e.g. Ladd and Schepman 2003 for duration and F0; Zhang and Francis 2010 for various parameters including vowel quality). These are just some examples of research carried out using Praat, but there are countless other ways the program has been and may be used which have not been addressed here.

Like Praat, EMU enables users to annotate and analyse speech samples. While there are some similarities between the programs in many of the types of acoustic analyses that may be carried out, the interface between the two programs is clearly different, as are many of the options offered to users. EMU originally evolved through developments made to a program called 'Acoustic Phonetics in S' at Edinburgh University by Gordon Watson and Jonathan Harrington (see Harrington et al. 2003). EMU's current format is based on an earlier version of the program called 'MU+' which was developed at Macquarie University (see Cassidy and Harrington 1996), and its primary role is 'creating, [complex] querying and analysing' large speech databases for phonetic analysis and laboratory phonology (see Harrington et al. 2003: 356).

Researchers involved in the development of EMU have lauded the superiority of some of Praat's functions, including its labelling and segmentation tools, as well as the signal manipulation (Harrington et al. 2003). However, they note that EMU's advantages are its hierarchical annotation structure and subsequent possibilities for complex querying of databases. In EMU, the possibilities of analysis are really only limited by what a user chooses. For example, users may choose to label prosodic phenomena along with syllable boundaries, phonemes, and fine-grained phonetic detail, all the while connecting these related phenomena (or forming a 'relationship' between them) in the labelling process. This makes it possible to explore various aspects of the data, such as the duration of all word initial /bi/ syllables compared to word final /bi/ syllables, or the hierarchical structure of utterances in which a certain type of lenition occurs (i.e. where the lenition tends to occur—perhaps at word boundaries, in weak syllables, utterance finally, or a combination of these). It is also possible to extract information more generally, for example to measure some aspect of all voiced stops in a corpus. While some queries can be carried out within EMU, the library 'EMU-R', used within the R programming language, can be employed for powerful statistical analyses and graphical representation of data. Harrington (2010) also provides detailed information on how to query databases, with plenty of other examples of some of the more complex questions that phoneticians may be interested in (see also §6.4).

EMU can also be used to label other types of linguistic information, with or without accompanying phonetic analyses. One example is a study by Evans et al. (2008), who studied non-isomorphism in the Australian language Dalabon, using EMU to combine phonetic and morphological analyses. Through analysis of word boundaries, intonational contours, and pause units researchers found a mismatch between grammatical and phonological words in Dalabon.

In another study, EMU was used to analyse fricated /p t k/ consonants in Australian English (Loakes and McDougall 2010). In that study, we were interested in individual variation in twins' speech. The EMU hierarchy involved tiers that had utterance, word, phoneme, and phonetic levels. At the phoneme level, a consonant /k/ would be labelled as such, whereas fine-grained phonetic detail (such as fricative [x] variants) was labelled on the phonetic tier. Through EMU, it was possible for us to search for all instances of /k/ realized as [x], and to exclude all other variants. While this was not a prosodic analysis *per se*, the utterance and word tiers were used to glean information about where the frication had occurred (at word boundaries, word-medially, etc.). The main findings of that study were that members of twin pairs display individual phonetic behaviour, and do so consistently. For example, in non-contemporaneous data we saw that one twin tended to realize /k/ as [x] whereas his brother did not. This is interesting first, because identical twin pairs are anatomically as similar as possible yet use different strategies for achieving a target phoneme (i.e. their speech has an element of individuality). Second, this idiosyncrasy was observed on more than one occasion, demonstrating that the speaker's phonetic behaviour was consistent.

Another advantage of EMU is that it allows users to simultaneously analyse acoustic and articulatory data. For example, EMU reads electropalatography (EPG) data, and it also reads electromagnetic articulography (EMA) data, both of which can then be analysed through EMU-R. EPG is a technique that tracks tongue–palate interaction (see §6.3 for more detail), and EMA is a system in which magnets are fixed to soft articulators and tracked continuously (see Ladefoged 2003: 187–9 for further information). Harrington (2010) presents a case study of stop–sonorant clusters as a means of explaining how to analyse EMA data in EMU-R, and some examples of recent studies using EMA in EMU are Tabain (2008), which analysed variability in tongue movement for Australian English /u/, and Tabain (2009), which analysed jaw movement in consonant production in the Australian language Arrernte.

In Fletcher et al. (2008), EPG data was analysed in EMU to investigate coarticulation of sonorant–stop clusters in the Australian language Warlpiri. In that study we used two tiers, 'word' and 'phonetic.' The phonetic level was used to label both vowels and consonants, assisted by the waveform, spectrogram, and EPG trace. Because we were interested in the degree of coarticulation in nasal and lateral clusters, we collected information from the phonetic tier such as the degree of consonantal contact in the anterior and dorsal regions of the palate in both the sonorant and obstruent portions of the clusters, as well as durational information. This allowed us to focus on anticipatory coarticulation by analysing the sonorant, as well as carry-over coarticulation through analysis of the obstruent. We observed some spatial and temporal coarticulation (primarily with lamino-palatal consonants), but this was limited compared to languages such as English—consistent with the notion that Australian languages have rich place-of-articulation contrasts which must be maintained by speakers (i.e. too much coarticulation in any direction would render the phonemes non-contrastive; see e.g. Butcher 2006). An example of the EMU interface with data from this study can be seen in Fig. 6.2. This example shows the utterance *mayi kinki* 'don't know devil' produced by a female speaker of Warlpiri, with an accompanying waveform, spectrogram, and EPG frame (from around the midpoint of the /n/ in *kinki*).

The EPG frame represents the areas of tongue–palate contact during the alveolar nasal segment. Harrington (2010) describes how to read EPG palatograms: essentially the top of the frame shows the region just behind the speaker's teeth, and the bottom of the frame the region between the hard and soft palates. The dark areas in the frame in

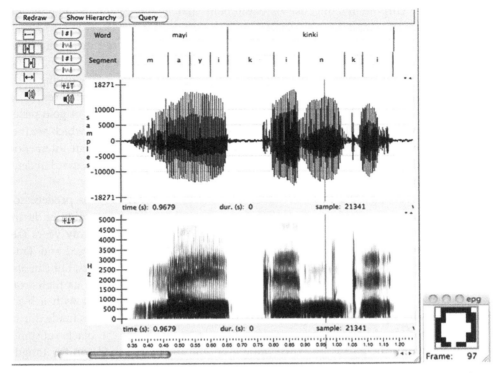

FIG. 6.2 Screen shot of the spectrographic display in EMU (version 2.3.0), including waveform and an EPG frame

Fig. 6.2 show where tongue–palate contact has occurred. Here, there is both anterior contact (typical for an alveolar nasal) and some dorsal contact (anticipation of the following /k/). Additionally, there is contact on the sides of the palate, due to coarticulation of the high-front /i/ vowels surrounding the /nk/ cluster.

As can be seen from the discussion in this section, Praat and EMU are very different types of software. However, there is now an interface between the two programs so that annotations can be read in both, in order to exploit the benefits of each of them (see e.g. Harrington et al. 2003, Harrington 2010).

6.3 ARTICULATORY SYSTEMS: EPG

Articulatory phonetics, introduced in the previous section, is another area in which the tools for phonetic research have developed rapidly. From collection and analysis of relatively small data samples using static records of vocal tract configuration during speech sound articulation (one example is direct palatography, described below) to much larger corpora making use of equipment that allows dynamic imaging and tracking of vocal tract configuration.

While only one type of articulatory tracking device is discussed in detail in this chapter, many more exist. Stone (2010) describes three types of laboratory techniques used for measuring speech: (1) imaging techniques that analyse internal working of the vocal tract without impeding it in any, way such as ultrasound and magnetic resonance imaging; (2) 'point-tracking measures of the vocal tract,' where magnetic or gold pellets are affixed to the articulators (which may include the tongue, face, or jaw) which are then tracked during speech, for example EMA, and (3) measures of tongue–palate interaction, which includes EPG. These, and other types of imaging techniques, are discussed in detail in Stone (2010).

Before discussing EPG in more detail, it is useful to understand its predecessor, direct palatography, which is a way of making a static record of the vocal tract during speech sound articulation. This method, which has been used for many years (see Abercrombie 1957), and particularly in phonetic fieldwork (see Ladefoged and Traill 1980, Ladefoged 2003), is used primarily for analysing lingual consonants, but can also be used to show areas of tongue–palate contact in other sounds such as high-front vowels (see Fig. 6.2). It involves speakers having their tongue coated with a black substance, and a photograph being taken of the palate where contact was made during speech sound production. Linguagrams are made similarly, by the black substance being applied to the palate, and then photographing the record made on the tongue. Palatography is still used today in fieldwork for its convenience (see Ladefoged 2003), and now the equipment required is far less obtrusive than it once was (see the image shown in Ladefoged and Traill 1980: 41). Numerous examples of how palatography can be useful for phonetic description are available in Ladefoged and Maddieson (1996), which shows impressions made from various speech sounds in the world's languages.

EPG is essentially the next stage in analysis of tongue–palate contact. It allows analysis of dynamic articulation through the use of an artificial palate, fitted with electrodes that track tongue movement, which is then recorded. How EPG works, and the types of systems available, are discussed in Harrington (2010: 220–22): essentially EPG systems provide the same information as palatograms and linguagrams, but in connected speech. Systems either print out frames of palate contact or show frames simultaneously with the acoustic display (as is the case in EMU) at timed intervals (see Hardcastle and Gibbon 2005: 41–2), with frames typically occurring around every 5–10 milliseconds depending on the system.

The earliest form of EPG was developed at Edinburgh University in the early 1970s by William Hardcastle under the supervision of John Laver (see Hardcastle 1972, 1975, Hardcastle and Gibbon 2005: 40). EPG was used first in phonetic research and is also now used in clinical applications (Hardcastle and Gibbon 2005: 40). In phonetic research, it is especially useful for investigating issues related to tongue–palate contact, for example coarticulation (as discussed in §6.2), gestural timing (Byrd 1996), and connected speech processes (Shockey and Gibbon 1993). An example of how EPG has been used in phonetic research has already been given (the degree of coarticulation in nasal and lateral clusters in an Australian language). One example of a clinical application is where a pathologist wearing a palate produces the speech sound in question and the patient (often a child), who is also wearing a palate, aims to produce the same pattern (examples are shown by Hardcastle and Gibbon 2005: 55, Wood et al. 2009: 67). EPG has been found to be highly effective in clinical settings when compared to therapy based on auditory transcription. This is primarily because the method allows direct evidence of articulatory movement (see the discussion in Wood et al. 2009), and often results in greater intelligibility in the patient. A bibliographical list of EPG-related papers, from both a phonetic and clinical perspective, is presented in Gibbon (2006). Further discussion of the merits and limitations of the method are provided by Ladefoged (2003) and Stone (2010).

6.4 PRAAT AND EMU IN ACTION

Advances in the tools used for phonetic research make it possible to address questions about the nature of speech in new ways. To this point, selected tools used for phonetic research, and some examples of their use, have been discussed. In this section, more detailed examples are given of research questions that have been addressed using both EMU and Praat.

Recent work involves objective analysis of Australian English vowel phonemes (see Loakes et al. 2010a, 2010b, 2010c). Using Praat and EMU, we are investigating a sound change in which /el/ sequences are realized as [æl] by some speakers (see also Cox and Palethorpe 2004). We are also interested in another, lesser known but possibly related change where /æl/ sequences are realized [el] (Loakes et al. 2011).

The /el/–/æl/ sound change is precisely the phenomenon that occurs in New Zealand English, where it has been researched in some detail (see Bayard 1987, Thomas and Hay 2006). The phenomenon also been reported to occur in other Englishes, such as Norfolk Island–Pitcairn English (Ingram and Mühlhäusler 2004) and in White South African English as well as the English spoken in Cape Flats in South Africa (Finn 2004, and references therein). To date, there is some evidence that the /el/–/æl/ sound change in Australian English may be confined to speakers from the south-east of the mainland, specifically in Victoria and its capital, Melbourne (Cox and Palethorpe 2004, Loakes et al. 2010a, 2010b, 2010c, 2011).

Our analysis of a sound change in progress means that we can use some of the tools discussed earlier to investigate the type of variability in the production of /el/ and /æl/ phonemes and how, in turn, listeners are responding to such variability in their input. We can also question why the sound change might be occurring in the first place. A sound change in progress is particularly interesting for linguistics because it affords an opportunity to investigate some of the unanswered questions about languages. There are broad questions such as how languages change and the forces that shape language structure, and narrower questions such as how speakers and listeners process spoken language, and what cues are important for speech units.

Ohala theorizes that sound changes occur due to listener hypocorrection: 'if the listener fails to correct the perturbations in the speech signal variation, then they will be taken at face value and will form part of [the listener's] conception of its pronunciation' (1993: 246). This means that listeners do not account for coarticulation, and a sound change ensues. Many examples of sound changes can be provided from phonetic and phonological literature. One example is Harrington et al. (2008), which specifically cites listener (mis)perception of contextual coarticulation as motivating change in the /u/ vowel in British English, seen clearly in the speech of the Queen and general public over time. They show that this vowel is the subject of a sound change in progress, whereby older and younger speakers are producing extremely different variants, and also responding differently when perceiving tokens produced by older compared with younger speakers. Similarly, our preliminary work has led us to hypothesize that the /el/–/æl/ sound change in Melbourne English is due to differences in listener (mis) perception leading to hypocorrection for some, in this case /el/ → [æl] → /æl/. This work has also led us to believe that shifts in both the vowels and lateral are responsible for listener confusion.

Regarding change in the vowels, it is well known that the context /V/ + /l/ is a common site for vowel differences and change due to the fact that velarized /l/ ([ɫ]) has significant coarticulatory effects, causing preceding vowels in different varieties of English to become lower and more retracted (see the discussion in Cox and Palethorpe 2004, and references therein). Regarding the lateral, Australian English /l/ can now be described as [ɫ] in most, if not all, contexts (cf. Wells 1982). While velarized /l/ is attributable to Australian English generally, the reason that the /el/–/æl/ sound change may be regionally defined may also be due to the fact that lax vowels in Melbourne/ Victoria are reported to be phonetically lower than elsewhere (see Loakes 2006a, b). We have seen evidence of change in both the vowel and lateral in our preliminary work on sound change.

Production studies that we have carried out, in which both EMU and Praat were used to measure formant frequencies, have led us to see that /e/ in /el/ sequences is actually lower and more retracted than /e/ in other contexts. For example, Loakes (2008) carried out some acoustic phonetic analysis of the /el/–/æl/ sound change using Praat, comparing Melbourne speech recorded in 1959/60 (1960s data) and in 2002. In that study, it was apparent that the lateral consonant, and the way vowels interact with /l/, appeared to be responsible for different vowel groupings. Analysis of the 1960s data indicated that speakers for whom /eC/ and /el/, and /æC/ and /æl/ patterned together (i.e. cases where prelateral vowels were no different to vowels in other contexts) were actually producing a more clear sounding [l], while the speakers who were merging prelateral /e/ and /æ/ were producing a darker sounding [ɫ]. None of the 2002 speakers produced clear [l] in any environment. In another study (Loakes et al. 2010a) we used some articulatory data analysed in EMU (EPG palatograms) to show that a female speaker of Australian English was actually using velarized /l/ in both onset and coda

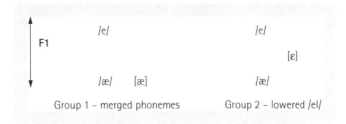

FIG. **6.3** Schematic diagram of prelateral vowels in the F1 dimension

position in the words *weller* and *welder*. In fact, a greater amount of tongue dorsum activity was found in *weller*.[6] While this is only limited data from one speaker, the observation accords with Wells's (1982) observation, as well as Loakes's (2008) acoustic data.

As well as our production work on laterals, we have also observed variability amongst prelateral /e/ and /æ/ tokens produced by speakers who do not merge the phonemes prelaterally. As well as the finding for laterals discussed above, Loakes (2008) found that for the 2002 data, there were also two clear groupings for the prelateral vowels. In the first type (group 1), the speakers merged /el/ and /æl/ pronouncing both as [æl], which is the /el/–/æl/ sound change. In the second type of grouping (group 2), speakers used three vowel categories /eC/ and /æl/, with /el/ in between. In another study (Loakes et al. 2010b), we saw that a speaker from Sydney, where the sound change is not reported to occur, nevertheless produced /el/ tokens which were much lower than /e/ in other contexts, like the second type of vowel grouping seen for Melbourne speakers in Loakes (2008). A schematic diagram of these two types of vowel groupings is presented in Fig. 6.3. As seen in the figure, /e/ in prelateral contexts is not the same as /e/ elsewhere, it is either lowered or produced in the same way as [æ].

These findings, which so far support Ohala's theory (1993) that sound changes occur due to listener hypocorrection, have all been possible using tools for phonetic research described above: acoustic analysis in Praat and EMU, and support from articulatory investigation through EPG. There is evidence that for some speakers /el/ → [æl] (group 1), and for other speakers /el/→ [ɛl] (group 2). We have also observed that some listeners interpret this lowered /el/ as /æl/ (Loakes et al. 2010a, 2010b, 2010c). Complicating this analysis are cases where /æl/ is realized as [el], and we are currently working on an account for this. It is possibly either hypercorrection or an unrelated sound coincidental change (see Loakes et al. 2011).

Tools used for phonetic research can also be used in applied domains such as forensic speaker comparison, where both acoustic and articulatory analyses are used to determine the identity of a speaker on a recording. Forensic speaker comparison involves analysis of a suspect sample where the speaker is known and a forensic sample

---

[6] See Scobbie and Pouplier (2010). /l/ in *weller* may in fact be ambisyllabic, but nevertheless /l/ in this context was more retracted than is often described for Australian English.

where the speaker is unknown. The suspect sample is often a recorded police interview, while the forensic sample varies widely—some examples are threatening voicemail messages or clandestine recordings made with bugging devices. Forensic phoneticians analyse a combination of phonetic variables across the speech samples to come to a decision about how likely it is that the samples were produced by the same or different speakers (see Rose 2002 for a detailed discussion of this field).

Two separate traditions of forensic speaker comparison can be traced from the beginning of the 1960s, one based on auditory analysis alone and one based on the examination of voiceprints (spectrograms, like the 'visible speech' discussed in §6.2). These techniques emerged from the UK and the US respectively. The tradition of forensic speaker identification by auditory analysis alone was used primarily in Britain between the 1960s and 1980s. Identity claims were made by phoneticians on the basis of auditory segmental and prosodic analysis of the particular speech samples, and instrumental phonetic techniques were not employed as a general rule (French 1994). An early description of the way forensic speaker comparison was perceived in this British tradition, and the aversion to instrumental analysis, is provided in Baldwin (1979).

In forensic speaker comparison today, auditory analysis is still seen to be necessary because it is thorough and descriptive (Rose 2002), but it is now seen as insufficient as the sole method of analysis. This is because ignoring the physical speech signal would mean that a large range of potential information is neglected. As such, consideration must also be given to instrumental methods of analysis, which allows for interpretation of aspects of the speech signal that the ear cannot detect (see the discussion in Nolan 1994).

One aspect of variation in one of the hoax call cases I have worked on illustrates how tools used for phonetic research may be used in an applied domain, and also addresses the complexity involved in forensic speaker comparison cases—although advances in technology, and in our understanding of variation in the human voice, have been very rapid. In this particular case, auditory analysis revealed that both the suspect sample (a recorded police interview) and the forensic sample (a call from a telephone box to the emergency services) had a markedly high pitch for a male speaker. Acoustic analysis of pitch (fundamental frequency, F_0), as well as a host of other features, was carried out on both samples using EMU. For this feature, a tier was created for all vowels, and F_0 was extracted from their midpoint (see the discussion in Loakes 2006b) using R. Summarized results are shown in Table 6.1.

Table 6.1 shows the number of observations drawn from each sample (628 in the forensic sample, 646 in the suspect sample), as well as the mean and median which are similar within each sample, the standard deviation (with more variation observed in the forensic sample), and the range. Additional measurements for a group of eight Australian English-speaking males is provided in the third column (from Loakes 2006b) so that comparison can be made. This average AusE pitch is almost the same as the average pitch of 106Hz for 100 male speakers of Standard Southern British English reported by Hudson et al. (2007). They note that pitch is only of interest

Table 6.1 Analysis of pitch (F0, measured in Hz) across a forensic and suspect sample

	Forensic	Suspect	Average AusE
No.	628	646	n/a
Mean	148.8	126.4	105.2
Median	145.7	125.9	103.1
Min.	119.7	89.7	91.0
Max.	220.8	188.6	120.7
S.D.	17.06	10.9	16.4

forensically for the 20 per cent of speakers whose average pitch falls outside the typical average, i.e. above 113Hz, or below 94 Hz.

The results in Table 6.1 show that the Fo for both the forensic and suspect sample fall well above the average for AusE-speaking males, confirming auditory observations. There is a large difference in pitch between the population mean and both the forensic and suspect sample, and there is also wide variation between the forensic and suspect sample. The disparity across the means is similar to an example shown by Butcher (2002: 5) in describing issues related to forensic speaker identification, where 'both the [forensic and suspect sample] differ markedly from the population mean and in the same direction.' That is, both samples are still much higher than the population mean. With a standard deviation of 17.06 Hz in the forensic sample and 10.9 Hz in the interview sample, Fo measurements are also more variable in the forensic sample. While there is a difference in mean pitch values across the samples, this cannot be counted as a difference as such, for the following reasons. First, it is known that while Fo is often relatively stable across one person's speech patterns, it is possible for a large amount of variation to occur. One example is provided in Loakes (2006b), where one speaker's average pitch varied between 99 and 125.7 Hz (26.7 Hz variation) on two separate occasions, which is slightly more than the 22.4 Hz variation observed here. Second, Hirson et al. (1995) and Gfroerer and Wagner (1995) report on research investigating Fo in male speech from forensic samples compared to suspect samples. The researchers reported that Fo taken from voices in police interviews is usually lower than the same voice recorded via telephone (Hirson et al. 1995), and similarly that Fo in forensic samples tends to be higher than in suspect samples recorded via telephone (Gfroerer and Wagner 1995). Gfroerer and Wagner (1995: 47) report excursions of up to 60 Hz between the samples, whereas the difference in this case was smaller at 22.4 Hz. Reasons given for pitch being higher in forensic samples are thought to be due to greater levels of stress or a heightened response, or possibly even due to the conditions in a telephone box, where speakers need to produce louder speech (Gfroerer and Wagner 1995). The effect of loudness was researched further by Jessen et al. (2005), who found that, of a sample of 100 speakers, all had a higher mean pitch when speaking loudly. The actual degree of Fo difference varied according to the speaker, but Jessen

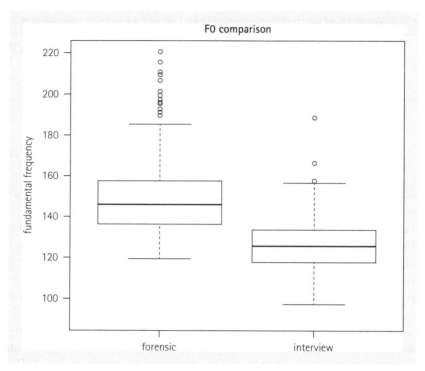

FIG. 6.4 Boxplots comparing Fo distribution across a forensic and suspect sample

et al. 2005 report that in their study and other similar studies the increase in mean Fo for male speakers is 15–40 Hz when speaking loudly.

It is useful to assess the distribution of Fo values in both the forensic and suspect samples, to better understand how the range of values observed, and to further demonstrate the type of data that can be generated in R, using EMU data. Fig. 6.4 shows boxplots of the Fo distribution in both forensic and suspect (interview) speech samples, in a graphical representation produced using R. Aside from showing the range of observations in the data more clearly, this figure shows that there are also a number of outliers observed in the forensic sample, all in the higher frequency range above approximately 185 Hz. This accords with the previous discussion, where higher Fo values are expected to occur in forensic samples.

While Fig. 6.4 gives a good indication of Fo distribution across the samples, Fig. 6.5 better indicate how the data is distributed by separating the data into 10Hz 'frequency bins' and showing how many tokens fall within each of these. These figures show that the tokens drawn from both samples are positively skewed (but more so for the forensic sample), which is common for Fo distribution (see Rose 2002). The Fo range is different in each figure to capture the range in which tokens fell, with 110–230Hz for the forensic sample and 80–190 Hz for the suspect sample. For the forensic sample, it can be seen that an almost equal number of tokens fall within the 130–140 and 140–150

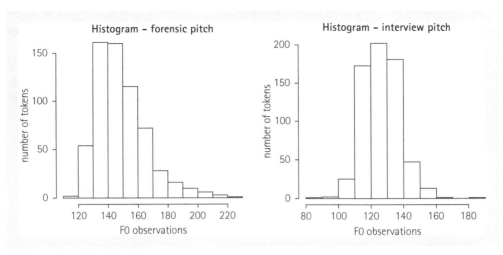

FIG. 6.5 Histograms comparing Fo distribution across a forensic and suspect sample

Hz range (more then 150 tokens in each case), while for the suspect sample the majority of tokens fall within the 120–130 Hz range (approx. 200 tokens), followed by the 130–140 Hz range (approx. 175 tokens), and then the 110–120 Hz range (approx 160 tokens). As such, there is overlap across the samples, especially in terms of the number of tokens falling within the 130–140Hz range. For the forensic sample this equates with 23.8 per cent of tokens, and 27.1 per cent of tokens for the suspect sample. There is also overlap seen in a number of other frequency ranges, but to a lesser degree. For these reasons, and also because the pitch of the two samples analysed falls well outside the population mean (i.e. the pitch of both samples is much higher than average), the 148.8 Hz observed in the forensic sample and 126.4 Hz in the suspect sample cannot really be considered a difference across the samples. Neither, of course, can they be considered as having come from the same speaker on the basis of this evidence alone. Rather, the Fo evidence must be seen to constitute just one part of the analysis. For this particular case, a host of other features were assessed before coming to a decision. Further understanding about Fo in forensic data can be gained from Rose (2002), who gives a different example of Fo analysed in forensic data, and Kinoshita (2005), amongst others, who illustrates Fo analysis using a Bayesian likelihood approach.

6.5 CONCLUSION

In this chapter, selected tools used for phonetic analysis and interpretation have been reviewed, and some examples of how they are employed to answer questions about the nature of speech have been provided. We saw that the International Phonetic Alphabet can assist users in making an indirect record of an utterance, from a broad through to fine-grained transcription. Software programs such as Praat and EMU give acoustic representations of the physical speech signal, and also provide users with opportunities for annotation and analysis. Finally, methods of articulatory analysis such as direct palatography, and more recently EPG, provide evidence of articulatory movement. We saw that the IPA has a longstanding history and is a mature system that rarely needs changing, as opposed to the rapidly advancing technology used for acoustic and articulatory analysis.

CHAPTER 7

NINETEENTH-CENTURY STUDY OF SOUND CHANGE FROM RASK TO SAUSSURE

KATE BURRIDGE

7.1 INTRODUCTION

We are all familiar with the notion of the nineteenth century as the heroic age of
linguistics, though, by now, we are equally familiar with its rejection. (Hoenigswald
1986: 174).

The nineteenth century heralded a new approach to the study of language and
languages and established 'linguistics' as a new science, distinct from literary studies
and philosophical enquiry. Outstanding theoretical and methodological breakthroughs
(particularly in the area of phonetics and phonology, the obsessions of the time)
created a clear break between the scholarship of this century and what had preceded
it. Jespersen (1922a: 32), himself a product of the time, summarizes the accomplishments in this way:

> The horizon was widened; more and more languages were described, studied and
> examined, many of them for their own sake, as they had no important literature.
> Everywhere a deeper insight was gained into the structures even of such languages
> as had been for centuries objects of study; a more comprehensive and more incisive
> classification of languages was obtained with a deeper understanding of their
> mutual relationships, and at the same time linguistic forms were not only described
> and analysed, but also explained, their genesis being traced as far back as historical
> evidence allowed, if not sometimes further. Instead of contenting itself with stating
> when and where a form existed and how it looked and was employed, linguistic

science now also began to ask why it had taken that definite shape, and thus passed from a purely descriptive to an explanatory science.

We can attribute to this nineteenth-century scholarship some of our basic methodological tools and labels; for example, glossing in modern (as opposed to classical) languages; asterisks for non-attested forms, comparative grammar, Indo-European (IE), protolanguage (*Ursprache*), strong vs weak, *Umlaut*, *Ablaut*, and many others. As Jespersen describes, the 'chief innovation' of the time was 'the historical point of view;' scholars equated the scientific study of language with an historical one, focusing on linguistic change and on the genetic relationships between languages that arose as a consequence of change. It was a legacy that shaped Jespersen's own work, as he makes clear in the preface to this same book:

> The distinctive feature of the science of language as conceived nowadays is its historical character: a language or a word is no longer taken as something given once for all, but as a result of previous development and at the same time as the starting-point for subsequent development.

The historicist view dominated the scientific investigation of language until, in the early twentieth century, Ferdinand de Saussure's separation of synchronic (static) and diachronic (historical) perspectives re-evaluated the role of historical data and shifted the bias to synchrony as the legitimate approach to language study.

7.2 THE SCHOLARS OF THE NINETEENTH CENTURY

....

> The novelty of the nineteenth century is the creation of a linguistic profession and a linguistic discipline which found their initial support in the research ethos of the German universities. (Davies 1998: xxiii)

A tremendous amount has been written about this period. In addition to accounts placed within the general histories of language and linguistic thought (e.g. Jespersen 1922, Amsterdamska 1987, Koerner and Asher 1995, Robins 1997, Seuren 1998, Allan 2010a), there have been numerous works on the specific theories, methods, and results of the time (e.g. Pedersen 1959 [1924], Jankowsky 1972, 1979,[1] *The Transactions of the Philological Society* 1978, Davies 1998), as well as discussions within general historical linguistics handbooks and monographs (e.g. Keiler 1972, Joseph and Janda 2003).

Trying to encapsulate nineteenth-century linguistic scholarship in one short chapter is something like trying to capture the contents of the sea in one small bucket. All this

---

[1] See also Ch. 28 below.

chapter can do is draw attention to some of the major linguistic developments, in particular the insights and contributions of those now seen as the major players, for the most part German-speaking linguists, who were setting the agenda at the time. The chapter addresses some of the general thoughts on the nature of language and language structure but, reflecting the nineteenth-century preoccupation with sounds and the oldest stages of languages, it concentrates on concepts to do with phonological change, the genetic relationship between IE languages, and the comparative method. While similar notions had been bandied about to some degree in earlier periods, these linguists are the ones credited with their discovery; certainly they gave coherence to these ideas, and their achievements went on to shape linguistic thinking in the twentieth century and beyond.

7.2.1 The Early Scholars

7.2.1.1 *Sir William Jones (1746–1794)*

> It would be superfluous to discourse on the organs of speech, which have been a thousand times dissected, and as often described by musicians or anatomists; and the several powers of which every man may perceive either by the touch or by sight, if he will attentively observe another person pronouncing the different classes of letters, or pronounce them himself distinctly before a mirror: but a short analysis of articulate sounds may be proper to introduce an examination of every separate symbol. (Jones 1786: 175)

Any account of nineteenth-century linguistics must begin with the middle of the previous century and the ideas of lawyer and amateur linguist Sir William Jones. During his famous lecture 'The Third Anniversary Discourse, on the Hindus', which he delivered to the Asiatick Society of Bengal on 2 February 1786, Jones argued that the classical languages Sanskrit, Ancient Greek, and Latin were related; moreover, he postulated the existence of a proto-language as the parent of most of the languages of Europe, south-western Asia, and northern India. Here is the very well-known and often-quoted philology passage:

> The Sanscrit language, whatever be its antiquity, is of a wonderful structure; more perfect than the Greek, more copious than the Latin, and more exquisitely refined than either, yet bearing to both of them a stronger affinity, both in the roots of verbs and the forms of grammar, than could possibly have been produced by accident; so strong indeed, that no philologer could examine them all three, without believing them to have sprung from some common source, which, perhaps, no longer exists: there is a similar reason, though not quite so forcible, for supposing that both the Gothick and the Celtick, though blended with a very different idiom, had the same origin with the Sanscrit, and the old Persian might be added to this family, if this were the place for discussing any question concerning the antiquities of Persia. (Jones 1807: iii: 34).

Jones's ideas were not new. Others had noticed the similarities between these languages; even the notion of a shared linguistic source was not novel. However, what Jones was arguing for here was an ancestral language that 'perhaps, no longer exists,' in other words, he was putting forward the idea of a parent that was not an extant language (usually Sanskrit) as others had assumed (though, as Murray forthcoming has pointed out, this idea had been outlined at least 100 years earlier by Andreas Jäger). It cannot be argued that Jones founded what later came to be known as 'the comparative method' (the technique for studying the evolution of languages via the meticulous feature-by-feature comparison of two or more languages). However, his words were certainly timely, and because of his considerable influence, he inspired others and thus contributed in some significant way to the growth of historical and comparative linguistics. Rather aptly, Hoenigswald (1986: 175) describes Jones as 'the quintessential precursor, destined to be forever judged according to the light of the professionals of a much later day.'

A coincidence of factors explains his success. There was his excellent reputation as oriental scholar, as founder and president of the Asiatic Society (established in 1784, and with transactions appearing in 1788), and as polyglot (with a knowledge of Greek, Latin, Persian, Arabic, Hebrew, Sanskrit). Jones's extensive publications ranged across many different aspects of oriental scholarship including history, geography, philosophy, religion, art, literature, and of course language; his collected works later appeared in thirteen volumes (*The Works of Sir William Jones*, 1807). Interest in Sanskrit was considerable at the time, and Jones's achievements in this area were numerous and well regarded (they included translations of significant Sanskrit texts and the transliteration of the Devanāgarī syllabary). It was also the case that Jones's speech captured the imagination of the time—the romantic spirit, general speculation about the origins of language, colonial expansion, and European scholars' fascination with Near Eastern and Indian studies.

As Jones's substantial work on sounds and writing systems would indicate, his knowledge of phonetics was substantial, according to Lehmann (1967: 7) comparable at least with that of Grimm's successors. In his 'Dissertation on the Orthography of Asiatick Words in Roman Letters' (1807: 175–228), Jones sought a scientific system of transliteration. Dissatisfied with the Latin orthography, unable even to represent adequately the sounds of English, he created a mini-phonetic notation, capable of rendering the sounds of several languages. He provided an analysis of each of his symbols, and on page 205 of the 'Dissertation' he illustrated his script with some lines of Joseph Addison's poem 'The Campaign':

> Só hwen sm énjel, bai divain cămánd,
> Widh rais'n tempests shécs a gilti land,
> Sch az ăv lét ór pél Britanya pást,
> Cálm and s'rín hi draivz dhi fyúryas blást,
> And, plíz'd dh'ālmaitiz ārderz tu perfórm,
> Raids in dhi hwerlwind and dairects dhi stărm.
> [So when some angel by divine command

> With rising tempests shakes a guilty land,
> Such as of late o'er pale Britannia passed,
> Calm and serene he drives the furious blast;
> And, pleas'd th' Almighty's orders to perform,
> Rides in the whirlwind, and directs the storm.]

Knowledge of articulatory and auditory phonetics was nonetheless rudimentary, and we still have some time to wait before any universal phonetic alphabet makes an appearance. Nonetheless, Jones's efforts in this direction should not be underestimated. Firth (1946: 119), in his appraisal of the history of phonetics in England, describes 'the immense stimulus given to phonetics and general linguistics by Sir William Jones.' Making the point that modern grammar and phonetics were founded on the analyses of Indian scholarship, Firth further writes: 'Without the Indian grammarians and phoneticians whom he [Jones] introduced and recommended to us, it is difficult to imagine our nineteenth century school of phonetics.'

7.2.1.2 *Friedrich von Schlegel (1772–1829) and August Wilhelm von Schlegel (1767–1845)*

Jener entscheidende Punct aber, der hier alles aufhellen wird, is die innere Structur der Sprachen oder die vergleichende Grammatik, welche uns ganz neue Aufschlüsse über die Genealogie der Sprachen auf ähnliche Weise geben wird, wie die vergleichende Anatomie über die höhere Naturgeschichte Licht verbreitet hat. [The decisive point, however, which will clarify everything here, is the inner structure of languages, or comparative grammar, which will give us completely new conclusions about the genealogy of languages in the same way as comparative anatomy has spread light over the higher history of nature.] (Friedrich von Schlegel 1808: 28)

Lehmann (1967: 21) describes Friedrich von Schlegel as a 'popularizer' rather than a 'scholar'—he did not create a methodology, but like Jones he did inspire. *Über die Sprache und Weisheit der Indier* (1808) was one of the most important works of early nineteenth-century linguistics, doing much to kindle further enthusiasm for Sanskrit and its role in linguistic comparison (especially among scholars in Germany).

Schlegel was particularly struck by the regular similarities between the words of Sankskrit and the European languages, pointing also to the correspondences of grammatical forms and structures. Though this book is credited with the first mention of the description *vergleichende Grammatik* (comparative grammar), it is probably more the case that he was the first to give it a genealogical twist, foreshadowing Schleicher's family tree model of genetic relationship (see Davies 1998: 66–76). In making an analogy with comparative anatomy, Schlegel, like many others of his time and later, drew on biology for his linguistic terminology and methodology; he was one of the first to use scientific metalanguage to portray the idea of language as a living organism (see Koerner 1995 on the impact of the natural sciences on nineteenth-century linguistics).

While he never went as far as establishing any rules for changes in 'letters' (sounds), Schlegel does make mention of some of the correspondences that later formed part of the sound shifts laid down by Rask and Grimm (later 'Grimm's Law'). As he explained in the first chapter of his book (1808: 607), he demanded absolute identity of vocabulary items as evidence of the genealogy, thus creating a firm footing for any etymological investigation.

> Wir erlauben uns dabei keine Art von Veränderungs- oder Versetzungsregel der Buchstaben, sondern fordern völlige Gleichheit des Worts zum Beweise der Abstammung. Freilich wenn sich die Mittelglieder historisch nachweisen lassen, so mag *giorno* von *dies* abgeleitet werden, und wenn statt des lateinischen *f* im Spanischen so oft *h* eintritt, das lateinische *p* in der deutschen Form desselben Worts sehr haüfig *f* wird und *c* nicht selten *h*, so gründet dieß allerdings eine Analogie auch für andre nicht ganz so evidente Fälle. [We permit absolutely no rules of change or transmutation of letters, but rather demand complete equivalence of the word as proof of descent. Indeed, if it is possible to prove historically the intermediate steps (of historically attested forms), then *giorno* may be derived from *dies*; and when instead of Latin *f* often *h* shows up in Spanish and if Latin *p* in the Germanic form of the same word very often becomes *f* and *c* not rarely *h*, this certainly establishes an analogy also for other not quite so apparent cases (where sounds correspond).]

Relevant here is the contribution made by Friedrich (as well as his older brother) towards a general typological classification, since this connects with the widely held view of sound change as deterioration (and proved to be one of the impediments to progress in historical phonology). On the basis of morphological criteria, he divided languages into two main types: the inflectional languages like Sanskrit (which he described as truly 'organic' and superior to other languages) and the rest, those that indicated grammatical relationships via word order and grammatical particles (and, true to his organic conception of language, these were viewed as being in various stages of decay). His brother August Wilhelm turned this bipartite classification into the more familiar tripartite classification that is still current today (though now augmented by more sophisticated classifications, catering also for 'exotic' non-IE languages). It distinguished between languages without morphology (isolating languages such as Chinese), those with affixes that have a constant meaning (agglutinating languages such as Turkish), and those whose affixes have composite meanings (inflectional languages such as Sanskrit, also assumed to be the highest state).

7.2.1.3 *Rasmus Rask (1787–1832)*

> If there is found between two languages agreement in the forms of indispensable words to such an extent that rules of letter changes can be discovered for passing from one to the other, then there is a basic relationship between these languages. (Rask 1818, transl. Lehmann 1967: 29)

The Danish linguist Rasmus Rask can be credited as being the true originator of the comparative method (Allan 2010a: 211), though writing in Danish meant that his ground-breaking ideas did not receive the wide attention they warranted. Collinge (1995: 203) summarizes his role:

> Rask's contribution was to insist that a defensible prehistoric stage can be reconstructed, that sounds are the central body of evidence, and that their vicissitudes (here especially of Germanic plosive and spirant consonants) must be properly reported.

It was Rask who first set out the notion of systematic sound correspondences; in other words, sounds that regularly occur in corresponding environments in sets of words that are similar in form and in meaning. Thus Rask introduced order into the ideas of philology by pioneering the idea of a coherent set of principles whereby languages could systematically be compared with respect to their vocabulary and sounds, thereby establishing genetic affinity (especially with the additional support of corresponding similarities in grammatical structures). In particular, Rask noted that stops in Greek and Latin regularly corresponded to the equivalent series of stops and fricatives in Icelandic and the Germanic languages in general.

In an award-winning essay on the origin of Old Norse (published in 1818), he argued for the inclusion of what we now label the Germanic languages as well as Greek, Latin, Slavic, and Lithuanian within one and the same language family. While he did not initially include the Celtic languages in this relationship, he was later to change his mind and, in a letter dated 11 June 1818 he wrote: 'I divide our family of languages in this way: the Indian (Dekanic, Hindostanic), Iranic (Persian, Armenian, Ossetic), Thracian (Greek and Latin), Sarmatian (Lettic and Slavonic), Gothic (Germanic and Skandinavian) and Keltic (Britannic and Gaelic) tribes' (quoted in Jespersen 1922a: 89). Around the same time, he also provided a classification for Finnish and Hungarian within a different family and 'Greenlandic' within a third. His later survey of the languages of India and Persia was one of the first Western works on ancient Iranian languages.

7.2.1.4 *Wilhelm von Humboldt (1767–1835)*

> [S]o kann es in ihr [die Sprache], ebensowenig, als in den unaufhörlich fortflammenden Gedanken der Menchen selbst, einen Augenblick wahren Stillstandes geben. [There can never be in language, just as there can never be in the continually blazing thoughts of men, a moment of true standstill.] (von Humboldt 1836b: 184)

As 'one of the profoundest and most original thinkers on general linguistic questions in the nineteenth century' (Robins 1997: 164), Humboldt clearly has a place in our survey of scholars.[2] His remarkable views on language ranged widely across different aspects of the humanities and his ideas still sound strikingly modern: the importance of

---

[2] See also §§28.3 and 29.2.1 below.

first-hand observation of living languages; the notion of linguistic creativity; the rise of inflectional morphology through the agglutination of syllables; grammaticalization of word order; genetic versus typological classification; the recognition of four abstract forms of language (flexional, agglutinative, incorporating, and isolating, which Humboldt claimed characterized all languages to a certain extent); the close link between language, culture, and thought; the importance of describing every new language for its own sake (i.e. not through the linguistic spectacles of IE). These ideas, and many more, are now firmly entrenched in modern linguistic thinking. However, since our focus is on the progress of historical phonology, we concentrate here on Humboldt the comparative philologist.

There is one passage that nicely captures Humboldt's views on basic historical methodology. It comes, not from one of his many publications, but rather from a letter to August Wilhelm von Schlegel (written 19 May 1822). In outlining the role of 'grammar' (in its broadest sense) to determine language relationship (typological vs genetic), it signals a fundamental shift from grammar as the reliable focus of comparison to sounds and the lexicon (previously thought too arbitrary).

> [H]alte ich den Schluss auf die Verwandtschaft aus dem grammatischen Bau, und wenigstens muss man dabei, dünkt mich, notwending genau die verschiedenen Teile unterscheiden, aus denen der grammatische Bau besteht. Man kann darin, meiner Erfahrung nach, unterscheiden: 1. dasjenige was bloss aus Ideen und Ansichten beruht, und wovon man eine Schilderung machen kann, ohne nur Einen Laut der Sprache zu erwähnen; z.B. ob die Sprache eigne Verba hat, oder jedes Wort als ein Verbum behandeln kann, ob das Pronomen bloss den Begriff der Person enthält, oder auch den des Seins und dadurch zum Verbum substantivum wird, ob es ein Passivum gibt, oder man das Passivum nur wie ein impersonales Activum behandelt u.s.f. 2. die technischen Mittel, die grammatischen Verschiedenheiten zu bezeichnen, ob durch Affixa, Umlaut, Silbenwiederholung u.s.f. 3. die wirklichen Laute, die grammatischen Bildungssilben, wie das *a* privativum, die Substantivendungen u.s.f. . . . Der letzte [Teil] hat eine sehr genaue Ähnlichkeit mit der Mitteilung wirklicher Wörter. Er gehört zum Teil zum lexikalischen Teil der Sprache [. . .] Dieser Teil der Grammatik scheint mir am meisten für die Verwandtschaft, oder dagegen zu beweisen, weil er der speziellste ist [. . .]

In a nutshell, what Humboldt is saying here is that one needs to distinguish different parts of grammatical structure: (1) that which rests exclusively on ideas and views and which one can describe perfectly well without mentioning a single sound of the language (e.g. whether the language has verbs or allows words to function as verbs, if it has a passive voice and so on); (2) the technical means to denote the grammatical distinctions (e.g. affixation, *Umlaut*, reduplication, and so on); and (3) the actual sounds of the grammatical elements (e.g. the negative *a* in Sanskrit and in Greek, the noun endings, and so on). In essence, Humboldt is distinguishing between grammatical categories and mechanisms (meaning or grammatical structure without phonological content) and the morphs themselves (the physical shape of the markers). This last and least abstract part of grammar bears, in Humboldt's estimation, a close resemblance to the transmission of real words, and bears on the lexical aspects of language. Since it is the most specific ('weil er der speziellste ist'), it is the most significant when it comes to deciding (for or against) genealogical relationship.

His wide-ranging and significant accomplishments set Humboldt apart from the historical linguists of the nineteenth century; yet among his achievements we can highlight the following contributions to historical and comparative linguistics: data-oriented investigations, the priority given to sounds and comparative evidence in establishing genetic affinity, actual reconstructions of the phonological shapes of morphs and the application of this methodology to the Malayo-Polynesian languages. It is notable that Davies (1998: 101) describes his 'Essay on the Best Means of Ascertaining the Affinities of Oriental Languages' (presented in 1828) as offering 'the most lucid explanation (and exemplification) of the basic principles of the comparative method.'

7.2.1.5 *Jacob Hornemann Bredsdorff (1790–1841)*

> When consonants are pronounced with less effort or more weakly, they commonly change into other consonants. (Bredsdorff 1821: 14; translated by Andersen 1982)

What distinguishes Bredsdorff is that he looked into the how and the why of change. Separating off external pressures (contact), he identified four main internal motivations for sound change:

1. Mishearing and misunderstanding. This factor he identified is not being as important as the others.

2. Imperfection of speech organs. As Murray (in press) describes, Bredsdorff offered here the beginnings of a theory of markedness. He recognized that some segments (such as [ð]) were more difficult to master than others and consequently were never properly learned. Here, he distinguished segmental changes from sequential changes involving 'combinations of consonants' (e.g. insertion *e* before *st*, *sk*, and *sp* in Spanish).

3. Indolence. Bredsdorff assigned 90 per cent of pronunciation changes (not attributed to foreign influences) to something akin to Zipf's 'principle of least effort;' he described in detail a number of phonological processes including assimilation ('letters change to those which are most easily pronounced together with their neighbors,' p. 9) as well as weakening. Indeed, in what could be described as a budding theory of lenition, he provided a number of different trajectories, corresponding precisely to the strengthening and weakening hierarchies of modern phonology.

4. The desire to be distinct. Foreshadowing something like Lindblom's theory of the interplay between the clear speech necessary for intelligibility (hyperarticulation) and the need for physiological economy (hypoarticulation), Bredsdorff sees this factor as compensating for the weakening and reductive changes caused by indolence. To this he added the concept of diphthongization of original long vowels, as well as a kind of chain shift theory of sounds change.

Jespersen (1922: 71) describes Bredsdorff as being 'head and shoulders above his contemporaries;' yet, as Andersen (1982: 24) describes, his forward-thinking work of 1821, *Om Aarsagerne til Sprogenes Forandringer*, was 'fated not to have any influence on the development of historical linguistics. Published in Danish in the Examination Program of the Cathedral School of Roskilde in 1821—in the wrong language and the wrong place, and at the wrong time, one might say—there was no chance of Bredsdorff's views contributing to the scholarly dialogue.'

7.2.1.6 *Jacob Grimm (1785–1863) and Wilhelm Grimm (1786–1859)*

> Die lautverschiebung erfolgt in der masse, thut sich aber im enzelnen niemals rein ab. Es bleiben wörter in dem verhältnisse in der alten einrichtung stehn, der strom der neuerung ist an ihnen vorbeigestoßen. [The sound shift is a general tendency; it is not followed in every case. There are words that stay put within the relations of the old set-up, the path of the innovation passing them by.] (Jacob Grimm 1822: 590)

The brothers Grimm will be remembered by many for their work across a range of fields, including Germanic dialectology, folklore, mythology, medieval literature, law, and of course linguistics. Their many publications include essays, volumes of fables and folk tales, editions of medieval texts, and extensive volumes such as *Deutsche Mythologie, Deutsche Rechtalterthümer, Geschichte der deutschen Sprache, Deutsches Wörterbuch* (up to the letter *F*; subsequent volumes appeared after their death), *Deutsche Grammatik*,[3] and most significantly its completely recast second edition of 1822 with an extra 596 pages devoted to phonology—*Erstes buch. Von den buchstaben.* In their collaboration, the more energetic brother was Jacob, and he is credited with doing most of the research work (Davies 1998: 136).

Though he never lost his admiration for inflecting languages as the benchmark of linguistic development, Jacob was in all his endeavours strikingly anti-prescriptive. His practical attention to the vernacular meant he broke well away from the traditions of classical philology; it meant too that he was open to a broader range of source material than had conventionally been the case. As he expressed in the preface to the second edition of his *Deutsche Grammatik, Beobachtung* (observation) was *die seele der sprachforschung* (the soul of linguistic science). In his biography, Wilhelm Scherer (1885: 152) expressed the brothers' anti-normative approach in this way:

> They discarded the aristocratic narrow-mindedness with which philologists looked down on unwritten tradition, on popular ballads, legends, fairly tales, superstition, nursery rimes [. . .] In the hands of the two Grimm's philology became national and popular; and at the same time a pattern was created for the scientific study of all the peoples of the earth and for the comparative investigation of the entire mental life of mankind, of which written literature is nothing but a small epitome. (Transl. Jespersen 1922: 41–2)

---

[3] *Deutsch* from *þuida* 'people' assumed the meaning 'vernacular' and should here be translated as 'Germanic'.

It was with his range of technical breakthroughs in phonology and morphophonology that Jacob Grimm made the greatest impact. Davies (1998: 42) described these discoveries in this way:

> In essence they are based on a mixture of philological data, acutely analysed, and on a new understanding of some basic principles of historical and comparative analysis, not all of which had been clearly defined before him.

'Grimm's Law,' now almost a household name in historical linguistics, is rather a misnomer. Nowhere in Grimm's work is there ever mention of a law, only a *Lautverschiebung* (sound shift). Moreover, as we have seen, Rasmus Rask had already uncovered the basis of such a law. In his presidential address to the Philological Society, phonetician Alexander Ellis referred to 'the law of Rask or Grimm' (Davies 1998: 150); Jespersen (1922: 43) even suggests it would more accurately be called 'Rask's Law.' However, it was Grimm's all-encompassing conception of the shift as a unit that had such a significant impact on his contemporaries; hence, it was Grimm who became the PR person for the new methodology.

He noted, for example, that where Gothic had *b*, the non-Germanic languages had some sort of 'aspirate' (Latin *f*, Greek *ph*, Sanskrit *bh*); when Gothic had *p*, the non-Germanic languages had *b*; where Gothic had *f*, Latin, Greek, and Sanskrit frequently had *p*. In order to account for these correspondences, Grimm postulated a *Kreislauf* 'rotation' in the prehistory of Germanic, in which Proto-Indo-European (PIE) voiced aspirates became voiced plosives in Germanic (note: Grimm included both aspirated stops produced with an accompanying audible puff of breath and fricatives produced with audible friction on account of incomplete closure in the vocal tract); voiced plosives became voiceless plosives and voiceless plosives became voiceless aspirates.

Though he was by no means a phonetician (evident in his conflation of aspirated stops and fricatives), Grimm was nonetheless able to account methodically for a considerable group of the IE and Germanic consonants, showing how the parallel changes in the voiced and voiceless stops and fricatives retained the overall symmetry of the phonological system. Grimm himself later showed that a second consonant shift (later known as the High German Consonant Shift or Second Germanic Consonant Shift) separated off High German from the other Western Germanic languages that did not undergo the shift. Whether his more systematic formulation of these changes actually altered the outcome is not clear, but its influence on the scholars of his day and later was considerable, and had significant consequences for linguistics and the history of language. Items not captured by his rule were considered exceptions and were made the object of research for the next half century. Grimm himself was not concerned with exceptions, and this was apparent in some of his own etymologies (though he did recognize the value of a rigorous application of 'letters' (i.e. sounds) to overcome the weaknesses of previous etymological endeavours, *wilde Etymologie*, as he expressed it). Like many of his contemporaries, Grimm was an ecologist and not a formalist. Furthermore, his study of the many different forms of human behaviour had led him to the view that language was subject to cultural wild-card factors that meant there could only ever exist tendencies and never strict laws.

Grimm is also important for the distinction he made between two different types of vocalic alternation designating grammatical distinctions: *Umlaut* (environmentally conditioned vowel change) and *Ablaut* (vowel gradation). Germanic *Umlaut* he revealed to be a purely phonetic phenomenon, a kind of predictable vowel harmony caused by a following palatal [j] or high front vowel [i] (for instance, the vowel alternation in English pairs such as *foot–feet* and *tooth–teeth* was triggered by a lost plural [i] ending). *Ablaut* phenomena were older, dating back to PIE; though possibly originating as assimilatory changes at a distance, they came down as phonologically unpredictable vowel alternations, as in the root vowels of Germanic verb forms such as *sing–sang–sung*.

7.2.1.7 *Franz Bopp (1791–1867)*

> Die Sprachen sind [. . .] als organische Naturkörper anzusehen, die nach bestimm-ten Gesetzen sich bilden, ein inneres Lebensprincip in sich tragend sich entwickeln und nach und nach absterben, indem sie sich selber nicht mehr begreifend, die ursprünglich bedeutsamen, aber nach und nach zu einer mehr äußerlichen Masse gewordenen Glieder oder Formen ablegen oder verstümmeln und misbrauchen. [Languages [. . .] are to be regarded as natural organisms which develop on their own according to specific laws, evolve carrying within themselves an inner life-principle, and die off little by little; in no longer comprehending themselves, members or forms, which were originally significant, they cast off or mutilate and misuse, and gradually turn into more of a superficial mass.] (Bopp 1836: 1)

Though Franz Bopp was overwhelmingly a grammar man, we include him here, together with Rask and Grimm, as one of the founders of modern historical linguistics. Bopp's main aim was to uncover the origins of grammatical inflections and his first work, *Über das Conjugationssystem der Sanskritsprache in Vergleichung mit jenem der griechischen, lateinischen, persischen und germanischen Sprache* (published in 1816), is probably of greatest interest, being the first truly comparative work on the IE languages. It served to shape his entire academic endeavour, in particular his magnum opus, *Vergleichende Grammatik des Sanskrit, Zend, Griechischen, Lateinischen, Lit-thauischen, Altslawischen, Gotischen und Deutschen* (appearing over nineteen years in six parts: 1833, 1835, 1842, 1847, 1849, 1852).

Assuming the kinship of the IE languages, Bopp aimed to trace the common origin of their grammatical morphology via comparison, an enterprise that had never before been attempted. Many have pointed out that in his pursuit of the grammatical origins of IE, he came across the importance of grammatical comparison and his undertaking marks 'the real beginning of what we call comparative linguistics' (Pedersen 1962 [1924]: 257). Early twentieth-century French linguist Antoine Meillet (1903: 389) likened his breakthrough to Christopher Columbus' discovery of America in his quest for a new route to India ('à peu près comme Christophe Colomb a découvert L'Amérique en cherchant la route des Indes'). Dane Jespersen (1922: 55) cannot resist embellishing the analogy: 'in the same way as Norsemen from Iceland had discovered America before Columbus, without imagining that they were finding the way to India, just so Rasmus Rask through his Icelandic studies had discovered Comparative Grammar before Bopp, without needing to take the circuitous route through Sanskrit.'

As the quotation above indicates, Bopp had adopted the biological view of language that was typical of his time. Linguistic change was explained by the fact that a language, like any natural body, developed according to a lifecycle that included birth, growth, procreation, and gradual deterioration (signalled by the loss of inflections). It changed according to inherent laws that were not susceptible to any intervention by their human hosts. True, Bopp's focus was on overwhelmingly on morphology; yet he is credited with uncovering the mystery of the Irish initial mutations, showing them to be relics of external old sandhi (or assimilation) rules, whereby final syllables in prehistoric Celtic caused the following consonants to become fricatives or nasals. This discovery established conclusively that the Celtic languages were part of the IE family. Moreover, he identified laws of phonological change, *Wohllautgesetze* (euphony laws), which he viewed as the instruments of a comparative investigation of any group of languages. Through the detailed historical analyses of grammatical forms, Bopp provided the first dependable materials for a comparative history of the languages. His ideas went on to be further formalized into the comparative method by Schleicher and others. Davies (1998: 133) summarizes his contribution thus:

> When he identifies [. . .] laws of phonological changes, or observes the re-creation of new grammatical forms according to the old patterns, or comments about the fact that apparently identical forms may be due to parallel innovations, he is in fact opening the way to an understanding of the how, if not the why, of language change.

7.2.2 The later scholars

7.2.2.1 *August Schleicher (1821–1868)*

> Wenn wir nicht wissen, wie etwas geworden ist, so kennen wir es nicht. [Unless we know how something came into being, we do not understand what it is like.] (Schleicher 1863: 10)

In many ways, the German linguist August Schleicher encapsulates the development of IE linguistic studies post William Jones; yet we are positioning him here, since it was his methodological breakthroughs that laid the foundations of Neogrammarian thinking. Indeed, Bynon (1986: 130) describes him as a Neogrammarian 'in spirit if not in name.' In terms of his output, Schleicher is best known for his *Compendium der vergleichenden Grammatik der indogermanischen Sprachen* (first published 1861/2), the first attempt to present an organized account of the historical phonology of the individual IE languages. A second edition appeared in 1871, and third and fourth editions were published posthumously from an annotated copy. In addition to his *Compendium*, he produced a number of other works including a morphology of Old Church Slavonic (1852) and a grammar of Lithuanian (1856–7).

Over his short life, Schleicher is credited with the introduction of techniques and fundamental methodological advances that set the scene for the next eighty years— among others, the primacy he gave to the scientific approach to language studies and his emphasis on sounds and forms, his phonological reconstruction of IE, and his model for displaying languages (the *Stammbaum* or family-tree model of language spread and language descent). However, his originality and influence are frequently overlooked, eclipsed by the dominance of the Neogrammarians who were to follow him. Probably his most significant contribution to the discipline was his insistence on the need to establish regular *Lautgesetze* 'sound laws.' In his *Compendium*, he described what he saw as the current two schools of Indo-Europeanists. The first (to which he belonged) recognized the explanatory power of sound laws and rigorously applied them to their work; those of the second group were less interested in phonological comparisons and did not allow such laws to get in the way of a good etymological story.

Schleicher was the first linguist to offer tentative reconstructed forms of the extinct 'common source' that Jones had envisaged; in other words, he offered reconstructed forms of a protolanguage that was not the earliest known form of an already attested language that had developed from it. For these reconstructed forms, he is also credited with the convention of the asterisk to indicate that they should be viewed as abstractions and not documented language material. In the introduction to his *Compendium*, he explained:

> In the present work an attempt is made to set forth the inferred Indo-European original language side by side with its really existent derived languages. Besides the advantages offered by such a plan, in setting immediately before the eyes of the student the final results of the investigation in a more concrete form, and thereby rendering easier his insight into the nature of particular Indo-European languages, there is, I think, another of no less importance gained by it, namely that it shows the baselessness of the assumption that the non-Indian Indo-European languages were derived from Old-Indian (Sanskrit), an assumption which has not yet entirely disappeared. (Lehmann's translation, 1967: 96)

While reconstruction was certainly not new (Bopp, Grimm, Rask, and others had provided reconstructed forms), Schleicher was the first to attempt a systematic reconstruction of the sounds and forms of IE, to the extent that he even attempted to recreate an actual text in the protolanguage, the 'Fable of the Sheep and the Horses':

Avis akvāsas ka
   Avis, jasmin varnā na ā ast, dadarka akvams, tam, vāgham garum vaghantam, tam, bhāram magham, tam, manum āku bharantam. Avis akvabhjams ā vavakat:

kard aghnutai mai vidanti manum akvams agantam. Akvāsas ā vavakant: krudhi
avai, kard aghnutai vividvant-svas: manus patis varnām avisāms karnauti svabhjam
gharmam vastram avibhjams ka varnā na asti. Tat kukruvants avis agram ā bhugat.
[A sheep that had no wool saw horses, one of them pulling a heavy wagon, one
carrying a big load, and one carrying a man quickly. The sheep said to the horses:
'My heart pains me to see a man driving horses.' The horses said: 'Listen, sheep, our
hearts pain us when we see this: a man, the master, makes the wool of the sheep into
a warm garment for himself, and the sheep has no wool.' Having heard this, the
sheep fled into the field.]

Though resoundingly criticized as a flight of fancy, these reconstructions established
Sanskrit more convincingly as collateral to the other languages of the IE family (rather
than a parent). They also offered a more compelling demonstration that words in the
ancestral language represented an association between form and meaning that was
carried into each of the daughter languages (if the item was retained), sometimes
despite considerable sound changes. Schleicher grouped existing languages together
on the basis of lexical correspondences and the results of sound changes, and captured
the relationships in a model of language classification which, inspired by biological
taxonomy, arranged them in a genealogical tree. He is the first linguist to use the family
tree as a way of graphically representing historical changes that, via a process of gradual
divergence over time, eventually resulted in the formation of new languages.

The widely held organistic view of language was further developed in Schleicher's
writings; as 'natural organisms,' independent of their speakers, languages underwent
periods of development, maturity, and decline. In addition to being governed by laws,
he believed that phonological changes (together with analogy) were equivalent to
processes of language decay; he saw languages as passing through a lifecycle that was
similar to the life cycle of human beings. In the first phase of development, languages
were simpler (isolating) and then, after a period of grammatical growth, they developed
into agglutinating and in turn inflecting. The higher state was then followed by a period
of decline, which was then balanced by a corresponding period of 'growth'—for his
model also allowed for the gradual development via agglutination of complex forms out
of simple ones. As Bynon (1986: 131) describes, Schleicher inferred the growth processes, not from the comparison of inherited substance as in European, but from a
comparison of the morphology of languages around the world. However, since sound
change was assumed to take place only during the historical period of 'decay,' this (and
the special status given to Sanskrit) would have stymied any advances towards a theory
of phonological change.

7.2.2.2 *Modifications to Grimm's Law: Hermann Grassmann*
(1809–1877) and Karl Adolf B. Verner (1846–1896)

Es muss eine Regel fur die Unregelmassigkeit da sein; es gilt nur, diese ausfindig zu
machen. [There must be a rule for the irregularity; it remains only to discover it.]
(Verner 1877: 101)

Despite further fine-tuning of Grimm's Law, there remained significant groups of exceptions. One was that Germanic [b] had different correspondences in Greek ([pʰ] ~ [p]) and in Sanskrit ([bʰ] ~ [b]). Hermann Grassmann made his mark in linguistics by showing that this variation was predictable. In what became known as 'Grassmann's Law,' he showed that if an aspirated consonant was followed by another aspirated consonant in the next syllable, the first one lost the aspiration. For example, in the reduplicated forms for the perfect tense in Greek and Sanskrit, the consonant is de-aspirated if the initial consonant is aspirated: [pʰu-ɔː] φύω 'I grow': [pe-pʰuː-ka] πέφυκα 'I have grown'. While energy expenditure is difficult to measure, there was later speculation that the motivation for this law was 'economy of effort'—the fact that aspirated consonants require considerable respiratory exertion means that successive aspiration will be difficult and therefore pruned back (originally Müller 1864; see Müller 1873, Ohala 2003: 680). Grassmann's discovery was of interest for a number of reasons: it further refined Grimm's Law by doing away with a group of exceptions; it demon-strated that dissimilation (usually sporadic like other minor phonological processes) could be regular; as an instance of 'dissimilation at a distance' (with space between the sounds), it showed the importance of considering entire forms and not individual segments. Grassmann had also demonstrated that Germanic possessed a conservative phonological pattern that placed it phonologically closer to PIE, thus further under-mining the position of Sanskrit as the source of the IE languages.

Grassmann was one of the great figures in linguistics and also mathematics (as the founder of linear algebra). Perhaps on account of this mathematical bent, he eschewed speculative theory beyond what the facts justified. He sought to understand how speech was produced and perceived, classifying speech sounds according to their organs of articulation. He insisted that only with a knowledge of articulatory phonetics could one properly understand phonological change, and his achievements in phonetics and physics were considerable for their time (see Ohala 2011).

Verner's famous contribution to the sound laws debate was to become, as Robins (1978) describes, a Neogrammarian triumph. Like Grassmann's input, the problem and its solution are well documented in historical linguistics textbooks; only the highlights are outlined here.

Grimm's law predicted that PIE *[t] evolved into the fricative [θ] (<þ>) in Germanic (e.g. Gothic tunþu-, English tooth, corresponding to Latin dent- and Sanskrit dant-); yet there were also times when it evolved into a voiced dental stop [d] (<d>) (e.g. Gothic þridja- and English third corresponding to Latin tertius and Sanskrit trtíya-). More-over, the law occasionally failed to apply across what were clearly related words within the same language (e.g. Gothic leiþan 'to lead' but laidja 'to cause to leave'); there was also inconsistency across parallel cases (e.g. Gothic broþar/fadar and Old English broþor/fædar compared to Latin frater and pater both showing the original medial [t]). In other words, there were two shifts:

PIE *t > Germanic þ and occasionally also *t > d

We have already seen that such exceptions did not concern Jacob Grimm. Verner's view, however, was that the variation in consonants was not capricious but regularly conditioned. The explanation he presented was a convincing one, showing a direct correlation between consonant variation and variation in accent. In Germanic, the stops were voiced internally when they preceded the accent, but not when they followed it. This accent was not the Germanic accent (which was syllable-initial) but rather the older free accentuation of IE that was preserved in Sanskrit; compare Sanskrit *bhrátar-* 'brother' and *pitár* 'father' which comes down into Germanic as internal *þ* and *d* respectively (Gothic *broþar/fadar* and Old English *broþor/fædar*). Similarly, pairs such as *leiþan* and *laidja* could be explained by the fact that the causative form showed the accent on the suffix rather than the root. As historians of linguistics have described, not only was this a convincing eradication of Grimm's residue (thus strengthening the belief in exceptionless sound change), it also showed the importance of taking into account suprasegmental factors.

7.2.2.3 *The Neogrammarians: the Gang of Four*

Aller Lautwandel, soweit er mechanisch vor sich geht, vollzieht sich nach ausnahmslosen Gesetzen. [All sound change, in so far as it proceeds mechanically, is carried out according to exceptionless laws.] (Brugmann in Osthoff and Brugmann 1878: xiii)

What contributed to the linguistic successes of the nineteenth century was continuity in scholarship. In contrast to the isolated and sporadic discoveries that characterized previous research, nineteenth-century scholars (usually either from Germany or trained in Germany) drew upon the inspirations of their contemporaries or their predecessors, either building upon their work on reacting against it (Robins 1997: 190). This is best illustrated by the so-called 'Neogrammarians,' a group whose German nickname *Junggrammatiker* is probably more accurately translated into 'Young Grammarians' (the name does not imply that their ideas were 'new,' but rather they were achieved by young scholars; compare the label 'young Turk' to refer to any rebellious member of an organization). The four most influential linguists who made up the original group were Slavist August Leskien (1840–1916), classicist Hermann Osthoff (1847–1909), Sanskritist Berthold Delbrück (1842–1922), and Germanist and Indo-Europeanist Karl Brugmann (1849–1919), often described as 'the ringleader' (Seuren 1998: 90). Brugmann, in a document co-signed by Osthoff, is credited with setting out the essence of the Neogrammarian position. In the preface to the first volume of their journal *Morphologische Untersuchungen* in 1878, he denounced abstraction—historical linguistics was about fact-finding, living dialects, and careful attention to phonetic detail:

[N]ur derjenige vergleichende sprachforscher, welcher aus dem hypothesentrüben dunstkreis der werkstätte, in der man die indogermanischen grundformen schmiedet, einmal heraustritt in die klare luft der greifbaren wirklichkeit und gegenwart, um hier sich belehrung zu holen über das, was ihn die graue theorie nimmer erkennen lässt, [. . .] nur der kann zu einer rightigen vorstellung von der lebens- und umbildungsweise der sprachformen gelangen und diejenigen methodischen principien gewinnen, ohne welche [. . .] im besonderen ein vordringen in die hinter der sprachüberlieferung zurückliegenden zeiträume einer meerfahrt ohne kompass gleicht. [Only that comparative linguist who for once emerges from the hypotheses-laden atmosphere of the workshop, in which the original Indo-Germanic (i.e. Indo-European) root-forms are forged, and steps into the clear air of tangible reality and of the present day, in order to obtain information about those things which foggy theory can never reveal to him, [. . .] and only he can arrive at a correct idea of the life and the transformations of linguistic forms and only he can acquire those methodological principles without which [. . .] any penetration into the periods of the past which lie behind the historical tradition of a language is like a sea voyage without a compass.] (Brugmann and Osthoff 1878 (1): ix–x)

Despite these fighting words, their general approach to linguistic science differed little from what had preceded them (cf. Robins 1978). Their view of language was historical, their methods included the systematic comparison of recorded word forms, and their focus was on language change and on the genetic relationships between languages. There were, however, two major tenets that distinguished the Neogrammarian position.

The first dictum, and the one most associated with this group, came to be known as the 'regularity hypothesis'—*die Ausnahmslosigkeit der Lautgesetze* 'absolute regularity of sound change.' Accordingly, the sound system of any language, as it developed through time, was subject to the operation of regular *Lautgesetze* 'sound laws.' These sound laws were understood to be absolutely regular in their operation, except under the influences of non-phonetic factors such as analogy (where words deviated from the true or proper patterns; e.g. *kine* changing to *cows* on analogy with *horses* and *pigs*; or *grine* to *groin* on analogy with *loin*). By the end of the nineteenth century, the principle of regular sound change had become the cornerstone of the comparative method, giving scholars proper licence to compare and to reconstruct ancestral forms.

While the most celebrated work of these Young Grammarians was in their discovery of sound laws, we have already seen that the concept of *Lautgesetz* was by no means the creation of this group. Rask had certainly written about 'rules of letter changes' as the means of determining genetic relationships between languages; others later, such as Bopp and Humboldt, had used *Lautgesetz* as a technical term. Recall that Schleicher (1861: 15–16) wrote about those who, like himself, adhered strictly to sound laws. His pupil, Johann Schmidt (1887: 304–5), attested:

Schleicher zuerst lehrte, dass alle Umgestaltungen, welche die indogermanischen Worte von der Urzeit bis auf den heutigen Tage erlitten haben, durch zwei Factoren verursacht seien, ausnahmslos wirkende Lautgesetze und die durchkreutzende falsche Analogie. [Schleicher taught first of all that all changes, which Indo-European words have undergone from the oldest time to the present day, were caused by two factors, sound laws operating without exception and by interfering (false) analogies.]

It is also the case that two of the most significant sound laws (Grassmann's Law and Verner's Law) had been proposed well before the Brugmann–Ostoff creed of 1878. Another illustration is the multiple recognition in the 1870s of the so-called *Palatalgesetz* 'law of palatals.' In Sanskrit, palatals alternated before an *a*-vowel without any apparent motivation, and a number of scholars, including at least Karl Verner, Johannes Schmidt, Hermann Collitz, and Ferdinand de Saussure, recognized that *c* [tʃ] was found in environments that corresponded to *e* in the European languages, while *k* occurred before *a*-vowels which corresponded to *a* or *o* in the IE languages. Hence, the ancestor of Sanskrit, Indo-Iranian, had an *e*-vowel which had triggered the palatalization of [k] > [tʃ], obscured then by a later change that saw the merger of [e], [a], [o] > [a]. While the exact number of scholars who made this discovery is still in dispute, clearly not all were dyed-in-the-wool Neogrammarians.

The second, equally powerful Neogrammarian dictum is something that is now referred to as the 'uniformitarian principle.' Appealing to uniformity was common practice among geologists and biologists of the time, though nineteenth-century geologist Charles Lyell is the one usually named in connection with this practice (see Janda and Joseph 2003: 27–31). While uniformitarianism has appeared in many different guises both in philology and geology (Christy 1983), Brugmann (and Ostoff) (1878: xiii) expressed it this way: 'the psychological and physiological nature of man as speaker must have been essentially identical at all epochs' (Collinge's translation, 1995: 205). Hence, the Neogrammarians viewed the development of languages as subject to precisely the same factors and controls at all periods; in other words, the processes of change are basic and constant, and what takes place in observable history can conceivably take place in all stages of linguistic development, including those of reconstructed languages such as PIE. Since no linguistic stage can be qualitatively different at different times in the process of evolution (i.e. viewed as growth or decay), Neogrammarian thinking clearly came into conflict with Schleicher's (and others') naturalistic conception of language. In rejecting the biological model for the historical development of languages, they shifted the emphasis from language to the speaking individual and society as a whole. Rather than a natural organism, language was the manifestation of human cognition and social behaviour; sound changes proceeded with physiological *blinde Naturnotwendigkeit* 'blind necessity,' as predicted by the 'regularity hypothesis,' but were at the same time changes in the linguistic habits of the speakers (i.e. did not occur independently of individuals). This then allowed the shift in focus from written languages to contemporary living languages and dialects as the most valuable sources for linguistic research.

Finally, important for our consideration of the evolution of phonological theory is Brugmann's famous article of 1876, 'Nasalis sonans in der indogermanischen Grundsprache.' This was one of the two scandalous articles that so ruffled the feathers of Brugmann's teacher Georg Curtius (1820–85), causing Brugmann to hook up with Osthoff in editing their own periodical *Morphologische Untersuchungen*. What caused the uproar was that Brugmann, calling into question the methodology and results of previous research, asserted a new set of phonemes in PIE, the so-called nasal sonants or vocalic nasals. This was significant in that it helped to clarify earlier problems identified for the IE family (e.g. the matter of *Ablaut*), thus lending further support to the Neogrammarian principles. As Lehmann (1967: 190) summarizes, this essay 'illustrates the growing control over articulatory phonetics; it reflects an awareness that the phonological and morphological levels of language are distinct, and that the one can be examined for insights into the other.'

7.2.2.4 *The Neogrammarians: subscribers and critics*

> [F]ür den Sprachforscher ist die Lautphysiologie nur eine Hülfswissenschaft. Für ihn hat nicht der einzelne Laut einen Werth, sondern die Lautsysteme der einzelnen Spracheinheiten, deren Verhältniss zu einander und ihre allmähliche Verschiebung. [For the linguist sound physiology is only an auxiliary science. For him, it is not the individual sound that matters but the sound systems of each linguistic unity, their relationship with each other and their gradual alteration.] (Sievers 1876: 1)

We now move to the contributions of the most notable contemporary adherents and critics of the Neogrammarians, specifically Eduard Sievers, Hermann Paul, William Dwight Whitney, Henry Sweet, Ferdinand de Saussure, and Johannes Schmidt. As the quotation from Sievers suggests, it is at this time that we begin to see a shift in emphasis from individual sounds to the sound system as a whole; also a much clearer recognition of allophonic variation in language and the necessary distinction between a phonological and phonetic approach to language study. While a quasi-phonemic approach was inherent in earlier work, this was more as a by-product of the attention paid to the letters of written sources. (Allan 2010a points out that some notion of the phoneme had been around since ancient times, but we must wait until the twentieth century for a theory of phonemes and a methodology for isolating them.)

Eduard Sievers (1850–1932) was, like many others of his time, a Germanist and Indo-Europeanist, but with a penchant for dialect study. He has been described as 'probably the most brilliant of the neogrammarians' (Lehmann 1967: 210) and 'the phonetician *par excellence*' (Davies 1998: 277), and we include him here because his *Grundzüge der Lautphysiologie zur Einführung in das Studium der Lautlehre der indogermanischen Sprachen* was such an important event in development of phonology. In his account of Sievers' scholarship, Murray (in press) concludes that his work 'touches on virtually all topics relevant to modern phonology.' Among his many great achievements was the early identification of the relationship between Germanic sound changes and pitch accent. He outlined the phenomenon in a letter written to Wilhelm Braune on 24 March 1874, though failed to formulate his discovery in the systematic way that Karl Verner had.

Hermann Paul (1846–1921) was a supporter of the Neogrammarians, though he avoided the controversy and confrontation that characterized the group (Seuren 1998: 93). His influential *Prinzipien der Sprachgeschichte* (first published in 1880 as *Principien der Sprachgeschichte*) is still considered to be the most measured and rigorous account of Neogrammarian thinking (though Paul also included a number of innovative ideas of his own). The impact of this work on many modern linguists, in particular Ferdinand de Saussure, is widely acknowledged (Koerner 2008; Allan 2010a). In this book (Paul 1880: 69) is probably the best explication of what is now known as the 'Neogrammarian Hypothesis.' It makes plain the idea that the regularity of sound change was the fall-out of the physiology of speech (phonetics).

> Wenn wir daher von konsequenter Wirkung der Lautgesetze reden, so kann das nur heissen, dass bei dem Lautwandel innerhalb desselben Dialektes alle einzelnen Fälle, in denen die gleichen lautlichen Bedingungen vorliegen, gleichmässig behandel werden. Entweder muss also, wo früher einmal der gleiche Laut bestand, auch auf den späteren Entwicklungsstufen immer der gleiche Laut bleiben, oder, wo eine Spaltung in verschiedene Laute eingetreten ist, da muss eine bestimmte Ursache und zwar eine Ursache rein lautlicher Natur wie Einwirkung umgebender Laute, Akzent, Silbenstellung u. dgl. anzugeben sein, warum in dem einen Falle dieser, in dem anderen jener Laut enstanden ist. [When we speak of consistent effects of sound laws, that can only mean that, given the sound change within the same dialect, all individual cases in which the same phonetic conditions are present will be handled the same. So, either wherever earlier the same sound stood, also in the later stages the same sound remains or, where a split into different sounds has taken place, there must be provided a specific cause and indeed a cause of a purely phonetic nature such as the effects of surrounding sounds, accent, syllable position, and the like to account for why in the one case this sound, in the other that one, has come into being.]

Though Paul generally eschewed abstraction in accounting for language phenomena, his concept of a *Lautbild* (sound picture) comes very close to the psychological definitions of the phoneme in the first part of the twentieth century and, as Koerner argues (2008: 128), is the likely inspiration for Saussure's 'image accoustique.' Paul wrote about the vast variability of sounds and the difficulty of dividing the sound spectrum into segments; accordingly, as a kind of idealized sound image, the *Lautbild* acted as a control to limit this variability. In his third chapter on sound change, he wrote how the 'Vorstellung des noch zu sprechenden Lautes' ('the idea of the sound that is to be spoken') influenced the changes brought about by such processes as progressive assimilation (1880: 49). Here he made the distinction between *Lautwandel* (the diachronic aspect of change over time) and *Lautwechsel* (the allophonic alternation capture by synchronic rules):

> Demgemäss dürfen wir auch den Ausdruck Lautgesetz nie auf den Lautwechsel beziehen, sondern nur auf den Lautwandel. [Accordingly we may never refer the expression sound law to sound alternation but only to sound change.]

We now move outside of Germany to William Dwight Whitney (1827–1894); though nineteenth-century in his thinking, he was very much a linguist of the following century. Whitney is best known for his two books *Language and the Study of Language* (first published in 1867) and *The Life and Growth of Language* (1875). Leonard

Bloomfield (1933: 16) says of them: 'These books were translated into several European languages. Today they seem incomplete, but scarcely antiquated, and still serve as an excellent introduction to language study.' Whitney was in some respects an old-style philologist with a passion for dead languages, and his *Sanskrit Grammar* (Leipzig and Boston, 1876) remains a standard work.

Whitney was greatly influenced by Schleicher's views on the growth and decay of linguistic forms. In going against the Neogrammarian position, he enthusiastically supported the agglutination theory and, projecting later findings within grammaticalization theory, he famously wrote:

> By all the known facts of later language-growth, we are driven to the opinion that every formative element goes back to some previously existing independent word. (1885: 769)

However, he did not go along with the concomitant notion that modern languages were but the poor relations of their linguistically rich and more perfect progenitors ('glottogonic speculation,' as it became known), nor, as a biologist, did he support the biological view of language as a natural organism (*Naturkörper*). For him, language was a social product or, as Jespersen (1922: 88) describes, 'a human institution that has grown slowly out of the necessity for mutual understanding.' Echoing the 'uniformitarianism' of the Neogrammarians, Whitney (1885: 766) wrote:

> All expressions, as all instruments, are at present, and have been through the known past, made and changed by the men who use them; the same will have been the case in the unknown prehistoric past.

With the reputation as 'the man who taught Europe phonetics' (Howatt and Widdowson 2004: 199), Henry Sweet (1845–1912) deserves a place in our potted account of nineteenth-century phonetics and phonology. In the preface to his *History of English Sounds from the Earliest Period with Full Word-Lists,* Sweet wrote (1888: xi), 'I was the first to welcome the "neo-philological" reformers [the Neogrammarians] who have rescued German philology from its earlier stagnation of methods' and he specifically acknowledged his debt to Paul's *Principien* and Sievers' *Phonetik* as inspiration for the ideas in his extensive chapter on sound change. Nothing much of note had happened in Britain since Sir William Jones; yet with Sweet (and, later, phonetician Daniel Jones and general linguist J. R. Firth), British linguistics 'went international' (Seuren 1998: 168). In Sweet's work, we see the concept of the phoneme beginning to emerge more clearly as a distinctive phonological unit. He recognized that the same phonetic differences could be contrastive in one language but not in another, and he argued that only the distinctive sounds needed to be captured in writing.

> [I]t is necessary to have an alphabet which indicates only those broader distinctions of sound which actually correspond to distinctions of meaning, and indicate them by letters which can be easily written and remembered. (1877: 103).

While he did not use the term 'phoneme,' his distinction between a broad and narrow transcription (his 'Broad and Narrow Romic') parallels precisely a phonemic and phonetic distinction, and this dual system of the Romic alphabet provided the basis of the standardized representation of sounds used by the International Phonetic Association (founded in 1886).

As 'the last great phonological work in comparative linguistics in the nineteenth century' (Allan 2010a: 223), we turn now to Ferdinand de Saussure's 300-page essay *Mémoire sur le système primitif des voyelles dans les langues indo-européennes*. Lehmann (1967: 217) describes Saussure's achievement here as 'phenomenal' and 'far in advance of his time.' In order to explain several puzzling irregularities in the development of certain vowels, Saussure applied the methodology of internal reconstruction to PIE, proposing two hypothetical sounds (*coefficients sonantiques*), neither of which was preserved in any known languages at the time. The consonants he suggested were later referred to as laryngeals and their existence was subsequently confirmed with the discovery of Hittite; the disappearance of these sounds triggered vocalic changes such as lengthening, backing, and insertion between consonants. This work formed the basis of the so-called laryngeal theory, which, as Seuren (1998: 145) describes, 'was destined to keep comparative philologists busy for the next one hundred years.' When the Danish scholar Hermann Møller (1850–1923) proposed that there was a correspondence between Saussure's sonorant coefficients and Semitic laryngeals, it paved the way for long-distance comparison well beyond the reconstruction of PIE (cf. the work of Holger Pedersen, Møller's student, on 'Nostratic,' a macrofamily comprising IE, Finno-Ugric, Hamito-Semitic, Altaic, and possibly also Basque and Caucasian: Pedersen 1903).

Finally we need to address some of the new thinking as regards the genealogical classification of languages. A number of scholars were growing dissatisfied with the family tree model to describe the development of languages—not only did it fail to accommodate the fuzziness of language and dialect boundaries, it also could not capture the fact that languages (related or otherwise) often through contact continued to influence each other over time. Most notably, Johannes Schmidt (1843–1901) proposed what has now come to be known as the 'wave model' or 'wave theory' (*Wellentheorie*). In his 1873 book, he claimed correctly that sound laws were in fact spatially restricted and in different ways. By showing that each sound law had its own territory, essentially what he was introducing here was the concept of the 'isogloss.' This wave metaphor captured the fact that new features of a language could spread from a central point in continuously weakening concentric circles, much like waves created when something is thrown into a body of water. Many of the Neogrammarians (notably, Leskien and Brugmann) argued that both the *Stammbaum* and *Wellen* models were compatible; Schmidt himself saw his model as supplementing the standard family tree, simply providing a more complicated version of the single splits offered by the *Stammbaum* (more severe criticism was to come from the specialists in dialectology; cf. the work of Hugo Schuchardt). As Seuren (1998: 102–3) points out, however, what Schmidt's waves of innovation could not capture were sociolinguistic facts to do with the spread and influence of national standard varieties at the expense of local vernacular varieties; for this we need to wait for the insights of sociolinguistics.

7.3 CONCLUSION

Aufgabe der genannten Wissenschten is es einmal, die Gesetze zu suchen, durch welche die einzelnen Vorgänge in der Natur auf allgemeine Regeln zurückgeleitet, und aus den letzteren wider bestimmt werden können. [The task of the physical sciences is, in the first place, to seek the laws by which the particular processes of nature can be traced back to and deduced from general principles.] (von Helmholtz 1847: 3).

We now risk not understanding any longer the motivation and the methodological assumptions of a number of results which are still valid, but are known only to a few historical linguists; however, we also fail to understand the intellectual background of those linguistic theories which [. . .] in spite of the later changes in attitude were—and are—still influential at a much later period. (Davies 1998: xxiii)

It is telling that two of the dates in our brief history here fall within Hockett's four most significant dates in the history of linguistics; in his presidential address to the Linguistic Society of America in 1964 he listed what he believed to be the real breakthroughs in linguistic theory over the previous two hundred years: 1786, Sir William Jones; 1875, the Neogrammarians; 1916, Ferdinand de Saussure; 1957, Noam Chomsky.

The nineteenth century saw the birth of a new discipline. Encouraged by the newly formed or recreated educational institutions, especially universities, the linguistic scholarship of this century represented a flow or development of thinking, rather than a series of individual achievements. This was the golden age of historical and comparative work, specifically the comparison of lexical items and morphology of different languages leading to the identification of law-like correspondences across languages (and within them), as well as the reconstruction of unattested ancestral forms (especially of the IE linguistic family). The approach was an empirical one, more data-oriented than philosophical, and it was scientific; linguists were *Naturwissenschaftler* (natural scientists) in their method and their results. And while we can tilt at the widely held organistic attitude to language and language change (à la Schlegel, Bopp and Schleicher), the attraction of this approach at this time is understandable. Given the infancy of the social sciences, it is not surprising that scholars were drawn for inspiration to the more established disciplines like biology and geology and their quest for law-like principles to account for natural phenomena (Janda and Joseph 2003: 6–10). Yet the rejection of organism and the emphasis once more on the role of speakers in language production also opened doors to the study of language as a social and psychological phenomenon. As Allan (2010a: 195) points out, with the late nineteenth and early twentieth century came contact and cross-fertilization between the newer disciplines 'as progress in human social sciences such as anthropology, psychology, and sociology coincided with advances in linguistics.' There was the exciting possibility that uncovering the principles and 'laws' of the non-physical life of humans would solve some of the mysteries associated with the adoption and spread of change, as well as the mysteries of those counter-agents to regular sound change (e.g. the association processes driving analogical reformulations), without threatening the validity of sound laws as mechanical physiological processes.

With the nineteenth century came a growing understanding that research in sound change required a basic knowledge of phonetics and a recognition of the phoneme as the fundamental unit of description. Following on from the impact of the Sanskritic Indian phonetic treatises came real advances in articulatory and acoustic phonetics and in the technological inventions for recoding speech and for acoustic measurement; these advances, together the practical demands of such things as spelling reform, foreign language teaching, and 'exotic' language description, paved the way for a more sophisticated and clearly articulated distinction between speech sounds and phonemes and the methods for their discovery. However, we must wait until the twentieth century for a more solid knowledge of phonetics and phonological theory, as well as advances in dialectology and sociolinguistic techniques of description and analysis that help us to track and to comprehend the progress of phonological changes both socially and geographically.

In methodology, theory, and results, it is clear that the work of the nineteenth century offered something very different from what had preceded it. Many of its breakthoughs remain part of everyday linguistic knowledge today:

- recognition of the primacy of the sounds (of living languages) over the letters (of dead languages);
- discovery that sound change is regular and phonetically conditioned;
- identification and refinement of sound changes and rules to account for them within and between languages;
- invention of a method to reconstruct unattested protolanguages;
- classification of languages by descent (*Stammbaumtheorie* and *Wellentheorie*);
- relatedness of languages like German and Sanskrit as the continuation of an earlier IE language;
- rejection of unsupported etymologies;
- discovery that 'yesterday's syntax is today's morphology;'
- the relevance of the present in studying the past and the principle that recon-structed languages must be the same as those we observe today (i.e. uniformitar-ianism).

While the twentieth century assimilated these ideas and continued much of the comparative and historical work of the previous century, the obvious contrast was the recognition that a scientific study of language did not have to take account of the past. With the shift in focus to synchrony, linguistics ceased to be thought of as essentially an historical discipline.

CHAPTER 8

....

DISCOVERERS OF THE
PHONEME

....

HARRY VAN DER HULST

8.1 OVERVIEW[1]

....

THE central insight that underlies the linguistic study of speech is that sounds which are objectively different can count as the same at some level of linguistic analysis (and most likely also in the mind of language users). The sameness is captured by the notion 'phoneme', an abstract notion that is manifested in a large (perhaps endless) variety of speech sounds. We usually associate the first explicit statements of this insight, which I will call 'the phonemic principle,' with the birth of phonology, but the idea as such is much more widespread and older. While earlier writers and traditions will be mentioned in the introductory §8.2, §8.3 will focus on developments that began toward the end of the nineteenth century with Jan Baudouin de Courtenay and Mikołai Kruszewski (the Kazan School), and the impact of Ferdinand de Saussure's structuralist ideas, which together culminate in the Prague School (with N. S. Trubetzkoy and Roman Jakobson as the leading figures), discussed in §8.4. §§8.5–8.7 discuss Louis Hjemslev's glossematic theory, the London School (the prosodic analysis of J. R. Firth), and various American structuralists (Franz Boas, Edward Sapir, Leonard Bloomfield, and the 'post-Bloomfieldians'), respectively. §8.8 reviews later developments in Europe and also covers work in the Soviet Union. §8.9 focuses on Generative Phonology, the theory of Noam Chomsky and Morris Halle, and developments of this approach up to the present time. §8.10 winds up with some conclusions.

Goldsmith and Laks (2000b) make a distinction between an external history (theories, dates, names) and an internal history of a subject; the latter deals with the personal motives, contacts, and general backgrounds that lie behind historical developments.

¹ I would like to thank Bernard Laks, Tobias Scheer, and Keith Allan for comments and help.

The present overview is more external than internal since the latter approach requires much more space and most of the research has yet to be done.[2] I have tried to include references to important and pivotal works, both those that are part of the history and those that reflect on it. In dealing with the history of a discipline, or any history for that matter, we cannot always speak of a straight line, and this certainly applies here, since different individuals and schools developed principles of phonological analysis, often with little cross-reference, although it remains to be seen how various scholars influenced each other and to what extent various issues that were 'in the air' developed independently.

My main sources for this overview up to and including the early phase of generative phonology are Fischer-Jørgensen (1975) and Anderson (1985), two excellent overviews which offer detailed discussions of the individual phonological schools. I also mention Kilbury (1976), who presents a thorough discussion of the development of 'morphophonemics'. Many introductions to linguistics (e.g. Dinneen 1967) and general works on the history of linguistics also contain valuable overviews of approaches to phonology (and phonetics). Several other shorter works offer important discussions of the development of phonology, such as Kortlandt (1972), Durand and Laks' (2002) discussion of the cognitive setting of phonology, various papers by John Goldsmith (2000, 2005, 2008), Laks (2001, 2005), (Allan 2010a: ch. 9), and Dresher (2009, 2011). In what follows, I will derive many of my points from (interpretations of) these various works, having made an effort to confirm these remarks from my reading of 'original' works that played a pivotal role in this history.[3] There are various important collections of seminal phonological articles or book chapters (or sometimes excerpts): Makkai (1972) contains many classical papers from the American structuralist school and early generative phonology. See also Joos (1957) for the structuralist period and Vachek (1964) for a reader with Prague School work. Fudge (1973) is a much smaller collection with a broader orientation. Dinnsen (1979) and Goyvaerts (1981) contain overviews of a variety of Generative Phonology that precedes the development of non-linear models for which various volumes edited by van der Hulst and Smith contain representative work (1982ab, 1985a, 1988a, b, c). See also Durand and Laks (1996) for an important collection. Goldsmith (1999) focuses on generative phonology and McCarthy (2004) focuses on Optimality Theory. Kreidler (2000) offers a huge collection of articles covering many different approaches. Very useful also are various handbooks in phonological theory such as Goldsmith (1995), de Lacy (2007), Goldsmith et al. (2011), Kula et al. (2011), and in particular van Oostendorp et al. (2011), which contains 120 long chapters each offering overviews of a different area of phonology. Since 1985 we have

---

[2] Goldsmith and Laks (2000a) contains a number of studies that focus on internal history, as do several essays by Jakobson (e.g. 1971) and various other reflective works by the key figures in the history of phonology. Fischer-Jørgensen (1975) and Anderson (1985) do much more than enumerate the facts. These works contain numerous insightful remarks and passages on connections, general political and scientific background, 'who talked to whom,' etc.

[3] Some works fulfil both functions in that they review preceding work and then add their own point of view.

had a journal (*Phonology*, from 1984 to 1987 the *Phonology Yearbook*, CUP) devoted to theoretical phonology. Since the early 1990s there have been a number of phonology conferences in Austria of which the proceedings (called *Phonologica* [followed by the year], e.g. Dressler and Pfeiffer 1977) display a broad array of approaches.

Finally, a note on the term 'phonology'. For many, this term stands in contrast to 'phonetics,' and indeed, much of the history of phonology is about its relationship to phonetics. Phonetics, the story goes, studies the physical aspect of speech, i.e. how speech is produced and perceived as well as its physical properties, while phonology studies how speech sounds function distinctively and how these functioning units enter into paradigmatic (systemic) and syntagmatic (sequential) relations. Ignoring for the moment that many phoneticians would argue that their research goes beyond the strictly physical, this leaves us without a term that covers both disciplines. In the view of some (notably the British linguists), phonology is just a branch of phonetics, which others (like André Martinet) designate as 'functional phonetics.' Another view (characteristic of the American schools) is to use phonology as the cover term for 'phonemics' and phonetics. Since, clearly, phonemes (i.e. distinctive units) form the fundamental concept for phonology, I believe that the American practice deserves general use, also because this gives us a term ('phonology') to refer to a continuum of phenomena and research, since the boundary between the 'physical' and the 'functional' is not always so clear. Here, however, in keeping with more common usage, I will use phonology (as phonemics) and distinguish it as such from phonetics.

8.2 INTRODUCTION

The earliest development that is relevant to the history of phonology (that we know about) is perhaps the development of writing, and especially of *phonographic*, more specifically *alphabetic* systems. Then, as today, phonographic writing systems tend to be phonemic in character, avoiding different symbols for linguistically non-functional, allophonic distinctions that are not relevant for differentiating lexical meanings. This is true whether systems are alphabetic or involve larger syllabic units. However, alphabetic systems specifically anticipate the modern view that phoneme-sized units are the pivotal *sequential* components underlying speech. Occasional diacritic characters representing sub-phonemic sound qualities may even be said to anticipate the notion of distinctive features.

Early grammarians in various (Greek, Roman, Indian, Arabic, Chinese)[4] traditions often show explicit awareness of the notion of speech sound (see Allan 2010a: ch. 9 and Chapters 2 and 5 above), and an implicit recognition of the need to abstract away from non-meaning differentiating phonetic properties, but no explicit early developments of

---

[4] For Greek and Roman see Robins (1953) and Allen (1981); for Indian see Allen (1953), Deshpande (1995), and Ch. 11 below; for Arabic and Hebrew see Semaan (1968); for Chinese see Halliday (1981).

the phonemic principle can be found in these works. Pāṇini's work on Vedic might be an exception (Kiparsky 1979; Chapter 10 below), although closer investigation of other older sources might reveal otherwise. An isolated obvious and well-known exception, discussed by Fischer-Jørgensen (1975: ch. 2) and more extensively in Allan 2010a: ch. 9), concerns the anonymous Icelandic linguist who, in the twelfth century, wrote what is now known as the 'First Grammatical Treatise' in which, in the course of proposing a new writing system, he demonstrated the existence of phonemes (without using this term) by listing sound differences that occurred in otherwise identical environments, thus effectively producing minimal pairs (or rather minimal sets) and using the commutation test which is the fundamental discovery procedure for establishing phonemic contrast. This work, unfortunately, did not attract the attention it deserved.

In the following centuries, to be sure, others addressed the matter of spelling of other languages, also relying on the recognition of *relevant* sound differences. In conjunction with these concerns, these scholars often provided detailed phonetic descriptions of speech sounds (e.g. in the work of Thomas Smith and John Hart in England). Allan (2010a: 199ff.) also mentions various other British scholars who were concerned with spelling and pronunciation. Firth (1946), Abercrombie (1948), Fromkin and Ladefoged (1981), Ohala (2004), and Allan (2010a) also discuss various early (forgotten) phoneticians[5] whose work involves understanding of the distinctive role of speech sounds (often referred to as 'letters') and the fact that these sounds can be analysed in articulatory gestures. Fromkin and Ladefoged refer to William Holder (who offered a detailed description of articulation to be able to teach speech to the deaf), John Wallis, and Francis Lodwick. These scholars developed systems of articulatory building blocks, often with the explicit intention of such inventories being universal. Fromkin and Ladefoged's specific point is that these scholars realized not only that sounds could distinguish meaning but that they perhaps were on the brink of locating this distinctive function with the smaller articulatory ingredients. Ohala (2004) mentions a variety of other phoneticians (Johan Conrad Amman, Wolfgang von Kempelen, Erasmus Darwin, Robert Willis, T. Hewitt Key, and others). Several of these scholars developed experimental methods or built speech-producing contraptions. Interestingly, Erasmus Darwin (as pointed out in Ohala 2004) proposed a system of 13 'unary features' (Darwin 1803).

The nineteenth century shows great developments in the comparative study of languages (usually called 'philology'), with an emphasis on the historical developments of individual sounds or groups of sounds (see Allan 2010a: 207ff.; Waterman 1963, Robins 1967). While such work may generally have not been very precise in making reference to the phonetic properties of these sounds, there are various exceptions, such as Karl Verner (1846–96). It must also be noticed that the numerous studies of the historical development of 'speech sounds' most certainly rested on the *implicit* recognition of phonemic units and

---

[5] See also Ch. 5 above.

distinctive sound properties, even though the distinction between relevant and irrelevant phonetic properties had not yet been made.

Meanwhile, phoneticians developed more sophisticated experimental methods, and toward the end of the nineteenth century these methods allowed them to observe a considerable variability in the realization of speech sounds. As a consequence it no longer seemed justified to speak about speech sounds as the alleged invariant building blocks of words. Clearly, certain differences between speech sounds were more important than others in that some would be negligible because they would not differentiate words, whereas other differences were important in precisely this respect. Once a distinction is made between sound differences that are distinctive and sound differences that are not, we are essentially making a distinction between the phonetic study of sound systems and the phonological (or rather, phonemic!) study of sounds. With this we also have introduced the notions 'phoneme' and 'allophone.' A phoneme is an abstract category that generalizes over a large (infinite) set of actual speech sounds which are its allophones.

It is interesting to note that the founding father of the International Phonetic Alphabet, Paul Passy (1859–1940), felt that an international phonetic alphabet was necessary, precisely to write down speech in terms of symbols that ignore the allophonic differences (Albright 1958, Kemp 1994a). Thus, his 'broad transcription' would essentially be a *phonemic* transcription. A narrow transcription was possible to capture additional phonetic, i.e. allophonic, detail which might be useful (especially as long as the linguist has not yet figured out which properties are distinctive), but runs into the potential problem of not being able to decide where to stop. Another figure who bridges phonetics and phonology was Henry Sweet (1845–1912), who, like Passy, was keenly aware of the fact that one has to recognize that only certain phonetic properties serve the purpose of differentiating between words. Sweet (quoted in Ohala 2004) felt that the new instrumental methods should not take the place of what he called the 'natural method' (based on the perceptual observation of the phonetician), and qualified instrumental phonetics as not being phonetics at all (see Sweet 1877). This makes sense because instruments are by definition not sensitive to a distinction between contrastive and non-contrastive properties while the phonetician (at least in considering his own language) is.

From this point on, phonetics and phonology/phonemics are involved in an ongoing love–hate relationship. Both want to be seen as independent, but neither can do without the other. Ohala (2004) makes a useful distinction between 'taxonomic phonetics,' which culminated in the development of the IPA system, a tool for classifying sounds and their transcription, and 'scientific phonetics,' which aims at understanding the processes underlying speech production and perception. Phonology could easily embrace the results of taxonomic phonetics which, as we have seen, anticipated the phonemic principle. However, phonology did not relate well to scientific phonetics, on the one hand, due to the idea that there is nothing interesting to know beyond identifying the distinctive properties and, on the other hand, because scientific phonetics developed its own set of goals, making use of the rapidly evolving technological possibilities. One might say that phonology focused on *langue* (or 'competence'), while phonetics, assuming the units of langue/competence, focused on *parole* (or 'performance'), but that would imply a misunderstanding about the appropriate scope of what phoneticians study, many of whom would not insist on this dichotomy to begin with. Ohala (2004) notes that around the 1950s the strict separation, which was rejected even before that or indeed never accepted by several scholars, was bridged by various trends such as the interest in speech synthesis and the rigid development of explicit acoustic and articulatory definitions of distinctive features by Roman Jakobson and others (see §8.4).

8.3 THE FOUNDING FATHERS OF PHONOLOGY

If we see the Prague School views as held by Nikolai Trubetzkoy and Roman Jakobson (and, of course, many other pivotal figures) as a culmination of certain preceding developments, we need to especially discuss two of these which are at least partially independent: the views of the Kazan School (Jan Baudouin de Courtenay and Mikołai Kruszewski) and the views of Ferdinand de Saussure. Fischer-Jørgensen (1975) also mentions other forerunners, such as Otto Jespersen (1860–1943), Adolph Doreen (1854–1925), Johan Forchhammer (1794–1865), and Jakob Winteler (in the late nineteenth century), who had all explicitly recognized that only certain differences between speech sounds were 'functional', being 'linguistically relevant' or 'carrying semantic differences.' This is not to say that the development of phonology was an exclusively European affair. Fischer-Jørgensen (1975) also refers to Edward Sapir as a forerunner who had, in the US, been preceded by Franz Boas (see §8.7).

8.3.1 The Kazan School (Baudouin de Courtenay and Mikołai Kruszewski)

Entirely independently from and prior to de Saussure's work on synchronic linguistics, Baudouin de Courtenay (1845–1929) had embarked on the synchronic study of sound *alternations* in morphologically related words; see Baudouin de Courtenay (1972b), and for a collection of his other work, (1972a). Baudouin de Courtenay worked very closely with Mikołai Kruszewski (1851–1887), an enormously influential student of his.[6] Their work influenced the Leningrad and the Moscow Schools of Linguistics (see §8.8.2) and the founders of the Prague School, but was largely unknown elsewhere in Europe or the

---

[6] See Silverman (2012) for a thorough discussion of Kruszewski's views, and Radwańska-Williams (1993).

US, although some of Baudouin de Courtenay's students, such as Lev Vladimirovič Ščerba (1880–1944) did come to influence, for example, Daniel Jones in his development of the phoneme concept. However, Baudouin de Courtenay and Kruszewski were aware of de Saussure's earlier work on Indo-European (de Saussure 1879); Baudouin de Courtenay had met de Saussure in 1881 and they subsequently corresponded. De Saussure recognized the resemblances in their work in his notes. Jakobson and other members of the Prague School were also familiar with and clearly influenced by the Kazan School.

Baudouin de Courtenay and Kruszewski recognized the unit phoneme as a generalization over non-distinctive phonetic varieties, but their work focused more on alternations in related words, i.e. what came to be known as 'morphophonology' (in Europe) and 'morphophonemics' (in the US). They acknowledged the distinction between alternations that are purely phonologically/conditioned (both allophonic and neutralizing) and those that rely on non-phonological information, and sometimes use the term 'phoneme' *only* for the units that underlie the former, a usage adopted by the Moscow school. For de Courtenay the phoneme was a psychological unit, and Kruszewski, like de Saussure, saw language as a system of syntagmatic and paradigmatic relations.

Both Kruszewski and de Courtenay developed detailed typologies of different kinds of alternations, essentially boiling down to a three-way distinction into (a) alternations that are governed by fully automatic, transparent, exceptionless, 'phonetic' or low-level rules (allophonic or neutralizing), (b) alternations that follow rules that are no longer fully phonetic but have acquired morphological conditioning (*electric* ~ *electricity*), and (c) alternations that by themselves encode morphological or semantic distinctions (*was* ~ *were*). In his detailed discussion of the progression from one type to the other, de Courtenay introduced the term 'phonologization' to refer to the transition of type (a) rules to type (b) rules. Clearly much of the discussion that unfolds in later models, specifically in later developments in generative phonology, was more than anticipated (although unfortunately not often informed) by the work of these two linguists (see §8.9). The Kazan school theories about alternations were known to Jakobson and Trubetzkoy, but, as Anderson (1985: 80) points out, they did not resonate in their work, at least not initially. Rather, the Prague School focused on the phoneme which, although recognized by the Kazan writers, was not their major interest as such, apart from being a relevant unit in the study of alternations.

Several writers (Jakobson 1971 [1960], Anderson (1985: 38, 66–8, Dresher 2011) have pointed out that the term 'phoneme' was invented by the French linguist A. Dufriche-Desgenettes (1804–78), meant as a French equivalent to the German *Sprachlaut*. In his later work de Saussure used the term in this sense, i.e. as standing for 'speech sound', but in his *Mémoire* (de Saussure 1879) it referred to the sound that occurs in the ancestor word for cognates in different languages. From this work Kruszewski adopted the term, but he then extended its use as a reference to pairs of sounds that stand in a synchronic alternation *within* one language. De Courtenay subsequently made a further step: for him a phoneme was an abstract ('psychophonetic') unit that engages in morphological alternations (allomorphy) and, subsequently, underlies the variable pronunciations of any speech sound, thus also including allophonic variation. De Courtenay did not see his phonemes as built out of smaller units, like features, and therefore did not think of his acoustic images as strictly redundancy-free units. Rather, they were fully specified basic variants (cf. Anderson 1985: 43ff.). De Courtenay's view of the phoneme as an invariable unit that underlies allomorphy and allophony would become the dominant one in the twentieth century, with the further restriction that only those allomorphic variants that are phonetically (later, phonotactically) governed are taken into account (as made explicit in the Leningrad School; see §8.8.2).

8.3.2 Ferdinand de Saussure

If previous writers had already seen the important difference between allophonic differences and distinctive differences, what did Ferdinand de Saussure (1857–1913) add to this appreciation in *Cours de linguistique générale* (1916), which contains his views as written down by some of his students based on their and his lecture notes? He distinguished between the concrete sound (for which he reserved the term 'phoneme,' whose study was part of the study of *parole*, what we call today 'phonetics' but was called 'phonology' by him) and the 'acoustic image' (part of the linguistic sign's form or *signifiant* and thus falling within the realm of *langue*). For de Saussure, phonemes are contextual realizations of 'phonetic species,' and the acoustic image that he speaks of is a mental representation of this idealized unit which forms the basis for speech production and speech perception (and for alphabetic writing). Phonetic species (which are close to the modern sense of the term 'phoneme,' and which, similarly to de Courtenay, are regarded as a psychological unit) are of interest to de Saussure because they constitute the differences between the perceptible forms of linguistic signs. As such, the focus of study is not on their intrinsic or contextual properties, but rather on the relations between them, which is the essential structuralist angle that de Saussure added to the study of language and, by extension, to the study of 'sound images.' By making a distinction between the image and the actual sound, de Saussure recognized a system of implementation rules (belonging to *parole* and not to *langue*) which accounted for allophony. Like de Courtenay, his images were not composed of features and thus not completely redundancy-free, a view radically different from that of the Prague School.

Unlike de Courtenay, de Saussure's primary concern, as Anderson (1985) puts it, was representation (the phonemes and the structure of words), while de Courtenay and Kruszewski directed their primary attention to rules.

8.4 Prague School Phonology
(N. S. Trubetzkoy and Roman Jakobson)

While the ideas of Baudouin de Courtenay (and Kruszewski) were pursued by his students in St Petersburg (and other Russian universities where he taught), a group of young linguists in Moscow worked on integrating the Kazan views and de Saussure's work into a new approach to the study of language. Several of these joined the Linguistic Circle of Prague, which, within an interdisciplinary intellectual climate that profited from both native and imported traditions and scholars, gave rise to the prolific Prague School which made its new approach to phonology as the centrepiece of the proper study of language, Nikolaj S. Trubetzkoy (1890–1938) and Roman Jakobson (1896–1982) being its most important members.[7]

The Prague School linguists felt that (a) phonology (and language in general), both from a synchronic and diachronic view point, needed to be studied in terms of systems of interrelated phonemes, rather than as units in isolation (like the nineteenth-century philologists); (b) that the focus should be on distinctive properties; and (c) that phonologists needed to formulate universal laws that govern sound systems. Jakobson wrote (and Trubetzkoy and Sergei Karcevskij, 1884–1955, co-signed) a set of theses presented at the First International Congress of Linguists, held in the Hague in 1928, which set a new direction for linguistic and specifically phonological research. Systems should be studied in terms of recurrent correlations, pointing to distinctive properties among sets of phonemes, such as voicing, and noting that these properties need to be understood as acoustic events. Here, Jakobson laid the foundation for the theory of distinctive features which he developed later.

The Prague School saw phonetics as entirely different from phonology. This strict, rather programmatic, separation was firmly embraced by some followers of the Prague School (such as Louis Hjemslev), but by no means by all. Various later proponents of this school took a more integrative approach.

The Prague School views were well advocated and dispersed, attracting notable followers elsewhere in Europe throughout the 1930s such as André Martinet, 1949) and Nicolas van Wijk, 1939). Just prior to his death, Trubetzkoy completed his *Grundzüge der Phonologie*, published in 1939, which is the most complete and fullest statement of the Prague School programme.

Trubetzkoy is very much focused on establishing the set of phonetic properties which can serve as a contrast between phonemes. In terms of these properties, phonemes form systems, which are governed by universal laws. The system was the important part of the analysis, and phonemes were primarily seen as points in this system which was a network of oppositions. If a phonological property corresponds to

---

[7] Works on Prague phonology are Vachek (1964) and Krámský (1974). A more general work on the Prague School is Toman (1995).

several phonetic properties, these, while different, cannot be distinctive. The phoneme is the sum of the phonologically relevant properties. The phoneme was first seen as a psychological unit, but for Trubetzkoy it later became a functional unit, a term in a phonological opposition. It forms part of language as a social system.

Since phonemes are specified for properties that are strictly contrastive, a phoneme that phonetically is a stop is only phonologically seen as a stop if there is another phoneme identical in all respects except for not being a stop. Although this comes close to speaking about phonemes in terms of distinctive features, Trubetzkoy did not think of the non-contrastive unit in question as underspecified, but rather as a complete phoneme. Thus, although Trubetzkoy did not speak of features as such, he proposed various classifications of phonological oppositions, one being a three-way distinction in privative (e.g. voicing, nasality), equipollent (e.g. front/back), and gradual oppositions (e.g., vowel height). Trubetzkoy also made a specific proposal for a set of suprasegmental (non-segmental) properties such as tone and accent.

A very important aspect of Trubetzkoy's phonological theory concerns the fact that there are positions in the word where oppositions are *neutralized*. A notorious case is the neutralization of the voice contrast among obstruents in final position in German. In final position we find the voiceless sound, but since there is no contrast, the underlying phonological unit has no voicing property at all. Trubetzkoy calls such a unit an 'archiphoneme.' The phonetic value that an archiphoneme acquires is the 'logically unmarked' value. In the case at hand, voicelessness is thus logically unmarked. It is, at the same time, also 'naturally unmarked' since Trubetzkoy thinks of voicing as constituting a privative opposition. In principle, the former can exist without the latter. If a gradual opposition between mid and high vowels is neutralized such that only high vowels occur in some position, high vowels would be logically, but not naturally, unmarked.

A characteristic trait of the Prague School, following from its emphasis on systems, is its typological orientation, providing many typologies of vocalic and consonantal systems.

After Trubetzkoy's death in 1938, Jakobson focused his attention on the development of a theory of distinctive features, breaking away from de Saussure's idea that the linguistic sign can only be divided sequentially and thus from the idea that phonemes are the smallest building blocks of phonological structure. He proposed to analyse *all* phonological oppositions (privative, equipollent, and gradual) in terms of binary features, which gave rise to the 'feature matrix.' For Jakobson, features were clearly building blocks and thus the true primitives of phonology; see Jakobson et al. (1952) and Jakobson and Halle (1956). In this he differed from Trubetzkoy, who had seen his phonological properties as *attributes* of phonemes.

In his choice of a rigid binary system, Jakobson reflected a deep influence from new theories of communication which had focused on the most economical transmission of information; see Cherry et al. (1952) and Goldsmith (2000).

Most characteristic of his approach was the goal to subsume related phonetic properties that were thought not to occur contrastively in any language under a single feature, which implied the notion that there could be a single universal set of features for both consonants and vowels. He thus achieved a great reduction in his system when compared to Trubetzkoy's. Jakobson achieved this reduction by emphasizing the auditory characterization of features so that different articulatory actions that have similar auditory effects can be joined into one feature. Jakobson did adopt Trubetzkoy's view that phonemes needed to be represented minimally, such that only properties that are strictly necessary to distinguish words from each other would be specified.

Jakobson also broke new ground by trying to discover phonological universals and taking into account not just evidence from normal speech but also deviant speech, developmental speech, and historical change. His *Kindersprache, Aphasie und allgemeine Lautgesetze* (1941) brings together facts from three domains into the proposal that there is an order in the utilization of the features, meaning that certain types of contrast take precedence (in language development and in languages as such) over others, which reveals the cognitive language development, rather than the development of the articulatory motoric system. He linked these stages to implicational universals and to processes of language change.

Roman Jakobson, and his student Morris Halle, form a transition from the Prague School approaches toward those of *SPE, The Sound Pattern of English* (Chomsky and Halle 1968), discussed in §8.9.

8.5 GLOSSEMATICS (LOUIS HJEMSLEV AND HANS JØRGEN UDALL)

Establishing a new discipline often involves aggressive separation, and emphasis on autonomy and depreciation of those that are outside the new field. As Durand and Laks (2002) show, some phonologists went further than seeing phonology as being more abstract than phonetics (generalizing over non-distinctive variants) and declared that phonology is completely and logically independent from phonetic substance. Although it is not obvious how in practice one could postulate phonological units without considering the substance first, it is of course true that phonology deals with entities that are not themselves speech sounds, but instead symbolic representations of speech sounds. The idea that phonological entities are not defined or definable in terms of phonetic substance is inherent to the structuralist programme which defines phonemes as points in a system of oppositions. But the most explicit on the strict separation between phonology (the study of form) and phonetics (the study of substance) was the Glossematic School of Louis Hjemslev (1899–1965) and Hans Jørgen Udall (1907–57), who proclaimed that phonological units are purely abstract and substance-free. (The same can be said of Šaumjan's model discussed in §8.8.2, which was inspired by glossematics.) In trying to study the relation between sound (and meaning) in terms of a level of analysis which had to be conceived without relying on either of these substances, Hjelmslev went against the empiricist nature of, for example, the American structuralists who base their analysis in the study of what can be perceived (i.e. sounds) alone. However, in practice, both approaches, of course, have to depart from the phonetic substance. The crucial difference between glossematics and the empiricist approach is that in the latter the analysis has to be motivated in terms of the phonetic substance that it is based on, whereas in glossematics this is not so. The motivation for the form analysis has to be entirely internal to the form dimension.

8.6 THE LONDON SCHOOL (DANIEL JONES AND J. R. FIRTH)

The phoneticians from the London School adopted the phoneme, because they needed this concept to cope with the fact that speech sounds occurred in a seemingly unlimited variety. Their use of this term was influenced by the Kazan School views. They did not see the discovery of this unit as the beginning of a new discipline, though. Rather, they continued to think of what they did as phonetics. Views in Great Britain built on a long tradition of precise work on the properties of speech sounds with specific reference to English, fuelled by practical rather than theoretical purposes. Thus, these views developed without much influence from older and newer continental or American approaches and in turn did not impact the development of phonology in these other parts of the world.

Alexander Melville Bell (1819–1905) developed a precise notation ('Visible Speech,' 1867) for the articulation of sounds in any language, which he hoped would be helpful in teaching the pronunciation of English and other languages (to, among others, deaf people). This approach anticipated the development of theories of subsegmental structure (see Halle 1983, 2005), although, as pointed out in §8.2.1, many earlier phoneticians had done so too. Henry Sweet (1845–1912) wrote a *Handbook of Phonetics* (1877) in which he advocated the distinction between broad and narrow transcription (in agreement with Paul Passy), the former aiming to have separate symbols only for contrastive segments. In doing so he adhered to the phonemic principle without using the term. Anderson (1985: 173) makes the important point that the mere recognition of distinctive speech sounds ('phonemes') does not put Sweet (and others before him who had done the same) in the same realm as de Saussure and the Prague School phonologists. These latter scholars not only recognized the phoneme as a contrastive unit but also, and perhaps more importantly, placed the phoneme in a coherent and organized system that is governed by recurrent use of oppositions (or distinctive features). Thus Sweet should perhaps be better seen as the founding father of phonetics as an independent academic discipline rather than as a founding father of phonology. Put differently, while the continental and American structuralists put great emphasis on theories about how to establish phonemes, others, such as the British phoneticians and indeed the earlier students of sound change, postulated or assumed the phoneme for practical purposes (such as writing or transcription) or simply because they took it for granted that allophonic variations were to be ignored.

8.6.1 Daniel Jones

Daniel Jones (1881–1967) learned from Henry Sweet and Paul Passy that phonetic transcription needed to focus on 'broad transcriptions,' and when he later encountered Baudouin de Courtenay's work (via Lev V. Ščerba) he fully came to appreciate the phoneme unit and its practical value for spelling design and language teaching; this was before he learned of de Saussure's work or the Prague School. For Jones, the phoneme was not a psychological but a physical unit, a family of related sounds, including the free variants in each position, as well as the variants that are in complementary distribution (Jones 1929). He makes no reference to meaning and thus no reference to distinctive function. The distinctive function, he says, is what phonemes *do*, not what they *are*. His major work on the phoneme (1950)[8] appeared very late in his career. It contains detailed analyses of a wide variety of languages with a keen eye for phonetic detail. As in the case of Henry Sweet, we cannot say that Jones developed a phonological theory. His focus was on phoneme inventories. He did not focus on systematic relations between phonemes in terms of systems or in terms of alternations, nor did he pay much attention to distributional restrictions. A noteworthy property of his view of the phoneme is that he excludes the possibility of one sound in some context being the realization of two different phonemes. Thus the sound [t] alternating with [d] as a result of final devoicing could not be analysed by him as belonging to the phoneme /d/; it has to be assigned to the phoneme /t/. His views on neutralization and phonemic overlap are thus very different from those of the Prague School (but not so different from those of Bloomfield and his followers). Another difference from the Prague School is that Jones only used the term 'phoneme' for segmental units, introducing other terms (e.g. 'chronemes,' 'tonemes,' and 'stronemes') for length, tones, and stress.

8.6.2 John Rupert Firth

Unlike Jones, John Rupert Firth (1890–1960) was interested in developing a theory of language. His views on phonology did not, however, see phonemes as the foundational units (though he did acknowledge them as a sound basis for writing systems). Rather, he put great emphasis on the fact that many phonetic features belong to larger units than the single segment (which he called the 'phonematic unit'). There are systems of phonematic units for the different positions in the word and Firth (again unlike Jones

---

[8] See the 3rd edn from 1967 with an essay on the history of the term 'phoneme.'

and the continental schools) saw no need to recognize an initial [n] and a final [n] as instances of the same unit, especially not if in initial position we would have a contrast [n]–[m]–[ŋ], and no contrast (only [n]) finally. (Twaddell 1935 makes the same point; see §8.7.2.1.) This forms part of the 'polysystematic' approach, which goes much further and includes the notion that analyses of different parts of the phonology or grammar need not all be compatible with each other. Firth made no clear distinction between phonetic properties and (contrastive) phonological properties. Nor did he preclude reference to grammatical aspects in the phonological analysis. Since prosodies capture, among other things, co-occurrences of properties between segments, they capture in a static fashion what in other models (generative phonology) would be captured in rules (e.g. a rule turning an oral vowel into a nasal vowel before a nasal consonant). This, as Anderson (1985: 188) points out, precludes rule ordering. Indeed, the Firthian approach is a no-rule representational one-level theory, that can be formalized in a modern-day declarative model which also has these properties (as shown in Ogden 1999) (see §8.9.2). There is also a link with Zellig Harris' theory of 'long components' (Harris 1944) (see §8.7.2.2).

The importance of the Firthian approach, which was never fully worked out or written down (Firth 1948 being the main source), lies in its recognition of suprasegmental properties. Robins (1967), Dinneen (1967: 299–325), and Langendoen (1968) provide expositions of this approach from the viewpoint of generative grammar. An important collection of papers is Palmer (1970). Firth's approach prefigured important aspects of 'autosegmental phonology' or, more broadly, non-linear phonology which emerged in the mid-1970s in the US (see van der Hulst and Smith 1982a,b). Anderson (1985) shows how Firth's analysis of Arabic is very similar to that of McCarthy (1981), including the distinctions between a CV structure and separate vowel and consonant sequences. The prosodies, of course, resemble the autosegments proposed in Goldsmith (1976a,b) and Clements (1980 [1976], 2000). It is unfortunate that approaches and theories conceived in Great Britain tend to stay in Great Britain.

8.7 AMERICAN APPROACHES

In this section we start our overview of the American structuralism with Franz Boas, whose work of course pre-dates structuralism. Boas's interest in language was primarily in precise descriptions of Native American languages. He believed that these descriptions should record phonetic detail, and he therefore was against a broad transcription system. A precise description would have to reveal all the phonetic segments and their possible combinations. Predictabilities in phonetic properties could be recorded in a separate set of rules which capture allophony, phonemic alternations, and even the phonological/expression of semantic categories. This set of rules would imply, one might say, recognition of distinctive and predictable properties, without overt recognition of the 'phonemic principle' in the transcription itself. In this sense, Boas favoured what one might call a phonotactic analysis of the phonetic level. Anderson (1985: 212) notes that Boas's thinking about processes contains the idea of rule ordering, albeit in a diachronic sense, when talking about historically prior phonetic forms.

8.7.1 Edward Sapir

The next grand figure is Edward Sapir (1884–1939), a student of Boas, from whom he inherited an intense interest in the relation between language and culture. Sapir sees language as a mental phenomenon in which he was, as we will see, very different from his contemporary, Leonard Bloomfield, whom we turn to in the next section. He was well aware of the Prague School ideas through his correspondence with Trubetzkoy, who in turn held Sapir's work in high esteem. With reference to phonology, his mentalistic viewpoint entailed for him that phonology was an inner system; see Sapir (1925, 1933). As such Sapir therefore almost regarded the specific phonetic properties of phonemes as epiphenomenal. This did not preclude him from being a meticulous descriptive linguist who, again like Boas, studied various Native American languages, and as such he did not disregard taking note of phonetic details. He did not think of phonemes as being composed of smaller elements, like features, but did stress that they form a system, based on their contrastive patterning, distribution, and participation in morphological alternations. In particular, Sapir's interest in sequential phoneme combinations is noteworthy, since this syntagmatic aspect of phonological structure had not been the focus of the Prague School. He also allowed that different phonemes (his basic variants) could have overlapping phonetic realizations. Phonemic representations (basic variants) were related to the phonetic varieties by a system of rules, and Anderson (1985: 236ff.) shows that Sapir's practice uses, on the one hand, rules that state regularities over the surface phonetic forms and, on the other, rules that alter basic variants to bring them in line with the surface constraints. In other words, Sapir had adopted a kind of constraint and repair system (as found in some recent developments of generative phonology: see §8.9.2). Also, Sapir alluded to the notion of rule ordering, this time not merely as a diachronic concept (cf. Kenstowicz 1975).

8.7.2 Structuralism

8.7.2.1 *Leonard Bloomfield*

Leonard Bloomfield (1887–1949) was a pivotal figure in American linguistics.[9] Through his book *Language* (1933) and his teaching he influenced a whole generation of structuralist linguists, who, despite the fact that they were all strong individual figures

---

[9] See also §18.2 below.

with their own ideas, share a common core of assumptions that can be traced back to his influence. Of specific importance was his desire to turn linguistics into an empirical science, using exact methods focusing on the observable. He also stressed that linguistics had to be independent of other fields of science (such as psychology and physics). In this empirical stance, Bloomfield was influenced by behaviourism, which was promoted by John B. Watson. This meant that meaning was defined in term of the context in which utterances were produced, rather than in terms of mental concepts. But as such, meaning did not belong to language proper. As a consequence, meaning was to play no role in the analysis of language, except in the marginal sense that to establish phonemic contrast, two speech events should differ in meaning.

Bloomfield himself did not, in fact, write a great deal on phonology, and his work on Menomini phonology, apart from a short paper in 1939, was only published in 1962, after his death (see Bever 1963). He was well aware of the trends in Europe, both neogrammarian and structuralist, and with Pāṇini's work on Sanskrit (Bloomfield 1927). He shared with the Prague School the belief that phonemes (which he did not see as being composed of features) were units that abstract away from predictable properties. Unlike the Prague School, his focus was not on paradigmatic relations between phonemes, but on syntagmatic relations (which included some attention to syllable structure, especially in the work of later scholars like Pike; see below). Phonemes were identified in terms of their combinatorial properties (an influence from Sapir). Bloomfieldians saw phonology as comprising phonemics (the study of distinctive units) and phonetics (the study of the phonetic realization). This does not mean that phonemics and phonetics are seen as independent activities: rather, phonemics is derived from phonetics. At the same time, phonetics was not really seen as part of linguistics *per se*.

Bloomfield made a clear distinction between phonetic variations of phonemes and alternations between phonemes (mostly referred to as morphophonemics by the (post-) Bloomfieldians). Alternations do no enter into the identification of phonemes, because that would violate the hypothesis that phonemes must be derivable from local phonetic properties of words, not from comparing different words. Rather, they are treated as post-phonemic, i.e. as part of morphology, and within the class of morphophonemic rules various subclasses would be distinguished, much along the lines of the Kazan School and Trubetzkoy's work on alternations. Bloomfield explicitly introduced the concept of an underlying form (or basic alternant) and the idea of ordered rules which derive the surface form, although he did not attribute a psychological reality to such analyses (see Goldsmith 2008 and Kenstowicz 1975 for discussions of rule ordering in the pre-generative period). It did not escape Bloomfield's attention that the underlying form might be similar to a historically earlier form, but he explicitly states that the underlying form and the ordered rules are part of the synchronic description. Clearly, Bloomfield's conception of morphophonemics influenced generative phonology, with the difference that in this latter model morphophonemics is seen as the core of the phonological component (see §§8.9 and 8.11).

8.7.2.2 *The post-Bloomfieldians*

A sizeable number of American structuralists developed Bloomfield's approach to phonology, which indeed left much room for elaboration, and as a consequence there are many differences in the views of the post-Bloomfieldians, among which we also find former students of Sapir. Despite their differences, the post-Bloomfieldians formed a group that developed a new standard and a common language to discuss the analysis of language; all this came with an emancipation of linguistics as an autonomous academic discipline in the US, where formerly linguistics had been regarded as a branch of anthropology.

Initially, in the 1930s, the focus of discussion was on the nature of the phoneme and the manner in which to establish phoneme inventories, with important contributions by Morris Swadesh (1909–67) and W. Freeman Twaddell (1906–82); see Swadesh (1934, 1935), contained in the Makkai (1972) collection of many important works from this period. Twaddell (1935) discusses various understandings of the phoneme, psychological (as for de Courtenay and Sapir) or physical (as for Jones and Bloomfield). He himself decides on an 'instrumental approach' (as did Zellig Harris later). With reference to the manner in which phonemes can be established, several linguists developed elaborate schemes to minimize reference to even the notion of meaning difference. Other criteria such as phonetic similarity and pattern congruity were also widely discussed. Twaddell's own views were not followed, and the Post-Bloomfieldian linguists mostly settled on a view of the phoneme as a class of non-contrastive sounds (with phonetic similarity and complementary distribution being the key criteria), much as Daniel Jones had done (see §8.6.1).

Various phonologists produced detailed analyses of the phoneme system of English, e.g. Bloch and Trager (1942), Trager and Smith (1951). Other very well-known linguists of this generation are Zellig S. Harris (1909–92), Charles F. Hockett (1916–2000), and Kenneth L. Pike (1912–2000). Harris' important contribution was his discussion of 'long components,' which resembles Firth's prosodies and foreshadows today's autosegments. Hockett (1955) followed the Prague School in a number of ways: in recognizing a sub-phonemic distinctive feature analysis (initially in the form of unary features, which he later exchanges for binary features), and an interest in the typology of phonemic systems and general laws governing their organization. Pike's contributions lie in his attention to fieldwork methods, the practical implication of phonemic analysis for the development of writing systems, his explicit recognition and development of the unit syllable, and his detailed work on tone and intonation (see Pike 1947a, b, 1943, Pike and Pike 1947). He was in several ways a critic of the prevailing structuralist views, being more open to the mixing of levels and the reference to meaning. He also developed a multidimensional view in which language utterances would have three hierarchies, the phonological, the lexical, and the grammatical, with the phoneme, morpheme, and tagmeme ('word') as its basic units. This, of course, prefigures the distinction between a prosodic and morphosyntactic partitioning of sentences that we see today in generative phonology (see §8.9.2).

The post-Bloomfieldians favoured a strict inductive approach to language analysis, aiming at pure description and staying away from trying to find explanations. From this we can understand their emphasis on *discovery procedures* which would allow the linguist to motivate his analysis starting from the phonetic signals and proceeding step by step to higher levels of analysis.

A big difference between the post-Bloomfieldian approach and generative grammar lies in the switch from this inductive bottom-up approach (phonetics > phonemics > grammar) to a deductive top-down approach (grammar > phonemics (phonology) > phonetics) which means that in generative grammar, which permits mixing levels, phonology can make reference to grammatical information.[10] Furthermore, generative grammar no longer postulates the *bi-uniqueness condition* according to which the phonemic units and (sets of) the phonetic units stand in a one-to-one relationship. Neither the thesis of separation of levels nor the prohibition of phonemic overlap was part of Bloomfield's views, but rather became typical of post-Bloomfieldians (see Bloch 1941, 1948). Another difference between Bloomfield's approach (with underlying form and ordered rules) and that of his followers signals a shift from an 'item-and-process analysis' to an 'item-and-arrangement analysis' (Hockett 1954). Bloomfield's item-and-process model was recaptured by the generative phonologists who reacted most fiercely to the post-Bloomfieldian doctrines and practices, while not fully acknowledging their own debt to Bloomfield's work.

8.8 Developments in Europe

Meanwhile, one might wonder what was happening in the old world after the Prague School had made its impact in the 1930s and 1940s. This section offers some brief remarks on the development in continental western Europe and in the Soviet Union, which were influenced by major political turbulences such as the Russian Revolution and the Second World War.

8.8.1 Western Europe

Most phonologists in various countries in continental western Europe continued in the footsteps of de Saussure and the Prague School. Several important contributions to the development of the structuralist approach were made by André Martinet (1908–99), specifically in the area of relating phonemic systems to patterns of phonological

---

[10] A strict adherence to the bottom-up view did lead to the postulation of so-called juncture phonemes which in fact encoded grammatical information into the phonemic representation, but this was in itself problematic, in the sense that such juncture elements would often not be directly deducible from the phonetic signal. See Scheer (2011) for extensive discussion of these issues.

change. He stressed concepts like functional load, distance between phonemes (dispersion), and systematic 'harmony resulting from economy' (i.e. maximal use of features), and the opposing force due to the asymmetry of the articulatory organs.

On the whole, there was no other specific new theoretical development or major methodological shift. Rather, we see many discussions on important themes regarding the various dichotomies that de Saussure had set up. Fischer-Jørgensen (1975: ch.12) points out that several important works were written (by people who were not always associated with a clearly defined school) that examined the relationship between *langue* (phonology) and *parole* (phonetics). Authors like Coseriu (1952), Malmberg (1964), Gunnar Fant (specifically on distinctive features), and Martinet favoured a less radical separation of these two activities. Another theme regards the parallelisms between the content (meaning) and expression planes, which were emphasized by Hjelmslev. Interesting in this respect is an analogy seen by Jerzy Kuryłowicz (1895–1978) between the syllable and the sentence (Kuryłowicz 1948). See also Malmberg (1972) on hierarchical structure in both phonology and syntax and Haugen (1956) for important work on the syllable. It would seem that a close examination of phonological activity in Europe from the 1930s to the 1960s, up to the emergence of generative phonology, is missing.

8.8.2 Soviet Union

Both Fischer-Jørgensen (1975: ch.11) and Kortlandt (1972) provide detailed overviews of phonology in the Soviet Union on which this section is based. Two schools dominate the linguistic scene, the Leningrad School and the Moscow School, both developing ideas of Baudouin de Courtenay. Fischer-Jørgensen (1975) also mentions that until the Russian Revolution there were extensive contacts between scholars in Russia and the rest of Europe. The leading scholar in the Leningrad School was Lev Vladimirovič Ščerba (1880–1944), a student of Baudouin de Courtenay, who was well acquainted with de Saussure's work. This school focused its attention not on alternations but on the nature of the phoneme, adopting de Courtenay's psychological stance (phoneme as sound image) and stressing its communicative (i.e. distinctive) function. The idea that phonemes unite sounds that are in complementary distribution was adopted, but the concept of neutralization was not, which meant that this school embraced the 'once a phoneme always a phoneme' principle (like Jones and the post-Bloomfieldians). After Ščerba's death, Lev Rafailovich Zinder took the leading part in this school. In the 1920s and 1930s the Moscow School rose to prominence, opposing the doctrines of the Leningrad School. This school took inspiration from de Courtenay's approach to alternations, although they considered only phonetically conditioned alternations as important. For them this made neutralization a cornerstone concept. Both schools did not want to sharply separate phonology and phonetics. The controversy between these two schools went on, although various attempts were made in the late 1940s to bridge the gap, among others by S. I. Bernstein.

On the whole, the 1920s, 1930s, and 1940s were dominated by suppressive tendencies due to the influence of the politically correct linguist Nicholas Jakovlevich Marr (1864–1934) and his followers, until, due to an intervention of Stalin in the early 1950s, Marr's ideas were rejected, opening up possibilities for the development of new ideas (although Western structuralism was still considered degenerate). This created an opportunity for Sebastian K. Šaumjan to break with both schools and establish a completely new approach which essentially neglected (except for criticizing it) all previous work in the Soviet Union and built instead (despite this being controversial) on Western structuralism, as well as on modern logic and cybernetics. Šaumjan proposes his two-level theory of phonology that separates the level of observation from the level of constructs, these levels being related by rules of correspondence. This idea, of course, recaptures the principled distinction between phonology and phonetics, which was stressed by Hjelmslev. Šaumjan's 1962 book in Russian was translated in 1968 as *Problems of Theoretical Phonology*. In his work on syllable structure he makes comparisons between this unit and the structure of sentences (as Kuryłowicz and Malmberg had done before him). During the 1960s more and more Western structuralist theories became available in translations which influenced scholars. Fischer-Jørgensen (1975) notes that generative grammar has not been very influential. On the whole, Soviet phonology takes a great interest in mathematical models and formalized description (see Kortlandt 1972), but this interest pre-dates the emergence of Chomsky's work, being rooted in cybernetics and information theory of the 1940s and 1950s.

8.9 GENERATIVE PHONOLOGY[11]

8.9.1 Early Developments

Generative phonology broke with the post-Bloomfieldian dogma that phonological analysis had to be based on the local information available in specific utterances. It firmly rejected the prohibition on mixing levels and the bi-uniqueness condition (see Chomsky and Halle 1965). Most notorious is the elimination of the phonemic level as a necessary step in between the morphophonemic level and the surface phonetic output. The postulation of this level entailed circumstances in which the same generalization needs to be stated twice. This occurs when, for example, a process is neutralizing in some cases but allophonic in others. Halle (1959) points out that this loss of generalization is undesirable. This argument has often been referred to as involving the abandonment of the phoneme, but this is incorrect. By eliminating the distinction between the morphophonemic level and the phonemic level, we end up with one level that is phonemic in the sense that it encodes the properties of segments that are distinctive,

---

[11] This section is partly based on van der Hulst (2004).

abstracting away from all contextually predictable properties. See Anderson (2000) for a discussion of the history of this argument and various other aspects of the manner in which generative phonology settled in. See also Encrevé (1997, 2000) for a critical evaluation of the manner in which Generative Phonology presented itself as breaking with the preceding structuralist tradition, while perhaps understating the continuities with earlier work in American structuralism, especially with Bloomfield's work, but (as shown in Goldsmith 2008) also with some of the post-Bloomfieldians.

Generative Phonology embraced the distinctive feature theory developed by Jakobson (with the modification that features were now seen as primarily articulatory units), and combined it with a model that was very similar to Bloomfield's early ideas, in which alternations were treated in terms of a single underlying form and surface forms were derived by ordered rules. In contrast to Bloomfield, though, this derivational model was not seen as a mere analytic tool but as a realistic model for how language users process language.

The phonological theory developed in the early days of generative phonology, culminating in Chomsky and Halle's (1968) *The Sound Pattern of English* (*SPE*) focused mostly on the derivational aspect, i.e. on rule format, rule application, and rule ordering; see also Halle (1962) and Chomsky (1967) for earlier statements. With respect to the representational aspect, *SPE*'s theory was deliberately minimal: a phonological representation was a linear sequence of unordered and unstructured feature bundles, provided with morphosyntactic bracketing and boundary symbols. The *SPE* system was also minimal in the sense of recognizing only two levels and one rule type that mediates between them, which was essentially a transformational rule type, like the so-called transformations in syntactic theory. The complexity of the rule system resulted from two factors. Firstly, since few restrictions were imposed on the *rule format*, the rules could get quite complicated, especially since various notational conventions allowed collapsing seemingly independent rules. Secondly, since rules could be extrinsically ordered and no restrictions were imposed on the distance between input and output, derivations could get quite long and underlying forms quite remote from the surface.

It can be said that the explanatory goal of *SPE* was to relate as many surface forms as possible, where 'relating' means 'deriving from the same input form.' Hence, with rules that could *do* anything and input forms that could *be* anything, only 'poverty of imagination' stood in the way of deriving pater*nal* (minus suffix) and *father* from the same input source (cf. Lightner 1972). The absence of a morphological theory that could place formal and *semantic* limits on the notion of relatedness stimulated the creative quest for rather abstract 'common' sources. Clearly, with so much freedom, chances to arrive at real explanatory accounts diminished in inverse proportion to the depth of the derivations that were proudly proposed; see Dresher (2005) and Durand (2006) for assessments of the achievements of Generative Phonology.

8.9.2 Post-*SPE* developments[12]

The dialectal back and forth that Anderson (1985) sees in the development of phonology at large repeats itself *within* the history of generative phonology. While *SPE* devotes considerable space to a motivation of a set of distinctive features and various issues arising with redundancy and feature specification, it also proposes an explicit model of phonological derivations, and it was this derivational aspect that led to much discussion and criticism during the seventies.

The mentalistic side of the *SPE* model was also criticized in its own right, quite independently from the kinds of formal considerations that we discussed above; see Derwing (1973) and Linell (1979) for critical assessments. Overall, experimental work offered little confirmation of the derivational aspects of *SPE* analyses that the more concrete approaches (such as Natural Generative Phonology) were seeking to dismantle. In other words, experimental research and concerns with the restrictiveness of theory were going in the same direction. The continuing trend to doubt the psychological validity of *SPE* led to further developments.

Meanwhile, proponents of the *SPE* approach, having channeled some of the discussions concerning rule ordering and depth of derivations into the development of lexical phonology (Kiparsky 1982, 1985), had shifted their attention to the representational properties of the *SPE*-model. As of the mid–late 1970s and continuing during a good deal of the 1980s, a flow of new ideas concerning various aspects of phonological representations started dominating the phonological scene (cf. van der Hulst and Smith 1982a,b,c). The incentive for some of these developments came from the rejection of *SPE*'s ban on syllable structure (criticized in Vennemann 1971 and Fudge 1969), as well as, to some extent, from pre-*SPE* models that had argued for a parallel or syntagmatic organization in phonological representations, alongside vertical, syntagmatic organization (cf. Firth's prosodic analysis, 1948; Harris's long components, 1944).[13]

The 1990s were dominated by the approach called Optimality Theory (OT), a non-derivational, constraint-based approach to phonology. At first sight, it may seem odd to introduce a non-derivational theory as the main player in a decade that is, according to the prediction of the dialectic model, supposed to focus on derivational issues. However, OT is a theory about the relationship between lexical forms and output forms, and in that sense it concerns the derivational side of the theory. The above reference to 'non-derivational' as a property of OT refers to the fact that OT does not recognize or need so-called intermediate levels, as a consequence of there being no extrinsically ordered rules or sub-components (such as a lexical and post-lexical component).

---

[12] In this chapter I will not review the developments within generative phonology in great detail. I refer to van der Hulst (1979, 2004), van der Hulst and Smith (1982c, 1985b), and, in particular, to Scheer (2011).

[13] Dinnsen (1979) offers a collection of papers which reflect the diversity of approaches that were part of the generative enterprise by the mid-1970s.

The history of constraints in phonology does not start with OT, however. Constraint-based phonologies (or proposals moving in that direction) have been around for a long time. For a historical perspective on constraints in phonology, see Paradis and LaCharité (1993) and Bird (1995). OT instantiates a particular version of this approach with the specific property that constraints are violable (or 'soft'). This softness of constraints results from the possibility of imposing an extrinsic ordering on the constraints, allowing them to be violated in the output if higher-ranked constraints enforce this.

What are the current trends? On the whole, it would seem that the idea that one can study phonology without any consideration of substance is not considered tenable (if it ever was), just as an exclusive focus on substance would make phonetic research aimless. It is generally recognized that a scientific investigation of the speech chain must recognize several levels of analysis, which, although perhaps not strictly separated, give room to more discrete symbolic phonological units and structures as well as to gradient units and structures, including various types of processes at and transitional processes between levels. As stated in Cohn (2011), this is simply what the cognitive science of speech comprises. There is nothing wrong with some researchers being focused on certain distinct properties of certain phases of this chain, while others focus on the correspondences and transitions between phases.

I conclude this section with a remark on the relevance of sign languages.[14] In Stokoe (1960) it is proposed that the form of signs in ASL can be decomposed into meaningless building blocks. Stokoe's primary motive was thus to be able to design an alphabet for writing down signs, not in the first instance as a writing system for practical use by users of sign languages, but rather as an equivalent to the IPA system for spoken languages. Henceforth phonetics and phonology thus must be understood as the study of the *form* of linguistic signs (whether their medium is sound or sight). I refer to van der Hulst (1993), Brentari (1998), and Lillo-Martin and Sandler (2006) for further discussions of this important line of research.

8.10 CONCLUSION

There are two fundamental motivations for recognizing phonemes. On the one hand, phonemes are necessary as abstractions over sets of allophones. Interestingly, it can be said that in this respect phonology (which is so fundamentally based on the notion of contrast and the *emic*) emerged in contrast to (or special focus of) phonetics (the *etic*). This, at least, seems to be the case for the development of de Saussure's views and the view of the British phoneticians. The second motivation for phonemes lies in alternations, in allomorphy, which de Courtenay and Kruszewski focused on, and here it can

---

[14] See Ch. 3 above.

be said that phonology emerged as a separate focus of morphology. Various scholars in the history of phonology associated mainly with one or the other aspect of phonology, but some schools, specifically the Prague School and Generative Phonology, united both aspects into one theory, the former keeping a clear distinction between them, the latter merging both into one format. A feature common to both motivations is to move beyond the observable properties of words to underlying, cognitive structures as well as the communicative function of language.

Throughout the history of linguistics, we see how developments in phonology lay the foundation for approaches to other aspects of grammar. This is evident in the Prague movement, American structuralism, and even in early generative grammar, which, while being dominated by work in syntax, has its roots in dealing with alternations in terms of underlying forms and transformational rules that alter these into surface forms in a series of steps. Today, at least in generative grammar, phonology has been downgraded to an evolutionary afterthought which developed so that human thought could be externalized in observable form. It is, however, not clear whether this external-ization system is 'just phonology' rather than both syntax and phonology, while the internal system (the organization of thought) is something entirely different. It would seem that in the view of most linguists both syntax and phonology are systems for the externalization and communication of thought, which then puts these two systems on an equal footing, making it likely that both are based on similar structural principles. In this sense, phonological theories can and should continue to inspire the development of syntactic theories, as they always have.

Finally, even though there is much repetition in the literature and endless discussion on procedural issues that do not always seem meaningful in retrospect, it must be said that the founding fathers of phonology (i.e. the prominent members of the Kazan and Prague Schools), as well as Americans like Sapir and Bloomfield and some of the post-Bloomfieldians (such as Twaddell, Hockett, and Pike), did much more than laying the foundation for subsequent developments of which current generative approaches are the culmination. Unfortunately, much work in contemporary phonology is done with at best indirect knowledge or hearsay of very well-developed theories of predecessors. This, in part, is due to the fact that textbooks are usually theory-specific, while works such as Fischer-Jørgensen (1975) and Anderson (1985) are not 'required literature' and thus not widely read. Even phonological handbooks (such as Goldsmith 1995, Gold-smith et al. 2011, deLacy 2007, Kula et al. 2011) often lack sufficient historical perspective. A recently published compendium, van Oostendorp et al. (2011), which offers 120 survey articles in the field of phonology, offers some hope that current and prospective students of phonology will be directed to earlier work and not just to what has been published over the previous ten years.

CHAPTER 9

A HISTORY OF SOUND SYMBOLISM

MARGARET MAGNUS

9.1 OVERVIEW

9.1.1 The Problem with Sound Symbolism

The fundamental thesis underlying the field of sound symbolism has always been controversial, because it appears to be so transparently wrong. The Sound Symbolic Hypothesis is that the meaning of a word is partially affected by its sound (or articulation). If the sound of a word affects its meaning, then you should be able to tell what a word means just by hearing it. There should be only one language. In spite of this, there has always been a fairly substantial group of linguists who do not dismiss the possibility that the form of a word somehow affects its meaning. Many of those who we think of as 'great' prewar linguists (Bloomfield, Jakobson, Jespersen, Sapir, Firth) wrote works proposing that either the sound or the articulation of words has a synchronic, productive effect on their meaning.

9.1.2 Evidence

What sort of evidence have sound symbolists had for maintaining this position? Consider, for example, Lewis Carroll's *Jabberwocky*. You seem to be able to glean something from the meaning of nonsense words:

> 'Twas brillig, and the slithy toves
> Did gyre and gimble in the wabe;
> All mimsy were the borogoves,
> And the mome raths outgrabe.

Sound symbolists have, more often than not, been influenced by poetry. There seems to be some power inherent in the sound of words which is particularly accessible in poetry.

However, the evidence cited most frequently in support of the hypothesis is the fact that the distribution of phonemes across semantic classes is not random. J Firth (1935) coined the term 'phonaesthemes' for classes of words which are confined to a particular semantic space and whose members also are constrained by a particular phonological form. Phonaesthemes have been shown statistically to be quite pervasive throughout the languages of the world. Consider some examples from English.

- INTENTION HINDERED: around 40 per cent of monosyllabic words starting with /st/: *stall, stand, (fixed) star, stare, starve, stash, staunch, stave, stay, stem (tide), stew, stick, stifle, still, sting, stint, stone, stop, strain, strand, strangle, strap, (go on) strike, strip, stub, stuff, stumble, stump, stun, stunt, stutter*
- STICKING TOGETHER or STRIKING: around 50 per cent of monosyllabic words starting with /kl/: *claim, clam, clamp, clasp, claw, cleave, clench, clinch, cling, clutch; clog, clot, clump; clang, clank, clap, click, clink, clop; clan, class, clique, club; close*

Because words of a given phonestheme are not in general cognate, some principle other than etymological derivation appears to be operative. Maurice Bloomfield (1895: 409) described the dynamic thus:

> Every word, in so far as it is semantically expressive, may establish, by haphazard favoritism, a union between its meaning and any of its sounds, and then send forth this sound (or sounds) upon predatory expeditions into domains where the sound is at first a stranger and parasite. A slight emphasis punctures the placid function of a certain sound element, and the ripple extends, no one can say how far. [. . .] No word may consider itself permanently exempt from the call to pay tribute to some congeneric expression, no matter how distant the semasiological cousinship; no obscure sound-element, eking out its dim life in a single obscure spot, may not at any moment find itself infused with the elixir of life until it bursts its confinement and spreads through the vocabulary a lusty brood of descendants. [. . .] The signification of any word is arbitrarily attached to some sound element contained in it, and then congeneric names are created by means of this infused, or we might say, irradiated, or inspired element.

The history of sound symbolism is the history of the attempt to resolve this fundamental paradox: on the one hand, if sound determines meaning, we should know what a word means just by hearing it; on the other hand, the distribution of phonemes across semantic domains is not arbitrary.

9.1.3 The Overgeneralizations

Much of the uninteresting literature surrounding this debate can be traced back to two related overgeneralizations: the conventionalist overgeneralization and the naturalist overgeneralization. The conventionalist overgeneralization is that we cannot predict the referent of a given word in a given language from its form. There is therefore no synchronous, productive correlation whatsoever between the sound of a word and its meaning. This view presupposes that just because we cannot immediately see a correlation, none exists. It also presupposes that word semantics is monolithic and can be completely reduced to word reference. At the very least, most people accept that a word has a connotation as well as a denotation. The naturalists have all too often drawn the converse and equally untenable conclusion: the naturalist overgeneralization is that because some aspects of word semantics are derivable from phonetics, therefore all word semantics is derivable from phonetics.

9.1.4 Overview of Trends and Issues

If sound affects word meaning then it does so only in part, and one or more of the following must be true:

A. Sound affects meaning only in some words.
B. Sound modulates the basic meaning of the word.
C. Sound predisposes words to prefer certain referents.
D. Word meaning is decomposable into discrete parts, and sound affects only some aspects of the word meaning.

A number of other debates have preoccupied sound symbolists as well. For example:

E. Is sound-meaning in words a function of context? Does it arise only in *parole*, or do free-standing linguistic elements have sound meaning?
F. How far down the hierarchy does the sound–sense relationship go? Do syllable onsets have meaning? Do individual phonemes? Do phonetic features?
G. Are some languages influenced by sound-meaning more than others?
H. What influence has sound symbolism had on the evolution and origin of language?

9.2 PHILOSOPHICAL UNDERPINNINGS

9.2.1 Mythic Origins

Like most sciences, linguistics, and sound symbolism in particular, finds its origins in the mystical literature of the various traditions. In many traditions archetypal meanings were associated with the letters of the alphabet and used in mantras or oracles— the Viking Runes, the Hebrew Kabbalah, the Arab Abjad, the Upanishads, and so on.

9.2.2 Plato Defines the Problem

The first work that took a critical approach to the subject was Plato's *Cratylus* dialogue. In the first half of the *Cratylus*, Socrates takes issue with Hermogenes, who holds that sound has no effect on word meaning. Socrates provides a number of somewhat patchy examples of sound–meaning correlations. In the second half of the dialogue, Socrates takes on Cratylus, who holds the opposite—that a word's meaning is wholly determined by its sound. Socrates argues, for example, that if sound determined meaning, then the word for everything in every language would simply be the sound that it makes.

This dialogue raises all the major issues that run through the ensuing literature, and explains why the scientific study of language has kept sound symbolism at a distance. Socrates concludes that the essential nature of the correlation does not lie in mere imitation, or in onomatopoeia. Rather, it is an imitation of the *essence* of the thing to which the word refers.

The *essence* of a word or thing cannot be quantified scientifically in any obvious way. Worse, Socrates proposes that we mimic the abstract 'essence' of a concept or object in a completely different medium—that of sound. It is hard to imagine what, for instance, the essence of a chair is, and harder still to imagine how that chair essence might be represented as a sound. Not until the twentieth century were systematic methods applied which could address this dilemma.

It seems a logical conclusion of the position that Cratylus takes that some languages have chosen the right sounds and are therefore better than others: that all linguistic arbitrariness is a perversion of some great mimetic Truth. The sound symbolic literature is riddled with arguments that one or another language (typically the author's native tongue) is superior to all others.

9.2.3 The Dry Centuries

In the two millennia after Plato and prior to the seventeenth century, the subject was discussed almost exclusively in religious and mythical texts, particularly in the Kabbalistic and Indian traditions, which ascribed special significance to the name of God. What little critical discussion of the matter that is to be found seems to have focused on the *Cratylus*.

9.2.4 Locke vs Leibniz

Clearly by the middle of the seventeenth century, the naturalist vs conventionalist debate had some currency among intellectuals, because in 1690, John Locke took sides. He wrote in his *Essay Concerning Humane Understanding*:

Words [. . .] come to be made use of by Men, as the Signs of their Ideas; not by any
natural connection, that there is between particular articulate Sounds and certain
Ideas, for then there would be but one language amongst all Men; but by voluntary
Imposition, whereby such a Word is made arbitrarily the mark of such an Idea.
(book III, chapter II, paragraph 1, p. 4)

In 1704, Gottfried Wilhelm Leibniz published a point by point critique of Locke's book,
entitled *New Essays on Human Understanding*. He replies to this passage as follows:

[On the relationship between words and things, or rather on the origin of natural
languages] We can't claim that there is a perfect correspondence between words
and things. But reference isn't completely arbitrary either. There must be a reason
for having assigned a particular word to a particular thing. Languages are naturally
rooted in the harmony between its sounds and the effect impressed on the soul by
the spectacle of things. I tend to think that this foundation can be seen not only in
the first language, but in the languages that arose subsequently, in part from the first
one, and in part from new usages taken on by man over time and scattered across
the earth. (Leibniz 1981 [1704]: 291)

9.2.5 Eighteenth- and Nineteenth-Century Support from Outside the Field

The eighteenth and nineteenth centuries saw an explosion of popular interest in the
subject. Many Romantic philosophers, poets, writers, and Hermetics expressed sym-
pathy or provided sporadic evidence for the Sound Symbolic Hypothesis. These
included Alexander Pope, Emanuel Swedenborg, Novalis, Johann Wolfgang Goethe,
Honoré de Balzac, Ernest Renan, Ralph Waldo Emerson, Victor Hugo, Henry David
Thoreau, Rudolf Steiner, Lewis Carroll, Joseph von Eichendorff, Arthur Rimbaud, Paul
Claudel, and Marcel Proust.

9.2.6 Mimesis in France

In the late eighteenth and early nineteenth centuries, there was also a scholarly
tradition of mimesis in France, the original manuscripts of which are hard to come
by. According to Gérard Genette and Earl R. Anderson, Charles de Brosses, in *Traité de
la formation mécanique des langages* (1765), argued that there existed a perfect primeval
language which was 'organic, physical and necessary' and in which the sound conformed wholly to the meaning of the words. It was corrupted with time, resulting in our
modern Babel. A few years later, in 1775, Antoine Court de Gébelin in *Origine du
langage et de l'écriture* took the position, like Cratylus, that all semantics is imitation.
Speculations of this nature got so out of hand that in 1866 the Société de linguistique de
Paris saw fit to ban research into the related debates on the origins of language.

9.2.7 Wilhelm von Humboldt

In 1836 Wilhelm von Humboldt published a very important work on sound symbolism entitled *Über die Verschiedenheit des menschlichen Sprachbaues und ihren Einfluß auf die geistige Entwicklung des Menschengeschlechts*. In it, he delineates three types of sound–meaning relationships in language. This distinction turns out to be very useful.

The first type is what is generally known as onomatopoeia. It is based in acoustics rather than articulation, and is limited to those referents which emit a sound. Because onomatopoeia is the most accessible form of sound meaning, it is the best known. But it is also the least pervasive form (von Humboldt 1999: 73).

> The directly imitative, where the noise emitted by a sounding object thing is portrayed in the word.

The second class most closely resembles Socrates' notion of sound symbolic imitation: imitation of a semantic 'essence' by the actual articulation of the speech sound. If this type of relationship could be shown to hold, it would have to hold universally (which is to say that all words would to some degree be affected by it, though of course not entirely determined by it) Humboldt's definition bears some resemblance to Charles S. Peirce's 'iconism' which later informed Roman Jakobson's thinking on sound symbolism, as well as to the phenomenon known as synesthesia (ibid.).

> The designation that imitates, not directly, but by means of a third factor which is common to both the sound and the object. [. . .] It selects, for the objects to be designated, sounds which, partly in themselves and partly by comparison with others, produce for the ear an impression similar to the that of the object upon the soul, as *stand, steady, stiff* give the impression of fixity; the Sanskrit *li* melt and dispersal, that of dissolution; *not, nibble* and *nicety* gives the impression of finely and sharply penetrating. In this way objects that evoke similar impressions are assigned words with predominately the same sounds such as *waft, wind, wisp, wobble* and *wish*, wherein all the wavering, uneasy motion, presenting an obscure flurry to the senses, is expressed by the w, hardened from the already inherently dull and hollow u. This type of designation, which relies upon a certain significance attaching to each individual letter, and to whole classes of them, has undoubtedly exerted a great and possibly exclusive dominance on primitive word-designation. Its necessary consequence was bound to be a certain likeness of designation throughout all the languages of mankind, since the impression of objects would have everywhere to come into more or less the same relationship to the same sounds. Much of this can still be observed in languages even today, and must in fairness prevent us from at once regarding all the likeness of meaning and sound to be encountered as an effect of communal descent.

Humboldt's third class of sound meaning is 'clustering,' to use Weinreich's (1963) terminology. It is clustering which gives rise to the phenomenon of phonaesthemes, and Humboldt points out that this phenomenon, unlike the former, can only be understood in terms of the system of language as a whole. Furthermore, it is arbitrary in the sense that the quality of the sound is not in general organically linked to the concept it represents (von Humboldt 1999: 74).

> Words whose meanings lie close to one another, are likewise accorded similar sounds; but in contrast to the type of designation just considered, there is no regard here to the character inherent in these sounds themselves. For it is true emergence, this mode of designation presupposes verbal wholes of a certain scope in the system of sounds, or at least can be applied more extensively only in such a system. It is, however, the most fruitful of all, and the one which displays with most clarity and distinctness the whole concatenation of what the intellect has produced in a similar connectedness of language.

Humboldt gave the following account of the sound symbolic process (p. 75).

> But since language-making finds itself here in a wholly intellectual region, at this point also there develops, in a quite eminent way, yet another, higher principle, namely the pure and—if the term may be allowed—quasi-naked *sense of articulation*. Just as the effort to lend meaning to sound engenders, as such, the nature of the articulated sound, whose essence consists exclusively in this purpose, so the same effort is working here towards a determinate *meaning*. This determinacy becomes the greater as the field of the designandum still hovers effectively before the mind; for the field is the soul's own product, though it does not always enter, as the whole, into the light of consciousness. The making of language can thus be more purely guided here by the endeavour to distinguish like and unlike among concepts, down to the finest degree, by choice and shading of sounds. The purer and clearer the intellectual view of the field to be designated, the more the making of language feels itself to be compelled to let itself be guided by this principle; and its final victory in this part of its business is that principle's complete and visible dominance.

9.3 THE EVOLUTION OF EMPIRICAL METHODS

Since the Sound Symbolic Hypothesis appears to be so transparently contradicted by the facts of language, the burden of proof has lain with those who would maintain it. To this end, the phenomenon had to be defined in such a way that statistical methods could be applied to it. These did not really evolve until the twentieth century. The language of Humboldt perhaps renders a better intuitive feel for the fundamental sound symbolic experience than most of the literature written in the twentieth century, but it did not provide the empirical foundation necessary to either prove or disprove the Hypothesis.

9.3.1 John Wallis: the First List of Phonesthemes

In 1653, John Wallis published a list of English phonesthemes in his *Grammatica linguae anglicanae*, including for example (according to Gennette 1976: 37):

- wr shows obliquity or twisting: wry, wrong, wreck, and wrist, 'which twists itself and everything else in all directions.'
- br points to a breach, violent and generally loud splitting apart: break, breach, brook.

Wallis argued that in some words, the bulk of their semantics could be analysed down to a combination of their phonaesthemes. For example, in the word *sparkle*, the initial 'sp' indicates dispersion (*spit, splash, sprinkle*); the medial 'ar' represents high-pitched crackling; the 'k' is a sudden interruption; and the final 'l', frequent repetition (*wiggle, wobble, battle, twiddle, mottle*).

9.3.2 Charles Nodier: the First Dictionary of Phonaesthemes

In 1808 the young Charles Nodier produced the first sound-symbolic dictionary—his *Dictionnaire raisonnée des onomatopées françaises*. The dictionary included such entries as (according to Gennette 1976: 132): BEDON [potbelly], onomatopoeia of the noise of a drum; BIFFER [to scratch out], noise made by a quill pen passed rapidly over paper; BRIQUET [tinder], noise of two hard bodies that violently collide with each other, breaking one into pieces. Nodier's dream was to create the perfect sound symbolic language. Plato felt that Greek was the most perfect language. Vedic scholars argue the same for Sanskrit. Wallis found English to be superior. De Brosses argued for a perfect *primordial* language (albeit closely resembling French). The Kabbalists claimed that Ancient Hebrew is the perfect tongue, and so on and so forth. Nodier's dream of a perfect language, however, lay in the future rather than in the past or present. By 1834, in his *Notions élémentaires de linguistique,* Nodier changes his mind about the possibility of a perfect language; he has by then joined Plato in making the disconcerting assumption that the sound affects not so much what the word refers to but rather what it is like.

9.3.3 Leonard Bloomfield: the First Comprehensive Lexical Analysis

In 1909 and 1910, Leonard Bloomfield wrote 'A Semasiological Differentiation in Germanic Secondary Ablaut.' It contained the first body of data which was sufficiently comprehensive that it could in principle disprove the Sound Symbolic Hypothesis. Leonard Bloomfield's list of Germanic roots is basically complete. It therefore cannot be maintained that he picked out certain words or phoneme combinations that supported his case and conveniently omitted the others. For the first time it became possible to quantify the degree of the correlation, and this was the first step toward broadening the discussion from philosophy and speculation to science. In fact, his results did not disprove the hypothesis, but supported it.

> If a word containing some sound or noise contains a high pitched vowel like i, it strikes us as implying a high pitch in the sound or noise spoken of; a word with a low vowel like u implies low pitch in what it stands for . . . Its far reaching effects on our vocabulary are surprising. It has affected words not only descriptive of sound like E[nglish] *screech, boom* . . . but also their more remote connotative effects. A high tone implies not only shrillness, but also fineness, sharpness, keenness; a low tone not only rumbling noise, but also bluntness, dullness, clumsiness; a full open sound like a, not only loudness, but also largeness, openness, fullness. (Bloomfield 1909, 1910: 249)

Bloomfield itemizes *all* the major roots in Germanic in order of the consonant sounds: first /pVp/ (Norwegian *pipla, pupla*; English *peep, pip, pipple*), then /pVf/ (Swedish *piff, paff, puff*; English *piff, piffle, piffer, paffle, puff*) and so on, and he demonstrates that these phonologically based groupings are not semantically random. Furthermore, the correlations he observes hold throughout the entire vocabulary of Germanic. In the end, he regarded sound meaning as so fundamental that he wrote in *Language* (1933: 27):

> Since in human speech, different sounds have different meaning, to study the coordination of certain sounds with certain meanings is to study language.

9.3.4 Additional Comprehensive Lexical Studies

Since Bloomfield, a variety of studies have been conducted which test sound–meaning correlations on the existing vocabulary of many languages, to name a few: Abelin (1998), Swedish; Cubrovic (1999), English; Etzel (1983), cross-linguistic; Hisao et al. (1998), Japanese; McCune (1985), Indonesian; McPherson (1995), English; Poldervaart (1989), Paiute; Lawler and Rhodes (1981–2006), English; Sadasivam (1966), Tamil; Veldi (1988), Estonian, English; Voronin (1969), English, Russian.

To my knowledge, all the empirical tests that have appeared in the literature in fact support the Sound Symbolic Hypothesis. Suitbert Ertel's (1972) work is a good example of a comprehensive study employing the inverse of Bloomfield's methodology. Like Bloomfield's, Ertel's survey was a cross-linguistic study of existing vocabulary. However rather than taking vocabulary as a starting point, Ertel started with semantic domains, and tested the degree to which the phonemes of words in these semantic domains were random or predictable. He selected four fairly narrow domains: verbs of sound, verbs of motion, verbs for actions performed with the mouth, and verbs for sound produced by animals. He then selected 175 German words in these four semantic classes, and had them translated into 36 languages covering most of the major language families of the world. Finally he counted the frequency with which phonemes occurred in each of these verbs, and found that certain sounds occurred much more frequently in conjunction with certain verbs than one would anticipate if the relationship between sound and meaning were arbitrary. For example, gargling is expressed predominantly with voiced velar sounds, spitting with labials and unvoiced plosives, and so on and so forth. Because Ertel's tests were applied across a broad range of languages, and not to the Germanic languages alone, they suggest that sound meanings are not mere side-effects of linguistic change, but that they are synchronically productive in modern languages and on some level universal. Three of the four classes of verbs that Ertel researched concerned the mouth—classes which one would perhaps expect to be especially strongly influenced by mimetics.

9.3.5 Psycholinguistic Experiments

The above-mentioned studies document sound–sense correlations in existing vocabulary. Throughout the twentieth century another type of empirical study has been conducted which investigates native speakers' intuitions about nonsense words or isolated sounds. These studies provide evidence that the phenomenon is a living principle which actively affects the use of language.

Edward Sapir began as a conventionalist who then converted to a naturalist position after running several such experiments. He was one of the first to query native speaker intuitions about nonsense or foreign words in order to determine whether there was a productive correlation between sound and meaning. He described the purpose of his inquiry thus:

> We may legitimately ask if there are, in the speech of a considerable number of normal individuals, certain preferential tendencies to expressive symbolism not only in the field of speech dynamics (stress, pitch and varying quantities), but also in the field of phonetic material as ordinarily understood... The main object of the study is to ascertain if there tends to be a feeling of the symbolic magnitude value of certain differences in vowels and consonants, regardless of the particular associations due to the presence of these vowels and consonants in meaningful words in the language of the speaker. (Sapir 1929: 228)

Sapir asked approximately 500 English-speaking subjects of all ages 60 questions of the following type: 'The word "mal" and the word "mil" both mean "table" in some language. Which type of table is bigger—"mal" or "mil"?' 83 per cent of the children and 96 per cent of adults consistently found 'i' to be smaller and 'a' to be bigger. Sapir did not believe the feeling-tone that exists in words to be inherent to them, but characterized it rather as a 'sentimental growth on the word's true body.'

By testing the intuitions of English-speaking subjects, Stanley Newman (1933) showed that English vowels could be placed on a scale of small to large, and that the size associated with each vowel reflected the size of the oral cavity during articulation. However, when he came to analyse 500 extant English words, he found no correlation between specific vowels and size. Maxime Chastaing (1962) ran twelve types of tests, all of which showed that people intuitively associate clarity with high front vowels and obscurity with low back vowels. Numerous other tests of this nature have been conducted. Tsuru (1934) had native English speakers guess the meanings of 36 Japanese antonyms, and found that they guessed correctly much more than 50 per cent of the time. Allport (1935) translated the Japanese words into Hungarian and repeated the experiment in order to filter out the possibility that Tsuru had subconsciously chosen words which bore some resemblance to related forms in English. The results were the same for Hungarian as for Japanese. Wissemann (1954) showed that when asked to invent words for noises which they heard, German speakers tended to associate certain phonemes with certain sounds rather than with others. Fischer-Jørgensen (1967) interviewed 150–200 students in various experiments asking them to classify Danish vowels, and found that people intuitively classify vowels as having brightness and hue, but not saturation. Others who undertook experiments of this type include Brown et al. (1955), Maltzmann et al. (1956), Brackbill and Little (1957), Baindurashvili (1957), Miron (1961), Weiss (1964), Péterfalvi (1965 [1970]), Smolinsky (2001).

9.4 TWENTIETH-CENTURY DETRACTORS

9.4.1 Structuralism: de Saussure

Although the contingency for a synchronic sound–meaning relationship prior to the Second World War was in general stronger than it has been for most of the latter half of the twentieth century, the field was by no means unified. The most celebrated opponent of the sound symbolic hypothesis was, of course, Ferdinand de Saussure (1916). In his chapter entitled 'Nature of the Linguistic Sign', the second section heading reads unabashedly '*First principle: the sign is arbitrary*.' He goes on:

> The link between signal and signification is arbitrary. Since we are treating a sign as the combinations in which a signal is associated with a signification, we can express this more simply as: the linguistic sign is arbitrary. There is no internal connection between the idea 'sister' and the French sequence of sounds s-ö-r which acts as its signal. The same idea might well be represented by any other sequence of sounds. This is demonstrated by differences between languages, and even by the existence of different languages. [. . .] The principle stated above is the organizing principle for the whole of linguistics.
>   The arbitrary nature of the linguistic sign was adduced above as a reason for conceding the theoretical possibility for linguistic changes. But more detailed

consideration reveals that this very same feature tends to protect a language against any attempt to change it. (de Sanssure 1962 [1916]: 67)

Saussure's assertion presupposes that word meaning is a single monolithic thing—the word's referent. Saussure himself made a hobby of sound symbolism. His notebooks are extensively cited in Jean Starobinski (1979). Thaïs Morgan writes in the introduction to the English translation of Genette (1976: xxv):

> Yet even Saussure, the founder of structural linguistics, who introduced the notion of 'arbitrariness' of the sign or its relative freedom from ties to the phenomenal world, also enthusiastically engaged in mimologics. Intrigued by what he called 'anagrams' and 'paragrams', Saussure filled many notebooks with eponymic analyses of Vedic and Homeric verses and inscriptions, discovering the names of ancient gods and heroes mysteriously concealed in letters and sounds.

9.4.2 The Generative Tradition

Whereas most linguists prior to the rise of transformational generative grammar probably held that some level of sound symbolism was operative in language, the field felt itself to be somewhat embattled throughout the last four decades of the twentieth century. This is primarily attributable to the fact that generative linguistics followed Saussure in denying any natural relationship between sound and meaning in language. This attitude was rooted in its emphasis on universals, its lack of emphasis on semantics, and its view that the function of linguistics is to study grammar rather than language.

Suitbert Ertel observes that sound symbolism is not easily reconcilable with Saussurian structuralism or with Chomskian generativism, for the reason that both of these view language as

> a product of the mind which can be separated from psychological reality [. . .] an objective image which transcends the individual, or as an autonomous generative system, which employs the mental organization of the individual merely as a vehicle. (Ertel 1972: 1)

In other words, one of the difficulties that certain branches of linguistics have had in accepting the Sound Symbolic Hypothesis is that sound symbolism presupposes a view of language in which semantics cannot be abstracted away from language itself.

Roman Jakobson was probably the most influential sound symbolist of the latter half of the twentieth century. He felt that many distinctions, including the distinction between form and meaning drawn by structuralists and generativists (whom he considered to be descendants of the structuralists), were not entirely valid. The interrelatedness of form and content was a theme that ran through all of Jakobson's later work.

Roman Jakobson and Linda Waugh wrote a major work entitled *The Sound Shape of Language* (1979) which was in some ways a response to Chomsky and Halle's *Sound Pattern of English* (1968), addressing what they felt had been overlooked in generative phonology. Because they did not consider form to be distinct from content, they could not agree with the structuralists and generativists that parole was secondary to langue. To Jakobson and Waugh, *langue* was as much influenced by *parole* as the converse. While the generativists were emphasizing innateness, they emphasized pragmatics—language exists for a reason, and that reason lies in the domain of *parole* more than *langue*. It was in context, in the activity of speaking, that the influence of form on content could most truly be recognized.

9.5 TWENTIETH-CENTURY SUPPORT FROM OUTSIDE THE FIELD

Edward Sapir and Benjamin Whorf established the principle of linguistic relativity—that the language you speak affects how you think—though the evidence that Whorf (1956) provided was not sound symbolic. Rather, he said that different languages impose different conceptual landscapes in terms of which we necessarily express ourselves. A number of leading philosophers who were born near the end of the nineteenth century or the beginning of the twentieth took issue with structuralism or the schism implied between signifier and signified. These included Ludwig Wittgenstein, Ernst Cassirer, Owen Barfield, and Jacques Derrida. They founded diverse movements and espoused diverse philosophies, but their systems of thought overlapped on this point.

9.5.1 Poets and Writers

Velemir Khlebnikov was a Russian futurist poet. His verse consisted mostly of words of his own invention, superficially similar to those in James Joyce's *Finnegans Wake*. However, he also wrote purely linguistic works outlining the correlations he had observed between Russian phonemes and their meaning. He even produced a list of Russian phonemes followed by a brief semantic characterization of each. For example: v—the return of one point to another (a circular path); m—the breaking up of volume into infinitely small parts; s—the departure of points from out of one immovable point; z—the reflection of light from a mirror (Khlebnikov 1987: 481).

9.5.2 Charles Sanders Peirce

Roman Jakobson referred to Peirce as 'the most universal and inventive of American thinkers.' Peirce provided Jakobson with the key that he could use to resolve the paradox of sound symbolism. He did this by distinguishing different levels of the sign—that is, by recognizing that the word embodies more than the obvious arbitrariness of word reference, and that word meaning can be divided into distinct types, some of which may be influenced by the word's form and others not. Peirce (1931) distinguished three types or levels of signs:

- *Level 1 or Firstness*: Iconic. On this level there is no distinction between what a thing is and what it represents.
- *Level 2 or Secondness*: Indexical. On this level, a sign by its nature points to something else, as smoke is an index of fire. But with Peirce, secondness runs much deeper than merely this. Secondness is quite generally the introduction of the 'other.'
- *Level 3 or Thirdness*: Symbolic. This in his view corresponded to the word's referent.

Only the third level is truly arbitrary. On the first and second levels, word meaning was, in fact, influenced by form. On the first level, the influence was direct and visceral, not learned, but immediate. Jakobson distinguished between a direct relation between sound and meaning focused in the right hemisphere of the brain, and 'double articulation,' or an indirect, left hemisphere relationship, such as one finds in poetry, mythology, sound symbolism, and synaesthesia, though he did not correlate these in any way with Humboldt's classification.

9.5.3 Synesthesia

Synesthesia is an involuntary neurological condition wherein the senses are intermingled. Many types of synesthesia have been documented. Synesthetes may associate sounds with particular motions or shapes, or they may associate colours with speech sounds. The phenomenon was first documented medically in the nineteenth century. Fechner (1871) did the first empirical study of 73 synesthetes who correlated colours with letters, and the field flourished briefly in the 1880s and 1890s (see e.g. Galton 1883, Binet and Philippe 1892, Calkins 1893). In the 1980s, the field experienced a flowering led by Lawrence Marks, Richard Cytowic, Simon Baron-Cohen, Sean A. Day and others. Today it is the subject of a whole branch of research. Synesthesia tends to run in families (Lauret 1887, Klinkowström 1890). It can be triggered by stroke, drug use, or epilepsy, and it is more prevalent in autistic people than in neurotypical people (Tammet 2007). A number of researchers have speculated that linguistic iconism—the capacity that we have to make sense of Lewis Carroll's *Jabberwocky*, for instance—is a form of synesthesia, that we all have a form of synesthesia, but that in some people it is conscious (see Day 2001, Ramachandran and Blakeslee 1998).

9.6 Trends in Twentieth-Century Sound Symbolism

9.6.1 Morphemes as Minimal Meaning-bearing Units

Throughout the history of the field, different views have been held as to what the smallest meaning-bearing units are. Bloomfield assigned meanings to consonant combinations within the syllable (see §9.3.3). Hans Marchand (1959) assigned them to individual phonemes, but he also found that the meaning of a phoneme depended on its position within the syllable. And Ivan Fónagy in *Die Metaphern in der Phonetik* (1963) documented the meanings which poets and philosophers have intuitively assigned to individual phonemes throughout history, finding that characterizations overlapped to a great degree. Humboldt said that meaning could be assigned to classes of sounds, and Jakobson assigned meanings all the way down to the phonetic features.

Dwight Bolinger of Harvard University was one of the primary Western proponents of sound symbolism through the late 1940s and 1950s. In 1949, he published 'The Sign Is Not Arbitrary,' and in 1950, 'Rime, Assonance and Morpheme Analysis,' in which he concluded that morphemes cannot be defined as the minimal meaning-bearing units, in part because 'meaning' is so ill-defined, and in part because in some situations smaller units are clearly meaning-bearing (p. 119).

> We need not limit ourselves to pairs, but may look for larger patterns. One tempting example is the cross-patterning of /gl/ 'phenomena of light' and /fl/ 'phenomena of movement' with (1) /itr/ 'intermittent', (2) /ow/ 'steady' and (3) /ur/ 'intense': glitter↔flitter, glow↔flow, glare↔flare [. . .] as for the terminal 'morphemes' in the above words, we find (1) evidenced also in titter, jitter, litter, iterate; (2) in slow, grow and tow and (3) in blare, stare and tear.

Bolinger argued that one should regard at least the assonance and the rime of a monosyllabic root as 'sub-morphemes,' on the basis that virtually all English assonances and rimes were found in the context of much narrower meanings than one would expect statistically.

Rhodes and Lawler (1981) pursued this line of reasoning further, suggesting that a word has an abstract meaning which consists of the meanings of their composite assonances and rimes. The assonance, they argued, serves as the modifier, and the rime serves as the head. As support for this proposal, they analyse several words in both Ojibwe and English in which the true semantics of a word as it is used in practice is not derivable from the sum of its concrete senses, but encompasses something broader than these from which the senses derive by a process of athematic metaphor.

Keith McCune was a student of Rhodes and Lawler. He applied their methods to an entire vocabulary and expanded on the theory of athematic metaphors. In McCune (1985), he demonstrated that virtually every word in Indonesian can be decomposed into assonances and rimes which are constrained in limited semantic domains. The basic underlying definition of a word was to be extended to individual senses by means of three well-defined semantic processes—subgroups, metaphors, and Levi extensions.

9.6.2 Sound Symbolism and Historical Linguistics

One of the most obvious arguments for the arbitrariness of the sign is that regular sound change would be impossible if it were constrained by linguistic iconism. If Latin /p/s correspond to Germanic /f/s, how can it possibly be maintained that /p/ means one thing and /f/ another, and that this distinction is largely based on articulation and is therefore essentially universal or cross-linguistic? Yakov Malkiel addressed this issue in a number of articles which reappeared in an anthology in 1990. He argued that, although there is regular sound change, a lot is going on behind the scenes in the process of sound change that is not generally acknowledged. For example, often when languages undergo dramatic sound shifts, much of the vocabulary also undergoes semantic shifts allowing the new forms to appear in contexts that they could not previously appear in. In some cases words fall out of the vocabulary once their phonological structure is no longer appropriate to its meaning, and new forms are picked up through various forms of analogy, metaphor, etc. from words which exist and have more appropriate phonological structures. Robin Allott (1995) also takes issue with some of the presumptions of historical linguistics by pointing out that without even taking this into consideration, a large portion of the basic vocabulary in English is of either unknown, questionable, or onomatopoeic origin.

9.6.3 African Ideophones

Westermann (1927) and Doke (1931) observed correlations between sound and meaning in African languages. Doke introduced the notion of the 'ideophone' for Bantu languages, which he called a 'radical' and which inspired a whole body of literature in African linguistics. The ideophones are a grammatical classification of words whose function is iconic. These words are not limited to sound imitation, but extend to people, manners, actions, states, colours, and so forth. Doke defines the radical as 'a word, often onomatopoetic, which describes a predicate or qualificative in respect to manner colour, sound, state or action.' He distinguished it from the adverb, which describes in respect to 'manner, place or time.' The radicals, he says, are found in great numbers in Bantu, and pattern differently syntactically and morphologically from other parts of speech.

William Samarin did a significant amount of ideophone research. He was particularly concerned with methods of identifying the specific meaning of an ideophone in a way that is comprehensible to non-native Bantu speakers. This proves to be a non-trivial task requiring very sophisticated lexicographic methods. Other major researchers in this field include Awolyale (1981), Childs (1988), Maduka (1988, 1981), Mamphwe (1987), Mphande and Rice (1989), and von Staden (1974).

Roger Williams Wescott was one of the most prolific researchers on the subject of linguistic iconism during the 1960s and 1970s. He published many articles about specific correlations between sound and meaning that he had observed in English and in African languages, primarily Bini and Igbo. He remains perhaps the only researcher who united the African tradition of linguistic iconism with the Western tradition of sound symbolism. Wescott was also a poet and an anthropologist. His research often goes into language origins, the relationship between animal communication and human speech, and orthographic iconism. Dwight Bolinger, in the introduction to *Sound and Sense* (Wescott 1980), describes him as having the 'most irrepressible imagination to be found among serious scholars.'

9.6.4 Poetics

Grammont (1930) conducted an empirical study of great poetry correlating moods with phonemes. His book is divided into various 'ideas'—repetition, accumulation, sorrow, joy, irony, silence, smallness, etc. Grammont provides examples from great poetry exhibiting each of these 'ideas' and shows how they are expressed with the same types of sounds in the poetry not only of France, but also of other countries. These correspondences, he felt, were not in most cases purely onomatopoeic. He describes his intentions thus (p. 195):

> What is the sound of an abstract idea or of a sentiment? With what vowels or with what consonants can the poet paint them? The very question seems absurd. But it isn't. [. . .] One can paint an idea with sounds: everyone knows that we do it in music, and poetry, though strictly speaking not music, actually is to a certain degree (as we shall later) a kind of music; vowels being musical notes of a sort.

Grammont observes that any ordinary French phrase can of course be rendered in any other language, but that an element of meaning prevails in poetry which makes it inaccessible to precise translation, and this he considers to be the contribution that sound makes to meaning. He therefore sees some utterances as more mimetic and therefore superior to others. He also, however, finds sound symbolism not only to be a function of *parole*; rather, the phonemes have meanings implicit in them. He argues at some length that the fact that a phoneme's meaning is very broad does not mean that it has no semantics at all: since there are so few phonemes, one would expect each to have a broad meaning.

Jakobson's view on the interrelatedness of sound and meaning was strongly influenced by his studies in poetics. He studied poetry throughout his life, and especially in later years, he wrote numerous analyses of poems, in which he sought to get at what it was about the interrelations and juxtapositions of sound that gave the poem its effect. Jakobson's thought resembled Grammont's in that to him, poetry existed when a writer was being attentive to the effect of form on content.

Poetics has always been a source of fascination for linguists. Its study tends to be focused on how the form of a poem affects its content, and its practitioners are both numerous and varied, including Barthes (1980), Chvany (1986), Fónagy (1961), Hiraga (1993, 2000), Hofstadter (1997), Oliver (1994), Pinsky (1999), Prokofieva (1995), Ross (1986, 1991), Tsur (1992), and Whissel (1999).

9.7 CONCLUSION

Only one full-length history of sound symbolism has ever been published—Genette (1976). In 450 pages, Genette colourfully details the evolution of linguistic iconism among both linguists and poets, in syntax, morphology, and phonology. He presents all the primary concepts and paradoxes that have determined the evolution of the field, and follows them over time. He also discusses a number of related issues—the preoccupation with orthography and language origins, the relationship between sound symbolism and etymology, the sociology of the field, and so forth. In writing this chapter, I have frequently relied on him, particularly for sources which are hard to get direct access to. I have also made much use of the historical overview in Earl R. Anderson's *Grammar of Iconism* (1998).

CHAPTER 10

....

EAST ASIAN
LINGUISTICS

....

KAREN STEFFEN CHUNG

10.1 BACKGROUND AND CONTEXT
....

THIS entry outlines the linguistic traditions of China, Korea and Japan, with special emphasis on China. Genetically, Chinese is a Sino-Tibetan language, unrelated to Korean and Japanese. Korean and Japanese are commonly lumped together in the 'Altaic' phylum ('phylum' being superordinate to 'family') of languages, with some scholars even believing they are distantly related to the Turkic, Mongolic, and Tungusic families, though there is little if any proof for this based on shared native vocabulary with regular phonological correspondences. On the other hand, all the languages in the Altaic phylum share great similarities in their syntactic structure; all are agglutinative.

The story of the development of linguistic thought in East Asia centers to a great extent on each country's response to influence from a respected non-related language. In the case of China before the period of European influence, it was Sanskrit, the language of the Buddhist scriptures; for Korea and Japan, it was Chinese, and to a lesser degree also Sanskrit. Both Korean and Japanese borrowed vocabulary extensively from Chinese, as well as the Chinese writing system, and in more recent times, Chinese has borrowed heavily back from Japanese (Chung 2001), reflecting the ebb and flow of power between the countries. Korean and Japanese both later developed their own writing systems. This account traces the transmission, acquisition, and subsequent development of writing, both as a tool in its own right and as a medium for spreading literature, religious ideas, and learning. Mention of one example of a philosophical text on language is included in the case of China. Short introductions are provided for China and Japan on the beginnings of Western-style grammar studies, which do not appear in any of the three cultures examined here until the nineteenth century, under European influence. Finally, a number of modern language-related issues, such as the establishment of a national language or writing system, are briefly touched on.

10.2 CHINA

The history of linguistic thought in China, as in any other culture that has reached a certain level of development, can be approached in two ways: by examining implicit, applied knowledge of language on the one hand, and by surveying records of self-conscious, explicit thought about language on the other. Much of the history of linguistics in East Asia must in fact be constructed from texts and examples of applied language rather than linguistic writings *per se*. And in China, certain subfields of linguistic thought, such as lexicography, poetic prosody, phonology, and character etymology, have from an early period received much more attention than other areas, such as syntax. Rather than trying to force a preset idea of what linguistic thought 'should' be, it perhaps makes more sense to examine whatever traditions have appeared and developed over history, even if some fall more into the area of philology rather than the history of linguistic thought *per se*.

A very rough periodization of the Chinese language, simplified from that of Wang Li, is offered here for reference:

Archaic Chinese: the period prior to the third century AD;
Middle Chinese: from the fourth to twelfth century AD;
Pre-Modern Chinese: thirteenth to nineteenth century;
Modern Chinese: the period from the 1919 May Fourth Movement to the present.

The only truly reliable information we have on China's earliest linguistic thought comes from written records, and the written symbols themselves. The earliest examples we currently have of written symbols in China date to the fifth millennium BC, the period of China's Neolithic Yǎngsháo 仰韶 culture. They come to us in the form of engravings on pottery unearthed from the Bànpōcūn 半坡村 archaeological site near Xi'an in northern China (Lin 1981: 3–6, 82–4). Scholars are still unsure of the purpose of the figures and what they mean, if anything. They do in any case seem to be some kind of primitive precursor of the Chinese writing system still in use today.

The next major extant type of early Chinese writing is engravings on tortoise shells and ox bones, called *jiǎgǔwén* 甲骨文 in Chinese, used mainly for divination. These were first discovered in the village of Xiǎotún 小屯 in Anyang, Henan province, starting around 1880 (Chen 1988: 2). Other materials were probably used for writing as well, but being more durable, the shells and bones were better able to survive the millennia. The engraved symbols have largely been deciphered, and clear lines of development have been drawn connecting them with their modern counterparts. These writings are a rich source of information on ancient Chinese religious and superstitious beliefs and rituals, political and social history, and—of special interest to us here—early character forms, variants, and methods of composition, in addition to the syntax of archaic Chinese, covering the period from about 1200 BC to the third century BC. Records of the continued evolution of character forms can be found in inscriptions on bronze vessels from the latter part of this period and later, and in writings on bamboo strips, silk, paper, and other materials after these. Cai Lun 蔡倫 (63–121 AD) is credited with the invention of paper, though he may actually only have improved an existing technology.

10.2.1 Education, Ancient Texts and Philology

The *Yìwénzhì* 藝文志 'Treatise on Arts and Letters' of the *Hànshū* 漢書 'Annals of the Han dynasty', written in the early third century AD, says that at the age of 8, children began their studies at a *Xiǎoxué* 小學 'Little School', where they were trained in the 'Six Arts': (1) the five rituals and rites, (2) the six styles of music, (3) the five styles of archery, (4) the five styles of cart driving, (5) the six principles of character composition, and (6) the nine numbers (Wang 1987: 2–4). So along with learning to read classical texts and to write, children were taught about the methods of character composition. This system of analysis and classification of the characters was a revered cultural achievement, and it is still taught in schools today. The six methods, along with the two examples originally given for each, are:

1. *Zhǐshì* 指事 ideographs: a symbolic depiction of the referent, often used for abstract notions; examples: 'above' *shàng*上, 'below' *xià*下.
2. *Xiàngxíng* 象形 pictographs: a drawing of a concrete object, e.g. 'sun' *rì* 日, 'moon' *yuè* 月.
3. *Xíngshēng* 形聲 phono-logographs: composed of a semantic plus a phonetic component. Due to historical sound changes and influence from varying dialects, the pronunciation of the phonetic component itself does not always match the modern pronunciation of the whole character. Whereas the previous two categories use character form as a mnemonic, *xíngshēng* characters have two aids to memory: a general semantic category, e.g. 'plant', 'female,' 'vision,' plus a phonetic reminder. It is notable that approximately 85 per cent of all Chinese characters are constructed according to this model, and it is the default method both for existing characters and for inventing new ones. Examples: '[larger] river' *jiāng* 江 [the semantic category component or 'radical' is 'water,' plus the phonetic: *gōng*, which reflects an earlier pronunciation], '[smaller] river' *hé* 河 ['water' radical plus phonetic *kě*].
4. *Huìyì* 會意: compound ideograph: composed of two or more components from the other character composition types, e.g. 'military arms' *wǔ* 武 [composed of the two elements 'dagger axe' + 'stop'], 'trust' *xìn* 信 ['person' + 'words'].
5. *Zhuǎnzhù* 轉注: Characters which have changed in form over history, e.g. *kǎo*考 is an earlier form of *lǎo*老 'old.' This category has many widely differing interpretations; the one adopted here is the more systematic and convincing one of Lu Shixian魯實先, which he backed up by many examples from the *Shuōwén*.
6. *Jiǎjiè* 假借: A character borrowed purely for its phonetic value, with no semantic connection, as was often done in the Egyptian hieroglyphics. The original two

examples were words used in an extended sense rather than as actual phonetic loans; more appropriate examples are *ér* 而, which originally meant 'beard'; the character was later borrowed for a homophone meaning 'and, however'; also the character *yāo*要 'waist' was borrowed to write the word for 'to want' *yào* 要; a 'flesh' radical was then added to the character used for *yāo* 腰 'waist,' which through this process became a *zhuǎnzhù* character. Lu emphasizes that *jiǎjiè* is not a method of character *creation per se*, but a type of character *usage* supplementing the other five methods.

Over time, the term *xiǎoxué* came to mean 'philology,' that is, (1) works on ascertaining character meanings, particularly obscure ones found in ancient texts; (2) character compendia, with an emphasis on the forms of the characters; and (3) rhyme books, primarily intended as a reference in poetry writing, but also doubling as ordinary dictionaries. Interest and work in *xiǎoxué* reach its height in the Qing dynasty (1644–1911 AD).

Literacy education needs were the source of China's first 'word books.' A number of them were in use starting from the Qin dynasty (221–207 BC) and earlier. The only one still extant today, however, is a character primer called the *Jíjiùpiān* 急就篇, *jí* 急 and *jiù* 就 being the first two characters of the work, along with fragments of another, entitled the *Cāng Jié Piān* 倉頡篇 (Cang Jie was China's legendary inventor of written characters), which was in fact a collection of a number of works of this type. Many expansions and similar works followed. These primers were written in a highly stilted style, and consisted mainly of 3-, 4- or 7-syllable rhyming lines. They were also designed to include as many different characters as possible, with little repetition, to maximize the children's exposure to and learning of new words. Literacy education was strongly emphasized since, according to the *Hànshū Yìwénzhì*, a knowledge of 9,000 characters was required to pass the test to become a government official. And once employed, an official was subject to punishment if he wrote a wrong character in a document.

A work following these primers was the *Ěryǎ* 爾雅, dating to about the second century BC. The original author is unknown, and it was expanded by later writers. It is basically a lexicon of words classified by subject. Its format is to list a series of words that are close in meaning, then to end it with a 1–3-character definition or description. It starts off with three chapters of miscellaneous words under the general category of 'language,' followed by such subject areas as family relationships, music, geography, and animals. Its main purpose was to explain unfamiliar characters found in earlier texts. More common characters are generally not treated, since they were assumed to be already known by the reader and their inclusion thus unnecessary.

Dialects were another focus of these early word books. The most representative work is the *Fāngyán*方言 'Dialects' by Han scholar Yang Xiong 揚雄 (53–18 BC). It features comparative lists of vocabulary items from different parts of China, along with the name of the region where each was in use. Language study in Chinese focused above all on the *written* language, even in works that collected dialect data. Again, the absence of a system of phonetic notation is a major drawback to this work, but the data it provides can be used to build up isogloss maps indicating the differences and overlaps in vocabulary use of the various regional dialects of the time.

The primers and related word books declined in importance with the appearance in approximately the year 121 AD of the *Shuōwén Jiězì* 說文解字 etymological dictionary by Han dynasty lexicographer Xu Shen 許慎. Xu established 540 'radicals' or categories based on character components, mainly for the purposes of indexing and easily retrieving individual characters when needed. These often coincided with the semantic marker (rather than the 'phonetic', i.e. phonetic marker) of *xíngshēng*-type or phono-logographic characters. Pronunciations were indicated either by the phonetic marker of the character entry, or with a homophone, preceded by the phrase, *dúruò* 讀若 'read as...'. While the *Shuōwén* contains inevitable errors, many character etymologies are now known thanks to this work, especially when it is examined in conjunction with the bronze inscriptions, much studied during the Song dynasty (960–1279 AD), and the oracle bone and shell inscriptions. The *Shuōwén* is China's first bona fide dictionary, and continues to be a highly valued reference work even today.

Starting in the Han dynasty, a frequently used method of defining an item was *shēngxùn* 聲訓 'use of a homophone or phonetically similar word to define another word.' The belief behind this was that phonetically close words were often also etymologically related and could thus offer insight into the definition of an item (Wang 1987: 10). For example, *zhèn, zhèn yě*, 震，振也 'earthquake: vibration.' Other *shēngxùn* are less straightforward and often quite forced, e.g. *rì, shí yě* 日，實 也 'sun: solid'; *yuè, quē yě* 月，闕也 'moon: waning'. This approach is frequently drawn on in the *Shuōwén*, and culminated in the compilation of the *Shìmíng* 釋名 'Explaining the Names,' a Han dynasty lexicon of the late second to early third century, attributed to Liu Xi 劉熙, which used this method extensively. In contrast to Western dictionaries, in which entries are arranged alphabetically (roughly, phonetically), and given straightforward semantic definitions, items in the *Shìmíng* and lexica like it are arranged by subject category and usually paired with a phonetically related definition, either a homophone or an alliterative or rhyming gloss. The above examples are found both in the *Shuōwén* and the *Shìmíng*. *Shēngxùn* definitions are generally far from rigorous and are often not even very informative. But they formed a consistent pattern of word definition, and were possibly also useful as a mnemonic.

10.2.2 Central Asia and Buddhism

Credit for opening up contact between China and Central Asia and India goes mainly to Han court envoy Zhang Qian 張騫 (*c*.164–114 BC), who endured extreme duress to visit and return from many countries of Central Asia, and India, between 138 and 115 BC.

Numerous new vocabulary items entered Chinese around this time to name some of the new things he discovered in his travels, particularly names of plants and foods, such as grapes, pomegranates, sesame, and alfalfa; animals, including lions; musical instruments; and other culturally valuable items, such as glass. In general, each syllable in Chinese constitutes a separate morpheme; Central Asian loanwords from this period, on the other hand, are notable because many are disyllabic single morphemes, such as *pútáo* 葡萄 'grapes' from Old Iranian *buduwa*, derived from *buda* 'wine,' and *mùsù* 苜蓿 'alfalfa' from Old Iranian *buksuk* or *buxsux* (Shi 2008: 518–19).

Buddhism was founded in India in the sixth to fifth century BC, and transmitted to other parts of Asia, particularly Central Asia, largely through the efforts of India's Ashoka the Great (*c.*304–232 BC). This is of interest in a linguistic history of China for two major reasons: first, because of the large amount of new vocabulary introduced through Chinese translations of the Buddhist sūtras and second, because the process of translation unavoidably raised awareness of the features of Chinese that differed from Sanskrit and the other source languages.

Translation of Buddhist sūtras from Sanskrit, Pāli, and various Central Asian languages into Chinese began around 58 AD. Translation was typically a team effort. The first step was for a native of the source language, who had come to China specifically for this task—perhaps a Sogdian, Khotanese, Kashmiri, Indian, or Yuezhi monk—to declaim the text, often apparently from memory. Then a bilingual interpreter, usually a native of a Central Asian state or India, or a descendant of same who grew up in China, would interpret the text orally to Chinese scribes, who then transcribed what they heard. Then the texts were carefully edited for accuracy, consistency, conciseness, and style, and proofread. Some translations were also done by Chinese who learned Sanskrit in China. Studies of phonetic equivalents used when going from the source language to Chinese seem to establish that in the early period, the texts were usually translated from a translation into a Central Asian language, called in Chinese *húyǔ* 胡語 'foreigners' language' or *súyǔ* 俗語 'common, popular language,' rather than directly from Sanskrit or Pāli; as time went on, translations were increasingly directly from Sanskrit or Pāli, and this was reflected in different phonetic transliterations. Translations from the early period also tended to be very literal, at the expense of good Chinese style, in an effort to ensure accuracy. The monks also tried to choose transparent descriptive translations in easily understandable Chinese, and to avoid phonetic transliterations of specialized Sanskrit terms as much as possible, though many transliterated Sanskrit and Pāli words did still appear, and are opaque to the uninitiated. Different translators had different styles, and sometimes used different Chinese words for the same term in the source language; and there were many other complicating issues. It is clear from this description that the translation process was highly susceptible to error and omission. Then, as now, linguistically sophisticated, highly skilled translators were in short supply. Translated sūtras in circulation were thus often corrupt and incomplete, so this occasioned some monks, such as Faxian 法顯, between 399 and 412 AD, to undertake arduous and dangerous journeys to India and other countries to learn Sanskrit, and to bring back the original manuscripts for painstaking translation, thereby deepening and solidifying the connections between Chinese and the languages of Buddhism (Ma 1998: 18–94; Boulnois 2004: 209–34).

Translating religious and philosophical concepts which often had no ready equivalent in Chinese was a challenging task. Many new terms had to be invented, either by coining them from existing Chinese morphosyllables, e.g. *yè* 業 'business, deed' or *yèzhàng* 業障 'business + obstacle' for 'karma'; or often a phonetic rendering of the Sanskrit was used, e.g. *púsà* 菩薩 for 'bodhisattva' and *póluómén* 婆羅門 for 'Brahmin.' These examples are strongly marked as religious loanwords from India. But some of the newly created vocabulary came into general use, and is not easily identified as coming from Buddhism, e.g. *shìjiè* 世界, previously referred to as *tiānxià* 天下 'heaven below' in Chinese, is now the standard word for 'world'; and *xiànzài* 現在, which used to be 見在 *jiànzài* 'what-you-can-see existing' in earlier Chinese, became the normal word for 'now' (Wang 1988: 674–5).

The diverse alphabets, word orders, conjugations, declensions, and agglutinative suffixation of the source languages of the scriptures, i.e. Central Asian languages, which mostly belonged to the Turkic family, and Sanskrit and the Prakrits, of the Indo-Iranian branch of Indo-European, all offered sharp contrasts to the spare, unencumbered morphology of Chinese. Sanskrit and other Indian languages, for example, tend to have SOV word order, though word order can also be flexible, while Chinese is basically an SVO language; Sanskrit is also a highly inflected synthetic language, while Chinese is the classic example of an isolating, analytic one.

The translation process also made the Chinese highly aware of the importance and nature of the tones in their language, in contrast to Sanskrit and the other source languages, which were not tone languages. From earliest times, Chinese was in contact with many non-Han languages, which in theory could have led to more insights about Chinese much sooner, but these languages were generally viewed with condescension or even contempt, due to China's sense of her own cultural superiority. (It should be noted that China was in these times most often a collection of independent principalities and states, and not a unified nation.) The position of Sanskrit was entirely different; it was a prestige language because it was the language of the Buddhist scriptures, and this made it worthy of translation and close study.

One outcome of this comparative philological study was the first major work dedicated to a description of the four tones, the *Sìshēngpǔ* 四聲譜 'Tables of the Four Tones,' unfortunately no longer extant, by Shen Yue 沈約 (441–513 AD). From this time on, poetry rhymes were also required to take tone as well as syllable finals into account, although awareness of the tones was already reflected in some earlier works (Wang 1988: 74–5). (It is to be noted that the original four Chinese tones were not the same as the modern Mandarin ones—they went through considerable merging, splitting, and rearrangement before settling into their current form. And other dialects have different numbers of tones: e.g. modern Cantonese, a much more conservative dialect in some aspects, has nine.)

The original four tone categories are described as *píng* 平, 'the level tone'; *shǎng* 上, 'the rising tone'; *qù* 去, 'the falling tone'; and *rù* 入, 'the entering tone,' which is used to refer to syllables ending with a /-p/, /-t/, /-k/ or a glottal consonant stop final. The tones came to have central importance in the rules for Chinese poetic prosody, which were highly evolved by the Tang dynasty. For prosodic purposes, the four tone categories were divided into just two categories, *píng* 平 'level' (the first tone) and *zè* 仄 'oblique' (the remaining three tones lumped together). Various verse forms generally required specific sequences of the two tone types in each line of poetry—for example, two of one tone type, then two of the other, then one of the first type. The following line, often semantically parallel, would have basically the same tone pattern in reverse; there were also some exceptional breaks in the pattern for flexibility and variety. See the poem in Table 10.1, §10.2.4 below, for a sample tone scheme.

In face of the lack of an alphabetic writing system to use for phonetic notation, the *fǎnqiè* 反切 system was developed to indicate character pronunciations. Under the *fǎnqiè* system, two relatively well-known characters, plus the word *fǎn* 反 or later mostly *qiè* 切, were given after a lexical item. The reader needed to take the initial of the first and splice it onto the final rhyme and tone of the second, to derive the pronunciation of the item being looked up. A typical entry is *dōng déhóng qiè* 東 德紅切, i.e. *dé* plus *hóng* in the *qiè* 切 system make *dōng*. (The second tone had not yet separated from the first at this time, thus the difference in tones.) One big advantage of the system is that the *fǎnqiè* characters were already familiar to any literate Chinese, so there was no need to learn a new set of symbols. The disadvantage is that there is no way to know with certainty the actual phonetic realizations of the syllables at the time.

Spurred by his knowledge of alphabetic writing systems, the tenth-century monk Shouwen 守溫, who was possibly not an ethnic Han, developed an 'alphabet' for phonetic notation of Chinese characters for use in the rhyme books. It is interesting that, in spite of having the Sanskrit Devanāgarī alphabet as a model, he did not develop an alphabet or syllabary, but instead chose 30 existing Chinese characters to represent consonant or vowel initials. They were arranged in an order similar to that of the Sanskrit alphabet, according to, for example, whether a sound was voiced, voiceless, or voiceless aspirated. This set was later expanded to 36. The lack of a set of symbols indicating the values of individual segments is a big drawback of the system, but it does give us valuable categorical information on Middle Chinese.

10.2.3 The Rhyme Books and Dictionaries

The rhyme books were the next genre to appear of philological works building on the early primers, lexica, and expanded phonetic awareness of the special features of Chinese. These were primarily intended as reference works for poets checking which character-syllables were permissible as rhymes in the various verse forms; but they also served as dictionaries, since they included *fǎnqiè* pronunciations and simple definitions. Two noteworthy early works are the *Yùpiān* 玉篇 'Book of Jade' by Liang through Chen dynasty (502–89 AD) scholar Gu Yewang 顧野王, and the *Jīngdiǎn shìwén* 經典釋文 'Explanations of Words used in the Classics' compiled by Tang scholar Lu Deming 陸德明 (550?–630 AD).

The Song dynasty edition of the *Guǎngyùn* 廣韻 'Expanded Rhymes', compiled by Chen Pengnian 陳彭年 (961–1017 AD) is the most complete extant example of an early rhyme book. Many previous works were combined and re-edited to produce this work. One of the key works on which it was based was the *Qièyùn* 切韻—now lost except for a small number of fragments—compiled by Lu Fayan 陸法言 and other Sui dynasty language scholars in the late sixth century. In the surviving preface of this work, Lu describes how the compilers made a conscious decision to be as inclusive as possible regarding historical and geographical variations:

> In the evenings, after having enjoyed our wine, our discussions always turned to phonology. Differences obtain between the pronunciations of the past and the present, and different principles of selection are followed by the various authors. In the [southern] regions of Wu and Chu the pronunciation is at times too light and shallow. In [the northern regions of] Yan and Zhao it is often too heavy and muted . . . And so we discussed the right and the wrong of South and North, and the prevailing and the obsolete of past and present. Wishing to present a more refined and precise standard, we discarded all that was ill-defined and lacked precision . . . A knowledge of phonology is necessary for any literary undertaking . . . And so, choosing from the various rhyme books and other lexica, old and new, and basing myself on my earlier notes, I organized the material into the *Qieyun* in five volumes, analysing minutiae and making fine distinctions. It is not that I have been the sole judge in these matters. I have merely related the opinions of my worthy colleagues. (Translation from Malmqvist 1994: 11–12).

While the *Guǎngyùn* brings together much valuable data, it is difficult to sort out from it a single, consistent variety of the Chinese of the time.

Rhyme grid books (*yùntú* 韻圖) were a subsequent development of the rhyme book tradition. These also show direct influence from how sounds are combined to form words in the Sanskrit Devanāgarī script. Rather than just giving a *fǎnqiè* pronunciation for each individual syllable, characters were arranged in grids according to tone, and presumably their different main vowel qualities and medials—there is as yet no consensus on how to interpret all of the categories distinguished in the rhyme grids. Perhaps the most representative rhyme grid book is the *Yùnjìng* 韻鏡 'Rhyme Mirror,' author unknown, dating to the tenth century AD.

As the Chinese language evolved, new rhyme books were produced to reflect its changing phonology. The *Zhōngyuán yīnyùn* 中原音韻, compiled in 1324 by Zhou Deqing 周德清, is our best systematic record of the transition between Middle Chinese and modern Mandarin. Rather than attempting to incorporate historical and dialectal material, it focuses only on the actual spoken language of the time, an innovation in this genre (Norman 1988: 49). It documents the disappearance of the entering tone (tones realized with a final stop) from Mandarin, the devoicing of voiced initials, and the split of the even *píng* 平 tone into two new tones, the *yīnpíng* 陰平 and the *yángpíng*

陽平, the first two tones of modern Mandarin. Syllables that originally had a voiced initial ended up in the *yángpíng* tone category, among other changes.

Returning briefly to the dictionary tradition: the comprehensive *Kāngxī Zìdiǎn* 康熙字典 'Dictionary of the Kangxi Emperor' was completed in 1716 after six years of compilation work. Its format and content were based mainly on two earlier lexica, the *Zìhuì* 字彙 'Collection of Characters' of 1615, an innovative dictionary with 33,179 entries that reduced Xu Shen's 540 radicals to the current 214, and arranged characters according to their number of strokes; and the *Zhèngzìtōng* 正字通 'Correct Character Mastery' of 1671, produced as a supplement to the *Zìhuì*. The *Kāngxī Zìdiǎn*, in spite of errors, is still the authority many turn to for obscure characters: it contains 47,035 entries (Liu 1963: 40–56).

Starting from the early 1900s, Swedish linguist Bernard Karlgren (Chinese name: Gāo Běnhàn 高本漢) blazed a trail for studies in Chinese historical phonology based on works such as the *Guǎngyùn* and other written records, together with extensive modern dialect data, which he himself collected. Since then, considerable scholarly energy has been devoted to the phonological reconstruction of Chinese as spoken in various historical periods.

10.2.4 Grammar

It is interesting to contrast the great influence Sanskrit had on Chinese in the area of phonology with the negligible mark it left in the area of Chinese grammar studies. Rather than a division into nouns, verbs, adjectives, and such, the main grammatical categories posited by Chinese for their own language, starting in the Wei-Jin and Northern and Southern Dynasties period (265–589 AD), were content ('solid') words, called *shící* 實詞, vs function ('empty') words, or *xūcí* 虛詞. This simple binary approach was in fact a very reasonable one, since Chinese has very little explicit morphological marking, and was, and continues to be, highly dependent on word order to indicate grammatical relations. Function words are one of the few visible and concrete features of the language on which to build a grammatical analysis. And this approach is a natural outgrowth of the traditional text explication method of studying the written language. Up to the present, entire books are written on the meanings and usages of these 'empty' structural particles, especially those used in Classical Chinese. Such a book would include, for example, explanations of the many functions and uses of the possessive or genitive particle *zhī* 之 in Classical Chinese, and *de* 的 in Modern Chinese. This is probably China's most representative native approach to syntactic analysis.

There is, however, plenty of evidence of *implicit* awareness of the parts of speech as known in the West, reflected in the parallelism found in many types of literary writings, such as poetry. Table 10.1 is an example by Tang dynasty poet Wang Zhihuan 王之渙 (688–742 AD), entitled *Dēng Guànquèlóu* 登鸛鵲樓 'Ascending Stork Tower'; this sample will also give readers who are unfamiliar with Chinese a good idea of how it works. (Reference translation into English:

Table 10.1 The poem 'Ascending Stork Tower'

白	日	依	山	盡	CHARACTER
bái	*rì*	*yī*	*shān*	*jìn*	PRONUNCIATION
white	sun	along/follows	mountains	disappears	ENGLISH GLOSS
adj	noun	prep/verb	noun	verb	PART OF SPEECH
O	O	L	L	O	L[EVEL TONE] O[BLIQUE TONE]
黃	河	入	海	流	
huáng	*hé*	*rù*	*hǎi*	*liú*	
yellow	river	into/enters	sea	flows	
adj	noun	prep/verb	noun	verb	
L	L	O	O	L	
欲	窮	千	里	目，	
yù	*qióng*	*qiān*	*lǐ*	*mù*	
if-you-want-to	exhaust	1000	0.3 miles	eye/see	
verb	verb	number	measure	noun	
O	L	L	O	O	
更	上	一	層	樓。	
gèng	*shàng*	*yī*	*céng*	*lóu*	
further	ascend	one	storey	building	
adverb	verb	number	measure	noun	
O	O	O	L	L	

The white sun sinks behind the mountains
The Yellow River flows into the sea;
If you wish to have a broader view
Just climb up one more storey.)

The application of European-style grammar to Chinese began with Qing dynasty language scholar Ma Jianzhong 馬建忠 (1845–1900), who studied in Paris and knew French and Latin. In his *Mǎshì Wéntōng* 馬氏文通, published in 1898, he analyses Classical Chinese—the spoken vernacular was not yet recognized as worthy of this kind of study—mainly according to Latin-style grammatical categories, though he shows considerable innovation in his system of Chinese syntactic categories. He still adheres to the traditional opposition between content and function words in his treatment of the parts of speech. His list of content words includes nouns, pronouns, verbs, adjectives ('quiet words'), and adverbs ('situation words'); included under 'function words' are prepositions, conjunctions, particles ('helping words'), and exclamations; under parts of a sentence are subject ('beginning words'), direct object ('ending words'), predicate ('speech words'), adjectival, nominal and pronominal predicate ('expression words'), verb complements, including prepositional phrases ('transfer words'), object of a preposition ('operating words'), and appositives ('additive words'). The work is marked by repetition and inconsistencies; yet it is impressive for its time and made a notable contribution to introducing European grammatical traditions to China. Its influence is still felt today. Subsequent grammarians have mostly taken English rather than French and Latin as their model for analysing Chinese.

10.2.5 Philosophy and Language

Reference is made here to just one representative essay as a sample of linguistic thought in Chinese philosophy, the chapter entitled 'Rectifying the Names' *Zhèngmíng* 正名 in the philosophical work *Xún Zǐ* 荀子 (313–238 BC). Presaging Saussure, its main point is that while the forms of words are arbitrary, and differ from culture to culture, names like 'ruler,' 'subject,' 'father,' and 'son' were originally tied to very specific and unambiguous definitions, and can be matched quite precisely with corresponding terms in other languages, using Chinese as the common standard where needed. With the passing of time, however, these terms became blurred in the minds of the people, causing roles to be confused, and eventually leading to an inability to tell right from wrong. The author uses this as a foundation to emphasize the importance of matching words to their intended reality, and of society sticking to firm moral principles.

10.2.6 Choosing a National Language

The need to establish an official national language was felt already in the early Qing dynasty, when the Manchu government launched a number of 'orthoepy [correct pronunciation] institutes' to teach standard Beijing pronunciation, particularly in the Cantonese and Fukienese-speaking southern provinces. These met with very limited success (Chung 1989: 35). In 1913, scholar Wu Zhihui 吳稚暉 was chosen to direct the task of creating a truly 'national' speech that would transcend locality and dialect. The Beijing dialect was the general foundation of the new National Language, but certain features of various local dialects were also incorporated; in fact, the pronunciation of each individual character was actually voted on by the Commission on the Unification of Pronunciation *Dúyīn Tǒngyīhuì* 讀音統一會 (Wu 1964: 7–30). The newly designated 'standard' pronunciations were recorded by linguist Yuen Ren Chao for public release on a vinyl record. The entire scheme, however, proved impractical, since Chao was the first to point out that he himself was the only one who could actually pronounce everything correctly in running speech (Qin 2011: 25). The Beijing dialect was subsequently adopted more or less wholesale as the basis of the new national language. This was of course easiest for the one-third or so of the country that already spoke a variety of northern Chinese, but the policy encountered more difficulties in areas where more divergent dialects are spoken, particularly in the southern provinces. Philologist Zhang Binglin 章炳麟, better known as Zhang Taiyan 章太炎, came up with a phonetic alphabet for Chinese, which later became the *Zhùyīn fúhào* 注音符號

'Mandarin Phonetic Symbols' (MPS). The Ministry of Education put out a character list with standard pronunciations, called the *Guóyīn Jiǎnzì* 國音檢字, later used by Wu as a basis to compile a dictionary, in which the characters were arranged according to the 214 radicals.

Another major linguistic event in Republican China was the launching in 1919 of the 'May Fourth' movement, which incorporated writer Hu Shi's 胡適 promotion of the use of the vernacular *báihuàwén* 白話文 rather than the often stilted and unnatural Classical Chinese *wényánwén* 文言文 previously in use for most kinds of writing. The effects were great on literary writing, such as novels, but even more far-reaching for literacy education and language use in society in general.

A branch of the National Language Promotion Commission, originally founded in 1945, was established in Taiwan in 1946, a year after its retrocession to Chinese sovereignty, following 50 years as a Japanese colony. Mandarin was subsequently strongly promoted on both sides of the Taiwan Straits in education and all areas of public life—often to the detriment of local dialects. The Mandarin Phonetic Symbols are still used in Taiwan to teach literacy to children, while the PRC eventually adopted the Hanyu Pinyin Romanization system instead, which in fact closely parallels the MPS structurally, and is now pretty much the world standard for representing Chinese in the Latin alphabet.[1]

10.3 KOREAN

In the absence of written records from an earlier period, Korea's linguistic history can be said to have begun with the introduction of the Chinese language and writing system into the country, which started perhaps as early as the second century BC. Large-scale importation into Korean of Chinese characters, called *hanja* 漢字, began at the end of the seventh century AD, during the Unified Silla period. Korean previously did not have its own writing system, and in spite of the availability of other writing systems they could have borrowed from, such as Mongolian, Jurchen, and 'Phags-pa, the adoption of Chinese was all but inevitable because of China's relatively high level of cultural development. Similar to the case of Japan, the Chinese writing system was very poorly matched to the needs of writing Korean. Chinese is an isolating, analytic language in which each syllable generally corresponds to a single morpheme and written character, while Korean is typologically an agglutinative language using cumulative suffixation of words.

[1] Additional sources: Chao (1965), Chung (1995), Itkonen (1991), Karlgren (1954), Li (1975), Pu (1990), Shao (2005), Wang (1974), Zhou (1988). A very useful list of influential Chinese linguists, particularly more recent ones, with links to articles on each: en.wikipedia.org/wiki/Category:Chinese_linguists. On Chinese etymology www.chineseetymology.org/CharacterEtymology.aspx

In the earliest period, the Koreans learned and adopted the Chinese language itself, together with its writing system, for use in document writing, roughly analogous to how Latin was used in religion and scholarship by speakers of many various languages in Europe during the Middle Ages and beyond. Eventually they tried different approaches to using Chinese characters to write in the Korean vernacular, all variants of what was called the *Idu* script system. It was awkward at best. The three main approaches employed were analogous to the ones adopted for Japanese in the evolution of its own writing systems:

1. *Hyangchal* 鄉札 향찰 'vernacular letters': use of Chinese characters in their original form, mainly to transcribe *Hyangka* 'vernacular poetry.' Basic words in the text were mostly native Korean, Korean word order was used, and each syllable, for both content and function words, was transcribed with a single Chinese character. This system was used into the fourteenth century.

2. *Idu* proper 吏讀 이두 'clerk reading': Chinese characters were employed for basic words, Korean word order was used, and grammatical elements written in *Idu* characters were inserted. The main purpose of *Idu* was to clarify government documents written in Chinese for average Korean readers, and it was also used in teaching the Chinese language. It lasted into the nineteenth century.

3. *To* 吐 토 'particle': the original Chinese word order was retained, and additional *itwu* characters, often abbreviated from standard Chinese characters, were added to indicate Korean particles, verbal suffixes, and basic verbs not in the Chinese texts (Sohn 1999: 125–8).

These were clearly makeshift expedients. Korea badly needed an efficient writing system adapted to its own needs—and finally got one, in the year 1446.

The story of the invention and popularization of the Korean alphabet, known as the *Hanguel* 한글 (also written *Hangul* or *Hankul*), is the *pièce de résistance* of Korea's linguistic history. It has been called 'the only alphabet completely native to East Asia' (Kim-Renaud 1997: ix). It was originally intended as a writing system for the masses who were not literate in Chinese.

The *Hanguel*, originally called the *Hunmin Jeongum* 'Correct Sounds for the Instruction of the People', was promulgated in 1446 by King Sejong (born in 1397, reigned 1418–50) of the Joseon (Chosun) kingdom or Yi dynasty. The original system contained 28 letters; of these, only 24 are still in use, due to phonological change. The scholarly commentary that originally accompanied the *Hunmin Jeongum*, not discovered until 1940, describes the linguistic and philosophical underpinnings of the alphabet and its usage.

The system shows clear influence from the Sanskrit Devanāgarī script, which reached Korea via China through the transmission of Buddhism. Like the various Japanese scripts, the *Hanguel* were also clearly influenced by Chinese. However, unlike the Japanese syllabaries, in which syllables are added continuously in linear fashion, the *Hanguel* system chunks Korean into individual syllables and represents each one as a separate, integrated unit of initial (optional), vowel, and final (optional), presented as a square shape similar to that occupied by a single Chinese character on a page.

What is truly remarkable about the *Hanguel*, however, is that the forms chosen to represent the sounds are basically conceptual diagrams of the position of the articulatory organs used to pronounce each sound. For example, the letter for velar /k/ is ㄱ, which indicates the back of the tongue being raised to touch the soft palate; /n/ is written ㄴ, indicating the alveolar ridge, to be touched by the tongue tip. This represents a highly original and innovative concept in alphabet design that is unique among the alphabets of the world.

The new system was not universally embraced; it was viewed as too simple to be taken very seriously. Chinese held onto its cachet as the language and writing of prestige. The *Hanguel* thus came to be used only by 'women and commoners' up through the end of the nineteenth century.

Chinese characters continued to be an integral part of Korean up until very recently, in spite of the brief rise of nationalism in response to aggression by colonial powers, including Japan and Russia (Song 2005: 164). Their use has been entirely phased out in North Korea, where the *Hanguel* have been used exclusively since 1949; Chinese characters are taught only as a separate class in schools in the North. Most writing in South Korea is in *Hanguel* as well, though the study of Chinese character writing continues to be cultivated, and *hanja* are sometimes used in abbreviations or for disambiguation. The future role of the *hanja* in South Korea is as yet unclear.

Like Japanese, Korean has ended up with an enormous number of Chinese loanwords in its vocabulary. *The Comprehensive Dictionary of Korean* places the number of Sino-Korean words at about 52.1 per cent of its total 164,125 entries, pure Korean words at 45.5 per cent, and other loanwords, 1.4 per cent. Since the Second World War, however, English has been the main source of foreign loans into South Korean, accounting for about 90 per cent of the total. Many of these came into Korean in Japanized form, which the Koreans have tried to purge from their language since the end of Japanese colonial rule in 1945, either by nativizing them or by replacing them with direct loans from English. Some English loans are in fact homemade Korean coinages, as is also the case for Japanese (Song 2005: 19).

Finally, a note on Romanization. South Korea, which previously used a modification of the McCune–Reischauer (MR) Romanization system, promulgated the Revised Romanization of Korean in 2000. Opinions vary on the new system, which is more phonemic than the previous one, and eliminates diacritics which many readers didn't understand; but the values of some of the new letters, like *c*, may not be immediately obvious to the uninitiated, and the concurrent use of competing systems can be confusing.[2]

---

[2] Additional sources: Kim (1987), en.wikipedia.org/wiki/Korean_romanization; en.wikipedia.org/wikiRevised/_Romanization_of_Korean.

10.4 JAPANESE

Japan and Korea, in addition to the strong structural affinity between their spoken languages, also have roughly parallel histories as regards the introduction and adoption of Chinese writing, the subsequent tweaking of written Chinese for their own use, and ultimately, the development of their own scripts well adapted to their respective languages. And contact with western European ideas led in the cases of all three East Asian cultures to the development of grammatical studies, first only of earlier forms of their respective languages, and closely following European models, but eventually of the modern spoken language as well, and showing an increasingly greater independent development.

There is no record of a native Japanese writing system before the introduction of Chinese around 400 AD. In order to read early Chinese texts, the Japanese developed the *kanbun* or *kambun* 漢文 'Chinese texts/literature' system of markings around written Chinese characters to indicate Japanese word order, grammatical particles, suffixes, and inflectional endings, reminiscent of the various *itwu* schemes for Korean. Japan's own earliest literary works were generally composed directly in Chinese, with some concessions to the local language. Japan's earliest surviving written record, the *Kojiki* 'Record of Ancient Matters,' completed in 713 AD during the Nara period, is basically written in Chinese, but occasionally a sentence would be rendered phonetically in Japanese to preserve a personal or place name, a particular phrase, or a poem in its native form. The language is more precisely described thus: 'It is not Japanese, and at the same time it is not Chinese, but a quasi-Chinese which (to quote Chamberlain) "breaks down every now and then, to be helped up again by a few Japanese words written phonetically, and is surely the first clumsy attempt at combining two divergent elements"' (Sansom 1928: 19). This was the beginning of a mixed phonetic and semantic use of Chinese characters to represent Japanese. A single character, like the Chinese possessive particle 之 *zhī*, was borrowed both for its meaning—which would be の *no* in Japanese—and for its sound, probably *shi*, useful for example in verb endings. Later, native Japanese morphemes and pronunciation were paired with Chinese characters, resulting in sequences of characters that looked odd in Chinese—because the text was in fact representing spoken Japanese.

Phonetic use of the characters was the rule in poetry, in which it was essential to maintain syllable count and rhythm. Japan's earliest collection of poetry, the *Man'-yōshū* 万葉集 'Myriad Leaves Collection,' uses characters mainly as phonetic symbols, and it is fairly easy to reconstruct the Japanese of the time on this basis; but characters were also sometimes used for their meaning. Using Chinese characters for the meaning of content words, and for the pronunciation of grammatical endings, in theory should have put the Japanese well on their way to creating the *kana*, their own native script. However, in Japan as in Korea, reverence for the Chinese culture and language kept scholars more focused on studying Classical Chinese rather than developing a native script for a vernacular literature. This meant that the Japanese had in the meantime to get by as best they could with a script full of pitfalls and gross inefficiencies, such as assignments of multiple Japanese equivalents to the same Chinese character (Sansom 1928: 7–40).

Parallel to how Chinese characters were often simplified in the Korean *to* system, cumbersome Chinese characters used phonetically in Japanese writing also began to be abbreviated, based on the 'grass' or cursive *cǎoshū* 草書 calligraphic style. According to Japanese tradition, Kobo Daishi 弘法大師, a famous priest who lived from 774 to 835 AD, chose 47 of these phonetic characters to form a syllabary called the *hiragana* 平仮名 'easy kana,' which went a long way to standardizing phonetic writing in Japanese. At about the same time, a second system came into use, called the *katakana* 片仮名 'side kana,' simplified from the square style of Chinese calligraphy. Chinese characters continued to be used, with either Chinese-based pronunciations, called *onyomi* 音読み, or Japanese pronunciations, called *kunyomi* 訓読み, mostly for content words, and Japanese grammatical syllables were written in *kana*, called *okurigana* 送り仮名, when used in combination with Chinese characters in the same word, e.g. the *mi*み in *kunyomi* 訓読み. Small *kana* written on one side, called *furigana* 振り仮名, were and still are used to indicate the pronunciation of the characters where needed. Chinese characters were often re-adopted in different historical periods, with different pronunciations, due to phonological change in Chinese; the three main layers of these varying pronunciations are (1) *go-on* 呉音, the older pronunciation of Chinese characters of the Nara and Heian periods used in particular for Buddhist and legal terms; (2) *kan-on* 漢音, readings of the Chang'an area borrowed from the seventh to ninth centuries, in the Nara period; and (3) *tōsō-on* 唐宋音, dating approximately to China's Song dynasty (960–1279 AD) and the mid-Heian to Edo periods in Japan. While the layers of inconsistencies made Japanese writing more and more complex, this in fact increased the attraction of the system for the elite who mastered it, as was also the case in Korea (Sansom 1928: 41–6).

Similar to China, though starting several decades earlier, grammatical study of Japanese began under the influence of intense contact with western European ideas in the period leading up to the Meiji Restoration (1868–1912). Japan maintained connections to the West via a Dutch outpost near Nagasaki, and in this way gained access to European learning, for which it had a ravenous hunger. Fujibayashi Fuzan 藤林普山 published a verbatim translation into Japanese of a Dutch grammar in 1815. Shinto priest and scholar Tsurumine Shigenobu 鶴峰戊申 applied the categories of Dutch to early Japanese in his *Gogaku Shinsho* 語学新書 'New Book of Language Study,' published in 1833, which described, for example, governing (nominative) and governed (local) cases. As with Chinese, the earlier language is what was considered most worthy of study. Toward the end of the nineteenth century, however, grammarians had begun focusing their attention on the modern vernacular rather than just the language of the ancient *waka* 和歌 poetry, and started incorporating the notions of parts of speech and other European grammatical concepts into their grammars. The first grammar of spoken Japanese written by a Japanese author is Baba Tatsui's 馬場辰

猪 *Elementary Grammar of the Japanese Language*, published in English in London in 1873. This was followed by Tanaka Yoshikado's 田中義廉 *Shōgaku Nihon Bunten* 小学日本文典 'Elementary Japanese Grammar,' published in 1875. Ōtsuki Fumihiko 大槻文彦 based his *Kō Nihon Bunten*広日本文典 'A Comprehensive Grammar of Japanese,' published in 1897, on both early indigenous studies and Western grammar; and many more similar works followed (Frawley 2003: 195–6). After the Meiji Restoration, Japanese grammar became a required subject for students at all levels, from elementary school through university (Liu 1993: 11).[3]

---

[3] Additional sources: Frellesvig (2011), Heinrich (2012), Shibatani (1987, 1990).

CHAPTER 11

....

LINGUISTICS IN INDIA

....

PETER M. SCHARF

Partial Indic language Romanization key			
ISO 15919	IPA	ISO 15919	IPA
ā	ɑː	ḍh	ɖh
ī	iː	ṇ	ɳ
ū	uː	ś	ç
ṛ	ɻ̩	ṣ	ʂ
ḷ	l̩	ḥ	h
ṅ	ŋ	ẖ	x
ñ	ɲ	ḫ	ɸ
ṭ	ʈ	ṃ	nasal fricative
ṭh	ʈh	ḻ	ɭ (Tamil)
ḍ	ɖ	ṉ	ɲ (Tamil)
ṛ	ɽ		

11.1 ORIGINS OF LINGUISTICS

....

A strong tradition of linguistic analysis developed in early India associated with the composition and preservation of the ancient Vedic hymns. By the end of the second millennium BCE, there were in existence already large collections of verse and prose texts learned aurally, the oldest of which is the *Ṛgveda*. Mnemonic techniques were developed to preserve the texts and their comprehension including by about the seventh century BCE the word recitation (*padapāṭha*) of the *Ṛgveda*. In the course of natural language change over a long period of time, the language in the preserved Vedic texts became less familiar to those who used and preserved it and more in need of deliberate study and explication. By the middle of the first millennium BCE six branches of knowledge ancillary to Vedic texts proper, and known as 'limbs of the the veda' (*vedāṅga*), included four concerned with linguistic analysis: metrics (*chandas*), etymology (*nirukta*), phonetics (*śikṣā*), and grammar (*vyākaraṇa*).

11.1.1 Metrics (*chandas*)

Specific names of meters mentioned even in the oldest layers of the Ṛgveda date the discipline of metrics (*chandas*) back into the second millennium BCE. Meters of two types are common in Sanskrit poetics: those that consist in a fixed number of syllables in certain verse segments, and those that consist in a fixed number of morae in certain verse segments.

11.1.2 Lexicography (*nighaṇṭu*) and Etymology (*nirukta*)

Etymological remarks appear in prose commentary on Vedic hymns and ritual practice called Brāhmaṇa composed early in the first millennium BCE. Brāhmaṇa authors use etymology liberally to justify significance they wish to attribute to certain terms found in ritual liturgy. The first such remark in the *Aitareyabrāhmaṇa* associated with the Ṛgveda, for instance, explains that a preliminary offering is called *iṣṭi* because the deities desired (*aicchan*) to set in motion (*praiṣam*) the ceremony (*yajña*) with the preliminary offerings (*iṣṭibhiḥ*) (*Aitareyabrāhmaṇa* 1.1.2). The author derives the term *iṣṭi* 'preliminary offering' from the verbal root *iṣ* 'desire' by using a finite form *aicchan* derived from that root in his statement of the reason that an *iṣṭi* is what it is. Such derivations demonstrate their authors' intentions, though they are erratic and often linguistically faulty. In the present example, the term *iṣṭi* is in fact derived from the verbal root *yaj* 'worship', not from the verbal root *iṣ* 'desire.'

In the middle of the first millennium Yāska composed a commentary principally on a thesaurus of Vedic terms called *Nighaṇṭu*. The first three chapters of the *Nighaṇṭu* contain lists of synonyms; the fourth contains three enumerated lists of polysemous words; and the fifth contains six lists of the names of deities. The *Nighaṇṭu* initiated a long and full tradition of lexicography described by Vogel (1979) in his contribution to Gonda's series on the history of Indian literature. Yāska's commentary stands at the beginning of a rich tradition of commentary upon such texts, including the *Rāmāśramī* on the famous *Amarakośa*. The *Nirukta* consists of twelve chapters plus an appendix that explain the meaning of the Vedic words. Each of the twelve chapters of the *Nirukta* proper comments upon one of the lists in the *Nighaṇṭu*. The *Nirukta* was expanded by the addition of an exposition of its explanatory method. Yāska's statement of the purpose of the *Nirukta* captures well the pedagogical purpose motivating the composition of this early linguistic work in the Vedic tradition. He states (1.20), 'Recent sages, tired of teaching, composed this book in order that subsequent Vedic scholars would be able to comprehend certain passages' (*upadeśāya glāyanto 'vare bilmagrahaṇāyemaṃ granthaṃ samāmnāsiṣuḥ*).

Etymological assertions in the *Nirukta* state that a certain nominal derives from a certain verbal root, for example,

> *cittaṃ cetateḥ* (*Nirukta* 1.6)
> *Cittam* (mind) is derived from (the root) *cit* (to know). (Sarup 1927: 10)

Some etymological assertions provide a familiar synonym for the obscure word in addition to an etymological derivation, for example,

> *vayāḥ śākhā veteḥ* (*Nirukta* 1.4)
> *Vayāḥ* means branches, (and) is derived from (the root) *vī* (to move). (Sarup 1927: 8)

Some etymologies in the *Nirukta* are less explicit; they utilize semantic statements from which a phonetic analysis is easily inferred. *Nirukta* 2.14 explains the six words contained in *Nighaṇṭu* 1.4. The first, *svar*, is explained as follows:

> *svar ādityo bhavati. su araṇaḥ. su īraṇaḥ. svṛtaḥ rasān. svṛtaḥ bhāsam jyotiṣām. svṛ taḥ bhāseti vā.*

Sarup (1920–27: part II, p. 30) translates, '*Svar* means the sun; it is very distant, it has well dispersed (the darkness), it has well penetrated the fluids, it has well penetrated the light of the luminaries, or it is pierced through with light.' Sköld (1926: 360) points out that the explanations imply derivation from the preverb *su* plus the word *araṇa* 'distant,' *īr* 'set in motion,' or the root *ṛ* 'go.' The word *araṇa* is itself a derivate of the verb *ṛ* 'go.' Although the semantic explanations do not make explicit statements about phonetics, the analysis using familiar derivates of common roots makes the inference of phonetic analysis obvious.

Although the etymologies in the *Nirukta* vary in their linguistic accuracy, the sections of the *Nirukta* that explicitly detail the method of the text already show a sophisticated awareness of phonetics and systematic linguistics. It is likely that these sections were added to an earlier *Nirukta* text after some of the developments in phonetics and grammar described below. In outlining this procedure and in distinguishing it from that of the grammarians, the author of the introduction to the *Nirukta* shows his familiarity with the concepts of derivation including original grammatical elements, affixation, sound changes, secondary derivatives, and compounds. He considers the verbal roots (*dhātu*) to be the original forms or bases (*prakṛti*), and nominal forms to be the modifications of them (*vikṛti*), and speaks of the latter as 'born' from the former. The procedure described recognizes the relationship between the final *h* of verbal roots and the voiced aspirated stops in their nominal derivatives, between semivowels and their corresponding vowels, and between vowels of different length. Finally, the procedure described recognizes the need to parse secondary nominal derivatives and compounds at their proper morphemic boundaries. The author of the *Nirukta* affirms the view of Śākaṭāyana and etymologists that all words are analysable into basic verbal roots, in disagreement with Gārgya, who holds that not all are (*Nirukta* 1.12).

11.1.3 Phonetics (*śikṣā*)

Sanskrit phonetics has been a topic of investigation since phoneticians analysed inter-word sound alterations in Vedic hymns at the beginning of the first millennium BCE. Śākalya composed the word recitation (*padapāṭha*) of the continuous recitation (*saṃhitāpāṭha*) of the Ṛgveda in the seventh century BCE. Similar analyses were undertaken of other Vedic hymn collections, and several additional modes of recitation were built upon them. The earliest texts in the discipline of Śikṣā consist of sets of phonetic rules that account for the derivation of saṃhitā texts from their corresponding padapāṭha texts. Early Śikṣā texts, composed during the sixth through fourth centuries BCE (Staal 1972: xxiv), were proper to particular branches (*śākhā*) of the Veda and hence are termed *prātiśākhya*. The Prātiśākhyas and later texts called *śikṣā* also systematically analyse phonetics, phonology, and prosody. While Varma (1929) evaluates early Indian phonetic observations, Allen (1953) provides, as he himself says (1953: iii), 'a guide to the appreciation of the earliest phoneticians.'

The phonetic and phonological analyses in these texts differ from each other and from that assumed for the operation of Pāṇinian grammatical rules (discussed below). Yet these analyses share a number of characteristics. Indian phoneticians generally classify sounds according to articulatory features including place of articulation in the vocal tract, stricture, voicing, aspiration, nasalization, length, and relative pitch. Indian phoneticians categorize the duration of segments by recourse to the measure of the short vowel. A short vowel measures one mora; long vowels, two morae; prolonged vowels, three morae; consonants, half a mora. In terms of pitch, Indian phoneticians categorize vowels as high-pitched, low-pitched, circumflexed, or monotone. A circumflexed vowel is described as dropping from high to low, and a series of syllables is monotone if devoid of relative distinction in pitch.

Some of the observations of the phoneticians are extremely acute. They describe nasals called *yama* that occur as transition sounds between an oral stop and a subsequent nasal stop. They describe another nasal segment called *nāsikya* (h̃) that occurs as a transition between *h* and a subsequent nasal stop *ṇ*, *n*, or *m*. They describe unreleased stops that occur before stops, and reduced semivowels corresponding to *y*, *l*, and *v* that occur word-finally; both are termed *abhinidhāna*. They describe firmer approximants *y* and *v* that occur word-initially, and lighter approximants *y* and *v* that occur word-finally in several dialects. They describe the rare short simple vowels *ĕ* and *ŏ* and slightly lengthened short vowels that occur in Vedic recitation. Phoneticians describe vowel segments called *svarabhakti* that break up certain consonant clusters. Vedic phonetic treatises also describe contextual variation of nasals and vowel pitches.

Ancient Indian treatises themselves report phonetic differences that reflect dialectal differences. For example, Ṛkprātiśākhya 1.45 states that *s*, *r*, and *l* are produced at the base of the teeth, but 1.47 reports that some teachers hold *r* to be produced at the alveolar ridge (*barsvya*). Differing from both, the Pāṇinīyaśikṣā classifies *r* as coronal. Alveolar, coronal, and velar places of articulation are reported for vocalic *ṛ*. Ancient treatises report differences concerning sandhi of *m* before semivowels, sandhi of the glottal fricative (*visarga*) before an initial consonant, sandhi of final *y* and *v*, epenthesis of an unvoiced stop between a spirant and following unvoiced stop, the relative duration of subsegments that compose diphthongs, types and durations of the nasal segment *anusvāra*, and tonal phonotactics. Varma (1929: 53–4) demonstrates that such differences found in Indian phonetic treatises reflect dialectal variation by showing that the reflexes of Sanskrit words in subsequent regional languages originate in them. He shows, for instance (pp. 8–9), that dental and coronal pronunciations of vocalic *ṛ* correlate to reflexes in regional Ashokan inscriptions and modern languages that developed subsequent dental vs retroflex geminate consonants respectively.

Ancient Indian phonetic treatises differ not just in the facts they report but also in their phonological systems. Different phoneticians analysed Sanskrit sounds in accordance with different structures of phonetic features. Phonetic treatises vary in the number of places of articulation, the number of degrees of stricture, and other features utilized to distinguish sounds. Hence while most phonetic treatises enumerate seven places of articulation, including the nasal cavity and distinguishing the velar region from the glottal, Pāṇini deals with just five—guttural, palatal, coronal, dental, and labial, combining glottal and velar places under the term 'guttural' (*kaṇṭhya*). He avoids having to posit different places of articulation for distinguishing between glottal and velar fricatives by referring to the segments instead. Pāṇinian grammarians consider nasality as a means, rather than a place, of articulation. Thereby they avoid complications that would result from considering all nasals (their distinct oral places of articulation notwithstanding) as homorganic.

Āpiśali includes a full set of eight stricture distinctions, including five degrees of openness, as opposed to just three—contact, slight contact, and open—used by Śaunaka. While most ancient Indian phoneticians recognize just two dispositions of glottal aperture—closed and open—Śaunaka recognizes an intermediate disposition, only recently recognized as accurate by modern phoneticians, to account for the production of voiced spirants and voiced aspirated stops. Also significant is Śaunaka's recognition of the implication of vocal fold disposition on pitch: stretched vocal chords imply high pitch, slack vocal chords imply low pitch, and a tossing (*ākṣepa*) in the disposition of the vocal chords implies declining pitch (*svarita*).

Significantly, certain Indian phoneticians give particular prominence to features. A few explicitly state that features are entities distinct from both articulatory processes and phonetic segments and serve as the elements of which the latter are composed. Such analyses directly inspired feature analysis in modern linguistics. Most conspicuously, Āpiśali explicitly describes the active articulators of sounds, anticipating the approach adopted by phonologist Morris Halle. Beyond classifying sounds according to their common features, the *Āpiśaliśikṣā* operates with the features associated with those sound classes. After classifying sounds according to their place of articulation, the *Āpiśaliśikṣā* explicitly associates these sound classes with articulators. This method of description gives an operative role to features beyond noting shared characteristics of segments.

The *Āpiśaliśikṣā* goes on to clarify that it establishes articulatory features intermediate between the articulatory processes themselves and sets of sounds with shared properties. After already categorizing sounds according to their common extrabuccal articulatory processes and resultant characteristics, the next section establishes that articulatory processes produce features that in turn produce other features. For instance, according to *Āpiśaliśikṣā* 8.7–8, the extrabuccal features that are associated with the glottis imply particular features of the larynx, which in turn imply voice features.

Other Indian phonetic treatises establish a hierarchy in their systems of features. Some features are restricted to a domain in which they are contrastive. The *Ṛk*- and *Taittirīyaprātiśākhya*s concur with the *Āpiśaliśikṣā* in restricting the features of voicing (*ghoṣa*) and non-voicing (*aghoṣa*) to consonants, while the former allow the feature contrast between breath (*śvāsa*) and voice (*nāda*) to apply to all phones. According to Śaunaka in *Ṛkprātiśākhya* 13.3–6, breath and voice are featural entities in their own right from which all speech segments are produced: breath is the material of voiceless segments; both breath and voice are the material of voiced aspirates and *h*; and voice is the material of the rest.

Certain sections in the *Ṛkprātiśākhya* and *Atharvaprātiśākhya* name both features and segments as the constituents of other segments. While at first glance they seem thereby to confuse features and segments, they demonstrate a penetrating phonological analysis in terms of constituents that are more fundamental than segments. *Ṛkprātiśākhya* 13.15 reports the view of others that the segments *a* and the nasal segment *anusvāra* constitute the voicing in non-nasalized voiced stops and nasal stops respectively. 13.6–17 attributes to others the view expressed in *Āpiśaliśikṣā* 4.9–10 that the unvoiced aspirates contain the fricative produced at the same place of articulation (i.e. *kh, ch, ṭh, th, ph* contain *[ḥ], ś, ṣ, s, [ḥ]*, respectively) and that the voiced aspirates contain *h*.

Similarly, the commentary on *Atharvaprātiśākhya* 1.10 reports that some consider there to be only five stops (the first in each series). These become differentiated by the addition of certain features. United with the unvoiced fricatives, they become the unvoiced aspirates; united with voicing, they become the voiced deaspirates; united with their corresponding fricative in addition, they become the voiced aspirates; and united with voicing and nasalization, they become nasal stops. These and similar issues are discussed at greater length by Scharf and Hyman (2011).

11.1.4 Grammar (*vyākaraṇa*)

The systematic analysis of utterances into words, and of words into morphemes, is evident already in Śākalya's word-by-word recitation (*padapāṭha*) of the *Ṛgveda*. Similar analyses were undertaken of the other three Vedic hymn collections, and several additional modes of recitation were built upon them for the purpose of preservation of the Vedic hymns. Such analysis is referred to in Pāṇini's grammar, as is the grammatical analysis of several predecessors whose work is no longer extant.

11.2 Pāṇinian Grammar

11.2.1 Literature

11.2.1.1 *Rules*

By the early fourth century BCE Pāṇini had composed the *Aṣṭādhyāyī*, consisting of nearly 4,000 rules in eight chapters (*adhyāya*) of four sections (*pāda*) each, that gives a precise and fairly complete description of late Vedic Sanskrit. Pāṇini drew upon the work of predecessors and mentions ten by name. Yet no independent pre-Pāṇinian grammatical treatise survives, and the few extant grammatical treatises attributed to pre-Pāṇini grammarians have been shown to post-date Pāṇini. The *Āpiśaliśikṣā* may well be authored by the same Āpiśali to whom Pāṇini refers, but extant grammatical treatises attributed to Śākaṭāyana and Kāśakṛtsna are later productions, and the attribution of statements to an Aindra grammar mistakenly reifies the participation of the god Indra in certain inherited legends.

In the fourth or third century BCE, Kātyāyana appended approximately 4,300 brief statements (*vārttika*s) to 1,245 of Pāṇini's rules. Kātyāyana's vārttikas examine the formulations of Pāṇini's rules, their relation to other rules, suggest modifications, and also address the fundamental principles presupposed. The *Aṣṭādhyāyī* and its accompanying lists as well as Kātyāyana's vārttikas were composed orally and received aurally, and hence adopt techniques to maximize brevity. The rules themselves are composed in brief aphorisms. They are organized to take advantage of ellipsis by expecting that terms in preceding rules recur in subsequent rules and by the use of recurring headings (*adhikāra*). They utilize short, artificial technical terms and indicatory markers. The fact that phonetic segments are employed as markers itself indicates that the linguistic system was composed and transmitted aurally. In the middle of the second century BCE, Patañjali composed his monumental commentary, the *Mahābhāṣya*, on Kātyāyana's vārttikas and independently on 468 sūtras of the *Aṣṭādhyāyī*. The work imitates and is clearly based upon the live interaction between teacher and students engaged in an investigation of the scope, formulation, and implications of rules.

Pāṇinian grammar has generated an abundant literature in the form of commentaries on the *Aṣṭādhyāyī* and sub-commentaries on them. Extant running commentaries on the *Aṣṭādhyāyī* include the *Kāśikā* of Vāmana and Jayāditya, written in the seventh century CE, the *Bhāṣāvṛtti* of Puruṣottamadeva in the early twelfth century, the *Vyākaraṇamitākṣara* of Annambhaṭṭa, and the detailed and interpretive but incomplete *Śabdakaustubha* of Bhaṭṭojidīkṣita in the early seventeenth century. The *Bhāgavṛtti* of Vimalamati, written in the ninth century, is no longer extant, and the *Durghaṭavṛtti* of Śaraṇadeva, written in 1172, focuses on the derivation of about 500 difficult forms. The *Rūpāvatāra*, written by the Śrīlaṅkan Buddhist Dharmakīrti in the tenth or eleventh century, the *Prakriyākaumudī* of Rāmacandra (*c.*1400), the *Prakriyāsarvasva* of Nārāyaṇabhaṭṭa (1616), and the *Siddhāntakaumudī* of Bhaṭṭojidīkṣita reorder and comment on rules of the *Aṣṭādhyāyī* in topics such as technical terms, metarules, sandhi, nominal inflection, feminine affixes, thematic roles, secondary nominal derivates, compounds, verbal inflection, secondary verbal derivates, and primary nominal derivates. The latter includes Vedic rules and accentuation omitted by Dharmakīrti and treated briefly by Rāmacandra.

Many of these commentaries on Pāṇini's *Aṣṭādhyāyī* generated their own traditions of sub-commentary, particularly the *Mahābhāṣya*, *Kāśikā*, and *Siddhāntakaumudī*. Unfortunately Bhartṛhari's *Mahābhāṣyadīpikā* commentary on the *Mahābhāṣya* (fifth century) exists only in a single fragmentary and corrupt manuscript (āhnikas 1–7 with lacunae). However, Kaiyaṭa's *Pradīpa* commentary on the whole of the *Mahābhāṣya* in the eleventh century incorporated much of Bhartṛhari's work and was itself the subject of Nāgeśa's *Uddyota* commentary in the late seventeenth or early eighteenth century. The *Pradīpa* was the subject of several other commentaries, and the *Uddyota* was commented on by Nāgeśa's student Vaidyanātha. The *Kāśikā* was commented upon in the *Kāśikāvivaraṇapañjikā* by Jinendrabuddhi in the eighth or ninth century and in the *Padamañjarī* by Haradatta in the thirteenth. Commentaries on Bhaṭṭojidīkṣita's *Siddhāntakaumudī* include his own *Prauḍhamanoramā* 'pleasing to the learned' and *Bālamanoramā* 'pleasing to students,' and the former was commented on in the *Bṛhacchabdenduśekhara* by Nāgeśa. The tradition of grammatical commentary continues in Sanskrit, Indian vernacular languages, and foreign languages right up to the present.

Staal (1974), Rocher (1975), and Scharfe (1977) have written general surveys of Indian linguistic literature. Dandekar's 1946–93 comprehensive bibliography of Indological research includes sections on śikṣā (sections VII.47–53), vyākaraṇa (VII.75), nirukta (VII.76), and chandas (VII.78), lexicography (XI.93), and grammatical philosophy (XIII.102) in each volume. Cardona (1976, 1999) provides a critical survey of research on Pāṇinian grammar and related fields, which is updated by Houben (2003).

Filliozat (1988) gives an excellent practical introduction to Pāṇinian grammar and its methods. Cardona (1997) gives a sophisticated overview of Pāṇini's derivational system and its foundational principles. Sharma (1987) discusses Pāṇini's linguistic conceptions and procedures as an introduction to his 1990–2003 translation and commentary on the *Aṣṭādhyāyī*, which replaces the still useful simpler translation and commentary of Vasu (1891). Böhtlingk (1887) is still a convenient edition, German translation, and analytic apparatus even if Katre (1987, 1968–9) provides the same in Romanization with English translation. Thieme's (1935) classic study of the relationship between Pāṇinian grammar and its predecessors cannot go without mention, nor can Filliozat's masterly beginning of a translation and explanation of Patañjali's *Mahābhāṣya* with its principal commentaries.

11.2.1.2 *Subsidiary Components*

Pāṇini's comprehensive system of linguistic description consists of several components besides the set of rules at its centre. The system additionally includes metarules, lexical lists, a phonological list, and a list of additional affixes not taught in the rule-set proper. The *Aṣṭādhyāyī* itself includes among its rules a number of metarules that govern the syntax of rules, and principles concerning rule application. Additional principles seen to be applicable in the *Aṣṭādhyāyī* that were not explicitly stated in the rule-set were formulated by commentators, in particular by Patañjali in his *Mahābhāṣya*. These principles were collected and commented upon in works such as the *Vyāḍīyaparibhā-ṣāvṛtti*, Puruṣottamadeva's *Laghuparibhāṣāvṛtti*, *c.*1150 CE, Sīradeva's *Bṛhatparibhāṣāv-ṛtti*, and Nāgeśa's *Paribhāṣenduśekhara*, *c.*1755 CE.

Pāṇini's rule-set makes reference to an accompanying sound catalogue (*akṣarasa-māmnāya*) and accompanying lexical lists (*gaṇa*) not itemized in the rule-set itself. The sound catalogue is used to form abbreviations that serve as an efficient system of reference. Some 282 minor lexical lists are referred to by their incipits in the rule-set. For example, by *Aṣṭādhyāyī* (hereafter abbreviated *A.*) 1.1.27 *sarvādīni sarvanāmāni*, speech forms in the list beginning with *sarva* 'all' are termed *sarvanāman* 'pronoun.' The members of the list are specified in full or by a paradigmatic set of examples in commentaries on the *Aṣṭādhyāyī*. The most extensive of the lexical lists is a root list (*dhātupāṭha*) incorporated into the *Aṣṭādhyāyī* by *A.* 1.3.1 *bhūvādayo dhātavaḥ*, which terms about 2,000 items in the list beginning with *bhū* roots (*dhātu*). Reference to members of the root list is then achieved generally by use of the term *dhātu*.

The Pāṇinian root list is known through numerous manuscripts as well as through several commentaries (Kunjunni Raja 1977: 287–8). Three complete commentaries composed in Sanskrit are extant: the *Kṣīrataraṅginī* of Kṣīrasvāmin (early twelfth century CE Kashmir), the *Dhātupradīpa* of Maitreyarakṣita (mid-twelfth century CE Bengal), and the *Mādhavīyadhātuvṛtti* of Sāyaṇa (fourteenth-century CE Vijayanagara, Karṇāṭaka). These commentaries provide examples and details of derivates and comment upon variants in the roots, their markers, and their ordering and placement in the various sublists within the root list.

A list of affixes beginning with *uṇ* is incorporated into the grammar by *A.* 3.3.1 *uṇādayo bahulam*, which states that the affixes occur variously after roots to form conventional terms, and *A.* 3.4.75 *tābhyām anyatroṇādayaḥ*, which allows these affixes in thematic roles other than those stated in the two previous sūtras. A treatise consisting of five chapters, called the *Pañcapādyuṇādisūtra*, contains specific rules providing affixes beginning with *uṇ* after certain roots. For instance, the conventional term *kāru* 'artisan' is formed by provision of the affix *uṇ* by the first sūtra. The affix consists of the phone *u* marked with *ṇ*. (The convention in this document is to set markers in bold.) A second treatise in ten chapters, called the *Daśapādyuṇādisūtra*, rearranges the five-chapter version with the affixes in alphabetical order. While Pāṇini did not compose either of these treatises as received and may not necessarily have known a set of rules such as they comprise, he at least knew of a list of such affixes and accepted derivations involving them as valid. (See Table 11.1)

11.2.2 Architecture

Pāṇinian grammar describes correct Sanskrit usage by restricting valid utterances to those derivable in accordance with general and specific generative rules. Just as earlier

Table 11.1 Components of Pāṇini's grammar

Rules	Metarules	Lexical lists	Phonological list
Aṣṭādhyāyī	metarules	dhātupāṭha	akṣarasamāmnāya
Uṇādisūtra	paribhāṣāsūtras	gaṇapāṭha	

phonetic treatises formulated rules to regenerate the continuous text of Vedic saṃhitās from their word-by-word analyses in padapāṭhas, Pāṇini's grammar generates utterances from basic elements under semantic and coocurrence conditions. The set of rules of the grammar itself presupposes an extremely comprehensive and detailed analysis of the Sanskrit language into basic elements. These basic elements are roots and nominal bases listed in the dhātupāṭha and other lists, those inferrable as being of the same kind in lists of paradigmatic elements (ākṛtigaṇa), those included by specific semantic criteria, and some 464 affixes attached to them by rules of the Aṣṭādhyāyī. Additional nominal bases are included as basic elements under the sole specification that they be meaningful. By A. 1.2.45 *arthavad adhātur apratyayaḥ prātipadikam*, meaningful speech forms *arthavat*) other than roots, affixes, and speech forms that end with them are termed *prātipadika* 'nominal base'.

From these basic elements, the rules of the *Aṣṭādhyāyī* construct derived roots and nominal bases, words, and utterances. Roots and nominal bases are generally referred to as preceding contexts in rules that provide affixes after them. Rules in the third chapter headed by A. 3.1.91 *dhātoḥ* provide affixes after roots, and rules in the fourth and fifth chapters headed by A. 4.1.1 *ṅyāpprātipadikāt* provide affixes after nominal bases, including after nominal bases ending in feminine suffixes added by A. 4.1.3–75. Verbal affixes include verbal terminations provided by A. 3.4.77–112 in place of variables (the abstract symbol *l* with indicatory markers attached), and nominal affixes include nominal terminations provided by A. 4.1.2. Speech forms ending in nominal and verbal terminations constitute words and are termed *pada* and retain that status even when terminations are modified. Derived verbal roots are formed by the provision of affixes after primary verbal roots, nominal bases, and words by A. 3.1.5–32. A. 3.1.33–90 provide verbal-stem-forming affixes between roots and subsequent verbal terminations. Derived nominal bases are formed from affixes added to roots, affixes provided by A. 4.1.76–5.4, and by compounding in accordance with rules in A. 2.1–2.2. These are termed *prātipadika* 'nominal base' by A. 1.2.46 *kṛttaddhitasamāsāś ca*. All such verbal and nominal stems are subject to modification by augmentation, deletion, and replacement in accordance with rules in A. 6.4–7.4. Speech forms are subject to accentual modification specified in A. 6.1.158–6.2 and to additional augmentation and prosodic changes specified in A. 6.1.72–157 and A. 8.2–8.4. The functioning of the rules is facilitated by the classification of elements in accordance with semantic and syntactic criteria and by principles, conventions of reference, and metalanguage articulated in the first chapter.

Table 11.2 Pāṇinian derivation

1.	Theodore cooks	
2.	*devadatta*[masculine, one, independent actor] *pac*[present time]	
3.	*devadatta*[masculine, one, kartṛ] *pac*[present time]	*A.* 1.4.54 *svatantraḥ kartā*
4.	*devadatta*[masculine, one, kartṛ] *pac-l*	*A.* 3.2.123 *vartamāne laṭ*
5.	*devadatta*[masculine, one, kartṛ] *pac-ti*	*A.* 3.4.78 *tiptasjhi . . .*
5a.		*A.* 1.3.78 *śeṣāt kartari parasmaipadam*
5b.		*A.* 1.4.22 *dvyekayor dvivacanaikavacane*
5c.		*A.* 1.4.108 *śeṣe prathamaḥ*
6.	*devadatta*[masculine, one, kartṛ] (*pac-a*)-*ti*	*A.* 3.1.8 *kartari śap*
7.	*devadatta-s* (*pac-a*)-*ti*	*A.* 4.1.2 *svaujhas . . .*
7a.		*A.* 1.4.22 *dvyekayor dvivacanaikavacane*
7b.		*A.* 2.3.46 *prātipadikārthaliṅgaparimāṇa-vacanamātre prathamā*
8.	*devadatta-s*[pada] (*pac-a*)-*ti*[pada]	*A.* 1.4.14 *suptiṅantam padam*
9.	*devadatta-ru*[pada] (*pac-a*)-*ti*[pada]	*A.* 8.2.66 *sasajuṣo ruḥ* (*padasya* 8.1.16)
10.	*devadattaḥ pacati*	*A.* 8.3.15 *kharavasānayor visarjanīyaḥ* (*padasya* 8.1.16)

The partial derivation of a simple sentence will suffice to illustrate the procedure. The process operates from the point of view of the speaker so begins with a conception the speaker wishes to express. To derive a sentence meaning 'Theodore cooks' (Table 11.2, step 1), one selects the basic speech elements that denote the object and action involved, namely, the nominal base meaning Theodore, and the verbal root meaning cook (Table 11.2, step 2). The independent actor in the action is termed *kartṛ* 'agent' by *A.* 1.4.54 (step 3). *A.* 3.2.123 introduces the abstract verbal affix *laṭ* after the verbal root *pac* on the condition that present time is to be denoted (step 4). By *A.* 3.4.78 the *l* is replaced by a basic verbal termination (step 5). The singular active third person termination *tip* is selected on the conditions that what is to be denoted is an agent, a single entity, and not denoted by a first or second person pronoun in accordance with *A.* 1.3.78, *A.* 1.4.22, and *A.* 1.4.108 respectively (steps 5a–5c). The verbal-stem-forming affix *śap* is added after the root before the verbal termination on condition that an agent is to be denoted (step 6). *A.* 4.1.2 provides a nominal termination after the nominal base *devadatta*. A singular nominal termination is selected on condition that one object is to be denoted (step 7a), and the nominative is selected on the condition that just the meaning of the base is to be denoted, since the agent has already been denoted by the verbal termination (step 7b). The items ending in nominal and verbal terminations now qualify to be termed *pada* 'word' by *A.* 1.4.14 (step 8), which allows word-final sound changes to take effect (steps 9–10).

11.2.3 Reference

Several rules in the *Aṣṭādhyāyī* explicitly establish conventions of speech-form reference used throughout the grammar. *A.* 1.1.68 establishes the general convention that speech forms mentioned in the grammar refer to themselves, except technical terms that conventionally refer to speech forms. The first such exception is that *A.* 1.1.69–70 permit vowels and semivowels to refer to all members of their class (regardless of length, pitch, and nasality), and vowels followed by a *t* to refer to those of the same length within that class. *A.* 1.1.9 establishes that sounds produced with the same stricture at the same place of articulation within the mouth belong to the same class, and *A.* 1.1.10 prohibits consonants and vowels from belonging to the same class. The inclusion of the latter prohibition indicates that Pāṇini, like Śaunaka and unlike Āpiśali, did not recognize a distinction in stricture between the articulatory features of vowels and spirants; otherwise the prohibition would have been unnecessary.

Another convention departing from the autonomous reference of speech forms is the use of markers. *A.* 1.3.2–8 specify that certain sounds in certain contexts serve as markers in basic elements explicitly taught in the rule-set and accompanying lists. Sounds used as markers include nasalized vowels; final consonants, except dental stops, *s*, and *m* in inflectional terminations; initial diphones *ñi*, *ṭu*, *ḍu*; palatal and retroflex stops and *ṣ* initial in affixes; and *l*, *ś*, and velar stops in affixes other than those termed *taddhita*. For instance, a nasalized *u* is attached as a marker to the first consonant in each of the series of consonants produced at the five oral places of articulation. In accordance with *A.* 1.1.69 *aṇudit savarṇasya cāpratyayaḥ*, a sound marked with *u* refers not only to itself but also to sounds of the same class. Thus *ku* denotes the five stops *k*, *kh*, *g*, *gh*, and *ṅ* produced at the velum. Besides facilitating reference, these markers serve to condition certain operations or to distinguish otherwise homophonous basic elements. For example, affixes marked with *ñ*, or *ṇ* condition stem-vowel strengthening, while affixes marked with *k* or *ṅ* inhibit strengthening. Deleted by *A.* 3.1.9 *tasya lopaḥ*, markers are absent in the form derived by the grammar.

Modifying an inherited ordering of sounds that grouped vowels, stops, semivowels, and spirants together and ordered them within those groups generally by place of articulation from the throat to the lips, Pāṇini's sound catalogue (shown in Table 11.3) lists sounds in a particular order to maximize efficient reference to sound segments. For instance, nasals are grouped together, voiced non-nasal stops are grouped before unvoiced non-nasal stops, and within these groups aspirates are grouped together. The catalogue arranges these sounds in fourteen aphorisms (*sūtra*), each terminating in a consonant which is termed a marker by *A.* 1.3.3. *A.* 1.1.71 lets a sound mentioned in the sound catalogue, taken together with one of the consonant markers that occur at the end of each of the fourteen sūtras in that catalogue, denote itself and all of the sounds listed between. For example, *ik* refers to the vowels *i*, *u*, *ṛ*, and *ḷ*; *ac* refers to all the vowels; and *yaṇ* refers to the semivowels *y*, *v*, *r*, and *l*. Finally, *A.* 1.1.72 lets a speech form refer to an item that ends in the mentioned speech form rather than to itself. Hence *ik* refers to any speech form that ends in a simple vowel other than *a*. These

Table 11.3 Pāṇini's sound catalogue: Pratyāhārasūtras

1.	*a i uṇ*
2.	*ṛ ḷk*
3.	*e oṅ*
4.	*ai auc*
5.	*ha ya va raṭ*
6.	*laṇ*
7.	*ña ma ṅa ṇa nam*
8.	*jha bhañ*
9.	*gha ḍha dhaṣ*
10.	*ja ba ga ḍa daś*
11.	*kha pha cha ṭha tha ca ṭa tav*
12.	*ka pay*
13.	*śa ṣa sar*
14.	*hal*

conventions of referring to speech forms establish an extremely powerful technical apparatus that supplements the explicit reference to phonetic features described in §11.1.3. The explicit establishment of such conventions was unprecedented in the history of linguistics, and was unmatched in technical literature until the comparable use of superscript and subscript indices as markers in modern technical notation, and the explicit introduction of brief technical terms in modern mathematics.

11.2.4 Principles, Metalanguage, and Rule Types

Rules in the *Aṣṭādhyāyī* are of seven types, as shown in Table 11.4. Most of the sūtras in the *Aṣṭādhyāyī* are vidhi sūtras; they specify that certain operations take place. For example, in step 5 in Table 11.2, *A.* 3.4.78 provides that a verbal termination replace the abstract verbal affix *l* after a root, and in step 7, *A.* 4.1.2 provides that a nominal termination occur after a nominal base. These rules, however, are general; they list numerous terminations and do not specify which one should occur under which

Table 11.4 Rule types in Pāṇini's Aṣṭādhyāyī

1.	Introduction of a technical term (*sañjñā*)
2.	Metarule (*paribhāṣā*)
3.	Provision (*vidhi*)
4.	Restriction (*niyama*)
5.	Extension (*atideśa*)
6.	Heading (*adhikāra*)
7.	Negation (*niṣedha*)

circumstances. *A.* 1.3.78, *A.* 1.4.22, *A.* 1.4.108, *A.* 2.3.46 are niyama sūtras that comple-ment *A.* 3.4.78 and *A.* 4.1.2. They specify which terminations occur under which conditions. Hence in steps 5a–5c in Table 11.2, the third person singular active verbal termination *ti* is selected from among the 18 verbal terminations provided by *A.* 3.4.78, and in steps 7a–7b, the nominative singular nominal termination is selected from among the 21 nominal terminations provided by *A.* 4.1.2.

When the statement of a provision is too broad, a negation carves out a subdomain in which the rule does not apply. In addition, negative compounds, of which there are 490 in the *Aṣṭādhyāyī*, may state negations. Indian linguists recognize that such compounds make known negations of two types: limiting negation (*paryudāsa*) and cancelling negation (*prasajyapratiṣedha*; see Wujastyk 1993: paribhāṣā 48, *Paribhāṣ-enduśekhara* 74). A limiting negation makes the positive statement of an operation limited to the domain different from but similar to what the nominal compounded with the negative particle denotes. A cancelling negation cancels an operation previ-ously provided for within the domain specified in the statement of the cancelling negation, but operates independent of the domain of the previous provision. Patañjali shows the application of the limiting negation to ordinary affairs using the term 'non-brāhmaṇa' as an example: When told, 'Bring a non-brāhmaṇa,' one brings what is other than but similar to a brāhmaṇa, namely, another person. One has not done what was asked if one has brought a lump of earth. The negative compound, while excluding a brāhmaṇa, limits reference to an object similar to a brāhmaṇa, namely, another person. Hence even aside from the negated object itself, the operation applies only to a restricted domain. In contrast, a prasajyapratiṣedha cancels an operation previously provided for. The cancellation of the operation is a separate statement from the operation's prior provision. Hence, the cancellation applies only to the domain stated in the negative compound. Outside that domain the operation applies unrestricted.

An extension rule (*atideśa*) treats an item like another, thereby extending to it properties it did not have or operations to which it would otherwise not be subject. The most far-reaching extension rule in the *Aṣṭādhyāyī*, *A.* 1.1.56 *stānivad ādeśo 'nalvidhau*, provides that replacements are treated like their substituends. For instance replacements for nominal terminations provided by *A.* 4.1.2 are also treated like nominal terminations. In the derivation of the dative singular form *puruṣāya*, preceded by the *a*-final stem *puruṣa* 'man,' the nominal termination *ṅe* is replaced by *ya* before which the final *a* of the stem is lengthened. The lengthening occurs before a nominal termination denoted by the abbreviation *sup* in accordance with *A.* 7.3.102 *supi ca*. However, since the replacement *ya* is not included in the list referred to by the abbreviation *sup*, the final *a* of the stem *puruṣa* would not be subject to lengthening by *A.* 7.3.102. *A.* 1.1.56 extends the status of the substituend *ṅe* to its replacement *ya* so that the latter is treated as belonging to the list *sup* and does condition the required lengthening.

In Table 11.2 above, *A.* 1.4.54, *A.* 1.4.14 are sañjñā sūtras. Pāṇini uses 116 technical terms 1,350 times to facilitate the formulation of general rules. While he adopts several terms from general or linguistic usage, such as those for vowel length (*hrasva, dīrgha,* and *pluta*), and gender (*strī, pums, napuṃsaka*) without explicit introduction, he explicitly introduces most of these technical terms for various classes of items. Besides the techniques of phonetic reference described in §11.2.3, Pāṇini introduces the terms *vṛddhi, guṇa*, and *samprasāraṇa* to denote various vowel grades. The vowels *ā, ai*, and *au* are termed *vṛddhi*; the vowels *a, e*, and *o* are termed *guṇa*, and the simple vowels *i, u, ṛ*, and *ḷ* are termed *samprasāraṇa*, terms for pitch (*udātta, anudātta, svarita*), terms for vowel weights in syllables (*laghu, guru*), and terms for a penultimate sound (*upadhā*) and for a final vowel plus its syllable coda (*ṭi*). He introduces a term for markers (*it*) and several terms for various types of deletion (*lopa, luk, ślu, lup*). He introduces terms for verbal and nominal bases (*dhātu, prātipadika*), for stems (*aṅga*), for compounds (*samāsa*) and their various types (*tatpuruṣa*, etc.), for active and middle terminations (*parasmaipada, ātmanepada*), for first, second, and third person terminations (*prathama, madhyama, uttama*), for various other classes of affixes (*kṛt, kṛtya, sarvadhātuka, ārdhadhātuka, gha, taddhita*), for classes of roots (*ghu*), for particles (*nipāta*), indeclinables (*avyaya*), preverbs (*gati*), prepositions (*karmapravacanīya*), and for thematic roles (*apādāna*, etc.). While many of the terms he explicitly introduces are specifications of meaningful words, others are extremely brief artificial ones such as *ghu, ku, ṭi*, and the most frequent term, *it* 'marker,' is used 80 times.

Rules in the *Aṣṭādhyāyī* are stated in sūtras ordered and placed under headings to utilize ellipsis to maximize brevity. Headings and terms from preceding sūtras are understood to recur in subsequent rules to supplement the explicitly stated terms to complete the statement of the rule. A rule that provides an operation in Pāṇinian grammar states that a certain item occurs in place of another item in the context of preceding and following items. The nominative case is used for the item that occurs, the genitive case for the item replaced, the ablative case for the item in the preceding context, and the locative for the item in the following context. The provision of an affix after a root or nominal base is achieved by stating the affix rules in chapters 3–5 under the headings A. 3.1.1 *pratyayaḥ* and A. 3.1.2 *paraś ca*. The first lets items subsequently stated in the nominative be termed 'affix,' and the second qualifies them as occurring after. The direction word *para* 'after' ordinarily governs an ablative (in accordance with A. 2.3.29), so that the affix is understood to occur after roots or nominal bases taught in the ablative case. Where the root or nominal bases are stated in the genitive instead of the ablative, similar syntax is assumed by virtue of the fact that other direction words (such as *paratas*) govern the genitive (in accordance with A. 2.3.30).

However, an explicit statement of the significance of the genitive, locative, and ablative case is required to resolve doubt in other rules. The genitive may indicate any one of a number of relations such as property, ownership, proximity, part, whole, etc. In order to resolve doubt where the genitive is not susceptible of a single interpretation in its context, Pāṇini states the principle in A. 1.1.49 *ṣaṣṭhī sthāneyogā* that a genitive (*ṣaṣṭhī* 'sixth-triplet nominal termination') is understood to designate one relation in particular, namely, that of substituend. Pāṇini regularly indicates items to be replaced in the genitive. For example, according to the following rules, the verbal root *as* 'be' is replaced by the verbal root *bhū* 'be' when an ārdhadhātuka affix is to be used, and a simple vowel is replaced by its corresponding semivowel when a dissimilar vowel follows in continuous speech:

> A. 2.4.52 *aster bhūḥ* (*ārdhadhātuka* 35).
> A. 6.1.77 *iko yaṇ aci* (*saṃhitāyām* 72).

In these rules, the unbound genitives *asteḥ* (*asti* is a citation form of the verbal root *as*) and *ikaḥ* (*ik* is a reference to the vowels *i, u, ṛ, ḷ*) are understood to be substituends by virtue of the metarule *A.* 1.1.49.

Augments, in contrast to affixes, are generally provided to items specified in the genitive rather than in the ablative. Commentators justify the genitive in the syntax of augmentation by reference to the metarule *A.* 1.1.46 *ādyantau ṭakitau.* According to this rule, a speech form marked with *ṭ* or *k* is added as the initial or final part respectively of an element in the genitive. Such a genitive is a partitive genitive signifying the whole of which the augment is a part. Consistent with ordinary Sanskrit syntax, metarules serve to help the student of the *Aṣṭādhyāyī* interpret rules when doubt concerning their interpretation occurs because the rules of ordinary Sanskrit syntax permit ambiguity.

Two additional metarules specify the context of the operation taught in a rule. According to *A.* 1.1.67 *tasmād ity uttarasya*, an ablative that is subject to competing interpretations in a rule signifies that the operation specified takes effect upon the following speech form. *A.* 1.1.66 *tasminniti nirdiṣṭe pūrvasya* similarly serves to interpret a locative not already subject to a definite interpretation as specifying that the operation specified takes effect upon the preceding item. The commentators Kātyāyana and Patañjali clarify that these rules restrict the use of the ablative and genitive to one among the specific senses these cases have in ordinary usage. Both the ablative and genitive are ambiguous as to whether they convey placement before or after. Hence in the rule

> A. 6.1.77 *iko yaṇ aci*

the locative *aci* and the ablative *ikaḥ* do not specify whether the vowel (*ac*) precedes or follows the simple vowel (*ik*). Hence, in the string *dadhi udakam*, where both the *i* and *u* are simple vowels (*ik*) and vowels (*ac*), there is doubt concerning whether by *A.* 6.1.77 the semivowel (*yaṇ*) replaces the sound preceding or following the vowel. One would not know whether to replace the *i* by *y* or the *u* by *v*. It is desired that *A.* 6.1.77 apply to the sound preceding the vowel. That will not happen without the explicit statement of the restrictions in *A.* 1.1.66–67.

Some forty metarules are explicitly stated in the *Aṣṭādhyāyī.* Besides those that specify the syntax of rules described above, metarules clarify additional conventions of replacement, let certain replacements have the status of their original and deleted items have persistent effects, allow the derivation of alternate utterances, establish certain conventions of rule precedence and suspension, and other such conventions. Noteworthy is the concept of the persistent effect of a nullified affix. *A.* 1.1.62 *pratyaya-lope pratyayalakṣaṇam* establishes the convention that even when an affix is deleted, the operations it conditions are still carried out. For example, *A.* 1.4.14 *suptiṅantam padam* terms *pada* 'word' a speech form that ends in a nominal or verbal termination. The speech form *somasut* 'one who has pressed soma' is still termed *pada* even though its nominative singular masculine termination *s* has been deleted by *A.* 6.1.68. The following rule, however, states a partial negation of this principle. *A.* 1.1.63 *na lumatāṅgasya* disallows operations conditioned by the deleted affix on the preceding stem if the deletion is taught with one of the three terms containing *lu*, i.e. *luk*, *ślu*, or *lup*. Thus *gargāḥ* 'descendants of Garga' does not undergo replacement of the initial vowel of its stem by the *vṛddhi* vowel *ā*, despite the fact that such a replacement is conditioned by the affix *yañ*. The affix *yañ* is provided after the stems in the list beginning with *garga* by *A.* 4.1.105 *gargādibhyo yañ* if a descendant is to be denoted. For example, *gārgyaḥ* denotes a descendant of Garga. However, in the plural, the affix *yañ* is deleted by *A.* 2.4.64 *yañañoś ca* (*luk* 58 *bahuṣu* 62) by the term *luk* which is understood to recur from *A.* 2.4.58.

11.2.5 Syntactic Relations

11.2.5.1 *Abstract Expressions*

Pāṇini uses abstract expressions to designate syntactic structures. A noteworthy feature of the statement of the principles in *A.* 1.1.66–7 described in §11.2.4 is the use of pronouns as variables in abstract expressions. The demonstrative pronoun *tad* in the locative (*tasmin*) in the former and in the ablative (*tasmāt*) in the latter stand for any item stated in the locative or ablative in a grammatical rule. The quotative particle *iti* serves to indicate a reversal of the norm for speech forms in the grammar: these pronominal forms refer to their meaning—x[locative] or x[ablative]—rather than the mentioned locative and ablative pronominal speech forms themselves. Declined forms of demonstrative pronouns are similarly used as variables in rules that specify the conditions under which affixes are provided to form derived nominal bases from nominal constituents. The demonstrative pronoun is used in various cases to indicate the syntactic relation that the derivate has to the base, thereby specifying the significance captured by the affix. *A.* 4.1.82 *samarthānāṃ prathamād vā* specifies that in the following rules the relevant affix or affixes optionally occur after the first of syntactically and semantically related words in the phrase modelled in the rule. Since the provision of the affix is optional, the derivate alternates with the expression modelled. For example, the first word in each of the six sūtras in Table 11.5 is a demonstrative pronoun in the accusative, instrumental, dative, ablative, genitive, or locative case respectively. The pronoun stands for any word in that case (compatible with other limiting conditions stated or understood in the rule) in syntactic construction with the second word in the sūtra. *A.* 4.2.59 repeats the accusative pronoun with a second verb. Thus *A.* 4.2.59 provides an affix after a word in the accusative to form a derived base meaning 'studies x' or 'knows x' which alternates with the stated phrases. *A.* 4.2.1

Table 11.5 Pronominal variables in taddhita–affixation

A. 4.2.59 *tad adhīte tad veda*	*vyākaraṇam adhīte* 'studies grammar'	*vaiyākaraṇaḥ* 'grammarian'
A. 4.2.1 *tena raktaṃ rāgāt*	*kaṣāyena raktaṃ* 'dyed with ochre'	*kāṣāyam* 'an ochre robe'
A. 5.1.5 *tasmai hitam*	*vatsebhyo hitaḥ* 'good for calves'	*vatsīyaḥ* 'a milkman good for calves'
A. 4.3.74 *tata āgataḥ*	*srughnād āgataḥ* 'come from Srughna'	*sraughnaḥ* 'Srughnan'
A. 4.1.92 *tasyāpatyam*	*upagor apatyam* 'descendant of Upagu'	*aupagavaḥ*
A. 4.3.25 *tatra jātaḥ*	*srughne jātaḥ* 'born in Srughna'	*sraughnaḥ* 'Srughnan'

Table 11.6 General Pāṇinian kāraka rules

Sūtra	Kāraka	Semantic condition	Vibhakti	Sūtra
A. 1.4.24	*apādāna*	fixed point of departure	5th	A. 2.3.28
A. 1.4.32	*sampradāna*	intended recipient of the object	4th	A. 2.3.13
A. 1.4.42	*karaṇa*	immediately most efficacious	3rd	A. 2.3.18
A. 1.4.45	*adhikaraṇa*	substrate	7th	A. 2.3.36
A. 1.4.49	*karman*	most desired to be attained	2nd	A. 2.3.2
A. 1.4.54	*kartṛ*	independent	3rd	A. 2.3.18
A. 1.4.55	*hetu*	agent's motivator		

provides an affix after a word in the instrumental case to form a derived base meaning 'dyed with x' on the condition that x is a colour. Similarly with the others.

11.2.5.2 *Thematic Roles*

In order to achieve the complex mapping of speech forms to syntactic and semantic relations, Pāṇini utilizes intermediate syntactic structures called kārakas. The term literally means 'actors' and denotes what has now become familiar in modern linguistics under the name 'thematic roles.' General rules assign participants playing certain roles in bringing about an action to certain thematic role categories on purely semantic criteria by giving them one of seven terms denoting those roles. The seven terms given to roles on purely semantic criteria are shown in columns 2 and 3 of Table 11.6. Specific rules modify assignments based upon co-occurrence conditions. The seven kāraka-terms are subsequently used as conditions for the provision of verbal terminations, primary nominal affixes provided after verbal roots, secondary nominal affixes provided after nominal bases, compounds, and nominal terminations. The kāraka terms *kartṛ* and *karman* serve as conditions for the provision of verbal terminations in active and passive constructions respectively. The term *hetu* serves as condition for derivation of causative forms by *A.* 3.1.26. Nominal terminations are provided where kārakas have not already been denoted by verbal terminations and other speech forms. Columns 4 and 5 of Table 11.6 show the nominal terminations conditioned by kāraka terms by general rules. The first seven vibhaktis are triplets of nominal terminations used to derive forms in the nominative (including vocative), accusative, instrumental, dative, ablative, genitive, and locative cases.

11.2.6 Rule Application

11.2.6.1 *General Rules and Exceptions*

Pāṇini's *Aṣṭādhyāyī* is a systematic treatise that utilizes generalization to capture common features, yet details specifics as well. The grammar states general rules and exceptions to them. The correct operation of the grammar depends upon determining which rules are exceptions to which. The most basic principle of determining rule precedence is that a rule that provides an operation in a narrower domain wholly included within the domain of another rule constitutes an exception to the rule with the broader domain and blocks it from operating in the narrower domain. For instance *A.* 6.1.77 (see §11.2.4) is the general rule that replaces a simple vowel other than *a* by its corresponding semivowel before a vowel. *A.* 6.4.77 *aci śnudhātubhruvāṃ yvor iyaṅ-uvaṅau* replaces certain stem-final vowels *i* and *u* occurring before a vowel instead by *iy* and *uv* respectively. Since the domain of the latter is entirely included within the former, *A.* 6.4.77 constitutes an exception to *A.* 6.1.77. While the principle that a rule that applies to a domain wholly included within the domain of another rule constitutes an exception to it is not explicitly stated in the *Aṣṭādhyāyī*, commentators point out that the principle is inferrable. The rule with the narrower domain would have no scope of application if it did not block the more general rule within its own domain. The very fact that wholly included rules have been stated demonstrates that Pāṇini operated with the principle that they constitute exceptions that take precedence over their related general rules. Several other principles of rule selection are operative in the grammar as described in the following sections.

11.2.6.2 *Overriding Conjoint Classification by Sequence*

In contrast to operations, classificatory rules (*saṃjñā sūtras*) generally operate concurrently, thereby allowing subclasses and overlapping classes. The same vowel, for instance may simultaneously be termed short (*hrasva*) by *A.* 1.2.27 *ūkālo 'j jhrasva-dīrghaplutaḥ* and high-pitched (*udātta*) by *A.* 1.2.29 *uccair udāttaḥ*. In order to classify certain items in disjoint classes, Pāṇini states the rules that classify them under the heading *A.* 1.4.1 *ā kaḍārād ekā saṃjñā*, which permits only one term to apply to the same entity at a time, and in the purview of the metarule *A.* 1.4.2 *vipratiṣedhe paraṃ kāryam*, which in cases of conflict between rules with overlapping domains has the latter rule apply. The kāraka rules occur in this section. Thus an object eligible for more than one classification is assigned exclusively the kāraka class name provided

subsequently unless explicitly stated otherwise by the use of the conjunction *ca* 'and.'
For example, Kātyāyana states in *A.* 1.4.1 vt. 31 and Patañjali explains, 'The term
karman by 1.4.38 *krudhadruhor upasṛṣṭayoḥ karma* blocks the term *sampradāna*'
(*Mahābhāṣya* (hereafter abbreviated *MBh.*) 1.302.22–3). Consider sentences (1) and
(2). In (1) Devadatta is termed *sampradāna* by *A.* 1.4.37 by virtue of being the one
toward whom anger is felt, which conditions the dative nominal termination in
accordance with *A.* 2.3.13. In (2) Devadatta is eligible to be termed *sampradāna* by
the same rule but is also eligible to be termed *karman* by *A.* 1.4.38, which provides the
term *karman* for the one toward whom anger is felt under the condition that a preverb
occurs with the root *krudh* 'be angry' or with the root *druh* 'be malicious.' The latter
rule alone applies in accordance with *A.* 1.4.1–2.

(1) *devadattāya krudhyati.*
     He is angry at Devadatta.
(2) *devadattam abhikrudhyati.*
     He is angry toward Devadatta.

11.2.6.3 *Bracketing*

As described in §11.2.2, Pāṇini's grammar presupposes an analysis of utterances into
constituent words (*pada*), words into stems and affixes, and derivable stems into their
components. When rules of the grammar apply to build utterances from basic constituents, a hierarchy is observed: internally conditioned (*antaraṅga*) operations take
precedence over externally conditioned (*bahiraṅga*) operations, that is, operations
within words take precedence over operations between words, and operations within
sub-word components take precedence over operations between such components. The
principle is formalized in *Vyāḍiparibhāṣā 73 asiddhaṃ bahiraṅgam antaraṅge.* In the
derivation of *kurutas* 'they two make,' the verbal termination *tas* occurs after the root
kṛ, and the stem-forming affix *u* occurs between. The root *kṛ* plus stem-forming affix *u*
as a unit is itself stem to the verbal termination *tas* such that units may be bracketed as
follows: (*kṛ-u*)-*tas*. An operation conditioned by the stem-forming affix *u* is therefore
more internally conditioned with respect to an operation conditioned by the verbal
termination *tas*. Consider the conditions causing and inhibiting replacement by a guṇa
vowel in this phonetic string. Replacement of *ṛ* final in the root *kṛ* by its corresponding
guṇa vowel in accordance with *A.* 7.3.84 *sārvadhātukārdhadhātukayoḥ* is conditioned
by the affix *u*. On the other hand, replacement of the penultimate vowel *ṛ* of the stem
kṛ-u by its corresponding guṇa vowel in accordance with *A.* 7.3.86 *pugantalaghūpadhasya ca* is prevented before the verbal termination *tas* because the verbal termination
tas is marked with *ṅ* by the extension rule *A.* 1.2.4 *sārvadhātukam apit* (*ṅit* 1).
Replacement by guṇa is negated before affixes marked with *ṅ* by *A.* 1.1.5 *kṅiti ca*. By
virtue of the principle that an internally conditioned operation takes precedence over
an externally conditioned operation, guṇa in accordance with *A.* 7.3.84 *sārvadhātukārdhadhātukayoḥ* conditioned by the stem-forming affix *u* takes precedence over the
inhibition of guṇa conditioned by the verbal termination *tas* (see Cardona 1998: 413).

11.2.6.4 *Bleeding Operations*

Operations that deprive other operations of their conditions take precedence over them if the latter would not likewise deprive the former of their conditions. Such operations are among those called 'bleeding operations' in today's terminology. Pāṇinians call an operation that deprives another operation of its conditions *nitya* with respect to the other operation if the other operation does not deprive it of its conditions. The other operation is termed *anitya* with respect to the first operation. For example, in the derivation of the third person singular present active indicative verb *tudati* ' . . . strikes' given *tud-ti* where the verbal root *tud* is followed by the verbal termination *ti*, the stem-forming affix *a* could be introduced by A. 3.1.77 *tudādibhyaḥ śaḥ*, or the penultimate vowel *u* of the root *tud* could be replaced by its corresponding guṇa vowel by A. 7.3.86 *pugantalaghūpadhasya ca*. Since replacements have the status of their constituents, guṇa replacement does not eliminate the conditions for the introduction of the stem-forming affix. Introduction of the stem-forming affix, on the other hand, eliminates the conditions for guṇa replacement, since the vowel *u* would no longer be the penultimate sound before the verbal termination *ti*. A. 3.1.77 is therefore nitya with respect to A. 7.3.86 and takes precedence over it.

11.2.6.5 *Suspension of Rules and their Effects*

Rules in the last three-quarters of the eighth chapter of the *Aṣṭādhyāyī* are ordered in such a way that prior rules should apply before subsequent ones, and an explicit statement is made in A. 8.2.1 *pūrvatrāsiddham* that subsequent rules are suspended with respect to former ones within that section as also the entire group is suspended with respect to the preceding seven and one quarter chapters. Pāṇini likewise provides for mutual suspension of the effects of rules in the section headed by A. 6.4.22 *asiddhavad atrābhāt*, and (by A. 6.1.86 *ṣatvatukorasiddhaḥ*) for the suspension of the effects of single replacement rules A. 6.1.84–111 with respect to the retroflexion of *s* (A. 8.3.59 *ādeśapratyayayoḥ*) and addition of the final augment *t* (A. 6.1.71–6). Suspension of rules serves preventing the undesired feeding to rules as well as preventing undesired bleeding from general rules. For example, in the sentence *ko'siñcat* 'Who watered?', the single replacement *o*, provided by A. 6.1.109 *eṅaḥ padāntād ati*, is considered the final sound of the preceding word as well as the initial sound of the following word in accordance with the principle for single replacements stated in A. 6.1.85 *antādivac ca*. The vowel *o* therefore would serve as the condition for the undesired retroflexion of the following *s* in accordance with A. 8.3.59. Suspension prevents it.

11.2.7 Indeterminism

Although Pāṇini's grammar constitutes a detailed and systematic generative apparatus that adheres to the several principles of rule precedence described in §11.2.6, these principles alone are not adequate to completely determine rule selection. The grammar depends upon specific statements of the early commentators Kātyāyana and Patañjali that specify which of these principles is operative in which sections. For example, assuming that the principle that the latter of two conflicting rules with overlapping domains takes precedence applies throughout the grammar rather than just in *A.* 1.4–2.4, Kātyāyana states that the augment *num* occurs in precedence over guṇa, vṛddhi, and certain other operations by virtue of the opposite principle, i.e. the principle that the prior rule applies in cases of conflict (*A.* 7.1.96 vt. 10, *MBh.* 3.275.23.). Moreover, Patañjali often comments that explanation is required to deliver the correct understanding of a rule (*vyākhyānato viśeṣapratipattiḥ. MBh.* 1.6.26 et alibi; *Vyāḍiparibhāṣā* 52), and that one doesn't understand speech forms just from the rules but also from explanation (*na hi sūtrata eva śabdān pratipadyante kiṃ tarhi vyākhyānataś ca, MBh.* 1.11.20–21 et alibi). The subsections 1 and 2 discuss two ways in which commentators recognize indeterminism in the grammar and resort to linguistic convention or prior knowledge of outcomes to determine derivational processes. Subsection 3 discusses rules in the *Aṣṭādhyāyī* itself that deliberately allow indeterminate variation, and the last subsection reveals theoretical disagreement as to how far grammatical specification should extend into the lexicon.

11.2.7.1 *Linguistic Convention (vivakṣā)*

§11.2.6.2 described how participants in action are assigned the kāraka term that occurs later in accordance with the principle stated in *A.* 1.4.2 that the later rule applies in cases of conflict between rules with overlapping domains. The example provided there shows a case in which a co-occurring speech form is a condition for the change in syntax reflected by the different kāraka classification. Kātyāyana and Patañjali adduce examples in which a change in syntax is due solely to a speaker's intention of participants in action in roles other than their proper ontological roles. Legitimate utterances in which items are spoken of in roles other than their proper ontological roles are derived by extending the semantic condition for the application of a kāraka term to one intended by a speaker. In sentence (3), for example, the bow (*dhanus*) is spoken of in its proper ontological role as the fixed point of departure from which the arrow (by means of which Devadatta pierces the target) emerges. As source, the bow is termed *apādāna* by *A.* 1.4.24 *dhruvam apaye 'pādānam* which conditions a fifth-triplet nominal termination by *A.* 2.3.28 *apādāne pañcamī* by virtue of which the word *dhanus* appears in the ablative case. In sentences (4) and (5), however, the word *dhanus* appears in the instrumental and nominative cases respectively. It was understood that the different cases embody different conceptions the linguistic community holds of the roles played by the denoted objects. Kātyāyana and Patañjali incorporate linguistic conception into the grammatical procedure that derives these syntactic structures. Kātyāyana adduces (4) and (5) as examples of the application of the principle that the later term applies stated in *A.* 1.4.2. Patañjali explains that in (4) and (5), the bow is still eligible for the class term *apādāna* by virtue of being the fixed point of departure. Yet in the derivation of (4) the term *karaṇa* 'instrument' provided by *A.* 1.4.42 and in (5) the term *kartṛ* 'agent' provided by *A.* 1.4.54 override the term *apādāna* 'source' provided by *A.* 1.4.24 because they are provided later (*MBh.* 1.302.11–1.303.5).

Later commentators, however, adduce examples that would violate the rule precedence principle stated in *A.* 1.4.2. Consider sentence (6). Helārāja, the tenth-century commentator on Bhartṛhari's *Vākyapadīya*, states, 'Although the pot in (6) is recognized as being adhikaraṇa "locus," it attains to being karaṇa "instrument" by a speaker's intention, by virtue of bringing about cooking more quickly because it is a thinner vessel.' Because the pot is the substrate of cooking, the term *adhikaraṇa* obtains by *A.* 1.4.45. Because it is intended as the most efficacious in cooking, the term *karaṇa* obtains by *A.* 1.4.42. By *A.* 1.4.1–2, only the latter term, *adhikaraṇa*, should apply. However, against the hierarchy of rules, the earlier term, *karaṇa*, applies. Bhartṛhari and his successors conclude from examples such as (6) that there is no hierarchy of kāraka rules, and that kāraka classification depends more loosely on a speaker's intention. Bhartṛhari writes (*Vākyapadīya* 3.7.3ab), 'The employment of the kārakas is dependent upon the attitude of the intellect' (*sādhanavyavahāraś ca buddhyavasthā-nibandhanaḥ*). The freer use of a speaker's intention as a criterion that overrides the stated rule-selection principle suggests that these later commentators do not consider the derivational process to be fully determined by explicit principles.

(3) *Devadattaḥ dhanuṣaḥ nirgatena śareṇa lakṣyaṃ vidhyati.*
   Devadatta pierces the target with an arrow emerged from his bow.
   (implied by Nāgeśa IB.286–87, 288 [Roh 2.315, 317])

(4) *dhanuṣā vidhyati.* (1.4.1 vt. 30; *MBh.* 1.302.11)
   He pierces (the target) with a bow.

(5) *dhanur vidhyati.* (1.4.1 vt. 30; *MBh.* 1.302.12)
   The bow pierces (the target).

(6) *sthālyā pacyate.* (*Vākyapadīya* 3.7.91)
   (Rice) is cooked by means of a pot.

11.2.7.2 *Rule vs Target*

As mentioned in §11.2.7, Kātyāyana assumed that the principle that the later of two conflicting rules with overlapping domains takes precedence applies throughout the grammar and specified exceptions to it. Without such an assumption and those specifications, the procedure of the grammar remains indeterminate, and one is required to rely upon knowledge of outcomes—that is, knowledge of the correct forms to be derived—in order to determine rule precedence. In order to avoid the necessity of stating Kātyāyana's specification of exceptions to the principle that the later rule applies in cases of conflict, Patañjali proposes to reinterpret the principle. He adduces evidence of the use of the term *para*, previously understood in *A.* 1.4.2 to mean 'later', instead to mean 'desired'. He thereby reinterprets the principle to specify that the most desired rule takes precedence where there is conflict between rules with overlapping domains (*MBh.* 1.306.4–10). By departing in this way from a mechanistic procedure for determining the application of rules, and relying rather on knowledge of the desired outcome of the generative grammar to determine rule ordering, Patañjali's proposal weakens the grammar. It would be circular for knowledge of correct speech forms to be required in order to comprehend what the grammar provided, since the grammar is meant to validate correct speech forms.

However, it is not necessarily the case that Pāṇini's grammar was intended to function in total independence from the guidance of those who know what constitutes correct Sanskrit usage. As a matter of fact, later grammarians criticize those who are single-minded in finding solutions to make the grammar operate entirely by rule. Nāgeśa uses the term *lakṣaṇaikacakṣuṣka* 'rule-one-eyed,' i.e. 'for whom the rules are their only eye,' in a derogatory manner for such people; they do not know the correct forms to be described by the rules (*lakṣya*) without depending upon the rules (*lakṣaṇa*).

11.2.7.3 *Interpretation and Indeterminate Variation*

Pāṇini himself formulated certain rules in such a way as to leave the grammar open-ended. §11.2.2 noted that certain basic elements are unlimited: nominal bases are included as basic elements under the sole specification that they be meaningful (*A.* 1.2.45). Verbal roots are also unlimited, since rules are included that derive verbal roots from nominal bases specified by general criteria (*A.* 3.1.8–11 et alia). Likewise, Pāṇini formulates numerous escape rules. Some of these, such as *A.* 3.2.101 *anyeṣv api dṛśyate*, state that affixes provided in specified circumstances 'are seen in others as well,' or similarly state that those provided after specific roots 'are seen after others as well,' for example *A.* 3.2.178 *anyebhyo 'pi dṛśyate*. Others state that there is transgression of certain previously stated rules with indeterminate variation, such as *A.* 3.1.85 *vyatyayo bahulam*. In some cases, such as regarding Vedic forms, deference may be made to other treatises that deal with the phenomena in greater specificity. Yet in other cases it may be that Pāṇini deliberately leaves room for productive processes and free variation in usage (see Cardona 2004).

11.2.7.4 *Limits of Analysis*

Unlike Śākaṭāyana and the etymologists who considered that all words were derivable from verbal roots (see §11.1.2), most grammarians recognized that some nominal forms are opaque to linguistic analysis and must be included in the lexicon anomalously. *A.* 1.2.53 *tad aśiṣyaṃ saṃjñāpramāṇatvāt* considers that anomalies of gender and number agreement for certain derivates such as fruit and place names are not to be taught as inherited from their derivational bases because these anomalies are understood by convention. Two subsequent rules, *A.* 1.2.54–5, eschew the derivation of such fruit and place names altogether; such words are to be included in the lexicon as independent underived conventional terms. *A.* 1.2.53, which though possibly an interpolation was part of the *Aṣṭādhyāyī* text received by Patañjali, and *A.* 1.2.54–7, which are commented upon by Jayāditya and Vāmana in the *Kāśikā* yet are very probably interpolations since they are not commented upon by Kātyāyana or Patañjali, are critical of the policy of deriving such conventional terms actually carried out in the *Aṣṭādhyāyī*. On the other hand, the *Aṣṭādhyāyī* contains numerous rules that derive conventional terms while insufficiently specifying their limited scope of application. Kātyāyana and Patañjali frequently defend such rules from charges of overextension by arguing that unwanted application of such rules is prevented by virtue of the fact that unwanted derivates simply happen not to be used to signify the given meaning (*anabhidhānāt*) (*A.* 3.2.1 vt. 5, *MBh.* 2.94.15). Indeed, one of the impressive features of Pāṇinian grammar is the deep lexical penetration of its systematic derivation.

11.3 NON-PĀṆINIAN SANSKRIT GRAMMAR

11.3.1 Rules

Even though they depend upon Pāṇini's work, a number of grammatical treatises are called non-Pāṇinian because they depart from his techniques in significant ways. The earliest such grammar known, by Kumāralāta, *c.*325 CE, is extant only in a single fragmentary manuscript discovered in Turkestan. Kumāralāta permits Middle Indo-Aryan forms commonly found in Buddhist scriptures (Scharfe 1977: 162). Perhaps the oldest extant, but of uncertain date, is the *Śabdakalāpa* grammar of Kāsakṛtsna. A shorter version of the *Śabdakalāpa* is found in the *Kātantra* grammar of Śarvavarman (*c.*400 CE), which itself was enlarged (*c.*800 CE) in Tibetan Tanjur. The grammar is less analytic and derivational than Pāṇini's in that, for example, it provides ready-made a full set of verbal terminations for the various tenses and moods rather than deriving them from basic terminations by substitution and augmentation. The description of phonetic change and the arrangement of the sound catalogue follow the Prātiśākhyas rather than the Pāṇinian description of speech form substitution, and the Pāṇinian rearrangement of the sound catalogue for the purpose of forming abbreviatory terms of phonetic reference (see §11.2.3). Śarvavarman's *Kātantra* grammar originally did not include sections devoted to deriving primary nominal derivates, secondary nominal derivates, and compounds. While such simplifications have often been considered to be solely for pedagogical purposes, they are motivated by a theoretical concern that has a long history: conventional terms are considered underivable (see Cardona 2008); they are to be included in an enlarged lexicon as opaque to derivation just as underived stems are included among basic elements in Pāṇinian grammar and just as verbal roots constitute the lexicon in the view of Śākaṭāyana and the etymologists.

The *Cāndra* grammar of the Buddhist Candragomin (fifth-century CE) avoids technical terms and dispenses with Pāṇini's kāraka class names. The *Jainendra* grammar of the Jain Devanandin (*c.* fifth–seventh century CE) closely follows the sequence of Pāṇini's rules while further condensing their formulation. The *Mugdhabodha* of Vopadeva (late thirteenth century CE, Maharashtra) similarly condenses rule formulation in a set of 1,184 sūtras in 26 sections. The rule set and commentary *Amoghavṛtti* of the Jain monk Śākaṭāyana (ninth century CE) are the foundation of the *Siddhahaima-candra* of the Jain Hemacandra Sūri (1089–1172 CE, Gujarat). A quarter of the 4,500 rules of the latter are transfer rules in the eighth book that derive Prakrit from Sanskrit basic forms (Scharfe 1977: 169). In 1042, Bhoja, king of Dhārā in western Madhya Pradesh, incorporated Kātyāyana's vārttikas, metarules, and other grammatical components in his *Sarasvatīkaṇṭhābharaṇa* grammar of more than 6,000 rules in a topical arrangement commented upon in the *Hṛdayahāriṇī* by Nārāyaṇabhaṭṭa. In the twelfth century Kramadīśvara wrote the *Saṃkṣiptasāra* arranged topically in 4,000 sūtras on which Jūmaranandin (thirteenth century) wrote the *Rasavatī*. In the first half of the twelfth century in Varanasi, Dāmodara wrote a grammar in 50 kārikās in Ārya metre arranged in five chapters that shows the relationship of Old Kosalī to Sanskrit. The last two chapters are devoted to letter writing. The Sārasvata grammar, extant in Anubhūtisvarūpācārya's (thirteenth–fourteenth centuries) *Sārasvataprakriyā* in 1,494 sūtras, generated a number of commentaries. In Mithila and Cooch in Bihar, Padmanābhadatta (fourteenth century) and Puruṣottama (sixteenth century) wrote the *Saupadma* and *Prayogaratnamālā* grammars.

11.3.2 Root Lists (*dhātupāṭha*s)

As in Pāṇinian grammar, a root list is an essential component of other Indian linguistic systems; hence root lists accompany the rule sets composed by other linguists. The *Śabdakalāpa* grammar of Kāsakṛtsna includes a root list on which Cannavīrakavi (*c.*1500 CE, Kuṇṭikāpura, Tumkur district, Karṇāṭaka) wrote a Kannada commentary *Kāsakṛtsna-Śabdakalāpadhātupāṭhakarṇāṭakaṭīkā*. The enlarged version of the *Kātantra* grammar was supplied with a root list. While the root lists associated with these grammars share a large common stock, each root list differs from that attached to other grammars by the addition, omission, alternative classification, and modification of roots in the list. Variation in the root list alters the linguistic description of the linguistic system that includes the root list. Roots may have been deliberately added by linguists or redactors to their root list in order to account for forms in the Sanskrit language as known to them. Such roots would account for new words not known to Pāṇini, or to other early grammarians, that may have come into Sanskrit due to historical sound change and from borrowings into Sanskrit from regional and foreign languages throughout the history of Sanskrit's presence in the subcontinent. In addition to sound change and borrowing, the linguistic process of analogy created new verb forms in Sanskrit to be accounted for by reclassification of roots within the root lists.

11.4 GRAMMARS OF LANGUAGES OTHER THAN SANSKRIT

11.4.1 Prakrit Grammars

The Bharata-*Nāṭyaśāstra* (written by the early centuries CE) contains a few verses written in Prakrit (17.6–9) that state phonetic rules to convert Sanskrit to Prakrit exemplified in subsequent verses written in Sanskrit (17.10–23). The *Prākṛtaprakāśa*, attributed to Vararuci, consists of 420 sūtras dealing with Mahārāṣṭrī. The text was commented upon in the seventh century by Bhāmaha, who adds a chapter on Paiśācī and a chapter on Māgadhī. A chapter on Śaurasenī was subsequently added. The grammar derives the Prakrit forms from strings of basic Pāṇinian grammatical elements in Sanskrit. Expansions of the text attributed to Vararuci include Puruṣottama's (twelfth-century) *Prākṛ-tānuśāsana*, Mārlaṇḍeya's *Prākṛtasarvasva* (seventeenth-century), and Rāmaśarman's (seventeenth century) *Prākṛtakalpataru*, which add treatment of Paiśācī and Apabhraṃśa. Hemacandra Sūri composed 1,119 rules that similarly derive these Prakrits and Ardhamāgadhī from Sanskrit basic elements in the eighth book of his Sanskrit grammar (see §11.3). Kramadīśvara likewise included a treatment of Prakrit in the eighth book of his Sanskrit grammar (see §11.3). The *Prākṛtaśabdānuśāsana* of the Jain Trivikrama (thirteenth century) in 1,036 sūtras depends heavily upon the work of Hemacandra Sūri.

11.4.2 Pāli

The oldest extant Pāli grammar is the *Kaccāyanavyākaraṇa*, written between the fifth and eleventh centuries in Pāli in 675 sūtras and commented upon first in the eleventh century in the *Nyāsa* by Vimalabuddhi. Its most prominent recast is the *Rūpasiddhi* of Buddhappiya dīpaṃkara (late thirteenth century). In 1154 in Pagan, Aggavaṃsa composed the *Saddanīti*, which drew upon the Sanskrit grammars of Kramadīśvara, Maitreyarakṣita, and Kaccāyana. During the reign of Parakkamabāhu I (1153–86), Moggallāna of the Thūpārāma monastery in Anurādhapura wrote the *Māgadha saddalakkhaṇa*, influenced by the work of Candragomin, which inspired a large body of grammatical literature. While these grammars were influenced in their techniques by the Sanskrit grammars, they do not derive Pāli forms from Sanskrit as do the Prakrit grammars.

11.4.3 Persian

Kṛṣṇadāsa wrote a grammar and glossary of Persian called *Pārasīprakāśa* under commission from the Moghul emperor Akbar, who ruled 1556–1605. The grammar, written in Sanskrit in 480 rules, derives Persian from Sanskrit basic elements.

11.4.4 Tamil

The Sangam literature in Tamil comprises about 2,300 poems, constituting about 29,300 lines arranged in eight anthologies, composed over a long period of time in part in the early centuries CE, while the names of kings mentioned in some of them appear in inscriptions of the third century BCE. Composed no earlier than the second century BCE and reaching the form in which it has been received in the fifth century CE, the oldest Tamil linguistic treatise, the *Tolkāppiyam*, consists of 1,600 verses in three books, each containing nine chapters, covering three topics: phonetics, words, and poetic subject matter. The text was commented upon in full by Iḷampūraṇar (tenth–twelfth centuries) and in part by Cēṉāvaraiyar (thirteenth–fourteenth centuries), Pēraciriyar (thirteenth century), Naccíṉārkkiṉiyar (fourteenth century), Teyvaccilaiyār (c. sixteenth century), Kallāṭaṉār (c. fifteenth–seventeenth centuries), and a later anonymous commentator. The language it describes differs only in minor respects from that of the Sangam literature. The first book includes graphic considerations in writing as well as phonetics, phonology, sandhi, and morphophonemics. The second book treats of morphology and syntax, especially case. While inspired by Pāṇinian kārakas, it utilizes exclusively Tamil terminology and adds two additional categories: time and purpose. It also treats the syntax of particles. The third book describes the conventions of amorous and martial poetry, sentiments, analogy, and metrics—topics found in Sanskrit literary theory texts. The composition of the *Tolkāppiyam* borrows from the Sanskrit phonetic, grammatical, and poetic traditions but does not adopt Pāṇinian techniques. Like the Prātiśākhyas, phonetic rules are framed in terms of change rather than substitution (as in Pāṇinian grammar), and accounting is made of permitted phonetic sequences and occurrence of sounds in initial and final position in words.

Of the *Avinayam* handbook composed before the ninth century, only fragments remain. The *Vīracōḻiyakkārikai*, written by the Buddhist king Puttamittiraṉ in the eleventh century, consists of 181 verses in five chapters covering five topics: phonetics, word, poetic subject matter, metrics, and poetics. The text introduces some Pāṇinian terminology and techniques such as the kārakas and zero suffixes. The text was commented upon soon afterwards by Peruntēvaṉār. The Jain Kuṇavīrapaṇṭitar wrote the *Nēminātam* at the beginning of the thirteenth century. The text consists of 95 verses in two sections: phonetics and word. At about the same time, the Jain Pavaṇanti wrote the *Naṉṉūl* consisting of 462 verses in three sections, including a preface in 55 verses which may be a later addition, and sections on phonetics and word. The text was first commented upon by Mayilainātar in the fourteenth century. In the beginning of the seventeenth century Cuppiramaṇiyatītcitar wrote the *Pirayōkavivēkam*, and towards the end of the same century Vaittiyanāta Nāvalar wrote the *Ilakkaṇaviḷakkam*.

The *Līlātilakam* (1375–1400 CE) is a grammar of Tamil consisting of 151 sūtras in Sanskrit with a commentary in Malayalam concerning a style that mixes Sanskrit with a vernacular language called *maṇipravāḷam* 'jewel and coral.' The text describes the phonetics and grammar of each language while disapproving of the use of Sanskrit terminations for Tamil words and vice versa. Chevillard (2000) supplies more detail about Dravidian linguistics.

11.4.5 Telugu

The *Āndhraśabdacintāmaṇi* in 82–90 verses containing 274 sūtras in Sanskrit ascribed to the poet Nannaya (eleventh century) was commented upon in Telugu by Elakūci

Bālasarasvatī (c.1550–1600), Appakavi (c.1600–1670), and Ahobalapati (c.1700). Yet Mūlaghaṭika Ketana (1220–1300) claimed that his *Āndhrabhāṣābhūṣaṇa* in 192 Telugu verses was the first Telugu grammar. At the beginning of the fourteenth century, Atharvaṇācārya composed the *Vikṛtiviveka*, a supplement to the *Āndhraśabdacintāmaṇi* in Sanskrit, and the *Triliṅgaśabdānuśāsana*, an essay on the origin of the Telugu language. In the nineteenth century, following the arrangement of Bhaṭṭojidīkṣita's *Siddhāntakaumudī*, Paravastu Cinnayasūri wrote his influential *Bālavyākaraṇamu* in Telugu sūtras, to which B. Sītārāmācāryulu wrote a supplement replete with examples, the *Prauḍhavyākaraṇamu*, published in 1885.

11.4.6 Kannada

Nāgavarma (c.1150) wrote the *Śabdasmṛti* in 96 verses in Old Kannada as part of his literary manual *Kāvyālocana*, and an independent work, the *Karṇāṭakabhāṣābhūṣaṇa* in 280 sūtras in ten sections with a commentary in Sanskrit. In the thirteenth century, Keśirāja wrote a comprehensive grammar, the *Śabdamaṇidarpaṇa*, in Old Kannada in 322 metrical sūtras with a commentary. In 1604, Bhaṭṭākaḷaṅka Deva wrote the *Karṇāṭakaśabdānuśāsana* in 592 sūtras with commentary in Sanskrit, often quoting the *Jainendra* grammar (see §11.3).

11.5. Semantics

11.5.1 Literature

Bhartṛhari's (fifth century CE) *Vākyapadīya*, which derives much of its substance from the semantic discussions in Patañjali's *Mahābhāṣya*, exerted a wide and lasting influence. The three major parts of the *Vākyapadīya* were the subject of commentaries: the *Vṛtti* on the *Brahmakāṇḍa*, debatably by Bhartṛhari himself, on which Vṛṣabhadeva (post-tenth century?) wrote the *Paddhati*; Puṇyarāja's *Ṭīkā* (post-tenth century?) on the *Vākyakāṇḍa*; and Helārāja's *Prakāśa* (tenth century) on the extensive *Padakāṇḍa* which consists of fourteen sections. The more recent works on semantics of Kauṇḍabhaṭṭa (seventeenth century) and Nāgeśa (late seventeenth–eighteenth century) are heavily indebted to the *Vākyapadīya*. Kauṇḍabhaṭṭa's compositions include the *Vaiyākaraṇabhūṣaṇa* and its abridgement, the *Vaiyākaraṇabhūṣaṇasāra*. Nāgeśa wrote the *Vaiyākaraṇasiddhāntamañjuṣā* and two abridgements to it: the *Laghumañjuṣā* and the *Paramalaghumañjuṣā*.

At least two other major systems of philosophy are concerned with semantic analysis: Nyāya 'logic' and Karmamīmāṃsā 'ritual exegesis.' It is not possible to survey the massive literature produced in these philosophical traditions here, but their foundations will be briefly mentioned. Gautama's *Nyāyasūtra*s, codified perhaps in the second century CE, and Vātsyāyana's commentary on them, written in the early fifth century CE, are the foundation of the Nyāya system. The most important ancient commentary to follow is Uddyotakara's *Nyāyavārttika*, written at the end of the sixth or beginning of the seventh century CE. Vācaspatimiśra wrote his *Tātparyaṭīkā* commentary on the *Nyāyavārttika* in the tenth century. An independent work differentiating the views of Nyāya from Buddhism and Karmamīmāṃsā is the *Nyāyamañjarī* of Jayantabhaṭṭa (*c.*900). In the eleventh century, the *Kiraṇāvalī* by Udayana, a commentary on Praśastapāda's *Padārthadharmasaṅgraha* (*c.*550), begins the unification of Nyāya and the philosophical school concerned primarily with ontology called *Vaiśeṣika*. Central in establishing the new Nyāya (*navyanyāya*) is Gaṅgeśa (*c.*1320), the author of the *Tattvacintāmaṇi*.

As would be expected for those concerned with the analysis and interpretation of statements and injunctions in ritual texts, semantics is a major concern in the tradition known as Karmamīmāṃsā. Growing out of a long tradition of Vedic exegesis and performance, the *Pūrvamīmāṃsāsūtra*s were codified in about the second century BCE, although they may have reached their final form somewhat later. They are attributed to Jaimini, but both his name and that of Bādarāyaṇa, to whom the *Uttaramīmāṃsāsūtra*s are attributed, are mentioned in particular sūtras. In the fourth or fifth century CE, Śabara composed his *Bhāṣya* commentary on the *Pūrvamīmāṃsāsūtra*s. This is the most ancient commentary extant on them, but Śabara mentions predecessors and cites a long passage from one Vṛttikāra in his commentary on 1.1.5. Śabara is followed by Kumārila, Prabhākara, and Maṇḍanamiśra in the seventh century. Kumārila has been the most influential of the three, but each of them had distinct ideas and gave rise to long and active independent traditions.

Subramania Iyer (1969) provides an extensive summary of the thought presented by Bhartṛhari in his *Vākyapadīya*, while Houben (1995) translates an important chapter, discusses principles for its interpretation, and provides access to recent work on this central figure of Indian philosophy of language. Kunjunni Raja (1963) gives a clear presentation of the major points of view in Indian semantics, while Bhattacharya (1962) is more textually oriented and Biardeau (1964) is more interpretive. Scharf (1996) and Aussant (2009) enter into the details of argumentation concerning the semantics of common and proper nouns respectively.

11.5.2 Issues

Sanskrit grammarians begin from the conception of speakers and end with speech. They all, from the ancient phonetic treatises proper to particular Vedic traditions (Prātiśākhyas; see §11.1.3) to medieval non-Pāṇinian grammars (§11.3) and early modern reworkings of Pāṇinian grammars (§11.2.1.1), derive actual speech from basic elements previously abstracted in accordance with an assumed prior analysis. The rules, constructed from the point of view of the speaker rather than of the listener, generate speech forms under semantic as well as co-occurrence conditions. Indian semantic treatises, however, based upon an analysis of the implications of generative rules, determine the cognition produced from the comprehension of speech forms from the point of view of a listener. They investigate the verbal cognition (*śābdabodha*) produced by sentences, words, and basic grammatical constituents.

Among the principal questions investigated are the status and segmentation of the speech form that conveys meaning. Bhartṛhari considers that what conveys meaning is in fact the sentence itself manifested by articulated sounds but understood in the awareness of the listener as an indivisible whole (*akhaṇḍavākyasphoṭa*), that the meaning it conveys is likewise an indivisible whole insight (*pratibhā*), and that segmentation into words and basic elements is merely posited artificially (*kalpita*) as a convenient means to describe correct usage. Knowledge of correct usage leads to insight into the undifferentiated level of speech that is the ultimate reality (*brahman*) and source of differentiation in the world. The Karmamīmāṃsā philosopher Kumārila, on the other hand, considers that individual speech units directly cause the recall of meanings, which the listener then synthesizes into cognition of the meaning of the sentence (*abhihitānvaya*). Between these views is that of another Karmamīmāṃsā philosopher, Prabhākara, who considers that words convey meaning only after they have been cognized in syntactic constructions (*anvitābhidhāna*).

Another major topic of debate is what the principal element is in the verbal cognition of a sentence. Nyāya philosophers consider the entity denoted by the nominative to be the principal element, and to be qualified by the action denoted by the verb. Grammarians, on the other hand, consider the action to be principal and to be qualified by various participants in it, including the agent denoted by the nominative in an active construction. The action itself was analysed as consisting of two parts: behaviour itself (*vyāpāra*) and its result (*phala*). The ritual exegete Kumārila considered that just the former, called the act of bringing about (*bhāvanā*), is denoted by the verbal termination, and is the principal element of cognition in Vedic injunctions to perform ritual acts.

Other topics of debate include the denotation of common nouns and proper names; the nature of denoted items such as generic properties, substances, qualities, gender and number, time, and action; the nature of the primary denoting relation, secondary relations, suggestion, and purport; whether the relation between speech forms and their meanings is natural or conventional; and how such relations are established and learned. Important considerations in the last-mentioned topic are avoiding infinite regress and deviation. For instance, it is argued that a common noun must denote a generic property rather than particular individuals because a single invariant relation can be established with the former but not with the latter. Opposing views argue that a generic property can act as a handle without actually entering the cognition produced, or can enter the cognition as a qualifier rather than the principal qualificand. These discussions produced a voluminous literature that included the fields of literary criticism and artistic appreciation as well as the disciplines already mentioned, and the topics continue to be debated in circles of traditional Indian learning.

CHAPTER 12

......

FROM SEMITIC TO AFRO-ASIATIC

......

EDWARD LIPIŃSKI

12.1 SEMITIC AND AFRO-ASIATIC

......

THE Oxford Handbook of the History of Linguistics aims at informing a larger audience of scholars and students than the group of specialists in the field of Semitic or Afro-Asiatic linguistics. Therefore, the first part of this chapter will offer a general view of the languages in question,[1] while its second part will concisely present the history of research in this multifaceted field.

The 'Semitic' languages were so named in 1781 by August Ludwig von Schlözer (1735–1809) because most of the people who spoke them were supposedly descended from Sem (Gen. 10: 21–31). They were spoken in Arabia, Mesopotamia, Syria, and Palestine, whence they spread into Ethiopia and later, with Islam, into Egypt and North Africa. The Semitic languages go back to a 'Proto-Semitic' bundle of dialects, the general structure of which can be derived from the historically attested features of various Semitic languages. No single Semitic tongue can be said to be the representative of the Proto-Semitic type. In phonology, Epigraphic South Arabian may come closest to Proto-Semitic, whereas Akkadian may be regarded as representative for certain morphological verbal features.

Since the Semitic languages go back to a common origin, the question of the location of the speakers of these Proto-Semitic dialects is of importance. Various areas have been so considered, but nowadays the likeliest region seems to be the present-day Sahara in North Africa (Lipiński 2001a: 43–8).

Semitic is in fact a branch of a larger language group, namely Afro-Asiatic, also called Hamito-Semitic, for Ham was supposed to be the ancestor of the African nations

---

[1] A more detailed survey is given by Lipiński (2001a: 21–99, 2001b).

(Gen. 10: 6–20). It is widely accepted today that the language families belonging to Afro-Asiatic are Semitic, Libyco-Berber, spoken in North Africa, ancient Egyptian, Cushitic—comprising the non-Semitic languages of East Africa and so called because Cush was a name for Ethiopia and Sudan—and finally Chadic, including about 150 different languages spoken in Sub-Saharan Africa. They have been termed 'Chadic' after the large inland Lake Chad. It has been suggested that also Meroitic, spoken in Sudan at least to the fifth century AD, belonged to the Afro-Asiatic group.[2] The interrelations between the five generally recognized branches of Afro-Asiatic is represented schematically in Fig. 12.1.

Broadly speaking, genetic relations among the various Afro-Asiatic languages is quite clear in phonology, morphology, and vocabulary. Whereas the relation between the various Semitic languages can be compared with that of, say, the various Germanic or Romance or Slavic languages, Afro-Asiatic would have more or less the role of Indo-European with a closer relation between Semitic and Libyco-Berber, and much weaker connections between Semitic and Chadic languages.

One should stress at this point that much remains to be done on the reconstruction of the individual branches, even in the case of Semitic and of ancient Egyptian, and that we still lack reliable data for many Afro-Asiatic languages, especially Chadic and Cushitic. This means that one must proceed cautiously when attempting comparison at the Afro-Asiatic level. Mass lexical comparison, extended even to the so-called 'Nostratic,'[3] is a premature and hazardous venture.[4] Some publications of

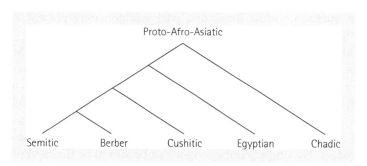

FIG. 12.1 Afro-Asiatic languages

---

[2] Militarev (1984); Rowan (2006a, 2006b). See further Lipiński (2011). Instead, Rilly (2010) regards Meroitic as an Eastern Sudanic tongue of the Nilo-Saharan language family. This group would include Nubian, Nara, Taman, Nyima, and Meroitic. Lexical relations with Semitic have barely been examined, as shown by the few lines in Rilly (2010: 99).

[3] 'Nostratic' is a macrophylum including Indo-European, Afro-Asiatic, Kartvelian, Uralo-Altaic, and Dravidian. Cf. Dolgopolsky (1999). The preparation of Dolgopolsky's *Nostratic Dictionary* is still in progress.

[4] Ehret's attempt to reconstruct not only Proto-Cushitic but also Proto-Afro-Asiatic is certainly premature: Ehret (1987, 1995). The same should be said about G. Takács' *Etymological Dictionary of Egyptian*: Takács (1999–2007).

this kind[5] may nevertheless serve as a basis for future research, but comparisons should take the changing sound correspondences into account, especially in the case of ancient Egyptian. It is noticeable, however, that few scholars nowadays feel sufficiently secure in relation to these languages to present anything like an overall synthetic perspective. That fact is in part the result of a tendency in the last quarter of the century towards ever narrower academic specialization, so that few Semitic scholars dare even to comment on the full range of linguistic problems linked to a particular group of Semitic languages.

The Semitic languages can be classified only geographically, since the hypothesis of a 'Central Semitic,'[6] based on 'shared innovations,' pays little attention to chronology and neglects significant phonological, morphological, and even syntactical facts. The factor of languages in contact has to be taken into account here.[7] East Semitic is represented by the various dialects of Akkadian, distinguished geographically (Babylonian and Assyrian)[8] and chronologically. Northwest Semitic includes Eblaic in the third millennium BC, a language still close to Old Akkadian,[9] then Amorite and Ugaritic in the second millennium BC, Canaanite with Hebrew (revived as 'Ivrit), Phoenician, Moabite, Ammonite, Edomite in the first millennium BC, Aramaic, attested as a spoken language for 3,000 years, down to the present-day dialects, and North Arabian, followed by Classical Arabic, Middle Arabic, and the dialects spoken nowadays in the Middle East and in North Africa. South Semitic includes Epigraphic South Arabian, also called Sayhadic,[10] the modern South Arabian dialects of Yemen, Oman, and Soqotra, and the Semitic languages of Ethiopia, both ancient (Ge'ez) and modern, often designated globally as Ethio-Semitic.

Akkadian is the oldest Semitic language. Its name comes from Akkad, the capital of the first known Semitic empire in Mesopotamia. Documents in the language, written in cuneiform script borrowed from the Sumerians, range from c.2400 BC to the beginning of the Christian era. There are various dialects and periods in its development. Old Akkadian is the language of the documents from c.2400 to c.1900 BC,[11] used side by side

---

[5] For instance, Diakonov et al. (1993–7), the English version of their Russian works, issued in 1981–3; Orel and Stolbova (1995), and a number of publications of Gábor Takács.

[6] The Central Semitic would have included Canaanite, Aramaic, and Arabic. This conception was first developed by Robert Hetzron. See Hetzron (1997: 8–11).

[7] Lipiński (2001a: §65.1–10, with the bibliography on pp. 651–6); St. Kaufman and O. Kapeliuk in Izre'el (2002: 297–340).

[8] Different spellings, especially gemination and lengthening of vowels, do not prove the presence of phonological differences (Reiner 1966: 44–6), but other particularities may argue for their existence, as assumed by Worthington (2010).

[9] An apparent lack of historical and geographic perspectives led John Huehnergard in 2006 to classify Eblaic as a separate branch of the East Semitic dialects of Mesopotamia.

[10] This appellation was proposed by Beeston (1984: 1). It does not seem that it will meet with general acceptance, since South Arabian culture covers a much wider area that the rim of the Sayhad desert in Yemen.

[11] Inclusive of the Akkadian of the Ur III period, which continues, to a certain extent, the language of the Sargonic period, as assumed by W. Sommerfeld in 2003. A different view was held by M. Hilgert in 2002 and R. Hasselbach in 2005 and 2007.

with Sumerian. The language of later periods is divided into Babylonian and Assyrian dialects. Within Babylonian one can distinguish the following periods: Old Babylonian (c.1900–1500 BC), Middle Babylonian (c.1500–1000 BC), Neo-Babylonian (c.1000–600 BC), and Late Babylonian (after 600 BC). In the latter period, Aramaic was the spoken tongue of Mesopotamia, while Late Babylonian was the literary language. The successive stages of Assyrian are: Old Assyrian (c.1900–1650 BC), Middle Assyrian (c.1500–1000 BC), and Neo-Assyrian (c.1000–600 BC). Because of the cultural prestige of Babylonia, Akkadian was also used in neighbouring countries such as Elam (Susa), the Hittite empire (Boghazköy), Mittanni (Nuzi), Syria (Mari, Emar, Ugarit), and Canaan (El-Amarna letters), and it was the international language of the Near East in the second half of the second millennium BC.

Eblaic is attested in the twenty-fourth century BC by tablets in cuneiform script, found at Tell Mardikh, ancient Ebla, in northern Syria; hence it is sometimes called 'Palaeosyrian.' It is followed chronologically by Amorite, known mainly from personal names occurring in Old Babylonian texts, then by Ugaritic, attested by alphabetic texts written in cuneiform script, found mainly at Ras Shamra, the site of ancient Ugarit, also in northern Syria. Documents in the language range from the fourteenth to the early twelfth century BC. Ugaritic has a close genetic relationship with Canaanite, whose name comes from Canaan, the ancient name for Cisjordan, Transjordan, Phoenicia, and southern Syria. Canaanite languages known through direct sources from the first millennium BC are: Phoenician, Hebrew, Moabite, Ammonite, and Edomite. The older stage of Canaanite is known indirectly through the El-Amarna letters, written basically in Middle Babylonian. Phoenician was current in the coastal cities of present-day Lebanon and adjacent areas, but many inscriptions have been found at the sites of ancient Phoenician colonies along the Mediterranean shores, in Cyprus, Malta, Sicily, Sardinia, Ibiza, in Carthage, and in other cities of North Africa, as well as in southeastern Anatolia. The linguistic stage of Phoenician on the North African coast is called Punic, and dates from the eighth century BC to the second century AD.

The Aramaic language is attested by documents ranging from the ninth century BC to the present day, with several still spoken dialects. It superseded various languages of the Near East and, beginning with the eighth century BC, became the international language of this region, from Persia and Mesopotamia to Egypt. The period of its greatest expansion was from about the fifth century BC to the seventh century AD, at which time it was supplanted by Arabic. Until Roman times there were no outstanding dialectal variations in the written language, but later documents show a distinction between West Aramaic and East Aramaic. The main dialects of West Aramaic are Jewish Palestinian Aramaic, Samaritan Aramaic, Christian-Palestinian Aramaic or Syro-Palestinian, Nabataean, Palmyrene, and Western Neo-Aramaic—which, in 2011, was still spoken in three villages to the north of Damascus—Maʿlūla (Christian), Baḥʿa and Ǧubbʿadīn (Muslim). East Aramaic includes Syriac with a rich Christian literature, Jewish Babylonian Aramaic, used in the Babylonian Talmud, Hatraean, Mandaic, and the Neo-Aramaic dialects still spoken in the regions between Lake Urmia and Lake Van, in the Tur Abdin (Turkey), in the region north of Mosul, and in various emigrant communities in Europe, North America, and Australia.

Today Arabic must be regarded as one of the important world languages. Its earliest written forms are provided by pre-Islamic North and East Arabian inscriptions using a variant of the South Arabian monumental script. The attested dialects are Liḥyānite or Dedanite in Hedjāz, Thamūdic in north-eastern Hedjāz, Safaitic in southern Syria and Jordan, Hasaean in the oasis of al-Ḥāsa', and Nabataean Arabic, represented by a few inscriptions in Aramaic script. Later pre-Classical Arabic dialects are described to a certain extent by early Arab philologists, while Classical Arabic goes back to the language of pre-Islamic poetry, probably based on an archaic form of the dialects of Nadjd, in Central Arabia. Neo-Arabic or Middle Arabic was the urban language of the Arab Empire from the eighth century AD on. It emerged from pre-Classical Arabic dialects, which continued developing in various linguistic ambient until the modern dialects, showing tremendous variations. Literary Arabic, used today for all written purposes and for certain formal kinds of speech, is substantially the Arabic of the Qur'ān and of the classical literature of the past. It is quite different from colloquial Arabic, which is used even in teaching.

South Arabian is represented by several ancient and modern dialects, spoken in Yemen, Oman, and on the island of Soqoṭra. Epigraphic South Arabian, attested by almost 10,000 inscriptions, some going back as far as the early first millennium BC, includes the main dialects of Saba and later Himyar (Sabaic), of Ma'in (Minaic), Qatabān (Qatabānic), Ḥadramautt (Ḥadramic), as well as the recently discovered two dialects of Oman, provisionally called Sa'kalhanic A and B. Modern South Arabian languages that are not Arabic include Mehri, with the closely related Ḥarsūsi and Baṭḥari dialects, Šhawri, also called Jibbāli, and Soqoṭri. Since they are surrounded by Arabic dialects, they are considerably influenced by them, especially in vocabulary.

Ethio-Semitic designates the language cluster spoken from the first millennium BC in Ethiopia and in Eritrea, a region the indigenous languages of which were Cushitic, and South Arabian script was introduced there later by colonists. Ethio-Semitic is divided into North Ethiopic, with ancient Ge'ez and modern Tigre and Tigrinya, and South Ethiopic, which includes Amharic, Argobba, Gafat, Harari, and the Gurage dialects. Ge'ez or ancient Ethiopic is no longer spoken, but it remains the language of the liturgy and is the language of the Bible, translated between the fourth and seventh centuries AD, and of the classical Ge'ez literature, dated between the thirteenth and seventeenth centuries AD. The oldest Ethiopic stone inscriptions, in unvocalized script, go back to the third century AD, but some form of cursive writing must have been used from the time of the South Arabian inscriptions found in Ethiopia and dated to the fifth–fourth centuries BC. Tigre and Tigrinya, spoken in northern Ethiopia and in Eritrea, are languages closely related to Ge'ez. Amharic is the national language of Ethiopia, and Argobba can be regarded as one if its dialects. Gafat disappeared completely in the twentieth century in favour of Amharic, and Harari is spoken in the city of Harar, in eastern Ethiopia. Gurage is a dialect cluster spoken to the south-west of Addis Ababa.

The Cushitic languages of Ethiopia exercised a strong influence on the phonology, morphology, syntax, and vocabulary of Ethio-Semitic.[12] Scarcely anything was known concerning this language family before the second half of the nineteenth century,[13] and none of its members possesses any written records or literature.[14] The Cushitic family comprises about seventy mostly little-explored languages. There is, as yet, little agreement concerning the identification and classification of these languages that are spoken from the Red Sea littoral to the area south of the Horn of Africa. They include Beja in Sudan,[15] Agaw in Eritrea and north-western Ethiopia,[16] Sidamo, Oromo in Ethiopia and northern Kenya, Somali, and Omotic,[17] regarded by some scholars as a distinct language family.

Libyco-Berber dialects form the Afro-Asiatic language family which is closest to Semitic. They were formerly spoken in all of North Africa, and written records in their 'Libyan' script, a variant of which is still used by Berber-speaking Tuaregs, go back to the mid-first millennium BC. Considerable interest in the spoken Berber dialects had developed by the middle of the nineteenth century, and continues unabated.

The ancient Egyptian language was the speech of the Nile valley to the north of the first cataract from the earliest historical times, which can now be dated c.3300 BC, until some time around AD 1500. Although there are evident similarities in phonology and lexical morphology between Egyptian and Semitic, these two branches were very distinct, especially in morphosyntax. The history of the Egyptian language for almost 5,000 years quite understandably involves phonetic and grammatical changes, while its vowel-less hieroglyphic script and the Egyptological transcriptions of Egyptian words and forms do not facilitate comparison with Semitic records. We distinguish the following phases in its development: Old Egyptian (down to c.2000 BC), Middle Egyptian, regarded as the classical stage of ancient Egyptian (c.2000–1300 BC), Neo-Egyptian or Late Egyptian (down from 1300 BC), Demotic (seventh century BC to fifth century AD), and Coptic (from the first century AD) with several dialects. The Sahidic dialect is the language of most Gnostic Nag Hammadi manuscripts, dating from the early fourth century AD and discovered from 1945–7. The Bohairic dialect is still the liturgical language of the Coptic Church. Coptic was still spoken in Upper Egypt in the fifteenth century AD.

[12] O. Kapeliuk in Izre'el (2002: 309–12) with former literature.

[13] Major collections of oral material and studies were the work of Leo Reinisch (1832–1919). A list of his main publications can be found in Lipiński (2001a: 646).

[14] Meroitic inscriptions cannot be related to Cushitic or Omotic on the ground of a few lexical analogies; cf. Rilly (2010: 29–30).

[15] Despite the opinion of Hetzron (1980: 78–101, 115–20). Beja would be the earliest offshoot of the family, apparently closer to Semitic.

[16] Various dialects of Agaw were the language spoken formerly by the Falashas or 'Black Jews' of Ethiopia, as shown by Agaw words and phrases included in their prayers in Ge'ez. In the 20th century, Agaw-speaking Falashas could still be found in some outlying villages in Quara and Semyen.

[17] Omotic languages, also known as Kaffa, are spoken in Ethiopia, in the region of the Omo river, which falls into Lake Turkana.

The Chadic family is a huge group of about 150 different languages, spoken in Sub-Saharan Africa.[18] Hausa speakers constitute the single most numerous group, and the language has become a lingua franca in northern Nigeria and in southern Niger. The appurtenance of Chadic to Afro-Asiatic is nowadays widely accepted, but it was not so until the mid-twentieth century. Although it represents half of the Afro-Asiatic language family, it has so far played a minor role in comparative linguistic studies. The particular interest of the Chadic languages lies in the fact that they have been separated from the other branches of the phylum for some 5,000 years. Therefore, on the one hand, they may better preserve some ancient features like the presence of a radical vowel in the verbal stem; on the other, however, their far-reaching transformation under the influence of Niger-Congo and Nilo-Saharan languages often makes it difficult to connect a particular Chadic idiom with Afro-Asiatic, at least seen from a Semitic point of view. Morphological and lexical correspondences nevertheless support the inclusion of Chadic in the Afro-Asiatic language family, as well as e.g. the morphosyntactic suggestion, made by Jungraithmayr in 2007, that the Chadic sub-junctive marker -*u* or -*o* is related to the Akkadian subordinate marker -*u*.

One should proceed very cautiously from Semitic to Afro-Asiatic, not forgetting that research should ultimately attempt comparison also at the Afro-Asiatic level.

12.2 RESEARCH ON SEMITIC LANGUAGES

Comparative historical grammar is a creation of the nineteenth century, but descriptive grammars of Semitic languages go back to the Middle Ages. Grammatical observers sought then, wherever possible, to go beyond the mere facts in order to classify and explain them. The field of Semitics enjoys 4,500 years of written records related to linguistics, beginning in the third or early second millennium BC, with some kinds of glossaries and comparisons of synchronic grammatical data.

12.2.1 Proto-history of Semitic Linguistics

The first lexicographic lists, in the shape of dictionaries with parallel columns of lexemes in two or more languages, at least one of them Semitic, date from the third millennium BC. They belonged to the essential implements of scribal schools, were used and copied until Late Babylonian times.[19] The bilingual lexical tablets found at Tell

---

[18] A useful survey of the names and categorizations of the Sub-Saharan languages is now provided by de Féral (2009). An inventory of the modern Chadic languages can be found in Jungraithmayr (1981: 265–76).

[19] Contributions by A. Cavigneaux and M. Civil in Ebeling et al. (1928: vi. 609–40); Sasson (1995: iv. 2305–14).

Mardikh-Ebla date from the twenty-fourth to twenty-third centuries BC, and list Old Sumerian and Eblaic (Palaeosyrian) words or phrases in parallel.[20] Quadrilingual dictionaries were used at Ugarit around the fourteenth to thirteenth centuries BC with the following languages: Sumerograms—Middle Babylonian—Hurrian—Ugaritic, for instance ZU—*a-mi-lu—tar-šu-wa-an-ni—bu-nu-šu* 'man.'[21]

The earliest properly grammatical works on a Semitic language appear in the eighteenth or seventeenth century BC. They concern the fixing of grammatically correct equivalences between Sumerian and Akkadian words and phrases. This is best illustrated by the composition of parallel verbal paradigms, by the morphological explanation of Sumerian terms, and by the lists of syllabograms consisting of a consonant followed by the vowels *u, a, i, e*. Hence it appears that these were the vocalic phonemes recognized by the grammarians. The grammatical terminology labels verbal forms and syllabograms either *marû* 'slow' or *ḥamṭu* 'rapid.' It seems that the concept 'slow' can imply the imperfect in Old Babylonian, thus the paradigm *iparras*, while 'rapid' denotes the preterit *iprus* or the perfect *iptaras*. The labels *rīqu* 'empty' and *malû* 'full' apparently indicate that an element is omitted in the phrase or that its formulation is complete. The meaning of other grammatical terms is as yet uncertain, but the large amount of material preserved on clay tablets reveals a high degree of abstraction from concrete grammatical facts.[22]

12.2.2 Aramaic

Aramaic has the longest continuous written record among the Semitic languages. Its older periods became better known thanks to discoveries in the twentieth century, but Middle Aramaic, especially Syriac, has a rich medieval literature, the language of which attracted close attention at least from the sixth century AD. Syriac enjoys a particularly strong grammatical tradition, with many classical and traditional treatises on its grammar surviving until the present time.[23] The earliest extant Syriac grammar is that of Jacob of Edessa (*c.*640–708). Grammars of Aramaic and Syriac begun to appear in Europe in the sixteenth century, but fundamental works in this field were published only in the second half of the nineteenth century. They concerned Syriac, as well as the Modern or Neo-Aramaic idioms.[24] Proper scientific studies started with Theodor

[20] Published by Pettinato (1982).

[21] Published by Nougayrol (1968: 199–251) with copies on pp. 409–24, nos. 109–42.

[22] See the contribution of D. O. Edzard in Ebeling et al. (1928: iii. 610–16).

[23] A survey is provided by Rosenthal (1939: 179–211).

[24] A survey of Neo-Aramaic idioms and of their study can be found in the updated English edition of Tsereteli (1978: 15–24), with a bibliography on pp. 100–102. See also O. Jastrow in Hetzron (1997: 334–77) and Izre'el (2002: 365–77).

Nöldeke (1836–1930),[25] whose grammatical work constitutes a milestone in Aramaic studies.[26]

A huge amount of epigraphic, papyrological, and literary material gave strong impetus to linguistic studies on Aramaic and generated a number of grammars and dictionaries, some pursuing practical aims, others purely academic.[27] This material included the discovery of Old Aramaic inscriptions in Syria, either engraved on steles or written on clay tablets, and dating from the ninth–seventh centuries BC; the publication of important Aramaic papyri and ostraca, found in Egypt and dating from the sixth to fourth centuries BC; more recent discoveries of Aramaic papyri, ostraca, and fragmentary scrolls from the fourth and second–first centuries BC, and first–second centuries AD in Central Asia, in Wadi Daliyeh, in Idumaea, at Qumran, and in the Judaean desert; the publication of numerous Palmyrene, Old Syriac, Hatraean, and other East Aramaic inscriptions from the Parthian and Roman periods; and the discovery of the Targum Neofiti 1.

12.2.3 Arabic

The study of Semitic grammar, Arabic, Syriac, or Hebrew, began with the driving need to establish a correct reading and a proper interpretation of the Holy Scriptures, the Qur'ān and the Bible, in both their formal and semantic dimensions. In the first centuries of Islam, the lack of a vowel system and of diacritical signs distinguishing some consonants, as well as the territorial expansion of the Arabs to countries with a population speaking other idioms, required a grammatical and semantic analysis of problematic passages in the Qur'ān[28] and the Hadith.[29] Besides, the Qur'ān was written in the Hidjazi idiom used in the Quraysh tribe for poetry and perhaps also for writing in general. Its language was regarded as close to a classical form of Arabic, the purity and clarity of which had to be preserved. It certainly exhibited differences from the spoken dialects, but also contained real or assumed dialectal words.[30]

---

[25] Nöldeke's publications dealing with Semitic linguistic topics, Aramaic, Arabic, Ethio-Semitic, are listed in his bibliography included in the volume offered to him in 1906, and re-edited with additions by Kuhn (1907), listing 628 books, articles, and critical reviews.

[26] It is not surprising, therefore, that an excellent survey of Aramaic studies since Nöldeke's publications appeared as Rosenthal (1939).

[27] See the bibliography in Lipiński (2001a: 623–8), and the surveys of Lipiński (1990) and Gzella (2008a), as well as Bélova et al. (2009: 414–96).

[28] The most comprehensive work on the Qur'ān was Nöldeke (1909–1938). See also the encyclopedia edited by McAuliffe (2001–6), with chapters on Qur'ānic exegesis, grammar, variant readings, and textual criticism.

[29] This other Islamic holy work was at least partly put into writing in the 8th century and probably earlier. Cf. Goldziher (1890: 1–274); Juynboll (2007).

[30] We must remember that it was often impossible for the Arabic script to express genuine dialect forms, just as it is inadequate today for writing the colloquials.

From this situation arose the endeavour of early Arab philologists to explain rare or difficult Qur'ānic words in works quoted later under the name *Kitāb al-luġāt*, 'Book on the Dialects,' or the like. We possess one of these monographs, the *Risāla* or 'Treatise on Dialect Words in the Qur'ān,' ascribed to Abū 'Ubaid Qāsim b. Sallām al-Herewī (d. 838 AD). *Risāla* was written when the study of Arabic grammar was already established as an independent discipline, traditionally represented by the Kufan and Basran schools.[31] The latter's main representative was Sībawayhi (d. *c.*793 AD, 177 AH), whose *Kitāb* was the first known full-scale Arabic grammar,[32] on which all the subsequent Arabic grammars were based.[33] Arabic grammatical tradition served as foundation to the modern European grammars of Classical Arabic.[34]

Arab scholars were active also in the field of lexicography. The fifteen volumes of Ibn Muqarran ibn Manẓūr's (1232–1311 AD) *Lisān al-'arab* contains about 80,000 entries, but a main organizing principle within the lemmas, representing a root, were semantic, with little or no attention to the morphology. The first large-scale modern Arabic dictionary since that of Jacobus Golius (Gool, 1625–67) and Georg Wilhelm Freytag's (1787–1861) lexica was the Arabic–English lexicon of Edward William Lane (1801–76), which has hardly been superseded.[35] However, the lexicon is incomplete: only sketches remain after the beginning of letter *kāf*. The International Congress of Orientalists considered the completion of the work as a matter of high priority, but only the letters *kāf* and *lām* have so far been published in order to fill the gaps in Lane's work.[36]

Grammatical study of Classical and Standard Literary Arabic represents only one aspect of Arabic linguistics as practised on a scholarly level since the twentieth century. Modern colloquial Arabic in its multiple forms, spoken from Central Asia (Uzbekistan) and the Persian Gulf to the Atlantic Ocean, is an important subject of modern linguistic research.[37]

---

[31] For a survey of the Arabic grammatical literature, see Sezgin (1984). For the early period, see Versteegh (1993); Talmon (2003). A bibliography concerning grammatical questions of classical and colloquial Arabic can be found in Lipiński (2001a: 628–36). There is a *Journal of Arabic Linguistics* (Wiesbaden), dealing with all the historical stages, as well as the regional and social variants of Arabic up to Modern Standard Arabic.

[32] Sībawayhi *Al-Kitāb fi'l an-naḥw*, 'The Book: A Grammatical Work,' published by Derenbourg (1881–9), and translated into German by Jahn (1894–1900). Another publication: Abū Bišr 'Amr 1316 AH.

[33] For a concise presentation of its form, see Owens in Hetzron (1997: 46–58) with further bibliography.

[34] A bibliography can be found in Fischer 2002 [1972]. Arabic grammatical tradition was probably developed from basic concepts of Aristotelian logic as known by early converts having access to Syriac translations, like that of *Categories*, which goes back to the 6th century AD. The possibility of Indian influence in early Arab phonetics was considered by Danecki (1985); Law (1990).

[35] Lane (1863–93). Parts 6–8 were edited by his nephew Stanley Lane Poole.

[36] Ullmann (1970). The letters still missing are *mīm*, *nūn*, *hā'*, *wāw*, and *yā'*.

[37] Fischer and Jastrow (1980) gives an idea of the extent of this field. There is a dictionary of the dialects spoken in the main Levantine centres, compiled by Barthélemy in 1935–69, with Arabic words printed in the International Phonetic Alphabet. For Yemen, a rather isolated Arab-speaking area, there is the dictionary of Piamenta, published in 1990–91 and complemented by Watson and Naïm. The *Wortatlas der arabischen Dialekte/Word Atlas of Arabic Dialects* in 3 vols will provide a survey of their lexical richness and diversity: Behnstedt and Woidich (2010).

12.2.4 Hebrew

The tradition of studying language as an independent discipline was also developed for Hebrew[38] and started, like the Arabic grammatical tradition, with lexicographic studies, best illustrated by the work of Sa'adiah Gaon (882–942), an important leader of Babylonian Jewry.[39] The interest in linguistic questions appears also in North Africa and in Andalusia. Judah ben David Ḥayyūǧ (c.945–1000) developed the view that all Hebrew roots are made up of three letters, one of which, however, may be elided or assimilated to a letter with a *dagesh*, when conjugated in certain forms.[40] The discovery of the tri-radicalism of the Hebrew verbs was revolutionary for Hebrew grammar and has had a great impact on Semitic grammar in general up to this day.[41] Ibn Barūn's work,[42] written in Spain c.1100, contains a section on the comparative grammar of Arabic and Hebrew.

Karaite grammatical thought originated in the ninth or even the eighth century (Khan 2000). It had its roots in Masoretic tradition and in the early works of Arab grammarians. Scholarly study of Karaite grammatical tradition was given new impetus a few years ago, when scholars got access to the second Firkovitch Collection housed in the National Library at St Petersburg, containing the bulk of extant Karaite linguistic manuscripts. Among the Karaite philologists one should mention Abū al-Faraǧ Hārūn ibn al-Faraǧ, active in the eleventh century. This grammarian and lexicographer from Jerusalem wrote an extensive work on Hebrew and Biblical Aramaic,[43] with a pioneering comparison of both languages. He held that all the Hebrew verbal forms are based on the infinitive, and he compared roots with a permuted order of the consonants, like *'br, 'rb, b'r, br', rb', r'b*. An abridged form of this treatise, preserved at St Petersburg and recently published, appears to be the work of an anonymous Karaite grammarian, perhaps the same as the author of another grammatical treatise.[44] Among the thirty-nine chapters or sections of the latter work one finds, for instance, chapters on transitive and intransitive verbs, on true verbs and pseudo-verbs, and on the functional categories of passive participles. Another Karaite work deserving special mention is the

---

[38] For the linguistic literature on Hebrew down to the 16th century, one can refer to the various works of Bacher, published towards the end of the 19th century, as well as to the article 'Linguistic Literature' by D. Tanne in the *Encyclopaedia Judaica*. See also Schippers in Hetzron (1997: 59–65).

[39] Cf. the article on 'Saadiah (ben Joseph) Gaon' in the *Encyclopaedia Judaica*; Skoss has published a hitherto unidentified fragment of Sa'adiah's Arabic work on Hebrew grammar.

[40] Judah ben David Ḥayyūǧ, *Kitāb al-afʿāl ḏawāt ḥurūf al-līn*, 'Book of the Verbs with Weak Letters,' and *Kitāb al-afʿāl ḏawāt al-matlayin*, 'Book of the Verbs with Reduplication.' The original Arabic text of the two treatises was published by Jastrow in 1897.

[41] A recent overview of the question is presented by Van de Sande (2008).

[42] Isḥaq Abū Ibrāhīm ibn Barūn, *Kitāb al-muwāzana bayn al-luǧa al-ʿibrāniyya wa-l-ʿarabiyya*, published by Kokovzov in 1893 and 1916.

[43] Abū al-Faraǧ Hārūn ibn al-Faraǧ, *Al-kitāb al-muštamil ʿalā l-uṣūl wa-l-fuṣūl fī-l-luǧa l-ʿibrāniyya*, 'Comprehensive Book on the Roots and the Derivatives in the Hebrew Language.'

[44] *Kitāb al-ʿuqūd fī taṣārīf al-luǧa l-ʿibrāniyya*, 'The Book of Rules Regarding the Grammatical Inflection of the Hebrew Grammar.'

extensive lexicon of Biblical Hebrew in Arabic by Dā'wīd ibn Ibrahim al-Fāsi (tenth century).[45] He quotes the Mishnah, the Talmud, the Targums, the masorah. This is an important work for the investigation not only of ancient Hebrew linguistics but also of Aramaic and Arabic, because of the great number of quoted parallels.

Abraham ibn Ezra (1089–1164) did not create any new grammatical system, but he was considered for generations one of the fathers of Hebrew grammar, because he collected the conclusions of early philologists of the East and of Spain, and wrote in Hebrew, bringing the results of their studies to the knowledge of Ashkenazi scholars (Bacher 1882). Their main representative was David Qimḥi (1160–1235), whose philological treatise *Miklol*, 'Magnificence,' offers a systematic arrangement of the material.[46] The vowels are divided into five long and five short, the *niphal* is treated as the passive of *qal*, the *dagesh lene* is duly recognized, the *wāw* consecutive is distinguished from the *wāw* conjunctive. Besides, Qimḥi recognizes the legitimacy of post-biblical forms, admitting a continued development of the language. Qimḥi had a profound influence on the Christian Hebraists.[47]

A new period of comparative historical grammar begins with Wilhelm Gesenius (1786–1842),[48] whose main field of interest was the scientific investigation of Biblical Hebrew based on comparison with other Semitic languages, even Maltese. Gesenius' grammar, dictionary, and monumental *Thesaurus* decidedly influenced the research on Hebrew language in the nineteenth and twentieth centuries.

The discovery and publication of the Qumran texts from 1947 on opened a new era in the study of Biblical Hebrew, since they provided written documents which were almost 1,000 years older than the Hebrew biblical manuscripts on which research was so far based. At the same time arose a major interest for the Samaritan tradition of Hebrew (Ben-Hayyim 1957–77) and for the linguistic study of Mishnaic Hebrew in the Roman period.

12.2.5 Ethio-Semitic

Ethiopian studies had begun in Europe in the sixteenth century. Their real founder was Job Ludolf (1624–1704).[49] His grammars and dictionaries of Ge'ez and Amharic are the outstanding works among the twenty-seven writings in the field of Ethiopic published

[45] Dā'wīd ibn Ibrahim al-Fāsi, *Kitāb ǧami' al-alfāz̧*, 'Comprehensive Book of Sounds.'

[46] The grammatical part of *Miklol*, published by Rittenberg at Łuck in 1862, was re-edited and translated by B. Chomsky. The first Bromberg edition of its second part, the lexicon known as 'Shorashim,' was published by Cornelius Adelkind in 1529. The best edition is supposed to be the one prepared by F. Lebrecht and J.H. Biesenthal in 1847.

[47] A long list of 'Hebraists, Christian (1100–1890)' can be found in the *Encyclopaedia Judaica*.

[48] On Gesenius and his work cf. Eissfeldt (1963: 430–42). His major works are listed in Lipiński (2001a: 620).

[49] The scientific literature on the Ethiopic languages up to 1965 was collected by Leslau (1965). See also Lipiński (2001a: 638–41).

during his lifetime. In the mid-nineteenth century, the name of August Dillmann (1823–94) emerges in the field of Ethio-Semitic with a grammar and a dictionary of Ge'ez.[50] His publications were soon followed by Franz Praetorius' (1847–1927) grammars of Ge'ez, Amharic, and Tigrinya.[51] Thus, three major Ethio-Semitic languages have been presented in scientifically conceived grammars and dictionaries. Ge'ez, traditionally called 'Ethiopic,' is no longer spoken; it is the language of the liturgy, and it continued to be the literary language of Ethiopia even when it ceased to be spoken sometime between the tenth and twelfth centuries. There is a traditional pronunciation of Ge'ez used by priests,[52] but it seems to be a reflection of the speech habits of various dialects. The scholar who in the twentieth century contributed most to our knowledge of Ethio-Semitic is undoubtedly Wolf Leslau (1906–2006).[53]

The modern languages closely related to Ge'ez are Tigrinya and Tigre. Tigrinya is spoken in northern Ethiopia and has a modern literature. Its verbal system has been studied by Rainer M. Voigt,[54] while Thomas L. Kane compiled a dictionary (Kane 2000). Tigre is mainly spoken in the lowland of Eritrea and in the border regions of the Sudan. Short Tigre grammars have been published by Leslau and Shlomo Raz, while E. Littmann and M. Höfner have prepared a dictionary.[55] South Ethiopic includes Amharic, which is the national language of Ethiopia,[56] Argobba, Harari, Gurage, and Gafat. Argobba, still spoken to the north of Addis Ababa, is closely related to Amharic and was studied by Leslau. There is no literature in this language. Harari is spoken in the city of Harar in eastern Ethiopia. Its vocabulary has many Amharic and Cushitic Oromo loanwords and there are religious texts in Harari written in Arabic characters (Wagner 1983, 2003). Harari has been studied by Enrico Cerulli and Leslau.[57] Gurage is a dialect cluster spoken to the south-west of Addis Ababa. There are three main groups of Gurage dialects, described by Leslau.[58] Gafat was spoken in the region of the Blue Nile, north-west of Addis Ababa. The language disappeared completely in favour of Amharic, and very few speakers remained when Leslau managed to describe their language.[59] There was a strong Cushitic, mainly Oromo and Sidamo, influence on the phonology, morphology, syntax, and vocabulary of Ethio-Semitic,[60] related on the other hand to the South Arabian languages.

---

[50] For the main bibliographical data, cf. Lipiński (2001a: 639).

[51] For the main bibliographical data, cf. ibid. 641.

[52] See Hetzron (1997: 260) and Lipiński (2001a: 638–41), s.v. Argaw, Mittwoch, and Ullendorff.

[53] His major works are listed in Lipiński (2001a: 639–40). See also the pertinent chapters in Hetzron (1997: 242–60, 424–549).

[54] See Lipiński (2001a: 641).

[55] See ibid. 640.

[56] For Amharic, see also Yushmanov, Starinin, Leslau, Hartmann, Kapeliuk, and Kane, all listed ibid. 639–41.

[57] For bibliographical data, cf. ibid. 638–40; see also Wagner in Hetzron (1997: 486–508), and Garad and Wagner (1998).

[58] For the bibliography, cf. Lipiński (2001a: 640); see also Hetzron (1977).

[59] For the bibliography, see Lipiński (2001a: 640).

[60] O. Kapeliuk in Izre'el (2002: 309–14) with further literature. One can find recent surveys of the Ethio-Semitic languages in Hetzron (1997: 242–60, 424–549).

12.2.6 South Arabian

The existence of South Arabian inscriptions was first reported in 1772 by Carsten Niebuhr (1733–1815), the sole survivor of the Royal Danish Expedition (1761–7) to Yemen and the Middle East (Niebuhr 1772: 93–5). A few years later, Ulrich Jasper von Seetzen (1767–1811) sent to Europe copies of five fragments of late Sabaic inscriptions, bought in 1810 at Ẓafār,[61] and in 1834–5 James Raimond Wellsted, an English navy officer, collected and brought back to Europe a dozen inscriptions from Ḥiṣn al-Ġurāb and Naqb al-Ḥaǧar.[62] He was followed by other English officers and travellers who brought some South Arabian inscriptions from Yemen (Grohmann 1963: 96–7), but it is to Joseph Halévy (1827–1917)[63] and Eduard Glaser (1855–1908)[64] that the greatest credit for their collection and publication must go. They visited the Yemen and took transcriptions and squeezes (moulded impressions of an inscription) in 1869–70 and 1882–94, respectively. In 1841, the thirteen then available inscriptions allowed Wilhelm Gesenius to decipher 20 out of the 29 Sabaic letters and to publish the results of his research. At the same time, Emil R. Rödiger (1801–74) reached a better understanding of the inscriptions, and in 1841 published his decipherment with a foreword from Gesenius.

The editions of South Arabian inscriptions are generally accompanied by grammatical comments, but a proper grammar was obviously needed. The first attempt to write an Epigraphic South Arabian grammar goes back to Fritz Hommel (1854–1936), who in 1893 added a *mināo-sabäische Grammatik* to his chrestomathy of South Arabian inscriptions. This soon outdated essay was replaced some thirty years later by Ignazio Guidi's (1844–1935) article, which appeared in 1925. The increasing number of South Arabian inscriptions required, however, a larger and more detailed presentation of the languages in question. Such a work was published in 1943 by Maria Höfner (1900–1992), who provided an important synthesis dealing with script, phonology, morphology, and syntax, while specifying—when necessary—the characteristics of the four main 'dialects': Minaic or Minaean, Sabaic, Qatabānic, and Ḥaḍramic.

The publication of new texts and progress in their study showed that we are faced with four languages, not dialects. The rapid increase of epigraphic material, especially Sabaic, prompted Alfred Beeston to publish a Sabaic grammar with an appendix noting the principal divergences of Minaic, Qatabānic, and Ḥaḍramic from Sabaic.[65]

---

[61] This is mentioned in his letter, dated 14.11.1811, to Joseph Freih. von Hammer-Purgstall, who published it in part with the fragments in *Fundgruben des Orients* II (Vienna, 1811), 275–83. The deciphered inscriptions are published in *Répertoire d'épigraphie sémitique* 2624–8.

[62] The deciphered inscriptions can be found ibid. 2633–6, 2640, 5082, 5091–3.

[63] The 686 inscriptions, copied partly by Halévy's Jewish Yemenite companion, were first published in Halévy (1875).

[64] Glaser was able to undertake four journeys to Yemen between 1882 and 1894, and he brought copies or squeezes of about 1,800 texts. Of particular importance was his third trip in 1888, during which he explored the area of Mārib, the Sabaean capital, and collected many inscriptions.

[65] Beeston (1984). Cf. also E. Kogan and A. V. Korotayev in Hetzron (1997: 220–41), and Stein (2003).

The lack of vocalization and of diacritical signs indicating gemination or stress leave open several questions, especially concerning the conjugation of the verbs, because stems, tenses, moods, and voice may be characterized by consonantal or vocalic lengthening, respectively by stress or a distinct vocalization. Lexicography was not forgotten in the research, although the dictionaries published in the 1970s and 1980s by A. Avanzini, A. F. L. Beeston, M. A. Ghūl, W. W. Müller, J. Ryckmans, J. C. Biella, and S. O. Ricks[66] lack the impressive presentation of Conti Rossini's glossary, printed in South Arabian characters and referring also to proper names and to corresponding words in other Semitic languages (Conti Rossini 1931: 99–261). The lexicographic publications are complemented by Rabin's and Ghūl's studies of South Arabian lexical and grammatical elements in Classical Arabic sources (Rabin 1951: 25–53; Ghūl 1993).

A new research field was opened by the discovery in 1970 of the first cursive or 'minuscule' South Arabian inscriptions (Ryckmans et al. 1994; cf. Ryckmans 2001). A completely unknown linguistic domain was brought to light in 1989 by epigraphic documents from Dhofar. Geraldine M. H. King recorded about 800 inscriptions during her expedition in 1992–3. Her unpublished study, as well as the book issued in 1994 by 'Alī Aḥmad Maḥaš al-Šaḥrī about these epigraphs, served as the basis for the study of Muhammed Abdul Nayeem (2001: 104–69). The latter provides a provisional transcription of the new Dhofar epigraphic material, termed by him Sa'kalhanic A and B. Its script is clearly related to Epigraphic South Arabian, but the texts seem to consist mainly of personal names. Nayeem assumes that they are archaic because they are written in vertical columns. These results should of course be regarded as provisional, also because the dating and the relation of these inscriptions to ancient and modern languages of South Arabia still remain problematic.

The main modern South Arabian language, spoken by some 100,000 people, is Mehri, with two varieties of dialects. Others are Ḥarsūsi, Baṭhari, Hobyōt, Jibbāli, and Soqoṭri, spoken on the island of Soqoṭra and on the neighbouring islets. The Soqoṭris form the second largest group, with some 50,000 speakers. Since the modern South Arabian dialects are surrounded, both in Yemen and in the Sultanate of Oman, by Arabic dialects, they are considerably influenced by them, especially in vocabulary.

The existence of such spoken languages was not noticed in Europe before the first half of the nineteenth century. One should here mention the lexical lists established by James R. Wellsted in his reports on the Island of Soqoṭra, published in 1835 and 1840, and the analyses of Mehri linguistic data found by Fulgence Fresnel (1795–1855) in Arabic records. The first oral material enabling the study of Mehri, Soqoṭri, and Šhawri (also called Jibbāli) was collected in 1898–9 by the South Arabian Expedition of the Austro-Hungarian Academy of Sciences in Vienna, led by David Heinrich Mueller (1846–1912). Its publication with glossaries and grammatical analyses followed without delay.[67] After the Austrian studies of the early twentieth century and the discovery of

---

[66] For bibliographical data, cf. Lipiński (2001a: 636–8).
[67] Publications concerning Modern South Arabian languages up to 1945 are listed and commented by Leslau (1946). See esp. M. Bittner, A. Jahn, D. M. Mueller. Cf. also Hetzron (1997: 421–3), and Izre'el (2002: 394–400).

Ḥarsūsi and Baṭḥari in 1929 by Bertram Thomas (Thomas 1937), many years went by until Hobyōt was identified by Thomas Muir Johnstone. Besides him one can mention in particular Marie-Claude Simeone-Senelle. Both provided a global descriptive presentation of the modern South Arabian languages.[68]

12.2.7 Decipherment of Egyptian Hieroglyphs

Nineteenth-century scholars did not just open the way to a more scientific approach to Semitic grammar and initiate the study of the South-Arabian languages; they also deciphered the Egyptian hieroglyphic script and the cuneiform writing system. Attempts made before 1800 to interpret the hieroglyphic inscriptions were completely unsuccessful, as the pictograms were believed to be mystical symbols. A definite clue to the decipherment of the hieroglyphs was at last provided by the discovery, in 1799, of the Rosetta Stone, with trilingual inscription in hieroglyphic Egyptian, Demotic, and Greek.

The first person who was actually able to read longer passages was the French scholar Jean François Champollion (1790–1832). He recognized that Demotic writing was developed from hieratic, which he knew from other documents, and that hieratic derived from hieroglyphic.[69] His *Précis du système hiéroglyphique* appeared in 1824, followed by his posthumous grammar and dictionary.[70] In the meantime, a new impetus was given to the study of hieroglyphs by Richard Lepsius (1810–84), who submitted Champollion's decipherment to a penetrating re-examination and declared in 1837 that its foundations were sound. Samuel Birch's (1813–85) dictionary was published in 1867, followed by the seven volumes of Heinrich Brugsch (1827–94). The year 1880 saw the appearance of two grammars of the highest importance, those of Adolf Erman[71] and Ludwig Stern (Stern 1880), providing a really scientific basis to our knowledge of the Egyptian language. Further study led to the publication of the monumental dictionary of Adolf Erman (1854–1937) and Hermann Grapow (1885–1967) (Erman and Grapow 1926–31), and of the great Coptic lexicon of W. E. Crum.[72]

---

[68] Johnstone (1975), Simeone-Senelle in Hetzron (1997: 378–473), and Izre'el (2002: 379–400).

[69] On identifying the name Cleopatra in Demotic, he transcribed it back into hieratic and then into hieroglyphic. He could check the results of his decipherment on the copy of an obelisk inscription written in both Greek and hieroglyphs, in which he found Cleopatra. However, Champollion was not convinced that hieroglyphs were regularly used in a phonetic way until he managed to decipher cartouches with the names of Ramesses and Tuthmosis in 1822. He knew then that he had the key to the ancient language itself.

[70] The grammar was published in 1836–41 by J. J. Champollion-Figeac and the dictionary was issued in 1841–4 by M. Villemain, both from Champollion's autographic manuscript.

[71] He deals with the idiom of the New Kingdom (1500–1100 BC). One should also mention K. Sethe's monumental work on the verb and his monograph on the nominal sentence, published in 1899–1902 and 1916.

[72] It was issued in 1964. Complements were published by R. Kasser in 1964 and by G. Roquet in 1973. A more detailed overview of the early period of Egyptology is given by Gardiner (1927: 10–18).

The existence of some affinities between Egyptian and Semitic was noticed in the nineteenth century. The first comprehensive study was written in 1892 by Erman, who dealt with phonetics, stem formation, morphology, syntax, lexical correspondences.[73] Comparisons of vocabulary and phonetic relations were pushed further by Aaron Ember in 1930 and by Franz von Calice in 1936, who nevertheless offered a critical evaluation of several etymologies. A step further was taken by Thomas W. Thacker (1911–84), who in 1954 compared Semitic and Egyptian verbal systems, as done also by Jozef Vergote in 1965, but the studies of Hans Jacob Polotsky (1905–91) and his followers resulted in a deeper understanding of their differences.[74] A larger group of related languages had been taken into account by C. Lottner in 1860–61, and R. Lepsius coined the appellation 'Hamitic,' applying it to Egyptian, Cushitic, and Libyco-Berber. In 1934, Werner Vycichl (1909–99) linked Hausa to Hamito-Semitic,[75] although Hausa is not the best representative of the Chadic language family. The latter was decisively included in Afro-Asiatic by Joseph H. Greenberg, who conceived Hamito-Semitic or Afro-Asiatic as a macrophylum consisting of several branches of more or less equal standing, without a particularly strong connection between Egyptian and Semitic (Greenberg 1950). The progress of studies on the relationship between ancient Egyptian and Semitic was recently presented by Helmut Satzinger, who is active in this particular research field.[76]

12.2.8 Decipherment of Cuneiform Scripts

Early comparisons of Egyptian with Semitic generally referred to Hebrew, sometimes to Arabic or Aramaic, and they mostly concerned lexicography and nominal patterns. The elements of the discussion changed when the older Semitic languages, viz. Akkadian and Ugaritic, were deciphered. The rediscovery and the decipherment of the cuneiform scripts was an achievement of the nineteenth and twentieth centuries. Paradoxically, the process began with the last secondary offshoots of cuneiform proper, the Old Persian inscriptions of the Achaemenid kings,[77] scattered examples of which had been brought to Europe by travellers in Persia since the seventeenth century. The name 'cuneiform' was first applied to the script in 1700 by the English philologist

See also the contribution of St G. H. James in Sasson (1995: iv. 2753–64). Since 1947, Egyptological bibliography has been compiled in the *Annual of Egyptological Bibliography*, listing the publications with a delay of two or three years.

[73] Linguistic affinities should of course be distinguished from loanwords, a recent survey of which was presented by Muchiki (1999).
[74] Satzinger in Izre'el (2002: 240–49), listing the main works of Hans Jacob Polotsky on pp. 255–6.
[75] Vycichl (1934), followed immediately by Marcel Cohen. However, a relation of Hausa to the Semitic languages was already assumed by Schön (1862: xii).
[76] Satzinger in Izre'el (2002: 227–61), with earlier literature.
[77] Old Persian cuneiform script was used in the fifth and fourth centuries BC for monumental writing and its remains were in many cases readily accessible without excavation.

Thomas Hyde (1636–1703).[78] Among the many inscriptions reported during the eighteenth century, those copied by Carsten Niebuhr (1733–1815) at Persepolis deserve a special mention.[79] It was recognized that they contained three different scripts, later identified as Old Persian, Elamite, and Babylonian. The first one, with about 40 different signs, seemed to reflect an alphabet, while the others with a much larger number of different characters were syllabaries or logograms.

Assuming that the first writing represented the Old Persian language, which would be related to Avestan and Sanskrit, and that a diagonal wedge served as word divider, Georg Friedrich Grotefend (1775–1853) initiated their deciphering in 1802.[80] His initial results were expanded and refined by other scholars.[81] Next the Elamite script of the trilinguals was attacked. It contained over 100 different signs, the value of which was gradually determined by applying the sound values of the Old Persian proper names to appropriate correspondences in the Elamite text. Some insight was gained into the language itself, but considerable obscurity still persists, also for Old Elamite. The third script of the Achaemenid trilinguals had in the meantime been identified with that of texts found in Mesopotamia, namely Akkadian or Assyro-Babylonian. Here also the proper names provided the first clues for a decipherment, but the difficulties were only gradually grasped. Once the Semitic character of the language had been established, the philological science of Assyriology developed rapidly, and Jules Oppert could demonstrate in 1856 that the Assyro-Babylonian cuneiform script derives from an older script, used for the non-Semitic language Sumerian.[82] He participated in 1857 at the successful competition organized in London by the Royal Asiatic Society for proving the correct decipherment of the cuneiform script.[83] In 1860, he published the first grammar of the Assyrian language.[84]

An important contribution to further grammatical research was provided by Friedrich Delitzsch (1850–1922), who wrote a grammar, a dictionary, and a manual for teaching.[85] Instead, the famous Babel–Bible controversy, in which he played a central role, had hardly any bearing on linguistic studies.[86] The main reference grammar of the

---

[78] He describes the wedges as *dactuli pyramidales seu cuneiformes*.

[79] For Niebuhr, see M.T. Larsen in Ebeling et al (1928: ix. 304–5).

[80] G. F. Grotefend reasoned that the introductory lines of the text were likely to contain the name, titles, and genealogy of the ruler, the pattern known from later Pahlavi inscriptions based on the Aramaic alphabet. The genealogy of Achaemenid rulers was known from Herodotus, and Grotefend found that the kings must be Darius I and his son Xerxes. This enabled the long proper names to be read and a number of sound values to be determined. For Grotefend and his deciphering of the cuneiform script, see e.g. R. Borger in Ebeling et al. (1928: iii. 655).

[81] Thus Henry Rawlinson (1801–95), who published in 1846 the trilingual Behistun inscription of Darius I, Edward Hincks (1792–1866), Jules Oppert (1825–1905), and Fox Talbot (1800–1877).

[82] Oppert had found bilingual syllabaries among the tablets from Nineveh in the British Museum: they gave ideograms with their phonetic value. In 1857 he published the first decipherment and translation of a monolingual Babylonian inscription.

[83] The results of the test have been published: *Inscription of Tiglath Pileser I, King of Assyria, BC 1150*, as translated by Sir Henry Rawlinson, Fox Talbot, Esq., Dr Hincks, and Dr Oppert (London, 1857).

[84] The history of Assyriology up to 1925 was written by Wallis (1925).

[85] His main publications are listed in Ebeling et al. (1928: ii. 198).

[86] For this controversy, see the contribution of M. T. Larsen in Sasson (1995: i. 95–106), with further bibliography.

Akkadian language was published in 1952 by Wolfram von Soden (1908–96) (von Soden 1952). Among the numerous linguistic studies dealing with Semitic cuneiform texts,[87] one can mention the grammar of Erica Reiner (1924–2005), who tried to apply principles of current linguistic research to Akkadian and to base her study on the literary dialect of Akkadian (Reiner 1966). Indeed, there is a need for studies on particular dialects and periods of Akkadian, and several works of the kind deal with genuine Akkadian idioms[88] or with 'peripheral' Akkadian, as written in West Semitic,[89] Hittite (R. Labat in 1932), Hurrian (G. Wilhelm in 1970; H.-P. Adler in 1976), and Elamite (L. De Meyer in 1962; E. Salonen in 1962).

In cuneiform lexicography, a major contribution was provided by Benno Landsberger (1890–1968), whose work laid the foundations of the monumental Chicago Assyriological Dictionary.[90] A more concise dictionary was published by Wolfram von Soden.[91] The entries of both dictionaries are divided, whenever possible and useful, according to dialectal and diachronic principles.

Excavations at Ras Shamra (Syria), started in 1929, unearthed the remains of Ugarit. Clay tablets with inscriptions in an unknown simple system of cuneiform signs were discovered. The low number of 30 different characters pointed at an alphabetic script, while the use of a vertical stroke as word-divider facilitated decipherment, based on the correct assumption that an early West Semitic dialect was involved. Thus the script was deciphered almost simultaneously in 1930 by Hans Bauer (1878–1937), Édouard Dhorme (1881–1966), and Charles Virolleaud (1879–1968), each working independently. It yielded a Northwest Semitic dialect of the Late Bronze Age (around the thirteenth century BC), named Ugaritic. Hurrian inscriptions in the same script were also found, as were texts in conventional Middle Babylonian cuneiform.

Fundamental research by Harold L. Ginsberg put the Ugaritic grammar on a solid scientific basis, and Cyrus H. Gordon made the first systematic presentation in 1940, 1947, 1955, and 1965,[92] adding a comprehensive glossary. However, the decisive recognition of two prefixed verbal forms *yíqtul* (accomplished) and *yiqáttal* (unaccomplished) in

---

[87] A bibliography can be found in Lipiński (2001a: 613–17). Assyriological bibliography is compiled yearly in the journal *Orientalia*, issued in Rome by the Biblical Institute Press.

[88] For Old Akkadian, for instance, see M. Hilgert in 2002; R. Hasselbach in 2005 and 2007; for Old Babylonian, see G. Buccellati in 1996; for Old Assyrian, K. Hecker in 1968; for Middle Assyrian, W. Mayer in 1971; for Neo-Assyrian, J. Hämeen-Anttila in 2000. Among similar older publications, see W. von Soden in 1932–6; I. J. Gelb in 1952; J. Aro in 1955. For bibliographical data up to 2000, see Lipiński (2001a: 613–17).

[89] The 'peripheral' dialect of Emar, on the Middle Euphrates, attested by texts from about the 13th century BC, was analysed by S. Seminara in 1998. Earlier grammars on 'peripheral' West Semitic Akkadian were published by A. Finet in 1956; G. Giacumakis in 1970; J. Huehnergard in 1989; W. H. van Soldt in 1991; Sh. Izre'el in 1991. The letters from Canaan, found at El-Amarna (Egypt), were analysed by A. F. Rainey in 1996. For Canaanite in general, see Bélova et al. (2009: 239–78).

[90] *Assyriological Dictionary of the Oriental Institute of the University of Chicago* (1956–2010), with 21 vols, some of which consist of two or three parts. It is now complete.

[91] Von Soden (1965–81). This work, based in part on the material previously collected by Bruno Meissner (1868–1947), reveals an excellent Semitic background.

[92] See the bibliography in Lipiński (2001a: 613–15).

Ugaritic poetry was due to Albrecht Goetze (1897–1971).[93] A big reference grammar of Ugaritic was published in 2000 by Josef Tropper[94], and the useful dictionary of Joseph Aistleitner (Aistleitner 1963) is now generally replaced by the English version of the lexicon prepared in Spanish by Gregorio del Olmo Lete and Joaquín Sanmartín.[95]

12.2.9 Comparative Semitic Linguistics

Lexical comparisons between Aramaic, Arabic, Hebrew, and even Berber words were already made by grammarians and lexicographers in the Middle Ages, but we had to wait for Gesenius to find a modern approach to historical comparative linguistics. After Theodor Nöldeke's sketch and William Wright's *Lectures*,[96] published in the late nineteenth century, there was the monumental grammar of Carl Brockelmann (1868–1956),[97] based essentially on Classical Arabic and lacking a historical perspective, though greater importance had already been given to Akkadian in the comparative grammar of Heinrich Zimmern, an Assyriologist (Zimmern 1898). Hans Bauer also paid a particular attention to the Akkadian verbal system, which should in fact be taken as a basis for the reconstruction of that in Proto-Semitic.[98]

A decisive step towards an Afro-Asiatic approach to grammatical questions was made in 1950, when Otto Rössler compared the verbal systems of Akkadian, Berber, and Beja.[99] A common basis was to be accepted also for Egyptian[100] and Chadic (Rössler 1979), but serious Chadic studies only started to appear in the 1970s.[101]

---

[93] Goetze (1938). Such a possibility was already considered hesitatingly by H. Bauer in 1936. See further Lipiński (2001a: §38.6, 2008: 303).

[94] Tropper (2000), as well as a smaller grammar: Tropper (2002). Extensive critical reviews were written by L. Kogan and D. Pardee. For Tropper's reply see Tropper 2001 (2002).

[95] Del Olmo Lete and Sanmartín (2003). An extensive review was written by Gzella (2007). The concise dictionary published by Tropper in 2008 was reviewed by Gzella (2008b).

[96] Nöldeke (1887); Wright (1890). Among the introductions to the Semitic languages one can mention Brockelmann (1906); Bergsträsser (1928); Gray (1934).

[97] Brockelmann (1908–13, 1908). On Brockelmann and his work, see e.g. Fück (1958).

[98] Bauer (1910), with some inaccuracies. See Bélova et al. (2009: 15–112).

[99] Several articles appeared in 1950, 1951, 1952, 1964 in which Rössler shows that Berber was typologically a 'non plus ultra' Semitic language, close to Proto-Semitic. A short reference to the Libyco–Berber–Akkadian relationship had already been made by Rössler in 1942. Bibliographical data can be found in Hetzron (1997: 256, 289). For the Akkadian–Beja relationship, see now Gragg (2006).

[100] Rössler (1971). However, some of Rössler's sound correspondences cannot be accepted without further analysis. For instance, Egyptian emphatic phonemes, e.g. $ḏ$, were originally pharyngealized dentals, like the Semitic ones (Lipiński 2001a: §10.9–10), not glottalized. Now, this explains precisely why Egyptian *nḏm* corresponds to Semitic *naʿim*, 'pleasant', and *psḏ* is possibly related to *tišʿ*. A similar correspondence occurs later in Semitic. Thus Hebrew *ṣʾn* and Aramaic *ʿn*, 'small cattle', go both back to *ḍʾn*. Pharyngealization can be lost, but can also supplant the basic dental articulation of the phoneme (Lipiński 2001a: §10.9). The rejection of Rössler's system by Takács (1999–2007: i. 333–93) goes too far.

[101] Vycichl (1934) had already tried to compare Hausa to ancient Egyptian, but a larger approach to Chadic languages was initiated only in the 1970s under the inspiring guidance of Herrmann

Morphosyntax seems to be the most stable and characteristic feature of languages, and a step forward was made in this research field in 1965, when Igor Diakonov (1915–99) recognized that Afro-Asiatic languages preserve some ergative features (Diakonov 1965, 1988, 1991) characterized by the predominance of intransitive verbs and the opposition of a *casus agens* and a *casus patiens*. The *casus agens* is used for the logical subject of transitive verbs and for the instrumental, while the *casus patiens* marks the logical object of transitive and the logical subject of intransitive verbs. Traces of ergativity appear in ancient Egyptian,[102] in Chadic languages, in Libyco-Berber dialects (Diakonov 1988: 111; Lipiński 2001a: §2.14; 32.1–3; 48.2) and in Semitic (Müller 1995; Lipiński 2001a: §32.1–7; 2001b: 8–9; Waltisberg 2002). The Semitic case system has shifted from the *casus agens*/*casus patiens* to a nominative/accusative opposition, to which a genitive was added.

The Afro-Asiatic frame and a historical perspective characterize, to various degrees, recent comparative grammars.[103] Authors try to give a description of the original grammatical structure with two prefixed conjugations and the distinction of the jussive *yíqtúl* from the indicative *yíqtul* (Hetzron 1969); they attempt to trace the phonetic laws and to investigate the origin, as well as the development of the grammatical forms.[104] An important and innovative feature of Bélova et al. (2009) is that it also contains accounts of the proto languages from which the historically attested languages are generally assumed to derive.

12.2.10 Phonology and Lexicography

Lexicography, lexical morphology, and phonology are closely related aspects of linguistic research. The phonology of the Semitic languages in historical periods is relatively well known,[105] despite the inadequate writing systems used for the ancient languages, especially Akkadian, with all its synchronic and diachronic varieties, and Aramaic, which has a long history of 3,000 years. The dictionary of Semitic roots, started in 1994 by David Cohen, has been continued (Cohen et al. 1994–2012). It adheres to a strictly alphabetic order, while the great Russian project focused on

Jungraithmayr, whose very partial bibliography is given by Lipiński (2001a: 650). Publications referring to this language family are listed ibid. 649–51.

    102 Satzinger in Izre'el (2002: 237–8).
    103 Moscati (1964); Stempel (1999); Lipiński (2001a); Kienast (2001). Brockelmann's mainly descriptive and rather static approach is followed by Grande (1972: 17–308).
    104 This general conception seems to go back to the comparative grammar of Indo-European languages by Franz Bopp (1791–1867).
    105 Lipiński (2001a: §9.1–27.30). Hypothetical phonetic re-evaluations of alphabetic and syllabic signs marking sibilants or gutturals, as found mainly in publications of Russian scholars, are not taken into account. Complementary data on the reflexes of gutturals in Assyrian can be found in Kouwenberg (2006).

etymology follows the semantic principle.[106] Cognate roots in other Afro-Asiatic languages are wisely added in separate sections and only when they are illuminating the sense of Semitic words. An earlier semantic approach to Semitic etymology was undertaken in 1964–71 by Pelio Fronzaroli, who dealt with words referring to anatomy and physiology, natural phenomena, forestry, the domestic setting, and food.

For a long period Marcel Cohen's essay (Cohen 1947) was the only comparative work in the Afro-Asiatic field. After half a century the situation has changed drastically, with the publication of descriptive and comparative dictionaries by a group of Russian scholars under the guidance of Igor M. Diakonov, on the one side,[107] and by the team of Victor E. Orel and Olga Stolbova, on the other (Orel and Stolbova 1995). They may appear hasty, because Diakonov developed a huge system of occlusive, fricative, and 'sonorant' proto-phonemes, next to only the two vowels *ə and *a. This calls to mind the North Caucasian languages, including Chechen, which are characterized by an extraordinary abundance of consonants. For Proto-Semitic, only some of the proto-phonemes proposed by Diakonov can be accepted.[108]

The posthumously published study of Nikolai Yushmanov (1896–1946) on Proto-Semitic phonology appeared only after the publication of the above-mentioned etymo-logical dictionaries.[109] Yushmanov had assumed that five 'archiphonemes' existed originally in Proto-Semitic: a dental (*t), a velar (*k), a liquid (*r/l), a labial (*p), and a nasal (*n). This means of course that a distinction of voiced, unvoiced, and emphatic or pharyngealized consonants represents a differentiation of the basic sounds in the course of a long prehistoric linguistic evolution. The same ought to be said about the spirantized occlusives, in which changes can occur merely in order to ease articulation. Yushmanov's hypothesis is thus basically diachronic. It should be reformulated now-adays in the broader frame of the Afro-Asiatic language family.

In 1926 Benno Landsberger pointed to a phenomenon noticeable in Semitic (Land-sberger 1926): there are groups of verbs having two radical consonants in common which express identical or similar meanings. Thus, for example, in Hebrew: *prd*, 'to separate,' *prm*, 'to tear,' *prs*, 'to split,' *prṣ*, 'to break down,' *prq*, 'to pull apart,' *prr*, 'to dissolve,' *prš*, 'to distinguish,' etc. All these verbs have the radical *pr* in common and they all express the basic notion 'to divide.' This phenomenon is widespread in the Semitic lexicon, and it raises the question whether many triconsonantal roots are not, in fact, derived from biconsonantal ones or, better, are basically monosyllabic.[110] This

---

[106] Militarev and Kogan (2000, 2005). The dictionary will consist of eight volumes, two of which have already been published. Some etymologies are far-fetched, and insufficient attention is paid to the changing values of sibilants.

[107] Diakonov et al. (1993–7), the English version of their Russian works dating from 1981–83.

[108] Voigt in Izre'el (2002: 272–9). Voigt favours Rössler's system of sound correspondences between Egyptian and Semitic (ibid. 289).

[109] Yushmanov (1998: 126–90). The manuscript was known to Igor M. Diakonov before its publication.

[110] This means that they consist of a vowel and one, two or three consonants, two of which form a cluster, for instance: -*lbas* 'dress!', -*ksir* 'break!', -*ktub* 'write!'.

question also applies to nominal roots.[111] The topic of bi- vs triradicality ushered in a new phase—in fact Proto-Afro-Asiatic—with Georges Bohas' theory on the 'matrix' and the 'etymon,'[112] i.e. the original linguistic sign with onomatopoeic origins, and the primitive, reversible biconsonantal basis C_1C_2. One might speculate that, in the twenty-first century, one task of comparative Afro-Asiatic linguistics will not be to discuss the bi- or triradicality of the roots, but to examine the question of their basic monosyllabism, reflecting a phonological system revealed by sound comparisons and resulting partly from nursery words and onomatopoeic sounds. The development of the verbal system with affixed forms, geminations, different stresses, and vowel lengths, as well as with internal apophony, will then be viewed in relation to this monosyllabic basis. Lexical morphology will pay more attention to the function of vocalic changes and of properly determined additional phonemes, while morphosyntax will scrutinize the transitivizing devices of the verbs and the passage from a *casus agens/patiens* opposition to a nominative/accusative case system.

[111] See e.g. Lipiński (2001a: §30.8–11).
[112] Bohas (1997, 2001); Bohas and Dat (2007); Gazov-Ginzberg (1965) can be regarded as a precursor of the theory.

CHAPTER 13

···

FROM PLATO TO PRISCIAN

Philosophy's Legacy to Grammar

···

CATHERINE ATHERTON AND DAVID BLANK

13.1 INTRODUCTION

···

THIS chapter will tell part of the story, not of grammar, but of the emergence from philosophy—a discipline far more ambitious and wide-ranging, in classical antiquity, than is its modern counterpart—of something that would one day be called 'grammar.' It finds its roots in specifically philosophical speculation about language's components, structure, origins, and function, although much of what is germane is actually about something rather different: *logos* or 'rational discourse.' A full, accurate reconstruction of all the original contexts of this material is crucial to a proper understanding of how 'grammar' came into being as a distinct discipline; and there is no one place to look for the antecedents to grammar in earlier Greek philosophy, just as there was no single, agreed account of what should fall within the philosopher's remit.

One context was more or less constant: philosophy's self-conscious, self-defining concern with argument, both in actual philosophical discussion and as a logical construct. Here the primary object of study was language as bearer of truth values and as signifier both of external *realia* and of our own internal states. But philosophers approached language in other ways too: as a vehicle of public persuasion; as a vehicle for ethical education, especially through the study of poetry; and as itself a source of information about the hidden properties and structures of the world, especially as evidence for or against a cosmic anthropocentric teleology.

A more distant ancestor of grammar is, unsurprisingly, the discipline concerned with instruction in reading and writing, or *grammatistikê* (a term first attested, probably, in the first century BCE). Pupils began with the names, shapes, and sounds of the 'letters' or 'letter-sounds' (*grammata*, sing. *gramma*); learned to write all their permissible combinations, in syllables; and then moved on to writing whole words, phrases, proverbs, slogans ('The unpunished boy does not learn'), and, finally, poetic verses. Children may have learned to write their names before they could read, and many did not get beyond this stage. The élite youth, however, went on to what was sometimes distinguished as *grammatikê*, a more advanced study of the poets as authorities for training the character, with a view to the duties of a citizen in peace and war, and as an entrée into the élite's shared cultural and social heritage.

The prominence of public speaking as the other enduring requirement of a political career in the classical West fostered the emergence, in the fifth century BCE, of itinerant professional teachers of oratory and of political activity generally, as well as of the interpretation of poetry: the 'sophists.' They presented themselves as competitors with more traditional educators—poets, sages, statesmen—and eventually with philosophers too; and it is on this disputed territory that Plato set his *Protagoras*. The sophist Protagoras has claimed to impart what Socrates sums up as 'political excellence' (319a), and also declares:

> I consider, for my part, that the greatest part of a gentleman's education is to be clever [*deinos*] on the subject of poetry; and that means, being able to understand things said by the poets, and to distinguish what is and what is not well done in them, and, when asked, to give an account [*logos*] of it. (*Protagoras* 338e–339a)[1]

We are shown the sort of thing he has in mind: identifying an apparent contradiction between two quotations—both ethical in content—from one poet, Simonides, and explaining the apparent falsity of a line from another, Pittacus. These feats of 'cleverness' win applause from the audience and mock discomfiture from Socrates at his 'defeat' (338e–347a). In real life, even the most famous line of all Greek poetry, 'Sing, goddess, the wrath of Achilles' (*Iliad* 1.1), was not safe from Protagoras, who disparaged Homer's choice of a grammatically feminine noun, *mênis* 'wrath,' to signify Achilles' assuredly masculine anger (Aristotle, *Sophistical Refutations* 14, 173b), and mocked the line as inappropriately issuing a command to a divinity (*Poetics* 19, 1456b). (Aristotle, typically, is unimpressed: no one will actually find Homer at fault.) But we should not interpret these as the first baby steps towards pragmatics, or as foreshadowing the criticism that *I order You to give us our daily bread* is an inappropriate deep structure for a prayer. Protagoras' concern was his own career as an authority who could turn even the most illustrious poetry into a showcase for his 'cleverness,' and teach others to do the same. What should be made of the implicit assumptions that some nouns 'ought' to be masculine, and that prayers and commands 'ought' to look different, was someone else's problem.

Plato's dialogues offer rhetorical displays and literary analysis and criticism, but for Plato to do philosophy is, at heart, to take part in a serious, generous, shared search for the truth, in the form of question-and-answer argumentation: in a word, dialectic. In such an environment, puzzles exploited by sophists merely to stump their opponents and impress their clients can be reinterpreted as serious philosophical challenges and made over into keys for unlocking the basic structures and properties of reality and of the language we (can or should) use about it, including the seminal distinction in the *Sophist* between an *onoma*, a noun or a subject of predicates, and a *rhêma*, a verb or a

---

[1] Authors' translation, here and throughout.

predicate (§13.3.2.2). This distinction now appears obvious, trite, almost naïve, only because of its enormous influence on philosophy, logic, and grammar, each of which interpreted and expanded on it in different ways and for different purposes.

Thus it is as a dialectician that Aristotle identifies the contribution made by the *onoma* and *rhêma* to what he identifies as the primary bearer of truth values (§§13.4.2.1, 13.4.2.3). Where Plato's Socrates delicately weaves the use of names to address people into a net to snare an unwary naturalist (§13.2.1.4), Aristotle bluntly banishes any *logos* that is not true or false to other specialisms—not, presumably, because poets or orators never say things that are true or false, but because this is not what is distinctive about their discourse. Other types of word, too, and other features of *onomata* and *rhêmata*, may be handed on: to poetics and rhetoric (*Int.* 17a4–7; cf. *Poetics* chs 19–22; *Rhetoric* 3) (see end of chapter, p. 338, for a list of abbreviations), which deal with 'parts' (*merê*), not of *logos*, but of linguistic expression; or to the discipline of 'delivery' (*hupokrisis*), later a fixture in rhetorical handbooks, which gives instruction in how to present a speech in front of an audience, including the framing of commands, prayers, and all the other 'formations of linguistic expression' (*skhêmata tês lexeôs*) that Aristotle thinks the poetry expert can safely neglect, whatever Homeric failures Protagoras may claim to have found (*Poetics* 19, 1456b).

The Stoa, in contrast, made both rhetoric and poetics the province of the philosopher, as, respectively, one-half of the division of philosophy concerned specifically with rational discourse, and a topic inside the other half, dialectic—the single most important source for what would become 'technical' grammar (§13.6.3). For the first time, *logos*, understood as one manifestation of human rationality and defined as 'significant linguistic expression,' was systematically divided up and located at the intersection of the physical and the non-physical: on the one side, the letter-sounds or 'elements' (*stoikheia*) of *lexis*, and the 'parts of speech' (*ta tou logou merê*), also sometimes called 'elements'; on the other, the incorporeal 'significations' of sentences and of some sentence parts (§13.6.8). This new classification of subject matter, both generally and in its details, reflected a fresh understanding of the scope of philosophical inquiry and a novel conception of the ideal range and structure of human knowledge.

As something called grammar gradually emerged as an independent discipline, this brilliant and complex philosophical framework was forgotten, but a cardinal feature of the Stoic approach to *logos* was not: the principle that there are certain linguistic phenomena—such as the similarities amongst inflected forms of words, or agreement in gender between noun and adjective—that are governed by rules; and that, if properly understood, apparent irregularity in these areas turns out to be explicable by reference to the norms underpinning those rules, through an application of the method of 'pathology,' that is, of giving a rational account, a *logos*, of the 'corruptions' or *pathê* in the objects of study (§13.8.3). The greatest exponent of this is the second-century CE technical grammarian Apollonius Dyscolus, whose debt to Stoic grammar does not diminish his remarkable achievement.

This sort of discourse about language was, therefore, normative, not descriptive. When, however, language was studied by orators or rhetoricians, or by professional 'grammarians' with a practical interest in view, it may well become the object of prescriptions, although it was not *everyday* usage or speech that had to be corrected, but always the language of a text (a poem, a speech, etc.); and correction was always done to serve a purpose beyond itself. In the case of oratory, what were wanted were tools of persuasion; accordingly, alongside proofs, the projection of an appropriate character, and the elicitation of a useful emotional response, Aristotle had defined a separate topic, *lexis* or linguistic expression, that became a fixture in later rhetorical handbooks. Yet it is implicit already in the teaching of the sophist Gorgias of Leontini (fifth century BCE), who, impressed by the power of poetry and of religious and medical incantations and spells to 'lead the soul' (*psuchagôgein*), prescribed a vocabulary tinged with poetic words and use of figures such as repetition, balancing clauses, and assonance. In the case of poetry, Aristotle's approach is similarly teleological: what he describes (*Poetics* 21–22, 1457a31–1458a18) are the kinds of diction and style that help it reach its goals, whether general—to be clear, but not commonplace—or attached to particular genres (tragedy, comedy, epic, etc.). His analysis includes a distinction between simple and compound nouns, and between nouns that are, in context, standard or in some way deviant, whether as exotic, metaphorical, ornamental, invented, lengthened, shortened, or altered.

The late third century BCE saw an important development: the emergence of specialized philologists, who compiled and corrected the texts of older literature, especially poetry, and who taught advanced students to read, analyse, use, and judge them. The beginnings of this profession are associated with Philitas of Cos (late fourth/third century BCE), first of a new generation of poets ('both poet and critic' for Strabo in the first century CE), who around 300 BCE came to Alexandria as a royal tutor. He trained Zenodotus of Ephesus, who became a tutor in his turn and then, in 285/4, director of the newly created Library in the *Mouseion* of Alexandria. Zenodotus focused on establishing the correct text of the genuine Homeric poems, which required comparison of manuscripts, analysis of the morphology and meaning of Homeric words, and study of Homeric syntax. The Homeric project was continued by his pupil Aristophanes of Byzantium (*c.*260–185 BCE), who applied his expertise to other poets as well, such as Hesiod, Pindar, Sophocles, and Euripides, and who compiled works on unusual or foreign words and on names found in older texts.

The greatest of the grammarians working under the Ptolemies in Alexandria was Aristophanes' pupil Aristarchus of Samothrace (*c.*216–144 BCE). His commentaries on Homer laid the foundation for the studies of later grammarians, particularly the so-called 'Four Men': Didymus, Aristonicus, Nicanor, and Herodian. In late antiquity, their treatises on the text of Homer were excerpted, and thereby came to be the basis of the marginal commentary in the great ninth-century manuscript of Homer (Venetus A), which in turn became the foundation of modern Homeric scholarship. It is clear from the mass of Homeric commentary deriving ultimately from Aristarchus that he had access to a fully developed system of grammatical concepts and categories; in particular, he uses the names of all eight of the word-classes that would eventually be called the 'parts of speech': noun, verb, participle (*metokhê*), article (*arthron*), pronoun (*antônumia*), conjunction (*sundesmos*), preposition (*prothesis*), and adverb (*epirr-hêma*). He also distinguished the various 'accidents' (*sumbebêkota*, sing. *sumbebêkos*) of these words, for example the voices of the verb and the 'cases' (*ptôseis*, sing. *ptôsis*, from *piptein* 'fall'; cf. Latin *casus* from *cado*) of nouns and participles.

An older contemporary of Aristarchus, Crates of Mallos, started a philological school of his own in Pergamon. He and his pupils, who called themselves 'critics' (*kritikoi*), combined textual studies with a kind of allegorical approach to Homeric interpretation, and Crates also made important contributions to the theory of poetry—so much so that he and Aristarchus were said to have 'perfected' grammar (S.E. *M* 1.44). The earlier Alexandrian grammarians (*grammatikoi*), as at least some of them called themselves, concentrated instead on textual criticism, and were greatly influenced by Peripatetic philosophy and its methods of solving 'questions,' 'problems,' or 'difficulties' in poetic texts.

The first general works systematizing the discipline of philology were written in the late second century BCE by students of Crates and Aristarchus, Tauriscus and Dionysius of Thrace. Tauriscus' book, now lost, may have been called *On Criticism*. It divides *kritikê* into three: the rational (*logikon*), empirical or experiential (*tribikon*), and historical (*historikon*) parts, dealing respectively with diction and figures; the dialects and various forms or types of style; and the pre-existing unordered raw material. Tauriscus apparently intended the first part to work out rational rules of combination, inflection, derivation, and syntax; the *tribikon* to make observations on dialectal usage and the styles of particular authors; and the *historikon* to identify the personages, places, myths, and so on in the 'unordered mass' of things mentioned in literary works. These studies, which belong to the grammarian, would be used in the judgment (*krisis*) of poems by the critic much as an apprentice is used by a master craftsman: for the critic is knowledgeable about the whole of 'scientific knowledge concerned with *logos*' (*logikê epistêmê*) (S.E. *M* 1.248–9, 79).

Dionysius' *Expertise of Grammar* (*Tekhnê grammatikê*), perhaps known rather as *Precepts* (*Parangelmata*, S.E. *M* 1.57), is also lost, although fragments are cited by later authors. The work transmitted under his name in a large number of manuscripts—not to mention in Syriac, Armenian, and other translations that laid the foundations for the first grammars of those languages—is actually a late antique compendium of grammatical rules appended to the introductory paragraphs of the original text, where its subject is defined as 'an experience [*empeiria*] for the most part of what is said in poets and prose-writers.' Its 'parts' (sometimes called 'duties' or 'tasks') prescribe how the grammarian is to approach and teach any text—just what we should expect from the pupil of Aristarchus. They comprise: 'practised reading respecting prosody; explication of the poetic tropes present [*sc.* in the text]; prompt elucidation of unusual words and histories [i.e. allusions to persons and places, etc., from myth and history]; discovery of etymology; calculation of analogy; and, the finest of everything in the expertise, judgment of poems.'

Dionysius' pupil Asclepiades of Myrlea seems to have understood these six parts to derive from a three-part system similar to the one he himself devised (S.E. *M* 1.250–52).

Like Tauriscus, he partitioned *grammatikê*, using epistemological criteria, into an expert (*tekhnikon*) part—corresponding to Tauriscus' rational part—and an historical part, corresponding to Tauriscus' empirical and historical parts together. The final, grammatical part is the equivalent of Tauriscus' criticism, as combining the results of the other parts (*M* 1.252). Asclepiades' tripartition survived in the Latin grammatical tradition, for example in Quintilian's (late first century CE) division of grammar into the 'knowledge (*scientia*) of correct speaking'; the 'explication (*enarratio*) of the poets'; and 'judgment' (*iudicium*) which is mingled (*mixtum*) with both of these (*Inst.* 1.4.2). The rationale (*ratio*) for speaking and the explication of authors he defines as methodical (*methodicê*) and historical (*historicê*) respectively (9.1). It may have been Varro (first century BCE) who transmitted this system from the Greek tradition into the Roman, perhaps relying on Asclepiades' book; and Quintilian may have learned it from his own teacher, Q. Remmius Palaemon.

This preoccupation with the internal organization and epistemological status of philology, whether as 'criticism' or as 'grammar,' is another powerful sign of indebtedness to philosophy, a constant concern of which is, of course, the nature, basis, and and varieties of knowledge. Plato's Socrates had argued that rhetoric is acquired by experience, but is something irrational (*alogon*), a mere knack or practice (*tribê*) and not a *tekhnê*, because it makes guesses about what may be pleasing, rather than trying to achieve knowledge about the good (*Gorgias* 463a–465d). This terminology, and the comparisons and contrasts it implies, were sharpened by the Stoa, whose founder, Zeno of Citium, defined a *tekhnê* as 'a system of cognitions unified by practice for some goal advantageous in life.' For Chrysippus, third head of the Stoa and perhaps its greatest philosopher, it is 'a state [*hexis, sc.* of the rational soul] that, with the aid of impressions, advances methodically' (LS 42A).

The 'scientific knowledge relating to *logos*' in Tauriscus' definition of the critic seems, however, to be something still more ambitious, perhaps a relative of Stoic *epistêmê*, which is a fixed rational disposition (*diathesis*) and so, unlike a mere state, does not admit of degrees and cannot be shaken by reasoning. Debates between rationalist (*logikoi*) and empiricist physicians about the cognitive status of medicine may also have provided material for the new discipline's self-definition. Here again Tauriscus' terminology is suggestive, for empiricist doctors laid claim to expertise that rested on 'practice'—the extension of practice through analogy—the methods of 'transition to the similar,' and on 'historical inquiry' (*historia*) into reports of particular cases (Galen, *Outline of Empiricism* 45.20, 48.25, 67.4).

Whatever its precise status, it is clear that the first part of grammar is claimed to be 'expert,' 'methodical,' or 'rational' because of its consistent application of a set of principles or 'canons'—usually comprising analogy, etymology, authority or antiquity, and usage—to establish correct pronunciation, spelling, morphology, and syntax. Correctness in these areas is *hellênismos* or *latinitas*, good Greek or Latin, and its violation is a *barbarismos*, in a single word, and a *soloikismos* in a combination of words. This part of grammar owes its origin to philology, but its concepts and categories came to be used, implicitly and explicitly, in other contexts: in grammatical primers, for example, which supplied lists of the letter-sounds and syllables and inflectional paradigms for memorization; in stylistic manuals for older boys on how to parse, paraphrase, or compose complete sentences; and of course in highly technical monographs on, for example, the parts of speech.

The interest in identifying rule-governed linguistic phenomena helped fuel a debate, not as to whether there is such a thing as linguistic regularity, for example in inflections (e.g. Varro, *LL* 10.68), but as to whether exceptions to it should be corrected, and if so, in which contexts. (The use by some orators of corrected forms, for example, was ridiculed as inappropriate and counterproductive.) Varro explicitly distinguishes the theses that regularities exist and that one ought to adhere to them in speech (9.4); yet his own presentation of the debate, which exaggerated the points of difference, gave rise to the misapprehension, regrettably widespread in modern scholarship, that the whole of ancient grammatical theory was divided between prescriptivists who wanted usage to be governed by regularity or 'analogy,' and 'anomalist' descriptivists who assumed that there are no rules governing language, and that observation of actual usage should be one's guide. Varro himself (9.1) makes Aristarchus the principal 'analogist' and Crates the principal 'anomalist,' and criticizes the latter for misunderstanding the sort of anomaly in which Chrysippus was interested—viz. the mismatch between linguistic forms and what they mean (§13.6.12, §13.7.1 below)—and for arguing that 'unlike' or 'irregular' forms should be preferred (10.1).

Yet it is clear from the sceptic Sextus Empiricus' presentation, in the second/third century CE, of a history of grammar that derives ultimately from Asclepiades, that Alexandrian and Pergamene philologists were in fundamental agreement on the nature of their discipline and its parts. Analogy, as both a linguistic phenomenon and a method for discovering what is correct by appropriate comparisons (say, of the form of a noun with forms of nouns of the same gender, syllabic structure, prosody, and/or meaning), formed, with etymology, the 'rational' basis of grammatical study (Quintilian *Inst.* 1.6.1): its *ratio* or *logos*. The remaining criteria of Hellenism and Latinity, such as dialectal usage, may be used when the 'rational' criteria do not produce a clear answer. The procedure of finding a word's original form by locating it in relation to its similars (e.g. Varro *LL* 5.5–6) was based on the assumption that language has a 'rational' structure that had once made it an excellent vehicle for representing both thoughts and the external world, and would have been easy to learn because, in the processes of inflection and derivation, it encoded family resemblances amongst related names and the names of related things: what shows clearly and memorably that *lego* 'I gather' and *legi* 'I gathered' are related, for example, is precisely their formal resemblance (3–6) (see §13.7.2).

Technical grammar began as part of a philologically oriented discipline, and was focused in first instance on texts—their constitution, correction, and interpretation—and not on the correction of everyday speech. The teaching of Greek and Latin to children and teenagers, in contrast with these (meta-)theoretical disagreements, was a wholly practical enterprise and thoroughly and unashamedly prescriptive. Both disciplines emerged with the transformation of the cultural, social, and political world after

Alexander's conquests in the third century BCE. As native speakers of Greek dialects became colonists in the conquered countries whose inhabitants began to learn the language of their new overlords, Greek itself changed, and there came into being a new lingua franca: *koinê*, the 'common' dialect. Rome's political and military expansion, including the diffusion of Latin as the lingua franca throughout Italy and then beyond, effected similar social changes, ensuring that teachers of good Latin, of the Greek classics and now the Roman ones too, and of the rudiments of composition, would be in demand in the West for centuries to come. But of course these changes created an ever-growing demand for such instruction only because it remained a constant in élite education and an unchallenged prerequisite for rhetorical training.

The distance travelled can be gauged by comparing a fourth-century BCE dialogue, the *Alcibiades*, with a sixth-century CE commentary on it. The young aristocrat argues (111a) that he has learned to be just as he learned to speak Greek: from people around him, not from any specialized teacher. The commentator Olympiodorus points out that there is speaking Greek and then there is speaking *correct* Greek, and for the latter you have to go to a *grammatikos* (*Commentary on Plato's Alcibiades 1*, 95.15–20). The *Alcibiades* may not be by Plato, but Plato's Protagoras teaches the same lesson (327e), and it would never have occurred to Plato, or to the real Protagoras, that learning one's native tongue could require instruction from specialists: to Olympiodorus, it is a self-evident fact.

There were, however, those who preferred Alcibiades' method to that of Olympiodorus. Sextus Empiricus speaks of two ways of learning to 'speak good Greek' (*hellênizein*): that of the expert, whose watchword is analogy, and that of the non-expert, who observes and imitates common usage and, when required, the usages of specialist groups such as philosophers and even grammarians (*M* 1.176, 179). Those who reject 'technical' analogy are neither grammarians nor experts, but sceptics, like Sextus himself, suspicious of all dogmatic theories and the disciplines based on them, or Epicureans with no time for so-called rules arbitrarily imposed by so-called experts. All think it worthwhile to learn grammar to the extent they need it to express themselves clearly and to avoid ridicule, and no further (*M* 1.232–5).

Sextus' sceptical attitude makes sense, of course, only if there are experts and jargons to joust with, and the rest of this chapter is, in a way, a history of the construction, first by philosophers, then by grammarians, of a metalanguage for language, on the shared basis that language is governed by rational rules and norms, and that secure knowledge of those rules and norms can therefore be had. We shall begin with a central component of this language (and thus of 'technical' Hellenism) with which Sextus was deeply familiar (*M* 1.142–53): discourse about the 'correctness of names.'[2]

---

[2] For further reading: Pinborg (1975) is an influential overview of the field; Taylor (1986) summarizes recent developments; Sluiter (1997) focuses on the role of semantics. On education in reading and writing, see Cribiore (2001). For Presocratic and sophistic debates about language, see Fehling (1965), Sluiter (1990). Nickau (1977) examines Zenodotus; Callanan (1987) studies linguistic theories in Aristophanes of Byzantium; Matthaios (1999) and Schironi (2004) collect many fragments of

13.2 WHAT'S IN A NAME? PLATO'S *CRATYLUS*

13.2.1 Introduction

Plato's *Cratylus* undoubtedly made the greatest contribution in antiquity to the form, and the persuasiveness, of the thesis that names are imposed, and imposed knowledgeably—although whether it was endorsed by Plato himself is another matter.[3] For the first time, it seems, the *Cratylus* brought together the questions of the correctness of names and of their origin, and offers a theory that yokes descriptive etymologies to a naturalist theory of naming that—at any rate in principle—leaves a space for expertise. Each element in this complex has precedents, but only in isolation.

Already in the sixth century BC the philosopher Parmenides could speak of the 'laying down [*katatithesthai*]' of different names for different things, a process he thinks grossly mistaken (28 B 8.39, 53; 19.3 DK). Plato's Protagoras claims that early men 'articulated vocal sound [*phônê*] and names expertly [lit. using *tekhnê*]' (*Protagoras* 322a), but does not say how, precisely, this expertise came in (or from). A passage in the *Cratylus* (391c, cf. 386cd) suggests the real Protagoras may have had views on the correctness of names, but we do not know what they were. Prodicus of Ceos, another sophist, seems to have been interested rather in correctness in the use of near-synonyms (384b, d cf. 337a–c).

In the *Cratylus* we hear of particular rival etymologies of religious terms (399d–400bc with 396d, 404c–406a), but of no rival theories about what makes names correct. A report about Plato's older contemporary Democritus, the atomist philosopher (Proclus *in Crat.* 16.23–36, fifth century CE), however, suggests the existence of a thesis that names are well matched with their *nominata* distributively or numerically, not descriptively—the descriptive thesis being the one that is examined in the *Cratylus* and that comes to dominate the debate to which Democritus is supposed to be contributing. By Proclus' day, that debate had come to be framed as an opposition between multiple varieties of *thesis* or 'imposition' and *phusis* or 'nature,' in which the questions of the

Aristarchus; Crates' fragments are treated by Broggiato (2001). On the organization of grammar, see Blank (2000). The standard edn of the *Tekhnê Grammatikê* attributed to Dionysius Thrax is Uhlig (1883); a newer edn with French translation and commentary is Lallot (1989/2003). That all but the beginning of it is actually a much later handbook is shown by Di Benedetto (1958–9), who summarizes his arguments in (2000). For early Roman grammarians, see Kaster (1995), Desbordes (1995), Taylor (2000); on the first Roman *artes*, Barwick (1922), Baratin (2000). Fehling (1956–7) first showed that the 'analogy vs anomaly' controversy was invented by Varro; further arguments in Blank (1982, 2005). For the conflict of empiricism and rationalism in grammar and philology and for any subject treated by Sextus Empiricus, see Blank (1998); also Atherton (1995). For Quintilian's paragraphs on grammar, see Ax 2011; for later Roman *artes*, see Schmidt (1989), Desbordes (2000). See also Ch. 34 below.

[3] An excellent discussion of the *Cratylus* and its philosophical problems is Sedley (2003), which ascribes to it a more optimistic view of the possibility of a science of etymology than the one in our treatment here. Another important study is Barney (2001). There is now a full commentary on the dialogue: Ademollo (2011).

origins of names and of what makes them correct had long since been (con)fused. Already in the first century BCE Philo can attribute the claim 'that the original imposers of names on things were wise' to 'the Greek philosophers' *en masse* (*Allegory of the Laws* 2.15; grammarians agreed, e.g. *Sch. Hom.* Il. p. I, 63.14–64.8 Erbse), which is why, perhaps, it was attributed to Pythagoras (Cicero *Tusculans* 1.62); in reality, the Stoics were its most forceful promoters (§13.7.1). So it may well be that Proclus' report, alongside the (re)classification of Democritus' position in the accepted terms (for imposition, against nature), preserves Democritus' own inference, from four varieties of quantitative (not qualitative) misassignment, that names are distributed randomly, by chance [*tukhê*]—a property quite independent both of their historical origin and of their contemporary correctness.

13.2.2 The Importance of the Debate

A question central to the *Cratylus* is whether, like rhetoric, navigation, and medicine, what would later be called 'etymology'[4] really is a *tekhnê*, with all the seriousness, prestige, and earning power that that implies, and whether an etymology is, as its name implies, a *logos* of what is *etumos*, 'genuine' or 'real.' If so, there will be only one way for a name to be correct, by its making clear what sort of thing its *nominatum* is (cf. 422d). Hence the importance of the thesis voiced by Cratylus, the 'naturalist' who gives his name to the dialogue: that the names things bear can teach us about the things, so that knowing the one entails knowing the other (435d–6d). And if 'things that come to be in accordance with nature'—as when a king's son becomes a king, or a good man has a good son (394a)—'must be given the same names' (394d), then conversely names, appropriately organized, can yield a genealogy of things. As a result, the etymologist, not the philosopher, will be able to tell us what the world is like. The stakes, then, could hardly be higher.

13.2.3 Hermogenes' 'Conventionalism'

Plato's response to this problem is, as always, complex, many-layered, and indirect, and the character of Socrates is critical, both openly and implicitly, of the positions he himself helps to construct. Socrates has been asked to mediate between Cratylus and Hermogenes, who, under Socrates' patient questioning (384d–385e), gradually expands on his initial assertion that a name is 'whatever people call a thing by, having made a convention to call it that, when they utter with regard to it [*epiphthengomenoi*] a bit of their own speech [*phônê*]' (383a), where *phônê* is nicely ambiguous between 'vocal

---

[4] It is not known when or by whom this term was invented. The Stoic scholarch Chrysippus (3rd century BCE) is credited with *Etymological writings* (*Etymologika*, DL 7.200); see §13.7.1.

sound' and 'language' or 'dialect.' (Cratylus' names, in contrast, are naturally correct in all languages, 383b.)

The relations amongst the various norms Hermogenes appeals to—convention//' (*nomos*); contract (*sunthêkê*); agreement (*homologia*); usage (*sunêtheia*); and habit (*ethos*)—are hardly perspicuous. Socrates' later interpretation of a habit as a contract a speaker makes with himself (435b) allows the possibility of conflict between public and private usage—for example, calling a man 'horse' or a horse 'man' (385a). Significantly, however, Hermogenes does at one point assume a distinction between laying down a rule and following it (384d).

Hermogenes also agrees—thereby opening the way to his acquiescence in the theory Socrates will advance—that each thing, and each action, has its own nature, independent of how it may strike us (386e–387b). If we want to cut something correctly, say, we must do it in accordance with the nature of cutting, and using what is naturally suited to cut that thing (386e–7a). This strongly realist principle is then applied to the actions of speaking (*legein*) and naming (*onomazein*), which is a part of speaking. Correctly performed naming is naming performed naturally, using the naturally correct tool or instrument (*organon*) for the job, viz. a name, by which 'we teach each other and divide up things as they are,' dividing being (*ousia*) much as a shuttle is a tool for separating the jumbled threads of warp and woof (387b–388c)—a comparison that, taken together with the cutting example, implies the possibility of failure for any *theoretical* division too.

Just as a shuttle is made by a craftsman at the behest, and under the guidance, of the weaver, who is the expert user of shuttles, so also with names: but here Socrates cleverly incorporates Hermogenes' thesis that names are bestowed by *nomos* (388d). The relevant expert must, therefore, be the *nomothetês*, the 'imposer of law/custom,' who is 'a master imposer of names' and also a name-maker (*onomatourgos*) (388d–389a); and whether he constructs new names or repurposes old ones, his own name suggests that what he really does is lay down the law.

This rapprochement between conventionalism and naturalism may be as unexpected as it is unconvincing (what has happened to the autonomy of speakers?); and we are in for three more surprises.

First, Hermogenes accepts the positing of ideal models—'forms' (*eidê, ideai*)—for ordinary artefacts (389b, d). In the case of names, it is left tantalizingly ambiguous whether there is but one model, or one for each (kind of) thing (389d–390e). Later on, Cratylus will accept the existence of ethical forms (439c–d). Second, the supervisor of the *nomothetês* and the expert user of names is the dialectician (*dialektikos*), who knows how to ask and answer questions (390b–d). Lastly, the *nomothetês*, again like any artisan, has a free hand in the selection of his raw materials, letters and syllables, only provided the names he makes are right for the job (389e–390a), which is why Greeks and barbarians can have quite different, but equally correct, names for the same things (cf. 390c).

This description of the craftsman's method, and his subordination to the user's superior knowledge, are reminiscent of a famous argument in *Republic* 10, except that nothing is said here of making by imitating, whether forms or anything else. Yet

Socrates' response to Hermogenes' request to see how this theory works in practice (390e–391a) rests ultimately on a scheme of mimetic relations (421e–427d)—not between names and forms, however, but between the mode of articulation of a letter-sound and the property of which it is both an imitation (*mimêsis*) and an indication (*dêlôma*) (423a–e). These 'primary names' or 'elements' go to form descriptive names, such as those, from myth, cosmology, theology, as well as from closer to home, decoded by Socrates in a lengthy, bravura series of etymologies (391b–3421d)—which must, however, come to an end somewhere if they are to be explanations at all (421d–e).

The primary names theory instead threatens the whole enterprise. Socrates is adamant that imitating the sound a thing makes is not naming it (423cd). Why, then, should imitating its being or nature count? For that is what descriptive names are supposed to do (423e–424b, cf. 393d, 396a, 429c). It is also what—supposedly—promises an expertise able to define *nominata* insofar as they are like their names (435e). Yet primary names can at best capture physical properties such as movements, so that the sliding of the tongue in pronouncing *l* fits it for indicating sleekness and smoothness (427b), for example. There is no guarantee any metaphorical extensions from these (as with *gliskhros*: 427b, cf. 414c, 435c) will be rule-governed, and the theory has nothing positive to say about how a sound-sequence is supposed to capture the structure of properties in an object, although it is not hard to see that mixing paints for a portrait (434a, de) is not an appropriate likeness. Finally, such rigid correspondences are hardly compatible with the free hand that the *nomothetês* is supposed to have with his material, and that Socrates actually has with his.

The names Socrates unpacks turn out to be, for the most part, disguised, distorted, and telescoped word-strings (*rhêmata, logoi*; cf. 421de, 425a), which, when expanded, form a phrase descriptive, or, optimally, definitive of the *nominatum*: *Dii philos* 'dear to God' is a *rhêma*, *Diphilos* 'Go(d-)dear' an *onoma*, for example (399a). The word *onoma* is itself 'like a name hammered together from a *logos* saying that "this is a being [*on*] into which an inquiry [*zêtêma*] is in being [*on*]"' (421a)—tools do have to be made, after all (cf. c). The name *Zeus* is 'like a *logos*' divided in two, since its two alternative accusative-case forms (as they would later be called), *Dia* and *Zêna*, 'when combined into one, indicate [*dêloi*] the god's nature,' viz. *di' (hon) zên*, 'through (whom) living' (396ab, an etymology later borrowed by Chrysippus). Hence the expertise that makes a *logos* out of names may be that of naming or that of oratory (425a)—uncertainty that is far from reassuring.

Moreover, Socrates drops frequent hints that his decodings may promise more entertainment than insight. The changes—adding, subtracting, and switching letter-sounds (393d, 395e, 418b), and altering syllable lengths (417c), breathings (417e), and accents (399ab), across dialects and languages (395de, 409d, 418b)—are chaotic, *ad hoc*, irregular: incompatible, in short, with the rules and norms of a genuine expertise. Socrates' account of the word *tekhnê*, significantly, involves a series of changes, from an original form *ekhonoê* 'condition of mind,' that Hermogenes thinks pretty fancy (*glischrôs*, 414bc). Socrates responds, alarmingly, that over time the first names have been manipulated into a lovely but unintelligible grandiloquence (414cd, cf. 404d,

421d). Similarly suspicious are the linked derivations of *mêkhanê* 'contrivance,' from *mêkos* 'length,' which 'signifies plenty [*to polu*], in a way [*pôs*]' (415a), and of *Hermês*, the name of the divine messenger, patron-god of travellers and salesmen, whom the *nomothetês*—not at all incidentally—'so to say sets to rule over us' (408ab): 'it seems to have something to do with *logos*, and being an interpreter [*hermêneus*], a messenger, a thief, a deceiver in *logoi* and a bargainer,' for it derives from the phrase *hos to eirein emêsato* 'he who contrived speech,' *via Eiremês*, which was 'prettified' into *Hermês* (407e–408b).

We cannot say we have not been warned. The *nomothetês* theory stipulated that what matters in a name is the form, not the matter. Similarly, a name's 'force' (*dunamis*) may be present in completely different sounds, as with *Hektôr* and *Astyanax*, the names of the Trojan hero and his son: although 'they have no letters but *t* in common, yet they signify the same thing,' viz. a king (392c–394c; cf. 383a). Thus the expert in names is like the doctor who can detect the same force in medicinal compounds despite differences in colour and scent (394ab); some names reveal their secrets only to the knowledgeable (395b; contrast d). Yet if changes are not rule-governed, and if the notion of 'signifying' is so vague and loose, no one, however expert, could retrace a name's history with any confidence. Moreover, contemporary names may be like those borrowed by epigones from their illustrious forebears (397b).

Little wonder that, with such bounty at his disposal, Socrates wants Hermogenes to play dialectician to his *nomothetês*—'but not with *too* much precision, please' (414d–415a); and in fact the ideal supervisor is nowhere in view. Little wonder too that Socrates distrusts his newfound 'wisdom' (428d, cf. 393c, 399a, 410e, 414b): like someone inspired (398e–399a, 409d, 428cd, cf. 411b), even if he is right he cannot say why, and in fact he may be talking plausible nonsense (393b, 399e, 401d, 421d) or simply making it up as he goes along (413d). Of the two interpretations—one serious, one playful—of the names of Dionysus and Aphrodite, patron gods of drinking and sex, Socrates knows only the jokey alternative (406b–d). He began with the names gods use because gods must 'call things correctly, by their natural names' (391d, cf. 400d), yet he is ignorant of both the gods and their names (400d–401a, d, cf. 319a–c, 407d); instead 'we are guessing at men's beliefs' about names (425c).

Socrates also reproaches himself and Hermogenes (393e, 425a, 418c, cf. 421c) for confusing their deconstructions with the work of the original imposers (401a, c, 411b, 426cd, 439c). The distinction between the *nomothetês* (393e, 429a) and historical imposers (411bc, 418ab, cf. 439c) likewise becomes blurred; Socrates even summarizes the whole naturalist construct as if it were the *nomothetês* theory plus the illustrations Hermogenes had asked for (427cd, cf. 391a). But the world(s) that names reveal may have been fashioned—albeit unwittingly—simply to match their makers' beliefs, which can be interesting and impressive (cf. 401b) and nonetheless false (411bc, cf. 439c), something we can know only by observing reality—which is what we should have been doing all along, investigating things 'through one another, if they are somehow related, and through themselves,' so far as we can (438e–439b), not through words and their supposed similarities to things (*cf.* 394a–d). Key terms such as *epistêmê, historia,* and *mnêmê* 'memory' (437a–c) 'are engaged in a civil war [*stasiasantôn*],' as Socrates puts it (438d), for they fit an Eleatic theory of cosmic stasis as snugly as a Heraclitean theory of cosmic flux, the ancestral world-view Socrates had hitherto detected (or so he says, 436e–438c; cf. 411a–412b, 414b), and which makes naming impossible (or so he says, 439b–440d; this verdict, especially as it regards forms, has generated a great deal of controversy that Socrates would no doubt say has largely missed the point again, like the argument over how justice got its name, 412c–413d).

In short, Socrates' explanations prove at best hermeneutic, not genuinely heuristic, so that, if we pay strict attention to names, they may not even deserve the name 'etymologies.' As Cratylus replaces Hermogenes as Socrates' interlocutor, all three agree on how difficult the subject is, and Socrates, who is, as always, ready to carry on the inquiry, adds: 'Indeed I myself would not confidently affirm any point in what I have said' (427d–428e, cf. 384bc, *Meno* 86b).

13.2.4 Cratylus' 'Naturalism'

It is now Cratylus' turn to have his theory turned upside down (428e–439c). Socrates first tries to pry him apart from the thesis that names are either perfect imitations of their *nominata* or not names at all. Both attack and defence are conducted by means of more likenesses, and Cratylus borrows a pair from two (other?) expertises, mathematics and orthography: a name resembles its *nominatum* as one number resembles another (432ab; yet perfect imitation is hardly practical for numbers, 435bc), or as a word being written resembles its 'target' word (430a–431c). Socrates' preferred likeness is a portrait, which may be more or less like Cratylus, say, while still being a portrait of him; similarly, even if a name or *logos* contains an inappropriate letter-sound or name respectively, 'the thing [*pragma*] is no less named and spoken' (432e). But his best point is that there must always be *some* difference between thing and imitation (430a–433b): after all, a perfect imitation of Cratylus would be, not Cratylus' name, but another Cratylus (432c). Cratylus is loath to abandon the all-or-nothing version of his theory (434d, 436c; cf. §13.3.1 below), however, and it takes two attempts to make him see what is really wrong with imitative naturalism.

The first (429de) turns on a misplaced address to 'Hermogenes, son of Smicrion'; he is actually son of Hipponicus (384a), and Cratylus has been adamant that 'Hermogenes' is not Hermogenes' name 'even if everyone calls him that' (383b, cf. 407e–408b, 429c). Cratylus judiciously qualifies the address as meaningless noise, like banging a bronze pot (perhaps to keep evil spirits away?). He thereby reveals—although not, as yet, to himself—that, as he has understood them perfectly well, these 'failed' names must be doing a pretty good job of naming *something*.

The second attempt (434c–435d) represents what is probably Socrates' most devastating argument. By rights, he says, the word *sklêros* 'hard' should not be used of hard things because it contains a smooth, soft *l* (434d, cf. 427b). Fatefully, Cratylus appeals to 'habit,' *ethos*, as an explanation (434e). Socrates then asks:

> [D]o you mean by a 'habit' anything other than that, whenever I make this utterance, I am thinking of that thing, and that you recognise [*gignôskeis*] that I am thinking of that thing? . . . If this is so, have you not made a contract with yourself [*autos sautôi sunethou*; note the pun]and for you the correctness of the name turns out to be a contract, seeing as both similar and dissimilar letter-sounds alike do indicate, when they have become habitual and conventional? And even if it is not at all the case that a habit is a convention, it would be right to say, not that likeness is an indication [cf. 423b], but rather that habit is. (434e–435b)

By this point Cratylus has, understandably, gone quiet.[5] Socrates says he 'will put your silence down [*thêsô*, from the same family as *sunthêkê*] as consent': it seems sharing our thoughts is possible without words of any kind.

Socrates' apparently regretful surrender to the commonplace ordinariness of custom, convention, and agreement (435c) may be ironic; just as the attraction of the naturalistic theory is 'clinging [*gliskhra*],' so are the blandishments of beauty, even where aesthetic considerations are irrelevant. The argument also suggests that, even if they have the dialectician's authority, the names fashioned by the *nomothetês* will be used, whether for 'dividing things up as they are' or, more humbly, as a means of communicating thoughts, only if they are accepted as names by a community (perhaps that of the gods, cf. 391d).

13.3 WHAT IS A NAME? PLATO'S *CRATYLUS* AND *SOPHIST*

13.3.1 The Problem

Dialectical 'names-in-use' certainly share one property with Hermogenes' 'conventional' names (§13.2. 3): they can take any phonetic shape, whereas Cratylus' natural names are constant across languages (383b). In fact, by the end of the dialogue the debate about the criterion of correctness for names is all but indistinguishable from a debate about what names really are; this problem is never attacked head-on, but it is kept before us from Hermogenes' definition of a name (383a) onward.

Thus the agreement that the *onoma* is the 'smallest part of (a) *logos*' (385c), and the working assumption that *onomata* are such familiar things as 'Socrates' (399e–400bc),

---

[5] Aristotle relates (*Metaphysics* 1010a10–15) that 'in the end, Cratylus thought one should say nothing at all, but would merely move his finger; and he used to reproach Heraclitus for saying that one cannot step into the same river twice: for he himself thought that <one cannot do it> even once.'

'fire' (409d), 'shameful' (416b), and 'false' (421b) are shaken by the later agreement that letter-sounds can be (primary) names (426b, cf. 422a). Socrates' etymologies treat *onomata* (which of course may not correspond to *names* or *words*) as almost infinitely malleable both phonetically and semantically (§13.2.1.3). General grounds have been given for doubting whether imitation of a thing is either sufficient or necessary for another thing's being its name (§13.2.1.4). As for the *nomothetês* theory, this can account, directly at least, for only some kinds of name (and for even fewer kinds of word generally). The theory also says nothing about grammatical functions and relations.

Also disquieting, in a dialogue concerned with names, is the fluidity of its semantic terminology. The now-familiar distinction between extensions and intensions, meanings, or senses (variously defined) is not made explicitly; instead, a name's 'signifying' or 'indicating' (cf. esp. 436e) or being a 'sign' (*sêmeion*) of (425c) a (kind of) thing are implicitly distinguished from its having a 'force' (*dunamis*) (405e, 406a), from indicating the 'thought' (*dianoia*) of its imposer (418c), and from its 'intending' (*boulesthai*) something. But other things have forces too (393e–394b, 404e–405a); a thing, its *ousia* (436e), its nature (396a), or that a *nominatum* is of a certain sort (399c, cf. 395b) may all be signified; and linguistic signifying, whether by words (e.g. 393a) or by people (e.g. 395de) is not marked off from other kinds (cf. 422e)

Similarly, syntactic distinctions and relations are not differentiated terminologically. A number of passages (399b, 421de, 424e–425a, 432e, cf. 396ab, 431b) must be combined to yield a graded sequence of utterances in ascending order of size: letter-sound > syllable > *onoma* > *rhêma* > *logos*. A *rhêma* (from *erô* 'I will speak') may be a verb or a phrase (399b, 421e), and, elsewhere in Plato, a single word (e.g. 'this,' *Timaeus* 49e; cf. *Symposium* 221e, with *onoma*) or, as in other authors (e.g. Pindar *Nemean* 4.6, 94; Aristophanes *Frogs* 821; Thucydices 5.3.3), simply 'something said' (e.g. *Protagoras* 343b). So, although in the *Cratylus logoi* are a 'composite' (*sunthesis*) from *onomata* and *rhêmata* (431c), and each is 'something whole (*holon ti*)' (425a), what makes them so is left unexplained; moreover, a *logos* can nonetheless be part of another *logos* (432de).

Another puzzle concerns what truth and falsity belong to. Hermogenes thinks that all the parts of a true *logos*—viz. its constituent names—are true as well (385bc), as if a true *logos* were a dessert all of whose slices are cake, whereas a false *logos* is at least one slice of something else—pie, maybe. And perhaps *A man is flying* is true iff 'is flying' is true of a thing that 'man' is true of; being true and being true *of* are still not the same thing. Cratylus' first and fall-back position is that names can be true but not false (§13.2.1.4). The same applies to *logoi*:

> SOCRATES: Is saying what is false completely impossible—is that what your theory [*logos*] means? For the people who say this, both now and in the old days, are pretty thick on the ground.
> CRATYLUS: How, Socrates, could someone not say what is, as long as he says what he says? Or isn't saying what is false saying the things that are not?
> SOCRATES: This theory is too clever for an old timer like me. (*Crat.* 429c–e)

We should recall Socrates' earlier warning that the name *logos* 'signifies everything and is constantly circling and on the move, and is double, both true and false at once' (408c).

A very similar argument to Cratylus' is wielded by a sophist in the *Euthydemus* (283e–284a) to help batter a prospective client into submission: one who speaks, speaks or says the thing the *logos* is about, and that thing is a thing that is; but one who says what is, is telling the truth; so how could someone speak, and not say what is and what is true? For example, if *Theaetetus is sitting* (*Sophist* 263a) talks about the sitting Theaetetus, then *Theaetetus is flying* ought to talk about the flying Theatetus—only there is no such thing, and so this (false) *logos* seems to be about nothing at all.

This puzzle takes advantage of two interlocking, unspoken assumptions: that speaking of or saying something is (very like) naming it; and that 'saying the thing that is not' is saying nothing at all. In Plato's earlier dialogues, some differentiation had been achieved in talk about truth, falsity, and saying what is (not). Thus Hermogenes agrees that a true *logos* says/speaks of the things that are *that* or *as* (*hôs*) they are, and *mutatis mutandis* for a false one (*Crat.* 385b), and in the *Theaetetus*, consideration of how it is possible to believe something false leads to an analogous distinction (188d). But the *Sophist* offers the first complete solution of the sophists' puzzle, and Plato's genius shows itself in seeing that the question that must be answered is: *What does a thing have to be like in order to be something that is true or false?*

His other innovation will be to forge a connection between this sort of puzzle and a challenge posed by one of the most august Presocratic philosophers, Parmenides of Elea (236d–237b). Parmenides had identified what seems to be a necessary condition for thought and language: 'What is there for speaking and thinking alike, must be: for it is there for being, but nothing is not <there for being>' (fr. 28 B 6.1–2 DK, cf. fr. 3). What you can think or talk about, must be. Suppose it is not: then what is it you are thinking or talking about? Suppose you think you have succeeded in talking about something that is not: your success shows that that something *is* after all, since 'you could not know . . . or mark in speech [*phrasais*] what is not' (fr. 2.7–8). The link to Parmenides' depth-charge transforms the sophists' superficial display (which nonetheless fosters a false belief in their non-existent wisdom, *Sophist* 239c–241a) into a serious threat to our cheerful everyday assumption that talk and thought represent the world (more or less) faithfully.

13.3.2 The Solution

13.3.2.1 *The 'greatest kinds'*

To solve the problem of falsehood, the *Sophist* offers a complex, many-layered analysis and resolution of a metaphysical conundrum—of how what is not can be—that require clarification of the web of relations amongst the 'greatest kinds' (*megista genê*): being and not being, sameness and difference, and change and stasis (250aff.).

The nature of these abstract, rather colourless kinds, and how they stand to the more familiar aesthetic, ethical, and biological 'forms' (*eidê, ideai*) of the earlier dialogues, remain highly controversial. Perhaps what the *Sophist* offers is a special application of the standard Platonic explanation of how objects get properties—viz. by 'partaking' in forms—to the highest-level metaphysical properties, those which anything, including a kind, must have if it is to be the one thing it is. Hence the 'greatest kinds' themselves variously partake in and 'mingle' with one another, so that (something like) partaking is no longer confined to (what were previously thought of as) particulars.

The first move towards the solution of the falsehood problem is therefore the rehabilitation of not-being as a kind like any other (260b): not absolute not-being (237b–239, 257bc), but the sort of not-being that is simply *being different from* something else (256de, 263b–d). For a thing not to be, is for it to partake in (the kind) 'different from' in relation to another thing.

13.3.2.2 *The First and Smallest Logos*

The second move is to determine the unique way in which this principle applies to *logos*, another kind (260ab). The key is that a *logos* is not formed by stringing together either *onomata* or *rhêmata*, for then 'the vocal sounds [*ta phonêthenta*] indicate neither an action nor an inaction nor the being either of something that is or of something that is not.' Things are different when someone says, for example, *A man learns*:

> ELEATIC VISITOR: For he thereby, I suppose, indicates something about things that are, or are coming about, or have come about, or are going to be, and he does not only name, but completes something, by weaving together [*sumplekôn*] the *ono-mata* with the *rhêmata*. For that reason we say that he is speaking, and not only naming, and furthermore we have given the name '*logos*' to this web [*plegma*]. (262d)

The *onoma* and the *rhêma* are now a 'double kind' (261e) of *onomata* in the old, loose sense, and are distinguished by their different semantic contributions to the 'first and smallest *logos*' (262c), which is itself reconceptualized as a web or a weaving together (*sumplokê*) of the two, as unlike either as a piece of cloth is unlike a skein of wool. These uses of *onoma* and *rhêma* are said to be drawn from ordinary usage (261e–262a), but Theaetetus, the young and inexperienced respondent, is brought to admit he has not actually grasped why the *logos*-complex can boast more than mere 'continuity' (*sune-kheia*) (261e, 262c, cf. a) or why some *onomata* (as yet undifferentiated) are able to fit together (*sunarmottein*) and others not, much like letter-sounds (261d, cf. 253ab, *Cratylus* 424d). A speaker of a *logos*, he learns, 'completes something [*perainei ti*].' Lists of *onomata* or of *rhêmata* can in principle go on to infinity (*eis apeiron*); but when one of each type is put together, a limit (*peras*) is reached, and nothing more can or need be added, for now the thing the *logos* 'belongs to' or 'is of' and is 'about [*peri*]' has not merely been named, but named *as* what is (or is doing or is undergoing) something (*Soph.* 262b–263a). This sequence is already, and thereby, something greater than the sum of its parts: a bearer of truth values (263b).

Here, then, the two theoretical frameworks overlap. A false *logos* is possible because a *rhêma* may be a sign of something (an action, a state) that 'is not'—read: is different from—any and all of the things that 'are with regard to' the thing of which the *onoma* is a sign (263b), but is a perfectly respectable 'thing that is' nonetheless. The new 'web' is even described as if one who says it is thereby combining real things: 'I shall now speak a *logos* for you, putting together an agent with an action by means of an *onoma* and a *rhêma*' (262e). And that is why false *logoi* are able to offer a (false, deceptive) world parallel to the real one: the *kind* of combination is the same in false as in true *logoi*.

The problem of how thinking what is false is possible is also solved:

> ELEATIC VISITOR: So thought [*dianoia*] and *logos* are the same; except that, to the inner dialogue of the soul with itself which takes place without vocal sound, we have given the name 'thought'.
> THEAETETUS: Absolutely.
> ELEATIC VISITOR: While the flow [*rheuma*] which comes from thought [*or:* from the soul], through the mouth, accompanied by noise [*phthongos*], is called *logos*?
> THEAETETUS: True. (263e; cf. 238bc, cf. *Tht.* 189e–190a)

Accordingly both saying (*phasis,* from *phêmi* 'I speak, say') and gainsaying (*apophasis*)—that is, assertion and denial—are also found in the soul, where they constitute belief (*doxa*) (263e–264a; cf. *Tht.* 189e–190a); and sense can now be made of the scandalous idea that a false belief is a belief that what is, is not, or that what is not, is (240d–241b).

13.3.2.3 *New Problems*

While some of the problems raised by the *Sophist* are peculiar to its Platonic context, especially the metaphysics of the 'mingling' of kinds, and how it is a necessary condition of *logos* (259e), the basic dichotomy of *onoma* and *rhêma* was taken over, in some shape or form, by all subsequent philosophers, and then by grammarians. That is why it seems so familiar; yet in reality it represents a remarkable innovation, and when admiring the brilliance and complexity of the edifices, logical and linguistic, that have been built on this foundation, we should not forget what underlies them.

The same applies to the shortcomings of the theory. The distinction between *onomata* and *rhêmata* is purely semantic, so that we can securely identify the constituents of at least some truth-valued *logoi* only if we already know that what we are looking at are, in fact, truth-valued *logoi*. This assumption, as well as the exclusive focus on such *logoi*, may tempt us to infer that not linguistic, but logical items are in question—subjects (arguments) and predicates, not nouns and verbs. Forcing this choice on the text would be anachronistic, however. Determining just when it was first made will be a delicate matter (see §§13.4.2.3, 13.6.8.3), as will assessment of Aristotle's and the Stoa's additions to and modifications of Plato's original (§§13.4.2.3–4, 13.6.8.2, 13.6.11).

The theory of a single *logos* with two faces will be as influential as the theory of the *logos* as a 'web.' If, however, *onomata* and *rhêmata* are defined as 'indicators by means of vocalization' and 'signs in vocalization' (261e, 262de), what shape will the components of internal *logos* take? Aristotle's and the Stoics' versions of the dual *logos* will be adaptions made, in part, precisely to meet this difficulty (13.4.2, 13.6.8.1).[6]

13.4 ARISTOTLE

13.4.1 Sources

A common feature of the work of all the philosophers we are examining is that it does not belong to just one subject area within their philosophy; equally, they may disagree over what counts as a fit topic for a philosopher. Aristotle's division of labour between philosophy and other disciplines is especially clear-cut (cf. §13.6.4). The theory of the *logos* as truth value bearer is set out in the work usually referred to as *On interpretation* [*Int.*] (*Peri hermêneias*; *On linguistic expression* would be less misleading), which expressly allocates to poetics or rhetoric every type of *logos* but the basic truth-valued one, the declarative (*apophantikos*) (*Int.* 17a4–7), also called a 'declaration' (*apophansis*, to be distinguished from *apophasis* 'negation,' as opposed to *kataphasis* 'affirmation,' 17b25–6).

13.4.2 *On Interpretation*

13.4.2.1 *Introduction*

On interpretation eventually came to be part of a sequence of Aristotle's works that was interpreted as expounding (something like) a system of philosophical and formal logic, where that was conceived of as the 'instrument' (*organon*) of philosophy and the special sciences. The theories constructed in the *Prior* and *Posterior Analytics* respectively of the syllogism (a valid deductive argument) and of proof (*apodeixis*) (a syllogism with premisses of a special kind) assume the availability of precise definitions of the relations amongst positive and negative premises or propositions, whether universal, particular, or unspecified, and these are indeed provided by *On interpretation*. But its original purpose was to help construct what might be called 'meta-dialectic': the systematic analysis and classification of the properties and contents of statements deployable for and against any given thesis in a formal or semi-formal debate, in which A opts to defend one or other of a contradictory pair of statements, and B tries to win, by means of a series of questions, A's assent to the other contradictory. The *Topics* collects and classifies the materials disputants might use, while *On interpretation* defines the various truth value bearers that they might assert or deny.

---

[6] Denyer (1991) gives a valuable overview of Greek philosophical discussion of language, truth and falsehood down to Aristotle. There is a large literature on the *Sophist*, to which Frede (1992) and Lesley Brown (2008) is a useful introduction.

The repurposing of this work (whether or not it was sanctioned by Aristotle) was made possible, in part, by the restrictions it imposes on its objects. Declaratives, as defined here, are those appropriate to a system of logic, the ultimate goal of which is to lay bare the characteristic structure of (scientific) knowledge, conceived of as the understanding of the necessary causes of a given range of phenomena. It takes the form of a system of demonstrations making appropriate use of essential predications, of the sort stated in definitions, which themselves optimally take genus+*differentia* form. Far less is said in the *Analytics* about inductive arguments (*epagôgai*), which 'move from the particular to the universal' (*Topics* 1.12, 105a13), but they, too, must arrive at the sort of general statements that help lay the foundations of the individual sciences, in the shape of principles that do not require demonstration and are the objects of another kind of knowledge, *nous* (*Posterior Analytics* 1.23, 2.19).

Identifying these principles will be the work of dialectic in its characteristically Aristotelian guise, as the discipline that marshals, analyses, criticizes, and, as far as possible, reconciles reliable relevant generalizations drawn from sense experience and from the 'reputable opinions' (*endoxa*) of experts and ordinary people on the topic in question. How this sort of dialectic is related to that which evolved in the Academy where Aristotle studied is controversial; but having a system for finding and organizing evidence for and against any given statement would be an advantage in any philosophical enterprise, and *On interpretation* contributes to this system by showing which features of a *logos* of a certain form are relevant to its truth value and to its logical relations with other statements.

The constituents of this sort of *logos* are treated in the first four chapters of the work. They set out what would (when combined with other material, above all from the *Categories*) become one of the most influential theories of meaning in the history of philosophy—which is ironic, since *On interpretation* is not, primarily, a contribution to semantics.

13.4.2.2 *Debts to Plato*[7]

Although Aristotle does not explicitly endorse the theory of internal and external *logos* (§13.3.3), he does assume that key structures are shared by (significant) vocalization and thought: in both, falsehood and truth exist in association with (*peri*) the processes or states that are combinations (*suntheseis*) and divisions (*diaireseis*) (*Int.* 16a12–14), and appear to consist in, respectively, affirming and denying a predicate of a subject (cf. 17a23–6). Hence making a judgement will be the silent, inner counterpart of a public assertion or denial, and public truth value bearers will have internal correlates the constituents of which are individual psychological states (lit. 'the *pathêmata* in the

---

[7] The indefinite (*aorista*) *onomata* and *rhêmata* (e.g. 'not-man,' 'not-walks,' 16a29–32, b11–15) may be descendants of the inactions (*apraxiai*) and 'not-beings' that are possible significations in the *Sophist* (262c), and/or of not-being considered as a kind of composite of whatever is 'different from' something else (cf. esp. 257cd, with §13.3.2.1 above). These terms play a role in fixing the logical relations of declaratives, but they do not substantially change Aristotle's componential analysis thereof.

soul') or thoughts (*noêmata*). It is of thoughts that vocalizations are primarily symbols or signs (16a3–16).

Thoughts, then, must be individuated and accessible by reflection independently of (public) language—an assumption, commonplace in classical philosophy, that seems hazardous today, just as it seems rash even to assume that it is clear what would count as evidence that thoughts are conjoined or disjoined independently of *logoi*. The direction of fit of the comparison of nouns and verbs to individual thoughts (16a13–14) implies that the latter ought to be informative about the former; but we hear no more about them here, Aristotle directing us instead to his *On the soul* for more information (8–9); psychological experience is, however, admissible as evidence relating to semantic properties (16b20–21, 24–5). The relation of predication appears to unify the declarative *logos* as it does Plato's 'first and smallest *logos*' (§13.3.2.2), and Aristotle shares with the *Sophist* the further assumption—hardly an uncontroversial one—that it is possible to determine, independently of its components, whether a thing has a truth value; for he argues that oblique forms (cases) of *onomata* are merely forms 'fallen' or derived from them on the grounds that, when combined with *is* or *was*, 'they do not say something true or something false' (16b1–5). Conversely, it is assumed to be clear which *logoi* are *not* truth-valued (17a4–7; see §13.4.2.3 below).

The assumption is also made that speech is for conveying our thoughts to one another (cf. *Crat.* 434e–435a). One puzzle will then be how vocal sounds signify things as well as thoughts about things; and the scholarly consensus is that a solution to this puzzle is contained in Aristotle's implicit distinction of semantic levels. A 'primary' signification will be the equivalent of (some variety of) a sense or intension, viz. the conceptual content that fixes an extension, which is in turn roughly equivalent to a 'secondary' signification.

13.4.2.3 *Constituents of the Declarative* Logos

Aristotle's accounts of the *onoma* and the *rhêma* differ in virtue of two semantic properties allocated exclusively to *rhêmata*.

First, the *rhêma* is 'a sign of things said of something else' (16b7) or 'of things that hold [*ta huparkhonta*], viz. of things <that hold> of [*kata*] a subject [*hupokeimenon*]' (9–10, cf. 17a23–4). This is broader than the *Sophist*'s definition, but suggestive of greater precision, and it is standardly filled in by reference to the metaphysical-cum-linguistic scheme of the *Categories*[8] (although it is merely implied that subjects are what *onomata* signify), the relation of predication being primitive in the theory of the declarative *logos*.[9] It is also, presumably, because of the metaphysical primacy of substances that Aristotle (like the Stoa: §13.6.5) defines *onomata* first, while the *Sophist*,

---

[8] Aristotle talks about categories in many ways: as modes of dividing being(s) or in which 'being is said'; as 'relations of the predication' (*skheseis tês katêgorias*) to a subject; sometimes (esp. in the *Topics*) as if they were predicate *expressions*. Debate about the subject-matter of the *Categories* continued for centuries (cf. §13.6.4).

[9] Something analogous holds of its Stoic correlate: §§13.6.8.1, 13.6.10.

beginning with intuitive groupings of actions and agents, had begun with *rhêmata* (§13.3.2.2).

Second, while an *onoma* is 'without time,' a *rhêma* 'in addition signifies [*prossêmainei*] time' (16b6–7). In case we are wondering, *In addition to what?*, Aristotle adds that a *rhêma* in itself must be an *onoma*—that is, a name (19–20) or a word (cf. a29)—since 'it signifies something,' which is in turn supported by psychological evidence (b20–1; cf. §13.4.2.2). 'Health' (*hugieia*) for instance, is an *onoma*, but 'is healthy' (*hugiainei*) is a *rhêma*, 'since it signifies in addition that it [*sc.* health, not the name 'health'] belongs' (b8–9) to someone or something.

Aristotle's 'defining' the two components is perhaps better understood as his making certain features of them salient against a background assumed to be already familiar. Shorn of its single illustration, to someone unacquainted with the *Sophist* and/or Aristotle's lectures, the definition of the *rhêma* (16b8–9) might be taken to imply that *a man at three o'clock*, for instance, is a *rhêma*, as it signifies time in addition. Infinitives are accommodated, but as *onomata* (e.g. 'To take a walk after dinner is beneficial,' *Posterior Analytics* 94b); participles find a home as *rhêmata*, that is when coupled, as *onomata* may be, with (present-tense indicative forms of) *einai* 'to be.'

This way of marking a predication is possible because *einai*, which 'is itself nothing, signifies in addition a kind of combination' (16b23–5), viz. of the two things signified by the *onoma* and by (the naming part or aspect of) the predicate, which is always a general term. The explicit opening up of the category of *rhêmata*, for which the *Sophist* had made room only implicitly (262d) will be crucial for the development of Aristotle's logic, in particular for the emergence of the familiar three-term syllogism;[10] indeed, in the *Analytics* components of *logoi* will be 'terms' (*horoi*) regardless of their role in any given premiss. Coupled with the stipulation that all forms but the nominative are 'cases' (cf. §13.4.2.2), just as all forms but the present indicative are 'cases' of a *rhêma* (16b9, 16–18), and with the absence of a distinction between *onomata* of individuals and of kinds, this expansion confirms that the task here is to determine the constituents, not of sentences generally, but of the truth value bearers that may be used as premisses in arguments of a certain kind (§13.4.2.1). The same task is what ultimately explains the unity of the declarative *logos*—not as a mere spatial or temporal sequence (17a14), but as the vehicle of predication, 'signifying one thing of one thing' (18a13–14, cf. 17a17–27) is not a mere temporal or spatial sequence (17a14)

While Aristotle's conception of his subject-matter makes irrelevant indexical words and features of words, and *logoi* that are unities in virtue of a conjunction (17a8–9, 15–16), they will be of intense interest to the Stoa (§13.6.10 below), along with propositions about past and future events, to which the *Sophist* had briefly alluded (262d) (§§13.6.6.3, 13.6.8–10). Aristotle's focus on universal propositions, the truth values of which are unchanging, may have shielded him from the problems thrown up by making truth value bearers linguistic items (*Int.* 17a23), whether tokens or types. Tomorrow's sea

---

10 See §34.2 below for more on Aristotle's syllogistic.

battle is of interest only because it threatens a possible exception to the general principle that one or other (but not both) of a contradictory pair of propositions must be true (18a24–19b4).

13.4.2.4 *Semantics*

A *rhêma*, as noted, 'signifies' in conveying information of two kinds: in addition to signifying something (the lexical content of the verb) in much the way an *onoma* does, it signifies that this thing belongs to the subject now. Hence what might be regarded as a syntactic function is conceived of as a semantic property—and as a bonus on top of, not as different in kind from, the other, *onoma*-like signifying that *rhêmata* also perform. In similar fashion, the quantifier *pas, pan* 'every' 'signifies, not the universal, but that <the predication is being made> universally' (17b12), so that in *Every man is mortal*, for example, 'every' carries the information, about being mortal, that it belongs to all men.

Aristotelian signifying, therefore, seems to amount to conveying, by means of conventionally fixed articulate vocalizations, more or less *any* kind of information about subjects and predicates, and Aristotle's vocabulary is notably free of semantic distinctions; even the difference between 'primary' and 'secondary' significations is nowhere explained (§13.4.2.2). The 'vocalisations' introduced at the start (16a3) as 'symbols' (4) and 'signs' (6) of things are almost immediately, and without further justification, whittled down to just two. *Onomata* signify, only we are not told what (§ 13.4.2.3), as do *rhêmata*, although on its own a *rhêma* 'does not yet signify if it is or is not' (16b21–2). A declarative *logos* is 'significant, about whether something belongs or not' (16b26, 34–17a1, 23–4). The parts of a *logos* signify as a saying of something and not as an affirmation or a negation (16b27–30; cf. §13.4.2.5). Each member of a contradictory pair 'signifies one thing of one thing' (18a13–14). A declaration, is one 'by indicating one thing' (17a16)—yet animal noises also 'indicate something' (16a28).

13.4.2.5 *Against the* Cratylus

Private psychological states are not useful things to which to assign truth values as part of meta-dialectic or philosophical logic, and we may wonder why Aristotle brings them in here. One plausible answer is: to criticize the *Cratylus*. This attitude would prove something of a stumbling-block for later commentators who wished to reconcile what they took to be the Platonic and the Aristotelian theories of the correctness of names.

For Aristotle it is mental states (or their objects), not vocalizations, that are (natural) 'likenesses' of things in the world (*Int.* 16a7) and are the same for all (6). Further, they must, like vocalizations, be put together in the right way if they are to have a truth value (12), for *onomata* and *rhêmata* do not in themselves amount to asserting or denying something (17a17–20), and the componential analysis of a *logos* need not be continued beyond this level: at any rate, this is where the dialectician's interest ends.

Thus it needs to be specified, not what kind of thing an *onoma* signifies, but that it— like the *rhêma* (16b6–7)—signifies *as a whole* (a18–20). Aristotle stipulates elsewhere (*Poet.* 1456b–1457a) that a letter-sound is something 'non-signifying' (*asêmos*), as is a syllable, the other parts of *lexis* all being put together out of these; but here his point is a different one. That the parts of the name *Beaulieu*, taken separately, signify 'fair' and 'place' in French, for example, may tell us why someone chose this name, but they cannot tell us what it is the name of, let alone what that thing is like. Perhaps Beaulieu is a hovel next to a rubbish tip: Beaulieu is its name nonetheless, if that is what the relevant community calls it, just as *Hermogenes* really is Hermogenes' name, despite his poor way with money or with words (§13.2.1.4).

Lest the anti-*Cratylus* message escape us, Aristotle now spells it out. The proviso 'by convention' is there 'because nothing is a name by nature, but when it becomes a symbol' (16a26–9). Symbols (28), strictly, are the halves of a token object taken away as proofs by each of the parties to a contract (cf. Plato, *Symposium* 191d); likewise, names are signs only because of (tacit) agreements to use them as such. Similarly, *logoi* cannot be 'instruments' (*Int.* 17a1–2)—as Plato's Socrates had called names (13.2.1.3)—presumably because tools are things deliberately invented for doing (or doing better) a job already identified, while *onomata* and *rhêmata* were not (with obvious exceptions) devised expressly to function as signs for this or that thing, like more efficient substitutes for the sign language Socrates imagines we might use were we mute (*Crat.* 423a; see §13.2.1.3). And yet it is not Hermogenes' version of conventionalism that Aristotle endorses. Hermogenes hoped he had identified *what makes names correct*: Aristotle is putting us right about *what makes names, names*, in effect short-circuiting the whole debate.The *Cratylus* is most decidedly shelved, as irrelevant to the actual workings of language.[11]

13.5 THE DEBATE ABOUT NAMES CONTINUED

13.5.1 The Afterlife of the *Cratylus*

One might reasonably expect, given the number, variety, and seriousness of the methodological objections to it that are raised in the *Cratylus* itself, and are so salient for the modern reader, that etymology would have been taken off the philosophical menu for good, even if philologists, literary critics, antiquarians, and historians might find some nourishment in it—as, indeed, they did (§13.7.3). Aristotle's criticisms of naturalism as an account of how language functions are curt but immensely effective. Nonetheless, Socrates' methods, and some of his actual explanations, came to be widely

---

[11] For Aristotle's views on *logos*, truth, and falsehood, see Nuchelmans (1973), Denyer (1991). Crivelli (2004, 2010) address Aristotle's views on the truth of sentences. Barnes (2007: 93–267) gives a lively discussion of predicates and subjects in ancient grammar and logic, including Aristotle and his later commentators. The best overall discussion of *De interpretatione* is Whitaker (1996). Charles (1994, 2000) are helpful on Aristotle's theory of names and meaning. For Aristotle's contribution to linguistics see Allan (2004).

accepted by many philosophers, especially within the later Platonic tradition, which recovered from the dialogue a single coherent theory, attributable to Plato himself (and not contradicted by Aristotle after all), that combines elements of *phusis* and *thesis* (the latter now identified with *nomos* and even *sunthêkê*) and explains the historical origins of names by reference to their natural appropriateness to their *nominata*. Proclus can even record the philosophers' dissatisfaction with the mess grammarians had made of etymology by reversing Plato's privileging of a name's phonetic matter over its form (*in Crat.* 90.1–6).

But the rehabilitation of etymology as a philosophical method had begun much earlier, in the Stoa, which also offered a replacement for the *Cratylus*' mimetic 'primary names' theory (§13.7.1). What is more, naturalism was given a complete overhaul by Epicurus, in the context of a continuing controversy over the origins of human civilization in general.

13.5.2 Epicurus: a New Form of Naturalism

The Epicurean explanation is that names first emerged from the vocal sounds uttered instinctively by primitive peoples in response to their different experiences of different (types of) things; at a later stage, communities made received names more efficient, and added others for new discoveries (LS 19A, B1–2, 6–7). Names can therefore have philosophical value, insofar as they mark objective distinctions amongst things and properties (19E)—the plain man's equivalents to Socrates' 'tools for dividing up being,' perhaps (§13.2.1.3). The theory's persuasiveness was enhanced by some very tart mockery of its impositional rival (e.g. 19B3–5, C).

What is perhaps most distinctive about this version of naturalism is its accommodation of the existence of different languages. Standardly this was a stumbling-block for naturalists (cf. S.E. *M* 1.145; Stephanus *in Int.* 9.34–5), and it continued to be argued, for example, that nominals having their genders 'by nature' (e.g. Varro *LL* 8.7–8; S.E. *M* 1.142–3) is incompatible with the same nominals in different Greek dialects having different genders (148–9). Criticism continued in Hellenistic and Imperial times, in particular from Pyrrhonist sceptics (apparently to very little effect[12]), but it is a pithy phrase of Aristotle's (*Nicomachean Ethics* 1134b26), repeated by Sextus (*M* 1.147), that sums up its core rationale best: 'fire burns both here and in Persia'—that is, what is natural is the same everywhere. Epicurus' response is that linguistic variety shows, not that names are not natural, but that the natures of human beings, and hence their experiences and vocalizations, vary as their environments do.

---

[12] Remarkably similar claims about gender (in e.g. [Theodosius] *Gram.* 131.27ff.) are still being criticized by Choeroboscus in the early 9th century CE (*Proleg.* 107.8–15). In the late 5th century CE, the Neoplatonist Ammonius (*in Int.* 35.21ff.) thinks 'not nature, but a rational soul's thoughtfulness [*epinoia*]' devised them.

13.5.3 Extreme Conventionalism: Diodorus Cronus

This naturalist stance marks a significant departure from that of Epicurus' venerable predecessor Democritus. His arguments that names are 'by chance' or 'by imposition' (§13.2.1) are supplemented by two more considerations in a late report that may stem from an Epicurean source (Ammonius *in Int.* 37.28–38.22); but the philosopher named in association with them is not Democritus but Diodorus Cronus, a member of one of the small and diverse 'Socratic' schools that flourished briefly in the late fourth and early third century BCE (DL 2.111–12).

The one concrete example that Plato's Hermogenes had offered of his conventionalism was that of changing slaves' names by *fiat* (*Crat.* 384d), as was customary when a new slave entered a household. Diodorus went one stage further: 'He gave his own slaves the names of conjunctions [which here include particles], calling them 'On the one hand' [*men*] and 'On the other hand' [*de*]' (Stephanus *in Int.* 9.22–4); another was named *alla mên* 'However,' in order 'to mock grammatical distinctions and those who claim names are natural' (Simplicius *in Cat.* 27.15–24, Ammonius *in Int.* 38.17–20).[13] To describe Diodorus' targets as 'grammatical' is anachronistic, but not very misleading; for while in his day such distinctions belonged more to philosophers—as with Chrysippus' distinction between proper and common nouns (§13.6.5)—later on they became the pride and joy of technical grammar (as well).

Diodorus' message is, of course, that these names 'take' despite a lack of descriptive or iconic appropriateness of any kind—although in another way they are not at all haphazard, having been carefully selected from what moderns would call a 'closed' word-class (and Varro a 'sterile' one, i.e. not giving rise to derived forms, *LL* 8.9–10). Diodorus and his slave will form a minimal linguistic community, like Hermogenes' household, perhaps (*Crat.* 385a)—although the slave has very little choice about taking part in it.[14]

13.6 STOICISM

13.6.1 Influence

The influence of the Stoa on technical grammar is hard to overestimate: it is also all too easy to misunderstand or misrepresent, not least because technical grammar tended to

---

[13] Another poor fellow may have been called *Autou*, i.e. either 'His' or 'There,' or even *Hautou* 'His own,' which is dizzyingly self-reflexive (fr. 115; text uncertain). A debate seems to have begun in the 4th century BCE as to whether genitives are ambiguous (cf. Aristotle, *Sophistical Refutations* 24, 179b–180a).

[14] There is an overview of Hellenistic philosophy of language in Schenkeveld and Barnes (1999). On the Epicureans, see Brunschwig (1994) and Atherton (2005, 2009). For Diodorus Cronus, see Sedley (1977) and Atherton (1993).

ignore the original theoretical contexts of the doctrines it borrowed or adapted. Stoic *logos* is an immanent divine, cosmic principle that gives the world and everything in it life, organization, and direction, and shows its special concern for us, as 'rational' (*logikoi*) animals, even in the details of the *logos* that is dialectic's particular object of study. Hence Stoic dialecticians enthusiastically and fruitfully embraced topics dismissed as trivial or extraneous by rival philosophers, but highly valued by the creators of technical grammar.[15]

It would hardly be original to claim that (Stoic) philosophy is the source of grammar's best offerings: already in the first century CE, Philo Judaeus was claiming that it gave *all* the specialized expertises their 'starting-points and seeds.' Reading and writing are taught by the less complete kind of grammar, *grammatistikê*; the more complete kind explains literary texts; and that is as far as either of them can go unaided.

> [W]hen [grammarians] give an account of the parts of speech, are they are not dragging off and turning to their own use the discoveries of philosophy? For it is [philosophy's] peculiar task to scrutinise what a conjunction is, what a noun, what a verb, what a common noun, what an individual noun; what is deficient in discourse, what full; what is assertable, what a question is, what an inquiry, . . . what a prayer is, what an oath: for <philosophy> is what puts together treatments of self-complete items and of propositions and of predicates. And as for seeing what a semivocalic element is, or a vocalic, or a completely non-vocalic one, and how each of these is called customarily, and the whole division concerned with vocal sounds and elements and the parts of speech—has this not been worked out and brought to completion by philosophy? But diverting tiny trickles from a torrent, so to say, and eking them out with their own still tinier souls, the thieves do not blush to proclaim what they have stolen their own. (Philo Judaeus 1898: 46–50)

Seneca (first century CE), in contrast, whose moral philosophy is heavily influenced by the Stoa, is nonetheless dissatisfied with *soi-disant* philosophers who 'descend to the grammarians' elements' (*Epistle* 108.11) and 'to the differences amongst syllables, and the properties of conjunctions and prepositions' (138.42). Philo, Seneca would say, has got it backwards: 'whatever is superfluous in the expertises' of grammar and geometry, philosophers 'have transferred to their own.' Similarly, the Platonist Ammonius (late fifth century CE) thinks that it is the grammarians, not philosophers, who 'busy themselves with metres and the formations [*skhêmatismoi*] of the primary words and their co-formations and side-formations and inflections and such like' (*in Int.* 65.7–9). Urbanely tolerant as ever, Dionysius of Halicarnassus finds the study of the speech-sounds 'more appropriate to grammar and metrics, and, if one likes, even to philosophy' (*Comp.* 30–3.).

---

[15] For the fragments of the Stoic philosophers we have referred to Long and Sedley (1987) (=LS); more extensive collections of fragments are: *Stoicorum Veterum Fragmenta*, ed. Hans von Arnim, i–iii, Leipzig: B. G. Teubner 1903 (iv, indices, by M. Adler 1924); *Die Fragmente zur Dialektik der Stoiker*, ed. Karlheinz Hülser, 4 vols, Stuttgart–Bad Canstatt: Frommann–Holzboog, 1987–8. The late antique or Byzantine commentaries on the *Tekhnê* are edited in Uhlig (1901).

13.6.2 Sources

The ideas and arguments of Plato and Aristotle have been analysed and evaluated on the basis of their own words: for the Stoa, in contrast, this is a rare luxury. Source material for much of Hellenistic philosophy is indirect, either hostile or uncomprehending, and often in the form of simplified summaries; and for the crucial early years, Stoic and grammatical texts alike survive, if at all, only in fragments, isolated quotations, or précis. Some Stoic doctrines are known to us thanks only to their critics—who may have failed to realize the enormous debts they owed to the Stoa—and many cannot be assigned to a particular philosopher, or even a particular stage in the school's history. But evidence of disagreements does survive, as we have just seen: between philosophers of different schools over what their territory should be; between grammarians and philosophers over shared territory; between grammarians; and even within the Stoa itself. Sometimes, though, philosophers are co-opted into almost whiggish accounts of the development of grammatical doctrines, as in Dionysius of Halicarnassus' neat little tale (*Comp.* 2) about how the parts of speech came to number eight (or nine).

13.6.3 Dialectic

Dialectic, the home of most of Stoic theorizing about language, was standardly one-half of logic, viz. the branch of philosophical discourse specifically concerned with *logos*. Fortunately, one ancient source (DL 7.48–83, cf. 43–8)[16] preserves a fairly comprehensive (if hardly impeccable) outline account of dialectic.

Dialectic's responsibility is identifying and classifying all the properties of rational discourse apart from those peculiar to public oratory, the province of the other half of 'logic,' rhetoric. Dialectic was defined as a practice, question-and-answer discourse, by reference to its Socratic origins, but also as, in ideal form, a branch of scientific knowledge that permits the confident distinction of truths from falsehoods, by guiding the application of the criterion of truth, the management of the constituents of *logos*, through conceptual analysis, and through the conduct of argument.

This last item was standardly assigned to the half of dialectic that embraced (what we would call) philosophical and formal logic, and that is concerned with things signified (*sêmainomena*), which include propositions (*axiômata*) and arguments. The others belonged to the half concerned with vocal sound or with signifiers (*sêmainonta*). This

---

[16] An informative collection of texts about Stoic dialectic (including selections from the account on DL) can be found in translation in Long and Sedley [LS] (1987), vol. I (esp. §§31–42) and in the original languages in LS vol. II, both with commentary; vol. I also has a list of sources and an *index locorum*, vol. II a bibliography. A text found in LS will be referred to by the LS system (*e.g.* '31A5' is group 31, text A, section 5; a lower-case letter indicates that a text is in vol. II only). Our translations of key terms may, however, be different from those in LS.

opens with two cardinal theories. One enumerates and classifies the elements of *lexis* (articulate vocal sound), viz. the sounds conventionally corresponding to the letters of the contemporary Greek alphabet. The other enumerates and classifies the 'parts of speech' in the traditional, unsatisfactory translation; for these are really the parts or elements of *logos*, i.e. significant *lexis*. There followed a classification of the 'excellences' (*aretai*, sing. *aretê*) of *logos*, of which 'pure Greek' (*Hellenismos*) is the first and apparently the most important—at any rate, the only two defects listed, barbarism and solecism, are offences against it, even though there are four more excellences: clarity (*saphêneia*), conciseness (*suntomia*), appropriateness (*prepon*), and ornament (*kataskeuê*).

Crucially, the definition of Hellenism, 'speech [*phasis*] faultless in the usage [*sunêtheia*] that is expert, not random,' obviously assumes that correctness can be captured by an expertise of some sort. No discrete portion of dialectic is marked out as such, and dialectic (in its ideal form at least) is a systematic body of knowledge that can be dismembered, but not bloodlessly compartmentalized. Moreover, some key doctrines relating to language are located in the *significata* half of dialectic, including the theory of syntax that underpins the definition of a solecism as 'a *logos* incongruously composed' (§ 13.6.10). Yet Chrysippus' most assiduous pupil, Diogenes of Babylon, wrote a (now lost) *Tekhnê* concerning vocal sound (*peri phônês*, Latin: *de voce*) and the two 'elements' theories do seem to represent Stoicism's most important legacies, in terms of organizational structures and key concepts and categories, to technical grammar.

An example can now be given of the historical realities of transmission and influence, which were far less straightforward than Philo allows (§13.6.2). After the excellences of *logos*, Stoic 'signifiers' dialectic proceeded to definitions of verse and poetry and of ambiguity (typically an offence against clarity, although not so described here). In between came accounts of two sorts of *logoi* so important they were sometimes assigned their own subject area inside 'logic': definitions and conceptual divisions (LS 32). The remarkable thing is that these *logoi* survive in some later Roman grammars (e.g. Charisius *Ars* 90.20–193.2 Barwick)—useless, unintegrated vestiges of their former selves.

13.6.4 Parts of *Logos*, Parts of *Lexis*

The Peripatetic Theophrastus (fourth century–early third century CE), we are told, anticipated the Stoic 'excellences' doctrine, with the exception of conciseness (considered a Stoic speciality). Modern scholarship has also credited him with the first formulation of the theory of the three types of style (lofty, plain, intermediate). Moreover, in keeping with his literary critical interests (cf. Cicero, *Orator* 39), Theophrastus is reported to have initiated the study of *lexeis qua lexis*, which asks:

> whether the noun and the verb are elements of rational discourse, or articles and conjunctions and suchlike are as well (even these are parts of linguistic expression, but <the parts> of discourse are noun and verb); and what is strict expression, and

what metaphorical; and what corruptions [*pathê*] it undergoes...which expressions are simple, which compound, which subcompound, and so on and so forth; and what is said on the subject of styles, what clarity in linguistic expressions is, what magnificence, what the pleasant and plausible. (Simplicius *in Cat.* 10.24–11.1)

This sequence should, as a whole, sound familiar. But it comes from a sixth-century CE commentary on Aristotle's *Categories* that had been shaped by centuries-long debates and exchanges between philosophers and grammarians; and it may rather be a sample of a tendency in the Aristotelian commentators to 'discover' Stoic innovations in Platonic and/or early Peripatetic texts.

Theophrastus, moreover, also distinguished two relations (*skheseis*) in which *logos* stands: to things in the world, the province primarily of the philosopher; and to an audience, where rhetoric and poetry are dominant (Ammonius *in Int.* 65.31–66.10). It is here, probably, that the topics in Simplicius' list belong; at any rate, the source is Theophrastus' (now lost) *On the elements of rational discourse*. Theophrastus did write books on *lexis*, but this may well be 'diction' or 'vocabulary' (cf. DH *Comp.* 16.90–93), not 'linguistic expression'—which is, however, what Simplicius means when he distinguishes it from *logos*.

This *logos* does not have, say, conjunctions as parts, for they 'are found in linguistic expression, but fall outside the scope of the predications [*katêgoriai*]; for they do not indicate any of the things that are, neither a substance nor a quality nor any other suchlike thing' (Simplicius *in Cat.* 11.27–9, citing Boëthus). That is, to signify is to signify some one thing, a subject or a predicate, or concepts of these things (§13.4.2.4). Other words rather indicate something about the ways in which predicates belong to subjects, or in which we think or feel about the matter; or else they contribute to non-declarative *logoi* (Ammonius in *Int.* 11.8–12.15; cf. §§13.4.1, 13.6.8.3).

This *logos/lexis* distinction was supposed to have Platonic and Aristotelian authority, and, in essence if not in name, it is known already to Plutarch (*c.*45–120 CE), who thinks other words than *onomata* and *rhêmata* simply make what we say more expressive (*QP* 1009E), and who compares conjunctions to textual and prosodic signs, as failing to signify linguistically (*lektikôs*) (1010D)—a parallel repeated by Simplicius, five centuries later (*in Cat.* 64.20–21, 26–9). Yet it undoubtedly owes something to the Stoic concepts of *lexis* and of *logos*, according to which signifying is making any sort of contribution to the signification of a *logos* (§13.6.11). In any event, the rendering of *ta merê tou logou* as 'the parts of speech,' especially in a Stoic context, is highly misleading. 'Parts of the sentence' is theoretically loaded, for the Stoa, in the wrong direction (§13.6.2). Again, 'element' was preferred to 'part' both by the founder of the Stoa, Zeno of Citium, for whom 'the philosopher's concerns are to know the elements of *logos*, what each of them is and how they are joined to each other, and their consequences [*or* 'concomitants,' *akoloutha*]' (31J), and also by Chrysippus (DL 7.193), who drew a parallel between speech elements, the four cosmic elements, and the elements of *logos*, in that they 'bring to perfection [*apartizei*]' syllables, bodies, and *logoi* respectively (SchDThr 356.1–4; see §13.8.3).

Not surprisingly, the Peripatetic/Neoplatonic *logos/lexis* distinction was rejected out of hand by technical grammarians (SchDThr 515.19–517.32)—who, however, criticised the Stoic theory too (517.33–521.5). Dionysius is therefore being his usual suave self when he manifests indifference as to whether one speaks of the parts or 'particles' (*moria*) or elements of *logos* or of *lexis* (*Comp.* 2.1–3, 17–18, 12.1). All four sides are, in a way, talking past one another. Dionysius had advice to give to budding orators on choosing and combining words. Technical grammarians classified the word forms encountered (primarily) in literary texts. Aristotle identified the components and structure of a certain kind of premiss (§13.4.2.3). Stoic interests were also typically dictated by wider philosophical concerns carrying no weight with grammarians, but they certainly looked beyond (the significations of) simple truth-valued sentences.

What is more, superficial Peripatetic and Stoic consensus on the status of *onomata* (e.g. Plutarch *QP* 1009C), perhaps as bona fide 'parts of speech,' masks sharp deeper disagreements. For the Stoics, there is not one part in question but two, the proper name (*onoma*) and the appellative (*prosêgoria*), neither of which, however, is explicitly defined as inflecting for case, although a third part is: the 'article' (§13.6.6). Moreover, while any one of these three may be found together with a *rhêma* (§13.6.7), in the truth-valued items that are the Stoic equivalents of Platonic and Aristotelian (declarative) *logoi*, we find instead 'cases' (e.g. 'this (male) (one),' *houtos*) and particles (e.g. 'someone,' *tis*) (§13.6.9). Truth value bearers belong to the 'significations' part of dialectic, specifically the theory of *lekta*—literally 'sayables' or 'things said,' from the same family as *logos, legein, lexis*—that lies at the heart of the Stoic understanding of rational thought and discourse (§13.6.8) and binds together all the apparently disparate topics embraced by Stoic dialectic. This web of connections shows how any Stoic thesis about language can be properly understood only within its philosophical framework.

13.6.5 Proper Names and Appellatives

A key metaphysical distinction in the Stoic system was that between individual and common qualities or qualified things. Socrates, for example, is an individual quality (*idia poiotês*) or an individually qualified thing (*idiôs poion*), viz. a unique bundle of common or shared (*koinai*) qualities, e.g. wisdom, humanness (LS 33M). Each such common quality is itself a unique body, being 'common' only insofar as it shares a character with similar qualities in other individual *qualia*. More transient properties also reduce to an individual qualified (in a more or less strict sense) thus-and-so (28N; cf. Simplicius *in Cat.* 66.32–67.8). Only bodies, strictly, speaking, can be said to be (real) (*einai*), since they alone can be causes or patients of actions (33H, 45B, 55B; see §13.6.8.1).

Features of contemporary inflectional and derivational morphology were adduced by the Stoics as evidence that the distinction between individual and shared qualities had been incorporated by our distant ancestors—if only unconsciously—into the names they were constructing (SchDThr 214.17–215.17; cf. §13.7.1). Features of the same kind were marshalled *against* the Stoic claim by Tryphon (356.21–357.18), and, perhaps as a result, more likely because the Stoic philosophical rationale buttered no parsnips for them, most grammarians (there were exceptions: 356.16–21) rejected it in favour of a genus *onoma* with two species distinguished semantically, the individual or 'proper' and the common or 'appellative' (e.g. 552.5–6; cf. 357.18–26).

13.6.6 Articles

13.6.6.1 *Introduction*

Conversely, the grammarians' pronoun and definite (*hôrismenon*) article correspond to the two species—definite and indefinite—of the Stoic article (ApD *pron.* 6.30–7.6, *adv.* 121.7–122.12, *synt.* 1.111, 94.11–13; SchDThr 518.33–519.25; Priscian *Inst.* 2, 54.12–16; 11, 548.7–14).[17] An *arthron* is usually a joint or point of articulation, but can also be a limb, as the Stoics pointed out in support of their subdivision (ApD *pron.* 5.15–18). Both Apollodorus of Athens, a pupil of Diogenes of Babylon, and Dionysius Thrax adapted it, calling pronouns 'deictic articles' (18–19); once again, however, these were exceptions.

13.6.6.2 *Indefinite Articles*

The Stoic nomenclature is plainly derived from the use of these articles in 'indefinite' constructions to yield generalizations (situationally indefinite sentences may perhaps be in view as well) that are equivalent to indefinite conditionals—e.g. 'The walking person moves (*ho peripatôn kineitai*)' to 'If someone (*tis*) walks, he moves,' as Apollonius points out in his criticism of the Stoic position (*adv.* 122.9–12, cf. *synt.* 4.6, 437.10–438.10, *pron.* 7.4–6). In effect this takes the form of a *reductio ad absurdum*: since what the Stoics call 'indefinite articles' really belong, like *someone*, in their category 'indefinite particles' (cf. §13.6.9), their theory leads to the bizarre conclusion that there are no such things as indefinite articles after all. This is probably why Apollonius concludes that the Stoics 'made use only of the name [*sc.* article], not of the thing itself as well' (9.1–2); he also plausibly suggests that the Stoics wanted simply to distinguish articles from pronouns, 'which are always definite' (*pron.* 7.5–6). Whether Apollonius knew it or not, the equivalence thesis he uses is Chrysippean (30I; see §13.7.1). A Stoic definition of the participle as a 'reflexive appellative,' apparently on the basis of its intersubstitutability with appellatives proper (Priscian *Inst.* 11, 548.14ff.; Plut. *QP* 1011CD), may have played a role here too.

Relative pronouns the Stoics also classified as indefinite articles (cf. Priscian *Inst.* 11, 548.7–9), and Greek grammarians continued to regard them as articles, specifically postpositive ones (*hupotaktika*). If, however, a relative pronoun picks up a definite article, why should it not count as definite too? More generally, a Stoic theory of

---

[17] Indefinite articles are the only ones listed at DL 7.58, one of several indications that this account of the parts of speech is incomplete.

anaphora is to be expected, especially in light of the equivalence thesis (see §13.7.1); yet little trace of it survives. The report that Stoics held that 'every pronoun is made definite by deixis or by anaphora' (SchDThr 518.39–519.3) is suspect to the extent that this is standard grammatical doctrine (cf. 256.20–27, 516.15–17). Nor is it known what later Stoics made of the absence of grammatical definite articles from Latin (grammarians substituted interjections, or indefinite pronouns[18]). Perhaps the moral drawn was that Greek is a more perfect, more 'rational' language (as the Epicurean Philodemus seems to have thought: *On the Gods* 3 [*PHerc.* 152/157] col. 4.8–13 Diels).

13.6.6.3 *Definite Articles*

The most salient and significant feature of Stoic definite articles is that they do not function as substitutes for nominals, the role assigned them by technical grammarians (and Peripatetics: e.g. SchDThr 515.33–4) and embodied in the labels *antônumia* and *pronomen*. The thesis that they substitute for definite articles/pronouns is supported by quotations from Homer (ApD *pron.* 5.21–6.6; indeed, Apollonius' severest criticism of the Stoics is for their ignorance of Homeric usage, 7.20–8.2), but a distinction holds between evidence adduced and what it is claimed to be evidence of. And it is quite clear that what made deixis interesting to Stoics was its bearing on their philosophical theories.

Most general is its role in epistemology, which left its mark on Stoic philosophical logic (LS 34H10; S.E. *M* 11.12–14). The foundation of Stoic epistemology is the 'appearance' (*phantasia*), or state of awareness of something external (39A; S.E. *M* 7.227–41), that is veridical, certain, and vividly detailed (31A1–3, 39A, 40, 41A, B, H, 61D, H). But an observer in a position to demonstrate something in her environment is also, typically, in a position to acquire such an appearance thereof. The point is well illustrated by Chrysippus' etymology of the personal pronoun *egô* 'I' (34J, K7), discussed in §13.7.2.

Deixis also played a central part in Chrysippus' response to a challenge to his definitions of the modalities and thereby to his theory of fate (38F), and in defending the Stoic formulation of negations.[19] If a female is being demonstrated, the argument went, then, regardless of whether she is walking, both <This (male one) is walking> and <This (male one) is not walking> are false, owing to the defective implicature (*mokhthêra paremphasis*) that the demonstrated thing is male (Alexander *in AnPr* 402.1–36). Hence the latter cannot be the negation or contradictory of the former.

In vivid contrast, Apollonius' interest in such examples (*synt.* 3.8, 273.9–276.9) is as a potential threat to the grammarian's expert status (cf. S.E. *M* I 212–13), in that these (alleged) single-word solecisms dissolve the distinction between a solecism, 'the combination [*sunthesis*] of incongruous word forms,' and a barbarism, a defect in a single word form (*lexis* in the Stoic definition at DL 7.59 must mean something different).

---

[18] This may be a survival of another Stoic theory (cf. Priscian *Inst.* 11, 548.9–15, with 2, 54.18–19); certainly some Stoics called definite articles 'articular pronouns' (548.9, 12–16).

[19] These logicians are not explicitly called Stoics, but *mokhthêros* is a characteristically Stoic term: cf. 36C1, 4, 'unsound'; S. E. *M* XI 10–11. On *paremphasis*, see §13.6.11.

13.6.7 Verbs

As for Aristotle, so for the Stoics, the primary property of *rhêmata* is semantic, to judge by the two extant definitions (LS 33M):

[V1] A part of rational discourse signifying a non-compound predicate [*katêgor-êma*].

[V2] An element of discourse uninflected for case [*aptôton*], signifying something (that can be) composed [*suntakton*[20]] around [*peri*] some thing(s).

[V1] assumes familiarity with another technical category, the predicate (§13.6.8.2). [V2] is vague, unless 'composable' has a technical meaning (see §13.6.10), and offers a specification that is not unique to the *definiendum*. Aristotle's definition of the *rhêma* added 'with time' to his definition of the *onoma*, but neither [V1] (by Diogenes of Babylon) nor [V2] (probably by his pupil Apollodorus: cf. 33G) mentions inflection for tense (or aspect)—almost certainly because, strictly speaking, verbs do not inflect: the things they signify do, viz. predicates, a species of *lekton*.

13.6.8 *Lekta*

13.6.8.1 *Philosophical Roles*

The mind and its states, being causally active (§13.6.5), are physical, and hence cannot be shared or, in any obvious way, have intentional content. The solution was to postulate incorporeal *lekta* as the contents of rational appearances (also called 'thoughts,' *noêseis*), viz. appearances the objects of which it is possible to 'present' (*parastêsai*) in or by *logos*. In consequence a *lekton* can be defined as 'that which subsists in relation to a rational appearance' (LS 33C, F2), subsistence, not existence, being the characteristic mode of being of incorporeals (27D; Plutarch, *Common Notions* 1074D). Items indivisible in physical reality, such as the wise Cato, are separable in rational thoughts, so that, for example, Cato's wisdom—a physical part of him (§13.6.5)—can be prised apart from, and simultaneously reconnected to, Cato, in a structure capturing the relation between them: viz. that of a predicate, e.g. <is wise (*sapit*)>,[21] assigned to a body that does or undergoes something or is in such-and-such a state (33E).

---

[20] Nouns ending in *-tos* are systematically ambiguous in this way; the same will hold of *lekton* (§13.6.8). Some texts use present passive participles instead, whether by way of clarification or of distinction is uncertain. The extent to which *lekta* are mind- and language-dependent is a problem for the Stoa that does not carry over into technical grammar, although it may bear on the difference in theoretical status between *lekta* and Apollonius Dyscolus' *noêta* (§13.8.4).

[21] Angle brackets '< >' will henceforth in this chapter enclose terms purportedly referring to *pragmata* or *lekta*.

This predicative structure was probably borrowed from Stoic aetiology, which postulated predicates as the effects of (most) causes (55B, C), i.e. as the incorporeal 'things done,' *pragmata* (from *prattein* 'do, make, act'; cf. *praxis* 'action'), by bodies to one another, *lekta* themselves being causally inert (27E). Predicates, which have a role too in the Stoic theory of action, as the objects of impulses (33J), were also called *lekta* (55C), and the relation between *lekta* and *pragmata* (cf. 33A) is still debated. Confusion in non-Stoic sources about Stoic terminology is, therefore, perfectly understandable.

Thus verbs also signify *pragmata* in grammatical theory (e.g. SchDThr 215.28–30; ApD *synt.* 1.130, 108.11–14, with 3.58, 323.9–324.9); these are actions, not Stoic *pragmata*, but, as they include passivities and states, Stoic influence is possible (as with the grammarians' use of *pragma* for incorporeal abstractions, e.g. Choeroboscus *Prolegomena* 105.29–36). The word *lekton* was used by non-Stoics to refer to a signifier that is 'sayable' (e.g. S.E. *M* 1.76–8; ApD *pron.* 59.5–6). Plutarch's assimilation of Stoic predicates and *pragmata* to Platonic *rhêmata* and *praxeis* respectively (QP 1009CD) is perhaps only a bit of mischief, but a report (SchDThr 356.10–11) that the Stoic term for the *rhêma* was *katêgorêma* is probably in good faith, given their close association (§13.6.7, §13.6.8.2.1).

For this is one way in which *lekta* contents and their parts are communicated via *logos*. In general, as one report has it: 'First comes the appearance; then the mind, being capable of talking [*eklalêtikê*], enunciates [*ekpherei*][22] in *logos* what is being done to it by the appearance' (33D). This (re-)combining of diverse elements is a version of the *Sophist*'s thesis that *logos* is a 'mingling of kinds,' although *lekta* do not so much reflect reality as refract it.

13.6.8.2 *Predicates*

Definitions

[P1] An incomplete *lekton* (that can be) composed with a nominative case to create a proposition.

[P2] The *pragma* said of [*agoreuomenon kata*] a thing, (that can be) composed around [*peri*] some thing(s).[23]

[V1] and [V2] (§13.6.7) differ markedly in content, yet neither fits [P1], which is purely compositional, and extremely narrow (see §13.6.10). [V2] goes well with [P2], but both are almost as vague as the *Sophist* passage to which they perhaps allude, where a *logos* is said to be 'of' or 'around' the thing named by it (262e–263a; cf. 13.3.2.2). A *pragma* here is clearly not the same thing as an action, however.

---

[22] Like *legein, ekpherein* became almost a technical term for 'bringing out' *lekta* in language, as opposed to the 'pronunciation' (*prophora* and cognate verbs) of speech sounds (33A), albeit not in Chrysippean usage, it seems. Nonetheless his *On singular and plural enunciations* appears in the *pragmata* section of his ancient bibliography (DL 7.192). Of the 311 'books' (equivalent in length, roughly speaking, to chapters) that Chrysippus wrote on 'logic,' legible fragments of just one have survived (PHerc. 307); hence the evidential value of this list of titles.

[23] Both in 33G. The first phrase of [P2] merely unwraps the Greek term *katêgorêma*, and we have adopted the emendation removing from the received text the word 'or' at the end of it.

At least two classifications of predicates were devised, apparently incompatible both with each other and with [P1] and [P2], although both implicitly distinguish between predicates that do and do not contain an oblique case.[24] The first, [C1] (DL 7.64–5), is broadly speaking semantic. In [C2],[25] in contrast, predicates (*sumbamata*,[26] from *sumbainein* 'happen, occur') are classified purely compositionally.[27] We will return to the classifications in §13.6.10.

13.6.8.3 *Self-complete* Lekta

What is identified in the *Sophist* as 'the first and smallest *logos*' is a truth value bearer, and Aristotle assigns non-declarative *logoi* to other disciplines (§13.4.1). Neither author, however, argues that a truth-valued *logos* is 'the first *logos*' *tout court*, or even that there is such a thing. Perhaps there are many 'first' *logoi*, all potentially of philosophical interest.

This is, in essence, the Stoic view, although the items in question are not *logoi* but what they signify, viz. self-complete (*autotelê*) *lekta*, such as propositions, orders, prayers, and oaths (DL 7.66–7; S.E. *M* 8.70–3), as opposed to predicates, which are 'deficient' (*ellipê*) *lekta* (LS 33F1, M). Stoic dialectic must define them all, for good epistemological and, ultimately, ethical reasons: we can respond appropriately to our appearances, including those produced in us by language, only if we know what their contents are, and *mutatis mutandis* for producing appearances in others (cf. 31B, R). Chrysippus wrote extensively on these *lekta* (DL 7.191; cf. Chrysippus' *Logical Questions* cols 11–12 in Marrone 1997, on imperatives) and disagreed with Cleanthes about oaths (Stobaeus *Anthology* 3.28.17–18).

It is tempting to identify this as a sort of speech-act theory, even though it does not posit a single content modifiable by different forces (assertoric, imperatival, etc.), for a proposition (*axiôma*) is defined by possession of a truth value, which is what makes it suitable for being 'the assertable *pragma*.' But at least some self-complete *lekta* were defined as what someone does when she says (*legei*) it, or what she says when she e.g. gives an order or makes a promise, as if these illocutionary acts were functions of a speaker's intentions on a given occasion of utterance, not of any particular form of words (unlike their Neoplatonic/peripatetic counterparts: see below). Perhaps, then, structures of *pragmata/lekta* and of vocalizations could come apart systematically, as Chrysippus thought with regard to definitions and fortune-tellers' rules (§13.7.1; cf. DH *Comp.* 8.2–13). We do not know, however, whether a classification of self-complete *lekta* would have been linked to a classification of inflections for mood, or whether

---

[24] This distinction surfaces in Diogenes' definition of the verb, 33M.

[25] [C2] has been almost completely lost from DL; fortunately, however, it (but not [C1], apparently) was known to Porphyry (LS 33q).

[26] The term is applied to both the genus and its most important species, a characteristically Stoic usage.

[27] The same contrast is found between the two known typologies of simple propositions: 34K5–7, which is explicitly compositional; H4-10, which is, broadly speaking, semantic.

there is Stoic ancestry to Apollonius' distinction of the morphosyntactic properties associated with mood from its semantic status (lit. its 'psychological disposition').

The evidence is lacking, sadly, for a full comparison of the self-complete *lekton* with its closest Platonic and Aristotelian counterparts (§13.3.2.2, §13.4.2.3). But self-completeness cannot reduce to predicative structure, since 'vocative' *pragmata* need not include a predicate (DL 7.67). Platonic, Aristotelian, and Stoic elements mingle in Ammonius' classification of 'species' (*eidê*) of *logoi* (5.1–17, 64.26–65.30), and the Peripatetic-Neoplatonic self-complete *logos* is almost certainly modelled on this Stoic original, although the Stoic scheme, of course, classifies *lekta*, not *logoi*, which have an 'enunciation' (*ekphora*) that is either perfected (*apêrtismenê*) or imperfect (*anapartistos*)[28] (31A7, 33F3, 34A; DL 7.65–8; cf.13.8.4). Given its apparent independence of a relation—that of predication—tied to logic rather than to grammar, an explanation would be welcome of how the Stoics thought the completeness of *lekta* gets determined, especially as the Stoic 'semantic triangle' (33B2–3) of signifier, signified *pragma/lekton*, and external object is non-psychologist *per se*, even if yoked to the minds of speakers via the *lekton* (and also, perhaps, through what must be non-natural semantic relations, to the community of speakers: cf. §13.7.1).

13.6.8.4 *Propositions*

Propositions are the most important of the self-complete *lekta*, for they are the contents of many of our appearances, and the constituents of arguments. The proposition also functions as the 'end-point' of the process of construction that begins with the verbal or non-compound predicate (§13.6.8.2, §13.6.10). Dialectical technicalities worked out on apparently mundane examples (e.g. LS 35A1) could be applied as needed, since the properties and relations in question remain constant. One such technical achievement was the theory of inflection (*enklisis*) of predicates and propositions for tense/aspect, number, and voice, which was put to work defining memory (Plutarch *Intelligence of Animals* 961C) and dismantling a theory of Diodorus Cronus' (cf. 13.5.2), that a thing can be said only to 'have moved' (LS 11i), by classifying propositions as singular or plural, and again as 'continuous' (*paratatika*)—containing predicates signified by present, imperfect, or aorist verbs—or 'perfect' (*suntelika*). Chrysippus' works on tensed items are listed in the *pragmata* section of the ancient bibliography (DL VII 190), and he was familiar with puzzles generated by inflection (*Logical Questions* frs. i–iii, cols 1–2 in Marrone 1997).

Dionysius' report (*Comp.* 6.38–9) that 'some people'—presumably Peripatetics—call *enkliseis* 'verbal (*rhêmatikai*) cases,' as if this usage were something of an oddity, shows the strength of the influence of inflection theory on grammarians. For Apollonius, there is inflection of both word forms and intelligibles (*noêta*) (§13.8.4), and this may well have a Stoic ancestor (cf. *synt.* 1.50, 43.15–17): at any rate, some Stoics defined a type of word, the participle, using the notion of inflection, as 'a verb inflecting for case' (*casuale*) or an inflection of the verb. It is a salutary warning against treating Stoic

---

[28] The relations between the use of this terminology here and in Stoic logic and metaphysics (32B1, 28N5–6, 'matching(ly)') remain obscure.

doctrine as monolithic that there are two more known Stoic definitions of the participle: a 'reflexive appellative' (see §13.6.6.2); and some (other) species of nominal
(SchDThr 548.15–19; Priscian *Inst.* 2, 54.9–11, 11, 548.14–549.7; Plutarch *QP* 1011D). At
the same time, there was general Stoic agreement that participles cannot constitute a
distinct part of speech, on the grounds that their forms are derivative and not
'primitive' (*prôtotupoi*), a principle applied to adverbs as well (SchDThr 365.15–16,
520.16–20; Priscian *Inst.* 2, 54.10–12).

13.6.9 Cases and Particles

Plutarch blithely, or mischievously, assumes that Plato's *onomata* are the same thing as
Stoic cases (*QP* 1009C). In fact it is not even clear whether the latter belong to the
'signifiers' part of dialectic (cf. LS 55C; Simplicius *in Cat.* 209.13) or are incomplete
lekta, like predicates. The Stoic classifications of ambiguities mark off a class of
'signifying particles' of *lexis* that certainly include (37Q7,[29] cf. Theon *Progymnasmata*
82.7–16) number words, prepositions (cf. DL VII 65), and relative pronouns, and
possibly the particles *Someone* and *No One* with which predicates are composed
(34K3, 7, cf. H5). But, if so, cases such as *This [male one]* and *Socrates*, with which
predicates are also composed (37K5–6, cf. H4, 6), must be word(form)s as well.
The problem then will be to explain how something incorporeal (e.g. a proposition)
can be generated from something incorporeal (e.g. a predicate, a proposition) and
something corporeal (e.g. a word form, or even the privative prefix *a-*: cf. 34K2, 4;
DL 7.65, S.E. *M* 8.73).

There is no direct evidence that Stoic cases are *lekta*, but it is easy to see that, in many
languages, a nominal's semantic contributions vary, roughly speaking, with its shape—
although shape is not what makes (all) the difference (cf. §13.6.12). Perhaps the cases
and particles found in *lekta* are word forms' contextualized significations, including
their context-dependent, non-lexical or non-referential content.[30] One pointer in this
direction is the Stoic defence of the thesis that the nominative is a case properly so
called (*sc.* a 'fall'), which links cases, rather mysteriously, to conceptions (33K, L).
Conceptions are not significations, as they are for Aristotle, but help constitute
linguistic ability. Indeed, according to Chrysippus, they turn mere vocal sound into
logos (*ap.* Galen, *PHP* 2.5.15, 20; *cf.* 53U7, 33H)—which explains his claim that parrots
and other 'talking' animals are able only 'to sort-of-talk [*ut loqui*]' (V. *LL* 6.56; the
original Greek was probably *hôsanei legein*, cf. Porphyry *Abstinence* 3.22.31–42).[31] But if

[29] The word translated 'element' here is *morion*.
[30] The quite different position has also been taken that Stoic cases are identical with qualities or
qualia (§13.6.5). This, however, seems incompatible with the Stoic theory of *lekta*, and lacks support in
the sources.
[31] Later Stoics may have adopted instead a distinction between 'pronunciative' *logos*, constituting
linguistic ability, and 'dispositional' (*endiathetos*) *logos*, embracing ethical and epistemological
capacities, which is exclusive to humans: *e.g.* S. E. *PH* 1.65–77; Porph. *abst.* 3.3ff.

a parrot uttering *Who's a pretty boy, then?* or *Polly wants a cracker* is not really producing a *logos*, and is certainly not asking a question or making a statement, neither can it use a case to represent something *as*, say, an agent, for which purpose the nominative is standard. For to do so it must have a conception of that thing *as such* (see §13.6.10).

The thesis that the nominative is a case was rejected by Peripatetics, as we would expect given Aristotle's own use of the term *ptôsis* (§13.4.2.3; cf. *Categories* 1a12–13, *Int.* 16a32–b1, 16–17, *Topics* 114a33–4, *Poetics* 1457a18–23). The grammarians, however, are said to have accepted it 'as if following the Stoics' (Ammonius *in Int.* 43.4–5); and this may well be an instance of a distinctively Stoic innovation torn from its theoretical moorings.

13.6.10 Syntax

Varro cites Chrysippus in support of the thesis that knowing a language involves knowing which word goes where (and adds that the Latin *locus* 'place' is the origin of *loqui* 'to speak,' *LL* 6.56). Syntax, for Stoics, is ultimately a relation between *lekta* (cf. Plutarch *Against Colotes* 1119F), and their classifications of predicates show that it was understood in terms of the combinatory potentials of units: specifically, the availability of predicates for composition with cases or particles.

In [C1] (cf. §13.6.8.2), predicates' compositional properties are determined by the meanings of the signifying verbs, for its core taxonomic principle is borrowed from the theory of action. Thus its first type, the 'straight' or 'direct' (*orthon*) predicate (e.g. <cuts>), reproduces the real-world direction of causation in being composed (*suntassomenon*) with an oblique case specifying the patient, to form a predicate (*sc.* a compound predicate, although curiously this is left implicit), which in turn 'is composed' with a nominative case specifying the agent. The nominative with which a reversed (*huption*) predicate is composed, in contrast, specifies the patient, e.g. <is cut>, and a 'reciprocal' predicate is both reversed and an act (*energêma*), viz. of the agent on herself, such as <gets her hair cut>, which is signified by a middle verb—but an *orthon* predicate may be too, such as *dialegetai* <converses (with)>.

In [C2], the compositional process, although it begins with a (verbal) predicate, soon diverges, for its next moves are to combine the predicate with a case that, in the examples at least, specifies an agent, and then to distinguish the deficient (*ellipes*) from the complete (*teleion*) predicate according as this sequence does or does not require an oblique case to make a proposition. Each type comes in two varieties, a novelty of [C2] being that impersonal constructions involving oblique cases alone are accommodated. ([C2] is, therefore, incompatible with [P1].) [C2] does not distinguish active from passive or reciprocal predicates, and so does not specify that passives are composed with the 'passive particle,' viz. the (signification of?) the preposition *hupo* 'by,' itself presumably composed with an oblique case specifying the agent; without this, it seems, the predicate is incomplete. Again, [C2] begins with a species for which the nearest counterpart in [C1] is classified by exclusion, as neither direct, reversed, nor reciprocal—although it is debatable whether [C1]'s categories are in fact mutually exclusive.

For taxonomic purposes, then, the starting-point of the compositional process is the (verbal/non-compound) predicate, the end-point is the proposition (§13.6.8.4). The syntax of *lekta* and that of the parts of speech were so closely linked, however, that this unit-based model came to be applied to the syntax of word(form)s as well, and was therefore passed on to technical grammar. The closeness of the two levels—signifiers and signified—is evident, for example, from Dionysius' huffy dismissal of Chrysippus' *On the syntax of the parts of speech* as 'containing, not rhetorical, but dialectical theory, about the syntax of both true and false propositions' and suchlike (*Comp.* 4.129–50). Several similar titles appear in Chrysippus' bibliography (DL 7.192–3) and show how the syntax of the parts of speech was intertwined with that of 'things said,' viz. *lekta* (cf. LS 30I1, 3, where 'meaning' translates *dunamis*, on which see §13.6.11). Cases and conjunctions may even be word(form)s themselves.

The familiar grammatical relation of 'rection' or 'governance' is, of course, absent from all ancient language theory,[32] and Stoic syntactic combination turns out to be a remarkably crude affair, as just one way for one thing 'to be composed with' (*suntattesthai*) another that can hold of predicates in relation to cases or particles (33G), of non-simple propositions in relation to simple ones (DL 7.72, cf. §13.6.8.3), and of the parts of a *logos* (59). Again, a variety of things may be constructed (*sunestos*) out of different units: not only simple propositions out of predicates and particles or cases (34K), but also conditionals out of simple propositions (35A1; cf. DL 7.68), and negative and privative propositions out of (potential) propositions and particles (34K2, 4, G).

A pair of telling assumptions about syntax emerges from the two extant Stoic classifications of ambiguity (13.6.9). First, two kinds of ambiguity occur when 'particles' (*sc.* of *lexis*) are variously composed to form word strings and words respectively, according as they do or do not signify, although one classification apparently envisages particles of both kinds being composed together. Second, the classifications make no (explicit) provision for the Aristotelian ambiguity type *amphibolia*. This occurs when several different grammatical relations can hold between lexically univocal elements, as in *epistatai ta grammata* '(He/she/it) knows (the) letters' and/or '(The) letters know' (Ar. *Sophistic Refutations* 4, 166a17–21, cf. 6–14). Here, what is unclear is not which signifying particles (to use the Stoic terminology) are composed with which, but how they go together.

The classifications of predicate types would be useful sources for differentiating the example's two significations—always supposing, of course, they were available. The example is one of syncretism, or what Apollonius calls 'coincidence' (*sunemptôsis*), 'conjunction' (*sunodos*), or 'formal identity' (*homophônia*), within or between lexemes,

---

[32] This terminology is found in linguistic contexts, e.g. DTSch. 552.8–9 (*kurieuein*), but not with this special force. S.E. *M* 8.109 (*epikratein*) is a logical context.

and the Stoics did recognize this phenomenon, at least in articles (ApD *pron.* 6.7–19; §
13.6.6.2; cf. Origen *Selections from On Psalms* 4.5, *PL* 12.1141.44–8), although, according
to Apollonius (*pron.* 7.23–8.2), they misinterpreted it, just as Posidonius did, he says, in
prepositions/conjunctions (*coni.* 214.18–21). The Stoic definition of ambiguity specifies
that multiple signifying must be done *lektikôs* (DL 7.62), but it is unclear what this is
supposed to exclude (perhaps signifying as a textual sign does: see §13.6.4).

Apollonius' own analysis of a similar example is strikingly different (*synt.* III 50–53,
315.16–319.2). The sequence **graphei hoi andres* *'The men draws,' he observes, is
obviously incongruous, but not so *graphei ta paidia* *'The children draws.' Like the
evil twin in a Bette Davis melodrama, it takes advantage of its outward identity with its
respectable sibling *graphei ta paidia* '(S/he) draws the children' to pass as good Greek.
Apollonius often uses coincidence to rehabilitate (apparently) incongruous constructions: here it explains how one of them, so to say, gets away with it.

13.6.11 Semantics

An explanation for the restricted Stoic notion of syntax can perhaps be found in two
interlocking factors.

First, the mental separation of objects from their properties and states (§13.6.8.1)
ensures that no further explanation is needed of the marital harmony between predicates and cases (and particles?), which is borrowed, only a little dimmed, by verbs and
nominals. Second, the cardinal distinction between *phônê* and *sêmainomena*—which,
on one influential view (LS 31A7; DL 7.62), structures the contents of dialectic itself, and
which confronts Chairemon when classifying expletives, and Apollonius when classifying the parts of speech (*synt.* 2.153, 248.1–9, *pron.* 67.6–7)—is also, in effect, an
exhaustive division of the properties of *logos*: some attach to it *qua logos*, others *qua*
mere *lexis*. Hence items, whether lexemes or formal properties, that might otherwise be
classed as having grammatical functions must instead count as semantic. What evidence there is, however, suggests that Stoic distinctions amongst types of signifying,
signifier, or *significatum* were not drawn with much finesse, terminologically at any
rate. Proper names 'indicate'; appellatives and verbs 'signify'; an ambiguous *lexis* does
either indifferently (37P); indefinite articles 'indicate anaphora too' (ApD *pron.* 5.21).

Conjunctions are a particularly intriguing case. Their logical role assured them new
status as a part of speech (DL 7.59; cf. Plutarch *QP* 1010D), and a conjunction (pair)
promises (*epangellesthai,* 35A1–4, 'declares'; S.E. *M* 8.111) that a certain logical relation
holds between the simple propositions (LS 34) it conjoins to form a non-simple one
(35)—an almost anthropomorphic characterization. That conjunctions 'signify' or
'indicate' was the view of the Stoics Chairemon (ApD *coni.* 247.30–248.13, cf. *pron.*
6.7) and Posidonius, whose reasoning shows (*coni.* 214.4–8) that he took conjunctions
to belong to the same part of speech as prepositions, the Stoic name for which was in
fact 'prepositive conjunctions' (*synt.* 4.5, 436.13–437.2; 4.27, 457.13–458.2). Posidonius

also identified a class of 'natural' conjunctions distinguished by their 'force' (ApD *coni.* 214.8–10, 18, 213.7; *cf.* S.E. *M* 11.7–8), but we do not know if this is different from their 'signification' or 'promise.' It is true that non-simple propositions are defined as constructed 'out of' (*ek*) propositions, but as put together 'through' (*dia*) or 'by' (*hupo*) a conjunction (pair). So perhaps signifying (etc.), for conjunctions, consists not in having a one-to-one lektal correlate, but in signifying (etc.), *about* the embedded propositions, *that* they are logically related thus-and-so. Aristotle gives an analogous account of quantifiers and the copula (§13.4.2.4), and it is tempting to adapt it to Stoic quantified propositions (34H5, 7, 10, K4, 7; 13.6.9) as well.

As for the semantic contributions of morphosyntactic features, the labels (*sum*)(*par*) *emphasis* '(co-)implicature'[33] and cognate verbs could be used, terminology that was passed on to the grammarians (e.g. ApD *synt.* 3.51, 317.10; DH *comp.verb.* 6.39–40). Demonstratives may have a 'defective implicature,' and Chrysippus' lost *On implicature* is listed with works on *pragmata* (DL 7.192). But Chrysippus preferred different terminology to describe a syllable 'involving a signification [*parensêmainousa*] of distance'; conversely, he characterized certain privative terms as having or signifying an additional 'implicature' in certain circumstances (Simplicius *in Cat.* 395.10–12)— a phenomenon crying out, to modern ears, for Gricean distinctions. There may also be Stoic roots to Apollonius' application of the 'implicature' terminology to non-lexically significant lexemes (e.g. definite articles: ApD *synt.* 1.48, 41.15).

Another semantic term that may be Stoic is 'co-signify' (*sussêmainen*), as when a verb signifies a predicate and a nominative case simultaneously (S.E. *PH* I 198–9). The term may have been borrowed by Peripatetics, for it is used to identify what, at best, parts of *lexis* do.

13.6.12 The Objects of Study

This brings us to an aspect of Stoic theorizing about language that is especially salient to us moderns. A *lexis* is corporeal (LS 33H) and perishable, and cannot change shape (e.g. inflect) without losing its identity. Similar *lexeis* may perhaps share a common quality (§13.6.5), but whether this could account for more than physical (*sc.* phonetic) similarity is debateable. Stoic metaphysics does not admit abstract objects such as universals (or sets, presumably), and one Stoic definition in philosophical logic (34H2; DL 7.68–9) suffers markedly from the lack of a type/token distinction. How, then, can Stoic dialecticians claim to make intelligible generalisations about *lexis*, *logos*, and their parts and elements?

One possible line of response is suggested by Chrysippus' comparison of inflectional relations to those between kin (Varro *LL* 10.59; 13.7.2), and by the Stoic theory of

---

[33] This translation is intended to avoid confusion with the logical terms 'imply,' 'implication,' not to mark a connection to Gricean semantics: although see main text, below.

'kinships' (*sungeneiai*) amongst the various verbal tenses/aspects (SchDThr 251.3–4, 6–9; cf. 249.33–250.25, on [Dionysius Thrax] *Art* 53.3–4). Suppose, then, that appropriately similar *lexeis* constitute one member, e.g. the genitive case, of a 'family' that constitutes a given word, e.g. *Socrates*, and that appropriately similar 'word families' collectively constitute a 'clan,' viz. a part of speech, while correlative members of these clans collectively constitute, for example, the genitive case.

First, however, the principle(s) by which members of word families are constituted must be fixed, and here our sources offer only a few obscure hints. Stoics may, for example, have accepted as ambiguous inscriptions the corresponding utterances of which are univocal (cf. 37Q7), a problem with which Aristotle was already familiar (cf. *Sophistic Refutations* 5, 166a35–8; 20, 177a8–177b9). Of course the inadequacies, for the grammarian's purposes, of the traditional Greek writing system were well known (cf. SchDThr 187.26–188.20, 496.11–26), though little was done about them: the question is whether the Stoics, for their own special purposes, got to grips with the need for (inter alia) cross-media identity criteria. Another important hint comes from an argument (SchDThr 523.9–27) that a nominal case must (also) be a signification, given that different word forms may belong to the same case, and the same word forms to multiple cases. Even if this is not a Stoic argument, the phenomena cited are certainly apt to catch Chrysippus' eye, given his interest in semantic anomaly (Varro *LL* 9.1), e.g. in privative expressions (§13.6.11). But this interest of his must be understood within another context: that of Stoic etymology and its philosophical justifications.[34]

13.7 LATER ETYMOLOGY

13.7.1 The Stoics

Already in the first century BCE, a philosopher and historian of philosophy could present etymology—'the explanation [*explicatio*] of words, that is, why each thing has the name it has'—alongside definition as a core activity of the earlier Academy (Cicero, *Academica* 1.32). These are the views of Antiochus, a member of the Academy, which, in the centuries after Plato's death, had turned sceptic; but Antiochus began to reverse the trend, and tried to locate his own school and the Stoa on a continuum philosophically and in a family tree historically. His validation of etymology suggests, therefore, that its exclusion from Stoic dialectic, as summarized in our most important source

[34] Fundamental for Stoic logic is Frede (1974). For Stoic philosophy of language, Atherton (1993) is essential, as are Long (1971) and Frede (1994a, 1994b); see also Gourinat (2000). For the relation of Stoic philosophy to grammar, see Frede (1987a, 1987b), Blank and Atherton (2003). For a treatment of 'connectors' in ancient philosophers and grammarians, see Barnes (2007: 168–263). For the development of the 'system' of the 'parts of speech,' see Matthaios (1999, 2002); also De Jonge (2008), especially on Dionysius of Halicarnassus' version of this development (cf. §13.6.2).

(31C2), may not have been the only view on the matter. Certainly the Stoa became famous—or notorious (cf. Cicero *Nature of the Gods* 3.62; Seneca *Benefits* 1.4.6, cf. 3.9)—for using etymologies in support of individual philosophical theories.

This strategy was presumably justified (little is known for certain of Stoic teaching in this area) by our distant ancestors' as yet uncorrupted relation with the world around them. Humans are unique amongst animals in being active foci of *logos*—the single, divine, cosmic principle that is identical with Zeus, Fate, and Providence—whose rationality includes the use of language (§13.6.1). Stoic cosmology and theology, which reconstrued the traditional gods and the myths and customs about them as aspects of and narratives about *logos*/Zeus, valued the divine names and epithets assigned intuitively by our distant ancestors and preserved by the older poets, such as Homer and Hesiod, because these encodings of ancient lore remain informative: early man's internal *logos*, being more in tune with the cosmic *logos*, yielded fuller, clearer, sharper insights into its many manifestations than we moderns—more sophisticated, but more corrupt—can enjoy.

Instead we must pursue philosophical inquiry (cf. Dio Chrysostom 12.27–34, 39–41; Seneca *Epistle* 90; Strabo, *Geography* 1.1.10), which yields such insights as that the key term *heimarmenê* 'Fate' (lit. 'what is allotted') is derived from *heirmos aitiôn* 'chain of causes' (e.g. Nemesius *Nature of Man* 37; cf. Cicero *Divination* 1.125). One of Chrysippus' etymologies of the name 'Zeus' (Stobaeus *Anthology* 1.31) follows the *Cratylus* closely (396ab; cf. 13.2.3), as does that of 'Hermes' (407e), from *hermêneia* 'linguistic expression' and thence from *logos* (Philo *Providence* 2.41). A Stoic-influenced authority who also made this connection tells us that Hermes is called *Argeïphontês* because '*logos* as a whole has a single nature that displays vividly [*ekphainei enargôs*] what is being thought' (Heraclitus, *Homeric Problems* 72.5, 11). For the Stoic Cornutus (*Nature of the Gods* 28.3ff.), the name of primordial moisture 'Khaos' comes from from *khusis* 'flowing, diffusion,' or from *kaos* 'burning,' because the original substance was fire (28.7–9).[35]

Amusing criticisms of such etymologies, whether as heuristic or as historiographical or anthropological resources, are almost certainly less familiar than is the Stoic admission that the origin of some words is hidden (Augustine *Dialectic* 6), or Chrysippus' cautious official evaluation of its epistemological and methodological status, which comes into focus in his use of them to support his theory that the locus of the mind (identifed with the self) is the chest. This cannot be perceived or, strictly speaking, proved, but it can nonetheless be made 'plausible' (*pithanon*) or 'reasonable' (*eulogon*) by argument (Galen *PHP* 2.5.15–18, cf. 3.5.22) and by other considerations, all having to do with language: poetry, commonplace turns of phrase, including those typical of women's speech,[36] and other (para)linguistic phenomena (cf. 2.2.5). Of this last type is Chrysippus' etymology of *egô* 'I' (9–11 [LS 34J]), which may in part be a response to the 'first names' articulatory theory of the *Cratylus*. We often point to the

---

[35] See also §24.1.1 on etymology in antiquity.
[36] Cf. Varro *LL* 8.56; Procl. *in Plat.Crat.* 86.

chest when saying 'I,' Chrysippus observes, 'with the deixis moving here naturally and appropriately'; yet even when we do not, 'we say the word *egô* nodding towards ourselves, the word *egô* itself being of this kind too [*i.e.* deictic] .... We utter *egô*, with regard to its first syllable, drawing the lower jaw downward toward ourselves demonstratively [*deiktikôs*].' And its second syllable, unlike the second syllable of *ekeinos* 'that (male one),' 'involves a signification (*parensêmainousa*) that has nothing to do with distance' (cf. §13.6.11).

Here, then, an observable movement having a known deictic purpose is interpreted as a model for an observable movement that proves deictic only when viewed in the right context, that of Chrysippus' theory; and it offers support for it not directly, in the way the hand gesture does, but by revealing the theory's explanatory power—the power to redescribe as semantic what had hitherto seemed arbitrary and meaningless. Chrysippus finds, in a single word, plausible evidence for a psychological theory, leaving unstated the implication that its appropriateness cannot be the work of chance. In contrast, Nigidius Figulus (first century BCE), in his grammatical notebooks, claimed to find in the articulation of all the Greek and Latin personal pronouns a consistent pattern of semantic appropriateness proving that words 'were made by a natural force and a rational principle of some kind' (Aulus Gellius, *Attic Nights* 10.4).

Chrysippus' circumspection is at least consonant with his recognition of semantic anomalies and inflectional irregularities (Varro, *LL* 10.59). Since the signification of a word was standardly taken to be a factor in determining what is to count as a pattern of analogous inflection for it, these phenomena are connected; the grammarian Aristophanes even wrote a book on analogy in words of similar meaning (68). Semantic anomalies may occur at the level of the single term, as with privatives (§13.6.11), or of the sentence, and some, at any rate, can be seen only through the lens of Stoic principles, as with Chrysippus' interpretations of definitions as indefinite conditionals in which (roughly speaking) the consequent picks up the referent of the antecedent (e.g. 'If something is a man, it [*sc.* that something] is a rational mortal animal') (S.E. *M* 11.10–13), and of divination's empirically based, general predictive 'rules' (*theorêmata*) as negated conjunctions instead of conditionals (Cicero *Fate* 15–17; cf. §§13.6.6.2, 13.6.8.3). These (re)readings of surface form are justified by the threat of false inferences (that universals exist, that the future is already determined). Such anomalies, and ambiguities too, may have been regarded as flaws in a once thoroughly regular system, and Chrysippus' awareness of them should, in principle, have alerted him to the fact that use of vocalizations as names is premised on current conventions, regardless of how specific vocalizations are selected; but this is speculative.

If Chrysippus used etymology to support a psychological theory, he may have used it in ethics too; for his works on the topic (now lost) are listed, not in the dialectical, but in the ethical section of his ancient bibliography, and are followed by titles on proverbs and poetry (DL 7.199–200). His interpretation of *egô* also shows that there must have been at least one rival to the etymological theory known to Augustine (*Dialectic* ch. 6),[37] because this has at its core, not articulatory phenomena, but onomatopoeia (dismissed by Plato's Socrates as irrelevant, *Crat.* 423c) and synesthesia, viz. similarity between a perceived property of a speech sound (e.g. harshness, smoothness) and some tactile or other sensory property of the *nominatum* (cf. DH *Comp.* 16.1–20). (Such theories could, therefore, be absent from Stoic dialectic because their home is psychology, inside natural philosophy.)

Of numerous possible objections to this theory, only one seems to have been met: that it can explain, even in principle, only a limited array of words. At any rate, two more modes of appropriate semantic relation were postulated. 'Contrariety' characterizes such notorious examples as a *lucus* 'grove' being so called because it is not well lit (*cf. lux, lucis* 'light'), an apparently bizarre principle that may be a recognition of the Greek apotropaic practice (disparaged as superstitious nonsense by Socrates, *Crat.* 403a, 404c–406a) of giving evil or dangerous things or persons flattering names. Proximity (*uicinitas*) characterizes a word transferred from a strict or primary extension to a (type of) object 'nearby,' as regards shape, function, etc.—a category so broad that Augustine also calls it 'impropriety' (*abusio, katakhrêsis*).

Some scholars have interpreted this category as evidence of the Stoic origin of the rhetorical system of tropes (metaphorical and other transferred expressions), in such a way that etymologies by proximity would correspond to the grammarian's elucidations of poetic tropes, which would be the fancy literary cousins of such homespun, ordinary-language habits as talking about the 'feet' of beds and mountains as well as of animals. This is, in fact, how Dionysius of Halicarnassus sees them (*Comp.* 16, 96; cf. Quintilian *Inst.* 8.3.30–31). Nature herself 'made us imitative [*mimêtikous*]' and therefore able to produce indications (*mênumata*), not only of the sounds things make, but of anything else about them too (18–20; for onomatopoeia as a poetic trope, cf. Eustathius *Commentary on Homer's* Iliad I, 63.12–14, and as lying on the cusp between articulate speech and mere noise, cf. Charisius *Gram.* 361.26ff.). Dionysius credits Plato with the first and most important discussion of etymology (*Comp.* 16.20–4), but his description of it fits Socrates' etymologies, not to mention the Stoic theory known to Augustine, far better than it does the *nomothetês* theory.

13.7.2 Varro

Such poetic etymologies are of less interest to Varro, as being less informative about the distant past he is trying to recover, than is the sort that explains the names invented by the kings of old (*LL* 5.9). But his justification of its usefulness as a window onto the past

---

[37] For Augustine's theory of language, see Kirwan (1994) and Bermon (2007). For his criticisms of the Stoic theory, see Atherton (1993). For his Stoicizing etymology and its relation to the *Cratylus*, see Long (2005).

first constructs a general account of the relations amongst names, before turning back to the past in order to explain the contemporary forms and meanings of particular words.

Chrysippus, who is one of Varro's two philosophical authorities in the field of etymology (6.1; the other is also a Stoic), had observed that inflected or derived forms of words can sometimes (*nonnumquam*) be worked out from their nominatives or primitives and vice versa, just as one can sometimes tell what a father is like by looking at his son, and vice versa (10.59). In fact, Varro says, oblique cases may give us a better lead than nominatives, and of course explanations must start from what is clearer, rather than what is prior: the plurals *trabes* 'beams,' *duces* 'leaders,' for instance, make the relations amongst the inflected forms of these words more evident than do the singulars *trabs*, *dux*. Such 'family' relations also hold between inflectional or derived forms of words that inflect 'analogously,' e.g. the nominatives and datives *lex* : *legi* :: *rex* : *regi* ('law' : 'to/for a law' :: 'king' : 'to/a king'), or the personal and abstract nouns *sodalis* : *sodalitas* :: *civis* : *civitas* ('fellow' : 'fellowship' :: 'citizen' : 'citizenship'). It is to keep the number of separately 'imposed' names, which have to be learnt one by one, at a minimum, that such primitives create related forms by 'inflection' (*declinatio*): thus the dative *Priamo* 'to/for Priam' is clearly related to *Priamus*; if the dative were *Hecuba* (the name of Priam's wife), say, the two forms would look and sound entirely unrelated (8.4), as 'kith' rather than 'kin.'

There are inflectional irregularities, of course, but what Varro calls 'natural inflection' (*declinatio naturalis*, for case, number, tense, mood, etc.) rests on the consensus of the language community and is more regular and predictable than derivation or 'voluntary inflection' (*declinatio voluntaria*), which results from the volition (*uoluntas*) of one person, guided rationally by the nature of the things named, coining a name for one thing from the name of another. There are, admittedly, instances of semantic anomaly that go back to 'those who first imposed names,' e.g. *scopae* (fem.pl.) 'broom'; but, crucially, *scopae* inflects just like other similar nouns (8.7–8). An expertise of these forms is required, but—and here we may recall Socrates' doubts about the etymological method—of the primitive, 'imposed,' words there is only piecemeal, *ad hoc* 'historical investigation' (*historia*) (8.6).

The greater freedom possible in derivation is a radical limitation on the scope and status of etymology; but Varro believes he can use it legitimately to advance his investigations into the origins of the Roman present by recovering traces of the Roman past left in texts, rituals, folklore, and vocabulary. The nub of his case is that, just as there are 'families' (*agnationes*) and 'noble clans' (*gentilitates*) among men, so there are among words (8.4); accordingly, the core of his method is that each word form must be located inside its 'kinship' groups of forms and also related to its two 'natures,' viz. the things *from* and *for* which it was coined. Each such piece of information then finds its rightful place in an indefinitely expanding system of interrelated names and *nominata* that enjoys the scope and mutually reinforcing consistency isolated etymologies could never provide, and that forms the net in which Varro snares his prey, the now lost *realia* of ancient Rome. 'The *Vinalia* cannot get going without *uinum*' (5.13), for example, means that the name *uinalia* 'wine festival' needs the name *uinum* 'wine' just as much as the actual wine festival needs its tipple. One of the first locative words Varro examines is *caelum* 'sky,' which his teacher, Aelius Stilo, had suggested gets its name from being *caelatum* 'raised,' or else by contrariety, viz. from (not) being *celatum* 'hidden' (which does not hide Stilo's Stoic training: cf. §13.7.1). Varro is dissatisfied with both explanations, and supports his own proposals with affinities both cosmic and humble, and both formal and real. The world began in what Hesiod calls *chaos* 'gaping emptiness,' from which came *choum*, then *cauum* 'hollow,' and, finally, as several poetic quotations confirm, *caelum*. More homely are *cauum* > *cauea, caull<a>e* 'hole'; *cauata uallis* 'hollowed valley' > *conuallis* 'enclosed valley'; and *cauernae* 'caverns,' which by *cauatio* 'hollowing' become a *cauum* (5.18–20).

Varro's procedure is legitimate, then, precisely because it is *not* heuristic, but hermeneutic, working out from the words they used what the inhabitants of early Rome ate, drank, wore, worshipped, believed, and so on. Consistency will be a virtue, despite Socrates' warning that it can characterize falsehoods as well as truths (*Crat.* 436cd), because Varro is not interested in whether the founders' world-view was true: he just wants to find out what it was.[38]

13.8 APOLLONIUS DYSCOLUS, HERODIAN, AND PRISCIAN

13.8.1 Transition

The Stoics had an enormous influence on grammarians in Greece and Rome. It can be seen above all in what survives of Dionysius Thrax's discussions of the parts of speech and of the work of the Roman grammarians of the first centuries BCE and CE, especially L. Aelius Stilo Praeconinus (*c.*150–85 BCE), who taught Varro and Cicero, and Quintilian's teacher Q. Remmius Palaemon (early first century CE), whose *Ars* was a major source for later Roman grammarians, such as Charisius (mid-fourth century CE, Constantinople). Stilo, who called himself a Stoic and may have studied with Dionysius Thrax in Rhodes, wrote a book on 'propositions' (*proloquia* = *axiômata*), presumably dealing with their syntax in a Stoic manner (Gellius, *Attic Nights* 16.8.2; cf. 16.8.9, which comes from Varro's lost *LL* 14).

---

[38] On Varronian etymology, see Blank (2008). On ancient and early medieval etymology see Allan (2010a).

13.8.2 Three Grammarians

Stilo's book points to a second major Stoic influence on grammar, the separation of sound and sense, of signifiers and things signified (cf. §13.6.11). This, along with a third major point, the emphasis on language as an orderly and regular system, are best seen in the first Greek grammatical treatises we can read in their original form, by Apollonius of Alexandria, nicknamed 'Dyskolos' or 'Grouch.' Happily for us, Apollonius and his son, Herodian, were thought to represent the highest development of grammar in Greece, and were called 'the technicians' (*hoi tekhnikoi*) by later commentators. A biographical sketch (Uhlig 1910: xi–xii) reports that Herodian lived in Rome during the reign of Marcus Aurelius (161–80 CE), while Apollonius remained in Alexandria and is thought to have been active under Antoninus Pius (138–61 CE). The pair were important sources of the early mediaeval commentaries on the supposed *Art of Dionysius Thrax*, and they were also the chief authorities of the last important Roman grammarian of late antiquity, Priscian.

Much of Apollonius' large output, which covered the whole range of grammar and philology (even false stories in literature) and included *Elements*, *Prosodic Markings*, *Forms*, *Division of the Parts of Speech*, *Voice*, *Orthography*, and *Dialects*, survives only in later quotations. Of his series of books on individual parts of speech, *Noun* and *Verb* were often cited by later commentators; the ones that survive are *Pronoun*, *Adverb*, and *Conjunction*. The most important of his works, which is also the last, the *Syntax* in four books, also survives almost intact; the last part of book 4, on the syntax of adverbs and conjunctions, is lost, except for ten pages that were incorporated into the manuscripts of *Adverbs*. Apollonius did not appear out of nowhere. He builds on Aristarchus' observations about Homeric language and on Stoic theory. He seems to recognize a couple of grammarians, particularly Tryphon (late first century BCE) and his pupil Habron, as predecessors working along similar lines to his own; but he only cites them where he disagrees.

The only work surviving in the form Herodian gave it is his *Uniquely Declined Words* (*peri monêrous lexeôs*, or 'On Lexical Singularity,' as Sluiter 2011 has it).[39] Otherwise his works survive only in excerpts and epitomes, which generally do not give much of an idea of their original organization, although one papyrus and two palimpsests may come closer to doing so. He published many important studies of the accentuation and aspiration of individual words in books on *Iliadic*, *Odyssean*, and *Attic Prosody*, and then a *General Prosody*. His works on *Corruptions*, *Derivations*, *Orthography*, and *Nominal Declension* were influential, as was a *Symposium*, perhaps a learned conversation about etymologies and other grammatical questions.

Priscian, a Mauretanian who taught in Constantinople in the early sixth century CE, covered all of grammar in his *Institutio de arte grammatica*, 'Textbook of the Art of

---

[39] Herodian is edited (not very reliably) in Lentz (1867–70). On Herodian, see Dyck (1993); for 'On Lexical Singularity,' see Sluiter (2011).

Grammar,' from 'vocal sound,' via letters and their combinations (book 1), syllables, words, and the sentence (2.1–14), and the parts of speech (2.15–16), to syntax (17–18). This is, of course, a grammar of Latin, but Priscian follows Apollonius and Herodian, whom he considers the greatest authorities (*Inst.* introduction §§2, 4, books 6.2, 17.1), very closely, frequently translating them directly or even citing them in Greek, while giving examples from Greek and Latin literature and sometimes drawing on earlier Roman grammarians. Often he also compares Latin phenomena with Greek, as if writing for pupils with a knowledge of both languages. He also wrote a *Textbook of the Noun, Pronoun and Verb*, which gave a brief, systematic treatment, referring frequently to the larger *Institutio*, of the inflectional classes of these parts of speech. Here we learn, for example, that the five Latin declensions are ordered according to the order of the vowels in their genitive cases: *-ae* for the first declension (*poetae*), *-i* for the second (*docti*), etc. Another of his works was for teaching Latin at a somewhat lower level: the *Partitiones* or 'Analyses of the first twelve lines of the *Aeneid*,' in which each word in these lines was minutely parsed in a question-and-answer format.[40] We will focus on Apollonius and Herodian.

13.8.3 Method

In a crucial inheritance from the Stoics' rationally ordered world, Apollonius and Herodian conceived of language as an ordered hierarchy of rule-governed systems. The letter sounds of the alphabet had a determined order; these combined only in certain orders to form syllables; and the parts of speech were ordered both when enumerated (first noun, then verb, etc.) and in their roles in the sentence. This ordered condition was one of the main senses of 'analogy,' and it was the linchpin of the grammatical theory of Apollonius and Herodian; for their basic method, 'pathology,' is the identification of the *pathê* or corruptions, such as repetition, ellipse, syncopation, transposition, lengthening, or shortening, to which all levels of language are subject. Obviously, these processes can be identified as *pathê* only insofar as there is a basic orderliness from which deviation is possible. The grammarian would establish a rule by observation and by collection of similars. Phenomena deviating from the rule were then explained by tracing the processes by which the original 'correct' or 'full,' 'healthy,' or 'natural' (*holoklêros, apathês, entelês, plêrês, hugiês, kata phusin*) form had been corrupted, and the order in which these corruptions had occurred.

We can see how this theory makes grammar possible when Apollonius announces his intention at the outset of his *Syntax* (1.1, 1.3–2.2) to explain with total accuracy 'the construction [*suntaxis*] arising from word forms [*phônai*] for the congruence

---

40 Priscian's shorter works are in Passalacqua (1987–93). The *Institutio de arte grammatica* is edited in Hertz (1855–60). A new edition of his syntactical books (*Inst.* 17–18), with commentary, is in progress: Ars Grammatica (2010). On Priscian and philosophy, see Luhtala (2005). For Priscian's use of Apollonius, see Schmidhauser (2009). See also Allan (2010a: ch. 6).

[*katallêlotês*] of the self-complete sentence [*autotelês logos*],' since this is absolutely necessary for the explication of poems. He continues:

> For what is mentioned first as the indivisible matter, viz. the elements, guarantees this [i.e., that accurate knowledge of syntax is needed for explaining poetry] at a much earlier stage, since it forms combinations of elements [*stoikheia*], not at random, but in the construction according to rule [*to deon*, 'what is necessary'], from which it also took its name [*stoikheia*, lit. 'items arrayed in order']. At the next level the syllable admits the same thing, since the constructions of these elements, completed according to rule, produce the word [*lexis*]. And it clearly follows [*akolouthon*] that words too, which are a part of the sentence that is self-complete in its construction, admit of congruence of construction. For the intelligible subsistent on each word is an element, as it were, of the sentence, and just as the elements produce syllables by their combinations, so too will the construction of the intelligibles produce syllables, so to say, by the combination of the words, and furthermore, just as the word comes from syllables, so does the self-complete sentence come from intelligibles. (*Synt.* 1.2, 2.3–3.2; cf. Priscian, *Inst.* 17.2–3)

Apollonius proceeds (1.3–7, 3.3–6.11) to show that combination at each of these levels is rule-bound by adducing corruptions of the same kind in each; for example, the reduplication of letters within a syllable (*ellaben < elaben* 'took'), of syllables (*pampan < pan* 'all'), of words (*barus barus sunoikos*, 'hard, hard companion,' from Sophocles), and of sentences ('when we repeat what was said, whether of necessity or not').

Consequently, just as there are faults in orthography obvious to the ear, but also faults apparent only to reasoning, which can compare them to the rationale (*logos*) of orthography (cf. §13.2.1.4), the same is true in sentences, where we call incorrect joining of words 'solecism' (1.8, 7.6–14), and knowledge of syntax is possible just as knowledge of correct writing is possible. Further, just as the letter sounds have their proper order in the alphabet (*alpha* first, thought to derive from *alphein*, 'to begin') grounded in reason (*logos*), so too in the metalanguage (1.13, 15.6 ff.) do the lists of the parts of speech (noun before verb etc.), and of their accidents (nominative before genitive, or present before imperfect).

The expertise of grammar therefore captures and reproduces the *logos* that structures language itself. This inheritance from the Stoic *logos*, which structures the whole world, is at the heart of Greek technical grammar. The confidence it gives the grammarian is perhaps best exemplified in Herodian's *On Uniquely Declined Words*:

> Of those words which are seen not to belong to a group [*mê plêthousai*] but to be isolated [*spaniôs*] . . . analogy makes the test [*elegkhos*], not forbidding their use, but indicating their isolation [*to spanion*]. For analogy, which has stewardship [*pronoia*] over all of Greek diction [*lexis*] and by her art [*tekhnéi*] contains, as it were in a net, the much divided utterance of the human tongue will know that the words used by the Greeks, though they are varied, are sometimes[41] uttered in groups based on similarity, or else isolated; analogy undertakes to subject to rule [*katorthoun*] the

---

[41] For this reading, see Sluiter (2011: 300 n 26).

natures of letter-sounds at the end of a word and those in penultimate position or at the beginning, concisely transmitting those that are isolated and abundant alike. (Lentz 1867–70: 2.909.12–23)

Herodian purposes in this treatise to examine those words that have escaped grouping (*ekphugousês to plêthos*), or lexical singularities among nouns, verbs, and adverbs, which sometimes do form groups of similar forms, so that he may test what is altered (*parêllagmenon*) or isolated by reference to the members of a given group (910.15–18). This is therefore not a matter 'of vilifying an immense number of very reputable words as being pronounced contrary to the laws of nature'; rather, 'we should readily accept the words nature produced for us, though she introduced them one, two, three, four at a time, or in an indefinitely large group.' His criterion for judgement (*krisis*) of these words is the preponderant usage of the ancients, with which the ordinary usage (*sunêtheia*) of his own day sometimes agrees (909.23–910.6).

This preface to *On Uniquely Declined Words* showcases the completeness of grammar's reach and ambition, as guaranteed by *analogia*. It also points to its two main methods: the collection of linguistic phenomena, followed by the association of similar forms, to constitute a rule, and, conversely, the dissociation of dissimilars; and pathology. The series of alterations responsible for any isolated form must then be traced. The result is the 'bringing to a successful conclusion' (*katorthoun*) or the 'setting in order,' 'establishment,' or 'regulation' (*kathistanai*) of the phenomenon under examination by 'bringing it under a rule' (*kanonizesthai*).

These methods are technical grammar's defence against empiricist arguments that simple observation of linguistic phenomena is the only legitimate basis for grammar, and that rules going beyond this are, even if possible, useless. For Apollonius, reason does not conflict with observation, and both are necessary for a science of grammar: he speaks (*synt.* 3.5, 270.10–11) 'not only on the basis of usage [*khrêsis*], but also of demonstration [*apodeixis*],' since grammar should proceed apodictically, according to the objective principles of natural consequence (*phusikê akolouthia*), reason, necessity (*to deon*), and *phusis*.

13.8.4 Linguistic Form and Content

Pathê affect only linguistic expression, the signifier, not its signified content (*adv.* 136.32), so that 'every word, no matter how it has suffered corruption, still has its own particular signification' (*pron.* 67.7). Apollonius structured his treatises on the parts of speech according to this distinction, dividing them (e.g. *adv.* 119.1) into accounts of their 'sense' or 'conception' (*ennoia*) and of the 'shape of the vocal sound' (*skhêma tês phônês*) that they possess. Under 'sense' comes a discussion, first, of the part's name, with a critique of names proposed by others, then of its definition: the name must suit the 'essence' (*ousia*) of the word class, and the *logos* of this essence is the definition. Next are listed the various types in the class (e.g. disjunctive and paradisjunctive conjunctions, different because they signify different things). Finally comes a discussion of syntax, since each part is used in a sentence because of 'its particular sense' (*synt.* 1.39, 35.11), and of whether certain words belong to that part or not. Under the 'shape of the vocal sound,' in contrast, come discussions of word forms and their prosody, especially of dialect forms, and the *pathê* that have resulted in these forms.

The basic Stoic distinction between sound and sense is also at the heart of the opening of the *Syntax*. The construction and the correctness of a spoken sentence depend upon the relations of the unheard intelligibles implicated by the word forms: 'the self-complete sentence comes from the congruence of the intelligibles' (*synt.* 1.2, 3.1–2). Word forms may be used together so long as their subsistent intelligibles accord with one another, are *katallêla*. The nominative second-person pronoun *su* 'you' cannot be added to *paideuô*, for example, because the second-person intelligible subsistent on it conflicts with the first-person intelligible implicit in *paideuô* '(I) teach.' The intelligibles are nowhere enumerated, but they apparently include person, number, gender, presentness and pastness, possession, and transitivity.

We have translated Apollonius' *noêton* as 'intelligible,' which permits a distinction between the corporeal and the incorporeal reminiscent of the Stoic opposition of the *lekton* to bodies; at the same time, we should note that Apollonius assimilates the *lekton* to an *ennoia* or 'conception,' which for the Stoics would be a psychological state, and therefore corporeal. Thus he argues (*adv.* 136.28–32) that the verb *phronô* '(I) am wise, (I) think' cannot have derived from *phrenô* '(I) instruct' by change of 'e' to 'o,' since the *ennoia* of the two verbs was not the same to begin with, and could not have changed along with the vowel: such 'corruptions belong to word forms, not to their senses [*lekta*].' This justification is repeated later (158.15) in different terms: 'items [i.e. word forms] that are complete [*entelê*], even when truncated or diminished, retain their indication [*dêloumenon*], for corruptions are of word forms, not of significations [*sêmainomena*].' Perhaps Apollonius is trying to avoid committing himself to a Stoic, as opposed to, say, Peripatetic idiom; certainly he defines the *logos* in non-Stoic terms as 'a composition of prose diction signifying a self-complete thought [*dianoia*]' (SchDThr 214.3, 354.7; Priscian, *Inst.* 2.53.28; cf. Ammonius' characterization [*in Int.* 64.32] of the self-complete *logos* as 'by itself signifying a perfected thought'). Perhaps he even intended a selective hybrid of theories, like the (admittedly misguided) reconciliation of Stoic and Peripatetic philosophy of language attempted by certain 'others,' who, according to Simplicius (*in Cat.* 9.31–10. 4), claimed that the *Categories* is concerned, not with significant vocal sounds or signified 'things' (*pragmata*), but with 'thoughts' (*noêmata*) or, as Aristotle made clear, 'things said' [*legomena*], which are the same thing, 'and things said and *lekta* are thoughts, which the Stoics also hold.' But Apollonius simply may not have been concerned to make distinctions which belong rather to metaphysics and the philosophy of language than to grammar, as long as *something* can be assumed to remain constant as word forms change.

13.8.5 Syntax

As we have seen (§§13.6.8, 13.6.10), Stoic syntax classified possible or required combinations of predicates with cases or particles (and probably also of particles with cases). Similarly, Apollonius conceives of syntax as the study of possible or required combinations of the noun (or its substitute, the pronoun) and the verb (or its permitted substitutes) with each of the other parts of speech (*synt.* 1.36, 33.9–34.2). His is a syntax of additions and their concord, therefore, not of dependence or rection, and he has no term for e.g. 'subject.'

The discussions that follow Apollonius' introductory pages do not constitute a systematic description, but rather deal on an individual basis with difficult or disputed points, questions (*zêtêmata*), first about the article (1.37–157), then the pronoun (2). The third book opens with a general discussion of 'correct construction' or 'congruence' (*katallêlotês*) and its opposites, *akatallêlotês* and the 'defect' of solecism (3.1–53), it then proceeds to the permissible additions to the verb (3.54–190). The syntax of prepositions is dealt with in what is left of book 4 (13.8.3).

The systematic rationality of language and its demonstration through the method of pathology dictate that the intelligible content of a sentence must always be in good, natural, rational or logical order, even though its spoken or written form may be corrupt. When the structures of utterances having the same content differ, the one better corresponding to the structure of the sense, broadly conceived, is prior and more correct, and helps to constitute the rule from which deviations have been produced by *pathê.* The very congruity of 'transposed' (*huperkeimenôn*) sentences suffers. Thus, while people may well say 'Today you I saw [*sêmeron se etheasamên*],' the original 'necessary fixed order [*hê deousa katastasis*]' (2.77, 183.9–184.7) 'suggests [*hupagoreuei*]' the word order 'Today I saw you [*sêmeron etheasamên se*],' with the adverb applied to the verb and the pronoun in the 'required position' of an enclitic. When Apollonius compares transposed sentences like *ho pais ho deipnêsas koimatai* (lit. 'the child the having-eaten sleeps') with 'more congruent [*katallêlotera*]' sentences such as *ho deipnêsas pais koimatai* (lit. 'the having-eaten child sleeps') (1.113, 95.8–14), he must think there is a principle requiring that the qualifier precede what it qualifies. Similarly, it is not the order in which the antecedent and consequent in a conditional happen to be put together by a speaker that determines the correctness of such a sentence, but rather their 'promise in terms of discursive argument [*têi diexodikêi epangeliai*],' which remains the same through transposition (184.8–14; cf. §13.6.11).

Since the rational order of language is the 'consequential order of nature' (*phusikê akolouthia*), the principle determining correctness may be extralinguistic. For example, congruence may be determined by the fact that cause–effect relations hold only of past events:

> Regarding things in the future, the construction with a causative conjunction could not occur; for causes are adduced for past things. Hence the causal conjunction turns out to be more congruent [*katallêloteros*] when past tenses follow it: after

'because I insulted Theon [*hina hubrisô Theôna*]' we shall not say 'Dion will be angry [*aganaktêsei Diôn*],' but 'he was angry [*êganaktêsen*].' (*synt.* 3.131, 382.7–383.1)

The extralinguistic connection of causation to the past makes the use of past tenses with causative conjunctions 'more congruent.' Apollonius could also have noted that this construction has things in 'their necessary place [*ton deonta topon*]' (*adv.* 126.11). The real-world facts of nature govern the linguistic facts, and the metalinguistic facts too, all being part of the same rational system. For example, Apollonius' discussion of predicates gives an ordering of different 'states' requiring case forms for their expression (3.147–157, 394.7–404.15): activity is expressed by the nominative case, passivity by the oblique cases, and since activity is prior to passivity (3.87, 345.10–13), the active is the first state. Similarly, Apollonius' treatment (*adv.* [*constr.*] 201.1–8) of the spatial adverbs ('where,' 'whither,' 'whence') gives them in an order that he justifies by reflection on the spatial relations they signify, the correct order being determined by the nature of local motion: in a place, to a place, from a place; and the word forms themselves follow this order, since from *pou* 'where' derive *pose* and *pothi* 'whither' and *pothen* 'whence.'

Apollonius' *katallêlotês* therefore clearly goes beyond mere 'congruence' in the usual sense of agreement of word forms in case, number, gender, etc., and even beyond agreement of the underlying intelligibles with one another, as laid down at the beginning of *Syntax*. It comprehends agreement with extralinguistic, real-world regularities, with logical rules, and with the rational rule system of language, and could therefore even be rendered 'regularity.' That is why Apollonius believes he can make the sweeping claims that 'the present investigation of *katallêlotês* will put in order [*katorthôsei*] what is in any way mistaken [*diapesonta*] in discourse' (1.60, 51.11–12), and that 'syntax has been demonstrated for this reason: so that even unnoticed [*lelêthota*] transpositions [*hyperbata*], which exist even in ordinary usage [*to sunêthes*], may keep their hold on rational consistency [*ekhêtai tou akolouthou logou*], and so that one should not assume they are only the exclusive property of poetry' (2.77, 183.14–184.1).[42]

Abbreviations

ApD   Apollonius Dyscolus; *adv.=On Adverbs*; *coni.=On Conjunctions*; *pron.=On Pronouns*; *synt.=On Syntax*
Crat.   *Cratylus* (Plato)

---

[42] Apollonius' texts form vol. II of *Grammatici Graeci*: the 'minor works' are edited, with interpretive commentary, in Schneider (1878). The *Syntax* is in Uhlig (1910); the fragments of lost works are in Schneider (1910). Newer edns, with translation and commentary, are: Lallot (1997), Dalimier (2001), Brandenburg (2005). On Apollonius in general, see Blank (1993). Study of Apollonius' *Syntax* should now begin with Lallot (1997) and its excellent commentary. Apollonius' method is studied in Blank (1982), Sluiter (1990), Allan (2010a); for pathology, see Wackernagel (1876) and Ax (1986) in general, Blank (1982), and Lallot (1995) on Apollonius; see also Atherton (1995, 1996).

DH   Dionysius of Halicarnassus; *Comp.=On Composition*
                  (*De compositione verborum*)
DK   Diels and Kranz (1951) (*Die Fragmente der Vorsokratiker*)
DL   Diogenes Laertius, *Lives of the Eminent Philosophers*
in AnPr   *Commentary on Aristotle's* Prior Analytics (Alexander of
                  Aphrodisias)
in Cat.   *Commentary on Aristotle's* Categories (Simplicius)
in Crat.   *Commentary on Plato's* Cratylus (Proclus)
in Int.   *Commentary on Aristotle's* On Interpretation (Ammonius,
                  Stephanus)
Inst.   *Instruction in the Art of Grammar* (*Institutio de arte grammatica*)
                  (Priscian); *Instruction in Oratory* (*Institutio Oratoria*) (Quintilian)
Int.   *On interpretation* (Aristotle)
LL   *On the Latin Language* (*De lingua Latina*) (Varro)
LS   Long and Sedley (1987)
M   *Against the Mathematicians* (Sextus Empiricus)
PH   *Outlines of Pyrrhonism* (Sextus Empiricus)
PHP   *On the Doctrines of Hippocrates and Plato* (Galen)
QP   *Platonic Questions* (Plutarch)
SchDThr   *Scholia on Dionysius Thrax's* Art of Grammar
Sch. Hom. Il.   *Scholia on Homer's* Iliad (Erbse 1969–88)
S.E.   Sextus Empiricus

CHAPTER 14

PEDAGOGICAL GRAMMARS
BEFORE THE EIGHTEENTH
CENTURY

ANNELI LUHTALA

14.1 INTRODUCTION

FOUR different types of grammars were produced in late antiquity: (1) grammars of the *Schulgrammatik* type, which cover the canonical eight parts of speech in a systematic manner, (2) *regulae* or *kanones*, 'rules,' which explore the formal features of some or all parts of speech, (3) *partitiones*, 'divisions' or parsing grammars, which identify and analyse individual head-words in a sentence, and (4) grammatical commentaries, which accompany the study of the *Schulgrammatik*-type grammar, spelling out the theoretical background of its doctrine. All of these genres are relevant for the development of pedagogical grammar.

The two most famous grammars of the Roman world, Donatus' *Ars minor* and *Ars maior*, belong to the *Schulgrammatik* type. They were studied continuously throughout the Middle Ages, and provided a model for numerous other works well into the early modern period. The more elementary *Ars minor* is a systematic presentation of the eight parts of speech, whereas the more advanced *Ars maior* has two additional sections. One deals with items smaller than the word (sounds, letters, syllables, metrical feet, and prosody), while the other discusses grammatical errors, barbarisms and solecisms, and lists tropes and figures relevant for the study of literature. The study of syntax fell outside the scope of these works, being introduced in Priscian's theoretical *Institutiones grammaticae* (*c*.500 AD).

Donatus' two works failed to provide a definition of grammar, but the standard definition associated grammar with the study of literature: 'Grammar is an art dealing with correct speech and the exposition of authors' (*ars recte loquendi, enarratio poetarum*). This definition is first attested in Quintilian, who depicts the study of grammar as propaedeutic for a higher aim, the study of rhetoric and the Liberal Arts. Isidore of Seville spelled out this wider context of study in his *Etymologiae* by defining grammar as the first of the Liberal Arts and their foundation. The definition of grammar underwent only minor modifications throughout the centuries. Some medieval authors left out its exegetical part, as did also many early modern scholars, who preferred to define grammar simply as 'the art of speaking (well)', *ars (bene) loquendi*.

The *Ars minor* is clearly an elementary work, but its definitions of the parts of speech are the same as those in the more advanced *Ars maior*, as are also their accidental properties. Thus, pedagogical grammars cannot properly be distinguished from works of a more advanced nature, and consequently the distinction between the statuses of the *Ars minor* and *maior* is far from clear. For instance, the letters and syllables, which were definitely the subject matter of elementary grammar, were discussed in the *Ars maior* rather than *minor*. The Middle Ages brought about a more radical break between theoretical and practical grammar, when the latter came to be known as *grammatica positiva* or *practica*. Then many topics of the *Ars maior* were indeed discussed in elementary grammars, such as letters, syllables and the tropes and figures. Moreover, the two levels continued to interact so that the developments in doctrine that took place in theoretical grammar were eventually reflected in pedagogical grammars. A case in point is the theory of syntax, which was initially a theoretical subject but entered pedagogical grammar in the Middle Ages.

14.2 THEORY OF THE NOUN IN DONATUS' *ARS MINOR*

Ancient grammars do not spell out their pedagogical views, which remain to be inferred from the works themselves. The *Ars minor* exhibits the following features that must have contributed to its enormous popularity as a teaching grammar: its orderly nature, rigorous hierarchical structure, conciseness, use of numbers as a memory aid as well as the question-and-answer form. Each part of speech is first defined, and then its various properties (*accidentia*) are treated in a fixed order. These properties include such basic categories as gender, derivation, composition, number, case, tense, person, mood, voice, and conjugation. The three parts of the *Ars maior* adhere to a hierarchical order of treatment from smaller units, letters, and syllables through words to complete expressions, and the work is structured around those four levels, which include neither phrase nor clause. The highest level, that of complete expression, is a literary work, such as Virgil's *Aeneid*.

The *Ars minor* was cast in question-and-answer form, which was in all likelihood an important part of elementary pedagogy. The teacher asked the question and the pupil answered. However, the way in which this method is used by Donatus hardly suggests the beginner's level, because its use presupposes a fair amount of knowledge of grammar in the pupil. Questions such as 'How many properties does the noun have?' cannot be answered by an untrained pupil, nor can he quote the definition of the noun as an answer to the question: 'What is a noun?' Thus, the method of interrogation appears to consist in memorizing something that has already been learnt. I will illustrate Donatus' grammatical theory by his treatment of the noun in the *Ars minor*.

Donatus uses definitions that are based on mixed formal and semantic features. He defines the noun as follows: 'The noun is a part of speech which has case and signifies either a material object (*corpus*) or an abstract thing (*res*), and is either proper or common' (see Holtz 1981: 585, ll. 7–8). He fails to explain the philosophical terms *corpus* and *res*, and it is left for the commentators or the teacher in the classroom to explain that a body is something that can be heard, touched, and seen, whereas an abstract thing can only be grasped by the intellect (cf. Servius *GL* 4: 406, ll. 29–31).[1] Donatus goes on to list the six properties (*accidentia*) of the noun: quality, comparison, gender, number, composition, and case, proceeding to treat their further subdivisions. The most important difference with respect to the theory of the noun in the *Ars maior* is the absence of the twenty-seven subtypes of common nouns, such as patronymical, possessive, generic, and specific nouns, discussed within quality in the *Ars maior*.

Donatus' approach is strikingly concise. For instance, he defines the common noun as 'the name of many individuals,' and the proper noun as 'the name of one individual,' without giving any examples. Some categories, by contrast, are described by simply quoting an example. For instance, the degrees of comparison are meant to be understood from the accompanying examples: 'Degrees of comparison are three: positive, like *doctus*, "knowledgeable," comparative, like *doctior*, "more knowledgeable," and superlative, like *doctissimus*, "most knowledgeable."'

In his discussion on gender, Donatus makes use of the demonstrative pronoun *hic, haec, hoc* as the token of gender: masculine, like *hic magister*, 'this teacher'; feminine, like *haec musa*, 'this muse'; neuter, like *hoc scamnum*, 'this bench'. Donatus also chose to base his account of the noun declension on gender, and he gave the following four paradigms, which exhaust his presentation: *hic magister*, 'this teacher,' *haec musa*, 'this muse,' *hoc scamnum*, 'this bench,' *hic et haec sacerdos*, 'this priest/priestess,' and *hic et haec et hoc felix* 'this happy man/woman/thing.' In the analysis of word structure, Late Latin grammarians did not have distinctly morphological tools available, such as 'root,' 'stem,' 'morpheme,' and 'suffix,' which began to be used only from the sixteenth century on. They simply spoke of adding or dropping 'syllables' or 'speech sounds.' Their method is known as a word and paradigm model. Thus, when Donatus described the forms of an inflecting word class, he chose an example and set out its forms one after the other in inherited order (Law 2003: 131–3).

---

[1] *GL* = *Grammatici latini*, ed. Heinrich Keil. 8 vols (vol. 8 ed. Hermann Hagen), Leipzig: Teubner, 1857–80.

A different pattern of noun declension based on the genitive endings was available in the works of Donatus' contemporaries, e.g. Diomedes (*GL* 1: 303, ll. 12–23). This model was also adopted in Priscian's *Institutio de nomine et pronomine et verbo*, in which an account is given of the formal features of the noun, pronoun, and verb. Noun inflection is described as follows: 'All the nouns which Latin eloquence employs are inflected according to five declensions whose sequence is derived from that of the vowels which form the genitive case. The first declension is thus that of which the genitive ends in the diphthong *ae*, as in *poeta*, genitive *poetae*; the second is that in which the aforesaid case ends in long *i*, as in *doctus*, genitive *docti*; the third ends in short *is*, as in *pater*, genitive *patris*; the fourth in long *us*, as in *senatus*, genitive *senatus*; and the fifth in *ei*, as in *meridies*, genitive *meridiei*' (ed. Passalacqua 1999: 5, transl. Law 2003: 87–8). This model was incorporated into several medieval works, but continued to compete with Donatus' gender-based framework up until the early modern period (Padley 1985: 130).

It is often claimed that the majority of examples in Donatus' works are drawn from Classical literature, and above all from Virgil. However, this is true only of the sections in the *Ars maior* dealing explicitly with literature (the sections on letters, syllables, metrical feet, as well as vices and virtues of speech), whereas its discussion on the parts of speech is practically devoid of literary examples. The *Ars minor* has no connection whatsoever with the study of literature.

14.3 Parsing Grammars

Priscian's *Partitiones duodecim versuum Aeneidos principalium*, 'Analyses of the Twelve First Lines of the *Aeneid*' is a unique example of a pedagogical method known as parsing (derived from the Latin word 'part') surviving from Antiquity. In this work, Priscian examines each word form in the first line of each book of Virgil's *Aeneid* in great detail, by raising a series of questions. In his analysis of the famous first line of the first book, *Arma virumque cano, Troiae qui primus ab oris* 'I sing of arms and a man who left the Trojan shore...', the question-and-answer method proceeds as follows: 'How many parts of speech does the verse contain? Nine. How many nouns? Six: *arma, virum, Troiae, qui, primus, oris*. How many verbs? One: *cano*. How many prepositions? One: *ab*. How many conjunctions? One: *que*' (ed. Passalacqua 1999: 48, ll. 15–19).

Priscian then runs through the properties of each headword, starting with the noun *arma* 'arms.' 'What part of speech? Which species: generic. Which gender: neuter. How do you know? Because all (nouns) which end in 'a' in the plural are no doubt neuter. (...) Which form is it? Simple. Make it a compound: *armiger, armipotens, semermis, inermus*' (ed. Passalacqua 1999: 48, l. 20–49, l. 20). Here the catechetical method is used to examine the knowledge of grammar that the pupil has already gained. The pupil is also encouraged to apply his knowledge to new contexts when he is asked to derive other forms of *arma*. For instance, he is supposed to memorize the final syllables of nouns, which are listed in some *regulae*-type material. This method anticipates principles of medieval derivational lexicography.

The homophonous case forms such as the neuter noun *arma* (which had the same form in the nominative and accusative plural) were a source of ambiguity that drew the ancient grammarians' attention. A replacement test is used in order to resolve this ambiguity:

> What case is it in? In the accusative. How is this certain? From its structure, that is from its ordering and combination with the following words; the verb *cano* is joined to the accusative. Whenever you come across such an instance, replace the neuter noun with a masculine or a feminine word (*cano virum*, 'I sing of a man,' or *cano illam rem*, 'I sing of that thing'), whose accusative case does not coincide with the nominative, and the case form can be identified. (49, l.21–50, l.8)

The method of parsing became popular in the Carolingian Renaissance. Texts of varying length began to appear at the beginning of the ninth century, and specimens of parsing were incorporated into grammatical works, such as the pedagogical grammar of Charlemagne's teacher Peter of Pisa. Two of the best-known texts of this kind are *Dominus quae pars* and *Ianua* from the later Middle Ages (see also Bayless 1993, Black 2001: 34–55, and *Remigius*). This kind of language study was in use until the end of the Middle Ages, and even Despauterius' popular Humanist grammar contains portions of this method (Law 1994: 94–5).

14.4 COMMENTARIES

The conciseness of Donatus' two *artes* must have been one of the keys to their success. However, they were concise to the extent of being incomprehensible in their own right, and as soon as they came into existence their study began to be accompanied by commentary. It now fell upon the commentators to expand Donatus' elliptical statements, explain the background of grammatical phenomena and justify the various hierarchical orders. It would be a mistake to think that commentary was a learned genre, and a platform for developing new ideas. Initially it was a pedagogical genre, as can be seen from the fact that the first Donatus commentary by Servius focused not only on the *Ars maior* but also on the more elementary *Ars minor*. Rather than introduce new doctrine, the ancient commentaries used the material available in the larger treatises like Diomedes' and Charisius' grammars in order to supplement Donatus' exposition.

The emergence of grammatical commentaries in the late fourth century is a puzzling phenomenon with far-reaching consequences. It appears that two textbooks were needed at an elementary level: one that presented the grammatical data in a systematic and memorable form, and another explaining what all these concepts and terms stood for. The attitude of the commentator towards Donatus' text was authoritative, justifying his views, which emerges from the following passage explaining why the parts of speech are discussed in a natural order: 'The noun correctly occupies the first place among the parts of speech, because the knowledge of all things originates in the noun. After the noun must come the pronoun, because it fulfills the function of the noun and cannot be divorced from its meaning. Thereafter comes the verb, because we say that we use it most frequently,' and so forth (Servius *GL* 4: 406, ll. 9–13).

In Late Antiquity, we can ascribe this development to the increasing importance of commentary as a pedagogical method in all fields of learning (Pollman 2009: 259), and, once this genre had established itself, it became a permanent feature of medieval scholarship that needed no justification. Learned commentaries, initially focusing on the *Ars maior*, also arose, such as Pompeius' and, later on, Priscian's massive *Institutiones grammaticae*. In the Middle Ages, commentaries gradually became the platform for developing new ideas.

From Servius on, a large number of teachers devoted themselves to the task of writing commentaries, e.g. Sergius, Cledonius, Pompeius, and Julian of Toledo. This method was used until the end of the Middle Ages, but afterwards declined radically in importance.

14.5 REGULAE

The term *regulae* is the Latin equivalent for the Greek term *kanones*, meaning 'rules, models, patterns, paradigms.' In ancient grammar this term was used in the description of formal patterns only. Grammars focusing on formal features exclusively were called *regulae*-type grammars. Such are, for instance, the grammars of Eutyches, Phocas, and pseudo-Augustine's and pseudo-Remmius' *regulae*, as well as the grammatical section in Martianus Capella's *Nuptiae Mercurii et Philologiae* 'The Marriage of Mercury and Philology.' Grammarians (e.g. Priscian) occasionally integrated portions of *regulae* into their *artes grammaticae*.

These grammars organized their materials according to various principles. Some set out the grammatical data as alphabetically organized reference works. For instance, Phocas lists every ending with which a noun may terminate in the nominative singular—*a, e, o, u, al, el, il, ol, ul,* and so on—and indicates what gender and declension is found with each termination. So if you come across an unfamiliar noun ending in 'a', this reference work will show you that it could belong to a masculine or a feminine noun of the first declension, or alternatively to a neuter noun of the third declension (Law 2003: 85).

14.6 FOUR KINDS OF SYNTAX

Ancient pedagogical grammars did not have a section on syntax, and they generally failed to explain what kind of a wider unit or 'speech' (*oratio*) the parts of speech (*partes orationis*) are parts of. It can be inferred, however, that there were at least three ways in which the ancient grammarians understood this wider unit: in terms of a literary work, like Virgil's *Aeneid*; in terms of a rhetorical composition consisting of *cola* and *commata*, like Cicero's speeches (Diomedes *GL* 1: 464, ll. 25f.); and in terms of simple sentences, comparable to the philosopher's logical proposition. It is this third kind of unit, introduced in the last two books of Priscian's *Institutiones*, that came to constitute the basis of the syntactical theory in our traditional grammars.

The point of departure for Priscian's syntactical description is the simple sentence (*oratio*), which expresses a complete thought, and is self-sufficient in that it can be understood without any other elements. The definition of sentence put forward by Priscian runs as follows: 'A sentence (*oratio*) is a congruent construction signifying a perfect meaning.' This kind of sentence consisted of at least a noun and a verb, e.g. *Socrates ambulat*, 'Socrates is walking,' or additionally involved another noun in the oblique case, as in *Socrates percutit Platonem*, 'Socrates is striking Plato.' These sentences were known as intransitive and transitive respectively. When described in terms of transitivity, a sentence expresses an action that passes over from the agent to the patient. Two additional tools entered into their description, namely concord (which takes place when the constituents refer to the same referent) and government (which involves different referents). The functional notions of subject and predicate are absent from this framework, which reminds us of dependency rather than constituency grammar.

The ancient theory of syntax was exhausted by the description of simple sentences, but it was not such minimal units of speech that the medieval pupils encountered in their study of Latin prose texts. On the contrary, they had to tackle very long sentences involving odd word orders and heavy rhetorical constructions for which the inherited works offered no tools of analysis. The medieval annotated manuscripts attest to the existence of various construe marks to facilitate the interpretation of complicated Latin prose texts. Various combinations of dots and strokes were used to indicate grammatical relationships, linking the adjective with the modified noun, the verb with its object, and so on. Another method was to rearrange the word order using letters of the alphabet to indicate a simplified word order. Two sophisticated treatises were dedicated to word order in the ninth century, which shows that the Carolingians' concern with construing Latin sentences goes beyond the stimulus given by the inherited works. Both treatises posit a SVO order for the simple sentence, and go on to expand this structure with various optional elements. In the absence of grammatical tools of analysis, one of the treatises, entitled *Quomodo VII circumstantiae rerum in legendo ordinande sint*, 'How the seven circumstances of things are to be ordered in reading' (see Grotans and Porter 1995), presses into service the rhetorician's argumentative *loci*, the seven circumstances, which serve to identify the various constituents of a sentence by asking a series of questions: 'Who? What? Where? Why? When? How? With what means?' The other treatise, edited by Thurot (1868: 87–8), also takes into account compound sentences and shows understanding of embedded constructions.

In these medieval treatises 'construction' came to be used in a new sense, in terms of techniques of construing Latin sentences. These techniques could be used in analysing an existing literary work or the Bible, or alternatively, they might help the pupil to produce a Latin sentence on his own, or to translate a Latin sentence into the vernacular. A section on this kind of construing was integrated into several medieval works, e.g. the *Doctrinale* (see §14.8). John Leylond's grammatical treatises include a short text entitled *Informacio*, which teaches how to translate a Latin sentence into English (Law 2003: 197). A short treatise, *Ordo constructibilium cum suis regulis*, is also included in the *Remigius*, a compilation of various grammatical texts from the end of the fifteenth century, printed in facsimile edition (Remigius 1982: 32–3). These texts circulated widely in the fifteenth century, and were printed in Lily and Colet's and Melanchthon's grammars, for instance. A concern with word order remained a permanent feature of medieval syntactical analysis.

14.7 MEDIEVAL PRACTICAL GRAMMAR

Medieval grammar was genre-based, and all the ancient grammatical genres found continuity in the Middle Ages. Donatus became the unrivalled authority for elementary grammar, Priscian for the more theoretical language study, and commentaries continued to be written on all levels of teaching. Some ancient, very short *artes* similar in length to Donatus enjoyed a brief popularity in the Carolingian Renaissance, but soon fell into disuse. Such include the grammars of Asper and Dositheus and Augustine's *Ars breviata*; only Maximus Victorinus' short grammar was widely used. Of the *regulae* grammars, those of Eutyches and Phocas continued to interest students, and became the focus of commentary themselves. The comprehensive grammars of Diomedes, Charisius, and Consentius, which contained much material not present in Donatus, enjoyed considerable popularity. Priscian's minor work *Institutio de nomine, de pronomine, de verbo* was universally known by the end of the seventh century, as was also Isidore's *Etymologiae* (636), which expanded the structure of Donatus' *Ars maior* with a large number of topics, e.g. orthography, analogy, etymology, glosses and *differentiae* (for Isidore, see Allan 2010a: 132–5).

The concerns of the grammarians of the first medieval centuries (600–800) were primarily pedagogical. Confronted with the challenge of infusing a knowledge of Latin into the Christianizing Western Europe, the grammarians took to transforming the inherited works so as to conform to the new requirements of language teaching. The literacy needs of the nations recently converted to Christianity were not satisfied by any of the late antique grammars designed for native speakers of Latin. Their most obvious shortcoming was the poor coverage of Latin morphology, which Donatus' pupils already commanded. Donatus offered the minimum of morphological paradigms, and medieval scholars began to compile their own descriptive grammars, based on the framework of one of Donatus' works, which they supplemented with a large amount of illustrative material. These developments are primarily associated with the British Isles, and the teaching grammars composed in insular circles are known as 'Insular grammars.' Many of these grammars, e.g. those of Tatwine (734) and Boniface (754), replaced Donatus' gender-based account of nominal inflection by the framework of Priscian's brief *Institutio*.

Collections of paradigms also began to circulate separately. Such texts, known as *Declinationes nominum, pronominum* or *Coniugationes verborum*, began to proliferate from the end of the seventh century. These paradigms included ecclesiastical vocabulary and Greek names, for instance, and the organizing principle in the presentation of nominal inflection was more often Priscian's declension than Donatus' gender. Alcuin's teacher, Peter of Pisa (*fl. c.776*), integrated an entire *Declinationes pronominum* tract into his *ars*. His descriptive grammar offered paradigms of sixteen nouns, twenty-seven pronouns, and four verbs. (By way of curiosity, it is worth mentioning that Peter became famous for coining an extraordinarily long word, *honorificabilitudinitas*, which he declined in all cases in his grammar.) Peter cast his grammar in question-and-answer format, which was popular with Carolingian masters. Alcuin developed this method towards a philosophical dialogue in his *Dialogus Saxonis et Franconis de octo partibus orationis*, whereby two pupils are conversing about elementary grammar. The teacher intervenes, encouraging the pupils to aim at a more advanced knowledge of things, which comes either from Priscian's *Institutiones* or from manuals of dialectic.

Donatus had the advantage of being the teacher of St Jerome, the translator of the Bible into Latin, which served to recommend his work to medieval students of grammar. The skills taught by the grammarian were vital for a Christian, who had to gain access to the sacred texts of his religion through the medium of Latin, and for a scribe, who wanted to transmit the precious texts to the following generations in as uncontaminated a form as possible. Medieval authors were faced with the problem of to what extent they ought to Christianize their grammar books, designed to accompany the study of Classical literature, and many early medieval treatises witness to efforts to Christianize grammar by replacing Donatus' examples with Christian ones. It is believed that a Christian version of the *Ars minor* was widely known during the pre-Carolingian era, although no copy of it has survived. Asper (*c.600*) is one of those who probably exploited such a grammar. He replaced Donatus' examples for proper (*Roma, Tiber*) and common nouns (*urbs, flumen*) with Christian ones: 'Michael, Peter, Stephen, Isaiah, Aaron, Ezechiel, angel, martyr, prophet, priest, king.' However, the conversion of grammar did not normally go beyond a partial substitution of the traditional examples for Christian ones, one notable exception being Smaragdus, who introduced some 750 Christian examples into his exegetical grammar. But many early medieval grammars failed to use Christian examples altogether (see Luhtala 2000b).

In the central Middle Ages (800–1100) the grammarians focused on writing commentaries, primarily on the grammars of Donatus, but later on several other ancient grammars as well. Among the most important are the works of Murethach (*c.*840), Sedulius Scottus (mid-ninth century), and Remigius of Auxerre (*c.*900). In the Carolingian renaissance, the study of Priscian's *Institutiones grammaticae* was revived, and this massive work became an object of commentary, which initially took the form of glossing but was later pursued in independent commentaries. Its study was always associated with dialectic, and the philosophical trend was reinforced during the following centuries. The term *grammatica positiva* or *practica* was introduced in the mid-thirteenth century to distinguish the traditional grammar (known until then simply as *grammatica*) from the philosophical (*theorica*), and the proponents of philosophical grammar occasionally even introduced new definitions of grammar.

Thus, from the ninth century onwards, there were two sufficiently distinct levels in the study of grammar, one based on Donatus and the other on Priscian. Alexander of Villa Dei intended his popular verse grammar to be studied at an intermediate level, after pupils had studied the *Ars minor*, but before they went on to study Priscian's *Institutiones Grammaticae*. However, the elementary level no longer covered only the topics of the *Ars minor* but also some of the *Ars maior*. Medieval grammar was divided into four parts, which reflect the structure of the *Ars maior*. The first part, *orthographia*, discusses letters and syllables, which are treated in the first part of the *Ars maior*, while the topics of the *prosodia* (metrical feet, accents and punctuation marks) come from its third part. *Ethimologia* is a traditional treatment of the parts of speech and their morphological properties, and *diasintastica* contains a major novelty in a pedagogical grammar, a syntactical theory, which leans heavily on Priscian.

In the High Middle Ages, the *Donatus minor* began to receive glosses in the vernacular languages, which suggests that the medieval teachers began to appreciate the role that the vernacular could play in the study of Latin (Law 2003: 196–7). Glossing of grammatical terminology gradually expanded into translations of entire passages, giving rise to a new kind of bilingual textbook. A continuous tradition of such bilingual textbooks established itself in the early fifteenth century (Ising 1970: 29–31). Donatus' *Ars minor* became so popular that the name 'Donatus' became a synonym for 'elementary textbook' (see Chase 1926). For instance, the Italian Paolo Camaldolese decided to name his grammar *Donatus* (*c.*1180), although it uses Priscian's definitions of the parts of speech and makes heavy use of the parsing method, but follows Donatus' order of the parts of speech.

Many medieval grammarians focused their attention upon lexicography and etymology. Papias (*fl.* 1040–1060) is the author of the first fully recognizable dictionary, the monolingual (Latin–Latin) dictionary *Elementarium*. Hugutio of Pisa (1130/1140–1210) dealt famously with etymologies in his *Derivationes*, and John of Garland is the author of *Synonyma*, *Aequivoca*, and a *Dictionarius* (after 1272), while John of Genoa's *Catholicon* (1286) contains an etymological dictionary of Latin, organized alphabetically. Lexicography grew in importance, and lexical meanings, such as possessive, derivative, and patronymical nouns, began to be regarded as belonging to the province of dictionaries rather than grammar during the early modern period (Padley 1985: 24).

14.8 GRAMMARS IN VERSE

Several verse grammars were produced in the Middle Ages, the most famous of which were Alexander of Villa Dei's *Doctrinale* (1199) and Edvard of Bethune's *Graecismus* (1212). These works were not self-contained treatises that can be understood on their own; they were rather designed to supplement the study of Donatus. The *Doctrinale* concentrated on such lexical and morphological features as were absent from the *Ars minor*: it adds Priscian's model of noun declensions, for instance, and teaches how to form the comparative and superlative. It also deals with syntax, which was absent from the *Donatus minor*, as well as the figures of speech, which traditionally belonged to the *Ars maior*. The *Graecismus* discusses figures of speech first, then prosody, orthography, etymology, and finally syntax. These works immediately became very popular. The *Doctrinale* has survived in over 400 manuscripts (and received more than 300 editions between 1470 and 1520), while the *Graecismus* was copied in over 200 manuscripts, but has only some twenty editions (Grondeux 2000: 600). Full-scale verse grammars were also produced; Henry of Avranches versified the entire *Ars minor* and wrote a few grammars of his own in verse, and John of Garland is the author of two extremely long versified grammars (Law 2003: 182–7).

It will be shown below that the verse form, though obviously a good memory aid, was not pedagogically unproblematical. The *Doctrinale* is not easy to follow, and not surprisingly, it soon became the object of commentary, the most famous tradition being known as *Admirantes* (see Thurot 1868: 33). As a matter of fact, medieval pedagogy is quite complex. In order to master the *Doctrinale*, one presumably had to learn three or four separate works: *Donatus minor* with a commentary, and the *Doctrinale* plus a commentary. On the more advanced level, the study of Priscian's *Institutiones* also involved reading a commentary. It is actually easy to understand that the traditional ways of teaching the trivium were found heavy, and that a conflict arose with newer ways of learning in the High Middle Ages (for this conflict, see Copeland and Sluiter 2009: 706–23).

14.9 SYNTAX IN PEDAGOGICAL GRAMMARS

Medieval scholars made significant contributions to the study of syntax, which began to interest them as soon as Priscian's *Institutiones* became widely available. In the mid-ninth century an anonymous Priscian commentator introduced the subject/predicate distinction into his copy of the *Institutiones*, using the vocabulary of Martianus Capella's *De dialectica*, *subiectivum* and *declarativum* (Paris, Bibliothèque Nationale, Ms. lat 7505, f. 26r, Luhtala 2000a: 168). However, we must wait until the twelfth century to find a treatment of syntax integrated into a pedagogical grammar. Such is Hugh of St Victor's *De grammatica* (*c.*1120). Among the first teaching grammars to employ the subject/predicate distinction were the *Doctrinale* and Pietro da Isolella's *Summa* (Fierville 1886) in the 1250s. Here and there early modern scholars, such as Despauterius (*c.*1460–1520) and Gerard Vossius (1577–1649), integrated this distinction into their works, but it was not until the late eighteenth century that the terms 'subject' and 'predicate' were assimilated into the mainstream grammatical tradition (Law 2003: 168).

The structure of Hugh's work is based on Donatus' *Ars maior* and Isidore's *Etymologiae*, and the syntactical section represents Priscian's doctrine, updated with some medieval innovations. Hugh starts by quoting Priscian's definition of sentence, and proceeds to give an account of the simple sentence, exploiting the key notions of Priscian's theory, concord, government, and transitivity. He also integrates into his syntax the substantival verb, marginal in Priscian's theory. Hugh's approach reflects the importance assigned to the verb *esse* in contemporary grammatico-philosophical speculation.

Hugh's theory of transitivity echoes recent developments by analysing a transitive sentence into two constructions. 'Every construction is completed by means of *transitio* and *intransitio*,' he argues. The first *intransitio* is between the noun in the nominative case and the verb, and the second is the *transitio* between the verb and the oblique noun. Thus, a sentence *Socrates percutit Platonem*, 'Socrates is striking Plato' consists of two constructions, *intransitio* (*Socrates percutit*) and *transitio* (*percutit Platonem*). This analysis also involves a typically medieval concern with the position of the elements before or after the verb.

Priscian had discussed complete sentences in terms of transitivity, whereas the medieval theory splits the transitive sentence into two constructions, thus dealing not only with sentences but even phrases. Indeed, the emphasis has moved from the simple sentence to its parts to the extent that transitivity now also applies to nominal constructions that do not involve a verb at all. The criterion used is whether or not the constituents pertain to the same referent. Hugh concludes his syntactical section by dealing with the various relations of government that the verbs have with the oblique cases, listing them by their semantic or syntactic force: possession, acquisition, transitivity, effect of the material cause, and so on, which became the standard way of organizing syntactical doctrine.

The syntactical doctrine that was incorporated into a verse grammar a few decades later is much more obscure. The *Doctrinale* starts the syntactical section by discussing the government (*regimen*) as follows:

The order [of treatment] demands that the government of words is to be treated. *Intransitio* demands that the nominative is the subject of the verb. You should understand that this concerns personal verbs. The vocative verb often wants to have a nominative case in the predicate position after it just like the substantive verb or other verbs with the same force. [Words] of this kind must be joined by a copula, when they pertain to the same person.

The passage fails to define any of the technical terms used. Their absence is all the more remarkable, as the *Donatus minor* has no syntactical section at all. Moreover, it lacks examples altogether. No doubt this passage was expected, to be rewritten by a commentator in prose, and that is what actually happened.

Having discussed the government of the nominative, the *Doctrinale* goes on to deal with the government of the oblique cases. It is only at the beginning of the next chapter that a general statement is made concerning construction: it consists of *transitio* and *intransitio*. The traditional point of departure, the formation of a simple sentence, is obscured in this account to the extent that the notion of sentence is absent from the syntactical section altogether; the closest the *Doctrinale* comes is 'a complete construction.' The much shorter treatment of syntax in the *Graecismus* similarly lacks the notion of sentence.

14.10 VISUAL AIDS

Grammatical texts were normally copied out continuously, without subtitles, and paradigms were written without any visual distinction from the surrounding text. Medieval readers introduced various aids to create a more memorable structure for grammatical works, especially Priscian's massive *Institutiones*, by writing paragraphs explaining the contents of each section, by numbering sections, or by drawing tree diagrams in the margins. Diagrams and tables gradually came to play an important part in the presentation of grammatical doctrine when a more definite shift towards the visual and material took place in the early modern period, and a tendency arose to consider both real world phenomena and the world of thought in terms of spatial models. Some pedagogical treatises made explicit statements to the effect that children learn more easily through the eye than through the ear (Padley 1985: 119), and grammar lent itself easily to being illustrated by means of dichotomies and other divisions. A Czech scholar, Comenius, wrote the first children's picture book, *Orbis pictus*, 'World in pictures' (*c*.1658), and the Englishman Mark Lewis taught children 'to look upon words as pictures' in his treatise *An Essay to Facilitate the Education of Youth, by Bringing Down the Rudiments of Grammar to the sense of Seeing* (*c*.1671). He further maintained that in learning 'progress is natural from the senses to the understanding, and from thence to the memory' (quoted by Padley 1985: 176–7).

From the thirteenth century onwards, syntactical doctrine was also discussed in several grammars compiled in Italy, such as Bene da Firenze's *Summa* (between 1218 and 1242), Pietro da Isolella's *Summa*, Sion or Simon da Vercelli's *Novum Doctrinale* (between 1244 and 1268), Tebaldo's *Regule* (between 1212 and 1250), Giovanni da Pigna's *Summa* (between 1237 and 1258), and the *Regule* of Francesco da Buti (between 1355 and 1378). (See Percival 1975: 233 and Black 2001: 92–6.)

14.11 TWO SPECIMENS OF HUMANIST GRAMMARS

Many ancient methods of pedagogy were still in use in early modern Europe, and ancient grammars continued to be a major source of inspiration for the Humanist grammarians, whose general aim was to restore the classical past. They rediscovered several works that had not been widely accessible in the Middle Ages—Varro, Diomedes, Servius, Sergius, and the *regulae* grammars of Phocas, Eutyches, pseudo-Palaemon, and pseudo-Augustine—and set out to study Donatus and Priscian in their authentic form, purged of the barbarities of scholasticism. Although they condemned the medieval innovations loudly, many medieval traits nevertheless survived in their grammars. The sixteenth-century authors, moreover, soon realized that the ancient grammars were no longer suited for their pedagogical needs, and took to compiling their own grammars. This situation is reflected upon in the prologue to the elementary grammar of the Bavarian theologian Johannes Cochleus (1479–1552), as follows:

> It may well seem superfluous to add a new grammar to the vast number by other people already in existence, with still further variations on the rules of one and the same art. But in fact anyone who gives careful consideration to the lot of German youth will realize that there is nothing available to facilitate and accelerate their studies. It is true that our teenagers are steeped in Alexander [of Villa Dei]'s short little verses from earliest childhood, but they are clumsy, both lacunose and repetitive, and encumbered with mile-long glosses. If you give them Priscian instead, you will find out that he is far too verbose and so cannot be had for a reasonable price. [...] Diomedes is a good deal more concise, but is quite difficult, and is too advanced. If you opt for Phocas, Caper or Donatus, you will find that they are too short. (Transl. Law 2003: 229)

I will conclude this chapter by introducing two very popular Latin grammars, which serve to illustrate some of the most salient new developments in the sixteenth century. One is Lily and Colet's *Short Introduction of Grammar* (1549), the official Latin grammar of England from the 1540s, and the other the German Philipp Melanchthon's *Grammatica latina* (1550), which became very influential in Protestant Europe. Lily and Colet's grammar is very short indeed (*c.*50 pages), while Melanchthon's work amounts to 400 pages in one of its revised editions. Both of them were designed to be self-contained and no longer needed to be studied with a commentary.

Both grammars first divide the parts of speech into declinable and indeclinable, which was a common practice in sixteenth-century grammars. They also exhibit a drift towards purely semantic definitions, and make use of formal marks in the definitions, which draw upon the pupil's knowledge of his mother tongue. These tokens provide the pupils with a ready means of identifying the parts of speech, and became very popular in later works. All the semantic subcategories of common nouns except the adjective are absent, together with the subcategory of 'quality' within which these properties were discussed by Donatus. This represents a general development of simplification; these subcategories were now understood as lexical properties that belonged to dictionaries rather than grammars. The adjective continued to be regarded as a subtype of the common noun, but in the later Middle Ages (*nomen*) *adiectivum* had largely come to stand on its own, being opposed to (*nomen*) *substantivum*. In some seventeenth-century grammars (e.g. in Mark Lewis's *Essay*), the further step was taken to regard it as a separate part of speech.

14.11.1 Lily and Colet's Latin Grammar in English

The definition of the noun in Lily and Colet's grammars is purely semantic: the noun is 'the name of a thing (*res*) that may be seen, felt, heard or understood.' Donatus' distinction between *corpus* and *res* is replaced by *res*, which is understood in a broad sense, and is now explained by the grammarian himself rather than a commentator. The authors divide nouns into substantives and adjectives, and substantives further into common and proper. They are defined in the traditional manner, and the examples continue to be joined to the demonstrative pronoun, as in *hic magister* and *hic, haec et hoc felix*. The examples are regularly translated into English.

Snippets of syntactical doctrine enter into the description of the parts of speech, and questions are asked to help identify the syntactical roles of cases, as follows: 'The nominative comes before the verb, answering the question "Who?" or "What?" as *Magister docet*, "The master teaches."' Moreover, English prepositions are used as tokens in describing the nominal cases: 'The genitive case is known by this token "of" and answers the question "Whose?" or "Whereof?", e.g., *doctrina magistri*, the learning of the master.' Like the *Doctrinale*, this work teaches how to form the comparative: 'The comparative is formed from the first case of the positive ending in *i*, by adding to it *or* or *us*, e.g. from *durus*: *duri*, *hic* and *haec durior* and *hoc durius*. Or from *tristis*: *tristi*, *hic* and *haec tristior* and *hoc tristius*.'

The section on syntax deals with two aspects of construction: one of a more traditional kind, based on congruence and government, and the other more practical, designed to provide an aid for translating an English text into Latin. In the practical account of sentence construction, the pupil is advised to look first for the principal verb. Having found it, the pupil is told to ask the question 'Who?' or 'What?' and the word answering the question will be the nominative case of the verb. This nominative is placed before the verb in Latin, the authors explain, except in questions and commands. The case form that comes after the verb and answers the questions 'Whom?' or 'What?' is normally the accusative case, although the verb can also govern other cases.

The traditional account of syntax is based on congruence and government, and the section on government treats the construction of each part of speech in turn. The discussion consists of lists of individual rules, often described semantically, and word order continues to play a prominent part in syntactical theory. Tokens are used, for instance, in describing the construction of the verb with the dative case: all kinds of verbs that are acquisitive and occur with the tokens *to* or *for* after them will have a dative case, as *non omnibus dormio*, 'I sleep not to all men' (thus in Lily and Colet). *Huic habeo, non tibi*, 'I have it for this man, and not for you.' Here and there the terms transitive and intransitive occur, but transitivity does not belong to the core of syntactical analysis in this grammar. The central concepts, such as concord or government, are not defined, and the focus on the individual parts of speech has obscured the basis of syntactical description to the extent that the definition of sentence is absent. Most tools of analysis, such as congruence, referentiality, transitivity, and government go back to antiquity, but the emphasis on word order is medieval, and the use of tokens is a recent development. The subject/predicate distinction is not used in this treatise.

The seventeen pages dedicated to syntax in Lily and Colet's grammar give a fairly good account of Latin construction, although by way of simplification some principles of the syntactical analysis have become blurred. Compilers of elementary grammars tended to avoid giving definitions, which they probably regarded as too abstract to be useful for their pupils. They also aimed at brevity, which often resulted in infelicities. Since writing commentaries was no longer a regular enterprise, the background information became marginal, and the 'Why?' questions no longer find answers in this textbook, which fails to give any justifications for such orders, as 'the first person is worthier than the second and the second worthier than the third' and 'the masculine gender is worthier than the feminine.' They are left to be provided orally by the teacher in the classroom.

14.11.2 Melanchthon's *Grammatica Latina* (1661)

Melanchthon (born Philipp Schwartzerdt, 1497–1560) wrote a Latin grammar, *Grammatica latina*, which appeared in 248 editions between 1525 and 1757. I will be using the one published in 1661. This comprehensive grammar, which is cast in a question-and-answer form, is more methodical than Lily and Colet's in that it defines the central principles of syntactical theory, such as the sentence, congruence, and government, as well as the art of grammar itself. Melanchthon divided grammar into the four medieval parts, orthography, prosody, etymology, and syntax. He simplified the grammatical exposition by dealing with the accidents of the parts of speech once and for all at the outset rather than repeatedly in the treatment of the individual parts (1661: 10–12). The accidents are divided into the most general ones (*generalissima*), valid for several or all parts of speech, such as *species* and *figura*, special ones (*specialiores*), pertaining only to the declinable parts, such as number and person, and the most special ones (*specialissima*), concerning only a few parts, such as gender and genus in the verb, noun declension, mood, conjugation, and tense. This is how Melanchthon introduces composition (*figura*) as a most general kind of accident: 'How many forms do words have? Two: simple, which cannot be divided into smaller significant parts, e.g. *doctus, ego, legens, raro, abs, nam*, and compound, which can be divided into significant parts, e.g. *indoctus, egomet, perlego, perlegens, peraro, absque, namque*.'

The noun is defined semantically, as 'a part of speech signifying a thing, not action and undergoing of action' (1661: 12–13), and only the special accidents, gender and case, are discussed in the noun section. The noun can be recognized from the German words *ein, der, die, das*. The category of noun is then divided into substantives and adjectives, and the substantive is that to which you cannot add *Mann, Weib, Ding* in German, e.g. *homo, equus*, and its meaning can be understood on its own. The adjective is defined as that to which you can add *Mann, Weib, Ding* in German. In the definition of person, he uses German pronouns as tokens: 'What is person? It is the demonstration of the signified thing subject to order, which takes place in German by means of *ich, du, er, sie, ihr, sie*.'

Syntax is defined as the part of grammar that teaches the theory of combining words or forming a sentence (1661: 239). Unlike Lily and Colet, Melanchthon offers a definition of the sentence and its obligatory constituents. He also states the general principles of construction by first dividing syntax into two parts, transitive and intransitive, identifying them as the domains of congruence and government respectively. 'What is intransitive syntax? It is the case when the words of which the sentence consists pertain to the same person, as *vir bonus, tu es Petrus*. It is also called the syntax of congruence. What is transitive syntax? It is when the words, of which the sentence consists, pertain to different persons. It is also called syntax of government' (p. 240). Then follow the syntactical rules, based on each part of speech, as in Lily and Colet, but Melanchthon's account is more detailed and methodical.

14.12 CONCLUDING REMARKS

The doctrine of pedagogical grammars changed very little in the course of the centuries, and novelties often had to do with the organization of inherited doctrine rather than the doctrine itself. This is the case when the accidents of grammatical categories came to be discussed once and for all at the outset, as in Melanchthon's grammar. Sometimes a novelty is a question of a new emphasis, as when the adjective steadily gained prominence and eventually established itself as a distinct part of speech, but continued to be defined in somewhat traditional ways. In spite of the fact that the development of pedagogical grammar is largely a story of continuities, there are also striking discontinuities. Such is the case when the subject/predicate distinction is first introduced into grammar in the ninth century, but it takes almost 1,000 years for it to establish itself in the mainstream grammar. A major novelty is the integration of syntax into pedagogical grammars, and the concern with practical techniques of construing sentences.

It emerges from the above survey that writing a pedagogical grammar was far from an easy task. A pedagogically oriented grammar ideally gave a skeleton of doctrine in a memorable form suited for learning by rote, but conciseness is a mixed blessing: simplifying the doctrine and dismissing definitions resulted in infelicities for the theory, as is the case when the notion of sentence is blurred in the treatments of syntax in pedagogical grammars. Moreover, the pupil ought to have the background information one way or another. Until the early modern period, this information was provided by the commentator, but this kind of pedagogy could become heavy too. A self-contained grammar that includes all the relevant information is inevitably a long grammar, such as Melanchthon's, but very short grammars such as Donatus' *Ars minor* and Lily and Colet's *Short Introduction* managed to be extremely popular. Since the students did not have textbooks of their own, considerable information was left to be given by the teacher in the classroom. Many aspects of ancient and medieval grammar teaching thus remain something of a mystery to us.

CHAPTER 15

VERNACULARS AND THE IDEA OF A STANDARD LANGUAGE

ANDREW LINN

15.1 IDEAS

> The greatest and most important phenomenon of the evolution of language in historic times has been the springing up of the great national common languages— Greek, French, English, German, etc.—the 'standard' languages.

So wrote Otto Jespersen (1946: 39), and the idea of a standard language has undoubtedly been one of the most seductive in the history of European linguistic thought. It has resulted in some of the most heated of debates on language matters, drawing in both academic and non-academic actors, and ranging from the learned *Questione della Lingua* in Italy around the turn of the sixteenth century (see below; also Engler 1993, Vitale 1960) to nineteenth-century debates on how best to standardise a newly independent Norwegian (Haugen 1966, Linn 1997), to the ongoing and often passionate discussions in homes and in bars throughout the modern world about 'right' and 'wrong' usage. The notion of a standard language has underpinned language teaching and learning since the Middle Ages, based as language teaching is on the acceptance that there is a right form of a language and a wrong form. The belief in a standard has motivated much of the grammar and dictionary writing, and has also been a central ideology in the emergence and reinforcement of the modern European nations. In the period following the Renaissance, national pride was expressed through the notion that the European vernaculars were as rich and as ordered as the Classical languages. Under the influence of Romanticism this idea of the richness of the 'national common languages' was increasingly linked to a sense of there being some sort of natural relationship between a people and their language, and indeed the perceived link between language and nation, for better or for worse, remains a strong one (cf. Wright 2000).

The key word in the title of this chapter is 'idea.' As Milroy and Milroy (1991: 23) put it, it is most appropriate to speak of 'a standard language as an idea in the mind rather than a reality—a set of abstract norms to which actual usage may conform to a greater or lesser extent.' A standard form by its very definition denies variation, striking an artificial line between forms in actual use when a language is spoken. A standard language does not exist in isolation from the processes which have brought it into being or the values which drive those processes. Standard languages, language standards, and the process of standardization have been subject to much theoretical scrutiny over the past 50 years. Until the rise of sociolinguistics, and specifically the work of Uriel Weinreich (Joseph 1987: 14) and Einar Haugen, standard languages had been largely treated as cultural givens, possessing the easy self-confidence of the big nineteenth-century dictionaries (the *Duden*, the *Littré*, the *OED*, etc.) and the cultural elites associated with them. Sociolinguistic analysis soon demonstrated that the standard languages were not cultural monoliths, there in perpetuity, but rather were the result of *processes* carried out by people intervening in the natural development of languages, of standardization, and, more than that, the standard languages served to perpetuate traditional and often outmoded social structures. The European elite classes had determined that their own usage was the most desirable and that it should therefore constitute the standard to which all should aspire, and the educational system throughout Europe conspired to reinforce the status quo by sanctioning the language of the elite as correct and other usage as incorrect or substandard. The political ideologies inherent in the idea of a standard language have been thoroughly investigated (e.g. Crowley 1991, 2003; Sledd 1986), at least for English, and it is no longer possible to be as triumphalist about the creation of standard languages as Jespersen was able to be in the 1940s. Joseph (1987: 43) sums up more recent thinking thus:

> The interaction of power, language and reflections on language, inextricably bound up with one another in human history, largely defines language standardization.

What is involved in standardisation as a generalizable phenomenon of language? Although only a handful of the languages of the world have undergone standardization (and Bailey 1986 maintains that English is not amongst them), the process of standardization has been theorised quite extensively. In 1963 Ray wrote that 'the operation of standardization consists basically of two steps, firstly, the creation of a model for imitation, and secondly, promotion of this model over rival models' (Ray 1963: 70). The first theory of language standardization, and (despite avowed limitations) the most productive, was however Haugen's (1959) four-stage process, involving successive stages of (1) norm selection, (2) norm codification, (3) norm implementation, and (4) norm elaboration. It has remained a helpful view of the process by which a language is transferred from existing in a series of dialects to having one or more formally agreed and codified written forms, and indeed Deumert and Vandenbussche, for example,

(2003) and Lodge (1993) base their analyses of the standardization of a range of languages on this model. The idea of a standard language is culturally very much a European one (Joseph 1987: x), but the challenge of creating a standard in the twentieth century migrated beyond the established nations of Europe to parts of the world where debates about language as 'capital' (Bourdieu 1990) or the ideologization of language (cf. Blommaert 1999) are very much secondary to practical language planning (Le Page 1963). During the past decades much has been written about *norms* in language (e.g. Bartsch 1987; the papers in Bédard and Maurais 1983; Omdal and Røsstad 2009), and since Haugen coined the term 'language planning,' the study of the process of intervention in and nurturing of language according to political and cultural ideology has developed into a subdiscipline all of its own (Language Policy and Language Planning). In this chapter we are concerned with such intervention in the past, the development of the idea that there is such a thing as a standard language and that it is something to aspire to. We cannot do this without first being aware of the view of twenty-first-century linguistics on the topic: that there is on the contrary no such immutable thing as a standard language and indeed that it is *not* something to aspire to. Without losing sight of this view, though, we now need to move back into European history and to look at the development of these ideas which, only in the course of the past half-century, have been so radically deconstructed.

While the idea of a standard language and the belief in language standards (norms of acceptability) may be social constructs, a *vernacular language* is something rather less culturally conditioned. In the context of this chapter, the vernacular languages are to be understood as those languages (and their later developments) which were spoken natively in medieval and Renaissance Europe, and which were felt by their speakers to be different from Latin. Latin was the language of education, of scholarship, of government and of religion, but the language of the home and the private space was something else; it has been suggested that Latin and those local spoken languages were in a diglossic relationship with one another (Fishman 1967a). For different reasons and at differing rates, the local languages began to be afforded a degree of prestige (high status in terms of diglossic relationships), and with prestige came a sense of pride and a commitment to studying, codifying, and teaching them, and so began the process of intervention delineated by Haugen. If the existence of vernacular languages alongside Latin may be more or less a verifiable fact in the history of European languages, and thus untroubled by linguistic ideologies, as soon as they were seen as something special and associated with particular social groups, they became bound up with ideologies and power struggles. Mattheier (1988: 4) writes:

> Die Herausbildung von Nationalsprachen bzw. die Sprachstandardisierung sind in diesem Zusammenhang gesellschaftliche Prozesse von erheblicher soziokommuni-kativer Bedeutung, die auf der grundlegenden Veränderung im Kommunikations-bedarf einer Gesellschaft basieren. [The development of the national languages or language standardization are in this context social processes of considerable

socio-communicative significance, based on the fundamental change in the communication needs of a society.]

It has been suggested that the development of the vernaculars vis-à-vis Latin is the
clearest sign from a linguistic point of view of the move from the Middle Ages to 'the
Modern Era,' and that 'developing a written standard is one of the most fundamental
institutional achievements of a society' (Schaefer 2006: 3). The existence side by side of
various written and spoken languages during the European Middle Ages is a historical
fact, but I would agree with those excitable commentators we have cited above who see
the manipulation of this situation as something of great cultural importance. Put
another way, one might suggest that once people started to plan languages, that was
the point at which it all started to go wrong, imposing a pressure on peoples and on
languages—pressures which in earlier times were seen by those who promulgated them
as social benefits, but which now, in our more ecologically minded times, we would
regard as social ills.

15.2 EMANCIPATION FROM LATIN

During the European Middle Ages, the serious study of language meant the study of
Latin. Latin was taught at the elementary level via the method established by Donatus
in his *Artes Grammaticæ* and later via the medium of Priscian's *Institutiones Grammaticæ*,[1] and in the majority of situations it was simply unreasonable to suggest that
other languages might be worthy objects of study. Classical Latin was of course the
standardized language *par excellence* and remains so. As Milroy and Milroy (1991: 22)
observe, 'the only fully standardized language is a dead language,' and an unchanging
standard for, say, English or French, is as unrealistic as it would be to deny language
change. The challenge for medieval teachers was not to codify Latin but to teach a
language which was more or less foreign to all Europeans, and an array of strategies
were devised in the ongoing push to teach Latin more effectively. Allan (2010a: 12)
suggests that Donatus's and Priscian's position in the history of linguistics is as
precursors to the field of applied linguistics. One strategy for teaching Latin more
effectively was to do so via the students' own mother tongue, and it is in this context
that we encounter perhaps the first example in the history of linguistics of a European
vernacular being explicitly preferred to Latin in a domain where Latin had hitherto
been entirely dominant.

The motivation is still very much the teaching of Latin—there is no sense in which
English should or could be studied as an end in itself—but the *Excerptiones de Arte
Grammatica Anglice* by Ælfric (*fl.* 987–1010) does at least allow the possibility that
grammar might be something relevant to a language other than Latin. Ælfric was

---

[1] See Chs. 13 and 14 above; Allan (2010a: ch. 6).

steeped in the monastic tradition; he lived and worked throughout his life in the south-west of England, studying at Winchester and later becoming the first abbot of the Benedictine monastery at Eynsham, west of Oxford. The grammar was based on a tenth-century edition of Priscian (see Porter 2002) and is, as far as we know, the first vernacular Latin grammar to be produced in Europe (see Law 1997). It was accompan-ied by a glossary, noteworthy for its onomasiological rather than alphabetical structure, and a colloquy, designed to help students improve their spoken Latin. As well as taking his pedagogical responsibilities seriously, Ælfric was committed to the development of English as a literary language, and his homilies (Godden 2000) and hagiographies, together with other writings on religious topics, make him the most prolific writer in Old English; valorization of the language involved more than just seeing its potential as a pedagogical tool. Ælfric did not teach English or suggest that the vernacular might be ranked alongside Latin as a scholarly language—indeed, he was apologetic about using the vernacular—but in his own practice he opened the minds of readers to the possibility that the vernacular might be worth a look.

Elsewhere in Europe there were those who felt that their own daily language was worth even more than that. From the eleventh-century Occitan, the Romance vernacu-lar of southern France and the northern parts of Spain and Italy, was developing an independent tradition of lyric poetry, associated with the troubadours, travelling performers in this rich genre (see Akehurst and Davis 1995; Gaunt and Kay 1999). The classical period of Occitan is generally taken to span the later Middle Ages (1100–1350), and in 1240 a grammar of the language was produced by one Uc Faidit, assumed to be the prolific writer of songs and of more scholarly prose works, Uc de Saint Circ (*fl.* 1217–53). Uc Faidit's *Donatz Proençals* 'Provençal Donatus' is written in both Latin and Occitan (the Latin version apparently by another author, cf. Marshall 1969: 65), and there are perhaps two principal observations to make about it. The first is that it followed Donatus' model very closely. Even though Occitan and Latin were both Romance languages, there were of course differences, points where Donatus' rules did not work, but Uc had no other model. Grammar was Donatus and Donatus was gram-mar, and if someone was going to write a pioneering grammatical description, it was going to be a 'Donatus.' Donatus would remain a model for grammar writers as late as the eighteenth century (cf. the anonymously published *Danish Donatus* of 1761 by Nicolai Engelhardt Nannestad, Anon. 1761). What was distinctive about Donatus' grammar was its pedagogical method, its question-and-answer structure, but for Uc this was not the key motivation, as this text was not intended for children but for other would-be troubadour poets, as was the case with the slightly later (fourteenth-century) and more ambitious Occitan *Leys d'Amors* (Anglade 1919–20). The second observation is a general one: that grammar writing is motivated by extralinguistic needs. No one writes a grammar just for the fun of it but rather to respond to some societal imperative. This has often meant a new pedagogical context, but, as with Uc, that is not always the case, nor in fact was it the case with the two other pioneering vernacular grammars of the late Middle Ages.

The context for Uc's grammar was a proud and independent literary tradition on the southern edge of Europe. Similarly proud and independent literary traditions were also to be found on the northern and western margins of the European area. Ireland and Irish scholars were at the forefront of Christian scholarship and of the Christianization of other parts of Europe during the Middle Ages, but at the same time heirs to a rich vernacular literary tradition dating back to the very beginning of the medieval period but associated perhaps most with bardic verse. It should not be surprising therefore that Irish scholars took a pride and interest in their language and that they saw it both from native, non-Christian and also Latin perspectives. The *Auraicept na n-Éces* 'The Scholars' Primer' (Ahlqvist 1982) is said to date back to the seventh century, which would make it the oldest surviving treatment of a European vernacular, but the text continued to be developed (rather like the *Technē Grammatikē* of Dionysius Thrax—such was the fate of manuscripts) over the course of the following centuries, and the oldest surviving manuscript is from around 1160. The *Auraicept* tells the story of the creation and superiority of the Gaelic language (according to the text the first language to be created after the destruction of the Tower of Babel), and it is also a good example of an *exegetical grammar*, consisting of excerpts from Donatus to which are added lengthy commentaries (Poppe 1999). Pride in the language and (usually spurious) arguments for its superiority above other languages are a common thread in the tradition of vernacular linguistics.

Iceland in the later Middle Ages also constituted a centre of literary activity, remote from the linguistic imperialism of the Roman empire and its legacy, where a pride in the native language could develop along with a sense of its difference from Latin. It was precisely the sense of difference, of the vernacular being something special—'because languages are all unlike one another, ever since they parted and branched off from one and the same language' (Haugen 1972: 13)—which led an anonymous Icelandic scholar to attempt a revised orthography for Icelandic some time in the mid-twelfth century. The manuscript of this orthographical treatise (the *Codex Wormianus*) is from a century later and contains the *Prose Edda* of Snorri Sturluson, a guide for poets, i.e. the same context as for the Occitan and Irish works. The *Codex Wormianus* also contains three other writings on language, and these four language treatises are simply referred to as the Four Grammatical Treatises, although only treatises three and four are on grammar proper and are, inevitably, based closely on Donatus' *Ars Maior*. The *First Grammatical Treatise* (and its author, named, by extension, the First Grammarian) is the one which has captured the imagination of modern linguists (especially since its greater accessibility in editions by Haugen 1972 and Hreinn Benediktsson 1972). The First Grammarian proposes an independent symbol for each meaningful sound in Old Norse, and he identifies the meaningful sounds by the use of something which to modern eyes looks like a commutation test, altering one sound in a word to see if another word of the language results, thereby confirming the phonemic status of the altered sound.

So these medieval skirmishes into languages other than Latin demonstrate a number of tendencies, characteristic of pioneering studies of the vernaculars and indeed going all the way back to Dionysius Thrax, in whose tradition they lie. Language studies serve a social or cultural need, and in all these cases the need is to preserve and teach the prized vernacular to subsequent generations. The language of a classical literature provides the data—there is no sense yet that the spoken language *per se* is worth studying or teaching. The model of Donatus and the spectre of Latin are never far away, and significantly it is those languages most closely related to Latin which are the first to be standardized as we enter the Renaissance. Up to this point treatments of the vernaculars have not had a specifically codifying agenda.

15.3 THE RENAISSANCE AND THE EMERGENCE OF STANDARDS

The cultural movement of the Renaissance spread slowly across the countries of Europe and was characterized by a collection of cultural shifts (some of them linguistic) rather than by particular events. In the history of linguistics we observe that countries have their day, dominating approaches to the study of language internationally for a while; it might be suggested, for example, that the nineteenth century was predominantly German and the twentieth predominantly American. The dominant cultural force of the European Renaissance was Italy, and it is therefore no surprise that the vernacularization of culture which is a feature of developments in Europe from the fourteenth to the seventeenth century should have found its inspiration here. Indeed, the figure perhaps most associated with the start of the Renaissance, Dante Alighieri (1265–1321), expounded strong views on the vernacular and provided the intellectual basis for later debates on the standardization of Italian.

Dante, inspired by the Occitan poets' regard for their language, wrote his *De vulgari eloquentia* 'On the Eloquence of the Vernacular' in 1304, although (significantly) it only became widely read after it was printed in Italian in 1529. In it he distinguishes between the first language (*locutio prima*), acquired naturally in childhood, and the secondary or *grammatical language* (in practice Latin), which not all people manage to acquire. While the grammatical language would generally have been regarded at the time as the nobler, Dante takes the opposite point of view, that the

> Vulgar Tongue is the nobler, as well because it was the first employed by the human race, as because the whole world makes use of it [. . .] It is also the nobler as being natural to us, whereas the other is rather of an artificial kind; and it is of the nobler form of speech that we intend to treat. (Ferrers Howell 1890: 2)

After surveying the properties of the different dialects of Italian, however, Dante concludes that none of them is appropriate for literature and that the poets must elaborate an appropriately literary standard themselves; and of course Dante practised what he preached in this respect. Along with the other great Tuscan poets of the fourteenth century, Petrarch and Boccaccio, Dante provided a prestigious model for other Italian writers to follow, a potential standard; but one of the few things that can be confidently stated about language standards is that they will provoke disagreement amongst users, who all have some form of vested interest, and the model of Dante, Petrarch, and Boccaccio provoked the Italian Language Question of the sixteenth century (Hall 1942).

Italy was not politically unified at the start of the sixteenth century, and the close link between language and identity meant that there were conflicting claims to be made in the choice of a standard language. Under the influence of Humanism, Latin had continued to develop as a written language at the expense of the Tuscan dialect elaborated by the fourteenth-century poets, and Latin had a strong claim as a viable standard, given its closeness to the contemporary Italian dialects. Other modern dialects (and indeed older forms of the language) had a claim too; but no matter which variety would be selected, there were further problems, such as what to call the standard (Florentine, Tuscan, or Italian?). These are questions which recur with local nuances wherever the need for a standard has been debated. The loudest voice in the debate was that of Cardinal Pietro Bembo (1470–1547) who, in his *Prose della volgar lingua* (published in 1525, but written in the first years of the century), championed the use of the Tuscan of Petrarch and his contemporaries. This form had been used for scholarly (as opposed to literary) writings as early as the 1440s in the work of Leon Battista Alberti (1404–72), who also wrote the first grammatical sketch of Italian, the *Regole della volgar lingua fiorentina*, in around 1443. This grammar was based on the view, not shared by all, that the common language did indeed possess rules and could therefore be subject to grammatical analysis (Grayson 1963).

Just as other new cultural currents were spreading out from Italy, so was pride in the vernacular, the view that it should be developed as the medium for serious forms of discourse, and the belief that it could be described and codified in grammars and dictionaries. In 1530 the Spanish theologian Juan de Valdés (c.1509–41) moved to Naples (a Spanish possession at the time), apparently to escape the Spanish inquisition, just five years after the publication of Bembo's *Prose della volgar lingua*, and his first work to be written there was essentially a Spanish counterpart to that work, the *Diálogo de la lengua* (c.1535, but only published in Madrid in 1737). For Valdés there was no distinction to be made between superior and inferior languages; it was through literary use that a language gained status and prestige. Indisputably the leading Spanish linguist of the period, and arguably the most ground-breaking linguist of the whole Renaissance, was, however, Antonio de Nebrija (1444–1522). Nebrija's *Gramática castellana* 'Castilian grammar' of 1492 was for a long time assumed to be the first modern grammar of a European vernacular, but this was to ignore Alberti's grammar, which was not available in a modern edition until 1908. While the pioneering vernacular linguists (like Alberti) tended, inevitably and often for strategic reasons, to base their descriptions and discussions on existing models, Nebrija (like the First Grammarian with Old Norse) looked at Castilian with fresh eyes. As well as the famous *Gramática castellana*, he also wrote grammars of Latin, both with Latin and with Castilian as the metalanguage. He wrote bilingual dictionaries and dictionaries of professional terms as well as orthographical and phonological studies of several languages; in short he was a true 'Renaissance man.' In the *Gramática castellana* Nebrija really does treat Castilian as something *sui generis*, devising a native (as distinct to Latin-derived) grammatical terminology (also a feature of the work of other nationally minded linguists, e.g. the Dane Rasmus Rask (1787–1832)) and including treatments of syntax and of Castilian for foreigners. A fate of such pioneering work may often be initial neglect or even hostility, and Padley (1988: 164–5) questions

> why even his contemporaries and immediate successors did not see fit to reprint a work that is now seen to be of such primary importance in the history of west European thought about language [. . .] indeed, a generation was to elapse before the *Gramática* received any attention, whether friendly or hostile.

Some comfort, I suppose, to those who feel that their work is yet to be accorded its full recognition! (For more on the history of linguistics in Spain, see Quilis and Niederehe 1986.)

Working our way west across southern Europe we come next to France, and it may be surprising to learn that the first treatments of French grammar were actually carried out by English writers. This was because there was during the late Middle Ages a local need for French grammars in England, where French was in use as an indigenous foreign language. This tradition of responding to opportunities presented by the peculiar position of French in England was continued in the late sixteenth century by the Protestant refugees from the Low Countries, who spotted a market opportunity to provide French–English language teaching during their period of exile in flight from the Counter-Reformation (Fernandez and Cormier 2010; Howatt and Widdowson 2004: ch. 2). However, as early as the beginning of the fifteenth century practical guides to French for speakers of English were appearing, such as the *Donait françois* 'French Donatus' of 1409, commissioned by John Barton (Merrilees 1993, Merrilees and Sitarz-Fitzpatrick 1993). As well as being the first (surviving) grammatical treatment of French, this work uses French rather than Latin (or indeed English) as its metalanguage, but note that again Donatus is the model and the motivation is practical ('applied' rather than 'theoretical'). The first complete (and immensely long) grammar of French was also written in England by an Englishman, John Palsgrave (*c*.1480–1554) (Stein 1997), who was tutor to various members of the royal family, bearing out another generalization of early studies of the vernaculars, that they were often serendipitous undertakings by individuals qualified to undertake a linguistic analysis only by the fact of their being well connected—e.g. the first grammar of English to be written in Denmark (Linn 1999). Palsgrave's *Lesclaircissement de la langue françoyse* of 1530 was dedicated to King Henry VIII. It was not long, however, before the wind of enthusiasm for the French language was blowing through the fields of France, an image pursued in the first appeal to 'mettre & ordonner par Reigle nostre langage François' (the evidence of it being as good as the 'ruled' language of Latin), the *Champ fleury* 'Flowery field' by Geoffroy Tory (*c*. 1480–1533), printed the year before Palsgrave's grammar (Smith 1993).

The study and description primarily of the morphology was then unleashed, with a rash of grammars of French both as a first and second language appearing in the course of the subsequent decades. Tory's pride in the language led him, well connected as he was in his capacity as royal printer, to advocate the printing of French texts (as opposed to Latin ones) and to advocate orthographic reform for French, also a key concern of the first grammarian of English. (For more on the early studies of the French language see Kibbee 1991.)

There are several reasons why the desire to advance the vernacular and to create a standard variety of it has not been the preserve of 'trained linguists.' The principal reason is that the scholarly study of the modern languages did not become possible in most of Europe until the middle of the nineteenth century and the emergence of the 'new' philology,[2] so there were no professional pundits for the vernacular languages until that time. Another reason is that gate-keeping for the language was quickly established as a cultural duty rather than a scholarly pursuit, a job for (self-appointed) culturally elevated people, those for whom (like Tory) language was a professional tool rather than object. So, when, for example, there was a call for an English dictionary in the mid-eighteenth century, it was to the essayist and literary man-about-town Samuel Johnson (1709–84) (see Lynch and McDermott 2005), who had famously failed to complete a university degree, that publishers turned. Even since the emergence of linguistics as a profession in the twentieth century, there have been few linguists willing to judge on and standardize the vernaculars. In fact, the unwritten code of professional conduct for many practitioners of linguistics means that straying into prescription is as professionally suicidal as being caught *in flagrante delicto* at the office Christmas party.

The gauntlet for English was picked up by proud Englishman William Bullokar (*c.*1531–1609). Bullokar was a former mercenary who in his later years turned to the ennoblement of his own language as a sort of national duty akin to that shown in his former career. His explicit aim was to demonstrate that English was 'a perfect ruled tongue, conferable to grammar art as any ruled long' (from 'W. Bullokar to the Reader' of his *Bref Grammar for English*, reprinted in Robins 1994). To this end he based his codification of English grammar on the official Latin grammar approved for use in schools by Palsgrave's dedicatee, King Henry VIII, the one attributed to William Lily (*c.*1468–1522). Consequently some grammatical categories were treated because they were part of the established structure of Latin, even though on an objective analysis they could not be shown to exist in English. For example, Bullokar states unequivocally that 'a substantiue is declined with fiue cases in both numbers,' and he sows confusion in the 1586 *Pamphlet for Grammar* in his treatment of the vowels by identifying <l>, <m>, <n> and <r> as half vowels which then allows for a category of triphthongs (as in *holm* or *elm*). As is the case with all these pioneer treatments of the vernacular, reading Bullokar one is struck by both the challenge and the excitement of embarking on uncharted seas. The modern reader faces the additional challenge with Bullokar's text

---

[2] See Chs 7 and 28, this volume.

of his revised spelling system, characterized by a series of digraphs and accents. Just as prescription has tended to be the preserve of the well-meaning armchair linguist, so has the tradition of spelling reform. The desire to reform spelling systems is fired by worthy cultural aims (e.g. facilitating learning by non-native speakers, saving money, increasing social mobility) but rarely receives the official support required to drive it through, although there have been some high-profile exceptions (for German, see Johnson 2005; for Turkish, Lewis 1999). Bullokar's reformed English metalanguage was a revolution too far, and on into the following century English grammars tended still to be written in Latin, even when formally they had broken away from Latin (e.g. Wallis 1653³). (For more on the history of English grammars, see Linn 2006, Michael 1987.)

After pedagogical requirements and admiration for a classical literature, it is religious motivations that have been the strongest driving force behind the description of the vernaculars and their standardisation. Missionaries have been responsible for numerous pioneering grammars and orthographies. The broader standardizing impact by missionaries on indigenous cultures has not always necessarily been a force for social good, especially where it has ironed out local customs or stigmatized practices which have not fitted in with the specifically Christian world-view. However, as Nowak (2006: 167) writes:

> [I]t is well known that most of the indigenous languages of North America and Australia today are at the verge of extinction or are already extinct. Sometimes their documentation by missionaries is the only one bearing testimony, providing today's scholars with invaluable information that otherwise would no longer be available.

Of course many of the missionary grammars are limited by the Western linguistic training of their authors. There was always a danger that typologically very different languages would be described as if they were Latin, but as we have seen, this is no different from the early fate of the European vernaculars. The issue motivating particularly Protestant missionaries was the translation of the Bible, 'the Word,' into the languages of the communities in which they proselytized, thus e.g. John Eliot's 1663 translation of the Bible into the now extinct Massachusett language, followed up in 1666 by a grammar, *The Indian Grammar Begun: or, An Essay to Bring the Indian Language into Rules, for the Help of such as desire to Learn the same, for the Furtherance of the Gospel among them* (Eliot 1666). Another well-attested example of the linguistic impact of missionaries is the establishment of the Vietnamese orthography by the Jesuit missionary Alexandre de Rhodes (*c.*1591–1660) through his trilingual Vietnamese–Portuguese–Latin dictionary of 1651, published under the auspices of the Roman Catholic missionary organization, the Propaganda Fide. Missionary linguistics has become a recognized sub-discipline of the broader historiography of linguistics and has been the subject of several conferences and publications (see the papers in the special issue of *Historiographia Linguistica* 36(2/3), 2009).

---

³ For the major ongoing project on the work of John Wallis (*Harmony and Controversy in Seventeenth Century Scientific Thought*), see: www.ling-phil.ox.ac.uk/wallisproject [accessed Sept. 2012].

The Protestant Reformation also had a significant impact on the valorization and standardization of the vernaculars of northern Europe. The first printed translation of the Bible in German dates from 1466, but the sixteenth-century translations by Martin Luther (the New Testament in 1522 and the complete Bible in 1534) are the ones with the real impact, both religious and linguistic. The northern European Reformation was very much a linguistic event, with the use of language as one of its key concerns. One of Luther's objections to the centralized power of the Roman Catholic Church was that the word of God, couched as it was in Latin, was incomprehensible to ordinary people, and in his translation of the Bible into High German Luther worked hard to use a variety of the language which would resonate with ordinary speakers and a style which was natural and comprehensible. As we have seen in the context of several languages, there was in the early days of vernacularization a general scepticism that the vernacular languages possessed the 'rules' of the Classical languages and so could be used for elevated discourse. The fact that the Bible, the most elevated text of all in a strongly Christian world, could be expressed in the vernacular without its being diminished was a major step forward in the reinforcement of the vernaculars. It is no accident that the first German grammar, the *Teutsche Grammatica* by Valentin Ickelsamer (*c*.1500–1541), should have appeared in the same year as Luther's Bible translation, and that it should have been inspired by pride in the status of German as a literary language, although this was less a grammar than a practical guide to usage. The first grammar proper, the *Teutsch Grammatick oder Sprach-Kunst* by Laurentius Albertus (*c*.1540–85) followed in 1573, and the most successful German grammar of the sixteenth century, the *Grammatica Germanicæ Linguæ* of 1578 by Johannes Clajus (1535–92), explicitly took the language of Luther as its model. The existence of a Bible in the vernacular also went hand in hand with the production of language works in the other countries which were feeling the wind of religious change at the Reformation. The pre-eminent Danish-language Bible, for example, used throughout the kingdom of Denmark-Norway, was published in 1550 under the auspices of Christian III, who brought the Reformation to that country. The translation was the work of Christiern Pedersen (1480–1554), who was also a lexicographer (author of a Latin–Danish dictionary), grammarian (of Latin), and printer. (Grammars of Danish did not appear until a century later, the first being the *Introductio ad Lingvam Danicam* from the early 1660s by Laurids Olufsen Kock (1634–91) and the *Grammatica Danica* of 1668 by Erik Eriksen Pontoppidan (1616–78)—see Hovdhaugen et al. 2000:7–75, Linn 2005: 168–71.) Likewise, the first authoritative treatment of Dutch, the *Twe-spraack van de Nederduitsche Letterkunst* of 1584 by Hendrik Spiegel (1549–1612), was part of that same movement of growing cultural and linguistic confidence which included the first complete translation of the Bible into Dutch inspired by Luther's model.

While it would be overstating the case to suggest that the appearance of the Bible and the resulting prestige of the northern European vernaculars led directly to standardization, there was undoubtedly a close link between the various cultural facets of the Reformation—religious independence, printing, translation, increased commercial wealth—and the codification of the national languages. We note again that standardization is not first and foremost about the language. It is about the reinforcement of a cultural idea. (For more on the history of linguistics in the Germanic languages, see the papers in Schmitter 2005; for more on the standardization of the Germanic languages, see Deumert and Vandenbussche 2003, Linn and McLelland 2002. For an overview of vernacular grammar writing in Europe from the Renaissance onwards, see Padley 1985, 1988.)

15.4 PRESCRIPTION AND INSTITUTIONS

Much of the early work in the history of European vernacular linguistics was done by individuals, in many cases inspired by patriotic or reforming zeal. However, in the post-Renaissance/Reformation world, it was not long before the maintenance of the language came to be seen as a corporate cultural duty. Correct standard language could not be left up to any old armchair language planner to cultivate. Standards had to be prescribed, and they had to be prescribed by those who knew where the boundaries of the norms lay. Hendrik Spiegel's 1584 Dutch grammar, the 'popular and influential grammar [. . .] usually seen as the real beginning of a tradition of prescriptive grammars in Dutch' (Willemyns 2003: 98) and which we have just mentioned, was published under the watchful eye of the *rederijkerskamer* 'De Eglantier'. A *rederijkerskamer* was a form of literary society, and the notion that maintenance of literary standards went together with the maintenance of linguistic standards, that standard and correct language was to be found in literature, has been a common view from the seventeenth century onwards.

In France, the *Académie Française* was founded in 1635 by Cardinal Richelieu with the task of rendering 'the French language not only elegant, but also capable of handling all the arts and sciences' (translation from Lodge 1993: 160). The *Académie* was formally required by its founding statutes to produce a dictionary, a grammar, a rhetoric, and a poetics of French—in short the cornerstones of a standard literary language, based on the usage of the powerful and the prestigious. Known internationally as the prescriptive body *par excellence*, the *Académie*'s influence on the language has perhaps been more symbolic than actual. The official grammar of the *Académie* only appeared in 1932 and was not well received. While the official dictionary (first edition 1694) has had greater standing, it should be noted that the *Académie*'s standards are only advisory and have no legal foundation. The twenty-first-century tendency towards destandardization (see next section) can only serve to loosen its grip on the language even further.

The *Académie Française* was in turn based on the Italian *Accademia della Crusca*, established in 1585 with the explicit intention of separating good language from bad. Early on it focused its attention on the production of a dictionary of 'good' Italian, rooted in the usage of the fourteenth-century Tuscan poets and, more than anything else, the 1612 *Vocabolario degli Accademici della Crusca* served to standardize Italian and provide a model for an institutionally produced standardizing dictionary. In England the Royal Society was set up in 1660 in parallel with the French *Académie*. Much of the early work of this scientific institution was in fact linguistic, fuelled by the needs of Empiricism and the desire to create a new universal philosophical language, as exemplified above all by the *Essay towards a real Character and a Philosophical Language* of 1668 by John Wilkins (1614–72) (Subbiondo 1992). Attempts to create universal languages represent the standardizing spirit taken to its extreme, espousing as they do the belief that all linguistic variety might be whittled down to one universally understood language. The paradox of the universal language, the impossibility of the pure standard, is summed up in the 1663 'Ballad of Gresham Colledge', mocking the activities of the new Royal Society:

> A Doctor counted very able [i.e. Wilkins]
> Designes that all Mankynd converse shall,
> Spite o' th' confusion made att Babell,
> By Character call'd Universall.
> How long this Character will be learning,
> That truly passeth my discerning. (Stimson 1932: 115)

While the Royal Society has remained the national institution for the sciences, there have been subsequent proposals in Britain for a dedicated language academy, along the lines of the French model. Serious proposals were advanced in the late seventeenth and early eighteenth centuries by some of the leading literary figures of the time. Daniel Defoe (*c.*1660–1731), author of *Robinson Crusoe*, wrote of the need to 'establish Purity and Propriety of Stile' in the face of 'all the Irregular Additions that Ignorance and Affectation have introduc'd' (Tieken-Boon van Ostade 2006: 241), and Jonathan Swift, the author of *Gulliver's Travels*, took up the baton in his 1712 *A Proposal for Correcting, Improving and Ascertaining the English Tongue*, bemoaning in the third paragraph the fact that 'our Language is less Refined than those of *Italy*, *Spain* or *France*' (Swift 1712). National pride mixes with a sense of shame in eighteenth-century England, and anxiety about the perceived debasement of the language results in a call for clear prescriptions about language use. Prescriptivism is nothing new in treatments of the vernaculars, of course, but in eighteenth-century England, this prescriptive undercurrent becomes a tidal wave, resulting in Johnson's *Dictionary* and in the grammars of Robert Lowth (1710–87) (Tieken-Boon van Ostade 2011) and Lindley Murray (1745–1826) (Tieken-Boon van Ostade 1996).

While British English may have failed to get a language academy to legislate and police its standard variety, and Bailey (1986: 81) takes the view that 'the success of English as a world language is due in no minor way to the fact that it has never been standardized,' it is highly unusual in this respect. The great linguistic task of the Modern period, the valorization, codification and advancement of the spoken vernaculars, has resulted in the majority of cases in institutionalization, and this is the case outside Europe too, where the European model has been followed. The language regulatory bodies internationally are too numerous to mention, but they are often linked with movements for purism or revival. (On the role of academies in language standardization, see Joseph 1987: 111ff.)

15.5 STANDARDIZATION AND DESTANDARDIZATION

The *idea* of standard languages has become established as a practical reality in most parts of the world, reinforced by official institutions, whether these be language planners or the stifling presence of big official repositories of language, typically dictionaries and grammars. In the quotation which opened this chapter, Jespersen writes of 'the *springing up* of the great national common languages,' but this is really the wrong image. The development of the standards has been a protracted process, a story of the gradual triumph of certain sets of values over others, of certain classes of people over others, and the practical reality this has created is something to which language users have been taught to cling. Standards are not simply enshrined in formal books and pronouncements, but they also loom large in the popular imagination (Davies and Langer 2006). Consequently, when the standard appears to be slipping, this can be a cause of anxiety and concern, and of course a standardized variety will always be in a state of slippage as it moves out of sync with change in the spoken varieties, hence the existence of usage guides to try to shore up the idea of unchanging language standards.

The story of standardization, 'a grand narrative of modernization' (Deumert 2010: 245), seemed by the mid-twentieth century to be complete, allowing the linear, teleological picture of the process set out by Haugen. It has been argued, however, that the grand narrative is now in reverse, that in practice there is an increasing move towards the acceptability of language variation in a process, driven from below, of *destandardization*, of the debasement of the capital of standard languages. The idea of language destandardization has been discussed for a range of languages (Erfurt and Budach 2008), and indeed in respect of periods other than the most recent (Hagland 2005), suggesting that standardization and destandardization may be cyclical processes. However, the 'death of the standard' in the late twentieth/early twenty-first century can be viewed as characteristic of the period which Bauman calls 'liquid modernity' (Bauman 2000). The standard language is not the only cultural monolith to have been pulled apart. The notion that marriage is a permanent contract between a man and a woman, that spirituality just means the acceptance of an official religion, that education is a process complete by young adulthood, that employment means one job for life— these are all ideas forged by the standardizing fetish of modernity, but ones which have been deconstructed in practice very rapidly. It is no surprise in the social world of the current century, where songs can be shuffled on your MP3 player and friends shuffled on your Facebook page, that scant regard should be paid to the dull presence of a standard language. Deumert (following Beck 2002) sees standard languages as zombies, the living dead, no longer real but nonetheless haunting 'the minds of speakers (and those linguists who believe in languages as unitary, well-defined, and countable objects)' (Deumert 2010: 258).

While standards continue to haunt both language users and the gatekeepers of languages (planners, teachers, publishers, journalists, etc.), they are real enough, and it is too soon to kill them off. How, anyway, do you go about killing something that is already dead? To end on a slightly less fanciful note, the history of Western linguistics has been driven by debates surrounding the use and teaching of standard languages, and a vast corpus of work has been produced in the service of standard languages and language standards. Consequently the idea of the standard is absolutely central to our understanding of the history of western linguistics.

CHAPTER 16

....

WORD-BASED MORPHOLOGY FROM ARISTOTLE TO MODERN WP (WORD AND PARADIGM MODELS)

....

JAMES P. BLEVINS

16.1 INTRODUCTION

....

THE dominant morphological models developed in the modern period can both trace their origins to ancient Indo-European grammatical traditions. Bloomfieldian models have their ultimate roots in the Sanskrit grammatical tradition, particularly as represented in the work of Pāṇini. These models adopt a formative-based perspective in which the central analytical task of morphology involves the disassembly of words into arrangements of sub-word units.[1] Modern word-based models likewise lie at the end of a continuous tradition that arose from attempts first to describe and subsequently to teach the grammar of ancient Greek and Latin. These models project morphological analysis primarily upwards from the word, and treat the association of words with paradigms or other sets of forms as the most fundamental morphological task. Sub-word sequences figure in the patterns of modification that related basic forms of an item to their 'inflected' variants. However, the classical model has no counterpart of morphemes—not even roots (Law 1998: 112)—and its proponents perceived no need for any unit intervening between sounds and words. The primacy of words in the

---

[1] The legacy of the Sanskrit grammarians is treated in more detail in ch. 11 of this volume, while aspects of the Bloomfieldian program are summarized in ch. 18.

Greco-Roman tradition had been encouraged and was further reinforced by an interest in etymology, which consisted in the main of word histories.

The classical word-based model has, moreover, been relatively stable through most of its history. The Alexandrine model attributed to Dionysus Thrax and Apollonius Dyscolus provides the basis for the Latin grammars of Donatus and Priscian, and in turn for subsequent descriptive and pedagogical treatments of classical grammar. An essentially classical word-based perspective survives into the Neogrammarian period and remains relevant to morphological analysis in the field of historical linguistics. It was not until Bloomfield threw off the yoke of his own classicist training and established an almost purely syntagmatic alternative that the classical model was eclipsed as a general model of analysis.

Yet the heyday of the neo-Pāṇinian morphemic model was remarkably short-lived. Little more than twenty years separate the first definitive presentation of the mature Bloomfieldian programme in Bloomfield (1933) from the last concerted effort to salvage the post-Bloomfieldian model of morphemic analysis in Hockett (1954). Before the end of the next decade, Hockett (1967) had ceased to see morphemic analysis as anything other than a linguist's shorthand for more psychologically plausible descriptions. These more 'realistic' alternatives comprised sets of word forms, organized into paradigms and extended by processes of analogy. Soon thereafter, Matthews (1972) reacquainted modern audiences with the types of morphological patterns that arise in a flectional language and with the classical models developed to provide descriptions and analyses of these patterns. The rehabilitation of these traditional insights in turn spurred the development of distinctively modern versions of word-based models.

In short, from at least the time of Aristotle through to the present, something like the word and paradigm model has occupied a central place in the approaches to morphological analysis developed within the Western grammatical tradition. The body of this chapter now traces this intellectual progression in more detail, focussing on the continuity between variants of word-based approaches.

16.2 ORIGINS OF WORD-BASED MODELS

On the basis of the surviving evidence about the pre-Socratic philosophers, their interest in language appears to have been linked to a broader interest in rhetoric. In Plato, questions concerning the structure and use of language likewise arose in the context of more general philosophical and logical investigations. Hence a number of terms that originate in Plato have, at least initially, a fundamentally logical usage and only gradually take on a strictly grammatical sense. In particular, when Plato suggests in *Sophist* that a *logos* can be analysed as an *onoma* and a *rhēma*, he can be understood as claiming that a 'proposition' or 'utterance' consists of a 'name' or 'noun phrase' and a 'predicate' or 'attribute.' Not until later did the grammatical meanings 'sentence,' 'noun,' and 'verb' come to predominate.

16.2.1 Aristotle and the Stoics

It is in Aristotle that the first recognizable precursor of a word-based model can be found. Indeed, to the contemporary observer, Aristotle seems remarkably modern in outlook. The fact that he never wrote a treatise devoted solely to grammar resonates with current efforts to reduce the isolation of linguistics within the cognitive and behavioural sciences. His view that words were organized into sets of basic forms and analogically similar inflected variants shares the same fundamental perspective as modern exemplar-based models. Even his insistence on distinguishing nouns from inflected forms of nouns anticipates the later contrast between word forms and lexemes (Matthews 1972: 161).

Some of Aristotle's clearest pronouncements regarding language are in a comprehensive treatment of the relation between logic and language that is usually known by its Latin name, *De Interpretatione* 'On Interpretation' (rather than by the Greek original *Peri Hermeneias*).[2] The discussion of meaning first identifies sentences as expressing propositions ('judgements') and then proceeds to define the word as the smallest meaningful part of a sentence.

> A sentence is a significant portion of speech, some parts of which have an independent meaning, that is to say, as an utterance, though not as the expression of any positive judgement... The word 'human' has meaning, but does not constitute a proposition, either positive or negative... But if we separate one syllable of the word 'human' from the other it has no meaning... In composite words, indeed, the parts contribute to the meaning of the whole; yet... they have not an independent meaning. (*De Interpretatione* 16^b, 27–36)

To Plato's *onomata* and *rhēmata*, Aristotle added a third category of *syndesmoi*, containing conjunctions (which are of particular logical importance) along with various other closed-class items that are sometimes grouped together as 'functional' categories. These word classes are notional rather than formal, so that it is reference to time that distinguishes *rhēmata* from *onomata*.[3]

> By a noun we mean a sound significant by convention, which has no reference to time, and of which no part is significant apart from the rest. (*De Int.* 16^a, 19–21)

> A verb is that which, in addition to its proper meaning, carries with it the notion of time. No part of it has any independent meaning, and it is a sign of something said of something else. (*De Int.* 16^b, 6–9)

---

[2] The quotations from Aristotle below are cited by the Bekker numbers in the translation of *De Interpretatione* by E. M. Edgehill in Ross (1926).

[3] Robins (1997: 33) warns in fact that 'the translation of *onoma* and *rhēma* by *noun* and *verb* at this stage in the development of Greek grammatical theory may be misleading.'

Although Aristotle did not use patterns of tense or case inflection to define word classes, he introduced a technical term, *ptōsis* 'fall,' to distinguish nouns and verbs (i.e. lexemes) from their inflected variants (word forms).

> The expressions 'of Philo', 'to Philo', and so on, constitute not nouns, but cases ['inflexions' in Ackrill 1987] of a noun. (*De Int.* 16^b, 1–2)

In the nominal domain, Aristotle singled out the category of gender, reflecting the influence of the previous classification of Protagoras and his own interest in meaning. It was the Stoics who first restricted the term *ptōsis* to apply solely to case forms (surviving in the German term *Fall* 'case'), and who then introduced a new term, *klisis* 'bend,' to apply to inflected variants in general.

The organization of Greek morphology into words and inflectional variants was governed by principles of analogy, in line with Aristotle's position on what is known as the 'analogy–anomaly' debate. This issue, which appears as the first strictly morphological debate in classical antiquity, was essentially a dispute about the role of regularity in language. On the one side, Aristotle and the subsequent Alexandrine school emphasized the systematicity of analogical patterns, principally within inflectional paradigms. On the other side, the Stoics attached particular importance to irregularities, within inflectional paradigms, but more pervasively within families of derivational formations in Greek.

The positions espoused by Aristotle and the classifications he proposed were significantly refined and elaborated by the Stoic and Alexandrine schools. The Stoics expanded his tripartite division to include additional word classes, and appear to have fired the first volley in the debate about the categorial status of names and common nouns.[4] The Aristotelian grammatical categories were likewise extended to distinguish verbal properties, including voice and transitivity, whose description in terms of 'upright' and 'bent' varieties paralleled the description of case forms. Even more innovative was the Stoics' use of case inflections to establish a formal contrast between *onomata* and *rhēmata*. The fact that adjectives inflected for case (and gender and number) in Greek led to a classification in which they were treated as a subclass of 'nouns' (Allan 2010a: 63f.). More significantly, the principle of distinguishing word classes according to form had been established (there appears to be no classical antecedent of purely distributional analysis) and was preserved in the Alexandrine grammatical tradition.

To a striking extent, the organization of a classical 'word and paradigm' model, consisting of words organized into sets of basic forms and analogically similar inflected variants, is fully present in Aristotle's time. The primacy of words resonated with the way that other linguistic issues were framed. For those on both sides of the analogy–anomaly debate, the critical evidence consisted of word forms, which either conformed to or deviated from general morphological patterns in Greek. The study of etymology,

---

[4] A debate which was revived in Montague Grammar (Thomason 1974) and lives on in contemporary discussions of the merits of noun phrases vs determiner phrases (Collinge 1998: 64).

which also dates from this period, was similarly word-based. The goals of these early etymological studies were closer to popular conceptions of etymology than to specialist historical or lexicographic views. The point of tracing the history of a word was to not to understand the ways that forms may change or meanings drift over time. Instead, this was designed to reveal the original or even authentic meanings of words. Although these early discussions had only limited direct influence on the subsequent grammatical tradition, the focus they placed on the properties of words and the regularity of relations between words reinforced a general word-based perspective that was carried forward into the classical word and paradigm model.

16.2.2 The Alexandrine Grammatical Tradition

Our understanding of the linguistic traditions that pre-date the appearance of the first written grammars is severely hampered by the fragmentary nature of the surviving materials. There is a particular risk of underestimating the influence of the Stoics, given how few of their own writings were preserved.

> No Stoic grammatical treatise of any period survives; indeed, only one text with what can be called, broadly, grammatical interests is extant in even something like its original form; in any case this book of Chrysippus' *Logical Questions* belongs rather in what moderns would call philosophical logic and the philosophy of language. (Blank and Atherton 2003: 310)

Hence in accepting the received view that the Alexandrine school served as the main conduit between the Greek and Latin traditions, one should not lose sight of the fact that the Stoic school remained active and influential during the period of Alexandrine ascendance. Stoic influences even provide key evidence bearing on the authenticity of the the the oldest surviving grammatical description of Greek, the *Technē grammatikē* 'art of grammar,' associated with the Alexandrine scholar Dionysius Thrax. It is widely accepted that there was a grammarian known as Dionysius Thrax (the Thracian), who taught in Alexandria around 100 BC, and that he was the author of a grammatical description of Greek. However, the authenticity of the version of the *Technē* that has come down to us is a matter of dispute, and the contemporary consensus appears to be that at most the first section can be securely attributed to Dionysius Thrax (Robins 1998: 15, Luhtala 2005: 28).[5] One source of scepticism derives from discrepancies between the views attributed to Dionysus in the historical record and the positions expressed in the later sections of the *Technē*. In particular, Dionysius is said by contemporaries to define verbs in terms of their function as predicates and to assign names and common nouns to distinct word classes (Robins 1998: 16f.). Both views

---

[5] It is instructive to compare Robins (1957) with the later discussion in the papers in Law and Sluiter (1998) and in Luhtala (2005), which re-evaluates the influence of Apollonius Dyscolus.

endorse Stoic positions, in contrast to the description in the *Technē*, which defines verbs mainly in terms of patterns of inflection and assigns names and common nouns to the same word class.

Reservations about the authenticity of the *Technē* clearly detract from its value as an accurate record of the grammatical assumptions current in Alexandria during the time of Dionysius. Nevertheless, given that the discrepancies reflect the effects of Alexandrinization, the *Technē* can be taken as a record of the grammatical assumptions current at a later stage of the Alexandrine school. From this perspective, what is again remarkable is the extent to which the *Technē* merely refines the Aristotelian conception. The sections dealing with *leksis* (12) and *logos* (13) echo the earlier passages from *De Interpretatione*. Sentences are again defined as meaningful units and words as their smallest parts.[6]

> A word is the smallest part of an ordered sentence.[7] (11, 1)

> A sentence is a prose expression that formulates a complete thought.[8] (11, 2)

The class of *onomata* is again defined as declinable elements, with the consequence that this class contains adjectives along with common and proper nouns. The class of *rhēmata* contains indeclinable elements that are marked for verbal properties. The accidents of nouns and verbs mix a range of inflectional properties with a category of 'species' (Gr. *eidos*), which designates types of derivational formations and 'form' (Gr. *schēma*), which distinguishes compounds.

> A noun is a declinable part of speech, signifying an object or an action ... There are five accidents of the noun: gender, species, form, number and case.[9] (12, 1–6)

> A verb is an indeclinable word, which marks time, person and number and which expresses the active and passive. There are eight accidents of the verb: mood, voice, species, form, number, tense, person and conjugation.[10] (13, 1–4)

The principal deviation from the Aristotelian conception is the formal definition of word classes in terms of declination. The extension of word classes and grammatical categories is largely an elaboration of Aristotle's classification. Moreover, the treatment of grammar in terms of 'an accurate account of analogies' in the initial (and presumably authentic) section is entirely Aristotelian.

---

[6] All translations below from French and German originals are my own (JPB). The references to the *Technē* cite the part and line number in Lallot (1989).

[7] 'Le mot (*léxis*) est la plus petite partie de la phrase (*lógos*) construite.'

[8] 'La phrase est une composition en prose qui manifeste une pensée complète.'

[9] 'Le nom est une partie de phrase casuelle désignant un corps ou une action ... Il y a cinq accidents du nom: le genre, l'espèce, la figure, le nombre, le cas.'

[10] 'Le verbe est un mot non casuel, qui admet temps, personnes et nombres, et qui exprime l'actif ou le passif. Il y a huit accidents du verbe: le mode, la diathèse, l'espèce, la figure, le nombre, la personne, le temps, la conjugaison.'

16.2.3 The Latin Grammarians

By the Alexandrine period, the die had been cast, and the classical model was to undergo only comparatively minor revisions until the modern period. The Roman grammarians were particularly conservative, and tended to see their role as adapting and applying the Greek model to Latin. Their attitude reflected the elevated position of Greek learning in the Roman world, together with the typological similarity of Greek and Latin. This assessment does not of course deny the real progress achieved within the Latin tradition, particularly in the domain of syntax, or undervalue the broader perspective afforded by expanding the scope of grammatical descriptions to include Latin as well as Greek. However, the general conception of morphological analysis was largely stable and essentially Greek during this time. The towering achievement of the Latin grammarians lay less in the innovations that they introduced than in their success in elaborating and codifying an inherited model in a form that could serve as the basis for the teaching of Latin from the Roman empire until the present day.

Some of the refinements introduced by the Latin grammarians nevertheless bring their model closer to modern conceptions of morphological analysis. The most obvious of these is a principled contrast between inflection and derivation, which is not observed in any general way within the Greek tradition. This distinction appears to originate with Varro, the earliest recorded Latin grammarian, who lived between 116 and 27 BC and was roughly contemporary with Dionysius Thrax (170–90 BC).[11] The way that Varro characterizes inflection in terms of implicational structure is almost arrestingly modern.

> This part of morphology [i.e. inflection] Varro called 'natural-word form variation;
> (dēclinātiō nātūrālis), because, given a word and its inflexional class, we can infer all
> its other forms. (Robins 1997: 63)

Varro's insight was only partially preserved in the subsequent tradition. One the one hand, the implicational relations that determine the analogical patterns within inflectional paradigms continued to play a role in the morphological rules of later grammars. The monumental *Institutiones grammaticae* 'Grammatical foundations' of Priscian (*c.*500 AD) exploits these interdependencies in the rules that derive inflected variants of nouns and verbs from their basic forms, which he assumed to be the nominative singular and first person singular indicative active. Yet on the other hand Priscian did not maintain a consistent distinction between inflectional forms and derivational formations.

From the standpoint of the development of the word-based model, the most salient feature of this tradition is again its stability. It is striking that the ancient grammarians, over the course of the millennium that runs from the earliest recorded discussions of language in Greece until the late Byzantine period, did not at any point perceive the

---

[11] Though see Matthews (1994) for a critical reappraisal of Varro's influence.

need to introduce units intervening between sounds and words. This possibility does not seem to have been entertained by the Greek grammarians. Moreover, to the extent that sub-word analyses occurred to those working in the later Latin tradition, they were roundly rejected.

> As with the rest of western Antiquity, Priscian's grammatical model is word and paradigm, and he expressly denied any significance to divisions, in what would now be called morphemic analysis, below the word. (Robins 1997: 70)

16.2.4 The Neogrammarian Turn

The Sanskrit grammarians had of course developed models of sub-word analysis to a high level of sophistication in the course of an even older linguistic tradition. Hence while the classical word-based model would continue to serve as the basis of Greek and Latin pedagogy from Priscian's time until the present, the Western rediscovery of Sanskrit ensured that it did not remain unchallenged as a general model of linguistic description. However, at least initially, there was no perception of a conflict between these models, and one can even see the consolidation of their 'external' and 'internal' perspectives on word structure as one of the factors that contributed to the extraordinary success of the Neogrammarian school. The morphotactic structure recognized by the Sanskritist grammarians contributed syntagmatic insights about the combination of formatives that complemented the paradigmatic analyses assigned by the classical model.

Thus, the dawn of the Neogrammarian period finds Schleicher 1859 echoing Aristotle and the *Technē* in again declaring that 'language consists of words'.[12]

> Language consists of words; thus to a first approximation, it is a matter of what kind of form a word can have and how we describe this form in a generally applicable way.[13] (p. 2)

Yet unlike classical grammarians, Schleicher then proceeds to outline an accompanying model of word-internal structure. He identifies roots (*wurzeln*) as expressions of lexical 'meaning' (*bedeutung*) and inflections (*beziehungslauten* 'relational sounds') as expressions of 'relations' (*beziehungen*) between meanings.

> The spoken expressions of meaning are called roots . . . The spoken expression of relations are relational sounds . . .[14] (p. 2)

---

[12] The footnoted originals of the following quotations preserve the spelling and capitalization of the source.

[13] 'Die sprache besteht auß worten; es handelt sich also zunächst darum: welcherlei form kann das wort haben und wie bezeichnen wir dise formen in einer algemeinen, für alle worte gültigen weise.'

[14] 'Den lautlichen außdruck der bedeutung nent man wurzel . . . Lautlicher außdruck der beziehung ist der beziehungslaut . . .'

The patterns formed by different combination of roots and inflectional affixes in turn provide the basis for a morphological typology. Although rudimentary, the significance of this type of morphotactic classification lies in the fact that is almost entirely without precedent in the classical tradition. It is also unlike the morphemic analyses of the later Bloomfieldian school, in that no particular grammatical importance appears to have been attached to the specific segmentations of word forms. As Davies (1998: 200) notes with respect to the notation that Schleicher uses to represent morphotactic structure, '[i]t is not clear that the symbolism is much more than a form of shorthand.'

This structural agnosticism survives through the Neogrammarian period and inter-acts with the models of proportional analogy developed during this period. As was observed at the time, assigning analogy a central role in reinforcing and extending the congruence of morphological systems was not original with the Neogrammarians. The basic outlook is, again, fundamentally Aristotelian. What was distinctively Neogram-marian was the interplay between analogy and their model of sound laws, and the view that these mechanisms could account for most if not all of language. A characteristic-ally bold pronouncement in the introduction to Leskien (1876) declares that the inflectional forms of a language at any particular point can be attributed either to sound change or to analogy.

> Both factors, sound change-driven reorganization and analogy, account in a defin-ite period for the declensional forms of a language, as with any type of inflection, and only these two factors come into consideration.[15] (Leskien 1876: 2)

Modern commentators are often inclined to regard analogy as a proxy for rules, as expressed in claims to the effect that 'the solution of an analogical equation is practically the same as the application of a word-based rule to a novel word' (Haspel-math 2002: 56). While this may apply to some uses of analogy, it is misleading in relation to the views of Neogrammarians such as Hermann Paul, as it attributes a significance to sub-word units that they expressly denied.

> Should we assume that analogy is simply another name for a set of rules which the speaker internalizes? Paul seems to reject this possibility mainly because any set of rules would operate in terms of abstractions to which he is not ready to attribute any validity. (Davies 1998: 257f.)

This structural agnosticism is reminiscent of the attitude towards sub-word sequences in the analogical correspondences of classical grammars.

> Priscian organized the morphological description of the forms of nouns and verbs, and of the other inflected words, by setting up canonical or basic forms . . . from these he proceeded to the other forms by a series of letter changes, the letter being

---

[15] 'Beide Momente, lautgesetzlich Umbildung und Analogie, erklären die in einer bestimmten Periode vorbandene Gestalt der Declination einer Sprache, wie jeder Art der Flexion, und nur diese beiden Momente kommen in Betracht.'

for him, as for the rest of western Antiquity, both the minimal graphic unit and the minimal phonological unit. (Robins 1997: 72)

In the work of the Neogrammarians, at least, this representational neutrality reflects a key insight. Just as the organization of words into paradigms in a classical model is driven by patterns of interdependence, the segmentation of individual forms is motivated by the predictive value of segments. There are no constraints on proportional analogies that would force them to cut forms 'at the joint' or to impose a stable and uniform head-thorax-abdomen analysis. Any patterns that are of use in predicting new forms provide a viable analogical base, without the need to attach any significance to their segments. Indeed, much of the attraction of their model of analogy derived precisely from the fact that

> it offered an algorithm for a structurally based form of morphological segmentation, without making any claims about the segments in question. More important perhaps is that Paul's concept of analogy and of analogical proportion is a definite attempt at providing a generalized account at a certain level of detail of how language production occurs and of how the speaker and hearer can produce and analyse an infinite number of forms and sentences which they have not heard before. (Davies 1998: 258f.)

Paul's account of the creative use of language is framed in essentially Aristotelian terms, in which previously encountered paradigms exert analogical pressures that guide the production (or, presumably, comprehension) of novel word forms.

> The creative activity of the individual is also very considerable in the domain of word building and even more so in inflection... We see the effect of analogy especially clearly in the grammatical acquisition of inflected forms of a foreign language. One learns a number of paradigms by heart and then memorizes only as many forms of individual words as is necessary to recognize their affiliation to this or that paradigm. Now and then a single form suffices. One forms the remaining forms at the moment that one needs them, in accordance with the paradigm, that is, by analogy.[16] (Paul 1920 [1880]: 112)

Analogy remains the cornerstone of the approaches developed by successors of the Neogrammarians, including de Saussure and, particularly, Kuryłowicz, who developed the most systematic account of the constraints on proportions.

> A proportion relates 'basic' forms to forms 'founded' on them and a relation of foundation $a \rightarrow b$ must exist in order for $a : b = c : d$ to be admissible as a proportion.

---

[16] 'Sehr bedeutend ist die schöpferische Tätigkeit des Individuums aber auch auf dem Gebiete der Wortbildung und noch mehr auf der der Flexion... Besonders klar sehen wir die Wirkungen der Analogie bei der grammatischen Aneignung der Flexionsformen einer fremden Sprache. Man lernt eine Anzahl von Paradigmen auswendig und prägt sich dann von den einzelnen Wörtern nur soviel Formen ein, als erforderlich sind, um die Zugehörigkeit zu diesem oder jenem Paradigma zu erkennen. Mitunter genügt dazu eine einzige. Die übrigen Formen bildet man in dem Augenblicke, wo man ihrer bedarf, nach dem Paradigma, d.h. nach Analogie.'

[I]f *b* is founded on *a*, this means that the existence of *b* presupposes the existence of *a*, rather than that *b* is constructed by starting with *a* and adding something. Thus, the stem of a paradigm is founded on the various fully inflected forms, rather than *vice versa*.[17] Kuryłowicz regards the grammar as a set of relations among full surface forms (much as de Saussure did: see Anderson 1985), rather than as a set of rules specifying the construction of complex forms from simple components. (Anderson 1992: 369)

The development of more explicit and restricted formats for expressing analogical proportions, like the recognition of word-internal structure, clearly represents a significant refinement to the classical model. Yet, for all that, the basic word-based model remains largely intact, and essentially Aristotelian.

16.3 THE MODERN REVIVAL OF WORD-BASED MODELS

It is not until the work of Bloomfield (a member of the last generation of general linguists to be trained in the Neogrammarian school) that an exclusively syntagmatic approach to morphological analysis takes hold, and eclipses the traditional model. However, the period of unchallenged dominance by the morphemic model was short-lived. Within a quarter-century after the pioneering work on morphemic analysis in Harris (1942) and Hockett (1947), Hockett had executed a complete volte-face and come to regard morphemic descriptions as shorthand for more psychologically realistic descriptions in traditional terms.

> To cover the complex alternations of Yawelmani by principal-parts-and-paradigms would take much more space than is occupied in the first sections of this paper by the morphophoneme-and-rewrite-rule presentation. But there would be a net gain in realism, for the student of the language would now be required to produce new forms in exactly the way the native user of the language produces or recognizes them—by analogy.... A correct principal-parts-and-paradigms statement and a correct morphophoneme-and-rule statement subsume the same actual facts of an alternation, the former more directly, the latter more succinctly. We ought therefore to be free to use the latter, provided we specify that it is to be understood only as convenient shorthand for the former. (Hockett 1967: 221f.)

---

[17] The notion that stems are abstracted from sets of fully inflected word forms is clear in the treatment of declension outlined by Kuryłowicz (1947: 159): 'Car la notion du thème est postérieure aux formes concrètes composant le paradigme: on trouve le thème en dégageant les éléments communs à toutes les formes casuelles du paradigme (quand il s'agit de la déclinaison)' [For the notion of the stem is dependent on the concrete forms composing the paradigm: one finds the stem in disengaging the elements that are common to all the case forms of a paradigm (when dealing with declension)].

In due course, the Transformationalists took over the morphemic model. However, their relation to the Bloomfieldians was akin to the Romans' relation to the Greeks, at least in morphological matters, as they were largely content to refine an approach they had inherited. One of the attitudes that came along with the Bloomfieldian model was disdain for traditional models and, indeed, for traditional grammar in general. Hence, with rare exceptions (Chomsky 1965: §2.2) the transformational tradition has been consistently morphemic in outlook.

Meanwhile, the classical, historical, and pedagogical traditions provided intellectual reservoirs that harboured the classical model until conditions were more favourable for a general reassessment of its merits. Although the first steps towards rehabilitation were tentative, each step nudged the classical model back towards to the linguistic mainstream. The modest mea culpa of Hockett (1954) provoked the more robust defence in Robins (1959), and both works are cited in the opening sentence of Matthews (1965), which offered the first theoretical reappraisal—and formalization—of the traditional model in a general linguistics journal. However, the first bridge between classical philology and modern linguistics was established by Matthews (1972), a dense and highly methodological monograph with the inauspicious-sounding title *Inflectional Morphology: A Theoretical Study Based on Aspects of Latin Verb Conjugation*. The first edition of Matthews' *Morphology* (1991) appeared two years later, in 1974, offering a modern introduction to the study of morphology that integrated a classical perspective.

16.3.1 The Flectional Challenge

In some sense, Matthews' studies are primarily concerned with the basis on which one arrives at and justifies morphological analyses. However, it was the issues that he raised in the course of exploring this question that ultimately had the greatest contemporary resonance. One set of issues were connected to a typology of the patterns that occur in flectional languages. A second set outlined the difficulties that these patterns present for models of morphemic analysis and clarified how they had influenced the development of the classical model.

Two empirical patterns that have since taken on particular importance for morphological models are cases of non-bi-unique exponence and Priscianic syncretism. The first pattern is illustrated by tangled feature–form associations in the classical Greek verb *elelýkete* 'you had unfastened,' in Fig. 16.1.

Within a classical model, the word form *elelýkete* is analysed as standing in a bi-unique relation to the second person past perfective indicative active cell in the paradigm of LYO 'unfasten.' But as Matthews observes, the realization of aspect and voice confounds any attempt to establish the bi-unique relation between features and sub-word units that is dictated by a morphemic model.

> But categories and formatives are in nothing like a one-to-one relation. That
> the word is Perfective is in part identified by the reduplication *le-* but also by the

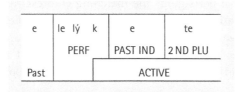

FIG. 16.1 Morphological analysis of Greek *elelýkete* (Matthews 1991: 173)

suffix *-k-*. At the same time, *-k-* is one of the formatives that help to identify the word as Active; another is *-te* which, however, also marks it as '2nd Plural'. (Matthews 1991: 173)

The features past, perfective, and active are all realized by multiple exponents in Fig. 16.1. The perfective exponents *le-* and *-k-* flank the root *lý*, and are themselves flanked by the past 'augment' *e-* and the past indicative suffix *-e-*, while active voice is expressed by *-k-*, *-e-* and *-te*. There is nothing exceptional about *elelýkete* within the inflectional system of classical Greek. On the contrary, the paradigm of LYO 'to unfasten' is treated as exemplary in traditional grammars such as Goodwin (1894). As Matthews (1991: 174) notes, this paradigm does not show 'any crucial irregularity' and it 'is in fact the first that generations of schoolchildren used to commit to memory.' Yet the features of *elelýkete* are realized at multiple points within this form, so that individual features cannot be correlated with single formatives. This tangle of extended and overlapping exponence presents a different challenge from the one posed by the 'cumulative' exponence exhibited by second person plural *-te*. This 'fusional' pattern shows that the 'units of content' that condition morphological exponence may also be larger than a single feature, so that biuniqueness is violated in both directions.

Patterns of Priscianic (or parasitic) syncretism present a different sort of challenge. The Latin example described below involves a regular correspondence between present active infinitives and imperfect subjunctives.

> For any Verb, however irregular it may be in other respects, the Present Infinitive always predicts the Imperfect Subjunctive. For the Verb 'to flower', *florere* → *florerem*; for the irregular Verb 'to be', *esse* → *essem*, and so forth without exception. (Matthews 1991: 195)

This correlation is expressed by the traditional proportional analogy in (1) below. One significant feature of these types of proportions is that they do not demand that any general meaning be associated with the shared 'units of form' *florere* and *esse*. The value of these elements resides in their predictive force, and it is only the full word forms in 0 below that are assigned grammatical meanings, in the context of their inflectional paradigms. A stem such as *florere* is non-meaning-bearing or 'morphomic' in the sense of Aronoff (1994). However, in this respect it is not fundamentally different from stems and formatives in any other proportional analogies. In the classical model, the grammatical features of exemplary word forms define their place in their paradigms, while the features of principal parts guide the matching with exemplary forms. There is no need to assign grammatical meanings to sub-word units, and cases like (1) suggest that it is counterproductive to try to impose meanings on shared units of form. This difficulty serves in fact to reinforce the traditional insight that the value of these units of form resides in the predictions that they sanction about other forms.

(1) florere : florerem = esse : X (X = essem)

The problems and insights that Matthews rescued from classical obscurity inspired the development of nearly all modern word-based approaches. Yet this tradition evolved in an intellectual climate that was, at least initially, not entirely conducive to a modern formalization of the exemplary patterns and (possibly sub-symbolic) processes of analogy that make up the classical model.

16.3.2 A Modern Adaption

Hence the formalization of the traditional model that Matthews outlines takes the form of a rule system that constructs complex forms from roots. The basic organization of this system can be understood by examining the analyses assigned to forms such as *elelýkete* and patterns such as *florere ~ florerem*.

Consider first patterns of extended exponence. These are characterized by a set of EXPONENCE rules that realize partially overlapping feature bundles. The point of departure for the analysis of *elelýkete* is the structure in Fig. 16.2, which combines the grammatical features of the surface form *elelýkete* and the root form *ly:* of the verb LYO 'unfasten'. This structure does not represent the root entry of LYO, which would only contain whatever intrinsic features are taken to characterize uninflected roots. The features in Fig. 16.2 instead characterize the abstract paradigm cell that is realized by the surface word form *elelýkete*.[18]

FIG. 16.2 Root and 2nd plural active paradigm cell of Greek LYO 'unfasten'

---

[18] Matthews (1991) also subscripts the category label 'V' to identify the word class of this form, though it turns out to makes no real difference whether features are considered part of the 'content' of a feature bundle or as specifying the 'context' in which the bundle is spelled out. Hence nothing hinges on whether category labels are included within feature bundles or subscripted to them.

$$\begin{bmatrix} \text{PERF} \\ \text{XV:} \end{bmatrix} \rightarrow \text{XV}$$

FIG. 16.3 Perfective 'shortening' rule

$$\begin{bmatrix} \text{PERF} \\ \text{CX} \end{bmatrix} \rightarrow \text{Ce} + \text{CX}$$

FIG. 16.4 Perfective reduplication rule

$$\begin{bmatrix} \text{ACT} \\ \text{PERF} \\ \text{X} \end{bmatrix} \rightarrow \text{X} + \text{k}$$

FIG. 16.5 Active perfective stem rule

Features	PERFECTIVE	PERFECTIVE	ACTIVE, PERFECTIVE
Rule	XV: → XV	CV: → Ce + CX	X → X + k
Output	*ly*	*lely*	*lelyk*

FIG. 16.6 Spell-out of the active perfective stem *lelyk*

The form *elelýkete* is obtained by applying rules that realize the features in Fig. 16.2 by successively modifying the root *ly:*. For the present illustration, the rules that define just the perfective active stem *lelyk* will suffice.[19] The shortening rule in Fig. 16.3 applies first. This rule realizes Perfective by reducing a long root vowel, shortening *ly:* to *ly*. The reduplication rule in Fig. 16.4 then repeats the initial stem consonant, obtaining *lely* from *ly*. The rule in Fig. 16.5 applies next, defining the perfective active stem *lelyk* by suffixing *-k* to *lely*. Fig. 16.6 summarizes the ordering of exponence rules in the 'derivation' of *lelyk*.

Matthews (1991: 178) demonstrates that a sequence of further exponence rules define the full word form *elelýkete*. However, the multiple realization of perfective in the derivation of *lelyk* suffices to show how realization rules admit patterns of extended exponence. The fact that spell-out neither alters nor consumes features allows each of

---

[19] Accent placement is suppressed, as it is predictable here (Goodwin 1894: 29).

the rules in Figs 16.3–16.5 to realize the same perfective feature. Hence vowel shortening, reduplication, and suffixation of /k/ can all function as exponents of the feature Perfective. One could seek grounds for identifying one of these as the 'primary' exponent and relegate the others to a supporting role. But there is no compelling reason to enforce this distinction.

More generally, the definition of *lelyk* identifies the fundamental building blocks of a modern stem and paradigm model. Abstract paradigm cells like Fig. 16.2 specify a set of distinctive features and a root form. Realization rules apply successively to define the surface form that realizes the features in a cell. The first rule in this sequence modifies the root *ly:* associated with the cell in Fig. 16.2 and the remaining rules modify the output of a previous rule. Many of the intermediate outputs in an analysis will underlie a family of surface word forms. Apart from cases of stem suppletion, roots will underlie the full conjugational paradigm of a verb. The reduplicated form *lely* likewise underlies perfective passive/middle forms of LYO, while *lelyk* underlies perfect and pluperfect active forms. At each point in the derivation of a surface form like *elelýkete*, there may then be a number of inflectional choices. In a modern stem and paradigm model, these choices correspond to the exponence rules applicable at that point.

As this treatment of cumulative and extended exponence shows, realization rules offer a flexible analysis of morphological patterns. Yet not all of the patterns described by traditional proportional analogies can be expressed as the spell-out of morphosyntactic features. The correspondence between present active infinitives and imperfect subjunctives in (1) is instructive. In the rule in Fig. 16.7, the form that realizes the present active infinitive defines the base for the imperfect subjunctive. However, the correspondence between the cells in Fig. 16.7 is purely at the level of form; there is no relation between the features of these cells and, in particular, no sense in which the features of the present active infinitive underlie or contribute to those of the imperfect subjunctive.

Relations of this nature plainly do not involve the spell-out of a paradigm cell. But, as in a proportional analogy, one feature–form pair in a morphological transformation PREDICTS another pair. Thus the features in Fig. 16.7 have essentially the same role that the features of a principal part do when they guide a process of matching the principal part against an exemplary paradigm.

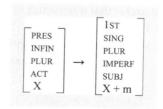

FIG. 16.7 Latin infinitive–imperfective correspondence (Matthews 1991: 194)

16.3.3 The Stem and Paradigm Model

Just as Bloomfield's work inspired approaches that adapted the Bloomfieldian model beyond all recognition, the word-based tradition that Matthews revitalized led off in a number of quite different directions. The Extended Word and Paradigm model (Anderson 1982)—subsequently A-Morphous Morphology (Anderson 1992)—combined an exponence-based perspective with a model of grammar in which feature bundles were relocated from abstract paradigms to the preterminal nodes of syntactic representations. The model of Paradigm Function Morphology (Stump 2001) moved in the opposite direction, attaching even greater importance to paradigms by assigning a central role to paradigm functions that mapped cell features and roots onto fully inflected forms. The descriptive challenge presented by patterns of Priscianic syncretism likewise prompted the general model of 'autonomous' morphology in Aronoff (1994).[20]

Despite differences in their theoretical orientation and device inventories, these modern approaches form a fairly cohesive block. They are all, in effect, theoretical hybrids that reject the most doctrinaire aspects of morphemic analysis, while adopting other prevailing ideas about the organization of a grammatical system and the composition of the lexicon. As should be clear from the preceding discussion, the most significant divergences from classical models lie in the treatment of content–form relations and in general morphotactic assumptions. Traditional models exhibit content–form correspondences by sets of exemplary patterns, together with proportional analogies that extend patterns to new items. In modern approaches, analysis is an interpretive process, in which bundles of distinctive features are spelled out by realization rules. Traditional and modern models can also both be described as 'word-based' in the sense that the word is the smallest grammatically meaningful unit. Yet traditional models are also morphotactically word-based. They treat surface word forms as the basic elements of a system, and, to the extent that they recognize roots, stems, and exponents at all, they regard these elements as abstractions over a lexicon of full word forms. In contrast, the morphotactic assumptions of modern models pattern more with those of morphemic approaches, in which surface word forms are assembled from more basic elements. Unlike Bloomfieldian models, they do not encapsulate formatives in discrete morphemes. But modern approaches still assume a model of the lexicon in which open-class items are represented by roots and/or stems, and surface word forms are constructed from these units though the successive application of realization rules. Thus, overall, modern approaches agree with morphemic models in treating surface words as derived units, but disagree about the nature of the devices that derive these units.

---

[20] Approaches that show a less direct influence include 'lexeme-based' or 'realization-based' models of Zwicky (1985) and Beard (1995) and the 'seamless' model of Singh and Starosta (2003).

More insidiously, although the use of a general mechanism for spelling out properties of abstract paradigm cells addressed some of the empirical challenges described by
Hockett (1947, 1954) and Matthews (1972), it also led to a natural expansion of the class
of morphosyntactic 'features' to be spelled out. The process seems to have begun with
the 'declension class features' proposed in the brief excursion into word and paradigm
morphology in Chomsky (1965: 171). Inflection class features are subsequently introduced without comment in Matthews (1972) and assumed in most subsequent word-
based models. As the tradition extended its empirical scope, the role of indexical
features expanded as well. Anderson (1992: 150) incorporates 'series indices' of the
form [±Series II] to govern case marking in Georgian. Indices for individual lexemes
are assumed in one form or another in most models, while stem indices are adopted in
analyses of Priscianic and other types of stem syncretism (Aronoff 1994, Stump 2001).
   In each of these cases, features or indices serve as assembly instructions that
determine the choice of an element from a set of alternatives, or trigger the application
of a particular rule. In languages where inflection class, series, or stem choice is not
predictable from grammatical or phonological properties, encoding class membership
as a separate morphological feature permits the selection of the appropriate stem or
exponents. By cross-referencing cells, entries, and rules, it is possible to introduce
elements of form that are underdetermined by grammatical features and a root (or
stem) form. Yet the use of indexical features radically changes the nature and orientation of a morphological model. It is not clear that exponence rules remain interpretive
in any meaningful sense if they can be taken to spell out class and series features and
stem indices.[21]

16.3.4 The Neo-classical Model

These contrasts between traditional and modern word-based models highlight the
profound ways in which the post-Bloomfieldian school had come to frame the form
in which morphological questions were posed and answers were formulated. Although
Robins, like Hockett (1954, 1967), had advocated a reassessment of the traditional
model, none of the models proposed between the initial publication of his defence of
WP in 1959 and its reprinting in 2001 attempted to formalize the exemplar-based
intuition of the classical model.
   Ironically, a framework for this formalization had already been developed during
Bloomfield's time, and had even attracted the early attention of Harris (1951) and
Hockett (1953). The theory of information pioneered by Shannon (1948) provided all
of the formal prerequisites for a modern formulation of the classical model. In

---

[21] Quarantining indexical features in class indices so that they provide the context rather than the
content of an exponence rule does not make any real difference as long as context and content both
condition the application of the rule.

particular, the use of entropy-based measures to model implicational structure offered solutions to a number of the seemingly intractable problems associated with classical and philological formulations of this model. Many of these problems reflect idealizations that arose from the pedagogical application of the classical model. Motivating the choice of principal parts and exemplary paradigms presents one set of problems, identifying valid proportions raises another set, and even the assumption that inflectional systems can be factored into a discrete number of inflection classes is problematic in its own way. Avoiding these problems by recognizing that they derive from practical idealizations rather than core properties of the classical model leaves a conception of paradigms as structured networks of interdependent elements

It is this interdependence that can be modelled by information theory. Specifically, each cell in a paradigm can be associated with a measure of variability or UNCERTAINTY that correlates with the number of realizations of the cell (and the frequency of those alternatives). A given cell is of diagnostic value in identifying the realization of another cell (or set of cells) if knowing the realization of the first cell reduces uncertainty about the realization of the second cell (or set). These intuitions can be formalized by regarding paradigm cells as random variables that take realizations as their values. The uncertainty associated with the realization of a cell C is then defined in terms of the ENTROPY (Shannon 1948) of the cell, $H(C)$. Example (2) adapts a standard definition of entropy, in which RC represents the set of realization outcomes for C, x represents outcomes in RC, and $p(x)$ represents the probability that C is realized by x.

$$(2) \quad H(C) = -\sum_{x \in R_C} p(x)\log_2 p(x)$$

Uncertainty is reduced in a system that has fewer 'choices,' either few outcomes in total or else outcomes with highly skewed distributions. The cumulative uncertainty associated with a paradigm P depends in turn on the uncertainty of its cells $C_1, C_2, \ldots, C_n$. On a traditional model, cells are generally assumed to be interdependent, so that the entropy of a paradigm, $H(P)$, will correspond to the JOINT ENTROPY of its cells, $H(C_1, C_2, \ldots, C_n)$. Given a general measure of uncertainty, the diagnostic value of an individual cell can be defined in terms of uncertainty reduction. The relevant notion can be based on CONDITIONAL ENTROPY, $H(C_2|C_1)$, which measures the amount of uncertainty that remains about C_2 given knowledge of C_1. It should be intuitively clear at this point how the traditional selection of principal parts is implicitly guided by entropy reduction. The more information that C_1 provides about C_2, the lower $H(C_2|C_1)$ will be. A fully diagnostic cell will reduce the uncertainty of the remaining forms in its paradigm to a value approaching 0. A fully non-diagnostic cell will preserve uncertainty. Most cells will fall between these extremes, reducing uncertainty about some cells while preserving the uncertainty of others.

The brief discussion so far has adopted what might be termed a speaker-oriented or production-based perspective, in which the choice of paradigm cell is fixed and what is uncertain is the realization of the cell. Inverting this perspective yields a hearer-oriented or comprehension-based standpoint. In this case, the realization is fixed and what is uncertain is which cell it realizes. This entropy measure is expressed in 0, in which r is a realization, C represents a cell in P, x, and $p(C)$ represents the probability that r realizes C.

$$(3) \quad H(r) = -\sum_{C \in P} p(C) \log_2 p(C)$$

The uncertainty associated with paradigms, and the uncertainty reduction attributable to knowing the cell realized by a given form are then defined as above.

Exactly the same notions of uncertainty reduction offer a means of validating proportional analogies. From either a hearer- or speaker-oriented perspective, the reliability of a proportion $a : b = c : X$ will correlate with the degree to which knowledge of a reduces uncertainty about b. In valid proportions, $H(b|a)$ will greatly reduce the uncertainty of b (whether this represents the realization of a given cell or the identification of the cell that a given form realizes), whereas in spurious proportions, the uncertainty of b will not be reduced.

This neo-classical model reflects the convergence of an implication-based tradition of morphological analysis (Wurzel 1984, Blevins 2006, Finkel and Stump 2007, Ackerman et al. 2009) with information-theoretic approaches to morphological processing (Moscoso del Prado Martín et al. 2004, Milin et al. 2009). A highly promising aspect of this approach is that it holds out the prospect of a unified model of morphological description. As Matthews (1972) notes, variation in the morphological systems of the world's languages poses acute challenges for any unified model of morphological analysis.

> Finally, it has become clear at least that different languages raise quite different problems in morphological analysis. It is therefore possible that they also require quite different sorts of description. (Matthews 1972: 156)

However a more uniform description can be assigned if the classical model is reconceptualized as an instantiation of a more general 'item and pattern' grammar (Blevins to appear) that analogically extends patterns that are of predictive value in a language. In many languages, words will be the most informative items and inflectional paradigms the patterns that sanction the most reliable deductions. But in other languages, sub-word units may be of predictive value.

16.4 CONCLUSION

There is general agreement that word structure constitutes the basic subject matter of morphology. There is, however, a fundamental split within the field concerning the nature and direction of this structure. Bloomfieldian models, with their roots in the Sanskritist tradition, take the central analytical task of morphology to involve the disassembly of words into formatives, so that word structure principally reflects combinations of sub-word units. The other dominant model, word-based morphology, approaches morphological analysis more as a classification task, and treats the association of words with paradigms or other sets of forms as the basis of the main grammatically distinctive structure in a morphological system. From its origins as a framework for the description of classical Greek to the present, this model has remained remarkably stable and useful, and even now may offer new insights into the structure of language.

CHAPTER 17

GENERAL OR UNIVERSAL GRAMMAR FROM PLATO TO CHOMSKY

JAAP MAAT

17.1 INTRODUCTION

FROM antiquity onwards, two distinct approaches to the study of language have been pursued: one philosophical, aimed at giving a general characterization of language as such, the other pedagogical, aimed at instructing pupils in the correct use of their native tongue, or of a foreign language. This chapter offers a necessarily eclectic overview of the history of the former, in the Western tradition. This type of language study has been given various names, such as 'philosophical,' 'general,' 'universal,' 'natural,' and 'rational' grammar. These labels sometimes reflect theoretical assumptions not necessarily shared by all grammarians and philosophers whose work can be considered as falling under this category, but for present purposes it is assumed that the often diverse theories covered by these labels form a sufficiently homogeneous trend to be treated together.

17.2 ANTIQUITY

17.2.1 Plato's Search for the Ideal Word

Plato was the first writer in the Western tradition to systematically consider the relationships between language, knowledge and the world. In his *Cratylus* he addressed a number of questions that have exercised both linguists and philosophers ever since.[1] The dialogue deals with the correctness of names, and explores the nature vs convention debate. The naturalists maintained that names can be correct as they represent the nature of the things they designate, whereas the conventionalists held that words are arbitrarily assigned to things. In examining this question, Plato had several purposes in mind: to safeguard the existence of absolute norms against relativism, and to investigate the philosophical significance of language study. He concluded that most of the issues raised in the *Cratylus* could not be resolved without further scrutiny, but he did find that investigating language is not a suitable method for investigating reality. Further, he made it clear that neither naturalism nor conventionalism could satisfactorily be brought into agreement with known facts about language.

A large part of the dialogue is taken up by detailed discussion of the etymology of a number of words of different sorts. Historically speaking, the method of linguistic analysis displayed in the *Cratylus* was important in that it followed a pattern that can be found in many theoretical approaches to grammar in subsequent centuries. It is characterized by the assumption that in order to understand how language works, one must take it apart and examine the bits of which it is ultimately composed. Further, it is assumed that in order to understand how language relates to the world and to the human mind, one must look under the surface of the linguistic forms encountered in language use. In the *Cratylus*, the focus is on 'names' and their constituents, i.e. syllables and letters, and the analysis proceeds in two steps. First, words are shown to be composed of other words from which the meaning of the analysed words is supposed to derive. Second, when the analysis reaches primitive words and the method used in the first step can no longer be applied, words are shown to derive their pictorial quality from the sound symbolism connected with the individual letters out of which they are composed.

Plato was well aware of the fact that there are many different languages. Yet he assumed that his conclusions, although based on Greek etymologies, were valid regardless of particular languages. The diversity of languages poses a challenge to universalist positions of all types, and in the context of the *Cratylus* this presents a particularly pressing problem. For if words show the nature of things, how can words for the same thing vary so enormously from language to language? Plato found a way out: it is only the ideal name that represents the nature of the thing perfectly, and this ideal name can be embodied in various materials. Just as the ideal instrument can be made of different pieces of iron, so can the ideal name be made of different syllables. In this way, Plato was led to develop the theoretical approach just mentioned: in order to find the forms or structures which are essential to language, one must ignore the immense variety of linguistic material found on the surface, and excavate the universal features hidden underneath. The method of digging that Plato examined, and ultimately dismissed, was etymological derivation aimed at finding the ideal word.

---

[1] See §13.3 and §34.2, this volume.

Subsequent theorists of universal grammar usually ignored individual words, and looked for the universal and essential in sentence structure and grammatical relations, but similarly assuming that in order to inspect what is general and universal in languages one must probe under the surface.

17.2.2 Aristotle Defines the Framework of Philosophical Grammar

Aristotle's writings defined the framework as well as many of the basic tenets of philosophical approaches to language study until well into the eighteenth century.[2] Among the writings which are relevant in this regard are those dealing with rhetoric and poetics, but also his treatises on metaphysics and physics. Most important, however, are a series of tracts which later became canonised as the 'organon,' and which are devoted to topics that came to be seen as the components of a coherent theory of logic. In the *Categories*, Aristotle considered 'uncombined words,' and provided a typology of predicates. In *On Interpretation*, he treated propositions, that is, words combined into statements. The *Prior Analytics* dealt with syllogisms, i.e. combinations of propositions. Together with the *Posterior Analytics*, the *Topics*, and *On Sophistical Refutations*, which dealt with various methods and materials for argumentation and proof, these treatises formed the basis of logical theory for more than two millennia.

Aristotelian logic was important for later philosophical grammars for a number of reasons. As it was organized according to a compositional pattern reflecting different levels of linguistic analysis (words, propositions, syllogisms), it provided a uniform framework for the analysis of meaning, and for the study of the relationships between language and mind, and between language and the world. Further, Aristotle emphasized that propositions consist essentially of the connection of two elements, a subject (*onoma*) and a predicate (*rhēma*), the former typically represented by a noun or common name, the latter by a verb, as in *A man walks* or *Socrates runs*. The observation that a combination of noun and verb is both necessary and sufficient for the formation of a complete proposition led many later theorists to claim that noun and verb, called 'categorematic terms,' are primary word classes, and that other words, 'syncategorematic terms,' are more marginal. A parallel distinction was that between words which have an independent meaning, apart from the sentence in which they occur, and words whose meaning cannot be established in isolation from others; the former were said to 'signify,' the latter to 'consignify.'

Aristotle's analysis of the proposition led to a distinction between the logical and grammatical form of sentences, although he did not use this terminology. He observed that the connection between the subject and the predicate of a proposition can be

---

[2] See §13.4 and §34.2, this volume.

expressed in various but equivalent ways: either the verb *to be* occurs, signifying the coupling of the subject and the predicate, or no such copula is explicitly expressed. In the latter case, one must assume that the copula is part of the verb. Thus, 'there is no difference between [. . .] "the man is walking" [. . .] and "the man walks"' (*Metaphysics*, V, vii, 5). In the footsteps of Aristotle, the majority of philosophical grammarians maintained that the copula is a necessary part of every sentence, whether explicitly expressed or not, and that consequently verbs should be analysed as consisting of the copula and a noun. It thus became a commonplace to assume that under the surface of linguistic forms lies the logical form of expressions, which often differs from them.

One passage in Aristotle's logical writings stands out for being particularly influential on philosophical grammar in later centuries. It occurs at the outset of *On Interpretation*, and reads as follows:

> Now spoken sounds are symbols of affections in the soul, and written marks symbols of spoken sounds. And just as written marks are not the same for all men, neither are spoken sounds. But what these are in the first place signs of—affections of the soul—are the same for all; and what these affections are likenesses of—actual things—are also the same. (*On Interpretation*, 16a, I)

This sketch of the relationships between the world, the mental realm, and language (spoken and written) remained largely unchallenged for many centuries to come. It drew a clear boundary between what is universal, namely the world and our perceptions and ideas about it, and what is diverse, namely the language we use to refer to the universally shared concepts. It suggested quite strongly that this diversity was of little consequence, since all languages have the same cognitive basis; different languages merely use different conventions in signifying the same set of concepts. Aristotle stated explicitly that nouns have meaning by convention, and that nature has no part in this (*On Interpretation*, 16a, II). Further, this account implied that thinking is independent of language: our concepts are likenesses of actual things; these concepts are formed before language comes into play, whose only role, it seems, is to signify the pre-existing concepts. However, in practice Aristotle often failed to observe a clear distinction between thought and its linguistic expression.

Two further Aristotelian doctrines became important for philosophical grammar. First, he distinguished four types of causes, traditionally termed material, formal, efficient, and final causes. Second, he used a distinction between the matter and the form of substances to account for a wide range of phenomena. Both doctrines were brought to bear on language by diverse theorists from the sixteenth century onwards.

17.2.3 A Standard Pattern of Grammar Takes Shape

In the following centuries, Greek scholars undertook to describe and systematize their own language. This led to a system of language description that remained a standard framework until the twentieth century. The *Technē Grammatikē* by Dionysius Thrax (around 100 BC) has long been regarded as the single most influential text containing the fundamentals of this framework. The *Technē* focused on what was called the 'parts of the sentence' (*meroi logou*), later usually called 'parts of speech.' Each of these parts was succinctly defined in the *Technē*, and their various characteristics were described. Eight of these parts were defined: noun, verb, participle, article, pronoun, preposition, adverb, conjunction. With respect to each of these word classes, so-called attributes were discussed, such as gender, number, and case with respect to nouns, and mood, voice, and tense with respect to verbs.

The framework as expounded in the *Technē* was expanded and modified by subsequent grammarians, while its basic pattern was retained. One of the most momentous additions to the system was made by Apollonius Dyscolus (second century AD). After Apollonius, syntax became an integral part of grammatical theory. However, the parts of speech remained the central component of grammar, while syntax was word-based and usually treated more briefly.

The model that had been developed for the Greek language was taken over by Roman grammarians and applied to Latin. The match was not perfect, but it proved to be quite possible to preserve the descriptive system with only minor adjustments. A comprehensive account of Roman grammatical theory was contained in the works of Donatus (fourth century AD), which were widely used in late antiquity and throughout the medieval period. The most canonical work on grammar during the Middle Ages and after was the *Institutiones Grammaticae* by Priscian (early sixth century AD). Virtually all philosophical or universal grammars to be produced in the later Western tradition until the twentieth century retained the basics of the descriptive model developed in antiquity.

17.3 THE MIDDLE AGES

During much of the Middle Ages, grammar was almost exclusively pedagogical in nature. But a philosophical attitude towards linguistic studies resurfaced in the scholastic period, when the need was felt to give grammar a theoretical foundation and people started looking for explanations of the grammatical categories that were inherited from the ancients. Leaving the categories themselves unquestioned, a number of grammarians sought to fit them into the system outlined by Aristotelian logic and metaphysics. This endeavour is known as speculative grammar. It was brought to the highest level of sophistication by the so-called Modistae, a group of grammarians who published a number of treatises on the 'modes of signifying,' around 1300.

Modistic grammar aimed to specify how linguistic categories connect with aspects of reality and with concepts in the mind. It was universalist in character, assuming that all languages are basically structured in the same way. This assumption was easily made, as any radical linguistic diversity went unnoticed in a time when most linguistic studies were focused on a single language, Latin. Sometimes Greek and Hebrew were also taken into account, but proved or seemed to be sufficiently similar. Moreover, it was necessary to assume that universal principles of grammar existed if grammar were to qualify as a science as opposed to a practical art. For according to Aristotle only the immutable characteristics of nature were eligible for scientific study. On this approach, all arbitrary and variable aspects of languages were irrelevant for a science of language. Accordingly, the Modistae disregarded speech sounds, and the whole apparatus concerning matters of spelling, pronunciation, and metrical patterns that were broadly set out in Priscian and the practical grammars derived from it.

Modistic grammarians developed an intricate technical vocabulary in order to describe the relations between language, the mind, and the world. A central term was the 'mode of signifying' (*modus significandi*). Each part of speech was assigned its own mode of signifying, which corresponded to a particular mode of being (*modus essendi*) and a particular mode of understanding (*modus intelligendi*). One of the most famous Modistic treatises was by Thomas of Erfurt, written in 1310. In this treatise, the mode of signifying of the noun is defined as 'the mode of signifying by means of the mode of an entity (*modus entis*).' This *modus entis* is the 'mode of state and permanence.' By contrast, the mode of signifying of the verb is defined as the 'mode of signifying by means of the mode of being (*modus esse*),' where the *modus esse* is the 'mode of flux and succession' (ch. 8, §15). The modes of signifying thus specify what features of the thing are indicated by words belonging to a certain part of speech. As Thomas claims, 'every active mode of signifying comes from some property of the thing' (ch. 2, §4). However, the link is not direct, for the modes of being are connected with the modes of signifying through the intermediate modes of understanding, i.e. by the properties of things as comprehended by the mind (ch.3, §7). The schema of Aristotle's *On Interpretation*, according to which words connect to the world through an intermediary mental level, was thus closely followed.

It was clear to Thomas that a strict isomorphism between world, mind, and language could not be maintained without difficulties. Already at the lexical level, some words seemed to distort the system as they could not be connected with anything in the world. Words for privations were of this kind, i.e. words indicating the lack of some property rather than its presence, such as blindness, and—a more extreme example—nothing, as well as words for nonexistents such as chimera. Thomas tried to solve this problem by appealing to the relation that the concepts expressed by such words have with other concepts which do derive from properties of things in the real world. Another problem was the fact that in some cases not every concept in the mind could be linked with a part or an aspect of its linguistic expression. An example of this is the imperative: e.g. *Read*. This problem was solved by the assumption that the imperative could be viewed as an abbreviation of a more explicit expression, *Read* being short for *I order you to read*. Thus, the method of reducing expressions to forms that supposedly display their logical structure, a trait of philosophical grammars since Aristotle, was applied to a range of instances.

Modistic grammar was not popular for very long. In the fourteenth century, it crumbled under the influence of nominalism.

17.4 THE RENAISSANCE

In the following centuries, a serious threat to any type of philosophical grammar was posed by the Humanist movement, which was hostile to scholasticism as a whole. But in the sixteenth century a form of philosophical grammar re-emerged in the work of Joseph Justus Scaliger. In his *De Causis Linguae Latinae* (1540) he claimed that grammar is a science and that language should be studied as a natural phenomenon. Scaliger thus approached language as a substance, to which the four 'causes' of Aristotelian physics are applicable. The material cause is concerned with the speech sound, and the formal cause with its meaning. The efficient cause can be identified with the one who imposes meaning on a speech sound, and the final cause with the end to which this is done. Scaliger revived a number of doctrines held by the speculative grammarians, like them formulating the relationships between language, the mind, and the world in terms of the Aristotelian schema set out in *On Interpretation*. He stated that things as well as the concepts we have of them are the same for everybody, whereas words and letters vary (p. 115). Just like the modistae, he characterized the difference between noun and verb as a difference in the mode of signifying.

Another sixteenth-century writer who can be seen as a representative of philosophical grammar is Sanctius, whose *Minerva, seu de causis linguae Latinae* of 1587 is primarily famous for its unusually lengthy treatment of syntax, and the important role it attributes to ellipsis in the analysis of sentence structure. The procedure of supplementing or paraphrasing expressions in order to bring out their semantic structure more clearly, used sporadically by a range of earlier authors, is here applied to an unprecedented range of instances. Sanctius not only devoted one of the four books that his work consists of to examples of ellipsis, but he offered a theoretical justification of what he calls the 'completing principle' (*doctrina supplendi*). In many cases, he argued, usage differs from what is grammatically correct: it is one thing to speak Latin, another to speak grammatically. Things are expressed more wittily as more is left to the hearer to understand. Thus in order to ensure that grammatical theory can be consistently applied it is often necessary to supplement elements that in actual usage are missing.

For example, the sentence from Virgil's *Aeneid* (IV, 39) *Nec venit in mentem, quorum consederis arvis?* 'And don't you realize in whose land you have settled?' reads, if spelled out grammatically: *Nec venit tibi, o Dido, in mentem recordatio illorum hominum, in quorum hominum arvis tu consederis?* 'And does not come to you, O Dido, the recollection in mind of those people, in the land of whose people you have settled?' (bk 4, cap. II). Sanctius did not explain why the longer sentence was grammatically more correct than the original one, probably assuming that the example was self-explanatory. In the longer sentence, he supplied the name of the person to whom the original sentence was uttered, 'Dido,' together with a sign of the vocative, *o*, and inserted the word *recordatio* ('recollection'), apparently so as to provide the verb *venit* with an overt subject. He further 'restored' the phrase *illorum hominum* ('of those people') in order to provide an antecedent to the relative pronoun *quorum* ('whose') and inserted *tibi, in, tu*, and another occurrence of *hominum*. The resulting sentence is in fact more amenable to grammatical analysis, but also contains elements which are superfluous in that respect (*o Dido, tu*), and which Sanctius probably added to make the semantic content or the pragmatic context as explicit as possible.

Although his *doctrina supplendi* thus looks somewhat arbitrary, Sanctius formulated several general rules for its application. For example, intransitive verbs such as *to live* should be supplied with an appropriate object, such as *a life*. And if an adjective or a genitive follows the copula, a noun should be added, for example: *hoc pecus est regis*, 'this herd is the king's' is transformed into *hoc pecus est pecus regis*, 'this herd is the king's herd.' Breva Claramonte (1983: 218–19) has distinguished four operations used by Sanctius in his account of the differences between grammatically correct sentences and those encountered in usage: substitution, deletion, addition, and permutation, adding a fifth, omission, in (1986: xl), and noting that deletion or ellipsis is the most common.

17.5 THE SEVENTEENTH CENTURY

17.5.1 Philosophical and General Grammar

At the beginning of the seventeenth century, Francis Bacon noted that grammar had two functions: the one 'popular,' for attaining languages and for understanding authors; 'the other philosophical, examining the power and nature of words, as they are the footsteps and prints of reason.' He added that philosophical grammar was 'very worthy to be reduced into a science by itself.' Bacon's proposal promoted a tendency in seventeenth-century linguistics to focus on the interrelationships between language and rational thought.

This tendency is discernible, for example, in Vossius' monumental *De Arte Grammatica* (1635). Vossius argued, on the Aristotelian assumption that there can only be science of eternal things, that grammar is an art rather than a science, as its subject matter is contingent and variable (liber I, caput II). Nevertheless, his grammar has many traits which it shares with philosophically oriented grammars. He defended the view that noun and verb should be seen as primary word classes—a term he preferred to the more usual 'parts of speech.' His main argument was that a combination of a noun and a verb is both necessary and sufficient for the construction of a complete sentence.

Unlike Vossius, the Italian philosopher Campanella treated grammar as one of the 'five parts of rational philosophy' (1638). Distinguishing, like Bacon, two types of grammar, the one 'civil,' the other 'philosophical,' he claimed that the latter was a science, concerned with rationality. Campanella's specific claims about how language relates to thought and to reality involved a conscious revival of speculative grammar, and incorporated a fair amount of scholastic terminology. He claimed that his own analysis of the modes of signifying was universally valid for all languages, and this led him to add a feature to his grammar that was a remarkable novelty: in an appendix to his work, he offered a concise list of instructions for the institution of a new language on a philosophical basis.

Another work on philosophical grammar was Caramuel's *Grammatica Audax* (1654), which claimed to discuss language in abstraction from particular languages, and in connection with metaphysical and theological issues. For example, the familiar distinction between *vox* (word viewed as speech sound) and *dictio* (word viewed as meaningful unit) was explained in terms of the theological concept of transubstantiation. In the sections in which the more common subject matter of grammar was treated (pp. 19–46), Caramuel merged this with elements from logical theory. Thus, most of the thirteen subtypes of the adjective he distinguished were characterized in terms of the Aristotelian categories (p. 21). Further, the verb was divided into substantive verb (copula) and adjective verb, and the equivalence between e.g. *Petrus legit* 'Peter reads' and *Petrus est legens* 'Peter is reading' was asserted (p. 31). Caramuel also used the method of expanding expressions so as to bring out their supposed logical form. Thus he explained the genitive as a way of making expressions shorter and more elegant. For example, the sentence *Hic est gladium Petri*, 'This is Peter's sword' is short for *Hic est gladium, qui pertinet ad Petrum*, 'This is the sword that belongs to Peter' (p. 26).

The most famous attempt in the seventeenth century to formulate a general theory of language resulted in the *Grammaire générale et raisonnée* (*GGR*) by Lancelot and Arnauld, two scholars from Port-Royal. The authors were concerned to show that what they claimed to be universal characteristics of language have a rational foundation, being consequences of the fact that language was made to express what goes on in a person's mind. Assuming that the structure of thought is the same with all people, it follows that all languages share structural features which reflect this. The *GGR* thus discussed the traditional parts of speech and the various grammatical categories associated with them, representing these as satisfying a need that naturally arose from the structure of the world and our ideas of it. Thus, languages have both proper names and common nouns because we have ideas both of single things and of several things resembling each other.

The attempt to represent grammatical categories as rational inventions did not succeed in all cases. Gender, for instance, is often purely whimsical, 'a usage without reason' (Lancelot and Arnauld 1660: ch. 5, p. 40). Although the *GGR* was primarily concerned to explain and justify the structure of language, it thus also displayed a tendency to criticize languages, assuming some normative principles by means of which they could be judged. These principles remained implicit, but can be gathered from the examples of 'caprice' and other supposed deviations from rationality provided in the *GGR*. Thus, grammatical distinctions which do not systematically correlate with semantic ones, such as gender, lack a rational basis. Further, redundancy is not what reason prescribes; more generally, words and categories should correspond one-to-one to meanings—a principle that prepositions and cases usually fail to follow.

The *GGR* further assumed that it is the rational foundation that accounts for universal characteristics of languages, and that language diversity is caused by, or is proof of, a lack of rationality. This assumption is at least almost explicit when they state that the 'usage without reason' with respect to gender distinctions brings it about that these vary among languages. Similarly, they claim that the syntax of government is almost completely arbitrary, and 'for this reason' is very different in all languages (ch. 25, pp. 154–5).

In explaining the rational underpinning of languages, the *GGR* relied on logical theory. The mental processes that form the foundation of grammar, according to the *GGR*, are the three operations traditionally distinguished in logic as the mental counterparts of linguistic units: conceiving, judging, and reasoning, which correspond to words or terms, sentences, or propositions, and discourse or syllogisms respectively. The grammar focuses on the second of these operations: judging. A judgement is expressed in a proposition, and this is what language is primarily used for. A proposition necessarily contains two terms, viz. a subject and, as the *GGR* has it, an attribute, and also a sign of the connection between these two. Further, all word classes can be divided according to whether instances of it are used to signify the objects of thought or the form and manner of thought. Nouns, together with articles, pronouns, participles, prepositions, and adverbs, belong to the former, and verbs, together with conjunctions and interjections, to the latter. The verb, indicating the form of thought, is analysed as consisting of copula + predicate. According to the *GGR*, the primary function of the verb is to mark a judgement, i.e. the connection between the two terms of a proposition, or in other words, to signify affirmation (ch. 13, pp. 95–6). As all verbs have this function, a single verb, *to be*, also called the 'substantive verb,' would have sufficed in each language. It is only because people have wanted to abbreviate speech that they have mixed other elements with the substantive verb. Often this is the predicate, as in *Pierre vit*, 'Peter lives,' which is the same as *Pierre est vivant*, 'Peter is alive,' but sometimes it is also the subject, e.g. *vivo*, 'I live,' which single word encloses all three elements of the proposition *je suis vivant*, 'I am alive' (ch. 13, pp. 96–7). Thus, with the *GGR* as with other contemporary philosophical approaches to grammar, it was assumed that there is an often implicit structure or form, to be established by the linguist or logician, to which expressions that are actually used are systematically related and to which they can be reduced.

The *GGR* claims that this form or structure is present in the mind, and reduces expressions encountered in language usage to this form in a number of instances. Words for professions like *king* and *philosopher* are claimed to be adjectives rather than substantives, because the substantive *man* is tacitly understood (ch. 2, p. 33). Sometimes even entire propositions are implicit. The *GGR* is thus quite liberal in postulating forms or structures that are present at the level of meaning, or equivalently in the mind, but that are not displayed at the linguistic surface. At one point, however, it formulates a constraint on this procedure, pointing out that it is unfounded to say that a word is tacitly understood when this word is never actually expressed in a similar context (ch. 21, p. 134). Thus, the authors of the *GGR*, like others before them, viewed what might be called the logical form of expressions not as a purely theoretical construct, but as a more fully articulated form, itself possibly used in certain contexts, of the expressions reduced to it. The difference between the two forms, in their view, results from contingencies of usage, such as the wish to abbreviate speech, or to avoid word combinations that are hard to pronounce.

The *GGR* acquired fame immediately after publication, and inspired a number of writers on general grammar in the eighteenth century.

17.5.2 Rational Grammar and Artificial Languages

Perhaps the most spectacular novelty in the study of language in the seventeenth century was the endeavour to create artificial languages. The first project to be published that was aimed at providing a complete and newly constructed language was Dalgarno's *Ars Signorum* (1661). Dalgarno claimed that logic and grammar are one and the same art, and explained that the use of his language would be based upon a logical analysis of thought. At the lexical level, this was achieved by an abundant use of compounds: a limited number of so-called radical words was defined, out of which words for things not designated by a radical were to be formed by the user. In this way, an analysis of concepts into constituent parts would be reflected in the compound words used to refer to them.

As for the grammar, Dalgarno claimed that in a truly logical language there is only one part of speech, namely the noun, which signifies the notion of a thing indefinitely. All determinations and aspects of things and notions are to be expressed by particles. The details of this view are intricate and not obvious, but it is clear that a basic distinction between radicals and particles was made, not unlike the *GGR*'s distinction between words for the objects of thought and words for the form of thought. A crucial further step in Dalgarno's reasoning was the insight that to express the latter type of meaning, radical words or nouns should be used rather than words belonging to a separate class of particles. This was because the meaning of particles is always derived from, and can be expressed by, a radical word. For example, the conjunction *because* is used to mention a cause. In Dalgarno's language, a radical word meaning 'cause' is consequently used for *because*. Similarly, Dalgarno noted, just like the *GGR*, that the copula is 'the *formal* part of the proposition, that is, the sign of the mental act of judging' (*Ars Signorum*, p. 63). Consequently, in his language the copula is expressed by a radical word meaning 'affirmation,' or by a word meaning 'negation,' depending on whether the proposition is affirmative or negative.

In this way, Dalgarno sought to abolish the distinction between actual sentences and their underlying logical form. In English, the word *is* reveals nothing about the act of affirming one is performing in uttering it. In using Dalgarno's language, the act of affirming coincides with mentioning that act, and this, he believed, contributes to his primary aim: to create a language which enables its speakers to express themselves so that 'the external logos is fully in accord with the internal one' (*Ars Signorum*, p. 68).

In 1668, a second scheme for an artificial language was published: *An Essay towards a Real Character and a Philosophical Language* by John Wilkins. The lexicon of the artificial language was based upon elaborate classificatory tables, so that the form of words reflected certain characteristics of the things named. Wilkins's scheme also contained a large chapter on 'Natural Grammar,' an abstract, a priori type of grammar, to be distinguished, as Bacon had done, from grammars dealing with particular languages, and put to use in specifying the morphological and syntactical rules of the artificial language.

Wilkins's natural grammar divided all words into 'integrals' and 'particles.' The integrals were the words listed in the classificatory tables, which signified 'some entire thing or notion.' Particles were 'less principal words, which may be said to consignifie.' Wilkins classified most of the traditional parts of speech as either integrals or particles, but with a few additions and omissions. The verb, in his view, should not be seen as a genuine word class in philosophical grammar: it is really an adjective and the copula 'affixed to it or contained in it' (p. 303). The copula was accordingly enumerated under the particles, as the one essential particle occurring in every complete sentence. Wilkins further created a novel kind of word, which he called 'transcendental particles.' They were intended to function like morphological affixes, changing lexical meanings in a systematic way. For example, the word for 'sheep' combined with the transcendental particle 'aggregate' yielded a word equivalent in meaning to *flock*.

Another conspicuous deviation from standard grammar was the introduction of a particle indicating tense, which could be used to modify not only the copula, but also nouns. This was because 'according to the true Philosophy of speech' (p. 316), tenses should be applied to substantives to the advantage of language. Thus, Wilkins made a deliberate attempt to improve on existing languages. The belief that it is possible to work out a theory of language independently of existing languages, and that such a theory indeed is better the more it is independent of actual languages, was a starting-point that was typical of the language planners such as Dalgarno and Wilkins, as was the assumption that such a theory could be used to judge the quality of particular languages. However, as mentioned, a similar normative trait can also be found in the *GGR*, and subsequent theories of universal grammar were rarely without it.

A project aimed at developing a rational grammar that was in many respects unique was carried out by Leibniz. It formed part of a grander scheme for an artificial language, which was never completed. The language that Leibniz envisaged was different from other schemes in that its principal use was as an instrument of reason: not merely reflecting and expressing thought, but serving as a means to facilitate and improve its operations. The language would be designed to make logical inferences transparent, and to guide the way to finding truths that would be hard to discover without the use of it. The rational grammar project was aimed at determining the types of expressions that such a logical language would have to contain. And the way to achieve this was to investigate the logical structure of existing languages, since these encompass all the relevant material. Leibniz thus did not start from a predetermined logical theory in order to create a philosophical language from scratch on its basis, but undertook to examine actual languages with a view to discovering their capacity for expressing logical relationships. This capacity, he perceived, was richer than what traditional logic could handle, so that rational grammar entailed an attempt to widen the scope of logic.

In some respects, Leibniz's rational grammar resembled contemporary philosophical grammars. Thus, he made a basic distinction between words and particles, the former concerning the matter of discourse and the latter the form of it. He also took the traditional parts of speech as a starting-point, and just like other language planners, he considered far-reaching modifications of the system. On the basis of the standard analysis of the verb as consisting of a copula and a participle, he noted that verbs could be dispensed with as a separate category.

Most of the work that Leibniz did in the context of rational grammar was focused on the analysis of 'formal particles,' which comprised prepositions, pronouns, a number of adverbs and conjunctions. And it is in this respect that his work differed most significantly from that of his contemporaries. For example, it had been noted that the genitive case is used to denote a number of different relations, part–whole, cause–effect, etc. The authors of the *GGR* had observed that this could lead to ambiguity (p. 47), and Dalgarno had insisted that such ambiguity should be removed, on each occasion, by the use of a particle indicating the specific relation that was intended by the speaker. For Leibniz, this was insufficient, as his aim was to reduce all expressions to a form such that they could be used in a proof system. Thus, he reduced a sentence like *The sword is Evander's* to two propositions: *the sword is property*, and *Evander is owner*, and connected these by a particle 'quatenus' ('in so far as'). Similarly, he reduced the expression *the hand of a man* to *the hand which is a part in so far as a man is a whole*. In this way, the genitive was eliminated, and replaced by a particle the logical properties of which he hoped he could account for at a later stage. Other examples of Leibniz's unique approach can be found in his analyses of specific prepositions and conjunctions, which were all aimed at determining their logical behaviour.

By the end of the seventeenth century, philosophical or general grammar had established itself as a separate branch of linguistic enquiry, to be distinguished from practical or pedagogical grammars. It purported to describe universal properties of language, and sometimes also to prescribe the properties of an artificial universal language. All of those writing on general grammar used the framework of traditional grammar as a starting-point, although deviating from it in various ways. The procedure of reducing expressions to an underlying form of some sort was widely used by these authors. They all assumed a strong relationship between language and thought, and logic and meaning were often more important to them than linguistic form. Sometimes actual languages were even criticized for not conforming to rational standards.

17.6 THE EIGHTEENTH CENTURY

In the eighteenth century, the concern with universal grammar was widespread. It had become commonplace to distinguish between universal and particular grammar. It was usual to characterize the former type as scientific, or theoretical, and the latter as constituting a practical art. However, the two types overlapped and interrelated in various ways.

Some of the fundamental tenets of seventeenth-century theories of philosophical grammar were present in much of the theoretical work produced in this period. The claim that all languages share a common foundation, to be explained by means of universal characteristics of human thought, was taken for granted by most theorists. Further, the traditional parts of speech continued to provide the framework for linguistic theory. It remained common to assume that sentences should be analysed in a logical fashion as consisting of a subject term a predicate term, and a sign indicating the connection between the two. This analysis required the reduction of grammatical surface structure to an underlying form, the existence and structure of which was postulated as a matter of course.

Nevertheless, eighteenth-century universal grammars differed from their predecessors in several respects. First, views of the relationship between language and thought changed drastically. Secondly, language was increasingly approached from a historical perspective. The origin of language became a widely discussed topic of speculation, and languages were supposed to have gone through distinct stages of development. The shift to a diachronic approach was also apparent in that several theorists, notably charles de Brosses and John Horne Tooke, assigned a central role to etymology. Thirdly, there was an increasing interest in the differences between languages and in language typology: theories of the specific 'genius' of a language and of the various 'excellencies' of languages gained prominence, although these were incorporated into a universalist framework.

17.6.1 France: the *Grammairiens Philosophes*

The main representatives of the French Enlightenment assigned an important role to the study of language, which became more and more intertwined with philosophical concerns. Philosophers speculated about the foundations of society and the origin of language, and grammarians focused on the thought processes believed to lie at the basis of language structure. The *GGR* formed a common frame of reference for the *grammairiens philosophes* who elaborated its main theses, often deviating from them or eventually defending opposite points of view. It was reprinted many times, and some of the editions were published with commentaries by Charles Pinot Duclos (1754) and L'Abbé Fromant (1756). The famous *Encyclopédie*, edited by Diderot and d'Alembert

(1751–72), contained numerous, often lengthy articles on language and grammatical theory, most of which were written by César Chesneau du Marsais and, after his death in 1756, by Nicolas Beauzée, himself the author of a voluminous work on general grammar (1767). Topics debated by these grammarians included questions concerning the *GGR*'s division of all words into words signifying the objects of thought and words signifying the manner of it, and questions concerning the *GGR*'s definition of the essence of the verb. Other questions were less directly related to the framework provided by the *GGR*, such as the much-debated problem of the 'natural order' of words (more on which below).

Answers to these questions were of course linked with views on the structure of thought. The tripartite framework of conceiving, judging, and reasoning, on which the *GGR* relied, no longer provided an unquestioned model of what thinking is. This was particularly clear in the work of Condillac (1746, 1775), who challenged the assumption, often made in Cartesian circles, that thought is complete and self-contained, and that language has no other function than to represent pre-existing thoughts. Condillac argued instead that thought by itself is confused and unanalysed, containing many ideas simultaneously. In discourse, by contrast, ideas are represented successively, and they can only be distinct if they are observed in isolation, one after the other. In order to make our thoughts known to others, we must first represent them to ourselves in this way. Language is thus required for the analysis of thought, and this must be carried out before communication is possible. Historically speaking, it is through the interaction between sensations and signs that abstract ideas have originated in the first place. Every language is an 'analytical method' which has developed alongside gradually growing knowledge and in answer to specific needs. Such a view, on which knowledge and thought are formed and structured conjointly with particular languages, opens up a perspective in which linguistic diversity may correlate with diversity in thinking, but this is not a consequence that Condillac considered. On the contrary, he emphasized the universal foundation of all languages: because all people have the same biological make-up and similar needs, all languages are built on the same principles. However, these principles determine the structure of languages only loosely, leaving open a number of different, and equally natural possibilities. Thus, he stressed, it is often custom rather than nature that makes us speak in one way and not in another. In particular, nature does not prescribe a specific way of ordering words in a sentence.

Condillac's rejection of the doctrine of the 'natural order' of words formed part of a debate in which a number of *grammairiens philosophes* took part (Ricken 1976). The doctrine had roots going back to antiquity, and it holds that logic prescribes that certain elements should be mentioned before others. For example, the noun that refers to the subject of a sentence should precede the verb, so that the subject is mentioned first, before the modification or quality of it referred to by the verb. Sentences in which this order is not observed are instances of inversion or hyperbaton. Du Marsais used the notion of a natural word order as a device in teaching Latin to French children (1722), and maintained that this natural order, more usually observed in French than in Latin, was common to all people, based as it was on a common logic. Against this, Batteux argued that on the contrary, inflected languages like Latin are more capable of displaying the order in which ideas occur in the mind, because this order is not determined by absolute logical categories, but varies with the intensity of sensations, so that in fact inversions are more frequent in French than in Latin (Batteux 1747–8). Diderot, in his *Lettre sur les Sourds et Muets* (1751) pointed out that neither Du Marsais nor Batteux could be right, since no general claims can be made about how frequently inversion occurs in the use of particular languages. For as inversion is a discrepancy between the order of words and the order of ideas, it depends on the characteristics of the person uttering a sentence and on the circumstances of utterance whether or not such discrepancy is present. Both Du Marsais (in his article 'Construction,' *Encyclopé-die* vol. 4, 73ff.) and Beauzée (1767: iii. 464ff.) subsequently wrote at length in defence of a natural order of words, which was claimed to form an indispensible and universal basis for mutual understanding.

Many theories propounded by the *grammairiens philosophes* included a historical perspective on language. Such a perspective was paramount in the work of de Brosses, who contributed to the *Encyclopédie* and produced a two-volume work on the 'mech-anical formation of languages' (de Brosses 1765), in which he employed etymology to support the theory that all languages share the same foundation, which itself is the result of a natural process following mechanical laws. This common foundation consists of a number of primitive words or 'roots,' the creation of which can be traced back to natural causes: the properties of the vocal organs, the characteristics of objects in the world, and the need to imitate these characteristics by the speech sounds used in representing them completely determine the form of these roots. It is only after the primitive language of roots has been formed in this way that convention and arbitrari-ness come into play: the root words are combined and altered so as to become almost unrecognizable, and this happens in numerous different ways, so that diverse languages are formed. In assigning a central role to sound symbolism and etymology, de Brosses's theory is reminiscent of the naturalist stance discussed in Plato's *Cratylus*. In empha-sizing the mechanical nature of root formation and in outlining a method for estab-lishing a genealogy of languages in order to identify a common ancestor, it bore some resemblance to the theoretical framework of nineteenth-century historical and com-parative linguistics. Most conspicuous perhaps from the point of view of universal grammar is the contrast with rationalist theories such as the *GGR* and that of Beauzée. In de Brosses's view, the universal basis of languages is provided by nature, not by the workings of the human mind, which precisely account for language diversity.

17.6.2 Universal Grammar in Eighteenth-century Britain

The first work specifically devoted to universal grammar to be published in England in the eighteenth century was James Harris's *Hermes, or, a Philosophical Inquiry concern-ing Universal Grammar* (1751). The work formed part of a wider endeavour to counterbalance the predominant influence of Locke's philosophy by restoring the wisdom to be found in ancient sources. Harris's treatment of universal grammar accordingly consisted in using a number of Aristotelian principles and tenets for a general account of language. He characterized universal grammar as an analytical activity, which uses two types of analysis: the first is to divide speech into its constituent parts, the second, to resolve speech into its matter and form.

The parts identified by the first type of analysis were simply the traditional parts of speech, but arranged and described in such a way that their connection with both the world and the mind is made clear. Just as Aristotle and the Modistae had done, Harris assumed a parallellism between the world, human thought, and language. According to Harris, all parts of speech belong to one of two categories, which he calls 'principals' and 'accessories.' The distinction parallels that made by many of his predecessors and separates off words 'significant by themselves' from words 'significant by relation.'[3] His analysis of the verb was also in line with earlier philosophical grammar: every verb contains, often latently, the substantive verb that expresses assertion. Harris's second type of analysis distinguished the matter of speech, i.e. speech sounds, from its form, i.e. their meaning. Speech sounds were treated in the abstract and briefly, and the chapters about meaning contained, aside from miscellaneous speculations with a Platonic ring, an argument supporting Aristotle's view that meanings are conventional, or as Harris has it, 'by compact' (327 ff.).

Harris's universal grammar differed deeply from contemporary work in France in its Aristotelianism, its almost complete neglect of syntax, and the absence of a historical perspective on languages. However, there was one respect in which it did resemble other eighteenth-century work, which is its attention to the distinctive qualities of particular languages: discussing the 'genius' of different languages, he sketched the peculiarities of English and Latin, and extolled the excellence of Greek.

The tendency to compare and evaluate languages in the context of universal grammar was also present in Joseph Priestley's *A Course of Lectures on the Theory of Language and Universal Grammar* (1762). Dealing with the scientific basis of all languages, Priestley devoted much of his attention to the traditional parts of speech, just like Harris and other general grammarians endeavouring to provide a rationale for their existence, repeating a number of standard observations, and taking the Aristotelian things–ideas–words schema for granted. However, Priestley distinguished a novel word class: words that are a compendium for other words (pp. 65–6). The distinction of this class was remarkable rather than standard, although the possibility of periphrasis on which it was based was often thought important in philosophical grammar. All adverbs belong to this class, as they are always resolvable into other expressions, e.g. *now* is short for *at this time*. Words of this sort, Priestley concluded, belong to the 'elegancies' rather than the 'necessaries of a language' (p. 62).

---

[3] This is reminiscent of Chinese *shící* 實詞 'content words' vs *xūcí* 虛詞 'function words'; see §10.2.4. [Ed.]

A further aspect of Priestley's theory that sets it apart from that of Harris is its historical approach. According to Priestley, the science of language should include an account of the origin of languages. He speculated that the first words that were invented would have been names for sensible objects, so that nouns substantive were the first class of words (p. 50). He also assumed that languages develop through various stages, from rude and barbarian beginnings to a stage of perfection until decline sets in (pp. 168ff.). Further, Priestley provided some criteria for evaluating languages: a perfect language is sufficiently rich in words, lacks ambiguity, and is pleasant to pronounce (p. 250). He also argued that the diversity of languages is advantageous: without it, mankind would have been more prejudiced, and would not have gained the deep insight into the nature of language that arises from the comparison of languages (pp. 192 ff.).

The origin and development as well as the evaluation of languages became the central focus of a six-volume work by James Burnett, Lord Monboddo, *Of the Origin and Progress of Language* (1773–92). This work was designed to be a universalist and comprehensive account of language, including rhetoric and poetics as well as grammar. The second volume treated universal grammar, in which Monboddo, who shared Harris's anti-Lockean sentiments, followed Harris in many respects. Like the latter, he used a primary distinction between the matter and form of language. He invoked Aristotle's authority to justify the claim that all words are either nouns or verbs, and that other word classes are subtypes of one of these. Monboddo included several chapters dealing with the question of the natural order of words, and maintained that the more liberty a language allows its users in ordering words, the more apt it is for the expression of intricate thoughts and images, which gives ancient languages an advantage over modern ones (vol. II, book III, chs 1–3).

Universal grammar as treated by Harris and Monboddo was the subject of severe criticism by John Horne Tooke, the first part of whose *Epea Pteroenta* [Winged Words], *or the Diversions of Purley*, appeared in 1786. Horne Tooke's criticism was directed at the obscurity and the contradictions he perceived in Harris's theory, not at universal grammar itself. On the contrary, he maintained that the study of general grammar was a necessary prerequisite for the attainment of knowledge of the mind. He himself proposed a universal grammar which, he claimed, was based upon an insight that had commonly been neglected: that language is used not only for communication, but for brief and efficient communication. Hence, the role of abbreviations in language is central; they are the 'wheels of language' which make it possible for communication to be carried on with the desired speed. The only indispensable parts of speech are noun and verb. Words of other types, traditionally called 'particles' and considered to lack independent meaning, are in fact etymologically derived from nouns or verbs, and retain much of their original meaning. Thus, the conjunction *if* is a corrupted form of the Gothic and Anglo-Saxon verb meaning 'to give,' and has the same meaning as the English imperative *Give* (p. 141). Horne Tooke offered numerous further etymologies to show that all conjunctions and prepositions are nouns or verbs that have been disguised by corruption, and that 'Etymology will give us in all languages, what

Philosophy has attempted in vain' (p. 344). It is unknown whether Horne Tooke knew Dalgarno's work, but there is a curious parallel in that what the latter saw as a distinctive advantage of his artificial language—that particles are meaningful expressions derived from nouns—was claimed, albeit unsustainably in view of present-day knowledge, by Horne Tooke to be realized in all languages.

17.6.3 General Grammar in Germany

In the first half of the eighteenth century, a number of universal grammars were published by German scholars, nearly all of which were written in Latin, e.g. Carpov (1735), Müller (1736), Canz (1737), Koch (1740) (see Weiss 1992 for description and analysis). Most of these grammars followed a pattern sketched by the leading philosopher Christian Wolff, who held that universal grammar belongs to philosophy as a subordinate discipline, which should be grounded in logic. Wolff (1703) took the three operations of the mind traditionally distinguished in logic—conceiving, judging, and reasoning—as a starting-point. He maintained that words, as signs of thoughts, are arbitrary, and defined nouns and adjectives in ontological terms as essential and accidental names, respectively. Further, he noted that the verb functions both as a copula and as a means to designate the condition or the essence of a thing. The details of this rather traditional framework were worked out in various ways by Wolff's followers, some emphasizing isomorphic relations between ontological and linguistic categories, others focusing on relations between mental and linguistic items (Weiss 1992: 34–50).

An influential and in some respects innovative work, written in German, appeared in 1781: *Versuch einer an der menschlichen Sprache abgebildeten Vernunftlehre oder philosophische und allgemeine Sprachlehre*, by Johann Werner Meiner. Distinguishing 'harmonical' and 'philosophical' doctrines of language, Meiner defined the former as describing linguistic rules common to many languages, obtained through comparison of various languages, whereas the latter deduces the linguistic rules from general properties of human thought, thus providing grounds for the rules described. Offering a philosophical doctrine of language himself, he emphasized the close connection between logic, considered as the theory of thought, and language. Meiner's theory covered most of the material usually found in philosophical grammars, such as the explanation of the function of the various parts of speech, but introduced some novel perspectives.

First, he took the sentence as the primary level of analysis, and went a long way towards defining the various parts of speech in terms of their possible contribution to sentences. He used a distinction between 'dependent' and 'independent' concepts to characterize the various types of words that are required to form a sentence, and observed that the predicate is always dependent, i.e. it designates a concept that needs reference to something other than itself to be complete. Meiner thus transformed the

Aristotelian ontological distinction between substances that exist on their own and accidents that require a subject of inhesion into a distinction of both logical and psychological nature, and used it for the analysis of sentence structure. The result bore a striking resemblance to Frege's analysis that forms the basis of modern predicate logic.

A second innovative feature of Meiner's theory was related to this: insisting on the importance of the distinction between absolute and relative concepts, he pointed out that predicates, typically expressed by verbs or adjectives, may be 'dependent' in various ways. If a predicate is 'one-sidedly dependent' (*einseitig unselbständig*), it can form a sentence by combining with a word designating an independent thing. But predicates can also be 'two-sidedly' or 'three-sidedly' dependent, in which case they designate relative concepts, and combination with two or three other words is required to make the sentence complete.

In the next few decades, quite a few universal grammars were produced in Germany, some of which were explicitly modelled on Kant's theory of categories, e.g. Roth (1795) and Bernhardi (1801–3) (Naumann 1996: 30–31). A work that acquired some fame was Johann Severin Vater's *Versuch einer allgemeinen Sprachlehre* (1801), which was set out on empirical and comparative principles and thus formed a harmonic theory of language in Meiner's terminology, but also contained an attempt to establish, by 'mere philosophical enquiry' (p. 258), what can be designated by language in general.

17.7 THE NINETEENTH AND TWENTIETH CENTURIES

At the beginning of the nineteenth century, general grammar was still popular. However, the number of works devoted to it gradually decreased in the course of the century, and the topic became more and more marginalized. This was related to two developments. First, historical and comparative linguistics as exemplified by the work of Bopp and Grimm, which was inductivist and rigorously empirical, established itself as the central discipline within the study of language. A preference for data collection paired with an aversion to a priori speculations about the nature of language in general became a dominant trait of linguistics. Second, those less disinclined to speculation tended to embrace a relativist perspective, emphasizing the strong connections between specific languages on the one hand and cultural phenomena and intellectual habits on the other. A perspective of this kind was sketched in the work of Johann Gottfried von Herder (1772) and can also be found in the writings of Wilhelm von Humboldt (1836b). In the twentieth century, both the data-oriented approach and the relativist perspective were carried to extremes, resulting in Bloomfieldian behaviourism and the Sapir–Whorf thesis, respectively.

In the mid-twentieth century, Chomsky argued forcefully and influentially against behaviourism, and for the restoration of universal grammar. Recognizing the seventeenth-century Cartesians and later universal grammarians as his intellectual ancestors, he made universal grammar (UG) the cornerstone of a new approach to linguistics, which revolutionized the field. A satisfactory linguistic theory as envisaged by Chomsky goes beyond description of particular languages, and provides an explanation of the human language capacity which underlies the structure of all languages. He believed that in order to achieve this, a number of idealizations are required.

First, a language is defined as a set of well-formed sentences, and a grammar as a set of rules that characterize these sentences. Many or even most of the utterances encountered in actual language use differ considerably from the idealized sentences generated by the grammar. The rules are not generalized from observed usage, but are formulated as hypotheses which are verified or falsified by grammaticality judgements of native speakers. Further, the finite set of rules is capable, through recursion, of generating an infinite set of sentences, thus capturing the capability of language users to produce, understand, and recognize as grammatical an unlimited number of sentences they have never heard before. A second idealization pertains to language users: linguistic theory is concerned with ideal speaker-listeners who are not distracted or hampered in any way in exercising their knowledge of the language. In other words, linguistics is not directly concerned with the performance of language users, but with their competence, which according to Chomsky results from an innate capacity, specifically geared towards language and uniquely found in humans. Ultimately, this capacity must be reducible to certain properties of the human brain.[4]

Chomskyan linguistics differed in at least one respect from the tradition of universal grammar in that it was relatively unconcerned with semantics, and for the most part disconnected from logic. An influential and successful attempt to establish a renewed connection between the study of language and logical theory was made by Richard Montague, who initiated a new field of research, aimed at developing a formal semantic theory of natural languages (see Montague 1974b). As in Leibniz's rational grammar, central notions in Montague's approach are truth and entailment. At present, approaches in formal semantics have diversified.

In the latter half of the twentieth century, Chomskyan linguistics dominated most branches of the field apart from semantics, although many alternative approaches were proposed. All of these alternatives share the assumption that a satisfactory linguistic theory is in principle applicable to all languages. In that sense, universal grammar is as alive today as it was in antiquity.

---

[4] See chapter 19 below.

CHAPTER 18

··

AMERICAN DESCRIPTIVISM ('STRUCTURALISM')

··

JAMES P. BLEVINS

18.1 A GENERAL REAPPRAISAL

··

FROM a contemporary standpoint, the period from the early 1940s to the late 1950s may appear as a minor interregnum between the Bloomfieldian and Chomskyan eras. It is difficult to identify any single work from this period with the iconic status of Bloomfield's *Language* (1933) or Chomsky's *Syntactic Structures* (1957a), and many of the works that are still cited from this time, such as Newman's 1944 grammar of Yokuts or Hockett's 1939 Potawotami studies, are referenced more for their descriptive content than for their theoretical insight. The breadth and diversity of the material covered in textbooks such as Gleason (1955) and Hockett (1958) can also make these works seem like relics of an era before scientific specialization took hold in the field. The assessments offered in transformational histories (Newmeyer 1986) and in critiques of what are sometimes termed 'taxonomic linguistics' (Chomsky 1964a) reinforce the impression of a period dominated by descriptive and methodological concerns that retain little current relevance.

Yet a re-examination of the work from this period shows the popular conception to be a crude caricature. By any objective measure, the decade between 1945 and 1955 was decisive for the development of modern linguistics. This period saw the ascendance of a distinctive American school of general linguistics that placed an explicit emphasis on synchronic analysis. Over the course of the decade, the focus of study within this school also shifted gradually from the description of languages to the investigation of methods, techniques, and theories about languages. Together, these developments ushered in an approach to the study of language which is now largely taken to define the field of linguistics.

Any attempt to assess the impact of the school that dominated American linguistics through most of the 1940s and 1950s must begin by acknowledging a number of striking anomalies. Although the members of this school identified themselves as 'descriptivist,' they have come to be known by a term, '(American) structuralist,' that was mainly applied to them by their detractors. They collectively looked on Leonard Bloomfield as a mentor and sought to develop a Bloomfieldian programme, but scarcely any of them studied with Bloomfield and virtually all quickly abandoned fundamental aspects of Bloomfield's model. Despite the fact that their own models laid the foundations for much of modern linguistics, the 'revolutionary' rhetoric of their Chomskyan successors denied them a role in the intellectual developments that they had set in motion.

A greater irony concerns their effect on the basic subject-matter of linguistics. Although the descriptivists admired Bloomfield for his mastery of languages, both ancient and modern, their efforts to redefine linguistics as a science effectively cut the field off from the older philological tradition in which Bloomfield had been trained. Within a generation, the focus of linguistics had shifted from the detailed study of languages by language specialists to meta-level investigations of the methods and devices employed in linguistic analysis.

For many contemporary linguists, this shift in focus is to be welcomed, as it is precisely what distinguishes what they see as the science of linguistics from other, ostensibly more humanistic approaches to the study of language. But this scientific shift was initially motivated—and has since been sustained—by the belief that the formal analysis of language would reveal fundamental commonalities and bring out a rich deductive structure that is masked by surface variation. By some measures, the field of linguistics is no closer to being a science that trades in these kinds of generalizations than it was in the 1940s (Blevins 2008), and may even be further away, insofar as the philological expertise required for detailed linguistic analysis is disappearing nearly as quickly as languages. So there is perhaps a further irony in the fact that any rehabilitation of the descriptivists must acknowledge that their largely uncredited contributions ultimately undermined the traditions out of which they had grown, without establishing a secure basis for a deductive science of language.

At the same time, some of the aspects of the descriptivists' programme that were most vigorously repudiated by their generative successors have received a new lease on life within current statistically and corpus-based paradigms. Although Chomsky's scepticism about the usefulness of corpora[1] and statistical models[2] came to set the tone for theoretic studies during the transformational period, his initial objections to statistical models have since been addressed in works such as Pereira (2002), while an entire subfield of corpus linguistics has grown up to provide a sustained argument for the value of corpora and corpus-based methods. The interest in information theory

[1] 'Any natural corpus will be skewed...The corpus, if natural will be so wildly skewed that the description [that it provides] would be no more than a mere list' (Chomsky 1962: 159).

[2] 'It would, incidentally, not be surprising if statistical models turn out to be of little relevance to grammar' (Chomsky 1957b: 224).

shown by Harris (1951) and Hockett (1953) likewise finds a contemporary resonance in the application of information theory in models of psychological processing (Moscoso del Prado Martín et al. 2004, Milin, Kuperman, et al. 2009) and, increasingly, in analyses of complex synchronic systems (Ackerman et al. 2009, Malouf and Ackerman 2010b).

18.2 THE BLOOMFIELDIAN LEGACY

In order to appreciate the breadth of the descriptivists' contributions and gauge their influence on the contemporary field of linguistics, it is useful to place their school in the intellectual context in which it arose, and identify the principal developments within this tradition. Despite the fact that a number of leading descriptivists were in fact trained by Edward Sapir, it is the work of Leonard Bloomfield that provides the point of origin for this school. Four broad tributaries lead off from the Bloomfieldian source. The first and best known is the theoretical tradition associated with figures such as Charles Hockett, Zellig Harris, and Bernard Bloch, among others. Since this group has had the greatest contemporary influence, they will be the primary focus of this chapter.

The development of Bloomfield's 'tagmemic' theory associated with Kenneth Pike is even more distinctive, though its influence is now largely confined to the Summer Institute of Linguistics. The two other main tributaries have since merged with more general linguistic currents. The first of these was devoted to theoretical and pedagogical treatments of English. Prominent members of this community included George Trager, Henry Lee Smith, and Charles C. Fries, though these linguists tended to have other linguistic interests as well, while figures such as Kenneth Pike, Eugene Nida, and Bernard Bloch also took an interest in English description and pedagogy. A second tradition applied methods of descriptive analysis to Algonquian and Austronesian languages, though this tradition is now largely remembered for its surviving descriptions and for the inscrutable nomenclature that Bloomfield bequeathed to Algonquian studies.

18.2.1 The Post-Bloomfieldians

In light of the shadow that the towering figure of Leonard Bloomfield casts over the entire descriptivist period, there is some justification in designating this tradition as 'Post-Bloomfieldian' (Matthews 1993). Many of the works that appeared in the first flush of descriptivism in the early 1940s had something of the character of Bloomfieldian exegesis. Throughout the period, Bloomfield's position on a range of issues continued to provide a standard point of departure for further discussion. To a large degree, this impact reflected the influence of Bloomfield's scholarship, particularly his monumental work *Language*, which served the dual function of a reference work and textbook from its publication in 1933. Bloomfield's influence on the teaching of linguistics was also amplified by his participation in Linguistic Institutes of the Linguistic Society of America.

Yet Bloomfield exerted far less influence through the students that he trained, initially at the University of Chicago and later at Yale. Charles Hockett, who was Bloomfield's literary executor and, in many ways, his intellectual heir, studied under Sapir at Yale. Zellig Harris, Hockett's opposite number at the University of Pennsylvania, originally trained there as Semiticist in the Oriental Studies department. Kenneth Pike, the only Descriptivist to take up the task of developing Bloomfield's tagmemic theory, studied with Sapir at the University of Michigan (where, however, Bloomfield served as a member of his dissertation committee). Eugene Nida also studied at Michigan, Stanley Newman again under Sapir at Yale, George Trager at Columbia, Rulon S. Wells III at Harvard, and Robert A. Hall Jr at the University of Rome. Bernard Bloch, nearly the only leading Descriptivist actually to have studied with Bloomfield, summed up Bloomfield's paradoxical influence in remarking, 'He had almost no students, yet most American descriptivists look up to him as a teacher' (Bloch 1941: 91).

The discrepancy between Bloomfield's direct and indirect influence goes a long way towards explaining his paradoxical impact on the descriptivist period. While looking on Bloomfield as a mentor, the descriptivists mostly found themselves in the position of extrapolating from his writings, which were then as now notoriously difficult to interpret. The scale of the challenge is reflected in the striking divergence between Bloomfield's own work and the elaborations of the 'Bloomfieldian' programme. In some cases, it was possible to sidestep interpretive difficulties by acknowledging a debt to Bloomfield's methods rather than to substantive principles or results. Thus one finds the opening footnote in Hockett (1942: 3) declaring: 'This paper . . . owes most to Bloomfield, though rather to the methodological rigor of his work than to his phonemic theories.' Fortunately, the descriptivists—with the exception of Harris—did not aspire to the same economy of expression that they professed to admire in Bloomfield.

Studies that explicitly aimed to clarify or develop Bloomfield's principles mostly ended up missing their mark and redefining the original principles beyond all recognition. The theory of tagmemics developed by Pike provides a celebrated example, but nearly all of the extensions of Bloomfield's programme have a similar character. Pike (1943) sets out initially to address problems of interpretation that faced students who attempted to use Bloomfield's *Language* as a model for descriptive analysis. Noting that this 'material proves more elusive in application than it did in appreciation,' Pike proceeds to suggest 'that part of the difficulty of Bloomfield's material for the beginning student was the lack of clarity in his statements of the relationship between taxemes and tagmemes, and the actual operation with these principles,' declaring his intention 'to point out this confusion, and . . . to outline a procedure which a student can apply to the easier stages of syntactic analysis' (p. 65). Yet the approach that Pike (1967) developed to 'clarify' these relationships was an entirely new theory, with little more than a terminological resemblance to Bloomfield's original model.

The difficulties that the descriptivists encountered in interpreting Bloomfield are candidly acknowledged in their claims at the time that his model seemed to them to contain 'contradictions' (Harris 1942: 169) or in later admissions that it 'didn't make sense' (Hockett 1968: 20). It is easy for today's observer to underestimate these difficulties, given that Bloomfield is in some ways more accessible now than he was to his immediate successors. This change is due in part to the anthologies that bring together a range of Bloomfield's writings (Hockett 1970) and in part to the secondary literature that has since grown up around Bloomfield (Matthews 1993, Fought 1999). In addition, Bloomfield's use of features of arrangement (or 'taxemes') to classify the properties of larger constructions ('tagmemes') resonates with construction-based perspectives. But to Bloomfield's successors, the model appeared convoluted and inconsistent, and they proceeded in their own work to isolate and develop the aspects which seemed to them to be most comprehensible and promising.

18.2.2 The Representational Turn

The invisibility of the descriptivist model is in part a reflection of its success. Many of the innovations that originated in the descriptivist period have come to define what it means to do linguistics, at least linguistics of a formal or theoretical nature. In particular, the practice of analysing language in terms of a set of REPRESENTATIONS, assigned to hierarchically organized levels, is a feature of the descriptivist model that has since been incorporated into most theoretical approaches. Yet this conception of linguistic analysis, like other aspects of the descriptivist model, cannot be understood in isolation. In essential respects, the descriptivist model is an attempt to clarify the model set out in Bloomfield (1933) or to solve problems that the Descriptivists perceived, perhaps unjustly (Matthews 1993), to arise within that model. Hence the descriptivist model must be interpreted in the context in which it evolved: as a development of, and reaction to, the conception of grammatical analysis in Bloomfield's model.

Two of the most influential aspects of Bloomfield's model are the separation of lexical form from grammatical arrangement and the recognition of a separate component, termed the 'lexicon,' which consists of minimal lexical forms.

> A linguistic form which bears no partial phonetic-semantic resemblance to any other form, is a SIMPLE form or MORPHEME ... The total stock of morphemes in a language is its LEXICON. (Bloomfield 1933: 161f.)

It is natural for a contemporary reader to anticipate later developments and interpret this passage in terms of a hierarchy of linguistic levels, one in which phonemes combine to form morphemes, morphemes combine to form words, words combine to form phrases, and so on. However, the Bloomfieldian conception is more intricate, closer in character to a construction-based approach.

The most challenging aspect of this model is the relation between 'forms' and 'arrangements.' Arrangements are the more transparent notion, corresponding to 'dimensions of grammatically distinctive variation.' Of the four types of arrangement that Bloomfield distinguished, three are relatively straightforward.

> The meaningful arrangements of forms in a language constitute its grammar. In general, there seem to be four ways of arranging linguistic forms. (1) ORDER is the succession in which the constituents of a complex form are spoken . . . (2) MODU-LATION is the use of phonemes which do not appear in any morpheme, but only in grammatical arrangements of morphemes . . . (3) PHONETIC MODIFICATION is a change in the primary phonemes of a form . . . (4) SELECTION of forms contributes a factor of meaning because different forms in what is otherwise the same grammatical arrangement, will result in different meanings. (Bloomfield 1933: 163f.)

The order of formatives is one obvious dimension of variation, and the suprasegmental properties (such as stress or intonation) that Bloomfield subsumes under modulation are another. His notion of phonetic modification likewise covers a range of contextually conditioned phenomena, including devoicing or sandhi patterns. Although arrangements do not form a classificatory system in later accounts, each arrangement type has a counterpart in descriptivist models.

The notion of 'selection' is what gives Bloomfield's model its distinctive character. The basic idea is simple, and even familiar to those accustomed to thinking in construction-based terms. Rather than treating forms solely as the sum of independently assembled parts, the Bloomfieldian model integrates a top-down perspective in which constructions are described in terms of characteristic choices of components. The reason that this is not merely a different perspective on the bottom-up assembly of forms from minimal elements is that selection is associated with a meaning (what Bloomfield calls an 'episememe') in addition to the meanings contributed by the parts selected (which he terms 'sememes'). As elsewhere, Bloomfield's terminology makes an already difficult conception even more obscure. However, the key feature of this conception is that meaningful 'units of form' do not just comprise segmental material, but include any distinctive characteristics that can be ABSTRACTED from a form. It is of course possible to think of minimal lexical forms, i.e. 'morphemes,' as being represented independently of the forms from which they are abstracted. But it is not possible to conceive of minimal units of grammatical form, i.e. 'tagmemes,' in the same way. In later post-Bloomfieldian accounts, the notion of selection is encapsulated in rules or complex lexical entries. But Bloomfield describes selectional taxemes with reference to forms or construction types that exhibit them. It is therefore misleading to think of Bloomfieldian analysis as consisting of the disassembly of complex forms into minimal units of lexical and grammatical form, and the assignment of these units to separate lexical and grammatical inventories. Analysis is more a process of classification in which complex forms perform a dual function, providing the data to which procedures of analysis are applied, and at the same time serving as the repository of units of grammatical form.

18.2.3 From Phone to Utterance

The attempt to combine both perspectives in a single model seems to have confounded even Bloomfield's own followers, and the various strands of descriptivist thought largely reflect different reinterpretations of Bloomfield's positions. A key simplifying assumption accepted by nearly all the descriptivists—apart from Pike—was the idea that units at one level of analysis were directly COMPOSED OF units at the next lower level of analysis. Hence, morphemes were composed of phonemes, complex forms composed of morphemes, etc. The justification for this assumption is set out most explicitly in Hockett (1961).

> The simplest and earliest assumption about the relation between morphemes and phonemes was that a morpheme is COMPOSED OF phonemes: the morpheme *cat* is composed of the phonemes /k/, /æ/, and /t/ in that arrangement. This put phonemes and morphemes in line with words, phrases, and sentences, since it was also assumed that a word consists of one or more morphemes (in a specified arrangement), a phrase of one or more words, and so on.

> This assumption is either explicit, or implicit but very close to the surface, in much of the early Prague discussion and in Bloomfield's postulates. The wording . . . clearly implies that morphemes are composed of phonemes. While Bloomfield does not say quite this, he does say . . . that 'The morphemes of a language can thus be analyzed into a small number of meaningless phonemes.' (Hockett 1961: 29)

As Hockett acknowledges, Bloomfield does not directly assert that morphemes are composed of phonemes; this claim is merely an inference that Hockett and his contemporaries drew from Bloomfield's sometimes opaque discussions of morphology. Bloomfield characteristically spoke of larger units being 'described by' smaller parts, as in the claim that '[a]ny utterance can be fully described in terms of lexical and grammatical forms' (Bloomfield 1933: 167). Description in this sense involves, as noted above, a general process of classification. The shift to a more decompositional part–whole perspective is clear in Hockett's restatement of a general principle of TOTAL ACCOUNTABILITY:

> Every morph, and every bit of phonemic material, must be determined by (i.e., predictable from) the morphemes and the tagmemes (if any) of which the utterance *is composed*. (Hockett 1947: 235, emphasis added)

This shift was the decisive step in the development of what came to be known as the 'item and arrangement' (IA) model (Hockett 1954). More generally, by reinterpreting Bloomfield's taxonomy of forms in terms of a hierarchy of part–whole relations, the descriptivists had arrived at a conception that was strikingly simple and transparent. At each linguistic level, elements could be organized into sequences that formed the primes for the next higher level.[3] The lowest, phonemic level assigned classes of phones

---

[3] A similar conception also underlies transformational models (Chomsky 1975a).

to phonemes. The morphemic level organized sequences of phonemes into morphemes. The syntactic level organized sequences of morphemes into larger constituents (Wells 1947). In this way, a uniform part–whole analysis could be extended from phone to utterance.

Uniformity was not regarded solely as an end in itself, but reflected the descriptivists' practical and methodological interest in general procedures of analysis. A model in which levels differ solely in the nature of the elements they contain is susceptible to analysis by means of general procedures of segmentation and classification. The resulting 'Russian doll' model is appealing in its sheer simplicity, so much so that it is still widely assumed in informal presentations of grammar and morphology, particularly in introductory textbooks.

However, in its most basic form, this model was immediately shown to be inadequate or, at the very least, incomplete. In the morphological domain, cases of 'morphologically conditioned allomorphy' presented an immediate problem. An example considered by both Harris (1942) and Hockett (1961) involves pairs such as *knife~knives* and *calf~calves*. Given that the singular form of each pair ends in a voiceless fricative, /f/, and the stem of the plural ends in the voiced counterpart, /v/, the singular and plural forms have no morphemes in common if morphemes are simply composed of phonemes. Characteristically, the descriptivists formulated a number of technical solutions to this fundamental challenge. On one alternative, explored by Harris (1942) and Hockett (1961), an analysis would introduce a morphophoneme '/F/, which represents /v/ before /-z/ "plural" and /f/ elsewhere, and say that there is but one English morpheme /najF/' (Harris 1942: 170). However, descriptivist phonemics suggested a solution which was more compatible with their general model. Hockett (1942) had earlier formulated principles of phonemic analysis that treated PHONEMES as abstract units, representing classes of PHONES with a non-contrastive distribution. Morphemic analysis could be established on exactly the same basis. A MORPHEME could be treated as an abstract unit, which represented classes of MORPHS with a non-contrastive distribution. Defining morphs as sequences of phonemes forged a more indirect link between morphemes and phonemes in a way that avoided the problems posed by morphologically conditioned allomorphy. In the earlier example, the morpheme {KNIFE} represents the two ALLOMORPHS /naif/ and /naiv/, and it is these morphs that are composed of phonemes.

The introduction of a morphophonemic level between morphological and phonological levels removed the main obstacle to the development of a general model of analysis based on classes and sequences. The descriptivists' policy of removing meaning from the grammar proper eliminated 'sememes' and 'episememes' from grammatical analyses. This led in turn to the collapse of Bloomfield's distinction between meaning-bearing tagmemes and sub-meaningful taxemes. What remained then were just two fundamental elements: morphemes, representing classes of morphs, and phonemes, representing classes of phones.

Most linguists agree on the existence, or at least on the inescapable utility, of two kinds of basic elements in a language: morphemes and phonemes. (Hockett 1961: 29)

18.2.4 Constituent Structure Analysis

Reducing Bloomfield's arrangements to selectional and ordering relations between elements produced a similar simplification at higher levels of the grammar (Matthews 1993: 148). Morphs consisted, as noted directly above, of sequences of phonemes. Words and larger syntactic constructions were likewise composed of sequences of morphemes. The model of grammar that emerges from these revisions is a recognizably modern, constituency-based model.

> We summarize this by asserting that every language has its own GRAMMAR. The grammar, or grammatical system, of a language is (1) THE MORPHEMES USED IN THE LANGUAGE, and (2) THE ARRANGEMENTS IN WHICH THESE MORPHEMES OCCUR RELATIVE TO EACH OTHER IN UTTERANCES. (Hockett 1958: 129)

The 'arrangements' of morphemes were conventionally represented by Immediate Constituent (IC) analysis. IC diagrams exhibited the structure of an expression by dividing the expression into parts (its immediate constituents), further subdividing these parts, and continuing until syntactically indivisible units (morphemes) were obtained. This style of analysis was motivated in part by a belief in the locality of syntactic relations, in particular the view that the most important relations held between immediate constituents.

> The process of analyzing syntax is largely one of finding successive layers of ICs and of immediate constructions, the description of relationships which exist between ICs and the description of those relationships which are not efficiently described in terms of ICs. The last is generally of subsidiary importance; most of the relationships of any great significance are between ICs. (Gleason 1955: 151)

Although again inspired by the programmatic remarks in Bloomfield (1933), models of IC analysis were principally developed by Bloomfield's successors, most actively in the decade between the publication of Wells (1947) and the advent of transformational analyses in Harris (1957) and Chomsky (1957a). Within this tradition, there was a fair degree of consensus regarding the application of procedures of IC analyses as well as about the analyses associated with different classes of constructions. The development of constituent structure analysis was held back by, among other things, the lack of a perspicuous format for representing syntactic analyses. The formats explored by the descriptivists were all somewhat cumbersome, ranging from annotated circuit diagrams through charts such as Fig. 18.1 to Chinese box arrangements like Fig. 18.2.

For the most part, these structures segmented an expression successively into subexpressions, each of which was annotated with a word class label and, usually, other

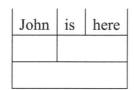

FIG. 18.1 Chart-based IC analysis (Hockett 1958: §17)

FIG. 18.2 Nested box-based IC analysis

types of information. For example, Fig. 18.2 expresses functional or dependency information that is absent from Fig. 18.1 in that 'the arrow points towards the head' in a modifier–head construction and 'the **P** always faces the predicate in a subject-predicate construction' (Gleason 1965: 157). But it was not until the early transformational accounts that procedures of IC analysis were made explicit in any general way, and the fact that these procedures were first formalized by the Bloomfieldians' successors had the effect of simplifying the procedures, much as the Descriptivists had themselves simplified Bloomfield's more intricate constructional perspective.

In Chomsky (1956), phrase structure grammars are proposed as 'the form of grammar [that] corresponds to [the] conception of linguistic structure' expressed by IC analysis (p. 111). Chomsky's insight consisted in recognizing how informal procedures for segmenting and classifying expressions could be recast in terms of rules of the form $A \rightarrow \omega$ that would 'rewrite' a single word class label A by a string ω (which could consist of labels along with words and formatives).

However, as in the move from the Bloomfieldian to the descriptivist model, the move from informal procedures of IC analysis to explicit phrase structure grammars achieved clarity at the cost of simplifying the original model. In particular, initial formulations of phrase structure grammars were incapable of representing the classes of discontinuous constituents recognized by the Bloomfieldians, a point that was conceded in initial models of transformational analysis.

> This [the treatment of 'long components' in the sense of Harris 1951] is an important question, deserving a much fuller treatment, but it will quickly lead into areas where the present formal apparatus may be inadequate. The difficult question of discontinuity is one such problem. Discontinuities are handled in the present treatment by construction of permutational mappings from **P** [the level of phrase structure, JPB] to **W** [the level of word structure, JPB], but it may turn out that they must ultimately be incorporated somehow into **P** itself. (Chomsky 1975a: 190)

The transformational tradition never did reconsider whether discontinuities could be handled better within a phrase structure analysis, and no general approach to this issue was explored within constituency-based grammars until much later.[4] Instead, this tradition sought to reinforce the case for 'permutational mappings' (i.e. transformations) by disputing the feasibility of applying procedures of IC analysis to 'derived' constructions such as polar and information questions.

> The case for indirect representation, not based on the relation of membership, becomes even stronger when we consider such sentences as 'did they see John' or 'whom did they see'. *These are sentences that no linguist would ever consider as the starting point for application of techniques of IC analysis*—i.e. no one would ask how they can be subdivided into two or three parts, each of which has several constituents, going on to use this subdivision as the basis for analysis of other sentences, and so on. Yet there is nothing in the formulation of principles of procedure for IC analysis that justifies excluding these sentences, or treating them somehow in terms of sentences already analyzed. (Chomsky 1962: 131f., emphasis added)

The emphasized passage in this quotation testifies to how thoroughly the descriptivist tradition was misunderstood and even misrepresented by its immediate successors. Virtually all leading American linguists of the time, including Hockett, Gleason, Nida, Pike, and Wells, not only considered applying but in fact *did* apply procedures of IC analysis to questions in English. In particular, the analysis of polar questions was regarded as a solved problem and presented as such in the introductory textbooks of the day. In the passage below, Gleason gives what he takes to be an uncontroversial IC analysis of polar questions to exemplify the notion of discontinuous constituents.

> In English, discontinuous constituents occur. One common instance occurs in many questions: *Did the man come?* This is clearly to be cut *did...come | the man.* (Gleason 1955: 142)

Hockett (1958) similarly uses polar questions as what he takes to be an uncontroversial illustration of semantically distinctive word order.

> On the other hand, two sentences may involve exactly the same constituents at all hierarchical levels, and yet differ in meaning because of different patterns...The difference [between *John is here* and *Is John here*] lies not in constituents, but in their arrangement: *John* respectively before or within *is here.* (Hockett 1958: 158)

The discrepancy between procedures of IC analysis and phrase structure grammars is of more than purely historical interest, given that one of the key criticisms levelled at phrase structure grammars turned on their inability to represent discontinuous dependencies, especially within auxiliary verb phrases.

---

[4] Descriptivist analyses are most systematically rehabilitated in the 'wrapping' analyses within the Montague grammar tradition, notably in Bach (1979) and Dowty (1982), in the work of McCawley (1982) and his students Huck (1985), Ojeda (1987), and subsequently in Head Grammars (Pollard 1984) and in linearization-based models of HPSG (Reape 1996, Kathol 2000).

> To put the same thing differently, in the auxiliary verb phrase we really have discontinuous elements...But discontinuities cannot be handled within [Σ, F] grammars [i.e. phrase structure grammars, JPB]. (Chomsky 1957a: 41)

Phrase structure grammars can be regarded as an extreme case of planned obsolescence in that they were designed with representational limitations that transformations (discussed in §18.3.3) were meant to overcome. It was pointed out almost immediately (Harman 1963) that these limitations could be overcome by a range of non-transformational means. However, the basic architecture had been established, and later models retained a simple part–whole constituent analysis, augmented by devices for relating non-contiguous elements.

18.3 DEVELOPMENT OF THE DESCRIPTIVIST MODEL

At each step in its progression through descriptivist models to current variants of constituency-based analysis, the Bloomfieldian model was simplified. With each simplification came the need for compensating elaboration elsewhere. In some cases, particularly in the area of morphology, the trade-off between the simplicity of the theoretical model and the auxiliary assumptions required to apply the model was apparent to the descriptivists. In other cases, notably in the domain of syntax, this kind of cost–benefit analysis was still at a fairly rudimentary stage when the descriptivists' influence declined abruptly in the 1960s.

18.3.1 Morphemic Analysis

The development of morpheme-based analyses of word structure shows how the descriptivists attempted to arrive at an honest accounting of the costs of theoretical parsimony. The atomistic perspective encapsulated in what is sometimes termed the 'structuralist' morpheme did not originate with the descriptivists. This perspective is present in an incipient form in Bloomfield's work, where it reflects the influence of the Sanskrit grammarians (Emeneau 1988).[5]

Nevertheless, Harris (1942) is the point of origin for a recognizably modern form of morphemic analysis. Subsequent models essentially refine his definitions of morphemes as groupings of morphs that '(a) have the same meaning (b) never occur in

---

[5] It was in general via Bloomfield that the insights of earlier philological traditions came to exert an influence on theoretical developments within the descriptivist school. Bloomfield's particular regard for the Sanskrit grammarians is reflected in his view that Pāṇini's Sanskrit description provided 'an indispensable model for the description of languages' (Bloomfield 1929).

identical environments, and (c) have combined environments no greater than the environments of some single alternant in the language' (Harris 1942: 179f.). Within five years, Hockett (1947) had begun to express reservations about morphemic analysis, at least as it had been formulated within what he later called 'item and arrangement' models. By the end of the decade (when most of Hockett 1954 was written), those reservations had led to a repudiation of the item and arrangement model and an initial formulation of an 'item and process' alternative, which rehabilitated the process-based perspective of Sapir (1921). Within twenty years of voicing his initial reservations Hockett (1967) had come to regard morphemic descriptions as nothing more than a 'convenient shorthand' for traditional descriptions in terms of paradigms and principal parts.

> A correct principal-parts-and-paradigms statement and a correct morphopho-neme-and-rule statement subsume the same actual facts of an alternation, the former more directly, the later more succinctly. We ought therefore to be free to use the latter, provided we specify that it is to be understood only as convenient shorthand for the former. (Hockett 1967: 222)

The ascendance of transformational models in the early 1960s, and particularly the treatment of morphology in Chomsky and Halle (1968), gave morphemic analysis a new lease of life, allowing variants of morpheme-based models to survive into the present day. In much the same way, the incorporation of phrase structure analyses into transformational models (as the format of the structures related by transformations) preserved a simplified variant of IC analysis. This restricted form of constituent analysis in turn provided the basis for Generalized Phrase Structure Grammar (Gazdar et al. 1985) and Head-driven Phrase Structure Grammar (Pollard and Sag 1994) and defined the structural backbone of Lexical Functional Grammar (Kaplan and Bresnan 1982).

18.3.2 Distributional Analysis

A common charge levelled against the descriptivists is that they neglected the study of meaning. Lyons covers more or less the entire tradition when he asserts, 'Many of the most influential books on linguistics that have appeared in the past thirty years devote little or no attention to semantics' (1968: 400). However, this neglect is less a descriptivist innovation than a more transparent representation of Bloomfield's own semantic agnosticism. Although Bloomfield had introduced 'sememes' and 'episemes' to represent lexical and constructional aspects of meaning, these 'units' are just placeholders in his model.

> The statement of meanings is therefore the weak point in language study, and will remain so until human knowledge advances very far beyond its present state. In practice, we define the meaning of a linguistic form, wherever we can, in terms of

some other science. Where this is impossible, we resort to makeshift devices. (Bloomfield 1933: 140)

As this passage also makes clear, Bloomfield's attitude towards semantics was agnostic rather than hostile. In other discussions of meaning, Bloomfield also emphasizes that the primacy accorded to form is largely a practical matter, reflecting the availability of techniques for describing and classifying forms.

> This re-enforces the principle that linguistic study must always start from the phonetic form and not from the meaning. Phonetic forms—let us say, for instance, the entire stock of morphemes in a language—can be described in terms of phonemes and their succession, and, on this basis, can be classified or listed in some convenient order, as, for example, alphabetically; the meanings—in our example, the sememes of a language—could be analyzed or systematically listed only by a well-nigh omniscient observer. (Bloomfield 1933: 162)

The idea that structural properties of language can be studied independent of meaning or function is of course developed more vigorously by Bloomfield's successors. Trager and Smith approach the description of English with the view that 'the syntax of a language like English can be constructed objectively, without the intervention of translation meaning or any sort of meta-linguistic phenomena' (1951: 68). It is however in the work of Harris that Bloomfield's practical caveats are elevated to a general methodological principal. The outset of the descriptivist period finds Harris proclaiming that 'the structures of language can be described only in terms of the formal, not the semantic, differences of its units and their relations' (Harris 1942: 701). By the time of the classic statement of distributionalism in Harris (1951), Harris had come to regard distributional analysis as defining an entire subfield of linguistics.

> Descriptive linguistics, as the term has come to be used, is a particular field of inquiry which deals not with the whole of speech activities, but with the regularities in certain features of speech. These regularities are in the distributional relations among the features of speech in question, i.e. the occurrence of these features relatively to each other within utterances . . . The main research of descriptive linguistics, and the only relation which will be accepted as relevant in the present survey, is the distribution or arrangement within the flow of speech of some parts or features relatively to others. (Harris 1951: 5)

The resulting model was purely distributional, concerned with the arrangement of observable units, without regard to any associated meaning or function. Where reference to meaning was unavoidable, this tended to be operationalized, as in the use of what came to be known as the 'paired utterance test' (Harris 1951: 32) for distinguishing phonemic contrasts. However, operational solutions reflected the practical orientation of the descriptivists, who, as Hockett stresses, developed their theories to serve the goals of linguistic description.

> [A]t the time we were all (except Chomsky) field-workers at heart; that is, we tended to express our theoretical notions operationally. The early followers of

Chomsky found fault with that, but without justification. To confuse theory and day-to-day field procedure would of course be a mistake, but to express theory in operational terms is not. (Hockett 1997a: 151)

The role of meaning and function in linguistic analyses remains a matter of contention, as does the status of semantic primitives and representations, participant roles, truth-conditional interpretations, and other components proposed to incorporate meaning into contemporary models. More importantly, to the extent that these components 'interpret' linguistic representations, or are segregated into separate representational levels, they fully with the Bloomfieldian and descriptivist view that at least some aspects of structure can be described independently of their meaning or function.[6]

18.3.3 Grammars and Transforms

One of the salient features of the descriptivist model is the degree to which it came to concern itself with representations, and with the procedures or devices that define those representations. The shift in focus from the study of the properties of languages to the study of the properties of the devices used to describe and analyse languages is one of the most enduring influences of the descriptivists, unleashing forces which gained even greater momentum during the transformational period. The change in the orientation and subject matter of the field is already implicit in Hockett's notion of a 'grammatical description,' which corresponds closely to a formal grammar in the modern sense.

> [a] grammatical description . . . sets forth principles by which one can generate any number of utterances in the language; in this sense, it is operationally comparable to that portion of a human being which enables him to produce utterances in a language; i.e., to speak. (Hockett 1954: 390)

Harris makes the same point in an even more modern form when he suggests that '[a] grammar may be viewed as a set of instructions which generates the sentences of a language' (Harris 1954b: 260). Although the descriptivists did not have a formal frame of reference in which to define applicable notions of 'description' or 'grammar,' the string rewriting systems developed in Post (1943, 1947) provided a good general model, as Scholz and Pullum note.

> The differences between Post's systems and the TGGs of Chomsky (1957a) lie mainly in the additional devices that Chomsky assumed, like rule ordering and obligatory application; but these turn out neither to restrict nor to enhance generative power. (Scholz and Pullum 2007: 718)

---

[6] Though see Matthews (2001) for a discussion of the fairly wide range of interpretations that have been associated with 'structuralism' and 'structural linguistics.'

The descriptivists initially welcomed the formalizations proposed in transformational models, seeing them as developments of their own models. Already by the early 1960s, introductory textbooks such as Gleason (1955) had been revised to incorporate discussions of rewrite interpretations of phrase structure rules (p. 180) and add chapters devoted to transformational analysis. Moreover, it is noteworthy that the notion of transformational analysis was already modelled on Chomsky (1957a) rather than on Harris (1957).

In Harris' original conception, transformations are equivalence relations between constructions in a corpus, employed to limit the role of IC analysis.

> If two or more constructions . . . which contain the same n classes . . . occur with the same n-tuples of members of these classes in the same sentence environment . . . , we say that the constructions are transforms of each other, and that each may be derived from any other of them by a particular transformation. For example the constructions N v V N (a sentence) and N's V*ing* N (a noun phrase) are satisfied by the same triples of N, V, and N (*he, meet, we; foreman, put up, list*, etc.); so that any choice of members which we find in the sentence we also find in the noun phrase and vice versa: *He met us, his meeting us . . . ; The foreman put the list up, the foreman's putting the list up . . .* Where the class members are identical in the two or more constructions we have a reversible transformation, and may write e.g. N_1 v V $N_2 \leftrightarrow N_1$'s V*ing* N_2 (and the set of triples for the first. the set for the second). (Harris 1957: 147)

Applying procedures of IC analysis to basic constructions first defined the 'kernel' of a language. The complex constructions of the language could then be obtained as transforms of basic constructions, avoiding the putative redundancy and inelegance entailed by extending IC analysis to cover passives and other constructions with a transparent relation to those in the kernel.

> The kernel is the set of elementary sentences . . . such that all sentences of the language are obtained from one or more kernel sentences . . . by means of one or more transformations. (Harris 1957: 335 [197])

The use of transformations to describe complex constructions, along with the kernel-transform split—and agnosticism about the constituent structure of transforms (Stockwell 1962)—survives into early models of transformational grammar (Chomsky 1957a, 1975a). However, Chomskyan models define transformations in terms of derivational relations between inputs and outputs.

> A grammatical transformation T operates on a given string (or, in the case of [generalized transformations], on a set of strings) with a given constituent structure and converts it to a new string with a new derived constituent structure. (Chomsky 1957a: 44)

This is the 'dynamic' conception that Gleason adopts when he explains: 'A transformation is a statement of the structural relation of a pair of constructions which treats that relation as though it were a process' (Gleason 1955: 172).

18.3.4 Discovery and Evaluation

Harris', work shows the greatest concern with methodological precision and explicit theory development (Matthews 1999), so it is unsurprising that the transformational lineage grew out of this branch of descriptivism. However, it is only in the transformational period that the primary focus of general linguistics shifts decisively from language description to theory construction. Whereas descriptivists tended to develop theories that were at least intended to be of use in improving the accuracy and uniformity of language descriptions, transformationalists approached language description almost purely as a means of obtaining evidence bearing on theoretic claims. This shift in perspective led the transformationalists to misinterpret and even misrepresent the descriptivists, nowhere more than in criticisms of the search for mechanical 'discovery procedures.'

As in the case of the designation 'structuralist,' the term 'discovery procedure' was never used by the descriptivists themselves, but was instead coined and applied by Chomsky, who regarded it as 'very questionable that this goal is attainable in any interesting way' (1957a: 53) and suggested that

> by lowering our sights to the more modest goal of developing an evaluation procedure for grammars we can focus attention more clearly on really crucial problems of linguistic structure and we can arrive at more satisfying answers to them. (Chomsky 1957a: 53)

The shift in methodological focus proposed by Chomsky reveals the extent of the change in perspective from the descriptivist to transformational paradigms. The descriptivists' interest in practical procedures for language analysis were not purely theoretical but grew naturally out of their descriptive concerns.

> It should be possible to establish a method of finding the best possible organization of any given utterance and of insuring comparable results with comparable material. This is the basic problem of syntax ... Unfortunately, the methodology has not as yet been completely worked out in a generally applicable form. (Gleason 1955: 132)

In contrast, the transformational tradition tended to regard the task of obtaining 'observationally adequate' descriptions as trivial, since they could be generated by Turing-equivalent devices, which incorporated the weakest assumptions about human languages: that they can be idealized as recursively enumerable sets of strings. Of course the assumption that any human language can be described by an unrestricted rewrite system or equivalent formalism is of no practical descriptive use. Moreover, there is an irony in the proposal that linguists should 'lower their sights' from discovery to evaluation. In the transformational literature, the search for evaluation metrics never progressed past the kinds of primitive symbol-counting metrics set out in Chomsky and Halle (1968). Meanwhile, Harris's work on what his detractors dismissed as 'discovery procedures' inspired a subfield of 'grammar induction' in which machine learning techniques are used to induce a grammatical description from a corpus.

The descriptivists' more general belief in the practical usefulness and theoretical relevance of corpora has also been confirmed by the range and fruitfulness of contemporary corpus-based research. Corpus-based grammars such as Biber et al. (1999) provide the first accurate synchronic snapshots, freezing languages in the course of their constant evolution. Despite the obvious limitations of current corpora as idealizations of a speaker's linguistic environment, the frequency information obtainable from corpora such as those in CELEX (Baayen et al. 1995) has proved useful for predicting response latencies and other behavioural responses. The descriptivists' early interest in information theory has turned out to be even more prescient. Information-theoretic measures provided the first general means of reconciling the type-sensitivity of derivation and the token-sensitivity of inflection (Moscoso del Prado Martín et al. 2004). Subsequent studies have confirmed the predictive value of other information-theoretic measures in models of psychological processing (Milin, Đurdjević, and Moscoso del Prado Martín 2009, Milin, Kuperman, et al. 2009). The fundamental grammatical importance of notions of uncertainty and uncertainty reduction has also become increasingly clear in synchronic analyses of complex morphological systems (Ackerman et al. 2009, Malouf and Ackerman 2010a, 2010b).

18.4 THE DESCRIPTIVIST LEGACY

In assessing the contribution of the descriptivists and their role in the history of linguistics, it is important to bear in mind the fact that ideas tend to outlive the traditions that initially hosted them and mutate during their own lifespans.

> It is ... worth stressing that ideas often persist, evolve and may be abandoned on a time scale that does not correspond to the transitory intellectual hegemony of one group of scholars or another. (Matthews 1993: 5)

Over time, the descriptivists repudiated or abandoned many of the innovations that they had formulated or come to be associated with. But they had unleashed forces, institutional as well as intellectual, that they were ultimately unable to control. The Chomskyan era saw the retrenchment and expansion of many of the most academically disruptive aspects of the descriptivist school. The descriptivists' general neglect of European scholarship and their casual disregard for traditional approaches had sown the seeds of an insular intellectual culture in which in which they in turn could be ignored by their Chomskyan successors. *Language*, which had functioned almost as a house journal for the descriptivists in the aftermath of the Second World War, came to reflect this shift in institutional power. By the mid-1960s, the descriptivists found themselves in the role of occasional contributors or, as in the case of Zellig Harris, seemingly ostracized.

[Harris 1965] was also, sadly, his last contribution to *Language*. I have not thought it my business to inquire into the circumstances; but from then on, for whatever reason, a journal for which he had written so much for a quarter of a century, and so much of such influence and importance, published him no more. (Matthews 1999: 114)

As the Chomskyan paradigm consolidated its hold over the emerging 'science' of linguistics, the metalinguistic focus on formal devices triumphed over descriptive concerns, and the study of languages was relegated to the role of providing evidence bearing on the choice between competing theories or toolkits. More than any other single innovation, this shift ushered in the modern era, by cutting off contemporary schools of linguistics from the older philological tradition. The distance that the field had moved is reflected in the sense of anachronism evoked in the modern reader by Bloch's eulogy for Bloomfield.

> Trained as an Indo-Europeanist in the great tradition of the neogrammarians, he had also a specialist's knowledge of at least four groups within the general field: Germanic, Indic, Slavic, and Greek. . . . Nor did he confine himself within the bounds of Indo-European; he had a wide acquaintance with languages in other families also. His first-hand investigation of several Malayo-Polynesian languages was one of the pioneer works in a little-known field. And as everyone knows, his descriptive and comparative studies of the Algonquian languages are among the classics of American Indian research. (Bloch 1949: 90f.)

The breadth of Bloomfield's expertise was remarkable even in someone of his generation. But what is perhaps most sobering is that this breadth of interests is not only less common but far less valued in the traditions that he spawned.

....

CHAPTER 19

NOAM CHOMSKY'S CONTRIBUTION TO LINGUISTICS

A Sketch

....

ROBERT FREIDIN

19.1 PRELIMINARIES[1]

....

OVER the past sixty years Noam Chomsky has produced a body of work on the study of language that includes over twenty-five books (some in their second and third editions) and over 100 articles in journals and book chapters. His work ranges from detailed technical studies of formal grammar (in phonology as well as syntax, see Chomsky and Halle 1968) to trenchant general discussions of foundational issues in philosophy and psychology concerning language and mind. In formal grammar, Chomsky pioneered the first work on (modern) generative grammar, laying the groundwork in his 1949 University of Pennsylvania undergraduate honours thesis on the morphophonemics of Modern Hebrew (revised and expanded as a 1951 master's thesis, a further revised 1951 version published 1979, henceforth *MMH*) and then developing the formal foundations with applications to English syntax in a 913 page manuscript, *The Logical Structure of Linguistic Theory* (henceforth *LSLT*, written 1955–6 and published in a somewhat shortened version in 1975[2]), which included a detailed theory of transformations. Since then and up to the present day, Chomsky has continued to develop the

---

[1] I am indebted to Howard Lasnik for discussions of some of the material developed in this chapter and to Noam Chomsky, Terje Lohndal, Katy McKinney-Bock, Carlos Otero, and Jon Sprouse for comments on a previous draft.

[2] See Chomsky's (1975a) preface to *LSLT* for details and discussion of the background of the manuscript.

theory of grammar, refining the formulations of grammatical mechanisms and the constraints on their operation and output as well as raising challenging general questions for linguistic theory (most recently in the form of the Minimalist Program of the past two decades). From the outset, Chomsky connected his work in linguistics to questions of epistemology and mind in philosophy and to learning and cognition in psychology, initially in his famous 1959 critique (1959b) of the behaviorist account of language and its acquisition in Skinner's *Verbal Behavior* (1957). In later years he extended that critique of an extreme form of empiricism to less extreme mainstream empiricist approaches to the study of language, including Wittgenstein and Quine (see e.g. Chomsky 1969 and more recently Chomsky 2000c: ch 3). In contrast, Chomsky's work engages the perspective of mentalism while rejecting dualism[3] and resurrects a theory of innate knowledge—Universal Grammar—to explain how speakers come to know so much about the language they speak that cannot be explained solely on the basis of their limited and impoverished experience (the contribution of their environment).

Chomsky has presented this work on generative grammar within the context of an intellectual history spanning several centuries. His historical commentary begins with a discussion of the seventeenth-century Cartesian roots of modern generative grammar (see Chomsky 1966/2009, 1968/2006) and expands to the history and philosophy of science more generally, focusing on the naturalistic approach from Newton to the present, 'the quest for theoretical understanding, the specific kind of inquiry that seeks to account for some aspects of the world on the basis of usually hidden structures and explanatory principles' (Chomsky 2000c: 134). His discussion shows how the study of language falls within the scope of naturalistic inquiry (hence the natural sciences), contrary to much philosophical debate in the opposite direction (see again Chomsky 2000c). Part of his achievement has been to align modern linguistics with the natural sciences, in particular as a sub-part of human biology, biolinguistics.

Chomsky's work has consistently moved the technical study of linguistic structure forward as well as deepened the general understanding of how the study of language fits into the larger investigation of human cognition (cognitive science) from the perspective of natural science. In the history of linguistics this achievement is unparalleled.

The first formulation of generative grammar developed in response to a suggestion by Chomsky's professor Zellig Harris that he construct a structural analysis of some language. Chomsky describes the origin of this work as follows:

> Harris suggested that I undertake a systematic structural grammar of some language. I chose Hebrew, which I knew fairly well. For a time I worked with an informant and applied methods of structural linguistics as I was then coming to understand them. The results, however, seemed to me rather dull and unsatisfying. Having no very clear idea as to how to proceed further, I abandoned these efforts

---

[3] See esp. his discussions of the mind/body problem, which he points out cannot be properly formulated because since Newton's demolition of the mechanical philosophy there is as yet no coherent theory of body (Chomsky 1988, 2000c, 2009). For a graphic demonstration, see Hoffmann (1993).

and did what seemed natural; namely, I tried to construct a system of rules for generating the phonetic forms of sentences, that is, what is now called a generative grammar. I thought it might be possible to devise a system of recursive rules to describe the form and structure of sentences, recasting the devices in Harris's methods for this purpose, [footnote omitted] and thus perhaps to achieve the kind of explanatory force that I recalled from historical grammar [footnote omitted, RF]. (*LSLT* p. 25)[4]

The methods Chomsky abandoned were basic taxonomic procedures of segmentation and classification applied to a limited, though supposedly representative, linguistic corpus.[5] Harris describes these analytic procedures in *Methods of Structural Linguistics* (1951), which Chomsky read as a manuscript in 1947 as his introduction to modern linguistics (see Harris's preface dated 1947, which acknowledges Chomsky's help with the manuscript).

> This volume presents methods of research used in descriptive, or more exactly, structural, linguistics. It is thus a discussion of the operations which the linguist may carry out in the course of his investigations, rather than a theory of the structural analyses which result from these investigations. The research methods are arranged here in the form of the successive procedures of analysis imposed by the working linguist upon his data. (1951: 1)

Harris applies these operations bottom-up from phonemes to morphemes on up to the level of the utterance. These operations yield a *grammar of lists*, taking the term 'grammar' to be some characterization of a language. In §20.21 Harris identifies two contrasting purposes of linguistic analysis: stating 'all the regularities which can be found in any stretch of speech, so as to show their interdependences (e.g. in order to predict successfully features of the language as a whole)' vs synthesizing 'utterances in the language such as those constructed by native speakers' on the basis of some minimal information (p. 365). The procedures presented in *Methods* are most naturally compatible with the former purpose. Moreover, as Chomsky notes in the 1975 introduction to the published version of *LSLT*, 'Harris did not elaborate on the suggestion

---

[4] The second footnote to this passage cites §56.2 for a brief mention of the historical analogy, which Chomsky credits as the source of his own work in generative grammar.

[5] To quote Harris: 'The basic operations are those of segmentation and classification. Segmentation is carried out at limits determined by the independence of the resulting segments in terms of some particular criterion. If X has a limited distribution in respect to Y, or if the occurrence of X depends upon (correlates completely with) the occurrence of a particular environment Z, we may therefore not have to recognize X as an independent segment at the level under discussion [footnote omitted, RF]. Classification is used to group together elements which substitute for or are complementary to one another [footnote omitted, RF]' (Harris 1951: 367). Harris elaborates in a footnote that 'the class of elements then becomes a new element of our description on the next higher level of inclusive representation.' These operations yield a grammar of lists. 'In one of its simplest forms of presentation, a synchronic description of a language can consist essentially of a number of lists' (p. 376). These include a segment-phoneme list, a phoneme distribution list, several morphophonemic lists, lists dealing with type and sequences of morphemes, a component and construction list, and a sentence list—the list of utterance structures.

that a grammar can be regarded as a device for "synthesizing utterances," an idea that does not, strictly speaking, seem compatible with the general approach of *Methods'* (p. 50 n. 45).

The formulation of generative grammar in *MMH* constitutes 'a theory of structural analyses' that Harris excludes as a focus in *Methods*.[6] Furthermore, its fundamental purpose is to synthesize utterances, 'the process of converting an open set of sentences—the linguist's incomplete and in general expandable corpus—into a closed [footnote omitted] set—the set of grammatical sentences—and of characterizing this latter set in some interesting way' (*MMH* p. 1), what Chomsky characterizes as 'a process of "description",' bypassing the 'process of "discovery" consisting of the application of the mixture of formal and experimental procedures constituting linguistic method' (p. 1). The footnote regarding the set of grammatical sentences notes that this set is 'not necessarily finite. Thus the resulting grammar will in general contain a recursive specification of a denumerable set of sentences' (p. 67). This shows that Chomsky had connected the notion of recursive function and language from the beginning.

It is worth recalling that Chomsky initially evaluated his work on generative grammar as unrelated to scientific linguistics.

> While I found this work intriguing and exciting, I thought of it as more or less of a private hobby, having no relationship to 'real linguistics.' Part of my skepticism about this work derived from the fact that as the grammar was improved in terms of its explanatory force and degree of generalization, it became more and more difficult to isolate anything approximating a phonemic representation, and I took for granted that phonemic analysis was the unchallengeable core of linguistic theory. More generally, I was firmly committed to the belief that the procedural analysis of Harris's *Methods* and similar work should really provide complete and accurate grammars if properly refined and elaborated. But the elements that I was led to postulate in studying the generative grammar of Hebrew were plainly not within the range of such procedures. (*LSLT* p. 29).

Chomsky notes that his evaluation of this work 'was reinforced by the almost total lack of interest in MMH on the part of linguists whose work I respect' (with the sole exception of Henry Hoenigswald) (p. 30).

The initial work on generative grammar in *MMH* Chomsky carried out virtually on his own, and for this he deserves sole credit. However, his work that followed benefited from the input of teachers, colleagues, and students (and their students, etc.)—in effect, a collaborative effort in a scientific enterprise that Chomsky's early work established in the 1950s.[7] Although the discussion that follows will focus on the specific proposals in Chomsky's publications, it should be kept in mind that this work responds to

[6] For some detailed discussion of how the analysis in *MMH* departs from the strictures of Harris (1951), see Freidin (1994).

[7] In particular, Chomsky's 1975 preface to *LSLT* credits Zellig Harris: 'While working on LSLT I discussed all aspects of this material frequently and in great detail with Zellig Harris, whose influence is

developments in linguistics based partially on the work of others and therefore belongs to a collaborative enterprise.

The preliminary sketch that follows contains four parts. The first characterizes the state of linguistics before Chomsky's first formulation of generative grammar in *MMH*. The second outlines the basic form of generative grammar that he postulated in *LSLT* and *Syntactic Structures* (1957a, henceforth *SS*). The third explicates the psychological interpretation of grammar that he developed in 1958–9 (see Chomsky 1982: 62), published seven years later as the first chapter of *Aspects of the Theory of Syntax*. The fourth sketches the current formulation of generative grammar under the Minimalist Program.

19.2 SYNTAX BEFORE GENERATIVE GRAMMAR

To fully appreciate Chomsky's contribution to linguistics, it is necessary to consider the state of American linguistics prior to 1957, the year his initial groundbreaking work reached a wide audience as the monograph *SS*. Consider for example the 1955 first edition of Henry A. Gleason's *An Introduction to Descriptive Linguistics*, a standard introduction to linguistics at that time. Linguistics is defined as 'the science which attempts to understand language from the point of view of its internal structure' (p. 2). The focus of discussion is primarily on phonology and morphology, concerned with phonemes and morphemes. Syntax occupies one thin chapter sandwiched between five chapters on morphology ('The Morpheme,' 'The Identification of Morphemes,' 'Classing Allomorphs into Morphemes,' 'Outline of English Morphology,' and 'Some Types of Inflection') and a sixth ('Some Inflectional Categories'). In chapter 5, morphology and syntax are linked together as 'not precisely delimitable' subdivisions under the heading of grammar (following Bloomfield 1914: 167, see also Bloomfield 1933: 184), which might account for the sandwiching of the chapter on syntax between two chapters about inflection.

At the beginning of the chapter on syntax, Gleason provides the following definition:

> Syntax may be roughly defined as the principles of arrangement of the constructions formed by the process of derivation and inflection (words) into longer constructions of various kinds. (1955: 128)[8]

---

obvious throughout' and mentions several other teachers and friends in Cambridge to whom he is indebted 'not only for their encouragement but also for many ideas and criticisms' (1975a: 4–5).

[8] In effect, syntax is concerned with the output of morphological processes, a definition that echoes Bloomfield (1933) where syntactic constructions 'are constructions in which none of the immediate constituents is a bound form' (p. 184) and also Bloch and Trager's *Outline of Linguistic Analysis* (1942), where syntax is limited to the analysis of constructions that involve only free forms (p. 71). Bloomfield (1933) attempts to separate syntax from morphology with the distinction between words and phrases. 'By the *morphology* of a language we mean the constructions in which bound forms appear among the

What these principles are is not made explicit. Gleason begins with a 'first hypothesis' that every word in an utterance 'has a statable relationship to each other word. If we can describe these interrelationships completely, we will have described the syntax of the utterance in its entirety' (p. 129).[9] To this end, Gleason introduces the concepts of construction ('any significant group of words (or morphemes'), constituent ('any word or construction (or morpheme) which enters into some larger construction'), and immediate constituent (IC) ('one of the two, or a few, constituents of which any given construction is directly formed') (pp. 132–3).[10] He goes on to identify word order (§1.13) and constituent classes (§1.14) as universal syntactic devices, defining the latter as 'any group of constituents (words or constructions) which have similar or identical syntactic function.'[11] However, none of this material solves what Gleason characterizes in §10.8 as 'the basic problem of syntax': 'to establish a method of finding the best possible organization of any given utterance and of insuring comparable results with comparable material' (p. 132). According to his assessment, 'unfortunately, the methodology has not as yet been completely worked out in a generally applicable form. Moreover, some of the best approximations to a general theory are beyond the scope of an introductory text' (p. 132). No references to these best approximations are given.

Compared to SS, the discussion of syntax in Gleason's 1955 textbook barely scratches the surface. In striking contrast, his 1961 revised edition, which references *Syntactic Structures* and thanks Chomsky for comments on the manuscript, discusses phrase structure rules and transformations, and contains three chapters on syntax

constituents. By definition, the resultant forms are either bound forms or words, but never phrases. Accordingly, we may say that morphology includes the constructions of words and parts of words, while syntax includes the construction of phrases' (p. 207). The approach is concerned with a strict separation of syntax and morphology—which is essentially abandoned in SS, e.g. in the syntactic analysis of the English verbal system. Generative grammar generally rejects the strict separation of levels, see for example the discussion of accent and juncture in Chomsky, Halle, and Lukoff (1956) about how higher levels of analysis can affect the choice of phonemic analysis.

  [9] In American structuralist linguistics this focus on the relationships between words goes back to Bloomfield (1914: 167): 'Syntax studies the interrelations of words in the sentence. These interrelations are primarily the discursive ones of predication and attribution, to which may be added the serial relation.' The perspective carries forward to Hockett's 1958 introduction to the field, *A Course in Modern Linguistics*, which states that 'syntax includes the ways in which words, and suprasegmental morphemes, are arranged relative to each other' (p. 177).

  [10] Gleason identifies immediate constituent as the most important concept. 'The process of analyzing syntax is largely one of finding successive layers of ICs and of immediate constructions, the description of relationships which exist between ICs, and the description of those relationships which are not efficiently described in terms of ICs. The last is generally of subsidiary importance; most of the relationships of any great significance are between ICs' (1955: 133).

  [11] Gleason discusses government (as it relates to case) and concord (agreement) as two other syntactic devices, presumably not universal, that indicate structural relations, but does not go beyond citing a few examples.

('Immediate Constituents,' 'Syntactic Devices,' and 'Transformations') followed by 'Language and Grammars.'

19.3 THE BIRTH OF MODERN GENERATIVE GRAMMAR

In marked contrast to the structuralist definitions of syntax cited above, Chomsky's definition in *SS* focuses instead on the grammatical mechanisms for constructing sentences. 'Syntax is the study of the principles and processes by which sentences are constructed in particular languages' (*SS* p. 11). One of the goals of syntactic investigation of a given language is 'the construction of a grammar that can be viewed as a device of some sort for producing the sentences of the language under analysis' (*SS* p. 11). In effect, Chomsky's definition shifts the focus of syntactic investigation from languages (viewed as a collection of sentences, superficially as a set of phonetic forms) to grammars, the mechanisms by which sentences of a given language are constructed. This is clarified further in Chomsky and Miller (1963).

> It should be obvious, however, that a grammar must do more than merely enumerate the sentences of a language (though, in actual fact, even this goal has never been approached). We require as well that the grammar assign to each sentence it generates a *structural description* that specifies the elements of which the sentence is constructed, their order, arrangement, and interrelations and whatever other grammatical information is needed to determine how the sentence is used and understood. A theory of grammar must, therefore, provide a mechanical way of determining, given a grammar G and a sentence s generated by G, what structural description is assigned to s by G. If we regard a grammar as a finitely specified function that enumerates a language as its range, we could regard linguistic theory as specifying a function that associates with any pair (G, s), in which G is a grammar and s a sentence, a structural description of s with respect to G; and one of the primary tasks of linguistic theory, of course, would be to give a clear account of the notion of structural description. (p. 285)

In this way, syntax is concerned with the grammatical mechanisms that construct structural descriptions for sentences, thereby specifying their internal structure.

The formulation of generative grammar developed in *LSLT* and *SS* contains two explicit grammatical mechanisms as the processes for constructing sentences: phrase structure rules and transformations. Phrase structure rules in a grammar are formulated as rewrite rules, where the grammar contains 'a sequence of conversion statements "$\alpha \rightarrow \beta$," where α and β are strings, and derivations are constructed mechanically by proceeding down the list of conversions' (*LSLT* p. 190).[12] The second appendix of *SS* provides the following simplified example (p. 111).[13]

(1)   (i)   Sentence → NP + VP
       (ii) VP → Verb + NP
       (iii) Verb → Aux + V
       (iv) NP → {NP$_{singular}$, NP$_{plural}$}
       (v)   NP$_{singular}$ → T + N + Ø
       (vi) NP$_{plural}$ → T + N + S
       (vii) Aux → C (M) (*have + en*) (*be + ing*)
       (vii) T → *the*
       (ix) N → *man, ball,* etc.
       (x)   V → *hit, take, walk, read,* etc.
       (xi) M → *will, can, may, shall, must*

Applying the rules in a sequence starting with the initial element 'Sentence' yields a set of strings, with a final string consisting entirely of terminal elements to which no phrase structure rule can apply. For example, one derivation of the sentence (2) from the grammar in (1) would produce a set of strings (3).

(2)   The man takes the books.
(3)   {Sentence, NP+VP, NP+Verb+NP, NP+Aux+V+NP, NP$_{singular}$+Aux+V+NP, NP$_{singular}$+Aux+V+ NP$_{plural}$, T+N+Ø+Aux+V+NP$_{plural}$, T+N+Ø+Aux+V+T +N+S, T+N+Ø+C+V+T+N+S, . . . , *the+man+Ø+C+take+the+books+S*}

---

[12] Phrase structure rules are first introduced in *MMH*, so Chomsky invented phrase structure grammar in his 1949 senior thesis at the University of Pennsylvania—including the rewrite mechanism utilized in their formulation. All the versions of *MMH* contained a rudimentary phrase structure grammar that was unaffected by changes in the later versions (Noam Chomsky, p.c.). It has been claimed that Chomsky's use of phrase structure rules comes from the work of Emil Post (see e.g. Scholz and Pullum 2007, which cites Post (1944) (as does Chomsky 1959a, see also Chomsky 2009b)). However, Chomsky's first exposure to Post was via Rosenbloom's *Mathematical Logic*, published in 1950, which Chomsky cites in chapter III of *LSLT*—referring to the second appendix 'Algebraic Approach to Language: Church's Theorem.' Post uses the rewrite notation to establish relations between strings and is not concerned with their hierarchical structure. The use of the notation for the analysis of phrase structure constitutes an intuitive leap.

[13] For ease of presentation the sequence of rules has been reorganized so that the rules that introduce single lexical items are listed as a block after the rules that specify phrases.
The phrase structure rules in *SS* are all formulated in context-free format, whereas *LSLT* also utilizes more complicated context-sensitive rules, where the application of the rewrite rule is restricted to a specific context or contexts. Chomsky (1959a) investigates the formal properties of grammars utilizing rewrite rules restricted to varying degrees and develops proofs concerning the equivalency between types of grammar and types of formal automata in terms of computational power, what is now referred to as the Chomsky Hierarchy. For example, grammars that allow only context-free phrase structure rules are equivalent to non-deterministic pushdown storage automata and grammars that allow context-sensitive phrase structure rules as well are equivalent to linear bounded automata, which are more powerful. For discussion of the significance of the Chomsky Hierarchy for transformational grammar, see Lasnik (1981) and Lasnik and Uriagereka (2011).

The ellipsis in (3) stands in for the subset of strings that would be produced by applying the lexical rules (vii–xi) one at a time to the string T+N+Ø+C+V+T+N+S. (3) constitutes a phrase-marker of the sentence which carries all the information about its constituent structure (see *SS* p. 87: n. 2, and *LSLT* §§53.2–54.1 for a more complicated and precise formulation). In practice, phrase markers are given equivalently as tree diagrams; in this case (3) would be represented as (4).

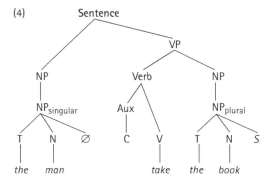

In Chomsky's earliest formulations, C marks the position of the element combining person/number agreement and tense (present vs past) that ultimately attaches to the finite verbal element in the sentence, in this case the main verb.[14] The separation of C from the verbal element it ultimately attaches to in phonetic form introduces a level of abstraction into the syntactic analysis of phrase structure, creating a distinction between abstract underlying form and concrete phonetic form. Chomsky motivates this analysis by demonstrating how it accounts for the distribution of periphrastic *do* in English. Chomsky's use of abstract structure to explain the patterns that occur in concrete phonetic form constitutes a large part of his legacy to linguistics.

In starting with the initial element Sentence, phrase structure grammar gives a top-down analysis whereby a phrase is subdivided into its constituent parts, each conversion specifying the immediate constituents of each phrasal element identified.[15] In this way the phrase structure rules provide an analysis of the internal structure of sentences, both the basic linear order of the lexical elements and also their hierarchical structure.

To get from the abstract underlying representation in (4) to the phonetic form of (2) involves the application of transformational rules, which are defined as mappings from one phrase marker to another. Under the grammar given in *SS* the derivation of (2) involves one transformation that has the effect of specifying C as a morpheme *S* (representing present tense and third person singular) and another (generally referred

---

[14] Because the specification of C can depend on the prior application of a transformation (e.g. the rule deriving passive constructions), it cannot be handled by a phrase structure rule.

[15] This rejects the bottom-up approach to constituent structure of Harris (1946), endorsed in Wells (1947 (cf. §48)).

to as Affix Hopping) that attaches C to the verb *take* (yielding *takes*). Thus the syntactic derivation of the simplest sentences will involve transformations as well as phrase structure rules.

Under the earliest formulations of transformational generative grammar the phrase marker (3–4) also serves as the underlying structure of the passive construction (5) corresponding to (2).

(5)   The books are taken by the man.

The derivation of (5) involves the application of a passive transformation as well as the two transformations required for the derivation of (2). The formulation of the passive transformation in *SS*, given in (6), is complex.

(6)   *Passive*—optional:
      Structural analysis: *NP—Aux– V—NP*
      Structural change:

$$X_1 - X_2 - X_3 - X_4 \rightarrow X_4 - X_2 + be + en - X_3 - by + X_1$$

It applies optionally, as opposed to the other two transformations, which must apply and are therefore obligatory. Thus transformations must be designated as obligatory or optional. Furthermore, it produces multiple changes in the phrase-marker (4), inverting the positions of the two NPs it analyses and inserting two lexical elements, the passive auxiliary *be+en* and the passive *by*. As formulated, (6) is specific to English and linked to a specific construction, the passive.

In deriving an active sentence and its passive counterpart from the same underlying representation, the transformational analysis provides a straightforward account of sentence relatedness. In the earliest transformational grammars, this extends to the relation between affirmative and negative sentences (e.g. (2) vs (7a)), and between declarative and interrogative sentences (e.g. (2) vs (7b)).

(7)   a. The man does not take the books.
      b. Does the man take the books?

Compounding the three basic distinctions (active/passive, affirmative/negative, declarative/interrogative) yields at least eight possible outcomes (e.g. affirmative-active-declarative (2) vs. negative-passive-interrogative (8)), all of which are derived from the same underlying structure (3–4).

(8)   Aren't the books taken by the man?

And given that (3–4) would also be the underlying structure for the wh-questions (9), the transformational account would extend to the relatedness between (2), (5), (7–8) and (9).

(9)   a. Who takes the books?
      b. What does the man take?

Thus in addition to a transformation that derives passive constructions, there would be transformations for deriving negative constructions and interrogative constructions—in the latter case one for yes/no questions and another for wh-questions.[16]

Another essential property of the early formulation of transformational grammars concerned the ordering of rules. For example, given (3–4) as the underlying phrase marker for the passive construction (5), if the transformation that determines the content of C applies before the passive transformation, then the deviant (10) results.

(10)   *The books is taken by the man.

However, if the passive transformation applies first, then C is mapped onto $\emptyset$ (representing the morpheme for third person singular and present tense) and the legitimate (5) is derived. Therefore early transformational grammars included statements about the necessary ordering of transformations.

The early formulation of transformational grammar involved two distinct types of transformations. Those involved in the derivation of simple sentences like (2) and (5) applied to a single phrase marker, the *singulary* transformations. The derivation of complex and compound sentences required another kind of transformation that operated on pairs of phrase markers to produce larger phrase markers, the *generalized* transformations. These transformations instantiate the recursive property of grammars by means of which an infinite class of structures can be generated. The ordering of these two types of transformations in a derivation was expressed as an ordering statement called a *transformation marker*. In this way, the ordering of transformations constituted a central focus of the earliest generative grammars.

While phrase structure rules in (2) provide an explicit and complete account of immediate constituent structure (for a finite set of sentences), the passive transformation (6) does not. Thus transformations formulated in terms of strings as in (6) raise the problem of derived constituent structure. As Chomsky notes in §82.1 of *LSLT*:

> It is necessary to study the internal effects of these transformations on strings in greater detail than we have done so far. The basic reason for this is that we must provide a *derived* constituent structure for transforms, for one thing, so that transformations can be compounded.

Each transformation contributes to derived constituent structure, so in derivations involving multiple transformations the compound effects on constituent structure need to be specified at each step. *LSLT* (p. 321) rejects the solution in which transformations are defined 'in so detailed a fashion that all information about the constituent structure of the transform is provided by the transformation itself, and that any constituent hierarchy can be imposed on any transform by an appropriate transformation' because

---

[16] While this analysis of sentence relatedness mirrors the transformational analysis proposed by Harris (see 1952 and 1957, esp. the first footnote), Chomsky's notion of transformation departs radically from Harris's in that it involves abstract underlying representations whereas in Harris transformations are formulated as relations between surface patterns. See Freidin (1994) for a detailed discussion.

it would make the definition of transformations 'extremely cumbersome' and also because some information is already provided by phrase structure grammar (e.g. the passive *by*-phrase which can be analysed as a PP). The alternative solution assumes the existence of general principles that determine derived constituent structure for the output of transformations.

Keeping to a minimal formulation of transformations, however, creates the possibility that transformations can (mis)generate deviant constructions. *LSLT* §95.3 cites the following examples, both of which would be derived from the same underlying phrase-marker:

(11)   a. Your interest in him seemed to me rather strange.
       b. *Whom did your interest in seem to me rather strange?

Chomsky notes that the deviance of (11b) cannot be attributed to the stranded preposition *in*, because it does not create deviance in other constructions, as illustrated in (12) (*LSLT* p. 437).

(12)   a. You lost interest in him (this year).
       b. Who did you lose interest in (this year)?

So the deviant (11b) is not blocked under the minimal formulation of the transformation that relocates the wh-phrase *whom* to clause-initial position from its underlying position where it occurs as the object of the preposition *in*. Consider the formulation of this rule in *SS* (rule 19 on p. 112), as given in (13) with details slightly modified for ease of exposition.

(13)   Structural analysis: $X - NP - Y$
       Structural change: $X_1 - X_2 - X_3 \rightarrow X_2 - X_1 - X_3$

In the structural analysis, X and Y are variables that range over strings (possibly the null string), whereas NP is a constant term. In this formulation, the displacement of NP to clause-initial position is over a variable, which without further constraints can represent a string of any size and internal structure. Note that the use of variables in the formulation of the wh-movement rule (13), which allows the misgeneration, contrasts with the formulation of the passive transformation (6), where all of the terms identified in the structural analysis are constants. One solution proposed in *LSLT* introduces a complicated constraint on both variables as part of the transformation, thus departing from minimal formulations. The alternative, developed several years later, starting with Chomsky's A-over-A Principle,[17] is to keep to minimal formulations by adding general

---

[17] The A-over-A Principle states that 'if a phrase X labeled as category A is embedded within a larger phrase ZXW which bears the same label A, then no rule applying to the category A applies to X (but only to ZXW)' (Chomsky 1964b: 931). The A-over-A Principle was originally proposed to restrict the ambiguous application of transformation (see Chomsky 1964b for details). It was not proposed to solve the problem of constructions like (11b). Note that if it applies to the structure underlying (11b), then it should also apply to the structure underlying (12b), thereby blocking the derivation of a legitimate sentence.

constraints ('hypothetical universals,' Chomsky 1964b: 931) that apply to the application of all transformations as part of a theory of transformations—i.e. not tied to
specific transformations or specific languages.

The model of grammar that emerges from *LSLT* contains a syntactic component
consisting of two subcomponents, a phrase structure grammar and a set of transformations where the output of the latter serves as the input of the former as
diagrammed in (14).

(14)   PS rules → transformations →

The output of the transformational component serves as input to the rules of morphology and phonology, which determine the phonetic form (PF) of sentences. In later
work beginning with Chomsky (1965), the outputs of these two syntactic subcomponents are treated as specific levels of representation: *deep structure* (later D-structure)
derived from the application of phrase structure rules and *surface structure* (later
S-structure) derived from the application of transformations. (See footnote 29 below
for further discussion.)

Although there is no discussion of semantic analysis in *LSLT*, the first sentence of the
preface distinguishes syntax from semantics as the major subdivisions of linguistic
theory, the former being 'the study of linguistic form'—which would naturally include
phonology and morphology (p. 57). According to *LSLT*, 'the goal of syntactic study is to
show that the complexity of natural languages, which appears superficially to be so
formidable, can be analyzed into simple components; that is, that this complexity is the
result of repeated application of principles of sentence construction that are in themselves quite simple' (a formulation that has been vindicated in a spectacular way in light
of the evolution of the current theory: see §19.5 below). In contrast, semantics 'is
concerned with the meaning and reference of linguistic expressions,' involving a
study of how natural language, 'whose formal structure and potentialities of expression
are the subject of syntactic investigation, is actually put to use in a speech community.'
LSLT views 'syntax and semantics as distinct fields of investigation,' and therefore
focuses on syntax as 'an independent aspect of linguistic theory' given that 'how much
each draws from the other is not known, or at least has never been clearly stated.'
Nonetheless, as Chomsky comments, 'syntactic study has considerable import for
semantics,' unsurprising because 'Any reasonable study of the way language is actually
put to work will have to be based on a clear, understanding of the nature of the
syntactic devices which are available for the organization and expression of content.'[18]

SS develops the discussion of syntax and semantics by examining the question of
how semantics might play a role in determining the form and function of a theory of
linguistic structure (see esp. chapter 9). In §9.3, Chomsky observes that core semantic
notions like reference, significance and synonymy play no role in the formulation of the
syntactic processes that construct sentences with their structural analyses. In Chomsky

---

[18] All quotes in this paragraph are from p. 57 of *LSLT*.

(1975b) this observation is reformulated as the restrictive thesis that the formulation of syntactic rules excludes all core notions of semantics—which Chomsky designates 'absolute autonomy of formal grammar' (p. 91). This formulation presupposes that the primitive notions of linguistic theory can be separated into distinct categories of formal vs semantic, where 'the choice of primitives is an empirical matter' (p. 91 n. 33). However, the thesis does not deny the existence of systematic connections between linguistic structure and meaning. Rather, it 'constitutes an empirical hypothesis about the organization of language, leaving ample scope for systematic form-meaning connections while excluding many imaginable possibilities' (p. 92). Chomsky (1975b) examines a representative sample of challenges to the absolute autonomy of formal grammar, concluding 'that although there are, no doubt, systematic form–meaning connections, nevertheless the theory of formal grammar has an internal integrity and has its distinct structures and properties, as Jespersen [1924] suggested' (pp. 106–7).[19]

From the outset, Chomsky's goals in proposing generative grammar transcend the development of new grammatical tools for syntactic analysis—i.e. phrase structure rules and transformations. *LSLT* identifies two interrelated general goals: the construction of both grammars for particular languages and a formalized general theory of linguistic structure.[20] *SS* extends the second goal to include an exploration of 'the foundations of such a theory' (p. 5). It also announces a further goal that in light of the

---

[19] For further discussion see various proposals from Generative Semantics, a line of work on generative grammar based on the hypothesis that underlying syntactic representations constituted the single level of semantic representation and therefore must be considerably more abstract than those Chomsky was positing. The disagreements between the two sides have been characterized somewhat hyperbolically as 'linguistics wars'—for a history of the period see Newmeyer (1986), and for further commentary Harris (1993) and Huck and Goldsmith (1995); for critical review of the latter, see Freidin (1997).

[20] Chomsky comments, 'Given particular grammars, we could generalize to an abstract theory. Given a sufficiently powerful abstract theory, we could automatically derive grammars for particular languages' (*LSLT* p. 78). The challenge of course is how to determine which grammars to choose as a basis for the abstract theory. *LSLT* discusses 'two factors involved in determining the validity of a grammar: the necessity to meet the external conditions of adequacy and to conform to the general theory. The first factor cannot be eliminated, or there are no constraints whatsoever on grammar construction; the simplest grammar for L will simply identify a grammatical sentence in L as any phone sequence. Elimination of the second factor leaves us free to choose at will among a vast number of mutually conflicting grammars' (p. 81). In effect, constructing the general theory solely on the basis of particular grammars cannot succeed because the formulation of particular grammars is going to be determined in part on the basis of some theoretical ideas. 'We can scarcely describe a language at all except in terms of some previously assumed theory of linguistic structure' (*LSLT* p. 78). Again to quote Chomsky: 'Actually, of course, neither goal can be achieved independently. In constructing particular grammars, the linguist leans heavily on a preconception of linguistic structure, and any general characterization of linguistic structure must show itself adequate to the description of each natural language. The circularity is not vicious, however. The fact is simply that linguistic theory has two interdependent aspects. At any given point in its development, we can present a noncircular account, giving the general theory as an abstract formal system, and showing how each grammar is a particular example of it. Change can come in two ways—either by refining the formalism and finding new and deeper underpinnings for the general theory, or by finding out new facts about languages and simpler ways of describing them' (*LSLT* p. 79). The fundamental problem for linguistics as for any scientific inquiry is that observation statements are

developments of the past two decades now stands as visionary. 'The ultimate outcome of these investigations should be a theory of linguistic structure in which the descriptive devices utilized in particular grammars are presented and studied abstractly, with no specific reference to particular languages' (p. 11). It took more than four decades of research to begin to understand how this goal might be realized within the Minimalist Program (see §19.5). Thus the conceptual shift in focus from describing the internal structure of languages to constructing formal grammars and their underlying formal theory, which marks the advent of modern generative grammar, was the first step toward this goal. The second involved the psychological interpretation of grammars and also the theory of grammar as discussed in the first chapter of Chomsky (1965).

19.4 KNOWLEDGE OF LANGUAGE

Beyond the initial formulation of modern generative grammars and the beginnings of an underlying general theory, Chomsky provides an essential interpretation of grammars and the theory of grammar that placed linguistics at the centre of cognitive revolution of the 1950s, which began to study human cognition in terms of computational models. Rather than treat a generative grammar as essentially an arbitrary conventional way to describe language data (cf. Harris 1951), the first chapter of Chomsky (1965) explores the interpretation of a generative grammar as a system of knowledge in the mind of the speaker (see Chomsky 1965: ch. 1).

Clearly, a child who has learned a language has developed an internal representation of a system of rules that determine how sentences are to be formed, used, and understood. Using the term 'grammar' with a systematic ambiguity (to refer, first, to the native speaker's internally represented 'theory of his language' and, second, to the linguist's account of this), we can say that the child has developed and internally represented a generative grammar, in the sense described (p. 25).

Furthermore, he proposes to treat linguistic knowledge as a separate entity of the faculty of language (henceforth FL), distinct from linguistic behavior—i.e. how that knowledge is put to actual use—thereby formulating a *competence/performance* distinction (see p. 4).

The interpretation of a generative grammar as a system of knowledge in the mind of a speaker raises four fundamental questions:[21]

intrinsically theory-laden (see Hanson 1958 for discussion). See ch. 2 of *LSLT* for further discussion of the relationships between particular grammars and the general theory.

[21] Chomsky (1986) mentions only the first three, formulated in terms of 'knowledge of language,' though it is clear from the discussion that this refers to specific generative grammars. Chomsky (1988) introduces the fourth question and formulates these questions in terms of a system of knowledge. More recently, Chomsky has added a fifth question about the evolution of language—how did such systems arise in humans? See Hauser et al. (2002) for some discussion and Larson, Deprez and Yamakido (2010) for further commentary.

(15)   a. What is the system of knowledge?
       b. How is it acquired?
       c. How is it put to use?
       d. What are the physical mechanisms that serve as the basis for this system
          and its use?

This interpretation connects generative grammar to epistemology and the philosophy of mind as well as cognitive psychology. The last question follows through on the assumption inherent in the first three that language is an intrinsic part of human biology and thus generative grammar should be understood as part of biolinguistics.[22]

Chomsky's answer to the first question has always been relatively straightforward: a computational system and a lexicon. What has changed significantly over the past half century are the formulations of the two components (see the next section for discussion). The second question can be interpreted in two ways: how is language acquisition possible versus how is it actually accomplished step by step. The possibility question involves what has been called *the logical problem of language acquisition*. The problem arises from the fact that what speakers come to know about their language cannot all be explained solely on the basis of the linguistic data they have encountered. Part of this knowledge involves distinguishing deviant from grammatical utterances. For example, English speakers know that (11b) is deviant and not a novel utterance,[23] a legitimate sentence of their language that they have not encountered before. English speakers can also make systematic judgements about relative deviance, where some constructions are judged to be more deviant than other deviant constructions. Consider for example (11b) compared to (16), which appears to be significantly worse.

(16)   *Whom did your interest in him seem to rather strange?

In both cases, the linguistic data provided by the environment is not sufficient to explain the linguistic knowledge attained, referred to as *the poverty of the stimulus*.[24] Chomsky's solution to the logical problem of language acquisition is to posit an innate

---

[22] See Chomsky (2000a) for discussion of the issues, especially the unification of linguistics and neuroscience. See also Poeppel and Embick (2005) on the disjointness of basic concepts in linguistics and neuroscience. Chomsky (2000a) notes, 'the recursive procedure is somehow implemented at the cellular level, how no one knows' (p. 19).

[23] Novel utterances result from one property of what Chomsky calls the creative aspect of language use, that language is innovative—i.e. that speakers are constantly creating sentences that are new to their experience and possibly to the history of the language. The other properties include that language is unbounded (there is in principle no longest sentence), free from stimulus control (speech is an act of free will), coherent, and appropriate to the situation. Chomsky notes that there has been no progress in finding an explanatory account for the creative aspect. 'Honesty forces us to admit that we are as far today as Descartes was three centuries ago from understanding just what enables a human to speak in a way that is innovative, free from stimulus control, and also appropriate and coherent. This is a serious problem that the psychologist and biologist must ultimately face and that cannot be talked out of existence by invoking "habit" or "conditioning" or "natural selection."' (2006 [1968]: 22–3). See Chomsky (1966/2009, 1968/2006) for further discussion.

[24] For further references and recent discussion, see Berwick et al. (2011).

component of the computational system, which would therefore be universal across the species—designated as Universal Grammar (UG). UG accounts for whatever linguistic knowledge cannot be explained solely on the basis of experience. Thus generative grammar bears on the debate about nature versus nurture. Given that the linguistic systems humans acquire are unique to the species, this innate component constitutes a core part of the definition of human nature.

Chomsky describes language acquisition as a transition between mental states of the FL, where the mind of a child starts out in a genetically determined initial state and on exposure to primary language data changes to a steady state involving a specific generative grammar—i.e. a specific formulation of the computational system and a specific lexicon. To the extent that the initial state places limits on the form and function of the generative grammar attained in the steady state, it provides an under-lying theory of grammar—that is, a theory of UG. In the early work on generative grammar Chomsky had suggested that a theory of linguistic structure could be achieved by 'determining the fundamental underlying properties of successful gram-mars' (SS p. 11). Thus it appeared that the first goal of linguistic research was the construction of generative grammars of specific languages from which the fundamental underlying properties could be discovered.[25] However, in the context of language acquisition, research into the initial state of the language faculty could proceed inde-pendently of attempts to characterize the steady state (i.e. construct generative gram-mars of specific languages) by solving specific poverty of the stimulus problems in a variety of languages using general constraints on the form and function of the computational system. As it turns out, this research path has yielded the greatest progress.

The cognitive interpretation of grammar has also had a fundamental effect on the concept of a language. Consider the definition of language in work that predates this interpretation. The term 'language' was not explicitly defined in LSLT, but in the 1975 introduction Chomsky notes that the 1955–6 manuscript takes a language to be 'a set (in general infinite) of finite strings of symbols drawn from a finite "alphabet"' (p. 5). SS defines a language as a set of sentences 'each of finite length and constructed out of a finite set of elements' (p. 13). In Chomsky (1986) such characterizations are designated 'as instances of "externalized language" (E-language), in the sense that the construct is understood independently of the mind/brain' (p. 20). If E-language is the object of investigation, then 'grammar is a derivative notion; the linguist is free to select the grammar one way or another as long as it correctly identifies the E-language' (p. 20). In contrast, the cognitive interpretation focuses on the representation of language in the mind of the speaker, thus the steady state of the language faculty attained on exposure to primary language data. This involves UG and the generative grammar of the language derived from it. Chomsky calls this concept 'internalized language' (I-language). Chomsky (1995b) takes 'I' to refer to 'individual' and 'intensional' as

---

[25] In practice, research produced fragments of grammars, never a complete generative grammar of any specific language. See also n. 20 above.

well as 'internal.' An I-language is a physical object in the world, a finite grammar consisting of a computational system and a lexicon. From this perspective the notion of a language as a set of sentences plays no role. Furthermore, the concept of I-language does not rely on a notion of 'an ideal speaker-listener, in a completely homogeneous speech-community, who knows its language perfectly and is unaffected by such grammatically irrelevant conditions as memory limitations, distractions, shifts of attention and interest, and errors (random or characteristic) in applying his knowledge of the language in actual performance' (Chomsky 1965: 3). This notion had been assumed in previous work, including Chomsky (1965), as standard for modern general linguistics.

19.5 GENERATIVE GRAMMAR IN 2011: THEORY AND ITS EVOLUTION

In the past sixty years the landscape of generative grammar has undergone a radical transformation. The two grammatical mechanisms for creating linguistic structure have been reduced to one, eliminating phrase structure rules (Chomsky 1995a) and reducing transformations to their simplest formulation as single elementary operations (see Chomsky 1976, 1980). This reduction unifies phrase structure and transformational rules under the simplest combinatorial operation. As discussed below, this reduction has been facilitated by the development of a system of constraints on the operation and output of transformations, formulated as general principles of grammar (and thus part of a substantive proposal about the content of UG). Since the 1990s Chomsky and others have been concerned with refining and reducing these constraints from the perspective of economy conditions on derivations and representations (see Chomsky 1991), ultimately as principles of efficient computation. The goal of this work is to show how the computational system for human language, a central part of a biological language faculty, incorporates properties of economy, simplicity, and efficiency— thereby revealing the optimal nature of language design.

As a concrete illustration, consider the derivation of (2) above. The structural analysis is derived via the elementary operation Merge,[26] which combines constituents (lexical items and/or constituents formed from lexical items) to form a new syntactic object with a syntactic label the matches the label of one of the constituents of the combination. Like generalized transformations of the earliest theory, this operation maps pairs of syntactic objects onto a single object. Thus *the* and *books* will be merged to form a syntactic object labelled N and that construct will be merged with *take* to form a phrase labelled V. The lexical item in a phrase that determines its label

---

[26] Merge is first proposed in Chomsky (1995a).

constitutes the *head* of the phrase.[27] Assuming that every phrase is endocentric (i.e. has a unique head), the derivation of (2) under Merge yields (17) where T stands for tense and contains tense and agreement features that are ultimately attached to the verb *take* (cf. Affix Hopping in §19.3).

(17)

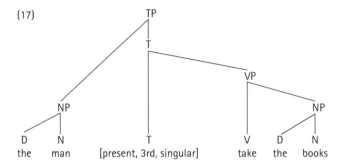

D	N		T		V	D	N
the	man		[present, 3rd, singular]		take	the	books

The category labels D, N and V are inherent features of the lexical items indicated orthographically as *the*, *man*, *take*, and *books*. The designations NP, TP, and VP indicate the maximal phrasal projection of the categories N, T, and V. In contrast to phrase structure rules, which construct a set of strings whose hierarchical structure is derived by an interpretive procedure of comparing adjacent pairs of strings in a phrase marker, Merge constructs the hierarchical structure directly but not a set of strings as in (3). Furthermore, under this model the lexicon is separated from the computational system as an autonomous component of the grammar (cf. the lexical phrase structure rules in (1)).[28]

Under Merge the derivation of the passive counterpart to (2) (i.e. (5)) involves the intermediate structure (18).

(18)   [$_T$ were [$_{VP}$ [$_V$ taken [$_{NP}$ the books]] [$_{PP}$ by [$_{NP}$ the man]]]]

The NP *the books* is merged with the verb *taken* as its logical object because it is in this position that the NP is assigned its semantic function by the verb. The NP *the man* is merged as the object of the passive P *by*, in which position it is interpreted as the logical subject of the verb. To derive (2) from (18), the NP *the books* must be merged with the phrase (18) to create the TP (19).

(19)   [$_{TP}$ [$_{NP}$ the books] [$_T$ were [$_{VP}$ [$_V$ taken [$_{NP}$ the books]] [$_{PP}$ by [$_{NP}$ the man]]]]]

---

[27] This concept lies at the core of the X-bar theory of phrase structure first proposed in Chomsky (1970). Although X-bar theory is fundamentally a bottom-up analysis of syntactic structure, it was nonetheless formulated in terms of top-down phrase structure rule schema. Merge incorporates the fundamental insight, eliminating the top-down implementation. It follows from Merge that all syntactic constructions are endocentric.

[28] The separation of the lexicon occurs in Chomsky (1965), allowing for the elimination of context-sensitive phrase structure rules, a reduction in the descriptive power of phrase structure rules. Note also that finite T in (17) would constitute an abstract item in the lexicon.

Chomsky distinguishes this application of Merge as 'internal Merge' (IM) as compared to 'external Merge' (EM), which applies in the derivation of (18). Like EM, IM joins two syntactic objects X and Y to form a new single syntactic object. In the case of IM a copy of X is contained in Y, whereas with EM X is not a part of Y. As Chomsky notes, 'Unless there is some stipulation to the contrary, which would require sufficient empirical evidence, both kinds of Merge are available for FL and IM creates copies' (2008: 140). Taking minimal computation as an overriding principle, the copy theory of IM is the null hypothesis.

The copy of the NP *the books* in the verbal object position is relevant to interpretation, but not pronunciation (i.e. phonetic form) and therefore is deleted (via another elementary operation Delete[29]) from the syntactic representation of phonetic form (PF) that interfaces with the sensory-motor components of the mind/brain. This leads to two distinct interface representations, PF and LF (which connects with the conceptual/intensional components of the mind/brain), yielding a derivational model (20) where a derivation bifurcates at some point, one part producing PF and the other LF.[30]

(20)

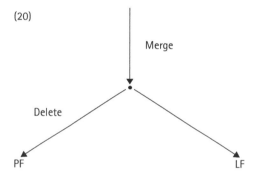

This model captures the phenomenon of displacement, where a constituent is interpreted in a different syntactic position than the one in which it is pronounced, a phenomenon that may be unique to natural language.

Replacing the passive transformation (6) with Merge eliminates the language-specific and construction-specific character of the operation that generates passive constructions. Employing IM generally for displacement phenomena eliminates transformations that compound operations (e.g. the double lexical insertion and the

[29] Delete accounts for ellipsis phenomena (e.g. VP-deletion in (i)) as well as eliminating multiple copies of a constituent at PF. *John has bought a new computer and Mary has ~~bought a new computer~~ too.* The strikethrough marks the VP that is interpreted in LF but not pronounced in PF.

[30] The original proposal occurs in Chomsky and Lasnik (1977) under a model that includes both phrase structure rules and a somewhat different formulation of transformations. Since Chomsky (1993) it has been assumed that the only levels of representation are the two interface levels, hence no level of deep structure, and no level of surface structure that is distinct from PF (see §19.3).

inversion of two NPs in (6)). Furthermore, it solves the problem of derived constituent structure because every application yields a distinct structure.

Merge generalizes to intra-clausal NP displacement, as illustrated in (21).[31]

> (21)   a. The man was reported to have taken the books.
>   b. The man is likely to have taken the books.

In (21a–b) the NP *the man* is interpreted as the subject of *taken*, its predicate-argument function, although it pronounced as the main clause subject. Thus in LF representation the infinitival subordinate clause has a covert NP subject *the man*, as illustrated in (22).

> (22)   a. [$_{TP}$ [$_{NP}$ the man] was [$_{VP}$ reported [$_{TP}$ [$_{NP}$ the man] to have taken the books]]]
>   b. [$_{TP}$ [$_{NP}$ the man] is [$_{AP}$ likely [$_{TP}$ [$_{NP}$ the man] to have taken the books]]]

The infinitival clause TP functions as an argument of the verb *reported* and the predicate adjective *likely* in the same way as the finite subordinate clauses in (23).

> (23)   a. It was reported that the man had taken the books.
>   b. It was likely that the man had taken the books.

The main clause subject position in these constructions is not assigned a predicate-argument function by the main clause predicate, as demonstrated by the occurrence of pleonastic and semantically null non-referential *it* in (23). Therefore, NP displacement in (21) involves one position that is assigned a predicate-argument function by a predicate and another that is not. This analysis also applies to cases of wh-displacement, as illustrated in (24).

> (24)   a. Which books did the teacher give to the student?
>   b. The books which the teacher gave to the student were on the list.
>   c. To whom did the teacher give the books?
>   d. The student to whom the teacher gave the books is in this class.

The interrogative phrase *which books* and the relative pronoun *which* are assigned a predicate-argument function as the direct object of *give*, but the clause initial position in which they are pronounced is assigned no such argument function. A similar analysis holds for *to whom*. In this way Merge replaces a special construction-specific wh-movement transformation (as actually formulated in *SS*) by generalizing across all displacement phenomena.

---

[31] In Chomsky's early work on this approach (see Chomsky 1976), NP displacement was handled by a rule called 'Move NP' where the operation was conceived as movement of an NP from one position to another, leaving behind an empty NP category called a *trace*. A separate rule 'Move *wh*' handled the displacement of wh-phrases in interrogatives and relative clauses. In Chomsky (1981b), these rules are replaced by the maximally general 'Move α.' The original formulation of Merge (Chomsky 1995a) distinguishes it from an operation Move. The distinction is eliminated in Chomsky (2004), where Move is recast as IM.

The massive reduction of the grammatical machinery of *LSLT/SS* to essentially two elementary operations, Merge and Delete,[32] was made possible by the development of a framework of constraints on the formulation of grammatical rules and on their operation in derivations and their output, the representations they produce. This system of constraints was postulated at the level of grammatical theory as principles of grammar, hence as part of UG. The development of this system focuses on the initial state of the language faculty (UG) (as opposed to complete grammars of particular I-languages), leading to the formulation of the Principles and Parameters framework in the late 1970s.[33] According to Chomsky (1981a: 61), 'The goal of research into UG is to discover a general system of principles and parameters such that each permissible core grammar is determined by fixing the parameters of the system.' The system of principles in Chomsky (1981b) includes constraints on (i) predicate/argument structure (the θ-Criterion, see below), (ii) the occurrence of NPs with phonetic content (the Case Filter, see below), (iii) the occurrence of silent copies resulting from IM (a) in terms of the syntactic distance from their antecedents (the Subjacency Condition) and (b) in terms of syntactic configuration characterized by a relation of government (the Empty Category Principle), and (iv) the syntactic relations between pairs of NPs construed in an anaphoric relation (principles of binding). In addition to the set of principles, UG also involves a set of parameters that account for cross-linguistic variation among languages. For example, some languages (e.g. Spanish and Italian) allow finite indicative clauses with covert pronominal subjects, whereas others (e.g. French, English, and German) do not; and further, some languages (e.g. French, Spanish, Italian, and German) allow yes/no interrogative construction where the finite main verb occurs clause-initially, whereas English does not. Chomsky (1981a: 38) summarizes as follows:

> The theory of UG must be sufficiently rich and highly structured to provide descriptively adequate grammars. At the same time, it must be sufficiently open to allow for the variety of languages. Consideration of the nature of the problem at a qualitative level leads to the expectation that UG consists of a highly structured and

[32] More recently Chomsky has proposed distinguishing two types of Merge: pair Merge, which applies to adjuncts, and set Merge, which applies to non-adjuncts. See Chomsky (2004, 2008) for details. Delete appears to be restricted to the externalization of linguistic expressions (i.e. PF), perhaps as a consequence of 'a principle of minimal computation (spell-out and pronounce as little as possible)' (Noam Chomsky, p.c.).

[33] This line of research begins with Chomsky's A/A Principle and continues with Ross's critique of the principle in his 1967 MIT dissertation (published as Ross 1986). Ross proposes to replace the A/A Principle with a new set of general constraints that identify 'syntactic islands' from which constituents may not be extracted. These island conditions extend the scope of constraints on the application of transformations. Chomsky (1973) proposes another set of constraints that generalize to NP displacement (Ross 1967 focuses primarily on wh-movement), some of which also account for binding relations between anaphors and their antecedents (see also Chomsky 1976). Chomsky (1991) and (1995b) attempt to reformulate the set of grammatical principles in terms of notions of economy of derivation and representation (see below for some discussion). See Freidin (2011) and Lasnik and Lohndal (2013) for some discussion of this history. For a detailed overview of the Principles and Parameters framework see Chomsky (1981a, 1981b), Chomsky and Lasnik (1993), and Freidin (1996).

restrictive system of principles with certain open parameters, to be fixed by experi-ence. As these parameters are fixed, a grammar is determined, what we may call a 'core grammar.'

UG provides a finite set of parameters (Chomsky 1981b: 11). Furthermore, 'The gram-mar of a particular language can be regarded as simply the specification of values of parameters of UG, nothing more' (p. 31).[34]

The system of general principles that has developed from the early 1970s sufficiently limits the operation and output of grammatical operations so that we can keep to their maximally simple formulations. Given the free application of Merge, various deviant constructions could otherwise be generated if not prohibited by general principles. For example, the failure of IM in the derivation of (21) could yield (25), where the main clause subject contains non-referential *it*.

> (25) a. *It was reported the man to have taken the books.
>   b. *It is likely the man to have taken the books.

The examples in (25) violate the Case Filter, which prohibits NPs containing phonetic features from occurring in a position that is not licensed for structural Case. The subject of the infinitival clause in (25) is not in a construction that licences structural Case and therefore the NP *the man* violates the Case Filter. The computational system thus prohibits the generation of deviant constructions like (25). Free Merge can also misgenerate constructions like (26), where instead of merging non-referential *it* as the main clause subject, a NP with semantic content is merged instead.

> (26) a. *The woman was reported that the man had taken the books.
>   b. *The woman was likely that the man had taken the books.

In (26), the NP *the woman* is not assigned a semantic function by any predicate and therefore violates the part of the θ-Criterion that prohibits NPs with semantic content that are assigned no semantic function by any predicate. Both the Case Filter and the θ-Criterion function as conditions on representations.

Comparing the legitimate constructions in (21) (where IM applies to the infinitival subordinate clause subject by creating a copy as the subject of the finite main clause) to the deviant constructions in (25) (where IM does not apply) demonstrates how Case motivates NP displacement—i.e. IM applies when it must. In contrast, consider (27) where unconstrained free Merge, as indicated in the analyses (27a.ii) and (27b.ii), produces another deviant result.

> (27) a. i. *The man was reported (that) has taken the books.
>   ii. [$_{TP}$ [$_{NP}$ the man] was [$_{VP}$ reported [$_{CP}$ (that) [$_{TP}$ [$_{NP}$ the man] to have taken the books]]]]

---

[34] Chomsky (1981a) discusses three cases of parameters that relate to the formulation of UG principles, hence the computational system. Chomsky (1991) raises the possibility that parameters of UG instead relate only to the lexicon, specifically functional (as opposed to substantive) elements like T (as opposed to substantive elements like N, V, A, and P), citing Borer (1984) and Fukui (1986, 1988).

b. i. *The man is likely (that) has taken the books.
    ii. [$_{TP}$ [$_{NP}$ the man] is [$_{AP}$ likely [$_{CP}$ (that) [$_{TP}$ [$_{NP}$ the man] to have taken the books]]]]

In (27), because the NP *the man* is licensed for Case as the subject of the finite subordinate clause, displacement of the NP to subject position of the finite clause via IM is not motivated by the Case Filter. If the application of IM in (27) is not required by any other UG principle, then the deviance of (27a.i) and (27b.i) would follow from a basic economy-of-derivation assumption 'that operations are driven by necessity: they are "last resort," applied if they must be, not otherwise' (Chomsky 1993: 31). Thus economy of derivations supports the minimal formulation of the grammatical operation Merge.

In tandem with economy constraints on derivations, Chomsky proposes a complementary constraint on representations: Full Interpretation (FI), which prohibits superfluous symbols in PF and LF, the two interfaces of syntax with systems of language use (see Chomsky 1986: 98, 1991: 437). Given that phonetic features are superfluous for the conceptual–intensional interface and that, correspondingly, semantic features are superfluous for the sensory–motor interface, FI requires a derivational point where phonetic and semantic features are separated onto distinct sub-paths via Spell-Out, thereby motivating the derivational model (20). Furthermore, FI subsumes the empirical effects of the portion of the θ-Criterion that prohibits (26), given that the NP *the woman*, having semantic content but filling no semantic function for any predicate in the sentence, would be presumably uninterpretable and hence superfluous at LF. Note also that the Case Filter might also be replaced by FI given that Case features on nouns are also uninterpretable under the analysis of Chomsky (1995b: ch. 4). Assuming that these features exist in the lexical entries for nouns that also have phonetic features, they must be eliminated during a derivation via a process of feature checking so that they will not occur in interface representations. The erasure of uninterpretable features results from an operation *Agree* that matches these features to corresponding interpretable features of another element in a construction.[35] In this way, FI requires minimal representations and at the same time provides a principled motivation for certain computational operations.

Another phenomenon that bears on the issue of minimal computation concerns the syntactic distance between pairs of adjacent copies created by IM, where shorter distances are preferred. Consider for example the following paradigm involving NP displacement in complex sentences.

(28) a. It seems that it has been reported that the student had taken the books.
      b. It seems to have been reported that the student had taken the books.

---

[35] For detailed discussion see Chomsky (2000b, 2001, 2004, 2005, 2008). Chomsky (2004: 114) states that IM requires Agree. Chomsky (2005: 17) proposes that uninterpretable features occur as unvalued in the lexicon and are valued and eliminated via Agree (see also Chomsky 2007, 2008). For an overview of Case theory, including its history, see Lasnik (2008).

    c. It seems that the student has been reported to have taken the books.

    d. The student seems to have been reported to have taken the books.

    e. *The student seems that it has been reported to have taken the books.

In the derivation of (28a) IM does not apply. This construction involves two syntactic positions to which a semantic function is not assigned, i.e. the subject of *seem* in the main clause and the subject of the passive predicate *reported*. This is demonstrated in (28a), where both positions are filled with pleonastic non-referential *it*. Also both positions can take displaced arguments, as illustrated in (28c) and (28d), where the NP *the students* is interpreted as the logical subject of the verb *taken*. (28b) shows that pleonastic elements can apparently also be affected by IM. However, displacement is blocked in (28e) where the distance between the subject of *taken* and the syntactic subject of *seems* crosses another subject position that does not contain a copy of the displaced NP. In contrast, the derivation of (28d) creates a chain of three copies of the NP *the students* where each link, consisting of a pair of adjacent copies, conforms to the shortest distance criterion. Chomsky (1995b) formulates this constraint as the Minimal Link Condition (MLC), interpreted 'as requiring that at a given stage of a derivation, a longer link from α to K cannot be formed if there is a shorter legitimate link from β to K' (Chomsky 1995b: 295). It follows from the MLC that long distance displacement (e.g. across multiple clauses) requires a series of local steps.[36] Thus the derivation of (28d) applies IM twice, as illustrated in (29) where **NP** indicates a copy of the displaced NP *the student*.

    (29) [$_{TP}$ The student seems [$_{TP}$ **NP** to have been reported [$_{TP}$ **NP** to have taken the books]]]

IM (as well as EM) applies here to successively larger structures, hence cyclically. Cyclic computation also contributes to the overall minimal character of the computational system.[37] In Chomsky's most recent work (2007, 2008) cyclic computation is enforced by the No Tampering Condition (NTC) that restricts Merge to the edges of the syntactic objects it combines.

    (30) NTC: Merge of X and Y leaves the two S[yntactic] O[bject]s unchanged.
          (Chomsky 2008: 138)

The NTC also constitutes a very narrow constraint on derived constituent structure, adhering to the principle of minimal computation and thereby contributing to a minimal account of representations. Note that the NTC entails the copy theory of IM.

---

[36] Regarding a more exact formulation of the MLC, note the comment in Chomsky (2008: 156): 'Just how small these local steps are remains to be clarified.'

[37] The cyclic application of transformations is first proposed in Chomsky (1965) as a means of reducing the descriptive power of the theory of grammar by eliminating generalized transformations and the related construct of T-markers. See Freidin (1999) and Lasnik (2006) for more detailed discussion of the history of the syntactic cycle.

Chomsky (2000b) introduces the Phase Impenetrability Condition (PIC) as another constraint on derivations that enforces a stronger form of cyclic computation.[38] The PIC is based on a conception of derivations as having multiple points where syntactic objects are transferred to the interfaces via Spell-Out. The syntactic objects transferred are called 'phases'; and 'Optimally, once a phase is transferred, it should be mapped directly to the interface and then "forgotten"; later operations should not have to refer back to what has already been mapped to the interface—again, a basic intuition behind cyclic operations' (Chomsky 2005: 17). As a result, derivation by phase imposes a high degree of locality, especially for the application of IM, and in this way contributes significantly to the goal of minimal computation.[39]

This focus on minimal computation derives most directly from Chomsky's concern for notions of simplicity and economy, which he had expressed on the first page and in first footnote of *MMH* (and repeated almost verbatim in the second footnote of chapter IV in *LSLT* again citing Goodman 1943 and adding Quine 1953):

> It is important, incidentally, to recognize that considerations of simplicity are not trivial or 'merely esthetic.' It has been remarked in the case of philosophical systems that the motives for the demand for economy are in many ways the same as those behind the demand that there be a system at all. (*MMH* p. 114)

The proposal of economy conditions on derivations and representations in Chomsky 1991 served as a prelude to the formulation of a minimalist program for linguistic theory (henceforth MP) in Chomsky (1993) (written a year earlier).[40]

Chomsky (1995b: 9) formulates the MP as a research program that addresses two interrelated questions.

(31) a. To what extent is the computational system for human language optimal?
      b. To what extent is human language a 'perfect' system?

These questions are interrelated to the extent that an optimal computational system is a reasonable prerequisite for establishing the perfection of human language as a system. Answers to these questions require precise substantive interpretations of the adjectives *optimal* and *perfect*. As discussed above, the characterization of the computational system under the Principles and Parameters framework does appear to be optimal to the extent that it focuses on minimal computation in terms of the minimal formulation of grammatical mechanisms, the minimal function of these mechanisms in derivations,

---

[38] See also Chomsky (2001, 2004) for more explicit formulations.

[39] However, as Chomsky (2004: 107) notes, 'It remains to determine what the phases are, and exactly how the operations work'—for example, whether the PIC replaces the MLC as it applies to block the derivation of (28e). Chomsky (2005: 17) adds a further cautionary comment about establishing a PIC: 'Whether that is feasible is a question only recently formulated, and barely explored. It raises many serious issues, but so far at least, no problems that seem insuperable.' See Chomsky (2008) for his most recent views on phases.

[40] For discussion of the roots of the minimalist approach in the history of generative grammar, see Freidin and Lasnik (2011), and for commentary on the evolution of linguistic theory that led to the MP, see Freidin and Vergnaud (2001).

and the minimal nature of the representations they produce. These formulations also conform to basic notions of simplicity, economy, and efficiency of computation.

If it turns out that the computational system for human language is in fact optimal, then it could also be true that human language is a 'perfect' system in some precise sense. Chomsky (1995b: 228) provides a single criterion.

> A 'perfect language' should meet the condition of inclusiveness: any structure formed by the computation (in particular, PF and LF) is constituted of elements already present in the lexical items selected for [the numeration] N; no new objects are added in the course of computation apart from rearrangements of lexical properties (in particular, no indices, bar-levels in the sense of X-bar theory, etc.).

This inclusiveness condition employs the lexicon to place significant constraints on the application and output of the computational system and thus contributes as well to minimal computation.

Ultimately the MP is an attempt to study the question of how well FL is designed, a new question that arises within the Principles and Parameters framework. 'The substantive thesis is that language design may really be optimal in some respects, approaching a "perfect solution" to minimal design specifications.'[41] These specifications concern the crucial requirement that linguistic representations are 'legible' to the cognitive systems that interface with FL, a requirement 'that must be satisfied for language to be usable at all' (Chomsky 2001: 1). Chomsky 2000b designates this as the strong minimalist thesis (SMT) and formulates it as (32).[42]

> (32)   Language is an optimal solution to legibility conditions. (p. 96)

Thus the SMT narrows the focus of UG to interface conditions, which may result in a significant reduction and simplification of UG.[43] Chomsky 2008 explains:

> If SMT held fully, which no one expects, UG would be restricted to properties imposed by interface conditions. A primary task of the MP is to clarify the notions that enter into SMT and to determine how closely the ideal can be approached. Any departure from SMT—any postulation of descriptive technology that cannot be given a principled explanation—merits close examination, to see if it is really justified. (p. 135)

From the perspective of the SMT there are three factors that affect the growth of language in the individual: data external to the individual (the contribution of experience), UG (the genetic endowment of the species), and principles that are not specific to FL. Chomsky (2004) subdivides UG into interface conditions ('the principled part') vs 'unexplained elements' (p. 106) and contrasts UG with general properties (the third

---

[41] Chomsky adds: 'The conclusion would be surprising, hence interesting if true' (2000b: 93).

[42] It is worth noting that Chomsky (2007) identifies SMT as holding 'that FL is "perfectly designed."' This suggests that there may be no significant difference between optimal design and perfect design.

[43] See e.g. the discussion above about how FI might replace the Case Filter and a part of the θ-Criterion.

factor, principles that are not specific to FL[44]), the latter elaborated in Chomsky (2005) as falling into two subtypes:

> (a) principles of data analysis that might be used in language acquisition and other domains; (b) principles of structural architecture and developmental constraints that enter into canalization, organic form, and action over a wide range, including principles of efficient computation, which would be expected to be of particular significance for computational systems such as language. It is the second of these subcategories that should be of particular significance in determining the nature of attainable languages. (p. 106)

Based on this three-way contrast, Chomsky (2004) proposes another formulation of the SMT where UG contains no 'unexplained elements' and therefore all parts of UG are principled.

> We can regard an account of some linguistic phenomena as principled insofar as it derives them by efficient computation satisfying interface conditions. We can therefore formulate SMT as the thesis that all phenomena of language have a principled account in this sense, that language is a perfect solution to interface conditions, the conditions it must at least partially satisfy if it is to be usable at all. (2004: 5)

Incorporating third factor considerations into the study of language leads to a second approach to the formulation of UG, as discussed in Chomsky (2007):

> Throughout the modern history of generative grammar, the problem of determining the character of FL has been approached 'from top down': How much must be attributed to UG to account for language acquisition? The MP seeks to approach the problem 'from bottom up': How little can be attributed to UG while still accounting for the variety of I-languages attained, relying on third factor principles? The two approaches should, of course, converge, and should interact in the course of pursuing a common goal. (p. 4)

Approaching UG from below shifts 'the burden of explanation from the first factor, the genetic endowment, to the third factor, language-independent principles of data processing, structural architecture, and computational efficiency, thereby providing some answers to the fundamental questions of biology of language, its nature and use, and perhaps even its evolution' (Chomsky 2005: 9). This third factor approach to language design opens the possibility that methodological considerations of simplicity and economy might be recast as empirical hypotheses about the world, thereby establishing more substantive connections between general biology and the biolinguistic perspective at the core of the MP within the Principles and Parameters framework.

---

[44] Interface conditions might plausibly be considered part of the third factor given that they are imposed by cognitive systems external to the FL.

19.6 Summing Up

The preceding sketch has attempted to convey the magnitude of Chomsky's contribution to linguistics by comparing his initial formulation of generative grammar with his structuralist predecessors' approach to syntax and then comparing that formulation to the current perspective. In the intervening six decades, Chomsky:

a. constructed a formal theory of grammar (leading to the discovery of abstract underlying linguistic structure) and explored its foundations;
b. developed a cognitive/epistemological interpretation of the theory, leading to an understanding of human language as a component of mind/brain with substantial innate content, hence a part of human biology;
c. contributed a series of major proposals for constraints on grammars (ongoing from the beginning) that resulted in a significant reduction in and simplification of the formal grammatical machinery;
d. re-evaluated the theory of grammar in terms of questions about language design, raising the possibility of empirical proposals about the language faculty as a biological entity with properties of economy, simplicity, and efficient computation.

From the beginning Chomsky's work placed linguistics at the centre of the cognitive revolution of the 1950s (see Miller 2003) and established the importance of the field for related fields concerned with the study of human language (e.g. philosophy, psychology, anthropology, computer science, and biology).[45] In redefining the science of language, Chomsky has wrought a revolution without precedent in the history of linguistics.

---

[45] See Fitch (in press) for an overview of the relevance of Chomsky's ideas for the biology of language.

CHAPTER 20

EUROPEAN LINGUISTICS SINCE SAUSSURE

GIORGIO GRAFFI

20.1 SAUSSURE AND THE *COURS DE LINGUISTIQUE GÉNÉRALE*

DESPITE Saussure's undeniable links with nineteenth-century linguistics (on which see Koerner 1973, Allan 2010a), the appearance of his posthumous *Cours de linguistique générale* (Saussure 1962 [1916/1922]) undoubtedly represented a radical change within the discipline, which exerted a powerful influence on subsequent scholars, especially within Europe (but, to a lesser extent, also in the United States). The main lines of Saussure's linguistic thought will therefore be discussed first in what follows. Subsequently, an overview of the several European linguistic schools more or less directly connected to it will be traced. This connection is especially close for the schools of continental linguistic structuralism, namely those of Geneva, Prague, and Copenhagen (see §20.2); it is somewhat looser for other scholars, such as the Frenchmen Guillaume and Tesnière, or the British linguists belonging to the so-called 'London school' (see §20.3). As will be seen, however, none of these scholars can avoid referring to some of Saussure's ideas and proposals: this is the reason for dealing with them under the same heading.

20.1.1 Saussure's Life and Work

Ferdinand de Saussure (1857–1913), born and educated in Geneva, subsequently studied historical-comparative linguistics at the University of Leipzig, which in that epoch (the end of the 1870s) was the centre of the Neogrammarian school. He obtained his Ph.D in 1880, but his scientific activity had already started a couple of years earlier, with a book devoted to the Indo-European vowel system (de Saussure 1879, actually published in 1878). It was analysed in a way so innovative that the book came to be fully appreciated by the scientific community only much later. After ten years of teaching in Paris, in 1891 Saussure became professor for Sanskrit and Indo-European Languages at the University of Geneva, where he remained until his death. During his Geneva years, he became more and more uncertain about his ideas and his results, as is witnessed by the fact that his publications were increasingly rare. His fundamental aim was a reconsideration of the methods and the goals of linguistics: 'montrer au linguiste ce qu'il fait' ('to show to the linguist what he is doing'), as he wrote in a letter of 4 January 1894 to his colleague and former student Antoine Meillet (1866–1936). Saussure first presented his ideas on such matters during three courses in general linguistics which he gave in the academic years 1906–7, 1908–9, and 1910–11. After his death, two of his former students, Charles Bally (1865–1947) and Albert Sechehaye (1870–1946), edited a book which they named *Cours de linguistique générale* 'Course in General Linguistics.' It first appeared in 1916, and the final edition in 1922. Since Bally and Sechehaye had never attended Saussure's courses in general linguistics, they based the text on the notes taken by other people: hence, their work was unavoidably arbitrary to some extent. In the second half of the twentieth century, an essential means for the knowledge of Saussure's authentic thought came from the work of two Swiss scholars, Robert Godel (1902–1984) and Rudolf Engler (1930–2003). Godel 1957 discovered the original notes from Saussure's lectures which had been the sources of Saussure 1922; Engler (1967–74) published such sources together with the text edited by Bally and Sechehaye. Starting from Godel's and Engler's work, Tullio De Mauro (b. 1932) added to his Italian translation of Saussure 1922 an extensive commentary which, since 1972, has also accompanied the original French version of the volume. A reader interested in deepening her/his knowledge of Saussure's thought should therefore refer to it.

20.1.2 The Saussurean Dichotomies

It is standard to summarize Saussure's thought by resorting to his four 'dichotomies,' i.e. four pairs of concepts opposed to each other: (1) *langue* 'language' vs *parole* 'speaking'; (2) synchrony vs diachrony; (3) *signifiant* 'signifier' vs *signifié* 'signified'; (4) syntagmatic vs 'associative' (later called 'paradigmatic') relations. This kind of exposition will also be adopted here, but Saussure's theories are much more complex than they appear from such a simplistic presentation. It has been maintained that traces of each of these four dichotomies can be found in the work of earlier linguists, from nineteenth-century scholars such as Hermann Paul (1846–1921) going back to the Stoics (from the fourth century BC: see Chapter 13 above): their essential novelty, however, cannot be denied. In particular, what distinguishes Saussure's thought from that of the preceding scholars is its *systemic* approach: every linguistic unit can be defined only by virtue of the system of relations it has with the other units. Another characteristic feature of Saussure's thought is his attempt at building an *autonomous* linguistics, namely independent from psychology, sociology, or any other discipline, contrary to the methods of most linguists immediately preceding him. Actually, this attempt was not completely carried out by Saussure: it however became the trademark of all later schools of European structural linguistics, together with the systemic approach to linguistics, as will be seen in the following sections.

20.1.2.1 Langue *vs* Parole

It is necessary to point out that the English word *language* has two different equivalents in French, namely *langage* and *langue*. According to Saussure (1959 [1922]), *langage* (rendered as 'speech' or 'human speech' in the English translation) 'is many sided and heterogeneous' and it has 'both an individual and a social side' (p. 8). The opposition between *langue* and *parole* as introduced in Saussure (1922) appears somewhat over-simplified with respect to its handwritten sources (cf. §20.1.1 above). In his class lectures, Saussure actually distinguished not two concepts, but three (*langue*, *parole*, and *langage*): the last concept is not only presented as a purely 'many sided and heterogeneous' phenomenon but, in a more positive way, also as the faculty which allows humans to acquire any language; and Saussure also speaks of a *faculté de langage* 'faculty of language,' a concept which appears rather close to the homonymous Chomskyan one (see e.g. Chomsky 1975c). However, Saussure only focuses on the *langue/parole* dichotomy. *Langue* is defined as the 'social side' of language (*langage*). It is the common code shared by all the speakers belonging to a given linguistic community: it is 'a storehouse filled by the members of a given community through their active use of speaking' (de Saussure 1959: 13). What Saussure calls *parole* 'speaking' denotes both (a) the usage of this common code by the different individuals and (b) the psycho-physical device which allows them to put such code into use (cf. de Saussure 1959: 14).

20.1.2.2 *Synchrony vs Diachrony*

In Saussure's own words, '*synchrony* and *diachrony* designate respectively a language-state and an evolutionary phase' (1959: 81). In itself, this opposition was nothing new: as Saussure himself recalls (p. 82), the 'programme' of traditional grammar, such as Port-Royal grammar, 'was strictly synchronic.' On the other hand, 'since modern linguistics came into existence, it has been completely absorbed in diachrony.' The difference between Saussure and earlier linguists therefore lies in their respective views of the opposition between synchrony and diachrony. Traditional grammar almost totally ignored diachrony; nineteenth-century historical-comparative grammar ('modern linguistics,' in Saussure's just quoted passage) subordinated synchrony to diachrony, stating that only a diachronic study of language can be really scientific (cf. Paul 1920: 20). Saussure's position is wholly opposite: 'it is evident that the synchronic point of view predominates, for it is the true and only reality to the community of speakers' and if the linguist 'takes the diachronic perspective, he no longer observes language (*langue*) but rather a series of events that modify it' (de Saussure 1959: 90). Synchronic facts cannot be accounted for in diachronic terms. For example, 'historically the French negation *pas* is identical to the substantive *pas* "step," whereas the two forms are distinct in modern French' (p. 91). Saussure's opposition between synchrony and diachrony can be condensed (as is standard) in the following way: synchronic facts are systematic and meaningful; diachronic facts are isolated and ateleological (i.e. without a goal). As will be seen below (§20.2.3), this polar opposition between synchrony and diachrony was rejected by some schools of European structuralism, especially by the Prague school, which attempted to overcome it: but Saussure's dichotomy had anyway the effect of producing a radical change in the goals and methods of twentieth-century linguistics with respect to those of nineteenth century. While the latter was mainly of a diachronic kind, the former preferred synchronic studies.

20.1.2.3 *Signifier vs Signified*

The signifier and the signified are the two 'sides of the linguistic sign' (de Saussure 1959: 66). Saussure (p. 67) states that 'the bond between the signifier and the signified is arbitrary. Since I mean by sign the whole that results from the associating of the signifier with the signified, I can simply say: *the linguistic sign is arbitrary*' (original emphasis). This is the so-called 'doctrine of the arbitrariness of the linguistic sign,' which has sometimes been misunderstood. First of all, it must be kept in mind that this doctrine not only states that the relationship between a given sequence of sounds (e.g. /buk/) on the one hand and a given object (a pile of printed sheets bound together) on the other has no natural basis, since it derives from a convention: such a 'conventionalist' conception of the linguistic sign can be found in many linguists before Saussure, and can be traced back at least to Aristotle's treatise *De interpretatione*. Saussure's conception is new and deeper: according to him, the relationship between the signifier and the signified is not, in the first place, a relationship between language and reality, but a relationship internal to language itself. What singles out a linguistic sign, in Saussure's perspective, is its *value*, namely its relationship with the other signs of the linguistic system to which it belongs. The signifier is the value from the point of view of the expression (of the 'sound,' in Saussure's words), the signified from that of the content (the 'concept'). The value of a sign is therefore not intrinsic, but is simply the outcome of its differences from the other signs belonging to the system. This 'differential' conception of the sign is the basis for the Saussurean notion of arbitrariness: '*arbitrary* and *differential* are two correlative qualities' (de Saussure 1959: 118). 'In language there are only differences. [. . .] differences *without positive terms*' (p. 121; original emphasis). For example,

> Modern French *mouton* can have the same signification as English *sheep* but not the same value, and this for several reasons, particularly because in speaking of a piece of meat ready to be served on the table, English uses *mutton* and not *sheep*. The difference in value between *sheep* and *mouton* is due to the fact that sheep has beside it a second term while the French word does not (pp. 116–17).

If linguistic signs are not simply conventional labels which designate a given reality, differing only in their sounds, but rather are values determined by their reciprocal relationships, what warrants them? The fact that they belong to a system shared by a social group, to a given language (*langue*): 'the social fact alone can create a linguistic system' (p. 113). However, as any other social fact, also a language is historically conditioned: the sign systems may change in the course of the time, as the opposition between synchrony and diachrony shows. This social and historical conditioning is the basic reason for the arbitrariness of the sign, in Saussure's sense.

20.1.2.4 *Syntagmatic vs Associative Relations*

This dichotomy may be exemplified by means of the word 'instruction.' The combination between the stem 'instruct-' and the suffix '-ion' is an example of a syntagmatic relation, namely of a combination between two signs. That between e.g. 'instruction' and 'education' is an example of an associative relation: each of the two words refers to the other, and any of them can replace the other in a given context (e.g. 'higher instruction' vs 'higher education'). The associative relations are surely considered by Saussure as belonging to a language (*langue*); the place of the syntagmatic ones is not wholly clear. Saussure states that the sentence, which is 'the ideal type of syntagm,' 'belongs to speaking (*parole*), not to language' (1959: 124). On the other hand, 'to language rather than to speaking belong the syntagmatic types that are built upon regular forms' (p. 125). De Mauro, in his commentary on Saussure's text (1972: n. 251), resorting to its handwritten sources, has come to the conclusion that Saussure considers also that sentences, insofar as they realize general patterns, also belong to *la langue*. This is probably the most accurate interpretation of Saussure's real thought: it is a fact, however, that the linguists immediately following Saussure, not having the handwritten sources at their disposal, maintained the view that the he ascribed the sentence to speaking (*parole*), and not to language (*langue*).

20.2 THE SCHOOLS OF GENEVA, PRAGUE, AND COPENHAGEN

20.2.1 General Features

The schools of linguistics most directly influenced by Saussure's thought differ considerably from each other, and such a differentiation often occurs even among scholars belonging to the same school. However, they share some significant ideas about the nature of language and the aims and methods of linguistics, which are essentially a critical development of some Saussurean basic insights. One such idea is the conception of the language as a *structure*, namely as set of entities defined not in themselves, but by virtue of their reciprocal relationships: it must also be stressed that the labels 'structure,' 'structural,' etc. became key terms of linguistics due to the work of post-Saussurean schools (Saussure very seldom employed 'structure,' rather speaking of 'system'). Another consistent development of Saussure's ideas by the European schools of structural linguistics, which marks their difference with respect to most preceding trends, is the abandonment of psychologism: according to such linguists, language has to be described only on the basis of its structure and its functions, without any reference to psychological entities or processes. This 'anti-psychologistic' attitude fully characterizes the Prague and Copenhagen schools, while some remnants of psychologism can still be detected among the Geneva scholars.

20.2.2 The Geneva School

It may seem somewhat paradoxical, but the first members of the Geneva school, Bally and Sechehaye (§20.1.1), were possibly the European structuralist linguists least influenced by Saussure's thought. This paradox is, however, only apparent: the views of Bally and Sechehaye were already formed when Saussure gave his classes on which the *Cours de linguistique générale* is based. As we hinted above, Bally's and Sechehaye's connection with pre-Sassurean linguistics is shown by their residual links to nineteenth-century psychologism.

A decidedly psychologistic attitude characterizes Sechehaye's first book, (Sechehaye 1908). For example, Sechehaye maintained that one of the major tasks of theoretical linguistics was the solution of what he called the 'grammatical problem,' which would consist in the investigation of the 'psychophysical basis' of the laws and of the functioning of the grammar (cf. Sechehaye 1908: 24). Actually, Sechehaye never solved this big problem: nevertheless, his analyses of many grammatical phenomena (especially those contained in Sechehaye 1926) are very insightful and still deserve attention. After the appearance of Saussure's *Cours*, Sechehaye also turned to more general problems, such as the relationship between the social and the individual sides of language. Detaching himself from Saussure's concept of *langue*, intended as a common code shared by a community of speakers, he denied the legitimacy of assuming an entity of 'a language in itself,' over and above the languages of the individuals (Sechehaye 1933: 65).

Bally's psychologism is especially to be found in the opposition between what he called the 'intellectual' and the 'affective' components of language. According to different circumstances, either of the two components can prevail over the other, but they always occur together: e.g. an affective (or 'emotional,' or 'expressive') element occurs even in the apparently most neutral utterances, such as 'it is raining' (cf. Bally 1926: 23). The reason for this lies in the fact that the concrete use of language always consists in a dialogical relation, where the speaker not only transmits some intellectual content to the hearer, but also expresses his own emotions, attempts to reach some goal, etc. (p. 33). Bally calls the discipline which has to deal with the combined effect of both the intellectual and the affective side of language 'stylistics.' In his sense, therefore, stylistics is not limited to the analysis of literary texts: e.g. to say *John, I cannot bear him* stylistically differs from *I cannot bear John*: the intellectual content is the same, but the affective element is stronger in the first sentence than in the second.

Bally's notion of stylistics is surely an original facet of his thought, which distinguishes it from Saussure's. Other notions directly derived from Saussure, in their turn, are somewhat modified by Bally. In particular, he reshapes the opposition between *langue* and *parole*: he defines *parole* as the 'actualization' of *langue*. All elements of *langue* are 'virtual,' and to be applied to the reality they have to be 'actualized': e.g. BOOK as an element of *langue* is a virtual concept, which becomes actualized by means of the 'actualizer' *this*, in a phrase such as *this book* (Bally 1965: §119). The phenomenon of actualization shows that *parole* follows *langue* from the point of view which Bally calls 'static.' From the 'genetic' point of view, however, this relationship is reversed: *parole* precedes *langue* in the genesis of language.

Among the scholars belonging to the second generation of Geneva linguists, we limit ourselves to quoting Bally's pupil Henri Frei (1899–1980). His most important work is Frei (1929), whose title ('The Grammar of Faults') is due to the fact that it deals with aspects of contemporary French normally treated as errors by French prescriptive grammars. Frei shows that such alleged errors are actually explained as effects of different needs, which he names 'assimilation,' 'differentiation,' 'shortness,' 'invariability,' and 'expressiveness.' In this same volume, Frei also worked out a 'syntagmatics' or theory of syntagms which resumed and developed Saussure's ideas about syntagmatic relations (§20.1.2.4 above). Frei's investigations in this domain were further deepened in some essays of the 1950s and the 1960s.

20.2.3 The Prague School: the Functional Approach and the Phonological Theory

The Prague school flourished in the 1920s and in the 1930s and was centred around the Prague Linguistic Circle, founded in 1926 by Vilém Mathesius (1882–1945), professor of English at the University of Prague. Mathesius' own work is especially important for his studies of the sentence structure, which he developed in an essentially communicative framework: from his earliest essays on this matter, Mathesius opposed the 'actual' to the 'grammatical' analysis of the sentence. The latter is the traditional analysis into subject and predicate; the former subdivides the sentence into 'theme' and 'enunciation' (later called 'rheme'; see Mathesius 1929). Both analyses are necessary, in Mathesius' view, since they do not always coincide: e.g. the theme is not always identical with the grammatical subject, nor the rheme with the grammatical predicate. The differences are also cross-linguistic: Modern English tends to make the subject coincide with the theme much more than do languages like Czech. Mathesius' investigations, which did not make any great impact at the time of their appearance, became instead very popular after the Second World War, under the label Functional Sentence Perspective.

Mathesius' organizational work was extremely important: the Prague Linguistic Circle counted among its members the most influential European structural linguists, among whom the Russians Roman Jakobson (1896–1982) and Nikolaj S. Trubetzkoy (1890–1938) are especially worthy of mention. The research fields of both scholars were very wide: Jakobson had also investigated folklore and was especially interested in poetic language; Trubetzkoy, after his early studies on ethnographic matters, turned to historical-comparative linguistics and eventually became professor of Slavic philology at the University of Vienna. He was always an active member of the Prague Linguistic Circle (for more information, see Toman 1995). Another important member of the Prague circle was Sergej Karcevskij (1884–1955), who had left Russia after the 1905 Revolution and migrated to Geneva, where he was in contact with Saussure: he can therefore be considered as the link between the school of Geneva and the Prague School. The link between the two schools became official at the First International Congress of Linguists, held in 1928 at The Hague, where both Bally and Sechehaye, on the one hand, and Jakobson, Karcevskij, and Trubetzkoy, on the other, expressed their reciprocal agreement on several points that emerged during the discussion.

On that occasion, Prague scholars stressed the importance of Saussure's conception of *langue* 'as a system of reciprocal values,' hence on the structural conception of language. In their view, however, Saussure's limitation lay in restricting this systematic, structural perspective to synchronic linguistics: a 'teleological' and 'systematic' view of linguistic change had therefore to replace Saussure's 'atomistic' one (cf. Jakobson et al. 1929: 35–6). This position was restated at the congress of Slavists held the following year in Prague, where the famous 'Theses of 1929' (see Steiner 1982) were presented by the members of the Prague Linguistic Circle. In particular, the need for overcoming the sharp opposition between synchrony and diachrony is restated in the first thesis: not only does linguistic change show a systematic character, but also any linguistic stage contains some traces of the preceding ones. Among the other arguments dealt with in the theses of 1929 (ten in total, but the most relevant for general linguistics are the first three), the distinction introduced in the second thesis between the sound considered as 'an objective physical fact' and as 'an element of a functional system' deserves special attention. This distinction became the basis of the opposition between phonetics and phonology, presented and developed in Trubetzkoy (1958 [1939]), which we will take up in a moment. The third thesis deals with the different functions of language: the Prague linguists maintain that the study of language, on both the synchronic and the diachronic plane, cannot be adequate if the different linguistic functions (communicative, referential, poetic, etc.) are not taken into account (the problem of the different functions of language and of their definition was returned to by Jakobson some decades later; see Jakobson 1960). The content of this thesis clearly illustrates the 'functional' view of language that already underlay Mathesius' kind of sentence analysis (see above) and can therefore be considered as the forerunner of the several 'functional frameworks' which developed in the second half of the twentieth century.

As has been alluded to above, the topic focused upon by the Prague linguists (and which gave them the greatest renown) was phonology; in their usage, phonology not only indicates a field of analysis, but also a specific theory, namely that worked out by them during the 1930s, and whose most detailed presentation—unfinished, because of the premature death of the author—is Trubetzkoy (1958 [1939]). Here only two aspects of Prague phonology will be presented: the distinction between phonetics and phonology and the notion of 'phoneme.'[1]

Trubetzkoy (1969 [1939]: 4) defines phonetics as the science of sounds 'pertaining to the acts of speech' (so, approximately, to Saussure's *parole*), and phonology the science of sounds 'pertaining to the system of language' (Saussure's *langue*). Actually, the opposition between the two sciences of linguistic sounds derives from their relationship with meaning: phonetics does not take it into account, while phonology singles out the sound differences which bring about differences in meaning (pp. 10–11). Hence phonetics only investigates 'the material side' of the linguistic sounds, their acoustic and articulatory properties, which instead concern phonology only insofar as they have a 'distinctive function' (they distinguish meanings). This distinctive function differs across languages: some different sounds which bring about a meaning difference in a given language do not produce it in another. It is on this possibility/impossibility of meaning that the opposition between 'sound' and 'phoneme' is based. 'Phoneme' was a term coined in the 1870s by a rather obscure French phonetician, A. Dufriche-Desgenettes, to contrast linguistic sounds with other kinds of sounds (e.g. those of music); it had also been employed by other linguists, including Saussure and Jan Baudouin de Courtenay (1845–1929), with a different meaning, which only partly anticipates Jakobson's and Trubetzkoy's. These latter scholars define phonemes as the units which, in a given language, bring about a meaning difference and cannot be analysed into smaller units. In other words, the phoneme is the smallest distinctive phonological unit in a given language (cf. Trubetzkoy 1969: 35). Hence phoneme is opposed to speech sound: the first entity only contains distinctive ('relevant' is Trubetzkoy's word) features, the latter the non-distinctive features as well (Trubetzkoy 1969: 36–7). This opposition is immediately related to that between phonetics and phonology: sounds are the 'material' entities, phonemes the 'functional' ones.

Trubetzkoy (1969: 46–65) works out several rules to discover the phonemes of a given language. Their effect can be summarized as follows: two sounds of a given language realize two different phonemes if (a) they occur in the same position; (b) they bring about a meaning change. So, for example, English /p/ and /f/ realize two different phonemes, since they distinguish at least two meanings: e.g. *pat* vs *fat* (a 'minimal pair,' it will later be called). Phonemes are always defined with respect to a given language, since some sounds can be distinctive in one language but not in another. As Trubetzkoy (p. 67) says, a phoneme is determined from its position in the system to which it belongs, namely from its relationships to the other phonemes to which it is opposed.

---

[1] See also §8.4 above.

Think e.g. of velar nasal consonants, like the final sound in English *sing* which distinguishes it from *sin*, with a final alveolar nasal. Velar nasal consonants also occur in Italian (e.g. in a word like *sangue*, 'blood'), but in this language there is no minimal pair brought about by the contrast between velar nasal vs alveolar nasal, like the English case just cited. Therefore the velar and the alveolar nasal consonants, in Italian, are not phonemes but, in Trubetzkoy's terms, 'variants' of the same phoneme: more exactly, they are called 'combinatory variants' (allophones, in American structural linguistics). The other kind of variants are 'optional variants': they do not differ according to the phonetic context in which they appear (like the Italian velar or alveolar nasals, which occur before velar or alveolar stops, respectively), but they are different sounds which may occur in the same position. One example of optional variants is Italian /r/: its standard realization is as an alveolar sound, but several Italian dialects realize it as a uvular phone (like in Parisian French).

The notions of system, phoneme, and variant lie also at the basis of historical phonology, which Prague linguists (especially Jakobson) worked out during the 1930s. Jakobson (1971 [1930]) lists four types of phonological change: (a) 'extraphonological,' i.e. when the change has no phonological effects, but only changes the number of the variants of a given phoneme; (b) 'dephonologization,' i.e. when the change deletes a phonemic opposition; (c) 'phonologization,' i.e. when two combinatorial variants become two different phonemes; (d) 'rephonologization,' i.e. the transformation of a phonological opposition into another, which has a different relationship to the phonological system (Jakobson 1971[1930]: 209). Actually, the notion of system is essential to account for any kind of phonological change: '*any modification must be treated as a function of the system within which it has occurred*' (p. 203; original emphasis, my translation). Jakobson's sketch of historical phonology was fully consistent with the Prague 1929 theses, namely the goal of superseding Saussure's neat opposition between synchrony and diachrony, and of showing the systematic character of the latter as well as of the former.

20.2.4 The Copenhagen School

The Copenhagen school was centred on the Copenhagen Linguistic Circle, but, in contrast to the Prague school, the Copenhagen school was not theoretically unified. The most important Copenhagen linguists, Viggo Brøndal (1887–1942) and Louis Hjelmslev (1899–1965) shared the structuralist approach to linguistics (strongly argued for in the opening article of the journal they founded together, *Acta Linguistica*: see Brøndal 1939), but their similarities do not go beyond this common core. In a nutshell: while Brøndal maintained that language is based on logic, and therefore attempted at analyse it by means of logic (largely borrowed from Leibniz), Hjelmslev's programme was that of basing linguistics on logic, in the sense of the 'logic of the science' worked out during the 1930s by the Neo-positivist philosophers. Since Hjelmslev became more celebrated than Brøndal, we will limit our presentation to Hjelmslev's theories; yet Brøndal's analyses are often very perceptive and therefore deserve attention (see esp. Brøndal 1943).

Hjelmslev's theory of language and linguistics was worked out mainly in the 1930s and 1940s. He coined for it the wholly new label 'glossematics' in order to distinguish it from preceding theories, which all (with a partial exception of Saussure's) shared the fault—as Hjelmslev saw it—of basing themselves on some discipline from outside linguistics, such as psychology, sociology, etc. They are therefore defined by Hjelmslev as 'transcendent' while his own theory, on the contrary, is 'immanent' (Hjelmslev 1961 [1943]: 4–5). The aim of linguistic theory, according to Hjelmslev, is the analysis of the system of dependences which form the structure of a given language (cf. pp. 21–8). Such dependences are called 'functions' (p. 33). As can be seen, this term is identical with that employed by Prague linguists, but its meaning is quite different for the two schools: for the Prague linguists, it designates something external to the structure of language (e.g. its poetic, or its communicative, function); in Hjelmslev's framework it denotes the internal dependencies which constitute the structure itself.

A function closely analysed by Hjelmslev (1961: 47–60) is the 'sign function,' the reciprocal dependence between expression and content. These notions approximately correspond to Saussure's signifier and signified, respectively (§20.1.2.3 above). Hjelmslev's starting point is Saussure's statement that the combination of such units '*produces a form, not a substance*' (de Saussure 1959: 113). Hjelmslev interprets this statement by assuming that the same 'factor common to all languages' (which he calls 'purport,' p. 50) can be differently shaped across languages, because of the different form that the sign function has in each of them. Lets us give an example both for expression and for content. On the expression plane, the articulatory space of the nasal consonants is differently partitioned in English vs Italian: English opposes three nasal phonemes /m/, /n/, /ŋ/, Italian only two /m/, /n/. On the content plane, consider the way in which some different languages denote the purport of matters to do with the trees: English and French employ *wood* and *bois* both for 'a collection of trees growing more or less thickly together' and 'the substance of which the roots, trunks, and branches of trees or shrubs consist.' German, instead, denotes the latter substance with a special word *Holz*, while the other meaning of English and French 'wood' is expressed in German by *Wald*. In its turn, German *Wald* covers also the meaning of English and French *forest/forêt* (cf. Hjelmslev 1961: 54).

Hjelmslev maintains that the expression plane and the content plane of natural languages, unlike other symbolic systems, are not 'conformal' (i.e. isomorphic) because there is no one-to-one correspondence between the minimal elements of each plane. If the two planes were conformal, there would be no reason to distinguish them: it would be a violation of the 'simplicity principle', which linguistic theory must strictly follow (Hjelmslev 1961: 18). Any system which is formed by two planes is called by Hjelmslev a 'semiotic': natural language is therefore a special case of semiotic. In a semiotic, a given plane (that of expression, that of content, or both) can in its turn consist of a semiotic. In the final part of his main theoretical work, Hjelmslev (1961: 114–27) works out a complicated hierarchy of the different kinds of semiotics which, in his view, should allow one to treat all scientific matters in a semiotic perspective. This enthusiastic conclusion appeared (and still appears) as too easily drawn: nevertheless, it exerted a great fascination on several scholars (e.g. Greimas 1966: 13–17).

20.2.5 Developments of European Structuralism after the Second World War: Jakobson's Binarism, Martinet, Benveniste

20.2.5.1 *Jakobson and Martinet*

With the outbreak of the Second World War, the activity of the Prague Linguistic Circle was put to an end: Trubetzkoy had died the year before, Jakobson was obliged to leave Czechoslovakia after the Nazi invasion, and Mathesius died in 1945. Nevertheless, the insights of the Prague school were subsequently developed, in different and often contrasting ways, by Jakobson and by another scholar who had been in close contact with the Prague circle during the 1930s, the Frenchman André Martinet (1908–99).

Jakobson's binaristic theory of phonology was presented for the first time in 1939, but its full development dates to the 1940s, when Jakobson settled in the United States. The final formulation of the theory is found in the first part of Jakobson and Halle (1956). Trubetzkoy had already observed that the phoneme is actually constituted of several 'features.' Jakobson's basic innovation is the statement that such features are binary, namely that the phonemes are uniquely characterized by the presence or the absence of given 'distinctive' features, respectively indicated with the signs + and −. Two such features are e.g. [± vocalic] and [± consonantal]: vocalic phonemes have the features [+vocalic] and [−]; consonantal ones the features [−vocalic] and [+consonantal]; liquid ones (/l/ and /r/ in languages like Czech, where they can form the nucleus of a syllable) have the features [+vocalic] and [+consonantal]; glides (i.e. /j/ and /w/), the features [−vocalic] and [−consonantal]. According to binary theory, any phonemic opposition is to be represented as an opposition of features values: e.g., /p/ and /t/ are both [−compact], and such feature opposes them to /k/, which is [+compact], while they are different from each other since /p/ is [+grave] and /t/ [−grave]. These binary features (twelve in the earlier formulations of theory, fourteen in the final ones) are the same both for vowels and consonants and they are assumed to be universal. In other words, the phonemes of any language cannot be constituted but by these features: cross-linguistic differences are accounted for by the fact that not all features occur in all languages, and that some phonemes can have a positive value in one language and the opposite value in another (e.g., /l/ is [+vocalic] in Czech, but [−vocalic] in Italian).

Binarism was fiercely opposed by Martinet. He allowed that the phoneme is not actually the minimal phonological unit, since it is further analysable into features, but he rejected Jakobson's assumption that such features have only a positive or negative value. According to Martinet, the binary hypothesis is aprioristic, i.e. not sufficiently proved (Martinet 1955: 74). On the other hand, Martinet shares with Jakobson the common Prague School assumption that diachrony is a system: he, however, tends to explain the phenomena of diachronic phonology already dealt with by Jakobson (§20.2.3 above) as due to the need for economy. This means that the phonological system of any language, in its changes across time, always tends to preserve a balance between the number of its members, which cannot be too high ('minimal effort'), and the need to keep the different signs distinct from each other ('communicative efficiency'; see e.g. Martinet 1955: 93–7).

20.2.5.2 *Benveniste*

Emile Benveniste (1902–76) can be considered the European structural linguist whose beliefs come most directly from Saussure (with the obvious exception of Bally and Sechehaye): at the Collège de France he was a student of Antoine Meillet, who in his turn had been a student of Saussure. Meillet was essentially an historical-comparative linguist, as was Benveniste, but his work also contains important theoretical insights which point in a different direction from the Prague scholars. His first important contribution to general linguistics was an essay devoted to Saussure's doctrine of the linguistic sign (Benveniste 1939; reprinted as Benveniste 1966: ch. 4), where he states that it is the relationship between the linguistic sign and the reality which is arbitrary, while that between the signifier and the signified is *necessary*. In this way, Benveniste contributed to the clarification of some issues which appeared somewhat obscure in the Saussure 1922 text edited by Bally and Sechehaye; today, on the basis of the handwritten sources (§20.1.1), it is possible to say that Saussure's authentic thought was close to Benveniste's interpretation. In the 1950s, Benveniste was the author of several essays which deal, among other things with the problem of performative utterances, which were investigated more or less contemporaneously by Austin (see especially those reprinted in Benveniste 1966: chs 18–23).

20.3 OTHER EUROPEAN SCHOOLS OF STRUCTURAL LINGUISTICS

20.3.1 Guillaume and Tesnière

The most significant works of the two French linguists Gustave Guillaume (1883–1960) and Lucien Tesnière (1893–1954) were published posthumously as Guillaume (1971–2010) and Tesnière (1959), respectively. Both scholars were essentially independent of the mainstream of European structural linguistics: this is also shown by the fact that both concentrated more on syntax than on phonology and morphology. This is the reason for dealing with them both within the same section. However they differ greatly from each other both in their systems of linguistic analysis as well as in their style, often obscure in Guillaume, extremely clear in Tesnière.

Guillaume starts from Saussure's assumption that language is a system, but he criticizes the Geneva linguist for not having worked out the proper technique to analyse this system. He therefore attempts to build a new theory of language which relates the notion of system to his own notion of time (possibly connected to that worked out by the French philosopher Henri Bergson): this theory is called by Guillaume 'psycho-mechanics.' Guillaume also reshapes the opposition between *langue* and *parole*: *langue* is 'potential,' while *parole* (which Guillaume proposes to replace with *discours*, 'speech') is 'actual.' Many different linguistic entities are opposed in this way: e.g. the word and the sentence are considered as the typical units of language and of speech, respectively, and morphology has to do with language, and syntax with speech. The language/speech dichotomy also opposes many categories of traditional grammar: e.g. nouns as a word class are the 'nouns of language,' while subordinate clauses with a nominal function are the 'nouns of speech.' Guillaume investigates not only intra-sentential syntactic phe-nomena but also inter-sentential relations: e.g. he opposes two sentences such as *I spoke to Peter* and *It is Peter I spoke to* as a 'basic sentence' vs a 'new expressive sentence' (Guillaume 1971–2010: iii. 175). This inter-sentential relationship is an example of what Guillaume names 'genetic syntax': to that, he opposes the 'syntax of result,' namely linear word order.

A partly similar distinction is traced by Tesnière, although in a very different conceptual framework. Tesnière is not particularly interested in developing a general doctrine of language, but in building a new system of syntactic analysis, which is characterized by a fundamental opposition: that between 'structural order' and 'linear order.' The latter consists of the linear sequence of words; the former derives from what Tesnière calls 'connection.' Connection is essentially a hierarchic fact: in the syntax of human languages, any two elements are in a dependency relation, since one of them is the governing element and other its subordinate. For example, in a sentence like *John speaks*, 'speaks' is the governing element and 'John' the subordinate one (Tesnière 1959: ch 2, §7). The hierarchic relations deriving from connection are represented by Tesnière in the format of tree diagrams (called by him 'stemmas'), the highest node of which is always the main verb. The verb is therefore the central category of syntax, according to Tesnière: and his classification of verbs according to the number of participant roles (*actants*) they can take is his best-known contribution to syntactic theory, his so called 'valency grammar.' So there are 'o-valency verbs' (such as the meteorological ones), '1-valency verbs' (the traditional intransitives), '2-valency verbs' (the traditional transi-tives), and '3-valency verbs' (such as the verbs of telling and giving).

Long after his death, Tesnière's syntactic model gained much greater success than Guillaume's: it had been worked out in the 1950s, hence more or less contemporarily with Chomsky's *Syntactic Structures*, and both maintain that human language syntax is organized along two dimensions, the hierarchic and the linear. However, Tesnière's model of grammar, unlike Chomsky's, fully overturned the traditional model of sentence analysis based on the dichotomy between the subject and the predicate in favour of the valency properties of the verb. It is for such reasons that Tesnière's dependency syntax was taken as a starting point for syntactic theories alternative to the Chomskyan generative grammar towards the end of the 1960s.

20.3.2 The London School

The label 'London school' in the strict sense refers to the group of linguists formed by John R. Firth (1890–1960) and his students at the School of African and Oriental Studies. Among the latter, M. A. K. Halliday (b. 1925) is the most influential, with his Systemic-Functional Grammar, one of the functionalist theories to present itself as an alternative to Generative Grammar in the second half of the twentieth century.

The London school shares the general features of British structural linguistics, which, while taking account of Saussure's and Prague School research, developed an autonomous framework. This autonomy can be seen in the work of scholars such as Daniel Jones (1881–1967) or Alan H. Gardiner (1879–1963). Jones, a leading phonetician, dealt with the notion of phoneme in the second decade of the twentieth century, earlier than Trubetzkoy and the other Prague linguists. Unlike Trubetzkoy, however, Jones did not define the phoneme in terms of 'relevance' (§20.2.3 above), but as 'a family of uttered sounds [...] in a particular language which count for practical purposes as if they were one and the same' (Jones 1957: 22). Gardiner, an outstanding Egyptologist, devoted a book to 'the theory of speech of language' (Gardiner 1951; 1st edn 1932), terms which respectively translated Saussure's *parole* and *langue*. However, while Saussure (1959: 14) defines *parole* as something 'accessory or more or less accidental,' the notion of speech is central for Gardiner: he defines it as 'a set of reactions' to external stimuli in order to obtain cooperation from other people (Gardiner 1951: 20).

In a rather similar vein, Firth's analysis of the communication process does not aim at discovering an abstract and over-individual structure such as *langue*, but rather at analysing the behaviour of individuals in particular special situations: and indeed the notion of 'context of situation,' which he borrowed from the anthropologist Bronislaw Malinowski (1884–1942), has a key role in his system. Firth therefore views language as a set of socially defined behaviours, of which it is possible to build a typology (cf. Firth 1957: 190). This attitude seems rather close to Bloomfield's and other American linguists' behaviourism, but one has to remark that Firth always declared himself neutral with respect to the behaviourism/mentalism controversy. Rather, his analyses seem to parallel some aspects of linguistic pragmatics which was beginning to develop in those same years (the 1950s) with the work of Austin and late Wittgenstein: for example, Firth's statement that meaning does not belong to words and/or sentences in themselves, but is a function of the context of situation of the speaker and the hearer, is surely close to Wittgenstein's (1953) view of meaning as use.

It is therefore not surprising that Firth's most original contributions, in the fields both of phonology and of syntax, are related to the notion of context. According to

Firth, Prague phonology restricted itself to a 'paradigmatic' approach, namely to the delimitation and classification of sounds and phonemes, while a 'syntagmatic' approach is also necessary, namely the analysis of the context where the sounds occur. 'Prosodies' are therefore to be added to phonemic entities (and actually Firth's model of phonology is named 'prosodic phonology'): by 'prosody,' Firth does not only mean accents, tones, or intonation, but also any other entity defined on the basis of its function within the spoken chain. For example, the English central vowel schwa (which occurs in words as *can* and *was* when they are unstressed) is not a phoneme but a prosody, the occurrence of which is determined by the rules of English syllabic structure. Hence, according to Firth, the sound chain is not formed by a simple combination of elements independent from each other, but is governed by autonomous rules: the syntagmatic axis crosses the paradigmatic one.

Firth's key notion in syntax is that of 'collocation,' which has a meaning different from 'context,' since it specifically applies to the syntactic environment, while context, as has been seen, more generally refers to the cultural and situational environment. Collocation is defined by Firth (1968: 181) as 'an order of mutual expectancy' between two or more words: e.g. a word like *ass* is (or was) often collocated with a word like *stupid*, in phrases such as *You stupid ass!* (Firth 1957: 195, 1968: 179).

20.4 CLOSING REMARKS

Coming back to Saussure's dichotomies, summarized in §§20.1.2.1–4 above, we can now ask ourselves: to what degree did each of them influence subsequent linguistic research? The dichotomy between signifier and signified seems to have been that most poorly understood and, as a consequence, that which had the least impact on the later linguists: only Hjelmslev and Benveniste appear to have fully realized its real meaning. On the contrary, the dichotomies between *langue* and *parole* and between synchrony and diachrony (and, to a lesser extent, those between syntagmatic and associative relations) opened a new era of linguistic thought. It has been seen that the interpretation of such dichotomies was not unanimous across the different schools of European structural linguistics: but it became impossible to avoid distinguishing between an abstract and a concrete aspect of language (*langue* vs *parole*) and between the analysis of a language at a given chronological moment and of the changes it underwent during its history (synchrony vs diachrony). This is therefore the most enduring heritage of Saussure's reflections about language and linguistics.

CHAPTER 21

FUNCTIONAL AND COGNITIVE GRAMMARS

ANNA SIEWIERSKA

21.1 INTRODUCTION

THE current consensus seems to be (e.g. Langacker 2007, Nuyts 2005, 2007, 2008, 2010, Butler 2009) that there is a functional-cognitive approach to language which is defined by more than just an anti-Chomskyan position on the nature of language and its relation to other aspects of human cognition.[1] The focus of functionalists is on language as a means of communication and how this communicative function has structured grammar both synchronically and diachronically. The hallmark of cognitive linguistics, on the other hand is, the relationship between language and cognition, how humans conceptualize the world around them, how they create and represent meaning and how this is reflected in language. Both approaches emerged as antidotes to Chomskyan generative grammar, albeit not concurrently but consecutively and somewhat removed in time.

Functionalism was first on the scene. As evidenced by the following quotation, its intellectual roots firmly lie in the Prague School, founded in 1926, and especially the work of Mathesius 1929, 1939.

> The new linguistics conceives language as something living; underneath the words it sees the speaker writer from whose communicative intention they have resulted. It realizes that in the large majority of cases the words are aimed at a hearer or reader. (Mathesius 1983[1929]: 122ff.)

---

[1] Chomskyan grammar is also portrayed as being cognitive, but in a different sense of the term from that used here, namely as merely residing in the human mind, being part of our human cognitive endowment but crucially not as being embedded in what is known independently about human cognition.

His views on topic > comment articulation and what came to be know as functional sentence perspective were developed further in Prague and Brno after the war by Daneš (1974), Firbas (1992), and with a formal twist also Sgal and Hajičova (Hajičova et al. 1994). In the West, functional approaches to syntax emerged in the 1960s in publications such as Halliday (1967/8), Martinet (1960, 1962a, b) and Dik (1968), and received somewhat fuller theoretical expositions in the course of the 1970s in Halliday (1973, 1978), Martinet (1975), and Dik (1978). Cognitive linguistics arrived nearly two decades later in the form of Fauconnier (1985), Lakoff (1987), Langacker (1987), and Talmy (1988), though Lakoff and Johnson's *Metaphors We Live By* (1980) and Langacker's (1982) space grammar are usually seen as precursors of the approach. Given the European origins of most strands of functionalism, it is not surprising that the stronghold of functionalism has been Europe, with centres in: The Netherlands (Amsterdam—Dik, Pinkster, Bolkestein, Mackenzie, Hannay); Belgium (Antwerp—Van der Auwera, Nuyts; Ghent—Simon-Vandenbergen; Leuven—Davidse); Denmark (Harder, Fortescue, Nedergard Thomsen); Finland (Enkvist, Östman, Virtanen); Germany (Cologne—Seiler, Lehmann, Sasse, Heine; Leipzig—Comrie, Haspelmath, Gil); Italy (Pavia—Ramat, Giacalone-Ramat); Spain (Cordoba—Minogorance; Granada—Faber; Madrid—Marial Usón); and the UK (London—Halliday; Cardiff—Fawcett; Liverpool—Thompson; Lancaster—Leech, Siewierska; York—Butler).[2] In the US, functional linguistics has been strongly tied to linguistic typology and the description of indigenous languages. Its practitioners have in the main been centred on the West Coast, in Stanford (Greenberg, Moravscik, Croft, Kemmer), Los Angeles (Comrie, Hawkins), Oregon (Givón, Payne, Gildea), Santa Barbara (Chafe, Mithun, Du Bois), and Berkeley (Li, Thompson, Hopper, Nichols) with very influential outliers in Albuquerque (Bybee) and Buffalo (Van Valin and Dryer).[3] Cognitive linguistics, on the other hand, is considered to be a rejuvenated and invigorated form of generative semantics, an offshoot of Chomskyan generative grammar of the late 1960s and early 1970s, and thus firmly North American in origin. In fact, virtually all of the original representatives of cognitive linguistics are in one way or another associated with Californian universities, especially Berkeley and San Diego. It took very little time, however, for cognitivism to spread to Europe, especially western Europe (Cuyckens, Dirven, Geeraerts, Rudzka-Ostyn, Verhagen) and Central Europe (Kalisz, Krzeszowski, Lewandowska-Tomaszczyk, Tabakowska), the first conference of the International Cognitive Linguistics Association being held in 1989 in Duisberg, Germany. Nowadays, European scholars working within the spirit if not the letter of cognitive linguistics are arguably more numerous than those representing any other framework.

---

[2] Some of the representatives of functional linguistics mentioned here, both from Europe and the US, may have subsequently shifted their allegiances, in the majority of cases to cognitive linguistics.

[3] Opinions are divided as to whether or not American functionalism developed independently of European functionalism or not. Key functionalists such as Jakobson (a member of the Prague School) and Martinet both resided in the US in the 1950s and 1960s and presumably shared their views with their colleagues. To what extent these had a wider impact is still being explored, most notably in Vykypěl (2009).

What distinguishes both functionalism and cognitivism from the formal approaches to grammar subsumed under the Chomskyan umbrella can be captured by Croft's (1995) notion of self-containedness as applied to both syntax and grammar. Self-containedness at the level of syntax relates to whether syntactic elements interact with semantic and discourse elements, i.e. whether the rules of syntax do or do not make reference to the semantic roles (e.g. agent vs patient or patient vs recipient), semantic features (e.g. animacy, countability), or discourse properties (e.g. definiteness, referentiality) of these elements. At the level of grammar, in turn, self-containedness relates to whether grammar is or is not dependent on other human cognitive capacities (e.g. attention, selection, ease of processing, categorization) and also on the social context of language use. Formalists view both syntax and grammar as being self-contained (and thus autonomous). They do recognize that there are connections between structure and function which are due to grammar being influenced by external factors in the course of language evolution (see Newmeyer 1998a: 26, 1998b). However, they do not see external factors as having a bearing on the form of synchronic grammar, let alone playing a role in syntactic description. Functionalists and cognitive linguists, by contrast, consider grammar and typically both syntax and grammar as being not self-contained, i.e. as being non-autonomous. They thus seek to identify the cognitive and discoursal factors that shape grammars both diachronically and synchronically and determine the extent to which these are reflected in the structural properties of language, functionalists focusing on the discoursal properties and cognitive linguists on the cognitive.

Needless to say, neither functional nor cognitive linguistics is internally uniform. Functionalism is a particularly broad church, encompassing within its scope a plethora of approaches to languages all of which profess to view some aspects of the structure of language as ultimately tied to its communicative function.[4] Where the approaches differ is in the aspects of the structure of language which are considered to be functionally motivated and what precisely is meant by communicative function. Some of the approaches which bear the label 'functional' are mere add-ons to a formal generative grammar. Kuno's (1987) and Prince's (1981) frameworks, which provide a series of functional constraints on the well-formedness of sentences, are two cases in point. Another is the more recent Functional Optimality Theory developed by Bresnan (Bresnan and Aissen 2001), in which the universal but violable constraints governing language structure are taken to be not innate but motivated by functional factors such as ease of production, perception, parsing, economy and iconicity. At the other extreme we have approaches which deny the arbitrariness of both structure and grammar and see all structure as being entirely based on function, and grammar as basically reducible

[4] There is even a broader interpretation of functionalism which includes approaches merely concerned with examining the various functions that language and or texts may fulfil irrespective of whether these functions do or do not have a bearing on language structure. Functionalism in this very wide sense of the term is essentially practiced in applied domains of linguistics such as stylistics, discourse analysis, etc. and will not be considered here.

to discourse. This version of functionalism, referred to in the literature as 'extreme functionalism' (Nichols 1984), originally advocated by North American West Coast linguists Hopper and Thompson (1984), Hopper (1987), and to some extent Givón (1979, 1984, 1990), is nowadays gaining ground and merging with more cognitively based approaches as reflected in the work of especially Bybee (2010) and other scholars featured in Bybee and Hopper (2001). Most functionalists, however, adopt a position somewhere in between the two extremes outlined above, and see both syntax and grammar as being to a large extent arbitrary but (crucially) not self-contained.

Cognitive linguistics is less broad than functional with respect to issues of autonomy; not only is grammar uniformly taken to be a reflection of general conceptual organization, but so is syntax, which is not seen to be separate from semantics. In fact, there is no clear demarcation of semantics as distinct from pragmatics, all linguistic meaning being identified (by most cognitive linguists) with conceptualization (Langacker 2007: 431–2).[5] Nonetheless, several strands within cognitive linguistics can also be discerned. Nuyts (2007) makes a distinction between core cognitive linguistics and functional-cognitive linguistics. Within the core there is what may be termed a more conceptual or semantic strand headed by Langacker and Talmy, and a construction-oriented strand originating in the work of Lakoff (1977) and Fillmore (1988). The construction strand has developed in two directions, a cognitive one, the primary drivers of which are Goldberg (1995, 1996, 2006) and Croft (2001), and a formal one which eschews the basic tenets of cognitive linguistics, while maintaining the superiority of construction-based over rule-based grammars, represented most notably in the Construction Grammar approach of Fillmore et al. (1988) and Head-Driven Phrase Structure Grammar of Pollard and Sag (1994) and their collaborators. The functional strand of cognitive linguistics, as the name suggests, blends into the cognitive approach ideas from functional linguistics, especially linguistic typology, information structure, discourse, textual analysis, and sociolinguistics. It encompasses a sizeable section of continental European cognitive linguistics including scholars such as Verhagen (1995, 2005), Geeraerts (1989, 1993, 1997), and Nuyts (2007) as well as American-based scholars, notably Kemmer (1993), Kemmer and Barlow (2000), and especially Croft (2001). An alternative subdivision of cognitive linguistics based more on chronological lines is suggested by Geeraerts and Cuyckens (2007: 7), who view cognitive linguistics as a category with a family resemblance structure, i.e. consisting of a cluster of overlapping approaches rather than a single theory. Around the core of the founding fathers, they posit two chronologically widening circles, the first emerging in the late 1980s and early 1990s consisting of the early collaborators and first students of the founding fathers, in both the US and Europe, and the second appearing throughout the middle and late 1990s involving a geographical expansion into southern Europe and Asia. No clear

---

[5] Langacker (2007: 432) points out that, contrary to what is sometimes claimed, cognitive linguistics does not deny the possibility of distinguishing semantics from pragmatics but rather recognizes the gradual nature of this distinction which also applies to lexical semantics and the difference between dictionary and encyclopedic knowledge.

demarcation of theoretical positions or primary topics of research interest are associated with these two waves, though perhaps one might say that the first wave was more strongly focused on the structural characteristics of natural language categorization, in particular prototypicality, cognitive models, metaphor, metonymy, etc., than the second.

Both the functional and cognitive research traditions subsume a large body of linguistic scholarship, theoretical, descriptive, empirical, and applied.[6] However, very little of this scholarship is directly concerned with developing actual models of grammar, be it functional or cognitive. Within the course of the last fifty years, various functionally oriented frameworks have been proposed but only three full-fledged models of grammar have gained currency: Halliday's Systemic Functional Grammar (SFG), Dik's Functional Grammar (FG), and Van Valin's Role and Reference Grammar (RRG).[7] SFG and FG have been mentioned previously. RRG, which, unlike SFG and FG, is an American product, was conceived of in the mid-1980s by Foley and Van Valin (1984) and subsequently developed by Van Valin (2005, 2008) and Van Valin and La Polla (1997). Butler (2003) has dubbed these three 'structural functional grammars,' and I too will refer to them as such. The dominant grammatical models to have emerged out of cognitive linguistics are Langacker's (1987, 1991a, b) Cognitive Grammar (CG), Goldberg's (1995, 2006) Cognitive Construction Grammar (CCG), and Croft's (2012) Radical Construction Grammar (RCG). The remainder of this chapter will be devoted to providing a brief characterization of these six models of grammar. §21.2 will deal with the similarities and differences obtaining among the three structural functional grammars and §21.3 with the major features of the three cognitive frameworks. Then in §21.4 a brief comparison of the two will be attempted.

21.2 Structural-Functional Grammars

SFG, FG, and RRG are three versions of integrated functional models of grammar with explicit sets of interlocking rules which can be employed to generate and comprehend utterances. SFG[8] is the most diverse of the three, as it occurs in a distinctive Sydney variety (Halliday 1985b, Matthiessen (1995), Martin (1992)) and a Cardiff variety (Fawcett 2000) and includes a Semiotic Grammar offshoot (McGregor 1997). FG too

---

[6] A good overview of a functionally oriented research in areas such as textlinguistics, psycholinguistics, sociolinguistics, and descriptive linguistics is provided in Dirven and Fried (1987). An even more comprehensive and up-to-date overview of cognitive linguistics is presented in Geeraerts and Cuyckens (2007).

[7] Bresnan's (1978, 2001) influential Lexical Functional Grammar is not included among the functional structural grammars as it does not express a commitment to the investigation of the communicative underpinnings of the structure of language but merely recognizes a layer of structural organization involving syntactic functions.

[8] See also Ch. 27 below on aspects of SFG.

has a cognitive instantiation in the from of Functional Procedural Grammar (Nuyts 1992, 2001), and a lexically oriented one in the guise of the Functional Lexemic Model (Faber and Mairal Usón 1999) as well as several discourse varieties, the most recent of which is Functional Discourse Grammar (FDG) (Hengeveld and Mackenzie 2008). FDG is presented by its creators as the successor to FG and will also be referred to below. The last of the three functional grammars, RRG, by contrast, has not spawned any serious internal subdivisions.

FG and RRG are much more similar to each other than either is to SFG with respect to both overall aims and architecture. As far as overall aims are concerned, while all three grammars seek to provide an account of human communicative competence and explicate the (competing) motivations that give rise to language specific structures, FG and RRG, as compared to SFG, are heavily committed to standards of typological adequacy. RRG, similarly to Croft's RCG (see §21.3), arose out of cross-linguistic work on basic clause structure, argument structure alternations, and clause linkage (Foley and Van Valin 1984), both of its founders having had a strong background in the description of indigenous languages of Papua and North America. This typological flavour has been not only maintained but expanded in subsequent renditions of the model, and is reflected in the impressive language coverage found in the publications of Van Valin and his collaborators. The RRG online bibliography (http://linguistics. buffalo.edu/people/faculty/vanvalin/rrg/RRGBib) features publications on such diverse languages as Amis, Beja, Bonggi, Danish, French, Ga, Hausa, Hay, Japanese, Karbadian, Korean, Mandarin, Polish, and Omaha. Equally impressive is the typological exploration of grammatical phenomena in RRG, especially grammatical relations, voice, reference-tracking mechanisms, clause linking, and information structure. FG too aims for typological adequacy and has engendered both explicit typological studies, most notably on parts of speech (Hengeveld 1992) and NP structure and order (Rijkhoff 2002) as well as analyses of a wide range of grammatical phenomena in a variety of European languages and also some non-European ones, such as Arabic, Sidamo, Turkish, and Kombai and Wambon (see http://home.hum.uva.nl/fg/publications_ papers.html). SFG has shown little interest in typological diversity despite Halliday's own early work on Mandarin. There have been only occasional mentions of languages other than English, McGregor's (1997) semiotic grammar, which deals in the main with Australian Aboriginal languages being a notable exception.

FG and RRG, again in contrast to SFG, strive for psychological adequacy which in both approaches is, however, very narrowly understood, especially when compared to cognitive linguistics (see §21.3). In RRG the cognitive dimension boils down to a commitment to provide an account of sentence structure consistent with online processing constraints, both with respect to production and comprehension. FG too seeks to be compatible with current theories of linguistic processing but in addition has the ambition for the grammar 'to relate as closely as possible to psychological models of linguistic competence and linguistic behaviour' (Dik 1997a: 13). However, strong doubts have been expressed, even within the FG community, as to the ability of the standard FG model to meet this expectation. Especially problematic is Dik's (1990: 234) claim that the representational language of FG underlying predications, which are tied to the argument structures of specific lexical predicates, constitutes a good approximation of conceptual structure. This runs against the prevailing view in artificial intelligence, the psychology of language, semantics and also cognitive linguistics which is that conceptual representations are not language based (or vision based) but much more abstract. As argued by Nuyts (1992: 223–36, 2005) among others, only such a language-independent view of conceptual structure can capture the apparent ability of humans to conceive of events normally expressed by different predicates as ultimately instantiating one and the same scene, i.e. as being at the conceptual level basically the same. This is generally illustrated with reference to the commercial event, first discussed in this context by Fillmore (1977b). The commercial event typically involves two human participants (A and D), an object of transaction (B), and money or the equivalent thereof (C), and can be expressed by a wide range of verbs with an array of argument structure patterns chief among them being: A *buying* B (from D for C); D *selling* B (to A for C); A *paying* C (to D for B); A *spending* C (on/for B); D *charging* A C (for B); B *costing* A C, etc. Needless to say, any identification of conceptual structure with linguistic structure renders each of the above instantiations of the commercial event as being by and large conceptually distinct. Nuyts' (1992, 2001) own model, Functional Procedural Grammar, is more cognitively plausible than Dik's both in regard to the relationship between linguistic structure and conceptual structure and in his dynamic approach to the production of discourse, as is also the successor to FG, FDG (see below). SFG has shown little interest in cognitive issues, preferring to see itself as a branch of sociology (Halliday 1978: 38–9) rather than of cognitive science. Even Halliday and Matthiessen (1999), which features cognition in its title, sees cognition as 'just a way of talking about language.' Nonetheless, aspects of the framework, especially the merging of the lexical and syntactic components and the recognition of the indeterminacy of linguistic categories, are very much in line with the positions adopted in cognitive grammars.

SFG's lack of ambition with respect to typological and psychological adequacy is compensated for by its systematic pursuit of pragmatic adequacy.[9] Crucially, whereas most functional approaches, including FG and RRG, content themselves with the analysis of sentences, SFG has taken on the analysis of actual texts (both written and spoken) as found in real sociocultural settings (e.g. service encounters, classroom interaction, quiz shows). From its inception SFG has been devoted to showing how the organization of real texts at the discourse semantic and lexicogrammatical levels relates to the different metafunctions of language (ideational, interpersonal, and textual). Thus, for example, the organization of a school class discussion is taken to

---

[9] Another characteristic of SFG which sets it apart from FG and RRG is the high store placed by Halliday (1985b) and some of his associates on the applicability of the model. SFG has been applied to text analysis, stylistics, computational linguistics, language pedagogy, and the study of language socialization. According to some, this has been at the cost of its descriptive adequacy (see Butler 2003 467–75).

involve discourse units such as exchanges, moves, and acts which relate to the inter-personal level. Lexical cohesive devices, on the other hand, are seen to relate primarily to the experiential component of the ideational metafunction, and conjunctive devices to the logical component of this metafunction. Particularly influential has been the SFG (Halliday and Hasan 1976) analysis of textual cohesion, i.e. of the relationships between the elements within texts (via anaphoric expressions or the above-mentioned conjunct-ive devices) and the flip side, how texts are linked to the situational context of use. The latter has been elaborated by means of the categories field (what the participants in the context of a situation are actually doing), tenor (the negotiation of social relationship among participants), and mode (the particular status that is assigned to the text) which subsequently gave rise to a more semantically based view of registers (Halliday 1978, Martin 1992) and genre.

Turning to the architecture of the three models, in his interim critical comparison of FG, RRG, and SFG, Butler (2003: ch. 6) highlights the similarities and differences between them on the basis of how they stand in relation to four points: (i) the nature of the postulated relationship between semantic, syntactic, morphological, lexical and prosodic levels of linguistic patterning, (ii) the type of mechanisms employed for specifying clause structure, (iii) the number and nature of layers or levels of clause structure proposed and (iv) the range of semantic, syntactic, and pragmatic functions recognized. In regard to levels of linguistic patterning, SFG again diverges from both FG and RRG in not making a distinction between the lexicon and grammar. The other two frameworks adhere to a fairly traditional view of the lexicon as consisting of an inventory of verbal, nominal, adjectival, and adverbial lexemes enriched with various prefabricated units, idioms, greetings, exclamations, and the like.[10] SFG is also the odd one out in recognizing only a partially specified higher semantic level. Both FG and RRG distinguish semantics from morphosyntax (not always consistently in the case of FG), and posit a level of pragmatic organization. Perhaps the most crucial difference between SFG on the one hand and FG and RRG on the other concerns the specification of clause structure. Whereas FG and RRG have basically a bottom-up orientation, deriving the structure of the clause from the properties of predicates and their arguments, SFG adopts a top-down approach; lexical items are the output rather than the input of the generation process, which involves a series of selections from an interlinked set of paradigmatic patterns.[11] A point of convergence between SFG and FG is that neither recognizes a distinctive level of syntactic representation, morpho-syntax being dealt with by a set of realization rules (SFG) or expression rules (FG), applied in the case of SFG to the output of the selection process and in the case of FG to the essentially semantic underlying representation. In RRG, by contrast, semantic representations are linked with syntactic templates (in the form of phrase markers)

---

[10] This traditional view of the lexicon is not, however, inherent to either FG or RRG. There is no obvious reason why it could not be extended to include partially schematic constructions in the cognitive linguistic sense of the term or compositional but entrenched items (see §21.3).

[11] A top-down approach is adopted in the new FDG, as discussed further below.

by a series of linking rules which differ depending on whether the mapping is from semantics to syntax or syntax to semantics. Turning to layering, while all three models of grammar assume that clausal structure is multilayered, the RRG layers refer to distinctions between syntactic units (nucleus vs core vs periphery), while the FG and SFG ones are semantic, inspired by Halliday's distinction between the representational and interpersonal functions of language. FG distinguishes at the lower representational level a predicate and predicational layer, and at the interpersonal level, a propositional and illocutionary layer. In SFG there is an ideational, interpersonal, and textual metafunctional layer. Again, however, FG converges with RRG in viewing the layers as being organized hierarchically (each higher layer including every lower layer), while SFG assumes that they exist in parallel. As a result of the above and the non-recognition of separate semantic and pragmatic components, SFG does not make a clear distinction between syntactic, semantic, and pragmatic functions. All three types of roles coexist at the same lexicogrammatical level. FG and RRG both recognize the three types of functions but differ with respect to how they interpret them. The RRG argument semantic functions are assumed to be predictable from their argument positions in logical structure, while their FG equivalents are by and large assigned (relative to states of affairs). RRG in addition to semantic functions recognizes the macro-roles of Actor and Undergoer which generalize across the more specific semantic functions (e.g. agent, patient, theme, experiencer effector) in a way determined by a set of universal principles. The RRG syntactic functions, referred to as privileged syntactic arguments, are construction-specific. The FG ones are assigned to whole languages, though relatively few languages actually qualify as having them, particularly an object function. The RRG repertoire of pragmatic functions consists of just the topic and focus, while FG posits various subdivisions within both types of functions.

The architecture of FG has been somewhat modified in the new Functional Discourse Grammar (Hengeveld and Mackenzie 2008), which has been elaborated to provide a better reflection of the discourse groundedness and cognitive adequacy of the model. The chief new features are: a top-down rather than bottom-up orientation; a conceptual and a contextual component in addition to a grammatical one; and, within the grammatical component, an expanded interpersonal layer reflecting a wider range of utterance types. The conceptual component is taken to be the locus of the communicative intention and its corresponding mental representation, and is seen to drive the formulation of the latter into a linguistic expression. The contextual component interacts with the interpersonal, representational, and morphosyntactic structure of linguistic units, which enables subsequent reference to various types of entities to be made as they are introduced into the discourse. The expanded interpersonal layer captures the linguistically relevant aspects of the interaction between the speaker and addressee in the form of a hierarchy of discourse units, the highest level of which is the move which may consist of several temporally ordered acts, which in turn may contain several temporally ordered contents, and these may feature multiple sub-acts of ascription or reference. FDG takes the act rather than the clause as the basic unit of grammatical description, and it is therefore the act which is embedded in one of three types of frames (illocutive, interpellative, and expressive), each of which has its own corresponding modifiers and operators and its component subacts to which pragmatic functions are assigned. The interpersonal structure then feeds into the representational, which corresponds more or less to that of FG outlined above.

Space precludes any illustration of the similarities and differences in how the three structural functional models of grammar actually deal with specific language phenomena. However, to dispel any potential misconceptions that might have arisen from the above discussion as to the nature of the clauses that they are capable of handling, I will end this discussion with a few words on the typology of complex sentences that each has developed. With respect to types of clause combining, FG distinguishes the traditional coordination and embedding, RRG, coordination, subordination, and co-subordination and SFG embedding, parataxis, and hypotaxis, as well as the logico-semantic relationships of expansion and projection. As for the units involved in the formation of complex sentences, in both F(D)G and RRG their characterization is tied closely to the hierarchically layered structure of the clause. Thus in F(D)G complements may be of the predicational, propositional, and clausal types (with various subtypes), and in RRG of the nucleus, core and clause types.

A particularly interesting approach to clause combining has been developed within SFG known as Rhetorical Structure Theory (Matthiessen and Thompson 1988), which views clause combining, and especially the grammar of so-called enhancing hypotaxis, as reflecting discourse-based hierarchies, in particular a hierarchy of rhetorically defined text spans. Though biased towards written language, Matthiessen and Thompson's approach has engendered much cross-fertilization between SFG and FG both in connection with its discourse roots and the important typological implication that is implicit in it: that clause combining may be expected to differ radically from one language to another.

21.3 COGNITIVE GRAMMARS

The three cognitive grammars, Langacker's Cognitive Grammar (CG), Goldberg's Cognitive Construction Grammar (CCG), and Croft's Radical Construction Grammar (RCG), have much in common. Although the term 'construction' does not appear in the title of Langacker's grammar, and only very rarely in his various expositions of it, CG, just like CCG and RCG, is a construction grammar model. Langacker's preferred term in place of 'construction' is 'conventional symbolic unit,' which he characterizes as an entrenched routine involving a form–meaning pairing conventionalized within a speech community (Langacker 1987: 57–63). This characterization corresponds in full to that of construction in the other two frameworks, though in the case of CCG, only to those of Goldberg (2006) and beyond (earlier formulation being more restrictive). It is important to note that, given their symbolic nature, constructions are by definition meaningful, meaning here being interpreted rather widely, as embracing both semantic and pragmatic meaning and, in the case of the former, image schemas, frames, conceptual metaphors, conceptual metonymies prototypes, blends, and the like. Thus the first feature which unites the three models is that they all consider constructions, conceived of as symbolic units, rather than rules, to be the primary objects of linguistic descriptions.

The second characteristic that the three models share is the assumption that linguistic structure can be exhaustively described in terms of constructions. This means that the notion of construction subsumes all conventional linguistic units, irrespective of their size or degree of complexity, including affixes, words, phrases, clauses, etc. Thus, for example, Goldberg (2006) analyses *A dozen roses, Nina sent her mother!* as involving the following eleven constructions: (a) ditransitive construction, (b) topicalization construction, (c) VP construction, (d) NP construction, (e) indefinite determiner construction, (f) plural construction, (g) *dozen, rose, Nina, send, mother* constructions. Constructions may vary not only in size and complexity but significantly also in their degree of schematicity (richness of detail), from the least schematic involving fully specified morphemes, as in the case of *dozen, roses* or *Nina* above or certain idiomatic expressions such as *kick the bucket*, via those requiring only some specific morphemes as in *the X-er, the Y-er* (e.g. *the bigger they come, the harder they fall*), to those of the highest level of schematicity with no specific morphemes at all, as in the case of the ditransitive construction or topicalization construction above. Moreover if all units are constructions of one type or another, there is no obvious basis for distinguishing between grammatical units and lexical ones. Accordingly, the third characteristic which unites the three models is the adoption of the syntax–lexicon continuum.

Finally, the constructions of a language are seen to form not just a list but rather a structural inventory or taxonomic network which represents different types of a speaker's knowledge of a language. While originally there were some differences between the three grammars both in the type of links between constructions that they allowed for and in how information at different levels of schematicity was distributed, nowadays there is considerable convergence on both of these matters. In addition to the taxonomic (schematic) relations linking the different constructions in the network, all three models allow for meronomic links (part–whole), prototype extensions (see e.g. Goldberg's 1995 analysis of the ditransitive construction), and metaphorical extensions (see e.g. Lakoff's 1987 analysis of *there*). All three grammars also allow for the redundant storing of grammatical information in the constructional taxonomy, i.e. for the same information to be stored several times at different levels of schematicity (the default inheritance or full entry model) rather than necessarily only once at the most superordinate level and then be inherited by instances at the lower levels (the complete inheritance model), on the grounds of psychological plausibility (Barsalou 1992: 180). However, the likelihood of redundant storage in less schematic constructions is seen to be tied to the degree of activation of these constructions and specifically their frequency of use, which in turn determines their degree of entrenchment (i.e. cognitive routinization). This view, called by Langacker (1987:

ch. 10) the usage-based model is nowadays widely adopted also outside of cognitive linguistics.[12]

Turning from areas of convergence to those of divergence, CG differs quite significantly from CCG and RCG in maintaining that all linguistic knowledge (semantic, pragmatic, discourse-functional, and crucially structural) is conceptual in nature, a part of semantic space 'the multifaceted field of conceptual potential within which thought and conceptualization unfold' (Langacker 1987: 76). As a consequence, all familiar grammatical constructs and categories (e.g. subject, noun, tense, complementizer, ergativity) receive a conceptual redefinition which often makes them quite opaque and only partially compatible with what is traditionally understood by the concepts or categories in question, and also the way these are employed in CGG and in RCG. While Goldberg (2006: ch. 10) sees this conceptual view of grammatical categories in CG as the sole most important factor distinguishing it from her CCG, Croft (2007) considers RCG as differing from both of the other two approaches in three important respects. First of all, unlike CG and CCG, RCG does not recognize any primitive relations or categories other than constructions (Croft 2001: 362). Thus, while for example the relations of subject and object are posited as atomic primitives in CCG and also CG, though in the latter not as syntactic relations but as semantic construals of the conceptual content of their denotations, in RCG they are derived from and defined in terms of constructions. There is thus no such thing as subject, but only a subject of some construction, for instance of an intransitive construction, a transitive construction, a passive construction, etc. Secondly, the structure of constructions is strictly meronomic and there are no direct syntactic relations between the elements of the same level in the meronomic hierarchy. This means that there is, for example, no syntactic relationship between a subject and verb, only a meronomic role of a part in a whole, here once again of a subject role in an intransitive construction. An important consequence of the above is that forms of encoding, e.g. case marking, agreement marking, and word order, which are typically assumed to encode syntactic relations are interpreted as encoding symbolic relations, i.e. as indicating how the given syntactic element fits into the semantic interpretation of a given construction and/or what it contributes to the identification of the construction as such (Croft 2001: 236–7). As noted earlier, in CG too there are no actual syntactic relations, these being reconceptualized as semantic construals. In CCG, by contrast, the issue is not directly addressed and the analyses provided are compatible with both a traditional syntactic and only meronomic interpretation of e.g. subject or object. The third difference between RCG and the other two models is that there are no universal construction types in RCG; all constructions are language-specific. Constructions can nonetheless be compared across languages, since the range of structural variation that they display is taken to define a multidimensional syntactic space on which language specific constructions can be plotted. Further, cross-linguistic universals can be formulated in terms of mappings

[12] A more detailed exposition of the usage-based approach is given in Langacker (1988), Barlow and Kemmer (2000), Bybee and Hopper (2001), and Bybee (2010).

between the syntactic space (defined by linguistic expressions) and the region in conceptual space whose grammatical expression is being examined.

The rejection of universal syntactic relations, categories, and constructions by RCG may be seen to follow to a large extent from the strongly typological orientation of the model. And indeed, the incorporation of a typological perspective is what some scholars, including Goldberg and Langacker, see as chiefly differentiating RCG from CG and CCG. CG has a strong Indo-European focus, the papers in Casad and Palmer (2003) being a laudable attempt to extend the language coverage of the theory. CCG, in turn, has been mainly English centred, cross-linguistic issues receiving attention only in chapter 9 of Goldberg (2006). The typological underpinnings of RCG and the concentration on English and other European languages in CG and CCG are also reflected in the linguistic phenomena that the respective frameworks have been primarily concerned with. RCG evolved out of an attempt to provide a typologically valid account of parts of speech, grammatical relations and voice phenomena, and only recently (Croft 2012) has been extended into the domain of argument structure patterns, aspectuality, and semantic roles. CCG has been concerned primarily with establishing the categorization relations between constructions, chiefly with argument structure relations, most notably the English ditransitive construction. CG has been devoted to providing a conceptual semantics for grammatical categories and relations and developing analyses of a wide range of conceptualization processes such as profiling, grounding, active zone, reference point scanning, and subjectification. In doing so it has also sought to provide cognitively based accounts of phenomena considered within the formal paradigm to be indicative of the necessity of recognizing the autonomy (self-containedness) of syntax such as constraints on pronominal anaphora, complementation, raising constructions, and empty categories (Langacker 2007: 447). Such a concern can also be detected in the range of linguistic topics taken up by Goldberg (2006), for instance, in providing a constructional mismatch analysis of Ross's (1967) island constraints or a prototype analysis within a radical network of subject auxiliary inversion. Croft, by contrast, has displayed little interest in engaging with the formalist agenda, his background in linguistic typology having revealed the very parochial and temporary nature of many of its concerns.

Unlike in the case of the three structural-functional grammars discussed in §21.3, there are no obvious standards of adequacy other than typological which may be invoked to distinguish the three cognitive models of grammar from each other. Though all three are usage-based models in the sense that they view speakers' linguistic systems as being fundamentally grounded in usage events, i.e. as both abstracted from actual instances of use and feeding back into new instances of use, to date none has shown much interest in the usage event as such.[13] There have thus been no attempts to model the dynamics of the interaction between speaker and hearer, let alone consider different

[13] The assumption that interest in actual usage events should follow from the usage-based approach may in fact be misguided if the usage-based approach is exclusively identified with non-redundant storage and frequency-based entrenchment (see e.g. Nuyts 2008). However, Langacker (1999: 376) clearly

types of texts or discourse. Even the analysis of information structure has received only modest attention. In other words, all three grammars are equally weak with respect to pragmatic adequacy. Nor, until very recently, has much store been placed on the inherently social nature of usage events, a matter lamented by Croft (2009) and being redressed by some of the research within what Kristiansen and Dirven (2008) term 'cognitive sociolinguistics,' especially that of Gries (2003), Grondelaers et al. (2008), and Hollmann and Siewierska (2007). With respect to psychological/cognitive adequacy, all three grammars also fare more or less the same. However, while by their proponents they are given high scores in this regard, this is not a unanimously accepted view. In fact it is precisely with respect to their cognitive credentials that CG, CCG, RCG, and cognitive linguistics have been most heavily criticized. Much of this criticism originates from the expectation that cognitive linguistics should be more closely tied to cognitive psychology and involve empirical methodologies (see Gibbs 2000, 2006). The argument seems to be that while the concepts which underpin cognitive linguistics, categorization, perception, schemas, prototypes, and the like are indeed ones that are central to cognitive psychology, little effort is made to provide any psychological plausibility to the details of the posited grammatical analyses themselves. These are in the main posited simply on the basis of introspection, the reliability and efficacy of which as a linguistic methodology has very clear limitations and is not subject to falsification. To give a very simple example, Peeters (2001) asks what the basis is for recognizing different idealized cognitive models or frames, such as the previously mentioned commercial event discussed by Fillmore (1977b). Should buying and selling be indeed associated with one ICM (idealized cognitive model), as we assumed earlier (and as is standard practice in cognitive linguistics), or with two? Why has no experimental or other empirical evidence of the type commonly used in psycholinguistics been adduced to substantiate this very commonly cited cognitive linguistic illustration?[14] The paramount importance of expanding the range of methodologies employed in cognitive linguistics and providing some empirical basis for the conceptual structures posited is now more generally appreciated. One reflection of this are the contributions in Gonzalez-Marquez et al. (2007), which present a range of empirical work in cognitive linguistics involving behavioural experiments, neural approaches, and corpus-based studies. Particularly important for improving the cognitive credentials of cognitive linguistics is entering into a dialogue with neurocognition, the absence of which is alleged to be the basic obstacle for cognitive linguistic research ever being considered seriously by cognitive scientists.

articulates the study of the dynamics of discourse and social interaction as belonging to the realm of CG, a sentiment which he reiterates in Langacker (2007).

[14] Some ERP (event-related potential) research has actually been carried out on the psychological reality of frames and ICMs which supports the claim of cognitive linguists that the presence of explicit frames facilitates language comprehension (see St Georges et al. 1994 and references in Coulson 2006). However, there has been no investigation of differences in comprehension suggestive of whether one or more than one frame might be involved.

21.4 TOWARDS A UNIFIED FUNCTIONAL-COGNITIVE GRAMMAR

As §§21.2 and 21.3 have suggested, there is nothing in the aims of the functional and cognitive models of grammar considered which would make them incommensurable. In line with their communicative orientation, functional grammars are clearly more concerned with the dynamics of discourse and especially its repercussions on grammar than are cognitive grammars. Nonetheless, of the three functional-structural grammars that we have discussed, only SFG has made an attempt to deal with the actual complexities (and realities) of discourse and take into account the relationship between discourse and context. FG in its newer guise of FDG is now more attuned to the dictates of discourse than its predecessor, in that it takes as its starting point the speaker's communicative intention, makes the act rather than the clause the basic unit of grammatical analysis, and allows for interaction with the context at all levels of analysis. However, the role played by discourse pragmatics in RRG is not much different from that in the cognitive models of grammar, being essentially confined to information structure, i.e. topic and focus articulation, the activation status of referents (and its effects on voice phenomena and argument structure alternations), and reference-tracking mechanisms. And significantly, in cognitive linguistics, as mentioned above, there is increasing recognition of the need to incorporate into grammatical analysis the dynamics not only of discourse interaction but also of social interaction. Thus commitment to reflecting the communicative function of language in grammar is more a matter of degree than a factor differentiating functional from cognitive approaches. *Mutatis mutandis*, the same holds for the cognitive dimension. Although the three cognitive grammars, CG, CCG, and RCG, are obviously deeply committed to cognitivisim, the scope of their cognitive concerns is not always considered to be entirely satisfactory. They show no interest in matters of online processing for example. Further, too little attention is devoted to substantiating the cognitive validity of the posited constructs and the assumed different *langue*–mind, and language–mind–body connections. The three functional grammars are clearly not 'cognitive' enough. Their cognitive concerns are directed only at linguistic systems and processes, at best at issues of storage, production, and comprehension. They leave basically untouched the central preoccupation of cognitive linguists: how the mind deals with meaning, i.e. the human conceptual system and its reflection in language. Among adherents of the functional approach there is, however, an increased interest in the relationship between language and conceptualization and in the appropriate localization of constructs at conceptual as opposed to linguistic levels. Therefore scholars who have looked closely at the two approaches see them as essentially complementary.

There is one area, however, with respect to which functional and cognitive approaches do differ in a perhaps more fundamental respect: the three functional grammars discussed are essentially process-oriented, the three cognitive ones construction-based. Ample discussion of the construction-based nature of CG, CCG, and RCG was provided in §21.3. The process orientation of the three functional grammars is reflected in the levels of organization that they display (minimally semantic vs morphosyntactic) and the rules or linking procedures which map the levels onto each other. According to Nuyts (2008), the process orientation of functional grammars makes them much better suited than construction-based grammars to capture the inherent dynamicity of language use. Nuyts (2008: 92) argues that commu-nication is a complex problem-solving activity requiring adaptation on the part of the speaker to new and changing circumstances, and thus that 'coding conceptual mean-ings into linguistic form (and vice versa) is not a self-obvious process, but something that must be worked out dynamically, time and again.' While at present functional grammars reflect this dynamism only imperfectly, in principle the meaning–form mappings that they posit could be made to more sensitive to contextual and conceptual factors and thus provide a better approximation of the inherent flexibility involved in speaking. Construction-based grammars, by contrast, offer a much more static per-spective on the process of communication. Simplifying the issue considerably, since grammar is a network of constructions, the process of speaking is either a matter of the selection of a ready-made constructions or alternatively of the unificational integration of a number of stored partial constructions. In either case, the implied view of communication is not very dynamic and clearly at odds with the laborious and often unsuccessful process sketched by Nuyts.

Langacker (1987: 57, 2007b: 237), while explicitly endorsing a process view of con-ceptualization, is very much against a process view of grammar. So is Croft (2001, 2003a). Yet most of their arguments are directed against a generative process approach where linguistic levels are independent modules which by definition are immune to the effects of other facets of cognition or to context and not aimed at functional grammars such as those discussed in §21.2. The other arguments are not so much against a processing approach as for the necessity of recognizing constructions, which in fact are not incompatible with functional grammars and do feature in them, albeit never exclusively. For example, both FG and RRG posit various types of templates; Hengeveld and Mackenzie's (2008) FDG represents argument structure patterns independent of predicates and RRG (Van Valin 2005: 131–5) recognizes constructional schemas for voice constructions. Van Valin (forthcoming) even suggests that it may well be the case that, while speakers operate within a projectionist system by mapping meaning to form, hearers may operate in a constructionsist manner, comprehension requiring co-composition. Thus the possibility exists that the process vs construction orientations may not be ultimately divisive, and that eventually some form of rapprochement between functional and cognitive grammars will emerge. One model of grammar which combines insights from functional grammars and cognitive ones, especially in the area of the semantics and pragmatics of predicate–argument relations, is the Lexical Constructional Model developed by Marial Usón and Faber (2007). Another is Nuyts' (2001) Functional Procedural Grammar. There is every reason to hope for more.

21.5 Concluding Remarks

Whether the relatively harmonious view of the relationship between functionalism and cognitivisim which I have presented in this discussion will stand the test of time remains to be seen. In the last couple of years, the scales seem to have shifted in favour of the cognitive as opposed to functional orientation. There are clearly more scholars now who consider themselves cognitive linguists than functional ones. In fact, many former functionalists are now firmly within the cognitive camp. By contrast, there seem to be no movements in the other direction, i.e. from within the cognitive community to the functional camp. This apparently unidirectional shift may subsequently give rise to a somewhat more nuanced view of the historical relationship between functional and cognitive models of grammar. Nevertheless, it seems to be the case that each approach has something to offer the other, and that linguistic theory is likely to benefit if the proponents of the respective approaches avail themselves of the opportunity to do so.

CHAPTER 22

....

LEXICOGRAPHY FROM EARLIEST TIMES TO THE PRESENT

....

PATRICK HANKS

22.1 WHAT IS A DICTIONARY?

....

A dictionary,[1] as Trench (1860) observed, is an inventory of the words of a language (with explanations of meaning and other information). All the world's major literary languages, as well as some less common ones, have evidently felt the need for such an inventory, and the trend has spread to rare and endangered languages. According to this view, lexicographers are, first and foremost, linguistic inventory clerks, but, as we shall see, there are other motives, too, for compiling a dictionary.

At first glance, the humble occupation of collecting words, defining them, and arranging them in some sort of order—usually, alphabetical—would not seem to call for any profound theoretical insight. However, when the activity begins to be under-taken in earnest, theoretical and practical linguistic questions begin to crowd in.

- What is the relationship between words and phrases? In traditional dictionaries of English and other European languages, a false dichotomy is presented between words and idioms (otherwise known, rather misleadingly, as 'fixed phrases'), as if there were some sharp dividing line between the two categories. During the past two or three millennia, dictionaries have tended to reinforce naïve theoretical reductionism as regards questions about where meaning resides. Recent advances,

---

[1] I would like to thank Xia Lixin, Rocky Miranda, Mohammad Resa Aslani, Elisabetta Jezek, Paz Battaner, Irene Renau Araque, and Araceli Alonso Campo for their comments on earlier drafts of this chapter. Any errors that remain are of course entirely my responsibility.

both in construction grammar (e.g. Goldberg 2006) and in corpus linguistics (e.g. Sinclair 2004, Hanks 2013), suggest that meaning resides not only in lexical items but also in phraseology.

- How far should a dictionary go in recording the millions of attested nominal phrases such as *fire escape* and *forest fire*, each of which has at least one unique meaning, which is very often not derivable from the sum of its parts? English dictionaries ignore most such combinations. Different languages deal with such compound concepts in different ways.

- How strictly should a dictionary confine its inventory to recorded usage? Should it be allowed to speculate about possible words and meanings in addition to recorded words and meanings? For example, is it a rule of English that adjectives have an adverb derivative ending in *-ly*? If this is right, should possible adverbs such as **saintlily* be recorded, even though there is little or no evidence that they have ever been used? The adjective *lame* has two senses: 'suffering from an injury to the leg' (e.g. *a lame horse*) and 'inadequate' (e.g. *a lame excuse*). Should two parallel senses be recorded for the adverb *lamely*, even if the available evidence suggests that the 'injured' sense is rare or nonexistent for the adverb?

- What can be said by way of definition of a word's meaning(s)? Can meanings be defined strictly and formally according to genus and differentia, as desired by Wilkins (1668) and Leibniz (see Couturat 1901)—or can they only be typified and hinted at?

- Can a spelling form be shared by more than one word? For example, should *record*, verb, and *record*, noun, be recorded as a single lexical entry (despite difference in pronunciations and meaning), or should there be two separate entries? What about *keep*, verb, and *keep*, noun? Should all lemmas that are used as two (or more) parts of speech have separate entries (homographs) for each part of speech? Different dictionaries adopt different policies with respect to such questions.

- What can be said about the origins and history of a word? This was a central topic in nineteenth-century European linguistics, following the gradual uncovering of the family of Indo-European languages, and it is still the main focus of the great historical dictionaries of European languages, such as *OED* and Grimm.

- How much attention should be paid to etymology in a synchronic dictionary? For example, philologists tell us that *weave* as an intransitive verb, meaning 'to move rapidly in and out,' has a different etymology from *weave* as a transitive verb, meaning 'to create cloth or a garment (by moving threads rapidly in and out on a loom)'. Is this a good reason for making them separate entries, in defiance of the common-sense perception that the two uses are somehow cognitively related and (whatever their history may be) can now be regarded as 'the same' word?

Questions such as these can have a profound effect on linguistic theory—our understanding of the way language works. Many such questions have been addressed by linguists, but others have been neglected, especially in the English-speaking world. In this chapter, we take a brief look at how dictionaries have developed in different cultures and related to linguistic theory.

22.2 ROOTS: LEXICOGRAPHY BEFORE PRINTING

22.2.1 China

The earliest dictionaries in the world were compiled in China during the Han Dynasty.[2] The history of Chinese lexicography has been summarized in English by Li Ming (2006), Yong and Peng (2008). For various reasons, not least the fact that Chinese writing is ideographic rather than alphabetical, there is room for debate about what counts as the earliest Chinese dictionary. Two works in particular may be mentioned here. It is generally agreed among Chinese scholars that the *Erya* (爾雅 'Near Correctness'), dating from the second or third century BC, must be classified as a work of encyclopedic lexicography: it contains explanations of the meanings of difficult words and phrases in the Chinese classics. The *Erya* falls somewhere between a thesaurus and a topically organized lexicon.[3]

During the Eastern Han Dynasty (first–second centuries AD), Xu Shen compiled the *Shuōwen Jiězì* (說文解字 'Origin of Chinese Characters'). This remarkable work of scholarship is the foundation of all subsequent Chinese lexicography and linguistics. It was presented to the emperor in AD 121, though actually completed many years earlier. It is recognizably a dictionary, even to Western readers. It contains entries for approximately 10,000 Chinese characters, with information about their origins, meanings, and pronunciation. It is organized in 540 sections according to the 'radicals' of each word. According to Boltz (1993), Xu's motives in compiling the *Shuowen* were pragmatic and political, rather than communicative, and sprang from the Confucianist belief that using the correct terms for things was essential for proper government. It is therefore a normative (prescriptive) dictionary rather than a descriptive one.

22.2.2 India and Persia

Sanskrit dictionaries and thesauruses were compiled over 2,000 years ago, and were the start of a long tradition of native lexicography in Indian languages. Three terms are particularly relevant to the Indian lexicographic tradition: *nighantu*, *kosha*, and *nirukta*.

---

[2] See also §10.2.3 above.
[3] Thanks to Karen Chung for advice on *Erya*.

Nighantu simply means 'lexicon.' The earliest known nighantu gives explanations of obscure words found in Vedic texts (sacred literature). In the second or third century BC, a scholar called Yaska, about whom nothing else is known, wrote an etymological commentary (*nirukta* 'explanation') on words found in a lexicon (nighantu).

A *kosha* is literally a storehouse or treasury. Unusually for lexicography, the earliest kosha was written in verse. It contains entries for nouns and indeclinable forms, but not verbs, and was intended for use by poets. The best-known such work is the *Amarakosha* by Amarasinha, a Buddhist scholar and poet who probably lived in the sixth century AD.

Throughout the medieval period there was much cultural interchange between India and neighbouring Persia (modern Iran), which intensified after the emergence of Islam, up to 1947, when Pakistan was established as an independent Islamic state between India and Iran. There is allusive evidence that Persian dictionaries existed during the Sassanid dynasty (third–seventh centuries AD), but these have not survived. The most important surviving dictionary of Persian before modern times is undoubtedly the *Loghat-e-Fors* 'Lexicon of Persian,' compiled by the epic poet Abu Mansur Ali ibn Ahmad Asadi Tusi (d. 1072). Asadi's declared aim was not only to record and explain words found in Persian poetry–words that might be unfamiliar to his contemporaries— but also to foster the continuation of Persian traditional literature. The entries are illustrated with citations from poetry; they are arranged according to the last letter of each entry word, in order to help poets find suitable rhymes—a practice also followed in medieval Arabic and Hebrew lexicography.

Another Persian work that must be mentioned is a lexicon compiled by Faxr-e-Qavas Qaznavi in India in 1291. This is the *Farhang-e-Panj Baxši* 'Culture in Five Sections,' so called because the entries are arranged hierarchically on semantic principles in five sections, on principles somewhat similar to those of Roget's Thesaurus 1852. For example, the fourth section of the book contains words for animals. It is subdivided into five 'varieties', of which the fifth concerns words for human beings, and this in turn is divided into two parts. The first part concerns human organs, and the second part is about humans and their environment. Each entry is presented with a verse from poetry as well as a definition. This type of dictionary is known in French as a *dictionnaire analogique*. The best-known example is the *Dictionnaire analogique de la langue française: répertoire complet des mots par les idées et des idées par les mots*, by Jean-Baptiste Prudence Boissière, published by Larousse in 1862.

The Persian lexicographical tradition continued mainly in India, where many Persian writers resided. Between the ninth and the nineteenth centuries, about 130 Persian dictionaries were compiled. The first Persian dictionary with explanations in Farsi was compiled in the fifteenth century, after the Mongol invasion. It contained about 2,300 lexemes and was written by Hendu Shah Nakhjavani, known as Shams-e-Monshi. A much larger work, *Borhan-e-Ghate*, with 20,000 entries, published by Mohammad Hossein Tabrizi in 1724, also belongs to this period of Persian and Indian history.

22.2.3 Classical Greece and Rome

The history of Greek lexicography has been summarized by Stathi (2006), who gives an account both of the efforts of Greek lexicographers in classical times and of the lexicography of ancient Greek since the Renaissance.

From the fifth century BC onwards, it was customary for Greek scribes to insert glosses into manuscript copies of the works of Homer and other earlier writers, explaining obsolete and unusual words. From the third century BC these glosses were compiled into separate glossaries by scholars at the library in Alexandria. All except a few fragments of these compilations have since been lost.

In the second century AD a different kind of Greek lexicography developed, as a result of the puristic linguistic movement known as 'Atticism.' The form of Greek that was used as a lingua franca throughout the eastern Mediterranean during the period of the Roman empire was regarded by literati as 'incorrect' or 'impure.' A dictionary was therefore needed that would present and define 'correct' words and terms, i.e. those that had been used by the great writers of Athens in the fourth to second centuries BC. Such a work was the *Eklogē* ('Εκλογὴ 'selection') of Attic words and phrases compiled in Byzantium in the second century by Phrynichos of Bithynia. This is a collection of Byzantine Greek words to which Phrynichos and his ilk had objections, the 'pure' or 'correct' Attic equivalents being given alongside the 'impure' colloquial forms. Ironically, the chief interest of this work to modern scholars is the light that it sheds on colloquial Byzantine Greek.

Lexicography in ancient Rome can be approached through the proceedings (Ferri 2011) of the 2008 conference in Pisa on 'The Latin of Roman Lexicography, from Verrius to the *Corpus glossariorum*,' and through the Festus project at University College London (www.ucl.ac.uk/history2/research/festus/index.htm). Ancient Latin linguists shared the general Roman predilection for classifying and imposing order on everything, and this is no doubt one reason why grammarians such as Priscian and Aelius Donatus had a profound influence on subsequent traditions in linguistics throughout Europe up to the mid-twentieth century, while Latin lexicographers are comparatively little known; works of classical Latin lexicography have been partly or wholly lost. It is known, too, that the Romans created bilingual Greek–Latin word lists, but these have likewise not survived.

An ambitious monolingual dictionary called *De Verborum Significatu* 'on the meaning of words' was compiled by the philologist and educationist Marcus Verrius Flaccus (*c.* 55 BC—20 AD), tutor to the grandsons of the emperor Augustus. By all accounts it was a huge work (the letter A alone took up four books) and was concerned with etymology and cultural history as well as word meaning. Entries were supported by citations from literature. In the second century AD, Sextus Pompeius Festus edited a revised version of this work, part of which (from letter M onwards) has survived in a single, seriously damaged manuscript. It is also known that Festus omitted obsolete and archaic words from his version of the dictionary and wrote them up in a separate work called *Priscorum verborum cum exemplis*, which, sadly, has been lost: it would have been a priceless source of information about early Latin. In the eighth century, the historian Paulus Diaconus created an abridged version of Flaccus' dictionary, and this has survived. It is our chief source of information about ancient Roman lexicography. The entries have a much greater emphasis on cultural practices and beliefs than modern readers of a dictionary would expect, and little or nothing is said about function words and grammar. Thus, it may be classified as a cultural rather than a linguistic compendium.

22.2.4 Arabic and Hebrew

Between the seventh and the thirteenth centuries AD a number of Arabic dictionaries were compiled, with a variety of different purposes, including regulation of 'correct' language, the facilitation of poetry, and deepening understanding of the words of the Qur'ān.[4] These developments are described by Haywood (1965), who comments, 'In the compilation of dictionaries and other lexicographical works, the Arabs . . . were second to none until the Renaissance, with the possible exception of the Chinese.' From Baghdad and Basra in the east to Granada and Cordoba in the west, the first five centuries of Islam witnessed an extraordinary flowering of literature. It is noteworthy that lexicographical activities of Muslim Spain, to the far west of the Mediterranean, are included here. As explained by Roth (1994), both Arabic and Hebrew lexicography flourished, along with many other modes of scholarship, under the enlightened regimes of the Muslim rulers in medieval Spain, before they were all swept away by the Christian 'reconquest,' culminating in the fifteenth century with the intolerant religious fundamentalism of Queen Isabella the Catholic and the Spanish Inquisition.

Latin and Greek enjoyed a universally accepted conventional alphabetical order from time immemorial, but the history of the conventional order of letters in the Arabic writing system is more complex. The complexity is compounded by the fact that in written Arabic normally only consonants are represented; readers are left to supply the vowels for themselves. For further details of written Arabic and indeed other writing systems, see Daniels and Bright (1996). Early Arab lexicographers experimented with various arrangements for ordering words: for example, both Al-Jawhariyy's *As-sihah* 'the Strong' (tenth century) and Ibn Manzur's monumental *Lisan Al-'Arab* 'Language of the Arabs' (thirteenth century) order words according to the last consonant, and arrange the consonants in an order that is determined to some extent by the mode of articulation. Modern Arabic dictionaries follow a different alphabetical order.

The most important work of medieval Arabic lexicography is the *Kitab Al-'Ayn* (literally, 'Book of the 'Ayn'), compiled by Al-Khalil ibn Ahmad in the eighth century. An 'ayn (ع)is a written symbol representing the Arabic voiced pharyngeal fricative

---

4 See also Ch. 12 above.

consonant /ʕ/, which has no equivalent in Latin or Greek. Al-Khalil used the name of this symbol as the title of his work, which in actuality is nothing less than a comprehensive dictionary of the Arabic language. It is claimed by some that this was the first systematic attempt anywhere to compile a comprehensive lexicon of any language.

The earliest known works of Hebrew lexicography were compiled in the Middle East in the tenth century AD (see Drory 2000, Cohen and Choueka 2006). Hebrew had already become rare or extinct during the Roman empire, so these were in effect dictionaries of a dead language. For two millennia Hebrew survived mainly (or only) as a liturgical and literary language, being preserved and cherished as a symbol of the ethnic and religious identity of Jews during the diaspora. From at least the second century AD it was no longer a medium of everyday communication. For that purpose, it was supplanted first by Aramaic and subsequently by Arabic.

Sefer ha-Egron (902) is a lexicon of approximately 1,000 Hebrew words for poetic purposes, compiled in Egypt by Sa'adiah ben Josef. Not all of it has survived. The words are presented in two arrangements: first, they are listed alphabetically, not for ease of reference as we might expect, but to help poets compile acrostic verses. The second list is of words according to their final consonant, in order to facilitate rhyming. Some years later Sa'adiah issued a version of his work with glosses in Arabic, to facilitate understanding of the meaning of Hebrew words. Sa'adiah was a scholar, philosopher, and theologian as well as a lexicographer; in 928, after many years' residence in Jerusalem, he was appointed gaon (spiritual leader) of the Jewish community in Sura, south of Baghdad; Gaon is often represented as his surname.

Kitab Jami al-Alfaz (*c.*945) is a Hebrew–Arabic dictionary of words in the Bible, compiled in Fez, Morocco, by David ben-Abraham El-Fasi.

According to Cohen and Choueka (2006), 'probably the finest achievement of medieval Hebrew lexicography is "the Book of Roots" by Yonah ibn-Janah.' Ibn-Janah, otherwise known as Abu al-Walīd Marwān ibn-Janāh, was a Jewish linguist and grammarian of the eleventh century who lived in Cordoba, Spain. His lexicon, *Kitab al-'usul*, is the second part of a work known as *Kitab al-Anqih* 'Book of Exact Investigation.' The first part is a Hebrew grammar with the exotic title *Kitab al-Luma* 'Book of the Multicoloured Flowerbeds.' The arrangement of the lexicon is based on the three-letter root system that is now recognized as universal for Semitic languages. The explanations or glosses are in Arabic. In the thirteenth century, a revised grammar and lexicon based on the work of Ibn-Janah was compiled in Narbonne by the Biblical scholar and philosopher Rabbi David Qimhi (1160–1235). This work, *Sefer Hashorashim*, was to be an influential source of Christian Old Testament scholarship.

22.2.5 Medieval Europe

In medieval Europe, lexicography originated (or rather, reinvented itself) in the form of interlinear vernacular glosses on words in medieval Latin manuscripts. These glosses came to be gathered up into separate works, sorted roughly into alphabetical order (see Murray 1900, Castro 1991, Hanks 2006, Kramer 2006). During the Middle Ages, a variety of manuscript lexicons of Latin with glosses in various vernaculars were compiled for use by novices in monasteries as they studied Latin—the universal European lingua franca of the Christian religion, of philosophy, and of scholarship. The earliest known example is the eighth-century *Glosses de Reichenau* (so called because the manuscript formed part of the library of the Benedictine Abbey on Reichenau Island in Lake Constance). This consists of over 5,000 words of the Latin Vulgate with glosses in Gallo-Roman medieval Latin, a precursor of Old French.

Probably the best-known example in England of such a glossary is the *Promptorium Parvulorum* 'Young People's Storeroom,' compiled in about 1440 by Galfridus Anglicus (alias Galfridus Grammaticus 'Geoffrey the Grammarian'), a Dominican friar living in Norfolk. Its 10,000 entries (words and phrases) were laboriously copied out by hand many times—the only means of dissemination possible before the invention of printing—and the copies transported to the libraries of other monasteries. Then, in 1499, something revolutionary occurred. The *Promptorium* was set in type and printed. This meant that identical copies of the work could be created and made available more or less immediately to anyone who wanted one and was able to pay for it. The role of the medieval scribe was at an end and immense new opportunities for ambitious lexicography opened up.

22.3 THE RENAISSANCE: THE IMPACT OF PRINTING ON LEXICOGRAPHY

Dictionaries are not only vast, systematic inventories of minutiae concerning lexical items; they are also vehicles that disseminate such information, thereby encouraging the growth and preservation of cohesive cultural and linguistic conventions in a language community. This disseminative role only began to realize its full potential with the invention of printing, so that identical copies of a work, however large, could be printed off and distributed within a very few days. Before the invention of printing in the mid-fifteenth century, each copy of a work had to be laboriously written out by hand. Thus, the invention of printing is of the greatest importance in the history of lexicography.

An equally important and related development was the revolution in typographical design and metal type-founding in Venice in the 1470s, which rapidly spread northwards, reaching Paris in the 1490s and England some decades later. The central figure here is Nicolas Jenson (1420–80), an expert in metals who had been master of the French royal mint in Paris before moving to Venice and setting up a printing business there. Jenson was a type-founder who introduced new standards of elegance and legibility, including skilful use of space on the page, with minute attention to the tiniest details of letter spacing, kerning, etc., and systematic distinctions between capital letters (based closely on Roman monumental inscriptions) and lower-case letters (based on Carolingian minuscules). Another important Venetian was the great Renaissance scholar Aldus Manutius, whose typographer, Francesco Griffo, faithfully observed Jenson's principles, adding further options such as the distinction between roman and italic type. The Venetian typographers abandoned the heavy, hard-to-read, space-consuming black-letter type of Gutenberg and other early printers, and set new standards for all future typography of printed books and journals in the Roman alphabet outside Germany. It is no exaggeration to say that the typographic achievements of Jenson, Griffo, and their immediate successors (notably Johann Froben in Basel and Claude Garamond in Paris) were a crucial factor, not only in the flood of classical texts that were rescued and printed during the Renaissance, but also in making modern lexicography possible, enabling lexicographers to cram vast quantities of information elegantly and legibly onto each page and to disseminate large numbers of identical copies of completed dictionaries quickly and efficiently. These developments are discussed in more detail in Hanks (2010). If we compare the black-letter type of *Promptorium Parvulorum* (1499), the earliest printed dictionary in England, whose type aimed at nothing more ambitious than replication of the letters used by scribes in monasteries, with Robert Estienne's masterly, elegant, and huge Latin *Dictionarium* (1531), we see a quantum shift in presentation, affecting both the quality and the quantity of information. Estienne's work would simply not have been possible in black-letter type. It would have been an unmanageable and unnavigable monster.

Estienne was a master printer in Paris, as well as a lexicographer and one of the leading intellectuals of his day. Even a casual inspection will show that his great work has most of the characteristics that present-day readers have come to expect of scholarly monolingual dictionaries, including:

- comprehensive list of words (lemmas);
- morphology: selected inflected forms for lemmas ('principal parts'), giving guidance on conjugations and declensions;
- clearly distinguished definitions, capturing an appropriate level of generalization for each meaning of each word;
- citations from literature (many of which were printed for the first time by Estienne himself), supporting each definition.

There is also a feature that has only very recently been revived by modern lexicographers:

- extensive selection of idiomatic phraseology.

Estienne's *Dictionarium* is a monolingual Latin dictionary: its definitions are in Latin, accompanied by occasional vernacular glosses in French for 'hard words.' It very clearly aims to be an inventory of the classical Latin language, or at least of the vocabulary of the classical Latin texts that were printed and published in Estienne's day. His motivation, according to Considine (2008), was to contribute to the preservation of the heritage of classical literature, and the same is true of the equally ambitious and equally monumental *Thesaurus Graecae Linguae*, published by his son Henri Estienne in 1572.

Two later dictionaries published by Robert Estienne show a different side of this great lexicographer. His main concern in 1531 was to cater to the needs of scholars and literati. But he was also sensitive to the needs of less erudite students and language learners. The *Dictionnaire Francoislatin* of 1539 is a practical work explicitly aimed at students learning to express themselves in Latin. A noticeable feature is the large number of idiomatic French phrases for which Latin equivalents are offered. To take just one rather striking example, the phrase *l'ordre et collocation des mots* is glossed as 'verborum constructio.' Here we have two words—*collocation* and *construction*—that are buzzwords in today's linguistics in the English-speaking world, as it slowly, painfully, and belatedly turns to the empirical and theoretical analysis of lexis and phraseology. Robert Estienne placed considerable emphasis on phraseology and context: it seems likely that he would have been sympathetic to and even excited by modern theories of collocation and construction grammar. A complementary and equally practical work is his *Dictionarium Latino-Gallicum* (1552). This is not a revised version of his 1531 work. Instead, it is a practical guide whose aim is to help students decode the meanings of Latin words and Latin texts into their native French—an early example of a bilingual dictionary.

One of the first monolingual European dictionaries devoted to a vernacular language (i.e. not Latin) was the *Tesoro de la lengua castellano o española* (Madrid, 1611) by Sebastian de Covarrubias, a sophisticated linguist and cultured humanist who included not only definitions and Latin etymons for words but also place-names and a number of subjective comments on lexical issues. This is a substantial work of over 1,400 beautifully typeset pages, in the best tradition of Robert Estienne. An online facsimile can be seen at fondosdigitales.us.es/fondos/libros/765/1275/tesoro-de-la-lengua-castel-lana-o-espanola.

22.4 POLYGLOT DICTIONARIES AND THE EMERGENCE OF BILINGUAL LEXICOGRAPHY

In terms of literature, the European Renaissance was primarily a revival of the literature and learning of ancient Greece and Rome, and (as suggested above) printed dictionaries of classical Latin and Greek played a substantial role. Linguistically, however, the Renaissance marked the beginning of the long, slow decline of Latin as an international lingua franca and the flourishing of vernacular languages as media for communication and culture throughout Europe. In these circumstances, one might have expected an exuberant growth of vernacular bilingual dictionaries, for example offering translations of words and phrases from Italian into French, Italian into English, French into Hungarian, or Spanish into German. Surprisingly, however, up to the end of the sixteenth century bilingual dictionaries of vernacular languages were few and far between. Instead, scholars, translators, travellers, and diplomats alike were constrained either to speak Latin or to rely on vernacular glosses appended to a rather inferior Latin dictionary. This was the *Dictionarium* of Ambrogio Calepino, an Augustinian friar living in Bergamo. Calepino's original edition (1502) was a Latin vocabulary, with glosses in Latin supported by citations, together with encyclopedic entries for the figures of classical mythology. In a second edition, glosses in Italian and French were added. By a process of accretion, the vocabularies of other languages, starting with Greek and Hebrew, were gradually added by others to successive editions of Calepino's original. In the words of Freed 2007, 'it evolved into the first polyglot dictionary.' By 1580 a dozen different editions, containing glosses in up to eleven different languages, all attributed to Calepino, were in print, published in locations as far apart as Reggio nell'Emilia, Venice, Paris, Strasbourg, Hagenau, Lyon, and Rome. In Paris alone, five competing editions appeared between 1524 and 1541. The 1573 edition printed and published in Venice includes the following comment in its front matter, quoted and translated by Freed:

> *In hac postrema editione, ut hoc dictionarium commodius exteris nationibus inservire possit, singulis vocibus latinis italicas, gallicas, & hispanicas interpretationes inseri curavimus.* [In this latest edition, in order that this dictionary might more fully serve foreign nations, we have taken care to insert Italian, French, and Spanish definitions among the lone Latin entries.]

By this time Ambrogio Calepino himself (1450–1510) was long dead and his book had become common property. Indeed, his very name had become common property. The *OED* has an entry for the obsolete English word *calepin*, supported by sixteenth and seventeenth century citations and glossed as:

> A dictionary (sometimes 'a polyglot'); *fig.* one's book of authority or reference; one's notebook or memorandum-book.

The *OED* also notes the French phrases 'je consulterai là-dessus mon calepin,' 'cela n'est pas dans son calepin,' 'mettez cela sur votre calepin' (i.e. make a note of that to serve as a lesson), and the obsolete English expression 'to bring someone to his calepin,' i.e. to the utmost limits of his information. Evidently, Renaissance readers expected a dictionary to be a comprehensive inventory.

The complex bibliographical history of Calepino's dictionary and its derivatives have been traced by Labarre (1975). This shows that multilingual editions really began to take off in the 1550s; by the 1580s they had come to include lexical items in up to 11 languages—not only Latin, Greek, Hebrew, Italian, French, and Spanish, but also outlandish tongues such as German, English, Polish, and Hungarian. By the end of the century, a Latin–Portuguese–Japanese 'Calepino' had appeared, supporting the missionary work of the Portuguese Jesuits who were at that time seeking to Christianize Japan. It has often been said that Calepino's original work is deficient in scholarly precision, while these polyglot derivatives are great cumbersome things, not suitable for carrying around and not particularly user-friendly. Nevertheless, these were the principal works that served for interpretation among vernacular languages in the sixteenth century.

The great English linguist and lexicographer John Palsgrave was French tutor to Mary Tudor, sister of Henry VIII, who was destined to marry the King of France. Palsgrave compiled a magnificent bilingual French–English dictionary and phrase book (in many cases with amusing and diverting illustrative phrases) as the major part of his general account of the French language, *Lesclaircissement de la langue francoyse* (1530). However, strangely, few scholars at the time followed Palsgrave's lead. The idea of bypassing Latin with bilingual dictionaries did not really catch on until the very end of the sixteenth century.

22.5 The Expectation that Etymology Guarantees Meaning

A hundred years later, during the European Enlightenment, it was increasingly felt there was a need to prescribe standards for living languages.[5] These standards were based on the ill-defended assumptions that earlier forms of a language are somehow more 'correct' that contemporary forms and that etymology guarantees meaning. A moment's thought will convince us that this assumption is incorrect. For example, none of the meanings of the modern word *subject* or its cognates in other modern languages have anything to do with the Latin etymology, which literally means 'something thrown under,' and the same is true of thousands of other words that have changed their meaning, in some cases many times, in the course of recorded history (not to mention reconstructed lexical prehistory). Nevertheless, the notion that etymology guarantees meaning was prevalent in Europe as the Renaissance developed into the Enlightenment, and indeed it was responsible for some remarkably fine scholarly lexicography. The notion was effectively refuted by Johnson (1755) in the preface to his dictionary, though it persists in a wistfully hankered-after form in some of the more conservative academies of Europe.

In 1612 (after over 20 years of work) the Accademia della Crusca published a *Vocabolario* for the Italian language, the aim of which was explicitly prescriptive, conservative, and indeed retrogressive, i.e. to establish the already old-fashioned Florentine dialect of the fourteenth century (as written in particular by Dante, Boccaccio, and Petrarch) as a gold standard for Italian. This was followed in 1640 for French by the first edition of the *Dictionnaire* of the Académie Française, whose aim was equally prescriptive and conservative: 'to give definite rules to our language and to render it pure.'

---

[5] See also Ch. 15 above.

The Real Academia Española was founded with similar aims in 1713, and still proudly announces that its mission is to regulate the Spanish language—'to fix the voices and vocabularies of the Castilian language with propriety, elegance, and purity.' The first edition of its dictionary, published under the title *Diccionario de autoridades* 'Dictionary of Authorities' in 1726. It is called a 'dictionary of authorities' because its definitions are supported by citations from literature. Unfortunately, in the mid-eighteenth century, it was decided that including citations is a waste of space in a dictionary whose role is to regulate the language. Since then, the *Diccionario de la lengua española de la Real Academia Española* (*DRAE*), the 23rd edition of which is available online, is extremely conservative. It is slow to admit neologisms and, at least up to 2006, had an inadequate system for labelling register, i.e. for distinguishing racist, sexist, and other offensive word uses from normal usage.

22.6 SAMUEL JOHNSON

In the early eighteenth century several English lexicography projects were proposed on the model of the French and Italian academy dictionaries, with the aim not only of inventorizing and defining all the words in English, but also of 'fixing' the language in its then supposed state of excellence. This aim eventually bore fruit in Samuel Johnson's *Dictionary* (1755), but with some interesting modifications of purpose, arising from Johnson's profound understanding of the nature of language.

Johnson was not only a lexicographer but also a major intellect: essayist, poet, biographer, critic, editor, and conversationalist. He set out with the aim, suggested to him by a consortium of booksellers, of 'fixing' the language, but in the course of the work, he came to recognize that a living language cannot be 'fixed': language change is inevitable. The lexicographer must therefore set out to observe and describe, rather than to pontificate and prescribe.

> Those who have been persuaded to think well of my design require that it should fix our language, and put a stop to those alterations which time and chance have hitherto been suffered to make in it without opposition. With this consequence I will confess that I flattered myself for a while; but now begin to fear that I have indulged expectation which neither reason nor experience can justify. When we see men grow old and die at a certain time one after another, from century to century, we laugh at the elixir that promises to prolong life to a thousand years; and with equal justice may the lexicographer be derided, who being able to produce no example of a nation that has preserved their words and phrases from mutability, shall imagine that his dictionary can embalm his language, and secure it from corruption and decay. (*Preface* to the Dictionary, Johnson 1755, §84)

The *Preface*, in particular, deals with many of the issues that concern modern lexicologists, as explained in Hanks (2005): issues that were not revisited until the work of twentieth century scholars—philosophers of language such as I. A. Richards, Ludwig Wittgenstein, and Hilary Putnam, anthropologists such as Bronislaw Malinowski and Eleanor Rosch, and linguists such as J. R. Firth and J. M. Sinclair. Johnson's recognition that language change is inevitable spared the English language the impertinence of an academy of learned men (and later women) impotently debating the acceptability or otherwise of behavioural phenomena (patterns of word meaning and word use) which in reality they have no power to alter.

Among Johnson's many merits and influences as a lexicographer are the following.

- Extensive use of illustrative citations from literature—not only to prove the existence of a particular sense of a word, but also to illustrate elegant usage and to delight and educate the reader.
- Arrangement of senses in a rational order, so that each dictionary entry stands as a coherent discourse, reflecting meaning development, influenced but not governed by etymology, and not just a list of senses in historical order.
- Extensive use of Aristotelian-Leibnizian principles of definition—stating first what kind of thing in general a word denotes and then adding carefully selected differentia.
- Respect for the vagaries of a living language—he recorded word meanings as he found them, not necessarily as he may have wished them to be. He confined his value judgments to a few acerbic comments (e.g. *clever*, 'a low word') and he observed, for example, that, although previous English lexicographers had found it convenient to define *ardent* as meaning 'burning,' this etymological sense of the word never made the transfer from Latin to English.
- Effective treatment of phrasal verbs.

Johnson's was the standard dictionary of English until the end of the nineteenth century, when it was superseded by the Philological Society's *New English Dictionary on Historical Principles* (*NED*, 1884–1928).

22.7 HISTORICAL PRINCIPLES

The *NED* was published by Oxford University Press and in the 1930s it was re-christened *The Oxford English Dictionary* (*OED*). It was followed by a shortened version, the *Shorter Oxford English Dictionary* (*SOED*), in two large volumes—whose title is sometimes wrongly thought to be some kind of joke, since it is so very much bigger than most other English dictionaries—and by a plethora of regional works on similar principles, including the *Dictionary of American English* (*DAE*), the *Dictionary of the Older Scottish Tongue* (*DOST*), the *Scottish National Dictionary* (*SND*), the *Australian National Dictionary* (*AND*), and the *Dictionary of South African English* (*DSAE*). It was also the supreme example of a general nineteenth-century European movement to compile historical dictionaries of national languages, which included the

Deutsches Wörterbuch of the brothers Grimm, the *Trésor de la langue française*, the *Woordenboek der Nederlandsche Taal*, and many others.

A dictionary on historical principles places the etymology at the start of each entry and traces the semantic development of the word by arranging senses in historical order. Thus, in the *Oxford English Dictionary*—a dictionary on historical principles— the entry for *camera* starts by explaining that the word is from classical Latin *camera*. The first sense is 'the department of the papal Curia dealing with finance; the papal treasury.' Sense 2 is 'an arched or vaulted roof, chamber, or building (also more generally: any room or chamber).' It is not until senses 4b and 4c respectively in the third edition that we get the familiar modern senses, 'a device for taking photographs' and 'a device for capturing moving pictures or video signals' (*OED* 3rd edition; entry revised and updated in 2010). In the first edition this sense was not present; this is not surprising, because cameras in the modern sense had only just been invented. Sense 4a is a cross-reference to the entry for *camera obscura*. All this faithfully reflects the chronological development of the word in English, though it is no doubt somewhat confusing to a naïve user who wants to know what *camera* means in modern English. Dictionaries on historical principles are of great value to literary scholars, social historians, historians of science, historical linguists, and others. However, they are not intended for language learners, translators, computational linguists, or casual inquirers into word meaning. Failure to make this simple typological distinction has resulted in considerable confusion and even misuse of great works of scholarship. It also resulted in mindless application of historical principles of lexicography to smaller one-volume dictionaries intended for general use.

Merriam Webster's *Third New International Dictionary* (*MWIII*, 1961) is a large American dictionary on historical principles, with impressive coverage of technical terminology in fields ranging from agriculture to zoology. Its definitions for everyday words are sometimes less than satisfactory, as a glance at entries such as *door, hotel, sugar*, and *mimosa* will show. The root of *MWIII*'s problematic definitions lies in a failure to distinguish word meaning from concept meaning, compounded by the editor's instruction to his staff that all explanations should be couched in terms of a single one-phrase definition.

> **sugar**: a sweet crystallizable substance that consists entirely or essentially of sucrose that is colorless or white when pure and usu. yellowish to brown otherwise, that occurs naturally in the most readily available amounts in sugarcane, sugar beet, sugar maple, sorghum and sugar palms, that is obtained commercially principally by processing the juice expressed from sugarcane or the aqueous extract of sliced sugar beets and refining so that the final product is the same regardless of the source, and that forms an important article of human food and is used chiefly as a condiment and preservative for other foods and for drugs and in the chemical industry as an intermediate. (*MWIII* 1961)

This starts well enough, defining the meaning of the noun *sugar* by stating a genus term ('a crystallizable substance') and adding differentiae ('sweet,' 'consists of sucrose').

However (setting aside any doubts we may have about whether sugar can be sugar before it is crystallized), we can see that the definition begins to go haywire after 'sucrose.' It is a rule of English grammar that a restrictive relative clause governed by *that* modifies the meaning of the preceding noun, but the natural interpretation of the relative clause in question would be incorrect, for it is not intended to distinguish one kind of *sucrose*, namely the colourless or white kind, from other kinds of sucrose; instead, it is a further differentia of 'crystallizable substance.' From here on the syntax, structure, and wording of the definition become increasingly bizarre until a mystical point of incomprehensibility is reached, culminating in a final homage to jargon (and insult to comprehensibility) with the use of the word *intermediate* in a sense that is highly specific to chemistry.

What went wrong? We may identify at least three principal problems, which (in less extreme forms) are pervasive in modern lexicography: (1) confusion of essential properties (e.g. 'sweet,' 'consists of sucrose'), which may reasonably be expected to contribute to a definition, with accidental properties (e.g. 'used as a condiment and preservative for other foods and for drugs'), which are incidental or indeed irrelevant to definition; (2) excessive reverence for scientific correctness coupled with indifference to making the text understandable by ordinary readers; (3) theoretical ignorance, in particular of the fuzzy and variable nature of word meaning. The latter problem is hardly surprising, as this dictionary was compiled in the 1950s, whereas the importance of prototype theory was not fully recognized until the 1970s. What is more surprising is that forty years later, many twenty-first-century lexicographers continue to display profound ignorance of prototype theory.

MWIII was savaged in America by journalists and pedants alike when it was first published, mainly because it was perceived as being insufficiently prescriptive (see Sledd and Ebbit 1962, Morton 1994). However, the weaknesses of definition, lack of an apparatus for describing register, and hard-to-read typography are more serious faults, though not the main subject of the general outcry.

The Merriam dictionaries trace their history back to the *American Dictionary of the English Language* compiled by the polemical lexicographer Noah Webster in 1828. It contains no fewer than 70,000 entries. Webster (1758–1843) was an indefatigable collector of words with a rare gift for definition writing. Only some of his definitions were taken directly from Johnson's dictionary, and he introduced some sensible spelling reforms (*color, center*) into American English, although unfortunately some of them (e.g. *tung* for *tongue*) did not achieve acceptance by the American public. At the same time, he added and defined Americanisms such as *caucus* and *wigwam*. A fuller account of this extraordinary man, his achievement, and his legacy will be found in Micklethwait (2000). Unfortunately, his etymologies were influenced by his belief that modern languages, including English, are derived from something called Chaldaean, which he believed was the language used by Adam and God for their conversations in the Garden of Eden and the immediate precursor of Hebrew. After his death, his successors—including his son-in-law, Chauncey H. Goodrich, and the redoubtable Noah Porter, president of Yale College—quietly abandoned the Chaldaean hypothesis and brought the etymologies into line with the findings of Germanic and Indo-European scholarship.

In continental Europe, the academies did not maintain a monopoly on dictionaries on historical principles. For French, *Le trésor de la langue française* is a massive dictionary, with nearly half a million citations from literature, of the French language as it developed from 1789 (the Revolution) to 1960. A modern Italian dictionary on historical principles equivalent to *OED* is Salvatore Battaglia's *Grande dizionario della lingua italiana* (1960).

22.8 THE RUSSIAN TRADITION

In the English speaking world since the nineteenth century, dictionary-making and linguistics developed in such a way that the two camps ended up having little common ground and being more or less incapable of having a sensible conversation with each other about matters that might be supposed to be of mutual interest. In the English-speaking world (America in particular), ignorance, arrogance, hostility, and suspicion have been prevalent on both sides, mixed with not a little mutual contempt. 'Twas not ever thus. In the Russian tradition, there has been a long and harmonious relationship between lexicography and linguistic theory. Vladimir Ivanovich Dal (1801–72) was a comparative linguist who did primary research on at least four of the Turkic languages of the Russian empire. Between 1862 and 1866 he published a massive four-volume *Explanatory Dictionary of the Living Great Russian Language*, of which new, expanded editions were regularly published after his death. The latest revision appeared in 1955 and has been reprinted many times since. It has also been used, with minor revisions, as the basic text for recent publications such as the *Illustrated Explanatory Dictionary of the Living Great Russian Language* (2007). Dal's dictionary achieved for the Russian language what the brothers Grimm were attempting to do for German at around the same time, but with a difference. Dal's interest was not only in language and its workings but also in culture, literature, and folklore expressed through language. He also published a collection of over 30,000 *Sayings and Bywords of the Russian People*. In keeping with the fashion of his time, he favoured coinages based on native Russian morphemes to express novel concepts, rather than foreign borrowings from Greek, Latin, or any other language.

Two successive revised editions of Dal's dictionary were prepared by Jan Niecisław Ignacy Baudouin de Courtenay (1845–1929), a Polish Slavicist of French extraction, also known in Russian under the name Ivan Aleksandrovič Boduen de Kurtene. Baudouin de Courtenay was a first-rate theoretical linguist, a founder member of the Prague Linguistic Circle. Among his many achievements was the development of the theory of the phoneme, later perfected by Roman Jakobson. Like his Swiss contemporary Ferdinand de Saussure, Baudouin de Courtenay was a champion of synchronic linguistics at a time when only historical Indo-Europeanist studies was regarded as academically respectable. Unlike Saussure, he was involved in practical lexicography, and he was able to bring a number of improvements to Dal's dictionary, systematically revising the methodology as well as the coverage.

The next Russian lexicographer-linguist who must be mentioned is Lev V. Ščerba (1880–1944). In contrast to Saussure, Ščerba identified three rather than two objects of study: speech activity, language system, and language material. In his theoretical work, he emphasized human linguistic creativity: the capacity of speakers to produce sentences never previously heard. He also emphasized the importance of experimentation in linguistics, particularly experiments yielding negative results—utterances that a language as a system does not allow—which of course can never be recognized through analysis of any corpus, however large.

Ščerba's pupil Sergei I. Ožegov (1900–64) was to become the editor of another standard Soviet dictionary, the *Dictionary and Culture of Russian Speech*, the editorship of which he inherited from Dmitri N. Ušakov (1873–1942). After Ožegov's death the dictionary was regularly updated by Academician Natalia J. Švedova (1916–2009), while in 2007 a competing revised edition by Leonid Ivanovich Skvortsov appeared. Despite reputedly being described by the novelist Vladimir Nabokov as 'moronic,' Ožegov's is still the most widely used Russian dictionary today. It is not clear whether Nabokov's objection is to dictionaries in general or Ožegov's work in particular. It is noteworthy that, in the best Russian tradition, Švedova not only maintained a major dictionary but also wrote a grammar of the Russian language.

Two of the most important recent Russian contributors to linguistic theory have been lexicographers, namely Jurij D. Apresjan (b. 1930) and Igor A. Mel'čuk (b. 1932). Apresjan was a bilingual lexicographer at the Russian Academy of Sciences in Moscow, who among other things compiled a *Dictionary of English and Russian Synonyms* (1979). His observations of regular semantic patterns in language led to his theory of regular polysemy (Apresjan 1973) and his book *Systematic Lexicography* (2000). Apresjan argues that lexicographers have a duty to represent the particular world view that is encoded in the lexicon of a particular language. This leads to an interaction between words (which represent beliefs) and idiomatic phraseology. Apresjan argues that a command of lexical synonyms and their subtle differences plays a vital role in enabling a speaker to express his or her thoughts in any language or culture. He says, for example:

> Each of the adjectives *healthy, healthful, wholesome, salubrious*, and *salutary* has the sense 'fostering the improvement or maintenance of health'. Thus, if we say *a salubrious diet, salubrious food, or a salubrious way of life*, we are making no semantic error: in principle the synonym selected is capable of expressing the required idea and we may be assured that we will be correctly understood. Nevertheless, none of the above collocations is fully correct (the best choices will be: *a healthy diet; wholesome food, a healthy way of life*). Each of them violates a co-occurrence constraint, which, though not binding, is observed in pedantic and literary discourse, and requires that *salubrious*, unlike all its synonyms, be used chiefly with the nouns *air* and *climate*. (Apresjan 2000: 5)

Here we see Apresjan, who did not have the advantage of corpus evidence and corpus tools, struggling, by using his intuitions to account for the phenomenon of collocational preferences, which no modern lexicographer can afford to ignore. The principle of collocational preference is correctly understood, but the details are sometimes wrong, because Apresjan did not have sufficient evidence at his disposal.

Mel'čuk, with co-workers who included Apresjan, compiled a fragment for an *Explanatory Combinatorial Dictionary* of Russian. A year after being forced to flee from the Soviet Union in 1976 for his support of political dissidents, Mel'čuk accepted a research and teaching post at the University of Montreal, Canada, where he set up an *Explanatory Combinatorial Dictionary* of modern French (*Dictionnaire explicatif et combinatoire du français contemporain*; (*DEC*, 1984, 1987, 1993). Despite its three volumes, this work does not offer anything like full coverage of the lexicon of French; instead it elaborates a theory: Meaning–Text Theory. According to this, a natural language is conceived as 'a specific set of correspondences between an infinite set of meanings and an infinite set of texts.' Mel'čuk's aim is to show that there is a wide range of lexical relations in text, which are governed by a finite set of lexical functions. For example, the lexical function *Magn*, which denotes the ways in which a lexical unit can be intensified, is realized by different words in different contexts: thus, the noun *maladie* 'illness' is intensified with the adjectives *sérieuse*, *grave*, etc., while the verb *remercier* 'to thank' is intensified with the adverbs *vivement*, *chaleureusement*, and *de tout coeur*. Part of Mel'čuk's importance as a linguistic theorist is simply that he assigned a central role to the lexicon in understanding the nature of language at a time when others were focused obsessively on syntax:

> Most current linguistic theories view a linguistic description of a language as a grammar; a lexicon is taken to be an indispensable but somehow less interesting annex to this grammar, where all the idiosyncrasies and irregularities that cannot be successfully covered by the grammar are stored. By contrast, Meaning–Text Theory considers the lexicon as the central, pivotal component of a linguistic description; the grammar is no more than a set of generalizations over the lexicon, secondary to it. (Mel'čuk 2006)

This all-too-brief summary section has given some indication of the relationship between lexicography and linguistic theory in the Russian tradition. It is now time to turn to the practical concerns of lexicography in the English-speaking world.

22.9 SYNCHRONIC PRINCIPLES

22.9.1 The American Tradition

In a dictionary on synchronic principles, the aim is to describe the current conventions of usage and meaning. The usual modern meaning of the word is placed first, followed by other, less frequent senses in some sort of logical order, and the etymology comes at the end. Thus, in the *(New) Oxford Dictionary of English* ((N)ODE,[6] 1998), *camera* is defined first as 'a device for recording visual images in the form of photographs or video signals.' The sense 'a chamber or round building' is recorded as a separate homograph—that is, it is regarded by the dictionary as a different word that just happens to have the same spelling.

The first dictionary to issue an explicit challenge to historical principles was Funk and Wagnall's *Standard Dictionary of the English Language* (F&W, 1894–97). F&W was conceived as a popular dictionary, albeit on a grand scale, and its editors therefore made little attempt to justify their innovations in scholarly terms or to draw attention to the difficulty of what they were doing. F&W recognized that most ordinary dictionary users are more likely to want to know what a word means in the contemporary language than to ask questions about its etymology and archaic or historical usages.

The *American College Dictionary* (ACD, 1947), edited by Clarence Barnhart, was a dictionary that set out quite explicitly to place the current meaning of each word first, following (without acknowledgement to F&W) the commonsensical principles of organization first adumbrated by Isaac Funk half a century earlier. ACD represented the best practices of American synchronic lexicography in the twentieth century, and it was to become the ancestor of a worldwide family of derivative dictionaries, including the *Random House Dictionary of the English Language* (RHD, 1966, 1987, American English); the *Hamlyn Encyclopedic World Dictionary* (1971, British English); and the *Macquarie Dictionary* (1981, Australian and New Zealand English). Lexicography is typically accretive—each new dictionary building on foundations laid by its predecessors.

In his preface to *ACD*, Barnhart explained his descriptive synchronic principles thus:

> This dictionary records the usage of the speakers and writers of our language; no dictionary founded on the methods of modern scholarship can prescribe as to usage; it can only inform on the basis of the facts of usage. A good dictionary is a guide to usage much as a good map tells you the nature of the terrain over which you may want to travel. It is not the function of the dictionary-maker to tell you how to speak, any more than it is the function of the mapmaker to move rivers or rearrange mountains or fill in lakes.... To select the words and meanings needed by the general user, we utilized the Lorge-Thorndike Semantic Count which measures the occurrences of various meanings in the general vocabulary. By using this count, which is based upon a reading of modern standard literature, we have been able to select the important meanings needed by the reader of today and to have some statistical assurance of the occurrence of the meanings. This count has also been of considerable importance in the arrangement of meanings, since it has enabled us to determine with some certainty which are the common meanings and to put them first.

---

[6] The word 'New' was dropped from the title of the second edition (2005).

Modern corpus-driven lexicographers may be forgiven a wry smile at Barnhart's glib assurances, for even with sophisticated computational techniques and corpora many times larger than that of Lorge and Thorndike, it is still difficult, for some words, to establish which meaning is the most frequent one. For example, what is the most frequent modern meaning of *admit*? Is it 'to say reluctantly,' or is it 'to allow to enter'? It is difficult to answer such questions with confidence, even with corpus evidence. Without it, we are merely guessing. Moreover, there are no generally agreed criteria for deciding where one meaning of a word ends and another begins, nor even for what counts as a meaning. Indeed, some lexicographers (see Kilgarriff 1997) go so far as to deny the very existence of word meanings. Hanks (1994) agrees that, strictly speaking, words do not have meanings, but goes on to argue that what dictionaries offer are statements of 'meaning potentials'—the potential of a word to make a given meaning when used in a particular context. Should launching a boat be a separate sense of the verb *launch* from launching a newly built ship? *ACD* has them as separate senses of the verb *launch*, but many people would say that they are one and the same. *ACD* (1947) does not record *launching a missile or rocket*: that sense developed later. Many people nowadays would regard this as the most literal sense, which should come first. The language has changed in this respect, and synchronic lexicographers must respond accordingly. Even when one meaning of a word has been successfully distinguished from another, it is by no means clear which one should be placed first. For example, *ACD* gives as definition 1 of the verb *launch*, 'to set (a boat) afloat; lower into the water.' Sense 4 is 'to set going: *to launch a scheme*.' Corpus analysis shows that sense 4 is much more common than sense 1, and the same was almost certainly true in 1947. Yet Barnhart's decision with regard to the arrangement of the senses of this word is defensible. The idea that launching is something that you do primarily to boats (or missiles) rather than schemes is cognitively salient for English speakers. For that reason it deserves first place, even in a synchronic dictionary. Senses involving 'imageable' concrete objects and events have cognitive preference over abstract notions. Thus, 'launching a boat or ship' can be seen as activating the most literal sense of this verb, while 'launching a scheme (or a new product)' can be interpreted as a metaphor exploiting the boat or missile sense. If the most frequent sense of a word is perceived as being a linguistic metaphor exploiting another, more literal sense, it takes second place in Barnhart's dictionary, regardless of frequency.

The leading present-day dictionary in America on synchronic principles is the *American Heritage Dictionary* (1969; 4th edn 2006), which may be regarded as carrying on the tradition of F&W and *ACD*, even though there is no formal relationship among these works.

22.9.2 The British Tradition

In Britain, synchronic principles were introduced from America, first by the *Hamlyn Encyclopedic World Dictionary* (1971) and subsequently by *Collins English Dictionary*

(*CED*, 1979), which greatly extended the lexicographic coverage of scientific and technical words compared with other dictionaries of the time. The one-volume *(New) Oxford Dictionary of English (NODE*, 1998; 2nd edn, *ODE* 2005; 3rd edn, 2010) is a one-volume dictionary on synchronic principles, more similar in design and structure to *RHD*, *AHD*, and Collins than to the great historical dictionary (*OED*) published by the same publishing house. It is based on an unrivalled body of citation evidence, for it is the only dictionary of English aimed at general users to use analysis of corpus evidence as an organizing principle for arranging and refining the definitions of complex words, as well as a source of citations of actual usage. For unusual words and senses, it draws on citations collected by the *OED*'s traditional reading programme. Among other things, (*N*)*ODE* adopts a more sophisticated approach to word grammar than most monolingual dictionaries aimed at the home market. It attempts, not always successfully, to identify 'core meanings' and group subsenses under a core meaning.

Some readers may wonder why America's favourite dictionary (if sales are anything to go by) has not been mentioned in this brief survey of synchronic dictionaries. The dictionary in question is *Merriam Webster's Collegiate*. The reason for this omission is simple: the *Merriam Webster Collegiate* is a dictionary based on historical principles; it is not a synchronic dictionary. It is based on Merriam's vast *Third New International Dictionary* of 1961 and its two predecessors. The current edition of the Collegiate is the 11th edition (2001). According to the publisher, a 12th edition is due to appear in 2014. It will be interesting to see whether this new edition will adhere to the long-standing Merriam preference for historical principles.

22.9.3 Synchronic Lexicography in Other Countries

In this section so far, examples of synchronic dictionaries have been taken from the English-speaking world. Only brief and selective mention can be made of modern synchronic dictionaries in other languages, sufficient perhaps to illustrate the variety of different social linguistic functions that a synchronic dictionary is expected to perform in different cultures.

22.9.3.1 *German-speaking Lands*

In 1880 the schoolteacher Konrad Duden published a spelling dictionary, *Die deutsche Rechtschreibung*, which became accepted as the de facto standard reference for German spelling in German-speaking lands. This was the first is a series of reference books on different aspect of the German language, including a synonym dictionary, a guide to usage, a pronunciation dictionary, a historical and etymological dictionary, and a children's dictionary. The publisher's flagship is the *Deutsches Universalwörterbuch*, the third edition of which was published in 2011 and is available on line. It is compiled on modern descriptive principles.

During the Communist era, state funding of lexicographical research was normal in central and eastern Europe. One of the finest works of synchronic lexicography created during this era was the *Wörterbuch der deutschen Gegenwartssprache* (*WDG*, 1964–77), edited by Ruth Klappenbach und Wolfgang Steinitz. If we can bring ourselves to ignore the occasional 'politically correct' entries for terms like *Kapitalismus* and *Sozialismus* and the extensive coverage of the terminology of the Volkspolizei, we find a very fine dictionary based on modern descriptive principles, making a real effort to account for the phraseology in which each word is used. Unfortunately, in the 1960s and 1970s, the editors did not have access to large electronic corpora, which had not yet been invented, so although their principles repay close examination, the details of the implementation is sometimes deficient. They had the same problem as Apresjan: insufficient evidence for the description of normal phraseology.

22.9.3.2 *Greece*

Throughout the nineteenth century, since Greece won independence from Turkey, attitudes to the modern Greek language have been divided between pragmatists, willing to accept the language as it is, and purists, with a desire to purify the language and in particular to expunge all the Turkish words which had come in since the Turkish occupation of the sixteenth–nineteenth centuries. In modern Greek, the triumph of *Dimotiki*, the everyday form of the language, over *Katharevousa*, the archaizing 'purified' form of the language, is now pretty well total, thanks in no small measure to the success of the dictionary of Giorgios Babinyiotis, which follows rigorously descriptive principles.

22.9.3.3 *Czech Republic and Slovakia*

In Czech, something very different has happened. Modern literary Czech is an artificially constructed language, harking back to the language of the sixteenth century, when Bohemia was a European great power. The Dictionary of the Standard Czech Language (*Slovník spisovného jazyka českého, SSJČ* 1960–71) therefore has a prescriptive function, legislating about correct vs. incorrect usage of words and occasionally inventing a word or a meaning to fill a lexical gap. A department of the Institute for the Czech Language has a similar prescriptive or advisory function. *SSJČ* is overdue for revision or replacement, and work started some years ago on a project that now seems to have been discontinued. There seems to be no general agreement on the principles on which a new Czech dictionary should be based. Neighbouring Slovakia, by contrast, is richly furnished with the up-to-date and ongoing products of a fine lexicographic tradition, including not only a great historical dictionary and a dialect dictionary, but also a fully descriptive Dictionary of Contemporary Slovak (*Slovník súčasného slovenského jazyka*), of which volumes 1 and 2 (A–G; H–L) have been published.

22.9.3.4 *Spain*

A fine dictionary of Castillian Spanish compiled on synchronic principles is the *Diccionario del español actual* (1999; 2nd edn 2011), compiled by Manuel Seco, Olimpia

Andrés, and Gabino Ramos, which gives a detailed and explicit account of contemporary Spanish, using evidence of contemporary usage culled from the Internet and other sources. Maria Moliner's *Diccionario de uso del español* (1966–7; 3rd edn 2007) is important because it was originally aimed specifically at repairing the deficiencies of the Royal Academy's dictionary (*DRAE*) in accounting for word usage in contemporary Spanish and this gave a new impetus to lexicography in Spanish.

22.9.3.5 *Catalonia*

The Catalan language plays a central role in the Catalan sense of national identity, so it is not surprising that the lexicon of Catalan and closely related languages has been painstakingly inventorized and defined in the *Diccionari català–valencià–balear: inventari lexicogràfic i etimologic de la llengua catalana* by Antoni M. Alcover and Francesc de Borja (1988).

22.9.3.6 *Italy*

Two important Italian dictionaries on synchronic principles are Tullio de Mauro's *Grande dizionario italiano dell'uso* (*GRADIT*, 1999–2000) and the *Dizionario Italiano Sabatini Coletti* (*DISC*, 1997).

22.9.3.7 *France*

French monolingual dictionaries tend to be more strongly influenced by historical principles than a modern British or Australian reader would expect, and a careful distinction is not made between literary French and practical modern French. An exception is *Le Petit Robert* (1967), which describes itself as 'une traitement moderne et soucieux de la réalité social du français.' Bilingual dictionaries in France generally adopt a thoroughly pragmatic synchronic approach to language description.

22.9.3.8 *Summary*

This rapid and superficial survey of synchronic dictionaries in various cultures is surely an inadequate treatment of the subject, but it should be sufficient to illustrate the growing emphasis on empirical description of the contemporary language that is characteristic of lexicography in many but by no means all languages and cultures in the modern world. Many of these dictionaries are aimed at helping foreign learners of a language, a subject to which we now turn.

22.10 DICTIONARIES FOR LANGUAGE LEARNING

During the 1930s a major development in English lexicography took place in Japan, a development that was eventually to have an effect on lexicography in other languages too. The linguist Harold Palmer, founder of the Institute for Research in English Teaching, the English teacher A. S. Hornby, and some other teachers of English in

Japan observed that the then-current dictionaries of English were not suitable for foreign learners of English and decided to do something about it. The result was the *Idiomatic and Syntactic Dictionary* (*ISED*), developed and tested in Japanese class-rooms and published by Kaitakusha just after the outbreak of the Second World War. This work was designed primarily as a dictionary for encoding purposes, that is, to help learners with their writing and speaking skills. It contains a deliberately limited selection of vocabulary—words that were in active use and that learners might be expected to know and to be able to use correctly and idiomatically. The apparatus gave a great deal of information about the syntactic structures associated with each word. Hornby's verb patterns in particular were in use among English language teachers for almost half a century before eventually being superseded by corpus-based research. *ISED* was republished unaltered in 1948 by Oxford University Press as *A Learner's Dictionary of Current English,* subsequently retitled the *Oxford Advance Learner's Dictionary of Current English* (*OALDCE*). A massive influx of additional vocabulary items was added to the second edition, which diminished rather than enhanced its original intention as an encoding tool for learners. The editors had ceased to ask themselves the unanswerable question, 'Does a learner need to know how to use this word idiomatically?' For, of course, different learners need different words for different circumstances. The sixth edition, edited by Sally Wehmeier (2000), was extensively revised using evidence from the British National Corpus, while adhering to the principle that vocabulary selection, definitions, and examples of usage must be driven by classroom needs rather than corpus evidence. It is therefore unabashed about using invented examples alongside or instead of text-derived examples of usage. 2011 saw its eighth edition.

In 1978, the supremacy of *OALDCE* in the marketplace for EFL (English as a foreign language) was challenged by the *Longman Dictionary of Contemporary English* (*LDOCE*, www.ldoceonline.com). This is the dictionary of choice for many researchers in computational linguistics. Like *OALDCE*, it is driven by perceived classroom needs, but was extensively revised in the 1990s using evidence from the British National Corpus. It devotes considerable attention to spoken English.

In 1987, with the publication of the COBUILD dictionary (an acronym for 'Collins Birmingham University International Language Database,' 1987, 1995), a radical new kind of lexicography emerged: the corpus-driven dictionary. COBUILD's innovations included examples selected from actual usage for naturalness, rather than invented by the lexicographer or teacher, while its unique defining style expresses links between meaning and use by encoding the target word in its most typical phraseology (e.g. 'when a horse gallops, it runs very fast so that all four legs are off the ground at the same time'). The editor-in-chief of COBUILD, John Sinclair, briefed his editorial team: 'Every distinction in meaning is associated with a distinction in form.' This was more a signpost for the future than a practical guideline for interpreting the then-available evidence. A great deal more research is required to determine exactly what counts as a distinction in meaning, what counts as a distinction in form, and what is the nature of the association. COBUILD was the first ever large-scale corpus-based dictionary research project. Its principles were set out in an associated book of essays (Sinclair 1987a). Unfortunately, a few years later the COBUILD research programme was cut short by News International, which had bought Collins, the publisher funding the work.

Another addition to the stock of corpus-based dictionaries for learners of English was the *Cambridge International Dictionary of English* (*CIDE*, 1995). Subsequent editions (2003, 2005, 2008) were published as the *Cambridge Advanced Learner's Dictionary* (dictionary.cambridge.org). This work has a number of associated data modules, such as lists of verb complementation patterns, semantic classifications of nouns, and semantic domain categories. The second edition and subsequent editions were re-titled *Cambridge Advanced Learners Dictionary* (*CALD*).

The most recent addition to the stock of such dictionaries published in Britain is the *Macmillan English Dictionary for Advanced Learners* (*MEDAL*, 2002). This dictionary is corpus-based but not corpus-driven. It makes eclectic use of some of the principles developed for other major lexicographical projects, and pays special attention to two things in particular: conventional metaphors and collocations. For the latter, it uses the Sketch Engine, a computer program that identifies statistically significant collocations of each target word, which the lexicographers were in many cases able to associate with specific senses of the target word.

In 2008 Merriam-Webster brought out *Merriam-Webster's Advanced Learner's English Dictionary*. This is a practical American work, with a sensible selection of currently used words and meanings in American English. It owes more to the definitions in rival British EFL dictionaries than to the Merriam tradition of historical lexicography and it pays little or no attention to primary research in phraseology, cognitive linguistics, or corpus linguistics.

In his (1987b) paper 'The Nature of the Evidence,' Sinclair stresses the importance of distinguishing significant collocations from random co-occurrences. The first attempt to undertake statistical analysis of collocations in a corpus for lexicographical and other purposes was by Church and Hanks (1990), but it was not until Kilgarriff, Rychlý, and their colleagues developed the Word Sketch Engine (Kilgarriff et al. 2004) that a user-friendly tool was made widely available for people to see at a glance how the meanings of a semantically complex word are associated with and indeed activated by its collocates.

22.11 THE IMPACT OF COMPUTER TECHNOLOGY ON MODERN LEXICOGRAPHY

§22.3 mentioned the impact of the invention of printing on Renaissance lexicography. A comparable impact has been made on modern lexicography by computational text processing. There are three aspects to this impact: compilation, evidence, and use.

22.11.1 Computers and Dictionary Compilation

In the 1960s and 1970s some adventurous lexicographers found that they could be freed by the computer from the tyranny of alphabetical order and proceed instead in a logical order, dictated by content rather than the vagaries of the alphabet. So, for example, the editor writing medical entries would work systematically through the field, starting, say, with definitions of terms denoting bones and organs of the body, before moving on to physiology, pathology, diseases, clinical psychology, and so on. Simultaneously, specialists in the arts could make their contributions by defining terms of, say, music, ballet, opera, and theatre, while others contributed the terminology of poetics, printing, and publishing. Meanwhile, a phonetician would write phonological transcriptions, while a team of etymologists summarized what is known about the origin and history of each word. It was no longer necessary for the special-subject editors to be polymaths with competence in grammar, phonology, and etymology. These various contributions were then slotted by computer into a framework of general definitions compiled by a team of general editors. A further group of editors would read through the text of each entry, correcting errors and inconsistencies, eliminating duplications, plugging gaps, and generally polishing up the work for publication. This, in very broad outline, is how the large one-volume synchronic dictionaries of the second half of the twentieth century, notably the *Random House Dictionary of the English Language, American Heritage Dictionary, Collins English Dictionary*, and *New Oxford Dictionary of English*, were compiled, with consequent improvements in quality and a dramatic reduction in elapsed time between start-up and publication. Because the text is compiled in a database or structured text file and because each dictionary entry has a basic uniformity of structure, the dictionary text can be run through a typesetting program to output page proofs in a matter of hours rather than months.

This aspect of lexicographical technology encouraged the editors of such dictionaries to ride roughshod over the traditional distinction between a dictionary and an encyclopedia, and to take the view instead that a dictionary is a sort of collective cultural index, which must summarize, for the practical benefit of users, all the most salient cognitive and social features associated with the meaning of every word and name that is in common currency.

22.11.2 Lexical Evidence

An even more important development, from the point of view of studying words and how they go together in idiomatic language use, was the emergence in the 1980s and 1990s of corpus linguistics. Up to that time, lexicographers had insufficient evidence to represent accurately the conventions of word meaning and word use. Corpus evidence changed the nature of lexicography. It demonstrated clearly that definitions in pre-corpus dictionaries had a tendency to be biased in favour of unusual rather than central and typical uses of words, and that introspection is not a good source of evidence. These developments have been fully described elsewhere, for example by Hanks (2009), and there is no need to repeat them here. Just one example will suffice to illustrate the radical impact that corpus technology has begun to have on lexicography. This concerns the meaning of the conventional metaphor *gleam*. Conventional metaphors are secondary senses of words and as such are (or ought to be) recorded in dictionaries. There is no disputing that the primary meaning of *gleam* is 'a faint or brief light,' but what is its secondary meaning, applied to an emotion appearing briefly in someone's eyes? Consulting their intuitions, cognitive linguists have invented examples such as *Amusement gleamed in his eyes* as a supposed realization of the conceptual metaphor HAPPINESS IS LIGHT. This hypothesis appears to be supported by the *OED*'s sense 2b of the noun *gleam*, 'a bright or joyous look.' But, as Deignan (2005) points out, corpus evidence shows that in the twentieth century (at any rate) a gleam in someone's eyes does not normally signal happiness, but rather cynical amusement, mischief, or even malice. And even the *OED*, a historical, pre-corpus dictionary *par excellence*, supports its definition with a citation from 1852 that might set alarm bells ringing in the head of an alert reader:

> 1852   H. B. Stowe *Uncle Tom's Cabin* vi. His black visage lighted up with a curious, mischievous gleam.

The following examples, selected from the British National Corpus (BNC), are typical of twentieth-century usage of this word in its secondary, metaphorical sense.

> Rosita looks at me indignantly, with a furious *gleam* in her eyes, a look of hatred.
> He had a zealot's *gleam* in his dishwater eyes.
> . . . the sardonic *gleam* in his eyes.
> . . . a rather nasty *gleam* in his blue eyes.
> [She] didn't understand the wicked *gleam* in his eye
> His eyes *gleamed* malevolently.

These are only six of sixty or more examples in BNC that could have been selected to illustrate this point. They are not matched by other examples designating happiness. These examples also illustrate another important contribution of corpus linguistics to lexicography: the identification of collocations. Collocations are recurrent co-occurrences of words in different texts. The word *gleam* collocates significantly with *eye*, but also with the adjectives *sardonic, mischievous, unsettling, predatory, manic, visionary, wry, wicked, amused, cynical, fierce*, and *mad*. And a *gleam* is (in descending order of statistical significance) a gleam of *amusement, malice, triumph*, or *humour*. It seems safe to predict that dictionaries of the future, in the age of the Internet and large corpora, will pay far more careful attention than previously to collocation and phraseology, using various measures of statistical significance to identify salient collocations, and that this new trend, marching arm in arm with other developments such as construction grammar, will continue to bring about a change that has already begun in perceptions among linguists of the relationship between words and meaning.

22.11.3 Online Dictionaries

Ironically, the revolution that has brought exciting new potential for lexical description has at the same time destroyed the business model that traditionally would have funded such work. Compiling a new dictionary is a huge, expensive, labour-intensive task, but if every well-educated member of a community feels the need to own a dictionary the financial incentives are likewise substantial. In the heyday of synchronic lexicography in the twentieth century, there were half a dozen dictionary publishers competing for market share. With the advent of the Internet, all that has changed. The market for dictionaries printed on paper has sharply declined. Dictionaries are typically used for rapid and uncritical look-up, for which the Internet is ideally suited, but the Internet offers a free-for-all, in which some very inferior and indeed inaccurate products jostle for position with some very sophisticated accounts of words and their meanings. The *OED* online must be singled out for mention as an example of the best that on-line lexicography can offer. The content of the dictionary is based on nineteenth-century principles (this fact alone is a tribute to the robustness of James Murray's linguistic insight and lexicographic skill), while the techniques of information retrieval and presentation are at the cutting edge of modern lexicographical technology. It remains to be seen whether new business models (or funding models) will emerge that will enable new lexicographical projects to undertake large-scale, detailed (and possibly cross-linguistic) investigations of words, their collocations, their phraseological patterns, and their meaning.

22.12 THESAURUSES AND ONTOLOGIES

Almost all the dictionaries mentioned so far are semasiological—that is, they start with a word or phrase and say how it is spelled, how it is pronounced, what it means, etc. Before concluding, brief mention must be made of an alternative approach to the lexicon, namely onomasiology, which starts with a concept and asks, is there a word or phrase to express it?

During the European Enlightenment, starting in the seventeenth century, attempts were made to arrange all human knowledge in conceptual hierarchies. Since concepts can only be represented by words, this is necessarily a quasi-lexicographical undertaking. The most important of these seventeenth-century conceptual and lexical models of the universe forms part of John Wilkins's *Essay towards a Real Character and a Philosophical Language* (1668), a vast and astonishing work (the term 'Essay' in the title is misleading), which contains among other things an attempt to summarize and organize all conceptual knowledge. The starting point is, for example, that a *dog* is a kind of *animal* and an *animal* is a kind of *physical object* and a *physical object* is a kind of *entity*. Wilkins assumed that all concepts could be arranged in hierarchies of this sort, applying this hierarchical schema to all words and concepts in a way that would be language universal. This central part of Wilkins's *Essay* is a forerunner of Roget's famous *Thesaurus* (1852), as Peter Mark Roget himself acknowledged. It is also a direct predecessor of WordNet (Miller 1985, Fellbaum 1998). In the words of Eco (1995), Wilkins' *Essay* was 'the most complete project for a universal and artificial philosophical language that the seventeenth century was ever to produce.' As a preliminary step, Wilkins undertook a review of all knowledge, 'to establish what the notions held in common by all rational beings really were.' The philosopher and logician Leibniz attempted an emulation in Latin of Wilkins' work, including a 'table of definitions,' but abandoned it after compiling only a few entries. The difficulty, in a world before Linnaeus, of building a satisfactory conceptual hierarchy of this sort can be illustrated with the word *dog*. Wilkins starts this part of his ontology by remarking that 'Beasts . . . may be distinguished by their several shapes, properties, uses, foods, their tameness or wildness, etc.' He lumps dogs together with cats as being 'rapacious' but not 'cloven-footed.' He distinguishes dogs from wolves because wolves howl but dogs bark, bay, or yelp. Here, as Eco remarked, Wilkins seems to be reaching for the modern concept of hypertext. 'Rapacious beasts of the dog-kind' include not only *dogs* and *wolves*, but also *foxes* and *badgers* and 'amphibious beasts of the dog-kind,' namely *seals*. (Seals bark, don't they?)

Only a person of overweening intellectual self-confidence and demented energy could have even dreamed of such an undertaking. One of many questions begged by it is: can a Wilkinsian hierarchy of concepts be equated with or represented satisfactorily by a lexical hierarchy? It must be admitted that badgers and seals have quite a lot in common with dogs, wolves, and foxes. However, any schoolchild nowadays will tell you that neither seals nor badgers are really 'of the dog-kind.' The place of dog in a post-Linnaean hierarchy such as WordNet is rather different from the place assigned to it by Wilkins.

The full conceptual hierarchy for *badger* in WordNet is:

> badger > musteline mammal > carnivore > placental mammal > mammal > vertebrate > chordate > animal > organism > living thing > whole > object > physical entity > entity

The conceptual hierarchy for *dog* begins with canine > carnivore. Thus, badgers are included in a set, not only with dogs, but also with all other carnivores, including felines (cats, lions etc.—'rapacious beasts,' in Wilkins's terminology) but also bears, 'procyonids' (whatever they may be—raccoons, apparently), and 'fissiped carnivorous mammals.' It will be readily seen that this conceptual hierarchy has little to do with everyday usage of language and very much to do with the organization of scientific concepts.

The great philosophers of the seventeenth century, including not only Wilkins and Leibniz but also Hobbes, Comenius, and others, took it for granted that the obvious vagueness and fuzziness of word meaning were defects of natural language, which ought to be rectified. It was not until the twentieth century, with the work of Wittgenstein,

Putnam, Rosch, and others, that an alternative view began to emerge, namely that vagueness and fuzziness might be essential properties—design features, we might say—of natural language. The natural human yearning for conceptual precision can easily be satisfied by creating stipulative definitions (e.g. I hereby assert that an *idea* is a kind of *concept* and not vice versa), but we should not imagine that such definitions can be equated with the meaning of terms in a natural language. The task of the present-day lexicographer is to account for the vague and variable conventions of word meaning in natural usage, not to build conceptual hierarchies.

Confusion between scientific concept meaning and natural-language word meaning continue to bedevil the study of meaning in language, and the false assumptions that it has generated must bear at least part of the responsibility for some of the failures of linguistics in Natural Language Processing. The attempt to make language precise was based on false assumptions about the relationship between scientific concepts and the everyday meaning of words, and these are with us to this day. Lexicography has, so far, been slow to respond to the challenges and insights of twentieth-century linguistic philosophy and anthropology.

22.13 CONCLUSION AND FUTURE PROSPECTS

In this brief survey of lexicography throughout the world from earliest times, I have tried to show how dictionaries have played a central role, not only in linguistics (the study and understanding of language), but also in the many and various conceptualizations of human cultures. A dictionary is an inventory of words, and an inventory of words is an inventory of basic beliefs. Such beliefs may or may not be well founded, and a dictionary may or may not do a good job of encapsulating them, but if the lexicographer does not take a stand and fashion a view of the beliefs of the culture that he or she is describing, then dictionary definitions cannot be written at all. A consequence of this is that definitions in monolingual dictionaries are necessarily circular: all words are defined in terms of other words. Logicians sometimes complain about this so-called circularity of dictionary definitions, and linguists such as Wierzbicka and Goddard (2002), following the lead of the Port-Royal grammarians (Arnauld and Nicole 1662), have attempted to break the vicious circle by selecting a small number of basic words as indefinable logical primitives, which are universals in terms of which the meanings of all other words in all language can be defined.

> It would be impossible to define every word. For in order to define a word it is necessary to use other words designating the idea we want to connect to the idea being defined. And if we wished to define the words used to explain that word, we would need still others and so on to infinity. Consequently, we necessarily have to stop at primitive terms which are undefined. (Arnauld and Nicole 1662)

The logic of this is impeccable, but it has nothing to do with either language or beliefs in the everyday world. In reality, it is certainly true that some words are broader in semantic scope than others—*say* is broader in scope than *whisper*, for example—but the steps from broad to narrow are more of a tangled hierarchy than an orderly progression. In practice, it is perfectly possible to compose a usable and true statement about any of the terms (such as *say*) identified by Wierbicka and Goddard as 'semantic primitives,' though only at the cost of circularity. The best that a practical lexicographer can hope to do is to accept the circularity but avoid direct reciprocity. If a dictionary defines a *helix* as a spiral and a *spiral* as a helix, it is vicious: something more must be said at one entry or the other, for example 'winding in a continuous curve . . .'.

Thus, dictionary definitions teeter uneasily on the sharp edge between the blindingly obvious and the philosophically profound. And then dictionaries nowadays are expected to give other information about words: most importantly about their orthography and morphology (inflections), but also about pronunciation, grammatical word class, and etymology or word history.

As a general rule, lexicography is accretive; one dictionary builds on another. Radical innovations do occur (*WDG*, for example, and COBUILD), but they are few and far between. We have seen that there are many motivations for compiling a dictionary. In recent centuries, the main motive has been to compile an inventory of the words of a language, with summary information about conventions of usage and belief associated with each word. In the past, the function of lexicography was perceived more strongly as being to control and regulate the language. Sometimes a dictionary may have an influence on social attitudes to language. For example, the highly practical Modern Greek dictionary of Babinyiotis was one more nail in the coffin of the movement to create a 'purified' language (*katharevousa*), expunging words of Turkish and other non-classical origin.

In the Arabic, Hebrew, Persian, and Indian traditions, a motivation for lexicography was facilitation of poetry, and this motivation is also found in the modern English-speaking world in a modest form with the publication of rhyming dictionaries. During the Renaissance in Europe, the principal motivation for some of the greatest dictionaries ever compiled was the preservation and understanding of culture and heritage, in particular the heritage of ancient Latin and Greek literature. Surprisingly, bilingual lexicography was a slow starter. In Europe from classical times up to the seventeenth century, it was expected that all educated and civilized people would be able to talk to one another in Latin, so vernacular words were merely appended to monolingual Latin dictionaries, in particular the series of dictionaries known as 'calpines' after Ambrogio Calepino.[7] It was not until the Enlightenment in Europe that the compilation of bilingual dictionaries became standard practice, although there were a few important precursors, notably Palsgrave (1530). In the twentieth century, bilingual lexicography

---

[7] See Ch. 14 above.

led the field in terms of understanding the importance of phraseology for language understanding.

More commercial motives arose in the twentieth century with the advent of dictionaries for second-language learners, a practical tradition founded by A. S. Hornby in the 1940s and now a multi-million dollar business worldwide.

In the twenty-first century the business model for dictionary publication is rapidly switching from paper to online formats, and the user community has expanded to include machines: lexicography has to include provision for the needs of computational linguists and programs for natural language processing. Lexicography is currently in a state of transition. The Internet affords unrivalled opportunities for new lexicographical research, but at the same time the traditional business model of funding new developments in lexicography from prospective sales has collapsed. The book trade itself, too, is in crisis, and many booksellers are going out of business. Hardback reference books no longer sell. The public has come to expect reference information to be free via the Internet, but unfortunately, this has opened the floodgates to a mass of free but inadequate, misleading, and even incorrect lexicographic information. Developments in electronic lexicography are surveyed from a variety of different viewpoints by a variety of authors in Granger and Paquot (2012).

....

CHAPTER 23

THE LOGICO-PHILOSOPHICAL TRADITION

....

PIETER A. M. SEUREN

23.1 THE PROPOSITION

....

HISTORY is not about the past but about understanding the present. This applies in particular to modern formal semantics, which cannot be understood without going back to at least its Aristotelian roots. Latching on to Plato's teaching, Aristotle developed his theory of truth as correspondence, basing it on his notion of *proposition*.

The notion of proposition has had many interpretations and definitions through the centuries (Nuchelmans 1973, 1980, 1983). Let us briefly summarize its origin. We find the *notion* of proposition, but not the *term*, first discussed at large in Plato's dialogue *The Sophist*, where Plato (427–347 BCE) discusses the notion of truth as correspondence between, on the one hand, the (possibly linguistically expressed) thought content of mentally assigning a property to an entity and, on the other, that which 'is'—the metaphysical notions of 'being' and 'not-being' taking up a large part of the text. This thought content then becomes by its very nature the bearer of a truth value, true or not true (false).

Aristotle (384–322 BCE), in his *On Interpretation* (*Int*) and *Prior Analytics* (*PrAn*), takes up some issues dealt with in Plato's *Sophist*, in particular the notion of the mental act of assigning a property to an entity, for which he then thinks up the Greek term *prótasis*, literally 'the act of putting forward,' or *propositio* in Latin. The term *prótasis* occurs for the first time on page one of Aristotle's *Prior Analytics* (written after *Int*), where it is defined as 'an affirmative or negative expression (lógos) that says something of something' (*PrAn* 24a16). Aristotle wavers between a verbal and a cognitive notion of proposition, but he always takes the proposition to be the primary bearer of a truth value. In his *Metaphysics* (1027b25) he clearly opts for the cognitive notion: 'For falsity and truth are not properties of actual things in the world . . . but properties of thought.'

So let us define a *proposition* as *the mental act of assigning a property to one or more entities.* A proposition differs from a sentence in that (a) a proposition is a *hic et nunc*, unique occurrence, whereas a sentence is a type-level linguistic unit, realizable as an utterance, and (b) a sentence type, as well as its expression as a token utterance, is more than a mere proposition, in that a sentence (utterance) must of necessity incorporate a proposition into a larger whole, the *intent*, in which a proposition is subordinated to a *speech act operator* of assertion, question, command, wish, etc. (Seuren 2009: ch. 4). This latter point was well known to Aristotle, who wrote (still using the term *lógos* instead of *proposition*) (*Int* 17a2–4):

> But not every *lógos* is an assertion. Only a *lógos* that has the quality of being true or false is an assertion. But this is not always the case. For example, a *lógos* can be a wish, in which case it is neither true nor false. We will disregard the others, as they are more properly dealt with in the study of rhetoric or poetry. Our present investigation concerns assertions only.

This is why the logico-philosophical tradition has, rightly or wrongly, always concentrated exclusively on the propositional aspect of grammar and semantics, leaving the speech act factor out of account. Since Austin (1962), speech act theory has been considered part of *pragmatics* rather than *semantics*, but this is justifiable only if semantics is equated with logic, or considered to be part of it, as is usually done in possible world semantics (PWS) introduced by Richard Montague during the 1960s. To the extent that semantics is not equated with the strictly formal logical framework of PWS but is more oriented towards the cognitive and socially binding aspects of sentences as linguistic types instantiated by utterance tokens, speech act theory comes into view as a separate chapter in semantics. In the present historical survey of the logico-philosophical tradition, speech act theory has no place, since it is not or hardly part of the logical or the philosophical tradition in language studies.[1] Speech act theory was first developed by philosophers (Lewis 1946, Austin 1962), but was soon appropriated by pragmaticists (Levinson 1983).

A proposition thus consists of an entity representation and a property representation. The former mentally represents that to which the property is assigned, Aristotle's *hypokeímenon*, Latinized as *subiectum* 'that which lies underneath'; the latter

---

[1] There is a small body of PWS literature on speech acts, notably Hintikka (1974), Hamblin (1976, 1987), Karttunen (1977), Stalnaker (1978), Hoepelman (1981), and Groenendijk and Stokhof (1984), but this literature focuses on the delimitation of sets of possible worlds in the context of information state modelling—a formal specification of what is asserted, asked, ordered, etc., and thus a study of propositions rather than of speech acts. Little or nothing, however, is said about what making an assertion, issuing an order, or asking a question actually amounts to in terms of socially binding human interaction and relations.

represents the property assigned, Aristotle's *katēgoroúmenon*, Latinized as *praedica-tum*.[2] The notion of proposition thus defined is of central importance to the study of language because the whole conglomerate of interrelated systems forming human natural language, what the French call *le langage*, is in the service of allowing speakers to commit themselves socially with regard to assigning properties to entities (of whatever nature) and expressing such assignments in some perceptible symbolic form under a speech act or commitment operator. If one does not understand the propositional principle, one will be unable to understand language.

23.2 DISCOURSE AND TOPIC-COMMENT MODULATION (TCM)

What was never realized until the 1850s is that the mental act of assigning a property to an entity is by definition context-bound, since the entity is selected from what the current thought is about and a new utterance tends to be presented as an answer to a question that has arisen, explicitly or implicitly, from what has been said before (Seuren 1985: 295–304). In modern terms: the entity forms the *topic* and the property assigned is the *comment*, and sentences are taken to have, besides a grammatically defined *syntactic structure*, a discourse-driven *topic-comment modulation* or TCM, usually but far from always expressed through intonational means.

Unaware of this discourse parameter, the first grammarians, working in ancient Alexandria from the third century BCE onward, transferred the Aristotelian *logico-philosophical* analysis of the proposition into subject and predicate to the *grammatical* analysis of sentences. From then on, a sentence was considered to consist of a *subject* constituent and a *predicate* constituent, the former referring to a world entity (of whatever nature or complexity), the latter to the property mentally assigned. The predicate constituent could encompass subsidiary terms such as a direct or indirect or prepositional object. With Greek and Latin as model languages, the subject term was thus definable as the term occurring in the nominative case, the direct object as the term occurring in the accusative case, etc.

---

[2] Note that the term *hypokeímenon* (*subiectum*) denotes the entity to which the subject term refers, while the *katēgoroúmenon* (*praedicatum*) is a constituent in a proposition, *casu quo* a sentence. Aristotle had no term for the sentence constituent we now call the *subject* (*term*). During the Middle Ages, the term *subiectum* came to be used mainly for the propositional or grammatical constituent, while the term *suppositum* 'that which has been placed below,' an alternative Latin translation of the Greek *hypokeímenon*, was mainly used for the world entity that the subject term refers to. Yet sometimes the terms *subiectum* and *suppositum* were used the opposite way. For a more detailed exposition see Seuren (1998: 121–3, 2009: 85–94).

During the 1850s, a number of (mostly German) scholars realized, however, that this grammatical analysis did not match the Aristotelian definition of the proposition. Steinthal (1823–99) formulated the problem thus (1860: 101–2):[3]

> One should not be misled by the similarity of the terms. Both logic and grammar speak of subject and predicate, but only rarely do the logician and the grammarian speak of the same word as either the subject or the predicate. [...] Consider the sentence *Coffee grows in Africa*. There can be no doubt where the grammarian will locate subject and predicate. But the logician? I do not think the logician could say anything but that 'Africa' contains the concept that should be connected with 'coffee grows.' Logically one should say, therefore, 'the growth of coffee is in Africa.'

Steinthal and his fellow scholars, such as Georg von der Gabelentz (1840–1893) or Wilhelm Meyer-Lübke (1861–1936), still failed to isolate the discourse parameter, but this was soon remedied by scholars like Philipp Wegener (1848–1916), Theodor Lipps (1851–1914), and above all the Cambridge scholar George Stout (1860–1944), who posited that a new assertive utterance tends to be meant and interpreted as an answer to an implicit or explicit question that has arisen in the current discourse.

Between roughly 1870 and 1930, the question of the incongruity of syntactic structure on the one hand and the original (discourse-bound) Aristotelian analysis of a proposition into subject and predicate on the other dominated the debate in the theory of language (as opposed to the theory of language change). Distinctions were made between linguistic, psychological, and logical subject and predicate, but no clear conclusions could be drawn owing to the imprecision of the concepts at issue. Around 1930, the debate petered out for lack of clarity and the general attention shifted to matters to do with formal linguistic structure rather than meaning.

Nowadays, some eighty years later, the nineteenth-century subject–predicate debate has been largely forgotten. Only in the Prague School of linguistics, led by Peter Sgall and Eva Hajičová, has knowledge of this tradition been preserved, partly because of the political and cultural isolation of eastern Europe between 1939 and 1990. It was here that term pairs were developed like *theme* and *rheme*, or, more commonly, *topic* (*focus*) and *comment*.

Around 1970, the issue was revived in the West in the guise of pragmatically oriented research into what is called *information structure*, a term meant to cover what is considered to be the vague border area of pragmatics and grammar, closely connected with TCM. Yet this revival took place without any awareness of the history preceding it and of its basic significance for the theory of language. The Aristotelian and nineteenth-century background to the notions of TCM and information structure has been completely forgotten. This has contributed to a state of affairs in which key notions such as TCM, topic, focus, comment are not properly defined. Knowledge of history would show the practitioners that *topic* and *comment* correspond to Aristotle's

---

[3] For a survey and ample discussion of the question of the incongruity between the Aristotelian notion of the proposition and syntactic structure, see Seuren (1998: 120–33, 2010: 378–91).

subject and *predicate*, respectively, though these terms are now reserved for standard grammatical analysis.

23.3 EUBULIDES AND THE PARADOXES

During Aristotle's own lifetime, his truth theory was attacked by the philosopher Eubulides (*c.*405–330 BCE), who came from Miletus in Asia Minor but taught philosophy in Megara, not far from Athens (Seuren 2005). He is one of the founders of the highly influential school of the Stoa, which lasted until the very end of antiquity, running over into early Christianity. He is the almost forgotten author of four so-called 'paradoxes,' known under different names, according to the sources, but reducible to the following four: *the Liar, Electra, Sorites*, and *the Horns*. They were all meant to show the inadequacy of Aristotle's theory of truth as correspondence. Aristotle, who was a bitter personal enemy of Eubulides, had no answer to these paradoxes and managed, using his enormous influence, to make the world believe that they were flippant pranks, of no value to philosophy. But for the Liar paradox, which was popular in medieval philosophy as an 'insoluble' and was rediscovered in modern logic but without attribution to Eubulides, the Eubulidean paradoxes have been largely forgotten or at best survive as mere anecdotal lore, even though they define central elements in twentieth-century semantics. William and Martha Kneale, in their book on the history of logic, express their doubt that

> Eubulides produced them in an entirely pointless way, as the tradition suggests. He must surely have been trying to illustrate some theses of Megarian philosophy, though it may be impossible for us to reconstruct the debates in which he introduced them. (Kneale and Kneale 1962: 114–15)

Yet despite the Kneales, the name Eubulides rings no bell among modern philosophers, logicians or semanticists.

The paradoxes are all illustrated with the help of one or more counterexamples to Aristotle's truth theory, which states (a) that every proposition is by nature either true or false, without any possible middle or any possible third truth value, and (b) that a proposition is true just in case it 'corresponds' with reality and false otherwise. Let us look at each paradox in turn.

The Liar paradox consists in the fact that a well-formed sentence like (1a), which refers to itself, must be false if true and true if false:

(1)   a. This very sentence is false.
       b. This very sentence is numbered (1b).

Modern logicians say that (1a) violates the principle that object language and metalanguage must not be mixed in one sentence. Since the phrase *this very sentence* belongs to the metalanguage, (1a) is illicit. However, natural language is replete with such 'violations' without any semantic difficulties: a sentence like (1b) also violates the principle but does not produce a paradox. The logicians' answer thus amounts to overkill.

The proper answer seems to be that (1a) is *uninterpretable* because it does not express a proposition: the predicate *false* in (1a) requires as part of its meaning description a proposition as reference object of its subject term, but the phrase *this very sentence*, when taken to refer to the proposition underlying (1a), leads to an infinite regress, so that no proposition comes about for lack of subject-term reference. In (1b), by contrast, the phrase *this very sentence* refers to the linguistic product, which is there, can be referred to and be numbered. This makes (1b) fully interpretable and, in fact, true.

The Electra paradox is illustrated by a story. On his return home from the Trojan war, Agamemnon, king of Mycenae, is killed by his wife Clytemnestra, who has set up house with a lover. This puts the son Orestes in a moral predicament, because he has to avenge his father's death by killing the murderer. But that means killing his mother, which again is a horrible crime. To make up his mind, he leaves Mycenae for a while and decides that he must kill his mother. He returns to the palace in Mycenae, disguised as a beggar. His sister Electra does not recognize him, and puts him in the kitchen with something to eat. Eubulides, the storyteller, now asks whether, given that (2a) is true, (2b) is also true:

(2)   a. Electra knows that the beggar is in the kitchen.
       b. Electra knows that her brother Orestes is in the kitchen.

According to Aristotle, (2b) must be true if (2a) is true, because the terms *the beggar* and *Orestes* refer to the same person and truth and falsity depend on how the world is, not on the words used to establish reference—the principle of *substitution salva veritate* (SSV) formulated by Leibniz around 1700. Yet natural intuition says that, in the story, (2a) is true but (2b) false. This problem, which was rediscovered by Frege in his famous 1892 article without his knowing about Eubulides, has been the central factor in the coming about of present-day formal semantics, whose practitioners are still, on the whole, unaware of the fact that Frege's discovery in 1892 was preceded by Eubulides' Electra paradox.

The Sorites paradox, or paradox of the heap (Greek *sōrós* 'heap'), is an attack on Aristotelian bivalence and a defence of 'vague' or 'fuzzy' truth values: one grain of sand does not make a heap; nor do two or three, but ten thousand do. Where exactly does it begin to be true that there is a heap of sand? Observations such as these have had wide repercussions in modern semantics and logic (for fuzzy logic see Zadeh 1975), even though the name Eubulides is hardly ever mentioned in this context.

The paradox of the horns lies at the basis of presupposition theory. It is illustrated by the following fallacy:

(3)   What you haven't lost you still have. You haven't lost your horns. *Ergo*: you still have horns.

If this were a correct argument, every person would 'have horns,' that is, be a cuckold.[4] Aristotle had no answer other than saying that this was silly. Modern presupposition theory (Seuren 2010: 311–77) tells us that *You have lost your horns* presupposes that the addressee had horns before and that its negation *You haven't lost your horns*, with unmarked *n't*, preserves this presupposition. Hence the, so far correct, conclusion. But the Greek (and English) negation word also occurs in a non-default, marked meaning that cancels any presuppositions. In this interpretation of *n't*, the conclusion does not follow. Since most people do not 'have horns' in whatever sense, they escape the conclusion by appealing to the non-default sense of the negation word. But this solution of the paradox involves two negations, giving distinct truth conditions and hence a non-bivalent logic.

Again, most modern presupposition theorists, including Frege (1892) and Strawson (1950, 1952, 1954, 1964), were or are unaware of the Eubulidean origin of presupposition theory. During the Middle Ages, presuppositions were not distinguished as a category in their own right but were treated under the rubric 'exponibles' (Seuren 2010: 314–16), in that a sentence like *I have lost my keys* is to be 'exposed' into the two sentences *I had my keys before* (the presupposition) and *I do not have my keys now* (the assertion). By that time, knowledge of Eubulides had already been lost.

The four Eubulidean paradoxes thus summarize the main problem areas that gave rise to modern formal semantics.

23.4 THE CORRESPONDENCE QUESTION

23.4.1 The Correspondence Question in the Middle Ages

When Aristotle says that a proposition is true just in case it corresponds with reality and false otherwise, the question arises of what is meant by the term 'reality' and what sort of mapping is intended by the term 'correspond.' The question of what constitutes reality has, of course, occupied metaphysics through the centuries. The question of correspondence, by contrast, became a central element in the philosophy of language around 1250 when, after a millennium of near-oblivion, Aristotle's texts became fully accessible to the Latin-speaking world first through translations into Latin from the Arabic and later through direct translations from the Greek originals.

The first and highly influential answer was given by the essentialist 'modist' school of philosophy, which flourished from *c.*1250 to *c.*1320, when it was superseded by the new nominalists (Bursill-Hall 1972, Covington 1982, Seuren 1998: 31–9). The modists held that there is, in principle, a one-to-one correspondence between the *ontological categories* of the world or 'modes of being,' the *cognitive categories* of the mind or 'modes

---

[4] It is safe to assume that Eubulides, who was versed in rhetoric and always up for a good laugh, chose this undignified example to irritate the extremely formal and prudish Aristotle.

of understanding,' and the *grammatical categories* of language (i.e. Latin) or 'modes of signifying.' This way, the correspondence relations between mind, language, and the world seem simple and transparent. But the doctrine required the acceptance of an extremely rich ontology comprising not only individual entities such as Socrates or the Eiffel Tower, but also universals such as mankind, complex entities such as the military-industrial complex or the average citizen, and even changeable entities such as my phone number or the prime minister, and, in order to accommodate predicate logic, quantified entities such as all humans or some children.

The modists produced a philosophical theory of grammar, *Grammatica Speculativa*, best known through the *Grammatica Speculativa* by Thomas of Erfurt, written around 1300 (Bursill-Hall 1972, Pinborg 1967).[5] To a large extent, speculative grammar was an effort at constructing an ontology that would fit the patterns of the Latin language and was supposed to be reflected as such in the mind. Language was thus regarded as the empirical key to the more remote areas of ontology and cognition.

The essentialist modist ontology, however, was too luxuriant for the taste of the nominalists, such as the Englishmen Walter Burleigh (*c*.1275–after 1344) or William of Ockham (1288–1347), or the Frenchman Jean Buridan (*c*.1300–after 1358). They insisted on a minimalist ontology without universals as ontological entities, and attributed the complexities of reference to a processing machinery in the mind. They thus created a complex theory of reference ('suppositio'),[6] according to which a term can do its reference work in a wide variety of ways.

It is important to realize that, for them, both the subject and the predicate count as 'terms,' so that predicates may 'refer' ('supposit') the way subject terms do, though, in principle, predicates 'refer' to entities of a higher order than the subject terms: predicates always 'refer' to classes.[7]

One thus finds a large number of, sometimes quite baroque, classifications or taxonomies of modes of reference. One such taxonomy, among many competing ones, is presented by Ockham in his *Summa Logicae* (in the example sentences, the terms at issue are printed in italics):

---

[5] The term 'speculative' should not be taken in its modern sense. It just means 'theoretical' (Covington 1982: 47–8). The link with Latin *speculum* 'mirror' (Lyons 1968: 15), as reality was seen as being 'mirrored' in language and cognition, seems to lack justification.

[6] The term *suppositio* 'placing below' in the general sense of 'relation between a term and an entity'— roughly equivalent to what we call 'reference,' or perhaps rather 'extension,' today—probably originates from the term *suppositum* 'that which has been placed below' or 'reference object' described in n. 2 above. Geach's conjecture that *suppositio* was 'apparently in origin a legal term meaning "going proxy for"' (Geach 1962: 56) may well apply to a later reinterpretation of the verb *supponere* (*supposit* in the modern medievalist English jargon). Ockham writes (*Summa Logicae* 193; translation mine): 'We use the word *suppositio* in the sense of "the placing <of a term> for something else," by which is meant that when a term in a proposition "stands" for something in the sense that it is used [. . .] for something that verifies its use, it takes the place of that something.'

[7] For this *term logic* (logica terminorum), see the masterful study De Rijk (1967).

Suppositio:

I personalis
  A *discreta* (*That man* is walking)
  B *communis* (*A man* is a human being)
    1 *determinata* (*Some man* is a human being)
    2 *confusa*
      a *confusa tantum* (Every man is *a human being*)
      b *confusa distributiva* (*Every man* is a human being)
        i *mobilis* (*Every man* is a human being)
        ii *immobilis* (*Every man except Jim* is a human being)
II *simplex* (*Man* is a species)
III *materialis* (*'Table'* is a noun)

The first thing that strikes one is that quantified terms are taken to 'refer.' Modern quantification theory has shown, to the satisfaction of most, that they do not, and that the logical and semantic analysis of quantification requires an analytical machinery with quantifiers and variables. Given such a machinery, the question of modes of reference is simplified considerably—though far from solved—in that the entire complex class of *suppositio personalis communis* (IB) can be dispensed with.

A complicating factor is, moreover, that Latin, unlike the modern European languages, has no articles: no form distinction is made between a noun phrase meaning 'the man' and one meaning 'a man' or 'some man' or simply 'man.' This linguistic idiosyncrasy has unnecessarily confused and complicated medieval theories of reference, while at the same time calling for such a theory.

One important reason for the new nominalists to lay the burden of explanation on the mind rather than on a luxuriant ontology was drawn from the fact that modes of reference are not automatically selected given the type of sentence (proposition) a reference is made in. Speakers and listeners *choose* a mode of reference through an act of interpretation. Mostly, the choice will be determined by the desire to let the sentence (proposition) be true. But an inappropriate selection may be made when a speaker intends the utterance to be a pun or a joke. In fact, as shown in De Rijk (1967), *fallacies* often arise through a silent change of the reference mode. Thus, when I say *'Table' is a noun* and *I bought a table*, the conclusion that *I bought a noun* is fallacious. Likewise, when I say *Some man is brave* and *Man is a species*, the conclusion that *A species is brave* is fallacious. It is clear that such reference mode changes are *mental* occurrences and cannot be explained in a modist framework, where the mind is a passive reflection of reality.

Nominalism has, on the whole, won the day. Modern philosophers are keen on minimizing their ontologies and attributing the complexities of language to the workings of the mind.

23.4.2 The Correspondence Question in the Twentieth Century

Between, say, 1600 and 1900, nothing much happened regarding the question of the correspondence relation between what is thought or said on the one hand and what is the case on the other. Since 1900, however, there has been a revival of the medieval debate, though no longer from the perspective of the triangular relation between language, thought, and reality but rather from the more restricted binary perspective of language and reality, the mind being largely ignored. The key names are Gottlob Frege (1848–1925) and Bertrand Russell (1872–1970).

23.4.2.1 *Frege*

For Frege, the cognizing mind was still an important factor, though he felt uneasy about it. Language was but a sideshow for him; his real interest lying in the development of formal arithmetic. Yet his contributions to natural language semantics have been monumental, for three main reasons: (a) his development of a formal logical language, (b) his (re)discovery of the blocking of SSV (*substitution salva veritate*) in intensional (partiscient) contexts, and (c) his broaching of the question of presuppositions. We deal with (a) and (b) here; the question of presuppositions is discussed in §23.5.

Frege developed a formal language to make explicit the logical processes of the properly thinking mind, and by implication their reflexes as found in natural language. The formal language he developed for this purpose, his *Begriffsschrift* (Frege 1879), was a direct inspiration for Whitehead and Russell in their *Principia*. The foremost innovation in these formal languages is the fact that they distinguish a new category of logical constants, the quantifiers.

Then, Frege presented some problems regarding SSV. SSV had been formulated by Leibniz (1646–1716) in various writings. Give or take a few textual variations, SSV runs as follows:

> Eadem sunt quae sibi mutuo substitui possunt salva veritate. [Entities are identical when terms referring to them can be mutually substituted without change in truth value.]

If truth consists in a correspondence between what is said and what is the case, as Aristotle wants it, it should make no difference whether term *a* or term *b* is used to refer to a given entity, as long as the entity is successfully referred to. Thus, whether I say (4a) or (4b), if the one is true the other is too and likewise for when they are false, precisely because the terms *morning star* and *evening star* refer to the same object, the planet Venus:

(4)   a. The morning star is inhabited.
      b. The evening star is inhabited.

Frege spotted two problems with regard to SSV. The first is to do with true identity statements such as (5):

(5)   The morning star is the evening star.

Substitution gives either *The morning star is the morning star* or *The evening star is the evening star*. But these two sentences are necessarily true, while (5) is only contingently true and may express an empirical discovery. This points to a complication.

The second problem, which restates Eubulides's Electra paradox, is even more unsettling. It consists in the fact that in clauses embedded under verbs with epistemic content (one may speak of *partiscient verbs*), SSV no longer holds. Thus (6a) may be true while (6b) is false and vice versa, depending on whether Harry does or does not know that the two 'stars' are the same object:

(6)   a.   Harry believes that the morning star is inhabited.
      b.   Harry believes that the evening star is inhabited.

This sentence pair corresponds directly with (2) above. Clauses under partiscient verbs such as *believe* or *know* are said to be 'intensional contexts' ('partiscient contexts' is a better term), and SSV fails to apply in such contexts. The question is: why? The whole framework of twentieth-century possible world semantics (PWS) was set up to answer this question.

Frege's answer was that one must distinguish between the 'extension' (*Bedeutung* reference) and the 'intension' (*Sinn* sense) of (a) terms, (b) predicates and (c) sentences, as in Fig. 23.1. He thus extended the traditional distinction between extension and intension from predicates to definite terms and sentences (propositions). Traditionally, a predicate's extension was (is) the class of entities it can be truthfully applied to, and its intension the conditions to be fulfilled for the predicate to yield truth when applied to, an entity. Frege extended this distinction to definite terms, whose extension he took to be the entity referred to and whose intension the procedure followed by the mind to arrive at the intended reference object, the mental 'search procedure,' and to sentences, whose extension he took to be their truth value and whose intension the underlying thought.

In addition, he posited the special category of clauses in intensional (partiscient) contexts, whose extension Frege took to be identical with the intension the clause would have if used independently: its underlying thought. The intension of a clause in a partiscient context Frege left undefined. Now, since *The morning star is inhabited* and *The evening star is inhabited* have different intensions (underlying thoughts), they have

	Extension	Intension
Definite term	entity	search procedure
Predicate	set of entities	concept (satisfaction conditions)
Sentence	truth value	thought
Clause in partiscient context	←	???

FIG. 23.1 Frege's position with regard to extensions and intensions

different extensions when used as subordinate clauses under a partiscient predicate, as in (6a, b). Therefore, these clauses, and *a fortiori* their subject terms, do not allow for SSV.

This analysis has been criticized mainly for two reasons. First, twentieth-century semanticists objected to the 'idealist' notions of thought and concept, replacing these with quasi-extensional notions of possible worlds and truth conditions defined in terms of them. Then, to take truth values as the extension of sentences goes against the nominalist minimalist conception of the world: truth values are not elements in the world we speak about. Frege, who was not a nominalist, could put up with this, but later generations of nominalist semanticists objected. The remedy proposed in PWS was to consider a proposition P to be the set of possible worlds in which P is true. However, as is widely known (Dowty et al. 1981: 175), this answer runs foul of the objection that sentence pairs like (7a,b) or (8a,b), whose embedded clauses express necessary truths, as in (7), or necessary falsities, as in (8), must be equivalent pairs because the extensions of their embedded propositions equal the set of all possible worlds (for (7)) or the null set of possible worlds (for (8)):

(7)   a. Harry believes that all bachelors are unmarried.
      b. Harry believes that the square root of 144 is 12.

(8)   a. Harry believes that all bachelors are married.
      b. Harry believes that the square root of 144 is 13.

This, of course, is not so in natural language: the (a)-sentences may be true and the (b)-sentences false or vice versa. This problem, known as the problem of propositional attitudes, has not been solved so far, which means that the possible world approach may have to be rejected *in toto*.

23.4.2.2 *Russell*

Russell never said anything much on the question of SSV in partiscient contexts. He concentrated on the question of reference to nonexisting entities, as in his famous sentence (9a), which he analysed as (9b) (Russell 1905):

(9)   a. The present king of France is bald.
      b. $\exists x \, [\text{KoF}(x) \land \text{Bald}(x) \land \forall y \, [\text{KoF}(y) \rightarrow x = y]]$
         (there is an x such that x is king of France and x is bald and for all y, if y is king of France, y is identical with x)

France having no king, now or in 1905, the question is: is (9a) true or false? The question is justified, as Aristotle requires every sentence (proposition) to be either true or false and nothing else (strict bivalence). Russell answered that it is false, because there is no x such that x is king of France, which suffices for the falsity of (9b). Flushed with enthusiasm over the discovery of the quantifiers and preparing for the seminal work *Principia Mathematica* he was to write a few years later together with Alfred North Whitehead (1861–1941), he dissolved the definite referring phrase *the present king of France* into a construction with quantifiers, dismissing the normal syntactic analysis of (9a) into a referring subject term and a predicate.

This analysis acquired the grand name of Russell's Theory of Descriptions. It quickly became standardly accepted among philosophers of language and formally inclined semanticists, despite the weighty arguments against it. One objection is that it eliminates the reference function of definite noun phrases—a central function of natural language. (9b) reads as *Some king of France is bald and identical to all kings of France*— not at all what (9a) means. Then, Russell's analysis fails to account for the maintenance of reference through texts, as appears from (10):

(10)   Harry believes that I bought a Ferrari and he fears that the Ferrari will be stolen.

If analysed according to Russell, there are at least two possibilities, depending on where the existential quantifier is placed. (For the sake of brevity, the uniqueness clause 'for all *y*, if *y* is king of France, *y* is identical with *x*' is omitted in (11a,b). The argument remains unaffected when it is properly incorporated.) In (11a), one quantifier stands over the whole sentence; in (11b), the quantifier occurs twice. Both violate the true meaning of the sentence. (10) is not about a specific really existing Ferrari, which is what (11a) says, nor does it say that Harry believes that I bought a Ferrari and fears that a Ferrari will be stolen, which is what (11b) says:

(11)   a. $\exists x$ [Ferrari(x) $\wedge$ Believe(H, Buy(I,x) $\wedge$ Fear(H, Be Stolen(x)]
         (there is an *x* such that (*x* is a Ferrari and Harry believes that I bought *x* and Harry fears that *x* will be stolen))
       b. Believe(H, $\exists x$ [Ferrari(x) $\wedge$ Buy(I,x)] $\wedge$ Fear(H, $\exists x$ [Ferrari(x) $\wedge$ Be Stolen(x)]
         (Harry believes that there is an *x* such that (*x* is a Ferrari and I bought *x*) and Harry fears that there is an *x* such that (*x* is a Ferrari and *x* will be stolen))

Further play with quantifier positions is possible, but no quantifier placement will render the meaning of (10).

A similar problem arises with sentences of the following types:

(12)   a. If Pedro has a donkey, he feeds it.
       b. All farmers who have a donkey feed it.
       c. If a farmer has a donkey, he feeds it.

Such sentences are called 'donkey sentences' because of their appearance in Peter Geach's influential book (1962).[8] Again, the problem is one of quantifier scope and variable binding. The overall conclusion must be that the celebrated Russellian formal language of predicate calculus is inadequate for the rendering of the meanings of natural language sentences.

---

[8] What is not generally known is that Geach took his donkey examples from Walter Burleigh, who, in his *De puritate artis logicae* of *c.*1328, gave examples like (Burleigh 1988: 92) *Omnis homo habens asinum videt illum* ('Every man owning a donkey sees it'). See Seuren (2010: 300–301) for further comment.

It took the best part of the twentieth century for the world of philosophy and semantics to realize that Russell's theory is untenable as an analysis of definite descriptions. The problem of donkey sentences made Hans Kamp and others realize that sentences have inbuilt devices that link them up with preceding discourse. In order to account for donkey sentences, he developed his Discourse Representation Theory or DRT (Kamp 1981, Kamp and Reyle 1993). DRT is one of a series of approaches, each positing a memory store for the representation of propositional content built up during previous discourse. Each new utterance is considered to be an addition, in the technical jargon an 'increment,' to the store as built up thus far. Apart from its failure to integrate cognition into natural language semantics (owing to its lasting allegiance to PWS), the main shortcoming of DRT is its failure to deal with presuppositions, without which no discourse-oriented semantic theory can be adequate (see §23.5).[9]

23.4.2.3 *Model-theoretic or Possible World Semantics*

Model-theoretic or possible world semantics (PWS) came about as an attempt to apply to natural language the method of model-theoretic semantics developed for logical languages around the middle of the twentieth century. The main figure, in this context, is Richard Montague (1930–71), who developed an ingenious method to reduce surface sentences of English to equivalent formulae in the Russellian language of predicate calculus and hence to compute their truth values for any set of worlds given term denotations and predicate extensions in each world (Montague 1970, 1973). In this method, the meaning of a sentence equals the proposition expressed by it, which again equals the set of possible worlds in which it receives the value 'true.'

During the 1970s and after, this theory was thought to constitute a breakthrough in the semantics of natural language and gained widespread popularity, mainly because of what was seen as its mathematical sophistication. Now, in the early twenty-first century, the initial enthusiasm has been subsided somewhat, mainly because it is becoming ever more apparent that this theory, though mathematically sophisticated, fails to account for the cognitive element in natural language, without which any semantic theory will fail. We have already seen, in §23.4.2.1, that PWS is essentially unable to solve the problem of propositional attitudes, a failure that is entirely due to the programme of reducing all cognitive content to sets of possible worlds and the inability to account for cognitive content in terms of cognitive content—that is, of virtual reality.

The philosophical and psychological foundations of PWS are shaky, as it considers the mind to be a mere reflection of the world and not an autonomous processing device whose output is input to language and language use. Being a branch of mathematics and not of linguistics, it professes the ideal of full formalization, not realizing that most elements of cognition are too complex to allow for formalization, given the techniques

---

[9] The attempt made by Van der Sandt (1992) to equate presuppositions with anaphora must be considered futile (for a detailed critique see Seuren 2010: 372–7).

available. The result is a stilted and artificial theory that may be useful in the context of computer languages but has little relevance for the semantics of natural language.

23.5 THE DISCOURSE FACTOR

That language is made for coherent texts and not just for isolated sentences is an insight that broke through relatively late. It has already been shown that the Aristotelian notion of proposition was, unbeknownst to Aristotle and the many generations after him, a discourse notion, closer to topic-comment than to syntactic subject-predicate structure. We have also seen that, around 1850, this led to a dilemma of two-tiered structure but that the analytical means available were insufficient, with the result that the subject–predicate debate petered out around 1930, though it came to life again around 1970, in the form of pragmatically oriented studies in 'information structure'— by which time the Aristotelian past had been totally forgotten.

During the same period it began to be clear that the discourse factor is essential from a semantic point of view. Natural language sentences are tailored to fit into certain contexts and not others: a sentence S imposes conditions on any preceding discourse D for D to remain coherent after the incrementation of S. This is manifest in three ways: (a) topic-comment modulation (TCM); (b) maintenance of reference relations (anaphora); (c) presuppositions.

TCM has been discussed above. It must be added that, contrary to widespread belief, TCM is of a semantic, not just a pragmatic, nature. This appears from the fact that TCM differences in clauses embedded under an emotive factive verb such as *be angry* or *be surprised* or *resent*, as in (13), or in factive clauses under *because* or *although*, as in (14), give rise to different truth conditions (see Seuren 2010: 406–8):

(13) a. Joan resented that HARRY had sold the car.
         (Joan resented that it was HARRY who had sold the car.)

      b. Joan resented that Harry had sold THE CAR.
         (Joan resented that it was THE CAR that Harry had sold.)

(14) a. Joan left the firm because HARRY had sold the car.
         (Joan left the firm because it was HARRY who had sold the car.)

      b. Joan left the firm because Harry had sold THE CAR.
         (Joan left the firm because it was THE CAR that Harry had sold.)

Clearly, (13a) may be true while (13b) is false, and vice versa, and likewise for (14a) and (14b). In emotive and motivational factive contexts, therefore, substitution of TCM makes a truth-conditional, and thus a semantic difference. This fact is as relevant as Frege's discovery that SSV in partiscient contexts makes a truth-conditional, and thus a semantic, difference. Yet it has not so far been incorporated into semantic theory.

As regards maintenance of reference or (external) anaphora relations, it has been shown above that the standard Russellian language of predicate calculus is unable to account for these phenomena, unless this language allows for definite terms (including definite pronouns). And even then it will not be up to this task. The reason is that maintenance of reference through texts cannot be captured in terms of a fully formalized system, since available world knowledge, as well as default and probability factors, play an important role. A sentence like (15), for example, is understood in such a way that the person referred to by the phrase *the 56-year-old bachelor* is identical with the person referred to by the phrase *a Swiss banker*:

(15)   Last night a Swiss banker was arrested at Heathrow Airport. The 56-year-old bachelor declared that he had come to Britain to kidnap the Queen.

Had the subject term of the second sentence been, for example, *the driver*, the sentence would have been uninterpretable, not for any formally definable reason but simply because our default knowledge makes no connection between a banker and a driver in the context given.

Like speech act theory, presupposition theory started late, around 1950. Both arose in the context of the so-called ordinary language philosophy practised at Oxford between 1945 and 1970. Attention was drawn to presuppositions in Frege's seminal (1892) article, but it was not until Strawson (1950) that modern presupposition theory came off the ground. Strawson rejected Russell's Theory of Descriptions and proposed that referring phrases should be recognised as such. For him, the existence entailment of a sentence like (9a) or (16a) is a matter of presupposition, not of existential quantification. For Strawson, an uttered sentence lacks a truth value when its presupposition is not satisfied. That this is not so follows from the examples given below.

Presuppositions are lexically defined coherence conditions of sentences on proper discourses (see Seuren 2010: ch. 10). Examples are given in (16), where the presupposition follows the » symbol.

(16)   a. John is bald » John exists
       b. John is divorced. » John was married before.
       c. John knows that it is raining » It is raining.
       d. Only John laughed. » John laughed.

One empirical test is that a presupposition followed by its carrier sentence after *and* or *but* gives a coherent bit of text:

(17)   a. John exists and he is bald.
       b. John was married before and/but he is divorced.
       c. It is raining and John knows it is.
       d. John laughed and only John laughed.

Another empirical test is that the presupposition is preserved under ordinary default negation:

(18)   a. John is not bald. » John exists
       b. John is not divorced. » John was married before.
       c. John doesn't know that it is raining » It is raining.
       d. Not only John laughed. » John laughed.

Yet in most but not all cases it is possible to insert an emphatic negation that cancels the presupposition and thus allows for the addition of the negated presupposition. This is possible for (18a,b,c), but not for (18d)—the reason being that the negation in (18d) occurs in a noncanonical position (before *only*):

(19)   a. John is NÓT bald. He does not exist!
       b. John is NÓT divorced. He never got married!
       c. John does NÓT know that it is raining. It ISN'T raining!
       d. *NÓT only John laughed.

The fact that grammatical and lexical conditions may prevent the occurrence of the presupposition-cancelling negation, as in (19d) and many other cases (Seuren 2010: 334–42), shows that this is not a matter of pragmatics, as maintained, for example, in Wilson (1975), but that there are two logically distinct negations: an unmarked default negation and a marked metalinguistic, discourse-correcting negation. It follows that the logic of language must be taken to be trivalent, with two distinct kinds of falsity: 'minimal falsity' for cases where the presupposition remains intact and 'radical falsity' for cases where the presupposition is cancelled—a conclusion independently reached in Dummett (1973: 425–6). The resulting trivalent logic is elaborated in Seuren (2010: 354–72).

   Like anaphora, presupposition does not allow for a fully formalized treatment, nor are they pragmatic consequences following from the use of sentences. This appears from the fact that presuppositions are retrievable from their carrier sentences regardless of context, which shows that they are part of the language system.[10] It follows that presuppositions can be inserted *post hoc*, a phenomenon usually called 'accommodation.' For example, when I utter (20a), I need not first say (20b), even though (20b) is a presupposition of (20a). The reason is that our world knowledge tells us that it is normal for people to have a nose:

(20)   a. John broke his nose.
       b. John had a nose.

When such a post hoc accommodation is not supported by world or contextual knowledge, the text becomes incoherent. Thus, accommodation of (21b) is blocked (the text becomes incoherent) unless the context has explained what John is doing with a wheel:

(21)   a. John broke his wheel.
       b. John had a wheel.

Accommodation is a powerful means made available by natural language to economize on the effort of speaking: presuppositions need not be explicitly uttered, as they are

---

[10] See also §26.4.2 below.

retrievable from their carrier sentences. But this implies that presupposition theory, like anaphora theory, is not fully formalizable. It is probably for this reason that 'standard' formal semantics, which insists on full formalization, has always preferred to leave anaphora and presupposition phenomena to pragmatics and has always resisted analyses that treat them as semantic phenomena.

CHAPTER 24

....

LEXICAL SEMANTICS FROM SPECULATIVE ETYMOLOGY TO STRUCTURALIST SEMANTICS

....

DIRK GEERAERTS

THE present chapter contains an overview of the development of word meaning research up to the era of structuralist semantics: after a brief introduction to the pre-nineteenth-century traditions, we have a closer look at historical-philological semantics, and at structuralist semantics, comprising lexical field theory, componential analysis, and relational semantics. Further developments in lexical semantics are included in Chapter 25 below. For a more detailed view of the history of lexical semantics, see Geeraerts (2010).

24.1 THE EMERGENCE OF LEXICAL SEMANTICS

....

Lexical semantics as an academic discipline in its own right originated in the early nineteenth century, but that does not mean that matters of word meaning had not been discussed earlier. Three traditions are relevant: the tradition of speculative etymology, the teaching of rhetoric, and the compilation of dictionaries. Let us see what each of the three traditions involves, and how it plays a role in the birth of lexical semantics as an academic enterprise.

24.1.1 The Etymological Tradition

To understand the tradition of speculative etymology that reigned before the birth of comparative philology in the beginning of the nineteenth century, we have to go back to classical antiquity. In Plato's dialogue *Cratylus* (which may be regarded as the oldest surviving essay in the philosophy of language),[1] Hermogenes argues with Socrates and Cratylus about the view that language is not conventional, but is rather subject to a criterion of appropriateness (Cratylus 383a, 383c–d). According to the naturalist theory defended by Cratylus, the names of things should be 'right' in a very fundamental sense: they express the natural essence of the thing named. Assuming that words are essentialist descriptions of the things they name, but at the same time taking for granted that the superficial form of the word as it has come down to us may hide its original constitution, etymological analysis takes the form of looking for the hidden original meaning of words. This type of speculative etymology, of which the work of Isidore of Seville (see Barney et al. 2006) is one of the best-known examples, was fully accepted up to the birth of comparative philology. (A detailed overview of the etymological tradition is found in Klinck 1970. A historical survey of etymological thinking in the past two centuries, in contrast with the practice of etymology in antiquity and the Middle Ages, is provided by Malkiel 1993.) An example may indicate the level of fancifulness reached in medieval etymological thinking. The etymologies for Latin *mors* 'death' suggested in antiquity associate the word either with *amarus* 'bitter' or with *Mars*, the god of war 'who inflicts death.' Medieval authors by contrast drew the explanation of the word from the realm of Christian theology. The fifth-century treatise *Hypomnesticon* is the first to link *mors* to *morsus* 'bite,' an etymology that would be repeated by many authors: in the Christian tradition, death became a reality for the human race when the serpent in the Garden of Eden persuaded Adam and Eve to take a bite of the forbidden fruit, and God subsequently expelled them from the earthly paradise for having eating from the Tree of the Knowledge of Good and Evil.

Such an analysis strikes us as fanciful, but what exactly is it that distinguishes a speculative etymology from a scientific one? Typically, the speculative etymologies have two specific characteristics. First, while they are based on a comparison of meanings (Allan 2010a suggests that the better ancient etymologists try to identify what we would now call lexical relations, as in §24.3.3 below), they take a lot of licence with the forms involved. Second, the entities they compare are words occurring within the same language. The etymological approach that fits into the comparative philological model that developed in the nineteenth century has exactly the opposite features. First, it is primarily based on a comparison of forms rather than a comparison of meanings, and second, it focuses on the comparison of related forms in different languages. In other words, the tradition of comparative philology with which scientific linguistics came into being in the late eighteenth and early nineteenth century

---

[1] See §13.3 above.

straightforwardly rejected the type of thinking about word meaning that was part of the tradition of speculative etymology.

At the same time, the birth of semantics within that young linguistic science was not just a question of completeness, but rather one of necessity. The study of meaning was not simply taken up out of a desire to study linguistic change in all of its aspects, but a thorough knowledge of the mechanisms of semantic change appeared to be a prerequisite for adequate historical investigations into the formal aspects of languages—and precisely, as a safeguard against curious and far-fetched etymologies. The methodology of comparative reconstruction requires that the word forms from different languages that are to be compared with each other, be semantically related. But such a relationship is not always obvious: considering a number of lexical forms as cognate requires that their semantic relationship can be plausibly established, and this in turn requires an overview of the regular mechanisms of semantic change. The development of diachronic lexical semantics, in other words, fits logically into the shift from speculative etymology to comparative historical linguistics.

24.1.2 The Rhetorical Tradition

We just saw that as a first factor in the birth of linguistic semantics, the age-old tradition of speculative etymologizing of word meanings was rejected, in favour of an approach that would identify and classify regular mechanisms of semantic change. But if this was the initial programme for lexical semantics, where could it start looking for those mechanisms? This is where the rhetorical tradition comes in. Rhetoric—the skill of using language to achieve a certain purpose, in particular, to persuade people—was a traditional part of the school curriculum from classical antiquity through the Middle Ages up to modern times. (For a history of rhetoric, see Kennedy 1994 for a discussion of the classical era and Fumaroli 1999 for the period from the fifteenth to the twentieth century. More directly relevant for the study of figures of speech is Lausberg 1990, a monumental overview of the concepts of classical rhetoric.)

Rhetoric was traditionally divided into five parts: invention (the discovery of ideas for speaking or writing), arrangement (the organization of the text), style (the formulation of the ideas), memorization, and delivery. From the point of view of semantics, it is the stylistic component that is particularly important. The tradition of rhetoric (which takes the physical form of a long series of treatises and textbooks) developed a large number of concepts to identify specific figures of speech, or 'rhetorical tropes': ways of formulation that would embellish a text or attract the attention of the audience. Some of these figures of speech are formal in nature, like alliteration, others are syntactic, like asyndeton, but a number of tropes refer to lexical and semantic phenomena, like euphemism, the substitution of an inoffensive or less offensive word for one that might be unpleasant. Metaphor and metonymy in particular are two fundamental semantic phenomena that will appear again and again in linguistic semantics, and that loomed large in the rhetorical tradition.

24.1.3 The Lexicographical Tradition

The emerging discipline of lexical semantics was faced with a task (to chart regular patterns of semantic behaviour) and came equipped with an initial set of descriptive concepts (the rhetorical tropes), but what was its descriptive basis? Where did the examples come from? One source of examples derived from philological research into older texts, specifically, classical and Biblical philology. Because the interpretation of the Greek, Latin, and Hebrew texts is often not immediately obvious, classical scholars naturally came across many intriguing instances of polysemy and semantic change. It is not a coincidence, from this perspective, that many of the earliest writers on semantic change were classical philologists. This holds for Karl Reisig, who may be credited with the oldest work in the historical-philological tradition (1839), but also for scholars like Haase, Heerdegen, Hey, and Hecht.

Another source of raw materials came from lexicography. Specifically, the nineteenth century witnessed the birth of the large-scale descriptive dictionary on diachronic principles, i.e. the historical dictionary that intended to chart the development of the language from the earliest origins to the present day. Major examples include the *Deutsches Wörterbuch* (started by Jacob and Wilhelm Grimm, 1854–1954), the *Dictionnaire de la langue française* (by Emile Littré, 1877), the *Oxford English Dictionary* (founded by James Murray, 1884–1928), and—the largest dictionary in the world by any count—the *Woordenboek der Nederlandsche Taal* (started by Matthias de Vries in 1864, finished 1998). Crucially, these grand historical dictionary projects derive from the same concern as diachronic lexical semantics: a fascination with the correct description of the historical development of words and meanings. They testify that the nineteenth-century interest in the semantic histories of words led to an hitherto unsurpassed amount of descriptive work. As another indication of the intellectual link between theoretical semantics and lexicographical practice, we may note that a number of important theoreticians in the field of diachronic lexical semantics were also editors of major dictionaries: Paul compiled a *Deutsches Wörterbuch* (1897), and Darmesteter co-edited a *Dictionnaire général de la langue française* (Darmesteter and Hatzfeld 1890).

24.2 HISTORICAL-PHILOLOGICAL SEMANTICS

The first stage in the history of lexical semantics as an academic discipline runs from roughly 1830 to 1930. Its dominant characteristic is the historical orientation of lexical

semantic research: its main concern lies with changes of word meaning—the identification, classification, and explanation of semantic changes. Although a wealth of
theoretical proposals and empirical descriptions was produced along these lines of
research, most of it is not well known to contemporary researchers. An aspect of this
lack of familiarity is that the tradition is not known under a standard name. We could
talk about 'traditional diachronic semantics,' if we want to highlight the main thematic
and methodological orientation, or about 'prestructuralist semantics' if we want to
focus on its chronological position in the history of the discipline, but I will opt here for
the term 'historical-philological semantics.'

The most accessible and comprehensive reference work about the period treated in
this section is Nerlich (1992). It individually discusses the various scholars of the
historical-philological era, for Germany, France, and the Anglo-Saxon world, with a
rich bibliography that points the way to many more primary and secondary publications than can be mentioned here. The older overviews of historical-philological
semantics remain valuable sources, though. Kronasser (1952) and Quadri (1952) provide
minute thematically organized summaries of existing research in semasiology and
onomasiology respectively, while Baldinger (1957) is a succinct outline of the tradition.

24.2.1 Dominant Features of Historical-philological Semantics

I have mentioned that when lexical semantics originates as a linguistic discipline,
speculative etymology serves as a negative role model; lexicography and textual philology provide an empirical basis of descriptive lexicological data, and the tradition of
rhetoric offers an initial set of terms and concepts for the classification of lexical
semantic phenomena. But what exactly does the new-born discipline do with these
starting-points? We may characterize the approach from a descriptive and a theoretical
perspective.

Descriptively speaking, classifications of semantic change are the main empirical
output of historical-philological semantics, and an in-depth study of the historical-
philological era would primarily take the form of a classification of such classifications.
Characteristically, the classificatory efforts of historical-philological semantics do not
stop at the level where we find high-level phenomena like metaphor and metonymy,
but also search for lower-level patterns of semantic development. While Albert Carnoy's 1927 and Gustaf Stern's 1931 classifications of semantic changes represent the final
stage of the heyday of historical-philological semantics, it is typical that in systems like
Stern's and Carnoy's, the classificatory depth is considerable: basic categories are
divided into subclasses, which may then be divided into further subclasses, and so
on, almost ad infinitum. As a consequence, works like Carnoy (1927) and Stern (1931),
but also Nyrop (1913) or Waag (1908), remain copious treasures of examples for anyone
interested in processes of semantic change: regardless of the classificatory framework
they employ, the wealth of examples amassed in these works continues to amaze.

Theoretically, the dominant conception of meaning of historical-philological semantics may be characterized in two ways. First, it is a psychological conception of meaning, in a double sense. Lexical meanings are considered to be psychological entities, that is to say, (kinds of) thoughts or ideas. Further, meaning changes are explained as resulting from psychological processes; the general mechanisms that are supposed to underlie semantic changes, and whose presence can be established through the classificatory study of the history of words, correspond with patterns of thought of the human mind. A concept like metonymy, for instance, is not just a linguistic concept, but also a cognitive capacity of the human mind.

To illustrate these points, we may refer to Bréal (1897), one of the theoretically crucial authors in this tradition. With regard to the first aspect of a psychological conception of meaning, Bréal thinks of meanings as psychological entities, i.e. (kinds of) thoughts or ideas: '(Le langage) objective la pensée [Language makes thought objective]' (Bréal 1897: 273). The mental status of lexical meanings links up directly with the overall function of thinking, i.e. with the function of cognition as a reflection and reconstruction of experience. With regard to the first aspect of a psychological conception of meaning, Bréal suggests that the general mechanisms of semantic change that can be derived from the classificatory study of the history of words constitute patterns of thought of the human mind. Bréal calls these mechanisms 'les lois intellectuelles du langage [the conceptual laws of language],' but he hastens to add that 'law' means something different here than in the natural sciences (1897: 338–9).

The second important feature of the theoretical position of historical-philological semantics is the importance it attaches to the contextual flexibility of meaning: meanings change over time, but in order to explain that change, we need to take into account how meanings change in specific contexts. For a clear theoretical formulation of the point, we may turn to the work of Hermann Paul, another highly influential figure in this tradition.

The first pillar of Paul's approach involves the distinction between the 'usual' and the 'occasional' meaning of an expression. The usual meaning (*usuelle Bedeutung*) is the established meaning as shared by the members of a language community. The occasional meaning (*okkasionelle Bedeutung*) involves the modulations that the usual meaning can undergo in actual speech (1920 [1880]: 75). If the *usuelle Bedeutung* is like the semantic description that would be recorded in a dictionary (fairly general, and in principle known to all the speakers of a language), then the *okkasionelle Bedeutung* is the concretization that such a general concept receives in the context of a specific utterance. The second pillar of Paul's conception of semantics is the insight that context is all-important in understanding the shift from usual to occasional meaning: it is precisely the interplay of contextual triggers and usual meanings can give rise to occasional meanings. Paul thus develops what we would now call a pragmatic, usage-based theory of semantic change: the foundation of semantic change is the modulation of usual meanings into occasional meanings, and if this happens often enough, the occasional one gets entrenched as a new usual one. So, the mechanisms of semantic change that semanticians are so eager to classify are essentially the same mechanisms that allow speakers to modulate those usual meanings.

24.2.2 Alternative Trends within Historical-philological Semantics

The conception of meaning that is so clearly expressed by Bréal and Paul is the mainstream view of historical-philological semantics: by and large, it is the view of writers like Wegener (1885), Hecht (1888), Hey (1892), Stöcklein (1898), Thomas (1894, 1896), Waag (1908), Erdmann (1910) in Germany, Paris (1887), Roudet (1921), and Esnault (1925) in France, Wellander (1917, 1921) in Sweden, Nyrop (1901–34, 1913) in Denmark, Van Helten (1912–13) in The Netherlands, Whitney (1875) and Oertel (1902) in the US. But it is not the only view, and it did not gain prominence immediately. Here, we will identify the main alternative tendencies within historical-philological semantics.

A. The psychological orientation did not emerge clearly before the middle of the century. In the first half of the nineteenth century, up to the 1860s, the focus lay on the mere identification of regular patterns of semantic development and the classification of those pathways of change, rather than on the cognitive background of such phenomena. This approach, which is often called 'logical-classificatory' or 'logical-rhetorical' in contrast with 'psychological-explanatory,' may be found in the work of Reisig (1839), Haase (1874–80), and Heerdegen (1875–81).

B. Whereas a psychological approach attributes agency to the individual language user, some approaches tend to talk metaphorically about the language as such as an agent of change, a perspective that is sometimes coupled to the idea of an organic 'life of the language.' Arsène Darmesteter's *La vie des mots* (1887, initial publication in English 1886) is a prominent example of such an organicist metaphor. Somewhat similarly, some approaches emphasize collective rather than individual agency, as in Wundt's *Völkerpsychologie* (or 'peoples' psychology'): given that language is a collective entity rather than a purely individual one, the mind that is expressed in the language is primarily the mind of a people—a *Volksgeist*, in other words, the typical 'spirit of a nation or people' that defines their specific identity. Wundt developed the *Völkerpsychologie* by focusing on three types of symbolic expression: language, myths, and customs. Not surprisingly, then, one of the ten volumes of his monumental *Völkerpsychologie* (1900) is devoted entirely to language and semantic change.

C. A number of scholars take a social rather than psychological perspective. The sociosemantic approach originates in the work of Antoine Meillet (1906); it is further represented by Vendryès (1921) and to some extent by Nyrop (1913). The essential idea is that the social group in which a word is used may differentiate between polysemous readings of a word, or may lead to meaning change. That is how Meillet explains the meaning 'to arrive' of French *arriver*, which etymologically means 'to reach the shore.'

Arriver is derived from Latin **ad-ripare*, in which *ripa* is 'shore.' Within the social group of sailors, disembarking has the consequence of reaching one's destination, and when the word is taken over by the larger community of language users, only the latter reading is retained.

D. Although basically concerned with semasiological changes, the major treatises from Reisig (1839) to Stern (1931) do not restrict themselves to purely semasiological mechanisms like metaphor and metonymy, but also devote attention to mechanisms of onomasiological change like borrowing or folk etymology. (The term 'onomasiology' itself was introduced by Adolf Zauner 1903 in his study on body-part terms in the Romance languages.) The onomasiological focus was not very systematic, though. A specifically onomasiological tradition emerged in the margin of the overwhelmingly semasiological orientation of historical-philological semantics, viz. the *Wörter und Sachen* ('words and objects') movement inaugurated by Rudolf Meringer (1909) and Hugo Schuchardt (1912). The principal idea is that the study of words, whether etymological, historical, or purely variational, needs to incorporate the study of the objects denoted by those words. As Meringer (1912) noted, in an article defining the scope and purpose of the journal *Wörter und Sachen* that he launched in 1909, 'Bedeutungswandel ist Sachwandel... und Sachwandel ist Kulturwandel [Semantic change is object change, and object change is cultural change].' The basic perspective is not so much 'What do words mean?' but 'How are things named and classified through language?'

24.2.3 The Impact of Historical-philological Semantics

Even though most of the work in historical-philological semantics has become inaccessible to a contemporary international audience, the intrinsic value of this tradition should not be underestimated. The empirical scope of the framework is remarkable, even by present-day standards: a multitude of examples from a wide variety of languages serves to illustrate and define a broad variety of theoretical concepts. Next to the contribution of historical-philological semantics to the study of particular lexicological phenomena, the approach has a lasting theoretical importance because it draws the attention to two concepts that play a fundamental role in the assessment of any theory of lexical semantics. First, historical-philological semantics highlights the dynamic nature of meaning: meanings are not immutable, but they change spontaneously and routinely as language is applied in ever new circumstances and contexts. Second, the historical-philological approach raises the question how language relates to the life of the mind at large.

On the downside, the predominantly semasiological and diachronic approach of historical-philological semantics implies that the synchronic structure of the vocabulary receives less attention. But then those aspects of semantics constitute the focal point of the structuralist tradition, which dominates the next phase in the development of lexical semantics.

24.3 STRUCTURALIST SEMANTICS

Taking its inspiration from the structuralist conception of language that is basically associated with the work of Ferdinand de Saussure, structuralist lexical semantics is the main inspiration for innovation in word meaning research from the 1930s until well into the 1960s. The central idea is the notion that language has to be seen as a system, and not just as a loose bag of words. Natural languages are symbolic systems with properties and principles of their own, and it is precisely those properties and principles that determine the way in which the linguistic sign functions as a sign.

Among the large variety of theoretical positions and descriptive methods that emerged within the overall lines set out by a structuralist conception of meaning, three broad strands may be distinguished: lexical field theory, componential analysis, and relational semantics. Broad overviews of (different kinds of) structuralist semantics—often as chapters in a work of broader scope—are provided by Lehrer (1974), Coseriu and Geckeler (1981), Kastovsky (1982), Lipka (2002). Introductions to and overviews of lexical field theory are provided by Öhmann (1951a, 1951b), Quadri (1952), Spence (1961), Hoberg (1970), Geckeler (1971a, 1971b). An advanced introduction to componential analysis is Leech (1974); for an introduction from a more descriptive point of view, see Nida (1975). For the relational approach, see Lyons (1963, 1977), Evens et al. (1980), Cruse (1986), and Murphy (2003).

24.3.1 Lexical Field Theory

The view that language constitutes an intermediate conceptual level between the mind and the world inspired the metaphorical notion of a lexical field: if you think of reality as a space of entities and events, language so to speak draws lines within that space, dividing up the field into conceptual plots. A lexical field, then, is a set of semantically related lexical items whose meanings are mutually interdependent and that together provide conceptual structure for a certain domain of reality. (We may note that the terminology of lexical field theory is relatively unstable. Mostly, 'lexical field,' 'semantic field,' and 'word field' are treated as synonyms, but some authors have suggested distinct readings among these items.) We first introduce the notion of lexical field as introduced by Trier, and then discuss two distinct forms of field analysis that emerged after Trier.

Although the theoretical basis of the lexical field approach was laid by Weisgerber (1927), the single most influential study in the history of lexical field theory is Jost

Trier's monograph *Der Deutsche Wortschatz im Sinnbezirk des Verstandes. Die Geschichte eines sprachlichen Feldes* (1931). In this work, Trier gives a theoretical formulation of the field approach, and investigates how the terminology for mental properties evolves from Old High German up to the beginning of the thirteenth century. In Trier (1932, 1934) an appendix was added which dealt with Middle High German, but the study which he originally anticipated, and which intended to trace the lexical field in question up to contemporary German, was never completed. Theoretically, Trier starts from the fundamentally structuralist insight that only a mutual demarcation of the words under consideration can provide a decisive answer regarding their exact value. Words should not be considered in isolation, but in their relationship to semantically related words: demarcation is always a demarcation relative to other words. Trier illustrates the idea with the image of a mosaic. The substance of human knowledge, the contents of cognition is divided by language into a number of adjoining small areas, in the way in which a mosaic divides two-dimensional space by means of contiguous mosaic stones (1931: 3).

To get an idea of how Trier brought this theoretical view into descriptive practice, we will focus on Trier (1934), in which a sub-area of the vocabulary concerning intellectual properties is dealt with, viz. the words denoting knowledge. At the beginning of the thirteenth century, courtly language possessed three core notions referring to types of knowledge: *wîsheit*, *kunst*, and *list*. The distinction between the latter two reflects the architecture of the medieval class society. *Kunst* conveys the knowledge and skills of the courtly knight (viz. courtly love, the chivalric code of honour, and the liberal arts), whereas *list* is used to indicate the knowledge and the skills of those which do not belong to the nobility (such as the technical skills of the craftsmen). *Wîsheit* is a general term which is used for the noblemen as well as for citizens; it was predominantly employed in a religious and ethical sense, similar to the Latin *sapientia*. One could say that *wîsheit* referred to the general ability to occupy one's position in society (whichever that might be) with the appropriate knowledge and skills. The general term *wîsheit* indicated that the distinct spheres of the noble *kunst* and the civil *list* were embedded in a common religious world order.

A century later, the division of the field had undergone considerable changes. *List*, which gradually acquired a derogative sense, somehow conveying 'artfulness, shrewdness,' was replaced by *wizzen*, which does not however have exactly the same meaning as the earlier *list*. *Kunst* and *wîsheit* as well acquired a different scope. *Wîsheit* ceased to be a general term. It conveyed a specific type of knowledge: instead of the original reading, referring to knowledge of one's own position in the predestined divine order and the skills required to occupy that position no longer matter, *wîsheit* now referred to religious knowledge in a maximally restricted sense, i.e. the knowledge of God. *Kunst* and *wizzen* indicated higher and lower forms of profane knowledge, without specific reference to social distinction. *Wizzen* gradually began to refer to technical skills, like the skills of a craftsman, whereas *kunst* started to denote pure forms of science and art.

Lexical fields as originally conceived are based on paradigmatic relations of similarity. One extension of the field approach, then, consists of taking a syntagmatic point of view. There are in fact two ways in which a syntagmatic analysis was suggested to be relevant for structuralist semantics. First, words may have specific combinatorial features which it would be natural to include in a field analysis. Traditionally, the possibilities for combining words with other words are looked at mainly from a purely syntactic point of view. The fact, for instance, that a word like *take* belongs to the syntactic category 'verb' implies that it can be combined with a noun as its subject. In 1934, however, the German linguist Walter Porzig pointed out that syntagmatic combinability has as much to do with aspects of meaning as with grammatical characteristics. If one asks someone: *Gehen sie oder fahren sie nach Hause?* 'Will you walk or drive home?,' the choice that person is faced with is between going on foot and going by car, since these are designated by German *gehen* and *fahren* respectively. To identify these syntagmatic lexical relations, Porzig introduced the term *wesenhafte Bedeutungsbeziehungen* 'essential meaning relations.' For a considerable period in the development of structural linguistics, these syntagmatic affinities received less attention than the paradigmatic relations, but in the 1950s and 1960s, the concept surfaced under different names in structuralist and generativist semantics: Firth (1957) uses the term 'collocation,' Katz and Fodor (1963) talk about 'selection restrictions,' Weinreich (1966) mentions 'transfer features,' and Coseriu (1967) discusses *lexikalische Solidaritäten* 'lexical solidarities.'

The second way in which the syntagmatics of lexical items could play a role in lexical field analysis is more radical than the mere incorporation of lexical combinatorics into the notion of lexical field: if the environments in which a word occurs could be used to establish its meaning, structuralist semantics could receive a firm methodological basis. The general approach of a distributionalist method is summarized by J. R. Firth's famous dictum: 'You shall know a word by the company it keeps' (1957: 11). A similar assumption is expressed by the 'distributional hypothesis' as formulated by Harris (1954a): words that occur in the same contexts tend to have similar meanings. We will see in Chapter 25 of this volume how this idea inspired the development of corpus-linguistic studies of word meaning. At this point, while we are still dealing with the earlier stages of structuralist semantics, we may refer to Apresjan (1966) for a concrete implementation of an early form of distributionalism; see also Dubois (1964).

Trier's use of the mosaic image was not a happy one. To begin with, the image suggests that the mosaic covers the whole surface of the field, i.e. that there are no gaps in the lexical field, that no pieces are lacking in the mosaic. This *Lückenlosigkeit* (absence of hiatuses) is contradicted by the existence of lexical gaps, i.e. gaps in the lexical field that occur when a concept that for reasons of systematicity seems to be a bona fide member of the conceptual field is not lexicalized. A further assumption that can be deduced from the image of the mosaic, is that fields are, internally as well as externally, clearly delineated, i.e. that the words in a field, like mosaic pieces, are separated by means of sharp lines, and that different fields link up in the same clear-cut way. The whole lexicon would then be an enormous superfield divided into huge but clearly delineated sets, which in turn break up into smaller field structures, and so on until we reach the ultimate level of the mosaic stone, the word. This compartmentalization of the lexicon was criticized from different angles. In a study that anticipates types of research that would become characteristic for cognitive semantics (see Chapter 25), Helmut Gipper (1959) points out that the borderline between concepts tends to be diffuse. As a consequence, it is often difficult to indicate exactly where a field ends; discreteness will usually only be found in the core of a field, whereas there is a peripheral transition zone around the core where field membership is less clearly defined.

In this respect, it is worth mentioning that Trier (1968), looking back on the development of lexical field theory, regrets that he failed to correct the mosaic image. This could have avoided, he admits, unnecessary confusion with regard to the character of lexical fields. The image of the closely fitting word and field boundaries, Trier suggests, should be substituted by a star-like conception of lexical fields in which the centre of the field sends out beams that are able to reach other cores with their extreme ends. Otto Ducháček (1959) proposes a graphical representation of a lexical field that nicely illustrates such a star-like conception.

24.3.2 Componential Analysis

Componential analysis, the second main approach that needs to be distinguished within structuralist semantics, is a logical development from lexical field theory: once you have demarcated a lexical field, the internal relations within the field will have to be described in more detail. It is not sufficient to say that the items in the field are in mutual opposition—these oppositions will have to be identified and defined. Componential analysis is a method for describing such oppositions that takes its inspiration from structuralist phonology: just as phonemes are described structurally by their position on a set of contrastive dimensions, words may be characterized on the basis of the dimensions that structure a lexical field. Componential analysis provides a descriptive model for semantic content, based on the assumption that meanings can be described on the basis of a restricted set of conceptual building blocks—the semantic 'components' or 'features.' Componential analysis was developed in the second half of the 1950s and the beginning of the 1960s by European as well as American linguists, largely independently of each other. Although both find a common inspiration in structural phonology, componential analysis in Europe grew out of lexical field theory, whereas in the United States, it originated in the domain of anthropological linguistics without any specific link to European field theory. Its major impact would not come from its European branch, but from its incorporation into generative grammar: the appearance of Katz and Fodor's famous article 'The Structure of a Semantic Theory' (1963) marked a theoretical migration of lexical semantics from a structuralist to a generativist framework. As this transition lay at the basis of major new developments in lexical semantics, it will be discussed in Chapter 25.

The American branch of componential analysis emerged from linguistic anthropology, in studies like Kroeber (1952), Conklin (1955), Goodenough (1956), and Lounsbury (1956). To illustrate, we will have a closer look at Goodenough's (1956) analysis of the kinship terms of the Micronesian language Truk. The first major step in the analysis consists of the identification of the referential denotata of the kinship expressions. Thus, *semenapej* refers to father, father's father, and mother's father: in an abbreviated notation Fa, FaFa, MoFa. The second major step is again similar to what happens in structuralist phonology: different phonemes are distinguished on the basis of distinctive features, with each feature occupying a specific position on a contrastive dimension. For the description of Truk kinship terms, Goodenough uses letters to identify nine relevant dimensions. For instance, A represents the general characteristic of being related to the reference person (ego). B indicates generation, with the values B_1 for a senior generation, B_2 for the same generation, and B_3 for a junior generation. These generations have a culture-specific definition that differs from the usual genealogical one, but the specifics of that definition need not detain us here. C is the sex of the relative, with C_1 for male and C_2 for female. J_1 is lineal. *Semenapej* can now be componentially defined as $AB_1C_1J_1$: it refers to all male members of an older generation than ego's of whom ego is a direct descendant (fathers and grandfathers).

In Europe, the first step in the direction of componential analysis can be found in the work of Hjelmslev (1961), but the full development does not occur before the early 1960s, in the work of Pottier (1964, 1965), Coseriu (1962, 1964, 1967), and Greimas (1966). For a brief illustration, we may refer to the work of Pottier. Pottier provides an example of a componential semantic analysis in his description of a field consisting, among others, of the terms *siège*, *pouf*, *tabouret*, *chaise*, *fauteuil*, and *canapé* (a subfield of the field of furniture terms in French). The word which acts as a superordinate to the field under consideration is *siège*, 'seating equipment with legs.' If we use the dimensions s1 'for seating,' s2 'for one person,' s3 'with legs,' s4 'with back,' s5 'with armrests,' s6 'of rigid material,' then *chaise* 'chair' can be componentially defined as [+s1, +s2, +s3, +s4, −s5, +s6], and *canapé* 'sofa' as [+s1, −s2, +s3, +s4, +s5, +s6]. The parallelism with Goodenough's method of description will be obvious: underlying dimensions structure the field, and the meaning of any single term in the field is established by the sum of the specific positions of the term on each of those dimensions.

As suggested, the European branch of componential analysis played a minor role in the further development of lexical semantics. This is predominantly due to the fact that approaches like those of Pottier and Coseriu penetrated with difficulty in the international forum of linguistics of the last decades, which had a decidedly Anglo-Saxon orientation. Even so, the predominant impact of American componential analysis did not prevent the European tradition from being further developed. Important names within this tradition are Heger (1964), Geckeler (1971a,b), and Baldinger (1980).

24.3.3 Relational Semantics

Relational semantics further develops the idea of describing the structural relations among related words, but restricts the theoretical vocabulary that may be used in such a description. In a componential analysis, descriptive features like gender and generation in a system of kinship vocabulary are real-world features; they describe the real-world characteristics of the referents of the described words. But structuralism is interested in the structure of the language rather than the structure of the world outside of language, and so it may want to use a different type of descriptive apparatus, one that is more purely linguistic. Relational semantics, as introduced by Lyons (1963), looks for such an apparatus in the form of sense relations like synonymy (identity of meaning) and antonymy (oppositeness of meaning): the fact that *aunt* and *uncle* refer to the same genealogical generation is a fact about the world, but the fact that *black* and *white* are opposites is a fact about words and language.

Instead of deriving statements about the synonymy or antonymy of a word (and in general, statements about the meaning relations it entertains) from a separate and independent description of the word's meaning, the meaning of the word could be defined as the total set of meaning relations in which it participates. A traditional (or perhaps naïve) conception of synonymy would, for instance, describe the meaning of both *quickly* and *speedily* as 'in a fast way, not taking up much time,' and then conclude to the synonymy of both terms on the basis of the identity in their content description. Lyons by contrast deliberately eschews such content descriptions, and equates the meaning of a word like *quickly* with the synonymy relation it has with *speedily*, plus any other relations of that kind (1963: 59). In a later work he clarifies: 'The question 'What is the sense of x?' . . . is methodologically reducible to a set of questions, each of which is relational: Does sense-relation R hold between x and y?' (1968: 444).

The main contribution to the study of sense relations after Lyons may be found in the work of Cruse, whose 1986 book is the main reference in the following pages. Murphy (2003) is a thoroughly documented critical overview of this research tradition and its current state.

24.3.4 The Impact of Structuralist Semantics

Structuralist thinking had a major impact on lexical semantics: it shifted the attention from an almost exclusive focus on semantic change to the description of synchronic phenomena, and it provoked a change from semasiological to onomasiological studies, i.e. it pushed through the recognition that the vocabulary of the language is not just an unstructured bag of words, but a network of expressions that are mutually related by all kinds of semantic links. The invention of a terminology to describe onomasiological structures is a principal and lasting achievement of structuralist semantics.

Critical points with regard to the structuralist tradition include the following. First, structuralist theorizing underestimates the importance of the semasiological level. In an extreme formulation of the structuralist creed, semasiological analysis as such would be superfluous: if the meaning of a lexical item is exhausted by the onomasiological position or positions it occupies, why bother about a separate analysis of the internal structure of the word? In actual practice, however, it would seem that a semasiological analysis precedes an onomasiological one. Establishing sense relations, for instance, assumes that we know which different meanings a word has (rather than that knowing the sense relations a word enters into establishes which meanings it has). In the post-structuralist era, then, questions involving polysemy will again receive more attention.

Second, the structuralist tenet that it is possible to identify an entirely language-internal level of semantic structure is open to debate. The crucial problem is one of demarcation: if there is an essential distinction between linguistic semantic knowledge as part of the language, and conceptual knowledge in general, as part of our knowledge of the world, where exactly do we find the boundary? Again, this is an issue that plays an important role in the post-structuralist developments that are covered in Chapter 25.

POST-STRUCTURALIST AND COGNITIVE APPROACHES TO MEANING

DIRK GEERAERTS

25.1 THE MAIN LINES OF POST-STRUCTURALIST SEMANTICS

THE present chapter continues the thread of Chapter 24, exploring the development of semantics (with an emphasis on lexical semantics) after structuralist semantics. As was the case for the previous chapter, a more detailed view of the history surveyed here may be found in Geeraerts (2010). The chapter consists of four sections. The first briefly describes the main lines of development of post-structuralist semantics. The second and third introduce the two main theoretical trends of late twentieth-century and early twenty-first century lexical semantics: neostructuralist approaches on the one hand, cognitive and functional ones on the other. The final section reviews some contemporary evolutions, with an emphasis on current methodological developments.

In Chapter 24 we saw how a componential analysis of meaning emerged in the context of a structuralist conception of semantics. The major breakthrough of componential analysis occurred outside the structuralist framework, however, when Katz and Fodor introduced componential analysis into generative grammar. Their paper 'The Structure of a Semantic Theory' (1963) is a landmark publication in the history of lexical semantics, not because it presented a model of description that is currently still widely used (although further developed in publications like Katz 1972, it has in fact been entirely superseded by other approaches) but because the discussions it engendered from its first formulation in the early 1960s up to the mid-1970s occupy a pivotal role in the development of lexical semantics. Characterized in a nutshell (more is beyond the scope of the present chapter), the Katzian model is a combination of a structuralist method of analysis, a formalist system of description, and a mentalist conception of meaning. While the first feature specifically takes the form of the adoption of componential analysis, the other two characteristics are singular additions of the Katzian approach: explicit attention for the description of meaning in the context of a formal grammar, and a renewed interest in the psychological reality of meaning. Both features were evidently and explicitly inspired by the emergence of Chomskyan generativism, and both play an important role in the further development of semantics—not just lexical semantics, but linguistic semantics in the broader sense. They raise new questions, and they suggest new adequacy criteria for the description of meaning. To what extent should it be a formal description, and if it is to be formalized, in what way? Should it take into account psychological criteria, and if so, how can it adequately do so? With regard to each of these issues, two broad developments may be distinguished.

With regard to the first issue, the interest in formalization contributed to the emergence of two ways of formalizing the semantics of natural language that lie outside the focus of our overview: computational semantics and formal semantics. (The two are not strictly separated: a considerable portion of computational approaches is based on logical formalisms.) 'Computational semantics' as meant here is the description of meaning in natural language in the context of computational linguistics. It is the attempt to simulate language-related knowledge and reasoning on a computer: how is meaning most adequately represented in a digital environment, and how can that formal representation be used in automated inferencing processes? 'Formal semantics' is the application of logical forms of description to natural language semantics. For computational approaches to language, see Chapter 32 of this volume; for the logical approaches, see Chapter 23.

Concerning the second issue (which is the one we will focus on in the following sections), a distinction needs to be made between maximalist and restrictive approaches to the cognitive reality of linguistic meaning. In both trends of research, the cognitive, ideational nature of linguistic meaning is taken for granted, but the two trends take a different stance with regard to the autonomy of linguistic meaning vis-à-vis cognition at large. These options derive from a certain tension that is inherent in the Katzian combination of a mentalist position and a componential descriptive framework. On the one hand, a decompositional method has a reductionist tendency: it reduces the semantic description to a set of primitive meaning components, and looks for a truly linguistic level of description, contrasting with an encyclopedic level world knowledge in the broadest sense. On the other hand, a theory that aims at psychological adequacy will inevitably have to face the fuzziness and flexibility of language use, where the phenomena are mostly less clearly delimited than then a system-oriented theory would suggest. So how far should semantic theory go in such a cognitive, usage-oriented rather than system-oriented direction?

A maximalist approach to semantic description abandons the idea (which is strongly present in structuralist and generativist theorizing) of achieving some form of autonomous semantics, and goes for a type of meaning description that radically embraces the idea that there are close and inseparable ties between 'word knowledge' and 'world knowledge.' This trend is most clearly embodied by the Cognitive Semantics movement that forms the subject matter of §25.3. Conversely, more restrictive approaches do try to create a space for encyclopedic knowledge and cognition in their overall model, but at the same time maintain the idea of a relatively autonomous semantic level of representation, as distinct from cognition at large. The most important of these restrictive models are introduced in §25.2. Given that such a more restrictive and autonomist approach is basically an inheritance from the structuralist tradition, we will present it under the heading 'neostructuralist' semantics.

25.2 NEOSTRUCTURALIST APPROACHES

The decompositional models of semantic description in this section basically represent three strategies of reconciling the reductionist tendency of componential analysis with the expansionist tendency of a perspective that takes cognition seriously. Aphoristically, the three positions are as follows: 'the mind is neat but the world is fuzzy,' 'conceptual knowledge is parsimonious, but perceptual knowledge is abundant,' and 'semantics is stable but pragmatics is flexible.' The first position is taken in Wierzbicka's Natural Semantic Metalanguage approach. It implies that the concepts we have in our head are clearly delineated, in spite of the fact that we have to apply them to a world that is essentially blurry. If we can just tap into the clarity that is in our own head, the unclarities of the world need not bother us. The second position is illustrated by Jackendoff's Conceptual Semantics. It implies that a sparse conceptual representation at the linguistic level can be combined with a rich and flexible representation at the perceptual level (or, in fact, at the level of various non-conceptual modes of knowledge). The decompositional description of meaning at the linguistic level can be kept tidy and well-delineated if we accept a close link between the conceptual level and vision, motor schemas, and other non-conceptual cognitive modes. The third position is typical of Pustejovsky's Generative Lexicon. It implies that well-defined semantic descriptions may be modulated or refined at the pragmatic level, under the influence of situational or contextual factors. If we can describe the mechanisms that engender such pragmatic specifications of meaning, we can safeguard the neatness of the semantic description. In the following pages, we will present these positions in more detail. The theories presented in this section do not exhaust the neostructuralist tendencies, but they do illustrate the main trends.

25.2.1 The Natural Semantic Metalanguage Approach

Componential definitions of meaning often come with the assumption that definitions are couched in a vocabulary of primitive concepts, i.e. concepts that are not themselves defined. The motivation for such an assumption is an epistemological one: if all the words in a language are defined by other words, we stay within the language and there is no relationship between language and world. The advantage of having definitional elements that themselves remain undefined resides in the possibility of avoiding circularity: if the definitional language and the defined language are identical, words are ultimately defined in terms of themselves—in which case the explanatory value of definitions seems to disappear as a whole. This motivation for having undefined primitive elements imposes an important restriction on the set primitive features. In fact, if achieving non-circularity is the point, the set of primitives should be smaller than the set of words to be defined: there is no reductive or explanatory value in a set of undefined defining elements that is as large as the set of concepts to be defined.

But what would those primitive concepts be? The Natural Semantic Metalanguage approach originated by Wierzbicka (1972) and developed in numerous books (among them Wierzbicka 1985, 1992, 1996, 2003, and Goddard and Wierzbicka 1994, 2002) is the most advanced attempt in contemporary semantics to establish an inventory of universal primitive concepts. Wierzbicka's model of semantic description rests on two pillars, in fact: the vocabulary of universal, primitive concepts, and a definitional practice characterized as 'reductive paraphrase.'

With regard to the first pillar, Wierzbicka insists on the requirement that definitions be written in natural, non-technical language, and not in some formalized representational language. Semantic primitives, then, to the extent that they are indeed universal, should be lexicalized in all languages of the world. Goddard, who is the main representative of the Natural Semantic Metalanguage framework next to Wierzbicka (Goddard 2006, 2008), defines this requirement as the Strong Lexicalization Hypothesis: primitives concepts are universally lexicalized (Goddard 1994: 13). The concepts that are universal (in contrast with culturally specific ones) are expressed in all languages, by a specific word or at least a specific expression.

The second pillar of the Natural Semantic Metalanguage is known as 'reductive paraphrase'—basically, writing definitions couched in the vocabulary of universal primitive concepts. Here, for instance, is Wierzbicka's definition of English *sad* (1996: 180):

X is sad =
X feels something
sometimes a person thinks something like this:
   something bad happened
   if I didn't know that it happened,
     I would say: I don't want it to happen
   I don't say this now
   because I know: I can't do anything
because of this, this person feels something bad
X feels something like this

Critical appraisals of the NSM approach focus on the alleged universality of the vocabulary of primitives, and on the restrictive nature of the reductive paraphrase technique: the rich polysemy and nuances that a word like *sad* receives in actual contexts of use fall outside the scope of the description. In the NSM view of things, however, it is the clear concept captured by the reductive paraphrase that constitutes the real and essential knowledge of language users; contextual nuances are in a sense epiphenomenal.

25.2.2 The Conceptual Semantics Approach

The Natural Semantic Metalanguage approach to lexical analysis smacks of idealism. Meanings are purely linguistic, and they are, as such, entirely conceptual: there is no explicitly described or acknowledged link between meaning and extralinguistic know-ledge. An entirely different approach to safeguarding a specifically linguistic level of semantic description, different from world knowledge in the larger sense, would be to consider linguistic meaning in combination with (rather than in opposition to) extra-linguistic knowledge, and to define a plausible division of labour between the two. In such a modular approach, linguistic meaning is still different from other forms of knowledge, like visual memory and perceptual knowledge in general, but at the same time, it would not need to carry the total burden of representing our knowledge of how to use words: part of that task could be delegated to other modules of cognition.

This is indeed the approach developed by Jackendoff (1972, 1983, 1990, 2002) in his model of Conceptual Semantics: the formal semantic representation does not contain all the information that is relevant to explain the language user's conceptual compe-tence. Rather, that information is to be situated on the level of 'conceptual structure'; within such conceptual structures, other modes of cognition, like perceptual knowledge and motor schemas, may play their role together with linguistic knowledge. Conceptual structure, in other words, acts as an interface between the formal structures of language and other, nonlinguistic modes of knowledge. With regard to phonology and syntax, Jackendoff adheres to the generativist, Chomskyan idea of an autonomous syntax, but at the same time, in an un-Chomskyan way, the autonomy of syntax does not mean than language can be studied autonomously: research into linguistic meaning implies doing cognitive psychology. Accordingly, Jackendoff consistently tries to confront his work on linguistic structure with psychological findings. The description of spatial language, for instance, is situated against the background of psychological theories of spatial language and visual cognition.

Practically speaking, this interface function is reflected in the form of lexical entries in Jackendoff's model, which take a decompositional form but pay considerable attention to the syntactic environment in which a word appears, represented by a subcategorization frame. The meaning of a verb like *put*, for instance, is formally described as an event in which one thing (the subject of the verb) causes an event in which another thing (corresponding to the direct object in the subcategorization frame) moves along a spatial path. *Run* expresses an event in which a thing (the subject) moves along the path optionally expressed by the prepositional phrase. At the same time, Jackendoff has devoted more attention to the interface between syntax and semantics than to the flexible use of words or to the detailed description of the interplay between conceptual structure and extralinguistic knowledge. The latter part of the model is not elaborated with the same formal rigour as the more grammar-oriented sections.

These explicit links between the syntactic and the semantic parts of the lexical entries is exemplary for a broader tradition of research into the interaction between semantics and grammar: how do the lexical semantic properties of words (specifically, verbs) correlate with their formal properties? From the point of view of formal grammar, a central question here is how the argument structure of verbs correlates with the semantics of those verbs; major work in this line is represented by Levin (1993) and Levin and Rappaport Hovav (2005). Again, the basic attitude is a restrictive one, in the sense that semantic description is curtailed by the perspective of the semantics–syntax interface.

25.2.3 The Generative Lexicon Approach

The most elaborate formalized componential model in contemporary semantics is the Generative Lexicon model introduced by Pustejovsky (1995). The overall position of the model is characterized by two features. First, more so than any of the approaches mentioned above, Pustejovsky is interested in the description of regular polysemy. Regular polysemy, as defined by Apresjan (1973), refers to the existence of polysemous patterns in the lexicon. Examples of regular polysemy (which is also called 'logical polysemy' by Pustejovsky) basically include all types of pattern-based polysemy that is traditionally studied in diachronic semantics, like part–whole metonymies. The essential idea of the Generative Lexicon is that such pattern-based polysemies should be derived by means of formal operations based on an underlying formalized entry for the meaning of a lexical item.

Second, then, with regard to the actual format of those formal representations, the Generative Lexicon explicitly links up with logical representations of meaning, and tries to provide a representational format that may be used in computational linguistics. In practical terms, the Generative Lexicon posits a number of procedures for generating semantic interpretations for words in particular contexts, starting from a formalized decompositional lexical entry that is encoded in the system for each lexical item. This encoded knowledge conforms to a general pattern with different types of information structure, the most important of which are the following: the argument structure specifies the number and nature of the arguments to a predicate; the event structure defines the event type of the expression, and possibly also the internal event structure; and the qualia structure is a structured set of descriptive characteristics that corresponds most closely to the more traditional kinds of componential definition of meaning. Among the procedures generating semantic interpretations on the basis of the formal entries, Type Coercion may be mentioned as an example. It ensures, for instance, that *beach* in *I could do with a big piece of beach now* is interpreted as a mass noun: the regular semantic type of *beach* is that of a count noun, but the expectations encoded in the entry for *piece* 'coerce' a mass noun reading of *beach*.

In the larger scheme of things, Pustejovsky's Generative Lexicon takes a big step towards a maximalist conception of semantics by its explicit attention to the contextual modulation of meaning. At the same time, the actual contexts effectuating such conceptual shifts are still very much linguistic ones, like the type conflicts that trigger coercion. How, for instance, world knowledge in the broadest sense intervenes in such processes of semantic contextualization is not envisaged. From this perspective, the Generative Lexicon model is one more example of a theory taking an intermediate position between the system-oriented approach of structuralism and a full-fledged usage-oriented theory.

25.3 COGNITIVE SEMANTICS

The tension between a maximalist and a minimalist understanding of lexical semantics, which we formulated in the context of Katzian semantics, takes many forms. It may relate to the borderline between word knowledge and world knowledge. It may involve the dividing line between semantics and pragmatics. Or it may surface as a methodological choice between a system-oriented or a usage-oriented mode of investigation. In the previous section, we came across a number of theories that tried in various ways to maintain the distinction. In the present section, I focus on an approach that explicitly embraces a maximalist position: one in which the distinction between semantics and pragmatics is not a major issue, in which language is seen in the context of cognition at large, and in which language use is the methodological basis of linguistics—at least in principle. Cognitive semantics emerged in the 1980s as part of cognitive linguistics, a loosely structured theoretical movement that opposed the autonomy of grammar and the secondary position of semantics in the generativist theory of language.

In the following subsections, *three specific* contributions of Cognitive Semantics to the study of word meaning will be presented: the prototype model of category structure, the conceptual theory of metaphor and metonymy, and frame semantics. Introductions to Cognitive Linguistics at large include Croft and Cruse (2004), Ungerer and Schmid (2006), Evans and Green (2006), and Kristiansen et al. (2006). Geeraerts and Cuyckens (2007) is a multi-authored handbook, while Geeraerts (2006b), and Evans et al. (2007) are collections with important articles in Cognitive Linguistics. In all of these works, ample attention is paid to semantics. More specifically, an indispensable textbook for semantic research within the framework of Cognitive Linguistics is Taylor (2003).

25.3.1 Prototype Theory

The prototype-based conception of categorization originated in the mid-1970s with Eleanor Rosch's psycholinguistic research into the internal structure of categories. (Overviews of the early developments may be found in Rosch 1978, 1988, and Mervis and Rosch 1981; further, see Taylor 2003.) From its psycholinguistic origins, prototype theory moved in two directions. On the one hand, Rosch's findings and proposals were taken up by formal psycholexicology, which tries to devise formal models for human conceptual memory and its operation: see Murphy (2002) for the current state of the field. On the other hand, prototype theory had a steadily growing success in linguistics from the mid-1980s. It is the latter development that we shall be concerned with here.

Rosch concluded that the tendency to define categories in a rigid way clashes with the actual psychological situation. Perceptually based categories do not have sharply delimited borderlines. Instead of clear demarcations between equally important conceptual areas, one finds marginal areas between categories that are only unambiguously defined in their focal points. Rosch developed this observation into a more general prototypical view of natural language categories, more particularly, categories naming natural objects. The theory implies that the range of application of such categories is concentrated round focal points represented by prototypical members of the category. The attributes of these focal members are the structurally most salient properties of the concept in question; conversely, a particular member of the category occupies a focal position because it exhibits the most salient features.

In the course of the linguistic elaboration of the model, it became clear that it was important to clearly distinguish between the various phenomena that may be associated with prototypicality. In this sense, theorists currently prefer to talk about various 'prototype effects' rather than a homogeneous 'prototype theory.' Specifically, the following four characteristics are frequently mentioned as typical of prototypicality. First, prototypical categories exhibit degrees of typicality; not every member is equally representative for a category. Second, prototypical categories exhibit a family resemblance structure, or more generally, their semantic structure takes the form of a radial set of clustered and overlapping readings. Third, prototypical categories are blurred at the edges. Fourth, prototypical categories cannot be defined by means of a single set of criterial (necessary and sufficient) attributes. These four features are not necessarily coextensive; they do not always co-occur. There is now a consensus in the linguistic literature on prototypicality that these characteristics are prototypicality effects that may be exhibited in various combinations by individual lexical items, and that may have very different sources.

Possibly the major theoretical innovation of the prototype model of categorization is to give salience a place in the description of semasiological structure: next to the qualitative relations among the elements in a semasiological structure (like metaphor and metonymy), a quantifiable centre–periphery relationship is introduced as part of the architecture. From a practical, descriptive perspective, this leads to the introduction of a 'radial set' model as a popular method for describing prototypically organized categories (see Lakoff 1987): the various readings and nuances with which a word appears are described as mutually linked extensions from one or more core senses. As such, a prototype approach provides a model for the description of the contextual flexibility of linguistic meaning, and accordingly also for the diachronic dynamics of meaning (see Geeraerts 1997 on diachronic prototype semantics).

To complete the picture, two models that are somewhat related to prototype theory need to be mentioned. First, the concept of salience can be transferred from the semasiological to the onomasiological domain, i.e. while semasiologically speaking we look at the meanings with which an item dominantly occurs, we can also, onomasiologically speaking, look at the categories that are dominantly used to talk about certain things in the world. In practice, such differences of onomasiological salience have so far been described primarily in terms of the 'basic-level hypothesis.' The hypothesis is based on the ethnolinguistic observation that folk classifications of biological domains usually conform to a general organizational principle, in the sense that they consist of five or six taxonomical levels (Berlin et al. 1973, 1974; Berlin 1976, 1978). One of these levels is dubbed the 'generic' level, and it is shown to be 'basic,' in the sense that it is, for instance, the default level for naming things; it is also the level which is learned first in language acquisition. The generic level, in other words, is onomasiologically salient: within the lexical field defined by the taxonomy, the generic level specifies a set of salient items and a set of naming preferences: given a particular referent, the most likely name for that referent from among the alternatives provided by the taxonomy will be the name situated at the basic level.

Second, an important aspect of the conception of meaning expounded in the philosopher Hilary Putnam's highly influential paper 'The Meaning of Meaning' (1975) is the notion of 'stereotype,' a concept that bears a superficial resemblance to that of prototype. The basis of the notion of stereotype is the recognition that not all members of a linguistic community are required to know the essential structure of the extension of an expression of their language. A division of linguistic labour ensures that there are societal experts who know that *water* is H_2O, that there is a difference between pyrites and gold, what the specific differences between elms and beeches are, and so on. On the other hand, laymen attune their own linguistic usage to that of the expert scientists and technicians. The members of the non-specialized group are not required to have expert knowledge, but they are supposed to know the *stereotype* connected with a category if they are to be regarded as full-fledged members of the linguistic community. A stereotype, then, is a socially determined minimum set of data with regard to the extension of a category. For the category *water* (H_2O), the stereotype includes the information that refers to a natural kind that is a colourless, transparent, tasteless, thirst-quenching liquid that boils at 100° Celsius and freezes when the temperature drops below 0° Celsius. For the natural kind *tiger* (*Felis tigris*), the stereotype includes the information that it is a yellowish, black-striped, catlike, dangerous predatory animal.

With regard to their descriptive content, stereotypes and prototypes are related: the information that is included in the stereotype is likely to correspond closely to the prototypical reading in for instance a radial network analysis. This correspondence should not blind us to the fact that the two concepts embody different, though possibly complementary, perspectives: stereotypes refer to a theory about the social distribution of information and meaning, while prototypes involve the cognitive structure of meaning in use (see Geeraerts 2008 for further analysis).

25.3.2 Conceptual Metaphor and Metonymy

The interest in the internal structure of lexical items, as illustrated and embodied by the research covered in the previous subsection, automatically entails an interest in the semantic relations that interconnect the various readings of an item. Within a radial set for instance, the elements are not only connected through the fact that a less prototypical sense derives from a more central one, but also through a specific mechanism of semantic extension: similarity, or metaphor, or metonymy—basically, any of the mechanisms of meaning change that constituted the focus of historical-philological semantics as discussed in Chapter 24. That is, overall, a major resemblance between Cognitive Semantics and historical-philological semantics: both embrace a psychological, encyclopedic conception of linguistic meaning, and both have a primary interest in the flexible dynamism of meaning.

Metaphor, in particular, constitutes a major area of investigation for Cognitive Semantics. The major impetus here came from George Lakoff and Mark Johnson's *Metaphors We Live By* (1980), a book that worked like an eye-opener for a new generation of linguists. In the linguistic climate of the 1970s, dominated by the formal framework of generative grammar, semantics seemed a peripheral issue, but *Metaphors We Live By*, more perhaps than the other foundational publications in Cognitive Semantics, was instrumental in putting semantics back on the research agenda.

Conceptual Metaphor Theory, the approach introduced by Lakoff, includes two basic ideas: first, the view that metaphor is a cognitive phenomenon, rather than a purely lexical one; second, the view that metaphor should be analysed as a mapping between two domains. (The standard formulation of the theory is Lakoff and Johnson 1980. Further central works are Lakoff 1987, and Lakoff and Johnson 1999, with Kövecses 2002 as a comprehensive and easily accessible introduction. An indispensable handbook for contemporary metaphor research is Gibbs 2008.)

To illustrate the first point, metaphor comes in patterns that transcend the individual lexical item. A typical example is the following. (Not all the examples given by Lakoff and Johnson are reproduced. It is customary for Conceptual Metaphor Theory to write metaphorical patterns in small caps.)

LOVE IS A JOURNEY
Look how *far* we've come. We are at a *crossroads*. We'll just have to go our separate *ways*. We cannot *turn back* now. We are *stuck*. This relationship is a *dead-end street*. I don't think this relationship is *going anywhere*. It's been a *long, bumpy road*. We have gotten *off the track*.

The second pillar of Conceptual Metaphor Theory is the analysis of the mappings inherent in metaphorical patterns. Metaphors conceptualize a target domain in terms of the source domain, and such a mapping takes the form of an alignment between aspects of the source and target. In the terminology introduced into literary studies by Richards (1936), the source domain corresponds to the *vehicle* of the metaphor, the target domain corresponds to the *tenor*, and mapping corresponds to the *ground*. For LOVE IS A JOURNEY, for instance, the following correspondences (adapted from Kövecses 2002: 7) hold.

Source	Domain
the travellers	the lovers
the means of transport	the relationship itself
the journey	the development of the relationship
the obstacles encountered	the difficulties experienced
decisions about which way to go	choices about what to do
the destination of the journey	the goals of the relationship

Conceptual metaphor theory has inspired a number of further developments. First, probably the biggest theoretical extension of Conceptual Metaphor Theory is the apparatus of blending theory. This analytic framework was introduced by Fauconnier and Turner (1995), as a development of earlier work by Fauconnier (1985). Further references to central works of blending theory include Fauconnier (1997) and Fauconnier and Turner (2002).

The descriptive model of conceptual integration (or blending, as it is commonly known), involves four spaces, instead of the two conceptual domains of standard Conceptual Metaphor Theory. Two of the four spaces, the input spaces, correspond to the source and target domain of Conceptual Metaphor Theory. The crucial addition of blending theory is the blend space, which represents the interaction of the input spaces: in the blended space, knowledge of source and target inputs combines into a coherent information structure that is temporarily activated in the mind of the language user. The fourth space in Fauconnier and Turner's analytic schema is the generic space, which contains schematic material shared by the two input spaces. To see how it works, we may look at one of the standard examples of a blend: the Grim Reaper, the traditional representation of death as a cloaked skeleton with a scythe. The image has death as a target domain, but there appear to be two source domains involved: that of the reaper and that of a killer. Death is personified as a reaper, but the reaper has lost his usual positive connotation. Reapers indeed harvest food, which is a positively evaluated action, whereas the Reaper in the image turns out to be a killer with negative intentions. Crucially, the blended space represents a novel conceptualization with regard to either the input domain(s) or the target domain: the Grim

Reaper does not as such belong to the target domain of death, but neither does he reside in the input space of farming and harvesting, because his grim features do not fit there.

Given the example, we may now identify the advantage of the blending model over a standard Conceptual Metaphor Theory representation: the blending approach highlights the interaction of source and target domains, clarifying that blended spaces contain features that belong to neither of the input domains. This emphasizes the constructive nature of metaphors: they do not just exploit perceived similarities, but also build meaningful structures.

A second major extension of Conceptual Metaphor Theory is the revival of the interest in metonymy. In Lakoff and Johnson (1980) already, metonymy figured next to metaphor as one of the conceptual mechanisms behind the semantic structure of language. That clearly should not come as a surprise: an approach that is interested in the semantic mechanisms behind language use and linguistic structures is likely to rediscover the traditional mechanisms of semantic extension. Lakoff and Johnson (1980: 38–9) list a number of metonymic patterns that might have been taken straightforwardly from a historical-philological treatise on semantic change of the type discussed in Chapter 24. Lakoff and Johnson emphasize that such metonymic patterns are conceptual and not purely linguistic, in much the same way that metaphorical concepts are. In the first place, metonymical concepts allow us to think of one thing in terms of its relation to something else. In that sense, we can distinguish a source and target in the description of metonymy just as we can for metaphors. In the second place, metonymies are systematic in the sense that they form patterns that apply to more than just an individual lexical item. In third place, metonymic concepts structure not just the language but also the language users' thoughts, attitudes and actions. For instance, saying that Nixon bombed Hanoi is not just a way of referring to the air force by means of its chief commander, but is also a way to think of Nixon as ordering the bombing and of holding him responsible for it, even though he may not have dropped the bombs himself.

From the late 1990s on (somewhat later than the rise in popularity of metaphor studies), the renewed interest in metonymy led to an upsurge of publications. Important collective volumes include Panther and Radden (1999), Barcelona (2003), Dirven and Pörings (2002), Panther and Thornburg (2003), and Benczes et al. (2011).

25.3.3 Frame Theory

The models presented in the previous two subsections illustrate two important features of Cognitive Semantics: interest in the contextual flexibility of meaning (as reflected in prototype-based models for describing polysemy and semantic nuances), and tight links between language and thinking in general (as illustrated by conceptual metaphor and metonymy research). A third feature of Cognitive Semantics that needs to be mentioned in this respect is its interest in the way our knowledge of the world is organized in larger 'chunks of knowledge,' and how these interact with language. The most articulate model in this respect is Fillmore's frame theory (Fillmore 1977a, 1985, Fillmore and Atkins 1992, 1994, 2000).

Frame theory is specifically interested in the way in which language may be used to perspectivize an underlying conceptualization of the world: it's not just that we see the world in terms of conceptual models, but those models may be verbalized in different ways. Each different way of bringing a conceptual model to expression, so to speak, adds another layer of meaning: the models themselves are meaningful ways of thinking about the world, but the way we express the models while talking adds perspective. This overall starting-point of Fillmorean frame theory leads to a description on two levels. On the one hand, a description of the referential situation or event consists of an identification of the relevant elements and entities and the conceptual role they play in the situation or event. On the other hand, the more purely linguistic part of the analysis indicates how certain expressions and grammatical patterns highlight aspects of that situation or event.

To illustrate, we may have a look at the standard example of frame theory, the COMMERCIAL TRANSACTION frame. This frame involves words like *buy* and *sell*. The commercial transaction frame can be characterized informally by a scenario in which one person gets control or possession of something from a second person, as a result of a mutual agreement through which the first person gives the second person a sum of money. Background knowledge involved in this scenario includes an understanding of ownership relations, a money economy, and commercial contracts. The categories that are needed for describing the lexical meanings of the verbs linked to the commercial transaction scene include Buyer, Seller, Goods, and Money as basic categories. Verbs like *buy* and *sell* then each encode a certain perspective on the commercial transaction scene by highlighting specific elements of the scene. In the case of *buy*, for instance, the buyer appears in the participant role of the agent, for instance as the subject of the (active) sentence. In active sentences, the goods then appear as the direct object; the seller and the money appear in prepositional phrases: *Paloma bought a book from Teresa for €30*. In the case of *sell*, on the other hand, it is the seller that appears in the participant role of the agent: *Teresa sold a book to Paloma for €30*.

In its further development, frame semantics was enriched, first, by the systematic use of corpus materials as the main source of empirical evidence for the frame-theoretical analyses, and second, by the development of an electronic dictionary with frame-theoretical descriptions. These two developments go together in the Berkeley FrameNet project (Johnson et al. 2002; Ruppenhofer et al. 2006).

25.4 CURRENT DEVELOPMENTS

The post-structuralist developments that were described in the previous pages reveal a certain tension between more restrictive interpretations of the post-structuralist 'cognitive turn,' and the Cognitive Semantics approach that rejects the structuralist legacy in a more outspoken way. However, one of the more interesting developments of the last decade points to a convergence between Cognitive Semantics and a sideshoot of structuralism: distributional semantics.

In §24.3.1, the distributional approach to semantics was introduced as an outcome of looking syntagmatically rather than paradigmatically at lexical–semantic relations. In the final decades of the twentieth century, major advances in the distributional approach to semantics were achieved by applying a distributional way of meaning analysis to large text corpora. John Sinclair, a pioneer of the approach, developed his ideas (see Sinclair 1991) through his work on the *Collins CoBuild English Language Dictionary* (Sinclair and Hanks 1987), for which a 20 million-word corpus of contemporary English was compiled.

The distributional analysis in the corpus-based approach is not restricted to constituents and syntactic classes, but takes into account the actual words in the context of which the target word appears. Firth (1957) remarked that part of the 'meaning' of *cows* can be indicated by such collocations as *They are milking the cows, Cows give milk*. This observation is taken as a methodological starting point: the words co-occurring with another one help to identify the properties of the word under scrutiny. An example (taken from Stubbs 2001: 15) may illustrate the basic idea. A classic example of homonymy in English is the item *bank*, which is either a financial institution or an area of sloping ground, specifically the raised ground on the side of the river or underneath a shallow layer of water. The sets of words that these two exemplars of *bank* normally occur with hardly overlap. Looking at compounds on the one hand, and on the other hand at co-occurring items within a few words to the left or right of *bank*, Stubbs comes up with the following lists:

> bank account, bank balance, bank robbery, piggybank
> cashier, deposit, financial, money, overdraft, pay, steal
> sand bank, canal bank, river bank, the South Bank, the Left Bank, Dogger bank, Rockall Bank, Icelandic Banks
> cave, cod, fish, float, headland, sailing, sea, water

The entities in the environment of the two homonyms appear to differentiate efficiently and effectively between the two meanings, and in that sense, a systematic analysis of the co-occurring items would appear to be an excellent methodological ground for lexical–semantic analysis. In theoretical terms, the essential concept here is that of 'collocation,' defined as 'a lexical relation between two or more words which have a tendency to co-occur within a few words of each other in running text' (Stubbs 2001: 24).

In Sinclair's original conception, a collocational analysis is basically a heuristic device to support the lexicographer's manual work. A further step in the development of the distributional approach was taken through the application of statistics. A decisive development took place when Church and Hanks (1990), working in the context of Sinclair's CoBuild project, introduced the Pointwise Mutual Information index (defined in terms of the probability of occurrence of the combination x,y compared to the probabilities of x and y separately) as a statistical method for establishing the relevance of a collocation. Once a statistical measure of association in the form of the Pointwise Mutual Information index was introduced, further possibilities opened up for quantifying the distributional approach. For instance, a whole variety of association measures has been suggested and researched, among which Dunning's (1993) log-likelihood ratio is one of the more popular. Also, the statistical turn in thinking about contextual distributions allowed for a rapprochement with the field of information retrieval and Natural Language Processing where so-called 'word space models' constitute an advanced form of distributional corpus analysis, applied to problems like word sense disambiguation and synonym extraction (see Agirre and Edmonds 2006).

Now, why would a quantitative distributional approach of the type described be relevant for Cognitive Semantics? In general, the corpus approach is attractive for any theoretical framework in lexical semantics, for the basic reason that it provides an unparalleled empirical basis for lexical research. The wealth of data contained in the corpora—regardless of what perspective they are analysed from—will simply benefit any research endeavour in lexical semantics, Cognitive Semantics no less so than other approaches. But more specifically and more importantly, there is a certain theoretical affinity between Cognitive Semantics and the distributional analysis of corpus data. Both approaches are explicitly usage-based. On the one hand, distributional corpus analysis takes a radical usage-based rather than system-based approach: it considers the analysis of actual linguistic behaviour to be the ultimate methodological foundation of linguistics. In the linguistic climate of the 1970s, when the scene of grammatical theory was dominated by the introspective methodology of Chomskyan linguistics, such a usage-based approach went against the grain of prevalent opinions; but with the advent of cognitive linguistics as an explicitly usage-based approach, the perspective definitely changes. On the other hand, it is difficult to see how Cognitive Semantics can live up to its self-declared nature as a usage-based model if it does not start from actual usage data and a methodology that is suited to deal with such data (see Geeraerts 2006a for an extended version of this argument).

It is no surprise to find then that younger scholars (as witnessed by the contributions in Gries and Stefanowitsch 2006 or Glynn and Fischer 2010) are combining the theoretical framework of Cognitive Semantics with the descriptive methods of quantitative corpus analysis. The descriptive potential of this combination is likely to be a major force in the future development of semantics.

CHAPTER 26

··

A BRIEF SKETCH OF THE HISTORIC DEVELOPMENT OF PRAGMATICS

··

JACOB L. MEY

26.1 EARLY ORIGINS OF PRAGMATIC THINKING

··

26.1.1 The Sophists

It may come as a surprise, even to the informed reader, that the modern interest in, or 'turn' to, pragmatics as a linguistic, or at least linguistically oriented, field of research did not originate with the linguists who controlled the field of language studies during most of the twentieth century. Instead, we have to look to the philosophers and psychologists in order to understand what such a 'pragmatic turn' is all about, and how it came to happen.

To start from classical history, the Greek Sophists developed their pragmatic philosophy of language in opposition to the received mode of moral instruction by storytelling. The *mythos* of Homer and the poets was replaced by the *logos* of persuasion and reasoning; Sophistic philosophy was also pragmatic in the modern sense. The Sophists were 'sophisticated' in that they turned their attention from mythological storytelling to real interaction—subsequently, they were blamed, as are many of today's pragmaticists, for advocating a view of language as a useful tool for action, rather than following the contemporary trends viewing language as a 'handmaid' to logic: a truth-functionally determined instrument for asserting and evaluating propositions (or 'judgements,' as they were called by the later Greek and subsequent medieval philosophers).

26.1.2 Rhetoric and Pragmatics

Unfortunately for the Sophists (who earned a rather bad repute on this account) and for us (who had to suffer through centuries or even millennia of sterile, rationalist, and essentialist philosophizing about language), their ideas were not particularly welcome in an environment that sought to liberate itself from its oral, narrative past to enter the world of written codification, in accordance with abstract, universalist principles. Thucydides, the historian, wanting to distance himself from the earlier anecdotal-narrative tradition of Herodotus (whose famous and very popular lectures he had attended in Athens when still a young man), decided that he would write the history of the wars between Athens and Sparta from the point of view of descriptive truth (and use this history as a tool for prediction about future developments).

But while sticking to the 'facts' of the wars, Thucydides could not help introducing practical, moral perspectives into his account; this he did by letting the protagonists of the two camps make speeches on various occasions (such as the famous funeral oratory that he had the Athenian leader Pericles deliver in the winter of 431 BC, while speaking at a commemorative ceremony for the soldiers who had fallen during the initial battles of the First Peloponnesian War; *Hist.* II: 35–46). Interestingly, Thucydides took care not to pretend that he was quoting Pericles verbatim; *élege toiáde* 'he spoke more or less as follows' is the Greek formula the author used to introduce this and other quoted official speakers.

In other words, the *pragmatic* purpose attributed to the speaker trumped the *descriptive* exigencies of the account: Thucydides was interested in the effect of Pericles' words on the mourners and the other citizens, who had to be motivated to continue shouldering the hardships of the war. Thucydides used the speeches, the words he put in the mouths of the leaders, to obtain an effect; like a good rhetorician, he manipulated the language, used the words, to fit his long-term, overarching agenda.

The rhetoric tradition and its practices can thus be said to be the place of origin for a pragmatic view on language—a view that was subsequently destined to remain in hibernation through centuries and millennia during which 'grammar,' the formally correct expression of one's thoughts, became the main focus of linguistic and philo-sophical reflection; rhetoric was relegated to an ancillary, practical function of getting things done (in today's business world, this would be called a 'pragmatic' view).

Also on the later, Aristotelian conception of rhetoric, the ways words and arguments were related to the person using them were not considered relevant; the pragmatic question of how the user obtained his arguments was of less importance than the way he organized them (that which Aristotle called the 'order,' *táxis*). In this way, the formal aspects of arguments (like the truth-functional aspects of propositions) were for the longest time thought to be all-important and decisive; thus, the stubborn assump-tion of some modern pragmaticists that one can separate the abstract proposition from its realization in speech acts (on which see below) has its origins in the mistaken view that the same propositional content can be expressed in different ways, by simply changing the 'force' of the acts—an idea I will proceed to criticize later on.

26.1.3 Medieval Philosophers/Linguists

Where the rhetoricians used a characteristic hands-on approach to language and its uses, the philosophers (and later the linguists), in contrast, tended to look at language as the embodiment of abstract ideas about the world, where propositions expressed an idealized state of affairs—one that could properly be assigned the predicate 'true' or its opposite. Most of the pre-medieval and medieval thinking about language turned around the problem of the extent to which one could represent the world through human speech, as in philosophy, or through divine revelation, as in theology.

The problem came to be extended to another, perpetual problem: not only how to speak about God, who (being eternal) in principle was unintelligible to time-bound humans, but how to think in universal, not to say eternal concepts. Between the unknowable God and the 'ineffable human individual' (as taught by the Scholastic philosophers), the language built an imperfect bridge. And the universal concepts of which language was the reflection came themselves under attack: were they 'spoken words' (*flatus vocis*)—mere replicas of the human classifying activity, as it was defended by the nominalists, who questioned the poets' and other normal mortals' glib, conceptualist assumption that 'words are for things' (*sunt verba rerum; pace* Virgil); or, alternatively, was speaking only about asserting the truth or falsity of propositions dealing with things, as it was preached by the realists and their successors and defenders?

Despite the scorn that the leading philosophers of the Middle Ages heaped on the nominalists, and the threats that were uttered against philosophers such as Roscellinus (thirteenth-century France) who risked his life at the stake and had to recant, it now seems that they were actually close to discovering a modern pragmatic truth about language: a proposition does not make sense until it is uttered (another take on *flatus vocis*); a word has no meaning except in its use (a thesis the philosopher Ludwig Wittgenstein later would try to establish, with varying degrees of success).

26.2 RECENT PRAGMATIC ANCESTRY

In more recent times, the famous American semiotician Charles Sanders Peirce is usually cited as having started pragmatics on its present track, bypassing or correcting earlier approaches. But Peirce only developed his ideas in the context of his philosophical speculations, and did not apply them to anything like real contexts such as the use of language in a concrete situation. Peirce never developed his rudimentary pragmatic insights consistently and in an encompassing fashion. His thoughts from the early 1860s are found mainly in some notebook notations; it was not until some forty years later that he was asked to write an encyclopedia article on the subject of 'Pragmatic: Pragmatism' (Fisch 1986: 114, Peirce 1932b). In the meantime, Peirce had had the opportunity to lecture on the subject in various connections, mostly as an unpaid university lecturer, but no coherent writings came out of this; hence the wholesale attribution of the origin of present-day pragmatics to Peirce is mildly dubious, and only serves the payment of an historic debt. Neither is the inclusion of pragmatics in the well-known tripartite distinction between syntax, semantics, and pragmatics due to Peirce himself (as many believe), but to Peirce's self-ordained acolyte and follower Charles Morris, who (also contrary to popular belief) never was a student of Peirce's and hardly had any contact with him during Peirce's last years (Peirce died in 1914, whereas Morris started his academic career only in the early 1920s).

26.2.1 Vico, Kant, Peirce: from Method in this Madness to Clear Ideas

Leaving historiographic niceties aside, one could ask: But wasn't there an important contribution that Peirce made to the development of pragmatic thought? It is important to remember (as Stanley Fisch suggests) that Peirce's 'pragmatic turn' may have been due to his early, persistent interest in Kant; actually, the word 'pragmatic' is probably borrowed from the latter's late lectures, bundled under the common title of *Anthropology from a pragmatic point of view* (1772); Peirce bought the entire Kantian *œuvre* (13 volumes in German) in 1865, prior to his notebook entries of that same year (Fisch 1986: 114).

But not only that: Peirce's pragmatic interests and ideas were, like those of some of his predecessors (the aforementioned Kant, and the eighteenth century Italian philosopher Giambattista Vico), mainly methodological. The question for Peirce was how to arrive at 'clear ideas'—here, he borrowed a Cartesian term (the famous *idées claires et distinctes*) minus their philosophical implications. And here the importance of Peirce's later pragmatic thinking becomes clear; like Kant, and earlier Vico, he relates the ideas to the person forming the ideas, just as Vico had postulated the necessary link between the 'true' and 'what people do.' As earlier for Vico, objects and actions are true for Peirce inasmuch as they are the result of a true *act* by an *actor*: 'the true is the made,' as Vico would express it (Fisch 1986: 207, Vico 1941[1710]: 131); and the made presupposes a maker, a user, as we would say in today's pragmatic terminology.

26.2.2 Peirce and Morris

As to the modern notion of pragmatics itself, it should not be identified with Peirce's 'pragmaticism' (or 'pragmatism,' as he called it sometimes, to distinguish his pragmaticism from that of the philosopher William James, his contemporary and sometime adversarial benefactor). In addition, it should not be assimilated with the term as it occurs in Charles Morris's work. Here, the triad consisting of syntax, semantics, and pragmatics was widely recognized, in line with the authors' own assertion, as 'an attempt to resolutely carry out the insight of Charles Peirce' (Morris 1946: 27, Biletzki 1996: 456). As Biletzki remarks, 'This self-alleged continuity is itself questionable and has come under attack. Nowhere does Peirce mention pragmatics (as opposed to pragmatism) and his division of semiotic is rather into pure grammar, logic proper, and pure rhetoric. It is not clear whether out of this distinction pragmatics, as Morris perceived it, can be gleaned' (Biletzki 1996: 456 n. 1; compare what I said earlier about the classic view of rhetoric and its connections to modern pragmatic approaches).

26.3 PRAGMATICS AND THE USER

In a wider historical perspective, our current view of pragmatics as a theory of language use, and more particularly of the language user as the central *auctor* of the linguistic activity (see Haberland and Mey 1977; 2002), was actually first adumbrated by classical, pre-structural historical linguists such as the Frenchmen Jean Vendryes and Antoine Meillet, who—in addition to their historical-linguistic interests—had something essential to say about the use of language as well. Vendryes remarks that 'the linguistic fact has to be considered in its totality, as a whole, such as it is realized *in its use*' (1933: 177; my translation and emphasis); Meillet alludes to Wilhelm von Humboldt's famous distinction when he writes that 'language is not a work, an *érgon*, but an *activity* [read: of the user], an *enérgeia*' (1934: 19; my translation and emphasis).

In another turn of the screw, the famous German psychologist Karl Bühler, in his ground-breaking work *Sprachtheorie* (1934), likewise squarely appeals to the concept of activity as the 'Ariadne's thread' that is uniquely able to lead us out of the labyrinth of conflicting and contradictory 'half-understood complexities' found in our thinking about language (1934: 52). More concretely, the 'guiding thread' he offers us is the notion of the speech act (in German: *Sprachhandlung*) several decades before the notion was taken up and developed by the Ordinary Language Philosophers such as John Austin and his followers (§26.8 below). And the US psychologist Grace Andres de Laguna had already, as early as 1927, stressed the 'social function' of the 'act of speaking' (1927: ix, 76; quoted by Nerlich and Clarke 1996: 140–41).

26.4 MODERN APPROACHES: FREGE ONWARDS

The two main modern approaches to pragmatics can be characterized as either 'inside out' or 'outside in.' Representatives of the first approach include Frege and his followers, including the majority of linguistic philosophers and linguists; among the members of the second group, we find mavericks such as Wittgenstein and Austin.

As to Frege, by many considered the true father of pragmatics (in contrast to Austin), his importance for the development of pragmatic thought is usually ascribed to his critical examination of the notion of meaning, and how it should be interpreted in context. A naive, realistic approach would tell us that meaning can be established by simply finding a link between a word and the thing it means. But right away, some doubts arise. Things are labelled differently by different people, and not everybody would use the same word for the same object such as a particular, potentially embarassing body part, or a certain tabooed activity; we are all familiar with euphemisms such as *brushing up one's Hebrew* (used by some Catholic priests to justify their afternoon naps) or *taking a leak* (to refer to micturition). Euphemism aside, sometimes we do in good faith refer to the same uncontroversial entity 'out there' by using different words, thereby consciously or unconsciously 'meaning' different objects, as when we refer to the planet Venus as either the Morning Star or the Evening Star (actually, this conundrum, often named 'Frege's puzzle' for the man who rediscovered it, was handed down to us from antiquity: Hesperus, the evening star, and Phosphorus, the morning star, were commonly thought of by unsophisticated Greeks as having to do with two different celestial bodies; this gave rise to Aristotle's famous remark that, while *Phosphorus is Hesperus* is a correct statement, *Hesperus is Hesperus* is vacuous).

26.4.1 Sense and Reference

Frege established the distinction between the 'sense' of an expression and its 'reference' (sometimes called, misleadingly, its 'meaning'). In modern pragmatic parlance, the sense is what we attribute to the object referred to: it is the way we use an expression when we ask about the morning star, but 'mean' Venus. The object referred to does not always have to be real, either; to use Frege's classic example: when I say *The King of France is wise*, this expression has a meaning even if there currently is no such object as a 'King of France.'

Frege's distinction has become important not only to the philosophers (for whom the problem of 'referring' always has been a true *crux*; see Allan 2010b), but mainly because of its role in the development of pragmatics, as it gave rise to the question of what we need to presuppose in order to be able to say things such as *the King of France is wise* (e.g. does there have to be a King of France?). However, Frege was not primarily interested in how and when such sentences were fit to use; as philosophers have done before and after him, Frege focused his thoughts on how and when the sentences could be *truthfully* uttered: his approach was truth-functional, semantic, rather than user-oriented, pragmatic. Nevertheless, as was soon discovered, one cannot properly study presupposition without at some time turning to pragmatics for an explanation. As we will see later in this chapter, the 'inside out' approach (from word to world) minimally needs to be complemented by an 'outside in' (from world to word) approach.

26.4.2 Presupposition

The earliest linguistic interest in presupposition was akin to that professed by the philosophers. Where the latter were keen to discover the truth or falsity of a particular expression, the linguists wanted to know in what ways a particular word or expression could be legitimately used in a certain language. In the American linguistic environment, for instance, the entire first decade of transformational theory (roughly, 1957–67), was mainly concerned with the set of correct sentences of a language—a set that ought to be derivable, and derivable to the exclusion of incorrect sentences, by generative-transformational rules *à la* Chomsky (1957a, 1965); the notion of correctness itself was modeled on the formal logicians' use of the 'well-formed expression.' This correctness had strictly to do with the syntactic conditions determining correct usage; it took fifteen years before linguists like George Lakoff (see §26.6.3 below) started to inquire about the semantic aspects of the problem, to be followed by considerations of a pragmatic nature.

Here is one of the classic examples. Suppose I ask a friend when he had stopped smoking. This question presupposes several things: that the person in question did indeed smoke at some time in the past; that he had quit smoking at some time prior to the moment of questioning; that I didn't know that exact time and wanted to be told; and so on. But suppose now that I change the question, or the frame in which the question is posed. To take the former first: If I had asked the same friend when he had stopped beating his wife, the answer would probably have been of a somewhat different nature; rather than coming up with a polite reply, the friend might just tell me to mind my own business and walk off (or sock me in the eye, in the worst-case scenario).

Similarly, when the insurance company asks me to fill out a standard application for life insurance, one of the questions asked will be if I am a smoker. If the answer is 'No,' the next questions may be 'Did you ever smoke?' and: 'If Yes, how long ago did you stop?' My answers will be dependent on the circumstances and background of the questions: my intention is to get a life insurance at the best possible conditions, but since I know that the company considers smokers to be a group at risk, and will impose higher premiums on them, my replies will be coloured by the desire to pay the lowest possible premium for the highest possible amount of insurance. Here, the truth is, within certain limits, more or less negotiable, even though at the end of the application I will have to sign a declaration that all answers have been true.

So what we are dealing with here is the question of external conditions: the frame of the question determines the answer to a certain (sometimes high) degree. In the case of my friend's supposed wife-beating, our common attitude is that such an activity is not to be permitted or condoned, and therefore not only carries a heavy social stigma in most civilized societies but often is considered an offence punishable by law. Such presuppositions to questions and their answers are not just semantic in nature—even though the insurance companies try to make us believe exactly that, every time they up the premiums by means of a 'terminological clarification' or an 'adjusted formulation'; what we are dealing with here is the way these presuppositions are being established

and put to a particular use in a particular society, in a special environment and for
special purposes. In other words, they are *pragmatic* presuppositions. (I will have more
to say on this subject later on).[1]

26.4.3 Presuppositions and Implicatures

In general, presuppositions are conditions on our use of language that precede (and
supersede) all other conditions; as the term indicates, they have to be there, being
posited as underlying, and prior to, all other possible constraints and restrictions. In
this way, they can be said to be 'transcendental,' in the sense of Kant: preconditions to
any proper use of language (because of this, some would count Kant among the
precursors of modern pragmatics, as also attested by his influence on Peirce, referred
to above; compare Nerlich and Clarke 1996: 150).

Presuppositions are often confused with another category of conditions, the
so-called 'implicatures.' The word itself did not belong to the standard linguistic-
philosophical terminology before it was canonized in its modern form by the philosopher H. Paul Grice, who is well known as one of the main protagonists of the Ordinary
Language movement in philosophy, to which John Austin and Ludwig Wittgenstein
also belonged.

Implicature is related to the verb *to imply*, from which the term *implication* is also
derived; in fact, Grice occasionally did not distinguish the two, but in the end decided
he needed to 'concoct' this new term (see Grice 1981: 184–5, Mey 2001: 336). An
implicature is something which arises in the course of language being used (as in
conversation); a presupposition is always already there, prior to our use (Caffi 2009:
762). If I say *I walked into a house*, the presupposition is that there is a house, that I was
walking, and so on; but what is implied is that normally, the house I walked into is not
my own—otherwise I would have said so: *I walked into my house*. Similarly, when I cut
my finger, I could report this momentous event to the world by saying *I cut a finger*
(example due to Horn 1984: 15; Mey 2001: 83); nobody would, under normal circumstances, believe that I was reporting on certain of my activities as a specially appointed
agent for my Japanese yakuza cell, in which a member's disobedience is routinely and
successively punished by the loss of up to 10 of the culprit's fingers.

Note especially that the 'implicature,' as Grice calls it, only arises in conversational or
other interpersonal use of language; by itself, the uttered sentences would not go
beyond what is explicitly conveyed: respectively, the acts of entering and cutting. It is
for this reason that Gricean implicatures are named 'conversational,' even if the term
may cause some confusion, as it diverts our attention to a very different subfield of
human language studies, namely conversation analysis (an area which will not be
covered in the present chapter). A conversational implicature is different from what

---

[1] See also §23.5 above.

we consider as logically implied: for one thing, it is much harder to contradict, to 'undo.' Once I am implied in conversation, I cannot escape; as a contemporary novelist, Jay McInerney, puts it, 'language implicates you in the lie right off' (1993: 108). Thus, when I say *Alexandra ate some of the raisins*, the conversational implicature is that she did not eat the whole package ('some, but not all'); only an unwilling or pernickety listener would claim that logically, she could have eaten the whole package ('some, maybe all'). The conversational point is that I would have said so if she indeed had eaten the whole package and not just some of its content; this kind of implicature is hard to duck in normal conversation (see Mey 2001: 48).

From this, we can see that what is needed in order to understand the functioning and practice of this kind of language behavior is the participants' willingness to follow the rules of the 'language game' (as Wittgenstein was wont to call it). Normally, we do not undo or cancel a conversational implicature except in cases of special need. In normal cases, the default assumption is that the conversational partners engage in *cooperation*. In order to capture this aspect of our language activities, Paul Grice has concocted yet another of his felicitous terms: the 'Cooperative Principle,' which will be the subject of the next section.

26.5 GRICE'S COOPERATIVE PRINCIPLE AND THE MAXIMS

In a way, the Cooperative Principle could be named the backbone of all of pragmatics. Even if Grice invented it to explain certain limited instances of human language work, its ramifications for the theory and practice of communication, seen from a pragmatic perspective, have been momentous. In its most general form, as stated by Grice, the Cooperative Principle looks deceptively simple:

> Make your contribution such as is required, at the stage at which it occurs, by the accepted purpose of the talk exchange in which you are engaged. (Grice 1975: 47)

As such, the principle doesn't seem to amount to more than a common-sense rule for making decent conversation, one might think. However, Grice takes care to make his principle more specific by adding the four conversational maxims (with attendant sub-maxims), for which he is rightly famous:

The maxim of *quantity*:
    Submaxim 1: Make your contribution as informative as required;
    Submaxim 2: Do not make your contribution more informative than required.
The maxim of *quality*:
    Submaxim 1: Do not say what you believe to be false;
    Submaxim 2: Do not say that for which you lack adequate evidence.
The maxim of *relation*:

Make your contribution relevant.
The maxim of *manner*:
    Be perspicuous, and specifically:
    Submaxim 1: avoid obscurity
    Submaxim 2: avoid ambiguity
    Submaxim 3: be brief
    Submaxim 4: be orderly. (Grice 1975: 47)

The question naturally arises why these maxims are proposed as instances of cooperative behaviour among language users. In fact, they seem to be no more than practical applications of some of Aristotle's venerated categories, applied to the individual's desire to get his or her intention successfully across. But consider this: if we take the maxim of quantity seriously, and refrain from providing either too much or too little information, we do indeed promote cooperation; this particular maxim expresses the desire, not to say the need, to maximize the interlocutors' successful interchange of information, such that essentials are not drowned in a sea of gossip and factoidal trivia, and that serious matter does not get left out because of the unwillingness of one of the partners to put the necessary facts on the table. And similar thoughts can be offered in illustration of the other maxims.

Another question is why the philosophers of language, beginning with Grice, restricted themselves to only four of the Aristotelian categories (the nine 'accidents' that pertain to the first category of substance, a.k.a 'the thing by itself'). Wouldn't it be possible to incorporate other accidents in addition to the four mentioned by Grice? What if we included a category such as action? Perhaps we then would be able to arrive at a more coherent vision of pragmatics, where the theory of speech acts (on which more later) would be properly contained within the Gricean maxims. I leave this suggestion for future consideration.

As to the four Gricean maxims themselves, they have been subjected to various efforts of simplification and reduction. For instance, Larry Horn has persuasively argued that we need only two conversational maxims: that of quantity ('tell as much as you can') and that of relation ('do not say more than you must'). In the case of my yakuza finger, mentioned earlier, any additional information that I may be tempted to offer will obscure the neutral fact of a finger having been cut, and lead people to falsely assume that I am a member of some obscure and dangerous Japanese gang. As to the maxim of quality, Horn assumes that this is the one 'accident' that needs no specification: if what I say has no value, then why should I say it—'idle words,' say no more! (cf. Matt. 12: 36). Quality is essential if we want to avoid a 'collapse of the entire conversational apparatus' (cf. Horn 1984: 12).

This leaves us with the two maxims that Horn has subsumed under his Q-maxim: manner and relation. Brigitte Nerlich and David Clarke (2001) have suggested an unexpected take on one of the submaxims, generally considered to be universal: that of being perspicuous. They point out that, in conversation, the point is to be knowledgeable, entertaining, humorous, and 'conspicuous,' rather than perspicuous. Here, They are in good company: Nietzsche reportedly once remarked that he always preferred an elegant error to boring correctness. Similarly, the submaxim that tells us to be brief has a very limited application in cultures where prolixity in rhetoric is thought of as a virtue; the seventeenth-century French culture of the *oraison funèbre* may serve as an example of the kind for which the 'eagle of Meaux,' Jacques-Bénigne Bossuet, is still regarded as the emblematic representative (his nickname referred to the location of his bishopric, but also alludes to the long and sometimes rather exorbitant flights of rhetoric for which his funeral oratory became famous). In other cultures such as the Malagasy, the maxim that tells us to be informative may be suspended, either generally or with regard to a particular situation (e.g. to avoid providing information that could be harmful to the people present or to their or others' spirits (see Ochs Keenan 1976; for a Navajo example, see Thomas 1996: 76–7).

26.5.1 Relation and Relevance

The Gricean maxim that has probably generated most interest and also controversy is that of relation, also called 'relevance.' When Dan Sperber and Deirdre Wilson published *Relevance: Communication and Cognition* in 1986, they could not have foreseen the impact that their work would have on generations of linguists both in Britain and abroad. What was at stake was a reformulation of the Gricean maxims by conflating all of them into one supermaxim or principle, that of 'Relevance.'

The 'presumption' of relevance, as Sperber and Wilson call it, means that we are ready to understand things in ways that are meaningful to us; we are prepared to recognize utterances that make sense, while those that do not are dismissed as irrelevant. Their example *George has a big cat* (1986: 168) makes sense for us if the cat we're talking about is of the Norwegian Forest race; one wouldn't expect the cat in question to be an Abyssinian, but neither would we assume that George kept a mountain lion in his backyard. To assume that, we need more information: the context in which the utterance occurs must be made more specific (George could be the director of the local zoo, or a circus performer). In other words, the utterance is only truly ambiguous in a neutered environment—quite the opposite of what we see when we observe a pragmatic perspective.

Sperber and Wilson have a point when they argue that natural language expressions, taken by themselves, are always ambiguous; but that need not deter prospective communicators. When people communicate, they have something in mind that is relevant to them, and presumably also to the hearer(s); ambiguity does not occur unless it is deliberately introduced, as in deceptive reasoning or in joke-telling. The principle of relevance captures this fact by stating that we, as communicators, 'do not "follow" the principle of relevance; [we] could not violate it even if [we] wanted to. The principle of relevance applies without exceptions' (Sperber and Wilson 1986: 162). For the same reason, we do not really need those protracted deliberations about quantity, quality, and so on: what is crucial in communication is the relevance of our message, evaluated in accordance with the proper 'mutual cognitive environment' (p. 193) that is available to the communicators.

While there is much that is of pragmatic interest in the Relevance Theorists' considerations (as also attested by the successful reception of the theory, sometimes even identified as the London School of Pragmatics), one major obstacle stands in the way of praising it as the last word in pragmatic theorizing (as many of its adepts are tempted to do). What is at stake here is the identity of the communicator as an individual, independent member of the speaking community, rather than as a communally bound representative of that community. As Mary Talbot has remarked,

> people are depicted as individuals who confront unique problems in communication. In the real world, however, people are social beings who are working within pre-existing conventions. In Sperber and Wilson's model, differences between people are depicted solely as differences between individuals' cognitive environments. These differences are assumed to stem from variations in physical environment and cognitive ability between people. Considerations of culture and society are notably absent in the characterization of individuals' cognitive environments. (1994: 3526)

For Relevance Theory to truly deserve the epithet pragmatic, it will have to reorient itself to the principle of principles in pragmatics: that of communication. The next sections will consider this and other 'principles' in more detail.

26.5.2 The Principle of Communication

Following its etymology, we could describe a principle as something from which everything else can be deduced or flows, like a river from its headwaters. Thus, the Machiavellian Prince (*Il Principe* in Italian) is the principal fountainhead of power from whom all other power derives, in the classic theory of government of the times. Similarly, both Euclid and Bertrand Russell called their major works 'Principles' (respectively 'of Geometry' and 'of Mathematics'); both works aim to furnish universally valid explanations, capable (with Plato in his *Timaios*) of saving the phenomena falling within their disciplines.

When it comes to pragmatics, there is one principle that has, so to say, navigated under the radar: the Principle of Communication. Even though indirect references abound, as in the case of the Principle of Relevance, the Principle of Communication has mostly not been explicitly formulated. In my book *Pragmatics: An Introduction*, I have introduced this principle as follows:

> People talk with the intention to communicate something to somebody; this is the foundation of all linguistic behavior. I call this the Communicative Principle. (Mey 2001: 68).

In this connection, too, I refer to the work of Paul Watzlawick and his associates (a 1960s California-based group of psychologists and communication researchers), who maintained that 'no matter how one may try, one cannot *not* communicate' (1967: 49). Clearly, their view of communication is at the very basis of all our work in pragmatics; consider that even the principle that has attracted most attention in pragmatics, Grice's Cooperative Principle, could not possibly function without the Communicative Principle. As Keith Allan expresses it, the Cooperative Principle holds whenever the participants in a communicative situation recognize that the other party/ parties have the intention to communicate, whether or not such an intention is explicitly formulated; this 'communicative presumption' (Allan 1986: 34; see also Bach and Harnish 1979: 62–5; Kecskes 2006) underlies all our collaborative efforts in communicating.

26.5.3 Other Principles

Even so, there are features of communicative behaviour that are not captured directly by the two principles referred to above. Linguists such as Geoffrey Leech have advocated the need to establish a Politeness Principle, by which we, all other things being equal, prefer polite expressions to impolite ones (Leech 1993: 81); in addition, Leech suggests a number of further principles and maxims such as those of tact, irony, or modesty, even to the point of self-mockingly accusing himself of 'risk[ing] to proliferate too many principles' (1983: 146).

26.6 POLITENESS AND FACE

Of all these principles, the one dealing with politeness has shown itself to be most robust; in fact, the sheer volume of studies on politeness, following the publication of Penelope Brown and Stephen Levinson's seminal study by that name (1978, reprinted 1987) has at times assumed the dimensions of a groundswell. For Brown and Levinson, the most important aspect of politeness is the protection of one's own and the other person's *face*—a concept that is vaguely oriental in its origins, but which has existed as such in Western societies for close to two centuries (see Thomas 1996: 168); its revival in modern times is probably due to the work of the sociologist Erving Goffman (1959).

A person's face has a double orientation: in its positive aspect, face relates to the desire to have one's personality favourably valued and appreciated by one's surroundings; in contrast, negative face has to do with one's person being unencumbered and free from intrusion. In accordance with these two aspects of face, politeness may be either positive (promoting positive 'face-work') or negative (ensuring that no adversarial action is taken that might endanger the interlocutor's face). Most clearly, these two aspects can be observed through the study of what has been called the 'face-threatening act' (FTA, Brown and Levinson 1978: 71ff.).

26.6.1 Face-threatening Acts (FTA)

An FTA is defined as an act on the part of the speaker that directly or indirectly threatens the (positive or negative) face of the conversational partner. Direct imperatives like *Shut the door* may be FTAs if produced inappropriately, e.g. when uttered to a person one is not familiar with; a non-FTA equivalent of the face-threatening *Shut the door* would be *Could you please shut the door?* (using an 'indirect speech act,' see §26.9.1 below). However, in a convivial context such as a birthday party, it is perfectly OK and non-face-threatening for the hostess to say to a guest: *Help yourself* (pointing to the buffet) or *Have a drink* (pointing to the array of bottles on the bar).

In addition, other cultures have different ideas about 'naked' imperatives than are valid in one's own. Anna Wierzbicka (1985) tells us how she, in the beginning of her Australian life, confused the Polish polite use of the naked imperative (*Sit!*) with the impolite English order *Sit down*. Even 'positively polite' expressions like those used for thanking (*No problem*) may be face-threatening in other cultures than those belonging to the Anglo cultural universe.

Likewise, an offer to be on a first-name basis (*Just call me Noam*), made during a softball game while you are diving for the same ball as your professor, butting heads in the process, would be highly inappropriate and face-threatening in the context of a formal awards reception, when addressing the president of a prestigious overseas university; see Scollon and Scollon (2001: 135–6) and Wierzbicka (2006: 305–6).

26.6.2 The Cultural Factor

With regard to cultural differences, it has been noted by researchers such as Sachiko Ide and her group of Japanese sociolinguists and pragmaticists (see Hill et al. 1986) that politeness in a Japanese context is quite a different kind of animal from the one we encounter in what Anna Wierzbicka (2006) calls 'the Anglo cultural world.' Without taking a position with regard to this somewhat controversial terminology, let me just point out that Wierzbicka has a valid case: there are cultural differences in language use, e.g. with regard to polite expressions like the use of the 'polished' vs the 'naked' imperative referred to above.

One of the first to remark on this fact was precisely Sachiko Ide herself in that early article (1982). In later work (1989), Ide centered her research around the Japanese concept of 'discernment' (*wakimae*), best understood as the ability to find one's proper place in society, linguistically and otherwise. The Japanese attitude of 'discernment' (which often, on the surface, looks very much like Anglo politeness) has less to do with the individual's conception of how to use words and expressions (which is often the focus of Western discussions on politeness, both in linguistics and in pragmatics) and much more to do with what Ide calls 'the speaker's [and I add: the hearer's] sense of place or role in a given situation according to [Japanese] social conventions' (Ide 1989: 229).

26.6.3 From Politeness to Truth and Beyond

Often, a polite expression or utterance is used to hide some unpleasant fact or mask a negative attitude. *You don't have to be polite* is often said as an admonition to speak our minds truthfully, even at the risk of offending our partner (as in the case of the Israeli *dugri* 'straightforward' speech; Katriel 1986). But truth is definitely not the whole story, neither in philosophy nor in pragmatics.

Rather than unilaterally targeting ways of truthfully and correctly asserting something by means of a proposition or a sentence (as was the primary concern of the logicians and philosophers, and later of the syntacticians among the linguists), pragmatics moves beyond true/false assertion and turns its attention to the problem of effectively sharing one's intentions with one's conversational or other text-sharing partners. The main insight here (which is not altogether new) is that asserting is more than formulating a proposition; it is an *act* of uttering. As early as 1885, the Austrian philosopher Franz von Brentano had told us that 'speaking is often brought into opposition with acting; but speaking itself is an acting; an activity' (Nerlich and Clarke 1996: 189, quoting Smith 1990: 42). And already Wilhelm von Humboldt, in the early years of the nineteenth century had expressed the famous opinion (referred to above) that language is not a thing done, but a continued activity ('not an *érgon*, but an *enérgeia*'); in modern parlance, not a product, but a process (see Hurford 2007: 158).

For the philosophers of the Ordinary Language variety, their original intention was to pursue a thought already formulated by John Locke three centuries earlier: that the candle of our intellect is bright enough by itself, and has no need of being assisted by the invention of cumbersome technical philosophical jargon. As Locke expresses it (in his 1700[1685] work *An Essay Concerning Human Understanding*), 'the candle that is set up in us shines bright enough for all our purposes' (book I: 1); it is by the light of this candle that the Oxonians endeavoured to unravel the mysteries of human language use. Rather than basing themselves on the analysis of individual linguistic items (words, phrases, grammatical constructions, etc.) and their correct uses, these philosophers directed their efforts towards grasping the *force* of a particular expression, as manifested by its effects on the environment (including, though not uniquely, those exemplary stalwarts, the speaker and the hearer). The difference was that the conversational partners were no longer visualized (as the introspecting linguists, beginning with Saussure, used to do) as disembodied talking heads (de Saussure 1962[1916]: 36; Mey 1985: 25). The heads were placed firmly in a context of use.

As an illustration, consider the following. The linguist George Lakoff once referred to his clever cat, 'who,' he said, 'loves to torment me' (1971: 329). By using the relative pronoun 'who' for this particular feline, Lakoff rightfully questions the legitimacy, in the case of his favourite beast, of maintaining the human/non-human distinction in the English relative pronoun (*who* for humans, *which* for animals, etc.). But he does this strictly within linguistics: Lakoff operates from the linguistic 'inside' outwards, asking 'Given this word (or utterance), what can it be used for?'

In contrast, a philosopher like John L. Austin, along with the pragmaticists, wants to know what words or utterances (or 'speech acts,' as Austin would call them; see §26.8) would be effective, given a situation of use. The question is not just one of establishing meaning or even correct use, but one of doing; one of process rather than of product. Austin operates from the outside inwards, asking: 'Given a particular situation, what words (or utterances) are possible and effective?' Doing so, Austin emphasized the *act* of speaking as the most important element in human language use, rather than the spoken words, taken by themselves; the question becomes 'how to do things with words,' as the title of his ground-breaking work has it; Austin 1962).

I will return to Austin later in this chapter, after a brief interlude where I introduce one of Austin's contemporaries, a person whose influence on pragmatics has gone mostly unnoticed: the Austrian/American philosopher Rudolf Carnap, one of the most influential thinkers in the pre-Second World War world.

26.7 INTERLUDE: A PRAGMATIC STEPFATHER

As I said earlier, a number of candidates have traditionally been proposed for the honorific title of 'father of pragmatics': Frege, Wittgenstein, Austin, Grice, to mention only the most prominent ones. But one name is seldom included in this pragmatic *anakeion*: that of Rudolf Carnap.

As early as 1942, in his *Introduction to Semantics*, Carnap wrote:

> [Linguistics] consists of pragmatics, semantics, and descriptive syntax. But these three parts are not on the same level; pragmatics is the basis for all of linguistics . . . seman-tics and syntax are, strictly speaking, parts of pragmatics. (1942: 13)

Carnap writes in the tradition of the Chicago School, the post-Neopositivist paradigm whose emblem was the star-crossed 'unification' of the sciences, embodied in its flagship, the *Encyclopedia of Unified Science* (of which only a few fascicles appeared); however, among the latter was the famous entry by Charles Morris (1938, 1946) in which he (re-)defined the Peirce–Morris triad of 'syntax, semantics, and pragmatics.'

What Carnap did was to snatch the linguistically relevant parts of the Peircean tradition and set them on a proper footing: pragmatics as the basis of linguistics. But he never elaborated on this sound principle; in fact, the only mention of pragmatics in a later work is to be found at the very end of his later classic treatise *Meaning and*

Necessity (1956), where he makes a passing, programmatic reference to pragmatics as of necessity including semantics (p. 248).

This is why I call Carnap a stepfather, rather than a true father (or even a strict uncle, in the Roman sense of *patruus*, whose 'whiplash words and tongue do make us fear and tremble'; Horace, *Odes* III: 12; cf. Mey 2005). Having played a somewhat fatherly role for some time, he then abandoned his offspring and left the baby in the care of others, most of whom saw fit to throw it out, along with the pragmatic bathwater. But who were these others, and what did they do (or what are they doing) with the (partially) rescued baby? And having thrown out the baby, where did they dump that water?

26.8 TRUE FATHERHOOD: JOHN AUSTIN

Above, I mentioned John L. Austin as the person who first put our thinking about language on a solid, pragmatic footing. As I also mentioned earlier, in today's literature Austin is often called the 'father of pragmatics.' As Nerlich and Clarke remark, a bit tongue-in-cheek, 'everybody knew that the father of pragmatics was Austin' (1996: 373); but they also insist on showing that there were many streams and rivulets that gathered together to break the containing dam of classical linguistics and open the floodgates for a new, revolutionizing approach to the study of language (the image is actually Talmy Givón's, himself a linguist who at one point decided to leave the linguistic mainstream and strike out on his own, even though he kept away from the after-effects of the pragmatic 'dam burst,' as he called it (1989: 25, Nerlich and Clarke 1996: 374)—to the point even of resigning his membership on the editorial board of the *Journal of Pragmatics* in 1989 in protest against the journal's lax interpretation of the pragmatics/linguistics divide.

But where does Austin's (imputed, rather than self-proclaimed) claim to pragmatic fatherhood stem from? As Jenny Thomas notes, Austin's original interest in language stemmed from the observation that 'we do not just use language to say things (to make statements), but to do things (to perform actions)' (1996: 31). In other words, the observational emphasis is shifted from truth-functionally interesting assertions to performatively important acts—'speech acts,' to use Austin's term.

26.8.1 Performatives and Things to Do

Looking around in the linguistic warehouse for things to do with words, Austin, using his Lockean candle, made another important observation: the English language itself offered copious examples of distinctions that were relevant to that shifted emphasis, such as seen in verbs that do not allow for truth-conditional evaluations. Take the verb *to wish*: how can an utterance such as *Condolences on your loss* be said to be either true or false? To be sure, such an utterance can be misplaced (or 'misfire,' as Austin was wont to call it), as when we offer condolences to a friend on the loss of her pet, jewel-encrusted tortoise ('There goes a package,' as Charles Ryder remarks to Julia in Evelyn Waugh's *Brideshead Revisited*)—an irregularity Austin would attribute to the felicity conditions for condolences not being observed; but that has nothing to do with truth or falsehood. The solution to this problem was, for Austin, to deny such verbs as *to apologize, to offer condolences*, etc. assertive status, naming them 'performatives' instead.

While this insight of course was not altogether new (similar ideas had been bandied about from ancient times by philosophers such as Aristotle and the Stoics and by grammarians such as Apollonius Dyscolus and his followers; on this, see Allan 2010a), it was Austin who reintroduced and revitalized it in the broader context of twentieth-century linguistic-philosophical thinking. It became further clear to Austin not only that those performatives did not obey truth conditions, but that in fact most of our utterances do not function in the truth value dimension. In fact, the only true thing about such utterances is that they can be said to have truly occurred: hence, a misfiring apology is still an apology, and an insult, even if retracted, does not exonerate the utterer from blame. Compare that a prospective applicant for a position at a major US university was denied the job because he had used the 'n-word' in his presentation, even though the user was not in any sense performing a racial slur by uttering *nigger*, but simply quoting from his field notes. The solution to the performative problem Austin found in his key concept of the 'speech act.'

26.8.2 Speech Acts

Speech acts were originally grouped by Austin into a few major categories, such as statements, promises, threats, and judgements. Later authors such as John Searle (on whom more below) have suggested refinements and changes, and there is no agreement either on the correct classification or on the actual number of speech acts.

What is important here is not the uniform division and watertight classification of speech acts (their number may vary greatly according to the preferences of the organizer, and overlaps cannot be avoided), but the understanding that speech acts are not the last word in the pragmatics of human language (even though they historically may have been among the first). Austin, along with his contemporaries and followers, realized that there is an inherent 'force' in our use of words; the concept of speech act expresses this notion in a more or less regularized way.

For Austin, the simple uttering of a sentence constitutes the 'locutionary' aspect of the speech act, seen as a neutral vehicle for expressing our thoughts and feelings. However, in order for us to make our point when speaking—that is, for the act to be a proper speech act—the locution must represent a particular intention (such as to make a promise); this is the 'illocutionary' aspect of the speech act, or its illocutionary point, or 'force' (which is what distinguishes the individual speech act from others, and permits its classification). And finally, we have to consider the effect of what we are saying: the 'perlocutionary' effect of the speech act (see Mey 2001: 95–6).

Austin's original discovery of the 'force' of our speaking was based on his reflections on certain verbs in English, for which he coined the term 'performatives' (as opposed to 'constatives,' which merely indicate a certain state of affairs). From the very beginning, a conceptual (or even natural) tie was thought to exist between a speech act verb and the corresponding speech act (the verb *to promise* seemed to be the natural, canonical expression of the promising act). But Austin himself was quick to realize (as many others have pointed out after him) that such an identification has its roots in a monolithic, essentialist view by which speech acts are deemed to be necessarily and sufficiently conditioned by the existence of a particular illocutionary verb. Or, in plain text: no promise without the verb *to promise* and conversely: the verb *to promise* always indicates a promise. This is called the 'Illocutionary Verb Fallacy' (see Leech 1983: 176; it is a special case of what John Searle earlier had dubbed the 'speech act fallacy' in philosophy; 1969: 136–41). However, as has been pointed out by many authors (e.g. Verschueren 1999), there is no clear-cut distinction between true speech act verbs and what is called a 'speech act formula': quasi-variations on a particular illocutionary theme (e.g. *to thank*, compared with *to express one's gratitude*: both serve the same purpose, and their 'force' is the same). Often, such expressions may be categorized under the label of 'indirect speech acts' (§26.9.1 below).

26.8.3 Appropriateness and Felicity

Consider this hypothetical event. On a dark and moonless night, I sneak up to the local shipyard, carrying a bottle of cheap champagne, which I proceed to throw at the bow of a ship, waiting to be launched the next day, while I pronounce the words: *I christen this ship the Imperial Battleship Mao* (Levinson's example, 1983: 229). Did I effectively perform an act of christening? Clearly not. But why not?

The question here is *what* makes a speech act 'felicitous' (Austin's expression) or successful. Austin specifies some of the conditions that have to be met for a speech act to be successful, such as that the person executing the act must be properly appointed, that the ship should not be named already, that the procedure be performed correctly, and so on (Austin 1962: 14–15, Levinson 1983: 228ff.). If any of these *felicity conditions* is not met, the speech act will fail, or misfire.

What is important here is to observe the institutional aspect of our acting. In cases like christening a ship, baptizing a baby, or performing a wedding, we immediately realize that the performer of the act needs to be one who has been authorized by the respective institutions governing such acts (the shipping company, the church, the registrar). But there is also an 'institutional' aspect to our less conscious activities of speaking—one which is often overlooked in public discourse. One is tempted to vary the Watzlawick dictum cited earlier: 'One cannot act non-institutionally'; by this, I mean that we all are placed under some authority, like the centurion in the Bible

(Matt. 8: 9). The parent rebuking a child, or a teacher prompting a student, all speak with the voice of the institution: the family or the school.

This point of view has consequences for how we view our public discourse: our public words are never frivolous or 'idle,' because they always are set in some institutional, social frame. Verbal abuse of authority may lead to other, even more serious abuses, so it is no wonder that most of the many recently revealed incidents of sexual abuse practised against minors have regularly (if not always) happened in institutional surroundings (schools, sports clubs, children's homes, and so on), where the words of the persons under authority have felicitously (but in the end disastrously) paved the way for the aggravated non-verbal abusive acts. I will revert to the theme of the societal institution in §26.10.1, where I deal with questions of societal pragmatics.

26.9 The Importance of Searle

It is impossible to talk about speech acts without mentioning the work of John R. Searle, Austin's probably most famous student at Oxford in the 1950s. Here, Searle also encountered another person, the man who in time, after Austin's untimely death in 1958, was to take up the pragmatics mantle: the philosopher H. Paul Grice (whose work I discussed in §26.5).

At Oxford, Grice had studied with Austin, but in 1968 he left Oxford for Berkeley, where he rejoined Searle. In a fascinating twist of history, the missing link joining these three famous pragmatic 'brand names,' Austin, Grice, Searle, is Gottlob Frege. Austin had translated one of Frege's major works into English early in his own career, and in addition had overseen the dissertation work of a promising American student of Frege, John Searle, who was writing on Frege's notions of 'sense' and 'reference' (see the discussion earlier in this chapter; Searle's Ph.D is the exception to the rule that dissertations don't make it into successful books; Searle 1969: vii). It is quite conceivable that Searle saw Frege as the true inspiring force behind Austin's pragmatic work because of his own engagement with the German philosopher; the latter's somewhat undeserved accolade as the father of pragmatics may have originated here, to be transmitted down the line to a number of Anglo-American philosophers and linguists, such as Larry Horn or Ken Turner.

Questions of genealogy and fatherhood aside, Searle's main work in pragmatics is embodied in this 1969 work, appropriately named *Speech Acts*. Austin had left his oeuvre unfinished and somewhat inconsistent (in the last chapter of his book, he disavows some of his initial assumptions about performatives). Neither was he ever able to oversee the printed edition of his lectures, which came out in 1962, a few years after his death. It was not until Searle's book hit the markets that the linguists began to pay serious attention to Austin and his earlier writings; in a way, Searle reinvented and to a certain degree re-created Austin in his own image, as Levinson, among others, has intimated (1983: 238, esp. n. 9).

Searle's account of speech acting, and especially his classification of speech acts, was to remain the staple of pragmatic theory for the next few decades. For instance, Searle codified some of the happy speech acts that Austin had talked about, by providing a set of nine conditions and five rules for the act of promising (Searle 1969: 57–64). In addition, he created the useful notion of an 'illocutionary force indicating device' (IFID), meant to capture the fact that speech acts are not always what they look like (as we saw in our earlier discussion of the illocutionary fallacy): Searle's IFID is neutral as to its manifestations (which can be fairly complex, 1969: 31). By not restricting the IFID to a particular linguistic manifestation ('illocutionary force indicating devices in English include *at least* word order, stress, intonation,' 1969: 30; my emphasis), Searle opens the way for a broader understanding of the act of speaking, something I will exploit later in this chapter when I talk about 'pragmatic acts.'

Searle provides a centrefold in his book, where he demonstrates various types of illocutionary acts (requests, questions, warnings, etc.), along with a conspectus of the various rules and conditions that apply (Searle 1969: 66–7). In later work (1979), Searle makes this classification more precise and also more categorical; it has become the generally received (albeit sometimes disputed) standard for describing speech acts. Searle distinguishes between representatives (also called 'assertions'), directives (e.g. when giving orders), commissives (like the act of promising we discussed earlier), expressives (as when we offer condolences), and declarations (statements that change the state of affairs by declaring something to be the case: e.g. *I declare this bridge to be opened*, one of Austin's original examples, and surely a case of saying it does make it so!).

But even with these five major classes more or less universally agreed on, there is no doubt that the classification could be extended or collapsed, multiplied or reduced; there is just no iron-clad procedure of determining the number of speech acts and their typology uniformly and *ex cathedra*. The pragmatic community does not recognize any institution-ally anointed keepers or defenders of the faith, as will become particularly evident when we move to the non-institutionalized fringes of the pragmatic territory where the indirect speech acts lead their hidden lives. (For further discussion, see Mey 2001: 120ff.)

26.9.1 Indirect Speech Acts

One of the thornier problems concerning speech acts is that there are certain 'indirect' ways of using words to obtain favours, make apologies, express thanks, etc. that do not seem to fit any of the pre-ordained types that the speech act theorists have confronted us with. Compare Stephen Levinson's remark that 'most requests . . . are indirect,' 'imperatives are rarely used to command' (1983: 264, 275); Jenny Thomas likewise observes that, when we invite somebody to our house, we seldom say something like *I hereby invite you to come and see me* (1996: 47). What we say, instead, is chosen from among a plethora of rather undefinable, indirect expressions. Thus, when your date says *Your place or mine?*, this may count as an invitation-cum-promise; the

quasi-obvious statement *It's getting late, John* may express wife Mildred's request/order
to her husband to interrupt the interesting conversation he has just struck up with the
new secretary, so Mildred can make hubby leave the departmental Christmas party
somewhat earlier than anticipated. The problem with all such formulas is precisely
their volatility: one cannot predict, sometimes not even post-construct, how a particular expression came to serve as the vehicle of a particular speech act. By their very
indirectness, indirect speech acts escape the focus of our pragmatic lens.

Two factors seem to be of importance here. The first is the force of tradition: a
particular expression may, over time, have acquired a meaning that is not inherent in
the words themselves, nor in the usual interpretation of the expression used. Thus,
thanking someone may take on an ironical meaning, such as when I say *Thank you for
sharing this with me*, meaning: 'I'm really not interested' (in response to the party bore
engaging me in information about his recent amorous conquests), while actually
thinking *Drop dead, you idiot*. In many Slavic cultures, greeting, or saying goodbye
to, a woman may be executed using an expression that literally means *I am kissing
[your] little hand* (thus in Slovak, one may say *ručku bozkávám*, without performing or
even gesture-sketching the kissing act). What is common to these expressions, as to all
other kinds of indirect speech acting, is that they depend for their correct understanding on the situation in which they are uttered; in many cases, they even define the
situation of use (as when the checker in the supermarket says *Hurry back*, as a way of
sending you off with the groceries). Such formulaic expressions or routine formulae, as
they used to be called (Coulmas 1981), have recently been studied under various names
such as 'situation-bound utterances' (Kecskes 2002): that is to say, expressions that
derive their essential meaning from the situation in which they are used; conversely,
they determine the situation as one of specific use. Another approach is that of the
situated speech acts, or pragmatic acts, on which see the next section.

The case of the indirect speech acts extends and redefines the classic Austinian
performative, often bound to only one type of institutionalized acting (such as
christening a ship). When it comes to non-institutional acting, the criterion of strict
performativity is inadequate. We construe our performance in accordance with the
situation we are in; only the 'total speech situation' (Austin 1962: 148) can give us the
ultimate answer to the question which speech acts are being, or have been, produced. In
the final analysis, as I say elsewhere, 'we will have to ask ourselves how speech acts relate
to our human activity as a whole: thinking "globally" while acting "locally", as the saying
goes' (Mey 2001: 95). Here, as elsewhere, the proof of the pudding is in the eating.

26.10 PRAGMATIC ACTS

As Austin already told us, 'words [and specifically, speech acts], in order to be
understood have to be "explained" by the "context" in which they were actually spoken'
(1962: 100). In a more robust version of this dictum (and omitting the scare quotes),

I contend that no speech act makes sense unless placed in the appropriate context (including, but not only, all the felicity conditions that we have talked about earlier). Speech acts, in order to have effect, must be *situated*. Thus, a situated speech act comes close to what the late Dell Hymes has called a 'speech event' (1972a): speech as embedded in a social, most often institutionalized, activity such as a visit to the hospital or a Japanese tea ceremony. The point of calling such activities 'pragmatic acts' is that they are not confined to particular words or individualized occasions, but pervade the entire gamut of our language use (and beyond). All speech acting depends on the situation: not only does the situation determine what speech acts are appropriate, but the situation strikes back, dialectically, by defining itself according to the speech being practised. The emphasis here is not on the individual speech act and how to describe or define it, but on the all-important question of what users in a particular situation have at their disposal in the way of speech acting in order to realize their interactional goals of apologizing, ordering, promising, etc.

A pragmatic approach to speech acting raises, as its most basic question, the matter of the user's access to words: how to use the appropriate language tools? However, the theory of pragmatic acts does not start out from those words (as is done in the classic theory of speech acts, and indeed, in most of linguistics at large). Rather than focusing on the individual speaker (properly idealized *à la* Chomsky 1957a, 1965) and his or her utterances, pragmatic acting is about speakers as well as hearers (in the widest possible sense) and about their interacting through language and other communicative means (such as gestures and body language in general). We are looking here at 'the construction of action through talk' in 'situated interaction' (Goodwin 2000: 1492), but at the same time we see how all 'talk in interaction' (Drew and Heritage 1992) depends on the framework of the situation (a girls' game of hopscotch in Goodwin's example) in order to be understood.

The interaction between speech and other human activity cannot be fully captured by a single-strand concept such as that of the 'speech act.' I have suggested the term 'pragmatic act' to identify the locus where all the various linguistic and other elements converge in order to create a holistic communicative event. As Bill Hanks has pointed out, 'meaning arises out of the interaction between language and circumstances, rather than being encapsulated in the language itself' (1996: 266). Instead of focusing on the *words* being spoken, we concentrate on the *things* being done. No speech act, taken by itself, makes sense: it has to be instantiated in a particular situation as a situated speech act or pragmatic act. Here, the emphasis is not on conditions and rules (as was the case for speech acts); the concept of the pragmatic act puts the spotlight on the environment in which both speakers and hearers find, and realize, their potential. The defining question for a pragmatic act is: 'What can successfully be uttered, given the current situation?' What we can say and what we can hear (or in general, successfully perceive) is a function of the situation we are in; moreover, the pragmatic act engages the whole communicative agent, not just his or her words: body language is an integrated part of the generalized prototype of pragmatic acting called the 'pragmeme.' (See further Allan 2010b, Capone 2010, Mey 2001: ch. 8, 2009, 2010.)

26.10.1 Towards a Societal Pragmatics

On the back cover of a recent book on pragmatics, one finds the following statement: 'At the present time, pragmatics is generally approached from the neo- and post-Gricean perspectives' (Moeschler 2010). For the readers who have followed the brief account of the history of pragmatics presented in the preceding pages, such a statement may appear somewhat surprising: Grice has indeed loomed large there, but his is definitely not the only approach we have been considering. In this final section of the present chapter, I want to sketch the development of another, more societally oriented way of thinking about, and doing, pragmatics. In other words, the statement quoted above is incomplete, to say the least.

But why should we bother about creating yet another sub-field of pragmatics? Isn't the notion of a 'societal pragmatics' somewhat oxymoronic, or at best pleonastic? Given that pragmatics, by definition, is social, one could legitimately raise the question: Why is it necessary to talk about 'societal pragmatics'?

The answer to this question can be found, once again, in the historical circumstances that have led to the development of pragmatics in the first place. The language and communication sciences have witnessed a reorientation over the past five decades, away from grammatical and philosophical speculations and towards a humanistic practice of using words. What has been called the 'pragmatic turn' in linguistics has been described as a 'shift from the paradigm of theoretical grammar (in particular, syntax) to the paradigm of the language user' (Mey 2001: 4). The need to testify to this pragmatic turn by putting the 'societal question' on the table in explicit and uncontroversial ways is clearly brought out when we consider the one-eyed view of pragmatics that emerges in the statement quoted at the beginning of this section. Implicit in this turn is, of course, the fundamental question of what is meant by saying that pragmatics by definition is social, and that this is a given.

As users of language, we are social beings, and hence we communicate, and use language, strictly on society's premises. This means that society not only *controls* our access to the linguistic and communicative means, but more importantly, it *enables* us, as language users, to use those very means. Generally speaking, 'pragmatics is defined as the study of language in human communication as determined by the conditions of society' (Mey 2001: 6); specifically, societal pragmatics scrutinizes those social conditions and inquires how they affect our language use. Societal pragmatics endeavours to determine in what ways the conditions under which we live facilitate or obstruct, perhaps even make or break, our use of language.

What I am arguing for here is a renewed consciousness of the human element in language use: an 'ecology' of language, we might call it. Since pragmatics focuses on language-in-use, the language user is its centre of attention. But users do not live in some abstract conservation environment, where one can control their movements and monitor their speech, and check that they do the right thing. The respect we pay to people should include our respect for their living conditions and our acceptance of their choices. Below, I will mention a case from recent practice, and draw some conclusions based on a societal pragmatic perspective.

During the past decades' heated international debates on whether or not to interfere in other nations' internal affairs (the former Yugoslavia and the conflict in the Darfur region of Sudan come to mind as instances). Here, the expression that many of the Western negotiators used in this context, viz. the 'right to interfere' in order to protect the people from their genocidal attackers, expresses an attitude that puts itself above other nations' sovereign aims and wishes; hence this way of dealing with the problems in former Yugoslavia and Sudan's Darfur is apt to generate considerable controversy in a variety of international and national fora. By contrast, if we define a possible military intervention, using language stating our international 'responsibility to protect' attacked people, we are able to express our feeling of obligation to assist other nations in safeguarding a respect for human rights and in building a democratic society. As a result, fewer people will be offended (both on the national and international level) by such a societal pragmatically motivated choice of language.

26.11 CONCLUSION

In the course of its brief history in modern times, pragmatics has managed to throw light on a number of issues that had been swept under the age-old rug of traditional linguistic and human communication studies, with their unique focus on the historical, grammatical, semantic, and informational aspects of language and its use. The return of the user and the renewed emphasis on his or her situation of language use (in Goffman's words, 'Felicity's conditions,' rather than just 'felicity conditions': 1983a: 54) has proved a valuable incentive for studies in a wide array of subfields and has yielded fascinating, often mind- and world-changing, results. As pragmatics unfolds in the decades to come, we can expect that it will extend to ever more fields of human communication, and help us understand the younger generations' innovative approaches to technology, by putting it to use in new, indeed revolutionizing ways. Dealing with modern communication requires an open-minded attitude, open both to the unconventional communicators themselves and to their often unexpected ways of using newfangled media. Practised in this way, a societal pragmatics can put light around pathways leading to a better recognition and enhanced understanding of such new developments and, not least, their users.

CHAPTER 27

....

MEANING IN TEXTS AND CONTEXTS

....

LINDA R. WAUGH, JOSÉ ALDEMAR ÁLVAREZ
VALENCIA, TOM HONG DO, KRISTEN
MICHELSON, AND M'BALIA THOMAS

27.1 INTRODUCTION

....

TWENTIETH-CENTURY linguistics began with approaches that, in general, equated meaning with lexical meaning and tended to study meaning (if they studied it at all) outside of contexts of use. Structuralism (formalist approaches), with its emphasis on an autonomous, synchronic *langue* (the common, monolithic code of a linguistic community—de Saussure 1962 [1916]), system (the inner patterning of language—Bloomfield 1933), grammar (abstract, decontextualized competence—Chomsky 1965), vs *parole*, performance (usage, the use of language in speaking), became the mainstream of American and some of European linguistics from 1920 to well into the 1970s (see Chapters 18–20 above). As a consequence, work on lexical meaning was approached from structuralist and neo-structuralist points of view (Chapters 24 and 25), which focused on the place of words and (lexical) semantics in the linguistic system. They assumed that words are well-defined Aristotelian categories with clear boundaries, and that the relationship between a word and its referent in the world is simple and direct. There was thus a dominance of interest in decontextualized meanings as would be found, for example, in a dictionary or a list of example sentences in a grammar book.

It was only slowly that attention turned to meaning in context—in spoken discourse and written texts as related to and influenced by contexts. This was largely through the agency of linguists who were interested in a dynamic, use-oriented view of language. This tradition has roots that go back to the nineteenth century and grew steadily through the twentieth century, helped by more functionalist approaches starting in the

1920s, and by the influence of other disciplines (e.g. anthropology, sociology, psychology, philosophy) after the Second World War and especially since the 1960s.

The differences between these two points of view with respect to meaning has centred on a variety of theoretical differences: (word) meaning as grounded in and referring to some language-independent reality vs language as a potential for creating meaning, and all elements of language, including non-referential ones (e.g. syntactic structure, word order, prosody) as both meaning-bearing and meaning-making. In the latter view, the definition of meaning is enlarged during the century to include not only referential (propositional) meaning, but also interpersonal, emotional, metalinguistic, poetic, textual, etc. meaning. The latter relate to a reality that is specifically human: intersubjectivity/interpersonal relations, based on various modes of social interaction.

Although linguistics in the twentieth century defined itself as focusing on the spoken language (vs literary studies, for example), for many decades structuralist/formalist linguistics did not grapple with an empirical approach to speech. Many believed that speech was unsystematic and thus intractable to serious study (Linell 1982, 2005). However, the more use-oriented linguists took the view that spoken (and written) language is worthy of study and is systematic in many aspects, and that language is dynamic, highly contextualized, an activity, a process, and linked to many linguistic and non-linguistic elements. An amalgam of multi/interdisciplinary approaches has widened the scope of work on language and, among other things, has insisted upon studying language in actual usage, in socially and culturally authentic communication, in texts, discourses, and contexts.

Meaning, in this perspective, is related to the linguistic context (also called 'co-text,' Catford 1965; van Dijk 1977), as well as the context of the speech event (Jakobson 1960, Hymes 1974) and the context of situation (Malinowski 1935, Firth 1957, 1968, Halliday 1973) in which language use occurs. Some linguists have a particularly broad definition of context, such that it includes the larger sociohistorical-cultural context and numerous facets of the social world (including social class, power structures, and historical factors). Scholars also moved from a unidirectional model (e.g. context influences language) to a model in which context and language co-constitute one another: e.g. it is through and with language that we build our sociocultural world, and at the same time it is this world that influences the specific way in which features of language use are understood (Hodge and Kress 1988, Hasan 2005b, Fairclough 2009).

27.2 WORK ON LEXICAL MEANING

As said above, the structuralists equated meaning with lexical meaning only and did not study how words are used. However, there was some work on meaning in general, and lexical meaning in particular, during this time period outside of this mainstream. As an example, we could cite *The Meaning of Meaning* by Charles Ogden and I. A. Richards (1923). Influenced by Charles Sanders Peirce (1960), they established a semiotic triangle (1923: 11) in which a linguistic symbol (e.g. a spoken word, e.g.

table) causes a visual image, a blurred outline, a thought or an act of reference in the mind, one of which is sufficient to identify a referent in the world (an actual table). Hence, the relation between language and the world is indirect and mediated by thought.

Somewhat later, Ludwig Wittgenstein, a philosopher of language, discussed what he called language games, in which the meaning of a word (e.g. *table*) 'is its use in the language' (1953: 43). His work eventually led to ordinary language philosophy, modern-day speech act theory, and pragmatics (see Chapter 26 and §27.4.2.4). Moreover, language use brings up issues that are difficult to resolve, such as e.g. polysemy—the multiple (typically contextualized) meanings of words. Wittgenstein (1953) tackled this problem by developing his 'family resemblance' theory of (lexical) meaning, in which he analysed 'game' (*Spiel*)—as in 'board games,' 'card games,' 'ball games,' 'Olympic games,' 'kid's games'—and showed that, much in the same way that members of an extended family share similarities, the various senses of the word 'do not share a set of common properties on whose basis games can be clearly distinguished from non-games' (Taylor 1995: 38–40). Rather they are structured 'by a criss-crossing network of similarities,' some of which are more central and others more peripheral to the concept of game.

While, as for Ogden and Richards, Wittgenstein's ideas had little impact at the time, his proposal finds echoes in prototype theory and the work of the psychologist Eleanor Rosch (1973, 1975) (see Chapter 25), who focused on natural and cultural categories like 'furniture,' 'fruit,' 'vehicle,' and 'bird,' and asked subjects to judge to what extent particular entities could be regarded as good examples of each one of these categories. The results showed that some members of a category are better (more focal, more prototypical) examples than other (more peripheral) members of the category. So, for a category like 'bird,' 'robin' is a good, prototypical type of 'bird,' whereas 'penguin' is a bad example (because it can't fly—a salient characteristic of the prototypical bird). Further work in this area has led to the idea of centre–periphery relationships, a radial model of the meanings of a word as emanation from a core sense (or senses) (Lakoff 1987), the notion of a basic or generic level for naming things (see Chapter 25 for more discussion), as well as the concept of fuzziness: in logic (Chapter 34), truth values (Chapter 23), structures (Chapter 33), the world (Chapter 25), and sets (Lakoff 1972).

Another influential outgrowth of this work is the analysis of extensions of meaning through metaphor and metonymy (see Chapter 25). George Lakoff and Mark Johnson's seminal book, *Metaphors We Live By* (1980), started a major area of investigation in what came to be known as Conceptual Metaphor Theory. Their claim was that metaphor is not peripheral or just literary or purely linguistic; rather it pervades all of language, because it is a conceptual (cognitive) phenomenon which underlies semantic patterns that can be seen across language use (their work typically dealt with sentences). In their approach, metaphors are given as simple equivalences (e.g. AN ARGUMENT IS A JOURNEY) based on sentences like *We have set out to prove that penguins are birds, This observation points the way to an elegant solution, We have arrived at a disturbing conclusion* (adapted from Lakoff and Johnson 1980: 90).

According to them, this sets up a mapping between an often more concrete and embodied source domain (JOURNEY) and a more abstract target domain (ARGUMENT). Since that original publication, conceptual metaphor theory has been extended into conceptual integration, or blending theory (Fauconnier and Turner 2002), in which not two domains, or spaces, are at issue, but four (see Chapter 25). It has also led to a revival of interest in metonymy as a separate figure that received little treatment in Lakoff and Johnson (see Jakobson 1956 for an earlier treatment) but has been taken up by modern-day European linguists, leading to a series of publications on metaphor and metonymy (e.g. Panther and Radden 1999, Barcelona 2003, Dirven and Pörings 2002). Others have looked at how metaphorical and metonymic patterns can be discerned in both spoken and written texts and can influence our thoughts, attitudes, and decisions (see the discussion of Critical Discourse Analysis below, §27.5.2.2).

27.3 FUNCTIONALIST APPROACHES

In our discussion of lexical meaning we have gone far from early twentieth-century work, but in order to understand other developments in the arena of meaning in texts (and contexts), we need to return to the 1920s and 1930s and the functionalist views of language mentioned above. Two groups called for a more functional approach to language which stressed its use for human communication and its role in interaction (see also Chapter 21): the Prague School in Czechoslovakia and the London School in Great Britain. The Prague School was heavily influential in Europe and also led to American functional approaches to linguistics, starting in the 1970s (Nichols 1984).The London School fostered the development of Systemic Functional Linguistics (SFL)[1] in the UK and Australia starting in the 1960s. Each of these has had many other offshoots, which cannot be covered in this short chapter.

27.3.1 Prague Functional-Structuralism: Theme–rheme, Functional Sentence Perspective

The Prague School (see also Chapter 20) comprised Czech linguists (the best-known being Vilem Mathesius) and Russian émigrés (Roman Jakobson and Nikolai Trubetz-koy) among others. They argued that linguistics had to study language use as well as language structure, since language 'serves for communication; from this fact comes the

---

[1] Although SFL is sometimes equated with Systemic Functional Grammar (SFG), it is important to notice that, while SFL is a theory of the architecture of language (Halliday 2003[1994], Matthiessen 2007a), SFG is one of its components that concentrates on the grammatical description of language (Halliday and Matthiessen 2004).

fundamental "need to analyze all the instruments of language from the standpoint of the tasks they perform." Language is a system with an internal *structure* suited to these communicative tasks' (Waugh and Monville-Burston 1990: 6).

Vilem Mathesius argued that, in addition to the traditional grammatical approach to the functions of constituents in a sentence (e.g. subject—predicate), there needed to be a functional and communicative approach which differentiates 'theme' (topic, what the sentence is about) and 'rheme' (comment, what is being said about the theme). He claimed that, in English, theme and subject and rheme and predicate are often (but not always) the same, whereas in Czech they are not. In addition, theme/rheme (topic/comment) is highly contextualized, being based on the viewpoint of the speaker, the interaction between speaker and addressee, as well as the linguistic, sociocultural, and experiential context of both. Mathesius' work was relatively unknown at the time, but it was developed after the war by the Czech Jan Firbas under the label of Functional Sentence Perspective (FSP) and, eventually, Communicative Dynamism (Mathesius 1964 [1928], Firbas 1964, 1986, 1992). It later came to influence work on functional grammar by M. A. K. Halliday (see below), André Martinet (1960, 1962), and Simon Dik (1978, 1997).

27.3.2 Prague Functional-Structuralism: Phonology and Morphology

In the 1920s and 1930s Jakobson and Trubetzkoy worked on phonology (see Chapters 8 and 20). Eventually Jakobson argued that phonemes and (grammatical) categories could be characterized by binary features, and that one of the terms differs from the other in possessing a special *mark* that the other one lacks (Jakobson and Waugh 1979: 90–92, 2002: 92–95). The unmarked term is less constrained and thus has more contextual variability and flexibility. 'Using this model as a basis, Jakobson developed a theory of form and meaning in morphology and elaborated fundamental principles for semantic analysis. He argued, in particular, that all categories contain an inseparable union of form and meaning, that grammar in itself is always meaningful, and that meaning is different from reference' (Waugh and Monville-Burston 1990: xvi). So, in the grammatical opposition of singular to plural, the plural is marked and refers to more than one entity (e.g. 'cats'), whereas the singular can refer to one entity in its basic meaning ('[a/the] cat'), as well as the category in general in its marginal, more context-bound meanings ('cat,' as in 'the cat is a small, carnivorous, domesticated animal'). These examples show the relation between (grammatical) meaning and context, and the importance of context in separating out the various meanings of (grammatical) elements into hierarchical relations. Jakobson sometimes used markedness for the lexicon: e.g. in autonomous pairs like *high—low, big—small, light—dark*, where the first word of each pair is unmarked, being more general in meaning (e.g. *How high is that table?*—see Jakobson and Waugh 1987[1979]: 181–203, Waugh 1982). However, he was less inclined to use features and markedness for all of lexical meaning, given Wittgenstein's work, polysemy, metaphor, metonymy, and so forth.

27.3.3 Prague School Functional-Structuralism: Functions of Language

The Prague School argued that the study of language is inadequate if the different functions of language are not taken into account. They were influenced by Karl Bühler (1934), who defined the speech act (event) as necessarily encompassing a speaker, an addressee and a thing referred to in the real world, and defined three functions on this basis: *depiction* of objects in the world (*representative* function), a *symptom* of the speaker (the *expressive* function), and a *signal* directed to a receiver and his/her behaviour (*appeal* or *accommodative* function). Jakobson added to this, the message (what is said) and a fourth function, the *poetic* (*aesthetic*) function, which focuses on the *properties of the message.*

In 1960 Jakobson published 'Linguistics and Poetics,' in which he developed this further (see also Jakobson 1990b: 69–79). He redefined each function as a set (*Einstellung*), a focus, on some factor of the speech event (1990b: 73). He generalized reference to the notion of context 'graspable by the addressee, and either verbal or capable of being verbalized,' including its spatio-temporal embedding as well as sociocultural factors. He defined focus on the context as the referential function (denotative, cognitive). He also said that there are two more 'inalienable' factors in speech communication: the code (more or less common to speaker and addressee) and the contact between them (a physical channel and psychological connection). The two additional functions are the metalinguistic (focus on the code) and the phatic (focus on the contact). Thus, for a focus on each factor (addresser, addressee, context, code, message, contact) there is a corresponding predominant function (emotive, conative, referential, metalingual, poetic, phatic), although other functions may be (and usually are) present in different hierarchical orders.

27.3.4 The London School (Firth and the Neo-Firthian Systemicists)

The London School of J. R. Firth (see Chapter 20), which developed in the 1940s and 1950s, established what R. H. Robins (1997) called, a 'contextual theory of language' (p. 246). Like Bloomfield and the American descriptivists (see Chapter 18), Firth drew on the work and thought of anthropologists, in his case Bronislaw Malinowski, who, 'faced with the task of translating native words and sentences in ethnographic texts . . . developed his theory of context of situation, whereby the meanings of utterances . . . and their component words and phrases were referred to their various functions in the particular situational contexts in which they were used' (Robins 1997: 246).

Context and meaning, in Firth's usage, is cultural and situational. Influenced by Wittgenstein, he defined meaning as the relation between language and the world of experience, as shown by the semantic functions of words, phrases, and sentences in different contexts of situation. Although Firth never wrote a comprehensive account of his approach to meaning, his student Michael Halliday, beginning in 1961, set out to develop what he called Systemic Functional Linguistics.

27.3.5 Systemic Functional Linguistics: Halliday and his Followers

While the primary source of Halliday's Systemic Functional Linguistics (SFL) is the work of J. R. Firth and other members of the London School (Hasan 1995, Butt 2001, Butler 2003; also see Chapter 20), it has roots in other linguistic traditions: the Prague School, glossematics (Hjelmslev, see Chapter 20), American anthropological linguistics (Chapter 29), French functionalism (Martinet, see Chapter 20) and linguistic work developed in China (Butt 2001, Butler 2003, Halliday 2003). Halliday's first publication in what would evolve into SFL, 'Categories of the Theory of Grammar', appeared in 1961, and from then on his conception of language as a social semiotic system which constitutes culture has been one of the main hallmarks of the theory. As a semiotic system, 'language is a resource for making meaning, and meaning resides in the systemic patterns of choice' (Halliday and Matthiessen 2004: 23) that are available to language users.

Halliday (2003) distinguishes four broadly defined levels/strata that are necessary for a description of language: context, semantics, lexicogrammar, and phonology. With regard to context, Halliday (1978) asserts that it corresponds to the situation, environment, and cultural milieu in which linguistic interaction takes place and that it interfaces directly with the semantic, lexicogrammar and phonological levels, since the happenings and conditions of the world with their social processes, along with the experiences of language users in interactional exchanges, are transformed into meaning (semantics); meaning is further transformed into wording (lexicogrammar) which is in turn realized in the form of speech production (phonology) (Halliday and Matthiessen 2004).

In order to account for the variation associated with language use in context, SFL developed the concept of register, viewed as the variables in the context of situation that impact a language event. They encompass field (the social process or the nature of the activity being engaged in), tenor (the social relationship between interacting communicators), and mode (the medium and role language is playing in the interaction—Halliday 1978, Halliday and Hasan 1989).

Halliday (1973, 1975, 2003) claimed that the semantic strata are organized in three functionally defined components labelled 'metafunctions.' The ideational metafunction is about the expression of experience, 'including both processes within and beyond the self—the phenomena of the external world and those of consciousness—and the logical relations deducible from them' (Halliday 1973: 91). The interpersonal metafunction enables the embodiment of social roles for establishing and maintaining personal and social relations; and the textual metafunction allows the building and recognition of texts that are discursively coherent and situationally relevant.

SFL has been used to analyse actual spoken and written texts in real settings, and has proved to have a wide scope of application in areas as varied as computational linguistics, stylistics, educational linguistics, translation, clinical linguistics, and artificial intelligence (Butler 2003, Hasan 2005a, Mathiessen 2007a, b, Halliday 2003). Recently an area that has gained wider application beyond SFL is multimodality, which, in addition to looking closely at the relationship between image and text/discourse in traditional domains such as educational materials, advertisements, and 3D objects (Kress and van Leeuwen 1996, van Leeuwen 2005, Kress 2010), has also studied architectural compositions (O'Toole 1994), music (van Leeuwen 1999), mathematical symbolism (O'Halloran 2005), and multimedia products (Baldry and Thibault 2006), among others.

27.4 ANALYSIS OF MEANING IN TEXTS AND CONTEXTS: SPOKEN LANGUAGE

The work of the functionalists set the stage for the expansion of linguistic analysis in general beyond the level of the clause or sentence to discourses and texts. Earlier approaches to this work came from rhetoric and oratory for spoken language and stylistics (plus philology) for written language.

27.4.1 Introduction: Rhetoric and Oratory

While rhetoric and oratory have a long history, the best-known approaches come from ancient Greece (especially the fifth century BCE) and the rise of the democratic polis, which depended on oratory and orality for many of its important governmental, business, political, and judicial functions. Producing and delivering effective speeches became essential, and the study of the art of persuasion acquired great importance. As interest in public speaking grew at that time, a theory of composing persuasive speeches became the educational cornerstone for the study of rhetoric (Kennedy 1994: 4–6, Bizzell and Herzberg 2001: 21–2). In his later treatise on rhetoric Aristotle identified three types of (artistic) proofs: *ethos*, developing a morally sound character and thus credibility; *pathos*, stirring an audience's emotions; and *logos*, the use of reasoning (logic), either inductive or deductive, to construct an argument.

With the political rise of the Roman republic, Roman orators (especially Cicero) copied and modified Greek techniques of public speaking, and instruction in rhetoric developed into a full curriculum of instruction in all areas of humanistic study (in the liberal arts, including philosophy), which continued through the Middle Ages and the Renaissance. While rhetoric was largely ignored by linguists, since they were not interested in public oratory nor planned speeches focused on persuasion, it has proved to be of interest to scholars in other domains, as will be shown below.

27.4.2 Work on Spoken Language

In the study of language from a discourse perspective, as Stubbs (1983: 1) reminds us, 'It is useful to understand the field broadly as the linguistic analysis of naturally occurring connected spoken or written discourse.' It will become clear in the exposition below that work on spoken language began in various disciplines but soon became interdisciplinary and was brought under what is now called discourse analysis (DA). We will discuss linguistic work, and then go to approaches that emanate from or were influenced by work in sociology, anthropology, and philosophy.

As was said in the Introduction, linguists originally did not believe in the orderliness of communication above the clause or sentence, especially in speech. However, the Prague School analysis of theme–rheme and FSP, and the London School and Halliday's interest in textual meaning led to renewed interest in ways of rigorously analysing spoken discourse. This was facilitated, in particular, by the ability to capture spoken usage through audio recordings; later, analysts were able to capture by film and video features of the speech event and the sociocultural context, all of which led to a widening of interest in the analysis of real spoken language and the construction of large databanks of spoken corpora (see Chapter 33).

One of the problems is that, while linguists professed to be interested in the spoken language, they approached it initially (and some still do now) from the viewpoint of written language (i.e. focusing on complete, grammatical sentences that are the norm in written language but rarely uttered in spoken discourse: see Linell 1982, 2005), but have been forced to consider the appropriate units of analysis: rarely is spoken discourse uttered in complete, grammatical sentences that are the norm in written language. Analysts often adopted the notion of 'utterance' (vs 'sentence'), and since spoken language is highly dialogic, the complete utterance may not be a text fashioned by one speaker, but rather a conversation with more than one participant, suffused with overlaps, interruptions, hesitations, false starts, negotiation of meaning, turn-taking, pairings of speakers' utterances (e.g. question–response), topic–comment structures, etc.

27.4.2.1 *Information Flow: Theme/rheme, Topic/comment, Given/new, etc.*

One of the topics covered in standard treatments of DA (e.g. Stubbs 1983, Brown and Yule 1983, Schiffrin 1994) is information structure (theme/rheme, topic/comment, given/new, topic or participant tracking), which was influenced by Prague School work as discussed above: 'information structure,' or 'flow,' is a cover term for various changes in the status of objects, states, and events within a discourse when language is produced and comprehended. Early on, theme–rheme was adapted by Halliday (1967/8, 1985a, b, Halliday and Matthiessen 2004) and applied to the sentence level: for Halliday, the subject and predicate of a sentence must be distinguished from the theme (the first part of a sentence) and rheme (the rest of the sentence). He related this to all three (ideational, interpersonal, and textual) metafunctions of language and also made the distinction between a given element (presented by the speaker as recoverable by the listener) and a new element (not recoverable, and often distinguished in speech by being given intonational prominence). Others in the SFL tradition (Hasan 1978, Hasan and Fries 1995) later applied 'theme' to the text (discourse) level.

In America, various linguists[2] from the mid-1960s on turned to the issue of meaning in language, first at the level of syntax and then at the level of discourse, citing the Prague School and Halliday. Dwight Bolinger (1952, 1977, 1979) argued for the semantic and pragmatic determinants of grammatical form and Charles Fillmore (1968) revived interest in the semantic roles of noun phrases in a clause (see Thompson 1992).[3] They worked on topic at the sentence and discourse levels, the difference between topic and subject (see Li 1976), as well as topic hierarchies (basic-level topics, subtopics, super-topics), topic shift, digressions (Grimes 1975, 1978), and a measure for determining the degree of continuity or accessibility of a referent (Givón 1983), and so forth.

This eventually became what is known as information flow, another aspect of which is the difference in narratives between events belonging to the story line, which are foregrounded, and those that are supporting events or states or provide clarification (Grimes 1975), which are backgrounded (Hopper 1979, Hopper and Thompson 1980, Tomlin 1987).

There was also lively interest in defining the basis of the difference between given–new information. Some argued for a 'given–new contract' between speaker and hearer: 'the speaker tries to the best of his ability, to make the structure of his utterance congruent with his knowledge of the listener's mental world' (Clark and Haviland 1977: 4). Others said that units of information are considered to be active, semi-active, or inactive in the listener's consciousness by the speaker (Chafe 1970, 1987, 1994). Finally, there was focus on the discourse and a hierarchy of types of assumed familiarity with discourse entities: new (first introduction into the discourse), evoked (already in the discourse), inferable (from something already said) (Prince 1981).

27.4.2.2 *Deixis*

What this work did was to bring into focus the issue of not just language itself but the immediate context in which it was embedded, namely, the speech event, and the

---

[2] At the beginning they were known as 'generative semanticists,' but later that group dissolved and split into functionalists, pragmaticists, discourse analysts, cognitive linguists, etc.

[3] Greenberg (1966, 1978) is also cited for an empirical approach to language universals and language typology.

important roles of the speaker and listener in determining how language is used—in short, the domain of pragmatics (see Chapter 26).

Ever since the early years of the twentieth century, various linguists have pointed out that the meaning of certain grammatical and lexical phenomena of language depends crucially on the coordinates of the speech event in which they are used, especially deictic categories (also called indexicals, shifters) like personal pronouns, verbal tense, mood, modality, temporal and spatial words like *now, here, yesterday, over there*. This led some linguists to widen the definition of meaning and semantics: for example, John Lyons (1968, 1975, 1979, 1981, 1987), who cites, among others, Bühler (1934), Benveniste (1946, 1956, 1958), Jakobson (1957), and Fillmore (1966, 1975). Lyons argued, for example, that deictic categories relate utterances to the 'spatiotemporal context created and sustained by the act of utterance' (1977: 637). Thus, pronouns like *I* and *you* necessarily bring in the context of their use for an understanding (*I* means the person who is speaking/saying 'I,' the referent of *I* is the person who is speaking/saying 'I,' etc.). All of this laid the groundwork for the close connection between semantics and pragmatics. Lyons also contended that reference to an object does not exist in the linguistic system, but can only be done through the action of referring on the part of a speaker (Lyons 1977: 177).

27.4.2.3 *The Difference Between Written and Spoken Language.*

Since language evolved as speech and since spoken language is a universal across all cultures, while written language is a late acquisition for humans and only a small portion of humanity is or has been literate, some linguists argued that we have to delve further into the nature of spoken language in order to develop a better understanding of what language is like. Instead of the written 'sentence,' which is based on grammatical structures like subject and predicate, they identify the spoken 'utterance' and use prosody—tone units (Halliday 1985c), intonation units, intonation groups, intonational phrases (Chafe 1994)—as the defining criterion. Thus, Halliday (1985c) claimed that writing does not incorporate all the meaning potential of speaking, since it leaves out prosodic and paralinguistic contributions to meaning (Halliday 1967/8); spoken language is a dynamic process with phenomena coming into being and then disappearing, while written language is a synoptic product; and speech and writing are used for different purposes in different contexts.

During the late 1970s and 1980s, according to Paul Hopper (1992, 1996), a number of linguists began to see grammatical structure as being closely integrated with discourse function. Discourse provides the motivation for grammar and structure (Hopper 1992: 364); regularity comes out of discourse and is shaped by discourse in an ongoing process (Hopper 1996: 156). Language is seen as indeterminate, constantly under construction, and structured only by emergent patterns that come and go as the forms that carry them are found useful for their speakers (1996: 172). Hopper (1992: 365) cites Givón (1979), who makes a distinction between more loosely organized pragmatic modes (spoken, informal, unplanned discourse), which achieve their goals more by means of pragmatic inference, and tighter, more structured syntactic modes

(written, formal, planned texts), which rely on explicit, grammatical, structural relationships.

While work was going on in linguistics about the nature of spoken language, other
disciplines—in particular, sociology, anthropology, and philosophy—were also grap-
pling with the nature of speech from different perspectives.

27.4.3 Approaches Mainly Influenced by Sociology

27.4.3.1 *Conversation Analysis (CA)*

One of the earliest trends in what was to become discourse analysis, Conversation
Analysis (CA), was pioneered within the field of sociology, particularly the ethnometh-
odological approach to language and communication (Garfinkel 1967, 1974, Heritage
1984), and originated with Sacks et al. (1974). CA set out to examine the structural
patterns of organization of social action and interaction and its relation to social and
institutional settings that are exhibited and contextually shaped in and through
naturally occurring talk (Heritage 1984, Atkinson 1988, Drew and Heritage 1992). In
CA, context and meaning in conversational exchanges stem directly from instances of
talk, and are analytically independent of any external social, political, cultural or
historical context and psychological characteristics of particular speakers (Heritage
1984, Schegloff 1991).

Conversation analysts collect recordings of mundane conversation and concentrate
on identifiable structural features of interaction including turn-taking (conventions
participants follow in taking turns at talk); adjacency pairs (the condition that certain
utterances such as greetings circumscribe a class of responses in a following turn);
overlapping talk (when more than one participant is speaking at the same time);
conversational repairs (strategies to sort out communication breakdowns due to
problems in speaking, hearing, or understanding); topic management and topic shift
(strategies of initiation, movement, and closure of topic frameworks); and preference
(socially preferred or expected responses following certain utterances, e.g. preference
for denials after accusations; see Sacks et al. 1974, Heritage 1984, Drew and Heritage
1992). Broadly speaking CA has been a major contributor to the understanding of talk
in a variety of private and public settings such as a medical consultation, the court-
room, the classroom, and radio talk-shows (see Atkinson and Drew 1979, Heritage
1984). Many discourse analysts have selectively adapted some of CA's techniques, such
as its fine-grained transcription procedures.

27.4.3.2 *Sociolinguistics (variation studies)*

Sociolinguistics has been defined as 'the study of language in relation to society'
(Hudson 1999: 4). It developed from the work of William Labov, who in the early
1960s conducted research on variation in language and its correlation with the social
life of members within a language community (see Labov 1963, Labov and Waletzky

1967; see Chapter 29 for a more detailed account). Drawing strongly on formal linguistics and quantitative research techniques, variationists established statistical correlations of linguistic forms (e.g. the presence or absence of [r] in postvocalic position: Labov 1972a,b) with non-linguistic features, either 'predetermined background demographic variables such as region, socioeconomic class, ethnicity, age, and sex' (Wolfram 2009: 41) or contextual variables including topic, setting, level of formality, etc. (Cameron 1997). Similar to CA, in the variationist paradigm data are collected from samples of casual speech produced mostly under ordinary conditions (Hudson 1999), and sometimes through questionnaires or in interviews.

27.4.3.3 *Oral Narrative*

A further aspect of Labovian studies comprises his work on oral narrative which, according to Schiffrin (1994: 286), constitutes an extension of the variationist 'beliefs about language structure to the analysis of texts' and thus purports 'to find out if there were correlations between the social characteristics of story tellers and the structure of their stories' (Renkema 1993: 120). Labov and Waletzky (1967) recorded and transcribed spontaneous personal narratives of speakers of African American Vernacular English (AAVE), and then looked for patterns and constraints within this unit of discourse. This work uncovered systematic organizational structures within narratives (at the level of the clause) and found that these clauses were 'temporally ordered independent clauses (along with their dependent subordinate clauses) that must occur in a fixed presentational sequence' (Toolan 2001: 145). Accordingly, Labov (1972b) posited that a fully-formed narrative contains several functional components in roughly the following order: a summary of the story (abstract); a group of clauses identifying the time, place, persons, and their activity in the situation (orientation); a series of narrative clauses that recapitulate the events occurred (complicating actions);[4] a justification for telling the story (evaluation),[5] the result of complicating actions (resolution); and a statement that indicates the end of the story (coda). Narrative texts are locally and socially situated due to their performative nature (Labov and Waletsky 1967), which means that the different contexts in which stories are told shape the language used in the narration and therefore meaning construction.

27.4.3.4 *Interactional Sociolinguistics*

Interactional sociolinguistics (IS) has developed from the combination of the ideas of the anthropologist John Gumperz and the sociologist Erving Goffman since the early 1960s (Schiffrin 1994, Kendall 2011, Gordon 2011). Unlike Labovian sociolinguistics, IS adopts a more 'qualitative,' 'micro,' or 'interactional' approach (Duranti 2009: 6) to 'exploring linguistic and cultural diversity in everyday talk' (Eerdmans et al. 2003: 105).

---

[4] Later, others added the notion of climax either as part of the complication action or as a separate category.

[5] Evaluation is the one component that can come at any moment in the story or at several different moments; and there may be different types of evaluation.

Going beyond the developing variationist sociolinguistics of the time, the work of Gumperz concentrated on multilingual settings (e.g. Gumperz 1958, 1960, 1964a, b, Blom and Gumperz 1972) with the aim of 'not only explicating the interpretive procedures underlying talk but also to address the consequences of real-life, everyday conversational misunderstanding between members of different cultural groups' (Gordon 2011: 70).

In order to analyse the variation present in multilingual interactions, in which interactants make use of several linguistic resources to shift between languages, dialects, styles, or registers, Gumperz proposed the concepts of repertoire and speech community, the former being the totality of linguistic resources that speakers have access to in the course of an interaction (Gumperz 1964b) and the latter 'any human aggregate characterized by regular and frequent interaction by means of a shared body of verbal signs and set off from similar aggregates by significant differences in language usage' (1982a: 219). Additionally, Gumperz (1982a, b, 1992) observed that speakers use signalling mechanisms or contextualization cues, mainly linguistic (phonology, morphology, lexicon, syntax), prosodic (intonation, stress, or accenting and pitch), and paralinguistic (tempo, pauses, hesitation), to indicate the semantic content and the force of their utterance. In turn, listeners are expected to make 'contextual presuppositions' and 'conversational inferences' (Gumperz 1977, 1982a) by drawing on situational context and cultural background knowledge in order to make meaning and provide an adequate response to an initiated communicative exchange. Conflicts in the interpretation of the contextualization cues, which cause miscommunication among speakers, has been one of the major research interests in IS in part due its ethical implications, since as Gumperz (1982a: 210) explains, conversational 'breakdowns lead to stereotyping and pejorative evaluations and may perpetuate social divisions.'

27.4.3.5 *Erving Goffman*

The work of Erving Goffman within the discipline of sociology—more particularly Interactional Sociology (Duranti 1997)—contributed greatly to the constitution of the interactional sociolinguistic approach to discourse (Schiffrin 1994). Like Gumperz Goffman focuses on situated meaning, but he provides a wider and richer framework to understand meaning in relation to context by allowing the analyst 'to more fully identify and appreciate the contextual presuppositions that figure in hearers' inferences of speakers' meaning' (Schiffrin 1994: 102). Drawing on elements from pragmatism, phenomenology, anthropology, and sociolinguistics (Kendall 2011), Goffman's 'ultimate interest is to develop the study of face-to-face interaction as a naturally bounded, analytically coherent field' (Goffman 1969: ix).

In attempting to determine the functional relationship between the structure of the self and the orderliness of interaction, Goffman (1959) adopted the metaphor of the theatrical performance to describe how the representation of the self in any occasion of face-to-face interaction unfolds in a performance tailored to the audience and the situation. This was enlarged with the concept of 'frame' (Goffman 1974), which acts as a schema of interpretation and allows the speakers and hearers to identify what type of communicational event is taking place (a joke, an invitation, casual talk among friends, etc.). Frames are negotiated in interaction through 'footings' of talk (Goffman 1974, 1981, 1983a, b), communicative resources through which interactants change interactional gears such as their status in the conversation or their language use: style, dialect, etc., among others. Successful communication takes place when participants attend to the tacit requirement of the system constraints and ritual constraints (Goffman 1981) in interaction. Both types of constraints operate on the basis of presuppositions, a shared body of 'assumptions, or implications, or expectations . . . defined very broadly as a state of affairs that we take for granted in pursuing a course of action' (Goffman 1983b: 1). While communicative system constraints make use of elements such as background knowledge, situational features, tone, turn exchange, and the like to avoid communication breakdowns, ritual constraints principally concern the interactants' mutual construction, maintenance and protection of their face or self-image, in other words, 'the positive social value a person . . . claims for himself' (Goffman 1955: 213). Regarding the dynamics of participation in communicational exchanges, Goffman (1981: 127) proposes the term 'participation status' to point to the relation each participant establishes with what is being said in an interaction, and the term 'participation framework' to define the configuration of all participation statuses. Within this framework Goffman distinguishes different modes of the speaker (the animator, the author, and the principal) and two complex types of listeners in conversation (ratified and unratified participants).

IS grew from the intersection of linguistics, anthropology, and sociology, facilitated mainly by Gumperz and Goffman. Gordon (2011: 30) states that the incorporation of 'insight from a range of fields has . . . formed a coherent framework of how meaning-making occurs in the interaction . . . [and] has propelled numerous research trajectories both within and beyond IS.'

27.4.4 Approaches Mainly Influenced by Anthropology

Much of the work discussed below is now part of what many call 'linguistic anthropology' (although 'anthropological linguistics,' Foley 1997, is sometimes used) and what was originally also called 'sociolinguistics.' Since the 1980s, sociolinguistics and linguistic anthropology have diverged enough that, while they overlap in certain ways, they also have strong 'methodological, analytical, and theoretical differences' (Duranti 2009: 7)—except perhaps in the area of language and gender. Nevertheless, what is common to both is their concern for language use in context and their contributions to discourse analysis, broadly defined.

27.4.4.1 *Ethnography of Speaking/communication*

Research on discourse analysis in the field of ethnography, which entails fieldwork (participant observation, an emic or insider's perspective) and social description

(Hymes 1971: 52), shares with anthropology a concern for situated, holistic explanations of meaning and behaviour. Ethnography of speaking (later, communication, see Chapter 29) is associated with the work of Dell Hymes (1966, 1972a, b, 1974) and John Gumperz (1964b), who challenged the centrality of the code in structural and generative grammar and 'pointed out that attention should be on people in the speech community, . . . speech events and the function of the speech in the community' (Ervin-Tripp 2009: 248). Transcending the concept of linguistic (especially grammatical) competence proposed by Chomsky (see Chapter 19) which is abstracted from language use (performance), Hymes postulates communicative competence (1972b), i.e. 'the tacit social, psychological, cultural, and linguistic knowledge governing appropriate use of language' (Schiffrin 1994: 8) as the essence of the ethnography of communication; the speech event as its unit of linguistic analysis (Hymes 1972a, 1974), based on Jakobson (1960), and the linguistic community (Gumperz 1962), later named 'speech community' (Gumperz 1968), 'based on speaker's shared norms' (Duranti 2009: 18). Hymes posited a functional analysis of eight factors that that are relevant to shaping and decoding the functional instance of language use (1972a: 65): settings, participants, ends, act sequences, keys, instrumentalities, norms, genres (SPEAKING).

In this discursive approach meaning is understood as created by larger cultural forces that influence linguistic choices and subsequent recognition and understanding of those linguistic choices. Context cannot simply be gleaned from the spoken discourse alone, but requires extensive study of the culture and a fine-grained analysis of the setting in which language occurs. Above all, there is a commitment to 'empirical description of how actual people speak in real social settings' (Hymes 1972a: 65). Hymes's work 'has inspired a considerable number of ethnographic studies of linguistic communities from the point of view of speech events' (Duranti 1997: 290).

27.4.4.2 Focus on Performance

At the same time that Hymes rethought Chomsky's notion of competence, he also raised the issue of performance: he viewed speakers as performers, and underscored that linguistic creativity was in how speakers 'adapt speech to the situation or the situation to speech' (Duranti 2009: 21). This led to work on the poetic nature of ordinary speech, the use of metaphor, and style in language (Friedrich 1986, Irvine 1986, Basso 1990, Sherzer and Urban 1986, Tannen 1989), 'newness and idiosyncrasy' (Johnstone 1996: 19) of language use, 'the role of the audience in the construction of messages and their meanings' (Duranti 2009: 22; cf. co-construction in CA), as well as other aspects of context (see Goodwin and Duranti 1992, Duranti 2009: 22).

27.4.4.3 Language in Verbal Art and Performance

Additionally, ethnography of communication has focused on verbal art forms, especially in oral traditions. For example, Hymes (1981) and others worked on the oral structures of narratives and myths from different Native American cultures and combined that with a 'fine-grained framework for describing verbal performance' (Hanks 1996: 190). Hymes's research in this area has added to the work developed by

Labov in narrative and led to much interest in what Richard Bauman called *Verbal Art in Performance* (1977). This also brought into focus the issue of indexicality, since the specialized nature of performance is an 'indexical reframing of the utterance relative to its immediate context' (Hanks 1996: 191; see also Silverstein 1976, 1992).

27.4.5 Philosophy and (Philosophical) Pragmatics

According to Jacob Mey (Chapter 26), the rhetorical tradition and its practices could be seen as a place of origin for a pragmatic view on language—a view that was subsequently destined to remain in hibernation through millennia during which grammar became ascendant. Chapter 26 gives a sketch of the historical development of pragmatics, in which Mey discusses the most important areas within this discipline that are foundational to discourse analysis. We will simply say here that discourse pragmatics encompasses many interlocking notions. The most important is that pragmatics looks at the meaningful functioning of language use in relation to the context of use, especially the co-text (linguistic context), the discourse context (speech event), and in some cases the larger context of situation. H. Paul Grice (1975) proposed various principles and maxims that are assumed to underlie conversation. The Gricean maxim of relevance has led to a trend in discourse analysis called relevance theory, based on Sperber and Wilson (1986), according to which people only say what is relevant to them and also, presumably, to their hearer(s). Another trend in discourse analysis comes from the focus on politeness and the strategies we use for the protection of face (see discussion of Goffman above; Brown and Levinson 1978): positive face (be favourably evaluated and appreciated) and negative face (unencumbered and free from intrusion), and the problem of face-threatening acts (Brown and Levinson 1978: 71ff.) by the speaker toward the hearer.

Ordinary-language philosophy had its beginnings in Wittgenstein's work (as noted above) and in the work of John Austin (1962), who insisted that we use language not only to say things but to do things, to perform actions. Austin's best-known contribution is the notion of 'performative,' as with expressions like *I apologize* or *I hereby pronounce you husband and wife*, which do not assert anything, but which are actions. He also focused on appropriateness and felicity conditions: e.g. the person who says *I hereby pronounce you husband and wife* has to be legally appointed to do the act, address people who are not already married, and perform the act correctly (Austin 1962: 14–15, Levinson 1983: 228ff.).

John Searle (1969), Austin's most famous student, interpreted Austin's work for the linguistic community and categorized speech acts into five classes according to a number of principles (although his classification is controversial since there is no procedure for completely determining the number of speech acts and their typology). He also developed the idea of indirect speech acts (1975), such as *It's cold in here*, intended and taken to mean in the right context: 'shut the window,' 'turn up the heat,' 'get me my sweater,' 'I want to leave,' etc. Thus, as Austin said, 'words [and specifically, speech acts], in order to be understood have to be "explained" by the "context" in which they were actually spoken' (1962: 100) and they may also define the situation of use.

27.5 ANALYSIS OF MEANING IN TEXTS AND CONTEXTS: WRITTEN TEXTS

While much of the emphasis of work in discourse was focused on spoken language (see Schiffrin et al. 2001, Jaworski and Coupland 2006, Gee 2011), at the same time there has been a call for discourse studies to analyse written texts. And indeed, there was work in stylistics which spanned the twentieth century.

27.5.1 Stylistics

The history of stylistics has been identified by some as starting with rhetoric (see above) and also as having ties with nineteenth-century work in historical philology. What occupied philologists the most was the comparative and historical study of languages, but eventually they turned to the study of literature. Most work in stylistics in the early part of the twentieth century focused on literary texts, as evidenced by Spitzer (1948), which is often seen as the forerunner of the stylistics movement that began in the 1960s (Wales 1989: 296–7). Others credit Roman Jakobson (Goatly 2008), whose article on 'Linguistics and Poetics' (1960), launched new interest in the poetic (aesthetic) function of language, which focuses on the specific way the poetic text is formed (see §27.3.3 above).

The different approaches to stylistics that have developed since have been divided into various categories depending on the analyst, but perhaps the simplest for our purposes is Bradford's (1997) division into 'textualist' vs 'contextualist' approaches. The former focus on the text and are more influenced by linguists; they include Russian Formalism, the New Critics, structuralism (Jakobson 1990b, Barthes 1966—see Culler 1983, Lodge 1986), and deconstruction (Culler 1994). The latter focus on the relation between the text and its context. There are many types of contextualists; what they have in common is the 'ways in which literary style is formed and influenced by its contexts' (Bradford 1997: 73). The contexts themselves are broad and diverse, and can perhaps be best understood by the labels these different groups took on: Marxism (ideology, the state), reader theory (reader response), feminism, postcolonialism, narratology, new historicism, cultural materialism, etc. While many of the contextualists (also called 'culturalists') have abandoned ties with linguistics and continue to develop new contexts to study (e.g. medical discourse, travel literature, cultural studies), those on the linguistic side have continued to expand their interest in the relation between language and literature into what they often call (modern) stylistics. These include

British-Australian traditions, which focus on linguistic aspects of literary texts and sometimes show influence from Firth's or Halliday's work, and the American-British tradition influenced by work in cognitive linguistics and pragmatics (see Chapters 21, 25, and 26).

27.5.2 Meaning in Texts and Contexts: Written Texts

There is a variety of approaches to written texts such as tagmemics, text linguistics, critical discourse analysis, narratology/text semiotics, literary stylistics, genre analysis, and text pragmatics.

27.5.2.1 *Tagmemics*

In North America, followers of the descriptive linguistic school such as Harris (1952) and Pike (1967) were taking the first steps towards discourse studies (van Dijk 1972, de Beaugrande, 1991). For instance, Summer Institute of Linguistics authors such as Pike (1966), Grimes (1975, 1978), and Longacre (1996) focused on structures above the sentence and at the textual level, and dealt with the issue of how to translate the Bible successfully from the Western cultural tradition to very different ones, using a large number of descriptions of indigenous languages from around the world in the tagmemic tradition. While they took on elements of other approaches (even formalist ones, such as Chomsky's), they have had little influence on linguistics in general.

27.5.2.2 *Textlinguistics*

The tradition of *textlinguistik*[6] took shape in the Netherlands and the two Germanys around 1960 (Fernández-Smith 2007, van Dijk 1972, 1980, 1985, 1997a, van Dijk and Kintsch 1983, de Beaugrande and Dressler 1981) and gained immediate currency, widened its scope and diversified, giving birth to different models: models based on sentence grammars, functional approaches, and pragmatic approaches[7] (Adam 1990, Fernández-Smith 2007). The models based on sentence grammar were aligned with the paradigm of generative grammar, and intended to describe supra-sentential relations of texts in order to 'state the formal rules that generate the underlying structure of all texts and of no non-texts or ungrammatical texts' (de Beaugrande 1997b: 60). Van Dijk, whose work moves along the continuum of the three text linguistic approaches, advanced the discussion about coherence, conceived as the result of the relations

---

6 De Beaugrande (1991, 1995, 2000) asserts that although text linguistics and discourse analysis emerged from different orientations, they have steadily merged into the same academic domain. Others, like van Dijk (1997a, b), distinguish between 'text' and 'talk' to refer to written and spoken modes of discourse, respectively (see also Schiffrin 1994).

7 In the interest of space, we limit the focus to the approaches that have received wider attention within these models. A description of other approaches such as the ones developed in the French tradition can be found in Adam (1990) and Rastier (2001).

between the propositional content in a text and its context, and introduced concepts such as macrostructure (structure of meaning of a text) and superstructures (text organization) (see van Dijk 1972, 1977, 1980, van Dijk and Kintsch 1983).

Further development came from functional and procedural approaches to text. Starting with the premise that text is 'a unit of meaning' (Halliday and Hasan 1976: 125), the functional perspective introduces the concept of 'texture' to define the property of a text that allows the listener to perceive a message as cohesive in relation to, first, the internal linguistic resources that hold it together and second, its extra-textual social and cultural context (Halliday and Hasan 1976, 1989). Two resources generate texture: (a) structural resources, involving thematic structures (theme and rheme) and information structure (given–new information); and (b) cohesive re-sources, elements such as conjunctions, reference, substitution and ellipsis, and lexical items. In line with the functional perspective, de Beaugrande and Dressler (1981) put forward the procedural approach to text which focuses on the pragmatic dimension of textual construction.

This orientation argues that text descriptions should draw on the context of com-municative occurrences, and thus it proposes principles of textuality that comprise exploring the attitudes of producers (intentionality) and receivers (acceptability); the conditions of communicative settings (situationality); the connections among linguistic forms (cohesion) and among meanings or concepts (coherence); the relations with other texts (intertextuality); and the communicative value of texts (informativity); see de Beaugrande and Dressler (1981, de Beaugrande 1995, 1997b).

27.5.2.3 *Critical Discourse Analysis (CDA)*

CDA is a multidisciplinary and multimethodical approach to social phenomena that is rooted in numerous linguistic, social, cultural, philosophical, and psychological trad-itions (Blommaert 2005, van Dijk 2008a, Wodak and Meyer 2009a). 'The text in CDA is often regarded as a manifestation of social action which again is widely determined by social structure' (Wodak and Meyer 2009b: 10). Although CDA researchers are best known for their work on written and multimodal texts, there is some work on interactional texts (dialogues), which are generally approached in the same way as written texts. CDA analysts are interested in 'de-mystifying ideologies and power through the systematic and retroductable investigation of semiotic data (written, spoken, or visual)' (Wodak and Meyer 2009b: 3). It adopts diverse approaches with the aim of critiquing and uncovering domination, ideologies, and power relations underlying language use in all spheres of social life (van Dijk 2008a, b, 2009, Weiss and Wodak 2003, Wodak and Meyer 2009a). The edited collection of articles by Wodak and Meyer (2009a) surveys the most prominent approaches of CDA: the Socio-Cognitive Approach, which focuses on 'the interface . . . between the mind, discursive interaction and society' (van Dijk 2009: 65); the Discourse-Historical Approach, which investigates the historical dimension of political and social discursive actions (Reisigl and Wodak 2009; Wodak 2009); and the Social Actors Approach, introduced by van Leeuwen (2008, 2009), focusing on the role of social action in constituting and reproducing social structure. Highly influenced by SFL and Social Semiotics is the Dialectical Relational Approach, which focuses on 'the relations between semiosis and other social elements ... in the establishment, reproduction and change of unequal power in ideological processes' (Fairclough 2009: 163; see also Fairclough 1995, 2003, 2006). Finally, the Corpus-Linguistic Approach and Dispositive Analysis respectively explore the potentialities of using concordance programs to enrich the analytical framework of CDA (Mautner 2009a,b) and the link between discourse and reality as mediated by social actors (Jäger and Maier 2009). There is also an approach that uses metaphor to explore the workings of the text (Santa Ana 2002, Charteris-Black 2004).

27.5.3 Approaches Influenced by Work on Literature

27.5.3.1 *Narratology/text Semiotics*

Prior to the work of Labov and Waletsky (1967) on oral narratives (see above), narratology had already been popularized as a field of inquiry through work by Vladimir Propp (1968 [1928]) on Russian fairy tales and Gérard Genette (1980 [1972]) on the French novel. Propp, who came out of the Russian formalist tradition, defined thirty-one elements of plot in a narrative. Genette was influenced by the French structuralist tradition and was interested in the *system* of narrative and the way that rules and structures govern what can be said. Subsequent work in narrative analysis from a linguistic standpoint includes work by Roland Barthes (1966) who focused on functions, actions, and narration (Toolan 2001) with emphasis on narrative sequence and its relation to reader/listener's prior knowledge (*schemas*) (Herman 1997). Finally, Algirdas J. Greimas (1966) the founder of the Paris School of Semiotics, whose theories were influenced by Propp and have been applied to literary and non-literary texts alike, focused on character analysis, actants, and their functions, with meaning arising from the functional roles played by the actants (Toolan 2001: 84).

27.5.3.2 *Literary Stylistics*

Similar to the way in which narrative analysis and narratology have comfortably straddled the disciplines of both linguistics and literature, stylistics has also been approached from both perspectives. When determining the objective for analysing a text, distinctions are made between literary stylistics and linguistic stylistics. Each stylistic mode serves a different function when applied to a text. In literary stylistics, the focus is on the interpretation of a literary text using linguistic techniques; linguistic stylistics, however, is concerned with testing or refining a linguistic model to further advance a linguistic theory (Wales 1989: 213, 438, Jeffries and McIntyre 2010: 2).

27.5.3.3 *Genre Analysis*

Genre analysis, an approach within discourse analysis (including spoken discourse, see above), also has roots in literary notions of genre (where emphasis is on the formal features of a text: (Bhatia 1993) but which has moved away from a focus on form toward a focus on texts as 'socially constructed, purposeful texts' (Johns 2002). As defined by Martin (1985: 251), genre is a 'staged, goal-oriented purposeful activity with its own schematic structures.' Most work in genre analysis has tended to fall within one of three distinct traditions: (1) the Sydney School, (2) English for Special Purposes (ESP)/ English for Academic Purposes (EAP)—so-called 'linguistic' approaches, and (3) New Rhetoric ('non-linguistic' approach) (Flowerdew 2002: 91). The Sydney School, taking its inspiration from SFL, foregrounds context as a way to interpret the text; ESP/ EAP sees genre as belonging to discourse communities and uses genre analysis for pedagogical purposes in L2 writing in academic contexts (Swales 1990) and for inter-pretation of legal (Bhatia 1993) or medical texts (Maher 1986). Finally, the New Rhetoricians take a more critical and more ethnographic approach rather than a linguistic one to the analysis of texts.

27.5.3.4 *Text Pragmatics*

Like genre analysis, text pragmatics also foregrounds context as integral to the meaning-making process; however, it places its analytical emphasis on the active construction of both written and spoken text through a dialectic, co-creative process between communicator and audience (Mey 2001 [1993]: 5, Mey 2006: 809, Togeby 1998: 1009). As in pragmatics broadly defined, authorial intention must also be clearly communi-cated through the text and be truthful and relevant so that an audience can add context (background knowledge, sociocultural environment) when interpreting a text, thus enabling effective communication (Togeby 1998: 1009).

27.6 CONCLUSION

Looking back at the development of linguistic theory and research during the last century, it is possible to observe that the lens through which language has been approached has greatly diversified. Linguistics has moved from a monologic view of the language faculty towards a more dialogical, pluralistic, dynamic, and integrative view of how speakers, texts, contexts, and meaning interplay. This has happened principally on account of the multidisciplinary dialogue that has facilitated the encoun-ter and applications of different theoretical and methodological perspectives in the study of how language is used and how it interrelates with culture and society. The survey presented here shows that bringing context to meaning has led the study of written and spoken language to transcend descriptivist approaches toward more interpretive and, more recently, critical views of how human communication unfolds.

CHAPTER 28

COMPARATIVE, HISTORICAL, AND TYPOLOGICAL LINGUISTICS SINCE THE EIGHTEENTH CENTURY

KURT R. JANKOWSKY

28.1 BEFORE THE EIGHTEENTH CENTURY

THE acknowledgment of speech as the distinctive feature separating *homo sapiens* from even his closest relatives in the animal world constituted the first essential stepping stone on the long road to a scientific analysis of language. The next equally crucial step that followed a multitude of centuries later was discarding the long-standing notion that the 'Three Holy Languages' (called 'Holy' because the inscription on the cross, according to the Gospel of Luke 23: 38, was composed in the three languages), Hebrew, Latin, and Greek were the only ones worth serious study, for which Gottfried Leibniz (1646–1716) deserves full credit. Subsequently, the eighteenth century prepared the stage for a rigorous scientific investigation which began to show promising results during the early decades of the nineteenth century.

Scientific investigation in general started taking shape with the pronouncement by Francis Bacon (1561–1626) that observation and experiment should be regarded as indispensable tools for any scholarly inquiry, thus effectively replacing, in the pursuit of knowledge, philosophical speculation with practical empiricism (see Schischkoff 1991). But even though his innovative thoughts proved to serve as a decisive impetus for subsequent developments and have quite justly earned him the *epiteton ornans* of 'father of empiricism,' Bacon himself by no means followed up his proclamation with

equally innovative actions. He had undoubtedly advocated a valuable scientific approach, but he left it to others to find and explore appropriate applications. In addition,
scientific investigation, as envisioned by him, was far from being focused on language
or any other specific subject matter. Language had not as yet acquired status as a
subject of principal importance, not for him nor even for Gottfried Leibniz. In the
overall research strategy of Leibniz, language was assigned the subsidiary role of (for
instance) helping him understand the workings of the human intellect:

> Ich glaube wirklich, dass die Sprachen der beste Spiegel des menschlichen Geistes
> sind und dass eine genaue Analyse der Bedeutung der Wörter besser als alles andere
> zeigen würde, wie der Verstand funktioniert. [I truly believe that languages are the
> best mirror of the human intellect and that a precise analysis of the meaning of the
> words would show better than everything else how the mind operates.][1] (Leibniz
> 1875: 313)

His significant advance in comparison to Bacon lies in his unequivocal endorsement of
natural scientific methodology for the investigation of language. And this endorsement
also involved replacing the time-honoured procedure of dwelling on older language
stages first and arrive from there at conclusions concerning the language stages of the
present time. For Leibniz it was imperative to proceed conversely: from the most
recent, hence most accessible and most comprehensively documented language
forms to the language material of the past, which of necessity will be available only
more or less fragmentarily. The following quotation from Leibniz spells out his attitude
regarding both items in great clarity:

> The study of languages must not be conducted according to any other principles but
> those of the exact sciences. Why begin with the unknown instead of the known? It
> stands to reason that we ought to begin with studying the modern languages which
> are within our reach . . . and then to proceed to those which have preceded them in
> former ages . . . and then to ascend step by step to the most ancient tongues, the
> analysis of which must lead us to the only trustworthy conclusions. (Leibniz 1768
> [1710]. Quoted after Müller 1880: 150)

Leibniz must certainly be given credit for having introduced, and dealt with elaborately,
two phenomena which constitute the fundamental ingredients of both historical and
comparative linguistics. The first one is the notion of genealogical relationship of
languages—as opposed to a relationship based on borrowing. The second, closely
related to the first, is the recognition that only by a thorough comparison of all aspects
of language will it be possible to gain insight into the true nature of language. In other
words, Leibniz had laid the solid foundation for both historical and comparative
linguistics. This claim seems fully justified even though Leibniz had never dealt with
language as an entity in itself, and had never made an attempt at investigating language
as a structure in itself. Language had always been viewed by him in its relationship to

---

[1] Translations into English here and elsewhere, unless stated otherwise, are mine—KRJ.

other objects of research. Important as it was for him, language had always been and always remained a means towards an end.

In keeping with his desire to replace speculation with scientifically established facts, he also dismissed the widely held belief that Hebrew was the oldest of all attested languages:

> There is as much reason...for supposing Hebrew to have been the primitive language of mankind, as there is for adopting the view of Goropius, who published a work at Antwerp, in 1580, to prove that Dutch was the language spoken in Paradise. (Quoted after Müller 1880: 149)

Leibniz entertained an extensive correspondence with the eminent Orientalist Hiob Ludolf (1624–1704). Leibniz and Ludolf most certainly exchanged and shared information on the nature of language relationships. Thus, it is safe to assume that Leibniz was aware of Ludolf's fairly elaborate distinction between the two most consequential types of language relationships:

> Si linguam alteri dicere affinem velimus, necesse est, non tantum ut ea contineat nonnulla cujusdam linguae vocabula, sed etiam ut Grammaticae ratio, maxima sui parte, eadem-sit, qualis convenientia cernitur-in Orientalibus-Ebraea, Syriaca-Arabica, et Aethiopica. [If we want to call one language related to another, it is necessary that the language not only contains some words of the other language, but that also the system of the grammar is to a very large extent the same, just as agreement is recognized in Oriental languages, Hebrew, Syriac, Arabic, and Ethiopian.] (Campbell and Poser 2008: 23)

Sharing individual words would amount to a language relationship based on borrowing, whereas high level of identity in grammatical structures would indicate what only much later was appropriately called 'genealogical relationship.' Neither Ludolf nor Leibniz employed the newly defined research tool in their own scholarly work, but the value of their theoretical framework was eventually recognized and became an integral part of all subsequent historical linguistic investigations.

28.2 LATE EIGHTEENTH AND EARLY NINETEENTH CENTURIES

Among the numerous scholars of the eighteenth century with noteworthy interest in linguistic investigations, Sir William Jones (1746–94) deserves to be assigned a very special role in the emergence of historical and comparative language studies.[2] Like most of his immediate predecessors, he did not engage in any linguistic research on his own. His importance, instead, is tied to gaining insight into historical language facts which

---

[2] See also §7.2.1.1 above.

had a profound impact on future linguistic work. Jones, appointed in 1783 to the Supreme Court of Justice in Calcutta as one of the three judges of the British Crown, one year later founded the Asiatick Society of Bangal in Calcutta. His address to the Society as its president, delivered on 2 February 1786, contained the following statement:

> The SANSKRIT language, whatever be its antiquity, is of a wonderful structure; more perfect than the Greek; more copious than the Latin and more exquisitely refined than either; yet bearing to both of them a stronger affinity, both in the roots of the verbs and in the forms of grammar, than could possibly have been produced by accident; so strong indeed, that no philologer could examine them all three without believing them to have sprung from SOME COMMON SOURCE, which, perhaps, no longer exists. (Jones 1788)

As is well known, what Jones enthusiastically proclaimed in 1786 had been stated several times before. Lyle Campbell (b. 1942) provides a partial list of those who have had something of substance to say on the subject involved: 'Giraldus Cambrensis 1194, Comenius 1657, Dante 1305, Gelenius 1537, Goropius 1569, Ihre 1769, Jäger 1686, J. J. Scaliger 1599 [1610], Stiernhielm 1671, Lhuyd 1707, among others' (Campbell 2007: 245). But whereas Jones—as Campbell correctly asserts—is far from being accurate in everything he says in matters of language relationships, the passage quoted not only is entirely free from any objectionable content, but also surpasses the statements of all previous scholars mentioned by having been widely acknowledged at the time of its publication as the very first pronouncement of its kind. The individual achievements of those silently passed over at their time still remain of course praiseworthy in each and every case. A *post festum* rearrangement of the 'when-becoming-effective' time line, however, does not seem to be a commendable procedure. To take refuge to an inimitable German set of terms: *wirkungsgeschichtlich* invariably supersedes *entstehungsgeschichtlich*.

For Christian Jacob Kraus (1753–1807), professor of history and political economy at the University of Königsberg in East Prussia, cultivating a passionate interest in the exploration of the historical development of language seemed to have been an almost obligatory expansion of his scholarly range. He used his critical discussion of *Vocabularium linguarum totius orbis comparativum, oder Vergleichendes Glossarium aller Sprachen und Mundarten*, edited by Peter Simon Pallas (1741–1811), to provide a rudimentary account of how comparative language studies should be conducted (cf. Kraus 1787). Pallas had been commissioned by Russian Czarina Catherine II (r. 1762–96) to edit what she had collected when she had 'shut herself up nearly a year, devoting all her time to the compilation of her Comparative Dictionary' (Müller 1880: 144). Catherine's amazing compilation effort was indirectly prompted by a suggestion which Leibniz had made to Czar Peter the Great (1672–1725) that he should take stock of all the languages spoken in his vast empire:

> Ich habe ... vorgeschlagen, die in Sr. Majestät Landen ... übliche viele, grossentheils bisher unbekannte und unausgeübte Sprachen, schriftbar zu machen ... und die Zehen Gebote Gottes, ... das Vater Unser und das Apostolische Symbolum

des Christlichen Glaubens, sammt andern Catechetischen Stücken, in solche Sprachen nach und nach versetzen zu lassen, ut omnia lingua laudet Dominum. [I
have . . . recommended to convert to writing those common numerous, mostly so
far unknown and unpractised languages in Your Majesty's lands . . . and by and by
put into such languages God's Ten Commandments, . . . the Our Father and the
Apostolic Symbolum of the Christian faith, together with other Catechetic pieces, so
that each language praises the Lord.] (Leibniz to Peter the Great, 26 Oct. 1713,
quoted in Adelung 1815: v–vi)

Czar Peter, though seemingly very supportive during his several personal meetings
with Leibniz, left it to Czarina Catherine to fulfil his promise of support.

The editorial work of Pallas was not exactly extensive. The *Vocabularium* appeared in
two volumes: the first in 1787, the second in 1789. There are some 300 Russian words
involved—supposedly constituting a basic vocabulary—with their equivalence given in
about 200 languages. Pallas arranged the words according to subject-matter categories,
which holds some prospect for meaningful comparison among languages. But otherwise,
what he published is basically a bare word list, without the addition of any type of
scholarly evaluation. Nevertheless, the list is to some extent unique, since the material it
provides had not been available before, and its very existence appears to have set off a
provocative incentive for action, even though the reaction also amounted to a great deal of
severe criticism and only to a lesser extent to generous applause. The reviewer Christian
Kraus dispenses both, and quite skilfully and convincingly at that. His thoroughness in
dealing comprehensively with every aspect of Pallas's lengthy exposition addresses additionally 'das Geschäft der kritischen Berichtigung' (Kraus 1787: col. 5) concerning
any type of language mistake which Pallas may have committed, insisting 'dass vor
allen Dingen Richtigkeit ein unerbittliches Erfordernis ist, weil die etwanigen [*sic*] Fehler
in den Angaben sich durch keine Vernunft verbessern lassen [that above all correctness is
an unrelenting requirement, since the potential mistakes in the data cannot be corrected
by whatever reason]' (col. 5). In this respect Kraus reaped a very positive comment by
Johann Christoph Adelung (1732–1806) on his 'meisterhafte Recension':

Diese Recension . . . (ALZ 1787. No. 235–237) . . . enthält die gründlichste aber auch
zugleich die schärfste Beurtheilung des vergleichenden Wörterbuches. . . . sie [griff]
den befolgten Plan im Allgemeinen, und einzelne Fehler der Ausführung im Besonderen mit tiefer Kenntniss des Gegenstandes und deutscher gründlicher Kritik so
offen und rücksichtslos an, dass ihre Erscheinung gewissermassen für fast eben so
merkwürdig angesehen wurde, als das ausserordentliche Werk, welches sie veran-
lasst hatte. [This review . . . contains the most detailed but at the same time also the
most pungent evaluation of the comparative dictionary . . . it (attacked) the inherent
plan in general, and individual mistakes of the implementation in particular with
deep knowledge of the subject and German thorough criticism in such an open and
relentless way that its appearance was regarded in a way as nearly as noteworthy as
the extraordinary work which had prompted it.] (Adelung 1815: 110–11)

Kraus is still far from producing a solid historical linguistic investigation, but his
guidelines for such an undertaking already focus, more or less precisely, on most of

the crucial ingredients. Concepts like 'Ursprache,' 'Geschlechtsverwandtschaft,' 'Stammesverwandtschaft' (Kraus 1787: 27–8) are brought into the discussion, and so is the emphasis on the need to differentiate between a language relationship based on mere similarity of words and on the similarity of grammatical structures. His envisioned approach to language comparison fails, however, to pay attention to the importance of the individual sound, and he endorses 'Bereicherung der Völkerkunde' (Kraus 1787: 15) as the main purpose of Pallas's collection. To pursue a language investigation for its own sake was, not surprisingly, outside his framework of thought.

Johann Christoph Adelung deserves mentioning, not as a major participant in the launching of comparative linguistics, but as an influential disseminator of essential information produced by others, mostly through the following two works: *Über den Ursprung der Sprachen und den Bau der Wörter, besonders der deutschen* (1781) and *Mithridates oder allgemeine Sprachenkunde*, of which only the first of the four volumes was published by Adelung 1806, the other three by Johann Severin Vater (1771–1826). *Mithridates*, mainly a compilation of the Lord's Prayer in about 500 languages, does not pass muster with Jacob Grimm, even though he does not spare praise concerning Adelung's general achievements:

> Hätte doch Adelung und Vater nur funken gehabt von solch universalem sprachtalent (wie Humboldt), so wäre der Mithridates was ganz anders! [If Adelung and Vater would only have had a fraction of such universal language talent (as Humboldt), then the Mithradates would have turned out as something totally different.] (Lefmann 1891: Anhang 179)

The last to be mentioned in the long list of those who helped pave the way for scientific language studies is Johann Gottfried von Herder (1744–1803). It is mainly due to his suggestive power—and certainly not due to a concrete implementation of what he had outlined *in nuce*—that at long last the concept of language study based on historical principles struck root and was solidified in the minds of his fellow linguists:

> [D]er erste Kopf, der an 'eine wahre Philosophie der Grammatik...' denkt, muss gewiss erst 'die Geschichte derselben durch Völker und Stuffen hinab' überdacht haben. Hätten wir doch eine solche Geschichte! Sie wäre mit allen Fortgängen und Abweichungen eine Charte von der Menschlichkeit der Sprache. [The first mind who thinks of 'a true philosophy of grammar...' must certainly first have considered 'its history down through peoples and stages.' If only we had such a history! It would constitute with all its developments and deviations a chart of the humankind of language.] (von Herder 1772: 134)

28.3 WILHELM VON HUMBOLDT

Wilhelm von Humboldt (1767–1835) occupies a remarkable position at the beginning of a new phase in linguistic research. His major contribution is, all the same, still one of designing theoretical guidelines by formulating insights which serve as additional enticements for empirical research. The difference among languages, he asserts, is not one of sounds or symbols, but is based instead on the different ways in which each language perceives the surrounding world. The function of language is not 'die schon erkannte Wahrheit darzustellen, sondern weit mehr, die vorher unerkannte Wahrheit zu entdecken [to present the truth already recognized, but much more, to discover the truth so far unrecognized]' (von Humboldt 1963 [1820]: 20). He defines, accordingly, what he calls the ultimate purpose of all language investigation:

> Die Summe des Erkennbaren liegt, als das von dem menschlichen Geiste zu bearbeitende Feld, zwischen allen Sprachen, und unabhängig von ihnen, in der Mitte; der Mensch kann sich diesem rein objectiven Gebiet nicht anders, als nach seiner eigenen Erkennungs- und Empfindungsweise, also auf einem subjectiven Wege, nähern. [The sum of what is recognizable lies, as the area to be worked upon by the human intellect, between all languages, and independent from them, in the middle; the individual cannot approach this purely objective area in any way other than according to his own cognitive and sensory faculties, that is, in a subjective way.] (p. 20)

For Humboldt, philosophical guidelines and empirical (for him identical with 'historical') research are inseparable and mutually dependable, which implies that new research results invariably bring about up-to-date changes in the preceding research agenda (cf. Humboldt 1963 [1827]: 114). This was by no means entirely new for his contemporaries, but its forceful proclamation by Humboldt has had undoubtedly a lasting effect.[3]

Just as Leibniz maintained lively contact with Ludolf by correspondence as well as personal meetings, Humboldt and Franz Bopp (1791–1867) became close friends from the time they met in London in 1818, when Humboldt served as Prussian Ambassador to the Court of St James. Young Bopp initiated Humboldt into the study of Sanskrit, and once he had returned to Berlin, it did not take Humboldt very long to achieve Bopp's appointment to the chair of Sanskrit and comparative grammar at the newly founded University of Berlin in 1821. With this successful intervention, Humboldt had not only secured a continued relationship with his valued friend, but also significantly facilitated and increased Bopp's influence upon the emerging new scientific discipline of comparative linguistics.

Widespread and important as Humboldt's influence may have been, its effect was undoubtedly curtailed by the circumstances which were characteristic of at least his written communication. He was under no obligation, professional or otherwise, to write for a particular clientele, nor did he seem to have contemplated the need for making sure that his message came across exactly as intended. He can afford to, and does, knowingly or unknowingly, write primarily for himself. There are of course other factors involved, some of them beyond his control. He performed an abundance of

---

[3] See also §7.2.1.4 and §29.2.1, this volume.

professional duties in the service of various governmental authorities and in his spare time pursued a great variety of individual interests, without focusing on a detailed and comprehensive presentation in any of them. His style remained for a long time largely enigmatic even to his most devoted pupil, Heymann Steinthal, who claimed that he came to a full understanding of Humboldt only after decades of intensive probing (cf. Steinthal 1884: 1–2). And Steinthal is not alone with his comments on how challenging it is to read and understand Humboldt's works. Karl Brugmann (1849–1919), for instance, in his review of Steinthal's edition, expresses his frustration with a polite remark: 'Humboldt, der der Interpretation so bedürftige [Humboldt, so much in need of interpretation],' followed by a rather harsh verdict:

> Den Humboldt'schen Text begleiten Fussnoten des Hrsgbr.'s, die . . . hauptsächlich dazu dienen, das grammatische Verständnis des (bei Humboldt's σκοτεινότης) oft ja nur schwer oder auch gar nicht zu verstehenden Textes zu fördern. [Humboldt's text is accompanied by footnotes of the editor, which . . . mainly serve the purpose of aiding the grammatical understanding of the text that is, after all (given Humboldt's σκοτεινότης [obscurity]) often only difficult—or even not at all—to understand.] (Brugmann 1883: 1315)

28.4 SCHLEGEL AND BOPP

It took team players like Friedrich von Schlegel (1772–1829) and Franz Bopp (1791–1867) to move linguistic exploration a decisive step further. Schlegel's sweeping fascination with Persian and most particularly with Sanskrit roused great enthusiasm among scholars.[4] He had learned Persian while staying in Paris for several years, beginning in 1802, but switched his enthusiastic acclaim for this language to Sanskrit after he gained new insights from the study of Sanskrit, having had Alexander Hamilton (1762–1824) as his teacher from 1803 to 1804. Through Hamilton he was provided with a personal link to the *Asiatick Society* of Sir William Jones, of which Hamilton had been a member in Calcutta.

The main result of Schlegel's sojourn in Paris was his prodigious treatise of 1808 *Über die Sprache und Weisheit der Indier: Ein Beitrag zur Begründung der Alterthumskunde.* Whereas in earlier years he had considered the Persian language as crucially important for the origin of languages, he is now convinced:

> Anfangs hat mich die Kunst und die persische Sprache am meisten beschäftigt. Allein jetzt ist alles vom Sanskrit verdrängt. Hier ist eigentlich die Quelle aller Sprachen, aller Gedanken und Gedichte des menschlichen Geistes; alles alles stammt aus Indien ohne Ausnahme. [Initially, the art and the Persian language had caught most of my attention. But now everything is replaced by Sanskrit. Here

---

[4] See also §7.2.1.2 above.

is truly the source of all languages, of all thoughts and poems of the human intellect; each and everything goes back to India without exception.] (Letter to Ludwig Tieck in Lüdecke 1930: 140)

That his fervour unavoidably gave rise to quite a number of notorious misstatements is regrettable, but Rudolf von Raumer overshoots the mark in his overall evaluation of Schlegel (von Raumer 1870: 361) when he claims that Schlegel mostly provides no more than general guidelines. Whenever he attempts to go beyond that, the result is negligible or full of mistakes. This harsh verdict does not tally with what von Raumer adds on at the next page: 'Aber trotz alle dem wird man die epochemachende Bedeutung dieser kleinen, aber inhaltsschweren Schrift nicht in Abrede stellen. [But in spite of all that, the epoch-making significance of this small but weighty treatise will hardly be denied]' (von Raumer 1870: 362). This juxtaposition of reproach and praise pleads for a bridging explanation, which von Raumer does not have. But, interestingly, he refers to remarks by Max Müller, obviously in search of a similar plus/minus evaluation to corroborate his own ambivalent verdict. Raumer does get indeed exactly what he was looking for, and also something he himself does not have: a bridging explanation. For Müller asserts:

> Schlegel was a man of genius; and when a new science is to be created, the imagination of a poet is wanted, even more than the accuracy of a scholar. It surely required somewhat of poetic vision to embrace with *one* glance the languages of India, Persia, Greece, Italy, and Germany, and to rivet them together by the simple name of Indo-Germanic. This was Schlegel's work; and in the history of the intellect, it has truly been called 'the discovery of a new world.' (Müller 1880: 165)

Schlegel's words fell on fertile ground. Now a set of solid criteria had been launched into orbit, to be utilized by those who were capable of implementing sound theoretical guidelines on appropriate language material. All decisive ingredients were there and were adequately interrelated; to establish the genealogy of languages requires comparative procedures as rigorous as those practised in the natural sciences. What is to be compared are elements of language structure, and not words whose similarity might be the result of mutual borrowing and not the result common origin. Although the term 'history' is not expressly cited, it is nonetheless clearly present as part of the term 'genealogy.' The exact wording of Schlegel's 'commandment':

> Jener entscheidende Punkt aber, der hier alles aufhellen wird, ist die innere Structur der Sprachen oder die vergleichende Grammatik, welche uns ganz neue Aufschlüsse über die Genealogie der Sprachen auf ähnliche Weise geben wird, wie die vergleichende Anatomie über die höhere Naturgeschichte verbreitet hat. [That decisive point, however, which will throw light on everything, is the inner structure of languages or the comparative grammar which will provide us entirely new information on the genealogy of languages in a way similar to what the comparative anatomy has made known on the higher natural history.] (von Schlegel 1808: 28)

Scholars like Franz Bopp and Jacob Grimm (1785–1863) seem to have been waiting for just such a signal to commence their anything but simple, stressful follow-up work;

Bopp for the Indo-European languages in general, Grimm specifically for the Germanic languages.[5] Obviously, their research could hardly have been as successful as it turned out to be without the parameters set by Schlegel. But it is equally important to emphasize that their meticulous large-scale endeavour did amount in each case to a magnificent achievement in its own right. They ventured out courageously and in good faith on uncharted territory, and could not possibly foresee what obstacles and setbacks they might encounter.

Bopp's masterpiece of 1816, *Über das Conjugationssystem der Sanskritsprache in Vergleichung mit jenem der griechischen, lateinischen, persischen und germanischen Sprache*, edited by his high-school teacher and long-term mentor Karl Joseph Windischmann (1775–1839), is introduced by the editor via a 46 page 'Vorerinnerungen.' In his praise for Bopp's 'erste Probe seiner Studien' (Bopp 1816: vi) Windischmann draws the attention of his readers to the unique impact which the work is bound to have on contemporary linguistics:

> Hiedurch wird allem Ohngefähr ein Ende gemacht und die Uebereinstimmungen oder Verschiedenheiten erhalten allmälig etwas Gesetzmässiges und Sicheres, was durch Vergleichung der Sprachelemente blos nach dem Gleichlaut oder wenigstens der Annäherung in Ton und Charakter nie erreicht, wohl aber befördert werden kann. [This puts an end to all by-chance matters, and the agreements and differences gradually acquire something regular and secure, which can never be reached by comparing linguistic elements merely by the identity or at least approximation in tone and character, but certainly be furthered.] (Bopp 1816: vii)

He is aware that at this stage no more than a most welcome beginning had been accomplished, but he is confident that more of the same will soon emerge. And it most definitely did.

The *Conjugationssystem* of the 26-year-old Bopp was followed by a number of no less important works, each of them being part of an overall plan whose strategy it was to continuously improve, supplement, and modify what he had been writing over the years. It also envisioned including new findings based on his own research as well as on what emerged from critical comments by both his friends and his opponents. After Paris, Bopp yearned to move to London, since it was the place next in importance to Paris for furthering his Sanskrit studies and tracking down additional Sanskrit manuscripts. His financial plight was overcome by a grant of 2,000 Gulden awarded to him by the Bavarian king on the recommendation of the Bavarian Academy of Sciences. He had qualified for the grant by an obligatory written examination, which he readily passed. While in London, Bopp published in 1819 an edition of *Nalus*, an episode from the third book of the *Mahabharata*, together with a Latin translation. Upon Bopp's request, Alexander Hamilton, whom he had come to know in Paris, wrote an extensive review, which covered not only *Nalus* but also the *Conjugationssystem*. The review was published the following year in the *Edinburgh Review* (Hamilton 1820: 431–42). It

---

[5] On Grimm see also §7.2.1.6, and on Bopp §7.2.1.7, this volume.

assigns to Bopp's writings a prominent place in the arena of contemporary Sanskritists, thus indicating that Hamilton regards Bopp's achievements as being second to none. And Hamilton's word carried considerable weight.

A second English-language publication appeared in 1820: *Analytical Comparison of the Sanskrit, Greek, Latin, and Teutonic Languages*. It is basically a translation of the *Conjugationssystem*, with some important changes. (A) All Sanskrit translations, which in the German edition appeared on pp. 159–312, were omitted. (B) The Persian language was excluded. In a six page 'Selbstanzeige [Self-Announcement],' (Bopp 1821: 530–5) Bopp explained that he wanted to concentrate more exclusively on Sanskrit relations. (C) He included three innovations: 1. The declensions become part of the language comparison. 2. He replaces the successive data arrangement with the side-by-side arrangement of data. 3. He moves further away from Schlegel's theory that inflectional endings emerged organically from the root and embraces instead the agglutination theory or, in Berthold Delbrück's (1842–1922) terminology: 'incorporating theory.' Wilhelm von Humboldt, in a lengthy letter to Bopp dated 4 January 1821, provides a six-page review of Bopp's *Analytical Comparison* which in his view is 'der erste so ausgezeichnete Versuch einer vergleichenden Analyse mehrerer Sprachen [the first and such an excellent attempt of a comparative analysis of several languages]' (von Humboldt 1889[1820]: 61). But even more important with regard to item 3 is the fact that Humboldt sides with Bopp's agglutination theory and calls Schlegel's diverging position 'ein aus mangelhafter Sprachkenntnis entstandener Irrtum [an error originating from too insufficient a knowledge of language (sc. Sanskrit)]' (p. 61).

Schlegel's reference to 'vergleichende Anatomie [comparative anatomy]' in 1808 had entailed, as it were, a binding directive for all linguistic practitioners to familiarize themselves with the by then well-proven methodology of the natural sciences, where scientific procedures are governed by the search for laws. This familiarization movement was initially rather slow and obviously hampered by a good amount of reluctance, scepticism, and doubt. The primary research interest in the humanities was, after all, to delve into the intellectual life of a community, of a nation, or of humankind as a whole. How could mechanical laws such as those employed in the natural sciences be of any help? Even Schlegel seemed to have been at a loss to provide a methodologically detailed procedure. Apart from the passage quoted above, he kept silent as to how the linguist should follow in the footsteps of the natural scientist. That he demanded strict adherence to rules does show that he was engaged in a serious search. However, he had to leave it to others to arrive at the longed-for solution.

Applying natural scientific principles to the investigation of language presupposed a determination of what integral component of language is part of nature and, hence, may meaningfully be probed by strict scientific laws. It was Wilhelm von Humboldt who in 1820, with his treatise *Über das vergleichende Sprachstudium in Beziehung auf die verschiedenen Epochen der Sprachentwicklung*, supplied the ground-breaking terminology by analysing the organism 'language' as consisting of one component—the physiology of the intellectual man, which is a product of nature (von Humboldt 1963 [1820]: 11).

28.5 RASK AND GRIMM

By that time, a number of skilful linguists had taken their chance at experimenting with data which they thought were relevant for moving language investigation closer to the prevailing scientific *modus operandi*. Franz Bopp has to be counted as one among them. He was joined by Rasmus Rask (1787–1832) and Jacob Grimm. For all three, reliance on introspection and conjecture played almost as great a role as did their adherence to hard-core facts ascertained via careful observation, quite understandably an obligatory intermediate stage to bridge over wide stretches of still unattainable facts with hypothetical conjectures.

Bopp has rightly been credited with having initiated language comparison, and Grimm with having pioneered the historical method (cf. Benfey 1869: 15). Yet neither would have been reluctant to acknowledge that for most of their progress the direct and indirect input of others—named or unnamed—was of immeasurable value. It would not require much effort to show that the publications from Schlegel (1808) to Bopp (1816) to Rask (1818) to Grimm (1819) are quite naturally interlinked by the succeeding publications profiting from the preceding publications.

The use of the term *Gesetz* (law) developed rapidly, having quickly replaced the less rigid term *Regel* (rule), which was much more susceptible to arbitrariness. But even *Gesetz* went through several stages of transformation, starting out from a position close to the indeterminate *Regel* until, via an intermediary stage of 'law with exceptions,' it finally reached the end stage of 'law without exceptions' with the advent of the Neogrammarian movement in 1875.

Here is a more detailed account of this development. Rask was a prolific writer whose first major publication, *Vejledning til det islandske eller gamle nordiske sprog* 'Introduction to the Grammar of the Icelandic and other Ancient Northern Languages,' appeared in 1811, when he was 24. As it was composed, like most of his works, in his native Danish, Rask's reputation outside Denmark was obviously slow to spread, even though Jacob Grimm and his brother Wilhelm maintained a lively correspondence with Rask from 1811 to 1826 (cf. Schmidt 1885: 84–126). Jacob Grimm, who had read the grammar almost immediately it appeared, commented on it rather favourably. Rask participated in a competition organized in 1811 by the Konglige Danske Videnskabers Selskab (Royal Danish Academy of Science), which had asked for a historical investigation to determine the origin of the ancient Scandinavian language (cf. Pedersen 1931a: 248). His essay *Undersögelse om det gamle Nordiske eller Islandske Sprogs Oprindelse* 'Investigation on the Origin of the Old Norse or Icelandic Language' was awarded the prize in 1814, but was not published until 1818. Among the numerous merits of the work, two items are of special relevance. One is that he clearly recognized the importance of sound laws to the relating of languages, even though he did not indicate a belief that they operate without exception. The second item of significance is that he established the genealogical relationships within the Germanic language family, without reference to Sanskrit, which at that time he did not know.

Jacob Grimm, before gaining well-deserved recognition as the originator of Historical Germanic Linguistics, had to learn a few lessons, from Rask among others. August Wilhelm von Schlegel could be very acerbic in his criticism, and he had a great deal of that in store for the Grimm brothers. When reviewing *Altdeutsche Wälder*, vol. 1 (1813), edited by the Grimm brothers, he cites a passage on 'Theut und Man,' written by Jacob Grimm (1813: 82): '*nemo* nicht contrahiert aus *ne homo*, sondern *ho* ein blosser Vorsatz und *mo* soviel als *mas, mans, Mann* [*nemo* not contracted from *ne homo*, but *ho* a mere prefix and *mo* as much as *mas, mans, Mann*]', then adding his harsh verdict: 'darüber werden alle Kenner einverstanden sein, dass wer solche Etymologien ans Licht bringt, noch in den ersten Grundsätzen der Sprachforschung ein Fremdling ist [all experts will agree on this that he who brings to light such etymologies, is still a stranger to the first principles of language research]' (von Schlegel 1847: 400). Slip-ups like these are not infrequent in Grimm's early writings, as Schlegel irrefutably substantiates. But it is equally incontestable that both Grimms were also quick learners.

When Jacob Grimm published in 1819 his *Deutsche Grammatik* (*Deutsch* here used as equivalent to 'Germanic'), he expressly mentioned 'Rasks treffliche, mir erst beinahe nach der Beendigung dieses Buches zugekommene Preisschrift [Rask's outstanding prize essay, which I received almost after concluding this book]' (Grimm 1819, 'Vorrede', i: xviii). A year earlier, in a letter to Georg Friedrich Benecke (1762–1844), dated 5 July 1818, he is somewhat more elaborate: 'Eine eben erhaltene Preisschrift von Rask ... ist voll der scharfsinnigsten und richtigsten Gedanken; es freute mich sehr, manches ebenso gefunden und gedacht zu haben. [A just received prize essay of Rask ... is full of the most astute and correct thoughts; I was very glad to have found and thought of a few things as well]' (W. Müller 1889: 97). Elmer H. Antonsen (b. 1929) has good reason to raise the question as to what extent Grimm's work on the *Deutsche Grammatik* is indebted to what Rask in his turn had 'found and thought of' while exploring the same subject between 1811 and 1818. Antonsen's article (Antonsen 1962: 183–94) presents a great deal of mainly circumstantial evidence and has to place his emphasis on Grimm's own acknowledgment that he had read Rask's *Undersøgelse* before his *Grammatik* went to the printer. More than that cannot be stated with certainty.

It is quite a different story with Grimm's 1822 edition. Although the title was not changed, this new edition looks like an altogether different book. Of the numerous and quite far-reaching changes, only one is of primary consequence here: the four-volume work now begins with a 595-page section in vol. I entitled: 'Von den Buchstaben. [On Letters].' It is this section that contains the formulation of what later came to be called 'Grimm's Law.' This massive insertion was almost certainly due to the influence of Rask's *Undersøgelse*. One might also assume, with good reason, that a note contained in the 'Nachtrag [Appendix]' of the 1819 edition which states that 'eine allgemeine Untersuchung der Laute [a general investigation of the sounds]' (Grimm 1819: 653) is planned for the next edition, was likewise due to the influence of Rask.

That a second edition was brought out so soon after the first can partly be explained by heavy demand for the book, leading to its near out-of-print status. But a much more important motivation for Grimm was his eagerness to make amends as speedily as possible for what he had recognized as a serious shortcoming ever since he had read Rask's extensive discussion of letters and sounds. With this new edition, Grimm had left his dependence upon Rask behind him for good, to some extent due to his own impressive growth. Rask by that time had expanded his range of interest enormously, but most of the languages that he was now focusing on, Asian languages, were out of Grimm's range. Grimm kept his research, to his great advantage, confined to the Germanic languages. That is why Grimm could achieve what Rask did not: recognize the interrelatedness of individual sound changes and discover a system of regularity, formulated as First and Second Sound Shift, which is the key to our understanding of the historical development of all Germanic dialects. He also backed up each and every theoretical finding with ample textual documentation.

Towards the mid-1800s, classical philology, for many centuries holding an unchallenged position in the area of language study, was sidelined by the advance of what was first called 'comparative grammar' or 'comparative philology' and later 'comparative linguistics.' Along with the attempt to determine the historically preceding and succeeding stage in a language family went the search for the protolanguage which necessitated linguistic reconstruction. The success of the processes involved was inevitably dependent upon the availability and quality of the so-called 'sound laws' (*Lautgesetze*). When *Lautgesetz* was used in the early nineteenth century, it was at best a rule valid for the majority of cases, but certainly no law in the generally accepted sense. Those working with the term were well aware that a good amount of wishful thinking was involved. Even Jacob Grimm had stated expressly in connection with the sound shift that his regularity rule or *Gesetz* was applied when items showed agreement 'in der Masse, thut sich aber im einzelnen niemals rein ab [in the majority, but does in singular instances never occur purely]' (Grimm 1822: 590).

This attitude could not prevail for very long. It was bound to be contradicted by a more thorough investigation of language facts, which eventually would lend credibility to what a number of linguists had dared to hope: that languages change according to laws that suffer no exception, thus establishing for one section of language research a rightful place among natural scientific disciplines.

28.6 MODIFICATIONS TO GRIMM'S LAW

August Schleicher (1821–68) made no special attempt to prove that sound laws operate without exception, because he seemed to be convinced that he had sufficient evidence to take this fact for granted, although he refrains from addressing it *expressis verbis*. In his *Sprachvergleichende Untersuchungen* of 1848, he elaborates on his belief of the closeness of language and nature: 'Wie sollte auch die Sprache, die durch so enge

Bande mit dem Geiste des Menschen verknüpft ist, einen anderen Weg gehen als dieser . . . [How it should be possible for language, being linked by such close bonds with the intellect of man, to proceed along a way different from the intellect . . .'] (Schleicher 1848: 2). He is more specific in one of his later works:

> Die Sprachen sind Naturorganismen, die, ohne vom Willen des Menschen bestimmbar zu sein, entstunden, nach bestimmten Gesetzen wuchsen und sich entwickelten. . . . Die Glottik, die Wissenschaft der Sprache, ist demnach eine Naturwissenschaft; ihre Methode ist . . . dieselbe wie die der übrigen Naturwissenschaften. [Languages are natural organisms, which, without being determinable by the will of man, came into existence, grew according to certain laws and underwent developments. . . . Glottology, the science of language, is therefore a natural science; its method is . . . the same as that of the other natural sciences.] (Schleicher 1863: 7)

Accordingly, he follows faithfully the natural scientific model: investigations have to proceed on the basis of conclusions derived from precise, objective observation of facts (Schleicher 1863: 6).

Schleicher's work is remarkable also in another respect. It is intrinsically connected with his determination to concentrate in the first place on the observation of facts. He wants to get away from earlier practices which started out with a particular system and then tried to make the facts conform to the preconceived system. He instead endorses a methodological approach in the opposite direction 'in der Überzeugung, dass . . . mit dem Versuch der Herstellung [eines Systems] gewartet werden müsse, bis . . . eine genügende Fülle zuverlässiger Beobachtungen . . . vorliegt [being convinced that . . . the attempt to establish (a system) would have to be postponed . . . until a sufficient number of reliable observations is available]' (Schleicher 1863: 9–10). This attitude is shared by numerous contemporaries and successors, for whom the detailed investigation of as many language facts as are attainable was a crucial intermediary step on the way to the establishment of a comprehensive structure, in which each item assumed a position that contributed towards the shaping of the systemic nature of the structure. An investigative framework like this turned out to be indispensable in the search for removing exceptions to the regularity feature in historical sound transitions.

It is a somewhat ironic coincidence that a trained mathematician, who turned to linguistics as a hobby, made a discovery which cleared away one of the perplexing exceptions to Grimm's sound law. Hermann Grassmann (1809–77), frustrated by lack of recognition for his important mathematical inventions, finally gained fame as a highly competent linguist with a paper entitled 'Über die Aspiration und ihr gleichzeitiges Vorhandensein im An- und Auslaute der Wurzeln,' published in 1863. Now known as 'Grassmann's Law,' his findings assert that if in Sanskrit and in classical Greek two aspirated consonants occur in one word, only the second one retains its aspiration.

A few years later, the Danish scholar Karl Verner (1846–96) succeeded in dispatching the last remaining obstacle that interfered with the exceptionless status of Grimm's first sound shift law by identifying Indo-European stress patterns as the cause for voiceless fricatives to develop into their voiced counterparts. His paper of 1877, 'Eine Ausnahme der ersten Lautverschiebung,' supplied extensive evidence that Germanic [f, t, x, s], created via the first sound shift from Indo-European [p, t, k, s], lose their voicelessness and become [β, ð, ɣ, z], if the immediately preceding vowel does not carry the main stress.

Verner utilized the compilation of all possible causes for the sound law exceptions which Carl Lottner (1843–73) had published in 1862. Lottner had mentioned a number of physiological conditions which he assumed might be the cause of the switch from voicelessness to voiced. He also included word accent as a possible cause, but left it at that, whereas Verner dug deeper. For him, *Zufall*, accidental occurrence, is a factor which comparative linguistics has to take into account, but there are limits, most definitely where 'die Fälle der unregelmässigen Verschiebung im Inlaute beinahe eben so häufig sind wie die der regelmässigen. Es muss in solchem Falle so zu sagen eine Regel für die Unregelmässigkeit da sein; es gilt nur diese ausfindig zu machen [The cases of irregular shift in medial sound are almost as frequent as those of the regular shift. In such cases there has to be present so to say a rule for the irregularity; it just has to be found]' (Verner 1877: 101). Such a viewpoint is markedly different from the frame of mind that was characteristic of the earlier decades of the nineteenth century. Now there is no place for doubt any more: if a law for sound transitions in the historical development of languages is solidly based on language facts, potentially emerging irregularities are declared as being caused by sound laws not yet discovered. With this, the parallelism of linguistic and natural scientific methodology was securely established.

28.7 THE NEOGRAMMARIANS

Verner's article is dated July 1875, two years before it was published. But its content were circulated long before publication. And that it was published at all was mainly due to the persistent urging of a friend and colleague, Vilhelm Thomson (1842–1927). Verner himself had an aversion to placing the results of his research before a wider public, being quite satisfied to discuss what he had found with his friends, as Karl Brugmann relates in an obituary note (Brugmann 1897). The year 1875 marked the beginning of the Neogrammarian movement, widely perceived as the onset of a type of language research where the axiom 'Sound laws suffer no exception' reigned supreme.[6] This is partially correct in that all of the principal Neogrammarians—the four Indo-Europeanists, Karl Brugmann, August Leskien (1840–1916), Hermann Osthoff (1847–1909), and Berthold Delbrück, and the four Germanists, Hermann Paul (1848–1921), Eduard Sievers (1850–1932), Friedrich Kluge (1856–1926), and Wilhelm Braune (1850–1926)—adhere faithfully to what they regard as an essential integral component of their work, but additionally, all of them were extremely productive scholars who covered an

---

[6] See also §7.2.2.3 above.

amazingly expansive range of subjects, of which the sound law principle is just one, though indispensably important, item. Historical and comparative linguistics were now embraced by a group of scholars who, although most of them individualists by nature, managed to coordinate their activities. Their influence on practically all aspects of language study was enormous, and continued to be a pervasive force throughout their life time and even far beyond. Since seven of them had either studied or held teaching positions at the University of Leipzig, this institution of higher learning became recognized as the focal point of Neogrammarian studies. Only Delbrück had no direct affiliation with Leipzig, but he had studied in Halle and in 1870 accepted a chair in Sanskrit and comparative linguistics at Jena, both places quite close to Leipzig. The fame of the Neogrammarians swiftly spread throughout Germany and to numerous other countries even outside Europe. A large number of foreign linguists were trained in Leipzig and incorporated a substantial amount of Neogrammarian thought into their own work as academic teachers and researchers.[7]

28.8 THE RISE OF LANGUAGE TYPOLOGY

During the early 1800s, simultaneous with the domineering trend to establish linguistic proof that there is a genealogical relationship between current languages and languages of the past, which gave rise to comparative and historical linguistics, another branch of language investigation was initiated. Friedrich von Schlegel, in addition to his comparative and historical approach, was the first to propose a language comparison on a non-historical basis: linguistic typology. Schlegel's initiation, morphological typology, identifies two kinds of language systems, the first characterized by inflection ('durch innre Veränderung des Wurzellauts' [via change of the root sound from within]), the second by affixation or agglutination ('durch ein eigenes hinzugefügtes Wort' [via the addition of a separate word]; von Schlegel 1808: 45).

The next step had much greater impact. It was taken by Friedrich's brother August von Schlegel (1767–1845), who introduced a supplementary categorization by devising a three-way classification of languages via structural criteria, thus formally launching a more comprehensive typological approach. He differentiates between (1) isolating languages, i.e. languages without grammatical structure (more accurately, with a low morpheme-per-word ratio); (2) agglutinative languages, i.e. languages using affixes; (3) inflecting languages, i.e. languages relying on inflection ('les langues sans aucune structure grammaticale, les langues qui emploient des affixes, et les langues à inflexions' (von Schlegel 1818: 14). For the inflecting group he proposes a further subdivision into analytical and synthetic languages, the former using particles instead of inflections, the latter identified by a high morpheme-per-word ratio (p. 16). August von Schlegel

---

[7] See details in Jankowsky (1972, 1990).

politely refers to his brother as the originator of typology: 'Cette classification fonda-
mentale des langues a été développé par mon frère dans son ouvrage sur la langue et
l'antique philosophie des Indiens' [This fundamental classification of languages has
been developed by my brother in his work on the language and ancient philosophy of
the Indians] (p. 85). Friedrich, it is true, had mentioned the subject matter first, but the
elaborations came from August.

A few years later,[8] Wilhelm von Humboldt revised and expanded Schlegel's
grouping by adding on the polysynthetic group, mainly to cover American Indian
languages. Peter S. Duponceau (1760–1844), who supposedly was the first to make use
of the term 'polysynthetic' in 1819, refers to American Indian languages as being 'rich in
grammatical forms and that in their complicated construction, the greatest order,
method and regularity prevail. . . . [T]hese complicated forms, which I call polysynthesis, appear . . . to differ essentially from those of the ancient and modern languages of
the old hemisphere' (Duponceau 1819: xxiii).

Typology based on morphological criteria lingered on for the remainder of the
nineteenth century and was even pursued exclusively during the first several decades
of the twentieth century. Edward Sapir (1884–1939) is generally recognized as one of its
most prominent representatives. Sapir's 'typologisches Raster' [typological grid] (cf.
Haase 2001a: 264) comprised a classification relying on 'isolating, agglutinative, fusional, and symbolic' which for him 'is a preferable scheme' (Sapir 1921: 144). This is an
improvement upon all previous classificatory attempts, but Sapir himself is convinced
that the results so far achieved and those that may be achieved in the future are, with
the available facilities, at best approximations of what is an acceptable goal: 'Strictly
speaking, we know in advance that it is impossible to set up a limited number of types
that would do full justice to the peculiarities of the thousands of languages and dialects
spoken on the surface of the earth' (Sapir 1921: 128). Relying as he had to on observed
language facts, he has good reasons for his pessimistic outlook: 'the historical study of
language has proven to us beyond all doubt that a language changes not only gradually
but consistently, that it moves unconsciously from one type towards another' (p. 128).
'A language may be both agglutinative and inflective, or inflective and polysynthetic, or
even polysynthetic and isolating' (p. 130). In his search to improve typological classifications, Sapir effectively put to rest the valuative and evolutionary aspect of language
development, which for the greater part of the nineteenth century had flourished in the
attitude of those linguists who divided languages according to evolutionary stages as
either 'imperfect' or 'perfect' languages. The isolating class was placed in the imperfect,
the inflecting class in the perfect group, and the agglutinating class held a middle
position. For Sapir, the hard evidence pointed into another direction: 'If . . . we wish to
understand language in its true inwardness we must disabuse our minds of preferred
"values" and accustom ourselves to look upon English and Hottentot with the same
cool, yet interested, detachment' (pp. 130–1).

---

[8] Cf. von Humboldt (1836b), posthumously published by his brother Alexander.

One of the proponents of historical language development from formally least to formally most sophisticated grammatical structure is Adelung. In his *Mithridates* he refers to Chinese as

> die Sprache, die unter den einsylbigen die einfachste, folglich der ersten Sprachbil-dung die nächste ist. Zwar ist sie nicht mehr blosser ungeschlachter Vocal-Laut, denn von diesem ersten rohen Versuche ist, ausser einzelnen Wörtern in allen alten Sprachen nichts mehr übrig, allein sie hat doch nächst diesen die höchste nur mögliche Einfachheit, welches mich denn bewogen hat, sie an die Spitze aller übrigen zu setzen. [The language that is among the one-syllable languages the least developed, hence the one nearest to the first language formation. This language is no more merely uncouth vowel sound, it is true, because of that first rough attempt is, apart from some single words in all old languages nothing left any more, but it has next to those the highest possible simplicity, which has led me to set it at the top of all others.] (Adelung 1806: 40)

Wild guesswork like this was not accorded a long life, due to the research of Jacob Grimm and others.

The typological work of Joseph Greenberg (1915–2001) constituted a remarkable turning point. He initially dwelled on the 'classical' morphological approach, and started out with a diachronic framework in which language genealogy and historical language development captured his interest. Early in his career he was engaged in fieldwork in Africa, which led him to experiment with classifying the languages he encountered that seemed to him to possess particularly striking and unusual typological features. In later years his attention was directed to Native American languages and, last but not least, also to the Indo-European language family. Greenberg was on the whole appreciative of the early nineteenth-century approach to language typology, which had mainly focused on the individual nature of languages and progressed from there to search for common characteristics. His extensive acquaintance with a great variety of vastly different lan-guages was a determining factor for him to go one decisive step further. Since the large number of existing languages makes it virtually impossible to devise an evaluative system with characteristics that uniformly pertain to all natural languages, he embraced as a way out a 'general' typology, in which he discards the emphasis on holistic grammatical description in favor of a selective characterization process. As a result he succeeded in documenting the fact that there is not, and cannot be, a set of descriptive values which could be meaningfully employed as a measuring rod for all languages.

Utilizing typology confirms the existence of language types; it cannot establish proof for the existence of one single type that would adequately describe key features shared by all languages. In choosing his strategy, Greenberg had implicitly raised the question of language universals, a topic which became a prominent item on his agenda as early as 1961 (cf. Greenberg 1966[1963]: 73–113). By then his range of formal features had widened from morphology to syntactical components and their interaction. He was quick to realize that an enormous amount of detailed research would have to be conducted both by himself and colleagues in order to arrive at results commensurate with the relevance of the project. To a large extent this research was carried out at Stanford University, where a special programme had been established under his leadership in 1961. Martin Haase (b. 1962) comments on the gathering at Dobbs Ferry, New York, in 1961: 'Die Eröffnungstagung ... wird als bahnbrechend für die moderne Linguistik angesehen [The inaugural meeting ... is regarded as epoch-making for modern linguistics]' (Haase 2001b: 281). Greenberg's influence was widespread, and most especially so in matters of typology. This fact is convincingly documented in an assessment by Martin Haase: 'Praktisch alle Richtungen zeitgenössischer typologischer Forschung sind von Greenbergs Arbeiten beeinflusst worden' [Practically all branches of contemporary typological research have been influenced by Greenberg's works] (Haase 2001b: 282). Among those who have conducted research along these lines either concurrently with Greenberg or after his death, Winfred P. Lehmann (1916–2007), Elizabeth C. Traugott (b. 1939), Bernd Heine (b. 1939), and Bernard Comrie (b. 1947) are some of the most notable. To determine in what way and to what extent their contributions further enriched the results in this area of studies would merit a separate investigation.

28.9 CONCLUDING REMARKS

This brief excursion into the wide field of the science of linguistics has dwelt on a matchless segment which, during its growth period over more than 200 years, rightly succeeded in captivating the full attention of innumerable first-rate researchers. Once the phenomenon of language had been discovered as an entity of enormous importance to be studied for its own sake, the slowly but steadily emerging results—few being anticipated, many more largely unexpected—evidently intensified the level of enthusiasm to dig further and deeper.

We have seen that the global expansion of historical linguistic studies not only led to a more precise comprehension of individual languages but also paved the way for securing essential insights into the very nature of language itself. A vital precondition for the achievement of unprecedented results was the early realization that language studies necessitated the alignment with the methodology of the natural sciences. For this, Humboldt had cleared the way by demonstrating that one component of the organism 'language' was a 'product of nature,' therefore requiring the employment of natural scientific procedures in its investigation.

Research is an ever-ongoing process. The 'completion' of one programme contains the germ for the beginning of the mandatory follow-up programmes. Historical linguistics spawned typological linguistics as one possible continuation of preceding endeavours. And typology in its turn will be the breeding ground for other, equally significant and interesting research agendas.

CHAPTER 29

....

LANGUAGE, CULTURE, AND SOCIETY

....

ANA DEUMERT

29.1 Socio-cultural Linguistics, or 'Working the Boundaries'

....

THE triad of language, culture, and society points to three separate fields of study (and their associated theories and methodologies): linguistics, anthropology, and sociology. Each of these fields has its own history and disciplinary gestation in the late nineteenth and early twentieth centuries. At the same time, boundaries between these disciplines have often been porous, and interdisciplinary interests have helped to create a research tradition 'that would put language at the center of social and cultural life' (Bucholtz and Hall 2008: 401). Bucholtz and Hall (p. 404) suggest the term 'socio-cultural linguistics' to refer to this larger cross-disciplinary project which they describe as an 'intellectual coalition for the study of language, culture and society'; a coalition, rather than a unified field, which has worked the interdisciplinary boundaries for over 150 years.

In the historical overview that follows I have quoted extensively from primary sources to show the modernity and relevance of writings published before the 1960s, i.e. before sociolinguistics emerged as a more or less well-defined area of enquiry (with its own textbooks, courses, and journals). I concur with Koerner (2002: 1) that a paucity of historical consciousness has at times led to exaggerated claims of 'novelty, discontinuity, breakthrough and revolution' in the history of linguistics. Rather than positioning revolutions—or Kuhnian paradigm shifts—I subscribe to the 'additive or meliorist model of scientific progress' (Andresen 1990: 144). Socio-cultural linguistics, just as any other intellectual enterprise, emerged step by step; always building on the work of others, not through revolutionary leaps and bounds.

The history of linguistics is closely associated with the birth of comparative historical linguistics in the nineteenth century. August Schleicher (1821–68), one of the protagonists of this new paradigm, carefully distinguished the newly emerging 'scientific' discipline of linguistics from its predecessor, philology: while linguistics is a natural science (*Natur-wissenschaft*) in Schleicher's conception of the field, philology is a hermeneutic and interpretive science (*Geisteswissenschaft*, 1850: 1).[1] This segregational approach was soon questioned by those who advocated a type of linguistics which recognizes the social and cultural dimensions of language use as essential, not peripheral, to the development of linguistic theory. Issues of agency, creativity, interaction, variation, language contact, and meaning are at the heart of these critiques and approaches.

This overview is necessarily selective. For the nineteenth century the focus in §29.2 is on Humboldt, Whitney, and Schuchardt as well as early dialectological work. §29.3 turns to the early twentieth century and considers Boas and Sapir in North America, as well as Bakhtin and Voloshinov in Russia. The consolidation of socio-cultural linguistics in the 1960s is the focus of §29.4, and three main approaches are discussed in detail: the sociology of language, variationist sociolinguistics, and the ethnography of communication.

29.2 THE NINETEENTH CENTURY: HISTORICAL ANTECEDENTS

29.2.1 Wilhelm von Humboldt: Language as Culture and Creativity

Closely associated with what Schleicher calls the philological approach is the work of the German amateur-linguist and philosopher Wilhelm von Humboldt (1767–1835). His views—which predate Schleicher's writings—are expressed programmatically in the posthumously published text *Über die Verschiedenheit des menschlichen Sprach-baues und ihren Einfluss auf die geistige Entwicklung des Menschengeschlechts*, 'On the diversity of human language structure and its influence on the intellectual development of humanity' (1836; the text constitutes the introduction to his three-volume treatise *Über die Kawi-Sprache auf der Insel Java*, 'On the Kawi language on the island of Java').

Humboldt critiques approaches to language which view it as mere collection of conventionalized signs; a tool (*Werkzeug*) for communication, which can be studied by linguists in isolation. Language, says Humboldt, is deeply integrated into human life: it is brought about by human beings, and brings about human beings through reflexivity. Language, thus, mediates between humanity and the world: 'Sprache is das bildende Organ des Gedanken' [language is the formative organ of thought] (Humboldt 1836b: 66, 1998: 180).

---

[1] On Schleicher see also §7.2.2.1 above.

The diversity of historical languages is the basis for Humboldt's reflections on the interactions of language, culture and thought. Thinking—i.e. reflection, attention, and abstraction—is not only dependent on language as such, but is inevitably shaped by the so-called 'inner' form of specific languages, i.e. their semantic and syntactic organization. This constitutes the core and purely 'intellectual' aspect of language (*intellectueller Theil der Sprache*: Humboldt 1836b[1998]: 211). The 'outer' form of language belongs to the realm of phonetics/phonology (*Lautform* 'sound form').

Human cognition and perception are historically and culturally embedded in the inner structures of specific languages, leading to a multiplicity of ways of seeing, conceptualizing, and assimilating the world around us (*Weltansichten* 'world views'). This diversity is not the curse of Babel, but a gift which enables numerous perspectives of reality (1812, cited in Di Cesare's edn of von Humboldt 1936b[1998]: 53).

> Alle Sprachen zusammen ähneln einem Prisma, an dem jede Seite das Universum unter einer anders abgetönten Farbe zeigt. [All languages taken together resemble a prism where each side shows the universe in differently tinted colour.]

A century later this view was re-articulated in the writings of Sapir and Whorf, and became known as the Sapir–Whorf Hypothesis (§29.3.1 below).[2]

Speakers, however, are not at the mercy of their languages: they are subjects and as such capable of agency and creativity. Individual speech acts simultaneously reproduce and transcend the system in which they operate. As a consequence language is always Janus-faced: it is *energeia* (formation) as well as *ergon* (form). Humboldt discusses this in a well-known section of *Die Verschiedenheit des menschlichen Sprachbaus* where he foregrounds the tension between the energy and force of the individual (*Kraft . . . Gewalt des Menschen*) and the power of language (*Macht der Sprache*).

> Die Sprache, in ihrem wirklichen Wesen aufgefasst, ist etwas beständig und in jedem Augenblick Vorrübergehendes . . . Sie selbst ist kein Werk (Ergon) sondern eine Thätigkeit (Energeia) . . . Die Sprache gehört mir an, weil ich sie so hervorbringe, als ich es thue; und da der Grund hiervon zugleich in dem Sprechen und Gesprochenhaben aller Menschengeschlechter liegt . . . so ist es die Sprache selbst, von der ich dabei Einschränkung erfahre . . . die Sprachuntersuchung muß die Erscheinung der Freiheit erkennen und ehren, aber auch gleich sorgfältig ihren Gränzen nachspüren. [Language, considered in its true nature, is something which is constantly and in every moment in transition . . . Language is not a product (Ergon) but an activity (Energeia). . . . Language belongs to me because I produce it in my very own way; and since the basis of this lies in the speaking and having-spoken of all previous generations . . . it is the language as such which limits me . . . the study of language must recognize and honour the phenomenon of freedom, but at the same time trace carefully its limits.] (von Humboldt 1836b [1998]: 174, 190, 191)

---

[2] However, as noted by Koerner (1995), this particular view did not start with Humboldt, but can be traced back to 17th- and 18th-century intellectuals such as Giambattista Vico and Johann Gottfried Herder. We might thus talk more aptly—but less elegantly—about the Vico–Herder–Humboldt–Sapir–Whorf Hypothesis.

As *energeia* language is not only dynamic but also dialogic. This is most clearly articulated in *Über den Dualis*, 'About the Dualis' (1963[1827]). Sociability (*Geselligkeit*) is part and parcel of the very nature of language; language exists in and through society.

> Besonders entscheidend für die Sprache ist es, dass die Zweiheit in ihr eine wichtigere Stelle, als irgendwo sonst, einnimmt. Alles Sprechen ruht auf der Wechselrede... Der Mensch spricht, sogar in Gedanken, nur mit einem Anderen, oder mit sich, wie mit einem Anderen... die Möglichkeit des Sprechens selbst wird durch Anrede und Erwiederung bedingt... das Wort gleicht, allein im Einzelnen geboren, so sehr einem blossen Scheinobjekt, die Sprache kann auch nicht vom Einzelnen, sie kann nur gesellschaftlich, nur indem an einen gewagten Versuch ein neuer sich anknüpft, zur Wirklichkeit gebracht werden. (1827, cited in Trabant's edn 1994: 164–5) [Particularly important for language is that duality plays a more crucial role in it than anywhere else. All speaking is based on dialogue... Humans speak, even in thoughts, only with the other, or with themselves as if they were the other... the potential for speaking presupposes address and reply... the word, born in solitude, too strongly resembles a mere imaginary object, language too cannot be realized by an individual, language can only be realized socially by connecting to a bold effort [of speaking] a new one.]

Humboldt's legacy is somewhat marred by his 'inflectional superiority thesis,' which claims that inflectional languages belonging to the Indo-European language family—with Sanskrit as his preferred example—enable more complex and profound thought than other types of languages (Manchester 1985: 125ff., Seuren 1998: 109f.). However, as noted by Nerlich and Clarke (2009: 178), 'Humboldt was a complex thinker,' and his notoriously ambiguous oeuvre provides evidence for 'linguistic chauvinism' (Seuren 1998: 111) as well as emancipatory, progressive thinking (Joseph 1999, Messling 2008).

29.2.2. Dialectology: Describing and Analysing Variation

The emergence of dialect geography—with its emphasis on fieldwork and empirical data collection—is commonly recognized as an important predecessor of modern sociolinguistic thinking (Malkiel 1976, Koerner 1995, 2002; §29.4.3 below). Germany and France were early intellectual centres for this line of research. Georg Wenker (1852–1911) initiated the *Deutscher Sprachatlas*, 'Atlas of the German Language,' which was published by Ferdinand Wrede (1863–1934), his successor at Marburg, from 1926 onwards. Similarly, in Paris, the Swiss Jules Gilléron (1854–1926), together with his assistant Edmond Edmont (1849–1926), established the foundations of French dialectology, and the *Atlas de la linguistique de France*, 'Linguistic Atlas of France' was published between 1902 and 1919.

The dialectologists' interest in variation—formal differentiation of a linguistic entity without change in referential meaning—was not limited to space, but also included social variation. An early programme for studying language variation in society was proposed by

Phillip Wegener (1848–1916) in 1880, drawing attention to speech differences between urban/rural as well as educated/uneducated. Just over twenty years later, in 1903, Ferdinand Wrede characterized Wegener's work as *Soziallinguistik* ('social linguistics'; Löffler 1994: 29). Reflections on language and society also occurred in other texts of the time such as Georg von Gabelentz' (1840–93) *Die Sprachwissenschaft* (The Science of Language, 1901), which notes variation not only according to region but also *Classe* (class), and draws attention to labour migration as a factor of language change (p. 288). Another example is Jacobus Van Ginneken's (1877–1945) *Handboek der Nederlandsche Taal* 'Handbook of the Dutch Language' (1913–14) which carried the subtitle *De sociologische structuur van het Nederlandsch*, 'The sociological structure of Dutch.'

Louis Gauchat's (1866–1942) socio-phonetic study of the Swiss village of Charmey (*L'unité phonétique dans le patois d'une commune*, 'Phonetic unity in the dialect of a village,' 1905) is an excellent example of (variationist) sociolinguistics *avant la lettre* (Labov 1972a: 23). Gauchat considers three social variables in his study of phonetic variation: age, gender, and mobility (in-migration from other villages). Phonetic change, the main interest of his study, shows clear age effects (p. 28):

> [L]a jeunesse se sépare de ceux qui l'ont élevée non seulement dans les us et coutumes, mais dans le details d'articulation de la langue. [The youth break away from those who have brought them up, not only in their habits and customs, but in the details of the articulation of the language.]

Although generally more qualitative than quantitative in orientation Gauchat paid due attention to numerical differences, i.e. relations of more or less, which became the cornerstone of Labovian quantitative analysis (§29.4.3 below). In Charmey, women led the sound change, and gender was thus just as important a variable as age:

> Comme toujours, les femmes se mettent plus facilement sur la voie de la diphtongaison que les hommes. Mme Rime, 63 ans, m'a offert trois fois autant de cas de *ae* que son mari, 59 ans. (p. 44) [As always, women move much more easily on the path of diphtongization than men. Mme Rime, 63 years, provided three times more cases of *ae* than her husband, 59 years.]

A key contribution of dialectological work was the emphasis placed on describing linguistic variation empirically, and the reluctance to evoke even idealized notions of homogeneity (in strict contrast to Chomskyan linguistics sixty years later). Thus, Gauchat explicitly notes the futility of searching for formal linguistic unity (p. 48), and heterogeneity thus becomes a defining feature of the speech community:

> Cependant il importe de constanter qu'à Charmey, où toutes les conditions sons plutôt favorables à l'unité, la diversité est beaucoup plus forte que je ne me le serais imagine après une courte visite . . . L'unité du patois the Charmey après un examen plus attentive, est nulle. [It is important to note that in Charmey, where all the conditions are rather favourable for unity (*i.e. very limited in-migration from other dialect areas, AD*), diversity is much greater than I would have imagined after a short visit . . . After careful investigation, the unity of the dialect proves to be zero.]

29.2.3 William Dwight Whitney: Language as a Social Fact

The American Sanskrit scholar and linguist William Dwight Whitney (1827–94) has received a mixed reception among historians of linguistics. Some have credited him with being among the first to promote a socially/culturally oriented view of language (Silverstein 1971, Labov 1972a, Joseph 2002, Alter 2005), and his influence on Saussure is now a matter of historical record (Koerner 1973, also Allan 2010a). Others, however, judged Whitney's work as 'non-innovative and traditional,' strongly committed to prescriptivist notions of correctness, and ultimately hostile to the study of Native American languages (Andresen 1990: 143). What is uncontested is that Whitney, who was appointed professor of comparative philology at Yale in 1869, exercised extensive authority and influence on the development of linguistics in the United States (Andresen 1990: 167).

Whitney's two major books, *Language and the Study of Language* (1867) and *The Life and Growth of Language* (1875), provide a synthesis of language study from a social perspective, and overtly challenge Schleicher's view of linguistics as a natural science. Although Whitney had little overt regard for Humboldt, whom he describes as 'one of the most impractical and unreadable philosophers of language' (Nerlich 1990: 27), his writings are permeated with Humboldtian ideas. Thus, Whitney borrowed from Humboldt not only the distinction between the 'outer' and 'inner' form of language, but also the idea that the structure of one's native language shapes an individual's 'experience and knowledge of the world' (1875: 22). Andresen (1990: 153) furthermore links his discussion of the agglutinative structures of American Indian languages as characterized by 'excessive and abnormal agglomeration...a character of time-wasting polysyllabism' (1867: 348) to Humboldtian evaluative linguistic hierarchies.

However, unlike Humboldt, who emphasized individual agency and creativity, Whitney foregrounds the social and consensual nature of language and language change. Language as a social institution is based on the egalitarian principles of democracy, and linguistic meaning is the result of conventional and, ultimately, arbitrary associations between form and idea 'under the guidance, and in obedience to the example, of those about us' (1867: 14). Language is thus a collective structure and possession, a social fact in the sense of Durkheim.

> [Language] has value and currency only by the agreement of speakers and hearers. It is in their power, subject to their will; as it is kept up, so is it modified and altered, so may it be abandoned, by their joint and consenting action, and in no other way whatsoever. The speakers of a language thus constitute a republic, or rather, a democracy, in which authority is conferred only by general suffrage and for due cause, and is exercised under constant supervision and control. Individuals are abundantly permitted to make additions to the common speech, if there be reason for it, and if, in their work, they respect the sense of community... Speech is not a personal possession, but a social; it belongs, not to the individual, but to a member of society. (1867: 35, 404)

At the same time, the importance Whitney assigns to actual language use as a force in language change allows individual variation to come into focus as a constant counterpoint to the centripetal, collective-consensual forces of language.

> [T]he English of no two individuals among us is the same; it is not the same in form; it is not the same in extent; it is not the same in meaning.... It is a mighty region of speech, of somewhat fluctuating and uncertain boundaries ... [a]lthough one language, it includes numerous varieties, of greatly differing kind and degree: individual varieties, class varieties, local varieties. (1867: 22)

It is in synchronic patterns of variation that we can see the direction of change, a theoretical view which foreshadows Labov's apparent-time approach (§29.4.3 below).

> [T]here must be in every existing language, at any time, processes of differentiation not yet fully carried out, words and forms of words in a transition, altering but not altered; words and phrases under trial, introduced but not general; words obsolescent but not yet obsolete ... the whole catalogue of possible linguistic changes. (1875: 154)

Methodologically, however, Whitney—true to his training in Sanskrit—remained closely linked to armchair methods of comparative philology. Instead of basing his social conception of language on comprehensive empirically collected data, he largely relied on what Labov (1972a: 269) criticized as 'thought-experiments' and 'series of anecdotes.'

29.2.4 Hugo Schuchardt: the Ubiquity of Language Contact

The German linguist and professor of romance philology Hugo Ernst Maria Schuchardt (1842–1927) is well known for his critique of the Neogrammarian doctrine of the 'absolute exceptionlessness of sound laws' (*absolute Ausnahmslosigkeit der Lautgesetze*), and his contribution to the early study of so-called mixed languages (*Mischsprachen*), i.e. the modern field of pidgin/creole studies and language contact (§29.4.1 below).

Schuchardt's 1885 text *Über die Lautgesetze: Gegen die Jungrammatiker* 'About Sound Laws. Against the Neogrammarians' outlines a socio-psychological approach to the science of language. It is precisely the emphasis Schuchardt puts on (individual) human consciousness that separates his thinking from those arguing for natural laws which sweep across a speech community without exception (1922 [1885]: 55).

> Ich werde daher wohl nicht fehlgehen, wenn ich mit dem Anteil den das Bewußtsein meines Erachtens am Lautwandel hat, die Ausnahmslosigkeit der Lautgesetze für unvereinbar halte. Welchen Einfluß übt nicht die Schule selbst da wo der öffentliche Unterricht die bescheidenste Rolle spielt? Wie weit verbreitet ist nicht unter den ungebildeten das Bedürfnis gebildet, under den Provinzialen das hauptstädtisch zu reden? [I will therefore probably not be mistaken if I consider the exceptionlessness of

sound laws to be irreconcilable with the influence consciousness has in my opinion on language change. What influence does the school not have even where public education plays only a marginal role? How widespread is the wish to sound educated among the uneducated, to sound metropolitan among those in the provinces?]

Thus, social factors—conscious and semi-conscious aspirations and 'acts of identity' (Le Page and Tabouret-Keller 1985)—are central forces in language use and change. Although any social grouping can drive change in language, Schuchardt maintains that the lower classes (*Unterschicht*) play the greatest role—even though their impact is hard to uncover and often denied (1922: 134; a point rearticulated fifty years later by Labov under the heading 'change from below'; §29.4.3). In addition, language contact and language mixing are omnipresent in language history, and need to be considered as central forces of change (1922: 56).

> Sprachmischung nehme ich . . . auch innerhalb der homogensten Verkehrsgenossenschaft an. [I assume language mixing . . . even within the most homogenous interactional community.]

Schuchardt's *Kreolische Studien* 'creole studies' (1882–8) were foundational to the discipline of creolistics and the study of language contact. In the late nineteenth century, when notions of racial, cultural and linguistic purity constituted the dominant discourse in Europe, Schuchardt established the despised creoles as worthy of academic study, and strongly emphasized the importance of creole studies for the theoretical development of linguistics. That is, their very hybridity, leading to a complex synchronic 'scale of crossings or transitions' (*Scala von Kreuzungen oder Übergängen*, *Kreolische Studien* II, 1883: 4), provides an important challenge for linguistic analysis (*Kreolische Studien* VIII, 1888: 3). Schuchardt's work foreshadows twentieth-century discussions on substrate/superstrate influence, the creole continuum, the unpredictability of the outcomes of language contact, and the role of foreigner talk in the genesis of creoles.

Schuchardt was explicit and emphatic about the need for fine-grained empirical analysis, the necessity to attend to the minutiae of language use, i.e. the 'small and smallest linguistic violations, imitations, explorations, and baubles' (*die kleinen und kleinsten sprachlichen Verstöße, Nachahmungen, Tastungen, Spielereien*, 1922: 133). Although Schuchardt did not travel for his *Kreolische Studien*—he obtained his data by extensive correspondence—he also was no armchair linguist, and carried out fieldwork on Basque in 1887 (in the village of Sara). In *Against the Neogrammarians* he issues a programmatic plea for empirical fieldwork (1922: 78).

> Linguisten sollten, dem Beispiele der Naturforscher folgend, häufiger irgendeiner Erscheinung oder Erscheinungsgruppe zuliebe Spaziergänge um die Welt machen. Es würde dabei auch auf das Besondere Licht fallen, vor allem freilich auf das allgemeine. [Linguists should follow the example of natural scientists and more frequently take walks around the world to explore a phenomenon or a group of phenomena. This would also throw light on the particular, but more especially on the general.]

And, indeed, fieldwork became a central focus of scholars interested in the intersections of language, culture, and society in the decades to come. The synchronic study of living languages—pioneered by the dialectologists—gained practitioners and firm institutional grounding in the early twentieth century, and by the 1920s the socio-historical perspective was well established in linguistic thinking.

29.3 THE EARLY TWENTIETH CENTURY: INDIVIDUAL AND SOCIETY

29.3.1 Franz Boas and Edward Sapir: Linguistic Anthropology in the United States

At the turn of the century North American anthropology had moved from a physical to a cultural orientation, and become a home for those interested in the study of (especially) American Indian Languages (Andresen 1990: 190ff.). A major figure in these early years was Franz Uri Boas (1858–1942), who had emigrated from Germany in the 1890s.[3]

The continuing influence of Humboldt on socio-cultural linguistic thought is evident in Boas' view of language as an integral part of cultural life, a 'manifestation of the mental[4] life of man' (1904: 518). However, unlike Humboldt, he strongly rejected linguistic hierarchies and argued for the fundamental functional equivalence of all languages, oral as well as written. Consequently, Boas established fieldwork as a central component of linguistics: under his guidance extensive linguistic data was collected, recorded, and stored, and descriptive grammars were produced for a great number of American Indian languages.

Although language and culture are deeply connected in Boas's thinking, they are also different: unlike other cultural practices, language always has a strong unconscious dimension (1911: 63).

> If the phenomenon of human speech seems to form in a way a subject in itself, this is perhaps largely due to the fact that the laws of language remain entirely unknown to the speakers, that linguistic phenomena never rise into the consciousness of primitive man, while other ethnological phenomena are more or less clearly subjects of conscious thought.

---

[3] Within European anthropology, a strong concern with language is evident in the work of Bronisław K. Malinowski (1884–1942) and Claude Lévi-Strauss (1908–2009): see Hymes (1964). Unfortunately these works cannot be discussed for reasons of space. Senft (2009a, b) provides a useful overview of Malinowski's theory of language which—focusing on context and the social bonding function of language ('phatic communion')—influenced the work of Firth in the UK (§29.4.1).

[4] As noted by Hymes and Fought (1981: 81), 'mental' in this context does not mean 'psychological', but 'intellectual' (as an equivalent to German geistig/Geist).

For Boas, language is thus simultaneously akin to and apart from other cultural practices; linguistics a discipline which is both separate from and united with the social sciences. Instead of Humboldt's creative, speaking subject whose agency and freedom is enabled as well as constrained by structure (linguistic and/or social), language use is conceptualized increasingly as 'automatic,' 'habitual,' and 'repetitive,' reflecting structure rather than creating and shaping it (Andresen 1990: 219).

Among Boas' students, Edward Sapir (1884–1939) stands out. A prolific field linguist, he documented thirty-nine different Amerindian languages (Darnell and Irvine 1997: 281), and his analyses and theoretical reflections have contributed significantly to the development of formal descriptive linguistics, especially phonology (Hymes and Fought 1981: 87); for an excellent collection of Sapir's oeuvre see Mandelbaum (1949). Like Boas, Sapir's thinking is grounded in a broadly Humboldtian stance, seeing languages as constituting and shaping reality (1929b: 209).

> Human beings ... are very much at the mercy of the particular language which has become the medium of expression for their society.

These ideas were further developed by Sapir's student Benjamin Lee Whorf (1897–1941; see n. 1 above).[5] However, Sapir's work goes well beyond a twentieth-century reformulation of Humboldt's *Weltansicht* theory, and his writings resonate strongly with the ethnography-of-communication paradigm as advocated by Dell Hymes from the 1960s onwards (§29.4.4).

Sapir's programmatic paper 'The Status of Linguistics as a Science' (1929b) emphasizes the necessary interdisciplinary linkages of linguistics to anthropology, sociology, and psychology; linkages which are ignored only by the 'somewhat unimaginative' linguist who continues to confine himself to the traditional subject-matter (p. 209).

> It is peculiarly important that linguists, who are often accused, and accused justly, of failure to look beyond the pretty patterns of their subject matter, should become aware of what their science may mean for the interpretation of human conduct in general. Whether they like it or not, they must become increasingly concerned with the many anthropological, sociological, and psychological problems which invade the field of language. (p. 214)

Although Sapir shares Boas' view that language is different from other cultural forms in that it is not usually subject to conscious reflection—it is 'of all the great systems of social patterning ... probably the one which is most definitely unconscious in its operation' (1927a: 423)—his interest in psychology and personality allowed him to transcend structuralism and to focus his attention on the interaction between cultural patterns (language form) and personal biography and experience, creativity and freedom.

---

[5] See also Joseph (2002: 71ff.), who attributes the intellectual pedigree of the Sapir–Whorf Hypothesis only indirectly to Humboldt, and emphasizes instead analytic philosophy (as synthesized by Ogden and Richards 1923) as a more direct and contemporary influence on Sapir.

[S]ociety has its patterns, its set ways of doing things . . . while the individual has his method of handling those particular patterns of society, giving them just enough twist to make them his and no one else's. (1927b: 894, 902)

For Sapir, language is not a Durkheimian-realist 'social *fact*' but an *abstraction,* a 'convenient summary' of numerous, historically-situated, individual human actions (1917: 446). And although individual behaviour is necessarily influenced by collectively constituted patterns, 'it is always possible . . . for the lone individual to effect a transformation of form or meaning which is capable of communication to other individuals' (Sapir 1938; cited in Johnstone 2000: 410). Sapir emphasizes style and voicing, the social symbolism of linguistic forms, and the ability of individuals to manipulate different linguistic levels and social personae simultaneously. The following extract from *Speech as a Personality Trait* reads decidedly modern in its emphasis on the strategic manipulation of linguistic resources by individuals as they project and negotiate identities in interaction:

[T]wo or more levels of a given speech act may produce either a similarity of expressive effect or a contrast. . . . In the case of the man with the lisp whom we termed a 'sissy', the essentially feminine type of articulation is likely to remain, but other aspects of his speech, including his voice, may show something of his effort to compensate. He may affect a masculine type of intonation, or, above all, consciously or unconsciously, he may choose words that are intended to show that he is really a man. (1927b: 904)

Sapir's concern with human agency is further linked to his interest in the poetic aspects of language. Being an accomplished poet himself, Sapir dedicated the final chapter of *Language* (1921) to this topic. Although a writer never has absolute freedom, being bound by the formal structures of the language used and social conventions present, '[t]he possibilities for individual expression are infinite' (p. 221). The challenge is thus to develop a theory which accommodates both the (conscious) individual and the (unconscious) social/collective/structural aspects of language use and change.

29.3.2 Soviet Linguistic Theory: Bakhtin and Voloshinov

The tension between the social and the individual in language are also at the heart of the work on language and meaning by Mikhail Mikhailovich Bakhtin (1895–1975) and Valentin Nikolaevich Voloshinov (1884/5–1936; for a comprehensive discussion of Soviet linguistic theory see Brandist and Chown 2010).

Voloshinov's *Marxism and the Philosophy of Language* (1973 [1929], possibly co-authored by Bakhtin; see Morris 1994: 1–4) is a seminal work in linguistic theory which foregrounds the importance of meaning in language. It is a critique of Saussurian structuralist/objectivist as well of individualist/psychological linguistics, and proposes a view of language not unlike that of Sapir, i.e. located in a complex interaction between the social (collective) and the individual (personal). The starting point of linguistic analysis is not the system—which, as for Sapir, is 'merely an abstraction arrived with a good deal of trouble' (1973: 67)—but the first-person experience of the speaker who creates meaning.

> What matters to him [the speaker] is applying a normatively identical form (let us grant there is such a thing for the time being) in some particular, concrete context. For him, the center of gravity lies not in the identity of the form but in that new and concrete meaning it acquires in the particular context . . . *what is important for the speaker about a linguistic form is not that it is a stable and always self-equivalent signal, but that it is an always changeable and adaptable sign.* (Voloshinov 1973: 68, emphasis in the original)

Just as generating meaning through speaking is context-dependent, so is the act of listening: the listener does not simply recognize an abstract linguistic form, but in the very act of understanding draws on the context in which the particular utterance is being produced. The listener *understands* the utterance's novelty and situated meaning, but does not *recognize* its formal identity and dictionary meaning.

> [T]he understander, belonging to the same linguistic community, . . . is attuned to the linguistic form not as a fixed, self-identical sign, but as a changeable and adaptable sign. (p. 68).

Language as experienced by speakers and hearers is always dialogic, a point argued earlier by Humboldt (§29.2.1); i.e. it is produced and understood in response to something. Individual utterances thus link into 'a continuous chain of speech performances' (p. 72). As a consequence of this, meaning does not reside in words or speakers' minds but is created in interaction.

> [T]here is no reason for saying that meaning belongs to a word as such. In essence, meaning belongs to a word in its position between speakers; that is, meaning is realized only in the process of active, responsive understanding. Meaning does not reside in the word or the soul of the speaker or in the soul of the listener. Meaning is the *effect of interaction between speaker and listener produced via the material of a particular sound complex.* (Voloshinov 1973: 102–3; emphasis original)

Language not only has meaning but also value, and every utterance exhibits an evaluative orientation, reflecting and evoking the perspectives, ideologies, and identities of particular social groups. The outcome of this is what Voloshinov calls 'a constant struggle of accents in each semantic sector of existence' (p. 106), and what Bakhtin (1994 [1935]) later calls 'heteroglossia.' This heteroglossia, or struggle of accents (i.e. socio-cultural forms of variation) is the source of language change as speakers transform these socially constituted forms through the act of speaking, and make them their own. In other words, heteroglossia, unlike mere variation, is not simply given—a relic of sociohistorical developments or a reflection of one's social upbringing—but is actively created by speakers through the appropriation not of a system, but of linguistic forms and meanings which, prior to their being spoken, existed only in 'other people's mouths.' This is expressed clearly in Bakhtin's seminal text 'The Dialogic Imagination' (1994 [1935]):

> Language is not a neutral medium that passes freely and easily into the private property of the speaker's intentions; it is populated—overpopulated—with the intentions of others. Expropriating it, forcing it to submit to one's own intentions and accents is a difficult and complicated process. (p. 77)

Thus, the constant struggle between the personal/collective and the social/individual is at the heart of Voloshinov's and Bakthin's conception of meaning in language. Freedom and individuality are possible, but do not come easily. The voices of others are always present, and have to be negotiated time and again by individual speakers and hearers in particular contexts. It is in this conception of individual voice vs the collective discourse (including forms of authoritative discourse) that structures of power are ever visible in language use.

29.4 THE SECOND HALF OF THE TWENTIETH CENTURY: 'SOCIOLINGUISTICS'

29.4.1 Consolidation, Dialogue and Emerging Research Traditions

From the 1950s onwards, the US emerged as an important centre for the development of socio-cultural linguists. Conferences, scientific committees, and meetings played a vital role in the formation and consolidation of what came to be known as 'sociolinguistics.'[6] These conferences brought together researchers from different disciplines (sociology, anthropology, linguistics), and created the conditions for prolonged and intense interdisciplinary dialogue (Murray 1998, Shuy 2003 [1990]; see also Paulston and Tucker 1997).

However, conferences and committees did not create a *unified* new discipline. In 1984 and 1990—twenty to twenty-five years after the heyday of the 1960s—Fasold published his introductory textbook in two volumes: *Sociolinguistics of Society* and *Sociolinguistics of Language*. He describes the first as a 'special kind of sociology,' the second as a 'about linguistics from a particular point of view' (1984: ix). And even within Fasold's *Sociolinguistics of Language*, there is an implicit distinction between variationist sociolinguistics (which grew out of dialect geography), and the ethnography of speaking (which

---

[6] The term 'sociolinguistics' has traditionally been attributed to Haver C. Currie (1908–93; Currie 1952). However, as noted by Joseph (2002: 108), the earliest attested use was probably by Thomas C. Hodson in 1939, in an article entitled 'Socio-linguistics in India' in the journal *Man In India* 19: 94–8.

emerged from the US tradition of anthropological linguistics; Gumperz and Cook-Gumperz 2008).

In addition to the triad of sociology (of language), (variationist) linguistics, and ethnography (of speaking), there were a number of research groupings and individuals whose work is less easy to classify. Joseph (2002: 107ff.) discusses the pioneering research of Paul Hanly Furgfey (1896–1991) and his students; a comprehensive history of the field should also include the work of J. R. Firth (1890–1960) in London, which informs the systemic-functionalist approach of M. A. K. Halliday (b. 1925; see Koerner (1995: 117); see also Murray (1998: 47ff.) on the work of the language-sociological work of the Chicago School). Of particular interest, and deserving a separate discussion, is the extensive work on language contact from the 1930s onwards. Seminal publications include John R. Reinecke's (1904–82) Ph.D dissertation 'Marginal languages: a sociological survey of the creole languages and trade jargons' (1937), Uriel Weinreich's (1926–67) *Languages in Contact* (1953), Einar Haugen's (1906–94) *The Norwegian Language in the United States* (1953), and the work carried out by Charles Ferguson, John Gumperz, and William Bright in India in the 1950s (see Ferguson and Gumperz 1960; Samarin 2000).

29.4.2 The Sociology of Language: Focus on Society

The period following the end of the Second World War was one of intense political engagement: Europe needed to be rebuilt, both physically and socially-ideologically, the civil rights movement in the US raised issues of socioeconomic and educational equality, and state formation in the highly multilingual former colonies brought questions of language planning and policy to academic attention (Ricento 2000, Gumperz and Cook-Gumperz 2008).

Joshua A. Fishman (b. 1926), the son of Yiddish language activists and a trained psychologist, has been most closely associated with the work commonly referred to as the 'sociology of language.' Multilingualism is at the heart of Fishman's research, a topic which he considers to be 'of great importance . . . for sociolinguistic theory' (1967: 597). In 1966 Fishman published a major study on language loyalty in the US, followed five years later by an equally significant work on urban multilingualism (Fishman et al. 1971). His interest in language shift/maintenance in multilingual communities culminated twenty years later in *Reversing Language Shift: Theory and Practice of Assistance to Threatened Languages* (1991). A second important figure was the linguist Charles Ferguson (1921–98), who is perhaps best known for his seminal paper on diglossia (1959). He also worked extensively on language contact/bilingualism, language standardization and language spread (see Spolsky 2010).

Methodologically, the sociology of language can be described as data-driven, macro-linguistic (focusing on language varieties not individual linguistic structures), and often quantitative, with a focus on counting languages and their speakers, identifying patterns of language use in different social domains (school, family, church, etc.), and understanding the attitudes of speakers towards specific languages and language varieties. Fishman (1972: 7, 9) provides a clear research programme in his preface to *Advances in the Sociology of Language*.

> [S]ociology of language implied a broader field of interest, and one that was less linguacentric, than did *sociolinguistics*... it seeks whatever level of linguistic sophistication may be necessary... to more fully explain variation in societally patterned behaviours pertaining to language maintenance and shift, language nationalism and language planning, etc. However, not only are supportive and adversary behaviours toward particular languages or language varieties close to the heart of the sociology of language but so are group self-identification behaviours, language attitudes and beliefs, etc.

Census and specialized survey data play an important role within this paradigm. An early example was the Ethiopian *Survey of Language Use and Language Teaching* which was conducted in the late 1960s under the leadership of Charles Ferguson (Bender et al. 1976). One of the papers which emerged from this collective work is a detailed quantitative analysis of language use in Ethiopian markets: language use in all markets was highly multilingual, and even though Amharic dominated quantitatively, it has not spread as a lingua franca (Cooper and Carpenter 1972). Information of this type provides important base-line data for language planning and policy decisions (including language in education).

Although not commonly associated with the US-based sociology-of-language paradigm, the UK sociologist Basil Bernstein (1924–2000) adopted a similar macro-sociological, variety-based approach in his neo-Marxist work on social class reproduction. His major study, *Class Codes and Control* (1971), which carries the subtitle *Theoretical Studies Towards a Sociology of Language*, introduces the well-known distinction between 'elaborated' and 'restricted codes,' two speech forms which are associated with different social classes (middle class and working class respectively). The two codes evoke different social meanings, with the former being privileged in educational environments. Bernstein's work is complex and theoretically sophisticated—for more detailed discussion see Atkinson (1985) and Ivinson (2010).

29.4.3 Variation Studies: Focus on Language

Variation studies or quantitative sociolinguistics is strongly associated with the work of William Labov (b. 1927). He was a student of Uriel Weinreich (§29.4.1), who in turn was trained by the French historical linguist André Martinet (1908–99). As argued by Koerner (1995, 2002), this genealogy is important, as much of Labov's thinking draws on earlier work in historical linguistics. A second important influence was the tradition of European dialectology (§29.2.2), which had shaped developments across the Atlantic from the 1930s onwards when Jacob Jud (1882–1952) and Paul Scheuermeier (1888–1973), both students of Gilléron, were invited by Hans Kurath (1891–1992) to train students in dialectological field methods for the *Linguistic Atlas of New England*.

Labov's main interest was the understanding of (phonetic) linguistic change in real time; i.e. 'the direct observation of a sound change in the context of the community life from which it stems' (Labov 1963: 273; also Weinreich et al. 1968). Labov's MA dissertation on sound change on Martha's Vineyard (1963) and his doctoral thesis, published as *The Social Stratification of English in New York City* (1966), established a methodological and epistemological blueprint for the sociolinguistic study of language change: first, the collection of interview data—eliciting formal as well as informal speech—from a large, socially stratified sample of individuals; second, the identification of linguistic variables in the data (i.e. formal linguistic sets consisting of two or more variants which have the same referential or structural meaning); third, the quantification of different variants for individual speakers; and finally, the correlation of this quantitative information with social group membership. Thus, in New York postvocalic /r/ has two variants: /r/ and no /r/ (rhotic and non-rhotic). /r/-full pronunciations are most common among younger speakers, those at the top of the social hierarchy and in more formal speech styles, thus marking the pronunciation of /r/ as prestigious.

Age, as already shown by Gauchat in 1905 (§29.2.2), is a particularly important factor in the study of language change. Labov's work directly challenges Bloomfield's (1933: 347) dictum that language change in progress cannot be observed. Through careful empirical analysis Labov is able to show that linguistic change is indicated in synchronic data by shifting frequencies between generations. This he calls 'change-in-apparent-time,' and contrasts it with 'change-in-real time,' i.e. a change in frequencies between two distinct time points. Labov's strong formal linguistic orientation is reflected most clearly in his concept of 'variable rules' which allow linguists to describe the systematic interaction of language-internal and language-external (social) constraints within the model of formal grammar. According to Labov, major linguistic changes typically come 'from below,' i.e. they originate in low status groups (Schuchardt's *Unterschicht*, §29.2.4) and are outside of the speakers' intentions and desires (below the level of consciousness). Changes 'from above,' on the other hand, originate in high-status groups and speakers tend to be aware of them (see Schuchardt's earlier description of the role of the school system and metropolitan varieties as driving aspiration-linked language change).

A further aspect of Labovian work is the systematic study of the evaluation of linguistic forms. This is typically done through the use of so-called matched-guise experiments using tape recordings of different pronunciations of a text as a stimulus. Different social groups, although showing diversity in their speech, generally agree on their evaluation of linguistic forms in terms of prestige or status. This empirical observation led Labov to conceptualize the speech community as being characterized by evaluative agreement ('homogeneity of interpretation') and socially stratified language use ('heterogeneity of production': Labov 1972a).

Although the variationist, quantitative approach has not escaped criticism (e.g. Cameron 1990), it has had enormous influence and is often seen as synonymous with sociolinguistics (see Chambers 2003 for an example). The sociolinguistic methods pioneered by Labov have since been applied (with some additional refinements) to communities as diverse as Norwich, Belfast, Montreal, Paris, Berlin, Buenos Aires,

Tunis, Sydney, Copenhagen, and Tehran. They have also been used successfully in the study of indigenous minority communities (see the papers in Stanford and Preston 2009). In addition to his work in social dialectology, Labov also contributed significantly to the study of narrative and African American Vernacular English (Labov 1972b).

29.4.4 The Ethnography of Speaking/communication: Focus on Culture and Interaction

The ethnography of speaking—later amended to the ethnography of communication—was developed by Dell Hymes (1927–2009) as a theoretical alternative to, especially, Chomskyan linguistics. It dislodges attention from language as an object to human beings as subjects who make strategic use not of 'language' but of complex linguistic repertoires and resources, creating multiple and diverse 'ways of speaking' (Hymes 1973: 67). Competence, according to Hymes, is about successful communication, not the production of grammatically correct utterances, i.e. it is 'a competence for use, involving the knowledge and ability to speak in ways that are both grammatical and socially appropriate' (Bauman and Sherzer 1974: 108). Hymes locates the socio-cultural study of language firmly within anthropology and suggests a clear division of labour:

> It is the task of linguistics to coordinate knowledge of language from the viewpoint of language. It is anthropology's task to coordinate knowledge about language from the viewpoint of *man*. (1964: xxiii; emphasis original)

Ethnography is central to Hymesian linguistics. It is not only a method of data collection—which allows researchers to develop emic understandings—but also brings with it a specific epistemological and ontological perspective on language as a locally embedded as well as emergent phenomenon (Hymes 1974: 5, Figueroa 1994: 37). The main unit of analysis is the 'event,' i.e. the actual performance of speaking within a particular culturally bounded context. Hymes locates his work as a continuation of functionalism (especially Roman Jacobson, 1896–1982), and draws on the notion of 'context of situation' as articulated by Firth (§29.4.1.), as well as the writings of Sapir.[7]

Hymes's publications in ethno-poetics are part and parcel of this larger research program. To understand a text, the reader needs to be able to read the text within its original context, i.e. be able to evoke and reconstruct the cultural functions, norms, and habits that originally produced its meaning. Hymes' functionalist perspective, emphasizing the complexity of linguistic repertoires, genres, and registers within a language, has practical consequences for applied issues such as language documentation:

---

[7] Although situated within ethnography, the ethnography-of-communication movement established important connections to sociology, i.e. the interactional work of Harold Garfinkel, Harvey Sacks, Emmanuel Schlegoff, and Erving Goffman (see Gumperz and Hymes 1972, Bauman and Sherzer 1974).

> sociolinguistic systems disappear before their languages, perhaps several gener-
> ations before. If salvage linguistics is urgent, salvage sociolinguistics is doubly
> urgent. (Hymes 1966a: 158)

Hymes provides an important new take on linguistic relativity—the Humboldt–Sapir–
Whorf Hypothesis discussed in §§29.2.1 and 29.3.1. Language, according to Hymes, is
not only an inherited structure which shapes human cognition and perception, but is
'in large part what users made of it' (1973: 60), a product of their creativity. Language
thus reflects a man-made world of 'social relationships . . . orientations towards persons, roles, statuses, rights and duties, deferences and demeanor' (Hymes 1996a: 45). In
addition, Hymes pushes Boas's dictum of the equality of all languages into the realm of
critical theory: while all languages are equal in principle, some are—for socio-historical
reasons—more equal than others. Thus, relationships of power and inequality limit 'the
theoretical potentiality of language in daily life' (1973: 73).

Also grounded within an ethnographic tradition is the interactional approach of
John J. Gumperz (b. 1922), who published with Hymes the seminal *Directions in
Sociolinguistics: The Ethnography of Communication* in 1972. Gumperz pays detailed
attention to micro-level language use in interactional encounters. Language is seen as
'communicating both content and metapragmatic or indexical information about
content' through the use of so-called contextualization cues. These are often prosodic
and/paralinguistic features which indicate how speakers 'mean' what they 'say' as they
engage in interaction, i.e. how they 'frame' a particular communicative situation.
Gumperz (1982a) advocates a strongly qualitative approach to linguistic analysis
which stands in opposition to the quantitative orientation of variationist sociolinguistics (§29.4.2).

29.5 CONCLUSION: THE TOTAL LINGUISTIC FACT

Socio-cultural linguistics has as its subject matter what Silverstein (1985: 220) has called
'the total linguistic fact', that is, an always unstable, emergent and ever-changing
interaction of linguistic *form*, situated language *use* and cultural *ideology*—the latter a
crucial mediating link between use and form. Those studying the 'irreducibly dialectic'
totality of language have consistently challenged attempts to establish linguistics as an
autonomous discipline which has 'language' as its sole object (from Schleicher to
Chomsky and beyond). Over the past 150 years their diverse and cross-disciplinary
work has given theoretical and empirical depth to the study of meaning and linguistic
variability, the understanding of the social matrix of linguistic change, the importance
of interaction in shaping language use, and the multiple roles language plays in social
organization. Many of the theoretical concerns of the past are still with us and continue
to drive academic debate: the limits of individual linguistic creativity, the role of human

consciousness, and the ontological status of the structural patterns of language (abstraction or social fact?).

Ongoing work within socio-cultural linguistics has drawn on and further developed social-science concepts such practice, performativity, indexicality, stance, identity, salience, and stylization, and there is an increasing interest in integrating the three traditions which developed in the 1960s, in particular bridging the gap between variation studies and ethnography (see e.g. Eckert 2005, 2008, Woolard 2008; also several of the papers in Fought 2004). A final but important point: in addition to being an intellectual project, work in socio-cultural linguistics has long had political implications, and continues to be deeply linked to concerns about social justice (Bucholtz and Hall 2008, Blommaert 2009).

CHAPTER 30

···

LANGUAGE, THE MIND, AND THE BRAIN

···

ALAN GARNHAM

30.1 INTRODUCTION

···

THE ability to use language is clearly a mental ability and thus, at least to modern sensibilities, one that is dependent on brain functioning. Although the crucial role of the brain in mental functioning has not always been recognized (e.g. by some Ancient Greek thinkers), its importance is now firmly established. However, a very recent trend (since about 1990), in both psychology and the philosophy of mind, has sought to broaden the role of the material in thinking about the mental. According to this view, cognition is said to be embodied, and thus dependent on the form of the human body and the way in which it interacts with the rest of the world. This idea has been applied in some detail in the domain of language and will be discussed further later in this chapter. In fact, there is an area of linguistics, namely phonetics, in which there is a strong history of relating the physical properties of the linguistic signal (acoustic phonetics), considerations of certain parts of the human body, in particular the vocal tract (articulatory phonetics), and the way in which sounds are categorized and distinguished (auditory phonetics). In other areas of linguistics, the corresponding links between the linguistic and the psycholinguistic are less concrete, to say the least, and it is only more recently, and with patchy interest from linguistics proper, that the connections are beginning to be made.

This chapter is concerned with the history of the links between language, mind, and brain, up to the present day. However, as has already been hinted, it will be considering the human brain as an organ within a human body, a body that may also be relevant to knowledge and use of language. The chapter begins with some very brief remarks about mind and brain, or mind and body, not in any attempt to make a definitive statement, but because the difficult and vexed nature of the relation between mind and body goes some way to explaining why investigations of the relation between language and mind and investigations of the relation between language and brain have developed relatively independently.

In the case of so-called low-level perception, which is pertinent to phonetics, a detailed understanding of the relation between speech sounds and their processing in the auditory system has emerged over the last 150 years. Thus the mapping between what might be regarded as psychological descriptions and what might be regarded as physiological descriptions is relatively clear. In a domain such as syntax, however, not only are the psychological facts less definitively established, but the physiology has until the recent advent of brain imaging techniques been extremely broad-brush and non-specific. Even imaging techniques typically allow only a somewhat more detailed account of which brain areas are involved in certain types of processing. They still say little or nothing about the processing of an individual stimulus.

Following this initial discussion, the chapter will turn to the history of the study of the links between, first, language and mind and then language and brain. It will conclude with a consideration of modern approaches, including cognitive neuroscience and embodied cognition, which attempt, in different ways, to bring the two threads together.

30.2 MIND AND BRAIN/BODY

The vocabularies we use to describe the mental and the material are largely distinct, and these different ways of talking give rise to the feeling that, in some not clearly defined sense, the mind and the body (including the brain) are two different things. This so-called substance dualism can be traced back at least as far as Plato (in his dialogue *Phaedo*), who derived the doctrine from more general metaphysical ideas, and in particular his notion of timeless Forms, which could not, according to his arguments, be material. In modern philosophy it is famously associated with the name of René Descartes. Aristotle rejected much of Plato's argument, though the exact interpretation of his writings remains the subject of debate. While he claimed on the one hand that the soul is the form of the body, which has been taken by some to be a materialistic argument, he argues elsewhere that the intellect must be immaterial, which is prima facie an argument in favour of dualism. Indeed, the predominant interpretation of Aristotle's writings is that he embraced at least a limited form of dualism.

In what has come to be called the Anglo-Saxon tradition, there are various monist responses to dualism. Modern versions—those developed in the last 100 years or so—tend to be physicalist, based on the assumption that the mental can be treated scientifically and that, at least in principle, psychological descriptions have to fit with biological, chemical, and physical ones. These modern versions include: behaviourism, mind–brain identity theory, functionalism, and various forms of nonreductive physicalism. All of these theories have their problems, and none denies that descriptions of events or states from a mental perspective are very different from those from a material perspective, though some accounts, such as the eliminative materialism of Patricia and Paul Churchland (e.g. Churchland 1981) and others, suggest that everyday mental descriptions are misleading and should eventually be discarded.

It is not the place of this chapter to attempt a solution to the so-called 'mind–body' problem, or to declare that it is a non-problem arising from conceptual confusion about the proper use of mental and physical vocabulary. Nor does the expertise of the author fit him to solve the problem. The relevance of the differences between mentalistic and materialistic vocabulary to this chapter is that these two different ways of picking out aspects of human beings and their behaviour that are relevant to linguistic enquiry have, almost inevitably, led to two largely separate bodies of work on the relation between language and mind and the relation between language and brain; it is to these bodies of research that the chapter now turns.

30.3 LANGUAGE AND THE MIND

As has already been suggested, the connections between language and the mind are many and various. Almost everyone learns at least one language, stores information about that language, and uses that information, in conjunction with other information—about the world, about what they are hearing and seeing, about what other people know—to produce and understand language in a variety of situations and for a variety of purposes. It might seem, then, that the study of language and the study of how the mind works would be inexorably intertwined. That this is not so is a remarkable fact about the history of linguistics that is in need of an explanation.

In fact, the systematic study of languages, in a form that can be seen as having similar aims to modern linguistics, predates by far the systematic scientific study of the mental representations and processes underlying language use (psycholinguistics). Work on the analysis of Sanskrit dates back at least 3,000 years, with detailed grammatical and phonetic descriptions being developed by 400 BC. Other traditions flourished in Ancient Greece, Ancient Rome, and China, and more recently in the Arabic-speaking world.[1] This work is, of course, based on recognizing patterns in language across multiple occasions of use, and is not directly concerned, as modern psycholinguistics is, with moment-to-moment language processing. And despite the fact that cognitive mechanisms are required both to extract information from individual instances of language use and to recognize the patterns across uses, the description of the patterns themselves typically does not make any direct reference to those mechanisms.

The discovery, in the West, of the Sanskrit tradition in particular led to the blossoming of the field of comparative philology and the proposal, by Sir William Jones, that Sanskrit, Ancient Greek, and Latin had a common linguistic ancestor, later

[1] See Chs 10, 11, 12, and 13 above.

dubbed Proto-Indo-European. The fields of comparative and descriptive linguistics were established, which led, by routes documented elsewhere in this volume, to modern linguistic practice.

Psychology, on the other hand, was not properly established as an empirical science, independent of philosophy, until the 1870s. However, as will be documented in the section on language and brain, important advances had been made in what might broadly be called medical science earlier in the nineteenth century. Wilhelm Wundt's psychological laboratory in Leipzig is usually regarded as the first proper psychological laboratory, and Wundt's own work ranged over a wide variety of topics within psychology, including language, which he regarded as part of *Völkerpsychologie* (usually translated as 'social psychology'). Although Wundt anticipated many modern themes in psycholinguistics, his work had relatively little influence in the Anglo-Saxon world. The reason was partly because the focus of attention had shifted to the United States by the early part of the twentieth century, and there behaviourism became the dominant approach to psychology, and partly because his works were either badly translated or not translated at all.

The two overarching themes in psycholinguistics, often studied separately, are language acquisition and language use in both production (speaking and writing) and comprehension (listening and reading). Wundt's ideas influenced early, detailed diary studies of language acquisition. Although people are used to raising children and experiencing their growing proficiency with language, they typically do not have the technical vocabulary needed to describe the changes taking place in their linguistic abilities, nor the motivation to register those changes, either in their heads or on paper. As is so often the case in psychology, an everyday occurrence needs detailed documentation by trained observers if it is to be described and then explained in a scientific way.

30.3.1 Language Acquisition

There is a long and honourable tradition of studying the details of language acquisition, in all of its aspects from phonetics through to pragmatics. However, since the 1960s a great deal of attention, if not always matched by research effort, has focused on an interrelated pair of general issues. These issues are the question of how much of our ability to acquire and use language depends on language-specific mechanisms that are built into humans (i.e. that are innate), and the so-called logical problem of language acquisition. The logical problem of language acquisition is as follows: given the data available to a person in the environment around them as they develop, how, in a very general sense, can they learn the rules of a particular language, given that those rules are rules of a certain well-specified kind (e.g. in the case of syntax, the rules of a transformational grammar, or the rules of a context-free phrase structure grammar)? The question is not about the detailed course of language acquisition, but about how acquisition is possible at all, given the nature of the information available and the complexity of what is eventually acquired. Two obvious facts suggest the problem might be a difficult one. First, at least in learning spoken language, very little explicit instruction is given to children. Second, the language that children hear around them is full of errors, hesitations, false starts, and utterances that would be acknowledged as incorrectly constructed, even if they are not corrected either by speakers or listeners. Furthermore, the generative linguistics of the 1960s, particularly the version inspired by Chomsky, suggested that adult grammars included certain rule-types that would, according to results by Gold (1967) and others, make them difficult to induce, particularly if it was assumed that the basic form of the data from which the rules had to be induced was positive instances of sentences of the language (mixed with some erroneous, but uncorrected, utterances), and not specific information that some strings of words do not constitute legitimate sentences. Problems, real or purported, with the input data for learning language are referred to as the Poverty of the Stimulus Argument (for innate-ness). If the available data are too poor to learn language from, then at least some knowledge about language structure must be built into the system(s) that learn it.

The argument made, by Chomsky and others, was that general learning mechanisms could not induce the kind of transformational grammar that Chomsky was proposing for human languages from positive instances only of sentences that the grammar generated. Hence, they claimed, an innate language-specific mechanism was suggested. According to Chomsky, this mechanism effectively encoded the rules of what he referred to as a Universal Grammar—a set of rules or principles that is common to the grammars of all natural languages, both actual and possible.[2]

In his book *Language and Mind* (1968) Chomsky traced the history of the idea of a Universal Grammar back to a rationalist, Cartesian tradition. He identified certain remarks by Descartes himself as hinting at the idea of Universal Grammar, and more specifically claimed to find precursors of his own ideas in the work of some of the so-called lesser Cartesians, in particular Cordemoy. More specifically, he stressed the importance of the Port-Royal Grammar (Lancelot and Arnauld 1660) in the history of the notion of Universal Grammar. However, the notion that the grammars of all languages show similarities can be traced back through a much wider variety of sources, at least as far as Roger Bacon in the thirteenth century (see e.g. Allan 2010a: 161–5).

After an early flirtation with psychology and psychologists such as George Miller, Chomsky quickly moved to describing language as a biological function, with the implication that the existence of a Language Acquisition Device (LAD) containing, in some sense, a Universal Grammar was something that required a biological explan-ation. However, Chomsky has been reluctant to commit himself to a standard Darwin-ian evolutionary account, or at least to give any hint of what he thinks the details of such an account might be. Although there are clearly difficult issues relating, for example, to timescale and to plausible precursors of a LAD, which has then become specific to humans, Chomsky's position on this issue has always sat highly uncomfort-ably with the professed view that language is a biological phenomenon. Psycholinguists

---

[2] See Chs 17 and 19 above.

of a broadly Chomskyan persuasion, such as Steven Pinker, have been more willing to endorse, in principle, a Darwinian account, even if its actual form remains unclear. Furthermore, over the last fifteen or twenty years there has been a growth of interest in the evolution of language, not just in grammar, narrowly construed, but in all the major aspects of language. Although general theories and, even more so, specific hypotheses in this domain remain difficult to test, some plausible ideas about the emergence of our linguistic facilities have emerged, and most people now believe that there is no obstacle in principle to explaining how language evolved.

Another result of Chomsky's flirtation with psychology was the founding of the discipline of psycholinguistics, or rather the establishment of the modern version of this discipline. A broadly Chomskyan position might be taken as suggesting that language use depends on language-specific aspects of the mind, and hence that psycholinguistics is or should be relatively independent of the rest of cognitive psychology. However, even in the modern era, there have been many psychologists who see the psychology of language (a term that many people of this persuasion prefer to 'psycholinguistics') as just one part of cognitive psychology. They see language use as depending largely, or perhaps in some cases even solely, on general cognitive mechanisms. When language acquisition is studied from such a perspective, general learning mechanisms must be invoked to explain language acquisition. A modern embodiment of such learning mechanisms can be found in connectionist systems, which have become increasingly popular in the psychology of language since the publication in the mid-1980s of Rumelhart and McClelland's two volumes on Parallel Distributed Processing (1986, 1986). Ironically, perceptrons, smaller-scale precursors of connectionist networks, had been deemed inadequate for many processing tasks, including language-based ones, by Minsky and Papert (1969) using abstract general arguments at the same level as those that Chomsky used against the idea that transformation grammars might be learned from positive evidence only without the use of a Universal Grammar. The publication of the Rumelhart and McClelland volumes in 1986 showed that connectionist networks were actually performing language-based tasks in a much more concrete way than previous psycholinguistic models, and were performing them reasonably well, at least to superficial observation.

In the domain of language acquisition, as the Chomskyans prefer to called it, or language learning, as those of an anti-innatist disposition are prone to say, particular attention focused on the learning of the past tenses of English verbs, which divide into the regulars, which basically take a -*ed* suffix on the stem of the verb, give or take a vowel, and the irregulars, which do not. One of the papers in the second (applications) volume of Rumelhart and McClelland (1986) presents a model of past tense learning, which attempts to deal with both regular and irregular forms using a single mechanism, and no language-specific assumptions about how learning occurs. There are two difficult problems about past tense learning, one of which gives succour to the anti-connectionists and one which gives succour to the connectionists. The connectionist learning mechanism is based, in a broad sense, on similarities between stems. However, the regular past tense rule applies to certain classes of verbs regardless of their form. So some derived verbs, e.g. *flied out* not *flew out* in baseball, and *grandstanded* not **grandstood*, even if they have the exact same form as irregulars have a regular past tense. It is difficult for a connectionist model to deal with this phenomenon, though there may be some complex way in which context, if it could be encoded properly, might determine when a verb was being used in its standard form and when it was being used by a derived form. A (non-connectionist) rule-based system can easily handle these cases. What rule-based systems have more difficulty in capturing, and hence responding to, is the complex and not clearly predictable (at least by rules) clusters into which the English irregular verbs form themselves—clusters that have similarly formed past tenses (e.g. *sting–stung, string–strung, stink–stunk, sink–sunk,* and *swing–swung*). Connectionist models have been shown to perform reasonably well in finding these clusters.

Whether connectionist models constitute existence proofs of non-language-specific language learning mechanisms is as yet, perhaps, undecided. However, a number of other criticisms have recently been made of the Poverty of the Stimulus argument. These range from relatively specific arguments about why the lack of specific negative evidence (e.g. being told that **Mary put the box the table* is ungrammatical) may not mean there is no negative evidence, to claims such as those of Geoffrey Sampson (e.g. 2005) that the purported facts about language that Chomsky and others rely on in making their arguments are not facts at all and that language can be learned just as anything else can.

A further line of argument in the nativist-empiricist debate, relating in particular to the idea that it is specifically human nature that nativists argue is relevant to language learning, stems from attempts to teach human languages to apes and other animals. Talking birds are, of course, primarily mimics, though African Grey Parrots show some remarkable abilities (see Pepperberg 2000). Apes have problems producing human speech sounds, as early ape language research projects by the Kelloggs and the Hayes confirmed. Apes are, however, adept at using their hands both to make signs similar to those used in human sign languages and to manipulate small shapes that can be designated as symbols in an analogue of written language. Apes and, indeed, other animals, such as the Grey Parrot, can learn associations between hundreds of these signs or symbols and concepts close to those of (some types of) human concepts. More controversial is their ability to deal with other aspects of language, and in particular syntax and pragmatics. Debates in this area have been heated, and not always enlightening. What is certainly true is that no other animal shows the facility with complex linguistic systems that humans do, and no other animal uses a communication system in their ordinary life for the wide variety of purposes that humans do.

30.3.2 Language Use: Comprehension and Production

The study of language use—the core topic of psycholinguistics—dates from the beginning of experimental psychological research in the late nineteenth century. As was previously mentioned, language was one of the many psychological topics investigated in depth by Wundt and his colleagues in Leipzig. Initially, psycholinguistic work in Wundt's laboratory and in other German laboratories attracted interest from both European and North American linguists. However, methodological differences among different groups of psychologists in Germany led to disillusionment among linguists about the contribution that psychology could make to the study of language. Before long, linguists such as Delbrück (1901) were arguing that linguists should return to their formal ways and work independently of psychologists. With the First World War and subsequent problems in Germany, the focus of psychological research quickly moved to the United States, where behaviourism became the dominant doctrine. Until the publication of B. F. Skinner's *Verbal Behavior* (1957), behaviourism had little to say about language, and the work of Wundt and the other great European investigator of language from a psychological point of view, Karl Bühler, was largely ignored. And although North American linguistics, particularly in the hands of Bloomfield (1933), dubbed itself behaviourist, it functioned almost entirely independently of psychology.

Modern (originally largely Anglo-Saxon) psycholinguistics began to emerge in the 1950s following two interdisciplinary seminars and the publication of Osgood and Sebeok's (1954) *Psycholinguistics: A Survey of Theory and Research Problems*. Part of the idea behind the seminars and the survey was to reunite linguistics and psychology. However, this attempted reunion quickly became caught up in the cognitive revolution, which added ideas from Artificial Intelligence (AI) to the mix. Furthermore, the Osgood and Sebeok survey was put together before the real impact of the Chomskyan revolution in linguistics became apparent, so the linguistics that psychology was eventually reunited with, albeit incompletely, was very different from the one assumed by Osgood and Sebeok. Those authors suggested that, in addition to the linguistic approach to language behaviour, two other approaches should be considered: learning theory and information theory. In the 1950s learning theory meant behaviourism, in its various manifestations. But no sooner had an extended attempt to apply behaviourist principles to language behaviour appeared (Skinner's *Verbal Behavior*) than an excoriating rebuttal of the whole venture (Chomsky 1959b) was published, from which it struggled to recover. Part of the argument, as we have already seen, was that language cannot be learned, at least not in the way that behaviourists envisaged, but is acquired with the help of a built-in language acquisition device, which already contained a lot of information about what the grammar of the language would be like. However, another part of the argument was that the concepts deployed in the behaviourist framework were inadequate for describing our language abilities. More specifically, at least in the Skinnerean version of behaviourism, the specific eschewal of mentalistic concepts was seen as a serious impediment to a satisfactory account of language behaviour.

Two themes underlying the cognitive revolution, often implicit in the early stages, were functionalism and the assumption of abstract symbol systems underlying cognitive behaviour. These ideas reinforced the notion that the link between language and mind was something that could be studied largely independently of specific brain mechanisms. Linguistic descriptions had always been symbolic. This idea was now amalgamated with the notion of a generative grammar. And although the term 'generative' is used here in an abstract way, it appeared to mesh will with psychological notions of constructing and analysing sentences. Furthermore, newly developing AI approaches allowed detailed modelling of how these processes might occur.

George Miller, an influential psychologist, who had earlier championed the Information Theory approach to psycholinguistics, took up Chomsky's ideas and suggested that the difficulty of putting together sentences when speaking and writing and analysing them as listeners and readers might be a function of the number of transformations in their derivation (an idea that was later dubbed the Derivational Theory of Complexity, DTC). During the 1960s there was a flurry of psycholinguistic work inspired more or less directly by Chomskyan linguistics, but it was confined to a relatively short period. On the one hand, Chomsky quickly became wary of the idea that there might be useful feedback from psychological work into linguistic theorizing. On the other, psycholinguistics could not make specific versions of Chomsky's theory work as the basis of processing models, and soon realized that the details of the theory were changing rapidly, but in ways that did not impinge directly on their concerns. Similarly, in AI, systems that appeared to have interesting language processing capacities, such as Terry Winograd's 1972 SHRDLU and Roger Schank's 1975 MARGIE, were not based directly on Chomskyan grammars.

In the following years, psycholinguistic research fell into three broad areas, lexical, syntactic, and meaning-based. Lexical research was not concerned with word meanings, which, where they were studied, were studied in relation to general issues about meaning, but with word identification and recognition (in comprehension) and retrieval (in production). The issues addressed in this field were, for the most part, not directly related to specific linguistic concerns, and this work, much more than other parts of the psychology of language, was regarded as a core part of cognitive psychology. Two types of model were considered. In the first type of model, cues (either perceptual in the case of comprehension or conceptual in the case of production) had direct access, in parallel, to a set of units (detectors in the case of perceptual input), roughly one corresponding to each word. In the second type of model, items in the mental lexicon were searched through in serial fashion for a match with the perceptual or conceptual input. However, with the advent of connectionism, a new breed of detector model was developed, and because some proponents of connectionism placed themselves in direct opposition to symbolic processing models, lexical processing became a topic that, although it aroused quite passionate disagreements and debates, was much better integrated into psycholinguistics in general.

Turning to higher levels of processing, after the early, transformation-based work of the 1960s, psycholinguists interested in syntax and parsing realized, on the one hand, that DTC could not be developed in a form that was viable either conceptually or empirically, and on the other hand that issues about transformations were, in any case, not the crucial issues in parsing research. Transformations were eliminated from some syntactic theories and in others they became more abstract and fewer in number— reducing to one (Move X) in one version of Chomsky's theory. But in any case, transformations or no transformations, a more critical issue in comprehension is deriving a surface structure description of incoming material. Bever (1970) suggested some heuristic methods of using superficial structure to get to underlying meaning, but a proper focus on surface structure parsing started with Kimball's (1973) seminal article 'Seven Principles of Surface Structure Parsing in Natural Language.'

Kimball's work led, via the Sausage Machine model of Frazier and Fodor (1978), to Frazier's later Garden Path Model, in which surface structures were derived according to two principles—Minimal Attachment and Late Closure—which made reference to structural considerations only and, hence, sometimes produced parses that needed to be revised because the combination of structure and content produced an analysis that did not make sense. Frazier's work on syntactic processing linked up, methodologically, with what had been a somewhat separate tradition of work on eye movements in reading. The advent of small, relatively fast computers and other technologies allowed the development of relatively easy to use eye-tracking devices, which, unlike those used by pioneers of eye movement monitoring research in the late nineteenth and early twentieth centuries, were also relatively comfortable to wear. These devices allowed the testing of predictions about moment-to-moment processing of sentences derived from the Garden Path Theory and its rivals. Frazier's work also came into conflict with rival theories, often loosely associated with connectionist ideas and parallel processing. These theories typically denied that reanalysis occurred, at least when sentences were used in appropriate contexts, and it became crucial to try to distinguish between cases of no reanalysis and cases of very rapid reanalysis. More recently, the visual-world paradigm (or, rather, a number of variants of this paradigm), in which people look at pictures or real scenes while listening to sentences, has provided evidence of rapid, word-by-word, syntactic and semantic analysis.

Psycholinguistic studies of meaning have looked at word meaning and also semantic and pragmatic aspects of text and discourse meaning. Until recently, studies of word meaning have been carried out relatively independently of work on lexical semantics in linguistics. If anything, from the 1960s to the 1980s at least, work in AI exerted a more powerful influence on this research. Perhaps the most important outcome of psychological work on lexical semantics was the notion that word meanings are embedded in folk theories about the world (the so-called theory theory of word meaning: Murphy and Medin 1985). More recently, there has been some interest in ideas about word meaning that derive from linguistics proper, for example in the work on metonymy by Traxler et al. (2002).

Work on the meanings of sentences and discourse and text has been much more varied, but again the influence of work from linguistics has been patchy. At the level of literal interpretation of sentences, or utterances in discourse, a broad parallel has been recognized (e.g. Garnham, 2001) between dynamic approaches to semantics, such as Kamp and Reyle's (1993) Discourse Representation Theory, and psycholinguistic theories of text meaning and interpretation based on discourse models. Other types of psychological theory, for example Kintsch's (1988) Construction–Integration model, focus to a greater extent on questions of processing, and there has not been an entirely satisfactory blending of the two types of approach.

Two sets of issues, often studied together, relate to the interpretation of (potentially) coreferential noun phrases (or anaphora more generally, though NP anaphora is by far the most widely studied aspect of anaphora in psycholinguistics) and inference (see Garnham 2001 for a summary of work to that date). In thinking about anaphora, psycholinguists have been influenced by linguistic work, such as the notion of C-command (see Reinhart 1983) and the distinction between deep (model-interpretive) and surface anaphora (ellipsis) (Hankamer and Sag 1976, Sag and Hankamer 1984). Inferences, however, are often based on knowledge (specific or general) about the world (real, abstract, or imaginary). Until recently linguists have fought shy of addressing questions about the impact of knowledge on interpretation, partly, presumably, because the conceptual framework required to understand such effects is not primarily a linguistic one.

Many other topics have been studied in the psycholinguistics of language comprehension and production by ordinary adults. From the present perspective, the important points are not the details of this work, but the broad perspective in which it has, for the most part, been carried out. Two aspects of this perspective are particularly worth noting. First, until the late 1990s, the dominant framework was a functionalist one that assumed the use of abstract symbol systems for representing and processing linguistic information. Links with brain mechanisms were largely ignored, and even where connectionist ideas impinged on work in sentence and discourse processing, the systems proposed were almost always hybrid ones with localist (symbolic) representations of content. Second, though ideas from linguistics were not unimportant, much of the work in psychology made only general use of such ideas. For example, descriptions of psycholinguistic work on parsing are peppered with phrase structure diagrams, but many, though not all, were uninfluenced by developments in syntactic theory after the mid-1960s. Given the hypotheses under investigation, and the fact that there were major disagreements among syntacticians about syntactic structure, this approach was perfectly reasonable, though it would be interesting if psycholinguistic investigations could help to resolve issues about the correct syntactic structure of natural language sentences.

30.4 LANGUAGE, THE BRAIN, AND THE BODY

Although it seems obvious to modern Western intuition that the brain is the seat of mental functioning, this intuition is not universal, and other organs, particularly the heart, have often been seen as the locus of the mental. Indeed, the link between the heart and the emotions remains strong in modern Western folk psychology. Although Plato identified the brain as the organ of the intellect, Aristotle, for example, thought the major function of the brain was to cool the blood. However, the Alexandrian biologists

Herophilos, who lived from 335 to 280 BC, and Erasisratus (304–250 BC) concluded, partly from anatomical investigations, that the brain was the seat of the intellect. They also gave the first proper account of the nervous system. Galen (b. 129 AD), to whom their work was known, confirmed and elaborated on their conclusions.

Knowledge of the link between language and the brain has been traced by to an Egyptian papyrus from the seventeenth century BC. However, modern thinking dates back little more than 200 years to the early part of the nineteenth century, when Gall, in the context of the now discredited theory of phrenology, located language functions in the frontal cortex. Gall's work, though based on a wholly inadequate evidential basis, marks the start of a clear interest in the precise location of different mental functions in the brain. Another early French pioneer was Jean-Baptiste Bouillaud, who in 1825 published his *Traité Clinique et Physiologique de l'Encéphalite, ou Inflammation du Cerveau* in which he, as did Gall, concluded that certain aspects of language function were localized in the frontal lobes. He further distinguished between language-specific deficits and motor problems affecting the articulators of the vocal tract. In 1836 another Frenchman, Marc Dax, concluded, on the basis of three case studies, that language is localized in the left, rather than the right, hemisphere of the cerebral cortex. We now know that things are much more complicated. Localization depends, not straightfor-wardly, on handedness (nearly all right-handers and around half of left-handers show left lateralization). Furthermore, there is continuing debate about what functions are localized in the left (or primary language) hemisphere and which are localized, or at least partly supported, in the other hemisphere (usually the right). There is also debate about the extent of individual variation in patterns of lateralization. These findings, and almost everything else that was known about the relation between language and the brain up to the late twentieth century, were based on studies of people suffering from language deficits (aphasias). It was not until the advent of brain imaging and related techniques that another major avenue to studying this relation was opened.

The two major milestones in aphasiology in the late nineteenth century were the reports by Paul Broca (1861) and Carl Wernicke (1874) of cases of, respectively, expressive and receptive aphasias, commonly known as Broca's and Wernicke's apha-sias. These aphasias are associated with brain lesions in the left hemisphere in, respectively, the posterior inferior frontal gyrus and the posterior part of the superior temporal gyrus, also known as Broca's area and Wernicke's area. Since Broca's aphasia presents more immediately and obviously as a difficulty with language, it is not surprising that the earlier reports, which located language function in the frontal lobes, were of this kind. However, while it is true that the most obvious symptoms of Broca's aphasia are language production problems (not attributable, as Bouillaud noted, to articulatory problems), and the most obvious symptoms of Wernicke's aphasia are comprehension problems, the full pattern of problems is neither as simple nor as consistent as the initial descriptions implied. Wernicke's work, too, has its predecessors, for example in the work of his mentor Theodor Meynert, published only a few years before his own case study.

In his 1874 publication, Wernicke had already begun to consider how the areas identified by him and by Broca might be linked in a brain network for language processing. According to this model, sensory inputs pass either via the primary auditory cortex to Wernicke's area, in the case of spoken language, or from the visual cortex via the angular gyrus to Wernicke's area, in the case of written language. From there information (about meaning) can pass to Broca's area via a nerve fibre bundle called the arcuate fasciculus and hence to the motor area, which is adjacent to Broca's area, and, eventually, the articulators. A version of Wernicke's model, known as Lichtheim's house, has remained important in medical training. Lichtheim also predicted, on the basis of his model, other types of aphasia caused by damage to components of the system, including the links from one area to another. To some extent his predictions have been borne out, but only within the context of an ever more complex picture of the relation between brain damage and aphasic symptoms.

For some of the same reasons that psycholinguistic studies were relatively neglected in the early part of the twentieth century—the dominance of behaviourism in the United States in particular—aphasiology was relatively neglected in that period also. Wernicke's model of aphasia was revived in the 1960s by Norman Geschwind, who, among other things, firmed up the notion of conduction aphasia, a specific type of aphasia postulated to be caused by damage to the arcuate fasciculus. The Wernicke–Geschwind model was important through the 1960s and 1970s, but as larger numbers of aphasic patients were studied it became apparent that, on the one hand, the model had some general problems and, on the other, the mapping between sets of symptoms and locations of lesions was not as clear-cut as the model suggested.

An alternative approach to neurological disorders in general, and aphasia in particular, emerged from the cognitive psychological tradition that developed after the cognitive revolution of the 1950s. This approach was known as cognitive neuropsychology (not to be confused with cognitive neuroscience, discussed below), and was particularly prominent in the UK. Cognitive neuropsychology is based on the functional (often boxological) models of cognitive neuropsychology, which analyse cognitive functioning independently of underlying brain mechanisms. Those models are then used to predict patterns of deficit and, most interestingly, complementary patterns of deficit in different patients (known as double dissociations). The deficits are predicted on the assumption that the boxes in the cognitive psychological models represented cognitive (and hence neural) modules that can be damaged. Some proponents of this approach placed particular emphasis on individual case studies, whereas others look at patterns across groups of patients. In the domain of language, this approach met with a number of successes, for example in the analysis of patterns of acquired dyslexia in terms of dual route models of adult reading. Such models propose a direct lexical route for reading words, in which perceptual information makes direct contact with information in the mental lexicon, and a route based on recoding using grapheme–phoneme correspondence rules followed by access to the lexicon using sound patterns.

Towards the end of the twentieth century, cognitive neuropsychology found itself in an at least partially false opposition to the different approach of cognitive neuroscience.

Cognitive neuroscience attempts to investigate the brain mechanisms underlying cognition. It was conceived, allegedly in a taxi-cab conversation between cognitive scientist George Miller (mentioned earlier) and neuroscientist Michael Gazzaniga, as a melding of those two disciplines. It was the functionalism of cognitive neuropsychology, which eschewed the study of specific brain mechanisms, that seemed at odds with the approach of cognitive neuroscience.

Cognitive neuroscience can be seen, and is seen by many, as being in direct succession to the work of Broca, Wernicke, Geschwind, and others on brain areas underlying language and other aspects of cognition. The modern discipline is, however, partly defined by a set of modern (and not so modern) techniques. The key techniques are modern brain-imaging techniques, borrowed and adapted from medical research and diagnosis, and in particular functional magnetic resonance imaging (fMRI), which relies on a complex and somewhat indirect measure of the increase in oxygenated blood flow in brain areas that are active. fMRI has reasonably good spatial resolution, but poor temporal resolution in relation to the speed at which cognitive processes typically occur. Partly for this reason it has lent itself to the localization of areas that contribute to various cognitive tasks, but has been less successful in allowing new insights into the functioning of the underlying cognitive systems—another reason for the conflict with the approach of cognitive neuropsychology. For an overview of recent language-related discoveries using fMRI, see Ferstl et al. (2008) and Price (2010). Other imaging techniques, such as Positron Emission Tomography (PET) and Single Photon Emission Computed Tomography (SPECT), have even poorer temporal resolution, and have been less important in the study of language.

Other cognitive neuroscience techniques include single-cell recording, though because of its intrusiveness this technique is relatively rarely applied in the study of human cognition, Transcranial Magnetic Stimulation (TMS) and electro- and magneto-encephalography (EEG and MEG). TMS, in which a relatively powerful magnetic field is applied above a small area of the scalp (and hence skull), is often characterized as producing the equivalent of a temporary lesion, as it interferes with the working of the part of the brain immediately below the scalp area to which it is applied. Its uses in the study of language processing are potentially very interesting. However, it is more intrusive than other techniques and must be used with caution. EEG and MEG are non-intrusive in the sense that they measure, respectively, electrical and magnetic activity at the scalp produced by the normal functioning of the brain—in fact they measure the linked electrical and magnetic changes in the same changing electromagnetic field. EEG and MEG are not imaging techniques, as the relation between electromagnetic activity at the scalp and the corresponding brain activity that it reflects is complex. There are methods (called source localization), which are not entirely reliable, that attempt to determine the underlying source of patterns of activity at the scalp, but many operators of EEG and MEG use known (or sometimes newly discovered) patterns of scalp activity that can be associated with specific cognitive functions. For example, about 400 milliseconds after a stimulus that does not fit with context, an enhanced negative going peak (the N400) is often seen. In language processing it can be detected, for example, at the last word in a sentence such as *He spread the warm bread with socks* (Kutas and Hillyard 1980). Because EEG is not so directly associated with localization of brain function, there is much less tension between the use of EEG as a technique (MEG is less commonly used, because it is so much more expensive to operate) and functionalist approaches, such as that of cognitive neuropsychology.

The most common use of EEG in language research uses Event-Related Potentials (ERPs) to investigate language processing. ERPs are characteristic patterns of scalp voltage change, with characteristic patterns of scalp topology, that follow events of various kinds, such as a word that does not fit into a sentence (as in the bread and socks example above) or a pronoun without a clear referent as in *The queen entered the room. He signalled for the crowd to sit.* After averaging electrical waveforms over many experimental trials, patterns of positive and negative peaks can be seen at approximately constant periods after the beginning of the crucial word. These peaks are modulated by the difficulty of the task, and particular peaks are associated with particular types of processing. In language research, two peaks are of particular interest: the already mentioned N400, a negative peak about 400 milliseconds after the word begins, and a positive peak at 600 milliseconds (P600). These peaks have been associated respectively with semantic and syntactic fit of a word into a sentence, though controversy remains over their exact interpretation, especially with respect to P600 being a syntactic marker.

In parallel with the renewed interest in the relation between language and the brain, a different strand of research, with very different originals, has looked at relations between the human body, and the ways in which it interacts with its environment, and language. Both Wittgenstein and the Oxford Linguistic Philosophers emphasized, in their different ways, the connection between meaning and use, and Wittgenstein (1953) in particular connected use with what he called forms of life. Later, in the precursors of what became cognitive linguistics, links were made between the meanings of abstract concepts and those of physical concepts that are more directly connected to human behaviour and interactions with the environment. It was further noted that the meaning of those more concrete concepts might best be explicated in terms of those interactions between people and their environment. Meanwhile, some cognitive psychologists were developing ideas that later became known as theories of embodiment or embodied cognition, though a variety of other terms have been used along the way. The idea of embodied cognition did not develop first in relation to language use, but in domains such as thinking and reasoning, in which, for example, external aids to problem solving were seen as intimately connected with mental processes. In the domain of language, a related idea developed: that meanings were not stored in the mind as abstract symbols, but in terms of the way people interact physically with the world. Ironically, the techniques of cognitive neuroscience lent support to this idea, by showing, for example, that areas of the brain that control movement are activated when simple sentences containing bodily action verbs are understood (Pulvermüller 2005).

30.5 CONCLUSIONS

Over the past 200 years much has been learned about the relations between language and the mind and between language and the brain (and the rest of the human body). Modern techniques and theories potentially provide new ways for drawing these two traditionally somewhat disparate research areas together. However, a genuine and satisfying synthesis remains elusive, and that fact is partly what makes research on these topics such a continuing and exciting challenge.

CHAPTER 31

TRANSLATION: THE INTERTRANSLATABILITY OF LANGUAGES; TRANSLATION AND LANGUAGE TEACHING

KIRSTEN MALMKJÆR

31.1 THE INTERTRANSLATABILITY OF LANGUAGES

31.1.1 Equivalence in Difference?

It takes but a moment's thought for a person exposed to two or more languages to realize that there are differences between them, and that what can be said in one language cannot be said using the same means in another. Nevertheless, the same individual may also feel that significant proportions of their experience can be described using any of their languages, despite the clear differences between them: that, as Jakobson (1987 [1959]: 430) puts it, there is 'Equivalence in difference' between languages. This phenomenon, according to Jakobson, 'is the cardinal problem of language and the pivotal concern of linguistics,' for three reasons: first, whoever receives a verbal message must, in a sense, translate it into their own language (even if it is what is usually thought of as the same language); secondly, to explain in a dictionary or grammar what a term or expression means involves translating it, in a sense, into other terms (of the same or another language); and thirdly, contrastive linguistics 'implies an examination of [the] mutual translatability' of the languages concerned. For example, if I wish to compare and contrast English and Danish ways of representing periods of time, I must first decide which sets of terms and expressions the two languages use to carry out this function. I will assert that terms like *second, hour, minute, week, month,* and *year* in English correspond closely to the terms *sekund, time, minut, uge, måned,* and *år* in Danish in the ways in which they are used to segment time, but that when it comes to the terms *day* and *fortnight,* the two languages differ: Danish has two terms corresponding to English *day*; one term, *dag,* is used to refer to the hours of daylight, and another, *døgn,* is used when the twenty-four hours that constitute a day and a night are at issue. Conversely, Danish has no term that exactly corresponds to the English *fortnight,* and must resort to the expression *fjorten dage* 'fourteen days' or *to uger* 'two weeks.' In this discussion, though, the fact of my selecting these two sets of terms to compare, as opposed to two different sets of terms, shows that I assume a degree of intertranslatability between the two languages with respect to these sets of terms. The assumption that there is translatability between languages must perforce also hover behind any foray into translation studies (what else would it be that we were studying?), where much effort has been expended in trying to establish what kind of equivalence there must be between two texts if one is to be counted as a translation of another. Within the philosophy of language, our right to the intertranslatability assumption has been put to the severest of tests: taking seriously the connection, which we saw Jakobson make above, between receiving a message and translating the message into your own language, Quine (1958, 1959, 1960) has suggested that since no evidence is available to us that would either support or counter this assumption, no theory of meaning, and therefore of translation, and therefore of language can be established.

Jakobson himself adopts two radically different approaches to the phenomenon of equivalence in difference. On the one hand, he maintains (1987: 431):

> All cognitive experience and its classification is conveyable in any existing language.
> ... No lack of grammatical devices in the language translated into makes impossible a literal translation of the entire conceptual information contained in the original.

On the other hand, he feels that certain text types cannot be translated, because the means of expression (which must perforce vary from language to language) are crucial to its result. As he puts it (1987: 434):

> In poetry, verbal equations become a constructive principle of the text. Syntactic and morphological categories, roots, and affixes, phonemes and their components (distinctive features)—in short, any constituent of the verbal code—are confronted, juxtaposed, brought into contiguous relation according to the principle of similarity and contrast and carry their own autonomous signification. Phonemic similarity is sensed as semantic relationship. The pun, or to use a more erudite and perhaps more precise term—paranomasia, reigns over poetic art, and whether its rule is absolute or limited, poetry by definition is untranslatable. Only creative transposition is possible.

Clearly, the juxtaposition of these two statements suggests that Jakobson thinks that what is conveyed in poetry is not, or is more than, cognitive experience; and it is instructive to recall that Jakobson also insists that the poetic function of language is by no means confined to poetry, but has a role in virtually any text (see Jakobson 1960). There is therefore a certain two-mindedness at play in Jakobson's writings on the issue of the intertranslatability of languages, and he seeks to alleviate this by distinguishing between, on the one hand, types of experience—cognitive and other—and, on the other, types of translation—literal and other.

Jakobson's duality of mind with regard to the intertranslatability question is by no means unique: most translation scholars probably live with it. It was shared by Edward Sapir, who, in his work on contrastive linguistics, spends an entertaining chapter (1921: ch. 5) detailing the thirteen distinct concepts expressed in the famous sentence *The farmer kills the duckling* and showing that languages differ considerably in how they choose to express them, that not all the concepts are in fact expressed in all languages, and that some languages need to express some different concepts in their nearest translation equivalent to the sentence. For example, in German, *Der Bauer tötet das Entelein*, it is necessary to express both number (singular) and grammatical gender (masculine and neuter, respectively) in the articles *der* and *das*; and in Yana:

> Literally translated, the . . . sentence would read something like 'kill-s he farmer he to duck-ling' in which 'he' and 'to' are rather awkward English renderings of a general third personal pronoun . . . and an objective particle which indicates that the following noun is connected with the verb otherwise than as subject. The suffixed element in 'kill-s' corresponds to the English suffix with the important exceptions that it makes no reference to the number of the subject and that the statement is know to be true. (Sapir 1921: 96)

This faith in literal translation belies Sapir's later insistence that 'The worlds in which different societies live are distinct worlds, not merely the same world with different labels attached,' because how would Sapir have been able to establish which features the different languages represented if not by recourse to something shared for the different labels to attach to? However, Sapir maintains equilibrium of thought by way of recourse to a distinction between types of world and reality—objective and social: just before the sentence just quoted, we read ([1929b] Mandelbaum 1949: 69):

> Human beings do not live in the objective world alone, nor alone in the world of social activity as ordinarily understood, but are very much at the mercy of the particular language which has become the medium of expression for their society . . . The fact of the matter is that the 'real world' is to a large extent built up on the language habits of the group. No two languages are ever sufficiently similar to be considered as representing the same social reality.

Of Jakobson's three reasons for taking equivalence in difference as the fundamental problem of linguistics, referred to above: (i) whoever receives a verbal message must translate it into their own language (even if it be the same language), (ii) to explain in a dictionary or grammar what a term or expression means involves translating it into other terms (of the same or another language), and (iii) contrastive linguistics 'implies an examination of [the] mutual translatability' of the languages, the first seems fundamental to the other two enterprises, so I will discuss it below, in an effort to establish the possibility of equivalence, albeit at a fairly fundamental level.

31.1.2 Equivalence? The View from the Philosophy of Language

In the philosophy of language, the intertranslatability of languages has been used to highlight what is arguably the fundamental question of semantics: whether it is possible to provide an account of meaning as something shared between any two language users, including those who believe they are using the same language (Davidson 1984 [1973]: 125):

> The problem of interpretation is domestic as well as foreign: it surfaces for speakers of the same language in the form of the question, how can it be determined that the language is the same? Speakers of the same language can go on the assumption that for them the same expressions are to be interpreted in the same way, but this does not indicate what justifies the assumption. All understanding of the speech of another involves radical interpretation. But it will help keep assumptions from going unnoticed to focus on cases where interpretation is most clearly called for: interpretation in one idiom of talk in another.

In the same article, Davidson also sets out succinctly what kind of evidence would serve to justify the sameness assumption:

> Kurt utters the words 'Es regnet' and under the right conditions we know that he has said that it is raining. Having identified his utterance as intentional and linguistic, we are able to go on to interpret his words: we can say what his words, on that occasion, meant. What could we know that would enable us to do this? How could we come to know it?

Both questions have to be answered satisfactorily, because it is not enough to explain what would serve to yield interpretations, if there is no way of explaining how speakers could become aware of it. This has been a major difficulty for numerous accounts of meaning across time. For example, Locke (1690, bk 3, ch. 2) considers that words are signs of the ideas that make up thoughts. This is a very common-sense reply to Davidson's first question about what would enable us to understand what Kurt's utterances meant, but it is an answer that falls foul of Davidson's second question, because short of telepathy, there is little chance of us coming to know what Kurt's thoughts and ideas are unless we have first interpreted his words; the thoughts and ideas cannot, therefore, themselves be used to explain how the understanding of the words comes about. Theories that assign parts of the world as references for words, along the lines implied by both Jakobson and Sapir (§31.1.1 above), might on the face of it seem to fare better, since we can at least all observe much of the objective world that

Sapir contrasts with the social world and from which we might gain the kind of cognitive experience that Jakobson contrasts with other forms of experience.

However, the objectivity of our cognitive experience of a real world has been severely challenged by Quine's (1958, 1959, 1960) claim that the fact that a person invariably utters a certain expression in the presence of a certain feature of the natural world is no guarantee that terms in that person's expression are translation equivalents of terms within an expression that another person might utter in the presence of that feature of the natural world.

> Given that a native sentence says that a so-and-so is present, and given that the sentence is true when and only when a rabbit is present, it by no means follows that the so-and-so are rabbits. They might be all the various temporal segments of rabbits. They might be all the integral or undetached parts of rabbits . . . And the case is yet worse: we do not even have evidence for taking the native expression as of the form 'A so-and-so is present'; it could as well be construed with an abstract singular term, as meaning that rabbithood is locally manifested. Better just 'Rabbiteth,' like 'Raineth.' (Quine 1969 [1958]: 2–3)

The implications of this for translation are drawn out especially clearly in Quine (1959), an article in a volume wholly devoted to the subject of translation. Here, Quine points out that a linguist engaged in radical translation, 'translation of the language of a hitherto untouched people' (p. 148), would segment the alien sentences into words and constructions which he or she would hypothetically equate to words and constructions of his or her own language, in an operation which Quine refers to as the formation of *analytical hypotheses* of translation' (1959: 165, italics original). The totality of such analytical hypotheses of translation would amount to a contrastive grammar and dictionary of the new language and the linguist's own, but the problem with it is that 'the supporting evidence remains entirely at the level of sentences,' and:

> Countless alternative over-all semantic correlations, therefore, are equally compatible with that evidence. If the linguist arrives at his one over-all correlation among many without feeling that his choice was excessively arbitrary, this is because he himself is limited in the correlations that he can manage . . . he has to assign them in some way that is manageably systematic with respect to a manageably limited set of repeatable speech segments . . . It is by his analytical hypotheses that our . . . linguist implicitly states (and indeed arrives at) the grand synthetic hypothesis which is his over-all semantic correlation of sentences. His supporting evidence, such as it is, for the semantic correlation is his supporting evidence also for his analytical hypotheses. Chronologically, the analytical hypotheses come before all that evidence is in; then such of the evidence as ensues is experienced as pragmatic corroboration of a working dictionary. (1959: 168–9)

Quine ends this article referring to the work of Usener, Cassirer, Sapir, and Whorf, comparing their view that 'deep differences of language carry with them ultimate differences in the way one thinks' (1959: 171) with his own indeterminacy thesis. But for Quine, the issue is not so much the fact that one culture believes something which another culture does not believe that is the problem—it is not a case of disagreement about something identifiable; Quine's pessimism pertains to the possibility of identifying anything beyond a speaker's words as evidence for their meaning—there simply is no fact of the matter as far as a theory of meaning (and therefore of translation and of language) is concerned. So

> it is only relative to an in large part arbitrary manual of translation that most foreign sentences may be said to share the meaning of English sentences, and then only in a very parochial sense of meaning, viz., use-in-English . . . most talk of meaning requires tacit reference to a home language in much the way that talk of truth involves tacit reference to one's own system of the world, the best that one can muster at the time.

For further reading on Quine's indeterminacy of translation thesis, see Quine (1960) and Hookway (1988).

There is, fortunately, relief from Quine's deep pessimism in the work of Donald Davidson, whom we have already met above. Given the indeterminacy of translation and the inscrutability of reference, Davidson (1973) selects a different starting point in his search for an account of translatability in the notion of holding an utterance true. This is an attitude of speakers (and hearers), not a property of language, and it is an attitude that it is not unreasonable to trust that speakers adopt towards their own utterances most of the time; so Davidson avoids, at least initially, the circle of belief and meaning that beset Quine's quest for non-linguistic evidence for the meanings of utterances: we have a speaker attitude to utterances that is independent of the meaning of the utterances (Davidson 1984 [1973]: 134).

Returning to Kurt's discourse on rain, we can now proceed as follows: Kurt, who belongs to a speech community which we call German, has a tendency to utter *Es regnet* if and only if it is raining near him at the time. We could take this, along with in principle infinitely many corroborating instances of observation of other speakers, as evidence for the statement (Davidson 1984: 135):

> 'Es regnet' is true-in-German when spoken by x at time t if and only if it is raining near x at t.

Or (Hookway 1988: 168)

> 'Gavagai' is true-in-L when uttered . . . iff there is a rabbit near x at t.

These statements—known as T-sentences—illustrate the importance of disquotation: to get at meaning, we need to relate linguistic items which are in quotation marks to show that their meaning is to be established, to linguistic items that are not in quotation marks because we already understand them—that is, we have a theory that can account for them. To see this point more clearly, consider the plight of a monolingual English speaker inquiring about the meaning of the Danish term ø, only to be told that it means 'Insel.' What this illustrates is that when we inquire what terms mean, we do not, ultimately, want to know what they mean the same as; being told what a term means the same as only helps if you already understand that other term (ø and *Insel* are the Danish and German terms, respectively, for 'island').

Were we to establish T-sentences for a large number of sentences of the language, we would be in a good position to interpret each individual sentence. The need for mass is highlighted by Evnine (1991: 121):

> being able to interpret a sentence is not simply knowing the appropriate T-sentence; it is knowing that some sentence is true iff some condition obtains *and* that that sentence is composed out of parts which feature in other sentences which are true iff other specified conditions obtain.

Of course, the efficacy of Davidson's mechanism rests on an assumption that other speakers are enough like us to be likely to hold true what we hold true in the same circumstances and to conceive of the circumstances in the same way that we do, which is what Quine doubts. But according to Davidson (1984: 137):

> The methodological advice to interpret in a way that optimizes agreement should not be conceived as resting on a charitable assumption about human intelligence that might turn out to be false. If we cannot find a way to interpret the utterances and other behaviour of a creature as revealing a set of beliefs largely consistent and true by our own standards, we have no reason to count that creature as rational, as having beliefs or as saying anything.

For Davidson, Wilson's principle of charity, according to which (Wilson 1959; quoted in Quine 1960: n. 2) 'We select as designatum that individual which will make the largest possible number of... statements true,' is not a principle that we can opt into for purely pragmatic reasons, as it is for Quine. Rather, it is fundamental to the very project of inquiry into meaning. Any attempt at comprehending the utterances of another implies an assumption that the person in question has one or a set of beliefs that they wish to convey. And since having beliefs is the same as holding something true, the question to be asked is whether it is possible for a creature to have a language which expresses what it holds true, but which is not translatable? But since the notion of truth (Tarski 1956) is defined in terms of translation between a sentence in quotation and its disquotated counterpart, the prospect of divorcing the two notions from one another is not good. In Davidson's account of translation, truth is taken for granted, reversing the direction of explanation from Tarski's; but the mutual dependency between the two notions remains.

As Davidson (1984: 139) points out,

> When all the evidence is in, there will remain, as Quine has emphasised, the trade-offs between the beliefs we attribute to speakers and the interpretations we give their words. But the remaining indeterminacy cannot be so great but that any theory that passes the [systematicity] test will serve to yield interpretations.

On this account, meaning is a relation between (at least) a speaker, a time, a state of affairs, and an utterance. It tells us that *S* means *P* iff *L* is a theory which makes the best overall sense of the community *C* and *L* yields the theorem: *S* is true iff *p*.

31.1.3 Equivalence: the View from Translation Studies

The 1960s saw the publication of two studies that both took seriously the problems posed for the development of a theory of translation by the tensions between equivalence and difference and which, by accepting difference and theorizing equivalence, albeit in radically different ways, can be considered to have laid the foundations for two of the major movements in twentieth-century translation studies, one oriented towards function and response, and the other primarily concerned with the relationship between theory and description in translation studies. The first study is that by Nida (1964) and the second is Catford's (1965).

Nida (1964) devotes a significant portion of his book to the analysis of meaning. He perceives a rough division into emotive, linguistic, and referential meaning, with more fine-grained dimensions brought into play 'when we attempt to determine the differences in the manner in which the source and the receptors understand a particular communication' (1964: 43). He makes much of the different ways in which different languages segment experience, pointing out for example, that

> In Totonac, spoken in Mexico, there are six basically different words for 'noise': (1) children yelling, (2) people talking loudly, (3) people arguing and turkeys gobbling, (4) people talking angrily, (5) a noise which increases constantly in volume, and (6) funeral noise. (Nida 1964: 50)

Furthermore, he also echoes Quine in stressing that since it is obviously true that

> each person employs language on the basis of his background and no two individuals ever have precisely the same background, then it is also obvious that no two persons ever mean exactly the same thing by the same language symbols. (Nida 1964: 51)

Nevertheless, Nida is especially impressed by the 'amazing degree of similarity in the use of language among members of the same speech community' (p. 51), and both this and communication across different speech communities and languages, he believes, are guaranteed by four basic factors: the similarity of mental processes of all peoples; the similarity of somatic relations, whether automatic, such as blushing, or semi-automatic, such as laughing and grimacing; the range of common human experience; and the capacity for adjustment to the behavioural patterns of others (pp. 53–5). Nida's faith in these universals allows him to develop an account of translation in terms of similarity of response to a text and its translation (see below) which might otherwise invite some scepticism. Adjusting Jakobson's (1987 [1960]: 66) six factors of speech events: addresser, message, addressee, context, code, and contact, to a set of five basic factors in communication: subject matter, participants, speech act or process of writing, code, and message, Nida (1964: 120) highlights what he terms 'the dynamic dimension in communication,' which is especially important when translation is at issue, because 'the production of equivalent messages is a process, not merely of matching parts of utterances, but also of reproducing the total dynamic character of the communication.' The figure of the translator is central in enabling this; he or she is 'the focal element in translating' (1964:

145), Nida being the first translation theorist to be quite so outspoken about the translator's role. The translator operates within 'the total cultural framework in which the communication occurs,' including the temporal and spatial distances between the interactants (p. 147). No receiver of a message can respond to it except within the cultural context in which they live; however, they can be enabled, within their own culture, to respond to the message in their own language 'in substantially the same manner as the receptor in the [original] culture responded, within the context of his own culture, to the message as communicated to him in his own language' (p. 149). This emphasis on equivalence of response enables Nida to live with the impossibility of obtaining 'absolute correspondence' or 'identity in detail' between a text and its translation (1964: 156). Instead, it is possible to decide on differing degrees of emphasis on similarity of content or form, depending on the nature of the message, the purpose of the author and translator, and the type of audience for which the message is intended. However, Nida identifies 'two fundamentally different types of equivalence: one which may be called formal and another which is primarily dynamic' (p. 149). Formal equivalence arises when the main focus is on the message itself in both form and content, and to measure it, the translation can be measured against the original for accuracy and correctness. Such a translation is oriented primarily towards the source culture and audience, and to understand it, the reader of the translation must identify as fully as possible with them. In contrast, where dynamic equivalence is sought, the translator must strive to provide a text which permits the audience to experience the same effect when reading the translation as the original readership experienced when reading the original text, and this may require substantial departures from the letter and style of the original text: expression in such a translation must be completely natural, and cultural elements must be made familiar to the audience. For example, Nida, whose primary focus is on Bible translating, suggests that Romans 16:16 'greet one another with a holy kiss' may be rendered 'give one another a hearty handshake all around' (1964: 160).

   In his focus on purpose and audience, Nida foreshadows more recent functional or *Skopos* oriented approaches to translation (see Vermeer 1978, Reiss and Vermeer 1984, Holz-Mänttäri 1984, Nord 1997) according to which the factor that more than any other should determine both the content and form of a translation is the purpose it has to fulfil for its audience: *Skopos* in Greek, used as a technical term in this approach. The audience may be very different from the audience for the original text, and the purposes of the two texts may also differ. For example, a technical description written by the designer of a product for distribution to sales outlets, to enable buyers to understand the design and function of the product, might be translated into a set of operating instructions for use by a child user group who would need to know less about the technical details than about how they might interact with the product for fun and entertainment. In this approach, therefore, there is less emphasis on linguistic issues than on cultural and commercial matters, and the translation task may merge with that of a copy writer. A similar situation pertains to aspects of website translation where internationalization of the appeal of products and services often goes hand in hand with localization, i.e. culturally focused adjustment of both text and illustration to suit a particular locale.

Like Nida, Catford (1965) is wary of claiming intertranslatability of languages, at least as far as meaning is concerned. Steeped as he is in Hallidayan and Firthian linguistics, Catford declares that meaning is 'the total network of relations entered into by any linguistic form,' and since these networks differ between languages, 'meaning . . . is a property of a language' (1965: 35). When we translate, therefore, it cannot be meanings that we translate. But whereas Nida turns inward to audience responses for his translational coin, Catford turns to context, in the sense of formal relationships that linguistic items enter into with other linguistic forms, and contextual relationships that they have with those aspects of context that are relevant to the linguistic interaction. The formal relationships are not replicated interlinguistically: 'every language is ultimately *sui generis*—its categories being defined in terms of relations holding within the language itself' (Catford 1965: 27), so only approximate formal correspondence can be established, in cases where a category in one language occupies as nearly as possible the same place in the 'economy' of its language as a category in another language occupies in the economy of its language. Similarly, contextual relationships that linguistic items enter into are 'rarely the same in any two languages.' For example (pp. 36–7), if we consider the deictic systems of north-east Scottish dialect and Standard English, the Scottish dialect has a three-term system devoid of a singular/plural distinction, consisting of *this* (proximal), *that* (distal), and *yon* (medial), while in English there are four terms, two of which are singular and two plural (*this, these, that, those*). So even though the two systems 'cover approximately the same total contextual field' (p. 37),

> It is clear that if we translate from Standard English to Scots we cannot 'transfer meaning.' There is no way in which, for example, Scots *that* can be said to 'mean the same' as English *that* or *this* or *these* or *those*. On a given occasion it may refer to, or be relatable to, the same feature of the situation as one of the English deictics—but its formal and contextual *meaning* is clearly different.

Translation equivalence, therefore, cannot be defined in terms of meaning. Rather, 'translation equivalence occurs when an SL [source language] and a TL [target language] text or item are relatable to (at least some of) the same features of substance' (p. 50).

This definition was built on by Gideon Toury, arguably the twentieth-century translation scholar who has done most to move the discipline forward by switching attention from the source text as the starting point for an examination of translation equivalence *per se*, to the target text as the staring point for an enquiry which goes beyond the textual to extrapolate socio-cultural norms which influence the types of target text choices through which translation equivalence is realized in particular cultures at particular times.

Toury adds to Catford's (1965: 50) definition of translation equivalence the notion of relevance: 'Translation equivalence occurs when a SL and a TL text (or item) are relatable to (at least some of) the same relevant features' (Toury 1980: 37). But relevance is relative to a point of view or a purpose, and in any given text, there may be hierarchies of relevance; in the case of pairs of texts of which one is a translation of the other, the hierarchies of relevance in which a given item and its translation find themselves are very likely to be different along with the places of the two items in their respective hierarchies.

The problem with previous translation theories, according to Toury (1980: 35), is that they are 'ST [Source Text]-oriented and, more often than not, even SL [Source Language]-oriented,' which makes them

> directive and normative in nature. They consider translation from the point of view of its being a reconstruction—in general a maximal (or at least optimal) reconstruction—of ST (i.e., the formalization of ST's systemic relationships), or even of SL, in TL [the Target Language], in such a way and to such an extent that TT [the Target Text] and ST are interchangeable according to some preconceived definition of this interchangeability.

This, he argues, makes such theories 'unable to supply a sound starting point and framework for a descriptive study of actual translations,' because the postulated optimal reconstruction of the original can never be reached, and we get statements like Jakobson's about untranslatability that we met in §31.1.1 above. These theories, then, define their object out of existence, and are unable to account for all those texts which in fact function as translations and are regarded as such by their users.

A better way of proceeding would be to accept those texts which are regarded as translations in a given culture as bona fide translations, available for empirical inquiry. The inquiry would work its way from the translation, in which features that the translator has assumed to be relevant for his or her readership will have been represented, to the original. In this way, segments of the translation can be matched up with segments of the original, and this will show the analyst actual relationships of equivalence: 'from TT's point of view, equivalence is not a postulated requirement, but an empirical fact, like TT itself: the *actual* relationships obtaining between TT and ST' (Toury 1995: 39, italics original). These relationships will not be the only ones possible, but regularities of choices will reveal translation norms that guide translators in their spatio-temporal communities in much the same way as Gricean maxims (Grice 1975) guide conversations, except that, unlike Grice's principle and its maxims, translation norms are subject to change over time and different sets of norms may be in competition with each other.

This framework invites extremely interesting comparisons between translations of the same original over time and across cultures, and has enabled textually oriented translation studies to engage with socio-cultural and historical studies to a much greater extent than had been possible previously.

31.2 TRANSLATION IN LANGUAGE TEACHING

31.2.1 Can Translation Exercises Help Students to Learn Languages?

In many parts of the world, translating forms a regular part of language teaching programmes, and students enjoy the exercises (see e.g. Carreres 2006). According to

Sewell (2004: 153), this is because translating exercises satisfy a learner's desire not to lose face and for confidence, self-esteem, reward, certainty, closure, and autonomy; and they are not as painful for introverts as are the role plays and active, public engagement demanded by communicative language pedagogy. When translating, the translator is not immediately responsible for the message, but is nevertheless in sole control of the translation being produced, and this product is an immediate reward of the effort that has gone into producing it. Furthermore, the product seems measurable against the original, and once measured, the task seems complete and the exercise closed. There is no risk of loss of face to other students during the exercise, and privacy remains with regard to its result.

This positive attitude to the use of translation in language teaching is generally shared among translation studies scholars and L2 educators. In a survey carried out by Källkvist of forty publications by scholars in these fields on the issue, only three expressed reservations (see Källkvist 2008: 184–5), and to this number we can now add the papers collected in Witte et al. (2009) and Cook's (2010) overwhelmingly positive discussion. Unfortunately, the few empirical studies of the direct effects on language learning of translation exercises that have been carried out (Berggren 1972, Slavikova 1990, Källkvist 1998, 2004, 2008) seem not to bear out this optimism. According to Källkvist (2008: 186), Berggren (1972), whose focus was on whether translation exercises had a negative effect on the learning of a second language, 'found no noticeable differences between a translation treatment and a close reading treatment,' and although

> Slavikova (1990) found statistically non-significant differences that she nevertheless interpreted as trends for the most part favoring a translation group over a no-translation group . . . neither study provides robust evidence and they both leave the issue of the effect of translation for the enhancement of L2 learning very much unresolved.

Källkvist herself addresses two main research questions:

> Do students who have been exposed to translation exercises for a substantial period of time perform equally well on morphosyntactic accuracy in English as students who have done exercises in the L2 only (but targeting the same structures) when (a) *translating writing* from Swedish into English, and b) [*sic*] *writing directly* in English?
>
> Do students who have had input through extensive reading and writing in English as an L2, but no explicit instruction in the use of morphosyntactic structures, perform equally well as students who have had 'translation exercises' or 'target-language-only exercises' on morphosyntactic accuracy when (a) *translating writing* from Swedish into English, and (b) *writing directly* in English? (Källkvist 2008: 186)

The treatment period was thirteen weeks. A group of fifty-five native Swedish speaking and Swedish-educated first-semester university students of English who had been learning English at school for nine or ten years, were divided into two groups on the basis of matched-pair random assignment, having had their grammar skills tested on their first day of the semester. Only students who missed no classes were included in the study, which meant that the two groups ended up, coincidentally, consisting of fifteen subjects each. The treatment was administered as follows:

> One group (the 'T' group, for 'Translation') was consistently engaged in translation exercises targeting structures presented in their grammar book and by their teacher. ... The second group (the 'NoT' group, for 'No Translation') performed fill-in-the-blank and transformation exercises in L2 targeting the same structures the same number of times. (Källkvist 2008: 188)

A third group, called the NoG (for No Grammar) group, consisting of high-school students, not randomized and taking other subjects as well as English, was included in order to address the second question above, but because this groups was different from the other two, Källkvist (2008: 189) points out that 'any differences in results between the NoG and the two experimental groups give rise to further hypotheses rather than conclusions.'

All the students were pre- and post-tested using first a multiple choice test, then a translation test (Swedish into English), and finally a written re-telling task (Källkvist 2008: 190), which allowed for relatively free production of tokens of the target structures (there were twenty-one tokens in the text to be retold), and the results of the tests were examined for pre-to-post test correct score increases.

For all three tasks, the T and the NoT groups showed significant gains, whereas the NoG group did not. The only significant difference between the groups' gains was between the T group and the NoG group, but Källkvist (2008: 192–3) attributes this lack of significance to the small number of test items and participants. The study therefore suggests that form-focused exercises (translation and fill-in-the-blank and transformation exercises) are more likely to enhance morphosyntactic accuracy in test situations than teaching that does not focus on form. However, the T group only excelled in comparison with the NoT group (and the difference only 'approached the level of significance' (p. 198)) in the translation tests, so there is no evidence of general enhancement of formal language skills by way of translation exercises. The study therefore 'does not provide support for form-focused courses for advanced learners that involve translation only' (p. 199), even though it does show that form focused translation exercises can enhance learners' grammar skills.

However, the kinds of exercise employed in Källkvist's studies can hardly be said to resemble real-life translation tasks, the benefits of which in language teaching have not to date been empirically tested. This is a shame, in light of the advocacy of the methodology referred to above. On the other hand, Källkvist's study does exonerate the use of even somewhat artificial translation exercises, since the study shows no evidence of the great harm that has been laid at their door by fierce opponents of the so-called grammar translation method in the nineteenth and twentieth centuries, whose arguments will be addressed in the final section of this article.

31.2.2 Can Translation Exercises Hinder Language Learning?

The arguments against the use of translating in language teaching made by members of the Reform Movement in the late nineteenth century and echoed in the mid- to late twentieth century by proponents of more or less communicative methods of language teaching need to be seen in the context of 'three major strands in the development of language teaching in the nineteenth century' (Howatt 1984: 129). The first of these was 'the gradual integration of foreign language teaching into a modernized secondary school curriculum,' which had concentrated on classical languages since the Middle Ages (Latin) and the Renaissance (Greek). The second was 'the expansion of the market for utilitarian language learning related to practical needs and interests,' which arose as a result of burgeoning internationalization from the middle of the nineteenth century. The third strand is the kind of thinking about language learning that led towards the Reform Movement in the 1880s (Howatt 1984: 130).

The traditional way for individuals to learn a modern foreign language in the eighteenth century was to study its grammar and read texts in the language, aided by a dictionary and by prior experience of learning classical languages. But such self-study methods were not well suited to mass education of school-aged students, and the method of language teaching often referred to as 'the grammar-translation method' arose as an adaptation of the traditional method for use with this clientele, initially in the state-run grammar schools (*Gymnasien*) in Prussia. In the new method, grammar remained focal and translation was still the favoured method; innovation lay in the use of individual sentences, instead of complete texts, to represent the new grammar and vocabulary to students in a graded manner (Howatt 1984: 132). In England, state involvement was anathema, and order was instead brought to the 'chaos of middle-class education (outside the ancient public schools)' (p. 133) by a system of public examinations controlled by the universities, the Oxford and Cambridge Local Examinations, established in 1858. Here, fear of modern languages being labelled soft options

> forced modern language teachers and textbook writers to ape the methods of the classics. French had to be made as 'demanding' as Latin, and German as 'intellectually disciplined' as Greek. Textbooks had to be 'thorough' . . . and based on selections from the 'best authors'. Spoken language was, at best, irrelevant and accuracy was elevated to the status of a moral imperative. (Howatt 1984: 135)

Interestingly, Howatt traces the reputation of the English as being bad at languages to an 'unholy alliance' between the public examination system and educational privilege: the public schools were able to opt out of the local examination and to keep teaching the classical languages, so that these, as opposed to modern languages, remained the sign of erudition. It is instructive to bear this in mind in the context of England in the early twenty-first century, where modern foreign languages are in danger of becoming confined to the most prestigious universities in the context of astronomical university fees.

The search for rigour and prestige eventually turned what began as a method for teaching languages to young schoolchildren employing nothing more radical than graded lessons containing grammar rules, vocabulary lists, and translation exercises, into what Howatt (1984: 136) describes as 'a jungle of obscure rules, endless lists of gender classes and gender-less exceptions, self-conscious "literary" archaisms, snippets of philology, and a total loss of genuine feeling for living language.' It was to this unfortunate state of affairs that the adherents of the Reform Movement turned their attention in the last two decades of the nineteenth century.

The Reform Movement is, according to Howatt (p. 169) 'unique in language teaching history.' Three of its main proponents, the phoneticians Viëtor in Germany, Passy in France, and Jespersen in Denmark, had all set out as language teachers, and they, together with Henry Sweet in England, were joined by many members of the profession in their quest for reform of language teaching across Europe. It began with the publication of Viëtor's (1882) pamphlet entitled *Der Sprachunterricht muss umkehren!* (Language teaching must change direction! reprinted in a translation by Howatt, David Abercrombie and Beat Buchmann as an appendix to Howatt 1984). A number of associations, including the International Phonetic Association (IPA), and journals were also founded under the auspices of the movement. The movement, according to Howatt (p. 171), 'was founded on three basic principles: the primacy of speech, the centrality of the connected text as the kernel of the teaching-learning process, and the absolute priority of an oral methodology in the classroom,' each of which was clearly in stark contrast to the grammar translation method, especially in its later manifestations. Viëtor argued that the method placed excessive demands on children and that they would learn languages more effectively if the spoken language was emphasized; and the new science of psychology lent weight to the argument for connected texts as opposed to individual sentences as the object of study, because it was centrally based on the notion of association. Finally, the movement advocated a more evidence-based, descriptive approach to learning: rather than selecting or constructing sentences to illustrate grammatical rules, the language of the more naturalistic texts being used should provide data for the formation of grammatical rules.

Sweet (1899) adopts associationism, the notion that learners need to form correct associations between linguistic elements through the use of full texts, and avoid 'cross-associations,' which might follow from the misuse of translations (Howatt 1984: 185); and further warnings about the dangers of translation were issued by proponents of the Natural, Conversational, Direct and Communicative methods of languages teaching in the late nineteenth and the twentieth century, including Berlitz (1907), Lado (1964), and Gatenby (1967). According to Malmkjær (1998: 6) these arguments include:

Translation
* is independent of the four skills which define language competence: reading, writing, speaking and listening;
* is radically different from these four skills;
* takes up valuable time which could be used to teach these four skills;
* is unnatural;

- misleads students into thinking that expressions in two languages correspond one-to-one;
- prevents students from thinking in the foreign language;
- produces interference;
- is a bad test of language skills; and
- is only appropriate for training translators.

However, Malmkjær (1998: 6–8) argues that these arguments do not hold for translation exercises that are or simulate the kinds of translation task that translators in fact undertake. Such tasks always have a purpose, and they will require focused reading and writing. It is also often necessary for the translator to discuss the task with clients and other professionals, so speaking and listening are regularly involved. It is also incorrect to say that translation is unnatural, both in light of the close connection which we have established in this article between it and what is normally considered interaction involving one language only (see §31.1.2 above) and in light of the fact that the majority of the world's population is not monolingual and lives in multilingual situations where translation is a fact of everyday life. Naturalistic translation tasks will also soon illustrate to learners that one-to-one relationships between terms in their languages are extremely rare; so rather than misleading them in this regard, it is likely to heighten their awareness of it. It is true that translation produces interference, but learning to cope with interference is probably one of the most useful skills that any language learner can acquire. Finally, since the translation and related professions are increasingly popular career choices for students of languages, introducing the requisite skills in their syllabuses can hardly be considered wasteful.

31.3 TO CONCLUDE

So much for surmise; the way ahead towards solving the difference of opinion with regard to the properly contextualized use of translation in language teaching has to lie in empirical research.

CHAPTER 32

....

COMPUTATIONAL LINGUISTICS

....

GRAEME HIRST

32.1 ORIGINS IN MACHINE TRANSLATION
....

THE field of computational linguistics (CL) has its origins in research on machine translation (MT) in the early days of computing in the 1940s. The founding moment of MT is traced to a widely circulated memorandum written in July 1949 by the American mathematician and science administrator Warren Weaver. Weaver's memorandum, which drew on ideas from a letter he had written to the cybernetician Norbert Wiener two years earlier, proposed the idea of automatic translation that would use the (assumed) common underlying logical structure of all languages and would resolve ambiguities in context. His proposal thus went beyond the idea of simple 'translations' based on lexical-substitution dictionaries and rudimentary analysis of accidence that Richard H. (Dick) Richens and Andrew Donald Booth had already begun experimenting with in England (Richens and Booth 1955,[1] Booth and Locke 1955).

The concept was greeted with much enthusiasm, scepticism, and research funding. Many MT research groups formed in the US, UK, USSR, and elsewhere in the 1950s; see Hutchins (1986) for a detailed list and a discussion of their technical work.[2] Given the early state of development of both software and hardware at the time, research on MT systems was inextricably bound up with research on more general problems in computer science and engineering, including the development of larger and faster physical storage media with more efficient data structures and indexes so that large

[1] Although published only in 1955, this paper was written in 1948 (Spärck Jones 2000).
[2] The early history of machine translation will not be recounted here in any detail, as it has been documented extensively elsewhere (Hutchins 1986, 2000a, Zarechnak 1979).

dictionaries could be stored.[3] While the work was truly interdisciplinary, bringing together researchers from fields as disparate as engineering, physics, cybernetics, and linguistics (Hutchins 2000b), much of it was also naïve with regard to the nature of language and translation. Thus in 1955, Booth and Locke could earnestly write, 'It is not possible to define a language in terms of its words alone. Its grammar must also be taken into account.'

Notable exceptions to this naïvety could be found in those groups that worked beyond MT on language processing more generally. The (University of) Cambridge Language Research Unit (CLRU), founded in 1954, was run by Margaret Masterman, a student of Wittgenstein whose broad interests and unorthodox (for the time) approaches led to the development of ideas, such as theories of synonymy and inter-linguas for MT (Richens 1958; see also Spärck Jones 2000), that were years ahead of their time (Wilks 2000, 2003). The CLRU was also home to important early research on information retrieval by Karen Spärck Jones (see §32.3.1.3 below). Similarly, at the RAND Corporation (Santa Monica, Calif.), the MT group led by David G. Hays followed the principle that more linguistic research was necessary before MT could be possible, believing that 'the broader field of computational linguistics deserved general attention' (Hays 1967: 15). Indeed, it was Hays who in 1962 coined the term 'computational linguistics' (Kay 2000).[4] Presaging the approaches of two decades later (§32.3 below), the RAND research had a strong empirical component, which included the creation of syntactically annotated corpora of Russian texts for descriptive analysis and grammar development (Hays 1967).

MT research in the USSR appears to have begun only in 1954, after Aleksej A. Ljapunov, a leading Soviet cybernetician, read about an American project (Kulagina 2000); but by the end of the 1950s, the USSR had more MT researchers than all other countries combined (Harper 1961). What the USSR lacked was sufficient computers, and MT was largely regarded as a 'thought-experiment' (Mel'čuk 2000: 216); systems were tested by having people who did not know the target language perform transla-tions by following flowcharts (Harper 1961). In such a situation, and in contrast to most US MT research, linguistic theory flourished, including the development of the mean-ing–text model of language (Mel'čuk and Žolkovskij 1970).[5]

---

[3] Booth (1955) estimated that a simple translating machine would require 6 physical components, including input and output magnetic tape units and a magnetic or optical drum for its dictionary and grammar, and would cost around $100,000 to build (about 50 times the price of an automobile). The relatively low cost was due to Booth's naïve assumption that a simple special-purpose letter-manipulating 'computer,' rather than a general-purpose central processing unit, would be sufficient.

[4] In 1960, Hays wrote, 'We are fretting under the MT label . . . [and] we petitioned for a change. Our new titles are *linguistic research* and *automatic language-data processing*. These phrases cover MT, but they allow scope for other applications and for basic research. Machine translation is no doubt the easiest form of automatic language-data processing, but it is probably one of the least important. We are taking the first steps toward a revolutionary change in methods of handling every kind of natural-language material' (published in Hays 1961: 24–5).

[5] For details of the theoretical approaches, see Rozencvejg (1974), a collection of English translations of papers on formal and theoretical linguistic aspects of Soviet MT published in the journal Машинный

By the early 1960s, it became clear that current approaches to MT were not successful. Critics included Hays, as noted above, and Yehoshua Bar-Hillel, who had worked in MT since 1951 (in fact as the first full-time researcher in the field: Booth and Locke 1955), but who in 1960 published an acerbic and highly critical survey of the field. Bar-Hillel argued that fully automatic high-quality translation—FAHQT, as he called it—would never be possible because ambiguity resolution often required encyclopedic world knowledge that a computer could never have; it was therefore necessary to accept either low-quality translation or the need for a human post-editor. In any case, he also argued, MT was not cost-effective compared to human translation.

The same conclusion was reached six years later by an interdisciplinary committee established by the US National Academy of Sciences. The Automatic Language Processing Advisory Committee was chaired by John R. Pierce;[6] Hays was one of its members, later claiming to have been a dissenter on the committee (Zarechnak 1979). The committee's report (1966), known generally as the ALPAC report, stated bluntly that 'there is no immediate or predictable prospect of useful machine translation' (p. 32), and that MT was not needed anyway. The report recommended that research funding should instead be directed to computational linguistics, both for its many other potential applications and for consequent better understanding of the nature of language itself.

The report attracted much furious criticism, claiming that it was too narrowly focused, as it concentrated almost solely on US government needs for translation from Russian (Hutchins 1996); that it severely underestimated the usefulness of low-quality translation (Friedrich Krollmann quoted in Josselson 1971[7]); that it contained serious factual errors and based its conclusions on out-of-date information (Titus 1967, Josselson 1971); and even that the committee had a 'hostile and vindictive attitude' and 'concealed' and 'willful[ly] omi[tted]' data and views inconsistent with its conclusions (Zbigniew L. Pankowicz quoted in Josselson 1971).[8] Nonetheless, funding for MT was cut drastically, and many projects were terminated—not just in the US but in Europe and the USSR (Titus 1967, Hutchins 1986, Mel'čuk 2000). In 1968, the young Association for Machine Translation and Computational Linguistics removed the words 'Machine Translation' from its name to avoid the taint (Hutchins 1986). MT research did not begin to revive until the mid-1970s (Hutchins 2000b); but by 1976, a seminar on MT sponsored by the US Foreign Broadcast Information Service could report cautious optimism on the feasibility of MT (Hays and Mathias 1976).

перевод и прикладная лингвистика (Machine Translation and Applied Linguistics) in the period 1957–70. For details of Soviet MT systems of the period, see Hutchins (1986).

   [6] Pierce was also known as a fierce critic of automatic speech recognition in the 1960s; see Church (2012).

   [7] Josselson misspells the name as 'Krollman.'

   [8] Winfred P. Lehmann, who was leader of MT research at the University of Texas, Austin, later wrote, 'I gave a presentation [to the committee] on 18 March 1964. . . . The effort was pointless. It's still difficult to forget the sneer on Pierce's face' (Lehmann 2000: 161).

32.2 SYMBOLIC METHODS, ARTIFICIAL INTELLIGENCE, AND NATURAL LANGUAGE UNDERSTANDING

32.2.1 Automatic Language Understanding as Artificial Intelligence

In 1950, in a seminal paper defending the concept of artificial intelligence (AI), Alan Turing proposed that if a computer had the ability to use language and converse knowledgeably about the world as well as any human, we should regard it as intelligent—a criterion that became known as the Turing test. The development of computational methods of natural language understanding, or NLU, thus became one part of the problem of building intelligent machines.

Nonetheless, little early work in AI addressed NLU. Only two papers in Feigenbaum and Feldman's (1963) representative collection concerned language; both involved largely unprincipled syntactic analysis of highly restricted English, but distinguished themselves from research in machine translation by their goal of complete semantic analysis, albeit within a trivial domain—kinship relations (Lindsay 1963) and questions about baseball statistics (Green et al. 1963). This work set the stage for computational linguistics, as it disentangled itself from machine translation, to be viewed as the facet of the then-glamorous field of AI whose primary goal was human-like language understanding. Given this goal, CL became more open to influence from linguistics and psycholinguistics.

32.2.2 Early End-to-end Systems

Early NLU was advanced by three important developments, all based on linguistic theory and purely symbolic, non-quantitative processing. The first was Procedural Semantics, a method developed by William (Bill) Woods (1968) for deriving an executable database query from a parse tree that represented a natural language query on the database. The second, to produce the necessary parse tree, was the Augmented Transition Network (ATN) parser, also developed by Woods (1970) (see also Woods 2010); ATN parsers had the power of a transformational grammar. The two coupled together could act as a natural language query system for a database, and in 1970, Woods and his colleagues were commissioned by NASA to build a 'natural language understanding system' (Woods 1973: 441) that would answer geologists' questions about samples brought back from the recent lunar missions, such as 'What is the average concentration of aluminum in high alkali rocks?' Although the system that was built (Woods 1973) never actually entered regular use by geologists, it was an influential proof-of-concept for subsequent research.

The third important development was also an end-to-end system billed as natural language understanding. Terry Winograd's 1972 SHRDLU system was based on early Hallidayan systemic grammar[9] and a procedural approach to semantics in which meanings were represented as executable procedures in a deductive problem-solving language named PLANNER. SHRDLU operated in the (simulated) world of a robot arm that could be ordered to manipulate a set of blocks on a table: 'Find a block which is taller than the one you are holding and put it into the box.' Just as Woods's systems could understand only utterances about the contents of their databases, and their replies were data, not sentences, SHRDLU relied on having perfect knowledge of its tiny world, and its responses were actions of the robot arm. Nonetheless, it was regarded as a tour de force, even as an indication that full NLU was close at hand.

32.2.3 The Representation of Knowledge as a Central Issue

The success of these systems focused attention on the need for research in artificial intelligence on computational representations of knowledge of the world—not just for language understanding but more generally for reasoning about and acting in the world. Moreover, a knowledgeable language understanding system would be able to read books and newspapers, and thereby gain more knowledge—learning by reading. It was necessary only to build a system just smart enough to get started.[10] Thus, an implicitly reader-based view of meaning was taken, in which systems would interpret new text in light of their present knowledge (Hirst 2007).

Early research by Marvin Minsky (1975) and by Eugene Charniak (1976, 1978) on the representation of knowledge emphasized recursive template-like slot-and-filler structures called 'frames.' Frames represented stereotypical or commonsense knowledge, could be arranged into default inheritance hierarchies, and could be used to make deductive and inductive inferences to answer questions about information that was not explicit in a text; for example, *Janet needed some money; she got her piggybank and started to shake it. Why did she shake the piggybank?* (Charniak 1973). Frames could be set to be invoked or triggered by certain keywords or concepts, or by the addition of new facts to the system. (In this respect, frames generalized Charniak's earlier (1973) approach in which inferences were made by snippets of knowledge characterized as 'demons' that were triggered by keywords or by prior inferences.) In many ways, frames resembled Fillmore's (1968) case structures in linguistics, although an explication of the relationship between the two came somewhat later (Charniak 1981).

---

[9] See Ch. 21 above.
[10] In fact, the so-called knowledge acquisition bottleneck remains a major problem in AI and CL. Contemporary CL includes the topics of 'knowledge acquisition from text' and 'learning by reading'; see §32.3.2 below.

A competing approach, known as conceptual dependency (CD), was developed by Roger Schank and his colleagues at Stanford University and subsequently at Yale University (Schank 1973, 1975). CD decomposed verbs and represented them as structures built from a small set of semantic primitives; a sentence was then represented as an instantiation of one or more such structures. Larger CD structures, known as scripts, represented stereotypical knowledge about situations and events (Schank and Abelson 1977); they were not dissimilar to frames but put a much greater emphasis on temporal sequence. Schank and his students built systems that could interpret paragraph-length stories, make inferences about the situations they described, and answer questions about them.

Although he had a Ph.D in linguistics, Schank deprecated linguistics and rejected the reality of syntax ('we have never been convinced of the need for grammars at all' (Schank 1975: 12)). The surface-form analysers in the systems that he and his students built created semantic structures directly, with no intervening syntactic representation. They were based wholly on heuristics and procedures invoked in response to the occurrence of particular words. (In this regard, the approach is similar to Charniak's described above, but at the surface level, not just in deeper understanding.)

Many other semantic representations were developed, almost all of which could be considered variations on the basic case-role-like theme of slot-and-filler. They included Yorick Wilks's (1975, 1978) 'preference semantics,' which contained mechanisms for using selectional restrictions to choose word senses and for backing off to non-literal meanings when selectional restrictions could not be satisfied, and John Sowa's (1984) 'conceptual graphs.' Often, the representations were motivated by research in cognitive psychology and were presented as psychological models, as evidenced by the subtitles of Schank and Abelson's (1977) and Sowa's (1984) books: *An Enquiry into Human Knowledge Structure* and *Information Processing in Mind and Machine*; copying how people do it was thought to be a good strategy for artificial intelligence. Indeed, many researchers in AI and CL regarded their work as part of the new discipline of cognitive science.

The systems that were built on all these theories typically had tiny vocabularies and knowledge bases whose domain was a minute sliver of the world. (CD researchers were frequently teased for their focus on the twin domains of interpersonal violence and eating in restaurants.) They were evaluated merely by demonstration on a handful of examples, with the tacit implication that if they could 'handle' a few representative examples, then all they needed in order to become useful was a realistically large knowledge base, which could be developed with some extra time and effort.[11] But almost without exception, these systems were equivalent to first-order predicate or propositional logic, and hence inherently inadequate as representations of the full expressivity of natural language. Concurrent research in formal semantics, such as the work of Richard Montague (1974b) and his successors (see §23.4.2.3 above), did not go unnoticed (e.g., Friedman et al. 1978b, Hobbs and Rosenschein 1977), but the higher-order and intensional logics that they required were computationally infeasible (Friedman et al. 1978a).

[11] See n. 10.

32.2.4 Parsing

By the early 1980s, the failure of syntax-free and syntax-lite approaches had become obvious (e.g. Lytinen 1985; for discussion, see Hirst 1987: 2–3), and those who rejected them in the first place had not been idle. In the 1960s, efficient algorithms for syntactic analysis were a topic of much interest. Much of this work took its cue from research in the analysis of formal languages such as programming languages. The Cocke–Kasami–Younger (or CKY or CYK) algorithm for parsing context-free languages in a time bounded above by the cube of the length of the input string was discovered independently by its three eponyms.[12] Earley's (1970) and Valiant's (1975) algorithms further improved efficiency, and laid the foundation for 'chart parsing,' in which a data structure known as a chart is used to store partially complete analyses of constituents for possible reuse in alternative analyses, greatly speeding up the process.

The belief of the time, following Chomsky (1957a), that context-free grammars were insufficient for natural languages led other researchers to develop more powerful approaches such as the transformation-based ATN parser (§32.2.2 above). Aravind Joshi's tree-adjoining grammars (TAGs), introduced by Joshi et al. (1975) and developed over a number of years by Joshi and his students (Abeillé and Rambow 2000), are mildly context-sensitive, and moreover were shown to be weakly equivalent (generating the same class of string languages) to three other independently developed formalisms of contemporaneous interest (Vijay-Shanker and Weir 1994). TAGs are unusual in that the primitives are not strings but trees, with distinguished root and foot nodes that enable operations of substitution and adjunction. TAGs were pioneers in the *lexicalization* of grammars to facilitate parsing—that is, associating each lexical item with one of a finite set of structures that may be composed by a set of operations (Schabes et al. 1988); lexicalization became particularly important later in the development of probabilistic parsers (§32.3.2 below).

Parsers for a number of other formalisms were also developed in this period, including lexical-functional grammars (Kaplan and Bresnan 1982), head-driven phrase structure grammars (HPSG) (Pollard and Sag 1987, 1994) (see §§8.3.1 and 21.1 above), and combinatory categorial grammars (Pareschi and Steedman 1987, Vijay-Shanker and Weir 1990). Many of these parsers were based on the operation of unification, which combines two partial descriptions of linguistic objects insofar as they are compatible. Unification permits the description of the grammar of a language to be largely declarative rather than process-based. It was developed independently (including the same choice of name) by both Martin Kay (1979) in the context of functional grammars and Alain Colmerauer and colleagues (e.g. Colmerauer 1978) in the context of applying logic and computational theorem-proving to parsing and machine

---

[12] John Cocke developed the algorithm in its earliest form in 1960 (Kay 2000), but did not publish it; it was first reported by Hays (1962). Younger's work appeared in 1967. Kasami's work was first reported in a 1966 technical report (cited by Younger 1967 in a last-minute footnote) and was published as Kasami and Torii (1969).

translation (see also Kay 1992, 2005, Colmerauer and Roussel 1993). Unification and theorem-proving were the basis of the logic-programming language Prolog, in which 'definite clause grammars' for natural languages could conveniently be written, with the programming language itself providing much of the operation of parsing; parsing thus was viewed as deduction (Pereira and Warren 1980, 1983; Pereira and Shieber 1987).

Most parsing algorithms, including those based on unification, are non-deterministic— i.e. the process must sometimes make a guess at what the next step in its analysis is, and, if subsequently stymied because the guess was wrong, must back up, throw away its work, and try a different guess. But in trying a different guess, the algorithm might recreate some of the work it did for the earlier guess, as parts of the analysis will be the same for both; this is a motivation for chart parsing (see above). A contrasting approach to parsing was inspired by research in psycholinguistics; people analyse a sentence even as it is being heard or read, and rarely if ever change their initial analysis. Mitchell (Mitch) Marcus (1980) developed the idea of deterministic parsing, in which syntactic structures, once built, could not be discarded or modified; and when making a structural decision at a point in a sentence, the parser could look only a certain distance further to the right. The definition of distance in structural terms modelled the fact that short so-called garden-path sentences such as *The horse raced past the barn fell* (Bever 1970) can lead people (and Marcus's parser) into unrecoverable errors of analysis, whereas much longer sentences ordinarily present no problems.

A parser by itself cannot decide which of the competing syntactic analyses of a sentence is the one intended in the context of utterance, even if it has an a priori preference for some structures over others. The syntactic disambiguation problem was taken to be one of semantics and, again, knowledge of the world, often interwoven with the problem of disambiguating polysemous and homonymous words (Hirst 1987).

The interest (and publications and sharing of software) of researchers in automatic syntactic analysis fell disproportionately on the largely language-independent process of parsing itself, rather than the development of computational grammars for the particular languages to be analysed. Published grammars were rarely larger than toy examples, and practical, broad-coverage grammars tended to be guarded as proprietary. One exception is the HPSG-based English Resource Grammar (Copestake and Flickinger 2000), which is freely available.

32.2.5 Discourse and Dialogue

Reflecting the assumption from AI that people would converse with intelligent machines in order to instruct them or to seek information or advice from them, determining the intent of a human interlocutor became an important theme in CL in the mid-1970s. Thus, in this work, a speaker-based view of meaning was taken (Hirst 2007); language understanding was construed as recognizing the goals and plans that underlaid a person's utterances to the machine. For example, a person who asks *Is there a coffee shop around here?* probably has the goal of buying coffee; a *yes/no* answer or the directions to a coffee shop known to be closed would not be appropriate responses. This work drew on research in the philosophy of language that viewed utterances as actions in the world (Austin 1962, Searle 1969) (see §26.8–9) and the meaning of an utterance as the speaker's intention in uttering it (Grice 1957). More generally, studies of linguistic pragmatics, including indirect speech acts (Searle 1975) (see §26.9.1), presuppositions (Wilson 1975) (see Chapter 23 and §26.4.2 above), and implicatures and maxims of conversation (Grice 1975) (§26.5), became very influential in computational linguistics.

To recognize an interlocutor's goals and plans from their utterances in order to construct an appropriate response, even though the utterances might be overly terse, or contain misconceptions, or only indirectly indicate what is wanted, requires reasoning about the interlocutor's beliefs, including their beliefs about one's own beliefs. James Allen, Philip Cohen, and Raymond Perrault developed systems that used plan recognition techniques to reason from first principles about the underlying intent of an utterance (Allen and Perrault 1980), and to construct appropriate utterances seeking action from others (Cohen and Perrault 1979), given initial beliefs about the interlocutor's beliefs. These ideas were further developed by Sandra (Sandee) Carberry (1990), who explicated the need for cooperative dialogue systems to construct and maintain, as the conversation progressed, a model of the user—the system's interlocutor—that includes not only inferences about their beliefs and intentions but anything else that might be relevant to the system's understanding and response.

The resolution of anaphora and of definite reference in general was another problem of conversation and discourse (Hirst 1981). Algorithms were developed to determine what elements of a text or conversation were available for reference at any particular point (Hobbs 1978, Sidner 1978). The problem of definite reference to implicitly invoked entities—for example, referring to *the wheels* after mention of *a car*—again pointed to the need for knowledge of the world. Research on coreference resolution converged with that on understanding intentions in discourse in an important paper by Barbara Grosz and Candace (Candy) Sidner (1986) that presented a general computational model of discourse segmentation taking into account both the intentions of the speaker and the focus or attentional state that the speaker of a segment associates with that segment. Within this model, the widely influential Centering Theory (Grosz et al. 1995)[13] developed rules that sought to relate focus of attention to the speaker's choice of referring expression and the consequent degree of coherence of the discourse; under the assumption that the speaker seeks to maximize coherence, these rules constrain the choice of antecedents in anaphor resolution.

Nonetheless, all this research was based on typewritten input from the human. While it was assumed that in due course, people would speak to computers, not type text to them, apart from an early project that brought computational linguists together with researchers working in signal processing and related fields (Woods et al. 1976; Wolf and Woods 1977),

---

[13] Although it was not published until 1995, earlier manuscript versions of this paper had circulated since 1983 and had been widely cited.

speech recognition itself remained a largely separate research field dominated by engineers and uninformed by linguistics and CL (see also §32.3.2 below).

32.2.6 Machine Translation

Despite the ALPAC report (§32.1 above), some work on machine translation did continue, mostly outside the United States. The TAUM-MÉTÉO system for the translation of weather forecasts from English into French (Chandioux and Guéraud 1981) entered daily use at the Canadian Meteorological Centre in 1977, translating millions of words each year (Thouin 1982, Hutchins 1986). In the European Community (as it then was), all twelve member states sponsored EUROTRA, a large and ambitious MT project for all nine EC languages that was firmly based on syntactic and semantic theory (Steiner et al. 1988).

32.3 EMPIRICAL COMPUTATIONAL LINGUISTICS AND NATURAL LANGUAGE PROCESSING

In the early 1990s computational linguistics underwent a revolution, becoming far more quantitative and data-oriented, and separating itself from artificial intelligence. While there are obvious parallels in the rapid development of corpus linguistics in the 1990s (see Chapter 33 below)—both, after all, involve computers and corpora—computational linguistics and corpus linguistics remained largely separate research fields with different motivations and methods of analysis.

32.3.1 The Rise of Empiricism

When it came, the transformation of computational linguistics from a rationalist enterprise inspired by artificial intelligence and armchair linguistics to an empiricist undertaking based on corpora and statistics was extremely rapid. In just a few years, the early 1990s, the character of research papers in the field changed radically: the number of papers on symbolic topics such as semantics and plan-based dialogue declined greatly, while those on empirical topics such as text classification and statistically based parsing (§32.3.2 below) showed a corresponding increase. This is depicted in Fig. 32.1, reproduced from the work of Hall et al. (2008), who documented these changes.[14] Of course, symbolic and deep formal approaches did not disappear

[14] Interestingly, Hall et al. used the methods of empirical computational linguistics to study the history of empirical computational linguistics. Because of a commitment to open-access publishing by the Association for Computational Linguistics, a corpus of all its conference and journal publications

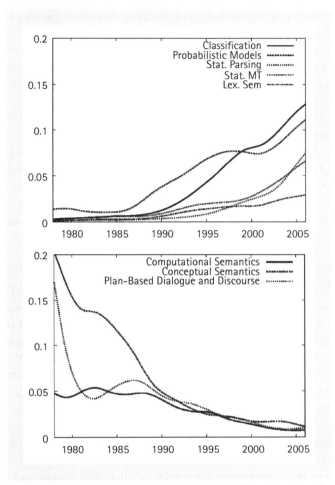

FIG. 32.1 Topics that became more prevalent (top panel) and less prevalent (bottom panel) in research papers in computational linguistics with the rise of empiricism. The y-axis is the probability that any given paper in a particular year included a particular topic. (From Hall et al. 2008)

overnight. Many researchers remained sceptical of empirical methods, and even those who saw their value did not immediately abandon their existing research. Nonetheless, as Fig. 32.1 shows, the displacement of the older approaches was quite rapid.

This new view of computational linguistics took language as a stochastic or probabilistic system. In this view, language understanding and its component tasks should not be viewed as processes deemed to have succeeded if they have returned the official

from 1965 onwards, 14,000 papers in total, was freely available for analysis. Treating the papers as bags of words, Hall et al. used topic models and latent Dirichlet allocation (Blei et al. 2003) (see §32.3.2) to cluster and classify them.

correct answer and to have failed if they have done otherwise; nor is a system that fails on some particular input refuted as if it were a mathematical theorem refuted by a counterexample. Rather, a system should use probabilistic methods to return what it believes to be the most likely answer; the more often a system is correct, the better it is, but perfection should not be expected and an imperfect system may still be very useful in practice (§32.3.2 below). Thus, the view is essentially Firthian (see this volume §§20.3.2, and 33.8) and explicitly anti-Chomskyan, repudiating Chomsky's famous (1957a) arguments against statistical models of language (see §33.3).[15] It has its roots in information-theoretic views of language and noisy-channel models of communication that had influenced Weaver (§32.1 above) but had themselves fallen out of favor for many years as a result of Chomsky's anti-statistical arguments (Liberman 2010). Its rise was the result of influential research within CL, advances in related areas of research and in computing, the increasing availability of online text, and other factors to be discussed below.

32.3.1.1 *Influential Research Within CL*

Perhaps the single most influential early piece of research in empirical CL was the IBM statistical model of machine translation. Frederick Jelinek and his research group at IBM Thomas J. Watson Research Center had used an information-theoretic noisy-channel model in the 1970s–80s to develop systems for speech recognition that were very successful for their day, and in 1987 began to apply the same methods to machine translation (Jelinek 2009). The result was a model of statistical machine translation based on correspondences derived from a parallel 'bitext'—a corpus that contains both a text and its translation into another language (Brown et al. 1990). The demonstration system was trained on 40,000 sentence pairs of English and the corresponding French (800,000 words of each language) from the bilingual proceedings of the Canadian Parliament (Hansard). The translations resulting from this method were at least as good as those of the contemporaneous systems that used syntax and semantics, and this was unsettling to many researchers who had worked long and hard on those systems. It seemed both impossible and unfair that translation could be accomplished by a system that had no knowledge of language[16] and had been constructed by researchers with no knowledge of linguistics.[17] The relative merits of rationalist and

---

[15] Nonetheless, Penn (2012) argues that Chomsky's views on syntax and language played a very significant role in laying the philosophical foundations of statistical parsing (see §32.3.2), which 'has obediently received a view of grammar that has been very carefully circumscribed to exclude any built-in symbolic apparatus for disambiguation, as well as most of the world knowledge or reasoning that might be useful for doing so.'

[16] In fact, the system had plenty of knowledge of language: it knew about correspondences between French and English and their probabilities, and latent within that was some knowledge of syntax and semantics. But its critics construed the absence of overt syntactic and semantic knowledge as no knowledge of language at all.

[17] The members of the IBM research team flaunted their ignorance of linguistics as if to taunt other researchers. Fred Jelinek is famously quoted as saying: 'Every time I fire a linguist from our project, the performance of our system gets better' (or words to that effect; Jurafsky and Martin 2009: 83). At the 1992

empiricist approaches were furiously debated at the 1992 TMI machine translation conference in Montreal.[18]

Kenneth Church and his colleagues at Bell Laboratories (later AT&T Research), especially William (Bill) Gale, were also early advocates for empirical CL. In particular, their papers on statistical analysis of lexical collocations (Church and Hanks 1990, Church et al. 1991) demonstrated the large amount of usable knowledge that can be derived from the word n-grams of a sufficiently large corpus. Church and colleagues also published influential work on part-of-speech tagging and on matching up ('alignment') of words and sentences in bitexts for training statistical machine translation systems (Church 1988, Gale and Church 1993).

A third influential researcher was Eugene Charniak, who had been one of the pioneers of knowledge-based approaches to NLU in the early 1970s (§32.2.3 above) and who was a co-author of two well-known textbooks on artificial intelligence. In 1993 Charniak published the first textbook on statistical methods for natural language processing, noting in the preface that it represented his own personal conversion from an artificial intelligence-based approach that 'is not going anywhere fast' (p. xvii–xviii).[19] The availability of this concise and easy introduction to help researchers master the new methods was certainly a factor in their rapid acceptance. By 1999, Charniak's small book had been superseded by Manning and Schütze's large introductory textbook, which could be used as the basis for a complete university course, and whose very existence indicated that statistical methods were now mainstream.[20]

32.3.1.2 *Advances in Computing*

Three advances in computing were instrumental in the rise of empiricism. The first, almost trivially, was the continuing exponential growth in the power of computers themselves; large corpora could be processed in a reasonable amount of time. The second was the parallel development of ever cheaper, ever denser storage media for files, which made the online storage of large corpora feasible. Moreover, the advent of the CD-ROM in the late 1980s brought a qualitative change, making the distribution of large corpora cheap and easy; suddenly, 650 Mb of data could be easily duplicated,

TMI conference (see n. 18), members of the research team presented a paper (Brown et al. 1992) showing that the results of the statistical model could be greatly improved by adding simple linguistic knowledge (such as basic morphological analysis), which they had gone to the library to read about in a book; they characterized this as a great advance, much to the frustration of other researchers present whose systems already included such elements and who regarded them as obvious.

[18] Formally, the Fourth International Conference on Theoretical and Methodological Issues in Machine Translation of Natural Languages, Montreal, 25–7 June 1992.

[19] In his speech accepting a Lifetime Achievement Award from the Association for Computational Linguistics in June 2011, Charniak said that he now regarded the research of the first half of his career, up to 1992, as not worth looking at.

[20] Nonetheless, the almost simultaneous appearance of another popular textbook, Jurafsky and Martin (2000), which put greater emphasis on symbolic approaches, served to retain these methods in university courses. Some instructors used both books, or divided their offerings into a 'Manning and Schütze course' and a 'Jurafsky and Martin course.'

stored on an extremely cheap medium, and mailed as an ordinary first-class letter, obviating the need for duplicating and shipping heavy reels or cartridges of magnetic tape. The third advance was the increasingly broad availability of the Internet,[21] as it was by then becoming known, permitting files of data of a reasonable size to be transferred directly over the network from machine to machine with the File Transfer Protocol (FTP).

32.3.1.3 *Advances in Related Fields*

Advances in the neighbouring research fields of information retrieval and machine learning were important factors in the development of empirical CL.

Early research in document and information retrieval had little to do with the contemporaneous research in computational linguistics (although a few key researchers, most notably Karen Spärck Jones, were involved in both areas). Rather, early systems for information retrieval were based on Boolean queries against bibliographic fields and keywords that were assigned to documents by human indexers (Liddy 2003). As it became feasible to store complete documents, and hence search the complete text, document representations were developed that sought to eliminate the need for a human indexer and a controlled indexing vocabulary. By far the most influential representation was Gerard Salton's vector-space model (Salton et al. 1975, Dubin 2004), in which a document is represented as a vector in a n-dimensional vector space, where n is the number of words in the vocabulary and the ith component of the vector is a weighted count of the number of times the ith word of the vocabulary appears in the document; the similarity between two documents, or between a document and a retrieval request similarly represented, is then measured as the cosine of the angle between the vectors. The vector-space model of text became the basis for much research in CL in which a text is treated as a bag of words or other features without order or structure and can thus be represented as a vector. Moreover, because many problems in empirical CL can be construed as retrieval problems (some linguistic objects are selected from a larger set and possibly are rank-ordered), two metrics used for evaluation in information retrieval, precision and recall, became commonly used for quantitative evaluation in empirical CL.

Empirical CL drew heavily on methods of machine learning, and became a consumer of research in that field in much the same way that symbolic CL was a consumer of research in knowledge representation (§32.2.3 above). The 1960s–80s had been a fertile period in machine learning, producing a number of methods and algorithms that subsequently became mainstays of CL, such as hidden Markov models, the Viterbi algorithm (Viterbi 1967, Forney 1973; see also Viterbi 2006), the EM (expectation-maximization) algorithm, and Bayesian networks (Mitchell 1997). Nonetheless, CL remained cool towards machine learning methods that were based on neural networks

---

[21] By 'Internet' here, I mean the Internet itself as a physical network, and not the World Wide Web, implemented by the Hypertext Transfer Protocol (HTTP) on this network, which arose a few years later (see §32.3.1.4) and which is often referred to metonymously as 'the Internet' by lay persons.

and spreading activation, which had some limited uptake in CL in the 1980s but which did not prosper, perhaps because Minsky and Papert's 1969 critique of the related notion of perceptrons (Rosenblatt 1958) led to general scepticism (Olazaran 1996), and perhaps because it was never clear how they could be used for complex linguistic tasks.

32.3.1.4 *Availability of Online Text*

By definition, empirical CL requires data—corpora of text in a machine-readable form. Previously, the largest online corpus was the laboriously built Brown Corpus of Present-Day Edited American English (Francis and Kučera 1964) (see §33.4 below), which at only one million words across many genres, though it had seemed large in 1964, was far too small for most work in empirical CL. However, the development of computerized typography and word processing in the 1980s allowed the relatively easy construction of large online corpora as a side effect; any text typeset this way would persist in a machine-readable form and could be compiled into a corpus, although much work might be needed to regularize the format of the data. (It was from such a source that Jelinek and colleagues obtained the data for their Canadian Hansard corpus.) Optical character recognition was also used for digitizing printed material.

However, it remained difficult in practice for researchers to get their hands on sufficient data; copyright in the text itself and proprietary rights in the compilation were among the barriers. In 1989, the Association for Computational Linguistics began its Data Collection Initiative (ACL/DCI) with the goal of at-cost distribution of corpora for non-profit scientific research, using appropriate licensing agreements to reassure rights holders (Liberman 1989). This in turn led to the establishment in 1992 of the Linguistic Data Consortium (LDC), housed at the University of Pennsylvania and led by Mark Liberman, for the collection and distribution of text and speech corpora, lexicons, and other linguistic resources in many languages.

A particularly influential early corpus obtained by the ACL/DCI was the *Wall Street Journal* corpus donated by Dow Jones Inc., 30 million words published in that newspaper in the years 1987–9, which became part of the LDC's first distribution in 1993. The corpus grew as later years of the newspaper were added. It was (and still is) used extensively in CL research. Parts of the *WSJ* corpus, along with the Brown Corpus, were selected as the textual basis of the Penn Treebank (Marcus et al. 1993) to be semi-automatically annotated with parts of speech and so-called 'skeletal' parse trees; subsequently 50,000 *WSJ* sentences (one million words) received more-detailed hand parsing for the Penn Treebank (Marcus et al. 1994), and this became the primary data for research in statistical parsing. The dominance of the *WSJ* corpus was such that CL was sometimes accused of studying not English but the language of English news reporting and of the *Wall Street Journal* in particular; it was not unusual for a system, especially a parser, that was trained on this corpus to perform well on new text from the *Wall Street Journal* but markedly less well on any other genre of English or even on the *New York Times*. The larger and more balanced (but rather more expensive) British National Corpus (Leech 1993, Burnard 1995, Aston and Burnard 1998; see also §33.5 below) was often used as an alternative.

The development of the World Wide Web from about 1995 onwards was another major boost, as it was quickly realized that the Web was itself a corpus and that corpora of many different genres, from literature to reviews of consumer products, could be easily created from its contents (Kilgarriff and Grefenstette 2003). Moreover, network bandwidth and the size of data storage media increased rapidly, enabling ever larger corpora. By 2005, multi-billion-word corpora were not unusual, and were motivated by the results of Banko and Brill (2001), who showed that, at least in some situations, the choice of algorithm for a system is a less important factor in the quality of its performance than the sheer volume of data on which it is trained.

32.3.1.5 *Quantitative Evaluation and Competitive Shared Tasks*

A backlash against the hand-waving proof-by-demo system evaluations that were common in symbolic CL research (§32.2.3 above) began in the later 1980s with a move towards more rigorous and quantitative evaluations. This was facilitated by the development of shared tasks and competitive evaluations, usually in conjunction with a workshop or conference. In a shared task competition, research groups are given a very specific problem, along with sample data and possibly some other relevant resources. The tasks are typically well-defined instantiations of unsolved problems—for example, finding antecedents of certain kinds of anaphors in certain kinds of texts—that are central to larger problems, so that breakthroughs or major improvements would have a large effect. Each group develops its own methods and software for the task, which is then run on data previously unseen by the competitors; at the subsequent event, quantitative results are released and each competitor discusses their system and its methods. Even after the competition, the datasets involved may continue to be used by researchers as training data and as test data to compare new systems with those of the original competition.

The first shared tasks in CL were associated with the Message Understanding Conference (MUC) series, beginning in 1989;[22] competing teams had to fill pre-defined templates with information extracted from military messages or, later, short news items (Grishman and Sundheim 1996). The Text Retrieval Conference (TREC), focusing on tasks related to document and information retrieval, followed in 1992 (Voorhees and Harman 2005). Participation in the shared tasks of these conferences was a requirement of some US government research-funding programmes (Crystal 1993), and poor performers could have their funding discontinued. However, many subsequent shared tasks and research challenges were not associated with funding but were voluntary and open to any interested researcher. Well-chosen shared tasks have spurred innovation in CL, and their necessary emphasis on quantitative evaluation and comparability of different systems and methods was another factor in the rise of empirical CL.

---

[22] The Message Understanding Conferences began in 1987, but it was only for the second MUC in 1989 that the essential characteristics of the shared task were developed (Grishman and Sundheim 1996). MUC ran until 1998.

32.3.2 The Development of Empiricism and Cross-disciplinary Influences

While some early empirical research in CL, as noted above, made a virtue of the complete absence of linguistic theory, this was not true in general. Rather, what was rejected was the idea that deep analysis, especially formal semantics, and complex representations of knowledge of the world are a necessary or desirable part of the solution of any practical problem in language processing. The new view was that many useful things can be done with surface form plus some linguistic analysis that could be shallow or deeper, depending on the problem. The syntactic analysis of a sentence that might be necessary could range from none at all, to part-of-speech tagging (e.g. Brill 1995, Ratnaparkhi 1996), to chunking into phrases ('partial parsing') (Abney 1991), to a complete parse tree. And the analysis itself could be carried out by a data-driven statistical process; great advances were made in the 1990s on probabilistic part-of-speech tagging and on parsing with probabilistic grammars derived from treebanks (§32.3.1.4 above)—in particular, lexicalized probabilistic grammars that thereby encode lexically conditioned structural preferences (Collins 1997, 2003). Interest in parsing with dependency grammars also increased markedly as a result of the development of a constraint-based approach to the problem (Maruyama 1990) and probabilistic parsing models (Eisner 1996) for these grammars (Kudo and Matsumoto 2000, Kübler et al. 2009). The data-driven constituent-based parsers of English by Charniak (2000) and Collins (1997, 2003) and the data-driven dependency-based MaltParser by Nivre et al. (2007), made available free to other researchers, were widely used.

Nor did interest in semantics and world-knowledge disappear. Rather, the new focus was on lexical semantics and the knowledge implicit in word meaning and word distribution. A particularly important development was the creation of WordNet (Fellbaum 1998) by George Miller and his colleagues at Princeton University. WordNet is a database of words and the lexical relations between them that gives primacy to word sense rather than word form; different senses of a word form are listed separately, and each separate sense of the form is grouped together in a so-called synset with synonymous senses of other word forms. Because synsets are connected by relations such as hyponymy, meronymy, and antonymy, WordNet encodes some taxonomic knowledge of the world. WordNets have now been developed or are under development for more than 50 languages.[23]

At the semantic levels above the lexical, considerable attention was given to the development of methods for semantic role labelling, i.e. determining the relationships asserted between the entities mentioned in a sentence by determining their thematic or case roles (Palmer et al. 2010). Learning by reading was revived as a topic of minor interest (Hovy 2006, Forbus et al. 2007), but it was also recognized that even if full text understanding could not be achieved, much knowledge could be systematically gleaned from texts for

---

[23] The Global Wordnet Association tabulates wordnets that comply with the standard design; see www.globalwordnet.org.

inclusion in knowledge-based resources and for use in tasks such as question answering. For example, from the text fragment *dachshunds and other small dogs* it can be learned that a dachshund is a small dog (Hearst 1998); from *bringing back her washed clothes* it can be learned that clothes may be washed (Schubert and Tong 2003).

Advances in machine learning continued to influence CL. In particular, support-vector machines[24] (SVMs), introduced by Cortes and Vapnik (1995), were rapidly adopted as a preferred method for classifying texts or other linguistic objects (Joachims 2002). Many applications of NLP can usefully be viewed as problems of text classification. For example, news articles gathered from a variety of sources may be grouped by each distinct topic or event; consumers' online reviews of a book or film may be classified as favourable or unfavourable, a task known as sentiment analysis (Pang and Lee 2008). Similarly, word sense disambiguation may be viewed as the classification of each occurrence of a word according to its set of possible senses. Two complementary developments in machine learning developed the idea of finding in a document the topics that are 'latent' in its words. Latent semantic analysis (Deerwester et al. 1990, Manning et al. 2008) reduces the number of dimensions in the vector-space representation of a set of documents, thereby implicitly bringing together documents on related topics, even if they happen to use different (synonymous or closely related) words for some concepts, while separating those on different topics that happen to use the same (homonymous) words. This idea was developed further in topic models and latent Dirichlet allocation (Blei et al. 2003, Blei 2012), in which a text is modelled as a Dirichlet distribution over a choice of topics and a topic is modelled as a distribution over a choice of words.

Despite its influences from research in information retrieval and in speech recognition, computational linguistics remained largely distinct from these other fields. Some US funding agencies recognized the overlap of interests and the potential for greater synthesis and practical applications in a convergence of the fields, and strongly pushed for this from their grantees in the three fields, holding workshops, first in 1993–4 and then again in 2001, to bring the fields together under the name Human Language Technologies (HLT). From 2003, this name was adopted as a subtitle for the North American conferences of the Association for Computational Linguistics, but the move had only limited success; while a greater number of researchers now do work that overlaps more than one of the fields, they still remain largely distinct research communities.

32.3.3 Applied Natural Language Processing

As computational linguistics further developed its empirical orientation, it became more concerned with practical and commercial applications of natural language

---

[24] Support-vector machines are not physical hardware but machines in the abstract sense. They are a class of algorithms for classifying points in a multidimensional vector space—e.g. documents represented by counts of words or other features—into two or more categories by deriving from training data the hyperplane that separates the classes with the least amount of error.

processing, and for good reason—component methods and resources had become mature and robust enough that useful applications were now in view, including many based on text classification, such as sentiment analysis (§32.3.2 above). In addition, funding agencies, especially in the US, emphasized the development of methods for finding, synthesizing, and succinctly presenting information from large document collections, including the World Wide Web itself. This included question-answering (see §32.4 below)—finding the right few words among billions, or summarizing the text of one or many documents (Maybury 2004).

The flagship application, however, remained automatic language translation. Machine translation systems had by this time been available for a number of years, often styled as assistants to professional translators rather than as end-user products. But in 1997 they became broadly available to the public over the Web when SYSTRAN's translator became the basis of AltaVista's Babel Fish service (Yang and Lange 1998), and they are now routinely sold as end-user software. SYSTRAN's system has evolved from being based purely on linguistic rules and dictionaries (Yang and Lange 1998) to a hybrid system incorporating statistical methods (Dugast et al. 2008). In 2006–7, Google began offering a competing service, Google Translate, based on purely statistical methods (Halevy et al. 2009, Koehn 2010).[25] Although the quality of their translations was often poor, these systems have improved demonstrably over time, and their extensive use vindicates the opinions of the critics of ALPAC who asserted that a low-quality translation may nonetheless have high utility.

32.4 COMPUTATIONAL LINGUISTICS TODAY

Kenneth Church (2004, 2012) has suggested that research in CL oscillates in twenty-year cycles between rationalism and empiricism: empiricist in the 1950s–60s, rationalist in the 1970s–80s, and empiricist again in the 1990s–2000s. This suggests that the field is due for a revival of rationalism in the 2010s as the limitations of present empirical methods are felt.[26] Certainly, a frequent criticism of the field in the last decade is that there is a lack of innovation—that too many papers merely report minor incremental work based on the innovations of the 1990s, following a sterile paradigm of annotate–learn–evaluate, and that the last decade of progress has been due to larger corpora and

---

[25] In an echo of Frederick Jelinek's comment about the deleterious effect of linguists on machine translation (see n. 17), Peter Norvig, Google's director of research, claimed in 2007 that Google's experiments had found that their translation system performed less well when explicit syntactic knowledge was incorporated. Nonetheless, subsequent research at Google (e.g. Xu et al. 2009, DeNero and Uszkoreit 2011) has investigated the use of syntactic components, which may themselves be derived from bitexts, within statistical MT.

[26] Church (2004) hypothesizes that the 20-year components of the cycle are due to students rebelling against their teachers. Church urges that students be taught not only current methods in CL but those of the previous cycle so that when they rebel, they do not simply repeat the mistakes of their teachers' teachers.

more powerful computers more than to any new conceptual breakthroughs. CL is also criticized for having abandoned its connections to theoretical linguistics and psychology (Reiter 2007, Spärck Jones 2007, Wintner 2009, Krahmer 2010), and for focusing too much on NLP and its applications rather than advancing the development of computational models of language and human language processing.

But an indication of the achievements of CL and NLP came in February 2011 when the Watson question-answering system, developed by a team at the IBM T. J. Watson Research Center, competed against two human champions on the American television game show *Jeopardy!*[27] and won (Kroeker 2011). Watson was based on IBM's DeepQA architecture for question-answering, which combines many different algorithms for analysing questions, finding possible answers in its knowledge sources, and selecting and computing its degree of confidence in a final answer (Ferrucci et al. 2010). When playing *Jeopardy!*, Watson was not connected to the Internet and relied solely on a large set of pre-analysed reference sources, such as encyclopedias, newswire articles, and additional material that it had earlier extracted from the Web (Ferrucci et al. 2010, Kroeker 2011).

The technologies developed for question-answering systems such as DeepQA have clear commercial applications in many professional and social domains for the kind of information needs which cannot be satisfied just by keyword searches that return lists of whole documents or passages of text through which the user then has to sift. A fortiori, Hirst (2008) has suggested that a likely direction for these applications will be a confluence of several streams of research in NLP and information retrieval to build systems that will construct a complete answer to a user's question by selecting and summarizing relevant information from many sources, and that, moreover, do so by 'considering each document or passage from the point of view of the user's question (and anything else known about the user)' (p. 7); that is, they act as an agent for the user, in effect taking a reader-based view of the meaning of the text. Some other applications, conversely, will take a writer-based or intention-based view of the text; this will include not just sentiment analysis (§32.3.2 above) but intelligence-gathering, in the broadest sense—systems that aim to determine the opinions, beliefs, and plans of the writer. Machine translation, by definition, attempts to preserve a writer's intent across languages, and as new research on statistical methods in MT supplements them with a semantic sensibility, it too may take on a more explicitly writer-based view of text and meaning (Hirst 2008).[28]

---

[27] In *Jeopardy!*, contestants are given an answer and its context, and must supply a corresponding question. For example, given the answer *Washington* and the context *Leaders of history*, a correct response could be *Who was the first American president?*, whereas in the context *National capitals*, a correct response could be *What is the capital of the United States?* The problems are generally more challenging, both in language and in the knowledge they require, than this example suggests; many involve wordplay (e.g. requiring a response that rhymes), and many implicitly require the solution of two separate problems (such as *The most northerly country with which the US does not have diplomatic relations*) (Ferrucci et al. 2010).

[28] For comments on, suggestions for, and discussion of this chapter, I am grateful to Ken Church, Joakim Nivre, Gerald Penn, and Nadia Talent. This work was supported financially by the Natural Sciences and Engineering Research Council of Canada.

CHAPTER 33

....

THE HISTORY OF CORPUS LINGUISTICS

....

TONY McENERY AND ANDREW HARDIE

33.1 INTRODUCTION

....

THIS chapter surveys the history of corpus linguistics. We will begin by surveying the very earliest work (before approximately 1955) that foreshadows features of modern corpus linguistics (§33.2), before discussing the motivation for and effects of the Chomskyan rejection of the corpus as a means of studying language (§33.3). We will then review the emergence of English Corpus Linguistics in the 1960s and 1970s, beginning at a number of key research centres (§33.4); it was within the community of corpus linguists studying the English language that the most basic techniques and principles of the contemporary field first emerged. The general position that we take in this chapter is that corpus linguistics—the study of language via computer-assisted analysis of very large bodies of naturally occurring text—is quite distinct from many other fields or subdisciplines of linguistics. Unlike such fields as phonology, the study of social variation in language, or the critical analysis of discourse, corpus linguistics is not directly *about* the study of any particular aspect of language. Rather, its focus is on a set of procedures, or methods, for studying language. Corpus linguistics is, then, a methodology that can be applied to some or many different fields of study within linguistics. One primary focus of English Corpus Linguistics in particular was enabling improved descriptions of English grammar, as we will outline in §33.5; we will also survey briefly a range of advances in corpus construction and annotation that were undertaken initially in support of this enterprise (§33.6). However, one critical aspect of the development of corpus linguistics has been the adoption of corpora and corpus-based methods as part of the 'toolkit' of other subdisciplines of linguistics. In §33.7 we will exemplify this by looking at the utilization of corpus methods within functionalist theoretical linguistics. By facilitating the exploration of linguistic theory in novel ways, corpus-based methods have proved their value to linguists of all stripes.

However, it bears noting that this methodologically oriented view of corpus linguistics is not the only approach; an alternative view of the field, developed by the neo-Firthian school of linguists under the leadership of John Sinclair, conceptualizes corpus linguistics not as a methodology, but as having a theoretical status in its own right—linking the findings of corpus analysis to an understanding of language in which words, their meanings in discourse context, and their collocation patterns are central. We will survey the work of this contrasting tradition in §33.8.

33.2 EARLY PRECURSORS

Corpus linguistics *per se*, considered as a method or as a subdiscipline of linguistics, is largely a phenomenon of the late 1950s onwards. This is in part because of its near-absolute dependence on computerized text—computer technology had to develop to the point where it could manage and manipulate large amounts of machine-readable text before anything like modern corpus linguistics could possibly emerge. That said, however, corpus linguistics did not appear *ex nihilo* in the late 1950s and 1960s; as with any other intellectual movement, precursors can be identified whose work in retrospect appears to have been building towards corpus linguistics in its modern form. In particular, approaches to language analysis based on natural usage data long predate modern corpus linguistics; wherever such approaches made use of especially large datasets, or focused on issues of quantitative analysis, we can see hints of what we might consider to be corpus linguistics *in utero*.

Much of this early research made use of one of the most basic of corpus analysis techniques, the frequency list—although compiling frequency lists from hundreds of thousands or millions of words of text was a much more challenging proposition before the advent of the computer. For example, Käding (1897) investigated letter-sequence frequencies in a corpus of 11 million words of German. A more common focus was the frequencies of words in lists used in foreign language teaching (see e.g. Thorndike 1921, Palmer 1933, Fries and Traver 1940, Bongers 1947, West 1953). But corpus data was put to other uses as well, for instance in Fries' (1952) corpus-based descriptive grammar of English, or in Eaton's (1940) study of the frequency of word meanings. Alongside this embryonic corpus-based work, some areas of investigation—such as field linguistics (e.g. Boas 1940) or the study of language acquisition (e.g. Stern 1924)—were based almost entirely on the analysis of collections of observed language data, an approach extremely similar in principle to that underlying corpus linguistics, though the datasets in question were mostly small by the standards of modern electronic corpora and were all manually analysed.

Analysis based on large text corpora moved onto computers almost as soon as computers existed—indeed, the first move was not to electronic computers but to the precursor technology of the punched-card machine. In 1951 Roberto Busa, working on a corpus of the poetry of Thomas Aquinas, used this technology to produce the earliest machine-generated concordances (Winter 1999). From Busa's pioneering work stems much of the field of humanities computing, or, as it is usually known today, *digital humanities*. Slightly later, equally groundbreaking research by Alphonse Juilland established some of the other major principles of work with corpora of electronic text, such as the importance of carefully balanced corpus sampling, or the importance of considering statistics of dispersion[1] alongside raw frequencies (see Juilland and Chang-Rodriguez 1964). The impact of Busa and Juilland's work on linguistics was, however, limited. At the same time as Juilland's pioneering work was taking place, linguistics as a field was retreating from corpus data, for reasons we will discuss in the next section. The main groups of linguists who did *not* participate in this retreat were working at UK universities on the English language; but neither Busa nor Juilland worked with English.

33.3 THE CHOMSKYAN REJECTION OF CORPUS DATA

The renowned American syntactician Noam Chomsky is a peculiarly central figure in the history of corpus linguistics—peculiar because his main contribution to the method was to vigorously oppose it. But the impact of Chomsky's opposition was so great that it is now impossible to develop a case in favour of corpus linguistics that does not address, implicitly or explicitly, the criticisms that Chomsky raised. It is worthwhile exploring the intellectual basis of Chomsky's dismissal of the corpus-based analysis of language. It is above all rooted in his attempted reorientation of the focus of linguistics, i.e. the explicandum of language science, away from language performance and towards language competence. Of course, the competence–performance distinction long predates Chomsky; de Saussure's *langue/parole* distinction is essentially equivalent. Chomsky's contribution was to argue that competence rather than performance—or in his later terminology, I(nternal)-language rather than E(xternal)-language—is the central phenomenon that a theory of language should explain. In the mind of a given individual speaker is an abstract knowledge of their language which does not correspond to any particular finite collection of observed utterances; it is this knowledge, for instance, which allows a speaker to know intuitively what is and is not a grammatical sentence in their language, completely independently of whether or not they have ever before heard the particular sentence they are judging. The native speaker's intuitive ability to generate an infinite number of valid sentence structures is what Chomsky believed linguists should be trying to account for. Chomsky did not merely relegate the

---

[1] Measures of dispersion move beyond simply noting the frequency of a word, to give some measure of how evenly spread, or dispersed, a word is in a given corpus. This allows us to distinguish readily e.g. between words which are used frequently and those which are used infrequently but which, when mentioned, are likely to be repeated reasonably often within a short space of text.

study of performance to a secondary priority, however. Rather, he actively argued that performance data can tell us little or nothing about competence, precisely because the number of possible sentences in a language is infinite, and any collection of performance data can represent no more than a finite (and skewed) subset of the language. Moreover, he considered naturally occurring language data to be of 'degenerate quality' (Chomsky 1965: 8), riddled with performance errors and ungrammatical forms that do not adequately reflect the competence of the speakers that produced them. Chomsky's opposition to observed language evidence has remained consistent in his thinking over the years as other aspects of his theories have evolved. For instance, when interviewed by Andor (2004: 97) he had this to say:

> Corpus linguistics doesn't mean anything. It's like saying suppose a physicist decides, suppose physics and chemistry decide that instead of relying on experiments, what they're going to do is take videotapes of things happening in the world and they'll collect huge videotapes of everything that's happening and from that maybe they'll come up with some generalizations or insights. Well, you know, sciences don't do this. But maybe they're wrong. Maybe the sciences should just collect lots and lots of data and try to develop the results from them. Well if someone wants to try that, fine. They're not going to get much support in the chemistry or physics or biology department. But if they feel like trying it, well, it's a free country, try that. We'll judge it by the results that come out.

For Chomsky, the linguist's equivalent to the chemist or physicist's carefully constructed laboratory experiments is the use of introspection. That is, explanations of the workings of the language system are arrived at via a native speaker linguist reflecting on their own knowledge of language and giving grammaticality judgements on artificially concocted sentences. This is very much a *rationalist* approach to language, as opposed to the *empiricist* views that typically underlie the use of corpora.

Chomsky's arguments contain many valid insights. For example, it is undoubtedly true that no corpus can completely represent a language; Chomsky's observation that the set of possible sentences is infinite is very valuable. The effect of these arguments was a shift within linguistics away from empirical usage data as found in corpora, and towards rationalism and reliance on intuition and introspection as primary data. This shift was not complete and definitive, of course. Fields such as phonetics, child language acquisition research, the study of language variation, and other forms of sociolinguistics all continued to rely on observed, natural data to a large extent. Likewise, the trend away from empirical data was not as pronounced in the east European tradition. A broadly empirical approach to linguistics survived in the former eastern bloc, especially in the so-called mathematical linguistics approach to language (see Papp 1966 for an overview).[2]

---

[2] Considering that the work in the Soviet Union in particular was a deliberate and conscious effort to provide linguistics in the USSR with an expressly scientific basis, in opposition to Marr's (1926) Marxist-Leninist approach to the subject, the overtly scientific and mathematical approach to linguistics in this historical context is understandable. And given that the anti-Marrist approach to linguistics was

But despite these exceptions, arguably the shift towards rationalism that did take place was ultimately greater than justified by Chomsky's arguments. For instance, a meaningful corpus analysis does not require that the corpus contain the entirety of the language being investigated, as Chomsky's objection implies. It merely requires the corpus to contain a representative sample of the language. Moreover, Chomsky's appeals to the natural sciences are founded on an inadequate acquaintance with how those sciences work. There exist entire fields in science which do indeed function by collecting and analysing massive bodies of observational data—for instance astronomy and geology. Perhaps because of these limitations to Chomskyan anti-corpus arguments, the pendulum eventually swung back towards empiricism—which ultimately meant a major expansion of corpus linguistics. Throughout the period when introspection was the dominant method of mainstream linguistic theory, small groups of researchers persisted in exploring the computer-based analysis of large text corpora—in many cases using these corpora as sources of frequency data, frequency being largely inaccessible to introspection. Later on, in the 1980s and 1990s, the use of corpus data in linguistics was substantially rehabilitated, to the degree that in the twenty-first century, using corpus data is no longer viewed as unorthodox and inadmissible. For an increasing number of linguists, corpus data play a central role in their research. This is precisely because they have done what Chomsky suggested—they have not judged corpus linguistics on the basis of an abstract philosophical argument, but rather have relied on the results the corpus has produced. Corpora have been shown to be highly useful in a range of areas of linguistics, providing insights in areas as diverse as contrastive linguistics (Johansson 2007), discourse analysis (Aijmer and Stenström 2004, Baker 2006), language learning (Chuang and Nesi 2006, Aijmer 2009), semantics (Ensslin and Johnson 2006), sociolinguistics (Gabrielatos et al. 2010), and theoretical linguistics (Wong 2006, Xiao and McEnery 2004b). As a source of data for language description they have been of significant help to lexicographers (Hanks 2009) and grammarians (Biber et al. 1999). It is now, in fact, difficult to find an area of linguistics where a corpus approach has *not* been taken.

Most notably, in this context, corpora have been used to show that Chomsky's native-speaker introspection data is in certain cases flatly wrong. For example, Pullum and Scholz (2002) use corpus data to demonstrate that interrogative sentences with embedded relative clauses are very common in English, whereas Chomsky had claimed that a person might go their entire life without being exposed to examples of this structure (Piattelli-Palmorini 1980: 40). Likewise McEnery and Wilson (2001: 11) show that Chomsky's personal intuition that the verb *perform* cannot have a mass-noun object is incorrect. Chomsky had said that 'one can *perform a task* but one cannot *perform labour*' (Hill 1962: 29); McEnery and Wilson, by contrast, find examples in the

endorsed by Stalin himself, the prominence of mathematical linguistics in the USSR is easily explicable. See Pollock (2006: 104–35) for a further description of Stalin's intervention in the development of Soviet linguistics; see Papp (1966: 38–55) for an outline of the broader context of mathematical linguistics in the USSR.

British National Corpus such as *perform magic*; and many examples of the exact phrase *perform labour* can nowadays easily be found via a web-search engine (e.g. 'the *lex generalis* of Geneva Convention III with regard to the labour of prisoners of war is that they may be *compelled* to perform labour,' Chifflet 2003: 529).

So the great impedance to the development of corpus linguistics as a field that Chomsky's opposition represented has by now nearly entirely dissipated. What, then, was the nature of the groups of researchers who pushed corpus research forwards when Chomskyan ideas were at the zenith of their influence, in the 1960s and 1970s? They were for the most part scholars of the English language, and research in this period into English Corpus Linguistics was thus critical to the emergence of modern corpus linguistics.

33.4 ENGLISH CORPUS LINGUISTICS

The early work we discussed above as precursors to corpus linguistics as a subdiscipline was varied in the languages it looked at. For example, Juilland produced frequency lists of Chinese, French, Romanian, and Spanish; and Busa worked with Aramaic and Nabatean as well as other, more familiar languages. But although this non-English work was important, ultimately English Corpus Linguistics (ECL) was the crucible in which the field of modern corpus linguistics was formed. The major, systematic contributions of corpus linguistics to the improved description of the lexis and grammar of language were made within ECL. It was also within ECL that key concepts such as collocation and corpus annotation were developed and refined.

The earliest phases of work in ECL were typically concentrated in particular research centres, often with key researchers at those institutions being responsible for a formal or informal research group that contributed to corpus-based language studies. Many of these groups were in regular contact with each other through an organization called ICAME (the International Computer Archive of Modern English),[3] founded in the 1970s. As Leech and Johansson's (2009) account of the formation and early years of ICAME relates, the organization provided an important framework for a network of scholars to cooperate in the development of ECL as a field. Importantly, ICAME also collected and distributed English corpora. A further contributing factor to the rapid development of ECL, and studies focused on British English in particular, is that not only were such corpora produced more frequently, but they were also amongst the first to be placed in an archive allowing relatively easy access to the resources by researchers other than their creators.

One of the most important corpora distributed by ICAME was the Brown Corpus. The Brown Corpus was actually created much earlier on, and only subsequently added to the ICAME archive. Its name refers to Brown University in the United States of America, where it was constructed, having originally been given the much more cumbersome

---

[3] It later became the International Computer Archive of Modern and Medieval English.

official title of 'A Standard Corpus of Present-Day Edited American English for Use with Digital Computers' (Francis and Kučera 1964). Notably, the Brown Corpus was built as an electronic corpus from the start; it did not begin on paper, as had the Survey of English Usage (SEU, see below), on which work had commenced some years earlier. In addition, Francis and Kučera paid close attention to two issues that concern corpus builders to this day, namely balance and representativeness, which were also prominent amongst the concerns of the Survey of English Usage. The Brown Corpus was constructed according to a careful sampling frame. The population of texts to be sampled was written American English published in books or periodicals in the year 1961, but excluded poetry and drama; each text sample was to be 2,000 words in length (or as close as possible to 2,000 words without breaking up a sentence), and the corpus was designed as containing 500 such samples for a total of one million words. This was a very large corpus for the time and remains a respectable size today, when corpora hundreds of times bigger can feasibly be manipulated. The 500 texts were split up across fifteen different genres. These included categories such as 'Press Reportage,' 'Press Editorial,' 'Science Fiction,' 'Popular Lore,' 'Learned' (i.e. academic/scientific), 'General Fiction,' and 'Humour.' Within these categories, texts were chosen randomly.

The Brown Corpus was massively influential. First, for a long time it remained the only publicly available corpus of American English, and as such was used in very many corpus linguistic studies as well as in corpus-based computational linguistics. Second, the model it provided of a meticulous sampling technique with a carefully designed genre breakdown set the parameters for one of the major trends in subsequent corpora, that of the sample corpus. A sample corpus aims to represent as carefully as possible a specified variety of a given language at a specified point in time—thus the alternative term for this type of corpus, a snapshot corpus. Some later corpora followed the Brown Corpus to the extent of employing the same genre breakdown and other design criteria to other varieties of English or other languages. For example, the Lancaster–Oslo–Bergen (LOB) Corpus applies the Brown Corpus sampling frame to British English from 1961 (Johansson et al. 1978); the Kolhapur Corpus applies it to Indian English from 1978 (Shastri et al. 1986); and the Lancaster Corpus of Mandarin Chinese (McEnery and Xiao 2004) does the same for Mandarin c.1991. Many of the subsequent corpora following the Brown sampling frame were also archived and distributed by ICAME.

The virtue of multiple corpora following the same sampling frame is in comparability. Comparative analysis, e.g. the comparison of different varieties of English, using two corpora is naturally more rigorous when the designs of those corpora are congruent in this way. A substantial amount of this type of comparative work has been done using the core four members of the so-called 'Brown Family' of corpora: Brown itself, LOB, and their successors, Frown and FLOB, which sample US and UK English respectively from 1991 rather than 1961 (Hundt et al. 1998, 1999) thus allowing for diachronic comparison as well as inter-varietal comparison (see Leech and Fallon 1992, Mair et al. 2002, Leech et al. 2009). Cross-linguistic comparison is also possible according to the same principle, as exemplified by Xiao and McEnery's (2004a, 2010) comparison of Chinese and English by contrasting LCMC and FLOB, among other datasets.

But even if the precise sampling frame of the Brown Corpus is not adopted, the same principle of a careful breakdown across text categories that the Brown Corpus and the contemporaneous SEU together popularized is typically still used when building a sample corpus—although the precise typology of categories, and the overall scope of the sampling, is of course often different. For example, the ARCHER corpus (Biber et al. 1993) applies that same principle of a balanced spread of genres diachronically— i.e. with the same breakdown in the sample for each different time period, putting cross-period comparison on a sounder basis. The ICE corpora (see below) also follow the same principle, but with texts sampled from the spoken language as well as the written language. Even some much larger corpora apply a very similar approach to sampling and the balance of content across different modes, genres and domains—a good example here being the British National Corpus (Aston and Burnard 1998).

Although an American institution (Brown University) was at the very forefront of early ECL, over the course of the 1960s and 1970s far more corpus linguistic research— including the work that spawned both major strands of corpus linguistics today, the methodologist approach, and the neo-Firthian school (see §33.8 below)—was undertaken in institutions in Europe and, especially, in the UK. American universities which today are hubs of corpus linguistic research (e.g. Northern Arizona University, the University of California Santa Barbara, the University of Michigan, and Brigham Young University) have established this activity largely during and since the 1980s. It is tempting to view the prominence of British research centres in the early emergence of corpus linguistics as a function of geography—since Britain was insulated by the width of the Atlantic from the Chomskyan school then so dominant in the US. But this temptation should be resisted. The insulation from Chomskyan ideas was probably more intellectual than geographical. The structuralist approach from which Chomskyan generativism emerged was never as strong in Britain as in North America, for a number of reasons: for instance American structuralism was shaped in part by the demands of fieldwork with a wide variety of Native American languages, obviously not a factor in the British Isles. Instead, researchers such as J. R. Firth, Randolph Quirk, and later Michael Halliday were at the centre of twentieth-century British linguistics. This tradition was a much more hospitable environment for the incubation of corpus linguistics than Chomskyan generativism could ever be, and so it is perhaps not surprising that much of the earliest work in corpus linguistics took place in the UK.

33.5 THE IMPACT OF CORPORA: GRAMMATICAL DESCRIPTION

To give an impression of the impact of corpus linguistics, we will focus here upon Randolph Quirk, because the credit for initiating corpus linguistics must go, in large part, to him. In 1959 Quirk founded the Survey of English Usage (SEU) at University

College London (UCL). The term SEU (or just 'the Survey') is used to refer both to the research unit that Quirk established and to the corpus whose construction was its initial project. This was the first attempt to provide an ongoing collection of present-day English. The SEU was a precursor of later corpora such as the British National Corpus and the American National Corpus (Ide and Reppen 2004), as it sought to balance its approach to the English language, recording both written and spoken English and sampling them in a range of genres and contexts. The SEU was very much a groundbreaker in corpus linguistics, its earliest phases preceding even the Brown Corpus. Initially the SEU corpus was not stored on a computer at all. It was stored on file cards and only later converted into a computerized form, the spoken part of which is available as the London–Lund Corpus (Svartvik 1990). When computerized, the corpus contained one million words of grammatically analysed modern British English. The team at UCL, led by Sidney Greenbaum, would later take the lead in developing what is still to date the largest corpus for the comparative study of varieties of English, the International Corpus of English (ICE; see Greenbaum 1996). This corpus includes a very wide variety of Englishes from around the world, including Australian, British, Hong Kong, Indian, and Irish English.

From its earliest days, one of the features that made the UCL contribution to corpus linguistics distinctive was its engagement with the parsing (detailed grammatical annotation) of corpus data. Given this salience of grammatical analyses in the UCL approach, it is not particularly surprising that one of the major contributions by the UCL team to demonstrating the utility of corpus linguistics was in the area of grammar production. The Quirk et al. (1972, 1985) reference grammars of English both arose from the work of the SEU. The 1985 grammar was also the first widely distributed modern corpus-informed grammar, making its publication something of a milestone in the development of corpus linguistics. Some earlier grammars had drawn on corpus evidence, notably that of Fries 1940. However, Quirk et al. (1985) set the scene for the grammars that followed.

The early UCL grammars had one notable shortcoming, however—they all had the written language as their principal focus, in spite of the fact that a great deal of effort was invested in the production of spoken corpus material by the Survey of English Usage. The grammars of this period were very much rooted in the attitude to speech that casts it as a debased form of language, mired in hesitations, slips of the tongue, and interruptions.[4] In this context it should be noted that until relatively recently, there were no large corpora of spoken English available on which to base a study of grammar in spoken English. Some pioneering early work, including Fries (1940), had used small collections of transcribed speech in order to explore grammar in spoken English, but until the creation of London–Lund Corpus, the spoken section of the British National Corpus, and the Santa Barbara Corpus of Spoken American English,[5] there were no

---

[4] While the grammars produced from the SEU did not focus on speech, the team at UCL did treat dysfluency as a feature of language, rather than an error to be excised from our account of language.

[5] See www.linguistics.ucsb.edu/research/sbcorpus.html.

substantial corpora of spontaneous speech. When such corpora were created, a spectrum of opinion regarding grammar in speech developed quite rapidly. One extreme may be characterized as the orthodox position—that grammar in speech is present only in some bastardized form, subject to interference from a host of irrelevant performance features. The advent of spoken corpora allowed an opposite extreme to develop—the view not only that speech is grammatical, but also that it has a grammar of its own which is quite distinct from writing. This latter position is most closely associated with Brazil (1995).[6] Brazil argues for a linear grammar of speech, a grammar which is not sentence-oriented and which does not have 'recourse to any notion of constituency of the hierarchically organized kind' (p. 4)—to put it simplistically, this kind of grammar involves no tree-style parsing. Brazil worked as part of the corpus research group at the University of Birmingham and was heavily influenced by John Sinclair (§33.8 below).

A middle ground in the spectrum of this debate was developed by linguists at the University of Nottingham, notably Ron Carter and Mike McCarthy. In their work, Carter and McCarthy (1997) used the 5 million word CANCODE corpus of spoken English developed for Cambridge University Press to explore the nature of grammar in speech. While initially seeming to adopt a position similar to that of Brazil (Carter and McCarthy 1995), Carter and McCarthy later took an approach that did not call for a distinct grammar of speech. Instead, their approach focused on those features of speech which appear most at odds with grammars taking the written language as their starting point. By shifting the focus from arguments in favour of the uniqueness of spoken grammar towards the distinctive features of spoken grammar, McCarthy and Carter developed a useful characterization of spoken English, given full expression in their recent *Cambridge Grammar of English* (Carter and McCarthy 2006). McCarthy and Carter have drawn particular attention to how the grammar of speech can vary by context and can be influenced by the relationship that exists between the speaker and hearer (McCarthy 1998). This observation informed much of the design and development of the CANCODE corpus (Carter 2004) and other corpora developed at Nottingham, notably the Nottingham Multi-Modal Corpus (Carter and Adolphs 2008, Knight et al. 2009). This latter corpus has grown directly out of Nottingham's focus on speech, which has led the Nottingham team to look at how speech, gesture, and prosody combine to create meaning, following on in particular from the work reported in Schmitt (2004).

The position developed at Nottingham in turn links clearly to the development of later grammars produced in the UCL tradition: if the work of linguists like Brazil, and more importantly McCarthy and Carter, can be viewed as having a distinct influence, it has been on grammars of English. While large grammars of English in the 1970s and 1980s rarely engaged with spoken language, grammars produced since then have done so routinely,

---

[6] In fairness to Brazil (1995: 12), he does believe that the grammar he produces may be as applicable to writing as speech. His work is perhaps best characterized as a grammar *proceeding* from speech, rather than a grammar proceeding from writing. The former type of grammar is likely to be quite distinct from the latter.

and moreover have done so in a way that closely resembles what McCarthy and Carter called for—an acknowledgement of the differences between grammar in speech and grammar in writing. The *Longman Grammar of Spoken and Written English* (*LGSWE*, Biber et al. 1999) is a perfect case in point. This grammar might reasonably be viewed as part of the UCL tradition discussed earlier in this chapter,[7] yet it engages fully with the differences between speech and writing. That said, the *LGSWE* moves more firmly to the middle ground than Carter and McCarthy did, by arguing that these grammatical differences are largely a matter of degree rather than absolute distinctions. So there has been a shift from a polarized debate about whether or not speech has a distinct grammar, towards the view now predominant in most schools of English descriptive grammar,[8] where the grammatical system is both flexible and dynamic—where, as Leech (1998: 13) argues, 'English grammar is common to both written and spoken language—but its shape can be moulded to the constraints and freedoms of each.'

The above discussion of the development of grammars in English is indicative of the general impact of corpus linguistics: it has enabled different approaches to linguistic data and in doing so it has pushed along debate. Prior to the availability of large spoken and written corpora and the ability to manipulate them rapidly and reliably, grammars were limited by a reliance on intuition and a limited number of citations. The exposure of grammars to corpus data has changed them, quite fundamentally, for the better.

33.6 DEVELOPMENTS IN CORPUS CONSTRUCTION AND ANNOTATION

Using once again the SEU as an important example of the development of corpus linguistics, it is possible to see how further developments in the field were spawned, albeit indirectly, by it. As well as making critical contributions to corpus construction and annotation practices, the SEU had one further impact on the field: it provided a steady stream of grammarians trained in the corpus approach to linguistics who went on to establish much more firmly the methodological basis of corpus linguistics. Notable corpus linguists who gained experience working on the SEU include Geoffrey Leech and Jan Svartvik, both of whom went on to develop corpus linguistics further, at Lancaster University (UK) and the University of Lund (Sweden) respectively.

At Lancaster, Leech extended the work of the Survey team in three important ways. First, he began to work with computer scientists, both to explore ways in which corpora

---

[7] While often viewed as the successor to grammars such as Quirk et al. (1972) and (1985), the *LGSWE* differs in that while those grammars used corpus data for the purpose of informing and illustrating English grammar, the *LGSWE* is a wholly corpus-based grammar, with *all* examples and observations attested from the corpus data itself.

[8] For a discussion of different perspectives and attitudes to the use of corpora in the production of grammars, see Aarts (2006).

could be used to develop computer applications and also to see how computer applications might help with the process of corpus building. Secondly, he initiated a process of extending the range of corpus annotation. Finally, due to his collaboration with computer scientists especially, he found that he was able to build much larger corpora than had been possible at the Survey. The research unit founded by Leech, UCREL,[9] developed two important resources: specialized tools for the editing and searching of corpus data, and tools for the automated annotation of corpus data. These enabled annotated corpus production on a scale not previously seen (see Garside and McEnery 1993: 38). Prominent among the annotation systems that emerged from Leech's collaboration with Garside was the first viable automated part-of-speech tagging program. While such software had been devised previously (notably by Greene and Rubin 1971), only with the creation in 1980 to 1982 of the CLAWS tagger (Garside et al. 1987: 42–56, *passim*) was a fully automated part-of-speech annotation system developed that worked well across a range of genres. Many other such systems were developed over the course of the next decade by different (teams of) linguists and computer programmers (see e.g. DeRose 1988, Cutting et al. 1992, Karlsson et al. 1995). The availability of automated tagging led to a fundamental change in corpus building. Rather than taking time to collect a corpus and then even more time to annotate it with basic word-class information, it was now possible to collect a corpus, annotate it while you had your lunch, and then work on the annotated corpus in the afternoon, so to speak. Later on the Lancaster team worked to expand the range of annotations undertaken on corpus data. As Garside et al. (1997) report, by the early 1990s the Lancaster team had developed and applied a very wide range of annotations, covering not only written corpora but also spoken corpora (Knowles 1993).

While Lancaster produced probably the widest variety of corpus annotations in the period up to the mid-1990s, it was far from the only centre engaged in this enterprise. There were other centres actively treebanking English corpus data at this time. Of particular note in this respect is the University of Nijmegen in the Netherlands, where Jan Aarts worked with colleagues such as Nelleke Oostdijk, Pieter de Haan, and Hans van Halteren to develop a parsed corpus (also known as a 'treebank'). Like Lancaster, that group also produced bespoke corpus editing tools, in the form of TOSCA (Tools for Syntactic Corpus Analysis, van den Heuvel 1988) which allowed them to treebank substantial volumes of data. Geoffrey Sampson, a member of the UCREL team, continued to develop treebanked corpora after he left Lancaster University, notably the SUSANNE corpus (Sampson 1995). Important work on treebanking also took place at the University of Pennsylvania (UPenn) in the US, beginning with the work of Mitch Marcus and his team (see Marcus et al. 1993), whose annotated corpora—most famously the Penn Treebank—are widely used in computational linguistics[10] in

---

[9] University Centre for Computer Corpus Research on Language; ucrel.lancs.ac.uk.

[10] To give a sense of how widely this resource is used in computational linguistics, a search of all of the literature published by the Association for Computational Linguistics on the ACL Anthology website (www.aclweb.org/anthology-new/, as of Feb. 2012) produced over 2,000 articles which mention the Penn Treebank.

particular. Since then, a major centre for corpus production, archiving, and distribution has been founded at UPenn—the Linguistic Data Consortium (LDC), which has
become a highly significant centre promoting the development of, in particular,
corpus-based computational linguistics in the US and around the world.

33.7 CORPORA BEYOND CORPUS LINGUISTICS

One especially salient feature of the recent history of corpus-based research is the
increasing number of researchers who would not identify themselves as corpus linguists, but who have started to adopt corpus-based methodologies in their work. The
impact of corpus methods in other fields of linguistics has thus been to provoke new
developments, new findings, and in some cases critical reflection on earlier work. The
corpus-based methodology has found especially fertile soil in the areas of functionalist
linguistic theory, cognitive linguistics, and psycholinguistics. To understand how
corpus linguistics has been utilized within the theoretical frameworks of these areas
of language study, let us consider as an example the adoption of corpus methods within
functionalist linguistics.

Much corpus-based research could be described as functionalist in the broadest
sense, in terms of its theoretical stance. This is evident in more ways than just corpus
linguistics and functionalist theory's shared rejection of (Chomskyan) formalism. The
primary enterprise of functionalism is to seek to understand linguistic structure relative
to the meanings it conveys and the functions it serves in usage.[11] This is a goal shared
by much corpus-based research. For example, Biber's (1988) multi-dimensional approach to text-type (register) variation seeks functional explanations for formal (grammatical) differences—exactly the major concern of functionalism. Likewise, the role of
grammaticalization in much corpus-based research into the history of the English
language makes such diachronic corpus linguistics likewise, in effect, a functionalist
enterprise. However, there is a growing body of work that exploits corpus-based
analyses within research addressing *core* aspects of functionalism.

A characteristic mode of investigation in functionalist linguistics is to look at one or
more particular grammatical structures, and to try to identify functional motivations
for their usage—i.e. semantic, pragmatic, or processing factors which can explain
aspects of grammatical form. One methodology found in many studies is to examine
a set of instances of the structure(s) in question, analysing each one for the presence or
absence of a range of such functional factors, and then to investigate whether there is a
(statistical) link between these factors and the syntactic form. A common application of
corpus data in functionalist linguistics has been to use queries of corpus resources as
the source of the set of examples to be analysed. This application of corpora emerged

---

[11] See Ch. 21 above.

gradually from the earlier practice of using less rigorously sampled sets of instances. For example, Birner's (1994) study of non-interrogative subject–verb inversion in English (sentences with the order XVS . . . instead of SV . . .) is based on 1,778 examples of this structure which Birner and others happened to encounter and notice in various written and spoken sources.[12] Notably, before corpus linguistics emerged as a widely known methodology, it was not uncommon for any set of linguistic examples—even one collected on an ad hoc or arbitrary basis—to be described as a 'corpus.' However, in some such studies using relatively small and arbitrary 'corpora,' particularly in the 1980s and 1990s, we see the beginnings of a movement towards the incorporation of corpus data (in the usual sense) into functionalist-theoretical analysis. For example, Carden's (1982) study of backwards anaphora (i.e. cataphora) is based on a 'corpus' of twelve texts (six children's books, a history book by Churchill, two adult fiction books, two newspapers, and a book of Yeats); although this is too small and too arbitrary a selection of texts to be considered balanced and representative in a meaningful sense, Carden's study clearly shows an awareness of the importance of representativeness.

From the mid- to late 1990s onwards, more functionalist studies have actually used large and/or standardized corpora of the kind familiar to corpus linguists. These may be divided on the basis of how comprehensively the corpus evidence is addressed. Some studies of syntax treat the corpus solely as a repository of examples, without taking a systematic approach to addressing the evidence of the corpus as a whole. For example, Declerck and Reed (2000) draw examples of English clauses marked by the conjunction *unless* from the COBUILD, Brown, LOB, and ICE corpora. Other research uses corpus data in a more systematic way. For instance, Valera (1998) examines the phenomenon of subject-oriented adverbs, i.e. adverbs which structurally speaking modify a predicative adjective but which function to describe an attribute of the subject (for example, *she was viciously unkind* implying *she was vicious and unkind*). Valera's dataset is drawn systematically and comprehensively from the LOB corpus. He investigates, in a partially quantitative way, if any syntactic factors influence whether an adverb–adjective combination has a subject-oriented meaning or not, concluding that in fact the lexical semantics of the words involved, and the compatibility of these meanings, is the major factor. Similar methods are used (to give some non-exhaustive examples) by McKoon and Macfarland (2000) to investigate the transitivity and subject/object-types of internally caused vs externally caused change-of-state verbs, using a combination of large English corpora, by Temperley (2003) in an enquiry into factors underlying the use of zero relative pronouns in English, using the Penn Treebank, and by Hollmann (2005) to look at the active and passive forms of the English periphrastic causative, using data extracted from the British National Corpus.

---

[12] This same general approach to the collection of relevant examples from running text is also sometimes adopted with individual texts taken from established corpora. In a study aiming to account for the use of definite articles in English using a theoretical framework termed the 'Givenness Hierarchy,' which classifies degrees of familiarity or identifiability of a referent in discourse, Gundel et al. (2001) use 321 examples collected from 10 different texts, 7 of which were drawn from published corpora.

Of course, as well as functionalist researchers adopting corpus-based methods, the opposite process—corpus specialists using, and/or extending, functional theories in order to adequately characterise their data—has also been observable. A good example of this is the work on situation aspect in Mandarin Chinese undertaken by Xiao and McEnery (2004a, b); another is the use by Stefanowitsch and Gries (2003) of the functional-cognitive theory of Construction Grammar as the basis for their technique of analysing the co-selection of grammatical structures and lexical items in corpus data. However, the impact of corpus data and methods on the research of functionalist theorists who have adopted it in service of their own research goals is clearly considerable. This phenomenon could equally well have been exemplified via any of a wide range of areas of linguistics. The key point here is not only that the corpus offers access to new perspectives on the analysis of language; it is also critical to note that many (intra-) disciplinary barriers to the widespread exploitation of corpus data have now fallen. Corpora can be used, fruitfully, in work on a wide range of problems in linguistics—not only by self-identified corpus linguists but also, and just as easily, by researchers who would not characterize themselves as corpus linguists but who are prepared to use corpus-based methods. The shift in the status of corpus linguistics that this represents is one of the most significant developments in the field over the past twenty or so years.

33.8 THE NEO-FIRTHIAN APPROACH TO CORPUS LINGUISTICS

The history of corpus linguistics we have outlined has been quite intentionally presented from the perspective of one particular approach to, or school of, corpus linguistics. This is the view in which corpus linguistics is primarily a *method* that may be used in a number of areas of linguistics, testing and refining existing findings but also enabling new approaches to basic problems in the subject. This is, however, not the only perspective from which the history of corpus linguistics can be viewed. Before we conclude this brief historical survey, it is worth exploring another, quite distinct approach to the use of corpora, that pioneered by John Sinclair. This approach emerged primarily at Sinclair's institution, the University of Birmingham, from the late 1960s and 1970s onwards—in parallel to the tradition then developing at UCL, Lancaster, and the other institutions whose contributions we considered earlier. Most notably, Sinclair's perspective considers corpus linguistics to have some theoretical status which elevates it above being solely a methodology. We will label this school 'neo-Firthian' due to the roots of Sinclair's work in the ideas of mid-twentieth-century linguist J. R. Firth (see e.g. Firth 1957), which the neo-Firthians extended by applying them to computer-aided corpus analysis (as Tognini-Bonelli 2001: 157 points out, Firth himself would probably not have subscribed to corpus methods). It is however worth noting that most identifiably neo-Firthian scholars do not use the term as a self-designation.

Typically, neo-Firthian corpus linguistics has the word and its discourse context as its central focus of investigation; thus, word and discourse meaning, phraseology, and collocation (i.e. the pervasive regular patterning of co-occurrence among words in corpus data) have been its major though not exclusive concerns. For instance, in the 1980s, Sinclair's COBUILD research unit drove forward the development of corpus lexicography, leading to the publication of a series of highly influential dictionaries; corpus data is today *the* central resource for lexicographers.[13] Slightly later, a neo-Firthian approach to English grammar was developed in which words and grammar are ineluctably bound, in what has been called 'lexicogrammar' (Halliday 1985b, Sinclair 1991—though Sinclair preferred the term 'lexical grammar'). And the phenomenon of collocation in particular has come to have not only descriptive but also theoretical significance in neo-Firthian thinking on language. In the remainder of this section, we will elaborate on some of these intellectual developments in the work of Sinclair and other scholars associated with this school.

Some neo-Firthian approaches go so far as to make the word, its phraseology, and its collocational features the keystone of linguistic description and theory, perhaps unsurprisingly in light of the school's roots in lexicography. A common trend in much neo-Firthian argumentation is that many features of language which had traditionally been explained in terms of grammar are instead explained in terms of the lexicon: this is the idea of lexicogrammar which we have already mentioned. While most neo-Firthians agree with this privileging of lexis over grammar in linguistic description, the basic insight has been captured in various ways. In Sinclair's writings, the centrality of collocation is linked above all to the centrality of meaning. Like the notion of collocation itself, the assignment of a central role in linguistics to 'meaning in context' ultimately derives from Firth but was developed extensively by Sinclair. Briefly, Sinclair (2004: 18–20) argues from the prevalence of collocation in corpus data that meanings in running text are not confined to individual words, but have wider extents—and the beginning and end points of the expression of a particular meaning may not be evident. From the prevalence of collocation also follows the notion that words are not individually selected by speakers. Rather, units of meaning are selected, and each unit of meaning brings along a stretch of several words. Sinclair (1991: 110) expressed this in terms of the 'Idiom Principle': the notion that a speaker 'has available to him or her a large number of semi-preconstructed phrases that constitute single choices, even though they might appear to be analysable into segments.'[14] The units Sinclair argues for, units which reach beyond the word and thus incorporate the collocations of words, are referred to either as 'extended units of meaning' or as 'lexical items' (Stubbs 2001: 60). Most instances of what may *seem* to be syntactically generated phrases are in fact

---

[13] See §22.11 and §32.3 above, Hanks (2013).

[14] Such multiword unit chunks have, of course, been studied by other linguists and have been defined in similar ways, though with different names, a number of times—so Wray (2002, 2008) talks of 'formulaic language,' Biber et al. (1999, 2004) talk of 'lexical bundles,' and De Cock et al. (1998) talked of 'the phrasicon.'

products of the retrieval of idioms and other collocational units from the lexicon, *not* the product of the operation of a mental set of rules 'on-the fly' (as proposed by many formalist models of grammar in particular). Only a minority of language is produced or comprehended in a rule-governed way, according to what Sinclair called the 'Open-Choice Principle.'

Other than Sinclair, researchers associated with the neo-Firthian school include Michael Halliday, whose approach to data shaped Sinclair's views (Sinclair 2004: vii), and Michael Stubbs, who developed an approach to the study of discourse in which collocation plays a central role (see Stubbs 1996). Linguists who collaborated with Sinclair at Birmingham include Susan Hunston, Michael Hoey, Bill Louw, Wolfgang Teubert, and Elena Tognini-Bonelli. Tognini-Bonelli (2001) is responsible for one of the most influential characterizations of the theoretical basis of the neo-Firthian approach in terms of 'corpus-driven' linguistics. Teubert (2004, 2005) is notable for his attempts to root the neo-Firthian approach in older traditions of philology and to explore its conceptual underpinnings. Louw (1993) is largely responsible for the promulgating the notion of semantic prosody (connotation), which is an important one in neo-Firthian approaches to word meaning and discourse analysis. Hunston and Hoey both worked to extend Sinclair's lexicogrammatical approach to language further; while Sinclair's view still invokes the lexicon and the grammar as two contrasting (implicitly separate) systems, Hunston's and Hoey's approaches go further—not only emphasizing the role of lexicon but also, in fact, *unifying* the description of lexis and grammar largely or entirely. Hunston's contribution to this development was Pattern Grammar, a model where language is built up as a series of linked sequences of fuzzy structures, within which collocation provides both structural coherence and meaning (Hunston and Francis 1999). Meanwhile Hoey (2005) developed the framework of Lexical Priming, the first comprehensive attempt to develop a theory of language on the basis of neo-Firthian ideas, with Hoey making specific claims about the link between frequency and collocation in text corpora, and the nature of language in the mind. In this view, words are primed to co-occur with other words, so that a person perceiving/ producing a given word X is then psychologically primed (i.e. predisposed in some way) to anticipate/produce one or more of the words that X is linked to in the mind. Hoey's theory of a psychological role for collocation is, however, at odds with the views of some other neo-Firthians, notably Teubert (2005: 2–3). For Teubert, collocation— and in fact corpus linguistics in general—is not a window into a mind-internal phenomenon; rather it is a tool for exploring meaning in discourse. The emergence of such contrasting views from a common root in Sinclair's ideas on collocation and lexicogrammar has been one of the primary features of the recent history of the neo-Firthian school of corpus linguistics.

Hoey was one of a number of key researchers who moved from Birmingham to the University of Liverpool in the 1990s. This created a new and vital centre for the study of corpus linguistics along the lines developed at Birmingham. The spread and popularization of Sinclair's ideas beyond his own institution was in part the result of moves such as this. So although the conceptual underpinnings of neo-Firthian corpus linguistics are markedly different from those of methodologist corpus linguistics, the overall story of how these two schools emerged is broadly the same: a pioneering centre in the postwar UK exploited emergent computing technologies to take a data-intensive approach to linguistics, using spontaneously occurring speech and writing as the basis for their investigation of language. Likewise, both neo-Firthian and methodologist schools have developed new insights into language and also successfully propagated their pioneering approaches, in part through the dissemination of ideas and techniques, and in part through the training of new generations of linguists who have gone on to further pursue that approach to the study of language.

33.9 Conclusion and Suggestions for Further Reading

In this brief overview of the emergence of corpus linguistics as a subdiscipline of linguistics, and its subsequent spread as a near-ubiquitous method, we have concentrated on the major trends and issues in the field as it developed. Despite early work by Juilland and Busa, we have seen that the roots of contemporary corpus linguistics are in pioneering research at institutions such as UCL in the 1960s, which was made possible at least in part by the intellectual insulation of UK-based English linguistics from the Chomskyan rejection of corpus-based and other empirical approaches to the study of language. We have surveyed the achievements of this field of English Corpus Linguistics—in terms of corpus design and construction, the development of annotation techniques, and the enabling of new approaches to the description of English grammar in particular—and its spread from the UK institutions where it emerged to centres of research in Europe, North America, and around the world; and we have seen the vital role played by enabling organizations such as ICAME. Corpora are now available for many varieties of English and for many languages other than English. For English, the International Corpus of English provides corpora of a range of varieties of English including Australian English, Hong Kong English, and New Zealand English.[15] Beyond English, corpora are increasingly available both for languages with many speakers such as Mandarin Chinese (McEnery et al. 2004) and Hindi (Baker et al. 2004) and for minority and endangered languages such as Basque,[16] Mansi (Bíró and Sipőcz 2009) and Sylheti (Baker et al. 2000).

The growing importance of corpus methods to other sub-fields of linguistics has been illustrated via the example of functionalist-theoretical linguistics, showing how the exploitation of corpus data has enabled functionalist analysts to address the central

---

[15] See www.corpora4learning.net/resources/corpora.html for an extensive list of corpora covering a variety of Englishes.

[16] See www.corpeus.org/cgi-bin/kontsulta.py to access a corpus of Basque via a web-based interface.

research questions of their discipline in novel ways. Finally, we have surveyed the separate tradition of neo-Firthian corpus linguistics, which assigns to corpus linguistics a theoretical status linked to an understanding of the nature of language in which words, their meanings in context, and their collocational behaviours are central.

We have not had space here to talk about very many important but more specialized aspects of the field, such as: work on the creation and analysis of learner corpora (see Granger 1993, Granger et al. 2002); contrastive cross-linguistic corpus analysis and the use of parallel and comparable corpora (see e.g. Aijmer et al. 1996, Borin 2002, Johansson 2007); corpora in (critical) discourse analysis and sociolinguistics (see Baker 2006, 2010); the intersection of corpus linguistics and computational linguistics (see McEnery and Wilson 2001 for an overview); applications of corpus data in the digital humanities (see McCarty 2005); corpus-based literary stylistics (e.g. Semino and Short 2004, Culpeper 2009, Mahlberg 2010); or a plethora of other issues and applications. We have elsewhere reviewed many of these trends in detail, as well as addressing in greater depth many of the findings, methodologies, and controversies that we have only been able to touch on briefly here (see McEnery and Hardie 2012); a deeper understanding of the historical development of the field may also be gleaned from collections of classic papers such as Sampson and McCarthy (2004) or from the regular volumes of proceedings from long-running conferences such as the annual ICAME conference (e.g. Leitner 1992, Kirk 2000, Nevalainen et al. 2008). Yet our outline of the history of corpus linguistics has hopefully been sufficient to indicate the main reasons why corpus usage has spread and has been found to be a crucial resource for linguistics in general.

CHAPTER 34

···

PHILOSOPHY OF
LINGUISTICS

···

ESA ITKONEN

34.1 INTRODUCTION

···

34.1.1 Purpose

Katz (1985) is a decent attempt to establish philosophy of linguistics as a field of its own. It seems eminently reasonable that this field should be 'conceived as a branch of philosophy parallel to the philosophy of mathematics, the philosophy of logic, and the philosophy of physics' (p. 1). What is less recommendable, however, is the openly expressed wish to single out those issues that might be of interest to philosophers at large. There is no need to convince any particular part of the general audience that philosophy of linguistics is valuable. Just like the philosophy of any other academic discipline, it possesses an intrinsic value.

34.1.2 Definition

The philosophy of linguistics is indistinguishable from the methodology of linguistics. Linguistics is not, however, a monolithic whole, but comprises several subdisciplines, which may overlap to a higher or lower degree: grammatical theory, typology, diachronic linguistics, sociolinguistics, psycholinguistics, and so on. The methodology of each of these subdisciplines has an equal right to be taken into account. To be sure, the greatest amount of philosophical reflection has been devoted to grammatical theory.

Philosophy of linguistics must not be confused with philosophy of language, as expounded e.g. in Blackburn (1984). The two overlap in semantics. To philosophy of linguistics, however, phonology is just as important as semantics, whereas philosophy of language (as this term is currently used) has no interest in phonology. Moreover, if in the domain of philosophy an analogue has to be found for philosophy of linguistics, it is not philosophy of language but philosophy of philosophy, or metaphilosophy (cf. Pap 1958, Cohen 1986, Wedgwood 2007).

34.1.3 A Question of Authorship

It goes without saying that history of linguistics concentrates on the leading representatives of each period. Thus, to put it bluntly, the history of linguistics deals with the *best* linguists.[1] (This entails that any purportedly value-free approach is doomed to failure.) It may seem self-evident that these very same personages will reappear in the history (or, rather, historiography) of the philosophy of linguistics. But this cannot be quite right. 'Philosophy of subject matter X' presupposes methodological self-awareness of what it means to study X and, in the historical context, some written record of this self-awareness. This means that the best linguists need not be the best philosophers of linguistics, for two reasons. First, one may have left no written record of one's methodology. Second, even where some record exists, it is not unusual for one to be a good linguist but a bad philosopher of linguistics.

It follows that in that type of history that will be dealt with here, the authorship of ideas is less clear-cut than in the history of linguistics. The 'philosophy of person Y' may have been formulated by Y him-/herself; or it may have been extracted from his/her writings by somebody else.

34.1.4 Choosing the Focus

There have been significant linguistic traditions outside of the West, especially in India and in Arabia (understood as a cultural rather than geographical area).[2] For reasons of space, these other traditions will not be treated here in their own right, but some of their contributions will be briefly mentioned in a proper context. For some 2,000 years, synchronic grammatical analysis constituted the sole type of linguistic inquiry in the West. Other linguistic subdisciplines, although just as important methodologically, will therefore be treated more succinctly or not at all.

34.1.5 First Beginnings

For a long time, the three traditions mentioned above have been monolingual, which means that they have not been brought into existence by awareness of cross-linguistic

---

[1] Which is why this chapter touches on matters dealt with in other chapters throughout this volume.
[2] See Chs 11 and 12 above.

differences (cf. Auroux 1989: 25–6). Rather, the original motivation for linguistic inquiry has been exegesis of some canonical text, even if grammar writing later established itself as an independent form of research (cf. van Bekkum et al. 1997: 287). It seems natural to think that the same hermeneutical interest may continue to imbue even modern-day linguistics to some extent. To be sure, in the West another impetus for linguistic inquiry came from general philosophy (see below).

The invention of writing has often been cited as the principal facilitating factor that enabled linguistics to come into being. This view, inspired by Goody (1977), certainly sounds plausible, but it overlooks some important facts. Pāṇini composed his grammar of Sanskrit around 400 BC, but there are no written records of either Sanskrit or its descendant Prakrit before the edicts of the emperor Asoka (c.250 BC). By comparison, the (Harappan) language of the Indus valley civilization (c.2200–1800 BC) has been preserved in numerous (albeit brief) documents carved on stone, metal, or bone. 'It is unheard of that any people having a script never use it on hard materials' (Masica 1991: 134). It follows that Pāṇini had no written medium at his disposal, a view confirmed by a visiting Greek who flatly stated c.280 that the Indians have no knowledge of written letters (p. 135).

It is customary to claim that Pāṇini could not have achieved his grammar without the aid of writing, but this is just another instance of Eurocentrism. 'Inference of the existence of writing from the feats of textual preservation and analysis accomplished by the ancient Aryans does an injustice to the remarkable mnemonic powers developed by them' (Masica 1991: 134). Some of the mnemonic techniques are discussed in Rubin (1995). The overemphasis put on literacy tends to conceal what the human mind is capable of (cf. Itkonen 1991: 13–14).

34.2 ANTIQUITY

In his dialogue *Cratylus*,[3] Plato (428–348 BC) raises the question concerning the nature of language: does it exist *nomōi* or *phusei*? These are dative forms of *nomos* and *phusis*, respectively. The former means 'law' and 'convention' while the latter means 'nature' in the sense of 'essence.' If language exists *nomōi*, it is conventional or arbitrary. If it exists *phusei*, it is an instrument that has been devised by a mythical or imaginary 'name-giver' (*onomathetēs* or *nomothetēs*) so as to reveal the essence of its referent; and this it can do insofar as it is a picture of the latter.

The actual examples that are marshalled to support the *phusei* view are rather unconvincing, as Plato (or his mouthpiece, Socrates) is himself willing to admit. Still, he claims that this is what language would be like in an ideal world: 'For I believe that if we could

---

[3] See also Ch. 13 above.

always, or almost always, use likenesses, which are perfectly apppropriate, this would be the most perfect state of language, as the opposite is the most imperfect' (435C).

Here the central question is whether or not there is something like 'correctness of names' (*orthotēs onomatōn*). It may be of some interest to note that the same question lies at the heart of the most influential philosophical doctrine in China, that of Confucius: whether or not it is possible to (re-)establish the situation consonant with *cheng ming*, generally translated as 'rectification of names' (cf. Fung Yu-lan 1952: 60).

In his dialogue *Sophist*, Plato formulates the first rudiments of sentence analysis. He notes that (correct) statements are not just strings of words like *Walks runs sleeps* or *Lion stag horse*. Rather, when one is uttering a (correct) statement of the 'simplest and shortest possible kind' like *A man understands*, one is 'putting a thing together with an action by means of a name and a verb' (*suntheis prāgma prāxei di' onomatos kai rhēmatos*). As a consequence, 'just as some things fit together, some do not, so with the signs of speech; some do not fit, but those that do fit make a statement' (262D–E).

Aristotle (384–322 BC) does not investigate language for its own sake but rather as part of his logic, rhetoric, or poetics. Here the emphasis will be placed on the connection with logic.[4]

Aristotle identifies logic with syllogistic. A syllogism is an inference with two premises and one conclusion. The premises and the conclusions are sentences with the core structure X is Y (see below). Both X and Y express (lexical) meanings ultimately definable in terms of ten categories. Thus, preliminary to his logic proper, expounded in *Analytica Priora* (to use the Latin name), Aristotle had to write the books on categories (= *Categoriae*) and sentences (= *De Interpretatione*). As documented by Arens (1984), the two or three opening pages of the latter book have had a lasting influence on the Western linguistic tradition.

The following three relations of signification are stated to exist: written language (*grammata*) → spoken language (*phōnai*) → mental experiences (*pathēmata* or *noēmata*) → things (*prāgmata*). The link between language and mental experiences is conventional (*kata sunthēkēn*, synonymous with *nomōi*). By contrast, mental experiences are pictures (*homoiōmata*) of things, which means that the two must be linked by a *phusei*-type connection. Unlike the linguistic expressions, the mental experiences and the things are common to the mankind. Even if the reality (as constituted by things) is always conceptualized or 'mind-penetrated,' mind and reality must nevertheless be postulated as two distinct realms. There has to be mind because there clearly are some mental experiences with no extramental counterparts. But there also has to be reality: 'that the substrata which cause the sensation should not exist even apart from sensation is impossible' (*Metaphysica* 1010b, 30).

There are different types of sentences, of which statements, i.e. those admitting of truth or falsity, are singled out as those needed in syllogistic. A statement has a subject (*onoma*, also 'noun') and a predicate (*rhēma*, also 'verb'); as we have seen, these terms

---

4 See also Ch. 23 above.

were already used by Plato. A statement is given both a semantic and an 'actionist' interpretation: the subject both signifies a substance and is that about which the predicate asserts something. The predicate is thought to contain an either implicit or explicit copula, which means that all statements are reduced to the canonical form *X is (not) Y* required by syllogistic. This entails that all types of predicate must, rather unnaturally, be reinterpreted as one-place predicates: e.g. *Socrates loves Plato* → *Socrates is Plato-loving, Socrates gives books to Plato* → *Socrates is books-to-Plato-giving*. The copula has no lexical meaning but only a grammatical meaning: it does not signify (*sēmainein*) but only consignifies (*prossēmainein*). An affirmative statement combines the meanings of X and Y, while a negative statement separates them.

As explained in more detail by Kneale and Kneale (1962, ii. 5–6), syllogistic deals with four distinct types of sentences, traditionally designated by the following letters:

A = Every S is P
E = No S is P
I = Some S is P
O = Some S is not P

These are the 'general' sentence-types, of which A and E qualify as 'universal' while I and O qualify as 'particular.' A and O, on the one hand, and E and I, on the other, are contradictories, while A and E are contraries. E and I are 'convertible': *No S is P = No P is S* and *Some S is P = Some P is S*. S and P can be understood as standing for 'subject' and 'predicate,' respectively. This choice of letters anticipates the conclusion of the syllogism, which has the form S—P. In addition to the conclusion, a syllogism contains two premisses such that one states a relation between S and a 'middle term' M and the other states a relation between M and P.

This issue is slightly complicated by a discrepancy between Aristotle's original formulations and their modern translations. In general, Aristotle uses a schema of the following type: 'If P is predicated of every M and M is predicated of every S, then it is necessary that P should be predicated of every S.' This particular schema may be exemplified by the following syllogism:

'Patriot' is predicated of every maniac
'Maniac' is predicated of every soldier
'Patriot' is predicated of every soldier

Furthermore, it is natural to summarize this syllogism in the following way:

P—M
M—S
P—S

This indeed illustrates Aristotle's original way of summarizing syllogisms (cf. Kneale and Kneale 1962: 68). But if the premisses and the conclusions are assumed to be copula sentences of the type *X is Y*, then both the subject–predicate order and the order of the premisses should be reversed:

Every soldier is a maniac	S—M
Every maniac is a patriot	M—P
Every soldier is a patriot	S—P

For a modern reader, this difference in presentation may be a needless obstacle to an adequate understanding of syllogistic.

There are four, and only four, possible ways, called 'figures,' in which S, M, and P may relate to one another in a syllogism. (Aristotle himself recognized only three figures.) The traditional presentation of these figures is something of a compromise: the order of letters has been changed from what it was in Aristotle's original formulation, but the order of the premisses has been retained (cf. Reichenbach 1947: 200). Evans (1982: 77), for instance, has changed also the order of the premisses. This is the new, non-traditional form of presentation:

(1)	(2)	(3)	(4)
S—M	S—M	M—S	M—S
M—P	P—M	M—P	P—M
S—P	S—P	S—P	S—P

The syllogism given above is an instance of figure (1). Moreover, each line of a syllogism must exemplify one of the four alternatives A, E, I, and O. A given constellation of these alternatives is called a 'mood.' For instance, our example has the mood AAA (with the traditional label *Barbara*); hence, its figure and mood label is 1-AAA or SAM and MAP and SAP. Each figure contains $4 \times 4 \times 4 = 64$ possible moods. Because there are 4 figures, there are 256 possible moods in all. Originally, Aristotle recognized only 14 moods that are valid in the sense that it is necessarily the case that, if the premisses are true, the conclusion is true (Kneale and Kneale 1962: 72–3). Valid conclusions of the form P—S are also possible, but they are not part of the Aristotelian syllogistic.

It is a characteristic of figure (1) that its four valid moods produce, exactly, four conclusions of the A, E, I, and O type. As we just saw, the Barbara mood produces an A conclusion. The other three moods are as follows: *If every S is M, and no M is P, then no S is P* (1-AEE, traditionally called *Celarent*); *If some S is M, and every M is P, then some S is P* (1-IAI); *If some S is M, and no M is P, then some S is not P* (1-IEO). Aristotle regarded only these valid moods of figure (1) as 'perfect' or intuitively self-evident. The validity of moods in other figures may indeed be quite difficult to grasp, for instance: *If some S is M, and no P is M, then some S is not P* (2-IEO); *If every M is S, and every M is P, then some S is P* (3-AAI); *If some M is S, and no P is M, then some S is not P* (4-IEO) (cf. Johnson-Laird 1983: 102–3).

A syllogism is demonstrated to be valid by being derived from (or reduced to) Barbara or Celarent. More informally, several generalizations have been stated about the premisses of a valid syllogism, for instance: (i) If one premiss is particular, the conclusion is particular. (ii) If both premisses are particular, there is no valid conclusion. (iii) If both premisses are affirmative, the conclusion is affirmative. (iv) If one premiss is negative, the conclusion is negative. (v) If both premisses are negative, there is no valid conclusion.

Aristotle's syllogistic is a logic of classes or, alternatively, of one-place predicates: 'That one term should be included in another as in a whole is the same as for the other to be predicated of all of the first' (*Analytic Priora* 24b, 25). The main difference vis-à-vis modern formal logic concerns the interpretation of A-sentences. For Aristotle, their truth presupposes the existence of some S, whereas the comparable universal sentence of modern logic, formalized as $\forall x(Sx \rightarrow Px)$, has no such existential import. Assuming that there are no ghosts, the sentence *All ghosts are friendly* is false for Aristotle and true for modern logic. It is only the existential import that justifies the validity of a syllogism such as 3-AAI above. The existential import also justifies the 'partial conversion' *Every S is P* $\rightarrow$ *Some P is S* (via *Some S is P*).

Aristotle's authority was pervasive and long-lasting. Writing in 1787, Immanuel Kant still claimed that in logical theory no progress at all had been achieved during 2,000 years because Aristotelian syllogistic is 'complete and perfect' (*geschlossen und vollendet*). From today's perspective, however, this kind of logic seems arbitrary insofar as it lacks its natural foundation, i.e. propositional logic, and ignores the existence of relations. Even as an analysis of its chosen topic, it has been characterized as 'unnecessarily complicated and unelegant' (Reichenbach 1947: 206). Yet it has its own justification: 'For many centuries all the relations asserted by Aristotle were accepted without much questioning by the thousands who studied his work. It is therefore likely that his work is a faithful reflection of the normal usage for sentences constructed with words like "every" and "some"' (Kneale and Kneale 1962: 59). Hence, little needs to be changed in the way that Aristotle described negation and quantification in natural language.

Aristotle's *Metaphysics* contains a 'Philosophical Lexicon' where e.g. the following conceptual distinctions are defined: one vs many, same vs different, quantity vs quality, necessary vs possible vs imposssible, prior vs posterior, active vs passive, part vs whole. It is not difficult to see that these overlap with grammatical meanings that every language of the world has to express in one way or another.

In sum, Allan (2010a: 58) seems eminently justified to say of Aristotle that 'his legacy is overwhelming.'

After Plato and Aristotle, the Stoics constructed an ambitious theory that was supposed to encompass the entire universe. It has three components: ethics, 'physics' (including psychology), and logic. Logic is in turn subdivided into dialectic and rhetoric. Within dialectic it is possible to further distinguish between grammatical analysis and the theory of valid inference. Unlike Aristotle, the Stoics investigated language for its own sake and not just as a precondition for doing logic.

In general, the Western tradition assumes that mental experiences are the meanings of linguistic forms, ascribing—rightly or wrongly—this view to Aristotle. The Stoic metaphysics is strongly materialistic in the sense that as many entities as possible (including qualities and relations) are interpreted as being of corporeal nature. It is therefore only the more remarkable that, according to the Stoics, linguistic meanings (*sēmainomena* or *lekta*) are incorporeal and thus clearly distinct from the corresponding mental experiences (*phantasiai*), which belong to 'physics.' Of course, linguistic forms (*sēmainonta*) too are part of 'physics.'

Distinct types of sentences are recognized insofar as they express different speech acts, for instance, statements, questions, and requests. A verb like *teaches* is an incomplete predicate (and an incomplete *lekton*); a verb phrase like *teaches Dion* is a complete predicate but an incomplete *lekton*. A statement like *Plato teaches Dion* is a complete *lekton*. A negation plus a statement forms a statement. Likewise, two statements conjoined form a statement. Because statements qua *lekta* are true or false while this cannot be said of sentence-meanings, it is only as a first approximation that *lekta* have been equated here with meanings. It would be more accurate to say that to a declarative sentence-form there corresponds, as its *lekton*, that which it asserts to be the case.[5]

Both verb and noun morphology have become objects of systematic analysis in the Stoic grammar. It influenced both Varro and Apollonius (see below).

Chrysippus (282–206 BC), the leading Stoic thinker, constructed a propositional logic, which Aristotle had failed to do. He assumed five inference schemas as basic. For simplicity, they will be presented here with the modern notation:

(1)	(2)	(3)	(4)	(5)
$p \rightarrow q$	$p \rightarrow q$	$\sim(p \wedge q)$	$p \vee q$	$p \vee q$
p	$\sim q$	p	p	$\sim p$
q	$\sim p$	$\sim q$	$\sim q$	q

Here $p \rightarrow q$ = 'if p, then q', $\sim q$ = 'not-q', $p \wedge q$ = 'p and q'. The schemas (1) and (2) are known as Modus Ponens and Modus Tollens, respectively. Taken together, the schemas (4) and (5) show that the disjunction 'or' (= $\vee$) is not inclusive, as in modern formal logic, but exclusive: 'p or q but not both'. Of course, the inferences (4) and (5) are also valid if the second premiss is either q or $\sim q$, with $\sim p$ and p as the respective conclusions. In schema (3) the negation (= $\sim$) and the conjunction (= $\wedge$) combine to define an inclusive disjunction ('not-p or not-q or both'). The inference is valid if the second premiss is either p or q, with $\sim q$ and $\sim p$ as the respective conclusions. But if the second premiss is $\sim p$, neither q nor $\sim q$ follows, because the truth of both is compatible with the truth of the premisses; and the same applies, mutatis mutandis, to $\sim q$ as the second premiss. The law of the excluded middle, i.e. $p \vee \sim p$, which is abandoned by some schools of logic, is unquestioningly endorsed by the Stoics.

The five basic or 'indemonstrable' schemas are used by Chrysippus and his followers as starting points from which an indefinite number of other valid schemas or sentences could be derived as theorems. (The Stoics were perfectly well aware that inference schemas can be transformed into conditional sentence-schemas, e.g. Modus Ponens into $[(p \rightarrow q) \wedge p] \rightarrow q$.) Thus, what they were trying to do was construct axiomatic (propositional) logic. On the basis of the extant evidence it is difficult to appreciate the

---

[5] See Ch. 13 above.

extent to which they actually carried out this program. At least the following theorems were proved (cf. Kneale and Kneale 1962: 165–9).

(i) If the first, then if the first, then the second; but the first; therefore the second = by two applications of schema (1): $[p \rightarrow (p \rightarrow q)]$ and p yield $(p \rightarrow q)$, and $(p \rightarrow q)$ and p yield q.

(ii) If the first and the second, then the third; but not the third; on the other hand the first; therefore not the second = by one application of schema (2) and one application of schema (3): $(p \wedge q) \rightarrow r$ and $\sim r$ yield $\sim(p \wedge q)$, and $\sim(p \wedge q)$ and p yield $\sim q$.

(iii) Either the first or the second or the third; but not the first; and not the second; therefore the third = by two applications of schema (5): $[p \vee (q \vee r)]$ and $\sim p$ yield $(q \vee r)$, and $(q \vee r)$ and $\sim q$ yield r.

(iv) If the first, then the first; but the first; therefore the first = by one application of the schema (1): $p \rightarrow p$ and p yield p.

(v) Either the first or not the first; but the first; therefore not not the second = assuming the law of the excluded middle and applying schema (4): $p \vee \sim p$ and p yield $\sim\sim p$.

(vi) Either the first or not the first; but not not the first; therefore the first = assuming the law of the excluded middle and applying the schema (5): $p \vee \sim p$ and $\sim\sim p$ yield p.

Taken together, theorems (v) and (vi) establish the equivalence $p \equiv \sim\sim p$. Theorem (iv) is important because it shows that the same methods must be applied to prove any non-basic schema, regardless of whether it is felt to be intuitively non-obvious or obvious. This is something that the critics of Stoic logic failed to understand. Apparently also the following theorem was proved: $[(p \rightarrow q) \wedge (p \rightarrow \sim q)] \rightarrow \sim p$. This is the all-important inference schema known as *reductio ad absurdum*, which says that a sentence is false if it contains a contradiction.

Although many aspects of Stoic logic survived in fragmentary comments, the basic insight, i.e. the invention of propositional logic, fell into oblivion. It was rediscovered only in the twentieth century, thanks to Łukasiewics (1935). Thus, it is part of the hidden history of the Western thought. While Stoic logic remained without genuine influence, Euclid's *Elements* provided the generally acknowledged model for axiomatic thinking until the end of the nineteenth century. It is interesting to note that Pāṇini's grammar too exemplifies the idea of axiomatics (cf. Itkonen 1991: ch. 2, esp. pp. 38–44). Comparable to the *Elements*, it was for more than 2,000 years the cornerstone of higher education in India.

After Plato and Aristotle, linguistic inquiry received two types of impetus. One came from Stoic philosophy; the other came from Alexandrian philology, starting in the third century BC. Marcus Terentius Varro (116–27 BC) was influenced by both lines of thinking. The aspect of Varro's methodology that will be singled out here is the notion of explanation in his book *De Lingua Latina*.

This is the crucial passage: 'The origins of words are therefore two in number, and no more: *impositio* and *declinatio*; the one is as it were the spring, the other the brook. Men have wished that imposed nouns should be as few as possible ... but derivative nouns (*nomina declinata*) they have wished to be as numerous as possible' (VIII, 5). *Impositio* designates the original act of name-giving, and Varro refers to 'those who first imposed names upon things [*illi qui primi nomina imposuerunt rebus*]' (VII, 7). This is Varro's counterpart to Plato's *nomothetēs*, with the difference that the Varro-type name-giver is an ordinary, occasionally fallible human being. *Declinatio* designates the process by which new words are produced from the original simple words. In practice it covers inflection and derivation. If *declinatio* is applied to e.g. 1,000 words resulting from *impositio*, millions of new words can easily be shown to result (VI, 36–39). First of all, it may be admitted that the original 1,000 words are unexplainable. Still, it is no mean feat for the grammarian to have explained such a large number of the new words. The term for 'explaining' is here either *ostendere* or *expedire*.

But secondly, this is not all that the grammarian can do. The very disproportion between few imposed words and many derived words is explained by the fact that it imposes a minimum load to memory. Such and similar functional explanations are ultimately based on the instrumental character of language: 'I grant that speech has been produced for utility's sake [*Ego utilitatis causa orationem factam concedo*]' (IX, 48; also VIII, 30). Now, language would be a very bad instrument if every word had to be learned separately.

Third, we need not admit that *impositio* operates in a totally arbitrary way: 'nature was the man's guide to the imposition of names' (VI, 3). On the one hand, the lack of plural forms in mass nouns is ontologically motivated (IX, 66). On the other, the lack of gender distinctions in the names of non-domestic (and thus less important) animals is functionally motivated (IX, 56). Varro is here outlining a moderate version of the *phusei* view.

Much of the discussion is carried out in terms of the 'analogy vs anomaly' dichotomy. For instance, inflection is correctly asserted to be more analogical and less anomalous than derivation. A phenomenon is explained by exhibiting its place in a larger analogical structure. For instance, Varro (X, 47–8) gives the following account of the Latin tense/aspect system:

INFECTUM		PERFECTUM	
Imperfect	Present	Pluperfect	Perfect
$\left\{\dfrac{legebam}{lego}\right.$	$\left.\dfrac{lego}{legam}\right]$ =	$\left\{\dfrac{legeram}{legi}\right.$	$\left.\dfrac{legi}{legero}\right\}$
Present	I Future	Perfect	II Future

The generalization implicit in the data is presented here by means of a complex analogy. On both sides, the first-level analogy is temporal: the relation of past to the present is the same as the relation of the present to the future. The two sides of each analogy share a common member, present, which means that each is an *analogia coniuncta*. Moreover, both INFECTUM and PERFECTUM contain the same (temporal) analogy, which means that they are analogous to each other at the second level. They have no common members, which means that each is an *analogia disiuncta*. This second-level analogy is aspectual. The only weakness of this elegant description is that the aorist function of the perfect remains unaccounted for.

The Varro-type analogy is not just language-internal, but extends—*phusei*-like—also to the relation between language and extralinguistic reality: 'The basis of all regularity [*analogia*] is a certain likeness, that, as I have said, which is wont to be in things and in spoken words and in both' (X, 72; also IX, 63). Finally, Varro (IX, 23) justifies analogy in language by referring to the ubiquity of analogy in general: *Quae enim est pars mundi quae non innumerabiles habeat analogias?* 'For what part of the world is there which does not have countless regularities?'

The oldest extant sentence analysis in the Western tradition is given in *Peri suntaxeōs* by Apollonius Dyscolus (*c*.80–160 AD). This title should not be translated as 'syntax', because the book deals equally with the meaning and the form of sentences. Apollonius exhibits considerable freedom in inventing and manipulating his data. Consider the following example (I, 14):

ho	*autos*	*anthrōpos*	*olisthēsas*	*sēmeron*	*kata-epesen*
art	pron	noun	participle	adv	prep-verb
The	same	man	slipping	today	down-fell

This sentence has been so constructed as to contain all word classes except the conjunction. The idea of name-giving (*thesis tou onomatos*) still survives, in the sense that the word classes are supposed to have been invented in the order of their importance: first the noun, then the verb, and so on. Now, it is of course Apollonius' own linguistic intuition that assures him of the correctness of this self-invented example sentence. Next, the words of this sentence are deleted one by one, on the correct assumption that only those words whose deletion results in incorrectness are necessary to sentencehood; and, again, the only criterion of incorrectness is Apollonius' own intuition. In this way the original sentence is reduced step by step to *anthrōpos epesen*. Looking back, we realize that it was Plato's intuition, and nothing else, that distinguishes the correct *The man understands* from the incorrect *Walks runs sleeps.

All this is self-evident if the data of grammatical analysis is taken to be the normal linguistic usage which is by definition accessible to intuition. The grammarians of antiquity, however, view the data in more complex terms. Varro distinguishes between usage (*consuetudo*) and reason (*ratio*), even if he admits that they often coincide: 'Therefore as each one ought to correct his own usage if it is bad, so should the people correct its usage. . . . [T]he people ought to obey reason, and we individuals ought to obey the people' (IX, 6). Hence a nation should correct its language if it is contrary to *ratio*, but an individual has no choice but to follow the *consuetudo* of his/her nation. Apollonius echoes the same view: 'I rely not merely on poetical citation . . . ., but on common everyday usage, the practice of best prose-writers, and *most of all*, on the force of theory' (II, 49; emphasis added). The resulting attitude vis-à-vis the data is somewhat 'warped.' One is forced to accept the usage as it is, but then one counteracts by trying to find a rational justification for it even where none exists in fact. 'This notion that everything in grammar must have a reason, that nothing is arbitrary or random, pervades A.D.'s work' (Householder 1981: 43).

As far as Apollonius' methodology is concerned, this is the crucial passage: 'So we'd better stop and explain what the actual cause of the ungrammaticality is, not by mere citation of examples as some linguists do, pointing out the ungrammaticality without explaining its cause. But if you don't grasp the cause, it is an exercise in futility to cite examples' (III, 6). The central explanatory notion is *akolouthia* (or *katallēlotēs*), translated as 'concordance.' It subsumes agreement and government, but is not re-stricted to these two. Examples are given throughout the book, the most revealing ones in III, 22–34. This is the general constraint: 'No part of speech [combined with another] can be ungrammatical with respect to a category which it fails to distinguish' (III, 51). Looking back, we realize that Plato's distinction between *A man understands* and **Walks runs sleeps* is based on pretheoretical use of *akolouthia*.

Apollonius makes extensive use of the descriptive apparatus deep structure–trans-formation—surface structure, connecting e.g. the following types of sentences: *N V1-ed and (then) he V2-ed, N V1-ed and V2-ed, N who V1-ed V2-ed, V1-ing N V2-ed.* He also postulates uniform performative deep structures for sentences expressing different speech acts. This just goes to show that the history of linguistics is shorter than one might have been led to think. The very ontology-*cum*-methodology of grammatical analysis must possess some peculiar feature that makes this possible.

Many of Apollonius' syntactic insights were subsequently lost in the Latin adapta-tion *Institutiones Grammaticae* by Priscian (*c.*500 AD), a fact also noted by Robins (1967: 60). Moreover, mastery of Classical Greek by no means secures an adequate understanding of *Peri suntaxeōs* that was written more than 400 years after Aristotle. As a result, this work has been known less well than it deserves: 'Surprisingly, perhaps, the literature dealing directly with *Syntax* is very modest in extent, most of it prior to [1878]' (Householder 1981: 1). Since the 1981 English translation by Householder, the situation has changed dramatically.

34.3 FROM THE MIDDLE AGES TO THE END OF THE EIGHTEENTH CENTURY

The scholastic grammarians, called Modistae (*c.*1250–1320), constructed a universal grammar (*grammatica universalis*) which had the following general structure.[6] First,

---

[6] On the modistae see also Chs 14, 17, and 23 above.

there are the ontological categories of thing, action, and quality, called the 'modes of being.' Second, there are the corresponding mental concepts, called the 'modes of understanding.' Third, there are the corresponding word classes, i.e. noun, verb, and adjective, called the 'modes of signifying.' There is a general iconicity between the three levels, but none of them is redundant: 'Although things cannot be understood apart from the modes of understanding, the human mind makes nevertheless a distinction between the things, on the one hand, and the modes of understanding, on the other' (Boethius de Dacia 1980 [c.1280]: 70). Considering the iconic relation between thing and noun, on the one hand, and action and verb, on the other, we now see that Plato would have been able to build a more convincing case for the *phusei* view, if he had been speaking about word classes instead of individual words.

According to Aristotle, both the reality and the mind are universally the same, whereas languages which express what's in the mind vary arbitrarily. The Modistae found this inconsistent, and correctly so. If universally valid distinctions are expressed by the various languages, these too must possess some universal core which is just hidden behind superficial differences.

The Modistic universal grammar is an ambitious theory insofar as the *modi significandi* are meant to be explained—via the *modi intelligendi*—by the *modi essendi*. This is language-external explanation. The *modi significandi* are meant to provide language-internal explanations in the sense of Apollonius-type *akolouthia*. There is a grave discrepancy between what the Modistae tried to achieve and what they achieved in fact. Because their data basis remained restricted to Latin, they were caught in a vicious circle: the existence of a linguistic category suggests the possible existence of a corresponding ontological category, which is then used to 'explain' the former. Furthermore, the levels of language and ontology came to be conflated in practice. The same confusion hampers Modistic syntax. On the one hand, the verb is thought to depend on the noun, because the action (*qua* the ontological counterpart of the verb) depends on the thing (*qua* the ontological counterpart of the noun). On the other hand, there is an attempt to separate linguistic criteria from ontological ones: 'The sentence is made complete by the word-class which governs the others and is governed by none, namely the verb' (Sigerus de Cortraco (Siger de Courtrai) 1977 [c.1330]: 51). Let it be mentioned that Sībawayhi (d. c.795), the founder of the Arab linguistic tradition, applied the notion of dependency systematically in a purely language-internal sense (see Owens 1988).

Plato and Aristotle had regarded thinking as a form of silent speaking. The Stoics assumed the existence of a mental language which is free from the quirks of the oral language. The Modistae took the existence of a mental language for granted. Perhaps the most precise definition of a mental sentence (*propositio mentalis*) is given by William Ockham (c.1285–1349) in his book *Summa Totius Logicae*. William assumes that there are no universal concepts like 'man' and 'white' (referred to by the corresponding terms S and P), but only individual men and, as it were, individual occurrences of whiteness (referred to by the corresponding individual-names S-i and P-j). Hence, the meaning normally expressed by *This man is white* ought to be expressed by an identity-sentence like S-7 = P-29. The Aristotelean general sentences are now transformed accordingly, in two steps. First, universally and existentially quantified sentences like *Every S is P* and *Some S is P* are reduced to simple or non-quantified sentences, i.e. either conjunctions *S-1 is P* and *S-2 is P* and . . . or disjunctions *S-1 is P* or *S-2 is P* or . . . . This was already 'an interesting novelty' (Kneale and Kneale 1962: 268). Second, subject~predicate schemas *X is Y* and *X is not Y* are replaced by identity schemas $X = Y$ and $X \neq Y$. As a result, the general sentences are given the following truth-conditional definitions (cf. Loux 1974: 28–31):

A) Every S is P [(S-1 = P-1) $\vee$ (S-1 = P-2) $\vee$ . . .] $\wedge$ [(S-2 = P-1) $\vee$ (S-2 = P-2) $\vee$ . . .] $\wedge$ . . .
E) No S is P [(S-1 $\neq$ P-1) $\wedge$ (S-1 $\neq$ P-2) $\wedge$ . . .] $\wedge$ [(S-2 $\neq$ P-2) $\wedge$ (S-2 $\neq$ P-2) $\wedge$ . . .] $\wedge$ . . .
I) Some S is P [(S-1 = P-1) $\vee$ (S-1 = P-2) $\vee$ . . .] $\vee$ [(S-2 = P-1) $\vee$ (S-2 = P-2 $\vee$ . . .] $\vee$ . . .
O) Some S is not P [(S-1 $\neq$ P-1) $\wedge$ (S-1 $\neq$ P-2) $\wedge$ . . .] $\vee$ (S-2 $\neq$ P-2) $\wedge$ (S-2 $\neq$ P-2) $\wedge$ . . .] $\vee$ . . .

Thus, the A-sentence is reanalysed as a (finite) conjunction of disjunctions of identity-sentences: this S coincides with this P *or* that P *or*, etc. *and* that S coincides with this P *or* that P *or* etc. *and*, etc. The E-sentence is reanalysed as a conjunction (of conjunctions) of negated identity-sentences. And so on. It goes without saying that this type of reanalysis (which is supposed to be metaphysically motivated) entails a huge gain in logical simplicity. Certainly, the analysis of sentences with proper names as subjects is less natural: asserting Socrates to be a man amounts to asserting that Socrates is identical with Socrates or with Plato or with Hermogenes, etc.

Next, sentences of increasing complexity are subjected to the same type of reanalysis. The logical structure of a complex sentence (*exponibile*) is revealed by reducing it to a set of simple sentences (*exponentes*) so as to ultimately reach the level of affirmative or negative identity-sentences. Consider the sentence *Socrates, insofar as he is a man, has a colour*. Mechanical rules are given to reduce it to the following more basic sentences: *Socrates has a colour*; *Socrates is a man*; *Every man has a colour*; *If a man exists, then something which has a colour exists*. This type of *expositio* analysis was also practised, even if less rigorously, by the Modistae. For instance, the sentence *Sedentem ambulare est impossibile* 'It is impossible for a sitting person to walk' was analysed as having the following three-level ('deep') structure: [[[*qui est sedens*] *ambulat*] *est impossibile*].

In its austerity William Ockham's metaphysics has strong affinities with the Stoic metaphysics and differs sharply from the one generally adopted by the Modistae. Since the existence of universal concepts is denied, it seems natural to assume that it is only by their names that things are kept together, as it were. Hence the designation 'nominalism.' As the redefinitions of the A, E, I, O sentences eloquently show, logical simplicity is achieved at the cost of extreme outward complexity. Certainly the language constructed by William could not function as a mental language in the sense of 'silent speaking.'

The Modistic universal grammar concentrates on ontological explanation of simple sentences, while logical linguistics as represented by William Ockham concentrates on truth-functional definition of complex sentences. In spite of their metaphysical disagreements, these two approaches should be thought of as complementing rather than contradicting each other. The linguistics of the Renaissance stays far behind what was accomplished in the Middle Ages. This teaches an important lesson. It is perfectly possible that people come to reject a theory not because they have cogent arguments against it, but just because they are—or think they are—fed up with it.

The Aristotelian/Modistic heritage was exploited by all non-pedagogical grammars written in the sixteenth and seventeenth centuries. For instance, *Grammaire générale et raisonnée*, or the Port-Royal grammar (1660), by Claude Lancelot and Antoine Arnauld, concentrates on the first two terms of the Aristotelean trichotomy concept—sentence—syllogism. Peter Abelard had already postulated three mental processes corresponding to these three levels (plus a specific process for forming disjunctive/conditional sentences). In the same vein, the Port-Royal grammarians and logicians (see below) postulate the three processes of conceiving (*concevoir*), judging (*juger*), and inferring (*raisonner*). Conceiving produces an 'idea,' and judging consists in combining two ideas to make an affirmation. (Inversely, a negation entails separating the two ideas.) A judgment is called a 'proposition'; what is affirmed is called 'attribute' while that about which it is affirmed is called 'subject'; the subject is combined with the attribute by means of an explicit or implicit copula. There are two basic ontological categories, substance and accident, with noun and adjective/participle as their linguistic counterparts.

If someone says *I just saw a dog*, what (s)he means is that (s)he saw a certain thing, not that (s)he saw an idea of this thing. In his authoritative formulation of the language—mind—reality trichotomy in *De Interpretatione*, however, Aristotle clearly states that words signify ideas (or 'mental experiences'), not things; it is by ideas that things are signified. This unfortunate formulation gave rise to misunderstandings which are still perpetuated in the philosophy of the seventeenth and eighteenth centuries, including the Port-Royal grammar. As against this, William Ockham echoes Peter Abelard in asserting quite explicitly that both spoken words and ideas (= 'mental words') signify things, even if the former do so 'in subordination' to the latter.

According to the Port-Royal grammarians, the complex sentence, or 'figurative construction,' *Dieu invisible a créé le monde visible* '[The] invisible God has created the visible world' is derived from the following 'simple constructions': *Dieu est invisible, Dieu a créé le monde, Le monde est visible*. This is a continuation of the medieval *expositio*. And of course, Apollonius Dyscolus had already noted the transformational relations between participle constructions, relative constructions, and co-ordinate constructions.

The three above-mentioned mental processes are dealt with in the first three parts of *La logique, ou l'art de penser*, or the Port-Royal logic (1662), by Antoine Arnauld and Pierre Nicole. In conformity with Descartes, innate ideas are assumed to be identical with those in God's mind. Ideas *qua* mental terms may be either singular or general, their linguistic counterparts being proper nouns and common nouns. The intension (*compréhension*) of a general term X is the set of attributes which constitute it. This encompasses not just the meaning of X but also what it entails. The extension (*étendue*) of X encompasses, somewhat inconsistently, both the subtypes of X and the individuals to which X applies. The intension and the extension of X are inversely proportional. The 'quasi-mathematical' presentation of syllogistic by Arnauld and Nicole 'continued to dominate the treatment of logic by most philosophers for the next 200 years' (Kneale and Kneale 1962: 319–20). The fourth part of the Port-Royal logic, which deals with general methodology, shows the influence of *Discours de la méthode* by Descartes. Special emphasis is placed on axiomatics: '[One ought] to prove all propositions which are at all obscure, using in the proof of them only preceding definitions, agreed axioms, and propositions already demonstrated.'

The tradition of the Port-Royal grammar was continued by César Chesnau Dumarsais (1676–1757) and by Nicolas Beauzée (1717–1789), each of whom produced his own version of general grammar.[7]

34.4 THE MODERN ERA

34.4.1 Diachronic and Typological Linguistics

August Schleicher (1821–1868) was a champion of diachronic linguistics: 'If we do not know how something has come into being, we do not understand it.' But he is no less a champion of typological linguistics: 'We do not comprehend the essence of a language unless we relate it to other languages.' In his 1850 *Linguistische Untersuchungen* (quoted from Arens 1969: 251–5) he follows the preceding tradition insofar as he divides the object of diachronic linguistics into two clearly separate parts. The prehistory of languages is characterized by progress whereas their documented history is characterized by decline. The former contains an ascending three-stage development monosyllabic structure (*Einsilbigkeit*) > Agglutination > Flexion, on the analogy of mineral > plant > animal. The latter contains a degeneration of synthetic into analytic languages, as had already been proclaimed by August von Schlegel (1767–1845) in 1818 (cf. Arens 1969: 189). In 1850 Schleicher regards diachronic linguistics as a natural science pure and simple, and in 1863 he reasserts this position. Methodological monism is unmistakeably the order of the day ('Die Richtung der Neuzeit läuft unverkennbar auf Monismus hinaus'; Arens 1969: 259).

In his 1875 book *The Life and Growth of Language* William Dwight Whitney (1827–94) too recognizes what is the *Zeitgeist* 'in these days when the physical sciences are filling men's minds with wonder at their achievements' (pp. 310–11). But he prefers to go against the current: 'There is no way of claiming a physical character for the study of [linguistic] phenomena except by a thorough misapprehension of their nature' (p. 311). Why is it a misapprehension? Because no linguistic change 'calls for the admission of

---

[7] See Ch. 17 above.

any other efficient force than reasonable action, the action for a definable purpose, of the speakers of language' (p. 144). And reasonable actions flow from 'the faculty of adapting means to ends, of apprehending a desirable purpose and attaining it' (p. 145). Every change is the result of a 'choice' prompted by the 'human will' even though all this happens 'without any reflective consciousness' (p. 146).

In essence, Hermann Paul's conception of linguistic change is the same as Whitney's. All languages share the goal (*Ziel*) of establishing a one-to-one correspondence between meanings and forms ('für das funktionell Gleiche auch den gleichen lautlichen Ausdruck zu schaffen,' 1880 [1920]: 227). But this 'symmetry of the form system' is constantly being destroyed by sound change. The principal means (*Mittel*) of mending the damages caused by sound change is analogy. Thus, from a bird's-eye view, the history of any language is an eternal tug-of-war, governed by a means–ends strategy, between two opposite tendencies, material and intellectual (p. 198). In the same spirit Roman Jakobson (1896–1982) later outlines a 'means–end model of language' (1990a).

Saussure (1916: 115–16) regarded linguistic change as affecting single units only, which means that diachronic linguistics, unlike synchronic linguistics, cannot be a systematic or structure-based discipline. This is clearly not true, as was noted by Roman Jakobson in his 1931 article 'Prinzipien der historischen Phonologie.' The prime example of diachronic structuralism is given by André Martinet (1908–99) in his 1955 book *Économie des changements phonétiques*, which adds an important correction to Paul's view of linguistic change. Instead of merely being a destructive force, sound change contains its own tug-of-war: on the one hand, there is the intellectual effort to maintain the 'stability' of phonological systems; on the other, due to 'the inertia and the asymmetry of the articulatory organs,' there is the tendency to disrupt this stability (1955: 89, 101). Martinet notes (pp. 67, 97) that he was to some extent anticipated by Trubetzkoy, who mentioned in 1933 that sound change is characterized by a 'tendency towards harmony.'

If linguistic change is explained as being a means that speakers (subconsciously) consider adequate for achieving a given goal, then the corresponding explanation must qualify as teleological. (Alternative designations are 'functional explanation,' 'explanation by reasons,' and 'rational explanation'.) This type of explanation may be difficult to accept because it is nonexistent in the natural sciences. This is why Martinet hesitates (1955: 18, 97) to call his explanations 'teleological,' although he otherwise agrees (pp. 16–17) with Paul that what he is trying to do is give causal explanations of linguistic change. There is another problem as well. Natural-science explanations are not just non-teleological, but they are also nomological, i.e. based on either deterministic or statistical laws. Thus Lass (1980), for instance, sees little or no value in diachronic linguistics because of its non-nomological character. The other option is, obviously, to accept the basic fact that linguistic behaviour (like intelligent human behaviour in general) is prompted by a non-nomological type of causation (see Itkonen 1983).

Since the 1990s it has become fashionable to view linguistic change in Darwinist terms. This is an interesting return to the position that Schleicher held in the 1860s. But the analogy between biological evolution and linguistic change is clearly defective.

In general, those who subscribe to Darwinism are willing to admit that linguistic change involves some sort of problem-solving. In maximally general terms, adopting a given means is a solution to the problem of attaining the end. But this produces a contradiction: 'No evolutionary change of any kind came about through the application of intelligence and knowledge to the solution of a problem' (Cohen 1986: 125).

Von der Gabelentz and Sapir are among the pioneers of typological thinking. The foundations of modern typological linguistics were laid by Joseph Greenberg (1915–2001) in the two books edited by him, *Language Universals* (1966) and the four-volume *Universals of Human Language* (1978). The basic thesis is that, as conjectured by Plato and Varro and confirmed by cross-linguistic regularities, grammatical categories and/ or constructions have been shaped, and should accordingly be explained, by the functions they serve. For instance, such explanatory notions have been proposed as iconicity, economy, cognitive salience, and animacy hierarchy (i.e. 1/2 person singular > human > animate > inanimate). It seems clear enough that the access to such notions is provided, ideally, by the linguist's empathy, or his/her capacity to reconstruct those thought processes that the speakers of the various languages must have undergone.

This view is as old as typological linguistics itself: 'we need to put ourselves precisely in the nomenclator's place, apprehending just his acquired resources of expression and his habits of thought and speech as founded on them; realizing just his insight of the new conception and his impulses to express it' (Whitney 1875: 143). According to Paul (1880: 349), such a process as suffixation must be made 'psychologically understand-able' (*psychologisch begreifbar*); this is what historical explanation amounts to in practice. Havers (1931: 211–12) demands that, however difficult it may be, one must get rid of the thought habits of one's mother tongue in order to achieve a 'total empathy (*Einfühlung*) with the mental reality of the alien language.' Hockett (1955: 147) correctly points out that 'we know of no set of procedures by which . . . a machine could analyze a phonologic system. . . . The only rules that can be described are rules for a human investigator, and depend essentially on his ability to empathize.' Talmy Givón (b. 1936) concludes this list of methodologically crucial citations: 'the scientist merely recapitu-lates the bio-organism' (2005: 204).

Whitney (1875) describes the genesis of new word forms as follows: 'suffixes of derivation and inflection are made out of independent words, which . . . gradually lose their independent character, and finally come to be . . . mere subordinate elements . . . in more elaborate structures' (p. 124). This process, which of course encompasses more than just suffixation, is called *Komposition* (= 'condensation') by Paul (1880), who characterizes it as 'the normal way that anything formal emerges in a language' (p. 325). Today it is called grammaticalization. It was the central topic of nineteenth-century linguistics, launched by Franz Bopp. Eclipsed by synchronic structural and/or genera-tive analysis during most of the twentieth century, it was rediscovered in the 1970s.

The process of grammaticalization has been shown to follow a large set of well-documented 'paths', many of which are listed by Heine and Kuteva (2002). This means that linguistic change, though still non-nomological, has become predictable at least to some extent. Now that grammaticalization theory has been integrated into typological linguistics, it is generally agreed that any synchronic description not embedded in a wider historical context is just as deficient as any description without typological background. 'The linguist who asks "Why?" must be a historian' (Haspelmath 1999: 205). Following the spiral (rather than cycle) of history, we have returned—on a higher plane—to Schleicher's and Paul's position.

34.4.2 The Modern European Tradition

From the beginning of the nineteenth century, the history of languages became the focus of attention. Karl Ferdinand Becker tried to revitalize the tradition of general or philosophical grammar in his *Organism der Sprache* (1827, 2nd edn 1841), but his work was largely ignored. The same is true of Anton Marty's (1847–1914) efforts to elicit the 'inner form' of language. Similarly, Edmund Husserl's (1859–1938) notion of a 'pure grammar,' as defined in his *Logische Untersuchungen* (2nd edn 1913), failed to have an impact on linguistics. Parret's (1976) interpretation of Marty and Husserl is informed by more recent developments in linguistics.

Hermann Paul (1846–1921) is a central figure at this juncture insofar as his methodology constitutes a synthesis of general linguistic theory and of diachronic linguistics. For quite some time, most of his successors in the field of general theorizing showed little interest in diachronic linguistics. Ultimately, however, there has been a massive *de facto* return to the position held by Paul.

The following account of Paul's views is based on the Introduction and chapters 1 and 2 of his *Prinzipien der Sprachgeschichte* (Principles of the History of Language) (1st edition 1880). Methodology (*Prinzipienlehre*) is the key for transcending the outdated dichotomy between philosophy and science. Each science has its own methodology. There are two basic types of science: nomothetic sciences (*Gesetzeswissenschaften*) and historical sciences (*Geschichtswissenschaften*). Experimental physics is a typical nomothetic science. Nomothetic science does not coincide with natural science, however, because there are also sciences that concentrate on the history of either inorganic or organic nature (in particular, evolutionary theory). All cultural sciences are historical sciences. Among the cultural sciences, linguistics has achieved the most exact results, which has created the misconception that linguistics is actually a natural science. Experimental psychology (which was just emerging) is the most important auxiliary science of linguistics;[8] although nomothetic in nature, it is separated from natural sciences by the presence of the 'psychic element.'

Historical grammar is scientific in the sense that it explains the causal connection (*Kausalnexus*) between successive states of language. No non-causal account can be genuinely explanatory. A given state of language (*Sprachzustand*) is described by a corresponding (synchronic) descriptive grammar, exemplified by Paul's own grammar

---

[8] See Ch. 30 above.

of Middle High German (Paul and Mitzka 1960 [1881]). Because states of language are abstractions, descriptive grammars are non-causal and prima facie non-scientific in character. Yet they qualify as scientific in a secondary sense insofar as their existence is presupposed by historical grammar. Any descriptive grammar remains insufficient until it is completed by a psychological grammar of the same state of language. Although the two sets may overlap, grammatical categories, which result from conscious reflection, must be clearly distinguished from psychological ones, which belong to the unconscious mind. For instance, grammatical subject and predicate are quite different from psychological subject and predicate (cf. Elffers-van Ketel 1991: 253–6). Apart from actual non-correspondence, the difference consists in the fact that grammatical structure is categorical ('either/or') whereas psychological structure exhibits a huge number of subtle gradations ('more or less'). Finally, grammatical structure must also be distinguished from (purely) logical structure. (Occasionally, 'psychological' and 'logical' are also used as synonyms.)

The subject-matter of a descriptive grammar is *Sprachusus*, i.e. the usage of a linguistic community, which averages (*Durchschnitt*) over idiolects. Linguistics differs from other cultural sciences insofar as there is no division of labour among its subjects apart from the speaker/hearer dichotomy. It is this homogeneity of the data that has made it possible for linguistics to achieve such exact results. It is for the same reason that the usage can be investigated in practice by concentrating on a single individual. When this is the grammarian him/herself, careful self-observation is needed.

Language usage is constantly renewed in social interaction. The language of every individual is influenced by the language of others. Unlike in biological evolution, 'parents can become children of their own children.' The contact between two minds is possible only by means of an external physical signal sent by one person and received by the other. What we know or assume about other minds is based on the analogy of our own mind. There is no collective mind in addition to individual minds. Finally, there is the central question of linguistic methodology: how do the social *Sprachusus* and the linguistic activity of an individual (*individuelle Sprechtätigkeit*) influence each other?

Georg von der Gabelentz (1840–93) raises the same question in his *Sprachwissenschaft* 'Linguistics' (1901 [1891]), assuming a dichotomy between *Einzelsprache* or *Sprachzustand* 'a language' and its concrete manifestation, i.e. *Rede* 'speech.' The former is a system whose parts are related in such an organic way that none can be changed or removed without affecting the whole (p. 481).

The same question is also raised by Ferdinand de Saussure (1857–1913) in *Cours de linguistique générale* (1916). For him the social aspect (*langue*) is clearly primary vis-à-vis the individual aspect (*parole*) and constitutes therefore the genuine subject-matter of linguistics. (Remember that according to Paul the equivalent of *langue* is the subject-matter of descriptive grammar which remains subordinated to historical grammar.) Yet it is enough to investigate the consciousness of individual speakers (i.e. their linguistic intuition) in order to elicit the properties of *langue*. Saussure uses the term *langage* to designate the superordinate concept which subsumes both *langue* and *parole*. *Langage* in turn issues from the language capacity (*faculté de langage*), which is natural rather than social (like *langue*) or mental (like *parole*). Moreover, since *parole* is characterized as an 'act' (of speaking and understanding), it must encompass the psycho-physiological performances on the one hand and the physical utterances, on the other. Saussure's overall conception is narrower than Paul's. Diachrony is of secondary importance only; *parole* is clearly subordinated to *langue*; and there is no room for psychological grammar as study of the unconscious mind. The 'linguistic sign' is characterized as a 'mental entity' (*entité psychique*) consisting of a 'concept' and an 'acoustic image,' also called 'signified' and 'signifier,' respectively. *Langue* is said to be constituted by linguistic signs, but this is inconsistent because *langue* is defined as 'a social institution' whereas, as we just saw, the linguistic sign is individual-psychological. The same contradiction recurs in the passages where *langue* is located 'in the brain.'

A further distinction is introduced within both components of the linguistic sign, namely that between 'substance' and 'form.' The substance of the signifier is constituted by the whole spectrum of vocal sounds, while the substance of the signified is something like thought without conceptual distinctions. By 'form' is meant the way that each language structures the two substances. The notion of form is defined more narrowly as that of 'value.' The values, or identities, of linguistic units are determined by their mutual relations. This is the core idea of structuralism.

Linguistic signs are simultaneously situated on two dimensions, syntagmatic and associative. The latter term is used in its etymological sense, i.e. as standing for the relation between a linguistic sign X and anything that X can make the speaker think of, due to the similarity of either form or of meaning. Thus, 'associative relation' is identical with what Paul called *Verbindung zwischen Vorstellungsgruppen*.

In his (1939) *Grundzüge der Phonologie* Nikolaj Sergeyevich Trubetzkoy (1890–1938) solves the contradictions that beset Saussure's language conception (see the sections 'Phonologie und Phonetik', pp. 5–17 and 'Zur Definition des Phonems', pp 37–41). Because *langue* (here called *Sprachgebilde*) is a social institution, its units—represented by the phoneme—cannot be reduced to psychological or physiological phenomena, which belong to *parole* (*Sprechakt*). As normative entities, phonemes belong to the 'world of relations, functions, and values,' and not to the 'world of empirical phenomena.' 'The norm . . . cannot be determined by measurement and computations. . . . The system of language is beyond "measurement and number". . . . [In] the natural sciences there is no equivalent for the dichotomy *Sprachgebilde* vs *Sprechakt*.' Because structure is created by function, structuralism *is* functionalism. It is regrettable that Trubetzkoy's philosophical contribution has remained either ignored or misunderstood.

In his (1961 [1943]) book *Prolegomena to a Theory of Language* Louis Hjelmslev (1899–1965) summarizes Saussure's language conception as the following set of dichotomies: system vs process, expression vs content, form vs substance, syntagmatic vs paradigmatic. These dichotomies are integrated into a closely knit theory, and three 'functions' are added between formally defined units, namely 'interdependence' (= if A, then B, and vice versa), 'determination' (= if A, then B or not-B, and if B, then A), and 'constellation' (= if A, then B or not-B, and vice versa). Hjelmslev seeks to use these three functions as the basis for constructing a universally valid descriptive technique tantamount to a universal grammar. First, grammars of particular languages and, second, all and only correct sentences of each language ought to be derived from the overall theory. This approach, called 'glossematics,' seems to result in a somewhat skeletal view of language.⁹ But it is precisely for this reason, on the other hand, that it provides a plausible framework for general semiotics. Glossematics is presented as an axiomatic theory. Therefore it is natural that when alternative descriptive techniques are evaluated, 'that procedure must be chosen which ensures the simplest possible result of the description' (Spang-Hanssen 1966 [1948]: 234). But there is no absolute notion of simplicity. Rather, 'the simplicity of a description... is a relative concept, which has significance only if the purpose to which the description is applied is indicated' (p. 235).

34.4.3 American Structuralism and its Aftermath

At this point we must go back to the beginning of the twentieth century in order to pick up the story of American structuralism.¹⁰ Franz Boas (1858–1942) edited the *Handbook of American Indian Languages*, the first volume of which appeared in 1911, and which laid the foundations of anthropological linguistics. The Introduction of this book entails an interesting tension. On the one hand, the purpose is to capture the 'inner form of each language,' with the consequence that 'no attempt has been made to compare the forms of the Indian grammars with the grammars of English, Latin or even among themselves' (Boas 1911: 81). On the other hand, it is clear that 'the occurrence of the most fundamental grammatical concepts *in all languages* must be considered as proof of the unity of the fundamental psychological processes' (p. 71; emphasis added).

The same tension is evident in Edward Sapir's (1884–1939) *Language*, published in 1921. In his sentence analysis (pp 35–6) Sapir unknowingly follows the example of Apollonius. Consider the sentence *The mayor of New York is going to deliver a speech of welcome in French*. This sentence can be simplified by deleting *of New York, of welcome*, and *in French*, but at this point the 'process of reduction' must stop. For instance **Mayor is going to deliver* would be incorrect. What remains is the familiar Aristotelian dichotomy of 'subject of discourse' and 'predicate,' which combine to constitute 'the linguistic expression of a proposition.' This is also the definition of 'sentence.' The sentence analysis has an ontological justification: 'We must have objects, actions, qualities to talk about, and these must have their corresponding symbols in independent words or in radical elements' (p. 93). While 'subject' and 'predicate' are functional notions, the corresponding formal notions are 'noun' and 'verb,' which have thing and action as their extralinguistic counterparts. Nothing seems to have changed since antiquity. However, the accumulated evidence from the study of Native American

---

⁹ See also §20.2.4 above.   ¹⁰ See Ch. 18 above.

languages induces Sapir to boldly assert that 'no logical scheme of parts of speech . . . is of the slightest interest to the linguist. Each language has its own scheme' (p. 119). But then the following concession has to be made immediately: 'No language wholly fails to distinguish noun and verb.' Like Hermann Paul, Sapir regards linguistics as a cultural science but, unlike Paul, he wishes to keep linguistics strictly separate from psychology: 'We can profitably discuss the intention, the form, and the history of speech . . . as an institutional or cultural entity, leaving the organic and psychological mechanisms back of it as something to be taken for granted' (p. 11). Let it be added that when Sapir (1933) deals with the 'psychological reality of phonemes,' what he has in mind is conformity with 'phonemic/phonological intuitions,' not some unconscious structure to be elicited by experimental psychology.

In his 1933 *Language*, Leonard Bloomfield (1887–1949) shares Sapir's view of the proper relation between linguistics and psychology: 'we can pursue the study of language without reference to any one psychological doctrine' (p. vii). 'The findings of the linguist, who studies the speech signal, will be all the more valuable for the psychologist if they are not distorted by any prepossessions about psychology' (p. 32). Indeed, Hermann Paul is criticized precisely for having tried to include psychological grammar in linguistics: '[Paul] accompanies his statements about language with a paraphrase in terms of mental processes which the speakers are supposed to have undergone. The only evidence for these mental processes is the linguistic process; they add nothing to the discussion, but only obscure it' (p. 17). This criticism applies with more justification to the Aristotelian-*cum*-Modistic tradition that preceded Paul than to Paul himself because, instead of just paraphrasing, he actually tried to show that 'mental processes' and 'linguistic processes' do not coincide. Certainly, as he freely admits, he was hampered in this attempt by the nascent state of experimental psychology.

Bloomfield has been hugely criticized for not heeding his own advice and thus dismissing the analysis of lexical meanings in the name of crude behaviouristic psychology. This agrees with his endorsement of 'logical empiricism,' or the prevalent philosophical doctrine of the 1930s, which advocated methodological monism, with physics as the model science. But the criticism is not quite accurate. Being a grammarian, Bloomfield is interested in grammatical rather than lexical meanings; and his treatment of grammatical meanings (= '[epi]sememes') is in no way distorted by any behaviourist prepossessions. This is just as true of an 'episememe' like 'action' (1933: 166) as it is of a 'sememe' like 'more than one thing' (1933: 216). Bloomfield's behaviourism merely exemplifies the all-too-common gulf between one's self-professed methodology and the methodology implicit in one's actual descriptive practice.

In principle, Bloomfield (1933) portrays grammatical description from the perspective of a field linguist who has to start from scratch: 'Suppose we hear a speaker say *John ran* and a little later hear him or some other speaker say *John fell.* . . . [I]f we are lucky, we may hear some one utter the form *John!* . . . we may later hear the form *Bill ran* . . . we may hear a form like *Dan fell*' (p. 159). In practice, however, no corpus of actually uttered sentences is ever used in this book. Rather, Bloomfield just lets his own linguistic intuition produce the data, as he did in the passage just cited. The practice of the ordinary working grammarian is sanctioned in the following way: 'In no respect are the activities of a group as rigidly standardized as in the forms of language.... A linguistic observer therefore can describe the speech-habits of a community without resorting to statistics' (p. 37). The implications of this fact for the general philosophy of science have been spelled out by Hymes and Fought (1981: 175): 'It was considered a decisive accomplishment to show the existence of qualitative structure in a sphere of human life.... Linguistics was a demonstration of the possibility of rigorous formal analysis of a sort not requiring sampling, statistics, or other techniques derivative of a natural science orientation.'

Zellig S. Harris (1909–92) and Charles F. Hockett (1916–2000) further develop the structuralist approach. For Bloomfield (1933: 247–51), a 'substitute' is a minimal unit (like *I* or *did*) that can replace any member of a given form-class. Harris (1946) concentrates on 'extending the technique of substitution from single morphemes (e.g. *man*) to sequences of morphemes (e.g. *intense young man*).' Expressions of whatever length that pass the 'substitution test' are members of one and the same 'substitution class.' Substitution classes constitute the basis for a bottom-up sentence analysis. Wells (1947) reformulates substitution as 'expansion.' For instance, the sentence *The king of England opened Parliament* is an expansion of the sentence *John worked*. Expansion is the inverse of, and conceptually equivalent to, reduction as practiced by Apollonius and Sapir. Expansion constitutes the basis for a top-down sentence analysis in terms of immediate constituents (= IC). Typically, the IC analysis is binary in the sense of breaking up a unit into two lower-level units, but a constituent may also have three (or more) parts, as in *A, B, and C*. Also discontinuous constituents are allowed: an indefinite number of adjectives may occur inside the constituent *the ... king*.

Harris (1946) recommends choosing those descriptive devices 'in terms of which we get the most convenient total description'. As in glossematics, the ultimate criterion for preferring one description to another is the overall simplicity.

Echoing Varro, Bloomfield (1933: 275) notes that, as far as speech forms are concerned, 'the possibilities of combination are practically infinite.' Hockett (1948) makes the same point: the linguist must 'account also for utterances which are NOT in his corpus ... he must be able to predict what OTHER utterances the speakers of the language might produce.' Hockett (1949) adds that grammatical description constitutes a 'recurrent cycle of prediction, checking, gathering of new data, modification of predictions, and rechecking.' Harris (1951: 17) agrees: 'when the linguist offers his results as a system representing the language as a whole, he is predicting that the elements set up for his corpus will satisfy all other bits of talking in that language.'

Bloomfield (1926) purports to present his language conception in the axiomatic format of metalinguistic 'assumptions' and 'definitions.' Similarly, Harris (1951: 372–3) assumes that his grammar-conception amounts to a 'deductive system with axiomatically defined initial elements and with theorems concerning them. The final theorems would indicate the structure of the utterances of the language.' Such a description would 'enable anyone to synthesize or predict utterances in the language.' In practice, Harris's 'deductive system' is much too intricate to be applied by just 'anyone'. Hockett (1954) uses the term 'generate' instead of 'synthesize.'

Harris (1951) views utterances as purely physical phenomena which should be described with no recourse to meaning. This position is so extreme that none of the contemporary reviewers of the book was willing to accept it wholesale (cf. Hymes and Fought 1981: 146–7). 'No one has ever really done linguistics in that way,' as Chafe (1994: 14) was to observe later.

Saussure (1916), Hjelmselv (1943), Sapir (1921), Bloomfield (1933), and Harris (1951) are not concerned with any of those psychological or biological mechanisms that support language. By contrast, Hockett (1948) claims that insofar as the linguist is acting like a genuine scientist, his 'analytical process thus parallels what goes on in the nervous system of a language learner, particularly, perhaps, that of a child learning his first language.' Thus, it is the speaker, and not the linguist, who creates linguistic structure: 'The child in time comes to BEHAVE the language; the linguist must come to STATE it.'

In the 1940s Harris was perceived as advocating a conception of 'linguistics as a game,' to such an extent that Hockett (1968: 35) could later refer to 'Harris's theoretical nihilism.' But Harris (1954) clearly involves a change of attitude: 'Mathematical and other methods of arranging data are not a game.' Nor is language viewed any more as an entirely self-contained entity: 'the position of the speakers is after all similar to that of the linguist.'

In his 1955 dissertation, Noam Chomsky (b. 1928) subscribes to Bloomfield's anti-mentalism (p. 86) and declares his concern with the 'physical properties of utterances' in the sense of Harris-type distributional analysis (p. 127, p.63 fn 1). Unlike his predecessors, he restricts his data to English. His 1957 *Syntactic Structures* is based on a set of thirty-nine self-invented sentences. Some of these are grammatical and either simple like *The man comes* or compound like *John enjoyed the book and liked the play*. Others are either just ungrammatical like *Lunch is eaten John* or very ungrammatical like ****Of admires John*. The grammar that he outlines has two components (apart from morphophonemics). Phrase structure (= PS) rules assign a tree-structure derivation to strings identifiable as simple sentences, while transformational (= T) rules operate either on one string with a specific derivation or on two such strings to generate more complex sentences. T-rules are needed because PS-rules (wrongly identified with IC analysis) cannot handle discontinuous constituents, active–passive relations, and *NP-and-NP* or *S-and-S* conjunctions: '[T-rules] lead to an entirely new conception of linguistic structure' (p. 44). The resulting bipartite grammar is supposed to give an adequate description to all grammatical sentences, whether simple or complex, of any language.[11]

But this is the real novelty: 'the set of "sentences" of some formalized system of mathematics can be considered a language [and vice versa]' (Chomsky 1957a: 13). More precisely, 'the idea of a generative grammar emerged from an *analogy* with categorial systems in logic. The idea was to treat grammaticality like theoremhood in logistic systems

---

[11] See Ch. 19 above.

and to treat grammatical structure like proof structure in derivations' (Katz 1981: 36, emphasis added). This is a striking illustration of how scientific discovery is driven by analogy (see Itkonen 2005: 16–19, 190–6). As a result, a generative grammar turns out to be, technically speaking, an axiomatic system (cf. Wall 1972: 197–212). The initial S-symbol qualifies as the sole axiom, while the function of inference rules is performed, first, by structure-expanding PS-rules and second, by structure-changing T-rules. It is only the terminal string of the entire derivation that is supposed to qualify as grammatical. (An axiomatic theory, by contrast, has a property, i.e. either empirical truth or validity, which is transferred from axioms to theorems by inference rules.) Thus, in *Syntactic Structures*, it is the formalization of morphosyntax that is genuinely new. The grammatical analysis itself is thoroughly traditional, starting with the Aristotelian *NP* + *VP* dichotomy.

What is the methodological status of generative description? This question is answered in very dissimilar ways. First, generative description is identified with conceptual analysis as practiced in philosophy: 'We thus face a familiar task of explication of some intuitive concept—in this case, the concept 'grammatical in English'' (Chomsky 1957a: 13). But then it is the natural sciences that provide the model: '[A chemical theory] might be said to generate all physically possible compounds just as a grammar generates all grammatically "possible" utterances' (p. 48). In the same vein, grammatical categories (like *NP* or *T*) are equated with hypothetical constructs (like 'electron'), and grammatical rules (like *NP* → *T* + *N* and *T* → *the*) are equated with laws of nature (p. 49).

Thus, Chomsky does not merely perpetuate the axiomatic tradition in linguistics, but makes it fully explicit. The commitment to axiomatics is also evident from the central role that he, like Hjelmslev, ascribes to simplicity: 'the only ultimate criterion in evaluation is the simplicity of the whole system' (1975a: 56). He even speculates (p. 51) about an algorithm (called 'evaluation procedure') for choosing the simplest grammar from among several alternatives. No such algorithm has been or, most probably, will ever been found: 'Let us call a theory which obeys Ockham's razor . . . functionally simple. . . . Ockham's razor seems difficult or impossible to formalize as an algorithm' (Putnam 1981: 133).

After 1957, the generative grammar of English as envisaged by Chomsky has undergone radical modifications. It has also been given radically new interpretations. In *Aspects of a Theory of Syntax* (1965) it became both a mentalistic theory and the basis for a universal grammar. In the mid-1970s it became a biological theory: now language is a module (or 'organ') of the biologically based mind, and syntax is the central module of language. Yet Chomsky's approach to data has not changed at all. In the twenty-first century he still investigates distributional properties of such English sentences as his own intuition deems to be either grammatical or ungrammatical.

For Paul (1880: esp. ch. 3), variation was a necessary part of linguistic change. While endorsing the non-statistical nature of synchronic grammatical description (see above), Bloomfield (1933) was fully aware that any realistic account of linguistic change would be statistical in character: 'These changes could be observed only by means of genuinely statistical observation through a considerable length of time; for want of this, we are ignorant of many matters concerning linguistic change' (p. 38). But the situation has changed dramatically since Bloomfield's time. In the mid-1960s sociolinguistics, through the 'variationist paradigm,' was developed to deal with exactly those types of phenomena that Bloomfield placed beyond the ken of linguistics.[12]

To be sure, what is at issue is not just variation in change, but variation in general. As formulated by William Labov (b. 1927), 'the problem is how observation and experiment are to relate to intuitive data' (1975: 54). He provides a balanced answer with many gradations, which may be summarized as follows. As far as the so-called clear cases are concerned, 'we can ... study the social aspect of language through the intuitions of one or two individuals' (p. 9). Consider these sentences: *That John told him was a shame* and **John told him was a shame*. Here the difference in grammaticalness is so clear-cut that 'no one has as yet found any disagreements that would move us to begin a program of observation and experiment' (p. 8). Outside the clear cases, however, linguistic intuition is not enough, and it is here that a statistical approach becomes a necessity. Two principal cases may be distinguished: either the data are so complex or otherwise indeterminate that intuitions diverge; or the data are constituted by frequencies of occurrence, and here intuition is unreliable by definition. Rather than being 'free,' variation typically turns out to be conditioned, and thus explained, by extraneous linguistic or non-linguistic factors.

For the most part, linguistic distinctions are not categorical but gradual. This is true of e.g. grammatical vs ungrammatical, obligatory vs optional, noun vs not-noun. (But notice that the difference between the two extremes of a continuum is absolute, not relative.) Just as categorical distinctions are based on two-valued logic, continuous distinctions are based on fuzzy logic (which is in turn a direct descendant of Jan Łukasiewics's many-valued logic; cf. Kosko 1994). Any adequate linguistic theory should be able to deal not just with variation but also with fuzziness.

These and similar concerns ensured that the methodological status of linguistics in general, and of generative linguistics in particular, became the object of intense controversy in mid- and late 1970s: see the collections of articles such as Cohen (1974), Cohen and Wirth (1975), and Perry (1980).

In the 1970s and 1980s Chomsky claimed that linguistics is part of cognitive psychology and cognitive psychology is part of biology. Montague (1974b) and Katz (1981) countered by claiming linguistics to be a branch of logic or mathematics. Many felt that generativism offered a much too impoverished view of what cognition is really about. As a result, the school of Cognitive Linguistics came into being: 'it opened language description to a rich new landscape of conceptual phenomena and mechanisms interrelated in multiple ways with the whole of human experience and shaped in accordance with patterns of human imagination' (Harder 2007: 1247–8).

The first-generation cognitivists like Lakoff (1987), Langacker (1987), and Talmy (2000a, b) make use of exactly the same data basis as their generativist predecessors, namely their own respective intuitions (almost exclusively of English).[13] To second-generation cognitivists, this is not enough. Rather, contacts have to be (re)established

---

[12] See Ch. 29 above.   [13] See Ch. 21 above.

with main-stream psychology by adopting a set of statistical-*cum*-experimental techniques (cf. Gonzalez-Marquez et al. 2007). On the other hand, the exclusive concern with the individual mind has to be transcended by squarely accepting the primarily social nature of language (cf. Zlatev et al. 2008).

34.5 CONCLUSION

The need for, and the nature of, explanation as well as the idea of axiomatics have been shown to be central themes in recounting the philosophy of linguistics. Katz (1981: 52, 64–8) outlines the notion of an 'optimal grammar' which, free from any non-grammatical (i.e. psychological, sociological or neurological) constraints, should be based on the notion of overall simplicity. Here 'optimal' clearly equals 'axiomatic', and Pāṇini's grammar, 'the most complete generative grammar of any language yet written' (Kiparsky 1993: 2912), is so far the most likely candidate for an optimal grammar. A few qualifications, however, need to be added.

Even within formal logic, axiomatics is by no means the only alternative. For instance, the so-called dialogical logic dispenses with the 'traditional recourse to the axiomatic method' (Lorenzen and Lorenz 1978: 19). Being a 'reconstruction' of the norms of everyday language and thus embodying the social nature not just of language but also of logic, it is clearly superior to axiomatic logic (see Itkonen 2003: ch. 4).

Within linguistics, furthermore, the axiomatic ideal applies only to the grammatical theory, i.e. the subdiscipline discussed in Itkonen (1978). Everywhere else, i.e. in diachronic linguistics, sociolinguistics, and psycholinguistics, causal explanation is to be preferred. This view was adumbrated by Hermann Paul, and also agrees with the more recent developments within the philosophy of the natural sciences: 'A scientific theory admits of many different axiomatizations, and the postulates chosen in a particular one need not, therefore, correspond to what in some more substantial sense might count as the basic assumptions of the theory' (Hempel 1970: 152). This 'more substantial sense' refers to the causal structure of the research object, to be described by a corresponding causal model.

Salmon (1984) comes to the same conclusion: 'It now seems to me that the statistical relationships specified in the S[tatistical]–R[elevance] model constitute the *statistical basis* for a bona fide scientific explanation, but that this basis must be supplemented by certain *causal factors* in order to constitute a satisfactory scientific explanation' (p. 34, original emphasis). It is this aspect of linguistics that is focused on in Itkonen (1983).

References

Aarsleff, Hans, 1982. *From Locke to Saussure: Essays on the Study of Language and Intellectual History*. Minneapolis: University of Minnesota Press.

Aarts, Jan, 2006. Corpus linguistics, grammar and theory: report on a panel discussion at the 24th ICAME conference. In Antoinette Renouf and Andrew Kehoe (eds), *The Changing Face of Corpus Linguistics*. Amsterdam: Rodopi: 391–401.

Abeillé, Anne, and Owen Rambow (eds), 2000. *Tree Adjoining Grammars: Formalisms, Linguistic Analysis and Processing*. Stanford, CA: CSLI.

Abelin, Asa, 1998. Swedish phonesthemes. *Proceedings of FONETIK 98*. Stockholm: Department of Linguistics, Stockholm University.

Abercrombie, David, 1948. Forgotten phoneticians. *Transactions of the Philological Society* 1–34.

Abercrombie, David, 1949. What is a 'letter'? *Lingua* 2: 54–63. [Repr. in Abercrombie (1965: 76–85).]

Abercrombie, David, 1957. Direct palatography. *Zeitschrift für Phonetik und allgemeine Sprachwissenschaft* 10: 21–5. [Repr. in Abercrombie (1965: 125–30).]

Abercrombie, David, 1965. *Studies in Phonetics and Linguistics*. London: Oxford University Press.

Abercrombie, David, 1981. Extending the Roman alphabet: some orthographic experiments of the past four centuries. In Ronald E. Asher and Eugénie J. A. Henderson (eds), *Towards a History of Phonetics*. Edinburgh: Edinburgh University Press, 107–224.

Abney, Steven P., 1991. Parsing by chunks. In Robert C. Berwick, Steven P. Abney, and Carol Tenny (eds), *Principle-Based Parsing: Computation and Psycholinguistics*. Dordrecht: Kluwer Academic, 157–278.

Abramson, Arthur. S., Theraphan L.-Thongkum, and Patrick Nye, 2004. Voice register in Suai (Kuai): an analysis of perceptual and acoustic data. *Phonetica* 61: 147–71.

Ackerman, Farrell, James P. Blevins, and Rob Malouf, 2009. Parts and wholes: implicative patterns in inflectional paradigms. In James P. Blevins and Juliette Blevins (eds), *Analogy in Grammar: Form and Acquisition*. Oxford: Oxford University Press, 54–81.

Ackrill, John L. (ed.), 1987. *A New Aristotle Reader*. Oxford: Clarendon Press.

Adam, Jean-Michel, 1990. *Éléments de linguistique textuelle: théorie et pratique de l'analyse textuelle*. Liège: Mardaga.

Adelung, Friedrich, 1781. *Über den Ursprung der Sprachen und den Bau der Wörter, besonders der deutschen. Ein Versuch*. Leipzig: Breitkopf.

Adelung, Friedrich, 1806–17. *Mithridates oder allgemeine Sprachenkunde*. 4 vols. Berlin: Vossische Buchhandlung. [Only the first volume is by Adelung; the other three are by Johann Severin Vater.]

Adelung, Friedrich, 1815. *Catherinens der Grossen Verdienste um die vergleichende Sprachenkunde*. St Petersburg: Friedrich Drechsler.

Ademollo, Francesco, 2011. *The* Cratylus *of Plato: A Commentary.* Cambridge: Cambridge University Press.

Agirre, Eneko, and Philip Edmonds, 2006. *Word Sense Disambiguation: Algorithms and Applications.* Berlin: Springer.

Ahlqvist, Anders, 1982. *The Early Irish Linguist: An Edition of the Canonical Part of the* Auraicept na n-Éces. Helsinki: Societas Scientiarum Fennica.

Aijmer, Karin, 2009. So er I just sort I dunno I think it's just because . . . : a corpus study of *I don't know* and *dunno* in learners' spoken English. In Andreas Jucker, Daniel Schreier, and Marianne Hundt (eds), *Corpora: Pragmatics and Discourse: Papers from the 29th International Conference on English Language Research on Computerized Corpora* (*ICAME 29*). Amsterdam: Rodopi, 151–68.

Aijmer, Karin, Bengt Altenberg, and Mats Johansson (eds), 1996. *Language in Contrast: Papers from a Symposium on Text-Based Cross-linguistic Studies. Lund, March 1994.* Lund: Lund University Press.

Aijmer, Karin and Anna-Brita Stenström, 2004. *Discourse Patterns in Spoken and Written Corpora.* Amsterdam: Benjamins.

Aistleitner, Joseph, 1963. *Wörterbuch der ugaritischen Sprache.* Berlin: Akademie. [4th edn 1974.]

Akehurst, F. R. P., and Judith M. Davis (eds), 1995. *A Handbook of the Troubadours.* Berkeley: University of California Press.

Aklujkar, Ashok, 2010. Where do *lakṣaṇaikacakṣuṣka* and *lakṣyaikacakṣuṣka* apply? Part 2. Author-circulated PDF.

Albright, Robert W., 1958. The International Phonetic Alphabet: its background and development. *International Journal of American Linguistics* 24.1, part 3. Bloomington: Indiana University Research Center in Anthropology, Folklore, and Linguistics. [Doctoral dissertation, Stanford University, 1953.]

Aldrete, Gregory S., 1999. *Gestures and Acclamations in Ancient Rome.* Baltimore, MD: Johns Hopkins University Press.

Alexander of Villa Dei. 1893. *Doctrinale*, ed. D. Reichling. Berlin: Hofmann.

Allan, Keith, 1986. *Linguistic Meaning.* 2 vols. London: Routledge & Kegan Paul.

Allan, Keith, 2004. Aristotle's footprints in the linguist's garden. *Language Sciences* 26: 317–42.

Allan, Keith, 2010a. *The Western Classical Tradition in Linguistics.* 2nd (expanded) edn. London: Equinox. [1st edn 2007.]

Allan, Keith, 2010b. Referring as a pragmatic act. *Journal of Pragmatics* 42: 2919–31.

Allen, James, and C. Raymond Perrault, 1980. Analyzing intention in utterances. *Artificial Intelligence* 15(3): 143–78. [Repr. in Grosz et al. (1986: 441–58).]

Allen, William S., 1953. *Phonetics in Ancient India.* London: Oxford University Press.

Allen, William S., 1965. *Vox Latina: A Guide to the Pronunciation of Classical Latin.* Cambridge: Cambridge University Press.

Allen, William S., 1981. The Greek contribution to the history of phonetics. In Ronald E. Asher and Eugénie J. A. Henderson (eds), *Towards a History of Phonetics.* Edinburgh: Edinburgh University Press, 115–22.

Allen, William S., 1987. *Vox Graeca: A Guide to the Pronunciation of Classical Greek*, 3rd edn. Cambridge: Cambridge University Press.

Allott, Robin, 1995. Sound symbolism. In Udo L. Figge (ed.), *Language in the Würm Glaciation.* Bochum: Brockmeyer, 15–38.

Allport, Gordon W., 1935. Phonetic symbolism in Hungarian words. MS, Harvard University.

Al-Nassir, Abdulmunim A., 1993. *Sībawayh the Phonologist: A Critical Study of the Phonetic and Phonological Theory of Sībawayh as Presented in His Treatise Al-Kitāb*. London: Kegan Paul.

Alter, Stephen G., 2005. *William Dwight Whitney and the Science of Language*. Baltimore, MD: Johns Hopkins University Press.

Amanuma, Yasushi, 1974. *Giongo-Gitaigo Jiten* [Dictionary of Sound and Manner-Imitative Words]. Tokyo: Tokyo Publishing House.

Amman(n), Jan C., 1692. *Surdus loquens*. Amsterdam.

Amman(n), Jan C., 1700. *Dissertatio de loquela qua non solum vox humana*. Amsterdam.

Ammon, Ulrich, Klaus J. Mattheier, and Peter H. Nelde (eds), 1988. *Standardisierungsentwicklungen in europäischen Nationalsprachen: Romania, Germania [. . .]*. Tübingen: Max Niemeyer.

Amsterdamska, Olga, 1987. *Schools of Thought: The Development of Linguistics from Bopp to Saussure*. Dordrecht: D. Reidel.

Andersen, Henning, 1982. Jakob Hornemann Bredsdorff, 'On the Causes of Linguistic Change'. English translation with commentary and an essay on J. H. Bredsdorff. *Historiographia Linguistica* 9: 1–41.

Anderson, David W., and Stephen R. Lightfoot, 2002. *The Language Organ: Linguistics as Cognitive Physiology*. New York: Cambridge University Press.

Anderson, Earl R., 1998. *A Grammar of Iconism*. Madison, NJ: Farleigh Dickinson University Press.

Anderson, Stephen R., 1982. Where's morphology? *Linguistic Inquiry* 13: 571–612.

Anderson, Stephen R., 1985. *Phonology in the Twentieth Century*. Chicago: University of Chicago Press.

Anderson, Stephen R., 1992. *A-morphous Morphology*. Cambridge: Cambridge University Press.

Anderson, Stephen R., 2000. Reflections on 'On the phonetic rules of Russian'. *Folia Linguistica* 34: 11–28.

Andor, Jozef, 2004. The master and his performance: an interview with Noam Chomsky. *Intercultural Pragmatics* 1: 93–112.

Andrén, Mats, 2010. *Children's Gestures from 18 to 30 Months*. Lund: Lund University Department of Linguistics and Phonetics.

Andresen, Julie T., 1990. *Linguistics in America 1769–1924: A Critical History*. London: Routledge.

Anglade, Joseph (ed.), 1919–20. *Las Leys d'Amors*. Toulouse: Privat.

Anon., 1761. *En dansk Donat for Børn, indeholdende de første og almindeligste Sprog-Grunde; viiste i det Danske, og tienende som en Forberedelse til at lære fremmede Sprog*. Copenhagen: Berling.

Antonsen, Elmer H., 1962. Rasmus Rask and Jacob Grimm: their relationship in the investigation of Germanic vocalism. *Scandinavian Studies* 34: 183–94.

Apollonius Dyscolus, 1981. *The Syntax of Apollonius Dyscolus*, transl. with a commentary by Fred W. Householder. Amsterdam: John Benjamins.

Apresjan, Jurij D., 1966. Analyse distributionelle des significations et champs sémantiques structurés. *Langages* 1: 44–74.

Apresjan, Jurij D., 1973. Regular polysemy. *Linguistics* 142: 5–32.

Apresjan, Jurij D., 1979. *Anglo-russkij sinonimičeskii slovar'* [Dictionary of English and Russian Synonyms]. Moscow: Russkij Jazyk.

Apresjan, Jurij D., 2000. *Systematic Lexicography*, transl. Kevin Windle. Oxford: Oxford University Press.

Arbib, Michael, 2005. From monkey-like action to human language: an evolutionary framework for neurolinguistics. *Behavioral and Brain Sciences* 28: 105–67.

Arens, Hans, 1969. *Sprachwissenschaft: Der Gang ihrer Entwicklung von der Antike bis zur Gegenwart*, Band 1. Frankfurt am Main: Athenäum. [1st edn 1955.]

Arens, Hans, 1984. *Aristotle's Theory of Language and its Tradition*. Amsterdam: John Benjamins.

Aristotle, 1984. *The Complete Works of Aristotle: The Revised Oxford Translation*, ed. Jonathan Barnes. Princeton, NJ: Princeton University Press.

Armstrong, David F., William C. Stokoe, and Sherman E.Wilcox, 1995. *Gesture and the Nature of Language*. Cambridge: Cambridge University Press.

Arnauld, Antoine, and Pierre Nicole, 1965 [1683]. *La Logique, ou L'Art de Penser: contenant, outre les règles communes, plusieurs observations nouvelles propres à former le jugement*. Éd. critique par Pierre Clair et François Girbal. Paris: Presses universitaires de France. [First published 1662, final version 1683. English translation by Jill Vance Burker, *Logic or the Art of Thinking*, Cambridge University Press, 1996.]

Aronoff, Mark, 1985. Orthography and linguistic theory: the syntactic basis of Masoretic Hebrew punctuation. *Language* 61: 28–72.

Aronoff, Mark, 1994. *Morphology by Itself: Stems and Inflectional Classes*. Cambridge, MA: MIT Press.

Ars Grammatica Groupe (eds), 2010. *Priscien. Grammaire. Livre XVII—Syntaxe, 1* (Histoire des Doctrines de l'Antiquité Classique XLI). Paris: J. Vrin.

Asper. *Ars*. In Keil (1961: v. 547–54).

Aston, Guy, and Lou Burnard, 1998. *The BNC Handbook: Exploring the British National Corpus with SARA*. Edinburgh: Edinburgh University Press.

Atherton, Catherine, 1993. *The Stoics on Ambiguity*. Cambridge: Cambridge University Press.

Atherton, Catherine, 1995. What every grammarian knows? *Classical Quarterly* 46: 239–60.

Atherton, Catherine, 1996. Apollonius Dyscolus and the ambiguity of ambiguity. *Classical Quarterly* 47: 441–73.

Atherton, Catherine, 2005. Lucretius on what language is not. In Dorothea Frede and Brad Inwood (eds), *Language and Learning*. Cambridge: Cambridge University Press, 101–38.

Atherton, Catherine, 2009. Epicurean philosophy of language. In James Warren (ed.), *The Cambridge Companion to Epicureanism*. Cambridge: Cambridge University Press, 197–215.

Atkinson, J. Maxwell, and Paul Drew, 1979. *Order in Court: The Organisation of Verbal Interaction in Judicial Settings*. London: Macmillan.

Atkinson, Paul, 1985. *Language, Structure and Reproduction: An Introduction to the Sociology of Basil Bernstein*. London: Methuen.

Atkinson, Paul, 1988. Ethnomethodology: a critical review. *Annual Reviews of Sociology* 14: 441–6.

Augustine. *Regulae*. In Keil (1961: v.496–524).

Auroux, Sylvain, 1989. Introduction. In Sylvain Auroux (ed.), *Histoire des idées linguistiques*, 1: *La naissance des métalangues en occident et en orient*. Liège: Mardaga, 13–37.

Auroux, Sylvain, E. F. Konrad Koerner, Hans-Josef Niederehe, and Kees Versteegh (eds), 2000–2006. *History of the Language Sciences*. 3 vols. Berlin: de Gruyter.

Aussant, Émilie, 2009. *Le nom propre en Inde: considérations sur le mécansime référentiel*. Lyon: ENS.

Austin, Gilbert, 1966 [1802]. *Chironomia or, a Treatise on Rhetorical Delivery*. London: T. Cadell & W. Davis. Ed. with a critical introduction by Mary Margaret Robb and Lester Thonssen, Carbondale: Southern Illinois University Press, 1966.

Austin, John L., 1962. *How to Do Things with Words*. The William James Lectures delivered at Harvard University in 1955, ed. J. O. Urmson. Oxford: Clarendon Press.

Automatic Language Processing Advisory Committee, 1966. *Language and Machines: Computers in Translation and Linguistics*. Washington, DC: National Academy of Sciences.

Awolyale, Y., 1981. Nominal compound formation in Yoruba ideophones. *Journal of African Languages and Linguistics* 3: 139–57.

Ax, Wolfram, 1986. Quadripertita ratio: Bemerkungen zur Geschichte eines aktuellen Kategoriensystems 'Adiectio—Detractio—Transmutatio—Immutatio'. *Historiographia Linguistica* 13: 191–214.

Ax, Wolfram, 2011. *Quintilians Grammatik (Inst. orat. 1, 4–8): Text, Übersetzung und Kommentar*. Berlin: de Gruyter.

Baayen, R. Harald, R. Piepenbrock, and H. van Rijn (eds), 1995. *The CELEX Lexical Database (Release 2, CD-ROM)*. Philadelphia: University of Pennsylvania Linguistic Data Consortium.

Bach, Emmon, 1979. Control in Montague grammar. *Linguistic Inquiry* 10: 515–31.

Bach, Kent, and Robert M. Harnish, 1979. *Linguistic Communication and Speech Acts*. Cambridge, MA: MIT Press.

Bacher, Wilhelm, 1882. *Abraham ibn Ezra als Grammatiker*. Strassburg: Trübner.

Bacon, Francis, 1996 [1620]. *The Advancement of Learning*. In Brian Vickers (ed.), *Francis Bacon: The Major Works*. Oxford: Oxford University Press.

Bailey, C.-J. N., 1986. Remarks on standardization, English, and possibilities in developed and developing countries. In Gerhard Nickel and James C. Stalker (eds), *Problems of Standardization and Linguistic Variation in Present-Day English*. Heidelberg: J. Groos, 80–1.

Baindurashvili, Akaki G., 1957. Experimental materials concerning the problem of naming. *The Works of the Academy of Science of Georgia, D. Uznadze Institute of Psychology* V: 11.

Bakalla, Muhammad H., 1994. Arab and Persian phonetics. In Ronald E. Asher and James M. Y. Simpson (eds), *The Encyclopedia of Language and Linguistics*. Oxford: Pergamon Press, 187–91.

Baker, Charlotte, and Dennis Cokely, 1980. *American Sign Language*. Silver Spring, MD: TJ Publishers.

Baker, Paul, 2006. *Using Corpora in Discourse Analysis*. London: Continuum.

Baker, Paul, 2010. *Sociolinguistics and Corpus Linguistics*. Edinburgh: Edinburgh University Press.

Baker, Paul, Kalina Bontcheva, Hamish Cunningham, Robert Gaizauskas, et al., 2004. Corpus linguistics and South Asian languages: corpus creation and tool development. *Literary and Linguistic Computing* 19: 509–24.

Baker, Paul, Mabel Lie, Tony McEnery, and Mark Sebba, 2000. Building a corpus of spoken Sylheti. *Literary and Linguistic Computing* 15: 419–31.

Bakhtin, Mikhail M., 1994 [1935]. The dialogic imagination. In Pam Morris (ed.), *The Bakhtin Reader: Selected Writings of Bakhtin, Medvedev, Voloshinov*. London: Arnold, 74–80.

Baldinger, Kurt, 1957. *Die Semasiologie. Versuch eines Ueberblicks*. Berlin: Akademie.

Baldinger, Kurt. 1980. *Semantic Theory*. Oxford: Blackwell.

Baldry, Anthony, and Paul J. Thibault, 2006. *Multimodal Transcription and Text Analysis*. London: Equinox.

Baldwin, J., 1979. Phonetics and speaker identification. *Medicine, Science and the Law* 19: 231–2.

Baldwin, James M. (ed.), 1901–5. *Dictionary of Philosophy and Psychology*. New York: Macmillan.

Bally, Charles, 1926. *Le langage et la vie*. Zürich: Niehans.

Bally, Charles, 1965. *Linguistique générale et linguistique française*, 4th edn. Bern: Francke.

Banham, Debby, 1991. *Monasteriales Indicia:The Anglo-Saxon Monastic Sign Language*. Pinner: Anglo-Saxon Books.

Banko, Michele, and Eric Brill, 2001. Scaling to very very large corpora for natural language disambiguation. *Proceedings of the 39th Annual Meeting of the Association for Computational Linguistics* (Toulouse), 16–33.

Barakat, Robert A., 1969. Gesture systems. *Keystone Folklore Quarterly* 14: 105–21.

Barakat, Robert A, 1987. Cistercian sign language. In Umiker-Sebeok and Sebeok (1987: 67–322).

Baratin, Marc, 2000. À l'origine de la tradition artigraphique latine, entre mythe et réalité. In Auroux et al., vol. 1 (2000: 459–66).

Barcelona, Antonio (ed.), 2003. *Metaphor and Metonymy at the Crossroads: A Cognitive Perspective*. Berlin: Mouton de Gruyter.

Bar-Hillel, Yehoshua, 1960. The present status of automatic translation of languages. *Advances in Computers* 1: 91–163. [Repr., slightly abridged, in Sergei Nirenburg, Harold Somers, and Yorick Wilks (eds), *Readings in Machine Translation* (Cambridge, MA: MIT Press, 2003), 45–76.]

Barlow, Michael, and Suzanne Kemmer (eds), 2000. *Usage-Based Models of Language*. Stanford, CA: CSLI.

Barnes, Jonathan, 2007. *Truth, etc.: Six Lectures on Ancient Logic*. Oxford: Clarendon Press.

Barnett, Deane, 1987. *The Art of Gesture: The Practices and Principles of 18th Century Acting*. Heidelberg: C. Winter.

Barney, Rachel, 2001. *Names and Nature in Plato's* Cratylus. New York: Routledge.

Barney, Stephen A., W. J. Lewis, J. A. Beach, and Oliver Berghof (eds), 2006. *The Etymologies of Isidore of Seville*. Cambridge: Cambridge University Press.

Baron-Cohen, Simon, and John E. Harrison, 1997. *Synaesthesia: Classic and Contemporary Readings*. Oxford: Blackwell.

Barsalou, Lawrence W., 1992. *Cognitive Psychology: An Overview for Cognitive Scientists*. Norwood, NJ: Lawrence Erlbaum

Barthélemy, Adrien, 1935–69. *Dictionnaire arabe-français. Dialectes de Syrie: Alep, Damas, Liban, Jérusalem*. Paris: Geuthner.

Barthes, Roland, 1966. Introduction à l'analyse structural des récits. *Communication* 8. [Trans. Stephen Heath as 'Introduction to the structural analysis of narratives', in Roland Barthes, *Image, Music, Text* (New York: Hill & Wang, 1977), 79–124.]

Barthes, Roland, 1980. Proust and names. In *New Critical Essays*. New York: Hill & Wang.

Bartsch, Renate, 1987. *Norms of Language: Theoretical and Practical Aspects*. London: Longman.

Barwick, Karl, 1922. *Remmius Palaemon und die römische Ars grammatica*. Leipzig: Dieterich.

Basso, Keith, 1990. *Western Apache Language and Culture: Essays in Linguistic Anthropology*. Tucson: University of Arizona Press.

Bates, Elizabeth, Laura Benigni, Inge Bretherton, Luigia Camaioni, and Virginia Volterra, 1979. *The Emergence of Symbols: Cognition and Communication in Infancy*. New York: Academic Press.

Bateson, Gregory, 1972. *Steps to an Ecology of Mind*. San Francisco, CA: Chandler.

Bateson, Gregory and Margaret Mead, 1942. *Balinese Character: A Photographic Analysis.* New York: New York Academy of Sciences.

Batteux, Charles, 1747–8. *Lettres sur la phrase françoise comparée avec la phrase latine.* In *Cours de belles lettres,* vol. 2. Paris: Desaint & Saillant.

Battison, R., and Jordan, I. K., 1976. Cross-cultural communication with foreign signers: fact and fancy. *Sign Language Studies* 10: 53–68.

Baudouin de Courtenay, Jan, 1972a [1895]. *A Baudouin de Courtenay Anthology: The Beginnings of Structural Linguistics,* ed. Edward Stankiewicz. Bloomington: Indiana University Press.

Baudouin de Courtenay, Jan, 1972b. An attempt at a theory of phonetic alternations. In Baudouin de Courtenay (1972a: 144–212).

Bauer, Hans, 1910. *Die Tempora im Semitischen.* Leipzig: Hinrichs. [Repr. 1967.]

Bauman, Richard, 1977. *Verbal Art as Performance.* Prospect Heights, IL: Waveland Press.

Bauman, Richard and Joel Sherzer (eds), 1974. *Explorations in the Ethnography of Speaking.* Cambridge: Cambridge University Press.

Bauman, Richard and Joel Sherzer, 1975. The ethnography of speaking. *Annual Review of Anthropology* 4: 95–119.

Bauman, Zygmunt, 2000. *Liquid Modernity.* Cambridge: Polity Press.

Bayard, Donn, 1987. Class and change in New Zealand English: a summary report. *Te Reo* 13: 3–36.

Bayless, Martha, 1993. *Beatus quid est* and the study of grammar in late Anglo-Saxon England. In Vivien Law (ed.), *History of Linguistic Thought in the Early Middle Ages.* Amsterdam: John Benjamins, 67–110.

Baynton, Douglas C., 1996. *Forbidden Signs: American Culture and the Campaign Against Sign Language.* Chicago: University of Chicago Press.

Baynton, Douglas C., 2002. The curious death of sign language studies in the nineteenth century. In David F. Armstrong, Michael A. Karchmer, and John Vickery Van Cleve (eds), *The Study of Signed Languages: Essays in Honor of William Stokoe.* Washington, DC: Gallaudet University Press, 13–34.

Beard, Robert, 1995. *Lexeme–Morpheme Base Morphology: A General Theory of Inflection and Word Formation.* Buffalo, NY: SUNY Press.

Beauzée, Nicolas, 1767. *Grammaire générale, ou exposition raisonnée des éléments nécessaires du langage, pour servir de fondement à l'étude de toutes les langues.* Paris: Barbou.

Beck, Ulrich, 2002. The cosmopolitan society and its enemies. *Theory, Culture and Society* 19: 17–44.

Becker, Karl F., 1841. *Organism der Sprache,* 2nd edn. Frankfurt am Main: G. F. Kettembeil.

Beckner, Clay, Richard Blythe, Joan Bybee, et al., 2009. Language is a complex adaptive system: a position paper. *Language Learning* 59 (suppl. 1): 1–26.

Bédard, Édith, and Jacques Maurais (eds), 1983. *La norme linguistique.* Québec: Gouvernement du Québec, Conseil de la langue française/Paris: Robert.

Beeston, Alfred F. L., 1984. *Sabaic Grammar.* Manchester: Manchester University Press.

Behnstedt, Peter, and Manfred Woidich, 2010. *Wortatlas der arabischen Dialekte,* 1: *Mensch, Natur, Fauna und Flora.* Leiden: E. J. Brill.

Bell, Alexander M., 1867. *Visible Speech: The Science of Universal Alphabetics, or, Self-Interpreting Physiological Letters, For The Writing Of All Languages In One Alphabet* London: Simpkin, Marshall.

Bellugi, Ursula, 1981. The acquisition of a spatial language. In Frank S. Kessel (ed.), *The Development of Language and Language Researchers: Essays in Honor of Roger Brown*. Hillsdale, NJ: Lawrence Erlbaum, 153–85.

Bélova, Anna G., et al., 2009. *Аккадский язык: Северозападносемитскиеязыки*. [Akkadian Language and North-West Semitic Languages]. Winona Lake, IN: Academia.

Benczes, Réka, Antonio Barcelona, and Francisco Ruiz de Mendoza Ibáñez (eds), 2011. *Defining Metonymy in Cognitive Linguistics: Towards a Consensus View*. Amsterdam: John Benjamins.

Bender, Lionel M., Donald J. Bowen, Robert L. Cooper, and Charles A. Ferguson (eds), 1976. *Language in Ethiopia*. London: Oxford University Press.

Benediktsson, Hreinn, 1972. *The First Grammatical Treatise*. Reykjavík: Institute of Nordic Linguistics.

Benfey, Theodor, 1869. *Geschichte der Sprachwissenschaft und orientalischen Philologie in Deutschland seit dem Anfange des 19 Jahrhunderts mit einem Rückblick auf frühere Zeiten*. Munich: Cotta.

Ben-Hayyim, Ze'ev, 1957–77. *The Literary and Oral Tradition of Hebrew and Aramaic amongst the Samaritans* 1–5 (in Hebrew). Jerusalem: Bialik Institute and Academy of Hebrew Language.

Benveniste, Émile, 1939. Nature du signe linguistique. *Acta Linguistica* 1: 23–9. [Repr. as Benveniste (1966: ch. 4).]

Benveniste, Émile, 1946. Structure des relations de personne dans le verbe. *Bulletin de la Société de Linguistique* 126: 1–12. [Repr. in Benveniste (1966: 225–36).]

Benveniste, Émile, 1956. La nature des pronoms. In Morris Halle, Horace G. Lunt, Hugh McLean, and Cornelis H. van Schooneveld (eds), *For Roman Jakobson: Essays on the Occasion of His Sixtieth Birthday, 11 October 1956*. The Hague: Mouton. [Repr. in Benveniste (1966: 151–257).]

Benveniste, Émile, 1958. De la subjectivité dans le langage. *Journal de psychologie normale et pathologique*: 257–65. [Repr. in Benveniste (1966: 158–266).]

Benveniste, Émile, 1966. *Problèmes de linguistique générale*, vol. 1. Paris: Gallimard. [English transl. by Mary E. Meek, *Problems in General Linguistics*, Coral Gables, FL: University of Miami Press, 1971.]

Benzoni, Gino, 1967. Giovanni Bonifacio erudito uomo di legge e devoto. *Studi veneziani* 9: 247–312.

Benzoni, Gino, 1970. Bonifacio, Giovanni. In *Dizionario biografico degli italiani*. Rome: Enciclopedia italiana Treccani.

Berggren, I., 1972. Does the use of translation exercises have negative effects on the learning of a second language? *Rapport* 14. Gothenburg: Department of English, Gothenburg University.

Bergsträsser, Gotthelf, 1928. *Einführung in die Semitischen Sprachen: Sprachproben und grammatische Skizzen*. Munich: Max Hüber. [English transl. by Peter T. Daniels, *Introduction to the Semitic Languages: Text Specimens and Grammatical Sketches*, Winona Lake, IN: Eisenbrauns, 1983.]

Berlin, Brent, 1976. The concept of rank in ethnobiological classification: some evidence from Aguarana folk botany. *American Ethnologist* 3: 381–400.

Berlin, Brent, 1978. Ethnobiological classification. In Eleanor Rosch and Barbara B. Lloyd (eds), *Cognition and Categorization*. Hillsdale, NJ: Lawrence Erlbaum: 9–26.

Berlin, Brent, Dennis E. Breedlove, and Peter H. Raven, 1973. General principles of classification and nomenclature in folk biology. *American Anthropologist* 75: 214–42.

Berlin, Brent, Dennis E. Breedlove and Peter H. Raven, 1974. *Principles of Tzeltal Plant Classification :An Introduction to the Botanical Ethnography of a Mayan-Speaking People of Highland Chiapas*. New York: Academic Press.

Berlitz, Maximillian D., 1907. *The Berlitz Method for Teaching Modern Languages*. New York: Berlitz.

Bermon, Emmanuel, 2007. *La signification et l'enseignement*. (Texte latin, traduction française et commentaire du *De magistro* de saint Augustin.) Paris: J. Vrin.

Bernhardi, August F., 1801–3. *Sprachlehre*, 2 Theile. Berlin: Heinrich Frölich.

Berwick, Robert, Paul Pietroski, Beracah Yankama, and Noam Chomsky, 2011. Poverty of the stimulus revisited. *Cognitive Science* 35: 1207–42.

Bever, Thomas G., 1963. Leonard Bloomfield and the phonology of Menomini. Ph.D dissertation, MIT.

Bever, Thomas G., 1970. The cognitive basis for linguistic structures. In John R. Hayes (ed.), *Cognition and the Development of Language*. New York: Wiley, 179–362.

Bhatia, Vijay K., 1993. *Analysing Genre: Language Use in Professional Settings*. London: Longman.

Bhattacharya, Bishnupada, 1962. *A Study in Language and Meaning: A Critical Examination of Some Aspects of Indian Semantics*. Calcutta: Progressive Publishers.

Biardeau, Madeleine, 1964. *Théorie de la connaissance et philosophie de la parole dans le brahmanisme classique*. Paris: Mouton.

Biber, Douglas, 1988. *Variation Across Speech and Writing*. Cambridge: Cambridge University Press.

Biber, Douglas and Susan Conrad, 1999. Lexical bundles in conversation and academic prose. In Hilde Hasselgard and Signe Oksefjell (eds), *Out of Corpora: Studies in Honour of Stig Johansson*. Amsterdam: Rodopi, 181–9.

Biber, Douglas, Susan Conrad, and Viviana Cortes, 2004. If you look at . . . : lexical bundles in university teaching and coursebooks. *Applied Linguistics* 25: 371–405.

Biber, Douglas, Edward Finegan, and Dwight Atkinson, 1993. ARCHER and its challenges: compiling and exploring a representative corpus of historical English registers. In Jan Aarts, Pieter de Haan, and Nelleke Oostdijk (eds), *English Language Corpora: Design, Analysis and Exploitation*. Amsterdam: Rodopi, 1–13.

Biber, Douglas, Stig Johansson, Geoffrey Leech, Susan Conrad, and Edward Finegan, 1999. *Longman Grammar of Spoken and Written English*. London: Longman.

Bickerton, Derek, 1981. *Roots of Language*. Ann Arbor, MI: Karoma

Bickerton, Derek, 1984. The language bioprogram hypothesis and second language acquisition. In William E. Rutherford (ed.), *Language Universals and Second Language Acquisition*. Amsterdam: Benjamins, 141–61.

Bickerton, Derek, 1990. *Language and Species*. Chicago: University of Chicago Press.

Bickerton, Derek, 1995. *Language and Human Behavior*. Seattle: University of Washington Press.

Bickerton, Derek, 2007. Language evolution: a brief guide for linguists. *Lingua* 117: 510–26.

Bickerton, Derek, 2010. *Adam's Tongue: How Humans Made Language, How Language Made Humans*. New York: Hill & Wang.

Biletzki, Anat, 1996. Is there a history of pragmatics? *Journal of Pragmatics* 25: 455–70.

Binet, Alfred, and Jean Philippe, 1892. Étude sur un nouveau cas d'audition colorée. *Revue philosophique* 33: 461–4.

Bird, Steven, 1995. *Computational Phonology: A Constraint-Based Approach*. Cambridge: Cambridge University Press.

Birdwhistell, Ray L., 1970. *Kinesics and Context: Essays in Body Motion Communication*. Philadelphia: University of Pennsylvania Press.

Birner, Betty J., 1994. Information status and word order: an analysis of English inversion. *Language* 70: 233–59.

Bíró, Bernadette, and Katalin Sipöcz, 2009. Language shift among the Mansi. In James Stanford and Dennis Preston (eds), *Variation in Indigenous Minority Languages*. Amsterdam: John Benjamins, 321–46.

Bizzell, Patricia, and Bruce Herzberg, 2001. *Rhetorical Tradition: Readings from Classical Times to the Present*, 2nd edn. Boston: Bedford Books of St. Martin's Press.

Black, Robert, 2001. *Humanism and Education in Medieval and Renaissance Italy: Tradition and Innovation in Latin Schools from the Twelfth to the Fifteenth Century*. Cambridge: Cambridge University Press.

Blackburn, Simon, 1984. *Spreading the Word*. Oxford: Oxford University Press.

Blank, David L., 1982. *Ancient Philosophy and Grammar*. Chico, CA: Scholars Press.

Blank, David L., 1983. Remarks on Nicanor, the Stoics and the ancient theory of punctuation. *Glotta* 61: 4–67.

Blank, David L., 1993. Apollonius Dyscolus. In Wolfgang Haase (ed.), *Aufstieg und Niedergang der römischen Welt*. Berlin: de Gruyter, vol. II.34.1, 708–30.

Blank, David L., 1998. *Sextus Empiricus Against the Grammarians*. Oxford: Clarendon Press.

Blank, David L., 2000. The organization of grammar in Ancient Greece. In Auroux et al., vol. 1 (2000: 400–17).

Blank, David L., 2005. Varro's anti-analogist. In Dorothea Frede and Brad Inwood (eds), *Language and Learning*. Cambridge: Cambridge University Press, 110–238.

Blank, David L., 2008. Varro and the epistemological status of etymology. *Histoire épistémologie langage* 30: 49–73.

Blank, David L. and Catherine Atherton, 2003. The Stoic contribution to traditional grammar. In Brad Inwood (ed.), *The Cambridge Companion to the Stoics*. Cambridge: Cambridge University Press, 310–27.

Blei, David M., 2012. Probabilistic topic models. *Communications of the ACM* 55(4): 77–84.

Blei, David M., Andrew Ng, and Michael Jordan, 2003. Latent Dirichlet allocation. *Journal of Machine Learning Research* 3: 993–1022.

Blevins, James P., 2006. Word-based morphology. *Journal of Linguistics* 42: 531–73.

Blevins, James P., 2008. The post-transformational enterprise. *Journal of Linguistics* 44: 723–42.

Blevins, James P., to appear. Word-based morphology. In Andrew Spencer (ed.), *The Handbook of Morphology*, 2nd edn. Oxford: Blackwell.

Blevins, James P. and Juliette Blevins (eds), 2009. *Analogy in Grammar: Form and Acquisition*. Oxford: Oxford University Press.

Bloch, Bernard, 1941. Phonemic overlapping. *American Speech* 16: 278–84. [Repr. in Joos (1957: 93–96). Also in Makkai (1972: 66–70).]

Bloch, Bernard, 1948. A set of postulates for phonemic analysis. *Language* 24: 3–46.

Bloch, Bernard, 1949. Leonard Bloomfield. *Language* 25: 87–94. [Repr. in Joos (1957: 524–32).]

Bloch, Bernard and George L. Trager, 1942. *Outline of Linguistic Analysis*. Baltimore, MD: Linguistic Society of America.

Blom, Jan-Petter, and John J. Gumperz, 1972. Social meaning in linguistic structure: code-switching in Norway. In Gumperz and Hymes (1972: 407–34).

Blommaert, Jan (ed.), 1999. *Language Ideological Debates*. Berlin: Mouton de Gruyter.

Blommaert, Jan, 2005. *Discourse*. Cambridge: Cambridge University Press.

Blommaert, Jan, 2009. Ethnography and democracy: Hymes's political theory of language. *Text and Talk* 29: 257–76.

Bloomfield, Leonard, 1909, 1910. A semasiological differentiation in Germanic secondary ablaut. *Modern Philology* 7: 245–88, 345–82.

Bloomfield, Leonard, 1914. *An Introduction to the Study of Language*. New York: Henry Holt. [Repr. with an introduction by Joseph Kess, Amsterdam: John Benjamins, 1983.]

Bloomfield, Leonard, 1926. A set of postulates for the science of language. *Language* 2: 153–64.

Bloomfield, Leonard, 1927. On some rules of Pāṇini. *Journal of the American Oriental Society* 47: 61–70.

Bloomfield, Leonard, 1929. Review of *Konkordanz Pāṇini-Candra* by Bruno Liebich. *Language* 5: 267–76. [Repr. in Hockett (1970: 219–26).]

Bloomfield, Leonard, 1933. *Language*. New York: Holt, Rinehart & Winston.

Bloomfield, Leonard, 1939. Menomini morphophonemics. *Travaux du Cercle Linguistique de Prague* 8 : 105–15.

Bloomfield, Maurice, 1895. On assimilation and adaptation in congeneric classes of words. *American Journal of Philology* 16: 409–34.

Boas, Franz, 1889. On alternating sounds. *American Anthroplogist* 2: 47–53.

Boas, Franz, 1899. Anthropology. *Science* 9: 93–6.

Boas, Franz, 1904. The history of anthropology. *Science* 20: 513–24.

Boas, Franz, 1911. Introduction. In *Handbook of American Indian Languages*, Bureau of American Ethnology, Bulletin 40, Part 1. Washington, DC: Smithsonian Institution, 1–83. [The Introduction was published separately as *Introduction to the Handbook of American Indian Languages*, Washington, DC: Georgetown University Press, 1963.]

Boas, Franz, 1940. *Race, Language and Culture*. New York: Macmillan.

Boas, Franz, Pliny E. Goddard, Edward Sapir, and Alfred L. Kroeber, 1916. *Phonetic Transcription of Indian Languages: Report of Committee of American Anthropological Association. Smithsonian Miscellaneous Collections 66(6)*. Washington, DC: Smithsonian Institution.

Boas, Norman F., 2004. *Franz Boas, 1858–1942: An Illustrated Biography*. Mystic, CT: Seaport Autographs.

Boersma, Paul, and David Weenik, 2010. *Praat: Doing Phonetics by Computer* [computer program, www.praat.org].

Boethius de Dacia, 1980 [c.1280]. *Godfrey of Fontaine's Abridgement of Boethius de Dacia's modi significandi sive quaestiones super priscianum maiorem*, ed., transl., and introduced by Charlene McDermott. Amsterdam: John Benjamins.

Bohas, Georges, 1997. *Matrices, étymons, racines: éléments d'une théorie lexicologique du vocabulaire arabe*. Leuven: Peeters.

Bohas, Georges, 2001. *Matrices et étymons: développement de la théorie (Séminaire de Saintes 1999)*. Prahins: Éditions du Zèbre.

Bohas, Georges, 2003. Radical ou racine/schème? L'organisation de la conjugaison syriaque, avant l'adoption de la racine. *Le Muséon* 116: 343–76.

Bohas, Georges and Mihai Dat, 2007. *Une théorie de l'organisation du lexique des langues sémitiques: matrices et étymons*. Lyon: ENS.

Böhtlingk, Otto, 1887. *Pāṇini's Grammatik*. Leipzig. [Repr. in 2 vols, Hildesheim: Olms, 1964.]

Bolinger, Dwight, 1946. Some thoughts on 'yep' and 'nope'. *American Speech* 21: 90–5.

Bolinger, Dwight, 1949. The sign is not arbitrary, *Boletín del Instituto Caro y Cuervo* 5: 56–62.

Bolinger, Dwight, 1950. Rime, assonance and morpheme analysis. *Word* 6: 117–36.

Bolinger, Dwight, 1952. Linear modification. *PMLA* 67: 1117–44.

Bolinger, Dwight, 1965. *Forms of English*, ed. Isamu Abe and Tetsuya Kanekiyo. Cambridge, MA: Harvard University Press.

Bolinger, Dwight, 1973. Getting the *words* in. In Raven McDavid, Jr and Audrey Duckert (eds), *Lexicography in English*. New York: New York Academy of Science, 8–13.

Bolinger, Dwight, 1977. *Meaning and Form*. London: Longman.

Bolinger, Dwight, 1979. Pronouns in discourse. In Talmy Givón (ed.), *Discourse and Syntax*. New York: Academic Press, 189–309.

Boltz, William G., 1993. Shuo wen chieh tzu. In Michael Loewe (ed.), *Early Chinese Texts: A Bibliographical Guide*. Berkeley, CA: Society for the Study of Early China, 429–42.

Bongers, Herman, 1947. *The History and Principles of Vocabulary Control*. Woerden: Wocopi.

Boniface, 1980 [754]. *Ars grammatica*, ed. G. J. Gebauer and B. Löfstedt. Turnhout: Brepols, 15–99.

Booth, A. Donald, 1955. Storage devices. In William N. Locke and A. Donald Booth (eds), *Machine Translation of Languages*. Cambridge, MA: Technology Press of the Massachusetts Institute of Technology, 119–23.

Booth, A. Donald and William N. Locke, 1955. Historical introduction. In William N. Locke and A. Donald Booth (eds), *Machine Translation of Languages*. Cambridge, MA: Technology Press of the Massachusetts Institute of Technology, 1–14.

Bopp, Franz, 1816. *Über das Conjugationssystem der Sanskritsprache in Vergleichung mit jenem der griechischen, lateinischen, persischen und germanischen Sprache*. Herausgegeben und mit Vorerinnerungen begleitet von K[arl] J[oseph] Windischmann. Frankfurt am Main: Andreäische Buchhandlung.

Bopp, Franz, 1819. *Nalus carmen Sanscritum e Mahābhārato edidit, Latine vertit, et Adnotationibus illustravit Franciscus Bopp*. Londini: Treuttel & Würtz.

Bopp, Franz, 1820. Analytical comparison of the Sanskrit, Greek, Latin, and Teutonic languages, shewing the original identity of their grammatical structure. *Annals of Oriental Literature*. (London) 1: 1–65. [Repr. in *Internationale Zeitschrift für allgemeine Sprachwissenschaft* 4, 1889: 14–60.]

Bopp, Franz, 1821. Franz Bopp über 'Analytical comparison of the Sanskrit, Greek, Latin, and Teutonic languages, shewing the original identity of their grammatical structure'. *Göttingische Gelehrte Anzeigen* 88: 530–5.

Bopp, Franz, 1833–52. *Vergleichende Grammatik des Sanskrit, Zend, Griechischen, Lateinischen, Litthauischen, Altslawischen, Gotischen und Deutschen*. 6 vols. Berlin: Ferdinand Dümmler.

Bopp, Franz, 1836. *Vocalismus, oder sprachvergleichende Kritiken über J. Grimm's Deutsche Grammatik und Graff's Althochdeutschen Sprachschatz : mit Begründung einer neuen Theorie des Ablauts*. Berlin : Nicolaische Buchhandlung.

Borer, Hagit, 1984. *Parametric Syntax*. Dordrecht: Foris.

Borin, Lars (ed.), 2002. *Parallel Corpora, Parallel Worlds: Selected Papers from a Symposium on Parallel and Comparable Corpora at Uppsala University, Sweden, 22–23 April, 1999*. Amsterdam: Rodopi.

Botha, Rudi P., 1992. *Twentieth Century Conceptions of Language: Mastering the Metaphysics Market*. Oxford: Blackwell.

Botterill, Steven (ed.), 1996. *Dante: De Vulgari Eloquentia*. Cambridge: Cambridge University Press.

Bouillaud, Jean-Baptiste, 1825. *Traité Clinique et Physiologique de l'Encéphalite, ou Inflammation du Cerveau*. Paris: J.-B. Baillière.

Boulnois, Luce, 2004. *Silk Road: Monks, Warriors and Merchants*, transl. Helen Loveday. Geneva: Odyssey Books.

Bourdieu, Pierre, 1990. *Language and Symbolic Power*. Cambridge: Polity Press.

Brackbill, Yvonne, and K. B. Little, 1957. Factors determining the guessing and meaning of foreign words. *Journal of Abnormal and Social Pychology* 54: 312–18.

Bradford, Richard, 1997. *Stylistics*. London: Routledge.

Brame, Michael K., 1970. Arabic phonology: implications for phonological theory and historical change. Ph.D dissertation, MIT.

Brandenburg, Philip, 2005. *Apollonios Dyscolos: Über das Pronomen. Einführung, Text, Übersetzung und Erläuterungen*. Munich: K. G. Saur.

Brandist, Craig, and Katya Chown (eds), 2010. *Politics and the Theory of Language in the USSR 1917 to 1938: The Birth of Sociological Linguistics*. New York: Anthem Press.

Branner, David Prager (ed.), 2006. *The Chinese Rime Tables: Linguistic Philosophy and Historical-Comparative Phonology*. Amsterdam: John Benjamins.

Brazil, David, 1995. *A Grammar of Speech*. Oxford: Oxford University Press.

Bréal, Michel, 1897. *Essai de sémantique: science des significations*. Paris: Hachette.

Bredsdorff, Jacob H., 1821. *Om Aarsagerne til Sprogenes Forandringer*. Copenhagen: Roskilde Katedralskole.

Brentari, Diane, 1998. *A Prosodic Model of Sign Language Phonology*. Cambridge, MA: MIT Press.

Bresnan, Joan, 1978. A realistic transformational grammar. In Morris Halle, Joan Bresnan, and George A. Miller (eds), *Linguistic Theory and Psychological Reality*. Cambridge, MA: MIT Press, 1–59.

Bresnan, Joan, 2001. *Lexical Functional Syntax*. Oxford: Blackwell.

Bresnan, Joan and Judith Aissen, 2001. Optimality and functionality: objections and refutations. *Natural Language and Linguistic Theory* 20: 81–95.

Breva Claramonte, Manuel, 1983. *Sanctius' Theory of Language. A Contribution to the History of Renaissance Linguistics*. Amsterdam: Benjamins.

Breva Claramonte, Manuel, 1986. Introduction to Sanctius' *Minerva, seu de causis linguae Latinae*. Stuttgart–Bad Canstatt: Frommann–Holzboog.

Brill, Eric, 1995. Transformation-based error-driven learning and natural language processing: a case study in part-of-speech tagging. *Computational Linguistics* 21: 543–65.

Brilliant, Richard, 1963. *Gesture and Rank in Roman Art: The Use of Gesture to Denote Status in Roman Sculpture and Coinage*. New Haven, CT: Memoirs of the Connecticut Academy of Arts and Sciences.

Broca, Paul, 1861. Remarques sur le siège de la faculté du langage articulé, suivés d'une observation d'aphémie. *Bulletin de la Société Anatomique de Paris* 36: 330–57.

Brockelmann, Carl, 1906. *Semitische Sprachwissenschaft*. Leipzig: G. J. Göschen. [2nd edn 1916; French edn by William Marçais and Marcel Cohen, *Précis de linguistique sémitique*. Paris: Geuthner, 1910.]

Brockelmann, Carl, 1908. *Kurzgefasste vergleichendeGrammatik der semitischen Sprachen: Elemente der Laut- und Formenlehre*. Berlin: Reuther & Reichard.

Brockelmann, Carl, 1908–13. *Grundriss der vergleichenden Grammatik der semitischen Sprachen*. Berlin: Reuther & Reichard. [Repr. Hildesheim: Olms, 1982.]

Broggiato, Maria, 2001. *Cratete di Mallo: i frammenti*. La Spezia: Agorà.

Brøndal, Viggo, 1939. Linguistique structurale. *Acta Linguistica* 1. 2–10. [Repr. in Brøndal (1943: 90–97).]

Brøndal, Viggo, 1943. *Essais de linguistique générale*. Copenhagen: Munskgaard.

Bronowski, Jacob, and Ursula Bellugi, 1970. Language, name, and concept. *Science* 168: 669–73.

Brookes, Heather, 2001. O clever 'He's streetwise.' When gestures become quotable: the case of the clever gesture. *Gesture* 1: 167–84.

Brookes, Heather, 2004. A repertoire of South African quotable gestures. *Journal of Linguistic Anthropology* 14: 186–224.

Brookes, Heather, 2005. What gestures do: some communicative functions of quotable gestures in conversations among Black urban South Africans. *Journal of Pragmatics* 37: 2044–85.

Brown, Gillian, and George Yule, 1983. *Discourse Analysis*. Cambridge: Cambridge University Press.

Brown, Lesley, 2008. The *Sophist* on statements, predication, and falsehood. In Gail Fine (ed.), *The Oxford Handbook of Plato*. New York: Oxford University Press, 383–410.

Brown, Penelope, and Stephen C. Levinson, 1978. Universals in language usage: politeness phenomena. In Esther Goody (ed.), *Questions and Politeness: Strategies in Social Interaction*. Cambridge: Cambridge University Press, 56–289.

Brown, Penelope and Stephen C. Levinson, 1987. *Politeness: Some Universals in Language Usage*. Cambridge: Cambridge University Press. [Revised and expanded from Brown and Levinson (1978).]

Brown, Peter F., John Cocke, Stephen A. Della Pietra, et al., 1990. A statistical approach to machine translation. *Computational Linguistics* 16: 79–85.

Brown, Peter F., Stephen A. Della Pietra, Vincent J. Della Pietra, et al., 1992. Analysis, statistical transfer, and synthesis in machine translation. *Proceedings of the Fourth International Conference on Theoretical and Methodological Issues in Machine Translation of Natural Languages* (Montreal), 83–100.

Brown, Roger W., A. H. Black, and A. E. Horowitz, 1955. Phonetic symbolism in natural languages. *Journal of Abnormal and Social Psychology* 50: 388–93.

Bruce, Scott G., 2007. *Silence and Sign Language in Medieval Monasticism: The Cluniac Tradition c.900–1200*. Cambridge: Cambridge University Press.

Brugmann, Karl, 1876. Nasalis sonans in der indogermanischen Grundsprache. *Curtius Studien* 9: 287–338.

Brugmann, Karl, 1883. Review of Humboldt, *Sprachphilosophische Werke*, ed. H. Steinthal. 1. Hälfte. *Literarisches Centralblatt für Deutschland* 37: 1315–16.

Brugmann, Karl, 1897. Karl Verner. *Indogermanische Forschungen* (Anzeiger) 7: 269–70.

Brunschwig, Jacques, 1994. Epicurus and the problem of private language. In Jacques Brunschwig (ed.), *Papers in Hellenistic Philosophy*. Cambridge: Cambridge University Press, 11–38. [= Épicure et le problème du 'langue privé', *Rev. sci. hum.* 43, 1977: 157–77.]

Bucholtz, Mary, and Kira Hall, 2008. All of the above: new coalitions in sociocultural linguistics. *Journal of Sociolinguistics* 12: 401–31.

Bugarski, Ranko, 1970. Writing systems and phonological insights. *Papers from the Sixth Regional Meeting.* Chicago: Chicago Linguistic Society, 453–8.

Bühler, Karl, 1934. *Sprachtheorie: die Darstellungsfunktion der Sprache.* Jena: G. Fischer.

Bullokar, William, 1580. *A Short Introduction Or Guiding To Print, Write, and Reade Inglish Speech: Conferred with the Olde Printing and Writing.* London: Henrie Denham.

Bullowa, Margaret (ed.), 1979. *Before Speech: The Beginning of Interpersonal Communication.* Cambridge: Cambridge University Press.

Bulwer, John B., 1644. *Chirologia; or the natural language of the hand.* London: R. Whitaker. [Repr. with *Chironomia or the Art of Manual Rhetoric,* ed. with an Introduction by James W. Cleary, Carbondale: Southern Illinois University Press, 1974.]

Bulwer, John B., 1648. *Philocophus: or the Deafe and Dumbe Man's Friend.* London: Humphrey Moseley.

Burke, Peter, 1992. The language of gesture in early modern Italy. In Jan Bremmer and Herman Roodenburg (eds), *A Cultural History of Gesture.* Ithaca, NY: Cornell University Press, 71–83.

Burkhardt, Armin (ed.), 1990. *Speech Acts, Meaning and Intentions: Critical Approaches to the Philosophy of John R. Searle.* Berlin: de Gruyter.

Burleigh, Walter, 1988. *Von der Reinheit der Kunst der Logik. Erster Traktat. Von den Eigenschaften der Termini* (De puritate artis logicae. De proprietatibus terminorum), transl. and ed. Peter Kunze, with introduction and commentary. Hamburg: Felix Meiner.

Burnard, Lou (ed.), 1995. *User's Reference Guide for the British National Corpus.* Oxford: Oxford University Computing Services.

Burnet, James (Lord Monboddo), 1773–92. *Of the Origin and Progress of Language.* Edinburgh: J. Balfour.

Burrow, John, 2002. *Gestures and Looks in Medieval Narrative.* Cambridge: Cambridge University Press.

Bursill-Hall, Geoffrey L., 1972. *Thomas of Erfurt Grammatica Speculativa: An Edition with Translation and Commentary.* London: Longman.

Butcher, Andrew R., 2002. Forensic phonetics: issues in speaker identification evidence. Paper presented at the Inaugural International Conference of the Institute of Forensic Studies: 'Forensic Evidence: Proof and Presentation', Prato, 3–5 July. prospero.fmc.flinders.edu.au/Staff/andy.htm

Butcher, Andrew R. 2006. Australian Aboriginal languages: consonant-salient phonologies and the 'place-of-articulation imperative'. In Jonathan M. Harrington and Marija Tabain (eds), *Speech Production: Models, Phonetic Processes and Techniques.* New York: Psychology Press, 187–210.

Butcher, Andrew R. and Marija Tabain, 2004. On the back of the tongue: contrasting dorsal sounds in Australian languages. *Phonetica* 61: 22–52.

Butler, Charles, 1634. *The English Grammar, or the Institution of Letters, Syllables, and Woords in the English Tung. Wher'unto Is Annexed an Index of Woords Lik' and Unlik'.* Oxford: William Turner.

Butler, Christopher S., 2003. *Structure and Function: A Guide to Three Structural- Functional Theories,* Part I: *Approaches to the Simplex Clause*; Part II: *From Clause to Discourse and Beyond.* Amsterdam: John Benjamins.

Butler, Christopher S., 2009. The lexical constructional model: genesis, strengths and challenges. In Christopher S. Butler and and Javier MartínArista (eds), *Deconstructing Constructions.* Amsterdam: John Benjamins, 117–52.

Butler, Harold E., 1922. *The Institutio Oratoria of Quintilian with an English translation by H. E. Butler.* London: William Heinemann.

Butt, David, 2001. Firth, Halliday and the development of systemic functional theory. In Auroux et al., vol. 2 (2001: 1806–38).

Butterfield, Herbert, 1931. *The Whig Interpretation of History.* London: Bell.

Bybee, Joan L., 2010. *Language, Usage and Cognition.* Cambridge: Cambridge University Press.

Bybee, Joan and Paul J. Hopper (eds), 2001. *Frequency and the Emergence of Linguistic Structure.* Amsterdam: John Benjamins.

Bynon, Theodora, 1978. The Neogrammarians and their successors. *Transactions of Philological Society* 76 (1): 111–23.

Bynon, Theodora, 1986. August Schleicher: Indo-Europeanist and general linguist. In Bynon and Palmer (1986: 129–50).

Bynon, Theodora and Frank R. Palmer (eds), 1986. *Studies in the History of Western Linguistics (in honor of R. H. Robins).* Cambridge: Cambridge University Press.

Byrd, Dani, 1996. Influences on articulatory timing in consonant sequences. *Journal of Phonetics* 24: 209–44.

Caffi, Claudia, 2009. Pragmatic presupposition. In Jacob L. Mey (ed.), *Concise Encyclopedia of Pragmatics.* Oxford: Elsevier, 759–67.

Calbris, Geneviève, 1990. *Semiotics of French Gesture.* Bloomington: Indiana University Press.

Calbris, Geneviève, 2003. From cutting an object to a clear cut analysis: gesture as the representation of a preconceptual schema linking concrete action to abstract notions. *Gesture* 3: 19–46.

Calbris, Geneviève, 2011. *Elements of Meaning in Gesture.* Amsterdam: John Benjamins.

Calkins, Mary W., 1893. A statistical study of pseudo-chromesthesia and of mental-forms. *American Journal of Psychology* 5: 439–64.

Callanan, Christopher K., 1987. *Die Sprachbeschreibung bei Aristophanes von Byzanz.* Göttingen: Vandenhoeck & Ruprecht.

Cameron, Deborah, 1990. Demythologizing sociolinguistics: why language does not reflect society. In John E. Joseph and Talbot J. Taylor (eds), *Ideologies of Language.* London: Routledge, 79–95.

Cameron, Deborah, 1997. Demythologizing sociolinguistics. In Nikolas Coupland and Adam Jaworski (eds), *Sociolinguistics: A Reader and Course Book.* Basingstoke: Macmillan, 55–67.

Campanella, Tommaso, 1638. *Philosophiae Rationalis partes quinque, videlicet: Grammatica, Dialectica, Rhetorica, Poetica, Historiographia.* Paris: Apud Ioannem Du Bray.

Campbell, Lyle, 2007. Why Sir William Jones got it all wrong, or Jones' role in how to establish language families. In Joseba Lakarra et al. (eds), *Studies in Basque and Historical Linguistics in Memory of R. L. Trask.* Bilbao: Universidad del País Vasco/Euskal Herriko Unibertsitatea, 245–64.

Campbell, Lyle and William J. Poser, 2008. *Language Classification: History and Method.* Cambridge: Cambridge University Press.

Canz, Israel Gottlieb, 1737. *Grammaticae universalis tenuia rudimenta.* Tubingen: Joseph Sigmund. [Repr. Stuttgart–Bad Canstatt: Frommann–Holzboog, 1982.]

Capone, Alessandro (ed.), 2010. *Pragmemes.* Special Issue of the *Journal of Pragmatics* 42(11).

Capone, Nina C., and Karla K. McGregor, 2004. Gesture development: a review for clinical and research practices. *Journal of Speech, Language and Hearing Research* 47: 173–86.

Caramuel y Lobkowitz, Juan, 1654. *Praecursor Logicus Complectens Grammaticam Audacem, cuius partes sunt tres, Methodica, Metrica, Critica.* Francofurti : Sumptibus Iohan.

Carberry, Sandra, 1990. *Plan Recognition in Natural Language Dialogue.* Cambridge, MA: MIT Press.

Carden, Guy, 1982. Backwards anaphora in discourse context. *Journal of Linguistics* 18: 361–87.

Cardona, George, 1976. *Pāṇini: A Survey of Research.* The Hague: Mouton/Delhi: Motilal Banarsidass.

Cardona, George, 1997. *Pāṇini: His Work and its Traditions*, vol. 1: *Background and Introduction*, 2nd edn. Delhi: Motilal Banarsidass.

Cardona, George, 1999. *Recent Research in Paninian Studies.* Delhi: Motilal Banarsidass.

Cardona, George, 2004. Pāṇinian Sūtras of the Type *anyebhyo 'pi dṛśyate.* In M. A. Dhaky and J. B. Shah (eds), *Jambūjyoti: Munivara JambÂvijaya Festschrift.* Ahmedabad: Shreshti Kasturbhai Lalbhai Smarak Nidhi, Sharadaben Chimanbhai Educational Research Centre, 91–107.

Cardona, George, 2008. Theoretical precedents of the Kātantra. In Mrinal Kaul and Ashok N. Aklujkar (eds), *Grammatical Traditions of Kashmir: Essays in Honour of Pandit Dinanath Yaksh.* New Delhi: D. K. Printworld, 300–67.

Carnap, Rudolf, 1942. *Introduction to Semantics.* Cambridge, MA: Harvard University Press.

Carnap, Rudolf, 1956. *Meaning and Necessity.* Chicago: University of Chicago Press.

Carnoy, Albert J., 1927. *La science du mot: traité de sémantique.* Louvain: Éditions Universitas.

Carpov, Jakob, 1735. *Meditatio philosophico-critica de perfectione linguae methodo scientifica adornata.* Jena: Melchior.

Carreres, Angeles, 2006. Strange bedfellows: translation and language teaching. The teaching of translation into L2 in modern languages degrees; uses and limitations. *Sixth Symposium on Translation, Terminology and Interpretation in Cuba and Canada*, December 2006. Canadian Translators, Terminologists and Interpreters Council: www.cttic.org/_06symposium.asp

Carroll, Lewis, 1962. *Alice's Adventures in Wonderland and Through the Looking-Glass.* London: Penguin.

Carstairs-McCarthy, Andrew, 1999. *The Origins of Complex Language: An Inquiry into the Evolutionary Beginnings of Sentences, Syllables, and Truth.* Oxford: Oxford University Press.

Carter, Ron, 2004. *Language and Creativity: The Art of Common Talk.* London: Routledge.

Carter, Ron and Svenja Adolphs, 2008. Linking the verbal and visual: new directions for corpus linguistics. In Andrea Gerbig and Oliver Mason (eds), *Language, People, Numbers: Corpus Linguistics and Society.* Amsterdam: Rodopi, 175–91.

Carter, Ron and Michael McCarthy, 1995. Grammar and the spoken language. *Applied Linguistics* 16: 141–58.

Carter, Ron and Michael McCarthy, 1997. *Exploring Spoken English.* Cambridge: Cambridge University Press.

Carter, Ron and Michael McCarthy, 2006. *Cambridge Grammar of English: A Comprehensive Guide.* Cambridge: Cambridge University Press.

Casad, Eugene H., and Gary B. Palmer, 2003. *Cognitive Linguistics and Non-Indo-European Languages.* Berlin: Mouton de Gruyter.

Cassidy, Steve, and Jonathan M. Harrington, 1996. EMU: an enhanced hierarchical speech database management system. In Paul McCormack and Allison Russell (eds), *Proceedings* of the Sixth Australian International Conference on Speech Science and Technology. Canberra: Australian Speech Science and Technology Association, 361–6.

Cassirer, Ernst, 1933. La langage et la construction du monde des objets. Journal de psychologie normale et pathologique 30: 18–44.

Cassirer, Ernst, 1946. Language and Myth. New York: Harper.

Castro, Americo, 1991. Glosarios latino-españoles de la Edad Media. Madrid: Consejo Superior de Investigaciones Cientificas.

Catford, John C., 1965. A Linguistic Theory of Translation: An Essay in Applied Linguistics. London: Oxford University Press.

Cavalli-Sforza, Luigi L., 2000. Genes, Peoples, and Languages. New York: North Point Press.

Chafe, Wallace L., 1970. Meaning and the Structure of Language. Chicago: University of Chicago Press.

Chafe, Wallace L., 1987. Cognitive constraints on information flow. In Russell Tomlin (ed.), Coherence and Grounding in Discourse: Outcome of a Symposium, Eugene, Oregon, June 1984. Amsterdam: John Benjamins, 11–51.

Chafe, Wallace L., 1994. Discourse, Consciousness and Time: The Flow and Displacement of Conscious Experience in Speaking and Writing. Chicago: University of Chicago Press.

Chafe, Wallace L. and Jane Danielewicz, 1987. Properties of spoken and written language. In Rosalind Horowitz and S. Jay Samuels (eds), Comprehending Oral and Written Language. New York: Academic Press, 83–113.

Chafe, Wallace L. and Deborah Tannen, 1987. The relation between written and spoken language. Annual Review of Anthropology 16: 383–407.

Chambers, Jack K., 2003. Sociolinguistic Theory: Linguistic Variation and its Social Significance, 2nd edn. Oxford: Blackwell.

Chandioux, John, and Marie-France Guéraud, 1981. Météo: un système à l'épreuve du temps. Meta: journal des traducteurs 26: 18–22.

Chao Yuen Ren, 1965. A Grammar of Spoken Chinese. Berkeley, CA: University of California Press.

Charisius, 1925. Flavii Sosipatri Charisii Artis grammaticae libri V, ed. Karl Barwick. Leipzig: Teubner.

Charles, David, 1994. Aristotle on names and their signification. In Stephen Everson (ed.), Companions To Ancient Thought 3: Language. Cambridge: Cambridge University Press.

Charles, David, 2000. Aristotle on Meaning and Essence. Oxford: Clarendon Press.

Charniak, Eugene, 1973. Jack and Janet in search of a theory of knowledge. Proceedings of the 3rd International Joint Conference on Artificial Intelligence (Stanford), 337–43. [Repr. in Grosz et al. (1986: 331–7).]

Charniak, Eugene, 1976. Inference and knowledge part 2. In Eugene Charniak and Yorick Wilks (eds), Computational Semantics. Amsterdam: North-Holland, 129–54.

Charniak, Eugene, 1978. On the use of framed knowledge in language comprehension. Artificial Intelligence 11: 225–65.

Charniak, Eugene, 1981. The case-slot identity theory. Cognitive Science 5: 285–92.

Charniak, Eugene, 1993. Statistical Language Learning. Cambridge, MA: MIT Press.

Charniak, Eugene, 2000. A maximum-entropy-inspired parser. Proceedings of the 1st Meeting of the North American Chapter of the Association for Computational Linguistics (Seattle), 132–9.

Charteris-Black, Jonathan, 2004. Corpus Approaches to Critical Metaphor Analysis. Basingstoke: Palgrave Macmillan.

Chase, Wayland J., 1926. *The Ars minor of Donatus: For One Thousand Years the Leading Textbook of Grammar*. Madison: University of Wisconsin.

Chastaing, Maxime (n.d.). La voyelle 'I' paraît-elle jaune? *Vie et langage*.

Chastaing, Maxime, 1958. Le symbolisme des voyelles: significations des 'i', I and II. *Journal de psychologie* 55: 403–423, 461–81.

Chastaing, Maxime, 1962. La brillance des voyelles. *Archivum Linguisticum* 14: 1–13.

Chen Mengjia 陳夢家, 1988. *Yīnxū Bǔcí Zōngshù* 殷虛卜辭綜述 [An Overview of Divination Writings from the Yin Ruins]. Beijing: Zhonghua Bookstore.

Cherry, E. Colin, Roman Jakobson, and Morris Halle, 1952. Toward the logical description of languages in their phonemic aspect. *Language* 29: 34–46.

Chevillard, Jean-Luc, 2000. The establishment of Dravidian linguistics. Die Anfänge der dravidischen Sprachforschung. La constitution de la linguistique dravidienne. In Sylvain Auroux and E. F. Konrad Koerner (eds), *Geschichte der Sprachwissenschaften/History of the Language Sciences*, 1: *An International Handbook on the Evolution of the Study of Language from the Beginnings to the Present*. Berlin: Mouton de Gruyter, 191–202.

Chifflet, Pascale, 2003. Recent legal developments: the judgement of the international criminal tribunal for the former Yugoslavia in *Prosecutor v. Mladen Naletilić and Vinko Martinović*. *Leiden Journal of International Law* 16: 525–39.

Childs, G. Tucker, 1988. The phonology of Kisi ideophones. *Journal of African Languages and Linguistics* 10: 165–90.

Chladni, Ernst F. F., 1802. *Die Akustik*. Leipzig: Breitkopf & Härtel.

Chladni, Ernst F. F., 1827. *Kurze Uebersicht der Schall- und Klanglehre: nebst einem Anhange die Entwickelung und Anordnung der Tonverhältnisse betreffend*. Mainz: B. Schott's Söhne.

Chomsky, Noam, 1951. Morphophonemics of Modern Hebrew. Master's thesis, University of Pennsylvania. [New York: Garland, 1979.]

Chomsky, Noam, 1955–6. The logical structure of linguistic theory. MS. Published as Chomsky (1975a).

Chomsky, Noam. 1955-6. *The Logical Structure of Linguistic Theory*. Manuscript.

Chomsky, Noam, 1956. Three models for the description of language. *Institute of Radio Engineers Transactions on Information Theory* II-2: 113–24. [Repr. in Luce et al. (1965: 105–24).]

Chomsky, Noam, 1957a. *Syntactic Structures*. The Hague: Mouton.

Chomsky, Noam, 1957b. Review of Hockett (1955). *International Journal of American Linguistics* 23: 223–34.

Chomsky, Noam, 1959a. On certain formal properties of grammars. *Information and Control* 2: 137–67.

Chomsky, Noam, 1959b. Review of Skinner (1957). *Language* 35: 26–58.

Chomsky, Noam, 1962. A transformational approach to syntax. In Archibald A. Hill (ed.), *Third Texas Conference on Problems of Linguistic Analysis in English*. Austin: University of Texas Press, 124–58.

Chomsky, Noam, 1964a. *Current Issues in Linguistic Theory*. The Hague: Mouton.

Chomsky, Noam, 1964b. The logical basis of linguistic theory. In Horace Lunt (ed.), *Proceedings of the Ninth International Congress of Linguistics*. The Hague: Mouton, 914–1008.

Chomsky, Noam, 1965. *Aspects of the Theory of Syntax*. Cambridge, MA: MIT Press.

Chomsky, Noam, 1966. *Cartesian Linguistics: A Chapter in the History of Rationalist Thought*. New York: Harper & Row. [3rd edn, New York: Cambridge University Press, 2009.]

Chomsky, Noam, 1967. Some general properties of phonological rules. *Language* 43: 102–28.

Chomsky, Noam, 1968. *Language and Mind*. New York: Harcourt Brace & World. [3rd edn, New York: Cambridge University Press, 2006.]

Chomsky, Noam, 1969. Some empirical assumptions in modern philosophy of language. In Sidney Morgenbesser, Patrick Suppes, and Morton White (eds), *Philosophy, Science, and Method: Essays in honor of Ernest Nagel*. New York: St. Martins Press, 160–285.

Chomsky, Noam, 1970. Remarks on nominalization. In Roderick A. Jacobs and Peter S. Rosenbaum (eds), *Readings in English Transformational Grammar*. Waltham, MA: Ginn, 184–221.

Chomsky, Noam, 1973. Conditions on transformations. In Stephen R. Anderson and Paul Kiparsky (eds), *A Festschrift for Morris Halle*. New York: Holt, Rinehart & Winston, 132–286.

Chomsky, Noam, 1975a [1955–6]. *The Logical Structure of Linguistic Theory*. New York: Plenum.

Chomsky, Noam, 1975b. Questions of form and interpretation. *Linguistic Analysis* 1: 75–109.

Chomsky, Noam, 1975c. *Reflections on Language*. New York: Pantheon.

Chomsky, Noam, 1976. Conditions on rules of grammar. *Linguistic Analysis* 2: 303–51.

Chomsky, Noam, 1980. *Rules and Representations*. New York: Columbia University Press.

Chomsky, Noam, 1981a. *Lectures on Government and Binding*. Dordrecht: Foris.

Chomsky, Noam, 1981b. Principles and parameters in syntactic theory. In David Lightfoot and Norbert Hornstein (eds), *Explanation in Linguistics*. London: Routledge, 32–75.

Chomsky, Noam, 1982. *The Generative Enterprise: A Discussion with Riny Huybregts and Henk van Riemsdijk*. Dordrecht: Foris.

Chomsky, Noam, 1986. *Knowledge of Language: Its Nature, Origin, and Use*. New York: Praeger.

Chomsky, Noam, 1988. *Language and Problems of Knowledge*. Cambridge, MA: MIT Press.

Chomsky, Noam, 1991. Some notes on economy of derivation and representation. In Robert Freidin (ed.), *Principles and Parameters in Comparative Grammar*. Cambridge, MA: MIT Press, 417–54. [Repr. in Chomsky (1995b).]

Chomsky, Noam, 1993. A minimalist program for linguistic theory. In Kenneth Hale and Samuel J. Keyser (eds), *The View from Building 20: Essays in Linguistics in Honor of Sylvain Bromberger*. Cambridge, MA: MIT Press, 1–52. [Repr. in Chomsky (1995b).]

Chomsky, Noam, 1995a. Bare phrase structure. In Héctor Campos and Paula Kempchinsky (eds), *Evolution and Revolution In Linguistic Theory*. Washington, DC: Georgetown University Press, 51–109.

Chomsky, Noam, 1995b. *The Minimalist Program*. Cambridge, MA: MIT Press.

Chomsky, Noam, 2000a. Linguistics and brain science. In Alec Marantz, Yasushi Miyashita, and Wayne O'Neil (eds), *Image, Language, Brain: Papers from the First Mind Articulation Project Symposium*. Cambridge, MA: MIT Press, 13–28.

Chomsky, Noam, 2000b. Minimalist inquiries: the framework. In Roger Martin, David Michaels, and Juan Uriagereka (eds), *Step by Step: Essays on Minimalist Syntax in Honor of Howard Lasnik*. Cambridge, MA: MIT Press, 89–155.

Chomsky, Noam, 2000c. *New Horizons in the Study of Language and Mind*. Cambridge: Cambridge University Press.

Chomsky, Noam, 2001. Derivation by phase. In Michael Kenstowicz (ed.), *Ken Hale: A Life in Language*. Cambridge, MA: MIT Press, 1–52.

Chomsky, Noam, 2004. Beyond explanatory adequacy. In Adriana Belletti (ed.), *Structures and Beyond: The Cartography of Syntactic Structure*, vol 3. Oxford: Oxford University Press, 104–31.

Chomsky, Noam, 2005. Three factors in language design. *Linguistic Inquiry* 36: 1–22.

Chomsky, Noam, 2007. Approaching UG from below. In Uli Sauerland and Hans-Martin Gärtner (eds), *Interfaces + Recursion = Language? Chomsky's Minimalism and the View from Syntax-Semantics*. Berlin: Mouton de Gruyter, 1–29.

Chomsky, Noam, 2008. On phases. In Robert Freidin, Carlos Otero, and Maria-Luisa Zubizarreta (eds), *Foundational Issues In Linguistic Theory*. Cambridge, MA: MIT Press, 133–66.

Chomsky, Noam, 2009. Concluding remarks. In Massimo Piatelli-Palmarini, Juan Uriager-eka, and Pello Salaburu (eds), *Of Minds and Language: A Dialogue with Noam Chomsky in the Basque Country*. Oxford: Oxford University Press, 379–409.

Chomsky, Noam, 2010. Some simple evo devo theses: how true might they be for language? In Larson et al. (2010: 45–62).

Chomsky, Noam, and Morris Halle, 1965. Some controversial questions in phonological theory. *Journal of Linguistics* 1: 97–138.

Chomsky, Noam, and Morris Halle, 1968. *The Sound Pattern of English*. New York: Harper & Row.

Chomsky, Noam, Morris Halle, and Fred Lukoff, 1956. On accent and juncture in English. In Morris Halle, Horace Lunt, Hugh Maclean, et al. (eds), *For Roman Jakobson*. The Hague: Mouton, 65–80.

Chomsky, Noam and Howard Lasnik, 1977. Filters and control. *Linguistic Inquiry* 8: 425–504.

Chomsky, Noam and Howard Lasnik, 1993. The theory of principles and parameters. In Joachim Jacobs, Arnim Von Stechow, Wolfgang Sternefeld, and Theo Vennemann (eds), *Syntax: An International Handbook of Contemporary Research*. Berlin: de Gruyter, 506–69. [Repr. in Chomsky (1995b).]

Chomsky, Noam and George A. Miller, 1963. Introduction to the formal analysis of natural languages. In Robert Duncan Luce, Robert R. Bush, and Eugene Galanter (eds), *Handbook of Mathematical Psychology*, vol. 2. New York: Wiley, 169–321.

Christy, T. Craig, 1983. *Uniformitarianism in Linguistics*. Amsterdam: John Benjamins.

Chuang Fei-Yu and Hilary Nesi, 2006. An analysis of formal errors in a corpus of Chinese student writing. *Corpora* 1: 251–71.

Chung, Karen Steffen, 1989. Language. In *Republic of China Yearbook*. Taipei: Kwang Hwa, 34–47.

Chung, Karen Steffen, 1995. Review of Giulio Lepschy (ed.), *History of Linguistics*, vol. 1: *The Eastern Traditions of Linguistics*. *Historiographia Linguistica* 22: 401–9. [http://homepage.ntu.edu.tw/~karchung/pubs/Lepschy_rev.pdf]

Chung, Karen Steffen, 2001. Some returned loans: Japanese loanwords in Taiwan Mandarin. In Thomas E. McAuley (ed.), *Language Change in East Asia*. Richmond, Surrey: Curzon, 161–79. [Revised version: http://homepage.ntu.edu.tw/~karchung/pubs/Japanloans_rev.pdf]

Church, Kenneth W., 1988. A stochastic parts program and noun phrase parser for unrestricted text. *Proceedings of the Second Conference on Applied Natural Language Processing* (Austin, TX), 136–43.

Church, Kenneth W., 2004. Speech and language processing: can we use the past to predict the future? In Petr Sojka, Ivan Kopeček, and Karel Pala (eds), *Text, Speech and Dialogue: Proceedings of the 7th International Conference (TSD 2004)*. Berlin: Springer, 3–13.

Church, Kenneth W., 2012. A pendulum swung too far. *Linguistic Issues in Language Technology* 6, article 5. [elanguage.net/journals/lilt/article/view/2581]

Church, Kenneth W., William Gale, Patrick Hanks, and Donald Hindle, 1991. Using statistics in lexical analysis. In Uri Zernik (ed.), *Lexical Acquisition: Exploiting On-Line Resources to Build a Lexicon*. Hillsdale, NJ: Lawrence Erlbaum, 115–64.

Church, Kenneth W. and Patrick Hanks, 1990. Word association norms, mutual information, and lexicography. *Computational Linguistics* 16: 22–9.

Churchland, Paul, 1981. Eliminative materialism and the propositional attitudes. *Journal of Philosophy* 78: 67–90.

Chvany, Catherine, 1986. Translating one poem from a cycle: Cvtaeva's 'Your Name is a Bird in my Hand' from 'Poems to Blok'. In Anna Lisa Crone and Catherine Chvany (eds), *New Studies in Russian Language and Literature*. Columbus, OH: Slavica, 49–58.

Cienki, Alan, and Müller, Cornelia (eds), 2008. *Metaphor and Gesture*. Amsterdam: John Benjamins.

Clark, Herbert H., and Susan Haviland, 1977. Comprehension and the given–new contract. In Roy O. Freedle (ed.), *Discourse Production and Comprehension*. Norwood, NJ: Ablex, 1–40.

Cleary, James, 1959. John Bulwer: Renaissance communicationist. *Quarterly Journal of Speech* 45: 391–8.

Cledonius. *Ars.* In Keil (1961: v.9–79).

Clements, George N., 1980 [1976]. *Vowel Harmony in Nonlinear Generative Phonology: An Autosegmental Model*. Bloomington: Indiana University Linguistics Club.

Clements, George N., 2000. Some antecedents of nonlinear phonology. *Folia Linguistica* 34 (1–2): 29–56.

Coblin, Weldon S., 2007. *A Handbook of 'Phags-pa Chinese*. Honolulu: University of Hawai'i Press.

Cocchiara, Giuseppe, 1932. *Il linguaggio del gesto*. Turin: Bocca.

Cochleus, 1514. *Grammatica Io: Cochlei, Norici Rudimenta ad usum latinae linguae necessaria continens*. Strassburg: Beck.

Cohen, Chaim, and Ya'akov Choueka, 2006. Hebrew lexicography. In Keith Brown (ed.), *Encyclopedia of Language and Linguistics*, 2nd edn, vol. 5. London: Elsevier, 168–272.

Cohen, Daniel (ed.), 1974. *Explaining Linguistic Phenomena*. Washington, DC: Hemisphere.

Cohen, Daniel and Jessica Wirth (eds), 1975. *Testing Linguistic Hypotheses*. Washington, DC: Hemisphere.

Cohen, David, Jérôme Lentin, François Bron, and Antoine Lonnet, 1994–2012. *Dictionaire des racines sémitiques ou attestées dans les langues sémitiques* 1–9. Paris: Peeters.

Cohen, L. Jonathan, 1986. *The Dialogue of Reason: An Analysis of Analytical Philosophy*. Oxford: Clarendon Press.

Cohen, Marcel, 1947. *Essai comparatif sur le vocabulaire et la phonétique du chamito-sémitique*. Paris: Leroux.

Cohen, Marcel, 1958. *La grande invention de l'écriture et son évolution*. 3 vols. Paris: Imprimerie Nationale.

Cohen, Philip R., and C. Raymond Perrault, 1979. Elements of a plan-based theory of speech acts. *Cognitive Science* 3: 177–212. [Repr. in Grosz et al. (1986: 423–40).]

Cohn, Abigail, 2011. Laboratory phonology: past successes and current questions, challenges, and goals. In Cécile Fougeron, Barbara Kühnert, Mariapaola D'Imperio, and Nathalie Vallé (eds), *Laboratory Phonology* 10. Berlin: Mouton de Gruyter, 3–29.

Coles, [James] Oakley, 1872. On the production of articulate sound (speech). *British Medical Journal* (17 Feb.): 181–2.

Collinge, N. E., 1978. Exceptions, their nature and place—and the Neogrammarians. *Transactions of Philological Society* 76: 61–86.

Collinge, N. E., 1995. History of historical linguistics. In E. F. Konrad Koerner and Ronald E. Asher (eds), *Concise History of the Language Sciences: From the Sumerians to the Cognitivists*. Oxford: Pergamon, 1–212.

Collinge, N. E., 1998. Dionusios Anomalos. In Law and Sluiter (1998: 55–71).

Collins, Beverley, and Inger M. Mees, 1999. *The Real Professor Higgins: The Life and Career of Daniel Jones*. Berlin: Mouton de Gruyter.

Collins, Michael, 1997. Three generative, lexicalized models for statistical parsing. *Proceedings of the 35th Annual Meeting of the Association for Computational Linguistics* (Madrid), 16–23.

Collins, Michael, 2003. Head-driven statistical models for natural language parsing. *Computational Linguistics* 29: 589–637.

Colmerauer, Alain, 1978. Metamorphosis grammars. In Leonard Bolc (ed.), *Natural Language Communication with Computers*. Berlin: Springer, 133–88.

Colmerauer, Alain and Philippe Roussel, 1993. The birth of Prolog. *ACM SIGPLAN Notices* 28: 37–52.

Comenius, Johann Amos, 1658. *Orbis sensualium pictus. Hoc est omnium fundamentalium in mundo rerum, et in vita actionum, pictura et nomenclatura/Die sichtbare Welt, das ist, aller vornehmsten Welt-Dinge und Lebensverrichtungen, Vorbildung und Benahmung*. Nuremberg: Michael Endter.

Condillac, Etienne Bonnot de, 1746. *Essai sur l'origine des connoissances humaines*. Amsterdam: Pierre Mortier.

Condillac, Etienne Bonnot de., 1775. *Cours d'étude pour l'instruction du Prince de Parme*, tome premier: *Grammaire*. Parme: Imprimérie Royale. [Repr. Stuttgart–Bad Canstatt: Frommann–Holzboog, 1986.]

Condon, William S., and William D. Ogston, 1967. A segmentation of behavior. *Journal of Psychiatric Research* 5: 221–35.

Conklin, Harold, 1955. Hanunóo color categories. *Southwestern Journal of Anthropology* 11: 339–44.

Considine, John, 2008. *Dictionaries in Early Modern Europe: Lexicography and the Making of Heritage*. Cambridge: Cambridge University Press

Conti Rossini, Karolus (Carlo), 1931. *Chrestomathia Arabica meridionalis epigraphica*. Roma: Istituto per l'Oriente.

Cook, Guy, 2010. *Translation in Language Teaching: An Argument for Reassessment*. Oxford: Oxford University Press.

Cooper, Jerrold S., 1999. Sumerian and Semitic writing in most ancient Mesopotamia. In Karel Van Lerberghe and Gabriela Voet (eds), *Languages and Cultures in Contact: At the Crossroads of Civilizations in the Syro-Mesopotamian Realm*. Leuven: Peeters, 61–77.

Cooper, Robert L., and Susan Carpenter, 1972. Linguistic diversity in the Ethiopian market. In Joshua A. Fishman (ed.), *Contributions to the Sociology of Language*, vol. 2. The Hague: Mouton, 155–267.

Copeland, Rita, and Ineke Sluiter (eds), 2009. *Medieval Grammar and Rhetoric: Language Arts and Literary Theory, AD 300–1475*. Oxford: Oxford University Press.

Copestake, Ann, and Dan Flickinger, 2000. An open-source grammar development environment and broad-coverage English grammar using HPSG. *Proceedings of the Second Conference on Language Resources and Evaluation (LREC-2000)* (Athens). www-csli.stanford.edu/~aac/papers/lrec2000.pdf

Corballis, Michael C., 2002. *From Hand to Mouth: The Origins of Language.* Princeton, NJ: Princeton University Press.

Corballis, Michael C., 2010. Did language evolve before speech? In Larson et al. (2010: 115–23).

Corbeill, Anthony, 2004. *Nature Embodied: Gesture in Ancient Rome.* Princeton, NJ: Princeton University Press.

Cortes, Corinna, and Vladimir Vapnik, 1995. Support-vector networks. *Machine Learning* 20: 273–97.

Coseriu, Eugenio, 1952. *Sistema, norma y habla.* Published 1975 as *Sprachtheorie und allgemeine Sprachwissenschaft.* Munich: Fink.

Coseriu, Eugenio, 1962. *Teoría del lenguaje y lingüística general: cinco estudios.* Madrid: Gredos.

Coseriu, Eugenio, 1964. Pour une sémantique diachronique structurale. *Travaux de linguistique et de littérature* 2: 139–86.

Coseriu, Eugenio, 1967. Lexikalische Solidaritäten. *Poetica* 1: 293–303.

Coseriu, Eugenio and Horst Geckeler, 1981. *Trends in Structural Semantics.* Tübingen: Gunter Narr.

Coulmas, Florian (ed.), 1981. *Conversational Routine: Explorations in Standardized Communication Situations and Prepatterned Speech.* The Hague: Mouton.

Coulmas, Florian, 1996. *The Blackwell Encyclopedia of Writing Systems.* Oxford: Blackwell.

Coulson, Seana, 2006. Electrifying results: ERP data and cognitive linguistics. In Monica Gonzalez-Marquez, Irene Mittelberg, Seana Coulson, and Michael J. Spivey (eds), *Methods in Cognitive Linguistics.* Amsterdam: John Benjamins, 400–23.

Court de Gébelin, Antoine, 1777. Origine du langage et de l'écriture. In *Le Monde primitif, considéré dans l'histoire naturelle de la parole,* nouvelle édition. Paris: l'Auteur; Boudet et al.

Couturat, Louis, 1901. *La logique de Leibniz.* Paris: Félix Alcan.

Covington, Michael A., 1982. Syntactic theory in the High Middle Ages: modistic models of sentence structure. Ph.D thesis, Yale University.

Cox, Felicity, and Sallyanne Palethorpe, 2004. The border effect: vowel differences across the NSW–Victorian Border. In Christo Moskovsky (ed.), *Proceedings of the 2003 Conference of the Australian Linguistics Society.* www.als.asn.au/proceedings/als2003/cox.pdf

Cribiore, Raffaella, 2001. *Gymnastics of the Mind: Greek Education in Hellenistic and Roman Egypt.* Princeton, NJ: Princeton University Press.

Critchley, Macdonald, 1939. *The Language of Gesture.* London: Edward Arnold.

Crivelli, Paolo, 2004. *Aristotle on Truth.* Cambridge: Cambridge University Press.

Crivelli, Paolo, 2010. Aristotle on signification and truth. In Georgios Anagnostopoulos (ed.), *A Companion to Aristotle.* Oxford: Wiley-Blackwell, 81–100.

Croft, William, 1995. Autonomy and functionalist linguistics. *Language* 71: 490–531.

Croft, William, 2000. *Explaining Language Change: An Evolutionary Approach.* London: Longman.

Croft, William, 2001. *Radical Construction Grammar.* Oxford: Oxford University Press.

Croft, William, 2003a. Lexical rules vs. constructions: a false dichotomy. In Hubert Cuyckens, Thomas Berg, René Dirven, and Klaus-Uwe Panther (eds), *Motivation in Language: Studies in Honour of Günter Radden.* Amsterdam: John Benjamins, 49–68.

Croft, William, 2003b. Social evolution and language change. MS.

Croft, William, 2007. Construction grammar. In Dirk Geeraerts and Hubert Cuyckens (eds), *Handbook of Cognitive Linguistics*. Oxford: Oxford University Press, 463–508.

Croft, William, 2008. Evolutionary linguistics. *Annual Review of Anthropology* 37: 219–34.

Croft, William, 2009. Toward a social cognitive linguistics. In Vyvyan Evans and Stéphanie Pourcel (eds), *New Directions in Cognitive Linguistics*. Amsterdam: John Benjamins, 395–420.

Croft, William, 2012. *Verbs: Aspect and Causal Structure*. Oxford: Oxford University Press.

Croft, William and D. Alan Cruse, 2001. *Construction Grammar*. Oxford: Oxford University Press.

Croft, William and D. Alan Cruse. 2004. *Cognitive Linguistics*. Cambridge: Cambridge University Press.

Crowley, Terry, 1991. *Proper English? Readings in Language, History and Cultural Identity*. London: Routledge.

Crowley, Terry, 2003. *Standard English and the Politics of Language*, 2nd edn. Basingstoke: Palgrave Macmillan.

Cruse, D. Alan, 1986. *Lexical Semantics*. Cambridge: Cambridge University Press.

Crystal, Thomas H., 1993. TIPSTER Program History. *Proceedings of the TIPSTER Text Program Phase I Workshop* (Fredricksburg, VA), 3–4.

Cubrovic, Biljana, 1999. *Onomatopoeic Words in English*. Belgrade: University of Belgrade.

Culler, Jonathan D., 1983. *Roland Barthes*. Oxford: Oxford University Press.

Culler, Jonathan D., 1994. *On Deconstruction: Theory and Criticism after Structuralism*. Ithaca, NY: Cornell University Press.

Culpeper, Jonathan, 2009. Keyness: words, parts-of-speech and semantic categories in the character-talk of Shakespeare's *Romeo and Juliet*. *International Journal of Corpus Linguistics* 14: 29–59.

Currie, Haver C., 1952. A projection of socio-linguistics: the relationship of speech to social status. *Southern Speech Journal* 18: 28–37.

Curtis, James F., 1954. The rise of experimental phonetics. In Karl R.Wallace (ed.), *History of Speech Education in America: Background Studies*. New York: Appleton-Century-Crofts, 348–69.

Cutting, Doug, Julian Kupiec, Jan Pedersen, and Penelope Sibun, 1992. A practical part-of-speech tagger. *Proceedings of the Third Conference on Applied Natural Language Processing. Trento, Italy*. Stroudsburg, PA: Association for Computational Linguistics, 133–40.

Cytowic, Richard E., 1989. *Synesthesia: A Union of the Senses*. New York: Springer.

Daines, Simon, 1640. *Orthoepia Anglicana: or, the First principall part of the English Grammar*. London: Robert Young & Richard Badger.

Dalgarno, George, 1661. *Ars Signorum, vulgo character universalis et lingua philosophica*. London: J. Hayes. [Text and English transl. by David Cram and Jaap Maat in *George Dalgarno on Universal Language: The Art of Signs (1661), The Deaf and Dumb Man's Tutor (1680), and the Unpublished Papers* (Oxford: Oxford University Press, 2001).]

Dalgarno, George, 1680. Didascalacophus, or the Deaf and Dumb mans Tutor. Oxford: At the Theatre.

Dalimier, Catherine, 2001. *Apollonius Dyscole. Traité des Conjonctions: introduction, texte, traduction et commentaire*. Paris: J. Vrin.

Dalton, Martha, and Ailbhe Ní Chasaide, 2005. Tonal alignment in Irish Dialects. *Language and Speech* 48: 441–64.

Dandekar, R. N., 1946–93. *Vedic Bibliography*. 5 vols. Pune: BORI.

Danecki, Janusz, 1985. Indian phonetical theory and the Arab grammarians. *Rocznik Orientalistyczny* 44: 127–34.

Daneš, František, 1974. Functional sentence perspective and the organization of the text. In František Daneš (ed.), *Papers on Functional Sentence Perspective*. Prague: Academia, 106–28.

Daniels, Peter T., 1990. Fundamentals of grammatology. *Journal of the American Oriental Society* 110: 727–31.

Daniels, Peter T., 1992a. The syllabic origin of writing and the segmental origin of the alphabet. In Pamela Downing, Susan D. Lima, and Michael Noonan (eds), *The Linguistics of Literacy*. Amsterdam: John Benjamins, 83–110.

Daniels, Peter T., 1992b. What do the 'paleographic' tablets tell us of Mesopotamian scribes' knowledge of the history of their script? *Mār Sipri: Newsletter of the Committee on Mesopotamian Civilization, American Schools of Oriental Research* 5: 1–4.

Daniels, Peter T., 2000a. On writing syllables: three episodes of script transfer. *Studies in the Linguistic Sciences* 30: 73–86.

Daniels, Peter T., 2000b. Syllables, consonants, and vowels in West Semitic writing. *Lingua Posnaniensis* 42: 43–55.

Daniels, Peter T., 2006. On beyond alphabets. *Written Language and Literacy* 9: 7–24.

Daniels, Peter T., 2007. *Littera ex occidente*: toward a functional history of writing. In Cynthia L. Miller (ed.), *Studies in Semitic and Afroasiatic Linguistics Presented to Gene B. Gragg*. Chicago: Oriental Institute of the University of Chicago, 53–68.

Daniels, Peter T., in press, a. Arabic writing. In Jonathan Owens (ed.), *Oxford Handbook of Arabic Linguistics*. Oxford: Oxford University Press.

Daniels, Peter T., in press, b. Three models of script transfer. *Word* 57(3). [Paper presented at the annual meeting of the International Linguistic Association, New York, 2004.]

Daniels, Peter T., and William Bright (eds), 1996. *The World's Writing Systems*. New York: Oxford University Press.

Darmesteter, Arsène, 1886. *The Life of Words as Symbols of Ideas*. London: Kegan Paul.

Darmesteter, Arsène., 1887. *La vie des mots étudiée dans leur significations*. Paris: Delagrave.

Darmesteter, Arsène and Adolphe Hatzfeld, 1890. *Dictionnaire générale de la langue française du commencement du XVIIe siècle jusqu'à nos jours*. Paris: Delagrave.

Darnell, John C., F. W. Dobbs-Allsopp, Marilyn J. Lundberg, P. Kyle McCarter, and Bruce Zuckerman, 2005. Two early alphabetic inscriptions from the Wadi el-Ḥôl: new evidence for the origin of the alphabet from the Western Desert of Egypt. *Annual of the American Schools of Oriental Research* 59: 63–124.

Darnell, Regna, 1990. *Edward Sapir: Linguist, Anthropologist, Humanist*. Berkeley: University of California Press.

Darnell, Regna and Judith Irvine, 1997. Edward Sapir 1884–1939. *Biographical Memoirs*, vol. 71. Washington, DC: National Academy of Sciences.

Darwin, Charles, 1871. *The Descent of Man and Selection in Relation to Sex*. 2 vols. London: John Murray.

Darwin, Charles, 1872. *The Expression of the Emotions in Man and Animals*. London: John Murray.

Darwin, Erasmus, 1803. Additional Notes, XV: Analysis of articulate sounds. In *The Temple of Nature; Or, the Origin of Society: a Poem. With Philosophical Notes*. London: J. Johnson, 107–20.

Darwin, George H., 1874. Professor Whitney on the origin of language. *Contemporary Review* 24: 894–904. [Repr. in Harris and Pyle (1996: 177–290).]

Davidson, Clifford (ed.), 2001. *Gesture in Medieval Drama and Art*. Kalamazoo: Western Michigan University Medieval Institute.

Davidson, Donald, 1973. Radical interpretation. *Dialectica* 27: 313–28. [Repr. in *Inquiries into Truth and Interpretation* (Oxford: Clarendon Press, 1984), 125–39.]

Davies, Anna Morpurgo, 1998. *Nineteenth Century Linguistics*. Vol. 4 of Lepschy (1994–8).

Davies, Winifred V., and Nils Langer, 2006. *The Making of Bad Language: Lay Linguistic Stigmatisations in German: Past and Present*. Frankfurt am Main: Peter Lang.

Davis, Jeffrey E., 2010. *Hand Talk: Sign Language among American Indian Nations*. New York: Cambridge University Press.

Davis, Martha, 1972. *Understanding Body Movement: An Annotated Bibliography*. New York: Arno Press.

Davis, Martha and Janet Skupien, 1982. *Body Movement and Nonverbal Communication: An Annotated Bibliography, 1971–1981*. Bloomington: Indiana University Press.

Day, Sean A., 1995. I remember her name was cool blue: synaesthetic metaphors, evolution, and memory. In Cary W. Spinks and John Deely (eds), *Semiotics*. New York: Peter Lang.

Day, Sean A., 2001. Trends in synesthetically colored graphemes and phonemes. mutuslab.cs. uwindsor.ca/schurko/misc/trends_in_synesthete_letters.htm

de Beaugrande, Robert A., 1980. Text and discourse in European research. *Discourse Processes* 3(4): 287–300.

de Beaugrande, Robert A., 1991. Text linguistics and new applications. *Annual Review of Applied Linguistics* 11: 17–41

de Beaugrande, Robert A., 1995. Text linguistics. In Jef Verschueren, Jan-Ola Östman, Jan Blommaert, and Chris Bulcaen (eds), *Handbook of Pragmatics: Manual*. Amsterdam: John Benjamins, 536–44.

de Beaugrande, Robert A., 1997a. *New Foundations for a Science of Text and Discourse*. Greenwich, CT: Ablex.

de Beaugrande, Robert A., 1997b. The story of discourse analysis. In Teun van Dijk (ed.), *Discourse as Structure and Process*. London: Sage, 35–62.

de Beaugrande, Robert A., 2000. Text linguistics at the millennium: corpus data and missing links. *Text* 20(2): 153–97.

de Beaugrande, Robert A. and Wolfgang U. Dressler, 1981. *Introduction to Text Linguistics*. London: Longman.

de Brosses, Charles, 1765. *Traité de la formation mécanique des langages et des principes physiques de l'étymologie*. Paris: Saillant, Vincent & Desaint.

De Cock, Sylvie, Sylviane Granger, GeoffreyLeech, and Tony McEnery, 1998. An automated approach to the phrasicon of EFL learners. In Sylviane Granger (ed.), *Learner English on Computer*. London: Addison Wesley Longman, 67–79.

de Féral, C. (ed.), 2009. *Le nom des langues III. Le nom des langues en Afrique sub-saharienne: pratiques, dénominations, catégorisations / Naming Languages in Sub-Saharan Africa: Practices, Names, Categorisations*. Leuven: Peeters.

de Gérando, Joseph-Marie, Baron, 1800. *Des signes et de l'art de penser considérés dans leurs rapports mutuels*. Paris: Goujon fils.

De Jonge, Casper C., 2008. *Between Grammar and Rhetoric: Dionysius of Halicarnassus on Language, Linguistics and Literature*. Leiden: Brill.

de Jorio, Andrea, 1832. *La mimica degli antichi investigata nel gestire napoletano*. Naples: Fibreno.

De Jorio, Andrea, 2000. *Gesture in Naples and Gesture in Classical Antiquity: A Translation of 'La mimica degli antichi investigata nel gestire napoletano' by Andrea de Jorio (1832) with an Introduction and Notes by Adam Kendon*. Bloomington: Indiana University Press.

de Lacy, Paul (ed.), 2007. *The Cambridge Handbook of Phonology*. Cambridge: Cambridge University Press.

de Laguna, Grace A., 1927. *Speech: Its Function and Development*. New Haven, CT: Yale University Press.

de Mauro, Tullio (ed.), 1972. *Corso di linguistica generale*, 4th edn with Addenda. Bari: Laterza.

De Rijk, Lambert M., 1967. *Logica Modernorum. A Contribution to the History of Early Terminist Logic*, vol. 2, part 1. Assen: Van Gorcum.

de Saussure, Ferdinand, 1879. *Mémoire sur le système primitif des voyelles dans les langues indo-européennes*. Leipzig: Teubner.

de Saussure, Ferdinand, 1959. *Course in General Linguistics*, transl. Wade Baskin. New York: McGraw-Hill.

de Saussure, Ferdinand, 1962 [1916, final edn 1922]. *Cours de linguistique générale*, ed. Charles Bally and Albert Sechehaye in collaboration with Albert Riedlinger. Paris: Payot.

de Saussure, Ferdinand, 1972. *Cours de linguistique générale, édition critique préparée par Tullio De Mauro*. Paris: Payot.

Deacon, Terrence R., 1997. *The Symbolic Species: The Co-evolution of Language and the Brain*. New York: W. W. Norton.

Declerck, Renaat, and Susan Reed, 2000. The semantics and pragmatics of *unless*. *English Language and Linguistics* 4: 205–41.

Deerwester, Scott, Susan T. Dumais, George W. Furnas, Thomas K. Landauer, and Richard Harshman, 1990. Indexing by latent semantic analysis. *Journal of the American Society for Information Science* 41: 391–407.

DeGraff, Michel, 2001. On the origin of creoles: a Cartesian critique of neo-Darwinian linguistics. *Linguistic Typology* 5: 213–310.

Deignan, Alice, 2005. *Metaphor and Corpus Linguistics*. Amsterdam: John Benjamins

del Olmo Lete, Gregorio, and Joaquín Sanmartín, 2003. *A Dictionary of the Ugaritic Language in the Alphabetic Tradition*. Leiden: E. J. Brill.

Delbrück, Berthold, 1901. *Grundfragen der Sprachforschung; mit Rücksicht auf W. Wundt's Sprachpsychologie*. Strassburg: Trübner.

DeNero, John, and Jakob Uszkoreit, 2011. Inducing sentence structure from parallel corpora for reordering. *Proceedings of the 2011 Conference on Empirical Methods in Natural Language Processing* (Edinburgh), 193–203.

Denyer, Nicholas, 1991. *Language, Thought and Falsehood in Ancient Greek Philosophy*. London: Routledge.

Derenbourg, Hartwig, 1881-9. *Le livre de Sibawayhi, traité de grammaire arabe*. Paris: Imprimerie Nationale. [Repr. Hildesheim: Olms, 1970.]

DeRose, Steven, 1988. Grammatical category disambiguation by statistical optimization. *Computational Linguistics* 14: 31–9.

Derrida, Jacques, 1976. *Of Grammatology*, trans. Gayatri Chakravorty Spivak. Baltimore, MD: Johns Hopkins University Press. [French original 1967.]

Derwing, Bruce, 1973. *Transformational Grammar as a Theory of Language Acquisition*. Cambridge: Cambridge University Press.

Desbordes, Françoise, 1995. Sur les débuts de la grammaire à Rome. *Lalies* 15: 125–37.

Desbordes, Françoise, 2000. L'ars grammatica dans la période post-classique: le *Corpus grammaticorum latinorum*. In Auroux et al., vol. 1 (2000: 466–74).

Deshpande, Madhav M., 1994. Phonetics, ancient Indian. In Ronald E. Asher and James M. Y. Simpson (eds), *The Encyclopedia of Language and Linguistics*. Oxford: Pergamon, 3053–8.

Deshpande, Mahdav M, 1995. Ancient Indian phonetics. In E. F. Konrad Koerner and Ronald E. Asher (eds), *Concise History of Language Sciences: From the Sumerians to the Cognitivists*. Oxford: Elsevier, 72–7.

Despauterius, 1537/8. *Commentarii grammatici*. Paris.

Deumert, Ana, 2010. *Imbodela zamakhumsha*: reflections on standardization and destandardization. *Multilingua* 29: 243–64.

Deumert, Ana and Wim Vandenbussche (eds), 2003. *Germanic Standardizations Past to Present*. Amsterdam: John Benjamins.

Di Benedetto, Vincenzo, 1958–9. Dionisio Trace e la Techne a lui attribuita. *Annali della Scuola Normale di Pisa, serie Lettere, Storia e Filosofia*, 2.27: 170–210 and 2.28: 87–118.

Di Benedetto, Vincenzo, 2000. Dionysius Thrax and the *Tékhnē Grammatikē*. In Auroux et al., vol. 1 (2000: 394–400).

Di Cesare, Donatella, 1994. Einleitung. In Wilhelm von Humboldt, *Über die Verschiedenheit des menschlichen Sprachbaues und ihren Einfluß auf die geistige Entwicklung des Menschengeschlechts*, ed. Donatella Di Cesare. Paderborn: Schöningh, 11–128.

Diakonov, Igor M., 1965. *Семитохамитские языки*. Moscow: Nauka. [English version: *Semito-Hamitic Languages* (Moscow: Nauka, 1965).]

Diakonov, Igor M., 1988. *Afrasian Languages*. Moscow: Nauka.

Diakonov, Igor M., 1991. Афразийские языки. In *Афразийские языки* I. *Семитскиеязыки*. [Afroasiatic languages, in Afroasiatic Languages I: Semitic Languages]. Moscow: Nauka, 5–69.

Diakonov, Igor M., Anna G. Bélova, Alexander Y. Militarev, Victor Y. Porhomovskij, and Olga V. Stolbova, 1993–7. Historical comparative vocabulary of Afrasian. *St. Petersburg Journal of African Studies* 2 (1993): 5–28; 3 (1994): 5–26; 4 (1994): 7–38; 5 (1995): 4–32; 6 (1997): 12–35.

Diderot, Denis, 1751. *Lettre sur les sourds et muets, à l'usage de ceux qui parlent*. Paris.

Diderot, Denis and Jean le Rond d'Alembert (eds), 1751–72. *Encyclopédie ou Dictionnaire raisonné des sciences, des arts et des métiers, par une Société de Gens de lettres*. Paris.

Diels, Hermann, and W. Kranz, 1951. *Die Fragmente der Vorsokratiker*. 3 vols. Berlin: Weidmann.

Dik, Simon C., 1968. *Coordination*. Amsterdam: North-Holland.

Dik, Simon C., 1978. *Functional Grammar*. Amsterdam: North-Holland.

Dik, Simon C., 1990. On the semantics of conditionals. In Jan Nuyts, A. Machtelt Bolkestein, and Co Vet (eds), *Layers and Levels of Representation in Language Theory: A Functional View*. Amsterdam: John Benjamins, 233–61.

Dik, Simon C., 1997a [1989]. *The Theory of Functional Grammar*, part 1: *The Structure of the Clause*, 2nd edn, ed. Kees Hengeveld. Berlin: Mouton de Gruyter.

Dik, Simon C., 1997b [1989] *The Theory of Functional Grammar*, part 2: *Complex and Derived Constructions*, 2nd edn, ed. Kees Hengeveld. Berlin: Mouton de Gruyter.

Dinneen, Francis P., 1967. *An Introduction to General Linguistics*. New York: Holt, Rinehart & Winston.

Dinnsen, Daniel (ed.), 1979. *Current Approaches to Phonological Theory*. Bloomington: Indiana University Press.

Diomedes. *Ars grammatica*. In Keil (1961: i. 199–529).

Dionysius Thrax, 1987. *The Tekhne Grammatike of Dionysius Thrax*, transl. Alan Kemp. In Daniel Taylor (ed.), *The History of Linguistics in the Classical Period*. Amsterdam: Benjamins, 169–89.

Diringer, David, 1968. *The Alphabet: A Key to the History of Mankind*, 3rd edn. New York: Funk & Wagnall.

Dirven, René, and Ralf Pörings (eds), 2002. *Metaphor and Metonymy in Comparison and Contrast*. Berlin: Mouton de Gruyter.

Dirven, René and Vilém Fried, 1987. *Functionalism in Linguistics*. Amsterdam: John Benjamins.

Dobson, Eric J. (ed.), 1957. *The Phonetic Writings of Robert Robinson*. London: Oxford University Press.

Dobson, Eric J., 1968. *English Pronunciation 1500–1700*, 2nd edn. Oxford: Clarendon Press.

Dodwell, C. Reginald, 2000. *Anglo-Saxon Gestures and the Roman Stage*. Cambridge: Cambridge University Press.

Doke, Clement M., 1931. *A Comparative Study of Shona Phonetics*. Johannesburg: University of the Witwatersrand Press.

Doke, Clement M, 1935. *Bantu Linguistic Terminology*. London: Longmans.

Dolgopolsky, Aharon B., 1999. *The Nostratic Macro-Family and Linguistic Palaeontology*. Cambridge: Cambridge University Press.

Donald, Merlin, 1991. *Origins of the Modern Mind: Three Stages in the Evolution of Culture and Cognition*. Cambridge, MA: Harvard University Press.

Donatus, Aelius. *De Partibus Orationis: Ars Minor*. In Keil (1961: iv. 355–66).

Dor, Daniel, and Eva Jablonka, 2010. Plasticity and canalization in the evolution of linguistic communication: an evolutionary developmental approach. In Larson et al. (2010: 135–47).

Downer, G. B., 1963. Traditional Chinese phonology. *Transactions of the Philological Society*, 127–43.

Dowty, David, 1982. Grammatical relations and Montague Grammar. In Geoffrey K. Pullum and Pauline Jacobson (eds), *The Nature of Syntactic Representation*. Dordrecht: Reidel, 79–130.

Dowty, David R., Robert E. Wall, and Stanley R. Peters, 1981. *Introduction to Montague Semantics*. Dordrecht: Reidel.

Dresher, B. Elan, 2005. Chomsky and Halle's revolution in phonology. In James McGilvray (ed.), *The Cambridge Companion to Chomsky*. Cambridge: Cambridge University Press, 102–22.

Dresher, B. Elan., 2009. *The Contrastive Hierarchy in Phonology*. Cambridge: Cambridge University Press.

Dresher, B. Elan., 2011. The phoneme. In Marc van Oostendorp, Colin J. Ewen, Elizabeth Hume, and Keren Rice (eds), *The Blackwell Companion to Phonology*, vol. 1. Oxford: Wiley-Blackwell, 141–266.

Dressler, Wolfgang U., and Oskar Pfeiffer (eds), 1977. *Phonologica 1976*. Innsbruck: Universität Innsbruck.

Drew, Paul, and John Heritage (eds), 1992. *Talk at Work: Interaction in Institutional Settings*. Cambridge: Cambridge University Press.

Dreyer, Günter, 1998. *Umm el-Qaab I: das prädynastische Königsgrab U-j und seine frühen Schriftzeugnisse*. Mainz: Zabern.

Drory, Rina, 1995. Bilingualism and cultural images: the Hebrew and the Arabic introductions to Saadia Gaon's Sefer ha-Egron. In Shlomo Isre'el and Rina Drory (eds), *Language and Culture in the Near East*. Leiden: E. J. Brill for Israel Oriental Studies, 11–23.

Drory, Rina, 2000. *Models and Contacts: Arabic Literature and Its Impact on Medieval Jewish Culture*. Leiden: E. J. Brill.

Du Bois-Reymond, Félix H., 1862. *Kadmus oder allgemeine Alphabetik vom physikalischen, physiologischen und graphischen Standpunkt*. Berlin: Ferdinand Dümmler.

Du Marsais, César Chesneau, 1722. *Exposition d'une méthode raisonnée pour apprendre la language latine*. Paris: Étienne Ganeau.

Du Marsais, César Chesneau, 1751–72. *Construction*. In Denis Diderot and Jean le Rond d'Alembert (eds), *Encyclopédie ou Dictionnaire raisonné des sciences, des arts et des métiers, par une Société de Gens de lettres*, vol. 4. Paris.

Dubin, David, 2004. The most influential paper Gerard Salton never wrote. *Library Trends* 52: 748–64.

Dubois, Jean, 1964. Distribution, ensemble et marque dans le lexique. *Cahiers de lexicologie* 4: 5–16.

Ducháček, Otto, 1959. Champ conceptuel de la beauté en français moderne. *Vox romanica* 18: 297–323.

Duclos, Charles P., 1754. *Commentaire*. In Claude Lancelot et Antoine Arnauld, *Grammaire générale et raisonnée*, 5th edn. Paris: Prault.

Dugast, Loïc, Jean Senellart, and Philipp Koehn, 2008. Can we relearn an RBMT system? *Proceedings of the Third Workshop on Statistical Machine Translation*, 175–8.

Dummett, Michael E., 1973. *Frege: Philosophy of Language*. London: Duckworth.

Dunbar, Robin, 1996. *Grooming, Gossip, and the Evolution of Language*. Cambridge, MA: Harvard University Press.

Dunbar, Robin and Louise Barrett (eds), 2007. *The Oxford Handbook of Evolutionary Psychology*. Oxford: Oxford University Press.

Duncan, Susan, Justine Cassell, and Elena Levy (eds), 2007. *Gesture and the Dynamic Nature of Language: Essays in Honor of David McNeill*. Amsterdam: John Benjamins.

Dunning, Ted, 1993. Accurate methods for the statistics of surprise and coincidence. *Computational Linguistics* 19: 61–74.

Duponceau, Peter S., 1819. Report of the corresponding secretary to the committee, of his progress in the investigation committed to him of the general character and forms of the languages of the American Indians: Read, 12th Jan. 1819. *Transactions of the Historical and Literary Committee of the American Philosophical Society, Held at Philadelphia, for Promoting Useful Knowledge*, vol. 1, pp. xvii–xlvi.

Durand, Jacques, 2006. La phonologie générative jusqu'en 1975. In Auroux et al., vol. 3 (2006: 1265–70).

Durand, Jacques and Bernard Laks (eds), 1996. *Current Trends in Phonology: Models and Methods*, vols. 1 and 2. Paris: CNRS/ESRI.

Durand, Jacques and Bernard Laks, 2002. Phonology, phonetics and cognition. In Jacques Durand and Bernard Laks (eds), *Phonetics, Phonology, and Cognition*. Oxford: Oxford University Press, 1–50.

Duranti, Alessandro, 1997. *Linguistic Anthropology*. Cambridge: Cambridge University Press.

Duranti, Alessandro, 2001. Linguistic anthropology: history, ideas, and issues. In Alessandro Duranti (ed.), *Linguistic Anthropology: A Reader*, 2nd edn. Oxford: Blackwell, 1–38.

Duranti, Alessandro, 2009. Linguistic anthropology: history, ideas, and issues. In Alessandro Duranti (ed.), *Linguistic Anthropology: A Reader*, 2nd edn. Oxford: Blackwell, 1–40.

Dutsch, Dorota, 2002. Towards a grammar of gesture: a comparison between the type of hand movements of the orator and the actor in Quintillian's *Institutio Oratoria*. *Gesture* 2: 259–81.

Dutsch, Dorota, 2007. Gestures in the dramas of Terence and late revivals of literary drama. *Gesture* 7: 39–71.

Dyck, Andrew R., 1993. Aelius Herodian: recent studies and prospects for future research. In Wolfgang Haase (ed.), *Aufstieg und Niedergang der römischen Welt*, vol. 2. Berlin: de Gruyter, 34.2, 772–94.

Earley, Jay, 1970. An efficient context-free parsing algorithm. *Communications of the ACM* 13: 94–102. [Repr. in *Communications of the ACM*, 1983, 26: 57–61.]

Eaton, Helen, 1940. *Semantic Frequency List for English, French, German and Spanish*. Chicago: Chicago University Press.

Ebeling, Erich, et al. (eds), 1928. *Reallexikon der Assyriologie*. Berlin: de Gruyter.

Eckert, Penelope, 2005. Variation, convention, and social meaning. Paper presented at the Annual Meeting of the Linguistic Society of America (Oakland, CA, 7 Jan.).

Eckert, Penelope, 2008. Variation and the indexical field. *Journal of Sociolinguistics* 12: 453–76.

Eco, Umberto, 1995. *The Search for the Perfect Language*, transl. James Fentress. Oxford: Blackwell.

Edison, Thomas A., 1878. The phonograph and its future. *North American Review* 126: 527–36.

Eerdmans, Susan, Carlo Prevignano, and Paul Thibault, 2003. *Language and Interaction: Discussions with John Gumperz*. Amsterdam: John Benjamins.

Efron, David, 1972 [1941]. *Gesture, Race and Culture*. The Hague: Mouton. [Originally published 1941 by King's Crown Press, New York.]

Ehret, Christopher, 1987. *Proto-Cushitic Reconstruction*. Hamburg: Helmut Buske.

Ehret, Christopher, 1995. *Reconstructing Proto-Afro-Asiatic (Proto-Afrasian)*. Berkeley: University of California Press.

Eisner, Jason M., 1996. Three new probabilistic models for dependency parsing: an exploration. *Proceedings of the 16th International Conference on Computational Linguistics (COLING-1996)* (Copenhagen), 340–5.

Eissfeldt, Otto, 1963. *Kleine Schriften* II. Tübingen: J. C. B. Mohr.

Ekman, Paul, and Wallace Friesen, 1969. The repertoire of non-verbal behavior: categories, origins, usage and coding. *Semiotica* 1: 49–98.

Elffers-van Ketel, Els, 1991. *The Historiography of Grammatical Concepts*. Amsterdam: Rodopi.

Eliot, John, 1666. *The Indian Grammar Begun: or, An Essay to Bring the Indian Language into Rules, for the Help of such as desire to Learn the same, for the Furtherance of the Gospel among them*. Cambridge: Marmaduke Johnson.

Ellis, Alexander J., 1845. *The Alphabet of Nature; or, contributions towards a more accurate analysis and symbolization of spoken sounds... Originally published in the Phonotypic Journal, June, 1844–June, 1845*. London: Pitman.

Ellis, Alexander J., 1873–4. First Annual Address of the President to the Philological Society (the Anniversary Meeting, Friday 17 May 1872). *Transactions of the Philological Society*, 1873–4: 1–34.

Emeneau, Murray B., 1988. Bloomfield and Pāṇini. *Language* 64: 755–60.

Emmorey, Karen, H. B. Borinstein, R. Thompson, and T. H. Gollan, 2008. Bimodal bilingualism. *Bilingualism: Language and Cognition* 11: 43–61.

Emmorey, Karen, David Corina, and Ursula Bellugi, 1995. Differential processing of topographic and referential functions of space. In Karen Emmorey and Judy S. Reilly (eds), *Language, Gesture and Space*. Hillsdale, NJ: Lawrence Erlbaum, 43–62.

Emmorey, Karen and Stephen McCullough, 2009. The bimodal brain: effects of sign language experience. *Brain and Language* 110: 208–21.

Encrevé, Pierre, 1997. L'ancien et le nouveau: quelques remarques sur la phonologie et son histoire. *Langages* 125: 100–23. [See Encrevé (2000).]

Encrevé, Pierre, 2000. The old and the new: some remarks on phonology and its history. *Folia Linguistica* 34: 57–85.

Enfield, Nicholas J., 2009. *The Anatomy of Meaning*. Cambridge: Cambridge University Press.

Engberg-Pedersen, Elisabeth, 1993. *Space in Danish Sign Language*. Hamburg: Signum Press.

Engel, Johann Jacob, 1785–6. *Ideen zu einer Mimik*. Berlin: Auf Kosten des Verfassers und in Commission bey August Mylius.

Engler, Rudolf, 1967–74. *Critical Edition of F. De Saussure, Cours de linguistique générale*. Wiesbaden: Harrassowitz.

Engler, Rudolf, 1993. La discussion italienne sur la norme et sa réception en Europe. In Pierre Knecht and Zygmunt Marzys (eds), *Écriture, langues communes et normes: formation spontanée de koinés et standardisation dans la Galloromania et son voisinage: actes du colloque tenu à l'Université de Neuchâtel du 21 au 23 septembre 1988*. Geneva: Droz, 105–225.

Ensslin, Astrid, and Sally Johnson, 2006. Language in the news: investigations into representations of 'Englishness' using *WordSmith Tools*. *Corpora* 1: 153–85.

Erbse, Hartmut, 1969–88. *Scholia in Homeri Iliadem (Scholia Vetera)*. 7 vols. Berlin: de Gruyter.

Erdmann, Karl-Otto, 1910. *Die Bedeutung des Wortes: Aufsätze aus dem Grenzgebiet der Sprachpsychologie und Logik*, 2nd edn. Leipzig: Avenarius.

Erfurt, Jürgen, and Gabriele Budach (eds), 2008. *Standardisation et Déstandardisation/Estandarización y desestandarizacion (Le français et l'espagnol au XXe siècle /El francés y el español en el siglo XX)*. Frankfurt am Main: Peter Lang.

Erman, Adolf, and Hermann Grapow, 1926–31. *Wörterbuch der ägyptischen Sprache I–V*, Leipzig: Hinrichs. [Repr. Berlin: Akademie, 1971.]

Ertel, Suitbert, 1969. *Psychophonetik: Untersuchungen über Lautsymbolik und Motivation*. Göttingen: Verlag für Psychologie C. J. Hogref.

Ertel, Suitbert, 1972. *Sinnvolle Artikulation: Statistische Untersuchungen zur Lautbedeutsamkeit mit 37 Sprachen*. MS, Universität Göttingen.

Ervin-Tripp, Susan, 2009. Hymes on speech socialization. *Text and Talk* 29(3): 245–56.

Esling, John, 2010. Phonetic notation. In William J. Hardcastle, John Laver, and Fiona E. Gibbon (eds), *The Handbook of Phonetic Sciences*, 2nd edn. Oxford: Blackwell, 678–702.

Esnault, Gaston, 1925. *Métaphores occidentales. Essai sur les valeurs imaginatives concrètes du français parlé en Basse-Bretagne comparé avec les patois, parlers techniques et argots français*. Paris: Presses Universitaires de France.

Essen, Otto von, 1962. *Allgemeine und Angewandte Phonetik*, 3rd edn. Berlin: Akademie.

Etzel, Stefan, 1983. Untersuchungen zur Lautsymbolik. Ph.D thesis, University of Frankfurt am Main.

Eutyches. *Ars de verbo*. In Keil (1961: v. 447–89).

Evans, Jonathan St B. T., 1982. *The Psychology of Deductive Reasoning*. London: Routledge & Kegan Paul.

Evans, Nicholas, Janet Fletcher, and Belinda Ross, 2008. Big words, small phrases: mismatches between pause units and the polysnthetic word in Dalabon. *Linguistics* 46: 89–129.

Evans, Vyvyan, Benjamin Bergen, and Jörg Zinken (eds), 2007. *The Cognitive Linguistics Reader*. London: Equinox.

Evans, Vyvyan and Melanie Green, 2006. *Cognitive Linguistics: An Introduction*. Mahwah, NJ: Lawrence Erlbaum.

Evens, Martha W., Bonnie E. Litowitz, Judith E. Markowitz, Raoul N. Smith, and Oswald Werner, 1980. *Lexical-Semantic Relations: A Comparative Survey*. Edmonton: Linguistic Research.

Evnine, Simon, 1991. *Donald Davidson*. Stanford, CA: Stanford University Press.

Faber, Pamela B., and Ricardo Mairal Usón, 1999. *Constructing a Lexicon of English Verbs*. Berlin: Mouton de Gruyter.

Fairclough, Norman, 1995. *Critical Discourse Analysis: The Critical Study of Language*. London: Longman.

Fairclough, Norman, 2003. *Analysing Discourse: Text Analysis for Social Research*. London: Routledge.

Fairclough, Norman, 2006. *Language and Globalization*. London: Routledge.

Fairclough, Norman, 2009. A dialectical-relational approach to critical discourse analysis in social research. In Ruth Wodak and Michael Meyer (eds), *Methods of Critical Discourse Analysis*. London: Sage, 163–86.

Fantham, Elaine, 2004. *The Roman World of Cicero's* De Oratore. Oxford: Oxford University Press.

Farnell, Brenda, 1995. *Do You See What I Mean? Plains Indian Sign Talk and the Embodiment of Action*. Austin: University of Texas Press.

Farrar, Frederick W., 1865. *Language and Languages, being 'Chapters on language' and 'Families of speech'*. New York: E. P. Dutton. [Excerpts published in Harris and Pyle (1996: 42–80).]

Fasold, Ralph, 1984. *The Sociolinguistics of Society*. Oxford: Blackwell.

Fasold, Ralph, 1990. *The Sociolinguistics of Language*. Oxford: Blackwell.

Fauconnier, Gilles, 1985. *Mental Spaces: Aspects of Meaning Construction in Natural Language*. Cambridge, MA: MIT Press. [2nd edn, 1994.]

Fauconnier, Gilles, 1997. *Mappings in Thought and Language*. Cambridge: Cambridge University Press.

Fauconnier, Gilles and Mark Turner, 1995. Conceptual integration and formal expression. *Journal of Metaphor and Symbolic Activity* 10: 183–204.

Fauconnier, Gilles and Mark Turner, 2002. *The Way We Think: Conceptual Blending and the Mind's Hidden Complexities*. New York: Basic Books.

Fawcett, Robin P., 2000. *A Theory of Syntax for Systemic Functional Linguistics*. Amsterdam: John Benjamins.

Fechner, T., 1871. *Vorschule der Aesthetik*. Leipzig: Breitkopf & Hartel.

Fehling, Detlev, 1956–7. Varro und die grammatische Lehre von der Analogie und der Flexion. *Glotta* 35: 214–70; 36: 48–100.

Fehling, Detlev, 1965. Zwei Untersuchungen zur griechischen Sprachphilosophie. *Rheinisches Museum für Philologie* 108: 212–29.

Feigenbaum, Edward A., and Julian Feldman (eds), 1963. *Computers and Thought*. New York: McGraw-Hill. [Repr. 1995, Menlo Park, CA: AAAI Press and Cambridge, MA: MIT Press.]

Fellbaum, Christiane (ed.), 1998. *WordNet: An Electronic Lexical Database*. Cambridge, MA: MIT Press.

Ferguson, Charles A., 1959. Diglossia. *Word* 15: 325–40.

Ferguson, Charles A. and Gumperz, John J., 1960. *Linguistic Diversity in South Asia: Studies in Regional, Social and Functional Variation*. Bloomington: Indiana University Research Center in Anthropology, Folklore, and Linguistics.

Fernandez, Heberto, and Monique C. Cormier, 2010. 'For the better understanding of the order of this dictionarie, peruse the preface to the reader': topics in the outside matter of French and English dictionaries (1580–1673). In John Considine (ed.), *Adventuring in Dictionaries: New Studies in the History of Lexicography*. Newcastle upon Tyne: Cambridge Scholars.

Fernández-Smith, Gerárd, 2007. *Modelos teóricos de la lingüística del texto*. Cádiz: Universidad de Cádiz.

Ferragne, Emmanuel, and François Pellegrino, 2010. Formant frequencies of vowels in 13 accents of the British Isles. *Journal of the International Phonetic Association* 40: 1–34.

Ferrein, Antoine, 1741. Sur l'organe immédiat de la voix et de ses différens tons. *Histoire de l'Académie Royale des sciences . . . avec les Mémoires de mathématique et de physique*, 51–6; De la formation de la voix de l'homme. *Histoire de l'Académie Royale des sciences . . . avec les Mémoires de mathématique et de physique*, 409–32. Paris: Imprimerie Royale.

Ferrers Howell, A. G., 1890. *Dante's Treatise* De Vulgari Eloquentia *Translated into English with Explanatory Notes*. London: Kegan Paul, Trench, Trübner.

Ferri, Rolando (ed.), 2011. *The Latin of Roman Lexicography*. Pisa: Fabrizio Serra.

Ferrucci, David, et al., 2010. Building Watson: an overview of the DeepQA project. *AI Magazine* 31: 59–79.

Ferstl, Evelyn C., Jane Neumann, Carsten Bogler, and D. Yves von Cramon, 2008. The extended language network: a meta-analysis of neuroimaging studies on text comprehension. *Human Brain Mapping* 2: 581–93.

Février, James-G., 1959. *Histoire de l'écriture*, 2nd edn. Paris: Payot.

Fierville, Charles (ed.), 1886. *Une grammaire latine inédite du XIIIe siècle, extraite des manuscrits No. 465 de Laon et No. 15462 de la Biobliothèque Nationale*. Paris: Imprimerie Nationale.

Figueroa, Esther, 1994. *Sociolinguistic Metatheory*. Oxford: Pergamon.

Filliozat, Pierre-Sylvain, 1975–86. *Le Mahābhāṣya de Patañjali avec le Pradīpa de Kaiyaṭa et l'Uddyota de Nāgeśa*. Pondichéry: Institut Français d'Indology.

Filliozat, Pierre-Sylvain, 1988. *Grammaire Sanscrite Paninéenne*. Paris: Picard.

Fillmore, Charles J., 1966. Deictic categories in the semantics of 'come'. *Foundations of Language* 2: 219–27.

Fillmore, Charles J., 1968. The case for case. In Emmon Bach and Robert Harms (eds), *Universals in Linguistic Theory*. New York: Holt, Rinehart &Winston, 1–88.

Fillmore, Charles J., 1975. *Santa Cruz Lectures on Deixis*. Bloomington: Indiana University Linguistics Club.

Fillmore, Charles J., 1977a. Scenes-and-frames semantics. In Antonio Zampolli (ed.), *Linguistic Structures Processing*. Amsterdam: North-Holland, 55–81.

Fillmore, Charles J., 1977b. Topics in lexical semantics. In Roger W. Cole (ed.), *Current Issues in Linguistic Theory*. Bloomington: Indiana University Press, 76–138.

Fillmore, Charles J., 1985. Frames and the semantics of understanding. *Quaderni di semantica* 6: 222–54.

Fillmore, Charles J., 1988. The mechanisms of construction grammar. *Berkeley Linguistic Society* 14: 35–55.

Fillmore, Charles J. and B. T. Sue Atkins, 1992. Toward a frame-based lexicon: the semantics of 'risk' and its neighbors. In Adrienne Lehrer and Eva Feder Kittay (eds), *Frames, Fields and Contrasts: New Essays in Semantic and Lexical Organization*. Hillsdale, NJ: Lawrence Erlbaum, 75–102.

Fillmore, Charles J. and B.T. Sue Atkins, 1994. Starting where dictionaries stop: the challenge of corpus lexicography. In B. T. Sue Atkins and Antonio Zampolli (eds), *Computational Approaches to the Lexicon*. Oxford: Oxford University Press, 349–93.

Fillmore, Charles J. and B.T. Sue Atkins, 2000. Describing polysemy: the case of 'crawl'. In Yael Ravin and Claudia Leacock (eds), *Polysemy: Theoretical and Computational Approaches*. Oxford: Oxford University Press, 91–110.

Fillmore, Charles J., Paul Kay, and Catherine O'Connor, 1988. Regularity and idiomaticity in grammatical constructions: The case of *let alone*. *Language* 64: 501–38.

Finkel, Raphael, and Gregory T. Stump, 2007. Principal parts and morphological typology. *Morphology* 17: 39–75.

Finn, Peter, 2004. Cape Flats English: phonology. In Kate Burridge and Bernd Kortmann (eds), *A Handbook of Varieties of English*, vol. 1: *Phonology*. Berlin: Mouton de Gruyter, 964–84.

Firbas, Jan, 1964. On defining the theme in functional sentence analysis. *Travaux linguistiques de Prague* 1: 267–80.

Firbas, Jan, 1966. Non-thematic subjects in contemporary English. *Travaux linguistiques de Prague* 2: 239–56.

Firbas, Jan, 1986. On the dynamics of written communication in the light of the theory of functional sentence perspective. In Charles Cooper and Sidney Greenbaum (eds), *Studying Writing: Linguistic Approaches*. Beverly Hills, CA: Sage, 40–71.

Firbas, Jan, 1992. *Functional Sentence Perspective in Written and Spoken Communication*. Cambridge: Cambridge University Press.

Firth, John R., 1935. The use and distribution of certain English sounds. *English Studies* 17: 8–18.

Firth, John R., 1946. The English school of phonetics. *Transactions of the Philological Society*: 92–132.

Firth, John R., 1948. Sounds and prosodies. *Transactions of the Philological Society*: 127–52. [Repr. in Palmer (1970: 1–26).]

Firth, John R., 1957. A synopsis of linguistic theory 1930–1955. In John R. Firth (ed.), *Studies in Linguistic Analysis*. Oxford: Philological Society, 1–32.

Firth, John R., 1957. *Papers in Linguistics 1934–1951*. Oxford: Oxford University Press.

Firth, John R., 1968. *Selected Papers of J. R. Firth 1952–59*, ed. Frank R. Palmer. London: Longmans.

Fisch, Max H., 1986. *Peirce, Semeiotic, and Pragmatism: Essays*. Bloomington: Indiana University Press,

Fischer, Renate, 1990. Sign language and the French enlightenment: Diderot's 'Lettre sur les sourds et muets'. In Siegmund Prillwitz and Tomas Vollhaber (eds), *Current Trends in European Sign Language Research*. Hamburg: Signum, 35–58.

Fischer, Renate, 1993. Language of action. In Renate Fischer and Harlan Lane (eds), *Looking Back: A Reader in the History of Deaf Communities and their Sign Languages*. Hamburg: Signum, 429–55.

Fischer, Susan D., 1974. Sign language and linguistic universals. In Christian Rohrer and Nicolas Ruwet (eds), *Actes du colloque franco-allemand de grammaire transformationnelle*. Tübingen: Niemeyer, 187–204.

Fischer, Susan D., 1978. Sign language and creoles. In Patricia Siple (ed.), *Understanding Language Through Sign Language Research*. New York: Academic Press, 309–31.

Fischer, Wolfdietrich, 2002 [1972]. *Grammatik des klassischen Arabisch*, 3rd edn. Wiesbaden: Harrassowitz.

Fischer, Wolfdietrich and Otto Jastrow, 1980. *Handbuch der arabischen Dialekte*. Wiesbaden: Harrassowitz.

Fischer-Jørgensen, Eli, 1967. Perceptual dimensions of vowels. In *To Honor Roman Jakobson: Essays on the Occasion of His Seventieth Birthday*, vol. 1. The Hague: Mouton, 667–71.

Fischer-Jørgensen, Eli, 1972. Kinaesthetic judgement of effort in the production of stop consonants. *Annual Report of the Institute of Phonetics of the University of Copenhagen, (ARIPU)* 6: 59–73.

Fischer-Jørgensen, Eli, 1974. *Almen Fonetik*. Copenhagen: Akademisk Forlag.

Fischer-Jørgensen, Eli, 1975. *Trends in Phonological Theory: A Historical Introduction*. Copenhagen: Akademisk Forlag.

Fischer-Jørgensen, Eli, 1978. On the universal character of phonetic symbolism with special reference to vowels. *Studia Linguistica* 32: 80–90.

Fishman, Joshua A., 1966. *Language Loyalty in the United States: The Maintenance and Perpetuation of Non-English Mother Tongues by American Ethnic and Religious Groups*. The Hague: Mouton.

Fishman, Joshua A., 1967a. Bilingualism with and without diglossia; diglossia with and without bilingualism. *Journal of Social Issues* 23(2): 29–38.

Fishman, Joshua A., 1967b. Review of J. O. Hertzler 'A Sociology of Language'. *Language* 43: 586–603.

Fishman, Joshua A., 1972. Advances in the sociology of language. In Joshua A. Fishman (ed.), *Advances in the Sociology of Language*. The Hague: Mouton, 7–11.

Fishman, Joshua A., 1991. *Reversing Language Shift: Theoretical and Empirical Foundations of Assistance to Threatened Languages*. Clevedon, UK: Multilingual Matters.

Fishman, Joshua A., Robert L. Cooper, Roxana Ma, et al. (eds), 1971. *Bilingualism in the Barrio*. Bloomington: Indiana University Press.

Fitch, W. Tecumseh, 2002. Comparative vocal production and the evolution of speech: reinterpreting the descent of the larynx. In Alison Wray (ed.), *The Transition to Language*. Oxford: Oxford University Press, 21–45.

Fitch, W. Tecumseh, 2010. *The Evolution of Language*. Cambridge: Cambridge University Press.

Fitch, W. Tecumseh, in press. Noam Chomsky and the biology of language. In Oren Harman and Michael Dietrich (eds), *Biology Outside the Box: Boundary Crosses and Innovation in Biology*. Chicago: University of Chicago Press.

Fletcher, Janet, Deborah Loakes, and Andrew R. Butcher, 2008. Coarticulation in nasal and lateral clusters in Warlpiri. In Janet Fletcher, Deborah Loakes, Roland Goecke, Denis Burnham, and Michael Wagner (eds), *Proceedings of Interspeech 2008, Incorporating SST08*. Brisbane: International Speech Communication Association, 86–9.

Flowerdew, John, 2002. Genre in the classroom: a linguistic approach. In Ann M. Johns (ed.), *Genre in the Classroom: Multiple Perspectives*. Mahwah, NJ: Erlbaum, 91–102.

Foley, William, 1997. *Anthropological Linguistics: An Introduction*. Oxford: Blackwell.

Foley, William and Robert D. Van Valin, 1984. *Functional Syntax and Universal Grammar*. Cambridge: Cambridge University Press.

Fonagy, Ivan, 1961. Communication in poetry. *Word* 17: 194–201.

Fonagy, Ivan, 1963. *Die Metaphern in der Phonetik*. The Hague: Mouton.

Fonagy, Ivan, 2001. *Language Within Language: An Evolutive Approach*. Amsterdam: John Benjamins.

Forbus, Kenneth D., Christopher Riesbeck, Lawrence Birnbaum, et al., 2007. Integrating natural language, knowledge representation and reasoning, and analogical processing to learn by reading. *Proceedings, 22nd AAAI Conference on Artificial Intelligence (AAAI-2007)* (Vancouver), 1542–7.

Forchhammer, Jørgen, 1928. *Die Weltlautschrift*. Berlin: Reichsdruckerei.

Forney, G. David, 1973. The Viterbi algorithm. *Proceedings of the IEEE*, 61: 268–78.

Fought, Carmen (ed.), 2004. *Sociolinguistic Variation: Critical Reflections*. Oxford: Oxford University Press.

Fought, John (ed.), 1999. *Leonard Bloomfield: Critical Assessments of Leading Linguists*. London: Routledge.

Fouts, Roger, and G. Waters, 2001. Chimpanzee sign language and Darwinian continuity: evidence for a neurological continuity for language. *Neurological Research* 23: 787–94.

Fowler, Harold N. (ed.), 1963. *Plato: Cratylus, Parmenides, Greater Hippias, Lesser Hippias*. London: Heinemann.

Francis, Nelson, and Henry Kučera, 1964. *Manual of Information to Accompany a Standard Corpus of Present-Day Edited American English for use with Digital Computers*. Providence, RI: Department of Linguistics, Brown University.

Franklin, Benjamin, 1779. *A Scheme for a New Alphabet and Reformed Mode of Spelling: with remarks and examples . . . and an enquiry into its uses, in a correspondence [Sept. 26 and 28, 1768] between Miss S[tevenso]n and Dr. Franklin, written in the characters of the alphabet*. In *Political, Miscellaneous and Philosophical Pieces*. London: J. Johnson, 467–78.

Franklin, Benjamin, 1972 [1768]. [Various pieces of correspondence in his phonetic alphabet]. In William B. Willcox et al. (eds), *The Papers of Benjamin Franklin*, vol. 15: *January 1 through December 31, 1768*. New Haven, CT: Yale University Press, 173–8, 216–20.

Frawley, William (ed.), 2003. *International Encyclopedia of Linguistics*, vol. 1. Oxford: Oxford University Press.

Frazier, Lyn, and Janet Dean Fodor, 1978. The sausage machine: a new two-stage parsing model. *Cognition* 2: 291–325.

Frede, Michael, 1974. *Die Stoische Logik*. Göttingen: Vandenhoeck & Ruprecht.

Frede, Michael, 1987a. The origin of traditional grammar. In Michael Frede (ed.), *Essays in Ancient Philosophy*. Oxford: Oxford University Press, 338–59. [Repr. from Robert E. Butts and Jaakko Hintikka (eds), *Historical and Philosophical Dimensions of Logic, Methodology, and Philosophy of Science* (Dordrecht: Reidel, 1977), 51–79.]

Frede, Michael, 1987b. Principles of Stoic grammar. In Michael Frede (ed.), *Essays in Ancient Philosophy*. Oxford: Oxford University Press, 301–37. [Repr. from John M. Rist (ed.), *The Stoics* (Berkeley: University of California Press, 1978), 17–75.]

Frede, Michael, 1992. Plato's Sophist on false statements. In Richard Kraut (ed.), *The Cambridge Companion to Plato*. Cambridge: Cambridge University Press, 397–424.

Frede, Michael, 1994a. The Stoic notion of a grammatical case. *Bulletin of the Institute of Classical Studies* 39: 13–24.

Frede, Michael, 1994b. The Stoic notion of a *lekton*. In Stephen Everson (ed.), *Companions to Ancient Thought* 3: *Language*. Cambridge: Cambridge University Press, 109–28.

Freeman, Edward A., 1881. *The Historical Geography of Europe*, vol. 1. London: Longmans, Green.

Freeman, Edward A., 1886. *Greater Greece and greater Britain; George Washington: The expander of England. Two lectures with an appendix.* London: Macmillan.

Frege, Gottlob, 1879. *Begriffsschrift. Eine der arithmetischen nachgebildete Formelsprache des reinen Denkens.* Halle a.S.: Louis Nebert.

Frege, Gottlob, 1892. Ueber Sinn und Bedeutung. *Zeitschrift für Philosophie und philosophische Kritik* 100: 25–50.

Frei, Henri, 1929. *La grammaire des fautes.* Paris: Geuthner.

Freidin, Robert, 1994. Conceptual shifts in the science of grammar: 1951–1992. In Carlos Otero (ed.), *Noam Chomsky: Critical Assessments.* London: Routledge, 653–90.

Freidin, Robert (ed.), 1996. *Current Issues in Comparative Grammar.* Dordrecht: Kluwer.

Freidin, Robert, 1997. Review of Huck and Goldsmith (1995). *Anthropological Linguistics* 39: 494–501.

Freidin, Robert, 1999. Cyclicity and minimalism. In Samuel D. Epstein and Norbert Hornstein (eds), *Working Minimalism.* Cambridge, MA: MIT Press, 95–126.

Freidin, Robert, 2011. A brief history of generative grammar. In Gillian Russell and Delia Graff Fara (eds), *A Companion to the Philosophy of Language.* London: Routledge, 894–915.

Freidin, Robert and Howard Lasnik, 2011. Some roots of minimalism in generative grammar. In Cedric Boeckx (ed.), *Handbook of Linguistic Minimalism.* New York: Oxford University Press, 1–26.

Freidin, Robert and Jean-Roger Vergnaud, 2001. Exquisite connections: some remarks on the evolution of linguistic theory. *Lingua* 111: 639–66.

Frellesvig, Bjarke, 2011. *A History of the Japanese Language.* Cambridge: Cambridge University Press.

French, Peter, 1994. An overview of forensic phonetics with particular reference to speaker identification. *Forensic Linguistics* 1: 169–81.

Fried, Daniel, 2007. Defining courtesy: Spenser, Calepine, and Renaissance lexicography. *Review of English Studies* 58: 229–44.

Friedman, Joyce, Douglas B. Moran, and David Scott Warren, 1978a. Explicit finite intensional models for PTQ. *American Journal of Computational Linguistics*, microfiche 74: 3–22.

Friedman, Joyce, Douglas B. Moran and David Scott Warren, 1978b. Evaluating English sentences in a logical model: a process version of Montague grammar. *American Journal of Computational Linguistics*, microfiche 74: 23–96.

Friedman, Lynn H. (ed.), 1977. *On the Other Hand: New Perspectives on American Sign Language.* New York: Academic Press.

Friedrich, Johannes, 1966. *Geschichte der Schrift.* Wiesbaden: Harrassowitz.

Friedrich, Paul, 1986. *The Language Parallax: Linguistic Relativism and Poetic Indeterminacy.* Austin: University of Texas Press.

Fries, Charles, 1940. *American English Grammar.* New York: Appleton Century.

Fries, Charles, 1952. *The Structure of English.* London: Longman.

Fries, Charles and Aileen Traver, 1940. *English Word Lists: A Study of their Adaptability and Instruction.* Washington, DC: American Council of Education.

Fromant, Abbé, 1756. *Réflexions sur les fondemens de l'art de parler pour servir d'éclaircisse-mens & de supplément à la grammaire générale et raisonnée.* Paris: Prault.

Fromkin, Victoria, and Peter Ladefoged, 1981. Early views of distinctive features. In Ronald E. Asher and Eugénie J. A. Henderson (eds), *Towards a History of Phonetics.* Edinburgh: Edinburgh University Press, 3–8.

Fück, Johann, 1958. Carl Brockelmann (1868–1956). *Zeitschrift der Deutschen Morgenlän-dischen Gesellschaft* 108: 1–13.

Fudge, Erik, 1969. Syllables. *Journal of Linguistics* 5: 253–86.

Fudge, Erik (ed.), 1973. *Phonology: Selected Readings.* Harmondsworth: Penguin.

Fujita, Takashi, et al., 1984. *Wa-ei giongo/gitaigo honyaku jiten* [Japanese/English: Mimesis/Onomatopoeia Translation Dictionary] Tokyo: Kinseidô.

Fukui, Naoki, 1986. A theory of category projection and its applications. Doctoral dissertation, MIT.

Fukui, Naoki, 1988. Deriving the differences between English and Japanese. *English Linguistics* 5: 249–70.

Fumaroli, Marc (ed.), 1999. *Histoire de la rhétorique dans l'Europe moderne 1450–1950.* Paris: Presses Universitaires de France.

Fung Yu-lan, 1952. *A History of Chinese Philosophy* I, transl. Derk Bodde. Princeton, NJ: Princeton University Press.

Gabrielatos, Costas, Eivind Torgerson, Sebastian Hoffmann, and Susan Fox, 2010. A corpus-based sociolinguistic study of indefinite article forms in London English. *Journal of English Linguistics* 38: 1–38.

Gale, William A., and Kenneth W. Church, 1993. A program for aligning sentences in bilingual corpora. *Computational Linguistics* 19: 75–102.

Galton, Francis, 1883. *Inquiries into the Human Faculty.* New York: Macmillan.

Garad, Abdurahman, and Ewald Wagner, 1998. *Harari-Studien: Texte mit Übersetzung, grammatischen Skizzen und Glossar.* Wiesbaden: Harrassowitz.

García, Manuel, 1855. Observations on the human voice. *Proceedings of the Royal Society of London* 7: 399–410.

Gardiner, Alan H., 1927. *Egyptian Grammar.* London: Oxford University Press. [3rd edn 1957.]

Gardiner, Alan H., 1951. *The Theory of Speech and Language.* Oxford: Clarendon Press. [1st edn 1932.]

Gardner, Allen, and Beatrice T. Gardner, 1969. Teaching sign language to a chimpanzee. *Science* 165: 664–72.

Gardner, Allen, Beatrice T. Gardner and Thomas E. Van Cantfort, 1989. *Teaching Sign Language to Chimpanzees.* Albany: State University of New York Press.

Garfinkel, Harold, 1967. *Studies in Ethnomethodology.* Englewood Cliffs, NJ: Prentice Hall. [Reissued 1984, Cambridge: Polity Press.]

Garfinkel, Harold, 1974. On the origins of the term 'ethnomethodology'. In Roy Turner (ed.), *Ethnomethodology: Selected Readings.* Harmondsworth: Penguin, 15–18.

Garnham, Alan, 2001. *Mental Models and the Interpretation of Anaphora.* Hove: Psychology Press.

Garside, Roger, Geoffrey Leech, and Geoffrey Sampson, 1987. *The Computational Analysis of English: A Corpus-Based Approach.* Harlow: Longman.

Garside, Roger, Geoffrey Leech and Tony McEnery (eds), 1997. *Corpus Annotation: Linguistic Information from Computer Text Corpora.* Harlow: Longman.

Garside, Roger and Tony McEnery, 1993. Treebanking: the compilation of a corpus of skeleton-parsed sentences. In Ezra Black, Roger Garside, and Geoffrey Leech (eds), *Statistically-Driven Computer Grammars of English: the IBM/Lancaster Approach*. Amsterdam: Rodopi, 17–35.

Gatenby, Edward V., 1967. Translation in the classroom. In William R. Lee (ed.), *ELT Selections 2: Articles from the Journal 'English Language Teaching'*. London: Oxford University Press, 65–70.

Gauchat, Louis, 1905. *L'unité phonétique dans le patois d'une commune*. Halle: Niemeyer.

Gaunt, Simon, and Sarah Kay (eds), 1999. *The Troubadours: An Introduction*. Cambridge: Cambridge University Press.

Gazdar, Gerald, Ewan Klein, Geoffrey K. Pullum, and Ivan A. Sag, 1985. *Generalized Phrase Structure Grammar*. Cambridge, MA: Harvard University Press.

Gazov-Ginzberg, Anatolij M., 1965. *Был ли язык изобразителен в своих истоках? (Свидетвльство прасемитского запаса корней)*. [Was Language Iconic in its Origins? Evidence from the Proto-Semitic Stock of Roots]. Moscow: Nauka.

Geach, Peter, 1962. *Reference and Generality: An Examination of Some Medieval and Modern Theories*. Ithaca, NY: Cornell University Press.

Geckeler, Horst, 1971a. *Strukturelle Semantik und Wortfeldtheorie*. Munich: Wilhelm Fink.

Geckeler, Horst, 1971b. *Zur Wortfelddiskussion*. Munich: Wilhelm Fink.

Gee, James, 2011. *The Routledge Handbook of Discourse Analysis*. London: Routledge.

Geeraerts, Dirk, 1989. Prospects and problems of prototype theory. *Linguistics* 27: 587–612.

Geeraerts, Dirk, 1993. Vagueness's puzzles, polysemy's vagaries. *Cognitive Linguistics* 4: 223–72.

Geeraerts, Dirk, 1997. *Diachronic Prototype Semantics: A Contribution to Historical Lexicology*. Oxford: Clarendon Press.

Geeraerts, Dirk, 2006a. *Words and Other Wonders: Papers on Lexical and Semantic Topics*. Berlin: Mouton de Gruyter.

Geeraerts, Dirk (ed.), 2006b. *Cognitive Linguistics: Basic Readings*. Berlin: Mouton de Gruyter.

Geeraerts, Dirk, 2008. Prototypes, stereotypes and semantic norms. In Kristiansen and Dirven (2008: 11–44).

Geeraerts, Dirk, 2010. *Theories of Lexical Semantics*. Oxford: Oxford University Press.

Geeraerts, Dirk and Hubert Cuyckens (eds), 2007. *The Oxford Handbook of Cognitive Linguistics*. New York: Oxford University Press.

Gelb, Ignace J., 1952. *A Study of Writing*. Chicago: University of Chicago Press.

Genette, Gérard, 1976. *Mimiologics*, transl. Thaïs Morgan. Lincoln: University of Nebraska Press.

Genette, Gérard, 1980. *Narrative Discourse*. Oxford: Blackwell. [French original 1972.]

Gfroerer, Stefan, and Isolde Wagner, 1995. Fundamental frequency in forensic speech samples. In Angelika Braun and J.-P. Köster (eds), *Studies in Forensic Phonetics*. Trier: Wissenschaftlicher Verlag Trier, 41–8.

Ghūl, Maḥmūd Alī, 1993. *Early Southern Arabian Languages and Classical Arabic Sources*. Irbid: Yarmouk University.

Gibbon, Fiona (ed.), 2006. Bibliography of electropalatographic (EPG) studies in English (1957–2006). www.qmuc.ac.uk///_biblio_2006_june.pdf

Gibbs, Raymond W., Jr, 2000. Making good psychology out of blending theory. *Cognitive Linguistics* 11: 347–58.

Gibbs, Raymond W. Jr., 2006. *Embodiment and Cognitive Science*. New York: Cambridge University Press.

Gibbs, Raymond W. Jr. (ed.), 2008. *The Cambridge Handbook of Metaphor and Thought*. Cambridge: Cambridge University Press.

Gil, Alexander, 1619, 1621. *Logonomia Anglica, quâ gentis sermo faciliùs addiscitur*. London: Johannes Beale.

Gipper, Helmut, 1959. Sessel oder Stuhl? Ein Beitrag zur Bestimmung von Wortinhalten im Bereich der Sachkultur. In Helmut Gipper (ed.), *Sprache, Schlüssel zur Welt: Festschrift für Leo Weisgerber*. Düsseldorf: Schwann, 171–292.

Givón, Talmy, 1979. *Understanding Grammar*. New York: Academic Press.

Givón, Talmy (ed.), 1983. *Topic Continuity in Discourse: A Quantitative Cross-Language Study*. Amsterdam: John Benjamins.

Givón, Talmy, 1984. *Syntax: A Functional Typological Introduction*, vol. 1. Amsterdam: John Benjamins.

Givón, Talmy, 1989. *Mind, Code and Context: Essays in Pragmatics*. Hillsdale, NJ: Erlbaum.

Givón, Talmy, 1990. *Syntax: A Functional Typological Introduction*, vol. 2. Amsterdam: John Benjamins.

Givón, Talmy, 1998. On the co-evolution of language, mind, and brain. *Evolution of Communication* 2: 45–116.

Givón, Talmy, 2002. The visual information-processing system as an evolutionary precursor of human language. In Givón and Malle (2002: 3–50).

Givón, Talmy, 2005. *Context as Other Minds: The Pragmatics of Sociality, Cognition and Communication*. Amsterdam: John Benjamins.

Givón, Talmy and Bertram F. Malle (eds), 2002. *The Evolution of Language out of Prelanguage*. Amsterdam: Benjamins.

Gleason, Henry A., 1955. *An Introduction to Descriptive Linguistics*. New York: Henry Holt. [Revised edn 1961.]

Gleason, Henry A., 1965. *Linguistics and English Grammar*. New York: Holt, Rinehart & Winston.

Glynn, Dylan, and Kerstin Fischer (eds), 2010. *Quantitative Methods in Cognitive Semantics: Corpus-Driven Approaches*. Berlin: Mouton de Gruyter.

Goatly, Andrew, 2008. *Explorations in Stylistics*. London: Equinox.

Goddard, Cliff, 1994. Semantic theory and semantic universals. In Goddard and Wierzbicka (1994: 7–30).

Goddard, Cliff, 2006. Ethnopragmatics: a new paradigm. In Cliff Goddard (ed.), *Ethnopragmatics: Understanding Discourse in Cultural Context*. Berlin: Mouton de Gruyter, 1–30.

Goddard, Cliff, 2008. *Cross-Linguistic Semantics*. Amsterdam: John Benjamins.

Goddard, Cliff and Anna Wierzbicka (eds), 1994. *Semantic and Lexical Universals: Theory and Empirical Findings*. Amsterdam: John Benjamins.

Goddard, Cliff and Anna Wierzbicka (eds), 2002. *Meaning and Universal Grammar: Theory and Empirical Findings*. Amsterdam: John Benjamins.

Godden, Malcolm, 2000. *Ælfric's Catholic Homilies: Introduction, Commentary and Glossary*. Oxford: Oxford University Press.

Godel, Robert, 1957. *Les sources manuscrites du Cours de linguistique générale de Ferdinand de Saussure*. Geneva: Droz.

Goetze, Albrecht, 1938. The tenses in Ugaritic. *Journal of the American Oriental Society* 58: 266–309.

Goffman, Erving, 1955. On face-work: an analysis of ritual elements in social interaction. *Psychiatry* 18: 213–31.

Goffman, Erving, 1959. *The Presentation of Self in Everyday Life*. New York: Doubleday.

Goffman, Erving, 1963. *Behavior in Public Places*. New York: Free Press of Glencoe.

Goffman, Erving, 1969. *Strategic Interaction*. Philadelphia: University of Pennsylvania Press.

Goffman, Erving, 1971. *Relations in Public*. New York: Basic Books.

Goffman, Erving, 1974. *Frame Analysis: An Essay on the Organization of Experience*. Cambridge, MA: Harvard University Press.

Goffman, Erving, 1981. *Forms of Talk*. Philadelphia: University of Pennsylvania Press.

Goffman, Erving, 1983a. Felicity's condition. *American Journal of Sociology* 1: 1–53.

Goffman, Erving, 1983b. The interaction order. *American Sociological Review* 48: 1–17.

Gold, E. Mark, 1967. Language identification in the limit. Information and Control 10: 447–74.

Goldberg, Adèle E., 1995. *Constructions: A Construction Grammar Approach to Argument Structure*. Chicago: University of Chicago Press.

Goldberg, Adèle E, 1996. Making one's way through the data. In Masayoshi Shibatani and Sandra A. Thompson (eds), *Grammatical Constructions: Their Form and Their Meaning*. Oxford: Clarendon Press, 19–53.

Goldberg, Adele, 2006. *Constructions at Work: The Nature of Generalization in Language*. Oxford: Oxford University Press.

Goldin-Meadow, Susan, 2003a. *Gestures: How Our Hands Help Us Think*. Cambridge, MA: Belknap Press.

Goldin-Meadow, Susan, 2003b. *The Resilience of Language*. New York: Psychology Press.

Goldsmith, John, 1976a. Autosegmental phonology. Ph.D dissertation, MIT.

Goldsmith, John, 1976b. An overview of autosegmental phonology. *Linguistic Analysis* 2: 23–68.

Goldsmith, John (ed.), 1995. *The Handbook Of Phonological Theory*. Oxford: Blackwell.

Goldsmith, John, 1999. *Phonological Theory: The Essential Readings*. Oxford: Blackwell.

Goldsmith, John, 2000. On information theory, entropy, and phonology in the twentieth century. *Folia Linguistica* 34: 85–100.

Goldsmith, John, 2005. Review of 'The legacy of Zellig Harris: language and information into the 21st century'. *Language* 81: 719–36.

Goldsmith, John, 2008. Generative phonology in the late 40s. *Phonology* 25: 37–59.

Goldsmith, John and Bernard Laks (eds), 2000a. The history of phonology in the twentieth century. *Folia Linguistica* 34(1–2).

Goldsmith, John and Bernard Laks, 2000b. Introduction. In Goldsmith and Laks (2000a: 1–10).

Goldsmith, John, Jason Riggle, and Alan C. L. Yu (eds), 2011. *The Handbook of Phonological Theory*, 2nd edn. Oxford: Wiley-Blackwell.

Goldziher, Ignaz, 1890. *Muhammedanische Studien* II. Halle: Niemeyer. [Repr. 1971, Hildesheim: Olms. English transl. C. R. Barber and S. M. Stern, *Muslim Studies* (Albany: SUNY Press, 1967).]

Gonzalez-Marquez, Monica, Irene Mittelberg, Seana Coulson, and Michael J. Spivey (eds), 2007. *Methods in Cognitive Linguistics*. Amsterdam: John Benjamins.

Goodenough, Ward H., 1956. Componential analysis and the study of meaning. *Language* 32: 195–216.

Goodman, Nelson, 1943. On the simplicity of ideas. *Journal of Symbolic Logic* 8: 107–21.

Goodwin, Charles, 1981. *Conversational Organization: Interaction Between Speakers and Hearers*. New York: Academic Press.

Goodwin, Charles, 1984. Notes on story structure and the organization of participation. In J. Maxwell Atkinson and John Heritage (eds), *Structures of Social Action: Studies in Conversation Analysis*. Cambridge: Cambridge University Press, 125–246.

Goodwin, Charles, 1986. Gesture as a resource for the organization of mutual orientation. *Semiotica* 62: 29–49.

Goodwin, Charles. 1992. Notes on story structure and the organization of participation. In J. Maxwell Atkinson and John Heritage (eds) *Structures of Social Action: Studies in Conversation Analysis*. Cambridge: Cambridge University Press, pp 125–246.

Goodwin, Charles, 2000. Action and embodiment within situated human interaction. *Journal of Pragmatics* 32: 1489–1522.

Goodwin, Charles, 2003. Pointing as situated practice. In Sotaro Kita (ed.), *Pointing: Where Language, Culture and Cognition Meet*. Mahwah, NJ: Lawrence Erlbaum, 117–241.

Goodwin, Charles, 2007. Environmentally coupled gestures. In Duncan et al. (2007: 195–212).

Goodwin, Charles and Alessandro Duranti (eds), 1992. *Rethinking Context: Language as an Interactive Phenomenon*. Cambridge: Cambridge University Press.

Goodwin, Marjorie H., and Charles Goodwin, 1986. Gesture and co-participation in the activity of searching for a word. *Semiotica* 62: 51–75.

Goodwin, William W., 1894. *Greek Grammar*. London: Macmillan.

Goody, John, 1977. *The Domestication of the Savage Mind*. Cambridge: Cambridge University Press.

Gordon, Cynthia, 2011. Gumperz and interactional sociolinguistics. In Ruth Wodak, Barbara Johns, and Paul Kerswill (eds), *The Sage Handbook of Sociolinguistics*. London: Sage, 67–84.

Gould, Stephen Jay, and Elizabeth S. Vrba, 1982. Exaptation: a missing term in the science of form. *Paleontology* 8: 4–15.

Gourinat, Jean-Baptiste, 2000. *La dialectique des stoïciens*. Paris: J. Vrin.

Goyvaerts, Didier (ed.), 1981. *Phonology in the 1980's*. Ghent: Story-Scientia.

Graf, Fritz, 1992. Gestures and conventions: the gestures of Roman actors and orators. In Jan Bremmer and Herman Roodenburg (eds), *A Cultural History of Gesture*. Ithaca, NY: Cornell University Press, 36–58.

Grafé, A. 1897. Note sur un nouveau cas de l'audition colorée. *Revue de médecine* 17: 192–5.

Gragg, Gene, 2006. The 'weak' verb in Akkadian and Beja. In G. Deutscher and Norbert J. C. Kouwenberg (eds), *The Akkadian Language in Its Semitic Context: Studies in the Akkadian of the Third and Second Millennium BC*. Leiden: Nederlands Instituut voor het Nabije Oosten, 19–29.

Grammont, Maurice, 1930. La psychologie et la phonétique. *Journal de psychologie* 27: 544–613.

Grammont, Maurice, 1933. *Traité de phonétique*. Paris: Delagrave.

Grande, Bentsion M., 1972. *Введение в сравнительное изучение семитских языков*. [Introduction to the Comparative study of Semitic Languages]. Moscow: Nauka.

Granger, Sylviane, 1993. The International Corpus of Learner English. In Jan Aarts, Pieter de Haan, and Nelleke Oostdijk (eds), *English Language Corpora: Design, Analysis and Exploitation*. Amsterdam: Rodopi, 57–69.

Granger, Sylviane, Joseph Hung, and Stephanie Petch-Tyson (eds), 2002. *Computer Learner Corpora, Second Language Acquisition and Foreign Language Teaching*. Amsterdam: John Benjamins.

Granger, Sylviane, and Magali Paquot, 2012. *Electronic Lexicography*. Oxford: Oxford University Press.

Grassmann, Hermann. 1863. Über die Aspiraten und ihr gleichzeitiges Vorhandensein im An- und Auslaute der Wurzeln. *Zeitschrift für vergleichende Sprachforschung auf dem Gebiete des Deutschen, Griechischen und Lateinischen* 12: 81–138

Gray, Louis H., 1934. *Introduction to Semitic Comparative Linguistics*. New York: Macmillan.

Grayson, Cecil, 1963. Leon Battista Alberti and the beginnings of Italian grammar. *Proceedings of the British Academy* 49: 291–311.

Green, Bert F., Jr, Alice K. Wolf, Carol Chomsky, and Kenneth Laughery, 1963. Baseball: An automatic question answerer. In Edward A. Feigenbaum and Julian Feldman (eds), *Computers and Thought*. New York: McGraw-Hill, 107–216.

Greenbaum, Sidney (ed.), 1996. *Comparing English Worldwide: The International Corpus of English*. Oxford: Clarendon Press.

Greenberg, Joseph H., 1950. Studies in African linguistic classification, IV: Hamito-Semitic. *Southwestern Journal of Anthropology* 6: 47–63.

Greenberg, Joseph H., 1966 [1963]. Some universals of grammar with particular reference to the order of meaningful elements. In Joseph H. Greenberg (ed.), *Universals of Language: Report of a Conference Held at Dobbs Ferry, New York, April 13–15. 1961*. Cambridge, MA: MIT Press, 73–113.

Greenberg, Joseph H., 1966. *Language Universals, with Special Reference to Feature Hierarchies*. The Hague: Mouton.

Greenberg, Joseph H., (ed.), 1978. *Universals of Human Language*, vols 1–4. Stanford, CA: Stanford University Press.

Greene, Barbara B., and Gerald M. Rubin, 1971. *Automatic Grammatical Tagging of English*. Providence, RI: Department of Linguistics, Brown University.

Greimas, Algirdas J., 1966. *Sémantique structurale: recherche de méthode*. Paris: Larousse. [Transl. as *Structural Semantics: An Attempt at a Method* (Lincoln: University of Nebraska Press, 1983).]

Grice, H. Paul, 1957. Meaning. *Philosophical Review* 66: 377–88.

Grice, H. Paul, 1975. Logic and conversation. In Peter Cole and Jerry Morgan (eds), *Speech Acts*. New York: Academic Press, 41–58.

Grice, H. Paul, 1981. Presupposition and conversational implicature. In Peter Cole (ed.), *Radical Pragmatics*. New York: Academic Press, 183–98.

Gries, Stephan Th., 2003. *Multifactorial Analysis in Corpus Linguistics: A Study of Particle Placement*. New York: Columbia University Press.

Gries, Stephan Th. and Anatol Stefanowitsch (eds), 2006. *Corpora in Cognitive Linguistics: Corpus-Based Approaches to Syntax and Lexis*. Berlin: Mouton de Gruyter.

Grimes, Joseph, 1975. *The Thread of Discourse*. The Hague: Mouton.

Grimes, Joseph (ed.), 1978. *Papers on Discourse*. Dallas, TX: Summer Institute of Linguistics.

Grimm, Jacob, 1819. *Deutsche Grammatik: Erster Theil*. Göttingen: Dieterichsche Buchhandlung.

Grimm, Jacob, 1822. *Deutsche Grammatik: Erster Theil. Zweite Ausgabe*. Göttingen: Dieterichsche Buchhandlung.

Grimm, Jacob, and Wilhelm Grimm, 1813. *Altdeutsche Wälder*, vol. 1. Cassel: Thurneissen.

Grishman, Ralph, and Beth Sundheim, 1996. Message Understanding Conference 6: a brief history. *Proceedings of the 16th International Conference on Computational Linguistics* (Copenhagen), 466–71.

Groenendijk, Jeroen A. G., and Martin B. J. Stokhof, 1984. On the semantics of questions and the pragmatics of answers. In Fred Landman and Frank Veltman (eds), *Varieties of Formal Semantics*. Dordrecht: Foris, 143–70.

Grohmann, Adolf, 1963. *Arabien*. Munich: C. H. Beck.

Grondelaers, Stefan, Dirk Speelman, and Dirk Geeraerts, 2008. National variation in the use of *er* 'there': regional and cognitive constraints on cognitive explanations. In Kristiansen and Dirven (2008: 153–203).

Grondeux, Anne, 2000. La grammatica positiva dans le Bas Moyen-Âge. In Auroux et al., vol. 1 (2000: 598–609).

Grosz, Barbara J., and Candace L. Sidner, 1986. Attention, intentions, and the structure of discourse. *Computational Linguistics* 12: 175–204.

Grosz, Barbara J., Aravind K. Joshi, and Scott Weinstein, 1995. Centering: a framework for modeling the local coherence of discourse. *Computational Linguistics* 21: 203–25.

Grosz, Barbara J., Karen Spärck Jones, and Bonnie L. Webber (eds), 1986. *Readings in Natural Language Processing*. Los Altos, CA: Morgan Kaufmann.

Grotans, Anna A., and David W. Porter, 1995. *The St. Gall Tractate: A Medieval Guide to Rhetorical Syntax*. Columbia, SC: Camden House.

Grützner, Paul, 1879. Physiologie der Stimme und Sprache. In Hermann Aubert, Ludimar Hermann, et al. (eds), *Handbuch der Physiologie*, Bd. 1, Theil 2. Leipzig: F. C. W. Vogel.

Guidi, Ignazio, 1925. Summarium grammaticae Arabiae meridionalis. *Le Muséon* 39: 1–32.

Guillaume, Gustave, 1971–2010. *Leçons de linguistique*. 20 vols. Québec: Presses de l'Université Laval.

Gullberg, Marianne, Kees de Bot, and Virginia Volterra, 2008. Gestures and some key issues in the study of language development. *Gesture* 8: 149–79.

Gumperz, John J., 1958. Phonological differences in three Hindi dialects. *Language* 34(2): 212–24.

Gumperz, John J., 1960. *Hindi Reader*, vol. 1. Berkeley: Center for South Asian Studies, University of California.

Gumperz, John J., 1962. Types of linguistic community. *Anthropological Linguistics* 4: 28–40.

Gumperz, John J., 1968. The speech community. In *International Encyclopedia of the Social Sciences*. New York: Macmillan, 381–6.

Gumperz, John J., 1964a. Hindi–Punjabi code-switching in Delhi. In Horace G. Hunt (ed.), *Proceedings of the Ninth International Congress of Linguistics*. The Hague: Mouton, 1115–24.

Gumperz, John J., 1964b. Linguistic and social interaction in two communities. In John J. Gumperz and Dell Hymes (eds), *The Ethnography of Communication*, Special Issue of *American Anthropologist* 66(6), II: 137–53.

Gumperz, John J., 1982a. *Discourse Strategies*. Cambridge: Cambridge University Press.

Gumperz, John J. (ed.), 1982b. *Language and Social Identity*. Cambridge: Cambridge University Press.

Gumperz, John J., 1992. Contextualization and understanding. In Alessandro Duranti and Charles Goodwin (eds), *Rethinking Context: Language as an Interactive Phenomenon*. Cambridge: Cambridge University Press, 129–252.

Gumperz, John J., and Dell Hymes (eds), 1972. *Directions in Sociolinguistics: The Ethnography of Speaking*. New York: Holt, Rinehart & Winston.

Gumperz, John J. and Jenny Cook-Gumperz, 2008. Studying language, culture, and society: sociolinguistics or linguistic anthropology? *Journal of Sociolinguistics* 12: 532–45.

Gumperz, John J. and Stephen C. Levinson (eds), 1996. *Rethinking Linguistic Relativity*. Cambridge: Cambridge University Press.

Gundel, Jeanette K., Nancy Hedburg, and Ron Zacharski, 2001. Definite descriptions and cognitive status in English: why accommodation is unnecessary. *English Language and Linguistics* 5: 273–95.

Gzella, Holger, 2007. Some penciled notes on Ugaritic lexicography. *Bibliotheca Orientalis* 64: 527–67.

Gzella, Holger, 2008a. Aramaic in the Parthian period: the Arsacid inscriptions. In Holger Gzella and Margaretha L. Folmer (eds), *Aramaic in its Historical and Linguistic Setting*. Wiesbaden: Harrassowitz, 107–30.

Gzella, Holger, 2008b. Review of *Kleines Wörterbuch des Ugaritischen* by Josef Tropper (Wiesbaden: Harrassowitz). *Journal of the American Oriental Society* 128: 351–3.

Haase, Friedrich, 1874–80. *Vorlesungen über lateinische Sprachwissenschaft, gehalten ab 1840*. Leipzig: Simmel.

Haase, Martin, 2001a. Sprachtypologie bei Edward Sapir. In Haspelmath et al. (2001: 164–265).

Haase, Martin, 2001b. Sprachtypologie und Universalienforschung bei Joseph H. Greenberg. In Haspelmath et al. (2001: 180–283).

Haberland, Hartmut, and Jacob L. Mey, 1977. Editorial: Linguistics and pragmatics. *Journal of Pragmatics* 1: 1–13.

Haberland, Hartmut, and Jacob L. Mey, 2002. Editorial: Linguistics and pragmatics, 25 years after. *Journal of Pragmatics* 34: 1671–82.

Hadamitzky, Wolfgang, and Mark Spahn, 1981. *Kanji and Kana: A Handbook and Dictionary of the Japanese Writing System*. Rutland, VT: Tuttle.

Hagland, Jan Ragnar, 2005. Language loss and destandardization in the Late Middle Ages and Early Modern times. In Oskar Bandle, Kurt Braunmüller, Ernst Håkon Jahr, Allan Karker, Hans-Peter Naumann, and Ulf Teleman (eds), *The Nordic Languages II*. Berlin: de Gruyter.

Haiman, John (ed.), 1985. *Iconicity in Syntax: Proceedings of a Symposium on Iconicity in Syntax, Stanford, June 24–6, 1983*. Amsterdam: John Benjamins.

Hajičová, Eva, Barbara Hall Partee, and Petr Sgall, 1998. *Topic-Focus Articulation, Tripartite Structures and Semantic Content*. Dordrecht: Kluwer.

Haldeman, Samuel S., 1860. *Analytic Orthography: An investigation of the sounds of the voice, and their alphabetic notation; including the mechanism of speech, and its bearing upon etymology*. Philadelphia: J. B. Lippincott.

Halevy, Alon, Peter Norvig, and Fernando Pereira, 2009. The unreasonable effectiveness of data. *IEEE Intelligent Systems* 24: 8–12.

Halévy, Joseph, 1875. *études sabéennes*. Paris: Imprimerie nationale. [Repr. from *Journal Asiatique*, 7th ser., 1 (1873), 1–98; 2 (1873), 305–65; 4 (1874), 497–585.]

Hall, David, Daniel Jurafsky, and Christopher D. Manning, 2008. Studying the history of ideas with topic models. *Proceedings of the 2008 Conference on Empirical Methods in Natural Language Processing* (Columbus, OH), 363–71.

Hall, Robert A., Jr, 1942. The significance of the Italian Questione della Lingua. *Studies in Philology* 39: 1–10.

Halle, Morris, 1959. *The Sound Pattern of Russian: A Linguistic and Acoustical Investigation*. The Hague: Mouton.

Halle, Morris, 1962. Phonology in generative grammar. *Word* 18: 54–72.

Halle, Morris, 1983. On distinctive features and their articulatory implementation. *Natural Language and Linguistic Theory* 1: 91–105.

Halle, Morris, 2005. Palatalization/velar softening: what is it and what it tells us about the nature of language. *Linguistic Inquiry* 36: 23–41.

Halliday, Michael A. K., 1961. Categories of the theory of grammar. *Word* 17: 241–92. [Repr. in Jonathan J. Webster (ed.), *On Grammar, vol. 1 of The Collected Works of M. A. K. Halliday* (London: Continuum, 2002), 37–94.]

Halliday, Michael A. K., 1967/8. Notes on transitivity and theme in English. *Journal of Linguistics* 3: 37–81, 199–244; 4: 179–215.

Halliday, Michael A. K., 1973. *Explorations in the Functions of Language*. London: Edward Arnold.

Halliday, Michael A. K., 1975. *Learning How to Mean: Explorations in the Development of Language*. London: Edward Arnold.

Halliday, Michael A. K., 1978. *Language as Social Semiotic: The Social Interpretation of Language and Meaning*. London: Edward Arnold.

Halliday, Michael A. K., 1981. The origin and early development of Chinese phonological theory. In Ronald E. Asher and Eugénie J. A. Henderson. (eds), *Towards a History of Phonetics*. Edinburgh: Edinburgh University Press, 123–40.

Halliday, Michael A. K., 1985a. Dimensions of discourse: grammar. In van Dijk (1985: 19–56).

Halliday, Michael A. K., 1985b. *Introduction to Functional Grammar*. London: Edward Arnold. [2nd edn 1994.]

Halliday, Michael A. K., 1985c. *Spoken and Written Language*. Geelong: Deakin University Press. [Republished 1989, Oxford University Press.]

Halliday, Michael A. K., 2003 [1994]. Systemic theory. In Jonathan J. Webster (ed.), *On Language and Linguistics*. Vol. 3 of *The Collected Works of M. A. K. Halliday*. London: Continuum, 433–42.

Halliday, Michael A. K., 2003. On the 'architecture' of human language. In Jonathan J. Webster (ed.), *On Language and Linguistics*. Vol. 3 of *The Collected Works of M. A. K. Halliday*. London: Continuum, 1–29.

Halliday, Michael A. K., 2006. *Studies in Chinese Language*. Vol. 8 of *The Collected Works of M. A. K. Halliday*, ed. Jonathan J. Webster. London: Continuum.

Halliday, Michael A. K., and Ruqaiya Hasan, 1976. *Cohesion in English*. London: Longman.

Halliday, Michael A. K., and Ruqaiya Hasan. 1985. *Language, Context, and Text: Aspects of Language in a Social-Semiotic Perspective*. Oxford: Oxford University Press.

Halliday, Michael A. K., and Ruqaiya Hasan. 2000. System and text: making links. *Text* 20(2): 201–10.

Halliday, Michael A. K., and Christian M. I. M. Matthiessen, 1999. *Construing Experience Through Meaning: A Language-Based Approach to Cognition*. London: Continuum.

Halliday, Michael A. K., and Christian M. I. M. Matthiessen. 2004. *An Introduction to Functional Grammar*, 3rd edn. London: Hodder Education.

Hamano, Shoko S., 1998. *The Sound Symbolic System of Japanese*. Tokyo: Kurosio.

Hamblin, Charles L., 1976. Questions in Montague English. In Barbara H. Partee (ed.), *Montague Grammar*. New York: Academic Press, 147–59.

Hamblin, Charles L., 1987. *Imperatives.*. Oxford: Blackwell.

Hamilton, Alexander, 1820. Review of Franz Bopp, 1: *Über das Conjugationssystem*; 2: *Nalus*. *Edinburgh Review* 33: 431–42.

Hamilton, Gordon J., 2006. *The Origins of the West Semitic Alphabet in the Egyptian Scripts*. Washington, DC: Catholic Biblical Association of America.

Hamp, Eric, Fred W. Householder, and Robert Austerlitz (eds), 1966. *Readings in Linguistics II*. Chicago: University of Chicago Press.

Hankamer, Jorge, and Ivan A. Sag, 1976. Deep and surface anaphora. *Linguistic Inquiry* 7: 391–428.

Hanks, Patrick, 1994. Linguistic norms and pragmatic exploitations, or, why lexicographers need prototype theory, and vice versa. In Ferenc Kiefer, Gabor Kiss, and Julia Pajzs (eds) *Papers in Computational Lexicography: Complex 94*. Budapest: Hungarian Academy of Sciences, 89–113.

Hanks, Patrick, 2004. Corpus pattern analysis. In G. Williams and S. Vessier (eds), *Euralex Proceedings*, vol. 1. Lorient: Université de Bretagne-Sud, 87–97.

Hanks, Patrick, 2006. English lexicography. In Keith Brown (ed.), *Encyclopedia of Language and Linguistics*, 2nd edn, vol. 4. Oxford: Elsevier, 184–94.

Hanks, Patrick (ed.), 2008. *Lexicology: Critical Concepts in Linguistics*. 6 vols. London: Routledge.

Hanks, Patrick, 2009. The impact of corpora on dictionaries. In Paul Baker (ed.), *Contemporary Approaches to Corpus Linguistics*. London: Continuum, 114–236.

Hanks, Patrick, 2010. Lexicography, printing technology, and the spread of Renaissance culture. In Anne Dykstra and Tanneke Schoonheim (eds), *Proceedings of the 14 Euralex International Congress*. Leeuwarden: Frisian Institute.

Hanks, Patrick, 2013. *Lexical Analysis: Norms and Exploitations*. Cambridge, MA: MIT Press.

Hanks, William F., 1996. Language form and communicative practices. In Gumperz and Levinson (1996: 132–270).

Hanks, William F., 1996. *Language and Communicative Practices*. Boulder, CO: Westview Press.

Hanson, Norwood R., 1958. *Patterns of Discovery: An Inquiry into the Conceptual Foundations of Science*. Cambridge: Cambridge University Press.

Hardcastle, William J., 1972. The use of electropalatography in phonetic research. *Phonetica* 25: 197–215.

Hardcastle, William J., 1975. Some aspects of speech production under controlled conditions of oral anaesthesia and auditory masking. *Journal of Phonetics* 3: 197–214.

Hardcastle, William J., and Fiona Gibbon, 2005. Electropalatography as a research and clinical tool: 30 years on. In William J. Hardcastle and Janet Mackenzie Beck (eds), *A Figure of Speech: A Festschrift for John Laver*. Mahwah, NJ: Lawrence Erlbaum.

Harder, Peter, 2007. Cognitive linguistics and philosophy. In Geeraerts and Cuyckens (2007: 1241–65).

Harman, Gilbert H., 1963. Generative grammars without transformational rules. *Language* 39: 567–616.

Harnad, Steven, Horst D. Steklis, and Jane Lancaster (eds), 1976. *Origin and Evolution of Language and Speech*. New York: New York Academy of Sciences.

Harper, Kenneth, 1961. Soviet research in machine translation. In H. P. Edmundson (ed.), *Proceedings of the National Symposium on Machine Translation Held at the University of California, Los Angeles, February 2–5, 1960*. Englewood Cliffs, NJ: Prentice Hall, 1–12.

Harrington, Jonathan, 2010. *The Phonetic Analysis of Speech Corpora*. Oxford: Blackwell.

Harrington, Jonathan, Steve Cassidy, Tina John, and Michel Scheffers, 2003. Building an interface between EMU and Praat: a modular approach to speech database analysis. In Maria Josep-Solé, Daniel Recasens, and Joaquín Romero (eds), *Proceedings of the 15th*

International Congress of Phonetics Sciences (ICPhS XV), Barcelona, Spain. Barcelona: Universitat Autònoma de Barcelona, 355–8.

Harrington, Jonathan, Felicitas Kleber, and Ulrich Reubold, 2008. Compensation for coarticulation, /u/ fronting, and sound change in standard southern British: an acoustic and perceptual study. *Journal of the Acoustical Society of America* 123: 2825–35.

Harris, James, 1751. *Hermes, or, a Philosophical Inquiry concerning Universal Grammar.* London: Woodfall.

Harris, Randy A., 1993. *The Linguistics Wars.* New York: Oxford University Press.

Harris, Roy, and Andrew Pyle (eds), 1996. *The Origin of Language.* Bristol: Thoemmes Press.

Harris, Roy, and Talbot J. Taylor, 1989. *Landmarks in Linguistic Thought: The Western Tradition from Socrates to Saussure.* London: Routledge.

Harris, Zellig S., 1942. Morpheme alternants in linguistic analysis. *Language* 18: 169–80. [Repr. in Joos (1957: 109–15).]

Harris, Zellig S., 1944. Simultaneous components in phonology. *Language* 20: 181–205.

—— 1946. From morpheme to utterance. *Language* 22: 161–83.

Harris, Zellig S., 1951. *Methods in Structural Linguistics.* Chicago: Chicago University Press.

Harris, Zellig S., 1952. Discourse analysis. *Language* 28: 1–30.

Harris, Zellig S., 1954a. Distributional structure. *Word* 10: 146–62.

Harris, Zellig S., 1954b. Transfer grammar. *International Journal of American Linguistics* 20: 259–70.

Harris, Zellig S., 1957. Co-occurrence and transformation in linguistic structure. *Language* 33: 283–340. [Repr. in Joos (1957: 143–210).]

Harris, Zellig S., 1965. Transformational theory. *Language* 41: 363–401.

Harris, Zellig S., 1981. *Papers in Syntax.* Dordrecht: Reidel.

Hart, John, 1569. *An orthographie: conteyning the due order and reason, howe to write or paint thimage of mannes voice, most like to the life or nature . . .* London: William Seres.

Hasan, Ruqaiya, 1978. Text in the systemic functional model. In Wolfgang U. Dressler (ed.), *Current Trends in Text Linguistics.* Berlin: Mouton de Gruyter, 128–246.

Hasan, Ruqaiya, 1995. The conception of context in text. In Peter H. Fries and Michael Gregory (eds), *Discourse in Society: Systemic Functional Perspectives.* Norwood, NJ: Ablex, 183–283.

Hasan, Ruqaiya, 2005a. Introduction: a working model of language. In Ruqaiya Hasan, Christian M. I. M. Matthiessen, and Jonathan J. Webster (eds), *Continuing Discourse on Language: A Functional Perspective*, vol. 1. London: Equinox, 37–52.

Hasan, Ruqaiya, 2005b. Language and society in a systemic functional perspective. In Ruqaiya Hasan, Christian M. I. M. Matthiessen, and Jonathan J. Webster (eds), *Continuing Discourse On Language: A Functional Perspective*, vol. 1. London: Equinox, 55–88.

Hasan, Ruqaiya, and Charles Fries, 1995. *On Subject and Theme: A Discourse Functional Perspective.* Amsterdam: John Benjamins.

Haspelmath, Martin, 1999. Optimality and diachronic adaptation. *Zeitschrift für Sprachwissenschaft* 18: 180–205.

Haspelmath, Martin, 2002. *Understanding Morphology.* London: Arnold.

Haspelmath, Martin, Ekkehard König, Wulf Oesterreicher, and Wolfgang Raible (eds), 2001. *Language Typology and Language Universals.* Berlin: de Gruyter.

Hasselbach, Rebecca, 2005. *Sargonic Akkadian. A Historical and Comparative Study of the Syllabic Texts.* Wiesbaden: Harrassowitz.

Hasselbach, Rebecca, 2007. The affiliation of Sargonic Akkadian with Babylonian and Assyrian: new insights concerning the sub-grouping of Akkadian. *Journal of Semitic Studies* 52: 21–43.

Haugen, Einar, 1950. *First Grammatical Treatise: The Earliest Germanic Phonology.* Baltimore, MD: Linguistic Society of America.

Haugen, Einar, 1953. *The Norwegian Language in the United States.* Philadelphia: University of Pennsylvania Press.

Haugen, Einar, 1956. The syllable in linguistic description. In *For Roman Jakobson: Essays on the Occasion of his 60th Birthday.* The Hague: Mouton, 113–21.

Haugen, Einar, 1959. Planning for a standard language in modern Norway. *Anthropological Linguistics* 1(3): 8–21.

Haugen, Einar, 1966. *Language Conflict and Language Planning: The Case of Modern Norwegian.* Cambridge, MA: Harvard University Press.

Haugen, Einar, 1972. *The First Grammatical Treatise.* London: Longman.

Hauser, Mark, Noam Chomsky, and W. Tecumseh Fitch, 2002. The faculty of language: what is it, who has it, and how did it evolve? *Science* 298: 1569–79. [Repr. in Larson et al. (2010: 14–42).]

Havers, Wilhelm, 1931. *Handbuch der erklärenden Syntax.* Heidelberg: Carl Winters.

Hay, Jennifer, Paul Warren, and Katie Drager, 2006. Factors influencing speech perception in the context of a merger-in-progress. *Journal of Phonetics* 34: 458–84.

Hayes, Francis C., 1957. Gestures: a working bibliography. *Southern Folklore Quarterly* 21: 218–317.

Hays, David G., 1961. Linguistic research at the RAND Corporation. In H. P. Edmundson (ed.), *Proceedings of the National Symposium on Machine Translation Held at the University of California, Los Angeles, February 2–5, 1960.* Englewood Cliffs, NJ: Prentice Hall, 13–25.

Hays, David G., 1962. Automatic language-data processing. In Harold Borko (ed.), *Computer Applications in the Behavioral Sciences.* Englewood Cliffs, NJ: Prentice Hall, 394–423.

Hays, David G., 1967. Computational linguistics: research in progress at the RAND Corporation. *T.A. Informations* 1: 15–20.

Hays, David G., and Jim Mathias, 1976. FBIS seminar on machine translation. *American Journal of Computational Linguistics,* microfiche 46. www.aclweb.org/anthology/J79-1046

Haywood, John A., 1965. *Arabic Lexicography: Its History, and Its Place in the General History of Lexicography.* Leiden: Brill.

Hearst, Marti A., 1998. Automated discovery of WordNet relations. In Christiane Fellbaum (ed.), *WordNet: An Electronic Lexical Database.* Cambridge, MA: MIT Press, 131–51.

Heath, Christian, 1984. Talk and recipiency: sequential organization in speech and body motion. In J. Maxwell Atkinson and John Heritage (eds), *Structures of Social Action: Studies in Conversation Analysis.* Cambridge: Cambridge University Press, 247–65.

Heath, Christian, 1986. *Body Movement and Speech in Medical Interaction.* Cambridge: Cambridge University Press.

Heath, Christian, 1992. Gesture's discrete tasks: multiple relevancies in visual conduct in the contextualization of language. In Peter Auer and Aldo di Luzio (eds), *The Contextualization of Language.* Amsterdam: John Benjamins, 102–27.

Hecht, Max, 1888. *Die griechische Bedeutungslehre: eine Aufgabe der klassischen Philologie.* Leipzig: Teubner.

Heerdegen, Ferdinand, 1875–81. *Ueber Umfang und Gliederung der Sprachwissenschaft im Allgemeinen und der lateinischen Grammatik insbesondere: versuch einer systematischen Einleitung zur lateinischen Semasiologie*. Erlangen: Deichert.

Heger, Klaus, 1964. *Monem, Wort, Satz und Text*. Tübingen: Max Niemeyer.

Heims, Steve J., 1975. Encounter of behavioral sciences with the new machine–organism analogies in the 1940s. *Journal of the History of the Behavioral Sciences* 11: 368–73.

Heims, Steve J., 1977. Gregory Bateson and the mathematicians: from interdisciplinary interaction to societal functions. *Journal of the History of the Behavioral Sciences* 13: 141–59.

Heine, Bernd, and Tania Kuteva, 2002. *World Lexicon of Grammaticalization*. Cambridge: Cambridge University Press.

Heine, Bernd and Tania Kuteva, 2007. *The Genesis of Grammar: A Reconstruction*. Oxford: Oxford University Press.

Heinrich, Patrick, 2012. *The Making of Monolingual Japan: Language Ideology and Japanese Modernity*. Bristol: Multilingual Matters.

Hellwag, Christophorus Fridericus, 1781. *Dissertatio Inavgvralis Physiologico Medica De Formatione Loqvelae Qvam . . . Praeside . . . Gottlieb Conrad Christiano Storr . . . Pro Licentia Conseqvendi Gradvm Doctoris Medicinae . . . Avctor respondens Christophorus Fridericus Hellwag*. Tubingae: Fues.

Hempel, Carl G., 1970. On the 'standard conception' of scientific theories. In M. Radner and S. Winokur (eds), *Minnesota Studies in the Philosophy of Science IV*. Minneapolis: University of Minnesota Press, 145–60.

Hengeveld, Kees, 1992. *Non-verbal Predication: Theory, Typology, Diachrony*. Berlin: Mouton de Gruyter.

Hengeveld, Kees and Lachlan Mackenzie, 2008. *Functional Discourse Grammar: A Typologically Based Theory of Language Structure*. Oxford: Oxford University Press.

Henning, Walter B., 1958. Mitteliranisch. In *Iranistik*. Leiden: Brill, 10–130.

Henry of Avranches, 1929. *Libellus Donati metrice compositus*. In J. P. Hieronimus and J. C. A. Russell (eds), *Two Types of Thirteenth Century Grammatical Poems*. Colorado Springs: Colorado College, 10–15.

Heritage, John, 1984. *Garfinkel and Ethnomethodology*. Cambridge: Polity Press.

Heritage, John, 2007. Territories of knowledge, territories of experience: (not so) empathic moments in interaction. Keynote speech at the 15th Symposium about Language and Society (SALSA), Austin, TX, 14 April.

Herlofsky, William J., 1981. *Phonetic Symbolism in Japanese Onomatopoeia*. Minneapolis: University of Minnesota.

Herman, David, 1997. Scripts, sequences, and stories: elements of a post-classical narratology. *PMLA* 112: 1046–59.

Hertz, Martinus (ed.), 1855–60. *Prisciani Institutionum Libri XVIII*. In *Grammatici Latini* II–III. Leipzig: B. G. Teubner.

Hetzron, Robert, 1969. The evidence for perfect **y'aqtul* and jussive **yaqt'ul* in Proto-Semitic. *Journal of Semitic Studies* 14: 1–21.

Hetzron, Robert, 1977. *The Gunnän-Gurage Languages*. Naples: Istituto orientale di Napoli.

Hetzron, Robert, 1980. The limits of Cushitic. *Sprache und Geschichte in Afrika* 2: 7–125.

Hetzron, Robert (ed.), 1997. *The Semitic Languages*. London: Routledge.

Hewes, Gordon W., 1973. Primate communication and the gestural origins of language. *Current Anthropology* 14: 5–24.

Hewes, Gordon W., 1996. A history of the study of language origins and the gestural primacy hypothesis. In A. Lock and C. R. Peters (eds), *Handbook of Symbolic Evolution*. Oxford: Blackwell, 571–95.

Hewes, Gordon, William C. Stokoe and Roger W. Wescott (eds), 1974. *Language Origins*. Silver Spring, MD: Linstok Press.

Hey, Oskar, 1892. Semasiologische Studien. *Jahrbücher für classische Philologie* 18: 83–212.

Hilgert, Markus, 2002. *Akkadisch in der Ur-III-Zeit*. Münster: Rhema.

Hill, Archibald A. (ed.), 1962. *The Third Texas Conference on Problems of Linguistic Analysis in English*. Austin: University of Texas Press.

Hill, Beverly, Sachiko Ide, Shoko Ikuta, Akiko Kawasaki, and Tsunao Ogino, 1986. Universals of linguistic politeness: quantitative evidence from Japanese and American English. *Journal of Pragmatics* 10: 347–471.

Hintikka, Jaakko, 1974. Questions about questions. In Milton K. Munitz and Peter K. Unger (eds), *Semantics and Philosophy*. New York: New York University Press, 103–58.

Hinton, Leanne, Johanna Nicols, and John J. Ohala, 1994. *Sound Symbolism*. Cambridge: Cambridge University Press.

Hiraga, Masako K., 1993. Iconicity in poetry: how poetic form embodies meaning. In Karen Haworth, John Deely, and Terry Prewitt (eds), *Semiotics 1990*. New York: University Press of America, 115–26.

Hiraga, Masako K., 2000. Iconicity as principle of composition and interpretation: a case study in Japanese short poems. In Patrizia Violi (ed.), *Phonosymbolism and Poetic Language*. Turnhout: Brepols, 147–69.

Hirata, Yukari, and Kimiko Tsukada, 2009. Effects of speaking rate and vowel length on formant frequency displacement in Japanese. *Phonetica* 66: 129–49.

Hirson, Alan, J. Peter French, and David M. Howard, 1995. Speech fundamental frequency over the telephone and face-to face: some implications for forensic phonetics. In Jack W. Lewis (ed.), *Studies in General and English Phonetics*. London: Routledge, 230–40.

Hirst, Graeme, 1981. *Anaphora in Natural Language Understanding*. Berlin: Springer

Hirst, Graeme, 1987. *Semantic Interpretation and the Resolution of Ambiguity*. Cambridge: Cambridge University Press.

Hirst, Graeme, 2007. Views of text-meaning in computational linguistics: past, present, and future. In Gordana Dodig-Crnkovic and Susan Stuart (eds), *Computation, Information, Cognition: The Nexus and the Liminal*. Newcastle upon Tyne: Cambridge Scholars, 170–279.

Hirst, Graeme, 2008. The future of text-meaning in computational linguistics. In Petr Sojka, Aleš Horák, Ivan Kopeček, and Karel Pala (eds), *Text, Speech and Dialogue: Proceedings of the 11th International Conference (TSD 2008)*. Berlin: Springer, 1–9.

Hjelmslev, Louis, 1961. *Prolegomena to a Theory of Language*. Bloomington: Indiana University Press. [Transl. of *Omkring Sprogteoriens Grundlaeggelse*. Copenhagen: Luno, 1943.]

Hjelmslev, Louis, 1985. *Nouveaux essais*. Paris: Presses Universitaires de France.

Hobbs, Jerry R., 1978. Resolving pronoun references. *Lingua* 44: 311–38.

Hobbs, Jerry R., and Stanley J. Rosenschein, 1977. Making computational sense of Montague's intensional logic. *Artificial Intelligence* 9: 287–306.

Hoberg, Rudolf, 1970. *Die Lehre vom sprachlichen Feld: ein Beitrag zu ihrer Geschichte, Methodik und Anwendung*. Düsseldorf: Schwann.

Hockett, Charles F., 1939. Potawatomi syntax. *Language* 15: 235–48.

Hockett, Charles F., 1942. A system of descriptive phonology. *Language* 18: 3–21. [Repr. in Joos (1957: 97–108).]

Hockett, Charles F., 1947. Problems of morphemic analysis. *Language* 23: 321–43. [Repr. in Joos (1957: 129–242).]

Hockett, Charles F., 1948. A note on structure. *International Journal of American Linguistics* 14: 269–71.

Hockett, Charles F., 1949. Two fundamental problems in phonemics. *Studies in Linguistics* 7: 29–51.

Hockett, Charles F., 1953. Review of *The Mathematical Theory of Communication* by Claude L. Shannon and Warren Weaver. *Language* 29: 69–93.

Hockett, Charles F., 1954. Two models of grammatical description. *Word* 10: 210–31. [Repr. in Joos (1957: 386–99).]

Hockett, Charles F., 1955. *A Manual of Phonology*. Bloomington: Indiana University Publications in Anthropology and Linguistics.

Hockett, Charles F., 1958. *A Course in Modern Linguistics*. New York: Macmillan.

Hockett, Charles F., 1959. Animal 'languages' and human language. *Human Biology* 31: 32–9.

Hockett, Charles F., 1961. Linguistic elements and their relation. *Language* 37: 29–53.

Hockett, Charles F., 1965. Sound change. *Language* 41: 185–204.

Hockett, Charles F., 1967. The Yawelmani basic verb. *Language* 43: 208–22.

Hockett, Charles F., 1968. *The State of the Art*. The Hague: Mouton.

Hockett, Charles F. (ed.), 1970. *A Leonard Bloomfield Anthology*. Chicago: University of Chicago Press.

Hockett, Charles F., 1987. *Refurbishing Our Foundations*. Amsterdam: John Benjamins.

Hockett, Charles F., 1997a. Approaches to syntax. *Lingua* 100: 151–70.

Hockett, Charles F., 1997b. Review of *The World's Writing Systems*, ed. Peter T. Daniels and William Bright. *Language* 73: 379–85.

Hockett, Charles F., 2003 [1951]. Two lectures on writing (ed. Peter T. Daniels). *Written Language and Literacy* 6: 131–75.

Hockett, Charles F., and Robert Ascher, 1964. The human revolution. *Current Anthropology* 5: 135–68.

Hodge, Robert, and Gunther Kress, 1988. *Social Semiotics*. Cambridge: Polity Press.

Hodges, Richard, 1644. *The English primrose: far surpassing al others of this kinde, that ever grew in any English garden, by the ful sight whereof, there wil manifestly appear, the Easiest and Speediest-way, both for the true spelling and reading of English, as also for the True-writing thereof: that ever was publickly known to this day. Planted (with no smal pains) by Richard Hodges, a School-master . . . for the exceeding great benefit, both of his own Countrey-men and Strangers.* London: Richard Cotes.

Hoenigswald, Henry M., 1984. Etymology against grammar in the early nineteenth century. *Histoire, épistémologie, langage* 6(2): 95–100.

Hoenigswald, Henry M., 1986. Nineteenth-century linguistics on itself. In Theodora Bynon and Frank R. Palmer (eds), *Studies in the History of Western Linguistics (in honor of R. H. Robins)*. Cambridge: Cambridge University Press, 172–88.

Hoepelman, Jaap, 1981. On questions. In J. A. G. Groenendijk, T. M. V. Janssen, and M. B. J. Stokhof (eds), *Formal Methods in the Study of Language*, vol. 1. Amsterdam: Mathematisch Centrum, 107–35.

Hoey, Michael, 2005. *Lexical Priming: A New Theory of Words and Language*. London: Routledge.

Hoffmann, Roald, 1993. *Chemistry Imagined*. Washington, DC: Smithsonian Press.

Höfner, Maria, 1943. *Altsüdarabische Grammatik*. Leipzig: Harrassowitz.

Hofstadter, Douglas, 1997. *Le Ton Beau de Marot: In Praise of the Music of Language*. New York: Basic Books.

Holder, William, 1669. *Elements of Speech: an essay of inquiry into the natural production of letters: with an appendix concerning persons deaf and dumb*. London: T.N. for J. Martyn.

Hollander, Lee M., 1990. *Sayings of the High One, The Poetic Edda*. Austin: University of Texas Press.

Hollmann, Willem B., 2005. Passivisability of English periphrastic causatives. In Gries and Stefanowitsch (2006: 193–223).

Hollmann, Willem B., and Anna Siewierska, 2007. A construction grammar account of possessive constructions in Lancashire dialect: some advantages and challenges. *English Language and Linguistics* 11: 407–24.

Holt, Robert (ed.), 1878. *The Ormulum: with the Notes and Glossary of Dr. R. M. White*. Oxford: Clarendon Press.

Holtz, Louis, 1981. *Donat et la tradition de l'enseignement grammatical: étude sur l'Ars Donati et sa diffusion (IVe–IXe siècle) et édition critique*. Paris: CNRS.

Holz-Mänttäri, Justa, 1984. *Translatorisches Handeln: Theorie und Methode*. Helsinki: Suomalainen Tiedeakatemia.

Hombert, Jean-Marie, and Gérard Lenclud, in press. *Comment le langage serait venu à l'homme*. Paris: Fayard.

Hookway, Christopher, 1988. *Quine: Language, Experience and Reality*. Oxford: Polity Press.

Hopper, Paul J., 1979. Aspect and foregrounding in discourse. In Talmy Givón (ed.), *Discourse and Syntax*. New York: Academic Press, 113–42.

Hopper, Paul J., 1987. Emergent grammar. In Jon Aske et al. (eds), *Proceedings of the Thirteenth Annual Meeting of the Berkeley Linguistics Society*. Berkeley, CA: Berkeley Linguistic Society, 139–57.

Hopper, Paul J., 1992. Emergence of grammar. In William Bright (ed.), *International Encyclopedia of Linguistics*. Oxford: Oxford University Press, 364–7.

Hopper, Paul J., 1996. Some recent trends in grammaticalization. *Annual Review of Anthropology* 25: 217–36.

Hopper, Paul J., 1998. Emergent grammar. In Michael Tomasello (ed.), *The New Psychology of Language: Cognitive and Functional Approaches to Language Structure*. Mahwah, NJ: Lawrence Erlbaum, 155–75.

Hopper, Paul J., and Sandra A. Thompson, 1980. Transitivity in grammar and discourse. *Language* 56: 251–99.

Hopper, Paul J., and Sandra A. Thompson, 1984. The discourse basis for lexical categories in Universal Grammar. *Language* 60: 703–52.

Horn, Laurence R., 1984. Toward a new taxonomy for pragmatic inference: Q-based and R-based implicature. In Deborah Schiffrin (ed.), *Georgetown Round Table on Languages and Linguistics 1984*. Washington, DC: Georgetown University Press, 11–42.

Horne Tooke, John, 1786. *Epea Pteroenta, or the Diversions of Purley*. London: Johnson.

Houben, Jan E. M., 1995. *The Sambandha-Samuddeśa (chapter on relation) and Bhartṛhari's Philosophy of Language*. Groningen: Egbert Forsten.

Houben, Jan E. M., 2003. Three myths in modern Pāṇinian studies. (Review of *Recent Research in Pāṇinian Studies*, by George Cardona.) *Asiatische Studien / Études Asiatiques* 57: 121–79.

Householder, Fred W., 1981. Commentary. *The Syntax of Apollonius Dyscolus*. Amsterdam: John Benjamins.

Houston, Stephen (ed.), 2004. *First Writing*. Cambridge: Cambridge University Press.

Hovdhaugen, Even, Fred Karlsson, Carol Henriksen, and Bengt Sigurd (eds), 2000. *The History of Linguistics in the Nordic Countries*. Helsinki: Societas Scientiarum Fennica.

Hovy, Eduard, 2006. Learning by reading: an experiment in text analysis. In Petr Sojka, Ivan Kopeček, and Karel Pala (eds), *Text, Speech and Dialogue: Proceedings of the 9th International Conference (TSD 2006)*. Berlin: Springer, 3–12.

Howatt, Anthony P. R., 1984. *A History of English Language Teaching*. Oxford: Oxford University Press.

Howatt, Anthony P. R., with Henry G. Widdowson, 2004. *A History of English Language Teaching*, 2nd edn. Oxford: Oxford University Press.

Huck, Geoffrey J., 1985. Discontinuity and word order in categorial grammar. Ph.D. thesis, University of Chicago.

Huck, Geoffrey, and John A. Goldsmith, 1995. *Ideology and Linguistic Theory: Noam Chomsky and the Deep Structure Debates*. London: Routledge.

Hudson, Richard, 1999. *Sociolinguistics*. Cambridge: Cambridge University Press.

Hudson, Toby, Gea de Jong, Kirsty McDougall, Philip Harrison, and Francis Nolan, 2007. F0 Statistics for 100 young male speakers of Standard Southern British English. In Jürgen Trouvain and William J. Barry (eds), *Proceedings of the 16th International Congress of Phonetic Sciences* (Saarbrücken), 1809–12.

Hugh of St Victor, 1966. *De grammatica*. In Roger Baron (ed.), *Hugonis de sancto Victore opera propaedeutica*. South Bend, IN: University of Notre Dame Press, 65–163.

Hundt, Marianne, Andrea Sand, and Rainer Siemund, 1998. *Manual of Information to Accompany the Freiburg–LOB Corpus of British English ('FLOB')*. Freiburg: Albert-Ludwigs-Universität, Englisches Seminar.

Hundt, Marianne, Andrea Sand, and Paul Skandera, 1999. *Manual of Information to Accompany the Freiburg–Brown Corpus of American English ('Frown')*. Freiburg: Albert-Ludwigs-Universität, Englisches Seminar.

Hunston, Susan, and Gill Francis, 1999. *Pattern Grammar: A Corpus-Driven Approach to the Lexical Grammar of English*. Amsterdam: John Benjamins.

Hurford, James R., 2006. Recent developments in the evolution of language. *Cognitive Systems* 7: 23–32.

Hurford, James R., 2007. *The Origins of Meaning*. Oxford: Oxford University Press.

Hurford, James R., 2008. The evolution of human communication and language. In Patricia D'Ettorre and David Hughes (eds), *Sociobiology of Communication: An Interdisciplinary Perspective*. Oxford: Oxford University Press, 149–264.

Husserl, Edmund, 1913. *Logische Untersuchungen I–II*, 2nd edn. Halle: Niemeyer. [1st edn 1901–2.]

Hutchins, W. John, 1986. *Machine Translation: Past, Present, Future*. Chichester: Ellis Horwood.

Hutchins, W. John, 1996. ALPAC: the (in)famous report. *MT News International*, no. 14. [Repr. in Sergei Nirenburg, Harold Somers, and Yorick Wilks (eds), *Readings in Machine Translation* (Cambridge, MA: MIT Press, 2003), 131–5.]

Hutchins, W. John (ed.), 2000a. *Early Years in Machine Translation: Memoirs and Biographies of Pioneers*. Amsterdam: John Benjamins.

Hutchins, W. John, 2000b. The first decades of machine translation: overview, chronology, sources. In Hutchins (2000a: 1–15).

Hymes, Dell H. (ed.), 1964. *Language in Culture and Society: A Reader in Linguistics and Anthropology*. New York: Harper & Row.

Hymes, Dell H., 1966a. Two types of linguistic relativity (with examples from Amerindian ethnography). In William Bright (ed.), *Sociolinguistics: Proceedings of the UCLA Sociolinguistics Conference, 1964*. The Hague: Mouton, 114–67.

Hymes, Dell H., 1966b. Introduction: toward ethnographies of communication. *American Anthropologist* 66(6): 12–25.

Hymes, Dell H., 1971. Sociolinguistics and the ethnography of speaking. In Edwin Ardener (ed.), *Social Anthropology and Language*. London: Tavistock, 47–93.

Hymes, Dell H., 1972a. Models of the interaction of language and social life. In Gumperz and Hymes (1972: 35–71).

Hymes, Dell H., 1972b. On communicative competence. In John B. Pride and Janet Holmes (eds), *Sociolinguistics*. Harmondsworth: Penguin, 169–93.

Hymes, Dell H., 1973. The origin and foundation of inequality among speakers. *Daedalus* 102: 59–85.

Hymes, Dell H., 1974. *Foundations in Sociolinguistics: An Ethnographic Approach*. Philadelphia: University of Pennsylvania Press.

Hymes, Dell H., 1981. *In Vain I Tried to Tell You: Essays in Native American Ethnopoetics*. Philadelphia: University of Pennsylvania Press.

Hymes, Dell H., 1996. *Ethnography, Linguistics, and Narrative Inequality:Toward an Understanding of Voice*. London: Taylor & Francis.

Hymes, Dell H., and John Fought, 1975. *American Structuralism*. The Hague: Mouton. [2nd edn 1981.]

Ide, Nancy, and Randi Reppen, 2004. The American National Corpus: overall goals and first release. *Journal of English Linguistics* 32: 105–13.

Ide, Sachiko, 1982. Japanese sociolinguistics: politeness and women's language. *Lingua* 57: 357–85.

Ide, Sachiko, 1989. Formal forms and discernment: two neglected aspects of universals of linguistic politeness. *Multilingua* 8: 223–48.

Ingram, John, and Peter Mülhäusler, 2004. Norfolk Island Pitcairn English: phonetics and phonology. In Kate Burridge and Bernd Kortmann (eds), *A Handbook of Varieties of English*, vol. 1: *Phonology*. Berlin: Mouton de Gruyter, 780–804.

Irvine, Judith, 1986. Status and style in language. *Annual Review of Anthropology* 14: 557–81.

Isidore of Seville, 1911 [636]. *Etymologiae: Isidori Hispalensis episcopi Etymologiarum sive originum libri XX*, ed. W. M. Lindsay. 2 vols. Oxford: Clarendon Press.

Ising, Erika, 1970. *Die Herausbildung der Grammatik der Volkssprachen in Mittel- und Osteuropa. Studien über den Einfluss der lateinischen Elementargrammatik des Aelius Donatus De octo partibus orationis ars minor*. Berlin: Akademie.

Itkonen, Esa, 1978. *Grammatical Theory and Metascience*. Amsterdam: John Benjamins.

Itkonen, Esa, 1983. *Causality in Linguistic Theory*. London: Croom Helm.

Itkonen, Esa, 1991. *Universal History of Linguistics: India, China, Arabia, Europe*. Amsterdam: John Benjamins.

Itkonen, Esa, 2003. *Methods of Formalization Inside and Outside Both Autonomous and Nonautonomous Linguistics*. Turku: University of Turku.

Itkonen, Esa, 2005. *Analogy as Structure and Process: Approaches in Linguistics, Cognitive Psychology and Philosophy of Science.* Amsterdam: John Benjamins.

Ivinson, Gabrielle, 2010. Bernstein: codes and social class. In Barbara Johnstone, Ruth Wodak, and Peter Kerswill (eds), *SAGE Handbook of Sociolinguistics.* London: Sage, 40–56.

Izre'el, Shlomo (ed.), 2002. *Semitic Linguistics: The State of the Art at the Turn of the Twenty-First Century.* Winona Lake, IN: Eisenbrauns.

Jackendoff, Ray, 1972. *Semantic Interpretation in Generative Grammar.* Cambridge, MA: MIT Press.

Jackendoff, Ray, 1983. *Semantics and Cognition.* Cambridge, MA: MIT Press.

Jackendoff, Ray, 1990. *Semantic Structures.* Cambridge, MA: MIT Press.

Jackendoff, Ray, 2002. *Foundations of Language.* Oxford: Oxford University Press.

Jackendoff, Ray, 2010. Your theory of language evolution depends on your theory of language. In Larson et al. (2010: 63–72).

Jäger, Andreas, 1686. *De lingua vetustissima Europae, Scytho-Celtica et Gothica.* Wittenberg: Typis C. Schrödteri.

Jäger, Siegfried, and Florentine Maier, 2009. Theoretical and methodological aspects of Foucauldian critical discourse analysis and dispositive analysis. In Ruth Wodak and Michael Meyer (eds), *Methods of Critical Discourse Analysis.* London: Sage, 34–61.

Jahn, Gustav, 1894–1900. *Sibawayhi's Buch über die Grammatik, übersetzt und erläutert,* Berlin: Reuther & Reichard. [Repr. Hildesheim: Olms, 1969.]

Jakobson, Roman, 1931. Prinzipien der historischen Phonologie. *Travaux du Cercle Linguistique de Prague* 4: 247–67.

Jakobson, Roman, 1956. Two aspects of language and two types of aphasic disturbances. Chapter 2 of Jakobson and Halle (1956). [Repr. in *Selected Writings II* (The Hague: Mouton, 1971), 139–259.]

Jakobson, Roman, 1957. Shifters, verbal categories and the Russian verb. In *Selected Writings II.* The Hague: Mouton, 130–47.

Jakobson, Roman, 1959. On linguistic aspects of translation. In Reuben A. Brower (ed.), *On Translation.* Cambridge, MA: Harvard University Press, 132–9. [Repr. in Jakobson (1987: 62–94).]

Jakobson, Roman, 1960. Linguistics and poetics. In Thomas A. Sebeok (ed.), *Style in Language.* New York: Technology Press, 350–77. [Repr. in Jakobson (1987: 428–35).]

Jakobson, Roman, 1966. Henry Sweet's paths toward phonemics. In C. E. Bazell et al. (eds), *In Memory of J. R. Firth.* London: Longmans, Green, 142–254.

Jakobson, Roman, 1968 [1941]. *Kindersprache, Aphasie und allgemeine Lautgesetze.* Transl. A. Keiler as *Child Language, Aphasia and Phonological Universals.* The Hague: Mouton

Jakobson, Roman, 1970. Subliminal verbal patterning in poetry. In Roman Jakobson and S. Kawomoto (eds), *Studies in General and Oriental Linguistics.* Tokyo: TEC, 302–8.

Jakobson, Roman, 1971 [1960]. The Kazan school of Polish linguistics and its place in the international development of phonology. In *Selected Writings II: Word and Language.* The Hague: Mouton, 394–428.

Jakobson, Roman, 1971 [1930]. Principes de phonologie historique. In *Selected Writings I: Phonological Studies.* The Hague: Mouton, 102–20.

Jakobson, Roman, 1976. *Six leçons sur le son et le sens.* Paris: Éditions de Minuit.

Jakobson, Roman, 1978. *Sound and Meaning.* London: MIT Press.

Jakobson, Roman, 1978. Sound symbolism and distinctive features. Paper given at a conference on Semiotics and the Arts, University of Michigan.

Jakobson, Roman, 1979. Speech sounds and their tasks. In Jakobson and Waugh (1979: 7–82).

Jakobson, Roman, 1981. *Poetry of Grammar and Grammar of Poetry*. Berlin: Mouton de Gruyter.

Jakobson, Roman, 1987. *Roman Jakobson: Language in Literature*, ed. Krystyna Pomorska and Stephen Rudy. Cambridge, MA: Belknap Press.

Jakobson, Roman, 1990a. Efforts towards a means–end model of language in interwar continental linguistics. In Jakobson (1990b: 56–61). [First published 1958.]

Jakobson, Roman, 1990b. *On Language*, ed. Linda Waugh and Monique Monville-Burston. Cambridge, MA: Harvard University Press.

Jakobson, Roman, C. Gunnar Fant, and Morris Halle, 1952. *Preliminaries to Speech Analysis*. Cambridge, MA: Acoustics Laboratory, MIT.

Jakobson, Roman, and Morris Halle, 1956. *Fundamentals of Language*. The Hague: Mouton.

Jakobson, Roman, Sergej Karcevskij, and Nikolaj S. Troubetzkoy, 1929. Quelles sont les méthodes les mieux appropriées à un exposé complet et pratique de la grammaire d'une langue quelconque? In Christianus C. Uhlenbeck (ed.), *Actes du Premier Congrès International de Linguistes à la Haye: du 10–15 avril 1928*. Leiden: Sijthoff, 33–6.

Jakobson, Roman, and Linda R. Waugh, 1979. *The Sound Shape of Language*. Bloomington: Indiana University Press. [2nd edn, 1987; 3rd edn, 2002; Berlin: Mouton de Gruyter.]

Janda, Richard D., and Brian D. Joseph, 2003. On language, change, and language change—or, of history, linguistics, and historical linguistics. In Joseph and Janda (2003: 3–180).

Jankowsky, Kurt R., 1972. *The Neogrammarians: A Re-evaluation of Their Place in the Development of Linguistic Science*. The Hague: Mouton.

Jankowsky, Kurt R., 1979. Typological studies in the nineteenth century and the Neogrammarian sound law principle. *Forum Linguisticum* 4: 159–73.

Jankowsky, Kurt R., 1990. Theoretical models of change: the Neogrammarian hypothesis. In Edgar Polomé (ed.), *Trends in Linguistics*. Berlin: Mouton de Gruyter, 123–239.

Jardine, Nick, 2003. Whigs and stories: Herbert Butterfield and the historiography of science. *History of Science* 41: 125–40.

Jaworski, Adam, and Nikolas Coupland, 2006. Introduction: perspectives on discourse analysis. In Adam Jaworski and Nikolas Coupland (eds), *The Discourse Reader*, 2nd edn. London: Routledge, 1–44.

Jeffries, Lesley, and Dan McIntyre, 2010. *Stylistics*. New York: Cambridge University Press.

Jelinek, Frederick, 2009. The dawn of statistical ASR and MT. *Computational Linguistics* 35: 483–94.

Jensen, Hans, 1969. *Sign, Symbol and Script*, transl. George Allen. New York: Putnam's.

Jespersen, Otto, 1889. *The Articulations of Speech Sounds Represented by Means of Analphabetic Symbols*. Marburg: Elwert.

Jespersen, Otto, 1890. *Danias lydskrift*. Copenhagen. [n.p.] [Repr. from *Dania: Tidsskrift for Folkemaal og Folkeminder* 1, 1890–92, 33–79.]

Jespersen, Otto, 1922a. *Language, Its Nature, Development and Origin*. London: Allen & Unwin.

Jespersen, Otto, 1922b. Lydsymbolik. *Nordisk Tidsskrift för Vetenskap, Konst och Industri* (II) (Stockholm), 122–31.

Jespersen, Otto, 1922c. The symbolic value of the vowel I. *Philologica* 1: 1–19.

Jespersen, Otto, 1924. *The Philosophy Of Grammar*. London: George Allen & Unwin.

Jespersen, Otto, 1933. Zur Geschichte der älteren Phonetik. In O. Jespersen, *Linguistica: Selected Papers in English, French and German*. Copenhagen: Levin & Munksgaard, 40–80.

Jespersen, Otto, 1946. *Mankind, Nation and Individual from a Linguistic Point of View.* London: George Allen & Unwin.

Jespersen, Otto, and Holger Pedersen, 1925. *Phonetic Transcription and Transliteration: Proposals of the Kopenhagen Conference, April 1925.* Oxford: Clarendon Press.

Jessen, Michael, Olaf Köster, and Stefan Gfroerer, 2005. Influence of vocal effort on average variability of fundamental frequency. *International Journal of Speech Language and the Law* 12: 174–210.

Joachims, Thorsten, 2002. *Learning to Classify Text Using Support Vector Machines.* Boston, MA: Kluwer Academic.

Johansson, Stig, 2007. *Seeing Through Multilingual Corpora: On the Use of Corpora in Contrastive Studies.* Amsterdam: John Benjamins.

Johansson, Stig, and Knut Hofland, 1994. Towards an English–Norwegian parallel corpus. In U. Fries, G. Tottie, and P. Schneider (eds), *Creating and Using English Language Corpora.* Amsterdam: Rodopi, 15–37.

Johansson, Stig, Geoffrey Leech, and Helen Goodluck, 1978. *Manual of Information to Accompany the Lancaster-Oslo/Bergen Corpus of British English, for Use with Digital Computers.* Oslo: Department of English, University of Oslo.

John of Genoa [Iohannes Balbus], 1495. *Catholicon.* Venice: Boneti Locatelli for Domino Octaviano Scoto.

Johns, Ann M., 2002. *Genre in the Classroom: Multiple Perspectives.* Mahwah, NJ: Erlbaum.

Johnson, Christopher R., Charles J. Fillmore, Esther J. Wood, et al., 2002. *FrameNet: Theory and Practice.* Berkeley, CA: International Computer Science Institute.

Johnson, Sally, 2005. *Spelling Trouble: Language, Ideology and the Reform of German Orthography.* Clevedon, UK: Multilingual Matters.

Johnson, Samuel, 1755. *A Dictionary of the English Language: in which the words are deduced from their originals, and illustrated by examples from the best writers. To which are prefixed, a history of the language, and an English grammar.* 2 vols. London: W. Strahan.

Johnson-Laird, Philip N., 1983. *Mental Models.* Cambridge: Cambridge University Press.

Johnston, Trevor A., 1989. Auslan: the sign language of the Australian deaf community. Doctoral dissertation, University of Sydney.

Johnstone, Barbara, 1996. *The Linguistic Individual: Self-Expression in Language and Linguistics.* New York: Oxford University Press.

Johnstone, Barbara, 2000. Individual voice in language. *Annual Review of Anthropology* 29: 405–24.

Johnstone, Barbara, 2008. *Discourse Analysis*, 2nd edn. Oxford: Blackwell.

Johnstone, Thomas Muir, 1975. The modern South Arabian Languages. *Afroasiatic Linguistics* 1(5): 93–121.

Jones, Daniel, 1929. Definition of a phoneme. *Le maître phonétique*, 43–4.

Jones, Daniel, 1957. The history and meaning of the term 'phoneme'. London: International Phonetic Association. [Repr. in Fudge (1973: 17–34).]

Jones, Daniel, 1967. *The Phoneme: Its Nature and Use*, 3rd edn, with an appendix on the history and meaning of the term *phoneme.* Cambridge: Heffer. [1st edn 1950.]

Jones, (Sir) William, 1786. *Dissertation on the Orthography of Asiatick Words in Roman Letters.* Repr. in *The Works of Sir William Jones*, vol. 1. London: G.G. & J. Robinson and R. H. Evans, 1799, 175–228.

Jones, (Sir) William, 1788. The Third Anniversary Discourse, Delivered 2 February 1786 [On the Hindus]. *Asiatick Researches, or, Transactions of the Society Instituted in Bengal for*

Inquiring into the History and Antiquities, the Arts, Sciences, and Literature, of Asia, vol. 1. Calcutta, 415–31.

Jones, (Sir) William, 1807. *The Works of Sir William Jones with the Life of the Author by Lord Teignmouth*, ed. John Shore, Baron Teignmouth. 13 vols. London: Stockdale, Walker.

Joos, Martin (ed.), 1957. *Readings in Linguistics*. Washington, DC: American Council of Learned Societies. [Reissued as *Readings in Linguistics I: The Development of Descriptive Linguistics in America 1925–56* (Chicago: University of Chicago Press, 1971).]

Joseph, Brian D., and Richard D. Janda (eds), *The Handbook of Historical Linguistics*. Oxford: Blackwell.

Joseph, John E., 1987. *Eloquence and Power: The Rise of Language Standards and Standard Languages*. London: Frances Pinter.

Joseph, John E., 1999. A Matter of Consequenz: Humboldt, race and the genius of the Chinese language. *Historiographia Linguistica* 26: 89–148.

Joseph, John E., 2002. *From Whitney to Chomsky: Essays in the History of American Linguistics*. Amsterdam: John Benjamins.

Joshi, Aravind K., Leon S. Levy, and Masako Takahashi, 1975. Tree adjunct grammars. *Journal of Computer and System Sciences* 10: 136–63.

Josselson, Harry H., 1971. Automatic translation of languages since 1960: a linguist's view. *Advances in Computers* 11: 1–58.

Joyce, James, 1939. *Finnegans Wake*. London: Faber & Faber.

Juilland, Alphonse, and Eugenio Chang-Rodriguez, 1964. *A Frequency Dictionary of Spanish Words*. The Hague: Mouton.

Julian of Toledo, 1973. *Ars Iuliani Toletani episcopi: una gramática latina de la Espana visigoda*, ed. M. A. H. Maestre Yenes. Toledo: Instituto Provincial.

Jungraithmayr, Herrmann, 1981. Soudan oriental du nord, 1: Tableau d'ensemble. 2: Le Daju de Dar Sila (Wadai, Tchad). In Jean Perrot, Gabriel Manessy, and A. Waldman (eds), *Les langues dans le monde ancien et moderne: Afrique subsaharienne, pidgins et créoles*. Paris: CNRS, 165–281.

Jurafsky, Daniel, and James A. Martin, 2009. *Speech and Language Processing*, 2nd edn. Upper Saddle River, NJ: Pearson Prentice Hall. [1st edn 2000.]

Justeson, John S., 1976. Universals of language and universals of writing. In Alphonse Juilland (ed.), *Linguistic Studies Offered to Joseph Greenberg on the Occasion of His Sixtieth Birthday*, vol. 1: *General Linguistics*. Saratoga, CA: Anma Libri, 57–94.

Juynboll, Gautier H. A., 2007. *Encyclopedia of Canonical Hadith*. Leiden: E. J. Brill

Käding, Friedrich W., 1897. *Häufigkeitswörterbuch der deutschen Sprache*. Steglitz: privately published.

Kaiser, Stefan, 1994. Japan: history of linguistic thought. In Ronald E. Asher and James M. Y. Simpson (eds), *The Encyclopedia of Language and Linguistics*. Oxford: Pergamon, 1800–1804.

Kakehi, Hisao, Lawrence Schourup, and Ikuhiro Tamori, 1998. *A Dictionary of Iconic Expressions in Japanese*. The Hague: Mouton.

Källkvist, Marie, 1998. How different are the results of translation tasks? A study of lexical errors. In Kirsten Malmkjær (ed.), *Translation and Language Teaching: Language Teaching and Translation*. Manchester: St Jerome, 77–87.

Källkvist, Marie, 2004. The effect of translation exercises versus gap-exercises on the learning of difficult L2 structures: preliminary results of an empirical study. In Kirsten Malmkjær (ed.), *Translation in Undergraduate Degree Programmes*. Amsterdam: John Benjamins, 163–84.

Källkvist, Marie, 2008. L1–L2 translation versus no translation: a longitudinal study of focus-on-formS within a meaning-focused curriculum. In Lourdes Ortega and Heidi Byrnes (eds), *The Longitudinal Study of Advanced L2 Capacities*. London: Routledge, 182–202.

Kamp, Hans, 1981. A theory of truth and semantic interpretation. In J. A. G. Groenendijk, Th. M. V. Janssen, and M. B. J. Stokhof (eds), *Formal Methods in the Study of Language*, vol. 1. Amsterdam: Mathematisch Centrum, 177–322.

Kamp, Hans, and Uwe Reyle, 1993. *From Discourse to Logic: Introduction to Model-Theoretic Semantics of Natural Language, Formal Logic and Discourse Representation Theory*. Dordrecht: Kluwer.

Kandhadi, Padmapriya, and Richard Sproat, 2010. Impact of spatial ordering of graphemes in alphasyllabic scripts on phonemic awareness in Indic languages. *Writing Systems Research* 2: 105–16.

Kane, Thomas L., 2000. *Tigrinya–English Dictionary*. Springfield, MD: Dunwoody Press.

Kaplan, Ronald M., and Joan Bresnan, 1982. Lexical-functional grammar: a formal system for grammatical representation. In Joan Bresnan (ed.), *The Mental Representation of Grammatical Relations*. Cambridge, MA: MIT Press, 173–281. [Repr. in Mary Dalrymple, Ronald M. Kaplan, John T. Maxwell III, and Annie Zaenen (eds), *Formal Issues in Lexical-Functional Grammar* (Stanford, CA: CSLI, 1995), 19–130.]

Karlgren, Bernard, 1954. *Compendium of Phonetics in Ancient and Archaic Chinese*. Stockholm: Museum of Far Eastern Antiquities, Bulletin No. 26. [Repr. Taipei: Southern Materials Center, 1988.]

Karlsson, Fred, Atro Voutilainen, Juha Heikkilä, and Arto Anttila (eds), 1995. *Constraint Grammar: A Language-Independent System for Parsing Unrestricted Text*. Berlin: Mouton de Gruyter.

Karttunen, Lauri, 1977. Syntax and semantics of questions. *Linguistics and Philosophy* 1: 3–44.

Kasami, Tadao, and Koji Torii, 1969. A syntax-analysis procedure for unambiguous context-free grammars. *Journal of the Association for Computing Machinery* 16: 423–31.

Kaster, Robert A., 1995. *C. Suetonius Tranquillus De grammaticis et rhetoribus*. Oxford: Clarendon Press.

Kastovsky, Dieter, 1982. *Wortbildung und Semantik*. Düsseldorf: Schwann.

Kathol, Andreas, 2000. *Linear Syntax*. Oxford: Oxford University Press.

Katre, Sumitra Mangesh, 1968–9. *Dictionary of Pāṇini*. Pune: Deccan College Postgraduate and Research Institute.

Katre, Sumitra Mangesh, 1987. *Aṣṭādhyāyī of Pāṇini: Roman Transliteration and English Translation*. Austin: University of Texas Press. [Repr. Delhi: Motilal Banarsidass, 1989.]

Katriel, Tamar, 1986. *Talking Straight: Dugri Speech in Israeli Sabra Culture*. New York: Cambridge University Press.

Katz, Jerrold J., 1972. *Semantic Theory*. New York: Harper & Row.

Katz, Jerrold J., 1981. *Language and Other Abstract Objects*. Oxford: Blackwell.

Katz, Jerrold J., 1985. Introduction. In Jerrold J. Katz (ed.), *The Philosophy of Linguistics*. Oxford: Oxford University Press, 1–16.

Katz, Jerrold J., and Jerry A. Fodor, 1963. The structure of a semantic theory. *Language* 39: 170–210.

Kay, Martin, 1979. Functional grammar. In Christine Chiarello et al. (eds), *The Fifth Annual Meeting of the Berkeley Linguistics Society*. Berkeley, CA: Berkeley Linguistics Society, 142–58. [Repr. in Kay (2010: 147–264).]

Kay, Martin., 1992. Unification. In Michael Rosner and Roderick Johnson (eds), *Computational Linguistics and Formal Semantics*. Cambridge: Cambridge University Press, 1–29. [Repr. in Kay (2010: 445–65).]

Kay, Martin., 2000. David G. Hays. In W. John Hutchins (ed.), *Early Years in Machine Translation: Memoirs and Biographies of Pioneers*. Amsterdam: John Benjamins, 165–70. [Repr. in Kay (2010: 563–7).]

Kay, Martin, 2005. A life of language. *Computational Linguistics* 31: 425–38. [Repr. in Kay (2010: 600–12).]

Kay, Martin, 2010. *Collected Papers of Martin Kay: A Half Century of Computational Linguistics*. Stanford, CA: CSLI.

Kay, Paul, and Charles J. Fillmore, 1999. Grammatical constructions and linguistic generalizations: the *What's X doing Y?* construction. *Language* 75: 1–33.

Kecskes, Istvan, 2002. A cognitive approach to situation-bound utterances. *Journal of Pragmatics* 32: 605–25.

Kecskes, Istvan, 2006. Communicative principle and communication. In Keith Brown (ed.), *Encyclopedia of Language and Linguistics*, 2nd edn, vol. 2. Oxford: Elsevier, 680–3.

Kegl, Judy, Ann Senghas, and Marie Coppola, 1999. Creation through contact: sign language emergence and sign language change in Nicaragua. In Michel DeGraff (ed.), *Language Creation and Language Change: Creolization, Diachrony, and Development*. Cambridge, MA: MIT Press, 179–237.

Keil, Heinrich (ed.), 1961. *Grammatici Latini*. 8 vols. Hildesheim: Georg Olms. [First published 1870, Leipzig: Teubner.]

Keiler, Allan R. (ed.), 1972. *A Reader in Historical and Comparative Linguistics*. New York: Holt, Rinehart & Winston.

Kelly, John, 1981. The 1847 alphabet: an episode of phonotypy. In Ronald E. Asher and Eugénie J. A. Henderson (eds), *Towards a History of Phonetics*. Edinburgh: Edinburgh University Press, 148–64.

Kemmer, Suzanne, 1993. *The Middle Voice*. Amsterdam: John Benjamins.

Kemmer, Suzanne, and MichaelBarlow, 2000. Introduction: a usage-based conception of language. In Barlow and Kemmer (2000: vii–xxviii).

Kemp, J. Alan, 1972. *John Wallis's Grammar of the English Language*. London: Longman.

Kemp, J. Alan, 1994a. Phonetic transcription: history. In Ronald E. Asher and James M. Y. Simpson (eds), *The Encyclopedia of Language and Linguistics*. Oxford: Pergamon, 3040–51.

Kemp, J. Alan, 1994b. Phonetics: precursors of modern approaches. In Ronald E. Asher and James M. Y. Simpson (eds), 1994. *The Encyclopedia of Language and Linguistics*. Oxford: Pergamon Press, 3102–16.

Kemp, J. Alan, 2001. The development of phonetics from the late eighteenth to the late nineteenth century. In Auroux et al., vol. 2.2 (2001: 1468–80).

Kemp, J. Alan, 2006. Phonetic transcription: history. In Keith Brown (ed.), *Encyclopedia of Language and Linguistics*, 2nd edn, vol. 9. London: Elsevier, 396–410.

Kendall, Shari, 2011. Symbolic interactionism, Ervin Goffman, and sociolinguistics. In Ruth Wodak, Barbara Johns, and Paul Kerswill (eds), *The Sage Handbook of Sociolinguistics*. London: Sage, 113–24.

Kendon, Adam, 1972a. A review of *Kinesics and Context* by R. L. Birdwhistell. *American Journal of Psychology* 85: 441–55.

Kendon, Adam, 1972b. Some relationships between body motion and speech: an analysis of an example. In A. Siegman and B. Pope (eds), *Studies in Dyadic Communication*. Elmsford, NY: Pergamon, 177–210.

Kendon, Adam, 1980. Gesticulation and speech: two aspects of the process of utterance. In Mary R. Key (ed.), *The Relationship of Verbal and Nonverbal Communication*. The Hague: Mouton, 107–227.

Kendon, Adam, 1981a. Geography of gesture. *Semiotica* 37: 129–63.

Kendon, Adam, 1981b. Introduction: current issues in 'nonverbal communication'. In Adam Kendon (ed.), *Nonverbal Communication, Interaction and Gesture: Selections from Semiotica* (vol. 41, Approaches to Semiotics). The Hague: Mouton, 1–53.

Kendon, Adam, 1983. Gesture and speech: how they interact. In John M. Wieman and Randall P. Harrison (eds), *Nonverbal Interaction*. Beverly Hills, CA: Sage, 13–45.

Kendon, Adam, 1984. Did gesture have the happiness to escape the curse at the confusion of Babel? In Aaron Wolfgang (ed.), *Nonverbal Behavior: Perspectives, Applications, Intercultural Insights*. Lewiston, NY: C. J. Hogrefe, 75–114.

Kendon, Adam, 1986. Some reasons for studying gesture. *Semiotica* 62: 3–28.

Kendon, Adam, 1988a. How gestures can become like words. In Fernando Poyatos (ed.), *Cross-Cultural Perspectives in Nonverbal Communication*. Lewiston, NY: C. J. Hogrefe, 131–41.

Kendon, Adam, 1988b. *Sign Languages of Aboriginal Australia: Cultural, Semiotic and Communicative Perspectives*. Cambridge: Cambridge University Press.

Kendon, Adam, 1990a. *Conducting Interaction: Patterns of Behavior in Focused Encounters*. Cambridge: Cambridge University Press.

Kendon, Adam, 1990b. Signs in the cloister and elsewhere. *Semiotica* 79: 307–29.

Kendon, Adam, 1992. Abstraction in gesture. *Semiotica* 90: 225–50.

Kendon, Adam, 1995. Gestures as illocutionary and discourse structure markers in Southern Italian conversation. *Journal of Pragmatics* 23: 247–79.

Kendon, Adam, 1997. Gesture. *Annual Review of Anthropology* 26: 109–28.

Kendon, Adam, 2002. Historical observations on the relationship between research on sign languages and language origins theory. In David Armstrong, Michael A. Karchmar, and John V. Van Cleve (eds), *The Study of Signed Languages: Essays in Honor of William C. Stokoe*. Washington, DC: Gallaudet University Press, 32–52.

Kendon, Adam, 2004. *Gesture: Visible Action as Utterance*. Cambridge: Cambridge University Press.

Kendon, Adam, 2007. On the origins of modern gesture studies. In In Duncan et al. (2007: 13–28).

Kendon, Adam, 2008a. Some reflections on the relationship between 'gesture' and 'sign'. *Gesture* 8: 348–66.

Kendon, Adam, 2008b. A history of the study of Australian Aboriginal sign languages. In William B. McGregor (ed.), *Encountering Aboriginal Languages: Studies in the History of Australian Linguistics*. Canberra: Pacific Linguistics, Research School of Pacific and Asian Studies, Australian National University, 383–402.

Kendon, Adam. 2008b. Some reflections on 'gesture' and 'sign'. *Gesture* 8: 348–66.

Kendon, Adam, and Stuart J. Sigman, 1996. Ray L. Birdwhistell (1918–94). *Semiotica* 112: 231–61.

Kennedy, George A., 1994. *A New History of Classical Rhetoric*. Princeton, NJ: Princeton University Press.

Kenstowicz, Michael, 1975. Rule application in Pregenerative American phonology. In Andreas Koutsoudas (ed.), *The Application and Ordering of Phonological Rules*. The Hague: Mouton, 159–282.

Key, Mary R, 1975. *Paralanguage and Kinesics (Nonverbal Communication)*. Metuchen, NJ: Scarecrow Press.

Key, Mary R., 1977. *Nonverbal Communication: A Research Guide and Bibliography*. Metuchen, NJ: Scarecrow Press.

Khan, Geoffrey, 2000. *The Early Karaite Tradition of Hebrew Grammatical Thought*. Leiden: E. J. Brill.

Khlebnikov, Velemir, 1987. *Tvorenia*. Moscow: Sovjetskij Pisatel'.

Kibbee, Douglas A., 1991. *For to Speke French Trewely: The French Language in England, 1000–1600: its Status, Description and Instruction*. Amsterdam: John Benjamins.

Kibbee, Douglas A. (ed.), 2010. *Chomskyan (R)evolutions*. Amsterdam: John Benjamins.

Kienast, Burkhart, 2001. *Historische semitische Sprachwissenschaft*. Mit Beiträgen von Erhart Graefe (Altägyptisch) und Gene B. Gragg (Kuschitisch). Wiesbaden: Harrassowitz.

Kilbury, James, 1976. *The Development of Morphophonemic Theory*. Amsterdam: John Benjamins.

Kilgarriff, Adam, 1997. I don't believe in word senses. *Computers and the Humanities* 31: 91–113.

Kilgarriff, Adam, and Gregory Grefenstette, 2003. Introduction to the special issue on Web as corpus. *Computational Linguistics* 29(3): 333–47. www.aclweb.org/anthology/J03-3001

Kilgarriff, Adam, Pavel Rychly, Pavel Smrz, and David Tugwell. 2004. The sketch engine. In G. Williams and S. Vessier (eds), *Euralex Proceedings*, vol. 1. Lorient: Université de Bretagne-Sud, 105–16.

Kim, Nam-Kil, 1987. Korean. In Bernard Comrie (ed.), *The World's Major Languages*. Oxford: Oxford University Press, 881–98.

Kimball, John P., 1973. Seven principles of surface structure parsing in natural language. *Cognition* 2: 15–48.

Kim-Renaud, Young-Key (ed.), 1997. *The Korean Alphabet: Its History and Structure*. Honolulu: University of Hawai'i Press.

Kingsley, Norman W., 1879. *Mechanism of Speech*. New York: D. Appleton.

Kingsley, Norman W., 1880. *A Treatise on Oral Deformities as a Branch of Mechanical Surgery*. New York: D. Appleton.

Kinoshita, Yuko, 2005. Does Lindley's LR formulation work for speech data? Investigation using long-term Fo. *International Journal of Speech, Language and the Law* 12: 235–54.

Kintsch, Walter, 1988. The role of knowledge in discourse comprehension: a construction-integration model. *Psychological Review* 95: 163–82.

Kiparsky, Paul, 1979. *Pāṇini as a Variationist*. Cambridge, MA: MIT Press and Pune: Centre of Advanced Study in Sanskrit, University of Poona.

Kiparsky, Paul, 1982. From cyclic phonology to lexical phonology. In van der Hulst and Smith (1982a: 131–77).

Kiparsky, Paul, 1985. Some consequences of Lexical Phonology. *Phonology Yearbook* 2: 85–138.

Kiparsky, Paul, 1993. Pāṇinian linguistics. In Ronald E. Asher and James M.Y. Simpson (eds), *The Encyclopedia of Language and Linguistics*. Oxford: Pergamon, 1918–23.

Kirby, Simon, 2007. The evolution of language. In Robin Dunbar and Louise Barrett (eds), *The Oxford Handbook of Evolutionary Psychology*. Oxford: Oxford University Press, 669–81.

Kirk, John (ed.), 2000. *Corpora Galore: Analysis and Techniques in Describing English*. Amsterdam: Rodopi.

Kirwan, Christopher, 1994. Augustine on the nature of speech. In Stephen Everson (ed.), *Companions to Ancient Thought 3: Language*. Cambridge: Cambridge University Press, 188–211.

Klima, Edward A., and Ursula Bellugi, 1979. *The Signs of Language*. Cambridge, MA: Harvard University Press.

Klinck, Roswitha, 1970. *Die lateinische Etymologie des Mittelalters*. Munich: Wilhelm Fink.

Klinkowström, A., 1890. Trois cas d'audition colorée dans la même famille. *Biologiska Föreningens i Stockholm Förhandlingar* 3: 117–18.

Kneale, William, and Martha Kneale, 1962. *The Development of Logic*. Oxford: Clarendon Press.

Knecht, Pierre, and Zygmunt Marzys (eds), 1993. *Écriture, langues communes et normes: formation spontanée de koinés et standardisation dans la galloromania et son voisinage*. Geneva: Droz.

Knight, Dawn, David Evans, Ron Carter, and Svenja Adolphs, 2009. HeadTalk, HandTalk and the corpus: towards a framework for multi-modal, multi-media corpus development. *Corpora* 4: 1–32.

Knowles, Gerry, 1993. From text to waveform: converting the Lancaster/IBM spoken English corpus into a speech database. In Clive Souter and Eric Atwell (eds), *Corpus-Based Computational Linguistics*. Amsterdam: Rodopi, 47–58.

Knowlson, James, 1965. The idea of gesture as a universal language in the 17th and 18th centuries. *Journal of the History of Ideas* 26: 495–508.

Knowlson, James, 1975. *Universal Language Schemes in England and France*. Toronto: University of Toronto Press.

Knox, Dilwyn, 1990a. Ideas on gesture and universal languages, c. 1550–1650. In John Henry and Sarah Hutton (eds), *New Perspectives on Renaissance Thought: Essays in the History of Science, Education and Philosophy in Memory of Charles B. Schmitt*. London: Duckworth, 101–36.

Knox, Dilwyn, 1990b. Late medieval and Renaissance ideas on gesture. In Volker Kapp (ed.), *Die Sprache der Zeichen und Bilder: Rhetorik un nonverbale Kommunikatio in der frühen Neuzeit*. Marburg: Hitzeroth, 11–39.

Knox, Dilwyn, 1996. Giovanni Bonifaccio's *L'arte de' cenni* and Renaissance ideas of gesture. In Mirko Tavoni (ed.), *Italia ed Europa nella linguistica del Rinascimento: confronti e relazioni. Atti del Convegno internazionale, Ferrara, 20–24 marzo, 1991*, vol. 2. Ferrara: Franco Cosimo Panini, 379–400.

Koch, Friedrich Christian, 1740. *Fundamenta linguae Hebraeae suis undique rationibus solide firmata seu Grammatica Hebraea philosophica in usum auditorum suorum adornata*. Ienae: Sumptibus vidvae Croekerianae.

Koehn, Philipp, 2010. *Statistical Machine Translation*. Cambridge: Cambridge University Press.

Koerner, E. F. Konrad, 1973. *Ferdinand de Saussure: Origin and Development of his Linguistic Thought in Western Studies of Language*. Braunschweig: Vieweg.

Koerner, E. F. Konrad (ed.), 1994. *Giulio Panconcelli-Calzia. Geschichtszahlen der Phonetik; Quellenatlas der Phonetik. New edition with an introduction*. Amsterdam: John Benjamins.

Koerner, E. F. Konrad, 1995. *Professing Linguistic Historiography*. Amsterdam: John Benjamins.

Koerner, E. F. Konrad, 2002. William Labov and the origins of sociolinguistics. *Folia Linguistica Historica* 12: 1–40.

Koerner, E. F. Konrad, 2008. Hermann Paul and general linguistic theory. *Language Sciences* 30: 102–32.

Koerner, E. F. Konrad, and Ronald E. Asher (eds), 1995. *Concise History of the Language Sciences: From the Sumerians to the Cognitivists*. Oxford: Pergamon.

Kohler, Klaus, 1981. Three trends in phonetics: the development of phonetics as a discipline in Germany since the nineteenth century. In Ronald E. Asher and Eugénie J. A. Henderson (eds), *Towards a History of Phonetics*. Edinburgh: Edinburgh University Press, 161–78.

Kortlandt, Frederik H., 1972. *Modelling the Phoneme: New Trends in East European Phonemic Theory*. The Hague: Mouton.

Kosko, Bart, 1994. *Fuzzy Thinking: The New Science of Fuzzy Logic*. London: HarperCollins.

Kouwenberg, Bert, 2006. The reflexes of Proto-Semitic gutturals in Assyria. In Guy Deutscher and Norbert J. C. Kouwenberg (eds), *The Akkadian Language in Its Semitic Context: Studies in the Akkadian of the Third and Second Millennium BC*. Leiden: Nederlands Instituut voor het Nabije Oosten, 150–76.

Kövecses, Zoltán, 2002. *Metaphor: A Practical Introduction*. Oxford: Oxford University Press.

Krahmer, Emiel, 2010. What computational linguists can learn from psychologists (and vice versa). *Computational Linguistics* 36: 285–94.

Kramer, Undine, 2006. German lexicography. In Keith Brown (ed.), *Encyclopedia of Language and Linguistics*, 2nd edn, vol. 5. London: Elsevier, 45–52.

Krámský, Jiří, 1974. *The Phoneme: Introduction to the History and Theories of a Concept*. Munich: W. Fink.

Kratzenstein, Christian Gottlieb, 1781. *Tentamen resolvendi problema ab Academia scientiarum imperiali petropolitana ad annum 1780 publice propositum: 1. Qualis sit natura et character sonorum litterarum vocalium a, e, i, o, u, tam insigniter inter se diversorum; 2. Annon construi queant instrumenta ordini tuborum organicorum, sub termino vocis humanae noto, similia, quae litterarum vocalium a, e, i, o, u, sonos exprimant...* Petropoli: Typis Academiae Scientiarum.

Kraus, Christian J., 1787. *Vocabularium linguarum totius orbis comparativum, oder Vergleichendes Glossarium aller Sprachen und Mundarten, gesammelt auf Veranstaltung der allerhöchsten Person. Erste Abtheilung, die europäischen und asiatischen Sprachen enthaltend*. Peter Simon Pallas ed. in *Allgemeine Literatur-Zeitung* 235–237b, Sp. 1–29.

Kreidler, Charles W., 2000. *Phonology: Critical Concepts*. London: Routledge.

Kress, Gunther, 2010. *Multimodality: A Social Semiotic Approach to Communication*. London: Routledge Falmer.

Kress, Gunther, and Theo van Leeuwen, 1996. *Reading Images: The Grammar of Visual Design*. London: Routledge.

Kristiansen, Gitte, and Rene Dirven (eds), 2008. *Cognitive Sociolinguistics: Language Variation, Cultural Models and Social Systems*. Berlin: Mouton de Gruyter.

Kristiansen, Gitte, Michel Achard, René Dirven, and Francisco Ruiz de Mendoza Ibáñez (eds), 2006. *Cognitive Linguistics: Applications and Future Perspectives*. Berlin: Mouton de Gruyter.

Kroeber, Alfred L., 1952. *The Nature of Culture*. Chicago: University of Chicago Press.

Kroeker, Kirk L., 2011. Weighing Watson's impact. *Communications of the ACM* 54(7): 13–15.

Kronasser, Heinz, 1952. *Handbuch der Semasiologie: kurze Einführung in die Geschichte, Problematik und Terminologie der Bedeutungslehre*. Heidelberg: Winter.

Kruse, Otto F., 1853. *Über Taubstumme und Taubstummenanstalten nebst Notizen aus meinem Reisetagebuch*. Bremen: Selbstverlag.

Kruszewski, Mikolai, 1993. *Writings in General Linguistics: On Sound Alternation. An Outline of Linguistic Science*. Amsterdam: John Benjamins.

Kübler, Sandra, Ryan McDonald, and Joakim Nivre, 2009. *Dependency Parsing*. San Rafael, CA: Morgan & Claypool.

Kudo, Taku, and Yuji Matsumoto, 2000. Japanese dependency structure analysis based on support vector machines. *Proceedings of the Joint SIGDAT Conference on Empirical Methods in Natural Language Processing and Very Large Corpora* (Hong Kong), 18–25.

Kuhn, Ernst, 1907. *Übersicht der Schriften Theodor Nöldeke's*. Giessen: Töpelmann.

Kula, Nancy, Kuniya Nasukawa, and Bert Botma (eds), 2011. *Continuum Companion to Phonology*. New York: Continuum.

Kulagina, Olga S., 2000. Pioneering MT in the Soviet Union. In W. John Hutchins (ed.), *Early Years in Machine Translation: Memoirs and Biographies of Pioneers*. Amsterdam: John Benjamins, 197–204.

Kunjunni Raja, K., 1963. *Indian Theories of Meaning*. Madras: Adyar Library and Research Center. [2nd edn 1969.]

Kunjunni Raja, K., 1977. *New Catalogus Catalogorum: An Alphabetical Register of Sanskrit and Allied Works and Authors*, vol. 9. Chennai: University of Madras.

Kuno, Susumo, 1987. *Functional Syntax*. Chicago: University of Chicago Press.

Kunzel, Hermann J., 2001. Beware of the 'telephone effect': the influence of telephone transmission on the measurement of formant frequencies. *Forensic Linguistics* 8: 80–99.

Kuryłowicz, Jerzy, 1947. La nature des procès dits 'analogiques'. *Acta Linguistica* 5: 121–38. [Repr. in Hamp et al. (1966: 158–74). English translation with introduction by Margaret Winters, 'The nature of the so-called analogical processes', *Diachronica* 12 (1995): 113–45.]

Kuryłowicz, Jerzy, 1948. Contributions à la théorie de la syllabe. *Bulletin de la Société polonaise de linguistique* 8: 80–114.

Kutas, Marta, and Steven Hillyard, 1980. Reading senseless sentences: brain potentials reflect semantic incongruity. *Science* 207: 203–5.

Kyle, James G., and Bencie Woll, 1985. *Sign Language: The Study of Deaf People and Their Language*. Cambridge: Cambridge University Press.

Labarre, Albert, 1975. *Bibliographie du Dictionarium d'Ambrogio Calepino*. Baden-Baden: Koerner.

Labov, William, 1963. The social motivation of a sound change. *Word* 19: 273–309.

Labov, William, 1970. *The Study of Nonstandard English*. Champaign, IL: National Council of Teachers of English.

Labov, William, 1972a. *Sociolinguistic Patterns*. Philadelphia: University of Pennsylvania Press.

Labov, William, 1972b. *Language in the Inner City: Studies in Black English Vernacular*. Philadelphia: University of Pennsylvania Press.

Labov, William, 1973. The linguistic consequences of being a lame. *Language in Society* 2: 81–115.

Labov, William, 1975. *What is a Linguistic Fact?* Lisse: Peter de Ridder.

Labov, William, and Joshua Waletzky, 1967. Narrative analysis: oral versions of personal experience. In June Helm (ed.), *Essays on the Verbal and Visual Arts*. Seattle, WA: American Ethnological Society, 12–44.

Ladd, D. Robert, and Astrid Schepman, 2003. 'Sagging transitions' between high pitch accents in English: experimental evidence. *Journal of Phonetics* 31: 81–112.

Ladefoged, Peter, 2003. *Phonetic Data Analysis: An Introduction to Fieldwork and Experimental Techniques*. Oxford: Blackwell.

Ladefoged, Peter and Ian Maddieson, 1996. *The Sounds of the World's Languages*. Oxford: Blackwell.

Ladefoged, Peter and Peter Roach, 1986. Revising the International Phonetic Alphabet: a plan. *Journal of the International Phonetic Association* 16: 22–9.

Ladefoged, Peter and Tony Traill, 1980. Instrumental phonetic fieldwork. *UCLA Working Papers in Phonetics* 49: 28–42.

Lado, Robert, 1964. *Language Teaching: A Scientific Approach*. New York: McGraw-Hill.

Lakoff, George, 1971 [1968]. Presupposition and relative well-formedness. In Danny Steinberg and Leon Jakobovits (eds), *Semantics: An Interdisciplinary Reader in Philosophy, Linguistics, and Psychology*. Cambridge: Cambridge University Press, 329–40.

Lakoff, George, 1972. Hedges: a study of meaning criteria and the logic of fuzzy concepts. In Paul M. Peranteau, Judith N. Levi, and Gloria C. Phares (eds), *Papers from the Eighth Regional Meeting of the Chicago Linguistics Society*. Chicago: Chicago Linguistics Society, 183–228. [Revised version in *Contemporary Research in Philosophical Logic and Linguistic Semantics*, ed. D. Hockney, W. Harper, and B. Freed (Dordrecht: Reidel, 1972), 121–71.]

Lakoff, George, 1977. Linguistic gestalts. In W. A. Beach et al. (eds), *Papers from the Thirteenth Regional Meeting, Chicago Linguistic Society, April 14–16, 1977*. Chicago: Chicago Linguistic Society, 236–87.

Lakoff, George, 1987. *Women, Fire and Dangerous Things: What Categories Reveal About the Mind*. Chicago: University of Chicago Press.

Lakoff, George, and Mark Johnson, 1980. *Metaphors We Live By*. Chicago: University of Chicago Press.

Lakoff, George and Mark Johnson, 1999. *Philosophy in the Flesh: The Embodied Mind and its Challenges to Western Thought*. Chicago: University of Chicago Press.

Laks, Bernard, 2001. Un siècle de phonétique et de phonologie: quelques questions permanentes. *Modèles linguistiques* 22 : 75–103.

Laks, Bernard, 2005. Approches de la phonologie cognitive. In Véronique Rey and Noël Nguyen (eds), *Nouvelles approches en phonétique et en phonologie*. Paris: Hermès, 191–319.

Laland, Kevin N., 2007. Niche construction, human behavioural ecology and evolutionary psychology. In Robin Dunbar and Louise Barrett (eds), *The Oxford Handbook of Evolutionary Psychology*. Oxford: Oxford University Press, 35–47.

Lallot, Jean, 1989. *La grammaire de Denys le Thrace*. Paris: Centre National de la Recherche Scientifique. [2nd edn 2003.]

Lallot, Jean, 1995. Analogie et pathologie dans la grammaire Alexandrine. *Lalies* 15: 109–23.

Lallot, Jean, 1997. *Apollonius Dyscole: De la construction (syntaxe)*. Paris: J. Vrin.

Lancelot, Claude, and Antoine Arnauld, 1660. *Grammaire Generale et Raisonnée*. Paris: Pierre Le Petit. [Stuttgart–Bad Canstatt: Frommann–Holzboog, 1966; Menston, UK: Scolar Press Facsimile, 1967; Geneva: Slatkin, 1968.]

Landsberger, Benno, 1926. Die Eigenbegrifflichkeit der babylonischen Welt. *Islamica* 2: 355–72.

Lane, Edward W., 1863–93. *Arabic–English Lexicon*. 8 vols. London: Williams & Norgate. [Repr. 1955–6, 1968.]

Lane, Harlan L., 1977. *The Wild Boy of Aveyron*. London: Allen & Unwin.

Lane, Harlan L., 1980. Historical: a chronology of the oppression of sign language in France and the United States. In Harlan L. Lane and François Grosjean (eds), *Recent Perspectives on American Sign Language*. Hillsdale, NJ: Lawrence Erlbaum, 119–61.

Lane, Harlan L., 1989. *When the Mind Hears: A History of the Deaf*. New York: Vintage Books.

Langacker, Ronald W., 1982. Space grammar, analysability, and the English passive. *Language* 58: 22–80.

Langacker, Ronald W., 1987. *Foundations of Cognitive Grammar*, vol. 1: *Theoretical Prerequisites*. Stanford, CA: Stanford University Press.

Langacker, Ronald W., 1988. A usage-based model. In Brygida Rudzka-Ostyn (ed.), *Topics in Cognitive Linguistics*. Amsterdam: Benjamins, 127–61.

Langacker, Ronald W., 1991a. *Concept, Image, and Symbol: The Cognitive Basis of Grammar*. Berlin: Mouton de Gruyter.

Langacker, Ronald W., 1991b. *Foundations of Cognitive Grammar*, vol. 2: *Descriptive Application*. Stanford, CA: Stanford University Press.

Langacker, Ronald W., 1999. *Grammar and Conceptualization*. Berlin: Mouton de Gruyter..

Langacker, Ronald W., 2000. A dynamic usage-based model. In Michael Barlow and Suzanne Kemmer (eds), *Usage-Based Models of Language*. Stanford, CA: CSLI, 1–63.

Langacker, Ronald W., 2001, 2nd edn. Berlin: Mouton de Gruyter.

Langacker, Ronald W., 2007a. Cognitive Grammar: a basic introduction. In Geeraerts and Cuyckens (2007: 421–62).

Langacker, Ronald W., 2008. *Cognitive Grammar: A Basic Introduction*. Oxford: Oxford University Press.

Langendoen, D. Terence, 1968. *The London School of Linguistics: A Study of the Linguistic Theories of B. Malinowski and J. Firth*. Cambridge, MA: MIT Press.

Larson, Richard, Viviane Déprez, and Hiroko Yamakido (eds), 2010. *The Evolution of Human Language: Biolinguistic Perspectives*. New York: Cambridge University Press.

Lasnik, Howard, 1981. Learnability, restrictiveness, and the evaluation metric. In Carl L. Baker and John McCarthy (eds), *The Logical Problem in Language*. Cambridge, MA: MIT Press, 1–21.

Lasnik, Howard, 2006. Conceptions of the cycle. In Lisa Lia-Shen Cheng and Norbert Corver (eds), *Wh-Movement: Moving On*. Cambridge, MA: MIT Press, 197–216.

Lasnik, Howard, 2008. On the development of Case theory: triumphs and challenges. In Robert Freidin, Carlos Otero, and Maria-Luisa Zubizarreta (eds), *Foundational Issues in Linguistic Theory*. Cambridge, MA: MIT Press, 17–41.

Lasnik, Howard, and Terje Lohndal, 2013. Brief overview of the history of generative syntax. In Marcel den Dikken (ed.), *Cambridge Handbook of Generative Syntax*. Cambridge: Cambridge University Press,

Lasnik, Howard, and Juan Uriagereka, 2011. Structure. In Ruth Kempson, Tim Fernando, and Nicholas Asher (eds), *Handbook of the Philosophy of Science*. New York: Elsevier,

Lass, Roger, 1980. *On Explaining Language Change*. Cambridge: Cambridge University Press.

Lass, Roger, 1997. *Historical Linguistics and Language Change*. Cambridge: Cambridge University Press.

Lasse, Bombien, Steve Cassidy, Jonathan M. Harrington, Tina John, and Sallyanne Palethorpe, 2006. Recent developments in the EMU speech database system. In Paul Warren and Catherine Watson (eds), *Proceedings of the 11th International Australian Conference on Speech Science and Technology*. Auckland: University of Auckland, 313–16.

Lauret, Duchaussoy, 1887. Un cas héréditaire d'audition colorée. *Revue philosophique* 23: 222–4.

Lausberg, Heinrich, 1990. *Handbuch der literarischen Rhetorik: eine Grundlegung der Literaturwissenschaft*, 3rd edn. Stuttgart: Steiner.

Law, Vivien, 1982. *The Insular Latin Grammarians*. Woodbridge: Boydell Press.

Law, Vivien, 1990. Indian influence on early Arab phonetics—or coincidence? In Kees Versteegh and Michael G. Carter (eds), *Studies in the History of Arabic Grammar* II. Amsterdam: John Benjamins, 115–227.

Law, Vivien, 1994. The study of grammar. In Rosamond McKitterick (ed.),*Carolingian Culture: Emulation and Innovation*. Cambridge: Cambridge University Press, 88–110.

Law, Vivien, 1997. Ælfric's *Excerptiones de arte grammatica anglice*. In Vivien Law (ed.), *Grammar and Grammarians in the Early Middle Ages*. London: Longman, 100–223.

Law, Vivien, 1998, The *Technē* and grammar in the Roman world. In Law and Sluiter (1998: 111–20).

Law, Vivien. 2003, *The History of Linguistics in Europe from Plato to 1600*. Cambridge: Cambridge University Press.

Law, Vivien, and Ineke Sluiter (eds), 1998. *Dionysius Thrax and the Technē Grammatikē*. Münster: Nodus.

Lawler, John M., and Richard R. Rhodes, 1981–2006. *Lawler–Rhodes Database of Simplex English Words* (version 7.4). www.umich.edu/~jlawler/monosyl.zip

Le Page, Robert B., 1963. *The National Language Question: Linguistic Problems of Newly Independent States*. London: Oxford University Press.

Le Page, Robert B., and Andrée Tabouret-Keller, 1985. *Acts of Identity: Creole-Based Approaches to Language and Ethnicity*. Cambridge: Cambridge University Press.

Ledyard, Gari, 1997. The international linguistic background of the correct sounds for the instruction of the people. In Young-Key Kim-Renaud (ed.), *The Korean Alphabet*. Honolulu: University of Hawai'i Press, 31–87.

Lee, Namhee, Lisa Mikesell, Anna D. L. Joacquin, Andrea W. Mates, and John H. Schumann, 2009. *The Interactional Instinct: The Evolution and Acquisition of Language*. Oxford: Oxford University Press.

Leech, Geoffrey, 1974. *Semantics*. Harmondsworth: Penguin.

Leech, Geoffrey, 1983. *Principles of Pragmatics*. London: Longman.

Leech, Geoffrey, 1993. 100 million words of English. *English Today* 9: 9–15.

Leech, Geoffrey, 1998. The special grammar of conversation. *Longman Language Review* 5: 9–14.

Leech, Geoffrey, and Roger Fallon, 1992. Computer corpora: what do they tell us about culture? *ICAME Journal* 16: 29–50.

Leech, Geoffrey, Marianne Hundt, Christian Mair, and Nicholas Smith, 2009. *Change in Contemporary English: A Grammatical Study*. Cambridge: Cambridge University Press.

Leech, Geoffrey, and Stig Johansson, 2009. The coming of ICAME. *ICAME Journal* 33: 5–20.

Leeds-Hurwitz, Wendy, 1987. The social history of the *Natural History of an Interview*: a multidisciplinary investigation of social communication. *Research on Language and Social Interaction* 20: 1–51.

Lefmann, Salomon, 1891–7. *Franz Bopp, sein Leben und seine Wissenschaft*. Berlin: Georg Reimer.

Lehmann, Winfred P., 1967. *A Reader in Nineteenth Century Historical Indo-European Linguistics*. Austin: University of Texas. www.utexas.edu/cola/centers/lrc/books/read08.html

Lehmann, Winfred P., 2000. My early years in machine translation. In W. John Hutchins (ed.), *Early Years in Machine Translation: Memoirs and Biographies of Pioneers*. Amsterdam: John Benjamins, 147–64.

Lehrer, Adrienne, 1974. *Semantic Fields and Lexical Structure*. Amsterdam: North-Holland.

Leibniz, Gottfried W., 1768 [1710]. *Brevis designatio meditationum de Originibus Gentium*. In Ludovic Dutens (ed.), *Opera omnia: Tomus quartus*. Geneva: Fratres de Tournes, 186–98.

Leibniz, Gottfried W., 1875. *Die philosophischen Schriften*, vol. 3, ed. Carl I. Gerhardt. Berlin: Weidmann.

Leibniz, Gottfried W., 1981 [1704]. *New Essays on Human Understanding*. Cambridge: Cambridge University Press.

Leibniz, Gottfried W., 1999. *Sämtliche Schriften und Briefe*. Berlin: Akademie.

Leitner, Gerhard, 1992. *New Directions in English Language Corpora: Methodology, Results, Software Development*. Berlin: Mouton de Gruyter.

Lentz, Augustus, 1867–70. *Herodiani Technici Reliquiae*. In *Grammatici Graeci* III.i–ii. Leipzig: B. G. Teubner.

Lenz, Rudolf, 1887. Zur Physiologie und Geschichte der Palaten. *Zeitschrift für Vergleichende Sprachforschung* 29: 1–59. Also: *Zur Physiologie und Geschichte der Palaten, Inaugural-Dissertation*. Gütersloh: C. Bertelsmann.

Leopold, Joan (ed.), 1999. *The Prix Volney: Its History and Significance for the Development of Linguistic Research*, vols 1a and 1b. Dordrecht: Kluwer Academic.

Lepschy, Giulio C. (ed.), 1994–8. *History of Linguistics*, vol. 1: *The Eastern Traditions of Linguistics*; vol.2: *Classical and Medieval Linguistics*; vol. 3: *Renaissance and Early Modern Linguistics*; vol. 4: *Nineteenth Century Linguistics*. London: Longman.

Lepsius, Carl R., 1854. *Das allgemeine linguistische Alphabet*. Berlin: W. Hertz.

—— 1863. *Standard Alphabet for reducing unwritten languages and foreign graphic systems to a uniform orthography in European letters*, 2nd edn. London: Seeleys. [1st edn 1855.]

Leskien, August, 1876. *Die Declination im Slavisch-Litauischen und Germanischen*. Leipzig: Hirzel.

Leslau, Wolf, 1946. Modern South Arabian languages: a bibliography. *Bulletin of the New York Library* 50: 607–33.

Leslau, Wolf, 1965. *An Annotated Bibliography of the Semitic Languages of Ethiopia*. The Hague: Mouton.

Levin, Beth, 1993. *English Verb Classes and Alternation: A Preliminary Investigation*. Chicago: University of Chicago Press.

Levin, Beth, and Malka Rappaport Hovav, 2005. *Argument Realization*. Cambridge: Cambridge University Press.

Levinson, Stephen C., 1983. *Pragmatics*. Cambridge: Cambridge University Press.

Lewis, Clarence I., 1946. *An Analysis of Knowledge and Valuation*. La Salle, IL: Open Court.

Lewis, Geoffrey, 1999. *The Turkish Language Reform: A Catastrophic Success*. Oxford: Oxford University Press.

Lewis, M. Paul (ed.), 2007. *Ethnologue, Languages of the World*, 15th edn. Dallas, TX: SIL International.

Lewis, M. Paul (ed.), 2009. *Ethnologue: Languages of the World*, 16th edn. Dallas, TX: SIL International. www.ethnologue.com

Li, Charles (ed.), 1976. *Subject and Topic*. New York: Academic Press.

Li Guoying 李國英, 1975. *Shuōwén Lèishì* 說文類釋 [Categories of the Shuowen Dictionary Explained]. Taipei: Quanqiu (self-published).

Li Ming, 2006. Chinese lexicography. In Keith Brown (ed.), *Encyclopedia of Language and Linguistics*, 2nd edn, vol. 2. London: Elsevier, 362–5.

Liberman, Mark, 1989. Text on tap: the ACL/DCI. *Proceedings of the Speech and Language Processing Workshop* (Philadelphia), 173–88.

Liberman, Mark, 2010. Obituary: Fred Jelinek. *Computational Linguistics* 36: 595–9.

Liberman, Mark, and Alan Prince, 1977. On stress and linguistic rhythm. *Linguistic Inquiry* 8: 249–336.

Liberman, Philip, Edmund S. Crelin, and Dennis H. Klatt, 1972. Phonetic ability and related anatomy of the newborn and adult human, Neanderthal man, and the chimpanzee. *American Anthropologist* 74: 287–307.

Liddell, Scott K., 1990. Four functions of a locus: re-examining the structure of space in ASL. In Ceil Lucas (ed.), *Sign Language Research: Theoretical Issues*. Washington, DC: Gallaudet University Press, 176–98.

Liddell, Scott K., 2003. *Grammar, Gesture, and Meaning in American Sign Language*. Cambridge: Cambridge University Press.

Liddy, Elizabeth D., 2003. Document retrieval, automatic. In Keith Brown (ed.), *Encyclopedia of Language and Linguistics*, 2nd edn, vol. 3. Oxford: Elsevier, 748–55.

Lieberman, Philip, 1984. *The Biology and Evolution of Language*. Cambridge, MA: Harvard University Press.

Lieberman, Philip, 2002. On the nature and evolution of the neural bases of human language. *Yearbook of Physical Anthropology* 45: 36–62.

Lieberman, Philip, 2006. *Toward an Evolutionary Biology of Language*. Cambridge, MA: Harvard University Press.

Lieberman, Philip, 2007. The evolution of human speech. *Current Anthropology* 48: 39–66.

Lieberman, Philip, 2010. The creative capacity of language: in what manner it is unique, and who had it? In Larson et al. (2010: 163–75).

Lightner, Theodore, 1972. *Problems in the Theory of Phonology*. Edmonton: Linguistic Research.

Lillo-Martin, Diane, and Wendy Sandler, 2006. *Sign Language and Linguistic Universals*. Cambridge: Cambridge University Press.

Lily, William, and John Colet, 1970. *A Short Introduction of Grammar 1549*. English linguistics 1500–1800. Menston, UK: Scholar Press.

Lin Shoujin 林壽晋, 1981. *Bànpōcūn Yízhǐ⊠ Zōngshù* 半坡村遺址綜述 [An Overview of the Banpocun Archaeological Site]. Hong Kong: Chinese University of Hong Kong Press.

Lindblom, Björn, 1990. Explaining phonetic variation: a sketch of the H&H theory. In William J. Hardcastle and Alain Marchal (eds), *Speech Production and Speech Modeling*. Dordrecht : Kluwer, 403–39.

Lindsay, Robert K., 1963. Inferential memory as the basis of machines which understand language. In Edward A. Feigenbaum and Julian Feldman (eds), *Computers and Thought*. New York: McGraw-Hill, 117–233.

Linell, Per, 1979. *Psychological Reality in Phonology*. Cambridge: Cambridge University Press.

Linell, Per, 1982. *The Written Language Bias in Linguistics*. Linköping : University of Linköping, Dept of Communication Studies.

Linell, Per, 2005. *The Written Language Bias in Linguistics: Its Nature, Origins and Transformations*. London: Routledge.

Linn, Andrew R., 1997. *Constructing the Grammars of a Language: Ivar Aasen and Nineteenth Century Norwegian Linguistics*. Münster: Nodus.

Linn, Andrew R., 1999. Charles Bertram's *Royal English–Danish Grammar*: the linguistic work of an eighteenth century fraud. In David Cram, Andrew Linn, and Elke Nowak (eds), *History of Linguistics 1996*, vol. 2. Amsterdam: John Benjamins, 183–91.

Linn, Andrew R., 2005. The Scandinavian languages: grammars and grammar writing to 1900. In Peter Schmitter (ed.), *Geschichte der Sprachtheorie 6/1: Sprachtheorien der Neuzeit III/1: Sprachbeschreibung und Sprachunterricht*, vol. 1. Tübingen: Gunter Narr, 162–99.

Linn, Andrew R., 2006. English grammar writing. In Bas Aarts and April McMahon (eds), *The Handbook of English Linguistics*. Oxford: Blackwell, 72–92.

Linn, Andrew R., and Nicola McLelland, 2002. *Standardization: Studies from the Germanic Languages*. Amsterdam: John Benjamins.

Lipiński, Edward, 1990. Araméen d'Empire. In Pierre Swiggers and Alfons Wouters (eds), *Le langage dans l'Antiquité*. Leuven: Peeters and Leuven University Press, 94–133.

Lipiński, Edward, 2001a [1997]. *Semitic Languages: Outline of a Comparative Grammar*, 2nd edn. Leuven: Peeters.

Lipiński, Edward, 2001b. *Języki semickie rodziny afroazjatyckiej: Zarys ogólny*. Poznań: Wydawnictwo Naukowe UAM.

Lipiński, Edward, 2008. Język ugarycki a hebrajszczyzna ksiąg biblijnych. *Studia Judaica* 11: 301–7.

Lipiński, Edward, 2011. Meroitic (review article). *Rocznik Orientalistyczny* 64(2): 87–104.

Lipka, Leonhard, 2002. *English Lexicology*. Tübingen: Gunter Narr.

Lipset, David, 1980. *Gregory Bateson: The Legacy of a Scientist*. Englewood Cliffs, NJ: Prentice Hall.

Liu Yaowu 劉耀武, 1993. *Rìyǔ Yǔfǎ Yánjiùshǐ* 日語語法研究史 [A History of Grammatical Research in Japan]. Beijing: Higher Education Publishers.

Liu Yeqiu 劉葉秋, 1963. *Zhōngguó Gǔdài de Zìdiǎn* 中國古代的字典. [Ancient Chinese Dictionaries]. Beijing: Zhonghua Bookstore. [Repr. Hong Kong: Hawaii Publishers, n.d.]

Loakes, Deborah, 2006a. A forensic phonetic investigation into the speech patterns of identical and non-identical twins. Ph.D thesis, University of Melbourne.

Loakes, Deborah, 2006b. Variation in long-term fundamental frequency: measurements from vocalic segments in twins' speech. In Paul Warren and Catherine I. Watson (eds), *Proceedings of the 11th Australian International Conference on Speech Science and Technology*. Canberra: Australian Speech Science and Technology Association, 105–210.

Loakes, Deborah, 2008. Phonetic evidence for neutralisation of prelateral /æ/ and /e/ in Melbourne English. Poster presented at the Laboratory Phonology 11 conference, Wellington, New Zealand, 30 June–2 July.

Loakes, Deborah, John Hajek, and Janet Fletcher, 2010a. The /el/–/æl/ sound change in Australian English: a preliminary perception experiment. In Yvonne Treis and Rik de Busser (eds), *Selected Papers from the 2009 Conference of the Australian Linguistic Society*. Melbourne: La Trobe University.

Loakes, Deborah, John Hajek and Janet Fletcher, 2010b. (Mis)perceiving /el/~/æl/ in Melbourne English: a micro-analysis of sound perception and change. In Marija Tabain, Janet Fletcher, D. Grayden, John Hajek, and Andy Butcher (eds), *Proceedings of the 13th Australasian Conference on Speech Science and Technology*. Melbourne: Melbourne University, 179–82.

Loakes, Deborah, John Hajek and Janet Fletcher, 2010c. Issues in the perception of the /el/~/æl/ contrast in Melbourne: perception, production and lexical frequency effects. In Marija Tabain, Janet Fletcher, D. Grayden, John Hajek, and Andy Butcher (eds), *Proceedings of the*

13th Australasian Conference on Speech Science and Technology. Melbourne: Melbourne University, 183–6.

Loakes, Deborah, John Hajek and Janet Fletcher, 2011. /æl/-/el/ transposition in Australian English: hypercorrection or a competing sound change? *Proceedings of the International Congress of Phonetic Sciences (ICPhS) XVII*. Hong Kong: ICPhS, 1290–3.

Loakes, Deborah, John Hajek, and Janet Fletcher. 2010a. The /el/-/æl/ sound change in Australian English: A preliminary perception experiment. In Yvonne Treis and Rik de Busser (eds) *Selected Papers from the 2009 Conference of the Australian Linguistic Society*. Melbourne: La Trobe University.

Loakes, Deborah and Kirsty McDougall, 2010. Individual variation in the frication of voiceless plosives in Australian English: a study of twins' speech. *Australian Journal of Linguistics* 30: 155–81.

Lock, Andrew (ed.), 1978. *Action, Gesture and Symbol: The Emergence of Language*. London: Academic Press.

Locke, John, 1700. *Essay Concerning Humane Understanding. The fourth edn, with large additions*. 4 vols. London: Printed for Awnsham and John Churchil et al. [1st edn 1690.]

Locke, William N., and A. Donald Booth (eds), 1955. *Machine Translation of Languages*. Cambridge, MA: MIT Press.

Lodge, David, 1986. *Working with Structuralism*. London: Routledge & Kegan Paul.

Lodge, R. Anthony, 1993. *French: From Dialect to Standard*. London: Routledge.

Lodwick [or Lodowyck], Francis, 1686. *An Essay Towards An Universal Alphabet*. London: [n.p.]. Early English Books Online. eebo.chadwyck.com

Löffler, Heinrich, 1994. *Germanistische Soziolinguistik*. Münster: Erich Schmidt.

Long, Anthony A., 1971. Language and thought in Stoicism. In Anthony A. Long (ed.), *Problems in Stoicism*. London: Athlone Press, 75–113.

Long, Anthony A., 2005. Stoic linguistics, Plato's *Cratylus*, and Augustine's De dialectica. In Dorothea Frede and Brad Inwood (eds), *Language and Learning*. Cambridge: Cambridge University Press, 36–55.

Long, Anthony A., and David N. Sedley, 1987. *The Hellenistic Philosophers*, vol. 1: *Translations of the Principal Sources with Philosophical Commentary*; vol. 2: *Greek and Latin Texts with Notes and Bibliography*. Cambridge: Cambridge University Press.

Long, J. Schuyler, 1910. The Sign Language: A Manual of Signs. Washington, DC: Gibson.

Longacre, Robert, 1996. *The Grammar of Discourse*, 2nd edn. New York: Plenum Press.

Lorenzen, Paul, and Kuno Lorenz, 1978. *Dialogische Logik*. Darmstadt: Wissenschaftliche Buchgesellschaft.

Lottner, Carl, 1862. Ausnahmen der ersten Lautverschiebung. *Zeitschrift für vergleichende Sprachforschung* 11: 161–205.

Lounsbury, Floyd, 1956. A semantic analysis of Pawnee kinship usage. *Language* 32: 158–94.

Louw, Bill, 1993. Irony in the text or insincerity in the writer? The diagnostic potential of semantic prosodies. In Mona Baker, Gill Francis, and Elena Tognini-Bonelli (eds), *Text and Technology: In Honour of John Sinclair*. Amsterdam: John Benjamins, 157–76.

Loux, Michael J., 1974. Ockham on generality. In *Ockham's Theory of Terms: Part I of the Summa Logicae*, transl. Michael J. Loux. South Bend: Notre Dame University Press, 13–46.

Luce, R. Duncan, Robert R. Bush, and Eugene Galanter (eds), 1965. *Readings in Mathematical Psychology 2*. New York: Wiley.

Lucretius Carus, Titus, 2003 [?54 BC]. *De rerum natura*, transl. Walter Englert as *On the Nature of Things*. Newburyport, MA: Focus.

Lüdeke, Henry (ed.), 1930. *Ludwig Tieck und die Brüder Schlegel: Briefe mit Einleitung und Anmerkungen*. Frankfurt am Main: J. Baer.

Luhtala, Anneli, 1993. Syntax and dialectic in Carolingian commentaries on *Institutiones grammaticae*. In Vivien Law (ed.), *History of Linguistic Thought in the Early Middle Ages*. Amsterdam: John Benjamins, 145–91.

Luhtala, Anneli, 2000a. Early Medieval commentary on Priscian's Institutiones grammaticae. *Cahiers de l'Institut du Moyen-Âge grec et latin* 71: 115–88.

Luhtala, Anneli, 2000b. Linguistics and theology in the Early Medieval West. In Auroux et al., vol. 1 (2000: 510–24).

Luhtala, Anneli, 2005. *Grammar and Philosophy in Late Antiquity*. Amsterdam: John Benjamins.

Łukasiewicz, Jan, 1935. Zur Geschichte der Aussagenlogik. *Erkenntnis* 5: 111–31.

Lundell, Johan A., 1879. *Det svenska landsmålsalfabetet: till lika en öfversikt af språkljudens förekomst inom svenska mål*. Stockholm: P. A. Norstedt.

Lynch, Jack, and Anne McDermott (eds), 2005. *Anniversary Essays on Johnson's* Dictionary. Cambridge: Cambridge University Press.

Lyons, John, 1963. *Structural Semantics*. Oxford: Blackwell.

Lyons, John, 1968. *Introduction to Theoretical Linguistics*. Cambridge: Cambridge University Press.

Lyons, John, 1975. Deixis as the source of reference. In Edward Keenan (ed.), *Formal Semantics of Natural Language*. London: Cambridge University Press, 61–83.

Lyons, John, 1977. *Semantics*. Cambridge: Cambridge University Press.

Lyons, John, 1979. Deixis and anaphora. In Terry Myers (ed.), *The Development of Conversation and Discourse*. Edinburgh: Edinburgh University Press, 88–103.

Lyons, John, 1981. *Language, Meaning and Context*. London: Fontana.

Lyons, John, 1987. Semantics. In John Lyons, Richard Coates, Margaret Deucher, and Gerald Gazdar, *New Horizons in Linguistics*, 2. London: Penguin.

Lytinen, Steven L., 1985. Integrating syntax and semantics. *Proceedings of the Conference on Theoretical and Methodological Issues in Machine Translation of Natural Languages* (Hamilton, NY), 167–78.

Ma Zuyi 馬祖毅, 1998. *Zhōngguó Fānyì Jiǎnshǐ: Wǔsì Yǐqián Bùfèn* 中國翻譯簡史：五四以前部分 [A Short History of Translation in China: The Pre-May Fourth Period]. Beijing: Zhongguo Duiwai Fanyi.

MacMahon, Michael K. C., 1986. The International Phonetic Association: the first 100 years. *Journal of the International Phonetic Association* 16: 30–38.

MacMahon, Michael K. C. 191996. Phonetic notation. In Peter T. Daniels and William Bright (eds), *The World's Writing Systems*. Oxford: Oxford University Press, 821–46.

MacNeilage, Peter F., 2008. *The Origin of Speech*. Oxford: Oxford University Press.

MacSweeney, Mairéad, Cheryl M. Capek, Ruth Campbell, and Bencie Woll, 2008. The signing brain: the neurobiology of sign language. *Trends in Cognitive Sciences* 12(11): 432–40.

MacWhinney, Brian, 2002. The emergence of language from body, brain, and society. In Mary Andronis, Erin Debenport, Ann Pycha, and Keiko Yoshimura (eds), *Proceedings from the Panels of Thirty-Eighth Meeting of the Chicago Linguistic Society*, vol. 38(2). Chicago: Chicago Linguistic Society, 147–71.

Maduka, Omen N., 1988. Size and shape ideophones in Membe. *Studies in African Linguistics* 19: 93–113.

Maduka, Omen N., 1991. Phonosemantic antecedents of some verbs in Igbo. *Journal of West African Languages* 21: 105–15.

Maher, John, 1986. English for medical purposes. *Language Teaching* 19: 112–45.

Mahlberg, Michaela, 2010. *Corpus Stylistics and Dickens's Fiction*. London: Routledge.

Maier-Eichhorn, Ursula, 1989. *Die Gestikulation in Quintilians Rhetorik*. Frankfurt am Main: Peter Lang.

Maine, Henry Sumner, 1875. *Effects of observation of India on modern European thought*. The Rede lecture, delivered before the University of Cambridge, 22 May. London: John Murray.

Mair, Christian, Marianne Hundt, Geoffrey Leech, and Nicholas Smith, 2002. Short term diachronic shifts in part-of-speech frequencies: a comparison of the tagged LOB and F-LOB corpora. *International Journal of Corpus Linguistics* 7: 245–64.

Makkai, Valerie Becker (ed.), 1972. *Phonological Theory: Evolution and Current Practice*. New York: Holt, Rinehart & Winston.

Malinowski, Bronislaw, 1935. *Coral Gardens and Their Magic*. London: Routledge.

Malkiel, Yakov, 1976. From Romance philology through dialect geography to sociolinguistics. *International Journal of the Sociology of Language* 9: 59–84.

Malkiel, Yakov, 1990. *Diachronic Problems in Phonosymbolism*. Amsterdam: John Benjamins.

Malkiel, Yakov, 1993. *Etymology*. Cambridge: Cambridge University Press.

Mallery, Garrick, 1972 [1881]. *Sign Language among North American Indians Compared with that among Other Peoples and Deaf Mutes*. First Annual Report of the Bureau of Ethnology to the Secretary of the Smithsonian Institution, 1879–80. Washington, DC: Government Printing Office. [Repr. The Hague: Mouton, 1972.]

Malmberg, Bertil, 1964. *New Trends in Linguistics*. Stockholm:Bibliotheca Linguistica.

Malmberg, Bertil, 1972. The hierarchic principle. *Proceedings of the 7th International Congress on Phonetics*, 1145–8.

Malmkjær, Kirsten, 1998. Introduction. In Kirsten Malmkjær (ed.), *Translation and Language Teaching: Language Teaching and Translation*. Manchester: St Jerome, 1–11.

Malmqvist, Gören, 1994. Chinese Linguistics. In Giulio Lepschy (1994–8: i. 1–24).

Malouf, Rob, and Farrell Ackerman, 2010a. Paradigm entropy as a measure of morphological simplicity. Paper presented at Workshop on Morphological Complexity: Implications for the Theory of Language, Harvard University.

Malouf, Rob and Farrell Ackerman, 2010b. Paradigms: the low entropy conjecture. Paper presented at Workshop on Morphology and Formal Grammar, Paris.

Maltzman, Irving, Lloyd Morrisett, and Lloyd O. Brooks, 1956. An investigation of phonetic symbolism, *Journal of Abnormal and Social Psychology* 53: 245–51.

Mamphwe, C. T., 1987. *The Ideophone in Venda*. Pretoria: University of South Africa.

Manchester, Martin L., 1985. *The Philosophical Foundations of Humboldt's Linguistic Doctrines*. Amsterdam: John Benjamins.

Mandelbaum, David G. (ed.), 1949. *Selected Writings of Edward Sapir in Language, Culture and Personality*. Berkeley: University of California Press.

Manning, Christopher D., Prabhakar Raghavan, and Hinrich Schütze, 2008. *An Introduction to Information Retrieval*. Cambridge: Cambridge University Press.

Manning, Christopher D., and Hinrich Schütze, 1999. *Foundations of Statistical Natural Language Processing*. Cambridge, MA: MIT Press.

Marchand, Hans, 1959. Phonetic symbolism in English word formation. *Indogermanische Forschungen* 64: 146–68.

Marcus, Mitchell P., 1980. *A Theory of Syntactic Recognition for Natural Language*. Cambridge, MA: MIT Press.

Marcus, Mitchell P., Grace Kim, Mary Ann Marcinkiewicz, et al., 1994. The Penn treebank: annotating predicate argument structure. *Proceedings of the Human Language Technology Workshop* (Plainsboro, NJ), 114–19.

Marcus, Mitchell P., Beatrice Santorini, and Mary A.Marcinkiewicz,1993. Building a large annotated corpus of English: the Penn treebank. *Computational Linguistics* 19: 313–30.

Margoliash, Daniel, 2010. Sleep, off-line processing, and vocal learning. *Brain and Language* 115: 45–58.

Margoliash, Daniel, and Howard Nusbaum, 2009. Language: the perspective from organismal biology. *Trends in Cognitive Science* 13: 505–10.

Marial Usón, Ricardo, and Pamela Faber, 2007. Lexical templates within a functional cognitive theory of meaning. *Annual Review of Cognitive Linguistics* 5: 137–72.

Marks, Lawrence E., 1974. On associations of light and sound: the mediations of brightness, pitch and loudness. *American Journal of Psychology* 87: 173–88.

Marks, Lawrence E., 1978. *The Unity of the Senses: Interrelations among the Modalities*. New York: Academic Press.

Marr, Nikolaj V., 1926. *Средства передвижения, орудия самозащиты и производства в до-истории. К увязке языкознания с историею материальной культуры.* [Means of Carriage, Tools of Production and Self-Defence in Pre-history: Towards Links between Linguistics and the History of Material Culture]. Leningrad.

Marrone, Livia, 1997. Le questioni logiche di Crisippo (PHerc. 307). *Cronache ercolanesi* 27: 83–100.

Marshall, John H. (ed.), 1969. *The Donatz Proensals of Uc Faidit*. London: Oxford University Press.

Marslen-Wilson, William, 2005. *Speech and Language: Research Review Written for the Foresight Cognitive Systems Project*. www.foresight.gov.uk/Cognitive%20Systems/_CogA4_SpeechLang.pdf

Martianus Capella, 1978. *De nuptiis Philologiae et Mercurii*, ed. Adolf Dick (Leipzig 1925); repr. with addenda and corrigenda by Jean Préaux. Stuttgart: Teubner.

Martin, James R., 1985. *Factual Writing: Exploring and Challenging Social Reality*. Geelong: Deakin University Press.

Martin, James R., 1992. *English Text: System and Structure*. Amsterdam: John Benjamins.

Martinet, André, 1949. Phonology as functional phonetics. *Publications of the Philological Society*: 1–27.

Martinet, André, 1955. *Économie des changements phonétiques: traité de phonologie diachronique*. Bern: Francke.

Martinet, André, 1960. *Éléments de linguistique générale*. Paris: Armand Colin.

Martinet, André, 1962a. *A Functional View of Language*. Oxford: Clarendon.

Martinet, André, 1962b. *Langue et fonction*. Paris: Denoël.

Martinet, André, 1975. *Studies in Functional Syntax*. Munich: Wilhelm Fink.

Marty, Anton, 1908. *Untersuchungen zur Grundlegung der allgemeinen Grammatik und Sprachphilosophie*. Halle: Niemeyer.

Maruyama, Hiroshi, 1990. Structural disambiguation with constraint propagation. *Proceedings of the 28th Annual Meeting of the Association for Computational Linguistics* (Pittsburgh, PA), 31–8.

Masica, Colin P., 1991. *The Indo-Aryan Languages*. Cambridge: Cambridge University Press.

Mathesius, Vilém, 1929. On linguistic characterology with illustrations from Modern English. *Actes du premier congrès international de linguistes* (The Hague, 10–15 April 1928). Leiden: Sijthoff, 56–63. [Repr. in Vachek (1964: 59–67).]

Mathesius, Vilém, 1939. O tak zvanem aktualnim cleneni vetnem [On the so-called actual bipartition of sentences]. *Slovo a Slovnost* 5: 171–4.

Mathesius, Vilém, 1964 [1928]. On linguistic characterology with illustrations from Modern English. In Vachek (1964: 59–67). [First published in *Actes du Premier Congrès International de Linguistes à La Haye, du 10-15 Avril, 1928* (Leiden: A. W. Sijthoff, 1928), 56–63.]

Mathesius, Vilém, 1975. *A Functional Analysis of Present Day English on a General Linguistic Basis*, ed. Josef Vachek and transl. Libuše Dušková. The Hague: Mouton.

Mathesius, Vilém, 1983 [1929]. Functional linguistics. In Josef Vachek, Libuše Dušková, and Philip A. Luelsdorff (eds), *Praguiana: Some Basic and Less Known Aspects of the Prague Linguistic School*. Amsterdam: John Benjamins, 45–64.

Matthaios, Stephanos, 1999. *Untersuchungen zur Grammatik Aristarchs: Texte und Interpretation zur Wortartenlehre*. Göttingen: Vandenhoeck & Ruprecht.

Matthaios, Stephanos, 2002. Neue Perspektiven für die Historiographie der antiken Grammatik: das Wortartensystem der Alexandriner. In Pierre Swiggers and Alfons Wouters (eds), *Grammatical Theory and Philosophy of Language in Antiquity*. Leuven: Peeters.

Mattheier, Klaus J., 1988. Nationalsprachenentwicklung, Sprachstandardisierung und historische Soziolinguistik. In Ulrich Ammon, Klaus J. Mattheier, and Peter H. Nelde *Sociolinguistica* 2. Tübingen: Niemeyer, 1–9.

Matthews, Peter H., 1965. The inflectional component of a word-and-paradigm grammar. *Journal of Linguistics* 1: 139–71.

Matthews, Peter H., 1972. *Inflectional Morphology: A Theoretical Study Based on Aspects of Latin Verb Conjugation*. Cambridge: Cambridge University Press.

Matthews, Peter H., 1991. *Morphology*. Cambridge: Cambridge University Press. [1st edn 1974.]

Matthews, Peter H., 1993. *Grammatical Theory in the United States from Bloomfield to Chomsky*. Cambridge: Cambridge University Press.

Matthews, Peter H., 1994. Greek and Latin linguistics. In Lepschy (1994–8: ii. 1–133).

Matthews, Peter H., 1999. Zellig S. Harris. *Language* 75: 112–19.

Matthews, Peter H., 2001. *A Short History of Structural Linguistics*. Cambridge: Cambridge University Press.

Matthiessen, Christian M. I. M., 1995. *Lexicogrammatical Cartography: English Systems*. Tokyo: International Language Sciences.

Matthiessen, Christian M. I. M., 2007a. The 'architecture' of language according to systemic functional theory: developments since the 1970s. In Ruqaiya Hasan, Christian M. I. M Matthiessen, and Jonathan J. Webster (eds), *Continuing Discourse on Language: A Functional Perspective*, vol. 2. London: Equinox, 505–61.

Matthiessen, Christian M. I. M., 2007b. Lexicogrammar in systemic functional linguistics: descriptive and theoretical developments in the 'IFG' tradition since the 1970s. In Ruqaiya Hasan, Christian M. I. M Matthiessen, and Jonathan J. Webster (eds), *Continuing Discourse on Language: A Functional Perspective*, vol. 2. London: Equinox, 765–858.

Matthiessen, Christopher M. I. M., and Sandra A. Thompson, 1988. The structure of discourse and subordination. In John Haiman and Sandra A. Thompson (eds), *Clause Combining in Discourse*. Amsterdam: John Benjamins, 275–329.

Maupertuis, Pierre Louis Moreau de, 1748. *Réflexions philosophiques sur l'origine des langues et la signification des mots.* Lyon: Jean-Marie Bruyset.

Mautner, Gerlinde, 2009a. Checks and balances: how corpus linguistics can contribute to CDA. In Ruth Wodak and Michael Meyer (eds), *Methods of Critical Discourse Analysis.* London: Sage, 122–43.

Mautner, Gerlinde, 2009b. Corpora and critical discourse analysis. In Paul Baker (ed.), *Contemporary Corpus Linguistics.* London: Continuum, 32–46.

Maybury, Mark T. (ed.), 2004. *New Directions in Question Answering.* Cambridge, MA: MIT Press.

McAuliffe, Jane Dammen (ed.), 2001–6. *Encyclopaedia of the Qur'ān* I–VI. Leiden: E. J. Brill.

McCarthy, John J., 1981. A prosodic theory of nonconcatenative morphology. *Linguistic Inquiry* 12: 373–418.

McCarthy, John J., 2004. *Optimality Theory: A Reader.* Oxford: Blackwell.

McCarthy, Michael, 1998. *Spoken Language and Applied Linguistics.* Cambridge: Cambridge University Press.

McCarthy, Robert C., David S. Strait, Frederick Yates, and Philip Lieberman, forthcoming. *The Recent Origin of Human Speech.*

McCarty, Willard, 2005. *Humanities Computing.* Basingstoke: Palgrave Macmillan.

McCawley, James D., 1968. *The Phonological Component of a Grammar of Japanese.* The Hague: Mouton.

McCawley, James D., 1982. Parentheticals and discontinuous constituent structure. *Linguistic Inquiry* 13: 91–106.

McClelland, Jay L., David E. Rumelhart, and the PDP Research Group, 1986. *Parallel Distributed Processing: Explorations in the Microstructure of Cognition,* vol. 2: *Psychological and Biological Models.* Cambridge, MA: MIT Press.

McCune, Keith M., 1985. *The Internal Structure of Indonesian Roots.* Jakarta: Badan Penyelenggara Seri Nusa, Universitas Katolik Indonesia Atma Jaya.

McDonough, Joyce, and Valerie Wood, 2008. The stop contrasts of the Athabaskan languages. *Journal of Phonetics* 36: 427–49.

McEnery, Tony, and Andrew Hardie, 2012. *Corpus Linguistics: Method, Theory and Practice.* Cambridge: Cambridge University Press.

McEnery, Tony, and Andrew Wilson, 2001. *Corpus Linguistics,* 2nd edn. Edinburgh: Edinburgh University Press. [1st edn 1996.]

McEnery, Tony, and Zonghua Xiao, 2004. The Lancaster corpus of Mandarin Chinese: a corpus for monolingual and contrastive language study. In Maria Lino, Francisca Xavier, Fátima Ferreire, Rute Costa, and Raquel Silva (eds), *Proceedings of the Fourth International Conference on Language Resources and Evaluation (LREC) 24–30 May 2004* (Lisbon), 1175–8.

McEnery, Tony, Zonghua Xiao, and Lili Mo, 2004. Aspect marking in English and Chinese: using the Lancaster Corpus of Mandarin Chinese for contrastive language study. *Literary and Linguistic Computing* 18: 361–78.

McGregor, William, 1997. *Semiotic Grammar.* Oxford: Oxford University Press.

McInerney, Jay, 1993. *Brightness Falls.* New York: Vintage Books.

McKoon, Gail, and Talke Macfarland, 2000. Externally and internally caused change of state. *Language* 76: 833–58.

McNeill, David, 1985. So you think gestures are nonverbal? *Psychological Review* 92: 350–71.

McNeill, David, 1992. *Hand and Mind.* Chicago: Chicago University Press.

McNeill, David, 2000. *Language and Gesture*. Cambridge: Cambridge University Press.

McNeill, David, 2005. *Gesture and Thought*. Chicago: Chicago University Press.

McNeill, David, Susan D. Duncan, Jonathan Cole, Shaun Gallagher, and Bennett Bertenthall, 2008. Either or both: growth points from the very beginning. In Michael Arbid and Derek Bickerton (eds), *Holophrasis vs Compositionality in the Emergence of Protolanguage*. Amsterdam: John Benjamins, 117–32.

McPherson, Brian, 1995. Establishing connections between emotions and speech sounds. MS, University of Arkansas for Medical Sciences.

McWhorter, John H., 1998. Identifying the creole prototype: vindicating a typological class. *Language* 74: 788–818.

McWhorter, John H., 2001. The world's simplest grammars are creole grammars. *Linguistic Typology* 5: 125–66.

Meier, Richard P., Kearsy A. Cormier, and David G. Quinto-Pozos (eds), 2002. *Modality and Structure in Signed and Spoken Languages*. Cambridge: Cambridge University Press.

Meigret, Louis, 1542. *Traité touchant le commun usage de l'escriture françoise . . . auquel est debattu des faultes, & abus en la vraye, & ancienne puissance des letters*. Paris: Ieanne de Marnef.

Meillet, Antoine, 1903. *Introduction à l'étude comparative des langues indo-européennes, suivi d'un aperçu du développement de la grammaire comparée*. Paris: Hachette.

Meillet, Antoine, 1906. Comment les mots changent de sens. *Année sociologique* 9: 1–38. [Repr. in Antoine Meillet, *Linguistique historique et linguistique générale* (Paris: Champion, 1921), 130–271.]

Meillet, Antoine, 1934. *Introduction à l'étude comparative des langues indo-européennes*, 7th edn. Paris: Hachette.

Meiner, Johann Werner, 1781. *Versuch einer an der menschlichen Sprache abgebildeten Vernunftlehre oder philosophische und allgemeine Sprachlehre*. Leipzig: Breitkopf. [Repr. Stuttgart–Bad Canstatt: Frommann–Holzboog, 1971.]

Meinsma, Gerrit L., 1983. *Phonetic Sciences in the Netherlands: Past and Present*. Dordrecht: Foris.

Melanchthon, Philipp, 1661. *Philippi Melanchthonis Grammatica Latina*. Wittebergae: Selfisch.

Mel'čuk, Igor A., 2000. Machine translation and formal linguistics in the USSR. In W. John Hutchins (ed.), *Early Years in Machine Translation: Memoirs and Biographies of Pioneers*. Amsterdam: John Benjamins, 105–226.

Mel'čuk, Igor A., 2006. The explanatory combinatorial dictionary. In Giandomenico Sica (ed.), *Open Problems in Linguistics and Lexicography*. Milan: Polimetrica, 125–355.

Mel'čuk, Igor A., André Clas, and Alain Polguère, 1995. *Introduction à la lexicologie explicative et combinatoire*. Louvain-la-Neuve: Duculot.

Mel'čuk, Igor A., and Aleksandr K. Žholkovskij, 1970. Towards a functioning 'meaning–text' model of language. *Linguistics* 57(8): 10–47. [Repr. in Viktor Jul'evič Rozencvejg (ed.), *Machine Translation and Applied Linguistics*, vol. 2 (Frankfurt am Main: Athenaion, 1974), 1–53.]

Meringer, Rudolf, 1909. Wörter und Sachen. *Germanisch-Romanische Monatsschrift* 1: 593–8.

Meringer, Rudolf, 1912. Zur Aufgabe und zum Namen unserer Zeitschrift. *Wörter und Sachen* 3: 22–56.

Merkel, Carl L., 1857. *Anatomie und Physiologie des menschlichen Stimm- und Sprach-Organs (Anthropophonik): nach eigenen Beobachtungen und Versuchen*. Leipzig: Ambrosius Abel.

Merkel, Carl L., 1866. *Physiologie der menschlichen Sprache, physiologische Laletik*. Leipzig: Wigand.

Merrilees, Brian, 1993. Donatus and the teaching of French in medieval England. In Ian Short (ed.), *Anglo-Norman Anniversary Essays*. London: Anglo-Norman Text Society, 173–291.

Merrilees, Brian, and Beata Sitarz-Fitzpatrick, 1993. *Liber Donati: A Fifteenth Century Manual of French*. London: Anglo-Norman Text Society.

Mervis, Carolyn B., and Eleanor Rosch, 1981. Categorization of natural objects. *Annual Review of Psychology* 32: 89–115.

Mesoudi, Alex, Andrew Whiten, and Kevin N. Laland, 2004. Is human cultural evolution Darwinian? Evidence reviewed from the perspective of *The Origin of Species*. *Evolution* 58: 1–11.

Messling, Marcus, 2008. Wilhelm von Humboldt and the 'Orient': on Edward W. Said's remarks on Humboldt's Orientalist studies. *Language Sciences* 30: 482–98.

Mey, Jacob L., 1985. *Whose Language? A Study in Linguistic Pragmatics*. Amsterdam: John Benjamins.

Mey, Jacob L., 2001. *Pragmatics: An Introduction*, 2nd edn. Oxford, MA: Blackwell. [1st edn 1993.]

Mey, Jacob L., 2005. Horace and colors: a world in black and white. In Dag Haug and Eirik Welo (eds), *Haptačahaptaitiš: Festschrift for Fridrik Thordarson on the Occasion of his 77th Birthday*. Oslo: Novus Forlag and Instituttet for sammenlignende kulturforskning, 163–76.

Mey, Jacob L., 2006. Focus-on issue: text pragmatics. *Journal of Pragmatics* 38: 809–10.

Mey, Jacob L., 2009. Pragmatic acts. In Jacob L. Mey (ed.), *Concise Encyclopedia of Pragmatics*. Oxford: Elsevier, 747–53.

Mey, Jacob L., 2010. Reference and the pragmeme. *Journal of Pragmatics* 42: 2882–8.

Michael, Ian, 1987. *The Teaching of English from the Sixteenth Century to 1870*. Cambridge: Cambridge University Press.

Micklethwait, David, 2000. *Noah Webster and the American Dictionary*. Jefferson, NC: Macfarland.

Milin, Petar, Dušica Filipović Ðurdjević, and Fermín Moscoso del Prado Martín, 2009. The simultaneous effects of inflectional paradigms and classes on lexical recognition: evidence from Serbian. *Journal of Memory and Language* 60: 50–64.

Milin, Petar, Victor Kuperman, Aleksandar Kostić, and R. Harald Baayen, 2009. Words and paradigms bit by bit: an information-theoretic approach to the processing of inflection and derivation. In James P. Blevins and Juliette Blevins (eds), *Analogy in Grammar: Form and Acquisition*. Oxford: Oxford University Press, 114–253.

Militarev, Alexander, 1984. Язык мероитской епиграфики [The language of Meroitic epigraphy], *Vestnik Drevney Istorii* 2: 153–70.

Militarev, Alexander, and Leonid Kogan, 2000, 2005. *Semitic Etymological Dictionary*, vol. 1: *Anatomy of Man and Animals*; vol. 2: *Animal Names*. Münster: Ugarit.

Miller, D. Gary, 1994. *Ancient Scripts and Phonological Knowledge*. Amsterdam: John Benjamins.

Miller, George A., 1985. WordNet: a dictionary browser. In *Proceedings of the First Conference of the UW Centre for the New Oxford English Dictionary*. Waterloo: University of Waterloo, 15–28.

Miller, George A., 2003. The cognitive revolution: a historical perspective. *Trends in Cognitive Sciences* 7: 141–4.

Milroy, James, and Lesley Milroy, 1991. *Authority in Language: Investigating Language Prescription and Standardisation*, 2nd edn. London: Routledge.

Minsky, Marvin L., 1975. A framework for representing knowledge. In Patrick H. Winston (ed.), *The Psychology of Computer Vision*. New York: McGraw-Hill, 111–277.

Minsky, Marvin L., and Seymour A. Papert, 1969. *Perceptrons: An Introduction to Computational Geometry*. Cambridge, MA: MIT Press.

Miranda, Rocky, 2006. Indian lexicography. In Keith Brown (ed.), *Encyclopedia of Language and Linguistics*, 2nd edn, vol. 5. London: Elsevier, 614–16.

Miron, Murray S., 1961. A cross-linguistic investigation of phonetic symbolism. *Journal of Abnormal and Social Psychology* 62: 623–30.

Mirzoeff, Nicholas, 1995. *Silent Poetry: Deafness, Sign and Visual Culture in Modern France*. Princeton, NJ: Princeton University Press.

Mitchell, Tom M., 1997. *Machine Learning*. Boston: McGraw-Hill.

Mithen, Steven, 2005. *The Singing Neanderthals: The Origins of Music, Language, Mind, and Body*. London: Weidenfeld & Nicolson.

Moeschler, Jacques, 2010. *Pragmatic Theory, Lexical and Non-lexical Pragmatics*. Berlin: Mouton de Gruyter.

Møller, Christen, and Peter Skautrup (eds), 1930. *De literis libri duo: Jacobi Matthie Arhusiensis ... Mit einer dänischen Übersetzung nebst einer Abhandlung über Text und Quellen von Franz Blatt*. Aarhus: Aarhus Stiftsbogtrykkeriet.

Montague, Richard, 1970. English as a formal language. In Bruno Visentini (ed.), *Linguaggi nella società e nella tecnica*. Milan: Edizioni di Comunità, 189–223.

Montague, Richard, 1973. The proper treatment of quantification in ordinary English. In K. J. J. Hintikka, J. M. E. Moravcsik, and P. Suppes (eds), *Approaches to Natural Language: Proceedings of the 1970 Stanford Workshop on Grammar and Semantics*. Dordrecht: Reidel, 121–42.

Montague, Richard, 1974a. Universal Grammar. In Montague (1974b: 122–246).

Montague, Richard, 1974b. *Formal Philosophy: Selected Papers of Richard Montague*, ed. Richmond H. Thomason. New Haven, CT: Yale University Press.

Montanus, Petrus, 1964 [1635]. *De spreeckonst; uitgegeven und ingeleid door W. J. H. Caron*. Groningen: Wolters. [Repr. of *Bericht van een niewe konst, genaemt de spreeckonst...*]

Mora-Marín, David, 2003. The origin of Mayan syllabograms and orthographic conventions. *Written Language and Literacy* 6: 193–238.

Mora-Marín, David, 2010. Consonant deletion, obligatory synharmony, typical suffixing: an explanation of spelling practices in Mayan writing. *Written Language and Literacy* 13: 118–79.

Moran, John H., and Alexander Gode (eds), 1966. *Two Essays on the Origin of Language*. Chicago: University of Chicago Press.

Morison, Stanley, 1973. *A Tally of Types*, ed. Brooke Crutchley. Cambridge: Cambridge University Press.

Morris, Charles W., 1938. *Foundations of the Theory of Signs*. Chicago: University of Chicago Press.

Morris, Charles W., 1946. *Signs, Language and Behavior*. New York: G. Brazilier.

Morris, Desmond, 1977. *Manwatching: A Field Guide to Human Behavior*. New York: Harry N. Abrams.

Morris, Desmond, Peter Collett, Peter Marsh, and Marie O'Shaughnessy, 1979. *Gestures: Their Origins and Distribution*. London: Jonathan Cape.

Morris, Pam (ed.), 1994. *The Bakhtin Reader: Selected Writings of Bakhtin, Medvedev, Voloshinov*. London: Arnold.

Morton, Herbert C., 1994. *The Story of Webster's Third: Philip Gove's Controversial Dictionary and its Critics*. Cambridge: Cambridge University Press.

Moscati, Sabatino (ed.), 1964. *An Introduction to the Comparative Grammar of the Semitic Languages: Phonology and Morphology*. Wiesbaden: Harrassowitz.

Moscoso del Prado Martín, Fermín, Aleksandar Kostić, and R. Harald Baayen, 2004. Putting the bits together: an information-theoretical perspective on morphological processing. *Cognition* 94: 1–18.

Moses, Elbert R., Jr, 1964. *Phonetics: History and Interpretation*. Englewood Cliffs, NJ: Prentice Hall.

Mphande, Lupenga, and Curtis Rice, 1989. Toward a phonological definition of the ideophone in ChiTumbuka. *Colloquium on Ideophones, Twentieth Conference on African Linguistics*, 20 (University of Illinois, Urbana–Champaign).

Muchiki, Yoshiyuki, 1999. *Egyptian Proper Names and Loanwords in North-West Semitic*. Atlanta, GA: Society of Biblical Literature.

Mufwene, Salikoko S., 2001. *The Ecology of Language Evolution*. Cambridge: Cambridge University Press.

Mufwene, Salikoko S., 2005. *Créoles, écologie sociale, évolution linguistique*. Paris: L'Harmattan.

Mufwene, Salikoko S., 2008. *Language Evolution: Contact Competition, and Change*. London: Continuum.

Mufwene, Salikoko S., 2010a. Language as technology: an evolutionary perspective. Paper presented at the Conference on Evolutionary Linguistics 2, Nankai University, Tianjin, China, 30 May–1 June.

Mufwene, Salikoko S., 2010b. 'Protolanguage' and the evolution of linguistic diversity. In Zhongwei Shen et al. (eds), *Festschrift for William Wang*. Shanghai Jiaoyu Chubanshe: Education Press, 183–310.

Mugdan, Joachim, 1984. *Jan Baudouin de Courtenay (1845–1929): Leben und Werk*. Munich: Wilhelm Fink.

Müller, [Friedrich] Max, 1873. Lectures on Mr. Darwin's Philosophy of Language. *Fraser's Magazine* 7: 525–41, 659–78; 8: 1–24. [Repr. in Harris and Pyle (1996: 147–233).]

Müller, [Friedrich] Max, 1880. *Lectures on the Science of Language*, vols 1 and 2. London: Longmans, Green. [1st series 1861, 2nd series 1864. Some lectures repr. in Harris and Pyle (1996: 7–41).]

Müller, Cornelia, 2004. Forms and uses of the palm up open hand: a case of a gesture family? In Müller and Posner (2004: 133–256).

Müller, Cornelia, 2008. *Metaphors Dead and Alive, Sleeping and Waking: A Dynamic Theory*. Chicago: University of Chicago Press.

Müller, Cornelia and Roland Posner (eds), 2004. *The Semantics and Pragmatics of Everyday Gestures: Proceedings of the Berlin Conference, April 1998*. Berlin: Weidler.

Müller, Gottlob Ernst, 1736. *Delineatio grammaticae philosophicae universalis*. Halle: Societas Latina Halensis.

Müller, Hanz-Peter, 1995. Ergative constructions in early Semitic languages. *Journal of Near Eastern Studies* 54: 261–71.

Müller, Wilhelm (ed.), 1889. *Briefe der Brüder Jacob und Wilhelm Grimm an Georg Friedrich Benecke aus den Jahren 1808–1829*. Göttingen: Vandenhoeck & Ruprecht.

Murethach, 1977. *Commentum in Donati Artem maiorem*, ed. Louis Holtz. *Grammatici Hibernici Carolini Aevi. Pars I.* Turnhout: Brepols.

Murphy, Gregory L., 2002. *The Big Book of Concepts.* Cambridge, MA: MIT Press.

Murphy, Gregory L., and Douglas L. Medin, 1985. The role of theories in conceptual coherence. *Psychological Review* 92: 289–316.

Murphy, M. Lynne, 2003. *Semantic Relations and the Lexicon: Antonymy, Synonymy, and Other Paradigms.* Cambridge: Cambridge University Press.

Murray, James A. H., 1900. *The Evolution of English Lexicography.* The Romanes Lecture. Oxford: Clarendon Press.

Murray, Robert W., in press. An history of historical phonology. In Patrick Honeybone and Joseph C. Salmons (eds), *The Handbook of Historical Phonology.* Oxford: Oxford University Press.

Murray, Stephen O., 1998. *American Sociolinguistics: Theory and Theory Groups.* Amsterdam: John Benjamins.

Naïm, Samia, 2009. *L'arabe yéménite de Sanaa.* Leuven: Peeters.

Nakano, Miyoko, 1971. *A Phonological Study in the 'Phags-pa Script and the Meng-ku Tsu-yün.* Canberra: Australian National University Press.

Naumann, Bernd, 1996. Die Tradition der Philosophischen Grammatik in Deutschland. In Peter Schmitter (ed.), *Geschichte der Sprachtheorie 5, Sprachtheorien der Neuzeit II: Von der Grammaire de Port Royal (1660) zur Konstitution moderner linguistischen Disziplinen.* Tübingen: Gunter Narr, 14–43.

Nayeem, Muhammed Abdul, 2001. *Origin of Ancient Writing in Arabia and New Scripts from Oman: An Introduction to South Semitic Epigraphy and Palaeography.* Hyderabad: Hyderabad Publishers.

Nebrija, Antonio de, 1492. *Gramática de la lengua Castellana.* Salamanca [n.p.]

Nerlich, Brigitte, 1990. *Change in Language: Whitney, Bréal, and Wegener.* London: Routledge.

Nerlich, Brigitte, 1992. *Semantic Theories in Europe 1830–1930: From Etymology to Contextuality.* Amsterdam: John Benjamins.

Nerlich, Brigitte, and David D. Clarke, 1996. *Language, Action and Context: The Early History of Pragmatics in Europe and America, 1780–1930.* Amsterdam: John Benjamins.

Nerlich, Brigitte, and David D. Clarke, 2001. Ambiguities we live by: towards a pragmatics of polysemy. *Journal of Pragmatics* 33: 1–20.

Nerlich, Brigitte, and David D. Clarke, 2009. Wilhelm von Humboldt. In Gunther Senft, Jan O. Östman, and Jef Verschueren (eds), *Culture and Language Use.* Amsterdam: John Benjamins, 173–83.

Nevalainen, Terttu, Irma Taavitsainen, Päivi Pahta, and Minna Korhonen, 2008. *The Dynamics of Linguistic Variation: Corpus Evidence on English Past and Present.* Amsterdam: John Benjamins.

Nevins, John B., 1895. *The Sign Language of the Deaf and Dumb.* Liverpool: Literary and Philosophical Society of Liverpool.

Newman, Stanley S., 1933. Further experiments in phonetic symbolism. *American Journal of Psychology* 45: 53–75.

Newman, Stanley S., 1944. *Yokuts Language of California.* New York: Viking Fund Publications in Anthropology.

Newmeyer, Frederick (Fritz) J., 1986. *Linguistic Theory in America: The First Quarter Century of Transformational Generative Grammar.* New York: Academic Press. [1st edn 1980.]

Newmeyer, Fritz J., 1998a. *Language Form and Language Function*. Cambridge, MA: MIT Press.

Newmeyer, Fritz J., 1998b. The irrelevance of typology for grammatical theory. *Syntaxis* 1: 161–97.

Newmeyer, Fritz J., 2002. Optimality and functionality: a critique of functionally-based optimality-theoretic syntax. *Natural Language and Linguistic Theory* 20: 43–80

Newmeyer, Fritz J., 2003. Grammar is grammar and usage is usage. *Language* 79: 682–707.

Nichols, Johanna, 1984. Functional theories of grammar. *Annual Review of Anthropology* 13: 97–117.

Nickau, Klaus, 1977. *Untersuchungen zur textkritischen Methode des Zenodotos von Ephesos*. Berlin: de Gruyter.

Nickel, Gerhard, and James C. Stalker (eds), 1986. *Problems of Standardization and Linguistic Variation in Present-Day English*. Heidelberg: Julius Groos.

Nida, Eugene A., 1964. *Toward a Science of Translating: with special reference to principles and procedures involved in Bible translation*. Leiden: E. J. Brill.

Nida, Eugene A., 1975. *Componential Analysis of Meaning*. The Hague: Mouton.

Niebuhr, Carsten, 1772. *Beschreibung von Arabien*. Copenhagen: N. Möller.

Nikolaidis, Katerina, 2005. IPA news. *Journal of the International Phonetic Association* 35: 261.

Nirenburg, Sergei, Harold Somers, and Yorick Wilks (eds), 2003. *Readings in Machine Translation*. Cambridge, MA: MIT Press.

Nivre, Joakim, Johan Hall, Jens Nilsson, et al., 2007. MaltParser: a language-independent system for data-driven dependency parsing. *Natural Language Engineering* 13: 95–135.

Nodier, Charles, 1834. *Notions élémentaires de linguistique*. Paris: Renduel.

Nodier, Charles, 1984 [1808]. *Dictionnaire raisonnée des onomatopées françaises*. Mauvezin: Trans-Europ-Repress.

Nolan, Francis J., 1994. Auditory and acoustic analysis in speaker recognition. In John Gibbons (ed.), *Language and the Law*. London: Longman, 319–45.

Nolan, Francis J., John H. Esling, et al. (eds), 1999. *Handbook of the International Phonetic Association: A Guide to the Use of the International Phonetic Alphabet*. Cambridge: Cambridge University Press.

Nöldeke, Theodor, 1887. *Die semitischen Sprachen. Eine Skizze*. Leipzig: Weigel.

Nöldeke, Theodor, 1906. *Orientalische Studien Theodor Nöldeke zum siebzigsten Geburtstag (2. März 1906) gewidmet von Freunden und Schülern und in Ihrem Auftrag herausgegeben von Carl Bezold*. Gieszen: A. Töpelmann.

Nöldeke, Theodor, 1909–38. *Geschichte des Qorāns*, 2nd edn by Friedrich Schwally, Gotthelf Bergsträsser, and Otto Pretzl. Indices by Anneliese Gottschalk-Baur. Leipzig: Dieterich. [3rd repr. Hildesheim: Olms, 2000.]

Nöldeke, Theodor, 2001 [1904]. *Compendious Syriac Grammar*, 2nd edn., transl. James A. Crichton. Winona Lake, IN: Eisenbrauns.

Nord, Christiane, 1997. *Translation as Purposeful Activity: Functionalist Approaches Explained*. Manchester: St Jerome.

Norman, Jerry, 1988. *Chinese*. Cambridge: Cambridge University Press.

Norvig, Peter, 2007. Theorizing from data: avoiding the capital mistake. Presentation, Google Developer Day. www.youtube.com/watch?v=nU8DcBF-qo4

Nougayrol, Jean, 1968. Textes suméro-accadiens des archives et bibliothèques privées d'Ugarit. In Claude F. A. Schaeffer (ed.), *Ugaritica V*. Paris: Imprimerie Nationale and Librairie Orientaliste Paul Geuthner, 1–446.

Nowak, Elke, 2006. Missionary linguistics. In Keith Brown (ed.), *Encyclopedia of Language and Linguistics*, 2nd edn, vol. 8. London: Elsevier, 167–70.

Nuchelmans, Gabriel, 1973. *Theories of the Proposition: Ancient and Medieval Conceptions of the Bearers of Truth and Falsity*. Amsterdam: North-Holland.

Nuchelmans, Gabriel, 1980. *Late-Scholastic and Humanist Theories of the Proposition*. Amsterdam: North-Holland.

Nuchelmans, Gabriel, 1983. *Judgment and Proposition: From Descartes to Kant*. Amsterdam: North-Holland.

Nuyts, Jan, 1992. *Aspects of a Cognitive-Pragmatic Theory of Language*. Amsterdam: John Benjamins.

Nuyts, Jan, 2001. *Epistemic Modality, Language and Conceptualization: A Cognitive-Pragmatic Perspective*. Amsterdam: John Benjamins.

Nuyts, Jan, 2005. Brothers in arms? On the relation between cognitive ad functional linguistics. In Francisco Ruiz de Mendoza and Sandra Pena (eds), *Cognitive Linguistics: Internal Dynamics and Interdisciplinary Interaction*. Berlin: Mouton, 69–100.

Nuyts, Jan, 2007. Cognitive linguistics and functional linguistics. In Geeraerts and Cuyckens (2007: 543–65).

Nuyts, Jan, 2008. Pattern versus process concepts of grammar and mind: a cognitive-functional perspective. *Jezikoslovije* 9(2): 87–107.

Nuyts, Jan, 2011. Pattern versus process concepts of grammar and mind: a cognitive-functional perspective. In Mario Brdar, Stefan Th. Gries, and Žic Fuchs (eds), *Cognitive Linguistic Converaence and Expansion*. Amsterdam, John Benjamins, 47–66.

Nyrop, Kristoffer, 1901–34. *Ordenes liv*. Copenhagen: Gyldendalske Boghandel Nordisk Forlag.

Nyrop, Kristoffer, 1913. *Grammaire historique de la langue française IV: Sémantique*. Copenhagen: Gyldendalske Boghandel Nordisk Forlag.

O'Connor, Michael, 1983. Writing systems, native speaker analyses, and the earliest stages of northwest Semitic orthography. In Carol L. Meyers and Michael O'Connor (eds), *The Word of the Lord Shall Go Forth: Essays in Honor of David Noel Freedman in Celebration of His Sixtieth Birthday*. Winona Lake, IN: Eisenbrauns, 439–65.

O'Halloran, Kay, 2005. *Mathematical Discourse: Language, Symbolism and Visual Images*. London: Continuum.

O'Toole, Michael, 1994. *The Language of Displayed Art*. London: Leicester University Press.

Ochs Keenan, Elinor, 1976. On the universality of conversational implicatures. *Language in Society* 5: 67–80.

Ockham, William, 1974. *Ockham's Theory of Terms: Part I of the Summa Logicae*, transl. Michael J. Loux. South Bend, IN: Notre Dame University Press.

Ockham, William, 1980. *Ockham's Theory of Propositions: Part II of the Summa Logicae*, transl. Alfred J. Freddoso and Henry Schuurman. South Bend, IN: Notre Dame University Press.

Odling-Smee, F. John, Kevin N. Laland, and Marcus W. Feldman, 2003. *Niche Construction: The Neglected Process In Evolution*. Princeton, NJ: Princeton University Press.

Oertel, Hans, 1902. *Lectures on the Study of Language*. New York: Charles Scribner's Sons.

Ogden, Charles K., and Ivor A. Richards, 1923. *The Meaning of Meaning: A Study of the Influence of Language upon Thought and the Science of Symbolism*. London: Kegan Paul.

Ogden, Richard, 1999. A syllable-level feature in Finnish. In Harry van der Hulst and Nancy A. Ritter (eds), *The Syllable: Views and Facts*. Berlin: Mouton de Gruyter, 651–72.

Ohala, John J., 1993. The phonetics of sound change. In Charles Jones (ed.), *Historical Linguistics: Problems and Perspectives*. London: Longman, 137–278.

Ohala, John J., 2003. Phonetics and historical phonology. In Joseph and Janda (2003: 669–86).

Ohala, John J., 2004. Phonetics and phonology then, and then, and now. In H. Quene and V. van Heuven (eds), *On Speech and Language: Studies for Sieb G. Nooteboom*. Utrecht: LOT, 133–40.

Ohala, John J., 2010. The relation between phonetics and phonology. In William J. Hardcastle, John Laver, and Fiona E. Gibbon (eds), *The Handbook of Phonetic Sciences*, 2nd edn. Oxford: Blackwell, 653–77.

Ohala, John J., 2011. Hermann Grassmann: his contributions to historical linguistics and speech acoustics. In Hans-Joachim Petsche, Albert C. Lewis, Jörg Liesen, and Steve Russ (eds), *Hermann Graßmann: From Past to Future*. Berlin: Springer, 345–52.

Ohala, John J., Arthur J. Bronstein, M. Grazia Busà, Julie A. Lewis, and William F. Weigel (eds), 1999. *A Guide to the History of the Phonetic Sciences in the United States*. Berkeley: University of California Press.

Ohmann, Suzanne, 1951a. Theories of the 'linguistic field'. *Word* 9: 123–34.

Ohmann, Suzanne, 1951b. *Wortinhalt und Weltbild: Vergleichende und methodologische Studien zu Bedeutungslehre und Wortfeldtheorie*. Stockholm: Norstedt.

Ojeda, Almerindo E., 1987. Discontinuity and phrase structure grammar. In Alexis Manaster-Ramer (ed.), *The Mathematics of Language*. Amsterdam: John Benjamins, 157–275.

Olazaran, Mikel, 1996. A sociological study of the official history of the perceptrons controversy. *Social Studies of Science* 26: 611–59.

Oliver, Mary, 1994. *A Poetry Handbook*. New York: Harcourt Brace.

Olson, Kenneth S, and John Hajek, 1999. The phonetic status of the labial flap. *Journal of the International Phonetic Association* 29: 101–14.

Omdal, Helge, and Rune Røsstad (eds), 2009. *Språknormering: i tide og utide?* Oslo: Novus.

Orel, V. E., and O. V. Stolbova, 1995. *Hamito-Semitic Etymological Dictionary: Materials for a Reconstruction*. Leiden: E. J. Brill.

Osgood, Charles E., and Thomas A. Sebeok, 1954. Psycholinguistics: a survey of theory and research problems. *Journal of Abnormal and Social Psychology*, Supplement 49. [Repr. Indiana University Press, 1965.]

Osthoff, Hermann, and Karl Brugmann, 1878. Preface to morphological investigations in the sphere of the Indo-European languages. In *Morphologische Untersuchungen auf dem Gebiete der indogermanischen Sprachen* I. Leipzig: S. Hirzel.

Oudeyer, Pierre-Yves, 2006. *Self-Organization in the Evolution of Speech*, transl. James Hurford. Oxford: Oxford University Press.

Owens, Jonathan, 1988. *The Foundations of Grammar: An Introduction to Medieval Arabic Grammatical Theory*. Amsterdam: John Benjamins.

Padden, Carol, 1988. *Interaction of Morphology and Syntax in American Sign Language*. New York: Garland.

Padley, George A., 1976. *Grammatical Theory in Western Europe 1500–1700: The Latin Tradition*. Cambridge: Cambridge University Press.

Padley, George A., 1985. *Grammatical Theory in Western Europe 1500–1700: Trends in Vernacular Grammar I*. Cambridge: Cambridge University Press

Padley, George A., 1988. *Grammatical Theory in Western Europe 1500–1700: Trends in Vernacular Grammar II*. Cambridge: Cambridge University Press.

Palmer, Frank R. (ed.), 1970. *Prosodic Analysis*. London: Oxford University Press.

Palmer, Harold E., 1933. *Second Interim Report on English Collocations*. Tokyo: Institute for Research in English Teaching.

Palmer, Martha, Daniel Gildea, and Nianwen Xue, 2010. *Semantic Role Labeling*. San Rafael, CA: Morgan & Claypool.

Palsgrave, John, 1530. *Lesclarcissement de la langue françoyse*. London: Richard Pynson. [Facsimile repr. Menston: Scolar Press, 1969.]

Panconcelli-Calzia, Giulio, 1921. *Experimentelle Phonetik*. Berlin: de Gruyter.

Panconcelli-Calzia, Giulio, 1957. Earlier history of phonetics. In Louise Kaiser (ed.), *Manual of Phonetics*. Amsterdam: North-Holland, 6–19.

Panconcelli-Calzia, Giulio, 1994 [1941]. *Geschichtszahlen der Phonetik and Quellenatlas der Phonetik. New edition with an English Introduction by Konrad Koerner*. Amsterdam: John Benjamins.

Pang, Bo, and Lillian Lee, 2008. *Opinion Mining and Sentiment Analysis*. Boston: NOW. [Originally published in *Foundations and Trends in Information Retrieval* 2 (2008): 1–135.]

Panther, Klaus-Uwe, and Günter Radden (eds), 1999. *Metonymy in Language and Thought*. Amsterdam: John Benjamins.

Panther, Klaus-Uwe, and Linda Thornburg (eds), 2003. *Metonymy and Pragmatic Inferencing*. Amsterdam: John Benjamins.

Pap, Arthur, 1958. *Semantics and Necessary Truth: An Inquiry into the Foundations of Analytic Philosophy*. New Haven, CT: Yale University Press.

Papp, Ferenc, 1966. *Mathematical Linguistics in the Soviet Union*. The Hague: Mouton.

Paradis, Carole, and Darlene LaCharité (eds), 1993. Constraint-based theories in multilinear phonology. *Canadian Journal of Linguistics* 38(2): 127–53.

Pareschi, Remo, and Mark Steedman, 1987. A lazy way to chart-parse with categorial grammars. *Proceedings of the 25th Annual Meeting of the Association for Computational Linguistics* (Stanford), 81–8.

Paris, Gaston, 1887. La vie des mots. *Journal des Savants* 52: 65–77, 149–56, 241–9.

Parkes, Malcolm B., 1993. *Pause and Effect: Punctuation in the West*. Berkeley: University of California Press.

Parpola, Asko, 1994. *Deciphering the Indus Script*. Cambridge: Cambridge University Press.

Parret, Herman, 1976. Le débat de la psychologie et de la logique concernant le langage: Marty et Husserl. In Herman Parret (ed.), *History of Linguistic Thought and Contemporary Linguistics*. Berlin: de Gruyter, 732–71.

Passalacqua, Marina, 1987. *Prisciani Caesariensis Opuscula, I: De figuris numerorum, De metris fabularum Terenti, Praeexercitamina*. Rome: Edizioni di storia e letteratura.

Passalacqua, Marina, 1999. *Prisciani Caesariensis Opuscula, II: Institutio de nomine et pronomine et verbo, Partitiones Duodecim Versuum Aeneidos Principalium*. Rome: Edizioni di storia e letteratura.

Patel, Purushottam G., 2007. Akṣara as a linguistic unit in Brāhmī scripts. In P. G. Patel, P. Pandey, and D. Rajgor (eds), *The Indic Scripts: Palaeographic and Linguistic Perspectives*. New Delhi: D. K. Printworld, 167–213.

Patterson, D., and Cynthia M. Connine, 2001. Variant frequency in flap production: a corpus analysis of variant frequency in American English flap production. *Phonetica* 58: 254–75.

Patterson, Francine G., 1978. The gestures of a gorilla: language acquisition in another pongid. *Brain and Language* 5: 72–97.

Paul, Hermann, 1880. *Prinzipien der Sprachgeschichte*. Halle: Niemeyer. [5th edn 1920.]

Paul, Hermann, 1897. *Deutsches Wörterbuch*. Halle: Max Niemeyer.

Paul, Hermann, and Walther Mitzka, 1960. *Mittelhochdeutsche Grammatik*. Tübingen: Max Niemeyer. [1st edn 1881.]

Paulston, Christina B., and Richard G. Tucker (eds), 1997. *The Early Days of Sociolinguistics: Memories and Reflections*. Dallas, TX: Summer Institute of Linguistics.

Payrató, Lluis, 2008. Past, present and future research on emblems in the Hispanic tradition: preliminary and methodological considerations. *Gesture* 8: 5–21.

Pedersen, Holger, 1903. Türkische Lautgesetze. *Zeitschrift der Deutschen Morgenländischen Gesellschaft* 57: 535–61.

Pedersen, Holger, 1931a. *The Discovery of Language: Linguistic Science in the Nineteenth Century*. Bloomington: Indiana University Press.

Pedersen, Holger, 1931b. *Linguistic Science in the Nineteenth Century: Methods and Results*, transl. from the Danish by John Webster Spargo. Cambridge, MA: Harvard University Press. [English translation of Danish original, 1924. Reprinted as Pedersen (1959).]

Pedersen, Holger, 1959 [1924]. *The Discovery of Language: Linguistic Science in the Nineteenth Century*, trans. John W. Spargo. Bloomington: Indiana University Press. [Paperback edn 1962. First published in Danish in 1924; published as Pedersen 1931b.]

Peeters, Bert, 2001. Does Cognitive Linguistics live up to its name? In René Dirven, Bruce W. Hawkins, and Esra Sandikcioglu (eds), *Language and Ideology: Theoretical Cognitive Approaches*. Amsterdam: John Benjamins, 83–106

Peirce, Charles S., 1905. Truth, falsity, and error. Repr. in Charles Hartshorne and Paul Weiss (eds), *Collected Papers of Charles Sanders Peirce*, vol. 5: *Pragmatism and Pragmaticism* (Cambridge, MA: Harvard University Press, 1934), 565–73.

Peirce, Charles S., 1931. *Collected Papers of Charles Sanders Peirce*. 8 vols. Cambridge, MA: Harvard University Press. [Repr. 1960.]

Peirce, Charles S., 1932a. What pragmatism is. In Charles Hartshorne and Paul Weiss (eds), *Collected Papers of Charles Sanders Peirce*, vol. 5: *Pragmatism and Pragmaticism* (Cambridge, MA: Harvard University Press, 1934): 411–37. [Originally in *The Monist* 15 (April 1905): 161–81.]

Peirce, Charles S., 1932b. Pragmatic; Pragmatism. In Charles Hartshorne and Paul Weiss (eds), *Collected Papers of Charles Sanders Peirce*, vol. 5: *Pragmatism and Pragmaticism* (Cambridge, MA: Harvard University Press, 1934): 1–4.

Penn, Gerald, 2012. Computational Linguistics. In Ruth Kempson, Nicholas Asher, and Tim Fernando (eds), *Handbook of the Philosophy of Science*, vol. 14: *Philosophy of Linguistics*. Oxford: Elsevier, 143–73.

Pepperberg, Irene M., 2000. *The Alex Studies: Cognitive and Communicative Abilities of Grey Parrots*. Cambridge, MA: Harvard University Press.

Percival, Keith, 1975. The grammatical tradition and the rise of the vernaculars. In Thomas A. Sebeok (ed.), *Historiography of Linguistics*. The Hague: Mouton, 131–275.

Pereira, Fernando C. N., 2002. Formal grammar and information theory: together again? In Bruce E. Nevin and Stephen B. Johnson (eds), *The Legacy of Zellig Harris: Language and Information into the 20th Century*, vol. 2: *Mathematics and computability of language*. Amsterdam: John Benjamins, 13–32.

Pereira, Fernando C. N., and Stuart M. Shieber, 1987. *Prolog and Natural-Language Analysis*. Stanford, CA: CSLI.

Pereira, Fernando C. N., and David H. D. Warren, 1980. Definite clause grammars for language analysis: a survey of the formalism and a comparison with Augmented Transition Networks. *Artificial Intelligence* 13: 231–78.

Pereira, Fernando C. N., and David H. D. Warren, 1983. Parsing as deduction. *Proceedings of the 21st Annual Meeting of the Association for Computational Linguistics* (Cambridge, MA), 137–44.

Perry, Thomas A. (ed.), 1980. *Evidence and Argumentation in Linguistics*. Berlin: de Gruyter.

Peter of Pisa. *Ars*. Excerpts in Keil (1961: viii. 161–71).

Péterfalvi, Jean-Michel, 1965. Les recherches expérimentales sur le symbolisme phonétique. *L'Année psychologique* 65: 439–74. [Repr. 1970, Paris: CNRS.]

Petrus Montanus. 1635. *Bericht van een niewe konst, genaemt de spreeckonst, ontdect ende beschreeven door Petrus Montanus van Delft: waer in verhandelt ende in't licht gebracht wort, den rechten en tot nuu toe verborgen aert van alle uitspraec: als met naemen, vande oude ende veel niewe letteren, vande woordleeden, woorden, reedensneen, reedenleeden, ende reedenen*. Delft: Ian Pietersz Waalpot.

Pettinato, Giovanni, 1982. *Testi lessicali bilingui della biblioteca L. 2769*. Naples: Istituto universitario orientale di Napoli.

Philippe, J. 1893. L'audition colorée des aveugles. *Revue scientifique* 1: 806–9.

Philo Judaeus, 1898. De congressu eruditionis gratia. In Leopoldus Cohn and Paulus Wendland (eds), *Philonis Alexandrini Opera quae supersunt*, vol. 3. Berolini: Georgii Reimeri, 72–109.

Phocas. *Ars de nomine et verbo*. In Keil (1961: v. 410–39).

Piamenta, Moshe, 1990–1. *Dictionary of Post-Classical Yemeni Arabic*. Leiden: E. J. Brill.

Piattelli-Palmarini, Massimo (ed.), 1980. *Language and Learning: The Debate between Jean Piaget and Noam Chomsky*. London: Routledge & Kegan Paul.

Pickering, John, 1820. *An Essay on a Uniform Orthography for the Indian Languages of North America: as published in the Memoirs of the American Academy of Arts and Sciences*. Cambridge [MA]: Univ[ersity] Press–Hilliard and Metcalf.

Pike, Kenneth L., 1943. *Phonetics: A Critical Analysis of Phonetic Theory and a Technic for the Practical Description of Sounds*. Ann Arbor: University of Michigan Press.

Pike, Kenneth L., 1943. Taxemes and immediate constituents. *Language* 19: 65–82.

Pike, Kenneth L., 1947a. *Phonemics: A Technique for Reducing Languages to Writing*. Ann Arbor: University of Michigan.

Pike, Kenneth L., 1947b. *Tone Languages*. Ann Arbor: University of Michigan Press.

Pike, Kenneth L., 1966. A guide to publications related to tagmemic theory. In Thomas A. Sebeok (ed.), *Current Trends in Linguistics 3*. The Hague: Mouton, 365–94.

Pike, Kenneth L., 1967. *Language in Relation to a Universal Theory of the Structure of Human Behavior*. The Hague: Mouton

Pike, Kenneth L., and Eunice Pike, 1947. Immediate constituents of Mazatec syllables. *International Journal of American Linguistics* 13: 78–91.

Pinborg, Jan, 1967. *Die Entwicklung der Sprachtheorie im Mittelalter: Beiträge zur Geschichte der Philosophie und Theologie des Mittelalters*. Band XLII, Heft 2. Münster: Aschendorff.

Pinborg, Jan, 1975. Classical Antiquity: Greece. In Thomas A. Sebeok (ed.), *Historiography of Linguistics*. The Hague: Mouton, 69–126.

Pinker, Steven, and Paul Bloom, 1990. Natural language and natural selection. *Behavioral and Brain Sciences* 13: 707–84.

Pinsky, Robert, 1999. *The Sounds of Poetry*. New York: Farrar, Straus & Giroux.

Plato, 1926. *Cratylus*. Cambridge, MA: Harvard University Press.

Plato, 1961. *Plato, the Collected Dialogues*, ed. Edith Hamilton and Huntington Cairns. Princeton, NJ: Princeton University Press.

Plato, 1987. *Theaetetus*, transl. with an essay by Robin A. H. Waterfield. Harmondsworth: Penguin.

Poeppel, David, and David Embick, 2005. Defining the relation between linguistics and neuroscience. In Anne Cutler (ed.), *Twenty-First Century Psycholinguistics: Four Corner-stones*. Mahwah, NJ: Lawrence Erlbaum, 103–18.

Poizner, Howard, Edward Klima, and Ursula Bellugi, 1987. *What the Hands Reveal About the Brain*. Cambridge, MA: MIT Press.

Poldervaart, Arie, 1989. Proto Uto-Aztecan subanalysis, Part III: Phoneme meanings. Informal notes, Friends of Uto-Aztecan Conference. Unpublished.

Pollard, Carl J., 1984. Generalized phrase structure grammars, head grammars and natural language. Ph.D thesis, Stanford University.

Pollard, Carl J., and Ivan A. Sag, 1987. *Information-Based Syntax and Semantics*, vol. 1: *Fundamentals*. Stanford, CA: CSLI.

Pollard, Carl J., and Ivan A. Sag., 1994. *Head-Driven Phrase Structure Grammar*. Chicago: University of Chicago Press.

Pollmann, Karla, 2009. Exegesis without end: forms, methods, and functions of Biblical commentaries. In Philip Rousseau (ed.), *A Companion to Late Antiquity*. Oxford: Oxford University Press, 158–269.

Pollock, Ethan, 2006. *Stalin and the Soviet Science Wars*. Princeton, NJ: Princeton University Press.

Pompeius. *Commentum Artis Donati*. In Keil (1961: v. 95–312).

Pompino-Marschall, Berndt, 1995. *Einführung in die Phonetik*. Berlin: de Gruyter.

Poppe, Erich, 1999. Latinate terminology in *Auraicept na nÉces*. In David Cram, Andrew Linn, and Elke Nowak (eds), *History of Linguistics*, vol. 1. Amsterdam: John Benjamins, 191–201.

Porter, David W., 2002. *Excerptiones de Prisciano: The Source for Ælfric's Latin–Old English Grammar*. Cambridge: D. S. Brewer.

Porzig, Walter, 1934. Wesenhafte Bedeutungsbeziehungen. *Beiträge zur Geschichte der deutschen Sprache und Literatur* 58: 70–97.

Poser, William J., 1992. The structural typology of phonological writing. Paper presented at the annual meeting of the Linguistic Society of America, Philadelphia.

Post, Emil L., 1943. Formal reductions of the general combinatorial decision problem. *American Journal of Mathematics* 65: 197–215.

Post, Emil L., 1944. Recursively enumerable sets of positive integers and their decision problems. *Bulletin of the American Mathematical Society* 50: 284–316.

Post, Emil L., 1946. A variant of a recursively unsolvable problem. *Bulletin of the American Mathematical Society* 52: 264–8.

Post, Emil L., 1947. Recursive unsolvability of a problem of Thue. *Journal of Symbolic Logic* 12: 1–11.

Potter, Ralph K, George A. Kopp, and Harriet C. Green, 1947. *Visible Speech*. New York: D. Van Nostrand.

Pottier, Bernard, 1964. Vers une sémantique moderne. *Travaux de linguistique et de littérature* 2: 107–37.

Pottier, Bernard, 1965. La définition sémantique dans les dictionnaires. *Travaux de linguistique et de littérature* 3: 33–9.

Price, Cathy J., 2010. The anatomy of language: a review of 100 fMRI studies published in 2009. *Annals of the New York Academy of Sciences* 1191: 62–88.

Priestley, Joseph, 1762. *A Course of Lectures on the Theory of Language and Universal Grammar*. Warrington: W. Eyres.

Prince, Ellen, 1981. Towards a taxonomy of given/new information. In Peter Cole (ed.), *Radical Pragmatics*. New York: Academic Press, 223–55.

Priscianus. *Institutiones Grammaticae*, ed. Martin Hertz. Leipzig: Teubner, 1855–9. [Repr. in Keil (1961: ii.1–597; iii. 1–377).]

Priscianus, 1999. *Prisciani Caesariensis opuscula. Institutio de nomine et pronomine et verbo. Partitiones duodecim versuum Aeneidos principalium*. Rome: Edizioni di storia e letteratura.

Prokofieva, Larissa, 1995. *The Color Symbolism of Sounds as a Component of Individual Style of Poets (on the material of A. Block, K. Balmont, A. Bely, V. Nabokov)*. Saratov: Saratov State University.

Propp, Vladimir, 1968. *Morphology of the Folktale*, 2nd edn. Austin: University of Texas Press. [Transl. from the Russian original of 1928.]

Pu Zhizhen 濮之珍, 1990. *Zhōngguó Yǔyánxué Shǐ* 中國語言學史 [History of Chinese Linguistics]. Taipei: Bookman. [Repr. of Shanghai Guji Publishers, 1987 edn.]

Pulleyblank, Edwin G., 1994. Phonetics, East Asian: history. In Ronald E. Asher and James M. Y. Simpson (eds), *The Encyclopedia of Language and Linguistics*. Oxford: Pergamon, 3095–9.

Pullum, Geoffrey K., and Barbara C. Scholz, 2002. Empirical assessment of stimulus poverty arguments. *Linguistic Review* 19: 9–50.

Pulvermüller, Friedemann, 2005. Brain mechanisms linking language and action. *Nature Reviews Neuroscience* 6: 576–82.

Pustejovsky, James, 1995. *The Generative Lexicon*. Cambridge, MA: MIT Press.

Putnam, Hilary, 1975. The meaning of meaning. In Hilary Putnam (ed.), *Mind, Language and Reality: Philosophical Papers II*. Cambridge: Cambridge University Press, 115–271.

Putnam, Hilary, 1981. *Reason, Truth and History*. Cambridge: Cambridge University Press.

Qin Huifang 秦慧芳, 2011. *Lǎo Guóyīn Yánjiù: Yǐ Wáng Pú 'Guóyīn Jīngyīn Duìzhàobiǎo' Wéi Zhōngxīn* 老國音研究：以王璞《國音京音對照表》為中心. [A Study of the Phonetic System of the Early National Language, with a Focus on Wang Pu's Comparative Table of the National Language System and the Beijing dialect]. MA thesis, National Pingtung Normal University, Taiwan. www.360doc.com/relevant/22696358_more.shtml

Quadri, Bruno, 1952. *Aufgaben und Methoden der onomasiologischen Forschung: eine entwicklungsgeschichtliche Darstellung*. Bern: Francke.

Quay, Suzanne, 1998. Monastic sign language in the Far East. Paper presented to the Sociolinguistics Symposium 12 (London, March).

Quilis, Antonio, and Hans-J. Niederehe (eds), 1986. *The History of Linguistics in Spain*. Amsterdam: John Benjamins.

Quine, Willard V. O., 1953. *From a Logical Point of View*. Cambridge, MA: Harvard University Press.

Quine, Willard V. O, 1958. Speaking of objects. *Proceedings and Addresses of the American Philosophical Association* 31: 5–22. [Repr. in *Ontological Relativity and Other Essays* (New York: Columbia University Press, 1969), 1–25.]

Quine, Willard V. O., 1959. Meaning and translation. In Reuben A. Brower (ed.), *On Translation*. Cambridge, MA: Harvard University Press, 148–73.

Quine, Willard V. O., 1960. *Word and Object*. Cambridge, MA: MIT Press.

Quirk, Randolph, Sidney Greenbaum, Geoffrey Leech, and Jan Svartvik, 1972. *A Grammar of Contemporary English*. London: Longman.

Quirk, Randolph, Sidney Greenbaum, Geoffrey Leech and Jan Svartvik, 1985. *A Comprehensive Grammar of the English Language*. London: Longman.

Rabin, Chaim, 1951. *Ancient West-Arabian: A Study of the Dialects of the Western Highlands of Arabia in the Sixth and Seventh Centuries A.D.* London: Taylor.

Radwańska-Williams, Joanna, 1993. *A Paradigm Lost: The Linguistic Theory of Mikolaj Kruszewski.* Amsterdam: John Benjamins.

Ramachandran, V. S., and Sandra Blakeslee, 1998. *Phantoms in the Brain.* New York: HarperCollins.

Rapp, Karl M., 1836. *Versuch einer Physiologie der Sprache,* 1: *Die vergleichende Grammatik als Naturlehre dargestellt.* Stuttgart: Cotta.

Raschellà, Fabrizio D., 1982. *The So-Called Second Grammatical Treatise: An Orthographic Pattern of Late Thirteenth-century Icelandic.* Florence: F. Le Monnier.

Rask, Rasmus K., 1811. *Vejledning til det islandske eller gamle nordiske sprog* [Introduction to the Grammar of the Icelandic and the Ancient Nordic Language]. Copenhagen: Schubothes Forlag.

Rask, Rasmus K., 1818. *Undersögelse om det gamle Nordiske eller Islandske Sprogs Oprindelse* [Investigation of the Origin of the Old Norse or Icelandic Language]. Copenhagen: Gyldendalske Boghandlings Forlag.

Rastier, François, 2001. *Arts et sciences du texte.* Paris: Presses universitaires de France.

Ratnaparkhi, Adwait, 1996. A maximum entropy model for part-of-speech tagging. *Proceedings of the Conference on Empirical Methods in Natural Language Processing* (Philadelphia), 133–42.

Ray, Punya Sloka, 1963. *Language Standardization: Studies in Prescriptive Linguistics.* The Hague: Mouton.

Reape, Mike, 1996. Getting things in order. In Harry Bunt and Arthur van Horck (eds), *Discontinuous Constituency.* Berlin: Mouton de Gruyter, 109–254.

Rée, Jonathan, 1999. *I See a Voice: Language, Deafness and the Senses: A Philosophical History.* London: HarperCollins.

Reichenbach, Hans, 1947. *Elements of Symbolic Logic.* New York: Free Press.

Reinecke, John, 1937. Marginal languages: a sociological survey of the creole languages and trade jargons. Ph.D dissertation, Yale University.

Reiner, Erica, 1966. *A Linguistic Analysis of Akkadian.* The Hague: Mouton.

Reiner, Erica, 2000. The Sumerian and Akkadian linguistic tradition. In Auroux et al., vol. 1 (2000: 1–5).

Reinhart, Tanya, 1983. *Anaphora and Semantic Interpretation.* London: Croom Helm.

Reisig, Karl, 1839. *Vorlesungen über die lateinische Sprachwissenschaft (abgehalten ab 1825).* Leipzig: Lehnhold.

Reisigl, Martin, and Ruth Wodak, 2009. The discourse-historical approach. In Ruth Wodak and Michael Meyer (eds), *Methods of Critical Discourse Analysis.* London: Sage, 87–121.

Reiss, Katerina, and Hans J. Vermeer, 1984. *Grundlegung einer allgemeine Translationstheorie.* Tübingen: Niemeyer.

Reiter, Ehud, 2007. The shrinking horizons of computational linguistics. *Computational Linguistics* 33: 283–7.

Remigius, Schleswig, 1982 [1486]. *A Latin Grammar in Facsimile Edition with a Postscript by Jan Pinborg.* Copenhagen: Munksgaard.

Remigius of Auxerre, 1902. *In Artem Donati minorem commentum,* ed.W. Fox. Leipzig: Teubner.

Remijsen, Bert, and Vincent van Heuven, 2005. Stress, tone and discourse prominence in the Curaçao dialect of Papiamentu. *Phonology* 22: 205–35.

Remmius Palaemon. *Ars.* Keil (1961: v. 533–47).

Renkema, Jan, 1993. *Discourse Studies: An Introductory Textbook*. Amsterdam: John Benjamins.

Rhodes, Richard A., and John M. Lawler, 1981. Athematic metaphors. *Papers from the 17th Annual Meeting of the Chicago Linguistics Society*. Chicago: Chicago Linguistics Society, 318–42.

Ricento, Thomas, 2000. Historical and theoretical perspectives in language policy and planning. *Journal of Sociolinguistics* 4: 196–213.

Richards, Ivor A., 1936. *The Philosophy of Rhetoric*. Oxford: Oxford University Press.

Richens, Richard H., 1958. Interlingual machine translation. *Computer Journal* 1: 144–7.

Richens, Richard H., and A. Donald Booth, 1955. Some methods of mechanized translation. In William N. Locke and A. Donald Booth (eds), *Machine Translation of Languages*. Cambridge, MA: MIT Press, 14–46.

Richerson, Peter J., and Robert Boyd, 2005. *Not By Genes Alone: How Culture Transformed Human Evolution*. Chicago: University of Chicago Press.

Ricken, Ulrich, 1976. Die Kontroverse Du Marsais und Beauzée gegen Batteux, Condillac und Diderot: ein Kapitel der Auseinandersetzung zwischen Sensualismus und Rationalismus in der Sprachdiskussion der Aufklärung. In Herman Parret (ed.), *History of Linguistic Thought and Contemporary Linguistics*, Berlin: de Gruyter, 460–87.

Rijkhoff, Jan, 2002. *The Noun Phrase*. Oxford: Oxford University Press.

Rilly, Claude, 2010. *Le méroïtique et sa famille linguistique*. Leuven: Peeters.

Roberts, David, 2011. A tone orthography typology. *Written Language and Literacy* 14: 82–108.

Robins, Robert H., 1953. *Ancient and Medieval Grammatical Theory in Europe*. London: G. Bell.

Robins, Robert H., 1957. Dionysius Thrax and the Western grammatical tradition. *Transactions of the Philological Society*. London, 67–106. [Repr. in Robins (1970: 113–54).]

Robins, Robert H., 1959. In defence of WP. *Transactions of the Philological Society*. London, 116–144. [Repr. in *Transactions of the Philological Society* 99 (2001), 116–44.]

Robins, Robert H., 1967. *A Short History of Linguistics*. London: Longmans, Green.

Robins, Robert H., 1970. *Diversions of Bloomsbury: Selected Writings on Linguistics*. London: North-Holland.

Robins, Robert H., 1978. The Neogrammarians and their nineteenth century predecessors. *Transactions of Philological Society* 76(1): 1–16.

Robins, Robert H., 1994. William Bullokar's *Bref Grammar for English*: text and context. In Günther Blaicher and Brigitte Glaser (eds), *Proceedings of the 1993 Anglistentag at Eichstätt*. Tübingen: Max Niemeyer.

Robins, Robert H., 1997. *A Short History of Linguistics*, 4th edn. London: Longman.

Robins, Robert H., 1998. The authenticity of the *Technē*. In Law and Sluiter (1998: 13–26).

Robinson, Robert, 1617. *The Art of Pronuntiation*. London: Printed by Nicholas Okes.

Rochberg, Francesca, 2011. Conceiving the history of science forward. Paper presented at the annual meeting of the American Oriental Society, Chicago.

Rocher, Rosane, 1975. India. In Thomas A. Sebeok (ed.), *Historiography of Linguistics*. The Hague: Mouton, 3–67.

Rogers, Henry, 2005. *Writing Systems: A Linguistic Approach*. Malden, MA: Blackwell.

Rosch, Eleanor, 1973. On the internal structure of perceptual and semantic categories. In Timothy E. Moore (ed.), *Cognitive Development and the Acquisition of Language*. New York: Academic Press, 111–44.

Rosch, Eleanor, 1975. Cognitive representations of semantic categories. *Journal of Experimen-talPsychology: General* 104(3): 192–233.

Rosch, Eleanor, 1978. Principles of categorization. In Eleanor Rosch and Barbara B. Lloyd (eds), *Cognition and Categorization*. Hillsdale, NJ: Lawrence Erlbaum, 17–48.

Rosch, Eleanor, 1988. Coherences and categorization: a historical view. In Frank S. Kessel (ed.), *The Development of Language and Language Researchers: Essays in Honor of Roger Brown*. Hillsdale, NJ: Lawrence Erlbaum, 373–92.

Rose, Philip, 2002. *Forensic Speaker Identification*. London: Taylor & Francis.

Rosenblatt, Frank, 1958. The perceptron: a probabilistic model for information storage and organization in the brain. *Psychological Review* 65: 386–408.

Rosenfeld, Sophia, 2001. *Language and Revolution in France: The Problem of Signs in late Eighteenth Century France*. Stanford, CA: Stanford University Press.

Rosenthal, Franz, 1939. *Die aramaistische Forschung seit Th. Nöldeke's Veröffentllichungen*. Leiden: E. J. Brill. [Repr. 1964.]

Ross, John R., 1967. Constraints on variables in syntax. Ph.D dissertation, MIT.

Ross, John R, 1982. Poems as holograms. *Poetics Journal* 2: 3–11. [Repr. in Peter C. Bjarkman and Viktor Raskin (eds), *The Real-World Linguist: Applications in the 1980s* (Norwood, NJ: Ablex), 46–56.]

Ross, John R., 1986. *Infinite Syntax*. Norwood, NJ: Ablex.

Ross, John R., 1991. FOG CAT FOG. In Robert Hoffman and David Palermo (eds), *Cognition and the Symbolic Process: Applied and Ecological Perspectives*. Hillsdale, NJ: Erlbaum, 187–205.

Ross, William D. (ed.), 1926. *The Works of Aristotle*. Oxford: Oxford University Press.

Rössler, Otto, 1971. Das Ägyptische als semitische Sprache. In Franz Altheim and Ruth Stiehl (eds), *Christentum am Roten Meer* I. Berlin: de Gruyter, 263–326.

Rössler, Otto, 1979. Berberisch-tschadisches Kernvokabular. *Africana Marburgensia* 12: 20–31.

Roth, Georg Michael, 1795. *Antihermes oder philosophische Untersuchungen über den reinen Begriff der menschlichen Sprache und die allgemeine Sprachlehre*. Frankfurt: Neue Buchhandlung.

Roth, Norman, 1994. *Jews, Visigoths, and Muslims in Medieval Spain: Cooperation and Conflict*. Leiden: E. J. Brill.

Roudet, Léonce, 1921. Sur la classification des psychologique des changements sémantiques. *Journal de psychologie normale et pathologique* 18: 676–92.

Rousseau, Jean-Jacques, 1755. *Discours sur l'origine et les fondements de l'inégalité parmi les hommes*. Amsterdam: M. M. Rey.

Rousseau, Jean-Jacques, 1782 [1755]. Essai sur l'origine des langues. In *Collection complète des œuvres de J. J. Rousseau*, vol. 8. Geneva: [Peyrou], 355–434.

Rousselot, Pierre-Jean, 1897. *Principes de phonétique expérimentale*. Paris: H. Welter. [Later edns 1908, 1924.]

Rowan, Kirsty, 2006a. Meroitic: an Afroasiatic language? *SOAS Working Papers in Linguistics* 14: 249–69.

Rowan, Kirsty, 2006b. Meroitic: a phonological investigation. Ph.D thesis, School of Oriental and African Studies, London University.

Rozencvejg, Viktor Jul'evič (ed.), 1974. *Machine Translation and Applied Linguistics*. 2 vols. Frankfurt am Main: Athenaion. [Also published as *Essays on Lexical Semantics* (2 vols), Stockholm: Skriptor.]

Rubin, David C., 1995. *Memory in Oral Traditions*. Cambridge: Cambridge University Press.

Ruby, Jay, 1980. Franz Boas and early camera study of behavior. *Kinesis Report* 3: 6–11,16.

Ruby, Jay, 1983. An early attempt at studying human behavior with a camera: Franz Boas and the Kwakiutl, 1930. In Niko C. R. Bogaart and Henk Ketelaar (eds), *Methodology in Anthropological Film Making*. Göttingen: Herodot, 15–38.

Ruesch, Jurgen, 1955. Nonverbal language and therapy. *Psychiatry* 18: 323–30.

Ruesch, Jurgen, and Gregory Bateson, 1951. *Communication: The Social Matrix of Society*. New York: Norton.

Ruesch, Jurgen, and Weldon Kees, 1956. *Nonverbal Communication: Notes on the Visual Perception of Human Relations*. Berkeley: University of California Press.

Ruhlen, Merritt, 1994. *The Origin of Language: Tracing the Evolution of the Mother Tongue*. New York: John Wiley.

Rumelhart, David E., Jay L. McClelland, and the PDP Research Group, 1986. *Parallel Distributed Processing: Explorations in the Microstructure of Cognition*. 2 vols. Cambridge, MA: MIT Press

Ruppenhofer, Josef, Michael Ellsworth, Miriam R. L. Petruck, Christopher R. Johnson, and Jan Scheffczyk, 2006. *FrameNet II: Extended Theory and Practice*. Berkeley, CA: FrameNet.

Russell, Bertrand, 1905. On denoting. *Mind* 14: 479–93. [Repr. in Robert C. Marsh (ed.), *Logic and Knowledge* (London: Allen & Unwin, 1956), 39–56.]

Ryckmans, Jacques, 2001. Origin and evolution of South Arabian minuscule writing on wood. *Arabian Archaeology and Epigraphy* 12: 223–35.

Ryckmans, Jacques, Walter W. Müller, and Y. H. Abdallah, 1994. *Textes du Yémen antique inscrits sur bois*. Louvain-la-Neuve: Institut Orientaliste.

Sacks, Harvey, Emanuel A. Schegloff, and Gail Jefferson, 1974. A simplest systematics for the organization of turn taking for conversation. *Language* 50: 696–735.

Sadasivam, M., 1966. *Olikkurippakarati* [Dictionary of Expressives in Tamil]. Madras: Pari Nilayam.

Saeed, John, Rachel Sutton-Spence, and Lorraine Leeson, 2000. Constituent structure in declarative sentences in Irish Sign Language and British Sign Language: a preliminary examination. Poster presented at TISLR 2000, Amsterdam.

Saenger, Paul, 2000. *Space Between Words: The Origins of Silent Reading*. Stanford, CA: Stanford University Press.

Sag, Ivan A., and Jorge Hankamer, 1984. Toward a theory of anaphoric processing. *Linguistics and Philosophy* 7: 325–45.

Salmon, Vivian, 1995. Some reflections of Dionysius Thrax's 'Phonetics' in sixteenth-century English scholarship. In Law and Sluiter (1998: 135–50).

Salmon, Wesley C., 1984. *Scientific Explanation and the Causal Structure of the World*. Princeton, NJ: Princeton University Press.

Salton, Gerard, A. Wong, and C. S. Yang, 1975. A vector space model for automatic indexing. *Communications of the ACM* 18(11): 613–20.

Samarin, William J., 1965. Perspective on African ideophones. *African Studies* 24: 117–21.

Samarin, William J., 1971. Survey of Bantu ideophones. *Africa Language Studies* 12: 130–68.

Samarin, William J., 2000. Sociolinguistics as I see it. *Journal of Sociolinguistics* 4: 303–19.

Sampson, Geoffrey R., 1995. *English for the Computer: The SUSANNE Corpus and Analytic Scheme*. Oxford: Clarendon Press.

Sampson, Geoffrey R., 2005. *The Language Instinct Debate*, 2nd edn. London: Continuum.

Sampson, Geoffrey R., and Diana McCarthy (eds), 2004. *Corpus Linguistics: Readings in a Widening Discipline*. London: Continuum.

Sanctius, Franciscus, 1986 [1587]. *Minerva, seu de causis linguae Latinae.* Stuttgart–Bad Canstatt: Frommann–Holzboog. [Reprint of the Salamanca 1587 edn.]

Sansom, George B., 1928. *An Historical Grammar of Japanese.* Oxford: Clarendon Press.

Santa Ana, Otto, 2002. *Brown Tide Rising: Metaphors of Latinos in Contemporary American Public Discourse.* Austin: University of Texas Press.

Sapir, Edward, 1917. Do we need a 'superorganic'? *American Anthropologist* 19: 441–7.

Sapir, Edward, 1921. *Language: An Introduction to the Study of Speech.* New York: Harcourt, Brace.

Sapir, Edward, 1925. Sound patterns in language. *Language* 1: 37–51.

Sapir, Edward, 1927a. Language as a form of human behavior. *English Journal* 16: 421–33.

Sapir, Edward, 1927b. Speech as a personality trait. *American Journal of Sociology* 32: 892–905.

Sapir, Edward, 1929a. A study in phonetic symbolism. *Journal of Experimental Psychology* 12: 225–39.

Sapir, Edward, 1929b. The status of linguistics as a science. *Language* 5: 207–14. [Repr. in David G. Mandelbaum (ed.), *Selected Writings of Edward Sapir in Language, Culture and Personality* (Berkeley: University of California Press, 1949), 160–6. Also in David G. Mandelbaum (ed.), *Culture, Language and Society: Selected Essays* (Berkeley: University of California Press, 1956), 65–77.]

Sapir, Edward, 1933. La réalité psychologique des phonèmes. *Journal de psychologie normale et pathologique* 30: 247–65. [English version: The psychological reality of phonemes. In David G. Mandelbaum (ed.), *Selected Writings of Edward Sapir in Language, Culture, and Personality* (Berkeley: University of California Press, 1949), 46–60. Repr. in Makkai (1972: 22–31).]

Sarup, Laksman (ed. and transl.), 1920–27. *The Nighaṇṭu and the Nirukta: The Oldest Indian Treatise on Etymology, Philology and Semantics.* [Repr. with 3 parts in 1 vol.: Delhi: Motilal Banarsidass, 1984.]

Sasson, Jack M. (ed.), 1995. *Civilizations of the Ancient Near East.* New York: Charles Scribner's Sons.

Sastri, Gaurinath, 1959. *The Philosophy of Word and Meaning: Some Indian Approaches with Special Reference to the Philosophy of BhartÁhari.* Calcutta Sanskrit College Research Series no. 5. [Repr. Calcutta: Century Press, 1983.]

Šaumjan, Sebastian K., 1968 [1962]. *Problems of Theoretical Phonology.* The Hague: Mouton.

Savage-Rumbaugh, Sue, Duane S. Rumbaugh, and Kelly McDonald, 1985. Language learning in two species of apes. *Neuroscience and Biobehavioral Reviews* 9: 653–65.

Sawada, Hideo, 2003. Tonal notation of Indic scripts in mainland Southeast Asia. In Peri Bhaskararao (ed.), *International Symposium on Indic Scripts Past and Future: Working Papers.* Tokyo: Research Institute for the Languages and Cultures of Asia and Africa, 318–49.

Scaliger, Joseph J., 1540. *De Causis Linguae Latinae.* Leiden: Seb. Gryphium.

Schabes, Yves, Anne Abeillé, and Aravind K.Joshi, 1988. Parsing strategies with 'lexicalized' grammars: application to tree adjoining grammars. *Proceedings of the 12th International Conference on Computational Linguistics (COLING '88)* (Budapest), 578–83.

Schaefer, Ursula, 2006. The beginnings of standardization: the communicative space in fourteenth century England. In Ursula Schaefer (ed.), *The Beginnings of Standardization: Language and Culture in Fourteenth Century England.* Frankfurt am Main: Peter Lang, 3–24.

Schaffner, Bertram (ed.), 1956. *Group Processes: Transactions of the Second Conference.* New York: Josiah Macy, Jr Foundation.

Schane, Sanford, 1968. *French Phonology and Morphology.* Cambridge, MA: MIT Press.

Schank, Roger C., 1973. Identification of conceptualizations underlying natural language. In Roger C. Schank and Kenneth M. Colby (eds), *Computer Models of Thought and Language.* San Francisco: W. H. Freeman, 187–247.

Schank, Roger C. (ed.), 1975. *Conceptual Information Processing.* Amsterdam: North-Holland.

Schank, Roger C., and Robert P. Abelson, 1977. *Scripts, Plans, Goals, and Understanding: An Enquiry into Human Knowledge Structures.* Hillsdale, NJ: Lawrence Erlbaum.

Scharf, Peter M., 1996. *The Denotation of Generic Terms in Ancient Indian Philosophy: Grammar, Nyāya, and Mīmāṃsā.* Philadelphia: American Philosophical Society.

Scharf, Peter M., and Malcolm D. Hyman, 2011. *Linguistic Issues in Encoding Sanskrit.* Providence, RI: The Sanskrit Library. Delhi: Motilal Banarsidass.

Scharfe, Hartmut, 1977. Grammatical literature. In *A History of Indian Literature*, vol. 5, fasc. 2. Wiesbaden: Otto Harrassowitz, 77–216.

Scheer, Tobias, 2011. Aspects of the development of generative phonology. In Bert Botma, Nancy C. Kula, and Kuniya Nasukawa (eds), *The Continuum Companion to Phonology.* New York: Continuum, 397–446.

Schegloff, Emanuel A., 1991. Reflections on talk and social structure. In Deirdre Boden and Donald Zimmerman (eds), *Talk and Social Structure: Studies in Ethnomethodology and Conversation Analysis.* Cambridge: Polity Press, 44–70.

Schembri, Adam C., 2003. Rethinking 'classifiers' in signed languages. In Karen Emmorey (ed.), *Perspectives on Classifier Constructions in Sign Languages.* Mahwah, NJ: Lawrence Erlbaum, 3–34.

Schembri, Adam C., Caroline Jones, and Denis Burnham, 2005. Comparing action gestures and classifier verbs of motion: evidence from Australian sign language, Taiwan sign language, and non-signers' gestures without speech. *Journal of Deaf Studies and Deaf Education* 10: 272–90.

Schenkeveld, Dirk M., and Jonathan Barnes, 1999. Language. In Keimpe Algra et al. (eds), *The Cambridge History of Hellenistic Philosophy.* Cambridge: Cambridge University Press, 177–228.

Scherer, Wilhelm, 1885. *Jacob Grimm.* Berlin: Weidmann.

Schiffrin, Deborah, 1994. *Approaches to Discourse.* Oxford: Blackwell.

Schiffrin, Deborah, Deborah Tannen, and Heidi Hamilton, 2001. *The Handbook of Discourse Analysis.* Oxford: Blackwell.

Schironi, Francesca, 2004. *I frammenti di Aristarco di Samotracia negli etimologici bizantini: introduzione, edizione critica e commento.* Göttingen: Vandenhoeck & Ruprecht.

Schischkoff, Georgi, 1991. Bacon, Francis (Baco von Verulam). In Georgi Schischkoff (ed.), *Philosophisches Wörterbuch.* Stuttgart: Alfred Kröner.

Schleicher, August, 1848. *Sprachvergleichende Untersuchungen*, vol. 1. Bonn: H. B. König.

Schleicher, August, 1850. *Die Sprachen Europas in systematischer Uebersicht.* Bonn: H. B. König.

Schleicher, August, 1859. *Zur Morphologie der Sprache*, vol. 1: *Mémoires de l'Académie de St Pétersbourg.* Leipzig: Leopold Voss.

Schleicher, August, 1861/62. *Compendium der vergleichenden Grammatik der indogermanischen Sprachen*. 2 vols. Weimar: H. Boehlau. [Repr. Krefeld: Minerva.]

Schleicher, August, 1863. *Die Darwinsche Theorie und die Sprachwissenschaft: Offenes Sendschreiben an Hern Dr. Ernst Häckel*. Weimar: Hermann Böhlau. [Repr. 1873.]

Schleiermacher, Andreas, 1835. *De l'influence de l'écriture sur le langage. Mémoire . . . Suivi de grammaires barmane et malaie, et d'un aperçu de l'alphabet harmonique pour les langues asiatiques, que l'Institut a couronné en 1827*. Darmstadt: J. W. Heyer.

Schleiermacher, Andreas, 1864. *Das harmonische oder allgemeine Alphabet zur Transcription fremder Schriftsysteme in lateinische Schrift, zunächst in seiner Anwendung auf die slawischen und semitischen Sprachen*. Darmstadt : G. Johghaus.

Schmidhauser, Andreas, 2009. Le *De pronomine* de Priscien et son modèle grec. In Marc Baratin, Bernard Colombat, and Louis Holtz (eds), *Priscien*. Turnhout: Brepols, 167–82.

Schmidt, Ernst, 1885. *Briefwechsel der Gebrüder Grimm mit nordischen Gelehrten*. Berlin: Ferdinand Dümmler.

Schmidt, Johannes, 1873. *Die Verwandtschaftsverhältnisse der indogermanischen Sprachen*. Weimar: Böhlau.

Schmidt, Johannes, 1887, 1892. Schleichers Auffassung der Lautgesetze. *Zeitschrift für vergleichende Sprachforschung* 28: 303–12; 32: 419–20.

Schmidt, Peter L., 1989. Grammatik und Rhetorik. In Reinhart Herzog (ed.), *Restauration und Erneuerung: die lateinische Literatur von 284 bis 374 n. Chr.* Munich: Beck, 101–58.

Schmidt, Wilhelm, 1907. Anthropos-Lautschrift. In *Anthropos: Internationale Zeitschrift für Völker- und Länderkunde*, 2.

Schmitt, Alfred, 1980. *Entstehung und Entwicklung von Schriften*, ed. Claus Haeber. Cologne: Böhlau.

Schmitt, Jean-Claude, 1990. *Il gesto nel medioevo*. Rome: Laterza. [Italian translation of *La raison des gestes dans l'Occident médiéval* (Paris: Gallimard, 1990).]

Schmitt, Norbert, 2004. *Formulaic Sequences: Acquisition, Processing and Use*. Amsterdam: John Benjamins.

Schmitter, Peter (ed.), 2005. *Geschichte der Sprachtheorie 6/1: Sprachtheorien der Neuzeit III/1: Sprachbeschreibung und Sprachunterricht, Teil 1*. Tübingen: Gunter Narr.

Schneider, Richardus, 1878. *Apollonii Dyscoli Quae Supersunt*, fasc. i: *Apollonii Scripta Minora*. In *Grammatici Graeci* II.i. Leipzig: B. G. Teubner.

Schneider, Richardus, 1910. *Librorum Apollonii Deperditorum Fragmenta*, ed. Richardus Schneider. In *Grammatici Graeci* II.iii. Leipzig: B. G. Teubner.

Scholz, Barbara C., and Geoffrey K. Pullum, 2007. Tracking the origins of transformational generative grammar. *Journal of Linguistics* 43: 701–23.

Schön, Jacob F., 1862. *Grammar of the Hausa Language*. London: CMS. [Repr. Farnborough: Gregg, 1971.]

Schubert, Lenhart K., and Matthew Tong, 2003. Extracting and evaluating general world knowledge from the Brown Corpus. *Proceedings of the HLT-NAACL 2003 Workshop on Text Meaning*, Association for Computational Linguistics, 7–13.

Schuchardt, Hugo, 1883. *Über das Indoportugiesische von Cochim*. Vienna: Kaiserliche Akademie der Wissenschaften.

Schuchardt, Hugo, 1885. *Über die Lautgesetze: Gegen die Junggrammatiker*. Berlin: Oppenheim.

Schuchardt, Hugo, 1888. *Über das Anamito-Französische. Kreolische Studien VIII*. Vienna: Kaiserliche Akademie der Wissenschaften.

Schuchardt, Hugo, 1912. Sachen und wörter. *Anthropos* 7: 827–39.

Schuchardt, Hugo, 1922. *Hugo Schuchardt-Brevier: ein Vademekum der Allgemeinen Sprachwissenschaft*, ed. L. Spitzer. Halle: Max Niemeyer.

Scobbie, James M., and Marianne Pouplier, 2010. The role of syllable structure in sandhi: an EPG study of vocalization and retraction in word-final English /l/. *Journal of Phonetics* 38: 240–59.

Scollon, Ron, and Suzanne Wong Scollon, 2001. *Intercultural Communication*, 2nd edn. Oxford: Blackwell.

Searle, John R., 1969. *Speech Acts: An Essay in the Philosophy of Language*. Cambridge: Cambridge University Press.

Searle, John R., 1975. Indirect speech acts. In Peter Cole and Jerry L. Morgan (eds), *Speech Acts*. New York: Academic Press, 59–82.

Searle, John R., 1977. A classification of illocutionary acts. In Andy Rogers, Bob Wall, and John P. Murphy (eds), *Proceedings of the Texas Conference on Performatives, Presuppositions, and Implicatures*. Arlington, VA: Center for Applied Linguistics, 17–45.

Searle, John R., 1979. *Expression and Meaning: Studies in the Theory of Speech Acts*. Cambridge: Cambridge University Press.

Sebeok, Thomas, A., Alfred. S. Hayes, and Mary C. Bateson (eds), 1964. *Aproaches to Semiotics*. The Hague: Mouton.

Sebeok, Thomas A., and Donna-Jean Umiker-Sebeok (eds), 1978. *Aboriginal Sign Languages of the Americas and Australia*, vol. 1: *North America: Classic Comparative Perspectives*; vol. 2: *The Americas and Australia*. New York: Plenum Press.

Sebeok, Thomas A. and Donna-Jean Umiker-Sebeok (eds), 1980. *Speaking of Apes*. New York: Plenum Press.

Sechehaye, Albert, 1908. *Programme et méthodes de la linguistique théorique*. Paris–Leipzig–Geneva: Champion–Harrassowitz–Eggimann.

Sechehaye, Albert, 1926. *Essai sur la structure logique de la phrase*. Paris: Champion.

Sechehaye, Albert, 1933. La pensée et la langue, ou: comment concevoir le rapport organique de l'individuel et du social dans le langage. *Psychologie du langage* [= *Journal de Psychologie* 1–4, 1933]: 57–81.

Sedley, David N., 1977. *Diodorus* Cronus and Hellenistic Philosophy. *Proceedings of the Cambridge Philological Society*, n.s. 23: 74–120.

Sedley, David N., 2003. *Plato's Cratylus*. Cambridge: Cambridge University Press.

Sedulius Scottus, 1977. *In Donati Artem maiorem*, ed. Bengt Löfstedt. Turnhout: Brepols.

Sefer Yetsirah, 1997. York Beach, ME: Samuel Weiser.

Segal, Judah B., 1953. *The Diacritical Point and Accents in Syriac*. London: Oxford University Press.

Segerdahl, Pär, William Fields, and Sue Savage-Rumbaugh, 2005. *Kanzi's Primal Language: The Cultural Initiation of Primates into Language*. New York: Palgrave Macmillan.

Semaan, Khalil I., 1968. *Linguistics in the Middle Ages: Phonetic Studies in Early Islam*. Leiden: Brill.

Semino, Elena, and Michael Short, 2004. *Corpus Stylistics: Speech, Writing and Thought Presentation in a Corpus of English Writing*. London: Routledge.

Senft, Gunther, 2009a. Bronislaw Kasper Malinowski. In Gunther Senft, Jan O. Östman, and Jef Verschueren (eds), *Culture and Language Use*. Amsterdam: John Benjamins, 110–225.

Senft, Gunther, 2009b. Phatic communion. In Gunther Senft, Jan O. Östman, and Jef Verschueren (eds), *Culture and Language Use*. Amsterdam: John Benjamins, 126–233.

Sergius. *Explanationes in Artem Donati*. In Keil (1961: iv. 486–534).

Servius [Sergius]. *Commentarius in Artem Donati*. In Keil (1961: iv. 405–28).

Seuren, Pieter A. M., 1985. *Discourse Semantics*. Oxford: Blackwell.

Seuren, Pieter A. M., 1998. *Western Linguistics: An Historical Introduction*. Oxford: Blackwell.

Seuren, Pieter A. M., 2005. Eubulides as a 20th-century semanticist. *Language Sciences* 27: 75–95.

Seuren, Pieter A. M., 2009. *Language from Within*, vol. 1: *Language in Cognition*. Oxford: Oxford University Press.

Seuren, Pieter A. M., 2010. *Language from Within*, vol. 2: *The Logic of Language*. Oxford: Oxford University Press.

Sewell, Penelope, 2004. Students buzz round the translation class like bees round the honey pot—why? In Kirsten Malmkjær (ed.), *Translation in Undergraduate Degree Programmes*. Amsterdam: John Benjamins, 151–62.

Sezgin, Fuat, 1984. *Geschichte der arabischen Schrifttums 9: Grammatik*. Leiden: E. J. Brill.

Shannon, Claude, 1948. A mathematical theory of communication. *Bell System Technical Journal* 27: 379–423, 623–56.

Shao Aiji 邵靄吉, 2005. '*Mǎshì Wéntōng' Biànzhèng*.《馬氏文通》 辨正 [A Critical Study of the *Mashi Wentong*]. Beijing: Commercial Press.

Sharma, Rama Nath, 1987. *The Aṣṭādhyāyī of Pāṇini*, vol. 1: *Introduction to the* Aṣṭādhyāyī *as a Grammatical Device*. New Delhi: Munshiram Manoharlal.

Sharma, Rama Nath, 1990–2003. *The Aṣṭādhyāyī of Pāṇini*, vols 2–6, *English Translation . . . with Sanskrit Text, Transliteration, Word-Boundary, anuvṛtti, vṛtti, Explanatory Notes, Derivational History of Examples, and Indices*. New Delhi: Munshiram Manoharlal.

Shastri, Sudhama V., Chetan T. Patilkulkarni, and Geeta S. Shastri, 1986. *Manual of Information to Accompany the Kolhapur Corpus of Indian English, for Use with Digital Computers*. Bergen: ICAME.

Sheridan, Thomas, 1780. *A General Dictionary of the English Language. One main object of which, is, to establish a plain and permanent standard of pronunciation. To which is prefixed a rhetorical grammar*. London: J. Dodsley; C. Dilly & J. Wilkie.

Sherzer, Joel, 1972. Verbal and nonverbal deixis: the pointed lip gesture among the San Blas Cuna. *Language in Society* 2: 117–31.

Sherzer, Joel, 1991. The Brazilian thumbs-up gesture. *Journal of Linguistic Anthroology* 1: 189–97.

Sherzer, Joel, 1993. Pointed lips, thumbs up, and cheek puffs: some emblematic gestures in social interactional and ethnographic context. *SALSA* I: 196–211.

Sherzer, Joel, and Greg Urban (eds), 1986. *Native South American Discourse*. The Hague: Mouton.

Shi Cunzhi 史存直, 2008. *Hànyǔshǐ Gāngyào* 漢語史綱要 [An Outline History of the Chinese Language]. Beijing: Zhonghua Bookstore.

Shibatani, Masayoshi, 1987. Japanese. In Bernard Comrie (ed.), *The World's Major Languages*. Oxford: Oxford University Press, 855–80.

Shibatani, Masayoshi, 1990. *The Languages of Japan*. Cambridge: Cambridge University Press.

Shockey, Linda, and Fiona Gibbon, 1993. 'Stopless' stops in connected English. *Speech Research Laboratory University of Reading Work in Progress* 1–7(1): 163–80.

Shuy, Roger W., 2003 [1990]. A brief history of American sociolinguistics, 1949–1989. In Charles B. Paulston and G. Richard Tucker (eds), *Sociolinguistics: The Essential Readings*. Oxford: Blackwell, 4–16.

Sidner, Candace L., 1978. The use of focus as a tool for disambiguation of definite noun phrases. *Proceedings of the Second Conference on Theoretical Issues in Natural Language Processing* (Urbana–Champaign, IL), 86–95.

Sievers, Eduard, 1876. *Grundzüge der Lautphysiologie zur Einfürung in das Studium der Lautlehre der indogermanischen Sprachen.* Leipzig: Breitkopf & Härtel. [4th edn 1893 with the title *Grundzüge der Phonetik zur Einführung in das Studium der Lautlehre der indogermanischen Sprachen.*]

Sievers, Eduard, 1878. Zur Accent- und Lautlehre der germanischen Sprachen, III: Zum vocalischen Auslautsgesetz. *Beiträge zur Geschichte der Deutschen Sprache und Literatur* 5: 63–163

Sigerus de Cortraco, 1977[c.1330]. *Summa modorum significandi. Sophismata*, new edn, with an introduction by Jan Pinborg. Amsterdam: John Benjamins.

Silverman, Daniel, 2012. Mikołaj Kruszewski: theory and vision, Part 1 and Part 2. *Language and Linguistics Compass* 6: 330–42, 296–309

Silverstein, Michael (ed.), 1971. *Whitney on Language: Selected Writings of William Dwight Whitney.* Cambridge, MA: MIT Press.

Silverstein, Michael, 1976. Shifters, verbal categories and cultural description. In Keith Basso and Henry Selby (eds), *Meaning in Anthropology.* Albuquerque: School of American Research, 11–55.

Silverstein, Michael, 1985. Language and the culture of gender: at the intersection of structure, usage and ideology. In Elizabeth Mertz and Richard J. Parmentier (eds), *Semiotic Mediation: Sociocultural and Psychological Perspectives.* Orlando, FL: Academic Press, 119–259.

Silverstein, Michael, 1992. The indeterminacy of contextualization: when is enough enough? In Peter Auer and Aldo DiLuzio (eds), *The Contextualization of Language.* Amsterdam: John Benjamins, 55–77.

Sims-Williams, Nicholas, 1981. The Sogdian sound-system and the origin of the Uyghur Script. *Journal asiatique* 269: 347–59.

Sinclair, John M. (ed.), 1987a. *Looking Up: An Account of the COBUILD Project in Lexical Computing.* Glasgow: Collins.

Sinclair, John M., 1987b. The nature of evidence. In Sinclair (1987a: 150–9).

Sinclair, John M., 1991. *Corpus, Concordance, Collocation.* Oxford: Oxford University Press.

Sinclair, John M., 2004. *Trust the Text: Language, Corpus and Discourse.* London: Routledge.

Sinclair, John M., and Patrick Hanks, 1987. *Collins Cobuild English Language Dictionary.* London: Collins.

Singh, Rajendra, and Stanley Starosta, 2003. *Explorations in Seamless Morphology.* London: SAGE.

Sittl, Kurt, 1890. *Die Gebärden der Griechen und Römer.* Leipzig: B. G. Teubner.

Skinner, Burrhus F., 1957. *Verbal Behavior.* New York: Appleton-Century-Crofts.

Sköld, Hannes, 1926. *The Nirukta. Its Place in Old Indian Literature. Its Etymologies.* Lund: C. W. K. Gleerup.

Slavikova, H., 1990. Translating and the acquisition of Italian as a second language. Ph.D dissertation. University of Toronto.

Sledd, James, 1986. Permanence and change in Standard American English: the making of 'literary crises'. In Gerhard Nickel and James C. Stalker (eds), *Problems of Standardization and Linguistic Variation in Present-Day English.* Heidelberg: Julius Groos, 59–70.

Sledd, James, and Wilma R. Ebbit (eds), 1962. *Dictionaries and* That *Dictionary.* Chicago: Scott Foresman.

Slobin, Dan I., 2002. Language evolution, acquisition, diachrony: probing the parallels. In Givón and Malle (2002: 375–92).

Sluiter, Ineke, 1990. *Ancient Grammar in Context: Contributions to the Study of Ancient Linguistic Thought*. Amsterdam: VU University Press.

Sluiter, Ineke, 1997. The Greek tradition. In Wout Jac. van Bekkum et al. (eds), *The Emergence of Semantics in Four Linguistic Traditions: Hebrew, Sanskrit, Greek, Arabic*. Amsterdam: John Benjamins, 149–224.

Sluiter, Ineke, 2011. A champion of analogy: Herodian's *On Lexical Singularity*. In Stephanos Matthaios, Franco Montanari, and Antonios Rengakos (eds), *Ancient Scholarship and Grammar: Archetypes, Concepts and Contexts*. Berlin: de Gruyter, 191–310.

Smail, William M., 1938. *Institutiones oratoriae. Quintilian on education: being a translation of selected passages from the Institutio oratoria, with an introductory essay on Quintilian, his environment and his theory of education*. Oxford: Clarendon Press.

Smith, Barry, 1990. Towards a history of speech act theory. In Armin Burkhardt (ed.), *Speech Acts, Meaning and Intentions: Critical Approaches to the Philosophy of John R. Searle*. Berlin: de Gruyter, 19–61.

Smith, John Maynard, and Eörs Szathmáry, 1995. *The Major Transitions in Evolution*. New York: W. H. Freeman Spektrum.

Smith, Pauline M., 1993. Le XVIᵉ siècle: les débuts de la standardisation du français moderne. In Pierre Knecht and Zygmunt Marzys (eds), *Écriture, langues communes et normes: formation spontanée de koinés et standardisation dans la Galloromania et son voisinage. Actes du colloque tenu à l'Université de Neuchâtel du 21 au 23 septembre 1988*. Geneva: Droz, 43–58.

Smith, (Sir) Thomas, 1568. *De recta et emendata linguae anglicae scriptione dialogus*. Lutetiae: R. Stephani.

Smolinsky, Stephanie, 2001. Brilliance and size in vowels: a cross-linguistic study of phonetic symbolism. Ph.D dissertation, City University of New York.

Sohn, Ho-min, 1999. *The Korean Language*. Cambridge: Cambridge University Press.

Sommerfeld, Walfred, 2003. Bemerkungen zur Dialektgliederung Altakkadisch, Assyrisch und Babylonisch. In *Festschrift für Burkhart Kienast*, ed. G. J. Selz. Münster: Ugarit, 569–86.

Song, Jae Jung, 2005. *The Korean Language: Structure, Use and Context*. London: Routledge.

Sowa, John, 1984. *Conceptual Structures: Information Processing in Mind and Machine*. Reading, MA: Addison-Wesley.

Spang-Hanssen, Henning, 1966. On the simplicity of descriptions. In Eric P. Hamp, Fred W. Householder, and Robert Austerlitz (eds), *Readings in Linguistics II*. Chicago: University of Chicago Press, 134–41. [First published 1948.]

Spärck Jones, Karen, 2000. R. H. Richens: translation in the NUDE. In W. John Hutchins (ed.), *Early Years in Machine Translation: Memoirs and Biographies of Pioneers*. Amsterdam: John Benjamins, 163–278.

Spärck Jones, Karen, 2007. Computational linguistics: what about the linguistics? *Computational Linguistics* 33: 437–41.

Spence, Nicol C. W., 1961. Linguistic fields, conceptual systems and the Weltbild. *Transactions of the Philological Society* 1961: 88–106.

Sperber, Dan, and Gloria Origi, 2010. A pragmatic perspective on the evolution of language. In Larson et al. (2010: 124–31).

Sperber, Dan, and Deirdre Wilson, 1986. *Relevance: Communication and Cognition*. Cambridge, MA: Harvard University Press. [2nd edn 1995.]

Sperber, Dan, and Deirdre Wilson, 2002. Pragmatics, modularity and mind-reading. *Mind and Language* 17: 3–23.

Spitzer, Leo, 1948. *Linguistics and Literary History*. Princeton, NJ: Princeton University Press.

Spolsky, Bernard, 2010. Ferguson and Fishman: sociolinguistics and the sociology of language. In Barbara Johnstone, Ruth Wodak, and Peter Kerswill (eds), *Sage Handbook of Sociolinguistics*. London: Sage, 11–23.

St George, Marie, Suzanne Mannes, and James Hoffman, 1994. Global semantic expectancy and language comprehension. *Journal of Cognitive Neuroscience* 6: 70–83.

Staal, Johan F., 1972. *A Reader on the Sanskrit Grammarians*.Cambridge MA: MIT Press

Staal, Johan F., 1974. The origin and development of linguistics in India. In Dell Hymes (ed.), *Studies in the History of Linguistics: Traditions and Paradigms*. Bloomington: Indiana University Press, 63–74.

Stalnaker, Robert C., 1978. Assertion. In Peter Cole (ed.), *Pragmatics*. New York: Academic Press, 315–32.

Stam, James H., 1976. *Inquiries into the Origin of Language: The Fate of a Question*. New York: Harper & Row.

Stammerjohann, Harro, et al. (eds), 2009. *Lexicon Grammaticorum: A Bio-bibliographical Companion to the History of Linguistics*, 2nd edn. Tübingen: Max Niemeyer.

Stanford, James N., and Dennis R. Preston, 2009. *Variation in Minority Languages*. Amsterdam: John Benjamins.

Starobinski, Jean, 1979. *Words Upon Words: The Anagrams of Ferdinand Saussure*, transl. Olivia Emmet. New Haven, CT: Yale University Press.

Stathi, Ekaterini, 2006. Greek lexicography, Classical. In Keith Brown (ed.), *Encyclopedia of Language and Linguistics*, 2nd edn, vol. 5. London: Elsevier, 145–6.

Steele, Joshua, 1775. *An Essay Towards Establishing The Melody And Measure Of Spech, To Be Expressed And Perpetuated By Peculiar Symbols*. London: J. Almon.

Steele, Joshua, 1779. *Prosodia rationalis: or, an essay towards establishing the melody and measure of spech, to be expressed and perpetuated by peculiar symbols*. London: J. Nichols.

Steels, Luc, 2011. Explaining the origins of complexity in language: a case study for agreement systems. Paper presented at the Workshop on Complexity in Language: Developmental and Evolutionary Perspectives, Collegium de Lyon.

Stefanowitsch, Anatol, and Stefan Th. Gries, 2003. Collostructions: investigating the interaction between words and constructions. *International Journal of Corpus Linguistics* 8: 209–43.

Stein, Gabriele, 1997. *John Palsgrave as Renaissance Linguist: A Pioneer in Vernacular Language Description*. Oxford: Clarendon Press.

Stein, Peter, 2003. *Untersuchungen zur Phonologie und Morphologie des Sabäischen*. Rahden: Marie Leidorf.

Steiner, Erich, Paul Schmidt, and Cornelia Zelinsky-Wibbelt (eds), 1988. *From Syntax to Semantics: Insights from Machine Translation*. Norwood, NJ: Ablex.

Steiner, Peter (ed.), 1982. *The Prague School: Selected Writings, 1929–1946*. Austin: University of Texas Press.

Steinthal, Heymann, 1860. *Charakteristik der hauptsächlichsten Typen des Sprachbaues*. Berlin: Ferdinand Dümmler.

Steinthal, Heymann, 1884. *Die sprachphilosophischen Werke Wilhelm von Humboldts*. Berlin: Ferdinand Dümmler.

Stempel, Reinhard, 1999. *Abriss einer historischen Grammatik der semitischen Sprachen.* Frankfurt am Main: Peter Lang.

Stern, Gustaf, 1931. *Meaning and Change of Meaning (with Special Reference to the English Language).* Göteborg: Elanders Boktryckeri Aktiebolag.

Stern, Ludwig, 1880. *Koptische Grammatik.* Leipzig: Weigel. [Repr. 1971, Osnabrück: Biblio.]

Stern, Wilhelm, 1924. *Psychology of Early Childhood up to Six Years of Age.* New York: Holt.

Stevens, Mary, and John Hajek, 2007. Towards a phonetic conspectus of preaspiration: acoustic evidence from Sienese Italian. In J. Trouvain and W. J. Barry (eds), *Proceedings of the 16th International Congress of Phonetics Sciences (ICPhS XVI)* (Saarbrücken), 429–32.

Stimson, Dorothy, 1932. Ballad of Gresham College. *Isis* 18: 103–17.

Stocking, George W., 1982. French anthropology in 1800. In George W. Stocking (ed.), *Race, Culture and Evolution: Essays in the History of Anthropology.* Chicago: Phoenix, 13–41.

Stocking, George W., 1982. *Race, Culture and Evolution: Essays in the History of Anthropology.* Chicago: Phoenix.

Stocking, George W., 1992. *The Ethnographer's Magic and Other Essays in the History of Anthropology.* Madison: University of Wisconsin Press.

Stöcklein, Johann, 1898. *Bedeutungswandel der Wörter: Seine Entstehung und Entwicklung.* Munich: Lindaursche Buchhandlung.

Stockwell, Robert P., 1962. Discussion of 'A transformational approach to syntax'. In Archibald A. Hill (ed.), *Third Texas Conference on Problems of Linguistic Analysis in English.* Austin: University of Texas, 158–69.

Stokoe, William C., 1960. Sign language structure: an outline of the visual communication systems of the American deaf. *Studies in Linguistics Occasional Papers* 8: 1–78. University of Buffalo. [Repr. Silver Spring, MD: Linstok Press, 1978.]

Stokoe, William C., 2001. *Language in Hand: Why Sign Came Before Speech.* Washington, DC: Gallaudet University Press.

Stone, Maureen, 2010. Laboratory techniques for investigating speech articulation. In William J. Hardcastle, John Laver, and Fiona E. Gibbon (eds), *The Handbook of Phonetic Sciences,* 2nd edn. Oxford: Blackwell, 9–38.

Strawson, Peter F., 1950. On referring. *Mind* 59: 320–44.

Strawson, Peter F., 1952. *Introduction to Logical Theory.* London: Methuen.

Strawson, Peter F., 1954. A reply to Mr Sellars. *Philosophical Review* 63: 216–31.

Strawson, Peter F., 1964. Identifying reference and truth-values. *Theoria* 30: 96–118.

Streeck, Jürgen, 2009. *Gesturecraft: The Manu-Facture of Meaning.* Amsterdam: John Benjamins.

Stubbs, Michael, 1983. *Discourse Analysis: The Sociolinguistic Analysis of Natural Language.* Chicago: University of Chicago Press.

Stubbs, Michael, 1996. *Text and Corpus Analysis: Computer Assisted Studies of Language and Culture.* Oxford: Blackwell.

Stubbs, Michael, 2001. *Words and Phrases: Corpus Studies of Lexical Semantics.* Oxford: Blackwell.

Stump, Gregory T., 2001. *Inflectional Morphology: A Theory of Paradigm Structure.* Cambridge: Cambridge University Press.

Subbiondo, Joseph L. (ed.), 1992. *John Wilkins and Seventeenth-Century British Linguistics.* Amsterdam: John Benjamins.

Subramania Iyer, K. A., 1969. *Bhartṛhari: A Study of the Vākyapadīya in the Light of the Ancient Commentaries.* Pune: Deccan College Postgraduate and Research Institute.

Supalla, Ted, 1986. The classifier system in American Sign Language. In Collette Craig (ed.), *Noun Classes and Categorization*. Amsterdam: Benjamins, 181–214.

Swales, John M., 1990. *Genre Analysis: English in Academic and Research Settings*. Cambridge: Cambridge University Press.

Svantesson, Jan-Olof, Anna Tsendina, Anastasia Karlsson, and Vivan Franzén, 2005. *The Phonology of Mongolian*. Oxford: Oxford University Press.

Svartvik, Jan (ed.), 1990. *The London–Lund Corpus of Spoken English: Description and Research*. Malabar, FL: Krieger.

Swadesh, Morris, 1934. The phonemic principle. *Language* 10: 117–29.

Swadesh, Morris, 1935. Twaddell on defining the phoneme. *Language* 11: 244–50.

Swadesh, Morris, 1971. *The Origin and Diversification of Language*. Chicago: Aldine. [2nd edn 2006.]

Sweet, Henry, 1877. *A Handbook of Phonetics, Including a Popular Exposition of the Principles of Spelling Reform*. Oxford: Clarendon Press.

Sweet, Henry, 1880–1. Sound notation. *Transactions of the Philological Society*, 177–235.

Sweet, Henry, 1888. *A History of English Sounds from the Earliest Period with Full Word-Lists*. Oxford: Clarendon Press.

Sweet, Henry, 1899. *The Practical Study of Languages: A Guide for Teachers and Learners*. London: Dent.

Sweetser, Eve, 1990. *From Etymology to Pragmatics: Metaphorical and Cultural Aspects of Semantic Structure*. Cambridge: Cambridge University Press.

Swift, Jonathan, 1712. *A Proposal for Correcting, Improving and Ascertaining the English Tongue*. Eighteenth century Collections Online, accessed 8 February 2011.

Tabain, Marija, 2008. Production of Australian English /uː/: language-specific variability. *Australian Journal of Linguistics* 28: 195–224.

Tabain, Marija, 2009. A preliminary study of jaw movement in Arrernte consonant production. *Journal of the International Phonetic Association* 39: 33–51.

Takács, Gábor, 1999–2007. *Etymological Dictionary of Egyptian* I–III. Leiden: E. J. Brill.

Talbot, Mary M., 1994. Relevance. In Ronald E. Asher (ed.), *Encyclopedia of Languages and Linguistics*. Oxford: Pergamon, vol. 6, 3524–7.

Tallerman, Maggie, 2007. Did our ancestors speak a holistic protolanguage? *Lingua* 117: 579–604.

Talmon, Rafi, 2003. *Eighth-Century Iraqi Grammar: A Critical Exploration of Pre-Halilian Arabic Linguistics*. Winona Lake, IN: Eisenbrauns.

Talmy, Leonard, 1988. The relation of grammar to cognition. In Brygida Rudzka-Ostyn (ed.), *Topics in Cognitive Linguistics*. Amsterdam: John Benjamins, 165–205.

Talmy, Leonard, 2000a. *Toward a Cognitive Semantics*, vol. 1: *Concept Structuring Systems*. Cambridge, MA: MIT Press.

Talmy, Leonard, 2000b. *Toward a Cognitive Semantics*, vol. 2: *Typology and Process in Concept Structuring*. Cambridge, MA: MIT Press.

Tammet, Daniel, 2007. *Born on a Blue Day*. New York: Free Press.

Tannen, Deborah, 1989. *Talking Voices: Repetition, Dialogue, and Imagery in Conversational Discourse*. Cambridge: Cambridge University Press.

Tarski, Alfred, 1956. *Logic, Semantics, Metamathematics: Papers from 1923 to 1938*. Oxford: Clarendon Press.

Tatwine, 1968 [734]. Ars. In Maria de Marco and F. Glorie (eds), *Tatuini Opera omnia*, vol. 1. Turnhout: Brepols, 1–93.

Taub, Sarah F., 2001. *Language from the Body: Iconicity and Metaphor in American Sign Language*. Cambridge: Cambridge University Press.

Taylor, Daniel J., 1986. Rethinking the history of language science in Classical Antiquity, *Historiographia Linguistica* 13: 175–90.

Taylor, Daniel J., 2000. Varro and the origin of Roman linguistic theory and practice. In Auroux et al., vol. 1 (2000: 455–8)

Taylor, John R., 1995. *Linguistic Categorization: Prototypes in Linguistic Theory*, 2nd edn. Oxford: Oxford University Press.

Taylor, John R., 2002. *Cognitive Grammar*. Oxford: Oxford University Press

Taylor, John R., 2003. *Linguistic Categorization*, 3rd edn. Oxford: Oxford University Press.

Techmer, Friedrich H. H., 1880. *Einleitung in die Sprachwissenschaft. 1,1, Phonetik: zur vergleichenden Physiologie der Stimme und Sprache, Bd. 1, Th.1. Text und Anmerkungen*. Leipzig: Engelmann.

Temperley, David, 2003. Ambiguity avoidance in English relative clauses. *Language* 79: 464–84.

Tervoort, Bernard T., 1953. *Structurele analyse van visueel taalgebruik binnen een groep dove kinderen*. Amsterdam: Noord-Hollandsche Uitgevers Maatschappij.

Tesnière, Lucien, 1959. *Éléments de syntaxe structurale*. Paris: Klincksieck.

Teubert, Wolfgang, 2004. Language and corpus linguistics. In Michael Halliday, Wolfgang Teubert, Colin Yallop, and Anna Čermácová (eds), *Lexicology and Corpus Linguistics: An Introduction*. London: Continuum, 73–112.

Teubert, Wolfgang, 2005. My version of corpus linguistics. *International Journal of Corpus Linguistics* 10: 1–13.

Thausing, Moriz, 1863. *Das natürliche Lautsystem der menschlichen Sprache: mit Bezug auf Brücke's Physiologie und Systematik der Sprachlaute dargestellt*. Leipzig: Engelmann.

Thieme, Paul, 1935. *Pāṇini and the Veda: Studies in the Early History of Linguistic Science in India*. Allahabad: Globe Press.

Thomas, Bertram, 1937. Four strange tongues from South Arabia: the Hadara group. *Proceedings of the British Academy* 23: 231–329.

Thomas, Brynmor, and Jennifer Hay, 2006. A pleasant malady: the Ellen/Alan merger in New Zealand English. *Te Reo* 48: 69–93.

Thomas, Jenny, 1996. *Meaning in Interaction: An Introduction to Pragmatics*. London: Longman.

Thomas, Robert, 1894. Über die Möglichkeiten des Bedeutungswandels I. *Bayerische Blätter für das Gymnasialschulwesen* 30: 705–32.

Thomas, Robert, 1896. Über die Möglichkeiten des Bedeutungswandels II. *Bayerische Blätter für das Gymnasialschulwesen* 32: 193–219.

Thomas of Erfurt, 1972 [1310]. *Grammatica Speculativa*, ed. and transl. Geoffrey L. Bursill-Hall. London: Longman.

Thomason, Richmond H. (ed.), 1974. *Formal Philosophy: Selected Papers of Richard Montague*. New Haven, CT: Yale University Press.

Thompson, Sandra A., 1992. Functional grammar. In William Bright (ed.), *International Encyclopedia of Linguistics*. Oxford: Oxford University Press, 37–40.

Thorndike, Edward L., 1921. *A Teacher's Wordbook*. New York: Columbia Teachers College.

Thornton, William, 1793. *Prize dissertation, which was honored with the Magellanic Gold Medal, by the American Philosophical Society, January, 1793. Cadmus: or A treatise on the elements of written language. Illustrating, by a philosophical division of speech, the power of each character, thereby mutually fixing the orthography and orthoepy [. . .]. With an essay on the mode of teaching the surd or deaf, and consequently dumb, to speak. Transactions of the American Philosophical Society* 3, 262–319. [Repr. as a separate publication, Philadelphia: R. Aitken & Son, 1793.]

Thouin, Benoît, 1982. The METEO system. In Veronica Lawson (ed.), *Practical Experience of Machine Translation*. Amsterdam: North-Holland, 39–44.

Thucydides, 1906 [431 BCE]. *Historiae*, ed. H. Stuart Jones. Oxford: Oxford University Press.

Thurot, Charles, 1868. *Extraits de divers manuscrits latins pour servir à l'histoire des doctrines grammaticales au Moyen Age*. Paris: Impr. Nationale.

Tieken-Boon van Ostade, Ingrid (ed.), 1996. *Two Hundred Years of Lindley Murray*. Münster: Nodus.

Tieken-Boon van Ostade, Ingrid, 2006. English at the onset of the normative tradition. In Lynda Mugglestone (ed.), *The Oxford History of English*. Oxford: Oxford University Press.

Tieken-Boon van Ostade, Ingrid, 2011. *The Bishop's Grammar: Robert Lowth and the Rise of Prescriptivism*. Oxford: Oxford University Press.

Tillmann, Hans G., 1994. Phonetics, early modern, especially instrumental and experimental work. In Ronald E. Asher and James M. Y. Simpson (eds), *The Encyclopedia of Language and Linguistics*. Oxford: Pergamon Press, 3082–95.

Titus, James P., 1967. The nebulous future of machine translation. *Communications of the ACM* 10(3): 189–91.

Togeby, Ole, 1998. Text pragmatics. In Jacob Mey (ed.), *Concise Encyclopedia of Pragmatics*. Amsterdam: Elsevier, 1008–10.

Tognini-Bonelli, Elena, 2001. *Corpus Linguistics at Work*. Amsterdam: John Benjamins.

Toman, Jindrich, 1995. *The Magic of a Common Language: Jakobson, Mathesius, Trubetzkoy, and the Prague Linguistic Circle*. Cambridge, MA: MIT Press.

Tomasello, Michael, 2008. *Origins of Human Communication*. Cambridge, MA: MIT Press.

Tomasello, Michael, Malinda Carpenter, Joseph Call, Tanya Behne, and Henrike Moll, 2005. Understanding and sharing intentions: the origins of cultural cognition. *Behavioral and Brain Sciences* 28: 675–735.

Tomkins, William, 1969. *Indian Sign Language*. New York: Dover.

Tomlin, Russell (ed.), 1987. *Coherence and Grounding in Discourse*. Amsterdam: John Benjamins.

Toolan, Michael J., 2001. *Narrative: A Critical Linguistic Introduction*, 2nd edn. London: Routledge.

Tosco, Mauro, 2000. Cushitic overview. *Journal of Ethiopian Studies* 33: 87–121.

Toury, Gideon, 1980. Translated literature: system, norm, performance: toward a TT-oriented approach to literary translation. In Gideon Toury (ed.), *In Search of a Theory of Translation*. Tel Aviv: Porter Institute for Poetics and Semiotics, 35–50.

Toury, Gideon, 1995. *Descriptive Translation Studies and Beyond*. Amsterdam: John Benjamins.

Trager, George L., and Henry L. Smith, 1951. *An Outline of English Structure*. Norman, OK: Battenberg Press.

Trautmann, Moritz, 1884–6. *Die Sprachlaute im allgemeinen und die Laute des Englischen, Französischen und Deutschen im besonderen*. Leipzig: Gustav Fock.

Traxler, Matthew J., Martin J Pickering, and Brian McElree, 2002. Coercion in sentence processing: evidence from eye-movements and self-paced reading. *Journal of Memory and Language* 47: 530–47.

Trench, Richard C., 1860. *On Some Deficiencies In Our English Dictionaries*. London: John W. Parker.

Trier, Jost, 1931. *Der deutsche Wortschatz im Sinnbezirk des Verstandes. Die Geschichte eines sprachlichen Feldes I. Von den Anfängen bis zum Beginn des 13. Jhdts*. Heidelberg: Winter.

Trier, Jost, 1932. Die Idee der Klugheit in ihrer sprachlichen Entfaltung. *Zeitschrift für Deutschkunde* 46: 625–35.

Trier, Jost, 1934. Das sprachliche Feld: eine Auseinandersetzung. *Neue Jahrbücher für Wissenschaft und Jugendbildung* 10: 428–49.

Trier, Jost, 1968. *Altes und Neues vom sprachlichen Feld*. Mannheim: Im Dudenverlag des Bibliographischen Institut.

Trissino, Gian Giorgio, 1524. *Epistola del Trissino de le lettere nuovamente aggiunte ne la lingua italiana*. Rome: Vicentino.

Tropper, Josef, 2000. *Ugaritische Grammatik*. Münster: Ugarit.

Tropper, Josef, 2001 (2002). Themen der ugaritischen Grammatik in der Diskussion. *Ugarit-Forschungen* 33: 621–39.

Tropper, Josef, 2002. *Ugaritisch. Kurzgefasste Grammatik mit Übungstexten und Glossar*. Münster: Ugarit.

Trubetzkoy, Nikolaj S., 1939. Gedanken über das Indogermanenproblem. *Acta Linguistica* 1: 81–9.

Trubetzkoy, Nikolaj S., 1958 [1939]. *Grundzüge der Phonologie*. Göttingen: Vandenhoeck & Ruprecht.

Trubetzkoy, Nikolaj S., 1969. *Principles of Phonology*, transl. C. A. M. Baltaxe. Berkeley: University of California Press. [German original: *Grundzüge der Phonologie*, Prague, 1939.]

Tsereteli, Konstantin G., 1978. *The Modern Assyrian Language*. Moscow: Nauka.

Tsur, Reuven, 1992. *What Makes Sound Patterns Expressive?* Durham, NC: Duke University Press.

Tsuru, Shigeto, 1934. Sound and meaning. MS, on file with Gordon W. Allport, Harvard University.

Turing, Alan M., 1950. Computing machinery and intelligence. *Mind* 59: 433–60. [Repr. in Edward A. Feigenbaum and Julian Feldman (eds), *Computers and Thought* (New York: McGraw-Hill, 1963), 11–35.]

Twaddell, W. Freeman, 1935. *On Defining the Phoneme*. Baltimore, MD: Waverley Press (for the Linguistic Society of America). [Repr. in *Readings in Linguistics*, ed. Martin Joos (Washington, DC: American Council of Learned Societies, 1957), 55–80.]

Tylor, Edward B., 1865. *Researches into the Early History of Mankind and the Development of Civilization*. London: John Murray. [2nd edn 1870.]

Tylor, Edward B., 1866. The origin of language. *Fortnightly Review* 4. [Repr. in Harris and Pyle (1996: 81–99).]

Tylor, Edward B., 1881. *Anthropology: An Introduction to the Study of Man and Civilisation*. London: Macmillan.

Tylor, Edward B., 1964 [1865]. *Researches into the Early History of Mankind and the Development of Civilization*, ed. Paul Bohannan. Chicago: Chicago University Press.

Uhlig, Gustavus, 1883. *Dionysii Thracis* Ars Grammatica. In *Grammatici Graeci* I.i. Leipzig: B. G. Teubner.

Uhlig, Gustavus, 1901. *Scholia in Dionysii Thracis Artem Grammaticam*. In *Grammatici Graeci* I.iii. Leipzig: B. G. Teubner.

Uhlig, Gustavus, 1910. *Apollonii Dyscoli De Constructione Libri Quattuor*, ed. Gustavus Uhlig, in *Grammatici Graeci* II.ii. Leipzig: B. G. Teubner.

Ullmann, Manfred, 1970. *Wörterbuch der klassischen arabischen Sprache* I, *kāf*, 1983–2002 II/1-4, *lām*. Wiesbaden: Harrassowitz.

Umiker-Sebeok, Donna-Jean, and Thomas A. Sebeok (eds), 1987. *Monastic Sign Languages*. Berlin: Mouton de Gruyter.

Ungerer, Friedrich, and Hans-Jörg Schmid, 2006. *An Introduction to Cognitive Linguistics*, 3rd edn. London: Pearson Longman.

Upanishads 1962. Transl. F. Max Müller. New York: Dover.

Vachek, Josef (ed.), 1964. *A Prague School Reader in Linguistics*. Bloomington: Indiana University Press.

Valera, Salvador, 1998. On subject-orientation in English *-ly* adverbs. *English Language and Linguistics* 2: 263–82.

Valiant, Leslie G., 1975. General context-free recognition in less than cubic time. *Journal of Computer and System Sciences* 10: 308–15.

van Bekkum, Wout, Jan Houben, Ineke Sluiter, and Kees Versteegh, 1997. *The Emergence*: John Benjamins.

Van de Sande, Axel, 2008. *Nouvelles perspectives sur le système verbal de l'hébreu ancien. Les formes *qatala, *yaqtul et *yaqtulu*. Louvain-la-Neuve: Institut Orientaliste/Leuven: Peeters.

van den Heuvel, Theo, 1988. TOSCA: an aid for building syntactic databases. *Literary and Linguistic Computing* 3: 147–51.

van der Hulst, Harry, 1979. Recent developments in phonological theory. *Lingua* 49: 207–38.

van der Hulst, Harry, 1993. Units in the analysis of signs. *Phonology* 10: 209–41.

van der Hulst, Harry, 2004. Phonological dialectics: a short history of generative phonology. In P. G. J. van Sterkenburg (ed.), *Linguistics Today: Facing a Greater Challenge*. Amsterdam: John Benjamins, 117–243.

van der Hulst, Harry, and Norval Smith (eds), 1982a. *The Structure of Phonological Representations*, part 1. Dordrecht: Foris.

van der Hulst, Harry, and Norval Smith (eds), 1982b. *The Structure of Phonological Representations*, part 2. Dordrecht: Foris.

van der Hulst, Harry, and Norval Smith, 1982c. An overview of autosegmental and metrical phonology. In van der Hulst and Smith (1982a: 1–46).

van der Hulst, Harry, and Norval Smith (eds), 1985a. *Advances in Nonlinear Phonology*. Dordrecht: Foris.

van der Hulst, Harry, and Norval Smith (eds), 1985b. The framework of nonlinear phonology. In van der Hulst and Smith (1985a: 3–59).

van der Hulst, Harry, and Norval Smith (eds), 1988a. *Autosegmental Studies on Pitch Accent*. Dordrecht: Foris.

van der Hulst, Harry, and Norval Smith (eds), 1988b. *Features, Segmental Structure and Harmony Processes*, part 1. Dordrecht: Foris.

van der Hulst, Harry, and Norval Smith (eds), 1988c. *Features, Segmental Structure and Harmony Processes*, part 2. Dordrecht: Foris.

Van der Sandt, Rob A., 1992. Presupposition projection as anaphora resolution. *Journal of Semantics* 9: 333–77.

van Dijk, Teun A., 1972. *Some Aspects of Text Grammars: A Study in Theoretical Linguistics and Poetics*. The Hague: Mouton.

van Dijk, Teun A., 1977. *Text and Context: Explorations in the Semantics and Pragmatics of Discourse*. London: Longman.

van Dijk, Teun A., 1980. *Macrostructures*. Hillsdale, NJ: Lawrence Erlbaum.

van Dijk, Teun A., (ed.), 1985. *Handbook of Discourse Analysis*, vol. 1: *Disciplines of Discourse*; vol. 2: *Dimensions of Discourse*. London: Academic Press.

van Dijk, Teun A., 1997a. The study of discourse. In Teun A. van Dijk (ed.), *Discourse as Structure and Process*. London: Sage, 1–34.

van Dijk, Teun, A., 1997b. Discourse as interaction in society. In Teun A. van Dijk (ed.), *Discourse as Social Interaction*. London: Sage, 1–37.

van Dijk, Teun A., 2008a. *Discourse and Power*. New York: Palgrave Macmillan.

van Dijk, Teun A., 2008b. *Discourse and Context: A Sociocognitive Approach*. New York: Cambridge University Press.

van Dijk, Teun A., 2009. Critical discourse studies: a sociocognitive approach. In Ruth Wodak and Michael Meyer (eds), *Methods of Critical Discourse Analysis*. London: Sage, 62–88.

van Dijk, Teun A., and Walter Kintsch, 1983. *Strategies of Discourse Comprehension*. New York: Academic Press.

Van Ginneken, Jacobus J. A., 1913–14. *Handboek der Nederlandsche Taal: De Sociologische Struktuur van het Nederlandsch*. 2 vols. Malmberg: s'Hertogenbosch.

Van Helten, Willem, 1912–13. Semasiologie. *Zeitschrift für deutsche Wortforschung* 14: 161–73.

van Leeuwen, Theo, 1999. *Speech, Music, Sound*. London: Macmillan.

van Leeuwen, Theo, 2005. *Introducing Social Semiotics*. London: Routledge.

van Leeuwen, Theo, 2008. *Discourse and Practice: New Tools for Critical Discourse Analysis*. New York: Oxford University Press.

van Leeuwen, Theo, 2009. Discourse as the recontextualization of social practice: a guide. In Ruth Wodak and Michael Meyer (eds), *Methods of Critical Discourse Analysis*. London: Sage, 144–61.

van Oostendorp, Marc, Colin J. Ewen, Elizabeth Hume, and Keren Rice (eds), 2011. *The Blackwell Companion to Phonology*. Oxford: Wiley-Blackwell.

Van Valin, Robert D., Jr, 2005. *Exploring the Syntax–Semantics Interface*. Cambridge: Cambridge University Press.

Van Valin, Robert D. Jr. (ed.), 2008. *Investigations of the Syntax–Semantics–Pragmatics Interface*. Amsterdam: John Benjamins.

Van Valin, Robert D. Jr., forthcoming. Lexical re-presentation, co-composition, and linking syntax and semantics. In James Pustejovsky et al. (eds), *New Developments in the Generative Lexicon*. Dordrecht: Kluwer.

Van Valin, Robert. D. Jr., and Randy J. LaPolla, 1997. *Syntax: Structure, Meaning and Function*. Cambridge: Cambridge University Press.

van Wijk, 1939. *Phonologie: Een hoofdstuk uit de structurele taalwetenschap*. 's-Gravenhage: Martinus Nijhoff.

Varma, Siddheshwar, 1929. *Critical Studies in the Phonetic Observations of Indian Grammarians*. London: Royal Asiatic Society. [Repr. Delhi: Munshiram Manoharlal, 1961.]

Varro, Marcus Terentius, 1938. *De lingua latina I–II: Varro on the Latin language*, transl. Roland G. Kent. London: Heinemann.

Vasu, Śriśa Chandra, 1891. *The Aṣṭādhyāyī of Pāṇini*. 2 vols. Allahabad. [Repr. Delhi: Motilal Banarsidass, 1980.]

Vater, Johann Severin, 1801. *Versuch einer allgemeinen Sprachlehre*. Halle: Rengersche Buchhandlung. [Repr. 1970, Stuttgart–Bad Canstatt: Frommann–Holzboog.]

Veldi, Enn, 1988. *English–Estonian Parallels in Onomatopoeia*. Tartu: University of Tartu.

Vendryes, Joseph, 1921. *Le langage: introduction linguistique à l'histoire*. Paris: La Renaissance du livre.

Vendryes, Joseph, 1933. Les tâches de la linguistique statique. *Journal de psychologie normale et pathologique* 30: 172–94.

Venn, Henry, 1848. *Rules for Reducing Unwritten Languages to Alphabetical Writing in Roman Characters: with reference especially to the languages spoken in Africa*. London: Church Missionary House.

Vennemann, Theo, 1971. Natural generative phonology. Paper presented at an LSA meeting, St Louis, MO.

Verhagen, Arie, 1995. Subjectification, syntax, andcommunication. In Dieter Stein and Susan Wright (eds), *Subjectivity and Subjectivisation: Linguistic Perspectives*. Cambridge: Cambridge University Press, 103–28.

Verhagen, Arie, 2005. *Constructions of Intersubjectivity: Discourse, Syntax and Cognition*. Oxford: Oxford University Press.

Vermeer, Hans J., 1978 Ein Rahmen für eine allgemeine Translationstheorie. *Lebende Sprachen* 23: 99–120.

Vermeerbergen, Myriam, 2006. Past and current trends in sign language research. *Language and Communication* 26: 168–92.

Vermeerbergen, Myriam, Lorraine Leeson, and Onno Crasborn (eds), 2007. *Simultaneity in Signed Languages: Form and Function*. Amsterdam: John Benjamins.

Verner, Karl, 1877. Eine Ausnahme der ersten Lautverschiebung. *Zeitschrift für vergleichende Sprachforschung* 23: 97–130.

Verschueren, Jef, 1999. *Understanding Pragmatics*. London: Edward Arnold.

Versteegh, Cornelis H. M., 1993. *Arabic Grammar and Qur'ānic Exegesis in Early Islam*. Leiden: E. J. Brill.

Versteegh, Kees, 1997. *The Arabic Language*. New York: Columbia University Press.

Vico, Giambattista, 1744. Principi di Scienza Nuova. Naples: Nella stamperia Muziana, a spese di Gaerano e Steffano Elia.

Vico, Giovanni Battista, 1941 [1710]. *Opere*, vol. 1, ed. Fausto Nicolini. Bari: Laterza.

Viëtor, Wilhelm (Quousque Tandem), 1882. *Der Sprachunterrichtung muss umkehren! Ein Beitrag zur Uberbürdungsfrage*. Heilbronn: Gebr. Henninger.

Viëtor, Wilhelm, 1884. *Elemente der Phonetik und Orthoepie des Deutschen, Englischen und Französischen mit Rücksicht auf die Bedürfnisse der Lehrpraxis*. Heilbronn: Gebr. Henninger.

Vijay-Shanker, K., and David J.Weir, 1990. Polynomial time parsing of combinatory categorial grammars. *Proceedings of the 28th Annual Meeting of the Association for Computational Linguistics* (Pittsburgh), 1–8.

Vijay-Shanker, K. and David J. Weir, 1994. The equivalence of four extensions of context-free grammars. *Mathematical Systems Theory* 27: 511–46.

Vitale, Maurizio, 1960. *La questione della lingua*. Palermo: Palumbo.

Viterbi, Andrew J., 1967. Error bounds for convolutional codes and an asymptotically optimum decoding algorithm. *IEEE Transactions on Information Theory*, IT-13(2): 260–9.

Viterbi, Andrew J., 2006. A personal history of the Viterbi algorithm. *IEEE Signal Processing Magazine*, 23(4): 120–2, 142.

Vogel, Claus, 1979. Indian lexicography. In *A History of Indian Literature*, vol. 5, fasc. 4. Wiesbaden: Otto Harrassowitz, 304–401.

Voigt, Rainer M., 1977. *Das tigrinische Verbalsystem*. Berlin: Dietrich Reimer.

Volney, Constantin-François Chassebœuf (Comte de), 1795. *Simplification des langues Orientales, ou méthode nouvelle et facile d'apprendre les langues Arabe, Persane et Turque, avec des caractères Européens. (Proverbes Arabes.)* Paris: L'Imprimerie de la République.

Volney, Constantin-François Chassebœuf (Comte de), 1819. *Discours sur l'étude philosophique des langues. Lu à l'Académie Française, dans la séance privée du premier mardi de décembre, 1819.* Paris: Baudouin frères.

Voloshinov, Valentin N., 1973 [1929]. *Marxism and the Philosophy of Language*, transl. L. Matejka and I. R. Titunik. Cambridge, MA: Harvard University Press.

Volterra, Virginia, and Carol J. Erting (eds), 1990. *From Gesture to Language in Hearing and Deaf Children*. Berlin: Springer.

von Brücke, Ernst W., 1856. *Grundzüge der Physiologie und Systematik der Sprachlaute für Linguisten und Taubstummenlehrer*. Vienna: Carl Gerold's Sohn.

von Brücke, Ernst W., 1863. *Über eine neue Methode der phonetischen Transscription. Mit einer lithographischen Beilage*. Vienna: Carl Gerold's Sohn.

von der Gabelentz, Georg, 1901. *Die Sprachwissenschaft: ihre Aufgaben, Methoden und bisherigen Ergebnisse*. Leipzig: T. O. Weigel Nachfolger. [1st edn 1891.]

von Foerster, Heinz, Margaret Mead, and Hans L. Teuber (eds), 1949–53. *Cybernetics: Circular, Causal and Feedback Mechanisms in Biological and Social Systems. Transactions of Conferences*. 5 vols. New York: Josiah Macy Jr Foundation.

von Helmholtz, Hermann, 1847. *Über die Erhaltung der Kraft*. Berlin: G. Reimer.

von Helmholtz, Hermann, 1863. *Die Lehre von den Tonempfindungen als physiologische Grundlage für die Theorie der Musik*. Braunschweig: J. Vieweg.

von Herder, Johann G., 1772. *Abhandlung über den Ursprung der Sprache*. Berlin: Voss. [Transl. in Moran and Gode (1966).]

von Humboldt, Wilhelm, 1836a. Einleitung. In von Humboldt (1836b).

von Humboldt, Wilhelm, 1836b. *Über die Verschiedenheit des menschlichen Sprachbaues und ihren Einfluss auf die geistige Entwickelungdes Menschengeschlechts*. Berlin: Ferdinand Dümmler. [Also ed. Donatella Di Cesare (Paderborn: Schöningh, 1998).]

von Humboldt, Wilhelm, 1889 [1820]. Wilhelm v. Humboldt an F. Bopp über *Analytic Comparison. Internationale Zeitschrift für allgemeine Sprachwissenschaft* 4: 61–6.

von Humboldt, Wilhelm, 1908. *Briefwechsel zwischen Wilhelm von Humboldt und August Wilhelm Schlegel*. Halle: Max Niemeyer.

von Humboldt, Wilhelm, 1960–4. *Werke in 5 Bänden*, ed. A. Flitner and K. Giel. Stuttgart: Cotta'sche Buchhandlung.

von Humboldt, Wilhelm, 1963 [1820]. *Ueber das vergleichende Sprachstudium in Beziehung auf die verschiedenen Epochen der Sprachentwicklung*. Leipzig: Meiner. [Repr. in von Humboldt (1960–4: Band 3, 1–15).]

von Humboldt, Wilhelm, 1963 [1827]. *Über den Dualis*. [Repr. in von Humboldt (1960–4: Band 3, 113–43). Also in J. Trabant (ed.), *Über die Sprache: Reden vor der Akademie* (Tübingen: Francke, 1994).]

von Humboldt, Wilhelm, 1999. *On Language*, ed. Michael Losonsky; transl. Peter Heath from *Einleitung: Über die Verschiedenheit des menschlichen Sprachbaues und ihren Einfluss auf die geistige Entwickelung des Menschengeschlechts*. [In *Über die Kawi-Sprache auf der Insel*

Java (Berlin: Druckerei der Königlichen Akademie der Wissenschaften, 1836).]. Cambridge: Cambridge University Press.

von Kempelen, Wolfgang, 1791. *Mechanismus der menschlichen Sprache nebst der Beschreibung seiner sprechenden Maschine*. Vienna: J. B. Degen.

von Raumer, Rudolf, 1870. *Geschichte der germanischen Philologie vorzugsweise in Deutschland*. Munich: R. Oldenbourg.

von Schlegel, August Wilhelm, 1818. *Observations sur la language et la littérature provençales*. Paris: Libraire Grecque-Latine, Allemande.

von Schlegel, August Wilhelm, 1847. Rezension: Jacob und Wilhelm Grimm, *Altdeutsche Wälder*. In *Sämtliche Werke*, ed. Eduard Böckling, vol. 12. Leipzig: Weidmann'sche Buchhandlung, 383–426.

von Schlegel, Friedrich, 1808. *Über die Sprache und Weisheit der Indier: ein Beitrag zur Begründung der Alterthumskunde*. Heidelberg: Mohr & Zimmer.

von Soden, Wolfram, 1952. *Grundriss der akkadischen Grammatik*. Rome: Pontificio Istituto Biblico. [Repr. 1969, 1995 with an *Ergänzungsheft*.]

von Soden, Wolfram, 1965–81. *Akkadisches Handwörterbuch* I–III. Wiesbaden: Harrassowitz.

von Staden, Paul M. S., 1974. Die Ideofoon in Zulu. *African Studies* 36: 195–224.

Voorhees, Ellen M., and Donna K. Harman, 2005. *TREC: Experiment and Evaluation in Information Retrieval*. Cambridge, MA: MIT Press.

Voronin, Stanislav V., 1969. *English Onomatopes: Types and Structure [Anglijskije onomatopy: Tipy i strojenije]*. Leningrad: Leningrad University Press.

Vossius, Gerardus Joannes, 1635. *De Arte Grammatica*. Amsterdam: Blaeu.

Vycichl, Werner, 1934. Hausa und Ägyptisch: ein Beitrag zur historischen Hamitistik. *Mitteilungen des Seminars für Orientalische Sprachen* 37(3): 36–116.

Vykypěl, Bohumil, 2009. *Empirical Functionalism and the Prague School*. Munich: Lincom Europa.

Waag, Albert, 1908. *Bedeutungsentwicklung unseres Wortschatzes: Ein Blick in das Seelenleben der Wörter*, 2nd edn. Lahr: Moritz Schauenburg.

Wackernagel, Jacob, 1876. *De pathologiae veterum initiis*. Basel: Schweighauser.

Wagner, Ewald, 1983. *Harari-Texte in arabischer Schrift: Mit Übersetzung und Kommentar*. Stuttgart: Franz Steiner.

Wagner, Ewald, 2003. *Harar: Annotierte Bibliographie zum Schrifttum über die Stadt und den Islam in Südostäthiopien*. Wiesbaden: Harrassowitz.

Wales, Katie, 1989. *A Dictionary of Stylistics*. London: Longman.

Walker, John, 1791. *A Critical Pronouncing Dictionary and Expositor of the English Language. In which Not only the Meaning of every Word is clearly explained, and the Sound of every Syllable distinctly shown, but where Words are subject to different Pronunciations, the Reasons for each are at large displayed, and the preferable Pronunciation is pointed out. To which are prefixed, principles of English pronunciation . . . Likewise rules to be observed by the natives of Scotland, Ireland, and London . . . and directions to foreigners . . .* London: G. G. J. & J. Robinson and T. Cadell.

Wall, Robert, 1972. *Introduction to Mathematical Linguistics*. Englewood Cliffs, NJ: Prentice Hall.

Wallis, Ernest A., 1925. *The Rise and Progress of Assyriology*. London: Hopkinson.

Wallis, John, 1653. *Grammatica Linguae Anglicanae. Cui præfigitur de loquela sive sonorum formatione, tractatus grammatico-physicus*. Oxford: Leon. Lichfield.

Wallis, John, 1972 [1653]. *A Grammar of the English Language*, transl. from Latin by Alan Kemp. London: Longman.

Wallman, Joel, 1992. *Aping Language*. Cambridge: Cambridge University Press.

Waltisberg, M., 2002. Zur Ergativitäthypothese im Semitischen. *Zeitschrift der Deutschen Morgenländischen Gesellschaft* 152: 11–62.

Wang Li 王力, 1987. *Zhōngguó Yŭyánxué Shĭ* 中國語言學史 [History of Chinese Linguistics]. Xindian: Gufeng. [Originally published in series in the journal *Zhōngguó Yŭwén*中国语文, issues 3–6 (1963) and issues 1 and 2 (1964).]

Wang Li 王力, 1988. *Hànyŭ Shĭgăo*漢語史稿 [A Draft History of the Chinese Language]. Vol. 9 of *Wáng Lì Wénjí*王力文集 [The Collected Works of Wang Li]. Ji'nan: Shandong Educational Publishers.

Wang, William S.-Y., 2011. Language and complex adaptive systems. Paper presented at the Workshop on Complexity in Language: Developmental and Evolutionary Perspectives, Collegium de Lyon.

Wang, William S.-Y., and Asher, Ronald E., 1994. Chinese linguistic tradition. In Ronald E. Asher and James M. Y. Simpson (eds), *The Encyclopedia of Language and Linguistics*. Oxford: Pergamon, 524–7.

Wang, William S.-Y., and Minett, James, 2005. The invasion of language: emergence, change and death. *Trends in Ecology and Evolution* 20: 263–9.

Wang Zhonglin 王忠林, 1974. *Xinyi Xun Zi duben* 新譯荀子讀本 [*Xun Xi*: A New Translation]. Taipei: Sanmin Bookstore.

Waterman, John T., 1963. *Perspectives in Linguistics*. Chicago: University of Chicago Press.

Watson, Janet C. E., 1996. *Ṣbaḥtū! A Course in Ṣanʿānī Arabic*. Wiesbaden: Harrassowitz.

Watson, Joseph, 1809. *Instruction of the Deaf and Dumb*. London: Darton & Harvey.

Watzlawick, Paul, Janet Beavin-Bavelas, and Don D. Jackson, 1967. Some tentative axioms of communication. In *Pragmatics of Human Communication: A Study of Interactional Patterns, Pathologies and Paradoxes*. New York: W. W. Norton.

Waugh, Linda R., 1982. Marked and unmarked: a choice between unequals in semiotic structure. *Semiotica* 38: 299–318.

Waugh, Linda R., 1987. On the sound shape of language, mediacy and immediacy. In *Roman Jakobson, Selected Writings*, vol. 8. Berlin: Mouton, 155–271.

Waugh, Linda R., and Monique Monville-Burston, 1990. Introduction: the life, work and influence of Roman Jakobson. In Linda R. Waugh and Monique Monville-Burston (eds), *Roman Jakobson on Language*. Cambridge, MA: Harvard University Press, 1–45.

Weaver, Warren, 1949. Translation. Memorandum. [Repr. in William N. Locke and A. Donald Booth (eds), *Machine Translation of Languages* (Cambridge, MA: Technology Press of the Massachusetts Institute of Technology, 15–23). Repr. in Nirenburg et al. (2003: 13–17).]

Wedgwood, Ralph, 2007. *The Nature of Normativity*. Oxford: Oxford University Press.

Wegener, Philipp, 1885. *Untersuchungen über die Grundfragen des Sprachlebens*. Halle: Max Niemeyer.

Weingarten, Rudiger, 2011. Comparative graphematics. *Written Language and Literacy* 14: 12–38.

Weinreich, Uriel, 1953. *Languages in Contact: Findings and Problems*. New York: Linguistic Circle.

Weinreich, Uriel, 1963. On the semantic structure of language. In Joseph Greenberg (ed.), *Universals of Language*. Cambridge, MA: MIT Press, 114–72.

Weinreich, Uriel, 1966. Explorations in semantic theory. In Thomas A. Sebeok (ed.), *Current Trends in Linguistics 3*. The Hague: Mouton, 395–477.

Weinreich, Uriel, William Labov, and Marvin Herzog, 1968. Empirical foundations for a theory of language change. In Winfred P. Lehmann and Yakov Makiel (eds), *Directions in Historical Linguistics*. Austin: University of Texas, 95–188.

Weisgerber, Leo, 1927. Die Bedeutungslehre: ein Irrweg der Sprachwissenschaft? *Germanisch-Romanische Monatsschrift* 15: 161–83.

Weiss, Gilbert, and Ruth Wodak, 2003. Theory, interdisciplinarity and critical discourse analysis. In Gilbert Weiss and Ruth Wodak (eds), *Critical Discourse Analysis: Theory and Interdisciplinarity*. Basingstoke: Palgrave Macmillan, 1–32.

Weiss, Helmut, 1992. *Universalgrammatiken aus der ersten Hälfte des 18. Jahrhunderts in Deutschland: Eine historisch-systematische Untersuchung*. Münster: Nodus.

Weiss, Jonathan H., 1964. Phonetic symbolism re-examined. *Psychological Bulletin* 61: 454–8.

Wellander, Erik, 1917. *Studien zum Bedeutungswandel im Deutschen 1*. Uppsala: Berling.

Wellander, Erik, 1921. *Studien zum Bedeutungswandel im Deutschen 2*. Uppsala: Almqvist & Wiksell.

Wells, Bryan K., 2011. *Epigraphic Approaches to Indus Writing*. Oxford: Oxbow.

Wells, George A., 1987. *The Origin of Language: Aspects of the Discussion from Condillac to Wundt*. La Salle, IL: Open Court.

Wells, John C., 1982. *Accents of English 3: Beyond the British Isles*. Cambridge: Cambridge University Press.

Wells, John C., 2006. Phonetic transcription and analysis. In Keith Brown (ed.), *Encyclopedia of Language and Linguistics*, 2nd edn, vol. 9. London: Elsevier, 396–410.

Wells, Rulon S., 1947. Immediate constituents. *Language* 23: 81–117.

Wernicke, Carl, 1874. *Der Aphasische Symptomencomplex: Eine Psychologische Studie auf Anatomischer Basis*. Breslau: Cohn & Weigert.

Wescott, Roger W., 1974. *Language Origins*. Silver Spring, MD: Linstok Press.

Wescott, Roger W., 1980. *Sound and Sense: Linguistic Essays on Phonosemic Subjects*. Lake Bluff, IL: Jupiter Press.

West, Michael, 1953. *A General Service List of English Words*. London: Longman.

Westermann, Diedrich, 1927. Laut, Ton und Sinn in westafrikanischen Sudan-Sprachen. In *Festschrift Meinhof: sprachwissenschaftliche und andere Studien*. Hamburg: Kommissionsverlag von L. Friederichsen, 315–28.

Whissel, Cynthia, 1999. Holding emotional and linguistic rulers up to the poetry of Robert Frost. *Psychological Reports* 85: 751–8.

Whissel, Cynthia, 2000. Rubaiyat of Omar Khayyam. *Empirical Studies of the Arts* 18: 135–49.

Whitaker, C. W. A., 1996. *Aristotle's* De Interpretatione: *Contradiction and Dialectic*. Oxford: Clarendon Press.

Whitehead, Alfred N., and Bertrand Russell, 1910–13. *Principia Mathematica*. 3 vols. Cambridge: Cambridge University Press.

Whitney, William D., 1867. *Language and the Study of Language: Twelve Lectures on the Principles of Linguistic Science*. New York: Scribner.

Whitney, William D., 1875. *The Life and Growth of Language: An Outline of Linguistic Science*. New York: D. Appleton. [Chapter on 'Nature and origin of language' repr. in Harris and Pyle (1996: 191–313).]

Whitney, William D., 1879. *A Sanskrit Grammar: Including both the Classical Language, and the Older Dialects, of Veda and Brahmana*. Cambridge, MA: Harvard University Press. [Repr. 1889.]

Whitney, William D., 1885. Philology, part 1: science of language in general. In *Encylopaedia Britannica*, 9th edn, vol. 18. Edinburgh: Adam & Charles Black, 765–80.

Whorf, Benjamin L., 1956. *Language, Thought and Reality: Selected Writings of Benjamin Lee Whorf*. Cambridge, MA: MIT Press.

Wierzbicka, Anna, 1972. *Semantic Primitives*. Frankfurt: Athenaeum.

Wierzbicka, Anna, 1985. Different languages, different cultures, different speech acts. *Journal of Pragmatics* 9: 145–78.

Wierzbicka, Anna, 1985. *Lexicography and Conceptual Analysis*. Ann Arbor, MI: Karoma.

Wierzbicka, Anna, 1992. *Semantics, Culture, and Cognition: Universal Human Concepts in Culture-Specific Configurations*. New York: Oxford University Press.

Wierzbicka, Anna, 1996. *Semantics: Primes and Universals*. Oxford: Oxford University Press.

Wierzbicka, Anna, 2003. *Cross-Cultural Pragmatics: The Semantics of Human Interaction*, 2nd edn. Berlin: Mouton de Gruyter.

Wierzbicka, Anna, 2006. *English: Meaning and Culture*. Oxford: Oxford University Press.

Wierzbicka, Anna, and Cliff Goddard, 2002. *Meaning and Universal Grammar: Theory and Empirical Findings*. Amsterdam: John Benjamins.

Wilkins, John, 1668. *An Essay towards a Real Character, and a Philosophical Language*. London: Sa[muel] Gellibrand & John Martyn.

Wilks, Yorick, 1975. A preferential, pattern-seeking semantics for natural language inference. *Artificial Intelligence* 6: 53–74.

Wilks, Yorick, 1978. Making preferences more active. *Artificial Intelligence* 11: 197–223.

Wilks, Yorick, 2000. Margaret Masterman. In W. John Hutchins (ed.), *Early Years in Machine Translation: Memoirs and Biographies of Pioneers*. Amsterdam: John Benjamins, 179–297.

Wilks, Yorick, 2003. Editor's introduction. In Margaret Masterman, *Language, Cohesion and Form*, ed. Yorick Wilks. Cambridge: Cambridge University Press, 1–17.

Willemyns, Roland, 2003. Dutch. In Ana Deumert and Wim Vandenbussche (eds), *Germanic Standardizations Past to Present*. Amsterdam: John Benjamins, 93–125.

Willis, Robert, 1830. On the vowel sounds, and on reed organ-pipes. *Transactions of the Cambridge Philosophical Society* 3: 231–68. [Repr. 1829, Cambridge: J. Smith.]

Wilson, Deirdre, 1975. *Presuppositions and Non-Truth-Conditional Semantics*. London: Academic Press.

Wilson, Neil L., 1959. Substances without substrata. *Review of Metaphysics* 12.4 (48): 521–39.

Wimsatt, William C., 2000. Generativity, entrenchment, evolution, and innateness. In Valerie Gray Hardcastle (ed.), *Biology Meets Psychology: Constraints, Connections, Conjectures* Cambridge, MA: MIT Press, 139–79.

Wimsatt, William C., and James R. Griesemer, 2007. Reproducing entrenchments to scaffold culture: the central role of development in cultural evolution. In Roger Sansom and Robert Brandon (eds), *Integrating Evolution and Development: From Theory to Practice*. Cambridge, MA: MIT Press, 127–323.

Winograd, Terry, 1972. *Understanding Natural Language*. New York: Academic Press. [Also published in *Cognitive Psychology* 3: 1–191.]

Winteler, Jost, 1876. *Die Kerenzer Mundart des Kantons Glarus in ihren Grundzügen dargelegt*. Leipzig: Winter.

Winter, Thomas N., 1999. Roberto Busa, S.J., and the invention of the machine-generated concordance. *Classical Bulletin* 75: 3–20.

Wintner, Shuly, 2009. What science underlies natural language engineering? *Computational Linguistics* 35: 641–4.

Wissemann, Heinz, 1954. *Untersuchungen zur Onomatopöie*. Heidelberg: Carl Winter.

Witte, Arnd, Theo Harden, and Alessandra Ramon de Oliveira Harden (eds), 2009. *Translation in Second Language Learning and Teaching*. Bern: Peter Lang.

Wittgenstein, Ludwig, 1953. *Philosophische Untersuchungen/Philosophical Investigations*. Oxford: Blackwell.

Wittgenstein, Ludwig, 2001. *Philosophical Investigations*. Oxford: Blackwell. [Ed. and transl. P. M. S. Hacker and Joachim Schulte (Oxford: Wiley-Blackwell, 2009).]

Wodak, Ruth, 2009. *The Discourse of Politics in Action: Politics as Usual*. Basingstoke: Palgrave Macmillan.

Wodak, Ruth, and Michael Meyer, 2009a (eds). *Methods of Critical Discourse Analysis*. London: Sage.

Wodak, Ruth, and Michael Meyer, 2009b. Critical discourse analysis: history, agenda, theory and methodology. In Ruth Wodak and Michael Meyer (eds), *Methods of Critical Discourse Analysis*. London: Sage, 1–33.

Wolf, Jared J., and William A. Woods, 1977. The HWIM speech understanding system. *Proceedings, IEEE International Conference on Acoustics, Speech, and Signal Processing (ICASSP '77)*, 784–7.

Wolff, Christian, 1703. *Disquisitio philosophica de loquela*. Magdeburg: Rengerianus.

Wolff, Christian, 1720. *Vernünfftige Gedancken von GOTT, der Welt und der Seele des Menschen, auch allen Dingen überhaupt*. Frankfurt and Leipzig.

Wolfram, Walt, 2009. Dialect in society. In Nikolas Coupland and Adam Jaworski (eds), *The New Sociolinguistics Reader*. Basingstoke: Palgrave Macmillan, 35–48.

Woll, Bencie, 2003. Modality, universality and the similarities among sign languages: an historical perspective. In Anne Baker, Beppie van den Bogaerde, and Onno Crasborn (eds), *Cross-linguistic perspectives in Sign Language Research: Selected Papers from TISLR 2000*. Hamburg: Signum, 17–30.

Woll, Bencie, and Paddy Ladd, 2011. Deaf communities. In Marc Marschark and Patricia Spencer (eds), *The Handbook of Deaf Studies, Language and Education*, 2nd edn. Oxford: Oxford University Press, 159–72.

Wollock, Jeffrey, 1996. John Bulwer's (1606–56) place in the history of the deaf. *Historiographica Linguistica* 23: 1–46.

Wollock, Jeffrey, 2002. John Bulwer (1606–56) and the significance of gesture in 17th-century theories of language and cognition. *Gesture* 2: 227–58.

Wong, May, 2006. Corpora and intuition: a study of Mandarin Chinese adverbial clauses and subjecthood. *Corpora* 2: 187–216.

Wood, Sara, Jennifer Wishart, William J. Hardcastle, Joanne Cleland, and Claire Timmins, 2009. The use of electropalatography (EPG) in the assessment and treatment of motor speech disorders in children with Down's syndrome: evidence from two case studies. *Developmental Neurorehabilitation* 12: 66–75.

Woods, Christopher, 2010. The earliest Mesopotamian writing. In Christopher Woods, Emily Teeter, and Geoff Emberling (eds), *Visible Language: Inventions of Writing in the Ancient Middle East and Beyond*. Chicago: Oriental Institute of the University of Chicago, 33–50.

Woods, William A., 1968. Procedural semantics for a question-answering machine. *AFIPS Conference Proceedings* 33 (FJCC), 457–71.

Woods, William A., 1970. Transition network grammars for natural language analysis. *Communications of the ACM* 13(10): 591–606. [Repr. in Grosz et al. (1986: 71–87).]

Woods, William A., 1973. Progress in natural language understanding: an application to lunar geology. *AFIPS Conference Proceedings* 42 (NCC), 441–50.

Woods, William A., 2010. The right tools: reflections on computation and language. *Computational Linguistics* 36: 601–30.

Woods, William A., Madeleine A. Bates, Geoffrey Brown, et al., 1976. *Speech Understanding Systems: Final Technical Progress Report*. Cambridge, MA: Bolt Beranek & Newman.

Woolard, Kathryn, 2008. Why *dat* now? Linguistic-anthropological contributions to the explanation of sociolinguistic icons and change. *Journal of Sociolinguistics* 12: 432–52.

Wörterbuch der deutschen Gegenwartssprache [WDG], 5 vols, 1961–77, ed. R. Klappenbach and W. Steinitz. Berlin: Akademie. Available on line at www.dwds.de

Worthington, Martin, 2010. A new phonological difference between Babylonian and (Neo-) Assyrian. *Zeitschrift für Assyriologie und vorderasiatischen Archäologie* 100: 86–108.

Wray, Alison, 2002. Dual processing in protolanguage: performance without competence. In Alison Wray (ed.), *The Transition to Language*. Oxford: Oxford University Press, 113–37.

Wray, Alison, 2002. *Formulaic Language and the Lexicon*. Cambridge: Cambridge University Press.

Wray, Alison, 2008. *Formulaic Language: Pushing the Boundaries*. Oxford: Oxford University Press.

Wright, Sue, 2000. *Community and Communication. The Role of Language in Nation State Building and European Integration*. Clevedon, UK: Multilingual Matters.

Wright, William, 1890. *Lectures on the Comparative Grammar of the Semitic Languages*. Cambridge: Cambridge University Press. [Repr. 1966.]

Wu Zhihui 吳稚暉, 1964. *Dúyīntǒngyīhuì Jìnxíngchéngxù* 讀音統一會進行程序 [Procedures of the Committee for the Unification of Reading Pronunciations]. In *Wú Zhìhuī Wénjí* 吳稚暉先生文集 [The Collected Works of Wu Zhihui], vol. 2. Taipei: Committee for the Compilation of Materials in the History of the Guomindang, Central Committee of the Guomindang, 7–30.

Wujastyk, Dominik, 1993. *Metarules of Pāṇinian Grammar: The Vyāḍīyaparibhāṣāvṛtti Critically Edited with Translation and Commentary*. 2 vols. Groningen: Egbert Forsten.

Wundt, Wilhelm, 1900. *Völkerpsychologie: Eine Untersuchung der Entwicklungsgesetze von Sprache, Mythus und Sitte*. Leipzig: Kröner.

Wundt, Wilhelm, 1973 [1921]. *The Language of Gestures*, transl. J. S. Thayer, C. M. Greenleaf, and M. D. Silberman. The Hague: Mouton.

Wurzel, Wolfgang U., 1984. *Studien zur deutschen Lautstruktur*. Berlin: Akademie.

Wyrod, Christopher, 2008. A social orthography of identity: the N'ko literacy movement in West Africa. *International Journal for the Sociology of Language* 192: 27–44.

Xiao, Zhonghua, and Tony McEnery, 2004a. *Aspect in Mandarin Chinese: A Corpus-Based Study*. Amsterdam: John Benjamins.

Xiao, Zhonghua, and Tony McEnery, 2004b. A corpus-based two-level model of situation aspect. *Journal of Linguistics* 40: 325–63.

Xiao, Zhonghua, and Tony McEnery, 2010. *Corpus-Based Contrastive Studies of English and Chinese*. London: Routledge.

Xu Peng, Jaeho Kang, Michael Ringgaard, and Franz Och, 2009. Using a dependency parser to improve SMT for subject–object–verb languages. *Proceedings of Human Language Technologies: The 2009 Annual Conference of the North American Chapter of the Association for Computational Linguistics* (Boulder, CO), 145–253.

Yang Jin and Elke D. Lange, 1998. SYSTRAN on AltaVista: a user study on real-time machine translation on the Internet. In David Farwell, Laurie Gerber, and Eduard Hovy (eds), *Machine Translation and the Information Soup*. Berlin: Springer, 175–285.

Yong Heming and Peng Jing, 2008. *Chinese Lexicography: A History from 1046 BC to AD 1911.* Oxford: Oxford University Press.

Younger, Daniel H., 1967. Recognition and parsing of context-free languages in time n^3. *Information and Control* 10: 189–208.

Yu, Alan C. L., 2007. Understanding near mergers: the case of morphological tone in Cantonese. *Phonology* 24: 187–214.

Yushmanov, Nikolai Vladimirevitch, 1998. *Избранные труды. Работы по общей фонетике семитологии и арабской классической морфологии.* [Selected Works: Work on General Phonetics, Semitic and Arabic Classical Morphology]. Moscow: Nauka.

Zadeh, Lotfi A., 1975. Fuzzy logic and approximate reasoning. *Synthese* 30: 407–28.

Zarechnak, Michael, 1979. The history of machine translation. In Bożena Henisz-Dostert, R. Ross Macdonald, and Michael Zarechnak (eds), *Machine Translation*. The Hague: Mouton, 3–87.

Zauner, Adolf, 1903. Die romanischen Namen der Körperteile: eine onomasiologische Studie. *Romanische Forschungen* 14: 339–530.

Zhang, Yanhong, and Alexander Francis, 2010. The weighting of vowel quality in native and non-native listeners' perception of English lexical stress. *Journal of Phonetics* 38: 260–71.

Zhou Binwu 周斌武, 1988. *Zhōngguó Gǔdài Yǔyánxué Wénxuǎn*中國古代語言學文選. [Selected Readings in Ancient Chinese Linguistics]. Shanghai: Shanghai Guji.

Zimmern, Heinrich, 1898. *Vergleichende Grammatik der semitischen Sprachen: Elemente der Laut- und Formenlehre.* Berlin: Reuther & Reichard.

Zlatev, Jordan, Timothy P. Racine, Chris Sinha, and Esa Itkonen (eds), 2008. *The Shared Mind: Perspectives on Intersubjectivity.* Amsterdam: John Benjamins.

Zwicky, Arnold M., 1985. How to describe inflection. In Mary Niepokuj, Mary Van Clay, Vassiliki Nikiforidou, and Deborah Feder (eds), *Proceedings of the Eleventh Annual Meeting of the Berkeley Linguistics Society*. Berkley, CA: Berkeley Linguistics Society, 372–86.

INDEX

functional sentence
   perspective (FSP) 476,
   486, 616, 617, 621
functional grammar 8, 41,
   431, 489, 490, 497, 499,
   500, 617, 713
functionalism 8, 9, 12, 483,
   485–8, 501, 613, 616, 619,
   620, 622, 668, 671, 676,
   682, 685, 688, 689, 727,
   739–41, 744, 767
fundamental frequency
   (F0) 127, 128, 136–9
fuzziness 163, 518, 533, 542,
   572, 573, 615, 743, 773

Gabelentz, G. 659, 764, 766
Gale, W. 719
Galen 288, 321, 327, 339, 686
Gall, F.J. 686
game 30, 595, 615, 771
Gardiner, A. 274, 483
Gardner, A. & B. 84, 85
Garnham, A. xii, 10, 675,
   684, 685
Garside, R. 738
Gauchat, L. 659, 670
Geʻez 261, 263, 264, 270, 271
Geckeler, H. 563, 567
Geeraerts, D. xii, 9, 486, 488,
   489, 555, 571, 577, 579,
   580, 585
gender 37, 241, 250, 257, 285,
   289, 308, 336, 338, 342–4,
   346, 349, 356, 357, 378,
   380, 401, 405, 406, 568,
   571, 627, 659, 693, 705, 756
genealogy 10, 145, 146, 149,
   155, 163, 276, 292, 412,
   567, 568, 606, 636, 637,
   643, 647, 651, 653, 669
general grammar 404, 407,
   409, 411, 413–16, 762
generalized
   transformation 434,
   449, 456, 463

generative grammar 7, 9, 38,
   180, 184, 186, 190, 202,
   249, 439–45, 448, 449,
   452–6, 464, 466, 467, 483,
   485–7, 566, 571, 580, 628,
   631, 683, 771, 772, 774
generative phonology 4,
   67, 167, 168, 173, 180–8,
   190, 203
generative semantics 38, 452,
   486, 622
Genette, G. 195, 202, 208, 633
Geneva 469, 470, 473–6,
   482, 732
genre 216, 218, 286, 341, 345,
   346, 363, 492, 628, 631,
   633, 634, 671, 721, 722,
   733–5, 738
German 21, 31, 65, 67–9, 105,
   115, 120, 121, 142, 143, 151,
   153, 157, 162, 165, 173, 176,
   200, 201, 234, 268, 354,
   357, 359, 365, 369, 370,
   378, 380, 415, 460, 479,
   512, 513, 519, 525, 540, 564,
   565, 590, 591, 606, 638,
   639, 645, 651, 656, 658,
   661, 663, 682, 693, 696,
   697, 704, 728, 766
Germanic 3, 146, 147, 150–2,
   156, 157, 160, 198, 199, 200,
   206, 260, 371, 437, 519,
   643, 644, 647, 648, 650
Geschwind, N. 687, 688
Gesenius, W. 270, 272, 278
Gesetz (law) 152, 154, 157–9,
   161, 164, 177, 646, 648,
   649, 661
gesture 1–3, 14, 19, 27, 30, 39,
   40, 42–4, 51, 71–89, 91,
   93–6, 98, 101, 102, 117,
   170, 328, 608, 609, 736
Gfroerer, S. 137
Gil, A. 113, 119, 486
givenness 621, 622, 632, 740
Givón, T. 43, 486, 488, 603,
   622, 623, 764

Gleason, H.A. 419, 427–9,
   434, 435, 443, 444
glossematics 167, 177, 178,
   479, 619, 768, 770
Goddard, C. 534, 574
Godel, R. 470
Goffman, E. 88, 599, 611,
   625–7, 629, 671
Goldberg, A.E. 488, 489,
   494–7, 504
Goldin-Meadow, S. 43, 86, 87
Goldsmith, J. 167, 168, 176,
   180, 182, 187, 190, 452
Goodenough, W. 567
Goodwin, Ch. 88, 609, 628
Google 11, 725
government 225, 241, 323, 352,
   353, 355–7, 392, 174, 175,
   183, 406, 444, 460, 482,
   484, 487, 518, 521, 758, 759
Graffi, G. xiii, 7, 469
grammatical category 6, 22,
   148, 218, 219, 317, 368, 378,
   380, 401, 405, 496, 497,
   544, 617, 764, 766, 772
grammatical meaning 48, 56,
   376, 387, 388, 617, 751, 753,
   769
grammatical theory 61, 289,
   318, 333, 343, 377, 401,
   403, 411, 460, 585, 747,
   774; see also theory of
   grammar
grammaticality/
   grammaticalness 11, 48,
   266, 417, 730, 758, 771, 773
grammaticalization 48, 148,
   162, 739, 764
grammatogeny 54–6, 63
Grammont, M. 105, 207, 208
Granger, S. 535, 745
Grassmann, H. 4, 10, 155, 156,
   159, 649
Greece 2, 5, 8, 9, 331, 332, 381,
   507, 512, 525, 620, 643, 677
Greek 4, 6, 17, 25, 53, 59, 62,
   64–6, 72, 78, 106, 108, 112,

Lightning Source UK Ltd.
Milton Keynes UK
UKOW07n0852100216

268083UK00018B/611/P